D0139511

AMERICAN RHETORICAL DISCOURSE

Second Edition

AMERICAN RHETORICAL DISCOURSE

Second Edition

Ronald F. Reid

WAVELAND
PRESS, INC.

Prospect Heights, Illinois

For information about this book, contact:
    Waveland Press, Inc.
    P.O. Box 400
    Prospect Heights, Illinois 60070
    (847) 634-0081
    www.waveland.com

Cover photo: Courtesy The Bettmann Archive.

Copyright © 1995, 1988 by Waveland Press, Inc.

ISBN 0-88133-839-7

All rights reserved. No part of this book may be reproduced, stored in a retrieval system, or transmitted in any form or by any means without permission in writing from the publisher.

Printed in the United States of America

14   13   12   11   10   9   8

The texts of the following speeches were printed from *American Public Addresses: 1740-1952*, ed. Craig Baird (New York: McGraw-Hill Book Co., 1956):

Jonathan Edwards, *Sinners in the Hands of an Angry God*
Patrick Henry, *Liberty or Death*
Abraham Lincoln, *Gettysburg Address*
Abraham Lincoln, *Second Inaugural Address*
Henry W. Grady, *The New South*
Booker T. Washington, *(Atlanta) Cotton States Exposition Address*
William Jennings Bryan, *Cross of Gold*
Theodore Roosevelt, *The Man with the Muck Rake*
Woodrow Wilson, *First Inaugural Address*
Woodrow Wilson, *War Message*
Robert LaFollette, *Senate Speech on Free Speech in Wartime*

The texts of the following speeches were printed from *American Forum: Speeches on Historic Issues, 1788-1900*, eds. Ernest J. Wrage and Barnet Baskerville (New York: Harper & Brothers, 1960):

Patrick Henry, *Speech at the Virginia Ratifying Convention Against Ratification*
James Madison, *Speech at the Virginia Ratifying Convention for Ratification*
Thaddeus Stevens, *Congressional Speech in Favor of Radical Republican Reconstruction Policy*
Henry Jarvis Raymond, *Congressional Speech in Favor of Johnson's Reconstruction Policy*
William Graham Sumner, *The Forgotten Man*
Albert Beveridge, *The March of the Flag*
William Jennings Bryan, *Acceptance Speech, 1900 (Imperialism)*

The texts of the following speeches were printed from David J. Brewer, *World's Best Orations*, Volumes 4, 5, 7 & 10 (St. Louis: Ferd. P. Kaiser, 1901):

George Washington, *Farewell Address*
Daniel Webster, *Bunker Hill Monument Address*
Robert Y. Hayne, *Webster-Hayne Debate on Foot's Resolution: Second Speech*
Daniel Webster, *Webster-Hayne Debate on Foot's Resolution: Second Speech*
Henry Clay, *Senate Speech on the Compromise of 1850*
Abraham Lincoln, *House Divided*
Abraham Lincoln and Stephen A. Douglas, *The Lincoln-Douglas Debate at Freeport*
Jefferson Davis, *First Inaugural Address*

The text of Martin Luther King, Jr.'s "I Have A Dream" speech was reprinted by arrangement with The Heirs of Martin Luther King, Jr., c/o Joan Daves Agency as agent for the proprietor. Copyright 1963 by Martin Luther King, Jr., copyright renewed 1991 by Coretta Scott King.

The text of Ronald Reagan's "A Time for Choosing" speech was reprinted from *Speaking My Mind: Selected Speeches*, copyright 1989 by Ronald W. Reagan. Reprinted by permission of Simon & Schuster, Inc.

Contents

SECTION V:
Changing Political Rhetoric of the Jacksonian Era   255

SECTION VI:
The Rhetoric of Religion, Reform and Counterreform, C. 1800–1850 323

SECTION X:
Post-Civil War America: Rhetoric of Regional Conciliation
and Racial Conflict   549

SECTION XI:
Post-Civil War America: Rhetorical Responses to
Socioeconomic Changes   579

SECTION XII:
Political Rhetoric and Socioeconomic Changes from Reconstruction to World War I

SECTION XIII:
Political Rhetoric from "The War to End Wars" to World War II

SECTION XIV:
The Rhetoric of Post-World War II America

Short Titles
(Arranged by Rhetorical Genres)

Notes

1. Although the term *genre* is defined variously, most critics say that discourses presented in similar rhetorical situations have similar rhetorical characteristics. The following set of genres is based primarily on situation, and readers are invited to study commonalities.
2. Because rhetorical characteristics sometimes change over time, the discourses are listed chronologically within genres.
3. A few discourses are listed in more than one genre.

Campaign Rhetoric: Speeches at Political Party Conventions

Campaign Rhetoric: General

Debates (limited to face-to-face encounters except for those marked with an asterisk, which involved an explicit response by the second party)

Commemorations, Celebrations and Eulogies

Lectures (persuasive in purpose, but advertised as "lectures" and repeated on the lecture circuit)

Legislative Speeches and Testimony (excluding debates listed above)

Pamphlets and Essays Addressed to the General Public (excluding those listed elsewhere)

Presidential Addresses: Inaugurals

Presidential Addresses (excluding those listed elsewhere)

Presidential War Messages

Public Meetings, Conventions and Rallies

Sermons

Acknowledgements

Printing (and therefore purchase) costs were reduced significantly because two copyright holders graciously permitted us to reproduce texts from their anthologies by direct photographic means; I wish to acknowledge my deep gratitude to them. First is Barnet Baskerville, Professor Emeritus of the University of Washington, who co-edited with the late Ernest J. Wrage of Northwestern University two excellent anthologies: *American Forum: Speeches on Historic Issues, 1788-1900* and *Contemporary Forum: American Speeches on Twentieth-Century Issues*. Originally published by Harper & Brothers in 1960 and 1962, they were later reissued by the University of Washington Press. Copyrights were held by the two editors during the life of the late Professor Wrage and are now the sole property of Professor Baskerville. Second is the McGraw-Hill Book Company, Inc., which published (1956) *American Public Addresses, 1740-1952*, edited by the late A. Craig Baird of the University of Iowa. These excellent anthologies served students and teachers (including myself) for many years but are now out of print.

Although the copyright has expired, I should acknowledge that *World's Best Orations From the Earliest Period to the Present Time* (St. Louis: Ferd. P. Kaiser, 1899 and 1901) was also used for direct photographic reproductions. Edited by the late David J. Brewer, a Justice of the United States Supreme Court, this ten-volume work continues to be a gold mine for scholars who wish to study masterpieces of rhetorical discourse.

Although no other published sources were reproduced photographically in the direct manner described above, other texts were duplicated to reduce the possibility of error and for the convenience of the editor and printer. The source of each text is always indicated, and I should like to acknowledge my gratitude to the publishers and editors whose material I used.

I should also like to thank the staffs of the libraries where I worked. The American Antiquarian Society (Worcester, Massachusetts) and the Massachusetts Historical Society (Boston) are two of the nation's leading repositories of colonial and antebellum publications. The following public and college libraries in Massachusetts also have excellent holdings: Amherst College (Amherst), Forbes Library (Northampton), Mount Holyoke College (South Hadley), Smith College (Northampton) and the University of Massachusetts (Amherst). Their friendly and efficient staffs were gracious in helping me solve problems and in honoring my requests, no matter how unreasonable.

Neil and Carol Rowe, owners and managers of Waveland Press, and their assistant editor, Steve Dungan, went far beyond what publishers usually do. They gave suggestions and took an interest in the scholarly quality, not just the market potential, of this anthology. Before the first edition was prepared, they conducted a survey of public address teachers to ascertain what discourses they would prefer to have in the book. A similar survey was taken more recently, with the result that a few discourses in the first edition have been replaced in this edition. Many teachers not only responded to the questionnaires, but also wrote detailed letters which I found extremely helpful. My only regret is that limitations of space and energy precluded adopting all their suggestions. All of these people deserve my warmest thanks.

As with all my projects, my wife, Dorothy, rendered invaluable assistance, but, as always, she refused to allow her name to appear as co-editor. Our daughter, Janice Reid, was helpful in more ways than she realizes. Our other daughter, Cheryl Momaney, typed several texts, and our son-in-law, Rev. Leon Momaney, was extremely helpful in tracking down information about Conwell's ''Acres of Diamonds'' and Winthrop's ''Model.'' Our grandchildren, Joshua and Jennifer Momaney, are too young to have helped with the anthology, but they make life worth living.

Introduction

This introduction discusses four questions that readers might like to have answered before studying the discourses in this anthology: (I) What is "rhetorical discourse"? (II) Why study rhetorical discourses of the past? (III) How should they be studied? and (IV) What guidelines governed the selection of discourses for this anthology?

I. What is "Rhetorical Discourse"?

Some academicians define *discourse* as any meaningful utterance, including a mere "Hello." Others restrict it to longer, more formal utterances, such as editorials and sermons. This anthology is restricted to longer, formal utterances.

A more difficult question is, What makes a discourse *rhetorical*? The word *rhetoric* has acquired many diverse meanings in its 2500-year history. We shall survey these meanings, beginning with the ancient Greeks. They thought of "rhetoric" as the teaching and practice of persuasive speaking about civic affairs. These speeches fell into three categories, one being those delivered at civic celebrations. Most ancient societies had speeches of this type, but the other two types grew out of the Greeks' unusual political situation. Greece was a collection of small, independent city-states, most of which were democratic in the sense that free male citizens (not slaves, women, or aliens) could participate *directly* in transacting public business. Speeches were delivered in the assemblies as citizens deliberated about public policy (for instance, whether taxes should be increased). There was no legal profession, and litigants did their own speaking in the courts, where decisions were rendered by juries of 500 or more.

Adapting to these civic needs, some enterprising sophists taught "rhetoric" and wrote how-to-do-it textbooks. Their textbooks have not survived, so we do not have their formal definitions of "rhetoric," but we know they taught students to speak persuasively on ceremonial occasions, in the assembly and in the courts. We also know that most sophists were skeptics; that is, they believed there is no Truth. There is only persuasion.

Unlike most sophists, Plato (428-348 B.C.) was not a skeptic. He believed in the Reality of True Ideas. Believing that the public was incapable of learning True Ideas, he scorned democracy and advocated an "ideal" government in which the populace would be ruled by "philosopher kings." This led him to

1

two definitions of "rhetoric." One, which defined the "rhetoric" that was being taught and practiced, was the "art of flattery." The second was an "Ideal" rhetoric that could presumably be practiced by philosopher-kings: they know Truth, define their terms and classify propositions. The nearest he came to compromising with the sophists was to permit the truth-tellers to adapt to popular audiences, or in his words, give simple speeches to simple souls and complex speeches to complex souls. Plato's influence on Western culture led to a widespread, informal definition of "rhetoric" as sleazy persuasion.

Aristotle (384-322 B.C.) spent two decades in Plato's school, first as a student and then as a teacher. He was a Platonist in his younger days, but he later rejected his mentor's concept of "Ideal Truth." To the older Aristotle, Ideas were not Real; they were abstractions created by the human mind. Yet he did not reject the concept of rationality. He deplored the sophists' skepticism and developed a complex system of logic, central to which was classification: individual things were placed in a class on the basis of their similarities; and classes were differentiated from one another on the basis of their differences.

Classification ran through all of Aristotle's theorizing, including his definition of "rhetoric." He differentiated "rhetoric" from two other classes of formal discourse. "Poetics" embraced fictional discourses, such as epic poetry and theatre. "Dialectic" embraced discourse between intellectuals. The third category, "rhetoric," was defined as "an ability, in each (particular) case, to see the available means of persuasion."[1] In Aristotle's scheme of classification, rhetoric and poetic were similar in that both involved popular audiences; but they differed because poetic was fictional, whereas rhetoric was non-fictional. (Even if a rhetorical discourse includes falsehoods, they are presented as fact, not fiction.) Dialectic was also non-fictional, but it involved learned audiences, whereas rhetoric involved popular audiences.

Continuing his penchant for classification, Aristotle categorized rhetorical discourses into three oratorical genres: (1) deliberative, in which audiences are urged to accept or reject a proposed policy; (2) forensic, in which audiences are urged to accept or reject a proposition about past actions; and (3) epideictic, in which persons are praised or blamed. In theory, Aristotle's scheme was more inclusive than the types of civic discourse that prevailed in Greek society. For example, we could interpret "forensic" to include a debate about the historical authenticity of the Bible. Yet Aristotle's lectures on rhetoric put so much emphasis on civic affairs that our generation of Aristotelians thinks of "rhetoric" as political persuasion and equates his genres with contemporary modes of political discourse: *deliberative* with legislative speaking; campaign oratory and other discourses dealing with policy-making; *forensic* with legal argument; and *epideictic* with ceremonial oratory.

Alert readers will have noticed a shift from the word *discourse* to *oratory*, but Aristotle's neglect of writing in his *Rhetoric* is understandable. Popular audiences in his day were generally illiterate. In our day, literacy is widespread (although some teachers have their doubts), and we can fit many written discourses into Aristotle's three genres. For example, newspaper editorials that advocate certain policies are deliberative; judicial opinions are forensic; and eulogistic biographies are epideictic.

Greece was conquered by Rome, which in turn was conquered by Greek culture. Unlike the Greek democracies, where free male citizens ruled *directly*, Rome had a republican government, in which free male citizens ruled *indirectly* by electing public officials. Unlike the Greek city-states, where litigants presented their own cases in court, Romans had a legal profession. Despite these differences, Romans saw the practical value of Greek rhetoric. They too defined ''rhetoric'' as the study of persuasive discourse about law and public affairs.

Many Roman textbooks still survive, and some were used in European schools until modern times. Thus the Greco-Roman definition of ''rhetoric'' has persisted to the present time, but a host of cultural changes inspired so many other definitions that much confusion now surrounds the word. One change was the rise of Christianity. Although many early Christians rejected rhetoric because of its pagan origins, the famous theologian, Augustine (who taught rhetoric before joining the priesthood) adapted rhetoric to preaching. After Augustine, many rhetoric textbooks classified oratorical genres as Aristotle's three, plus the sermon. By implication, ''rhetoric'' encompassed religious as well as political persuasion.

The history of Western culture has involved vast fluctuations in the extent to which governments were democratic. For centuries after the fall of the Roman Republic, rhetoricians repeated the old theory of the three genres, but they often said little about deliberative oratory. Some went so far as to ignore all the genres. They adapted to the nobility's desire to speak ''eloquently'' by teaching only the stylistic devices. Eager to set themselves apart from the ''common herd,'' aristocrats wanted ''rules'' about how to dress and behave, many of which involved an ''elegant'' or ''eloquent'' style of speaking. This was especially true during the Renaissance, when some teachers explicitly restricted their definition of ''rhetoric'' to style and delivery. The modern revival of democracy revitalized the Greco-Roman view, but the long tradition of restricting ''rhetoric'' to style, especially an ''elegant'' style, is still reflected in many current definitions.

New communication technologies also influenced definitions of ''rhetoric,'' but in ways that both broadened and restricted the term. Printing gave rise to many new genres of written discourse. The novel, for example, is sometimes included under the heading of ''rhetoric,'' even though Aristotle would have classified novels as ''poetic.'' On the other hand, many modern rhetoricians became so absorbed with the teaching of writing that they ignored the ancients' emphasis on public speaking. Some writing instructors concentrated on teaching grammatical correctness, thereby limiting ''rhetoric'' still further.

The importance of written discourse is now being undermined by many recent technologies, such as photography and television, which are pictorial as well as verbal. Whereas Aristotle's contemporaries voted on policy matters after hearing deliberative orations, we look at newspaper cartoons, posters, films, and television commercials. The psychological effects of the pictorial media are unclear, but some scholars speculate that contemporary audiences have been so inundated by pictorial media that we are less able, or at least less willing, than our ancestors to follow a complex chain of argument in a long, formal discourse. Although this speculation is debatable, it is obvious that complex arguments which can be presented in a Senate speech or magazine article cannot be presented in a cartoon or television commercial. This has implications for defining "rhetoric." Some scholars, adhering to the traditional idea that "rhetorical discourse" involves extended verbal argument, exclude visual discourses such as cartoons from their definition. Others, emphasizing the increased importance of visual media, include them.

A fairly recent cultural change that has influenced the meaning of "rhetoric" is increased specialization. Until recently, most men were farmers and most women were housewives. The few who attended college received basically the same undergraduate education. Thus they needed to develop the same kinds of communication skills. Until around the middle of the nineteenth century, American undergraduates took a prescribed curriculum that placed heavy emphasis on rhetoric because it was assumed that they would enter a profession that required speaking and writing skills (law, teaching, preaching or medicine) and that they would become opinion leaders in the political world.

Starting around the middle of the nineteenth century, most colleges established specialized courses-of-study and adopted an elective system. The teaching of communication skills was adapted accordingly, and the result was a hodgepodge of definitions of "rhetoric." In many cases, beginning courses, sometimes called "rhetoric" and sometimes labeled by terms such as "communication" or "composition," dealt only with the communication skills deemed necessary for all specialized professions, such as grammar and exposition. Advanced courses were designed to meet the needs of specialists. Sometimes the courses received labels that did not include the word "rhetoric" (courses in preaching are usually called "homiletics," for example), but sometimes they were called "Rhetoric and . . ." (such as "Rhetoric and Composition," "Rhetoric and Argument," or "Rhetoric and Literature"). Running through this confusion was one commonality: the old concept of "civic humanism" diminished, and with it came a de-emphasis of rhetoric as political persuasion. Curriculum planners no longer took it for granted that graduates would play a major role in civic affairs.

Specialization also affected college administrative structures, which in turn affected definitions of "rhetoric." During the late nineteenth century, departments of "rhetoric" developed into departments of "English," and "Speech" departments later split off from English Departments. English professors often think of "rhetoric" as written composition, while Speech teachers often think of "rhetoric" as public speaking.

If readers are now confused about *the* meaning of "rhetoric," they are not alone. Neither this writer nor anyone else can provide *the* meaning. Any definition is arbitrary, but in the case of this anthology, we shall define "rhetoric" in neo-Aristotelian terms. We shall consider "rhetorical discourses" to be formal writings and speeches that attempt to persuade popular audiences about matters concerning civic affairs. A few sermons are included in the anthology because American history has been influenced strongly by what historians often call "civic religion," a concept that hopefully will be clarified in later sections of this book.

II. Why Study Rhetorical Discourses of the Past?

Implicit in this question is another, Why study *anything* about the past? Readers of this book probably have their own answers, and this writer will simply state a couple of basic assumptions. First, irrespective of our specialized occupation, everyone is a citizen and ought to be concerned about civic affairs because we live in a democratic society. Second, understanding contemporary civic affairs requires a knowledge of the past.

Assuming, then, that history is important, we turn to the question of how studying old rhetorical discourses helps us understand the past. To begin, we should remind ourselves that "understanding" involves more than factual knowledge, such as dates of events. Factual knowledge is essential, but "understanding" means more. It means discovering and explaining trends, seeing changes and continuities. It means interpreting facts.

No clearly formulated theories of interpretation exist to guide historians, but some of them are clearly identifiable, albeit loosely defined. The value of studying rhetorical discourses depends largely on which of these "theories" we accept. I shall begin with two nineteenth-century views that are diametrically opposed. One emphasizes the *personal* forces that guide history, while the other emphasizes *impersonal* ones. Thomas Carlyle emphasized personal forces when he proclaimed that "the history of what man has accomplished in this world, is at bottom the History of the Great Men who have worked here."[2] Great men "accomplish miracles," he said, because "they persuade men."[3] If we subscribe to Carlyle's view, studying rhetorical discourse helps in two ways. First, it helps us understand the extent to which a leader's power arose from persuasive ability and the extent to which it arose from non-rhetorical factors, such as administrative and military skills. Second, the application of general rhetorical principles helps explain *why* a leader was persuasive. However, Carlyle unfortunately fails to justify studying "great" women or persuaders below the level of "great."

The other nineteenth-century view, often called "Scientific History," focused on general historical "laws," *impersonal* forces that guide historical change. In this spirit, Karl Marx found the dominant force to be economics. To Marx, history is a class struggle, the specific nature of which at a given historical moment is determined by the means of production. In agrarian societies, landowners and peasants struggle against one another; in industrial societies, capitalists and workers are the antagonists. Marx was so confident about his theory that he predicted the future: the struggle between capitalists and workers will lead to revolution and a classless, communist society.

Marx's *Communist Manifesto*, which urged workers to "throw off your chains and revolt,'' was a persuasive discourse, and his denouncement of religion as the ''opiate of the people'' implied that religion was a rhetorical tool to keep workers contented in their dismal state. Yet Marx never theorized about the role of rhetoric in history. Economics was the ultimate determinant.

Paradoxically, Marx's impact on American historians has been both limited and extensive. It was limited because he has had only a few avowed followers, and even the ''New Left'' historians have not been able to interpret the past in strict Marxist terms. Instead, as one of their severest critics observes, they have ''danced their way around the [historical] data in a visionary haze.''[4] Marx's impact was extensive because it encouraged an interpretation known as ''economic determinism,'' which was popular in the years between the two world wars and is still influential.

Economic determinists often disagree with Marx about the inevitability or desirability of capitalism's collapse, and they do not confine their study to the conflicts between workers and capitalists. Yet they agree on the importance of economic forces in the flow of history, and whatever rhetorical discourses they bother to study are usually seen as a gloss to cover the economic motivations of the speaker or writer. For example, in contrast to ''Great Man'' interpreters, who usually attribute the Civil War to the rhetoric of antislavery polemicists such as Lincoln, economic determinists usually attribute it to the competing economic interests of the agrarian South and the industrialized North. Debates about the legality of secession are dismissed as ''mere rhetoric.''

Few scholars today interpret history in terms of either great leaders or economics, although most (including this writer) agree that both are important. Believing that history is too complex to be interpreted by any one factor, most adopt what one historian calls ''a pluralistic vision in which more factors are seriously taken into account.''[5] Pluralism makes rhetoric one, but not the only, historical factor; and it leads to our next question.

III. How Should Rhetorical Discourse be Studied?

Inasmuch as history can be interpreted pluralistically, discourse can be studied from different perspectives. Before turning to them, we shall consider two common problems: textual authenticity and selecting texts.

(A) Textual authenticity and selecting texts. Although beginning students are usually content with the texts of discourses in anthologies such as this, they should be sensitive to textual problems. Countless numbers of speeches went unrecorded and have been reconstructed after the fact. For example, Patrick Henry's famous ''Liberty or Death'' speech was delivered at a meeting of the Virginia legislature (formally known as the Virginia Convention), which made no provision for recording the debates. It was reconstructed (accurately?) over a quarter-century later by his biographer, who generated a text based on interviews with a few listeners.

Many speeches have been read from manuscript or typescript, and if the script is available, the student probably has an authentic text. Yet speakers often depart from their script, sometimes in major ways.

Textual authenticity has been less of a problem since the advent of shorthand reporting and tape recording. Yet even recorded speeches are sometimes published differently. Congressional speeches, for example, are recorded, but legislators have the option of revising the recorded text before its publication in the *Congressional Record*. Speech texts in newspapers are usually based on press releases distributed prior to presentation and therefore do not reflect the speaker's "ad libbing." Similarly, written discourses are often revised from one edition to another. Thus, we have variant texts of a "single" discourse.

Deciding which of several texts to study depends largely on the critic's purpose. Suppose, for example, that a Senator delivered a commencement address from manuscript but that the Senator substantially revised the text for publication during her re-election campaign a year later. If the critic wishes to study the speech given to the immediate audience, the manuscript (although not perfect) is probably the "best" text. If the critic wishes to study the Senator's re-election campaign, the published version will be "best."

The "best" text is not always available, and the critic must "make do" as best he can. Yet a good student will remember the limitations and qualify his interpretations accordingly. The need to be careful about drawing conclusions increases when a critic selects a broad topic for research, such as antislavery discourse or Populist rhetoric. Some topics are so broad that not all relevant discourses can be studied in a single lifetime, and critics must be content to select only a sample of discourse. Careless critics give little thought to sampling, but careful ones make sure they are studying a large and representative sample.

The importance of sampling is illustrated by a classic study conducted by Merle Curti. Before his work on the subject, ideological historians "knew" that antebellum Americans had abandoned the eighteenth-century belief in Natural Law. Suspecting that this "fact" rested on studying the discourses of a few intellectuals (who often do not represent public opinion), Curti studied hundreds of Fourth of July orations delivered by a wide variety of speakers to a wide variety of audiences at various times during the antebellum period and corrected the misapprehension.[6]

Having selected a good sample of the best available texts, a student's next task is to make insightful critical interpretations. We should keep in mind that a pluralistic view of history leads to various worthwhile critical approaches.

(B) Ideological Approaches. An ideological interpreter studies a discourse (or set of discourses) to ascertain the ideas of the speaker or writer and/or the audience(s) to whom the discourse was addressed. Note our assumptions. If we are studying a speaker's ideas, we are assuming that the ideas in the discourse were really his (for example, he was not lying when he said he believed in X). If we are studying the audience's ideas, we are assuming that the ideas in a discourse reflected those of the audience.

Studying ideology involves more than isolating the ideas that were actually expressed in a discourse. Look, for example, at the long debate over woman suffrage—when proponents argued that women would cleanse American politics of its corruption, and opponents replied that its corruption made politics an unfit place for women. Implicit in both arguments was an unstated belief in the moral superiority of women.

A technical rhetorical device that is helpful in locating unstated ideas is Aristotle's enthymeme, which he described as the counterpart of a logical (or dialectical) syllogism. So let us begin with the syllogism, which was an elaborate scheme for analyzing the logical validity of various kinds of deductive reasoning, but we shall ignore complexities by simply looking at his oft-cited example:

> Major premise: All men are mortal.
>
> Minor premise: Socrates is a man.
>
> Therefore: Socrates is mortal.

In this syllogism, the major premise is a statement in which one category (men) is classified within a broader category (mortal beings). The minor premise is a statement in which the particular (Socrates) is placed within the category, men. It follows logically, therefore, that Socrates falls within the broadest category, mortal beings.

Aristotle recognized that speakers rarely articulate their premises in the formal way noted above. They might not even be aware of their premises; nor do they necessarily start from premises that dialecticians consider to be true. A rhetorical syllogism, or enthymeme, therefore, is simply an informal syllogism with popularly-accepted premises that might or might not be articulated.

Because unstated premises tell us a great deal about a speaker's or writer's (and perhaps the audience's) ideology, critics should make a special effort to look for them. Critics should also keep in mind that describing the ideology within a discourse(s) does not necessarily reveal how persuasive it was. After all, a speaker's premises might be acceptable to some audiences but unacceptable to others. To study the persuasiveness of discourse, we shall adopt a neo-Aristotelian rhetorical approach.

(C) Neo-Aristotelian rhetorical criticism goes beyond studying the text of a discourse. We must know what the speaker or writer was trying to accomplish. We must know as much as possible about the audience, because a text that is persuasive to one audience might be unpersuasive (or even counterpersuasive) to another. Obtaining such knowledge is called *extrinsic criticism* because it is extrinsic to the text. We shall consider it before turning to the *intrinsic criticism* of the text(s).

(1) Extrinsic criticism begins by asking, What was the speaker's or writer's persuasive purpose? Incidentally, a few (but fortunately not many) literary critics would object to this question on the grounds that an author's "meaning" is "indeterminate," but this view is ridiculous. In some cases, the purpose is obvious. A political candidate's campaign rhetoric is obviously designed to get votes. In some cases, the speaker or writer stated the purpose in the discourse.

Yet ascertaining purpose is sometimes a little tricky. For example, as you read Henry Clay's "American System" speech, you will note that he said nothing about the upcoming presidential election. You might therefore conclude that his purpose was simply to persuade his congressional hearers to vote for a high protective tariff. However, if you remember that Clay was a presidential candidate and that the speech was distributed nationwide as a pamphlet, you will probably conclude that the speech had two purposes: to persuade congressmen to vote for the tariff and to persuade voters to support his candidacy.

Among the extrinsic data available for determining purpose(s) are: statements made by the speaker or writer in his or her private papers, and inferences that can be deduced from the general context (or what some theorists call the "rhetorical situation") surrounding a discourse.

A second question is, What were the audience's pre-existing attitudes toward the author's purpose? Were they sympathetic, hostile, or undecided? The answer will become important when the critic turns to internal criticism. If attitudes were sympathetic, intrinsic criticism will focus on how the speaker or writer reinforced pre-existing attitudes. If attitudes were hostile or undecided, it will focus on how the persuader identified his or her ideas with the audience's values (or what Aristotle called major premises). But before intrinsic criticism can be meaningful, the critic must ascertain the audience's pre-existing views.

Ascertaining predispositions is complicated by three factors: (1) An audience might be divided; some were sympathetic, some hostile, some indifferent. (2) Audience predispositions differ in degree as well as in kind; one hostile listener might be extremely hostile while another might be mildly so. (3) A discourse might have been addressed to more than one audience. In our own day, for example, presidential State of the Union addresses are delivered to Congress, but television viewers are another (perhaps more important) audience. Many of the speeches in this anthology were published soon after delivery, thus giving them an immediate listening audience and a wider reading audience.

The extrinsic sources that can be used for ascertaining audience predispositions are pretty much the same as those available for determining a speaker's or writer's purpose. The same sources can also be used for answering a third question: What were the audience's attitudes toward the speaker or writer (as distinguished from his purpose)? This question is important because a persuader's reputation is an influential factor in his or her persuasive success or failure.

In assessing the "pre-discourse" reputation, critics should avoid confusing reputation and biographical accuracy. To illustrate, let us return to Clay's "American System." Biographers know he was born into a prosperous Virginia family, but contemporaries regarded him as a poor boy who went West and became a self-made man (a reputation he cultivated).

Critics should also avoid confusing a persuader's pre-discourse reputation with a future reputation. For example, Abraham Lincoln now has a reputation of being an abolitionist because of the Emancipation Proclamation, but when you read his Cooper Union Address (later in this anthology) you should remember that he had not yet proclaimed Emancipation. In fact, one of the reasons that the speech helped him get the presidential nomination was that he used it to build a reputation of moderation.

A final question for external criticism is, What audience attitudes constituted *available* means of persuasion? Even hostile audiences usually share some attitudes with the person who is trying to persuade them. These attitudes can be thought of as major premises which a persuader could use as starting points in a persuasive effort. Later, when the critic turns to internal criticism, he can compare the available means of persuasion with those actually used in order to assess the persuader's rhetorical skill. For example, when you read Sarah Grimke's public letter in this anthology, it will be obvious that her audience was partially hostile, but she based much of her argument on religion. This was a good rhetorical technique because her audience was favorably disposed toward religion. How does a critic know the available means of persuasion? By reading exhaustively in the field of history, especially ideological history.

Armed with an understanding of the speaker's or writer's purpose, the audience's attitudes toward the purpose, the speaker's or writer's reputation with the audience, and audience values in general, the critic can turn from extrinsic to intrinsic criticism.

(2) Intrinsic criticism is the close analysis of the text of discourse(s), but it is more than just describing the discourse. It involves relating the ideas, arguments and symbols within the discourse(s) to the kinds of information discussed above in order to assess its persuasive potential. This requires insight, and rigidly following an analytical system can often hinder insight. Yet insightful interpretation requires a systematic approach. In other words, a good critic strikes a balance between rigidly following a system and having no system at all.

One useful analytical system is a modification of the one that Greco-Roman rhetoricians told students to use for preparing and presenting persuasive speeches. It was a process-oriented system that took speakers through five stages: (1) invention (finding possible persuasive appeals), (2) disposition (selecting and organizing appeals), (3) style (wording the discourse), (4) memory (memorizing the speech), and (5) delivery.

Critics can proceed through the same stages, but they usually modify this system. Critics usually ignore memory, partly because modern speakers rarely memorize texts, partly because it is virtually impossible to determine how a speaker memorized a text (even *if* it was memorized) and partly because it does not seem to be a particularly important aspect of discourse to analyze. Delivery is not amenable to internal criticism unless the text exists in visual form (a videotape, for instance). Critics must study delivery via extrinsic sources, such as comments by observers.

Strictly defined, invention is finding possible appeals, which we· discussed earlier as an aspect of extrinsic criticism. Strictly defined, disposition includes the selection of possible appeals, but most neo-Aristotelian rhetorical critics blend their study of invention with an analysis of appeals that were actually within the discourse. This brings us to Aristotle's three ''modes,'' or types, of persuasive appeals: ethos, pathos, and logos. Aristotle defined ethos as the character, wisdom, and goodwill of a speaker as it appears to the audience. Some modern rhetoricians rephrase these aspects of ethos as competency and integrity. Irrespective of the terminology, the critic examines the methods used in a discourse to enhance the speaker's or writer's ethos. We have already mentioned a couple of examples of ethos enhancement: Clay's self-portrayal as a poor boy who made good and Grimke's implicit self-portrayal as a religious person. Readers will find many other techniques of ethos enhancement in this anthology, but they should do more than describe them. They should ask whether the techniques were adapted well to the audience's predispositions. If so, why? If not, why not? Were some potentially good ethos-raising techniques not used?

What Aristotle named pathos is what moderns usually call emotional appeals. Critics will ask: To what emotions did the speaker or writer appeal? How were the appeals made? Were they the best appeals to use? Did the persuader overuse or underuse emotionalism?

The Greek word "logos" is usually translated as "logic," but Aristotle did not mean that logic in rhetorical discourse is the same as logic in scientific demonstration or dialectic. Rhetorical logic is what seems reasonable to the audience. The speaker must base arguments on premises that the audience finds acceptable.

Critics often find it helpful to diagram arguments in the form of an enthymeme, especially when the major premise was unstated. For example, the recent debate over sending U.S. troops to Bosnia featured the opposing argument, "Sending troops will lead to another Vietnam." Although the major premise was unstated, we can diagram the argument as follows:

> Major premise: Anything that leads to another Vietnam is bad.
>
> Minor premise: Sending troops to Bosnia will lead to another Vietnam.
>
> Therefore: Sending troops to Bosnia would be bad.

Such diagrams help critics isolate the unstated premises undergirding an argument, but critics should also ask: Would the premises have been acceptable to the audience? What, if anything, did the speaker or writer do to persuade the audience to accept questionable premises?

Critics should not limit themselves to looking for premises that undergird formally stated arguments. Slogans and stylistic choices (if they are persuasive) also rest on audience-approved premises. For example, political campaign rhetoric often includes the word "new," as in Wilson's "New Freedom," Roosevelt's "New Deal" and Reagan's "New Beginning." As we shall see later in this book, America's Puritan heritage has left us with a faith that new is better. The faith need not be articulated by a persuader because audiences "know" it is true. Similarly, the "Declaration of Sentiments" issued by the women's movement in 1848 was stylistically similar to the Declaration of Independence, and its effectiveness rested on the unstated premise that the Declaration of Independence was wonderful.

Thus far, our discussion of logos has been limited to the enthymeme, but Aristotle also discussed examples. In his theory, enthymemes involved deductive reasoning, whereas examples involved induction (reasoning from particulars within a class to generalizations about the class). From a strictly logical, or dialectical, perspective, critics should ask whether the examples were sufficiently representative of the class to justify the conclusion. Unfortunately, audiences do not always ask this question. They often respond favorably if an example is consistent with their own personal experiences and if the example is presented in a way that is vivid and emotionally appealing. Critics therefore should assess examples within a discourse in terms of persuasive potential as well as logical merit.

Unfortunately, Aristotle's discussion of logos did not include a detailed treatment of some argumentative patterns that modern rhetoricians consider important. These include (followed by one example of each pattern): arguments from authority (Abortion is moral or immoral because authority X says so); arguments from analogy (A single-payer system of health insurance will work, or not work, in the U.S. because it is, or is not, working in Canada); statistically-based arguments (Congress should, or should not, adopt the president's proposed budget because it has a deficit of X number of dollars); and arguments involving cause-effect relationships (Teen-age pregnancy is, or is not, caused by poverty). Assessing the persuasive potential of all these types of arguments involves the same kinds of questions, previously discussed, that critics should raise about enthymemes and examples.

Rhetorical disposition involves the organizational pattern of a text. Organizational patterns vary, and critics should consider whether the pattern actually used in a discourse was best for the audience. For example, some of the sermons in this anthology follow the Puritan format (which will be explained later), while other follow a narrative mode. Which would have been most persuasive to the audience? Irrespective of which organizational pattern was employed, critics should assess whether the discourse was clear. If so, what made it clear (summaries, enumerations, well-worded transitions)? If not, why not?

Finally, the critic should turn to style, or the wording of a discourse. Ancient rhetoricians gave much attention to what are commonly called the "stylistic virtues." Although the "virtues" varied from one rhetorician to another, they usually included grammatical correctness and appropriateness to the audience, the speaker, the subject, and the genre. Aristotle also said a speech should be more dramatic than a written discourse, making use of devices that arouse an audience's emotions by "bringing things before the eyes." He described stylistic devices that could bring things before the eyes of the audience, including puns, riddles, proverbs, hyperboles, antitheses, and metaphors.

Critics can assess a discourse in terms of these stylistic virtues, but many recent rhetoricians complain that ancient theory, although not wrong, is inadequate. This complaint has given rise to some new approaches to stylistic analysis, especially "metaphorical criticism." Unfortunately, "metaphor" is defined differently by different scholars. To Aristotelians, a "metaphor" is a symbol that either states or implies that one thing is similar to another ("He's a pig"). Metaphorical critics concentrate on locating the metaphors that predominated in a text or set of texts and then asking whether they helped the persuader(s) achieve his or her purpose. For example, critics have noted that war metaphors predominated in many discourses about domestic policy during the 1960s and 1970s, such as Johnson's "War on Poverty" and Ford's "War on Inflation." Did war metaphors help them achieve their purpose?

Metaphorical criticism is only one modification of neo-Aristotelian criticism. Many others have emerged during the last two or three decades. However, many presuppose a definition of "rhetoric" that differs from Aristotle's and are of marginal value in analyzing the *persuasiveness* of rhetorical discourse. Others, such as those devised by Kenneth Burke, a literary-rhetorical critic whose theories have been both praised and belittled by other critics, are too complex to summarize adequately in a few pages. I shall summarize only three modifications of neo-Aristotelian rhetorical criticism: generic, movement, and social criticism.

(1) Generic criticism seeks to refine Aristotle's theory of genres and to apply that theory to the analysis of specific discourses. Although acknowledging the value of Aristotle's set of genres, generic critics say the modern world has seen the rise of so many new genres that Aristotle's system is inadequate. For example, presidential war messages and campaign speeches are both deliberative, but each has its own singular features.

What are generic features? Answers vary, but generic critics believe that the commonalities of a rhetorical situation (such as a funeral, a declaration of war, or an inauguration) impose "restrictions" that "require" (or at least result in) discourses given on those occasions having common rhetorical characteristics. They also believe that assessments of individual discourses should be in terms of these general characteristics and restrictions. For example, this writer once did an exploratory study of war rhetoric to see what appeals are commonly used in persuading the "home front" to support a war.[7] Similarly, Ware and Linkugel studied a group of discourses that speakers delivered in self-defense after their integrity had been attacked.[8] In both cases, the critics used their generalizations about commonalities to analyze individual discourses.

Few rhetoricians deny completely the idea of generic commonalities, but skeptics have two reservations: (1) Individual discourses within a genre have differences as well as similarities. (2) The alleged "restrictions" and commonalities of a genre provide an inadequate standard for analyzing individual discourses. For example, many of the essays in a recent book about presidential inaugural addresses focus on the differences between discourses in order to correct what the authors regard as erroneous statements made by earlier critics about commonalities.[9]

(2) Movement criticism involves assessing the persuasiveness of a set of discourses which collectively constitute a "movement." As is the case with generic criticism, rhetoricians disagree about the value of this approach. This

writer thinks that movement criticism is very valuable because it adds an important dimension to the context of discourse.

Scholars also disagree about definitions. Even the term *movement* is defined in varying ways, but the following is common: a movement is a more-or-less organized effort by a group of people to bring about or prevent some kind(s) of social and/or political change. This definition does not equate a "movement" with established institutions (such as labor unions, churches and political parties), but it does include more-or-less organized efforts to seize control of an established institution (as when opponents of the Vietnam War took over the Democratic party). We think of a movement as a semi-organized group or set of groups, such as Woman Suffrage, Abolitionism, Populism, Right-to-Life, Gay Rights or the New Right.

Although the definition is admittedly ambiguous, it is precise enough to permit rhetorical critics to study discourses produced by members of a particular movement in terms of certain theoretical presuppositions about the nature of movements. What are these presuppositions? Movement theorists have yet to develop an agreed-upon set of presuppositions, but they generally agree that movements go through a series of stages, which I call (1) dissent, (2) inception, (3) maturation, (4) termination and (5) post-termination. Each stage poses particular problems for a movement and imposes certain rhetorical requirements if the movement is to succeed. Critics must analyze the discourses of each stage accordingly.

Dissent is not, strictly speaking, a stage because nothing has been done to organize the movement. It is simply a time when discontent is spreading and, because reasons for discontent vary, critics must analyze the precise reason(s) if they are to understand the rhetoric of later stages. Unfortunately, no one knows all the reasons for discontent, but the following list, phrased in general terms (followed in each instance by a parenthetical example) is useful: (1) unfulfilled economic expectations (people expect to be prosperous but are not); (2) a perceived inconsistency between their own values and those of society (a value which says that abortion is immoral at a time when it is widely practiced); (3) a fear of some catastrophe (fear of another ice age); (4) unhappiness with the status of their group (some students complain that big universities treat them like numbers instead of people). Although various rhetorical discourses reflect one or more kinds of discontent during the dissent stage, leaders have not yet emerged, and discontented people have not yet been brought together.

Eventually, some leaders emerge to organize the discontented. This is the inception stage. In the real (as opposed to the theoretical) world, the process of inception is often more messy than I have just described it. Various groups with similar, but different, complaints might get organized by different leaders at various times and places, thus making it difficult for a critic to isolate precisely the "inception."

A naive critic might think that organizing the discontented would be easy, but organizers often face a host of problems. Potential followers might be lethargic; lack respect for the self-appointed leaders; fear legal repression; fear social disapproval; disagree with other discontented people about the nature of, or solutions to, the problem; be pessimistic about the possibility of success; or simply be unaware of the existence of the movement. Leaders, therefore, face special rhetorical tasks during inception. They must attract attention, establish their own ethos, build a sense of unity, arouse enthusiasm, and develop a sense of optimism. The rhetorical critic who studies discourses from a movement perspective must, therefore, study those of the inception period to determine how, and how well, they achieved these particular tasks.

Once a movement is fairly well organized, it enters the maturation stage, when leaders must gain a broader following. This implies two types of audiences: (1) the original followers, who often are militant and uncompromising; and (2) potential followers, who often are less militant, more compromising and satisfied with partial remedies. If the movement tempers its extremism, it risks alienating the original following; but if it does not, it risks failure with the larger public.

The maturation stage also brings other tasks. First, the movement must develop a set of *positive* goals. In earlier stages, it is enough to have a negative rhetoric (attacking devil figures who are allegedly causing the problem), but the persuasiveness of negative rhetoric declines as time goes by. The necessity of a positive rhetoric often leads to a second task—the prevention of splintering within the movement. Third, a movement that is showing signs of success usually generates a countermovement to which the movement must respond. The antislavery movement is a good example of all three tasks. Most of the early rhetoric was against slavery, and some of it was against the "Slavepower Conspiracy." Only later did the movement develop positive goals, but it splintered in the process. Moderates wished only to stop the spread of slavery, but extremists demanded total abolition. Even Northern extremists were split between those who demanded that the North secede from the Union (William Lloyd Garrison, for one) and those who did not (such as Frederick Douglass). Meanwhile, a vigorous proslavery countermovement developed. In cases such as this, critics should assess how, and how well, the movement overcame these problems.

Movements eventually terminate, sometimes in clear and sometimes in confusing ways. They might succeed or fail or do some of both. Sometimes non-rhetorical factors, such as an improving economy, remove the sources of discontent, and the movement simply withers away. At other times, growing popular support for a movement motivates established institutions to co-opt it. For example, the Populist movement, which attracted growing support from economically-depressed farmers during the 1890s, was co-opted by the Democratic party (see Bryan's "Cross of Gold" in this anthology). Then it withered away as prosperity returned to the farms.

The relationship between post-termination and rhetorical discourse is not very clear, and it constitutes an interesting area for future research. Sometimes the movement is forgotten. Sometimes it is eulogized with a plethora of epideictic discourse, as for example the now-current ceremonial rhetoric about the Civil Rights movement on the birthday of its major leader, Martin Luther King,

Jr. Sometimes even unsuccessful movements are eulogized, as for example when post-Civil War Southern speakers commemorated the "Old South" and the "heroes" of the "lost cause."

Although post-termination rhetoric is predominately epideictic, it can serve other important functions. It sometimes rebuilds social unity after it was disrupted. For example, the Gettysburg commemoration of 1903 brought together thousands of aged veterans who had fought one another fifty years earlier. The event was highly publicized and presumably helped unify North and South.

Another function is to provide favorable public images and myths for other movements and institutions. For example, abolitionists of the antebellum period capitalized on the favorable image of the American Revolution by holding Fourth of July celebrations, at which orators analogized the two movements. The Democratic party of today still calls itself the "Party of Jefferson" (even though its "activist government" philosophy is antithetical to Jefferson's). A movement critic attempts to determine whether a post-termination rhetoric appeared and, if so, to assess its nature and persuasive functions.

(3) Social criticism is such an extremely broad term that some scholars consider it too ambiguous to be useful. However, because it is a widely-used term and and has generated a considerable amount of controversy in Academe, I shall express a few opinions that readers might wish to consider, irrespective of whether they agree or disagree.

Our earlier discussion of persuasive *purpose* assumes that the author of a discourse intended to have a certain effect on the audience. However, a discourse or set of discourses probably has unintended effects as well. For example, a political candidate might put a short commercial on television for the persuasive purpose of getting votes, but the rise of this new rhetorical form has led some social critics to ask about its unintended effects. Do commercials lessen our ability to comprehend a complicated line of argument? Do they lessen public interest in civic affairs? Do they blur the distinction between entertainment and serious discussion of public issues?

My personal opinion is that the kinds of questions listed above are important, although they are difficult to answer. So are similar questions about other rhetorical practices. For example, some historians and critics dismiss ceremonial oratory (such as Fourth of July speeches and inaugural addresses) as trivial, whereas others say it functions to build social unity. Who is right? Again, some observers say that the common rhetorical practice of arguing that "my" group has certain "rights" is disrupting social unity, whereas others say this is not true. Who is correct?

Another type of social criticism consists of making judgments about discourse, not on the basis of its persuasiveness, but on the basis of the individual critic's personal opinions about the ideas and rhetorical characteristics of the discourse. This type of criticism has become extremely popular in Academe during the last few decades, especially among feminists, "new left" scholars and other "politically correct" writers in the humanities and social sciences. I confess that I do not know why this kind of criticism has become so popular, but I suspect that several factors are involved: (1) the increased popularity of "revisionist history" (which emphasizes the bad features of our past, such as slavery and imperialism); (2) increased political activity among academicians; and (3) the uncomfortable feeling that critics get when their rhetorical analysis tells them that a discourse was persuasive, yet they think it was morally reprehensible.

Supporters of this kind of social criticism argue that they fail in their social responsibility if they do not evaluate discourse in terms of morality, philosophy, and truth. They add that their knowledge of rhetoric makes them uniquely competent to distinguish "good" from "bad" persuasion.

Opponents of this kind of social criticism say that their rhetorical expertise gives scholars no more authority to present personal evaluations about the moral worth of a discourse than anyone else. They add that assessing discourse on the basis of subjective standards actually distorts our understanding of the past. It constitutes what many historians called "presentism"—looking at the past through the eyes of the present.

This is not to suggest that opponents of "presentism" (of whom I am one) have no personal opinions or are capable of totally keeping subjectivity out of judgments about the past. We try as best we can. For example, I belong to that minority of critics who has a strong personal dislike of Franklin Roosevelt and his New Deal rhetoric, but I try to avoid mixing my personal opinions with my judgments about his mastery of the rhetorical art and the social significance of the New Deal. Being human, we cannot avoid confusing different kinds of judgments, but we ought to try to avoid mixing personal opinions with analytical judgments.

IV. Selecting Discourses for This Anthology

Although most of the guidelines which were followed in preparing this anthology should be obvious from previous sections, a brief explanation might help readers get a better idea of the book's purpose, strengths, and limitations. Selections were made on the basis of Aristotle's definition of rhetoric as persuasion about civic affairs. The book is limited therefore to discourses dealing with civic affairs. Its primary purpose is to provide texts for introductory survey courses in the history and criticism of American public discourse. Therefore it covers a wide range, too wide to provide readers with enough material for definitive studies of specialized topics. It is a survey.

Inasmuch as it is a survey, it seemed appropriate to include mostly discourses of well-known leaders, such as Lincoln and Roosevelt, who represent dominant views. However, because I do not subscribe to the Great Leader theory of history, some lesser lights are included. I also believe that an adequate understanding of history requires an examination of the "losers" as well as the "winners." Losers tend to be forgotten with the passage of time, but they were often so important in their own day that the winners cannnot be understood properly without seeing them in the context of the losers' opposition. Readers therefore will find some discourses by Loyalists as well as American Revolutionists, pro-slavery as well as anti-slavery polemicists, "isolationists" as well as "internationalists."

Believing in the value of movement criticism, many of the discourses in this anthology were selected to demonstrate the development of some important movements in American history, such as anti-slavery and woman suffrage. In the process, some discourses were selected to illustrate common problems of movements, such as splintering and counter-rhetoric.

Because of the availability of many good anthologies covering the recent past, this book is weighted towards earlier historical periods. Fearing that readers sometimes lack sufficient historical background to appreciate the context of individual discourses, each is preceded by a brief (admittedly somewhat superficial) commentary. The commentary is not a rhetorical analysis of the discourse. It simply puts the discourse in its context. Most commentaries are organized by first sketching the general context and then the immediate situation. Information about the author is not to provide a biography per se, but to provide a sense of his or her reputation at the time. Textual authenticity is discussed only when it constitutes a problem, as it occasionally does. Although preferring to include complete texts, I used excerpts when the discourse was too important to omit but too long to present in its entirety. In such cases, the commentary includes an overview of deleted passages.

Hopefully, this introduction provides you with a fairly clear idea of what this anthology is all about. Hopefully, you will find the discourses interesting and profitable to study.

NOTES

[1] Aristotle, *On Rhetoric*, translated with commentary by George A. Kennedy (New York: Oxford University Press, 1991), book I, chp. 2, p. 36.

[2] Thomas Carlyle, *On Heroes, Hero-Worship, & the Heroic in History* (New York: D. Appleton, 1841), p. 1.

[3] Carlyle, p. 184.

[4] Oscar Handlin, *Truth in History* (Cambridge, MA: Belknap Press, 1979), p. 104. For a conflicting view, see G. A. Cohen, *Karl Marx's Theory of History: A Defence* (Princeton: Princeton University Press, 1978).

[5] Ernest R. May, cited by Michael Kammen in his introduction to *The Past Before Us: Contemporary Historical Writing in the United States* (Ithaca, NY: Cornell University Press, 1980), p. 40.

[6] Merle Curti, "The Great Mr. Locke: America's Philosopher, 1783-1861," *Huntington Library Bulletin* (1937), 11:107-51.

[7] Ronald F. Reid, "New England Rhetoric and the French War, 1754-1760: A Case Study in the Rhetoric of War," *Communication Monographs* (1976), 43:259-86.

8 B. L. Ware and Wil A. Linkugel, "They Spoke in Defense of Themselves: On the Generic Criticism of Apologia," *Quarterly Journal of Speech* (1973), 59:274-83. Reprinted in Sonja K. Foss, *Rhetorical Criticism: Exploration & Practice* (Prospect Heights, IL: Waveland Press, 1989), pp. 122-34.

9 Halford Ryan, editor, *The Inaugural Addresses of Twentieth-Century American Presidents* (Westport, CT: Praeger, 1993).

Puritan Preaching
and the
American Mission

A Model of Christian Charity

John Winthrop

Commentary

The English Puritans who came to America brought a religious faith that was secularized into what is often called our "civic religion." As we shall see in various sections of this anthology, our civic religion has profoundly affected our political rhetoric.

Central to Puritanism was a millenarian faith. History was a struggle between God's Agents and the Forces of Antichrist. It would culminate in an apocalyptic battle. Good would prevail, and a thousand years (a millennium) of peace and prosperity would last until the end of the world.

Puritanism was a movement within the English (Anglican) Church that earned its name because it wished to "purify" the Church by reforming its "false" theology and internal corruption. It gathered strength during the late 1500s and early 1600s, especially among small businessmen, skilled workers, and the lesser nobility. As we noted in the Introduction, movements often splinter. Puritanism splintered into the "separatists" (who established a *New* England at Plymouth, Massachusetts in 1620) and a more moderate group who tried to reform the English Church from within.

The moderates faced increasingly serious obstacles after Charles I mounted the English throne in 1625. He dissolved Parliament (which contained a fairly strong contingent of Puritans) so he could rule arbitrarily. He tolerated Church corruption, suppressed dissent and began persecuting Puritans. Many Puritans were convinced that Antichrist was now ruling England and that the final apocalyptic battle was at hand.

Meanwhile, a group of Puritan clergymen and businessmen formed the Massachusetts Bay Company, which received its charter of incorporation on March 19, 1628. The company's purpose was partly economic (it traded with the Indians and exported American timber and fish to Europe) and partly religious. A year after its founding, it decided to transfer the company headquarters from London to Massachusetts to keep its activities far away from the prying eyes of King Charles's "Antichristian" agents.

The company elected John Winthrop (1588-1649) as the Governor who would

23

lead what historians now call the "Great Migration." During the winter of
1629-30, he recruited one thousand immigrants. In the process, he circulated
a manuscript entitled *General Considerations for the Plantation in New England*. It
alluded to the King's recent actions and said the new plantation would serve
as "a bulwark against the kingdom of Antichrist."

General Considerations was not printed because Winthrop feared that too much
publicity would result in the King's revoking the corporation's charter and
preventing the migration. Similar fears prompted Winthrop to depart (with
the charter in hand) on March 22, 1630, even though only four of the eleven
ships were ready. The others could come later.

Bad winds forced the four ships into a nearby port. Still faced with the
possibility of having the charter revoked, Winthrop and other leaders issued
a public statement (April 7, 1630) disavowing any intention of "separating"
from the Church of England. This statement also served two additional
rhetorical functions. It helped calm some non-separatist Puritans who feared
that the enterprise was under "separatist" control. It also helped protect
corporation members who remained in England but might be arrested for
having supported the venture. The next day the four ships set sail. The others
followed soon. The "Great Migration" had begun.

Winthrop was a lawyer, not a preacher, but it was appropriate for the
Governor to deliver a "lay sermon" while aboard the flagship *Arbella*. Conscious
of the mission that his Puritan audience was undertaking, he explicated the
kind of society they were duty-bound to create when they reached the New
World. The mission is highlighted by the word, *model* and the oft-quoted line,
"We shall be as a city upon a hill."

Winthrop read his lay sermon from manuscript, this being the standard
practice of preachers. The text was not published during his lifetime, but
manuscript copies circulated in Massachusetts and England. Only one copy
survived. Like most seventeenth-century manuscripts, it contains numerous
abbreviations and occasional lapses in punctuation and spelling, which are
deliberately reproduced in the Massachusetts Historical Society's edition of
the *Winthrop Papers* (1929). The Society's purpose was to provide scholars with
a printed text that is faithful to the manuscript, but most other printings silently
correct "errors" and modernize the text because they are designed for non-
specialists. Unfortunately, many printings go so far in correcting and
modernizing that they change meanings and/or delete important sections of
the text (often without saying so).

Being designed for non-specialists, the following text has been edited so that
abbreviations are spelled out, and punctuation, spelling and a few words are
modernized. Although edited, this version remains faithful to the original in
terms of meaning and style. It is a complete text that is based on the Society's
edition. Any added material, such as the inclusion of missing words or biblical
sources, is printed within brackets.

Winthrop's use of biblical sources requires special comment. He frequently
(but not always) cited sources (with the source preceding the material used),
but the manuscript has no quotation marks. Many modern printings provide

quotation marks, but this version does *not*. My reason? Many of what seem at first glance to be quotations are actually paraphrases. Although the King James translation (1611) was available to Winthrop, his biblical quotations and paraphrases are closer to the so-called Geneva Bible. It was an English translation made by Puritan exiles in Geneva during the reign of Bloody Mary (1553-58) and first published in England in 1560. It was preferred by Puritans throughout the 1600s. Winthrop (or the manuscript copyist) made a few errors in citing the Bible. The errors are reproduced in the following version, but are corrected in endnotes. Readers who wish to pursue Winthrop's use of the Bible are encouraged to compare the citations provided here with the facsimile publication of the 1560 edition of the Geneva Bible (Madison: University of Wisconsin Press, 1969).

Christian Charity

A Model Hereof

God Almighty, in His most holy and wise providence, has so disposed of the condition of mankind, as in all times some must be rich, some poor, some high and eminent in power and dignity; others mean and in subjection.

The Reason Hereof

1. Reason: *First*, to hold conformity with the rest of His works, being delighted to show forth the glory of His wisdom in the variety and difference of the creatures and the glory of His power, in ordering all these differences for the preservation and good of the whole, and the glory of His greatness, that as it is the glory of princes to have many officers, so this great King will have many stewards counting Himself more honored in dispensing His gifts to man by man, than if He did it by His own immediate hand.

2. Reason: *Secondly*, that He might have the more occasion to manifest the work of His Spirit: first, upon the wicked in moderating and restraining them, so that the rich and mighty should not eat up the poor, nor the poor and despised rise up against their superiors and shake off their yoke; secondly, in the regenerate in exercising His graces in them, as in the great ones, their love, mercy, gentleness, temperance, etc., in the poor and inferior sort, their faith, patience, obedience, etc.

3. Reason: *Thirdly*, that every man might have need of other[s], and from hence they might be all knit more nearly together in the bond of brotherly affection. From hence it appears plainly that no man is made more honorable than another or more wealthy, etc., out of any particular and singular respect to himself but for the glory of his Creator and the common good of the creature, man. Therefore, God still reserves the property of these gifts to himself as [stated in] Ezekiel 16.17. He there calls wealth His gold and His silver, etc. [In] Proverbs 3.9 He claims their service as His due; honor the Lord with thy riches,

etc. All men being thus (by divine providence) ranked into two sorts, rich and poor. Under the first, all comprehended all such as are able to live comfortably by their own means duly improved; and all others are poor according to the former distribution. There are two rules whereby we are to walk one towards another: JUSTICE and MERCY. These are always distinguished in their act and in their object, yet may they both concur in the same subject in each respect; as sometimes there may be an occasion of showing mercy to a rich man in some sudden danger of distress, and also doing of mere justice to a poor man in regard of some particular contract, etc. There is likewise a double law by which we are regulated in our conversation one towards another in both the former respects, the law of nature and the law of grace, or the moral law or the law of the gospel, to omit the rule of justice as not properly belonging to this purpose otherwise then it may fall into consideration in some particular cases. By the first of these laws man as he was enabled so withall [is] commanded to love his neighbor as himself. Upon this ground stands all the precepts of the moral law, which concerns our dealings with men. To apply this to the works of mercy this law requires two things. First, that every man afford his help to another in every want or distress. Secondly, that he perform this out of the same affection, which makes him careful of his own good according to that of our Saviour. Matthew [7.12] Whatsoever ye would that men should do to you. This was practiced by Abraham and Lott in entertaining the angels and the old man of Gibea.

The law of grace or the Gospel has some difference from the former, as in these respects. First, the law of nature was given to man in the estate of innocence; this of the Gospel in the estate of regeneracy. Secondly, the former propounds one man to another, as the same flesh and image of God; this as a brother in Christ also, and in the communion of the same spirit, and so teaches us to put a difference between Christians and others. [Galatians 6.10] Do good to all, especially to the household of faith. Upon this ground the Israelites were to put a difference between the brethren of such as were strangers though not of the Canaanites. Thirdly, the law of nature could give no rules for dealing with enemies, for all are to be considered as friends in the state of innocence, but the Gospel commands love to an enemy. Proof. [Romans 12.20] If thine enemy hunger feed him. Love your Enemies do good to them that hate you. Matthew 5.44.

This law of the Gospel propounds likewise a difference of seasons and occasions. There is a time when a Christian must sell all and give to the poor as they did in the Apostles' times. There is a time also when a Christian (though they give not all yet) must give beyond their ability, as they of Macedonia. Corinthians 2.6.[1] Likewise community of perils calls for extraordinary liberality and so does community in some special service for the church. Lastly, when there is no other means whereby our Christian brother may be relieved in this distress, we must help him beyond our ability, rather than tempt God, in putting him upon help by miraculous or extraordinary means.

This duty of mercy is exercised in the [following] kinds: giving, lending, and forgiving.

QUESTION: What rule shall a man observe in giving in respect of the measure?

ANSWER: If the time and occasion be ordinary, he is to give out of his abundance—let him lay aside, as God has blessed him. If the time and occasion be extraordinary, he must be ruled by them; taking this withall, that then a man cannot likely do too much, especially if he may leave himself and his family under probable means of comfortable subsistance.

OBJECTION: A man must lay up for posterity. The fathers lay up for posterity and children and [1 Timothy 5.8] he is worse than an infidel that provides not for his own.

ANSWER: For the first, it is plain that it being spoken by way of comparison, it must be meant of the ordinary and usual course of fathers and cannot extend to times and occasions extraordinary. For the other place, the Apostle speaks against such as walked inordinately, and it is without question that he is worse than an infidel who through his own sloth and voluptuousness shall neglect to provide for his family.

OBJECTION: The wise man's eyes are in his head (said Solomon) [Ecclesiastes 2.14] and foresees the plague. Therefore we must forecast and lay up against evil times when he or his may stand in need of all he can gather.

ANSWER: This very argument Solomon used to persuade to liberality. Ecclesiastes [11.1-2] Cast thy bread upon the waters, etc. for thou knowest not what evil may come upon the land. Luke 16.[9] Make you friends of the riches of iniquity. You will ask how this shall be? Very well. First, he that gives to the poor lends to the Lord, and He will repay him even in this life a hundred fold to him or his. The righteous is ever merciful and lends, and his seed enjoys the blessing; and besides we know what advantage it will be to us in the day of account, when many such witnesses shall stand forth for us to witness the improvement of our talent. And I would know of those who plead so much for laying up for time to come, whether they hold that to be gospel. Matthew 16.19[2] Lay not up for yourselves treasures upon earth, etc. If they acknowledge it, what extent will they allow it? If only to those primitive times, let them consider the reason whereupon our Saviour grounds it. The first is that they are subject to the moth, the rust, [and] the thief. Secondly, they will steal away the heart; [Matthew 6.21] where the treasure, is there will the heart be also. The reasons are of like force at all times. Therefore the exhortation must be general and perpetual, which [applies] always in respect of the love and affection to riches and in regard of the things themselves when any special service for the church or particular distress of our brother do call for the use of them. Otherwise it is not only lawful but necessary to lay up as Joseph did to have ready upon such occasions, as the Lord (whose stewards we are of them) shall call for them from us. Christ gives us an instance of the first, when he sent his disciples for the ass and bids them answer the owner thus, [Matthew 21.2-3] the Lord hath need of him. So when the tabernacle was to be built His [servant] sends to his people to call for their silver and gold, etc. and yields them no other reason but that it was for His work. When Elijah comes to the widow of Zarephath and finds her preparing to make ready her pittance for herself and family, he bids her first provide for him; he challenges first God's part which she must first give before she must serve her own family. All these [Biblical examples] teach us that the Lord looks that when He is pleased to call for His right in anything we have, our own interest we have must stand aside, until His turn be served. For the other we need look no further than to that of John 1.[3] He who hath this world's goods and sees his brother to need, and shuts up his compassion from him, how dwells the love of God in him. Which comes punctually to this conclusion: if thy brother be in want and thou can help him, thou need not make doubt what thou should do. If thou loves God, thou must help him.

QUESTION: What rule must we observe in lending?

ANSWER: Thou must observe whether thy brother has present or probable or possible means of repaying thee. If there be none of these, thou must give him according to his necessity rather then lend him as he requires. If he has present means of repaying thee, thou art to look at him not as an act of mercy, but by way of commerce, wherein thou art to walk by the rule of justice. But if his means of repaying thee be only probable or possible then is he an object of thy mercy. Thou must lend him, though there be danger of losing it. Deuteronomy 15.7[-9] If any of thy brethren be poor, etc. thou shalt lend him sufficient. That men might not shift off this duty by the apparant hazard, he tells them that though the year of jubilee were at hand (when he must remit it, if he were not able to repay it before) yet he must lend him and that cheerfully. [Deuteronomy 15.7-11] It may not grieve thee to give him (says he) and because some might object, why so I should soon impoverish myself and my family, he adds, with all thy work, etc. for our Saviour. Matthew 5.42 From him that would borrow of thee turn not away.

QUESTION: What rule must we observe in forgiving?

ANSWER: Whether thou did lend by way of commerce or in mercy. If he has nothing to pay thee [thou] must forgive him (except in cause where thou has a surety or a lawful pledge). Deuteronomy 15.2. Every seventh year the creditor was to quit that which he lent to his brother if he were poor, as [it] appears in verse 8:[4] Save when there shall be no poor with thee. In all these and like cases Christ was a general rule. Matthew 7.22[5] Whatsoever you would that men should do to you do you the same to them also.

QUESTION: What rule must we observe and walk by in case of community of peril?

ANSWER: The same as before, but with more enlargement towards others and less respect towards ourselves and our own right. Hence it was that in the primitive church they sold all [and] had all things in common. Neither did any man say that that which possessed was his own. Likewise in their [the Jews'] return out of the [Babylonian] captivity; because the work was great for the restoring of the church and the danger of enemies was common to all, Nehemiah exhorts the Jews to liberality and readiness in remitting their debts to their brethren, and disposes liberally of his own to such as wanted and stands not upon his own due, which he might have demanded of them. Thus did some of our forefathers in times of persecution here in England, and so did many of the faithful in other churches whereof we keep an honorable remembrance of them. And it is to be observed that both in Scriptures and later stories of the churches that such as have been most bountiful to the poor Saints, especially in these extraordinary times and occasions, God has left them highly commended to posterity, as [for example] Zacheus, Cornelius, Dorcas, Bishop Hooper, the Cuttler of Brussells and diverse others. Observe again that the Scripture gives no caution to restrain any[one] from being over liberal this way; but all men to the liberal and cheerful practice hereof by the sweetest promises as to instance one for many. Isaiah 58.6[-9] Is not this the fast that I have chosen to loosen the bonds of wickedness, to take off the heavy burdens, to let the oppressed go free and to break every yoke, to deal thy bread to the hungry and to bring the poor that wander into thy house, when thou sees the naked to cover them, etc. Then shall thy light break forth as the morning, and thy health shall grow speedily, thy righteousness shall go before thee, and the glory of the Lord shall embrace thee, then thou shall call and the Lord shall answer thee, etc. 2.10[6] If thou power out thy soul to the hungry, then shall thy light spring out in darkness, and the Lord shall guide thee continually, and satisfy thy soul in draught, and make fat thy bones, thou shall be like a watered garden, and they shall be of thee that shall build the old vast places, etc. On the contrary most heavy curses are laid upon such as are straightened towards the Lord and his people. Judges 5.[23] Curse ye Meroshe because the[y] came not to help the Lord, etc. Proverbs [21.13] He who shuts his ears from hearing the cry of the poor, he shall cry and shall not be heard. Matthew 25[.41-42] Go ye cursed into everlasting fire, etc. I was hungry and ye fed me not. 2 Corinthians 9.16[7] He who sows sparingly shall reap sparingly.

Having already set forth the practice of mercy according to the rule of God's law, it will be useful to lay open the grounds of it also, being the other part of the Commandment; and that is the affection from which this exercise of mercy must arise. The Apostle tells us that this love is the fulfilling of the law. Not that it is enough to love our brother and so no further, but in regard of the excellency of his parts giving any motion to the other as the Soul to the body and the power it has to set all the faculties on work in the outward exercise of this duty—as [for example] when we bid one make the clock strike, he does not lay hand on the hammer, which is the immediate instrument of the sound, but sets on work the first mover or main wheel, knowing that will certainly produce the sound which he intends. So the way to draw men to the works of mercy is not by force of argument from the goodness or necessity of the work. For though this course may enforce a rational mind to some present act of mercy, as is frequent in experience, yet it cannot work such a habit in a Soul as shall make it prompt upon all occasions to produce the same effect, but by framing these affections of love in the heart which will as natively bring forth the other, as any cause does produce the effect.

The definition which the Scripture gives us of love is this, [Colossians: 3.14] Love is the bond of perfection. First, it is a bond or ligament. Secondly, it makes the work perfect. There is no body but consists of parts, and that which knits these parts together gives the body its perfection because it makes each part so contiguous to other [parts] as thereby they do mutually participate with each other, both in strength and infirmity, in pleasure and pain. To instance in the most perfect of all bodies, Christ and his church make one body. The several parts of this body considered apart before they were united were as disproportionate and as much disordering as so many contrary qualities or elements; but when Christ comes and by his spirit and love knits all these parts to himself and each to [the] other[s], it is [has] become the most perfect and best proportioned body in the world. Ephesians 4.16 Christ by whom all the body being knit together by every joint for the furniture thereof according to the effectual power which is in the measure of every perfection of parts a glorious body without spot or wrinkle. The ligaments hereof being Christ or his love; for Christ is love. 1 John 4.8 So this definition is right, Love is the bond of perfection.

From hence we may frame these conclusions.

First, all true Christians are of one body in Christ. 1 Corinthians 12.12,13,17[8] Ye are the body of Christ and members of [their] part.

Secondly, the ligaments of this body which knit together are love.

Thirdly, no body can be perfect which wants [lacks] its proper ligaments.

Fourthly, all the parts of this body being thus united are made so contiguous in a special relation as they must need partake of each other's strength and infirmity, joy and sorrow, weal and woe. 1 Corinthians 12.26 If one member suffers, all suffer with it; if one be in honor, all rejoice with it.

Fifthly, this sensibleness and sympathy of each other's conditions will necessarily infuse into each part a native desire and endeavor to strengthen, defend, preserve and comfort the other.

To insist a little on this conclusion being the product of all the former, the truth hereof will appear both by precept and pattern. 1 John 3.10[9] Ye ought to lay down your lives for the brethren. Galatians: 6.2 Bear ye one another's burdens and so fulfill the law of Christ.

For patterns, we have that first of our Saviour who out of his good will in obedience to his father, becoming a part of this body, and being knit with it in the bond of love, found such a native sensibleness of our infirmities and sorrows as He willingly yielded Himself to death to ease the infirmities of the rest of His body, and so healed their sorrows. From the like sympathy of parts did the Apostles and many thousands of the Saints lay down their lives for Christ again. The like we may see in the members of this body among themselves. 1 Romans 9 Paul could have been contented to have been separated from Christ that the Jews might not be cut off from the body. It is very observable which he professes of his affectionate partaking with every member. [2 Corinthians 11.29] Who is weak'' (says he) ''and I am not weak? Who is offended and I burn not? And again, 2 Corinthians 7.13 ''Therefore we are comforted because ye were comforted. Of Epaphroditus he speaks, Philippians 2.30 that he regarded not his own life to [do] him service. So Phebe and others are called [in Romans 16.1] the servants of the church. Now it is apparent that they served not for wages or by constraint but out of love. The like we shall find in the histories of the church in all ages: the sweet sympathy of affections which was in the members of this body one towards another, their cheerfulness in serving and suffering together, how liberal they were without repining, harborers without grudging, and helpful without reproaching; and all from hence they had fervent love among them, which only make[s] the practice of mercy constant and easy.

The next consideration is how this love comes to be wrought. Adam in his first estate was a perfect model of mankind in all their generations, and in him this love was perfected in regard of the habit; but Adam rent in himself from his Creator, rent all his posterity also one from another. Whence it comes that every man is born with this principle in him, to love and seek himself only; and thus a man continues till Christ comes and takes possession of the soul and infuses another principle: love to God and our brother. And this latter having continual supply from Christ, as the head and root by which he is united get the predominency in the soul, so by little and little expels the former. 1 John 4.7 Love cometh of God and everyone that loveth is born of God, so that this love is the fruit of the new birth, and none can have it but the new creature. Now when this quality is thus formed in the souls of men it works like the spirit upon the dry bones. Ezekiel 37[.7] Bone came to bone. It gathers together the scattered bones of perfect old man Adam and knits them into one body again in Christ whereby a man is become again a living soul.

The third consideration is concerning the exercise of this love which is twofold, inward or outward. The outward has been handled in the former preface of this discourse. For unfolding the other we must take in our way that maxim of philosophy, "Simile simili gaudet," or "Like will to like." For as it is things which are carved with disaffection to each other, the ground of it is from a dissimilitude or arising from the contrary or different nature of the things themselves, so the ground of love is an apprehension of some resemblance in the things loved to that which affects it. This is the cause why the Lord loves the [human] creature; so far as it has any of His image in it, He loves His elect because they are like Himself. He beholds them in His beloved son; so a mother loves her child because she thoroughly conceives a resemblence of herself in it. Thus it is between the members of Christ. Each discerns by the work of the spirit his own image and resemblance in another, and therefore cannot but love him as he loves himself. Now when the soul which is of a sociable nature finds anything like to itself, it is like Adam when Eve was brought to him. She must have it one with herself. This is flesh of my flesh (says she) and bone of my bone. She conceives a great delight in it. Therefore she desires nearness and familiarity with it. She has a great propensity to do it good and receives such content[ment] in it, as fearing the miscarriage of her beloved she bestows it in the inmost closet of her heart. She will not endure that it shall want any good which she can give it. If by occasion she be withdrawn from the company of it, she is still looking towards the place where she left her beloved. If she hear[s] it groan, she is with it presently. If she find[s] it sad and disconsolate, she sighs and mourns with it. She has no such joy as to see her beloved merry and thriving. If she see[s] it wronged, she cannot bear it without passion. She sets no bounds of her affections, nor has any thought of reward. She finds recompense enough in the exercise of her love towards it. We may see this acted to life in Jonathan and David. Jonathan, a valiant man endowed with the spirit of Christ, so soon as he discovers the same spirit in David had presently his heart knit to him by this linement of love, so that it is said he loved him as his own soul. He takes so great pleasure in him that he strips himself to adorn his beloved. His father's kingdom was not so precious to him as his beloved David. David shall have it with all his heart, himself desires no more but that he may be near to him to rejoice in his good. He chooses to converse with him in the wilderness, even to the hazard of his own life, rather than with the great courtiers in his father's palace. When he sees danger towards him, he spares neither care, pains, nor peril to divert it. When injury was offered his beloved David, he could not bear it, though from his own father, and when they must part for a season only, they thought their hearts would have broke for sorrow, had not their affections found vent by abundance of tears. Other instances might be brought to show the nature of this affection, as of Ruth and Naomi and many others, but this truth is clear enough. If any shall object that it is not possible that love should be bred or upheld without hope of requital, it is granted but that is not our cause; for this love is always under reward. It never gives, but it always receives with advantage. First, in regard that among the members of the same body, love and affection are reciprocal in a most equal and sweet kind of commerce. Secondly, in regard of the pleasure and content that the exercise of love carries with it as we may see in the natural body. The mouth is at all the pains to receive and mince the food which serves for the nourishment of all the other parts of the body, yet it has no cause to complain; for first, the other parts send back by secret passages a due proportion of the same nourishment in a better form for the strengthening and comforting the mouth; secondly, the labor of the mouth is accompanied with such pleasure and content[ment] as far exceeds the pains it takes. So is it in all the labor of love among Christians; the part loving reaps love again as was shown before, which the soul covets more than all the wealth in the world. Secondly [thirdly], nothing yields more pleasure and content[ment] to the soul than when it finds that which it may love fervently. For to love and live beloved is the soul's paradise, both here and in heaven. In the state of wedlock there be many comforts to bear out the troubles of that condition; but let such as have tried the most say if there be any sweetness in that condition comparable to the exercise of mutual love.

From the former considerations arises these conclusions.

First, this love among Christians is a real thing, not imaginary.

Secondly, this love is as absolutely necessary to the being of the body of Christ as the sinews and other ligaments of a natural body are to the being of that body.

Thirdly, this love is a divine spiritual nature: free, active, strong, courageous, permanent, undervaluing all things beneath its proper object; and of all the graces this makes us nearer to resemble the virtues of our heavenly Father.

Fourthly, it rests in the love and welfare of its beloved. For the full and certain knowledge of these truths concerning the nature, use, [and] excellency of this grace, that which the Holy Ghost has left recorded [in] 1 Corinthians 13 may give full satisfaction which is needful for every true member of this lovely body of the Lord Jesus to work upon their hearts by prayer, meditation, continual exercise at least of the special [power] of this grace till Christ be formed in them and they in him all in each other knit together by this bond of love.

It rests now to make some application of this discourse by the present design which gave the occasion of writing of it. Herein are four things to be propounded: first the persons; secondly, the work; thirdly, the end; fourthly, the means.

First, for the persons. We are a company professing ourselves fellow members of Christ in which respect only though we were absent from each other many miles, and had our employments as far distant, yet we ought to account ourselves knit together by this bond of love and live in the exercise of it, if we would have comfort of our being in Christ. This was notorious in the practice of the Christians in former times, as is testified of the Waldenses from the mouth of one of the adversaries, Aeneas Sylvius: "mutuo [solent amare] pene antequam norint;" "they use to love any of their own religion even before they were acquainted with them."

Secondly, for the work we have in hand. It is by a mutual consent through a special overruling providence, and a more than an ordinary approbation of the churches of Christ to seek out a place of cohabitation and consortship under a due form of government both civil and ecclesiastical. In such cases as this, the care of the public must oversway all private respects by which not only conscience, but mere civil policy does bind us. For it is a true rule that particular estates cannot subsist in the ruin of the public.

Thirdly, the end is to improve our lives to do more service to the Lord. The comfort and increase of the body of Christ whereof we are members that ourselves and posterity may be the better preserved from the common corruptions of this evil world to serve the Lord and work out our salvation under the power and purity of his holy ordinances.

Fourthly, for the means whereby this must be effected. They are twofold, a conformity with the work and end we aim at. These we see are extraordinary. Therefore we must not content ourselves with usual ordinary means whatsoever we did or ought to have done when we lived in England. The same must we do and more also where we go. That which the most in their churches maintain as a truth in profession only we must bring into familiar and constant practice, as in this duty of love. We must love brotherly without dissimulation. We must love one another with a pure heart fervently. We must bear one another's burdens. We must not look only on our own things, but also on the things of our brethren. Neither must we think that the Lord will bear with such failings at our hands as He does from those among whom we have lived, and that for three reasons.

First, in regard of the more near bond of marriage between Him and us, wherein He has taken us to be his after a most strict and peculiar manner, which will make Him the more jealous of our love and obedience. So He tells the people of Israel [in Amos 3.2], You only have I known of all the families of the earth. Therefore will I punish you for your transgressions.

Secondly, because the Lord will be sanctified in them that come near Him. We know that there were many that corrupted the service of the Lord, some setting up alters before His own, others offering both strange fire and strange sacrifices also. Yet there came no fire from heaven or other sudden judgment upon them as [it] did upon Nabad and Abihu, who yet we may think did not sin presumptuously.

Thirdly, when God gives a special commission, He looks to have it strictly observed in every article. When He gave Saul a commission to destroy Amalek, He indented [agreed] with him upon certain articles; and because he failed in one of the least, and that upon a fair pretense, it lost him the kingdom, which should have been his reward if he had observed his commission. Thus stands the cause between God and us. We are entered into covenant with Him for this work. We have taken out a commission. The Lord has given us leave to draw our own articles. We have professed to enterprise these actions upon these and these ends. We have here upon besought Him of favor and blessing. Now if the Lord shall please to hear us and bring us in peace to the place we desire, then has He ratified this covenant and sealed our commission, [and God] will expect a strict performance of the articles contained in it. But if we shall neglect the observation of these articles which are the ends we have propounded, and dissembling with our God, [we] shall fall to embrace this present world and prosecute our carnal intentions, seeking great things for ourselves and our posterity, the Lord will surely break out in wrath against us, be revenged of such a perjured people and make us know the price of the breach of such a covenant.

Now the only way to avoid this shipwreck and to provide for our posterity is to follow the counsel of Micah [6.8], to do justly, to love mercy to walk humbly with our God. For this end, we must be knit together in this work as one man. We must entertain each other in brotherly affection. We must be willing to abridge ourselves of our superfluities for the supply of others' necessities. We must uphold a familiar commerce together in all meekness, gentleness, patience and liberality. We must delight in each other, make others' conditions our own, rejoice together, mourn together, labor and suffer together, always having before our eyes our commission and community in the work our community as members of the same body. [Ephesians 4.3] So shall we keep the unity of the spirit in the bond of peace. The Lord will be our God and delight to dwell among us, as His own people and will command a blessing upon us in all our ways, so that we shall see much more of His wisdom, power, goodness, and truth than formerly we have been acquainted with. We shall find that the God of Israel is among us, when ten of us shall be able to resist a thousand of our enemies [and] when He shall make us a praise and glory that men shall say of succeeding plantations: "The Lord make it like that of New England;" for we must consider that we shall be as [Matthew 5.14] a city upon a hill. The eyes of all people are upon us; so that if we shall deal falsely with our God in this work we have undertaken and so cause Him to withdraw His present help from us, we shall be made a story and a by-word through the world. We shall open the mouths of enemies to speak evil of the ways of God and all professors for God's sake. We shall shame the faces of many of God's worthy servants, and cause their prayers to be turned into curses upon us till we be consumed out of the good land where we are going. And to shut up this discourse with that exhortation of Moses, that faithful servant of the Lord, in his last farewell to Israel. Deuteronomy 30[.15-20] Beloved there is now set before us life and good, death and evil in that we are commanded this day to love the Lord our God, and to love one another to walk in His ways and to keep His commandments and His ordinance, and His laws, and the articles of our covenant with Him that we may live and be multiplied, and that the Lord our God may bless us in the land where we go to possess it. But if our hearts shall turn away so that we will not obey, but shall be seduced and worship other gods our pleasures, and profits, and serve them, it is propounded unto us this day, we shall surely perish out of the good land whither we pass over this vast Sea to possess it.

> Therefore let us choose life,
> that we and our Seed
> may live by obeying His
> voice and cleaving to Him,
> for he is our life and
> our prosperity.

Notes

[1] Citations in Winthrop's text should be corrected as follows:
> [1] 2 Corinthians 9.6.
> [2] Matthew 6.19.
> [3] 1 John 3-17.
> [4] Deuteronomy 15.4.
> [5] Matthew 7.12.
> [6] Isaiah 58.1-11.
> [7] 2 Corinthians 9-16.
> [8] 1 Corinthians 12.12, 13, 27.
> [9] 1 John 3.16.

A Brief Recognition of New-England[']s Errand into the Wilderness

Samuel Danforth

Commentary

In England, the word *Puritan* was first used pejoratively by orthodox Anglicans to insult those who wished to "purify" the established Church, but soon the non-orthodox proudly accepted the label. All Puritans wished to cleanse the Church of England of the "popish superstitions" and rituals which remained from the days that it had been under papal authority. They disagreed among themselves about theology and church organization, but most of those who emigrated to America subscribed to the Calvinist theological principles of man's utter depravity and salvation by predestination. Most American Puritans also subscribed to a view of church organization called "independent" or "congregational." Rejecting hierarchy, they established independent congregations which ordained their own ministers and conducted religious services in simple "meetinghouses" (not "churches") that were devoid of "popish" rituals. The sermon was the central feature.

American Puritans brought from England a standard mode of preaching which grew out of their objections to the typical Anglican sermon. They charged that its ornate style and classical allusions were inappropriate for average audiences and inconsistent with theology. The one and only infallible source of Truth was the Holy Bible. Those who were predestined for salvation (the "elect" or "regenerate") had to have a deep understanding of biblical doctrines; thus, English Puritans developed a standard preaching method that has often been compared to a legal brief. Once in the New World, it predominated for over a century in spite of theological changes. Traces of it still remain.

The Puritan sermon was characterized by a standard organizational method. The preacher began with a biblical quotation, or *text*, which, to ensure its being understood by the audience, was *explained* by sketching its

36

historical context, defining key words or some such approach. Then the preacher summarized and developed the *doctrine(s)*, which was (were) implicit in the text or logically deducible from it. Sometimes the doctrines were divided into "branches" (as in Danforth's sermon) and sometimes supported with "reasons" (as is one of Danforth's "branches"). Regardless of the method of development, the doctrines were general theological principles. Variously called *Applications, Uses* or *Improvements,* the last section was to bring the abstract doctrines down to a practical level. Doctrines were "applied" so that listeners could "use" them and thereby "improve" their lives.

The rigidly organized sermon was filled with biblical citations and characterized by frequent summaries, careful enumeration of points and a plain style. Suspicious of emotionalism, the lawyer-like preacher rarely tried to arouse emotions, but when he did, he usually warned his audience in advance, saying something like, "Let the last improvement be by way of exhortation." Puritan audiences were expected to improve their lives, but improvements had to rest on an intellectual understanding of theology.

One of the most important theological principles was the "prophetic" or "literal" interpretation of Scripture. Firmly convinced that Scripture "prophesied," or predicted, a coming Millennium, Puritans believed that God had chosen them as His instrumentalities in protecting the True Faith and bringing about the Millennium. The Puritans' flight from England to the American Wilderness was not an historical accident. It was part of the Divine Plan of History and gave the Chosen People a Special Mission.

Making no distinction between religious and secular life, the idea of Mission dominated the Puritans' entire view of the world. Although now secularized, it still permeates American ideology and provides persuaders with a variety of premises and appeals. First, it undergirded the famous Puritan social ethic, which is now declining but still remains. Only by thrift, hard work and honesty could the Chosen fulfill their Divine Mission. Second, it undergirded the still prevalent American faith in progress and social perfectability. Third, it reinforced the Puritan sense of duty and instilled a sense of guilt for failure to perform one's divinely ordained duties (their distrust of emotionalism notwithstanding).

Preachers used several sermonic genres to keep their audiences' eyes fixed intently on their Mission. Regular Sunday sermons were supplemented by those on special occasions. When a crisis arose (e.g., an Indian uprising), Fast Day sermons were delivered, and when it passed (e.g., the Indians were defeated), it was time for a Thanksgiving sermon.

Another genre was the Election Day sermon, in which preachers reminded their audiences that public business was God's business. Immediately before the lower house of the Massachusetts legislature elected members to the upper house, they listened to an invited preacher remind them of their grave responsibilities. Election Day sermons were usually published, and the following one, delivered in 1670, is reproduced from the edition published the next year by "S.G. and M.F." of Cambridge and is now in the possession of the American Antiquarian Society. It was presented by Samuel Danforth

(1626-1674), who emigrated from England as a youngster and ministered to the congregation in Roxbury.

A Brief Recognition of New-England[']s Errand into the Wilderness

Matth. 11:7,8,9.
What went ye out into the wilderness to see? A reed shaken with the wind?
But what went ye out for to see? A man clothed in soft raiment?
behold, they that wear soft clothing, are in Kings houses.
But what went ye out for to see? A Prophet? yea, I say unto you, and more than a Prophet.

These words are our Saviour's Proem to his illustrious Encomium of John the Baptist. John began his Ministry, not in Jerusalem, nor in any famous City of Judea, but in the wilderness, i.e. in a woody, retired and solitary place, thereby withdrawing himself from the envy and proposterous zeal of such as were addicted to their old Traditions, and also taking the people aside from the noise and tumuk of their secular occasions and businesses, which might have obstructed their ready and cheerful attendance unto his Doctrine. The Ministry of John at first was entertained by all sorts with singular affection: There went out to him Jerusalem and all Judea, and all the region round about Jordan, Mat. 3.5. but after awhile, the people's fervour abated, and John being kept under restraint divers moneths, his authority and esteem began to decay and languish, John 5.35. Wherefore our Saviour, taking occasion from Johns Messengers coming to him, after their departure, gives an excellent Elogie and Commendation of John, to the intent that He might ratifie and confirm his Doctrine and Administration, and revive his Authority and Estimation in the hearts and consciences of the people.

This Elogie our Saviour begins with an elegant Dialogism, which the Rhetorician calleth Communication: gravely deliberating with his Hearers, and seriously enquiring to what purpose they went out into the Wilderness, and what expectation drew them thither. Wherein we have, 1. The general Question, and main subject of his Inquisition. 2. The particular Enquiries. 3. The Determination of the Question.

The general Question is, What went ye out into the Wilderness to see? He saith not, Whom went ye out to hear, but what went ye out to see? The phrase

---

The original printing of this address included extensive use of italics and numerous printer's errors and printing conventions that are different from those of our time (e.g., frequent use of small case at the beginning of sentences, non-use of apostrophes to show the possessive, use of a series of periods instead of dashes). To facilitate reading, the italics have been eliminated, but to give a flavor of colonial printing, other mannerisms (including errors) have been faithfully reproduced.

agrees to Shows and Stage-playes; plainly arguing that many of those, who seemed well-affected to John, and flock'd after him, were Theatrical Hearers, Spectators rather than Auditors; they went not to hear; but to see, they went to gaze upon a new and strange Spectacle.

This general Question being propounded, the first particular Enquiry is, whether they went to see A reed shaken with the wind? The expression is Metaphorical and Proverbial. A reed when the season is calm, lifts up itself and stands upright, but no sooner doth the wind blow upon it, but it shakes and trembles, bends and bows down, and then gets up again: and again it yields and bows, and then lifts up itself again. A notable Emblem of light, empty and inconstant persons, who in times of peace and tranquillity, give a fair and plausible Testimony to the Truth; but no sooner do the winds of Temptation blow upon them, and the waves of Troubles roll over them, but they incline and yield to the prevailing Party; but when the Tempest is over, they recover themselves and assert the Truth again. The meaning then of this first Enquiry is, Went ye out into the Wilderness to see a light, vain and inconstant man, one that could confess and deny, and deny and confess the same Truth? This Interrogation is to be understood negatively and ironically; q.d. Surely ye went not into the desert to behold such a ludicrous and ridiculous sight, A man like unto a reed shaken with the wind. Under the negation of the contrary levity, our Saviour sets forth one of John's excellencies, viz. his eminent Constancy in asserting the Truth. The winds of various temptations both on the right hand and on the left, blew upon him, yet he wavered not in his testimony concerning Christ, He confessed and denied not, but confessed the truth.

Then the general Question is repeated, But what went ye out for to see? and a second particular Enquiry made, Was it to see a man clothed in soft raiment? This Interrogation hath also the force of a negation, q.d. Surely ye went not into the Wilderness to see a man clothed in silken and costly Apparel. The reason of this is added, Behold, they that wear soft clothing, are in Kings houses. Delicate and costly Apparel is to be expected in Princes Courts, and not in wilde Woods and Forrests. Under the negation of John's affectation of Courtly delicacy, our Saviour sets forth another of John's excellencies, viz. his singular gravity and sobriety, who wore rough garments, and lived on course and mean fare, Mat. 3.4. which austere kinds of life was accommodated to the place and work of his Ministry. John Preached in the Wilderness, which was no fit place for silken and soft raiment. His work was to prepare a people for the Lord, by calling them off from worldly pomp and vanities, unto repentance and mourning for sin. His peculiar habit and diet was such as became a penitentiary Preacher.

Thirdly, the generall Question is reiterated, But what went ye out for to see? and a third particular Enquiry made, Was it to see a Prophet? This Interrogation is to be understood affirmatively, q.d. no doubt but it was to see a Prophet. Had not John been a rare and excellent Minister of God, you would never have gone out of your Cities into the desert to have seen him. Thus our Saviour sets forth another of John's admirable excellencies, viz. his

Prophetical Office and Function. John was not an ordinary Interpreter of the Law, much less a Teacher of Jewish Traditions, but a Prophet, one who by the extraordinary Inspiration of the holy Ghost, made known the Mysteries of Salvation, Luke 1. 76, 77.

Lastly, our Saviour determines and concludes the Question, He, whom ye went out to see was more than a 'Prophet, much more, or abundantly more than a Prophet. This he confirms by his wonted Asseveration, Yea, I say unto you, and much more than a Prophet. How was John much more than a Prophet? John was Christs Herould sent immediately before his face, to proclaim his Coming and Kingdome, and prepare the people for the reception of him by the Baptism of Repentance, ver. 10. Hence it follows ver. 11 Among all that are born of women, there hath not risen a greater Prophet than John. John was greater than any of the Prophets that were before him, not in respect of his personal graces and virtues, (for who shall perswade us that he excelled Abraham in the grace of Faith, who was the father of the faithful, or Moses in Meekness, who was the meekest man on earth, or David in Faithfulness, who was a man after God's own heart, or Solomon in Wisdome, who was the wisest man that ever was or shall be?) but in respect of the manner of his dispensation. All the Prophets foretold Christs Coming, his Sufferings and Glory, but the Baptist was his Harbinger and Forerunner, that bare the Sword before him, Proclaimed his Presence, and made room for him in the hearts of the people. All the Prophets saw Christ afar off, but the Baptist saw him present, baptized him, and applied the Types to him personally. Behold the Lamb of God. He saw and bare record that this is the Son of God, Joh. 1.29,34. But he that is least in the Kingdome of Heaven, is greater than John. The least Prophet in the Kingdome of Heaven, i.e. the least Minister of the Gospel since Christ's Ascension, is greater than John, not in respect of the measure of his personal gifts, nor in respect of the manner of his Calling, but in respect of the Object of his Ministry, Christ on the Throne, having finished the work of our Redemption, and in respect of the degree of the revelation of Christ, which is far more clear and full. John shewed Christ in the flesh, and pointed to him with his finger, but the Ministers of the Gospel declare that he hath done and suffered all things necessary to our Salvation, and is risen again and set down at the right hand of God.

> Doct.
> Such as have sometime left their pleasant Cities and Habitations to enjoy the pure Worship of God in a Wilderness, are apt in time to abate and cool in their affection thereunto: but then the Lord calls upon them seriously and throughly to examine themselves, what it was that drew them into the Wilderness, and to consider that it was not the expectation of ludicrous levity, nor of Courtly pomp and delicacy, but of the free and clear dispensation of the Gospel and Kingdome of God.

This Doctrine consists of two distinct Branches; let me open them severally.

Branch I. Such as have sometime left their pleasant Cities and Habitations, to enjoy the pure Worship of God in a Wilderness, are apt in time to abate and cool in their affection thereunto. To what purpose did the Children of Israel leave their Cities and Houses in Egypt, and go forth into the Wilderness? was it not to hold a Feast to the Lord, and to sacrifice to the God of their fathers? That was the onely reason, which they gave of their motion to Pharaoh, Exod. 5. 1, 3. but how soon did they forget their Errand into the Wilderness, and corrupt themselves in their own Inventions? within a few moneths after their coming out of Egypt, they make a Calf in Horeb, and worship the molten Image, and change their glory into the similitude of an Ox that eateth grass, Psal. 106. 19, 20. Exod. 32. 7, 8. yea for the space of forty years in the Wilderness, while they pretended to Sacrifice to the Lord, they indeed worshipped the Stars and the Host of Heaven, and together with the Lords Tabernacle, carried about with them the Tabernacle of Moloch, Amos 5. 25, 26. Acts 7. 42, 43. And how did they spend their time in the Wilderness, but in tempting God, and in murmuring against their godly and faithful Teachers and Rulers, Moses and Aaron? Psal. 95. 8. To what purpose did the Children of the Captivity upon Cyrus his Proclamation, leave their Houses which they had built, and their Vineyards and Oliveyards which they had planted in the Province of Babylon, and return to Judea and Jerusalem, which were now become a Wilderness? was it not that they might build the House of God at Jerusalem, and set up the Temple-worship? But how shamefully did they neglect that great and honourable Work for the Space of above forty years? They pretended that Gods time was not come to build his House, because of the rubs and obstructions which they met with; whereas all their difficulties and discouragements hindred not their building of stately houses for themselves, Hag. 1. 2, 3, 4. To what purpose did Jerusalem & all Judea, & all the region round about Jordan, leave their several Cities and Habitations, and flock into the Wilderness of Judea? was it not to see that burning and shining light, which God had raised up? To hear his heavenly Doctrine, and partake of that new Sacrament, which he administred? O how they were affected with his rare and excellent gifts! with his clear, lively and powerful Ministry! The Kingdome of Heaven pressed in upon them with a holy violence, and the violent, the zealous and affectionate hearers of the Gospel, took it by force, Mat. 11. 12. Luk. 16. 16. They leapt over all discouragements and impediments, whether outward, as Legal Rites and Ceremonies, or inward, the sense of their own sin and unworthiness, and pressed into the Kingdome of God, as men rush into a Theatre to see a pleasant Sight, or as Souldiers run into a besieged City, to take the Spoil thereof: but their hot fit is soon over, their affection lasted but for an hour, i.e. a short season, Joh. 5. 35.

Reas. 1.   Because the affection of many to the Ministry of the Gospel and the pure Worship of God, is built upon temporary and transitory grounds, as the novelty and strangeness of the matter, the rareness and excellency of Ministerial Gifts, the voice of the people, the countenance of great men, and the hope of worldly advantage. The Jews had lien in ignorance and darkness a long time, being trained up under the superstitious observances of their old Traditions, which were vain, empty and unprofitable Customes, and the

Church wanted the gift of Prophecy about four hundred years, and therefore when John the Baptist arose like a bright and burning light, shining amongst them with admirable gifts of the Spirit, and extraordinary severity and gravity of manners, proclaiming the Coming and Kingdome of the Messias, (which had been oft promised and long expected) and pressing the people to Repentance and good works; O how they admire and reverence him? especially, when grown popular, and countenanced by Herod the Tetrarch. What sweet affections are kindled! what great expectations are raised! what ravishing joy is conceived! Hoping (as its probable) to make use of his Authority to call off the Roman yoke, and recover their Civil Liberties, Riches and Honours. But after a little acquaintance with John, (for he was a publick Preacher but a year and half) his Doctrine, Administrations and Prophetical Gifts, grew common and stale things, and of little esteem with them; especially, when they saw their carnal hopes frustrated, the Rulers disaffected, and Herods countenance and carriage toward him changed.

Reas. 2.   Because Prejudices and Offences are apt to arise in the hearts of many against the faithful Dispensers of the Gospel. The Pharisees and Lawyers came among others to the Baptism of John, but when they hear his sharp reprehensions of their Viperous Opinions and Practices, they nauseate his Doctrine, repudiate his Baptism, calumniate his Conversation, Luke 7. 30. Herodias hath an inward grudge and a quarrel against him, because he found fault with her incestuous Marriage, Mar. 6. 19. Yea, that very Age and Generation of the Jews, were like to a company of surly, sullen and froward children, whom no Musick can please, they neither dance after the Pipe, nor make lamentation after the mourner. They inveigh against John's austerity, saying that he was transported with diabolical fury, and was an enemy to humane society: and they do as much distaste and abhor Christ's gentleness and familiarity, traducing him, as being a sensual and voluptuous person, given to intemperance and luxury, and a Patron and Abettor of looseness and profaneness, Mat. 11. 16-19. Thus doth the frowardness and stubbornness of man, resist and oppose the wisdome and goodness of God, who useth various wayes and instruments to compass poor sinners, but they through their folly and perverseness, frustrate, disanul and abrogate the counsel of God against themselves. The evil spirit that troubled Saul, was quieted and allayed by the sweet Melody of David's Harp: but the mad and outragious fury that transports men against the Truth and the Ministry thereof, cannot be quieted and allayed by the voice of the Charmers, charm they never so wisely.

Branch II.   When men abate and cool in their affection to the pure Worship of God, which they went into the Wilderness to enjoy, the Lord calls upon them seriously and throughly to examine themselves, what it was that drew them into the Wilderness, and to consider that it was not the expectation of ludicrous levity, nor of Courtly pomp and delicacy, but of the free and clear dispensation of the Gospel and Kingdome of God. Our Saviour knowing that the people had lost their first love and singular affection to the revelation of his grace by the Ministry of his Herauld John, He is very intense in examining them, what expectation drew them into the Wilderness: He doth not once nor twice, but thrice propound that Question, What went ye out into the Wilderness to see? Yea, in particular he enquires whether it were to see a man that was like to a Reed shaken with the wind? or whether it were to see a man clothed like a Courtier, or whether it were to see a Prophet, and then determines the Question[s], concluding that it was to see a great and excellent Prophet, and that had not they seen rare and admirable things in him, they would never have gone out into the Wilderness unto him.

The Reason is, Because the serious consideration of the inestimable grace and mercy of God in the free and clear dispensation of the Gospel and Kingdome of God, is a special means to convince men of their folly and perverseness in undervaluing the same, and a sanctified remedy to recover their affections thereunto. The Lord foreseeing the defection of Israel after Moses his death, commands him to write that Prophetical Song, recorded in Deut. 32. as a Testimony against them: wherein the chief remedy, which he prescribes for the prevention and healing of their Apostacy, is their calling to remembrance Gods great and signal love in manifesting himself to them in the Wilderness, in conducting them safely and mercifully, and giving them possession of their promised Inheritance, ver. 7-14. And when Israel was apostatized and fallen, the Lord to convince them of their ingratitude and folly, brings to their remembrance his deliverance of them out of Egypt, his leading them through the Wilderness for the space of forty years, and not onely giving them possession of their Enemies Land, but also raising up, even of their own sons, Prophets, faithful and eminent Ministers, and of their young men Nazarites, who being separated from worldly delights and encumbrances, were Paterns of Purity and Holiness: all which were great and obliging mercies. Yea, the Lord appeals to their own Consciences, whether these his favours were not real and signal, Amos 2.10, 11. The Prophet Jeremiah, that he might reduce the people from their backslidings, cries in the ears of Jerusalem, with earnestness and boldness declaring unto them, that the Lord remembred how well they stood affected towards him, when he first chose them to be his people and espoused them to himself, how they followed him in the Wildnerness, and kept close to him in their long and wearisome passage through the uncultured Desert; how they were then consecrated to God, and set apart for his Worship and Service; as the first-fruits are wont to be sequestred and devoted to God: and thereupon expostulates with them for their forsaking the Lord, and following after their Idols, Jer. 2. 2, 3, 5, 6. Surely our Saviour's Dialogism with his Hearers in my Text, is not a meer Rhetorical Elegancy to adorn his Testimony concerning John, but a clear and strong conviction of their folly in slighting and despising that which they sometime so highly pretended unto, and a wholesome admonition and direction how to recover their primitive affection to his Doctrine and Administration.

USE I.   Of solemn and serious Enquiry to us all in this general Assembly, Whether we have not in a great measure forgotten our Errand into the Wilderness. You have solemnly professed before God, Angels and Men, that the Cause of your leaving your Country, Kindred and Fathers houses, and transporting your selves with your Wives, Little Ones and Substance over the vast Ocean into this waste and howling Wilderness, was your Liberty to walk in the Faith of the Gospel with all good Conscience according to the Order of the Gospel, and your enjoyment of the pure worship of God according to his Institution, without humane Mixtures and Impositions. Now let us sadly consider whether our ancient and primitive affections to the Lord Jesus, his glorious Gospel, his pure and Spiritual Worship and the Order of his House, remain, abide and continue firm, constant, entire and inviolate. Our Saviour's reiteration of this Question, What went ye out into the Wilderness to see? is no idle repetition, but a sad conviction of our dulness and backwardness to this great duty, and a clear demonstration of the weight and necessity thereof. It may be a grief to us to be put upon such an Inquisition; as it is said of Peter, Joh. 21. 17. Peter was grieved, because he said unto him the third time, Lovest thou me? but the Lord knoweth that a strict and rigid examination of our hearts in this point, is no more then necessary. Wherefore let us call to remembrance the former dayes, and consider whether it was not then better with us, then it is now.

In our first and best times the Kingdome of Heaven brake in upon us with a holy violence, and every man pressed into it. What mighty efficacy and power had the clear and faithful dispensation of the Gospel upon your hearts? how affectionately and zealously did you entertain the Kingdome of God? How careful were you, even all sorts, young and old, high and low, to take hold of the opportunities of your Spiritual good and edification? ordering your secular affairs (which were wreathed and twisted together with great variety) so as not to interfere with your general Calling, but that you might attend upon the Lord without distraction. How diligent and faithful in preparing your hearts for the reception of the Word, laying apart all filthiness and superfluity of naughtiness, that you might receive with meekness the ingraffed word, which is able to save your souls; and purging out all malice, guile, hypocrisies, envies, and all evil speakings, and as new-born babes, desiring the sincere milk of the word, that ye might grow thereby? How attentive in hearing the everlasting Gospel, watching daily at the gates of Wisdome, and waiting at the posts of her doors, that ye might finde eternal life, and obtain favour of the Lord? Gleaning day by day in the field of Gods Ordinances, even among the Sheaves, and gathering up handfuls, which the Lord let fall of purpose for you, and at night going home and beating out what you had gleaned, by Meditation, Repetition, Conference, and therewith feeding your selves and your families. How painful were you in recollecting, repeating and discoursing of what you heard, whetting the Word of God upon the hearts of your Children, Servants and Neighbours? How fervent in Prayer to Almighty God for his divine Blessing upon the Seed sown, that it might take root and fructifie? O what a reverent esteem had you in those days of Christ's faithful Ambassadors, that declared unto you the Word of Reconciliation! How beautiful were the feet of them, that preached the Gospel of peace, and brought the glad tidings of Salvation! you esteemed them highly in love for their works sake. Their Persons, Names and Comforts were precious in your eyes; you counted your selves blessed in the enjoyment of a Pious, Learned and Orthodox Ministry: and though you ate the bread of adversity and drank the water of affliction, yet you rejoyced in this, that your eyes saw your Teachers, they were not removed into corners, and your ears heard a word behind you, saying, This is the way, walk ye in it, when you turned to the right hand and when you turned to the left, Isa. 30. 20, 21. What earnest and ardent desires had you in those dayes after Communion with Christ in the holy Sacraments? With desire you desired to partake of the Seals of the Covenant. You thought your Evidences for Heaven not sure nor authentick, unless the Broad-Seals of the Kingdome were annexed. What solicitude was there in those dayes to seek the Lord after the right Order? What searching of the holy Scriptures, what Collations among your Leaders, both in their private Meetings and publick Councils and Synods, to finde out the Order, Which Christ hath constituted and established in his House? What fervent zeal was there then against Sectaries and Hereticks, and all manner of Heterodoxies? You could not bear them that were evil, but tried them that pretended to New Light and Revelations, and found them liars. What pious Care was there of Sister-Churches, that those that wanted Breasts, might be supplied, and that those that wanted Peace, their Dissentions might be healed? What readiness was there in those dayes to call for the help of Neighbour-Elders and Brethren, in case of any Difference or Division that could not be healed at home? What reverence was there then of the Sentence of a Council, as being decisive and issuing the Controversie? According to that ancient Proverbial Saying, They shall surely ask counsel at Abel, and so they ended the matter, 2 Sam. 20. 18. What holy Endeavours were there in those dayes to propagate Religion to your Children and Posterity, training them up in the nurture and admonition of the Lord, keeping them under the awe of government, restraining their enormities and extravagancies; charging them to know the God of their fathers, and serve him with a perfect heart and willing minde; and publickly asserting and maintaining their interest in the Lord and in his holy Covenant, and zealously opposing those that denied the same?

And then had the Churches rest throughout the several Colonies, and were edified: and walking in the fear of the Lord, and in the comfort of the holy Ghost, were multiplied. O how your Faith grew exceedingly! you proceeded from faith to faith, from a less to a greater degree and measure, growing up in him, who is our Head, and receiving abundance of grace and of the gift of righteousness, that you might reign in life by Jesus Christ. O how your Love and Charity towards each other abounded! O what comfort of Love! what bowels and mercies! what affectionate care was there one of another! what a holy Sympathy in Crosses and Comforts, weeping with those that wept, and rejoycing with those that rejoyced!

But who is there left among you, that saw these Churches in their first glory, and how do you see them now? Are they not in your eyes in comparison thereof, as nothing? How is the gold become dim! how is the most fine gold changed! Is not the Temper, Complexion and Countenance of the Churches strangely altered? Doth not a careless, remiss, flat, dry, cold, dead frame of spirit, grow in upon us secretly, strongly, prodigiously? They that have Ordinances, are as though they had none; and they that hear the Word, as though they heard it not; and they that pray, as though they prayed not; and they that receive Sacraments, as though they received them not; and they that are exercised in the holy things, using them by the by, as matters of custome and ceremony, so as not to hinder their eager prosecution of other things which their hearts are set upon. Yea and in some particular Congregations amongst us, is there not in stead of a sweet smell, a stink? and in stead of a girdle, a rent? and in stead of a stomacher, a girding with sackcloth? and burning in stead of beauty? yea the Vineyard is all overgrown with thorns, and nettles cover the face thereof, and the stone wall thereof is broken down, Prov. 24.31. yea, and that which is the most sad and certain sign of calamity approaching, Iniquity aboundeth, and the love of many waxeth cold, Mat. 24.12. Pride, Contention, Worldliness, Covetousness, Luxury, Drunkenness and Uncleanness break in like a flood upon us, and good men grow cold in their love to God and to one another. If a man be cold in his bed, let them lay on the more clothes, that he may get heat: but we are like to David in his old age, they covered him with clothes, but he got no heat, 2 Sam. 1. 1. The Lord heaps mercies, favours, blessings upon us, and loads us daily with his benefits, but all his love and bounty cannot heat and warm our hearts and affections. Well, the furnace is able to heat and melt the coldest Iron: but how oft hath the Lord cast us into the hot furnace of Affliction and Tribulation, and we have been scorched and burnt, yet not melted, but hardened thereby, Isa. 63. 17. How long hath God kept us in the furnace day after day, moneth after moneth, year after year? but all our Afflictions, Crosses, Trials have not been able to keep our hearts in a warm temper.

Now let me freely deliberate with you, what may be the Causes and Grounds of such decayes and languishings in our affections to, and estimation of that which we came into the Wilderness to enjoy? Is it because there is no bread, neither is there any water, and our soul loatheth this light bread? Numb. 21. 5. Our soul is dried away, and there is nothing at all, besides this Manna, before our eyes, Numb. 11. 6. What, is Manna no bread? Is this Angelical food, light bread, which cannot satisfie, but starves the Soul? Doth our Soul loath the bread of Heaven? The Lord be merciful to us: The full soul loatheth the honey-comb, Prov. 27. 7.

What then is the cause of our decayes and languishings? Is it because the Spirit of the Lord is straitned and limited in the dispensers of the Gospel, and hence our joyes and comforts are lessened and shortned? O thou that art named the house of Jacob, is the Spirit of the Lord straitned? are those his doings? Do not my words do good to him that walketh uprightly? Mic. 2. 7. Surely it is not for want of fulness in the Spirit of God, that he withholds comforts and blessings from any; neither doth he delight in threatnings and judgements, but his words both promise and perform that which is good and comfortable to them that walk uprightly. The Spirit is able to enlarge it self unto the reviving and cheering of every man's heart; and that should we experience, did not our inquity put a barre. 2 Cor. 6. 11, 12. O ye Corinthians, our mouth is open unto you, our heart is enlarged: Ye are not straitned in your own bowels. The Spirit of God dilateth and enlargeth the heart of the faithfull Ministry for the good of the people; but many times the people are straitned in their own bowels, and cannot receive such a large portion, as the Lord hath provided for them. What then is the cause of our coolings, faintings and languishings? The grand and principal cause is our Unbelief: We believe not the Grace and Power of God in Christ. Where is that lively exercise of faith, which ought to be, in our attendance upon the Lord in his holy Ordinances? Christ came to Nazareth with his heart full of love and compassion, and his hands full of blessings to bestow upon his old Acquaintance and Neighbours, among whom he had been brought up, but their Unbelief restrained his tender mercies, and bound his Omnipotent hands, that he could not do any great or illustrious Miracle amongst them. Mat. 13. 58. Mark 6. 5, 6. He could do there no mighty work — and he marvelled because of their unbelief. Unbelief straitens the grace and power of Christ, and hinders the communication of divine favours and special mercies. The word preached profits not, when it is not mixed with faith in them that hear it, Heb. 4. 2. We may pray earnestly, but if we ask not in faith, how can we expect to receive any thing of the Lord? Jam. 1. 6, 7.

But though Unbelief be the principal, yet it is not the sole cause of our decayes and languishings: Inordinate worldly Cares, predominant Lusts, and malignant Passions and Distempers stifle and choak the Word, and quench our affections to the Kingdome of God. Luke 8. 14. The Manna was gathered early in the morning, when the Sun waxed hot, it melted, Exod. 16. 21; It was a fearful Judgement on Dathan and Abiram, that the earth opened its mouth and swallowed them up. How many Professors of Religion, are swallowed up alive by earthly affections? Such as escape the Lime-pit of Pharisaical Hypocrisie, fall into the Coal-pit of Sadducean Atheism and Epicurism. Pharisaism and Sadduceism do almost divide the Professing World between them. Some split upon the Rock of Affected ostentation of singular Piety and Holiness, and others are drawn into the Whirpool, and perish in the Gulf of Sensuality.and Luxury.

If any question how seasonable such a Discourse may be upon such a Day, as this; let him consider, Hag. 2. 10-14. In the four and twentieth day of the ninth moneth, in the second year of Darius, came the word of the Lord by Haggai the Prophet, saying, Thus saith the Lord of Hosts, Ask now the Priests concerning the law, saying, If one bear holy flesh in the skirt of his garmet, and with his skirt do touch bread, or pottage, or wine, or oyl, or any meat, shall it be holy? And the Priests answered and said, No. Then said Haggai, If one that is unclean by a dead body, touch any of these, shall it be unclean? And the Priests answered and said, It shall be unclean. Then answered Haggai and said, So is this people, and so is this nation before me, saith the Lord; and so is every work of their hands, and that which they offer there is unclean. It was an high and great day, wherein the Prophet spake these words, and an holy and honourable Work, which the people were employed in. For this day they laid the Foundation of the Lords Temple, ver. 18. nevertheless, the Lord saw it necessary this very day to represent and declare unto them, the pollution and uncleanness both of their persons and of their holy Services, that they might be deeply humbled before God, and carry on their present Work more holily and purely. What was their uncleanness? Their eager pursuit of their private interests, took off their hearts and affections from the affairs of the House of God. It seems they pleased themselves with this, that the Altar stood upon its Bases, and Sacrifices were daily offered thereon, and the building of the Temple was onely deferred untill a fit opportunity were afforded, free from disturbance and opposition: and having now gained such a season, they are ready to build the Temple: but the Lord convinceth them out of the Law, that their former negligence was not expiated by their daily Sacrifices, but the guilt thereof rendred both the Nation and this holy and honourable Work, which they were about, vile and unclean in the sight of God. And having thus shewn them their spiritual uncleanness, he encourageth them to go on with the work in hand, the building of the Temple, promising them from this day to bless them, ver. 18.

USE II. Of Exhortation, To excite and stir us all up to attend and prosecute our Errand into the Wilderness. To what purpose came we into this place, and what expectation drew us hither? Surely, not the expectation of ludicrous Levity. We came not hither to see a Reed shaken with the wind. Then let not us be Reeds, light, empty, vain, hollow hearted Professors, shaken with every wind of Temptation: but solid, serious and sober Christians, constant and stedfast in the Profession and Practice of the Truth, Trees of Righteousness, the planting of the Lord, that he may be glorified, holding fast the profession of our faith without wavering.

Alas, there is such variety and diversity of Opinions and Judgements, that we know not what to believe.

Were there not as various and different Opinions touching the Person of Christ, even in the dayes of his flesh? Some said that He was John the Baptist, some Elias, others Jeremias, or one of the old Prophets. Some said he was a gluttonous man, a wine-bibber, a friend of publicans and sinners: others said He was a Samaritan, and had a Devil; yet the Disciples knew what to believe. Whom say ye that I am? Thou art Christ, the Son of the living God, Mat. 16. 15, 16. The various heterodox Opinions of the people, serve as a foil or tinctured leaf to set off the lustre and beauty of the Orthodox and Apostolical Faith. This is truly commendable, when in such variety and diversity of Apprehensions, you are not byassed by any sinister respects, but discern, embrace and profess the Truth, as it is in Christ Jesus.

But to what purpose came we into the Wilderness, and what expectation drew us hither? Not the expectation of Courtly Pomp and Delicacy. We came not hither to see men clothed like Courtiers. The affectation of Courtly Pomp and Gallantry, is very unsuitable in a Wilderness. Gorgeous Attire is comely in Princes Courts, if it exceed not the limits of Christian Sobriety: but excess in Kings houses, escapes not divine Vengeance. Zeph. I. 8. ---- I will punish the Princes and the Kings children, and all such as are clothed with strange

Apparel. The pride and haughtiness of the Ladies of Zion in their superfluous Ornaments and stately gestures, brought wrath upon themselves, upon their Husbands, and upon their Children, yea and upon the whole Land, Isa. 3. 16-26. How much more intolerable and abominable is excess of this kinde in a Wilderness, where we are so far removed from the Riches and Honours of Princes Courts?

To what purpose then came we into the Wilderness, and what expectation drew us hither? Was it not the expectation of the pure and faithful Dispensation of the Gospel and Kingdome of God? The times were such that we could not enjoy it in our own Land: and therefore having obtained Liberty and a gracious Patent from our Sovereign, we left our Country, Kindred and Fathers houses, and came into these wilde Woods and Deserts; where the Lord hath planted us, and made us dwell in a place of our own, that we might move no more, and that the children of wickedness might afflict not us any more, 2 Sam. 7. 10. What is it that distinguisheth New-England from other Colonies and Plantations in America? Not our transportation over the Atlantick Ocean, but the Ministry of Gods faithful Prophets, and the fruition of his holy Ordinances. Did not the Lord bring the Philistines from Caphtor, and the Assyrians from Kir, as well as Israel from the land of Egypt? Amos 9 7. But by a Prophet the Lord brought Israel out of Egypt, and by a Prophet was he preserved, Hos. 12. 13. What, is the Price and Esteem of Gods Prophets, and their faithful Dispensations, now fallen in our hearts?

The hardships, difficulties and sufferings, which you have exposed your selves unto, that you might dwell in the House of the Lord, and leave your Little Ones under the shadow of the wings of the God of Israel, have not been few nor small. And shall we now withdraw our selves and our Little Ones from under those healing Wings, and lose that full Reward, which the Lord hath in his heart and hand to bestow upon us? Did we not with Mary choose this for our Part, to sit at Christs feet and hear his word? and do we now repent of our choice, and prefer the Honours, Pleasures and Profits of the world before it? You did run well: who doth hinder you, that you should not obey the truth? Gal. 5. 7.

Hath the Lord been wanting to us, or failed our expectation? Micah 6. 3. O my people, what have I done unto thee, and wherein have I wearied thee? testify against me. Jer. 2. 5. What iniquity have your fathers found in me, that they are gone far from me? and ver. 31. O generation, see ye the word of the Lord: have I been a wilderness unto Israel? a land of darkness? May not the Lord say unto us, as Pharaoh did to Hadad, I King 11. 22. What hast thou lacked with me, that behold, thou seekest to go to thine own Country? Nay, what could have been done more, then what the Lord hath done for us? Isa. 5. 4.

How sadly hath the Lord testified against us, because of our loss of our first love, and our remissness and negligence in his Work? Why hath the Lord smitten us with Blasting and Mildew now seven years together, superadding sometimes severe Drought, sometimes great Tempests, Floods, and sweeping Rains, that leave no food behinde them? Is it not because the Lords House lyeth waste? Temple-work in our Hearts, Families, Churches is shamefully neglected? What should I make mention of Signes in the Heavens and in the Earth, Blazing-Stars, Earthquakes, dreadful Thunders and Lightnings, fearful Burnings? What meaneth the heat of his great Anger, in calling home so many of his Ambassadors? In plucking such burning and shining Lights out of the Candlesticks; the principal Stakes out of our Hedges; the Cornerstones out of our Walls? In removing such faithful Shepherds from their Flocks, and breaking down our defenced Cities, Iron Pillars, and Brazen-Walls? Seemeth it a small thing unto us, that so many of Gods Prophets (whose Ministry we came into the Wilderness to enjoy) are taken from us in so short a time? Is it not a Sign that God is making a way for his Wrath, when he removes his Chosen out of the Gap? Doth he not threaten us with a Famine of the Word, the Scattering of the Flock, the Breaking of the Candlesticks, and the turning of the Songs of the Temple into howlings?

It is high time for us to remember whence we are fallen, and repent, and do our first works. Wherefore let us lift up the hands that hang down, and strengthen the feeble knees, and make straight paths for our feet, lest that which is lame, be turned out of the way, but let it rather be healed, Heb. 12. 12, 13. Labour we to redress our Faintings and Swervings, and address our selves to the Work of the Lord. Let us arise and build, and the Lord will be with us, and from this day will he bless us.

Alas, we are feeble and impotent; our hands are withered, and our strength dried up.

Remember the man that had a withered hand: Christ saith unto him, Stretch forth thy hand; and he stretched it forth; and it was restored whole, like as the other, Mat. 12. 13. How could he stretch forth his hand, when it was withered, the Blood and Spirits dried up, and the Nerves and Sinews shrunk up? The Almighty Power of Christ accompanying his Command, enabled the man to stretch forth his withered hand, and in stretching it forth, restored it whole, like as the other. Where the Soveraignty of Christ's Command takes place in the Conscience, there is effectual grace accompanying it to the healing of our Spiritual Feebleness and Impotency, and the enabling of us to perform the duty incumbent on us. Though we have no might, no strength, yet at Christ's Command, make an essay. Where the word of a King is, there is power.

But alas, our Bruise is incurable and our Wound grievous, there is none to repair the Breach, there is no healing Medicine.

The Lord Jesus, the great Physician of Israel, hath undertaken the Cure. I will restore health unto thee, and I will heal thee of thy wounds, saith the Lord, Jer. 30. 17. No case is to be accounted desperate or incurable, which Christ takes in hand. If he undertake to heal Jairus his daughter, he will have her death esteemed but a sleep, in reference to his power. She is not dead, but sleepeth, Mat. 9. 24. When Christ came to Lazarus his grave, and bade them take away the stone, Martha saith, Lord, by this time he stinketh; for he hath been dead four dayes: But Christ answereth, Said I not unto thee, that if thou wouldest believe, thou shouldest see the glory of God? Joh. 11. 40. Let us give glory to God by believing his word, and we shall have real and experimental manifestations of his glory for our good and comfort.

But alas, our hearts are sadly prejudiced against the Means and Instruments, by which we might expect that Christ should cure and heal us.

Were not the hearts of John's Disciples leavened with carnal emulation and prejudices against Christ himself? They would not own him to be the Messias, nor believe their Master's Testimony concerning him: insomuch that the Lord saw it necessary that John should decrease and be abased, that Christ might encrease and be exalted: and therefore suffered Herod to shut up John in Prison, and keep him in durance about twelve moneths, and at length to cut off his head, that so these fondlings might be weaned from their Nurse; and when John was dead, his Disciples resort to Jesus, acquaint him with the calamity that befell them, and were perfectly reconciled to him, passing into his School, and becoming his Disciples, Mat. 14. 12.

But alas, the Times are difficult and perillous; the Wind is stormy, and the Sea tempestuous; the Vessel heaves and sits, and tumbles up and down in the rough and boisterous waters, and is in danger to be swallowed up.

Well, remember that the Lord sitteth upon the flood, yea the Lord sitteth King for ever, Psal. 29. 10. His way is in the sea, and his path in the great waters, and his footsteps are not known, Psal. 77. 19. He stilleth the noise of the seas, the noise of their waves, and the tumult of the people, Psal. 65. 7. He saith to the raging Sea, Peace, be still: and the wind ceaseth, and there is a great calm, Mark 4. 39. Yea, he can enable his people to tread and walk upon the waters. To sail and swim in the waters, is an easie matter; but to walk upon the waters, as upon a pavement, is an act of wonder. Peter at Christ's call came down out of the ship and walked on the water to go to Jesus, Matth. 14. 29. and as long as his Faith held, it upheld him from sinking; when his Faith failed, his body sunk: but he cried to the Lord, and he stretched forth his hand and caught him, and said unto him, O thou of little faith, wherefore didst thou doubt?

But what shall we do for bread? The encrease of the field and the labour of the Husbandman fails.

Hear Christ's answer to his Disciples, when they were troubled, because there was but one Loaf in the ship. O ye of little faith, why reason ye, because you have no bread? perceive ye not yet, neither understand? have ye your heart yet hardened? having eyes, see ye not? and having ears, hear ye not? and do ye not remember? Mark 8. 17, 18. Mat. 16. 8, 9. Those which have had large and plentiful experience of the grace and power of Christ in providing for their outward Sustenance, and relieving of their Necessities, when ordinary and usual Means have failed, are worthy to be severely reprehended, if afterward they grow anxiously careful and solicitous, because of the defect of outward supplies. In the whole Evangelicall History, I finde not that ever the Lord Jesus did so sharply rebuke his Disciples for any thing, as for that fit and pang of Worldly care and solicitude about Bread. Attend we our Errand, upon which Christ sent us into the Wilderness, and he will provide Bread for us. Math. 6. 33. Seek ye first the Kingdome of God, and his Righteousness, and all these things shall be added unto you.

But we have many Adversaries, and they have their subtile Machinations and Contrivances, and how soon we may be surprized, we know not.

Our diligent Attention to the Ministry of the Gospel, is a special means to check and restrain the rage and fury of Adversaries. The people's assiduity in attendance upon Christ's Ministry, was the great obstacle that hindred the execution of the bloody Counsels of the Pharisees. Luk. 19. 47, 48. He taught daily in the Temple, but the chief Priests and the Scribes, and the chief of the people, sought to destroy him, and could not finde what they might do: for all the people were very attentive to hear him. If the people cleave to the Lord, to his Prophets, and to his Ordinances, it will strike such a fear into the hearts of enemies, that they will be at their wits ends, and not know what to do. However, in this way we have the promise of divine Protection and Preservation. Revel. 3. 10. Because thou hast kept the word of my Patience, I also will keep thee from the hour of Temptation, which shall come upon all the world, to try them that dwell upon the earth. Let us with Mary choose this for our Portion, To sit at Christ's feet and hear his word; and whosoever complain against us, the Lord Jesus will plead for us, as he did for her, and say, They have chosen that good part, which shall not be taken away from them, Luk. 10, 42. AMEN.

FINIS

Abraham's Offering Up his Son Isaac

George Whitefield

Commentary

The adherence to the "True Faith" gradually subsided as the years went by. Some Congregationalists strayed from Calvinist theology, and adherents of other faiths arrived. Life became more secularized as people seemed more interested in money, luxuries and politics. In 1691, representative of this social change, the Massachusetts charter was replaced by one which based voting rights on property qualifications rather than church membership.

The secular drift worried preachers of all faiths, not just Puritans. By the 1730s, rhetorical efforts were under way to "revive" or "reawaken" religious fervor. Preachers conducted "revivals" or "awakenings" in their own parishes, and unusually good preachers were invited to conduct them in other communities. Their efforts were marked by a new form of preaching known to them as "enthusiastical" and to us as "evangelical" or "revivalist." Believing that religion was more a matter of the heart than the head, "enthusiasts" paid little attention to theology and relied heavily on emotional appeals.

Although several "awakenings" occurred earlier, the "Great Awakening" came with the tour of George Whitefield (1714-1770). A native Englishman ordained in the Church of England, he got into trouble with the hierarchy for supporting the Wesley brothers' efforts to initiate ecclesiastical reforms. The Wesleyan movement, which culminated in the new Methodist denomination, was characterized by "enthusiastical" preaching. Although Whitefield was only twenty-five when his American tour began, colonial newspapers had already enhanced his ethos by reporting his tremendous success as a revivalist in England and his work with an orphanage in Georgia.

Whitefield's fifteen-month tour (October 1739-January 1741) was made to raise money for the orphanage, but local preachers welcomed him to "reawaken" religion and publicized his coming well in advance. Moving quickly from place to place, Whitefield traveled over 5000 miles and delivered over 500 sermons, usually to large crowds that included people from nearby communities and which could be accommodated only in an open field. He used various organizational schemes, but often (as in the following text) he built his sermons around a (somewhat embellished) narrative of a biblical event, which (being something of a ham actor) he acted out.

Being on tour, Whitefield repeated each sermon many times. He did not speak from manuscript, and a few surviving texts were either published in England before he came to America (but repeated here), written by him weeks after delivery or transcribed by someone during delivery (badly, according to his complaints). Surviving texts can only be regarded as representative of his method. The most complete collection was compiled by John Gillies shortly after Whitefield's death. The following is reproduced from a later edition of Gillies' *Memoirs and Sermons of Rev. George Whitefield* (Philadelphia: Leary & Getz, 1854), pp. 373-84.

Abraham's Offering
Up His Son Isaac

GENESIS XXII. 12.

> And he said, Lay not thine hand upon the lad, neither do thou any thing unto him; for now I know that thou fearest God, seeing thou hast not withheld thy son, thine only son from me.

The great apostle Paul, in one of his epistles, informs us, that "whatsoever was written aforetime, was written for our learning, that we through patience and comfort of the holy scripture might have hope." And as without faith it is impossible to please God, or to be accepted in Jesus, the Son of his love; we may be assured, that whatever instances of a more than common faith are recorded in the book of God, they were more immediately designed by the Holy Spirit for our learning and imitation, upon whom the ends of the world are come. For this reason, the author of the epistle to the Hebrews, in the eleventh chapter, mentions a noble catalogue of Old Testament saints and martyrs, "who subdued kingdoms, wrought righteousness, stopped the mouths of lions, &c. and are gone before us to inherit the promises." A sufficient confutation, I think, of their error, who lightly esteem the Old Testament saints, and would not have them mentioned to Christians, at persons whose faith and patience we are called upon more immediately to follow. If this was true, the apostle would never have produced such a cloud of

---

The original printing of this address included extensive use of italics and numerous printer's errors and printing conventions that are different from those of our time (e.g., frequent use of small case at the beginning of sentences, non-use of apostrophes to show the possessive, use of a series of periods instead of dashes). To facilitate reading, the italics have been eliminated, but to give a flavor of colonial printing, other mannerisms (including errors) have been faithfully reproduced.

witnesses out of the Old Testament, to excite the christians of the first, and consequently purest age of the church, to continue steadfast and immovable in the possession of their faith. Amidst this catalogue of saints, methinks, the patriarch Abraham shines the brightest and differs from the others, as one star differeth from another star in glory; for he shone with such distinguished luster, that he was called the friend of God, the father of the faithful; and those who believe on Christ, are said to be sons and daughters of, and to be blessed with, faithful Abraham. Many trials of his faith did God send this great and good man, after he had commanded him to get out from his country, and from his kindred, unto a land which he should show him; but the last was the most severe of all, I mean, that of offering up his only son. This, by the divine assistance, I propose to make the subject of your present meditation, and, by way of conclusion, to draw some practical inferences, as God shall enable me, from this instructive story.

The sacred penman begins the narrative thus; verse 1. "And it came to pass, after these things, God did tempt Abraham." "After these things," that is, after he had underwent many severe trials before, after he was old, full of days, and might flatter himself perhaps that the troubles and toils of life were now finished; "after these things, God did tempt Abraham." Christians, you know not what trials you may meet with before you die; notwithstanding you may have suffered, and been tried much already, yet, it may be a greater measure is still behind, which you are to fill up. "Be not high-minded, but fear." Our last trials, in all probability, will be the greatest: and we can never say our warfare is accomplished, or our trials finished, till we bow down our heads, and give up the ghost. "And it came to pass, after these things, that God did tempt Abraham."

"God did tempt Abraham." But can the scripture contradict itself? Does not the apostle James tell us, that God tempts no man; and God does tempt no man to evil, or on purpose to draw him into sin; for, when a man is thus tempted, he is drawn away of his own heart's lust, and enticed. But in another sense, God may be said to tempt, I mean, to try his servants; and in this sense we are to understand that passage of Matthew, where we are told, that "Jesus was led up by the Spirit (the good Spirit) into the wilderness, to be tempted of the devil." And our Lord, in that excellent form of prayer which he has been pleased to give us, does not require us to pray that we may not absolutely be led into temptation, but delivered from the evil of it; whence we may plainly infer, that God sees fit sometimes to lead us into temptation, that is, to bring us into such circumstances as will try our faith, and other Christian graces. In this sense we are to understand the expression before us, "God did tempt or try Abraham."

How God was pleased to reveal his will at this time to his faithful servant, whether by the Shechinah, or divine appearance, or by a small still voice, as he spoke to Elijah, or by a whisper, like that of the Spirit to Philip, when he commanded him to join himself to the Eunuch's chariot, we are not told, nor is it material to inquire. It is enough that we are informed, God said unto him, Abraham; and that Abraham knew that it was the voice of God: for "he said, behold, here I am." O what a holy familiarity (if I may so speak) is there between God and those holy souls that are united to him by faith in Christ Jesus! God says, Abraham; and Abraham said, (it should seem without the least surprise,) "Behold, here I am." Being reconciled to God by the death and obedience of Christ, which he rejoiced in, and saw by faith afar off; he did not, like guilty Adam, seek the trees of the garden to hide himself from, but takes pleasure in conversing with God, and talketh with him, as a man talketh with his friend. O that Christless sinners knew what it is to have fellowship with the Father and the Son! They would envy the happiness of saints, and count it all joy to be termed enthusiasts and fools for Christ's sake.

But what does God say unto Abraham; verse 2. "Take now thy son, thine only son Isaac, whom thou lovest, and get thee into the land of Moriah, and offer him there for a burnt-offering upon one of the mountains which I shall tell thee of."

Every word deserves our particular observation. Whatever he was to do, he must do it now, immediately, without conferring with flesh and blood. But what must he do? Take now thy son. Had God said, take now a firstling, or choicest lamb or beast of thy flock, and offer it up for a burnt-offering, it would not have appeared so ghastly: but for God to say, "Take now thy son, and offer him up for a burnt-offering," one would have imagined, was enough to stagger the strongest faith. But this is not all: It must not only be a son, but thine only son Isaac, whom thou lovest. If it must be a son, and not a beast, that must be offered, why will not Ishmael do, the son of the bond-woman? No, it must be his only son, the heir of all, his Isaac, by interpretation laughter, the son of his old age, in whom his soul delighted; whom thou lovest, says God, in whose life his own was wrapped up: And this son, this only son, this Isaac, the son of his love, must be taken now, even now without delay, and be offered up by his own father, for a burnt-offering, upon one of the mountains of the which God would tell him.

Well might the apostle, speaking of this man of God, say, that against hope he believed in hope, and, being strong in faith, gave glory to God: For, had he not been blessed with faith which man never before had, he must have refused to comply with this severe command. For how many arguments might nature suggest to prove that such a command could never come from God, or to excuse himself from obeying it? "What! (might the good man have said) butcher my child! it is contrary to the very law of nature: Much more to butcher my dear son Isaac, in whose seed God himself has assured me, that all the families of the earth shall be blessed. But supposing I could give up my own affections, and be willing to part with him, though I love him so dearly, yet, if I murder him, what will become of God's promise? Besides I am now like a city built upon a hill; I shine as a light in the world, in the midst of a crooked and perverse generation: How then shall I cause God's name to be blasphemed, how shall I become a by-word among the heathen, if they hear that I have committed a crime which they abhor! But, above all, what will Sarah my wife say? How can I ever return to her again, after I have imbued my hands in my dear child's blood? O that God would pardon me in this thing, or take my life in the place of my son's!" Thus, I say, Abraham might have argued, and that too seemingly with great reason, against complying with the divine command. But, as before by faith he considered not the deadness of Sarah's womb, when she was past age, but believed on him, who said, "Sarah thy wife shall bear thee a son indeed;" so now being convinced that the same God spoke to, and commanded him to offer up that son, and knowing that God was able to raise him from the dead, without delay he obeys the heavenly call.

O that unbelievers would learn of faithful Abraham, and believe whatever is revealed from God, though they cannot fully comprehend it! Abraham knew God commanded him to offer up his son, and therefore believed, notwithstanding carnal reasoning might suggest many objections. We have sufficient testimony, that God has spoken to us by his son; why should we not also believe, though many things in the New Testament are above our reason? For, where reason ends faith begins. And, however infidels may style themselves reasoners, of all men they are the most unreasonable: For is it not contrary to all reason, to measure an infinite by a finite understanding, or think to find out the mysteries of godliness to perfection?

But to return to the patriarch Abraham. We observed before what plausible objections he might have made; but he answered not a single word. No, without replying against his Maker, we are told, ver. 3. that "Abraham rose up early in the morning, and saddled his ass, and took two of his young men with him, and Isaac his son, and clave the wood for the burnt-offering, and rose up and went unto the place of which God had told him."

From this verse we may gather that God spoke to Abraham in a dream, or vision of the night: For it is said, he rose up early. Perhaps it was near the fourth watch of the night, just before break of day, when God said, Take now thy son; and Abraham rises up early to do so; as I doubt not but he used to rise early to offer up his morning sacrifice of praise and thanksgiving. It is often remarked of people in the Old Testament, that they rose early in the morning; and particularly of our Lord in the New, that he rose a great while before day to pray. The morning befriends devotion: and if people cannot use so much self-denial as to rise early to pray, I know not how they will be able to die at a stake (if called to it) for Jesus Christ.

The humility, as well as piety of the patriarch, is observable. He saddled his own ass (great men should be humble;) and to show his sincerity, though he took two of his young men with him, and Isaac his son, yet he keeps his design as a secret from them all: nay, he does not so much as tell Sarah his wife: for he knew not but she might be a snare unto him in this affair; and, as Rebecca afterwards, on another occasion, advised Jacob to flee, so Sarah also might persuade Isaac to hide himself; or the young men, had they known of it, might have forced him away, as in after ages the soldiers rescued Jonathan out of the hands of Saul. But Abraham sought no such evasion, and therefore, like an Israelite indeed, in whom there was no guile, he himself resolutely "clave the wood for the burnt offering, rose up and went unto the place of which God had told him." In the second verse, God commanded him to offer up his son

upon one of the mountains which he would tell him of. He commanded him
to offer his son up, but would not then directly tell him the place where. This
was to keep him dependent and watching unto prayer: For there is nothing
like being kept waiting upon God; and, if we do, assuredly God will reveal
himself unto us yet further in his own time. Let us practice what we know,
follow providence as far as we can see already; and what we know not, what
we see not as yet, let us only be found in the way of duty, and the Lord will
reveal even that unto us. Abraham knew not directly where he was to offer up
his son; but he rises up and sets forward, and behold now God shows him; and
he went to the place of which God had told him. Let us go and do likewise.

Ver. 4. Then on the third day, Abraham lifted up his eyes, and saw the
place afar off.

So that the place, of which God had told him, was no less than three days'
journey distant from the place where God first appeared to him, and
commanded him to take his son. Was not this to try his faith, and to let him
see what he did, was not merely from a sudden pang of devotion, but a matter
of choice and deliberation? But who can tell what the aged patriarch felt
during these three days? Strong as he was in faith, I am persuaded his bowels
often yearned over his dear son Isaac. Methinks I see the good old man
walking with his dear child in his hand, and now and then looking upon him,
loving him, and then turning aside to weep. And perhaps, sometimes he stays
a little behind to pour out his heart before God; for he had no mortal to tell
his case to. Then, methinks, I see him join his son and servants again, and
talking to them of the things pertaining to the kingdom of God, as they
walked by the way. At length, on the third day, he lifted up his eyes and saw
the place afar off. And, to show that he was yet sincerely resolved to do
whatsoever the Lord required of him, he even now will not discover his design
to his servants, but said, verse 5. to his young men, (as we should say to our
worldly thoughts when about to tread the courts of the Lord's house) "abide
you here with the ass; and I and the lad will go up yonder and worship, and
come again to you." This was a sufficient reason for their staying behind;
and, it being their master's custom to go frequently to worship, they could
have no suspicion of what he was going about. And from Abraham's saying,
that he and the lad would come again, I am apt to think he believed God
would raise him from the dead, if he permitted him to offer his child up for a
burnt offering. However that be, he is yet resolved to obey God to the
uttermost; and therefore,

Ver. 6. "Abraham took the wood of the burnt offering, and laid it upon
Isaac his son; and he took the fire in his hand, and a knife, and they went
both of them together." Little did Isaac think that he was to be offered on
that very wood which he was carrying upon his shoulders; and therefore, ver.
7, Isaac innocently, and with a holy freedom (for good men should not keep
their children at too great a distance) spake unto Abraham his father, and
said, My father; and he (with equal affection and holy condescension) said,
Here am I, my son. And to show how careful Abraham had been (as all
christian parents ought to be) to instruct his Isaac how to sacrifice to God, like

a youth trained up in the way wherein he should go; Isaac said, Behold the fire and the wood; but where is the lamb for a burnt offering? How beautiful is early piety! How amiable, to hear young people ask questions about sacrificing to God in an acceptable way! Isaac knew very well that a lamb was wanting, and that a lamb was necessary for a proper sacrifice: Behold the fire and the wood; but where is the lamb for a burnt offering? Young men and maidens, learn of him.

Hitherto, it is plain, Isaac knew nothing of his father's design: but I believe, by what his father said in answer to his question, that now was the time Abraham revealed it unto him.

Verse 8. "And Abraham said, my son, God will provide himself a lamb for a burnt offering." Some think that Abraham by faith saw the Lord Jesus afar off, and here spake prophetically of that Lamb of God already slain in decree, and hereafter to be actually offered up for sinners. This was a lamb of God's providing indeed (we dared not have thought of it) to satisfy his own justice, and to render him just in justifying the ungodly. What is all our fire and wood, the best preparation and performances we can make or present, unless God had provided himself this Lamb for a burnt offering? He could not away with them. The words will well bear this interpretation. But, whatever Abraham might intend, I cannot but think he here made an application, and acquainted his son with God's dealing with his soul; and at length, with tears in his eyes, and the utmost affection in his heart, cried out, "Thou art to be the lamb, my son; God has commanded me to provide thee for a burnt offering, and to offer thee upon the mountain which we are now ascending." And, as it appears from a subsequent verse, Isaac, convinced that it was the divine will, made no resistance at all: for it is said, "they went both of them together;" and again, verse 9, when we are told that Abraham bound Isaac, we do not hear of his complaining, or endeavoring to escape, which he might have done, being (as some think) near thirty years of age, and it is plain, was capable of carrying wood enough for a burnt offering. But he was partaker of the like precious faith with his aged father, and therefore is as willing to be offered, as Abraham is to offer him; and so they went both of them together.

Verse 9. At length "they came to the place of which God had told Abraham. He built an altar there and laid the wood in order, and bound Isaac his son, and laid him on the altar upon the wood."

And here let us pause awhile, and by faith take a view of the place where the father has laid him. I doubt not but the blessed angels hovered round the altar and sang, Glory be to God in the highest, for giving such faith to man. Come, all ye tender-hearted parents, who know what it is to look over a dying child. Fancy that you saw the altar erected before you, and the wood laid in order, and the beloved Isaac bound upon it: Fancy that you saw the aged parent standing by weeping. (For, why may we not suppose that Abraham wept, since Jesus himself wept at the grave of Lazarus? O what pious endearing expressions passed now alternately between the father and the son! Josephus records a pathetic speech made by each, whether genuine I know not; but methinks I see the tears trickle down the patriarch Abraham's cheeks; and, out of the abundance of the heart, he cries, Adieu, adieu, my son; the Lord gave thee to me, and the Lord calls thee away; blessed be the name of the Lord; adieu, my Isaac, my only son, whom I love as my own soul; adieu, adieu. I see Isaac at the same time meekly resigning himself into his heavenly Father's hands, and praying to the most High to strengthen his earthly parent to strike the stroke. But why do I attempt to describe what either son or father felt? It is impossible; we may indeed form some faint idea of, but shall never fully comprehend it, till we come and sit down with them in the kingdom of heaven, and hear them tell the pleasing story over again. Hasten, O lord, that blessed time! O let thy kingdom come!

And now, ver. 10. The fatal blow is going to be given. "And Abraham stretched forth his hand, and took the knife to slay his son." But do you not think he intended to turn away his head, when he gave the blow? Nay, why may we not suppose he sometimes drew his hand in, after it was stretched out, willing to take another last farewell of his beloved Isaac, and desirous to defer it a little, though resolved at last to strike home? Be that as it will, his arm is now stretched out, the knife is in his hand, and he is about to put it to his dear son's throat.

But sing, O heavens! and rejoice, O earth! Man's extremity is God's opportunity; for behold, just as the knife, in all probability, was near his throat, ver. 11, "the angel of the Lord, (or rather, the Lord of angels, Jesus Christ, the angel of the everlasting covenant,) called unto him, (probably in a very audible manner,) from heaven, and said, Abraham, Abraham. (The word is doubled, to engage his attention; and perhaps the suddenness of the call made him draw back his hand, just as he was going to strike his son.) And Abraham said, Here am I."

And he said, verse 12. "Lay not thine hand upon the lad, neither do thou any thing unto him; for now know I that thou fearest God, seeing thou hast not withheld thy son, thine only son from me."

Here then it was that Abraham received his son Isaac from the dead in a figure. He was in effect offered upon the altar, and God looked upon him as offered and given unto him. Now it was that Abraham's faith, being tried, was found more precious than gold purified seven times in the fire. Now as a reward of grace, though not of debt, for this signal act of obedience, by an oath, God gives and confirms the promise, "that in his seed all the nations of the earth should be blessed," verse 17, 18. With what comfort may we suppose the good old man and his son went down from the mount, and returned unto the young men! With what joy we imagine he went home, and related all that had passed to Sarah! And above all, with what triumph is he exulting now in the paradise of God, and adoring rich, free, distinguishing, electing, everlasting love, which alone made him to differ from the rest of mankind, and rendered him worthy of that title which he will have so long as the sun and the moon endure: "The father of the faithful!"

But let us now draw our eyes from the creature, and do what Abraham, if he was present, would direct; I mean, fix them on the Creator, God blessed for evermore.

I see your hearts affected, I see your eyes weep, (and indeed, who can refrain weeping at the relation of such a story?) But, behold, I show you a mystery hid under the sacrifice of Abraham's only son, which, unless your hearts are hardened, must cause you to weep tears of love, and that plentifully too. I would willingly hope you even prevent me here, and are ready to say, "it is the love of God, in giving Jesus Christ to die for our sins. Yes, that is it." And yet perhaps you find your hearts at the mentioning of this, not so much affected. Let this convince you, that we are fallen creatures, and that we do not love God or Christ as we ought to do: for, if you admire Abraham offering up his Isaac, how much more ought you to extol, magnify, and adore the love of God, who so loved the world, as to give his only begotten Son, Christ Jesus our Lord, "that whosoever believeth on him should not perish, but have everlasting life?" May we not well cry out, Now know we, O Lord, that thou hast loved us, since thou hast not withheld they Son, thine only son from us? Abraham was God's creature, (and God was Abraham's friend) and therefore under the highest obligation to surrender up his Isaac. But O stupendous love! Whilst we were his enemies, God sent forth his Son, made of a woman, made under the law, that he might become a curse for us. O the freeness, as well as the infinity, of the love of God our Father! It is unsearchable: I am lost in contemplating it; it is past finding out. Think, O believers, think of the love of God, in giving Jesus Christ to be a propitiation for our sins. And when you hear how Abraham built an altar, and laid the wood in order, and bound Isaac his son, and laid him on the altar upon the wood; think how your heavenly Father bound Jesus Christ his only Son, and offered him upon the altar of his justice, and laid upon him the iniquities of us all. When you read of Abraham's stretching forth his hand to slay his son, think, O think, how God actually suffered his Son to be slain, that we might live for evermore. Do you read of Isaac carrying the wood upon his shoulders, upon which he was to be offered? Let this lead you to Mount Calvary, (this very mount of Moriah where Isaac was offered, as some think,) and take a view of the antitype Jesus Christ, that son of God, bearing and ready to sink under the weight of that cross on which he was to hang for us. Do you admire Isaac so freely consenting to die, though a creature, and therefore obliged to go when God called? O do not forget to admire infinitely more the dear Lord Jesus, that promised seed, who willingly said, "Lo, I come," though under no obligation so to do, "to do thy will," to obey and die for men, O God! Did you weep just now when I bid you fancy that you saw the altar, and the wood laid in order, and Isaac laid bound on the altar? Look up by faith, behold the blessed Jesus, our all-glorious Immanuel, not bound, but nailed on an accursed tree: see how he hangs crowned with thorns, and had in derision of all that are round about him: see how the thorns pierce him, and how the blood in purple streams trickles down his sacred temples! Hark! how the God of nature groans! See how he bows his head, and at length humanity gives up the ghost! Isaac is saved, but Jesus, the God of Isaac dies; a ram is offered up in Isaac's room, but Jesus has no substitute; Jesus must bleed, Jesus must die: God the Father provided this Lamb for himself from all eternity. He must be offered in time, or man must be damned for evermore. And now where are all your tears? Shall I say, refrain your voice from weeping? No, rather let me exhort you to look to him whom you have pierced, and mourn, as a woman mourneth for her first born: for we have been the betrayers, we have been the murderers of this Lord of glory; and shall we not bewail those sins, which brought the blessed Jesus to the accursed tree? Having so much done, so much suffered for us, so much forgiven, shall we not love much? O! let us love him with all our hearts, and minds, and strength, and glorify him in our souls and bodies; for they are his. Which leads me to a second inference I shall draw from the foregoing discourse.

From hence we may learn the nature of true justifying faith. Whoever understands and preaches the truth as it is in Jesus, must acknowledge, that salvation is God's free gift, and that we are saved, not by any or all the works of righteousness which we have done or can do: no; we can neither wholly nor in part justify ourselves in the sight of God. The Lord Jesus Christ is our righteousness; and if we are accepted with God, it must be only in and through the personal righteousness, the active and passive obedience of Jesus Christ his beloved Son. This righteousness must be imputed, or counted over to us, and applied by faith to our hearts, or else we can in no wise be justified in God's sight: and that very moment when a sinner is enabled to lay hold on Christ's righteousness by faith, he is freely justified from all his sins, and shall never enter into condemnation, notwithstanding he was a fire-brand of hell before. Thus it was that Abraham was justified before he did any good work: he was enabled to believe on the Lord Christ; it was accounted to him for righteousness; that is, Christ's righteousness was made over to him, and so accounted his. This, this is gospel; this is the only way of finding acceptance with God: good works have nothing to do with our justification in his sight. We are justified by faith alone, as saith the article of our church; agreeably to which the apostle Paul says, "By grace ye are saved, through faith; and that not of yourselves; it is the gift of God." Notwithstanding good works have their proper place: they justify our faith, though not our persons; they follow it, and evidence our justification in the sight of men. Hence it is that the apostle James asks, was not Abraham justified by works, (alluding, no doubt, to the story on which we have been discoursing,) that is, did he not prove he was in a justified state, because his faith was productive of good works? This declarative justification in the sight of men, is what is directly to be understood in the words of the text: "Now know I," says God, "that thou fearest me, since thou hast not withheld thy son, thine only son from me." Not but that God knew it before; but this is spoken in condescension to our weak capacities, and plainly shows, that his offering up his son was accepted with God, as an evidence of the sincerity of his faith, and for this, was left on record to future ages. Hence then you may learn, whether you are blessed with, and are sons and daughters of faithful Abraham. You say you believe; you talk of free grace, and free justification: you do well; the devils also believe and tremble. But has the faith which you pretend to, influenced your hearts, renewed your souls, and, like Abraham's, worked by love? Are your affections, like his, set on things above? Are you heavenly-minded, and like him, do you confess yourselves strangers and pilgrims on the earth. In short, has your faith enabled you to overcome the world, and strengthened you to give up your Isaacs, your laughter, your most beloved lusts, friends, pleasures, and profits for God? If so, take the comfort of it; for justly may you say, "We know assuredly, that we do fear and love God, or rather are loved of him." But if you are only talking believers, have only a faith of the head, and never felt the power of it in your hearts, however you may bolster yourselves up, and say, "we have Abraham for our father, or Christ is our Savior;" unless you get a faith of the heart, a faith working by love, you shall never sit with Abraham, Isaac, Jacob, or Jesus Christ in the kingdom of heaven.

But I must draw one more inference, and with that I shall conclude.

Learn, O saints! from what has been said, to sit loose to all your worldly comforts; and stand ready prepared to part with every thing, when God shall require it at your hand. Some of you perhaps may have friends, who are to you as your own souls, and others may have children, in whose lives your own lives are bound up: all I believe have their Isaacs, their particular delights of some kind or other. Labor, for Christ's sake, labor ye sons and daughters of Abraham, to resign them, daily in affection to God, that, when he shall require you really to sacrifice them, you may not confer with flesh and blood, any more than the blessed patriarch now before us. And as for you that have been in any measure tried like unto him, let his example encourage and comfort you. Remember, Abraham your father was tried so before you: think, O think, of the happiness he now enjoys, and how he is incessantly thanking God for tempting and trying him when here below. Look up often by the eye of faith, and see him sitting with his dearly beloved Isaac in the world of spirits. Remember, it will be but a little while, and you shall sit with them also, and tell one another what God has done for your souls. There I hope to sit with you, and hear this story of his offering up his son from his own mouth, and to praise the Lamb that sitteth upon the throne, for what he hath done for all our souls, for ever and ever.

Sinners in the Hands of an Angry God

Jonathan Edwards

Commentary

The Great Awakening set off a bitter controversy in the colonies, especially New England. It highlighted theological disputes that had been brewing for decades and generated fierce disputes about ministerial education and preaching methods. Whitefield was imitated by many ordained ministers. He was also imitated by some poorly educated and unordained "preachers," who "invaded" communities without being invited, dismissed doctrines by saying religious truths were easily understood and proclaimed that education had created a "cold-hearted" ministry. Preachers at the other extreme retained the traditional sermonic form (although not always the traditional theology) and dismissed "enthusiastical" sermons as the ignorant ravings of the insane. In rhetorical terms, it was a battle between the new Pathos and the old Logos; between the new narrative form and the old deductively organized sermon that went from general doctrines to specific applications; between the new unscripted sermon that was delivered emotionally and the old, carefully prepared sermon that was read quietly from manuscript.

A central figure in the controversy was Jonathan Edwards (1703-1758), who succeeded his famous grandfather in the Northampton pulpit shortly after graduating from Yale (a newer, but more Calvinist, school than the older, but more "heretical" Harvard). A brilliant intellectual, Edwards can best be explained as a paradox. Thoroughly conversant with the secular Englightenment philosophy that was coming from Europe and undermining the old Calvinism, Edwards retained the old faith. He expounded it in his traditionally organized sermons, which included an extremely complicated interpretation of doctrines.

Yet Edwards was a thoroughgoing revivalist. He had an "awakening" in Northampton even before Whitefield's tour. He invited Whitefield to his community and later wrote several pamphlets to defend "enthusiasm." He even suggested that the Awakening marked the advent of the long-awaited

Millennium. He went to nearby communities to deliver revival sermons, which combined the traditional Puritan sermon with intense emotional appeals (especially an appeal to fear). Unlike many revivalists, he spoke from manuscript, thus leaving reasonably authentic texts for future generations.

Although not Edwards' own favorite, the following was well-known in its own day. Delivered first in Enfield, Massachusetts (now Connecticut) it was repeated elsewhere. It is unquestionably best known to future generations because of frequent reprintings. The following is reproduced photographically from A. Craig Baird, *American Public Addresses, 1740-1952* (New York: McGraw-Hill, 1956), pp. 16-28.

Sinners in the Hands of an Angry God

Their foot shall slide in due time. Deut. xxxii, 35.

In this verse is threatened the vengeance of God on the wicked un-believing Israelites, that were God's visible people, and lived under the means of grace; and that not withstanding all God's wonderful works that he had wrought towards that people, yet remained, as expressed in verse 28. . . . void of counsel, having no understanding in them. Under all the cultivations of heaven, they brought forth bitter and poisonous fruit; as in the two verses next preceding the text.—The expression I have chosen for my text, *Their foot shall slide in due time,* seems to imply the following things, relating to the punishment and destruction that these wicked Israelites were exposed to.

1. That they were always exposed to *destruction;* as one that stands or walks in slippery places is always exposed to fall. This is implied in the manner of their destruction coming upon them, being represented by their foot sliding. The same is expressed, Psalm lxxiii, 18. "Surely thou didst set them in slippery places; thou castedst them down into destruction."

2. It implies, that they were always exposed to *sudden* unexpected destruction. As he that walks in slippery places is every moment liable to fall, he cannot foresee one moment whether he shall stand or fall the next; and when he does fall, he falls at once without warning: Which is also expressed in Psalm lxxiii. 18, 19. "Surely thou didst set them in slippery places; thou castedst them down into destruction: How are they brought into desolation as *in a moment!*"

3. Another thing implied is, that they are liable to fall *of themselves,* without being thrown down by the hand of another; as he that stands or walks on slippery ground needs nothing but his own weight to throw him down.

4. That the reason why they are not fallen already, and don't fall now, is only that God's appointed time is not come. For it is said, that

when that due time, or appointed time comes, *their foot shall slide*. Then they shall be left to fall, as they are inclined by their own weight. God won't hold them up in these slippery places any longer, but will let them go; and then, at that very instant, they shall fall into destruction; as he that stands on such slippery declining ground, on the edge of a pit, he can't stand alone, when he is let go he immediately falls and is lost.

The observation from the words that I would now insist upon is this.— "There is nothing that keeps wicked men at any one moment out of hell, but the mere pleasure of God"—By the *mere* pleasure of God, I mean his *sovereign* pleasure, his arbitrary will, restrained by no obligation, hindered by no manner of difficulty, any more than if nothing else but God's mere will had in the least degree, or in any respect whatsoever, any hand in the preservation of wicked men one moment.—The truth of this observation may appear by the following considerations.

1. There is no want of *power* in God to cast wicked men into hell at any moment. Men's hands cannot be strong when God rises up. The strongest have no power to resist him, nor can any deliver out of his hands.—He is not only able to cast wicked men into hell, but he can most easily do it. Sometimes an earthly prince meets with a great deal of difficulty to subdue a rebel, who has found means to fortify himself, and has made himself strong by the numbers of his followers. But it is not so with God. There is no fortress that is any defence from the power of God. Though hand join in hand, and vast multitudes of God's enemies combine and associate themselves, they are easily broken in pieces. They are as great heaps of light chaff before the whirlwind; or large quantities of dry stubble before devouring flames. We find it easy to tread on and crush a worm that we see crawling on the earth; so it is easy for us to cut or singe a slender thread that any thing hangs by: thus easy it is for God, when he pleases, to cast his enemies down to hell. What are we, that we should think to stand before him, at whose rebuke the earth trembles, and before whom the rocks are thrown down?

2. They *deserve* to be cast into hell; so that divine justice never stands in the way, it makes no objection against God's using his power at any moment to destroy them. Yea, on the contrary, justice calls aloud for an infinite punishment of their sins. Divine justice says of the tree that brings forth such grapes of Sodom, "Cut it down, why cumbereth it the ground?" Luke xiii. 7. The sword of divine justice is every moment brandished over their heads, and 'tis nothing but the hand of arbitrary mercy, and God's mere will, that holds it back.

3. They are already under a sentence of *condemnation* to hell. They don't only justly deserve to be cast down thither, but the sentence of the law of God, that eternal and immutable rule of righteousness that God has fixed between him and mankind, is gone out against them, and stands against them; so that they are bound over already to hell. John iii. 18. "He that believeth not is condemned already." So that every unconverted

man properly belongs to hell; that is his place; from thence he is, John viii. 23. "Ye are from beneath:" And thither he is bound; 'tis the place that justice, and God's word, and the sentence of his unchangeable law assign to him.

4. They are now the objects of that very same *anger* and wrath of God, that is expressed in the torments of hell. And the reason why they do not go down to hell at each moment, is not because God, in whose power they are, is not then very angry with them; as angry as he is with many of those miserable creatures that he is now tormenting in hell, and do there feel and bear the fierceness of his wrath. Yea, God is a great deal more angry with great numbers that are now on earth: yea, doubtless, with many that are now in this congregation, who it may be are at ease, than he is with many of those who are now in the flames of hell.

So that it is not because God is unmindful of their wickedness, and don't resent it, that he don't let loose his hand and cut them off. God is not altogether such an one as themselves, though they may imagine him to be so. The wrath of God burns against them, their damnation don't slumber; the pit is prepared, the fire is made ready, the furnace is now hot, ready to receive them; the flames do now rage and glow. The glittering sword is whet, and held over them, and the pit hath opened her mouth under them.

5. The *devil* stands ready to fall upon them, and seize them as his own, at what moment God shall permit him. They belong to him; he has their souls in his possession, and under his dominion. The scripture represents them as his goods, Luke xi. 12. The devils watch them; they are ever by them at their right hand; they stand waiting for them, like greedy hungry lions that see their prey, and expect to have it, but are for the present kept back. If God should withdraw his hand, by which they are restrained, they would in one moment fly upon their poor souls. The old serpent is gaping for them; hell opens its mouth wide to receive them; and if God should permit it, they would be hastily swallowed up and lost.

6. There are in the souls of wicked men those hellish *principles* reigning, that would presently kindle and flame out into hell fire, it it were not for God's restraints. There is laid in the very nature of carnal men, a foundation for the torments of hell. There are those corrupt principles, in reigning power in them, and in full possession of them, that are seeds of hell fire. These principles are active and powerful, exceeding violent in their nature, and if it were not for the restraining hand of God upon them, they would soon break out, they would flame out after the same manner as the same corruptions, the same enmity does in the hearts of damned souls, and would beget the same torments as they do in them. The souls of the wicked are in scripture compared to the troubled sea, Isa. lvii. 20. For the present, God restrains their wickedness by his mighty power, as he does the raging waves of the troubled sea, saying, "Hitherto shalt thou come, but no further," but if God should withdraw that restraining power, it would soon carry all afore it. Sin is the ruin

and misery of the soul; it is destructive in its nature; and if God should leave it without restraint, there would need nothing else to make the soul perfectly miserable. The corruption of the heart of man is immoderate and boundless in its fury; and while wicked men live here, it is like fire pent up by God's restraints, whereas if it were let loose, it would set on fire the course of nature; and as the heart is now a sink of sin, so if sin was not restrained, it would immediately turn the soul into a fiery oven, or a furnace of fire and brimstone.

7. It is no security to wicked men for one moment, that there are no visible means of death at hand. It is no security to a natural man, that he is now in health, and that he does not see which way he should now immediately go out of the world by an accident, and that there is no visible danger in any respect in his circumstances. The manifold and continual experience of the world in all ages, shows this is no evidence, that a man is not on the very brink of eternity, and that the next step will not be into another world. The unseen, unthought-of ways and means of persons going suddenly out of the world are innumerable and inconceivable. Unconverted men walk over the pit of hell on a rotten covering, and there are innumerable places in this covering so weak that they won't bear their weight, and these places are not seen. The arrows of death fly unseen at noon-day; the sharpest sight can't discern them. God has so many different unsearchable ways of taking wicked men out of the world and sending them to hell, that there is nothing to make it appear, that God has need to be at the expense of a miracle, or go out of the ordinary course of his providence, to destroy any wicked man, at any moment. All the means that there are of sinners going out of the world, are so in God's hands, and so universally and absolutely subject to his power and determination, that it does not depend at all the less on the mere will of God, whether sinners shall at any moment go to hell, than if means were never made use of, or at all concerned in the case.

8. Natural men's prudence and care to preserve their own lives, or the care of others to preserve them, don't secure them a moment. This divine providence and universal experience do also bear testimony to. There is this clear evidence that men's own wisdom is no security to them from death; that if it were otherwise we should see some difference between the wise and politic men of the world, and others, with regard to their liableness to early and unexpected death: but how is it in fact? Eccles. ii. 16. "How dieth the wise man? as the fool."

9. All wicked men's pains and *contrivance* which they use to escape hell, while they continue to reject Christ, and so remain wicked men, do not secure them from hell one moment. Almost every natural man that hears of hell, flatters himself that he shall escape it; he depends upon himself for his own security; he flatters himself in what he has done, in what he is now doing, or what he intends to do. Every one lays out matters in his own mind how he shall avoid damnation, and flatters himself that he contrives well for himself, and that his schemes will not fail. They

hear indeed that there are but few saved, and that the greater part of men that have died heretofore are gone to hell; but each one imagines that he lays out matters better for his own escape than others have done. He don't intend to come to that place of torment; he says within himself, that he intends to take effectual care, and to order matters so for himself as not to fail.

But the foolish children of men miserably delude themselves in their own schemes, and in confidence in their own strength and wisdom; they trust to nothing but a shadow. The greater part of those that heretofore have lived under the same means of grace, and are now dead, are undoubtedly gone to hell; and it was not because they were not as wise as those who are now alive: it was not because they did not lay out matters as well for themselves to secure their own escape. If we could speak with them, and inquire of them, one by one, whether they expected, when alive, and when they used to hear about hell, ever to be the subjects of that misery: we doubtless, should hear one and another reply, "No, I never intended to come here: I had laid out matters otherwise in my mind; I thought I should contrive well for myself: I thought my scheme good. I intended to take effectual care; but it came upon me unexpected; I did not look for it at that time, and in that manner; it came as a thief: Death outwitted me: God's wrath was too quick for me. Oh, my cursed foolishness! I was flattering myself, and pleasing myself with vain dreams of what I would do hereafter; and when I was saying, Peace and safety, then suddenly destruction came upon me."

10. God has laid himself under *no obligation*, by any promise to keep any natural man out of hell one moment. God certainly has made no promises either of eternal life, or of any deliverance or preservation from eternal death, but what are contained in the covenant of grace, the promises that are given in Christ, in whom all the promises are yea and amen. But surely they have no interest in the promises of the covenant of grace who are not the children of the covenant, who do not believe in any of the promises, and have no interest in the Mediator of the covenant.

So that, whatever some have imagined and pretended about promises made to natural men's earnest seeking and knocking, it is plain and manifest, that whatever pains a natural man takes in religion, whatever prayers he makes, till he believes in Christ, God is under no manner of obligation to keep him a moment from eternal destruction.

So that, thus it is that natural men are held in the hand of God, over the pit of hell; they have deserved the fiery pit, and are already sentenced to it; and God is dreadfully provoked, his anger is as great towards them as to those that are actually suffering the executions of the fierceness of his wrath in hell, and they have done nothing in the least to appease or abate that anger, neither is God in the least bound by any promise to hold them up one moment; the devil is waiting for them, hell is gaping for them, the flames gather and flash about them, and would fain lay hold on them, and swallow them up; the fire pent up in their own hearts is struggling to break out: and they have no interest in any Mediator, there are no means within reach that can be any security to them. In short, they have no refuge, nothing to take hold of; all that preserves them every moment is the mere arbitrary will, and uncovenanted, unobliged forbearance of an incensed God.

Application

The use of this awful subject may be for awakening unconverted persons in this congregation. This that you have heard is the case of every one of you that are out of Christ.—That world of misery, that lake of burning brimstone, is extended abroad under you. There is the dreadful pit of the glowing flames of the wrath of God; there is hell's wide gaping mouth open; and you have nothing to stand upon, nor any thing to take hold of; there is nothing between you and hell but the air; 'tis only the power and mere pleasure of God that holds you up.

You probably are not sensible of this; you find you are kept out of hell, but do not see the hand of God in it; but look at other things, as the good state of your bodily constitution, your care of your own life, and the means you use for your own preservation. But indeed these things are nothing; if God should withdraw his hand, they would avail no more to keep you from falling, than the thin air to hold up a person that is suspended in it.

Your wickedness makes you as it were heavy as lead, and to tend downwards with great weight and pressure towards hell; and if God should let you go, you would immediately sink and swiftly descend and plunge into the bottomless gulf, and your healthy constitution, and your own care and prudence, and best contrivance, and all your righteousness, would have no more influence to uphold you and keep you out of hell, than a spider's web would have to stop a fallen rock. Were it not for the sovereign pleasure of God, the earth would not bear you one moment; for you are a burden to it; the creation groans with you; the creature is made subject to the bondage of your corruption, not willingly; the sun does not willingly shine upon you to give you light to serve sin and Satan; the earth does not willingly yield her increase to satisfy your lusts; nor is it willingly a stage for your wickedness to be acted upon; the air does not willingly serve you for breath to maintain the flame of life in your vitals, while you spend your life in the service of God's enemies. God's creatures are good, and were made for men to serve God with, and do not willingly subserve to any other purpose, and groan when they are abused to purposes so directly contrary to their nature and end. And the world would spew you out, were it not for the sovereign hand of him who hath subjected it in hope. There are black clouds of God's wrath now hanging directly over your heads, full of the dreadful storm, and big with thunder, and were it not for the restraining hand of God, it would immediately burst forth upon you. The sovereign pleasure of God, for the present, stays his rough wind; otherwise it would come with fury, and your destruction would come like a whirlwind, and you would be like the chaff of the summer threshing floor.

The wrath of God is like great waters that are damned for the present; they increase more and more, and rise higher and higher, till an outlet is given; and the longer the stream is stopped, the more rapid and mighty is its course, when once it is let loose. 'Tis true, that judgment against your evil works has not been executed hitherto; the floods of God's vengeance have been withheld; but your guilt in the mean time is constantly increasing, and you are every day treasuring up more wrath; the waters are constantly rising, and waxing more and more mighty; and there is nothing but the mere pleasure of God, that holds the waters back, that are unwilling to be stopped, and press hard to go forward. If God should only withdraw his hand from the flood-gate, it would immediately fly open, and the fiery floods of the fierceness and wrath of God, would rush forth with inconceivable fury, and would come upon you with omnipotent power; and if your strength were ten thousand times greater than it is, yea, ten thousand times greater than the strength of the stoutest, sturdiest devil in hell, it would be nothing to withstand or endure it.

The bow of God's wrath is bent, and the arrow made ready on the string, and justice bends the arrow at your heart, and strains the bow, and it is nothing but the mere pleasure of God, and that of an angry God, without any promise or obligation at all, that keeps the arrow one moment from being made drunk with your blood. Thus all you that never passed under a great change of heart, by the mighty power of the Spirit of God upon your souls; all you that were never born again, and made new creatures, and raised from being dead in sin, to a state of new, and before altogether unexperienced light and life, are in the hands of an angry God. However you may have reformed your life in many things, and may have had religious affections, and may keep up a form of religion in your families and closets, and in the house of God, it is nothing but his mere pleasure that keeps you from being this moment swallowed up in everlasting destruction. However unconvinced you may now be of the truth of what you hear, by and by you will be fully convinced of it. Those that are gone from being in the like circumstances with you, see that it was so with them; for destruction came suddenly upon most of them; when they expected nothing of it, and while they were saying, Peace and safety: now they see, that those things on which they depended for peace and safety, were nothing but thin air and empty shadows.

The God that holds you over the pit of hell, much as one holds a spider, or some loathsome insect over the fire, abhors you, and is dreadfully provoked: his wrath towards you burns like fire; he looks upon you as worthy of nothing else, but to be cast into the fire; he is of purer eyes than to bear to have you in his sight; you are ten thousand times more abominable in his eyes, than the most hateful venomous serpent is in ours. You have offended him infinitely more than ever a stubborn rebel did his prince; and yet it is nothing but his hand that holds you from falling into the fire every moment. 'Tis to be ascribed to nothing else, that you did not go to hell the last night; that you was suffered to awake again in this world, after you closed your eyes to sleep. And there is no other reason to be given, why you have not dropped into hell since you arose in the morning, but that God's hand has held you up. There is no other reason to be given why you han't gone to hell, since you have sat here in the house of God, provoking his pure eyes by your sinful wicked manner of attending his solemn worship. Yea, there is nothing else that is to be given as a reason why you don't this very moment drop down into hell.

O sinner! Consider the fearful danger you are in: 'Tis a great furnace of wrath, a wide and bottomless pit, full of the fire of wrath, that you are held over in the hand of that God, whose wrath is provoked and incensed as much against you, as against many of the damned in hell. You hang by a slender thread, with the flames of divine wrath flashing about it, and ready every moment to singe it, and burn it asunder; and you have no interest in any Mediator, and nothing to lay hold of to save yourself, nothing to keep off the flames of wrath, nothing of your own, nothing that you ever have done, nothing that you can do, to induce God to spare you one moment.

And consider here more particularly several things concerning that wrath that you are in danger of.

1. *Whose* wrath it is: it is the wrath of the infinite God. If it were only the wrath of man, though it were of the most potent prince, it would be comparatively little to be regarded. The wrath of kings is very much dreaded, especially of absolute monarchs, that have the possessions and lives of their subjects wholly in their power, to be disposed of at their mere will. Prov. xx. 2. "The fear of a king is as the roaring of a lion: Whoso provoketh him to anger, sinneth against his own soul." The subject that very much enrages an arbitrary prince, is liable to suffer the most extreme torments that human art can invent, or human power can inflict. But the greatest earthly potentates in their greatest majesty and strength, and when clothed in their greatest terrors, are but feeble, despicable worms of the dust, in comparison of the great and almighty Creator and King of heaven and earth. It is but little that they can do, when most enraged, and when they have exerted the utmost of their fury. All the kings of the earth, before God, are as grasshoppers; they are nothing, and less than nothing: both their love and their hatred is to be despised. The wrath of the great King of kings, is as much more terrible than theirs, as his majesty is greater. Luke xii. 4, 5. "And I say unto you, my friends, Be not afraid of them that kill the body, and after that, have no more that they can do. But I will forewarn you whom you shall fear: fear him, which after he hath killed, hath power to cast into hell: yea, I say unto you, Fear him."

2. It is the *fierceness* of his wrath that you are exposed to. We often read of the fury of God; as in Isaiah lix. 18. "According to their deeds, accordingly he will repay fury to his adversaries." So Isaiah lxvi. 15. "For behold, the Lord will come with fire, and with his chariots like a whirlwind, to render his anger with fury, and his rebuke with flames of fire." And in many other places. So, Rev. xix. 15. we read of "the wine press of the fierceness and wrath of Almighty God." The words are exceeding terrible. If it had only been said, "the wrath of God," the words would have implied that which is infinitely dreadful: but it is "the fierceness and wrath of God." The fury of God! the fierceness of Jehovah! Oh, how dreadful must that be! Who can utter or conceive what such expressions carry in them! But it is also "the fierceness and wrath of *Almighty* God." As though there would be a very great manifestation of his almighty power in what the fierceness of his wrath should inflict, as though omnipotence should be as it were enraged, and exerted, as men are wont to exert their strength in the fierceness of their wrath. Oh! then, what will be the consequence! What will become of the poor worms that shall suffer it! Whose hands can be strong! And whose heart can endure! To what a dreadful, inexpressible, inconceivable depth of misery must the poor creature be sunk who shall be the subject of this!

Consider this, you that are here present, that yet remain in an unregenerate state. That God will execute the fierceness of his anger, implies, that he will inflict wrath without any pity. When God beholds the ineffable extremity of your case, and sees your torment to be so vastly disproportioned to your strength, and sees how your poor soul is crushed, and sinks down, as it were, into an infinite gloom; he will have no compassion upon you, he will not forbear the executions of his wrath, or in the least lighten his hand; there shall be no moderation or mercy, nor will God then at all stay his rough wind; he will have no regard to your welfare, nor be at all careful lest you should suffer too much in any other sense, than only that you shall *not suffer beyond what strict justice requires.* Nothing shall be withheld, because it is so hard for you to bear. Ezek. viii. 18. "Therefore will I also deal in fury: mine eye shall not spare, neither will I have pity; and though they cry in mine ears with a loud voice, yet I will not hear them." Now God stands ready to pity you; this is a day of mercy; you may cry now with some encouragement of obtaining mercy. But when once the day of mercy is past, your most lamentable and dolorous cries and shrieks will be in vain; you will be wholly lost and thrown away of God, as to any regard to your welfare. God will have no other use to put you to, but to suffer misery; you shall be continued in being to no other end; for you will be a vessel of wrath fitted to destruction; and there will be no other use of this vessel, but to be filled full of wrath. God will be so far from pitying you when you cry to him, that 'tis said he will only "laugh and mock," Prov. i. 25, 26, etc.

How awful are those words, Isa. lxiii. 3, which are the words of the great God. "I will tread them in mine anger, and will trample them in my fury, and their blood shall be sprinkled upon my garments, and I will stain all my raiment." 'Tis perhaps impossible to conceive of words that carry in them greater manifestations of these three things, *viz.* contempt, and hatred, and fierceness of indignation. If you cry to God to pity you, he will be so far from pitying you in your doleful case, or showing you the least regard or favour, that instead of that, he'll only tread you under foot. And though he will know that you can't bear the weight of omnipotence treading upon you, yet he won't regard that, but he will crush you under his feet without mercy; he'll crush out your blood and make it fly, and it shall be sprinkled on his garments, so as to stain all his raiment. He will not only hate you, but he will have you in the utmost contempt: no place shall be thought fit for you, but under his feet to be trodden down as the mire of the streets.

3. The *misery* you are exposed to is that which God will inflict to that end, that he might show what that wrath of Jehovah is. God hath had it on his heart to show to angels and men, both how excellent his love is, and also how terrible his wrath is. Sometimes earthly kings have a mind to show how terrible their wrath is, by the extreme punishments they would execute on those that would provoke 'em. Nebuchadnezzar, that mighty and haughty monarch of the Chaldean empire, was willing to show his wrath when enraged with Shadrach, Meshech, and Abednego; and accordingly gave orders that the burning fiery furnace should be heated seven times hotter than it was before; doubtless, it was raised to the utmost degree of fierceness that human art could raise it. But the great God is also willing to show his wrath, and magnify his awful majesty and mighty power in the extreme sufferings of his enemies. Rom. ix. 22. "What if God, willing to show his wrath, and to make his power known, endure with much long-suffering the vessels of wrath fitted to destruction?" And seeing this is his design, and what he has determined, even to show how terrible the unrestrained wrath, the fury and fierceness of Jehovah is, he will do it to effect. There will be something accomplished and brought to pass that will be dreadful with a witness. When the great and angry God hath risen up and executed his awful vengeance on the poor sinner, and the wretch is actually suffering the infinite weight and power of his indignation, then will God call upon the whole universe to behold that awful majesty and mighty power that is to be seen in it. Isa. xxxiii. 12–14. "And the people shall be as the burnings of lime, as thorns cut up shall they be burnt in the fire. Hear ye that are far off, what I have done; and ye that are near, acknowledge my might. The sinners in Zion are afraid; fearfulness hath surprised the hypocrites," etc.

Thus it will be with you that are in an unconverted state, if you continue in it; the infinite might, and majesty, and terribleness of the omnipotent God shall be magnified upon you, in the ineffable strength of your torments. You shall be tormented in the presence of the holy angels, and in the presence of the Lamb; and when you shall be in this state of suffering, the glorious inhabitants of heaven shall go forth and look on the awful spectacle, that they may see what the wrath and fierceness of the Almighty is; and when they have seen it, they will fall down and adore that great power and majesty. Isa. lxvi. 23, 24. "And it shall come to pass, that from one new moon to another, and from one sabbath to another, shall all flesh come to worship before me, saith the Lord. And they shall go forth and look upon the carcasses of the men that have transgressed against me; for their worm shall not die, neither shall their fire be quenched, and they shall be an abhorring unto all flesh."

4. It is *everlasting* wrath. It would be dreadful to suffer this fierceness and wrath of Almighty God one moment; but you must suffer it to all eternity. There will be no end to this exquisite horrible misery. When you look forward, you shall see a long forever, a boundless duration before you, which will swallow up your thoughts, and amaze your soul; and you will absolutely despair of ever having any deliverance, any end, any mitigation, any rest at all. You will know certainly that you must wear out long ages, millions of millions of ages, in wrestling and conflicting with this almighty merciless vengeance; and then when you have so done, when so many ages have actually been spent by you in this manner, you will know that all is but a point to what remains. So that your punishment will indeed be infinite. Oh, who can express what the state of a soul in such circumstances is! All that we can possibly say about it, gives but a very feeble, faint representation of it; it is inexpressible and inconceivable: For "who knows the power of God's anger?

How dreadful is the state of those that are daily and hourly in the danger of this great wrath and infinite misery! But this is the dismal case of every soul in this congregation that has not been born again, however moral and strict, sober and religious, they may otherwise be. Oh that you would consider it, whether you be young or old! There is reason to think, that there are many in this congregation now hearing this discourse, that will actually be the subjects of this very misery to all eternity. We know not who they are, or in what seats they sit, or what thoughts they now have. It may be they are now at ease, and hear all these things without much disturbance, and are now flattering themselves that they are not the persons, promising themselves that they shall escape. If we knew that there was one person, and but one, in the whole congregation, that was to be the subject of this misery, what an awful thing would it be to think of! If we knew who it was, what an awful sight would it be to see such a person! How might all the rest of the congregation lift up a lamentable and bitter cry over him! But, alas! instead of one, how many is it likely will remember this discourse in hell! And it would be a wonder, if some that are now present should not be in hell in a very short time, even before this year is out. And it would be no wonder if some persons, that now sit here, in some seats of this meeting-house, in health, quiet and secure, should be there before to-morrow morning. Those of you that finally continue in a natural condition, that shall keep out of hell longest will be there in a little time! Your damnation does not slumber; it will come swiftly, and, in all probability, very suddenly upon many of you. You have reason to wonder that you are not already in hell. 'Tis doubtless the case of some whom you have seen and known, that never deserved hell more than you, and that heretofore appeared as likely to have been now alive as you. Their case is past all hope; they are crying in extreme misery and perfect despair. But here you are in the land of the living and in the house of God, and have an opportunity to obtain salvation. What would not those poor damned hopeless souls give for one day's opportunity such as you now enjoy!

And now you have an extraordinary opportunity, a day wherein Christ has thrown the door of mercy wide open, and stands in calling and crying with a loud voice to poor sinners; a day wherein many are flocking to him, and pressing into the kingdom of God. Many are daily coming from the east, west, north and south; many that were very lately in the same miserable condition that you are in, are now in a happy state, with their hearts filled with love to him who has loved them, and washed them from their sins in his own blood, and rejoicing in hope of the glory of God. How awful is it to be left behind at such a day! To see so many others feasting, while you are pining and perishing! To see so many rejoicing and singing for joy of heart, while you have cause to mourn for sorrow of heart, and howl for vexation of spirit! How can you rest one moment in such a condition? Are not your souls as precious as the souls of the people at Suffield,[1] where they are flocking from day to day to Christ?

Are there not many here who have lived long in the world, and are not to this day born again? and so are aliens from the commonwealth of Israel, and have done nothing ever since they have lived. but treasure up wrath against the day of wrath? Oh, sirs, your case, in an especial manner, is extremely dangerous. Your guilt and hardness of heart is extremely great. Don't you see how generally persons of your years are passed over and left, in the present remarkable and wonderful dispensation of God's mercy? You had need to consider yourselves, and awake thoroughly out of sleep. You cannot bear the fierceness and wrath of the infinite God. —And you, that are young men, and young women, will you neglect this precious season which you now enjoy, when so many others of your age are renouncing all youthful vanities, and flocking to Christ? You especially have now an extraordinary opportunity; but if you neglect it, it will soon be with you as with those persons who spent all the precious days of youth in sin, and are now come to such a dreadful pass in blindness and hardness.—And you, children, that are unconverted, don't you know that you are going down to hell, to bear the dreadful wrath of that God, that is now angry with you every day and every night? Will you be content to be the children of the devil, when so many other children in the land are converted, and are become the holy and happy children of

---

[1] A town in the neighborhood.

the King of kings?

And let every one that is yet of Christ, and hanging over the pit of hell, whether they be old men and women, or middle aged, or young people, or little children, now hearken to the loud calls of God's word and providence. This acceptable year of the Lord, a day of such great favours to some, will doubtless be a day of as remarkable vengeance to others. Men's hearts harden, and their guilt increases apace at such a day as this, if they neglect their souls; and never was there so great danger of such persons being given up to hardness of heart and blindness of mind. God seems now to be hastily gathering in his elect in all parts of the land; and probably the greater part of adult persons that ever shall be saved, will be brought in now in a little time, and it will be as it was on the great out-pouring of the Spirit upon the Jews in the apostles' days; the election will obtain, and the rest will be blinded. If this should be the case with you, you will eternally curse this day, and will curse the day that ever you was born, to see such a season of the pouring out of God's Spirit, and will wish that you had died and gone to hell before you had seen it. Now undoubtedly it is, as it was in the days of John the Baptist, the axe is in an extraordinary manner laid at the root of the trees, that every tree which brings not forth good fruit, may be hewn down and cast into the fire.

Therefore, let every one that is out of Christ, now awake and fly from the wrath to come. The wrath of Almighty God is now undoubtedly hanging over a great part of this congregation: Let every one fly out of Sodom: "Haste and escape for your lives, look not behind you, escape to the mountain, lest ye be consumed."

Excerpt from Joy and Salvation by Christ; His Arm Displayed in the Protestant Cause (Peace of 1763)

Samuel Haven

Commentary

The secularization of American society did not end the Millenarian faith. To the contrary, the doctrine became secularized, as it is today when, for example, we proclaim an idea "good" because it is "new." By the early 1700s, many Americans had come to believe that the Millennium would arrive not after a Final Battle between Christ and Antichrist, but slowly and in stages. Working through His Chosen People, Christ was gradually winning the battle against Antichrist, and His victories meant a progressive improvement in secular, as well as religious, affairs.

Nowhere is this semi-religious, semi-secular view of Progress and Mission more apparent than in the Thanksgiving sermons which celebrated the conquest of Canada in 1760 and the peace treaty of 1763. The war was the last of four bloody colonial conflicts with France, and their prophetic reading of Scriptures told New Englanders that the "Popish French" were Satan's agents in the long struggle between Christ and Antichrist. The victory meant that God's Chosen had reached an important milestone on the road to the Millennium.

This view was articulated in countless Thanksgiving sermons, many of which were published amidst the euphoria of victory. The following excerpt is reproduced from a sermon by a lesser known pastor, Samuel Haven (of the South Church in Portsmouth), published by the local printer (Daniel Fowle, 1763) and now housed in the American Antiquarian Society.

Organized in traditional form, the sermon began with a text from Isaiah, which, as Haven explained, involved the Jews' return from the Babylonian captivity. Isaiah's praise of the Lord, he further explained, concerned not only the immediate success of God's Chosen, but also prophesied future successes. From this text, Haven drew the doctrine that God "hath made bare his holy arm from age to age, while he has maintained the cause of his church...."

Haven developed the doctrine by recounting history, showing how God had "made bare his holy arm" in support of ancient Israel, the early Christian church and the Protestant Reformation. He started his third point by telling how the Pope, being the earthly agent of Antichrist, had tried to destroy the Reformation by sending Catholic and tyrannical nations against the Protestant and liberty-loving British. He continued by turning to the history of British America, and it is this portion of the sermon that is reproduced below (pp. 26-33).

Excerpt from Joy and Salvation by Christ; His Arm Displayed in the Protestant Cause. A Sermon Preached in the South Parish of Portsmouth; Occasioned by the Remarkable Success of His Majesty's Arms in the Late War, and by the Happy Peace of 1763.

But in this review we cannot fail to observe the dispensations of divine providence towards this country. "We have heard with our ears, O God, our fathers have told us what works thou didst, in their days, in the times of old, how thou didst drive out the heathen with thy hand, and plantest them, how thou didst afflict the people and cast them out. For they got not the land in possession by their own sword, neither did their own arm save them; but thy right hand and thine arm, and the light of thy countenance, because thou hadst a favour unto them." When a cloud was gathering over England and began to discharge itself upon our father's, hither the divine hand of providence led them...here they sought an asilum, and took their abode among savage beasts and more savage men.

They left their dear native country, their pleasant habitations, and indured a train of hardships, scarce credible to their posterity, that they might worship God according to their consciences, and maintain the protestant religion free from those corruptions which the high-church party had introduced at home.

When we reflect on their design, it appears truly noble, becoming the

---

The original printing of this address included extensive use of italics and numerous printer's errors and printing conventions that are different from those of our time (e.g., frequent use of small case at the beginning of sentences, non-use of apostrophes to show the possessive, use of a series of periods instead of dashes). To facilitate reading, the italics have been eliminated, but to give a flavor of colonial printing, other mannerisms (including errors) have been faithfully reproduced.

disciples of Christ, who has taught his followers, "to call no man master on earth," nor to receive for "doctrines the traditions of men;" but when we consider the difficulties which were opposed to this design, meer reason surely represents it altogether impracticable. For a handful of men, poorly accommodated to come into an howling wilderness...on a dangerous coast in a difficult season...into a wilderness, not desolate indeed...but far worse...full of cruel men, void of humanity, subtil, inured to want, expert in cruelty, &c. what surprizing attempt in this! yet the most High succeded it; he prepared room for this his British vine, swept away thousands of Indians by an epidemical sickness the preceeding year, and overuled those that survived; so that many of their tribes assisted the new settlement of our fathers, when (humanly speaking) it was in their power to have frustrated the whole design, and cut all off at one blow.

Then the pure gospel of Jesus the saviour visited this new world and the glorious sun of righteousness arose on these benighted ends of the earth: then the waste places of America broke forth into joy, "the wilderness began to blossom as a rose" and "the trees of the forest sang together."

But these tranquil scenes soon closed, and numerous tribes combined together, (many of them in open violation of their plighted faith) to make an utter end of the English in America. So few and defenceless were our settlements at that time; and so remote from their mother-country, that human probability devoted them an easy prey to their adversaries: and surely our fathers "had fainted had they not believed to see the salvation of the Lord," But the puisiant Jehovah was on their side. "He taught their hands to war, and their fingers to fight;" so that in them the promise made to Israel, was almost literally verified, viz. that "five shall chase an hundred, and an hundred put ten thousand to flight." Then the holy arm of the Lord was made bare in the eyes of all these Indian nations; and the infant church of Christ in America saw the salvation of God.

The righteous sovereign, in whose hand the wicked are often the rod of his anger," has indeed suffered the savages to shed much English blood, and sorely scourge the British colonies, even as the Canaanites afflicted Israel of old; yet HE has greatly restrained their rage, deminished their numbers, and enlarged the borders of his church. nor can we reflect without astonishment on the happy change this land has undergone in the course of one centry: the aboriginals have been most remarkably declining: they have melted away, as snow before the southern breaze and scorching sun; while the churches of Christ have been greatly increasing, and are now become numerous in these teritories of the Prince of darkness. The Lion of the tribe of Judah has displayed his strength, and the holy arm of Jesus has bound "the strong man armed" and spoiled him of much of his armory wherein he trusted; so that our colonies have long since had little to fear, from the unassisted natives.

But while the Indian tribes were diminishing, a more dangerous enemy has been increasing, and incroaching upon us. Canada has been the Carthage of New England; and the French have long endeavoured both by artifice and arms to drive us from this good land which the Lord God gave unto our fathers.

How have they fomented strife, and sent forth their Indians on our frontiers! while they have been fostering new claims, and drawing a chain of forts around us. Together with these, they were incircling us with the chains of France and the superstition of Rome.

What just apprehensions of danger spread thro' our land, when (besides land forces) a formidable fleet of French ships under the command of Duke D'Anville actually arrived on our coast, and according to human probability, were within a few days of executing their bloody design, and spreading desolation and death all along our sea coasts.

But God blew with his wind and discomfited them: the stars in their courses fought against them. Our God broke their ships, and sent his destroying angel, who slew thousands of them; then, the arm of the Lord was made bear before the enemy, while the language of divine providence to us was, in a strain like that to Israel under the hand of Moses (that eminent tipe of Christ) "stand still and see the salvation of God:" this is an event never to be forgot: so remarkable was our deliverance, that even our popish enemies were obliged to confess the finger of God in it. Then the Lord redeemed his Israel and comforted his people, while his salvation was appointed instead of walls and bulworks around our coast.

These are all remarkable interpositions in favour of the protestant church, and glorious displays of the holy arm of the Almighty in our defence....

But later than these demand out attention, and should excite our gratitude

For

At the commencement of the late war, the dangerous union of the two houses of Burbon and Austria; who likewise called to their assistance Russia and Sweden, might well alarm England and Prussia, against whom this powerful alliance was formed. The grounds of our alarm must have risen much higher, on a view of the internal state of our nation at that time; our reigning principles and manners being such as in a great measure destroyed the natural strength of the nation. To behold Britons sinking all their natural prowess, and loosing the true British spirit, in effeminacy...wisdom and integrity forsaking the great,...love of money and party interest reigning where true patriosm [sic] should have glowed in the most fervent manner,... our officers unskilful...our troops irresolute, and the main body of the nation by almost every kind of abomination, calling aloud for the righteous vengeance of heaven, to behold, I say, all this was dreadful indeed! surely such a view of our public character might well presage the event of war. Accordingly, what a melancholly prospect did more than two years of the war present before us, while our fleets were inactive,...our armies flying...our men slaughtered...our forts surrendering...America and Hanover in danger of being totally conquered...and England threatned with an invasion! How black was the cloud which then hung over the protestant church! how solemn, how tremendous the view! how did the many, who wantoned in their liberties and luxuries, turn pale thro' fear; and the few who love our Lord Jesus Christ, and are praying for the prosperity of his Zion (with good old Eli) tremble for the Ark of the Lord? (Note: The use of multiple periods appears in the original as a form of emphasis such as that achieved by the use of dashes. They are not ellipses.)

But God surprized us with his mercy, and suddenly shifted the important scene.

He presides in all human Affairs, and will be acknowledged as supreme Ruler in the kingdom of providence. He turned to us the brigh[t] side of the cloud, which, like the pillar of fire and cloud of old, afforded light to us, but was portending blackness and dispair to our enemies: He, inspired our ministry with wisdom, our officers with military skill and braveness, and our armies and navy with true valour. He divided the councils of our enemies, spread darkness before them, and "turned back the weapons of war in their hands." He has, in a manner which will surprize posterity, and is indeed, little short of miraculous, supported the cause of our ally of Prussia: that little principality had to meet three of the most powerful states in Europe in the field, who, trusting to their great superiority in numbers, forstalled the pleasures of intire conquest, and cantonned his dominions among them. But he who was with Prussia is the God of armies, who always preponderates the doubtful scale of victory, & claims all the praise. The famous battles of Rosback and Lissa, of Crevelt and Zorndorff greatly display the holy arm of God in favour of our Allies, and the protestant church. By a series of remarkable interpositions and signal victories Prussia has been delivered from the very brink of ruin, and is at this time in very respectable circumstances.

The same divine hand is visibly displayed, in saving our nation from the ambitious designs of our enemies: "the Lord hath been our shield and buckler, our high tower and rock of defence." Nay! he has much more than saved us: he has made us every where victorious; so that we, who were destined by Burbon and Austria to be the tail, are, by the holy arm of our God, become the head of the nations; and our English monarch shines with distinguished lustre among all the crowned heads in Europe.

To recount the particular instances of our success in the late war, and point out the remarkable circumstances and wonderful interpositions of divine providence in our favour, is too copious a subject to fall within the compass of our present design: it is hoped, some able hand will do justice to this agreeable subject; that our children's children may be taught the loving kindness of the Lord towards his British Israel, in these memorable years, and "talk of all his wonderful works."

Our success in both the Indies, and on the African coast, the destruction of the French shipping at Cherburge and of their fleet at Villain, the demolishing of Luisburg, and total reduction of all Canada, are such instances of divine goodness to us, and such displays of his holy arm, as must have made the most lasting impressions on such as have any proper regard for liberty, religion, and their country.

Nor may we omit, in our review, the merciful hand of God towards us in regard to the court of Spain, who, unprovoked opened a war with us; leagued with our enemies; and afforded them all the assistance in their power. But, the most high has brought their councils to nought; and given into our hands the vast riches and strength of .e Havannah, and the Spanish navy there: so that Spain, after augmenting our fleet with a considerable part of their navy, and inriching us with milions in the compass of one year, is glad to accept such terms of peace as Briton generously proposes. May we not, without arrogating any merit to ourselves, speak on this occasion, in the language of inspiration and say, "the Lord is known by the Judgements which he executeth": the kings of the earth set themselves, and the rulers took council together, against the Lord, and his English Israel; but the Lord had them in derision: "the Lord of host hath been with us, the everlasting Jehovah has been our refuge:" all praise to him who hath thus maintained our right...frustrated the designs of these powerful popish states, comforted his people, and defended the cause of his protestant church.

As God is to be acknowledged in these remarkable successes, which have raised the british glory to an unusual hight, and will mark the Annals of England with the most resplendent lines; so we are likewise to adore his governing providence in the present happy and glorious PEACE.

Founding a Nation
Rhetoric of the
American Revolution

Declarations

Stamp Act Congress

Commentary

The euphoria that swept the colonies after the last French war was matched by goodwill toward the mother country, but the colonies and Britain were at war a dozen years later. The Revolution has been so mythologized that many twentieth-century Americans misunderstand this dramatic shift in opinion. Many believe that the colonies had long been tyrannized by the King, got tired of the abuse, developed a new democratic ideology and went to war. However, the political rhetoric of the 1760s and 1770s shows the myth to be wrong. It was the British Parliament, not the King or colonies, that initiated a so-called New Colonial Policy. The colonies, after trying unsuccessfully to persuade Britain to restore the Old Colonial Policy, finally revolted. Admittedly, colonists disagreed among themselves, but the rhetoric which failed to persuade Parliament was generally persuasive in America.

The Old Colonial Policy was developed during the late seventeenth and early eighteenth centuries. Although it theoretically gave Britain much control over the political and economic life of the colonies, its practical operation gave the colonies considerable home rule. London appointed colonial judicial and executive officials, including governors (except in Connecticut and Rhode Island), and London occasionally vetoed legislation passed by colonial legislatures. In most colonies, governors appointed the upper houses of the legislatures, but the lower houses, elected by male citizens who met the minimal property qualifications, had considerable power. They levied taxes and decided expenditures (including the salaries of their governors, who usually went along with what the legislatures wanted).

The Old Colonial Policy entailed a series of trade laws which Parliament enacted to ensure that the agricultural economies of the colonies benefited Britain. With a few exceptions, the laws did no damage to America. Far too complex to describe in detail, the trade laws were of three types. First, the Staple Act required that colonies purchase most of their manufactured goods from Britain and that Oriental goods (such as tea and spices) come to the colonies by way of Britain. Second, the Enumerated List consisted of Southern agricultural products (primarily tobacco) that had to be exported to Britain. The Enumerated List did not include lumber and grain, which northern colonies, especially New England, exported to the West Indies in exchange for molasses, which was converted to rum. Rum provided the foreign exchange for manufactured and Oriental goods that came from Britain. New Englanders traded with both the British and French West Indies. In 1733, Parliament enacted a third type of trade law, the Molasses Act. It imposed a tariff of six pence a gallon on "foreign" (in effect, French) molasses, and the tax was to be collected in American ports.

Although all trade laws eventually became involved, the Molasses Act was to play an especially important role in later rhetoric. Britain would cite it as a precedent to support its claim that Parliament had the constitutional authority to tax the colonies. Colonists would reply correctly that it was never designed to raise revenue. Being approximately a 100% tax, its purpose was to stop trade with the French Indies. However, colonists would neglect to mention that they avoided the tax, primarily by bribing customs officials. When a customs officer tried to enforce the law, he usually lost. He had to take his case to a colonial Vice Admiralty court (one for each colony), where decisions were rendered by a judge who was usually a colonial shipper and himself a smuggler.

Like Mopsy, the Old Colonial Policy "just growed." The fundamental legal question about parliamentary authority over the colonies had seldom been raised before the 1760s because both Britain and the colonies were reasonably well satisfied with political and economic arrangements.

While the largely independent colonies prospered under the Old Colonial Policy, three political ideologies evolved. All of them would affect rhetorical responses to the New Colonial Policy. Ironically, all were imported from Britain and grew out of events in Britain. First, the Glorious Revolution of 1688-1689, in which the British Parliament invited William and Mary to rule as joint monarchs under a set of limitations known as the "Bill of Rights," was extremely popular in America. By the time that Parliament began its New Colonial Policy in the 1760s, Americans had a long rhetorical tradition of referring respectfully to the British constitution, especially its Bill of Rights. Second, John Locke's famous Natural Law philosophy of government, written in the 1690s to justify the Glorious Revolution, was quickly accepted in the colonies. Quoting the "Great Mr. Locke" was another time-honored rhetorical tradition long before the American Revolution. Third, as eighteenth-century British monarchs lost power to Parliament, a loosely knit group of British writers, known as "Real Whigs" or "Commonwealthmen," verbally assailed the Whigs who dominated Parliament. "Real Whigs" emphasized individual liberty by arguing for greater democratization of Parliament, denouncing political corruption and exposing governmental "conspiracies" (both real and imagined). Although having little influence in Britain, "Real Whig" ideas spread like wildfire in America long before the American Revolution.

Central to all three ideologies was a deep respect for individual liberty and a profound distrust of government, which were encouraged by various factors. The Puritans had been driven into the wilderness by a tyrannical government. The heritage of congregationalism discouraged respect for central authority, which was intensified by revivalist preaching against the authority of "cold-hearted ministers." The Puritan emphasis on "God's Law" meshed easily with Locke's Natural Law, and the Puritan view of history, with its emphasis on satanic forces conspiring against the Chosen, encouraged Americans to look for conspiracies everywhere — including governmental conspiracies to destroy people's liberties. A small population of farmers being spread over a wide area made laws difficult to enforce and encouraged individualism. Thus, when Parliament instituted an authoritarian New Colonial Policy, colonists were predisposed to oppose it. Although they did not think of themselves as "Americans," their common ideology was a foundation for building a new nation.

Printing also spread long before the Revolution. Although the first press was established in 1636, most seventeenth-century publications were either non-controversial (e.g., educational materials) or about religious disputes. By the early eighteenth century, political pamphlets and newspapers became increasingly popular. Only the well-to-do could afford to purchase them, so tavern owners subscribed to papers and purchased a few pamphlets for the benefit of their customers. Meanwhile, religious meetings (sermons), town meetings and a growing number of private organizations (such as merchants' associations) continued; thus, when colonial opinion leaders objected to Parliament's New Colonial Policy, they had an efficient communications network at their disposal. They could communicate not only with audiences in their own colonies, but also with other colonies and the mother country.

In short, the New Colonial Policy was doomed to failure. Largely unaware of colonial matters, Parliament decided that the end of the French war was a time for "reform." Faced with a much-enlarged empire to govern and serious financial difficulties, it was time to tighten London's control over the largely independent colonies and to raise a revenue in America. The new policy was enunciated clearly in 1764, when Parliament announced its intention of imposing a stamp tax on Americans in the near future and revised the trade laws, the preamble to which said explicitly that the new American (or Sugar) Act was designed to raise revenue as well as regulate trade. Based on the mistaken assumption that smuggling cost shippers three pence a gallon (in reality, it was around half a pence), the law reduced the tariff to three pence, which British leaders thought Americans would be willing to pay. Just to be sure that the tax was collected, enforcement procedures were tightened. Under the existing judicial system, all cases except those involving shipping were tried by juries in "common law" courts. Inasmuch as smuggling involved shipping, customs officers had to take their cases to a colonial Vice Admiralty court (one in each colony), where cases were decided by judges, not juries. Judges, being colonists, were usually sympathetic to the defendant. The new law provided for a single Vice Admiralty court with jurisdiction over all the colonies and was to be staffed by Britons.

Seven colonial legislatures promptly dispatched petitions to Parliament and the King, asking either that the new trade law be repealed, that the stamp tax not be imposed or both. The petitions, which were sometimes circulated as pamphlets in the colonies, had three basic rhetorical appeals, two of which were merely unpersuasive in London but the third (and most important) of which aroused Parliament's hostility. All were well received by colonial audiences. First, they argued that colonists would be impoverished by additional taxes, which would decrease the demand for British goods and injure British exporters. Despite the adaptation to British readers, Parliament was unpersuaded, but colonists liked it. Second, they argued that the new Court of Vice Admiralty was inconvenient and violated the British right of trial by jury. This argument made little sense in Britain, where the Admiralty Court was a time-honored fixture, and Parliamentarians familiar with America knew that each colony already had a Vice Admiralty court. However, the prospect of the Molasses Act being enforced alarmed shippers, and the lack of juries alarmed colonists in general. Finally, and most importantly, they argued that Parliament had no constitutional authority to tax the colonists, who were already taxed by their own legislatures. This argument had obvious overtones of colonial independence, and Parliament was incensed. Colonial response, on the other hand, was generally (though not entirely) favorable.

Scornfully disregarding colonial petitions, Parliament passed the Stamp Act in early 1765. It required that colonial legal documents and newspapers be affixed with stamps that were to be purchased from a stamp distributor (one for each colony). Unlike the law of the previous year, the stamp tax was intended solely to raise revenue and had nothing to do with regulating trade. Because shippers had to fill out many legal documents before clearing port, they would be the major taxpayers. The law also applied directly to lawyers, printers and even preachers (who had to fill out marriage certificates, etc.). In short, Parliament inadvertently ensured the opposition of colonial opinion leaders, most of whom were convinced that Parliament had no constitutional authority to impose the tax.

News of the Stamp Act, which was to take effect on November 1, 1765, began arriving in April and May. The intervening months saw one of the most dramatic protest movements in American history. Legislative petitions, which contained much the same arguments as those of the previous year, were again dispatched to London, but there was much more militancy and a greater sense of unity than in 1764. Militant extra-legal groups, although organized independently, corresponded with one another and adopted a common name: Sons of Liberty. They urged the colonial public to ignore the law. They employed violence and threats of violence to force stamp distributors to resign their posts.

Although opposition to the Stamp Act was almost universal (coming even from future Loyalists), colonial legislators were divided about what to do. Some supported the violence while others did not. None dared to endorse it officially. Colonial politicians also disagreed about what kind of rhetoric they should use in their petitions to Britain. Some wished to argue that the colonies historically had the "privilege" of not being taxed by Parliament (thus implying that Parliament had the constitutional "right" to do so), but most favored using the argument of unconstitutionality. Despite these differences, nine legislatures accepted the invitation from Massachusetts to send delegates to a "congress," though three could not do so because their governors refused to convene an election assembly. This was the first time that an intercolonial congress had been held since 1754, when a few colonies met (and failed) to take united action against the French. The "Stamp Act Congress" endorsed a boycott of British imports (thereby legitimizing peaceful coercion) and composed several rhetorical documents that were similar but adapted and dispatched to individual British audiences (the King and the two houses of Parliament). They were accompanied by the "Declarations," and the complete set was included in a pamphlet that circulated in Britain and the colonies. The essence of the argument was contained in the "Declarations," which is reproduced from the American Antiquarian Society's copy of the *Proceedings of the Congress at New York* (Annapolis, 1766), pp. 15-16.

Declarations

The Members of this Congress, sincerely devoted, with [the war]mest Sentiments of Affection and Duty to his Majesty's Person [and] Government, inviolably attached to the present happy Establishment of the Protestant Succession, and with Minds deeply impressed by a Sense of the present and impending Misfortunes of the British Colonies on this Continent; having considered as maturely as Time will permit, the Circumstances of the said Colonies, esteem it our indispensable Duty, to make the following Declarations of our humble Opinion, respecting the most Essential Rights and Liberties of the Colonists, and of the Grievances under which they labour, by Reason of several late Acts of Parliament.

I.   That his Majesty's Subjects in these Colonies, owe the same Allegiance to the Crown of Great-Britain, that is owing from his Subjects born within the Realm, and all due Subordination to that August Body the Parliament of Great-Britain.

II.   That his Majesty's Liege Subjects in these Colonies, are entitled to all the inherent Rights and Liberties of his Natural born Subjects, within the Kingdom of Great-Britain.

The original printing of this address included extensive use of italics and numerous printer's errors and printing conventions that are different from those of our time (e.g., frequent use of small case at the beginning of sentences, non-use of apostrophes to show the possessive, use of a series of periods instead of dashes). To facilitate reading, the italics have been eliminated, but to give a flavor of colonial printing, other mannerisms (including errors) have been faithfully reproduced.

III.   That it is inseparably essential to the Freedom of a People, and the undoubted Right of Englishmen, that no Taxes be imposed on them, but with their own Consent, given personally, or by their Representatives.

IV.   That the People of these Colonies are not, and from their local Circumstances cannot be, Represented in the House of Commons in Great-Britain.

V. That the only Representatives of the People of these Colonies, are Persons chosen therein by themselves, and that no Taxes ever have been, or can be Constitutionally imposed on them, but by their respective Legislature[s].

VI.   That all Supplies to the Crown, being free Gifts of the People, it is unreasonable and inconsistent with the Principles and Spirit of the British Constitution, for the People of Great-Britain, to grant to his Majesty the Property of the Colonists.

VII.   That Trial by Jury, is the inherent and invaluable Right of every British Subject in these Colonies.

VIII.   That the late Act of Parliament, entitled, An Act for granting and applying certain Stamp Duties, and other Duties, in the British Colonies and Plantations in America, &c. by imposing Taxes on the Inhabitants of these Colonies, and the said Act, and several other Acts, by extending the Jurisdiction of the Courts of Admiralty beyond its ancient Limits, have a manifest Tendency to subvert the Rights and Liberties of the Colonists.

IX.   That the Duties imposed by several late Acts of Parliament, from the peculiar Circumstances of these Colonies, will be extremely Burthensome and Grievous; and from the scarcity of Specie, the Payment of them absolutely impracticable.

X.   That as the Profits of the Trade of these Colonies ultimately center in Great-Britain, to pay for the Manufactures which they are obliged to take from thence, they eventually contribute very largely to all Supplies granted there to the Crown.

XI.   That the Restrictions imposed by several late Acts of Parliament, on the Trade of these Colonies, will render them unable to purchase the Manufactures of Great-Britain.

XII.   That the Increase, Prosperity, and Happiness of these Colonies, depend on the full and free Enjoyment of their Rights and Liberties, and an Intercourse with Great-Britain mutually Affectionate and Advantageous.

XIII. That it is the Right of the British Subjects in these Colonies, to Petition the King, or either House of Parliament.

Lastly, That it is the indispensable Duty of these Colonies, to the best of Sovereigns, to the Mother Country, and to themselves, to endeavour by a loyal and dutiful Address to his Majesty, and humble Applications to both Houses of Parliament, to procure the Repeal of the Act for granting and applying certain Stamp Duties, of all Clauses of any other Acts of Parliament, whereby the Jurisdiction of the Admiralty is extended as aforesaid, and of the other late Acts for the Restriction of American Commerce.

Letter II *in Letters from a Farmer in Pennsylvania to the Inhabitants of the British Colonies*

John Dickinson

Commentary

Parliament's repeal of the Stamp Act in 1766 was not due to American rhetoric. It resulted from lobbying by British exporters, who were alarmed by the colonial boycott, and a new administration's desire to extricate itself from the impossible task of enforcing the law. Aware of Parliament's anger at having its constitutional authority challenged, the new administration shrewdly preceded its proposal to repeal the Stamp Act with a Declaratory Act, which proclaimed Parliament's authority over the colonies "in all cases whatsoever."

Amidst the euphoria that came with repeal, colonists generally overlooked the Declaratory Act and drew some conclusions that were partly right and partly wrong. Most colonists attributed their success to the combination of coercion and rhetoric. Although there were some afterthoughts about the violence, the boycott was praised. All this was to have a profound effect on subsequent colonial strategies.

Largely oblivious to colonial opinion and chafing from its defeat, Parliament persisted in trying to enforce the New Colonial Policy, most notably by passing the Townshend Acts (1767). They imposed tariffs on tea and a few manufactured goods, which under the Staple Act could be imported legally only from Britain. Thus its obvious intent was to raise revenue, not regulate trade.

Townshend apparently hoped that colonists would accept tariffs. In some of the earlier rhetoric, colonists had referred to the Stamp Act as an "internal tax." He apparently thought that they would not extend the argument of unconstitutionality to "external taxes" (i.e., tariffs). After all, the molasses tariff had been around for years.

Townshend was partly right but mostly wrong. Opposition grew more slowly than in 1765. Some colonists were apparently unsure about what Parliament's constitutional authority actually was. The premise that citizens had to be represented in Parliament before its laws were legally binding would, if taken to its logical conclusion, mean that Parliament had no authority over the colonies whatsoever, but no one was ready yet to accept such a conclusion. Yet the Townshend Acts were unwelcome because they were revenue-raising. By the end of 1767, American merchants were forming Non-Importation Associations to pressure Britain with another economic boycott.

A major leader in the non-importation movement was John Dickinson (1732-1808), a wealthy landowner and Philadelphia lawyer. He generated public support with a series of "letters" that were published widely in colonial newspapers and collected into a pamphlet that went through several editions. The pamphlet's title, *Letters from a Farmer in Pennsylvania, to the Inhabitants of the British Colonies,* was linked to his self-portrayal in the first letter as a "gentleman farmer." It was a rhetorical masterstroke, identifying him with America's most common occupation and yet identifying him as one who had the leisure to study all (and he said "all") British laws relating to the colonies.

Taken as a whole, the "letters" built to a rhetorical climax and can be thought of as a single discourse. Yet each letter was complete in and of itself. The second one was especially important because it resolved the confusion about the constitutional authority of Parliament. It is reproduced from the American Antiquarian Society's copy of the first pamphlet edition (Philadelphia: Hall & Sellers, 1768), pp. 7-13, and is complete except for the omission of its voluminous footnotes.

Letter II in *Letters from a Farmer in Pennsylvania to the Inhabitants of the British Colonies*

My dear COUNTRYMEN,

THERE is another late act of parliament, which appears to me to be unconstitutional, and as destructive to the liberty of these colonies, as that mentioned in my last letter; that is, the act for granting the duties on paper, glass, &c.

THE parliament unquestionably possesses a legal authority to regulate the trade of Great-Britain, and all her colonies. Such an authority is essential to the relation between a mother country and her colonies; and necessary for the common good of all. He, who considers these provinces as states distinct from the British Empire, has very slender notions of justice, or of their interests. We are but parts of a whole; and therefore there must exist a power somewhere, to preside, and preserve the connection in due order. This power is lodged in

---

The original printing of this address included extensive use of italics and numerous printer's errors and printing conventions that are different from those of our time (e.g., frequent use of small case at the beginning of sentences, non-use of apostrophes to show the possessive, use of a series of periods instead of dashes). To facilitate reading, the italics have been eliminated, but to give a flavor of colonial printing, other mannerisms (including errors) have been faithfully reproduced.

the parliament; and we are as much dependant on Great-Britain, as a perfectly free people can be on another.

I HAVE looked over every statute relating to these colonies, from their first settlement to this time; and I find every one of them founded on this principle, till the Stamp-Act administration. All before, are calculated to regulate trade, and preserve or promote a mutually beneficial intercourse between the several constituent parts of the empire; and though many of them imposed duties on trade, yet those duties were always imposed with design to restrain the commerce of one part, that was injurious to another, and thus to promote the general welfare. The raising a revenue thereby was never intended. Thus the King, by his judges in his courts of justice, imposes fines, which all together amount to a very considerable sum, and contribute to the support of government: But this is merely a consequence arising from restrictions, that only meant to keep peace, and prevent confusion; and surely a man would argue very loosely, who should conclude from hence, that the King has a right to levy money in general upon his subjects. Never did the British parliament, till the period above mentioned, think of imposing duties in America, FOR THE PURPOSE OF RAISING A REVENUE. Mr. Greenville first introduced this language, in the preamble to the 4th of Geo. III. Chap. 15 [i.e., the American Act], which has these words — "And whereas it is just and necessary that A REVENUE BE RAISED IN YOUR MAJESTY'S SAID DOMINIONS IN AMERICA, for defraying the expences of defending, protecting, and securing the same: We your Majesty's most dutiful and loyal subjects, THE COMMONS OF GREAT-BRITAIN, in parliament assembled, being desirous to make some provision in this present session of parliament, TOWARDS RAISING THE SAID REVENUE IN AMERICA, have resolved to GIVE and GRANT unto your Majesty the several rates and duties herein after mentioned," &c.

A FEW months after came the Stamp-Act, which reciting this, proceeds in the same strange mode of expression, thus — "And whereas it is just and necessary, that provision be made FOR RAISING A FURTHER REVENUE WITHIN YOUR MAJESTY'S DOMINIONS IN AMERICA, towards defraying the said expences, we your Majesty's most dutiful and loyal subjects, the COMMONS OF GREAT-BRITAIN, &c. GIVE and GRANT," &c. as before.

The last act, granting duties upon paper, &c. carefully pursues these modern precedents. The preamble is, "Whereas it is expedient THAT A REVENUE SHOULD BE RAISED IN YOUR MAJESTY'S DOMINIONS IN AMERICA, for making a more certain and adequate provision for defraying the charge of the administration of justice, and the support of civil government in such provinces, where it shall be found necessary; and towards the further defraying the expenses of defending, protecting and securing the said dominions, we your Majesty's most dutiful and loyal subjects, the COMMONS OF GREAT-BRITAIN, &c. GIVE and GRANT," &c. as before.

Here we may observe an authority expressly claimed and exerted to impose duties on these colonies; not for the regulation of trade; not for the preservation or promotion of a mutually beneficial intercourse between the several constituent parts of the empire, heretofore the sole objects of parliamentary institutions; but for the single purpose of levying money upon us.

THIS I call an innovation; and a most dangerous innovation. It may perhaps be objected, that Great-Britain has a right to lay what duties she pleases upon her exports, and it makes no difference to us, whether they are paid here or there.

To this I answer. These colonies require many things for their use, which the laws of Great-Britain prohibit them from getting any where but from her. Such are paper and glass.

THAT we may legally be bound to pay any general duties on these commodities, relative to the regulation of trade, is granted; but we being obliged to her laws to take them from Great-Britain, any special duties imposed on their exportation to us only, with intention to raise a revenue from us only, are as much taxes upon us, as those imposed by the Stamp-Act.

WHAT is the difference in substance and right, whether the same sum is raised upon us by the rates mentioned in the Stamp-Act, on the use of paper, or by these duties, on the importation of it. It is only the edition of a former book, shifting a sentence from the end to the beginning.

SUPPOSE the duties were made payable to Great-Britain?

IT signifies nothing to us, whether they are to be paid here or there. Had the Stamp-Act directed, that all the paper should be landed at Florida, and the duties paid there, before it was brought to the British colonies, would the act have raised less money upon us, or have been less destructive of our rights? By no means: For as we were under a necessity of using the paper, we should have been under the necessity of paying the duties. Thus, in the present case, a like necessity will subject us, if this act continues in force, to the payment of the duties now imposed.

WHY was the Stamp-Act then so pernicious to freedom? It did not enact, that every man in the colonies should buy a certain quantity of paper — No: It only directed, that no instrument of writing should be valid in law, if not made on stamped paper, &c.

THE makers of that act knew full well, that the confusions that would arise from the disuse of writings, would COMPEL the colonies to use the stamped paper, and therefore to pay the taxes imposed. For this reason the Stamp-Act was said to be a law THAT WOULD EXECUTE ITSELF. For the very same reason, the last act of parliament, if it is granted to have any force here, WILL EXECUTE ITSELF, and will be attended with the very same consequences to American liberty.

SOME persons perhaps may say, that this act lays us under no necessity to pay the duties imposed, because we may ourselves manufacture the articles on which they are laid; whereas by the Stamp-Act no instrument of writing could be good, unless made on British paper, and that too stamped.

SUCH an objection amounts to no more than this, that the injury resulting to these colonies, from the total disuse of British paper and glass, will not be so afflicting as that which would have resulted from the total disuse of writing among them; for by that means even the Stamp-Act might have been eluded. Why then was it universally detested by them as slavery itself? Because it presented to these devoted provinces nothing but a choice of calamities, imbittered by indignities, each of which it was unworthy of freemen to bear. But is no injury a violation of right but the greatest injury? If the eluding the payment of taxes imposed by the Stamp-Act, would have subjected us to a more dreadful inconvenience, than the eluding the payment of those imposed by the late act; does it therefore follow, that the last is no violation of our rights, tho' it is calculated for the same purpose the other was, that is, to raise money upon us, WITHOUT OUR CONSENT?

THIS would be making right to consist, not in an exemption from injury, but from a certain degree of injury.

BUT the objectors may further say, that we shall suffer no injury at all by the disuse of British paper and glass. We might not, if we could make as much as we want. But can any man, acquainted with America, believe this possible? I am told there are but two or three Glass-Houses on this continent, and but very few Paper-Mills; and suppose more should be erected, a long course of years must elapse, before they can be brought to perfection. This continent is a country of planters, farmers, and fishermen; not of manufacturers. The difficulty of establishing particular manufactures in such a country, is almost insuperable. For one manufacture is connected with others in such a manner, that it may be said to be impossible to establish one or two, without establishing several others. The experience of many nations may convince us of this truth.

INEXPRESSIBLE therefore must be our distresses in evading the late acts, by the disuse of British paper and glass. Nor will this be the extent of our misfortune, if we admit the legality of that act.

GREAT-BRITAIN has prohibited the manufacturing iron and steel in these colonies, without any objection being made to her right of doing it. The like right she must have to prohibit any other manufacture among us. Thus she is possessed of an undisputed precedent on that point. This authority, she will say, is founded on the original intention of settling these colonies; that is, that she should manufacture for them, and that they should supply her with materials. The equity of this policy, she will also say, has been universally acknowledged by the colonies, who never have made the least objection to statutes for that purpose; and will further appear by the mutual benefits flowing from this usage, ever since the settlement of these colonies.

OUR great advocate, Mr. Pitt, in his speeches on the debate concerning the repeal of the Stamp-Act, acknowledged, that Great-Britain could restrain our manufactures. His words are these — "This kingdom, as the supreme governing and legislative power, has ALWAYS bound the colonies by her regulations and RESTRICTIONS in trade, in navigation, in MANUFACTURES — in every thing, except that of taking their money out of their pockets, WITHOUT THEIR CONSENT." Again he says, "We may bind their trade, CONFINE THEIR MANUFACTURES, and exercise every power whatever, except that of taking their money out of their pockets, WITHOUT THEIR CONSENT."

HERE then, my dear countrymen, ROUSE yourselves, and behold the ruin hanging over your heads. If you ONCE admit, that Great-Britain may lay duties upon her exportations to us, for the purpose of levying money on us only, she then will have nothing to do, but to lay those duties on the articles which she prohibits us to manufacture — and the tragedy of American liberty is finished. We have been prohibited from procuring manufactures, in all cases, any where but from Great-Britain (excepting linens, which we are permitted to import directly from Ireland.) We have been prohibited, in some cases, from manufacturing for ourselves; and may be prohibited in others. We are therefore exactly in the situation of a city besieged, which is surrounded by the works of the besiegers in every part but one. If that is closed up, no step can be taken, but to surrender at discretion. If Great-Britain can order us to come to her for necessaries we want, and can order us to pay what taxes she pleases before we take them away, or when we can land them here, we are as abject slaves as France and Poland can shew in wooden shoes, and with uncombed hair.

PERHAPS the nature of the necessities of dependent states, caused by the policy of a governing one, for her own benefit, may be elucidated by a fact mentioned in history. When the Carthaginians were possessed of the island of Sardinia, they made a decree, that the Sardinians should not raise corn, nor get it any other way than from the Carthaginians. Then, by imposing any duties they would upon it, they drained from the miserable Sardinians any sums they pleased; and whenever that oppressed people made the least movement to assert their liberty, their tyrants starved them to death or submission. This may be called the most perfect kind of political necessity.

FROM what has been said, I think this uncontrovertible conclusion may be deduced, that when a ruling state obliges a dependant state to take certain commodities from her alone, it is implied in the nature of that obligation; is essentially requisite to give it the least degree of justice; and is inseparably united with it, in order to preserve any share of freedom to the dependant state; that those commodities should never be loaded with duties, FOR THE SOLE PURPOSE OF LEVYING MONEY ON THE DEPENDANT STATE.

UPON the whole, the single question is, whether the parliament can legally impose duties to be paid by the people of these colonies only, FOR THE SOLE PURPOSE OF RAISING A REVENUE, on commodities which she obliges us to take from her alone, or, in other words, whether the parliament can legally take money out of our pockets, without our consent. If they can, our boasted liberty is but *Vox et praeterea nihil.* A sound and nothing else.

A FARMER.

Boston Massacre Oration— March 5, 1774

John Hancock

Commentary

Parliament's refusal to repeal the Townshend Acts put the economic boycott to a severe test. Merchants who continued importing could prosper at the expense of their boycotting competitors. Violence against these "smuggling merchants" became common, especially in Boston. Determined to teach the rebellious upstarts a lesson, Britain sent four regiments to Boston in late 1768. It was an unwise move. British law prohibited the army from quelling civilian riots unless invited to do so by civilian authorities, and Boston officials had no intention of issuing such an invitation. So the soldiers did nothing — except irritate Bostonians by their presence. On March 5, 1770, an incident occurred on King's Street (later State Street) in which several civilians were killed.

Most of the blame lay with the mob. Even though the soldiers were tried in civilian (rather than military) court, most were acquitted, and only two were convicted of manslaughter (not murder, as charged). Unencumbered by anything as trivial as the truth, a Boston town meeting officially endorsed the report of an investigating committee, which denounced the "Horrid Massacre." The report was issued as a pamphlet, thereby publicizing legally endorsed factual misrepresentation.

Although troops were withdrawn and the Townshend Acts partially repealed, many New England towns held annual commemorations of the "Massacre," each of which featured an oration by a distinguished "patriot." The commemorations were held on March 5 until after the Revolutionary War, when the date was changed to July 4. The Boston orations were published as pamphlets. They reinforced popular resentment during the short period of calm which prevailed after the partial repeal of the Townshend Acts and functioned as a powerful emotional appeal during the tense years ahead.

When Bostonians met on March 5, 1774, tensions had reached a new high.

During the previous year, Parliament had passed the Tea Act, which led to the famous "Tea Party" of December 16, 1773. When news of the party reached Parliament in January, 1774, it began work on a series of laws that would become known in the colonies as the "Intolerable Acts" and lead to the first intercolonial congress since Stamp Act days, the "Continental Congress."

News of only the first act had reached Boston when citizens met "to commemorate the bloody tragedy of the fifth of March 1770" — but it was terrifying news indeed. The Boston Port Bill closed the port to the import-export trade until Boston paid for the destroyed tea. If enforced, the law meant economic disaster for a town which lived off trade. Previous British efforts to enforce parliamentary laws had never amounted to much, but terrified citizens feared that this one would. Everyone knew that the current governor was leaving, and rumors circulated that his replacement would be an army general who was bringing soldiers with him.

For the first time in the Revolutionary Movement, the spectre of war permeated the atmosphere. It was in this rhetorical situation that Boston's wealthiest merchant and distinguished patriot, John Hancock (1737-1793), delivered his "Massacre" oration. But he did not speak only to the thousands of Bostonians who heard him. His oration went through five pamphlet editions and was read throughout the colonies. It is reproduced here from a later printing in *The Magazine of History, with Notes and Queries*, vol. 24, no. 95 (1923), pp. 125-36.

Boston Massacre Oration—March 5, 1774

MEN, BRETHREN, FATHERS AND FELLOW-COUNTRYMEN!

THE attentive gravity, the venerable appearance of this crouded audience, the dignity which I behold in the countenances of so many in this great assembly, the solemnity of the occasion upon which we have met together, joined to a consideration of the part I am to take in the important business of this day, fill me with an awe hitherto unknown, and heighten the sense which I have ever had of my unworthiness to fill this sacred desk; but, allured by the call of some of my respected fellow-citizens, with whose request it is always my greatest pleasure to comply, I almost forgot my want of ability to perform what they required. In this situation I find my only support in assuring myself that a generous people will not severely censure what they know was well intended, though its want of merit should prevent their being able to applaud it. And I pray that my sincere attachment to the interest of my country, and hearty detestation of every design formed against her liberties, may be admitted as some apology for my appearance in this place.

I HAVE always, from my earliest youth, rejoiced in the felicity of my fellow-men; and have ever considered it as the indispensable duty of every member of society to promote, as far as in him lies, the prosperity of every individual, but more especially of the community to which he belongs; and also, as a faithful subject of the state, to use his utmost endeavors to detect, and having detected, strenuously to oppose every traitorous plot which its enemies may devise for its destruction. Security to the persons and properties of the governed is so obviously the design and end of civil government, that to attempt a logical proof of it, would be like burning tapers at noon-day to assist the sun in enlightening the world; and it cannot be either virtuous or honorable to attempt to support a government of which this is not the great and principal basis; and it is to the last degree vicious and infamous to attempt to support a government, which manifestly tends to render the persons and properties of the governed insecure. Some boast of being *friends to government*; I am a friend to *righteous* government, to a government founded upon the principles of reason and justice; but I glory in publicly avowing my eternal enmity to tyranny. Is the present system which the British administration have adopted for the government of the colonies, a righteous government or is it tyranny? — Here suffer me to ask (and would to heaven there could be an answer) what tenderness, what regard, respect or consideration has *Great-Britain* shown in their late transactions, for the security of the persons or properties of the inhabitants of the colonies, or rather, what have they omitted doing to destroy that security? They have declared that they have, ever had, and of right ought ever to have, full power to make laws of sufficient validity to bind the colonies in all cases whatever: they have exercised this pretended right by imposing a tax upon us without our consent; and lest we should shew some reluctance at parting with our property, her fleets and armies are sent to enforce their mad pretensions. The town of Boston, ever faithful to the British crown, has been invested by a British fleet: the troops of George the III. have cross'd the wide Atlantick, not to engage an enemy but to assist a band of TRAITORS in trampling on the rights and liberties of his most loyal subjects in America, — those rights and liberties which, as a father, he ought ever to regard, and as a king, he is bound in honor to defend from violations, even at the risque of his own life.

LET not the history of the illustrious house of Brunswick inform posterity that a king, descended from that glorious monarch George the II. once sent his British subjects to conquer and enslave his subjects in America; but be perpetual infamy entail'd upon that villain who dared to advise his master to such execrable measures; for it was easy to foresee the consequences, which so naturally followed upon sending troops into America, to enforce obedience to acts of the British parliament which neither God nor man ever empowered them to make. It was reasonable to expect that troops, who knew the errand they were sent upon, would treat the people whom they were to subjugate, with a cruelty and haughtiness which too often buries the honorable character of a *soldier,* in the disgraceful name of an *unfeeling ruffian.* The troops, upon their first arrival, took possession of our senate-house, and pointed their cannon against the judgment-hall, and even continued them there whilst the supreme court of judicature for this province was actually sitting to decide upon the lives and fortunes of the king's subjects. Our streets nightly resounded with the noise of riot and debauchery; our peaceful citizens were hourly exposed to shameful insults and often felt the effects of their violence and outrage. But this was not all: as though they thought it not enough to violate our civil rights, they endeavored to deprive us of the enjoyment of our religious privileges; to violate our morals, and thereby render us deserving of destruction. Hence the rude din of arms which broke in upon our solemn devotions in your temples, on that day hallowed by heaven, and set apart by GOD himself for his peculiar worship. Hence impious oaths and blasphemies so often tortur'd your unaccustomed ear. Hence all the arts which idleness and luxury could invent, were used to betray our youth of one sex into extravagance and effeminacy and of the other to infamy and ruin; and did they not succeed but too well? did not a reverence for religion sensibly decay? did not our infants almost learn to lisp out curses before they knew their horrid import? did not our youth forget they were Americans, and regardless of the admonitions of the wise and aged, servilely copy from their tyrants those vices which finally must overthrow the empire of Great-Britain? and must I be compelled to acknowledge that even the noblest fairest part of all the lower creation did not entirely escape the cursed snare? When virtue has once erected her throne within the female breast, it is upon so solid a basis that nothing is able to expel the heavenly inhabitant. But have there not been some, few indeed, I hope, whose youth and inexperience have render'd them a prey to wretches whom, upon the least reflection, they would have despised and hated as foes to GOD and their country? I fear there have been some such unhappy instances; or why have I seen an honest father cloathed with shame; or why a virtuous mother drowned in tears?

BUT I forbear, and come reluctantly to the transactions of that dismal night, when in such quick succession we felt the extremes of grief, astonishment and rage; when heaven in anger, for a dreadful moment, suffer'd hell to take the reins; when Satan with his chosen band open'd the sluices of New-England's blood, and sacrilegiously polluted our land with the dead bodies of her guiltless sons. Let this sad tale of death never be told without a tear: let not the heaving bosom cease to burn with a manly indignation at the barbarous story, through the long tracts of future time: let every parent tell the shameful story to his listening children 'til tears of pity glisten in their eyes, and boiling passion shakes their tender frames; and whilst the anniversary of that ill-fated night is kept a jubilee in the grim court of pandaemonium, let all America join in one common prayer to heaven that the inhuman, unprovoked murders of the fifth of March, 1770, planned by Hillsborough and a knot of treacherous knaves in Boston, and executed by the cruel hand of Preston and his sanguinary coadjutors, may ever stand in history without a parallel. But what, my countrymen, witheld the ready arm of vengeance from executing instant justice on the vile assassins? Perhaps you fear'd promiscuous carnage might ensue, and that the innocent might share the fate of those who had performed the infernal deed. But were not all guilty? were you not too tender of the lives of those who came to fix a yoke on your necks? but I must not too severely blame a fault which great souls only can commit. May that magnificence of spirit which scorns the low pursuits of malice; may that generous compassion which often preserves from ruin even a guilty villain, forever actuate the noble bosoms of Americans! — But let not the miscreant host vainly imagine that we fear'd their arms. No; them we despis'd; we dread nothing but slavery. Death is the creature of a poltroon's brains; 'tis immortality to sacrifice ourselves for the salvation of our country. We fear not death. That gloomy night, the pale-faced moon and the affrighted stars that hurried through the sky, can witness that we fear not death. Our hearts, which at the recollection glow with a rage that four revolving years have scarcely taught us to restrain, can witness that we fear not death; and happy 'tis for those who dared to insult us, that their naked bones are not now piled up an everlasting monument of Massachusetts' bravery. But they retir'd, they fled; and in that flight they found their only safety. We then expected that the hand of public justice would soon inflict that punishment upon the murderers which, by the laws of GOD and man, they had incurred. But let the unbiass'd pen of a Robertson, or perhaps of some equally fam'd American, conduct this trial before the great tribunal of succeeding generations. And though the murderers may escape the just resentment of an enraged people; though drowsy justice, intoxicated by the poisonous draught prepared for her cup, still nods upon her rotten seat, yet be assured, such complicated crimes will meet their due reward. Tell me, ye bloody butchers! ye villains high and low! ye wretches who contrived, as well as you who executed the inhuman deed! do you not feel the goads and stings of conscious guilt pierce through your savage bosoms? Though some of you may think yourselves exalted to a height that bids defiance to the arms of human justice, and others shroud yourselves beneath the mask of hypocracy, and build your hopes of safety on the low arts of cunning, chicanery and falsehood; yet, do you not sometimes feel the knawings of that worm which never dies? do not the injured shades of Maverick, Gray, Caldwell, Attucks and Carr attend you in your solitary walks, arrest you even in the midst of your debaucheries; and fill ever your dreams with terror? but if the unappeased *manes* of the dead should not disturb their murderers, yet surely even your obdurate heart must shrink, and your guilty blood must chill within your rigid veins when you behold the miserable Monk, the wretched victim of your savage cruelty. Observe his tottering knees which scarce sustain his wasted body; look on his haggard eyes; mark well the death-like paleness on his fallen cheek, and tell me, does not the sight plant daggers in your souls? Unhappy Monk! cut off in the gay morn of manhood from all the joys which sweeten life, doom'd to drag on a pitiful existence, without even a hope to taste the pleasures of returning health! yet Monk, thou livest not in vain; thou livest a warning to thy country, which sympathizes with thee in thy sufferings; thou livest an affecting, an alarming instance of the unbounded violence which lust of power, assisted by a standing army, can lead a traitor to commit.

FOR us he bled, and now languishes. The wounds by which he is tortur'd to a lingering death, were aimed at our country! surely the meek-eyed charity can never behold such sufferings with indifference. Nor can her lenient hand forbear to pour oil and wine into these wounds; and to assuage at least, what it cannot heal.

PATRIOTISM is ever united with humanity and compassion. This noble affection which impels us to sacrifice everything dear, even life itself, to our country, involves in it a common sympathy and tenderness for every citizen, and must ever have a *particular feeling* for one who suffers in a public cause. Thoroughly persuaded of this, I need not add a word to engage your compassion and bounty towards a fellow-citizen who, with long protracted anguish, falls a victim to the relentless rage of our common enemies.

YE dark designing knaves, ye murderers, parricides! how dare you tread upon the earth which has drank in the blood of slaughtered innocents shed by your wicked hands? how dare you breathe that air which wafted to the ear of heaven the groans of those who fell a sacrifice to your accursed ambition? but if the labouring earth doth not expand her jaws; if the air you breathe is not commissioned to be the minister of death; yet hear it, and tremble! the eye of heaven penetrates the darkest chambers of the soul, traces the leading clue through all the labyrinths which your industrious folly has devised; and you, however you may have screen'd yourselves from human eyes, must be arraigned, must lift your hands, red with the blood of those whose death you have procur'd at the tremendous bar of GOD.

BUT I gladly quit the gloomy theme of death, and leave you to improve the thought of that important day, when our naked souls must stand before that Being from whom nothing can be hid. I would not dwell too long upon the horrid effects which have already followed from quartering regular troops in this town: let our misfortunes teach posterity to guard against such evils for the future. Standing armies are sometimes (I would by no means say generally, much less universally) composed of persons who have rendered themselves unfit to live in civil society; who have no other motives of conduct than those which a desire of the present gratification of their passions suggests; who have no property in any country; men who have lost or given up their own liberties, and envy those who enjoy liberty; who are equally indifferent to the glory of a George or a Lewis; who for the addition of one penny a day to their wages, would desert from the Christian cross, and fight under the crescent of the Turkish Sultan; from such men as these, what has not a state to fear? with such as these, usurping Caesar passed the Rubicon; with such as these he humbled mighty Rome, and forced the mistress of the world to own a master in a traitor. These are the men whom sceptered robbers now employ to frustrate the designs of GOD, and render vain the bounties which his gracious hand pours indiscriminately upon his creatures. By these the miserable slaves in Turkey, Persia, and many other extensive countries, are rendered truly wretched, though their air is salubrious, and their soil luxuriously fertile. By these France and Spain, though blessed by nature with all that administers to the convenience of life, have been reduced to that contemptible state in which they now appear; and by these Britain — — but if I was possessed of the gift of prophecy, I dare not, except by divine command, unfold the leaves on which the destiny of that once powerful kingdom is inscribed.

BUT since standing armies are so hurtful to a state, perhaps my countrymen may demand some substitute, some other means of rendering us secure against the incursions of a foreign enemy. But can you be one moment at a loss? will not a *well-disciplined militia* afford you ample security against foreign foes? we want not courage; it is discipline alone in which we are exceeded by the most formidable troops that ever trod the earth. Surely our hearts flutter no more at the sound of war than did those of the immortal band of Persia, the Macedonian phalanx, the invincible Roman legions, the Turkish Janissaries, the Gens des Armes of France, or the *well known Grenadiers of Britain.* A well disciplined militia is a safe, an honorable guard to a community like this, whose inhabitants are by nature brave, and are laudably tenacious of that freedom in which they were born. From a well regulated militia we have nothing to fear; their interest is the same with that of the state. When a country is invaded, the militia are ready to appear in its defence; they march into the field with that fortitude which a consciousness of the justice of their cause inspires; they do not jeopard their lives for a master who considers them only as the instruments of his ambition, and whom they regard only as the daily dispenser of the scanty pittance of bread and water. No, they fight for their houses, their lands, for their wives, their children, for all who claim the tenderest names, and are held dearest in their hearts, they fight *pro aris et focis,* for their liberty, and for themselves, and for their GOD. And let it not offend, if I say that no militia ever appear'd in more flourishing condition than that of this providence now doth; and pardon me if I say, — of this town in particular. — I mean not to boast; I would not excite envy, but manly emulation. We have all one common cause; let it therefore be our only contest, who shall most contribute to the security of the liberties of America. And may the same kind providence which has watched over this country from her infant state, still enable us to defeat our enemies. I cannot here forbear noticing the signal manner in which the designs of those who wish not well to us have been discovered. The dark deeds of a treacherous cabal have been brought to public view. You now know the serpents who, whilst cherished in your bosoms, were darting their envenom'd stings into the vitals of the constitution. But the representatives of the people have fixed a mark on those ungrateful monsters, which, though it may not make them so secure as Cain of old, yet renders them at least as infamous. Indeed it would be affrontive to the tutelar diety of this country even to despair of saving it from all the snares which human policy can lay.

TRUE it is, that the British ministry have annexed a salary to the office of the governor of this province, to be paid out of a revenue raised in America, without our consent. They have attempted to render our courts of justice the instruments of extending the authority of acts of the British parliament over this colony, by making the judges dependent on the British administration for their support. But this people will never be enslaved with their eyes open. The moment they knew that the governor was not such a governor as the charter of the province points out, he lost his power of hurting them. They were alarmed; they suspected him, have guarded against him, and he has found that a wise and a brave people, when they know their danger, are fruitful in expedients to escape it.

THE courts of judicature also so far lost their dignity, by being supposed to be under an undue influence, that our representatives thought it absolutely necessary to resolve that they were bound to declare that they would not receive any other salary besides that which the general court should grant them; and if they did not make this declaration, that it would be the duty of the house to impeach them.

GREAT expectations were also formed from the artful scheme of allowing the East-India company to export tea to America upon their own account. This certainly, had it succeeded, would have effected the purpose of the contrivers, and gratified the most sanguine wishes of our adversaries. We soon should have found our trade in the hands of foreigners, and taxes imposed on every thing which we consumed; nor would it have been strange if, in a few years, a company in London should have purchased an exclusive right of trading to America. — But their plot was soon discovered. The people soon were aware of the poison which with so much craft and subtility had been concealed: loss and disgrace ensued: and perhaps, this long-concerted master-piece of policy may issue in the total disuse of tea in this country, which will eventually be the saving of the lives and the estates of thousands — yet while we rejoice that the adversary has not hitherto prevailed against us, let us by no means put off the harness. Restless malice, and disappointed ambition, will still suggest new measures to our inveterate *enemies*. Therefore let *us* also be ready to take the field whenever danger calls; let us be united and strengthen the hands of each other, by promoting a general union among us. Much has been done by the committees of correspondence for this and the other towns of this province, towards uniting the inhabitants; let them still go on and prosper. Much has been done by the committees of correspondence for the houses of assembly, in this and our sister colonies, for uniting the inhabitants of the whole continent, for the security of their common interest. May success ever attend their generous endeavours. But permit me here to suggest a general congress of deputies, from the several houses of assembly on the continent, as the most effectual method of establishing such an union as the present posture of our affairs requires. At such a congress, a firm foundation may be laid for the security of our rights and liberties; a system may be formed for our common safety, by a strict adherence to which we shall be able to frustrate any attempts to overthrow our constitution; restore peace and harmony to America, and secure honor and wealth to Great-Britain, even against the inclinations of her ministers, whose duty it is to study her welfare; and we shall also free ourselves from those unmannerly pillagers who impudently tell us that they are licensed by an act of the British parliament, to thrust their dirty hands into the pockets of every American. But I trust, the happy time will come when, with the besom of destruction, those noxious vermin will be swept forever from the streets of Boston.

SURELY, you never will tamely suffer this country to be a den of thieves. Remember, my friends, from whom you sprang — Let not a meanness of spirit, unknown to those whom you boast of as your fathers, excite a thought to the dishonor of your mothers. I conjure you by all that is dear, by all that is honorable, by all that is sacred, not only that ye pray, but that you act; that if necessary ye fight, and even die, for the prosperity of our Jerusalem. Break in sunder, with noble disdain, the bonds with which the Philistines have bound you. Suffer not yourselves to be betrayed by the soft arts of luxury and effeminacy, into the pit digged for your destruction. Despise the glare of wealth. That people who pay greater respect to a wealthy villain, than to an honest upright man in poverty, almost deserve to be enslaved; they plainly shew that wealth, however it may be acquired, is in their esteem, to be preferred to virtue.

BUT I thank GOD that America abounds in men who are superior to all temptation, whom nothing can divert from a steady pursuit of the interest of their country; who are at once its ornament and safeguard. And sure I am, I should not incur your displeasure, if I paid a respect so justly due to their much-honoured characters, in this place; but when I name an ADAMS, such a numerous host of fellow-patriots rush upon my mind, that I fear it would take up too much of your time should I attempt to call over the illustrious roll: but your grateful hearts will point you to the men; and their revered names, in all succeeding times shall grace the annals of America. — From them let us, my friends, take example; from them let us catch the divine enthusiasm; and feel, each for himself, the GOD-like pleasure of diffusing happiness on all around us; of delivering the oppressed from the iron grasp of tyranny; of changing the hoarse complaints and bitter moans of wretched slaves, into those cheerful songs which freedom and contentment must inspire. There is a heart-felt satisfaction in reflecting on our exertions for the public weal, which all the sufferings an enraged tyrant can inflict will never take away; which the ingratitude and reproaches of those whom we have saved from ruin, cannot rob us of. The virtuous assertor of the rights of mankind merits a reward, which even a want of success in his endeavors to save his country the heaviest misfortune which can befall a genuine patriot, cannot entirely prevent him from receiving.

I HAVE the most animating confidence that the present noble struggle for liberty will terminate gloriously for America. And let us play the man for our GOD, and for the cities of our GOD; while we are using the means in our power, let us humbly commit our righteous cause to the great LORD of the universe, who loveth righteousness and hateth iniquity. — And having secured the approbation of our hearts, by a faithful and unwearied discharge of our duty to our country, let us joyfully leave her important concerns in the hands of HIM who raiseth up and putteth down the empires and kingdoms of the world as HE pleases; and with cheerful submission to HIS sovereign will, devoutly say,

Although the fig-tree shall not blossom, neither shall fruit be in the vines; the labour of the olive shall fail, and the fields shall yield no meat; the flock

shall be cut off from the fold, and there shall be no herd in the stalls: yet we will rejoice in the LORD, we will joy in the GOD of our salvation."

Excerpts from Free Thoughts on the Proceedings of the Continental Congress

Samuel Seabury

Commentary

Parliament followed the Boston Port Bill by revising the Massachusetts charter to increase gubernatorial powers. From a strictly legal perspective, the legislature's response marks its first revolutionary act, for it retreated to the countryside and continued to govern, as best it could, under the old charter. Meanwhile, Parliament enacted several other "Intolerable Acts," which applied to all the colonies. Several colonial legislatures promptly elected delegates to a "Continental Congress," which met in Philadelphia in September, 1774. The Congress was of questionable legality because some legislatures elected delegates after gubernatorial orders to dissolve, and other colonies elected them at local and county conventions.

Most Americans during 1774-1775 did not realize that they were on the verge of founding a new nation. Even militants indignantly (and probably sincerely) denied British allegations that the Congress was illegal and that they wanted independence. Supporters of the Congress argued that their meeting was legal under British law and that endorsing Massachusett's actions was legal because Parliament had no constitutional authority to ·revise colonial charters. Moreover, they argued that other congressional actions (petitioning the King to mediate its dispute with Parliament and endorsing another economic boycott) were in accord with legal precedent. Congress did nothing to prepare for war. It simply adjourned after agreeing to meet the following spring, when the King's response would be known, and after issuing its declarations in the name of the "United Colonies."

Just how united were the "United Colonies"? Whereas earlier historians generally believed that only an active minority supported the Revolution, most recent scholars subscribe to a "consensus" interpretation. Yet no one denies that a band of Loyalists existed. Unfortunately, the old cliché that "winners write history" has never been illustrated better than in the case of the

Loyalists. We know little about them, though we know that the term *Loyal* had long been a rhetorical god word used by various politicians to enhance their ethos as defenders of the British constitution. It was not until 1774 that "Loyalist Associations" were formed to oppose the Continental Congress and other "illegal" acts. Prior to that time, some future Loyalists had supported British policy while others had opposed it. Just why former opponents refused to join the budding rebellion is not altogether clear, but existing evidence points to various factors: membership in the Church of England, belief that Parliament had the constitutional authority to tax the colonies, fear of war, and psychological ties to the "mother country."

Being in the minority when passions were intense, Loyalists faced public pressure, mob action and little help from the press. One New York printer was a Loyalist, but mobs soon put him out of business. After fighting began, Loyalists were silenced completely. Even during 1774-1775, only a few managed to get anything into print.

One was Samuel Seabury (1729-1796), an Anglican minister who wrote a series of pamphlets whose title pages said they were "By a Farmer." Seabury's basic rhetorical strategy was to portray the Revolutionists as merchants without concern for the hard-working farmers who would suffer from the economic boycott that the Congress had endorsed. The following excerpts from the first pamphlet, which include his opening paragraph, illustrate this strategy. The excerpts are reproduced from the original pamphlet (1774), which is housed at the American Antiquarian Society, pp. 1, 9-11.

Excerpts from Free Thoughts on the Proceedings of the Continental Congress... in a Letter to the Farmers, and Other Inhabitants of North America in General, and to Those of the Province of New-York in Particular

My Friends and Countrymen,

Permit me to address you upon a subject, which, next to your eternal welfare in a future world, demands your most serious and dispassionate consideration. The American Colonies are unhappily involved in a scene of confusion and discord. The bands of civil society are broken; the authority of government weakened, and in some instances taken away: Individuals are deprived of their liberty; their property is frequently invaded by violence, and not a single Magistrate has had courage or virtue enough to interpose. From this distressed situation it was hoped, that the wisdom and prudence of the Congress lately assembled at Philadelphia, would have delivered us. The eyes of all men were turned to them. We ardently expected that some prudent scheme of accommodating our unhappy disputes with the Mother-Country, would have been adopted and pursued. But alas! they are broken up without ever attempting it: they have taken no one step that tended to peace: they have gone on from bad to worse, and have either ignorantly misunderstood, carelessly neglected, or basely betrayed the interests of all the Colonies.

The next thing I shall take notice of, is the advanced prices of goods, which will, not only probably, but necessarily, follow, as soon as the non-importation from Great Britain, &c. shall take effect. This is a consequence that most nearly concerns you; nor can you prevent it. You are obliged to buy many articles of clothing. You cannot make them yourselves; or you cannot make them so cheap as you can buy them. You want Woollens for your winter clothing. Few of you have wool enough to answer the purpose. For notwithstanding the boasts of some ignorant, hot-headed men, there is not wool enough on the continent, taking all the colonies together, to supply the inhabitants with stockings. Notwithstanding all the home-spun you can make, many of you find it difficult, at the year's end, to pay the shop-keeper for what the necessities of your families have obliged you to take up. What will you do when the prices of goods are advanced a quarter, for instance, or an half? To say that the prices of goods will not be raised, betrays your ignorance and folly. The price of any commodity always rises in proportion to the demand for it; and the demand always increases in proportion to its scarcity. As soon as the importation ceases in New-York, the quantity of goods will be daily lessened, by daily consumption; and the prices will gradually rise in proportion. "But the merchants of New-York have declared that, they will demand only a reasonable profit." Who is to judge what a reasonable profit is? Why, the merchants. Will they expose their invoices, and the secrets of their trade to you, that you may judge whether their profits are reasonable or not? Certainly they will not. and if they did, you cannot understand them; and, consequently, can form no judgment about them. You have therefore nothing to trust to in this case but the honour of the merchants. Let us then consider how far we have reason to trust to their honour.

Not to raise the price of a commodity when it is scarce, and in demand, is contrary to the principles and practice of merchants. Their maxim is, to buy as cheap, and sell as dear, as they can. Will they let you have a piece of goods for twenty shillings, which will fetch twenty-five? When the stores and shops are full, and a price is demanded which you think unreasonable, you will ask an abatement. If you are refused, you will look elsewhere. But when there are few goods and many buyers, no abatement can be expected. If you won't give the price, your neighbour perhaps is in greater necessity, and *must* give it. Besides, the merchant knows that no more goods can be imported. He knows that the necessities of the country are increasing, and that what you refuse now at twenty shillings, you will be obliged to take, by and by, at twenty-five.

But no argument is like matter of fact. You have had one trial of a non-importation agreement some years ago. Pray how did you like it? Were the prices of goods raised on you then? You know they were. What remedy had you? A good Christian remedy indeed, but a hard one — patience — and patience only: The honour of the merchants gave you no relief — confound their honour — it obliged me — it obliged many of you, to take old moth-eaten cloths that had lain rotting in the shops for years, and to pay a monstrous price for them.

Some, indeed, I confess it with gratitude, had honour enough to attempt to regulate the price of Tea, at that time. Did they succeed? No. There was not honour enough in the body of merchants to bring it to effect. Messrs.
declared at the Coffee-House, that they would be bound by no regulations. They would have their own price for their tea. They had it. And common bohea tea was sold at the enormous price of nine shillings the pound. Will you again trust to the honour of these men? You had better trust to the mercy of a Turk.

I know not how it happens, but not only the merchants, but the generality of citizens, treat us *countrymen* with very undeserved contempt. They act as though they thought, that all wisdom, all knowledge, all understanding and sense, centered in themselves, and that we farmers were utterly ignorant of every thing, but just to drive our oxen, and to follow the plough. We are never consulted, but when they cannot do without us. And then, all the plans are laid in the City before they are offered to us. Be the potion they prepare for us ever so nauseous, we must swallow it down, as well as we can. It is not many years since the Mayor, Aldermen, and Commonalty of the city, shewed their contempt of us, in the most insulting manner. They passed a law to regulate the prices of our produce; and instead of protecting us in their markets, we were exposed to continual abuse and insults. We could not carry a quart of milk, a duck, a chicken, — I think not an egg, — I am sure not a quail or *snipe*, to market, in peace. If they were scarce, we durst not ask an advanced price; for if we did, a fine — or imprisonment, was our portion. — — Did they also fix the price of *shop-goods?* catch them at that, and I will humbly ask their pardon. — — Where was honour at this time? Troth I cannot tell: But were it necessary, I could easily tell you where she was *not*.

Liberty or Death

Patrick Henry

Commentary

The winter of 1774-1775 was tense, but Revolutionary leaders were not yet ready to start a revolution. Although several colonial legislatures continued meeting in defiance of gubernatorial orders to dissolve, they carefully avoided appearing too rebellious by adopting names which implied limited authority. For example, the Virginia legislature called itself the "Virginia Convention" instead of using its formal name, "House of Burgesses."

The prevalent belief that America could remain peacefully within the British Empire was founded on a mixture of sensible reasoning and wishful thinking, information and misinformation, fear and courage — a mixture that is common in crisis situations. Clutching at straws, many colonists hoped that the King would settle the dispute before Congress met again in May, 1775.

As the months dragged by, nothing was heard from the King, but rumors persisted that he had responded favorably to the petition. Meanwhile, British naval forces appeared. Rumors circulated that foreign mercenaries were on their way and other rumors told of how British opposition to the New Colonial Policy was about to result in a change of administrations.

Amidst the uncertainty, a few legislatures began preparing for war, but it was not until March 23, 1775 (less than a month before Lexington and Concord) that Patrick Henry (1736-1799) proposed that the Virginia Convention do so. Henry faced an ambivalent audience. A poorly educated lawyer from the newly settled western part of the colony, he had been crossing verbal swords with elite Tidewater politicians for over a decade. His legislative colleagues shared his long-standing opposition to British policies, but his militancy, which dated back to Stamp Act days, made some think him too hawkish. In addition to his mixed ethos, his audience had reasons for believing that Britain was ready for reconciliation and reasons for believing that it was not.

Henry's speech in support of his proposal earned a favorable reputation in his own day; however, no one recorded it at the time. No written version appeared until Henry's admiring biographer, William Wirt, reconstructed the speech by interviewing people who had heard it over a quarter-century before. We cannot be sure how much of it represents what Henry actually said and how much is what Wirt wished he had said, but Wirt's version is all we have. Wirt integrated his version of the speech into his narration of events, thus using the past tense and the third person. As the speech became a classic, editors modified it to use the present tense and first person. Except for these minor modifications, they followed Wirt. The following is reproduced photographically from A. Craig Baird, *American Public Addresses, 1740-1952* (New York: McGraw-Hill, 1956), pp. 29-36.

Liberty or Death at the Virginia Legislature

MR. PRESIDENT: No man thinks more highly than I do of the patriotism, as well as abilities, of the very worthy gentlemen who have just addressed the House. But different men often see the same subjects in different lights; and, therefore, I hope that it will not be thought disrespectful to those gentlemen, if, entertaining as I do, opinions of a character very opposite to theirs, I shall speak forth my sentiments freely and without reserve. This is no time for ceremony. The question before the House is one of awful moment to this country. For my own part I consider it as nothing less than a question of freedom or slavery; and in proportion to the magnitude of the subject ought to be the freedom of the debate. It is only in this way that we can hope to arrive at truth, and fulfill the great responsibility which we hold to God and our country. Should I keep back my opinions at such a time, through fear of giving offense, I should consider myself as guilty of treason toward my country, and of an act of disloyalty toward the majesty of heaven, which I revere above all earthly kings.

Mr. President, it is natural to man to indulge in the illusions of hope. We are apt to shut our eyes against a painful truth, and listen to the song of that siren, till she transforms us into beasts. Is this the part of wise men, engaged in a great and arduous struggle for liberty? Are we disposed to be of the number of those who, having eyes, see not, and having ears, hear not, the things which so nearly concern their temporal salvation? For my part, whatever anguish of spirit it may cost, I am willing to know the whole truth; to know the worst and to provide for it.

I have but one lamp by which my feet are guided; and that is the lamp of experience. I know of no way of judging of the future but by the past. And judging by the past, I wish to know what there has been in the conduct of the British ministry for the last ten years to justify those hopes with which gentlemen have been pleased to solace themselves and the House? Is it that insidious smile with which our petition has been lately received? Trust it not, sir; it will prove a snare to your feet. Suffer not yourselves to be betrayed with a kiss. Ask yourselves how this gracious reception of our petition comports with these warlike preparations which cover our waters and darken our land. Are fleets and armies necessary to a work of love and reconciliation? Have we shown ourselves so unwilling to be reconciled, that force must be called in to win back our love? Let us not deceive ourselves, sir. These are the implements of war and subjugation; the last arguments to which kings resort. I ask gentlemen, sir, what means this martial array, if its purpose be not to force us to submission? Can gentlemen assign any other possible motives for it? Has Great Britain any enemy, in this quarter of the world, to call for all this accumulation of navies and armies? No, sir, she has none. They are meant for us; they can be meant for no other. They are sent over to bind and rivet upon us those chains which the British ministry have been so long forging. And what have we to oppose to them? Shall we try argument? Sir, we have been trying that for the last ten years. Have we anything new to offer on the subject? Nothing. We have held the subject up in every light of which it is capable; but it has been all in vain. Shall we resort to entreaty and humble supplication? What terms shall we find which have not been already exhausted? Let us not, I beseech you, sir, deceive ourselves longer. Sir, we have done everything that could be done to avert the storm which is now coming on. We have petitioned; we have remonstrated; we have supplicated; we have prostrated ourselves before the tyrannical hands of the ministry and parliament. Our petitions have been slighted; our remonstrances have produced additional violence and insult; our supplications have been disregarded; and we have been spurned, with contempt, from the foot of the throne. In vain, after these things, may we indulge the fond hope of peace and reconciliation. There is no longer any room for hope. If we wish to be free—if we mean to preserve inviolate those inestimable privileges for which we have been so long contending—if we mean not basely to abandon the noble struggle in which we have been so long engaged, and which we have pledged ourselves never to abandon until the glorious object of our contest shall be obtained, we must fight! I repeat it, sir, we must fight! An appeal to arms and to the God of Hosts is all that is left us!

They tell us, sir, that we are weak; unable to cope with so formidable an adversary. But when shall we be stronger? Will it be the next week, or the next year? Will it be when we are totally disarmed, and when a British guard shall be stationed in every house? Shall we gather strength by irresolution and inaction? Shall we acquire the means of effectual resistance by lying supinely on our backs, and hugging the delusive phantom of hope, until our enemies shall have bound us hand and foot? Sir, we are not weak, if we make a proper use of the means which the God of nature hath placed in our power. Three millions of people, armed in the holy cause of liberty, and in such a country as that which we possess, are invincible by any force which our enemy can send against us. Besides, sir, we shall not fight our battles alone. There is a just God who presides over the destinies of nations; and who will raise friends to fight our battles for us. The battle, sir, is not to the strong alone; it is to the vigilant, the active, the brave. Besides, sir, we have no election. If we were base enough to desire it, it is now too late to retire from the contest. There is no retreat but in submission and slavery! Our chains are forged! Their clanking may be heard on the plains of Boston! The war is inevitable—and let it come! I repeat it, sir, let it come!

It is in vain, sir, to extenuate the matter. Gentlemen may cry peace, peace—but there is no peace. The war is actually begun! The next gale that sweeps from the North will bring to our ears the clash of resounding arms! Our brethren are already in the field! Why stand we here idle? What is it that gentlemen wish? What would they have? Is life so dear, or peace so sweet, as to be purchased at the price of chains and slavery? Forbid it, Almighty God! I know not what course others may take; but as for me, give me liberty, or give me death!

Excerpt from Common Sense

Thomas Paine

Commentary

When the Virginia Convention endorsed Patrick Henry's call for military preparedness in the spring of 1775, a war for independence was virtually certain. It became more certain after the Massachusetts legislature (or "provincial congress," as it called itself) resisted Governor Gage's unsuccessful attempt to seize its military supplies at the battles of Lexington and Concord (April 19, 1775). Yet the colonies did not declare independence for another year.

After Lexington and Concord, the New England colonies sent volunteers to join the Massachusetts militia, who besieged Boston to prevent Gage from renewing his attacks. On May 10, 1775, Vermont volunteers captured Fort Ticonderoga and seized a vast quantity of military supplies for use in the siege of Boston. The Continental Congress reconvened on the same day, and it soon organized a "continental army" under George Washington's command to join the siege. Before Washington arrived in Massachusetts, British forces captured Breed's Hill (across the river from Boston) at what is mistakenly called the "Battle of Bunker Hill" (June 17) but failed to break the siege. In the fall, Congress responded to rumors that Britain was forming an army in Canada to "invade" New York by authorizing what turned out to be an ill-fated attempt to capture Quebec.

Despite these military actions, Congress tried once again to avoid all-out war by sending an "Olive Branch petition" to London. The King refused to receive it. On August 23, 1775, he proclaimed the colonies to be in rebellion. On December 23, 1775, he issued a royal proclamation closing all colonial ports to all commerce.

Prior to these royal proclamations, the British King had made no public statements regarding the disputes between Parliament and the colonial legislatures. Previous colonial rhetoric had been directed against Parliament, never the King, and several petitions had been sent to the King to mediate the dispute with Parliament. By the end of 1775, however, it was becoming increasingly apparent that the King was supporting Parliament, not the colonists.

Yet attacking the King was tantamount to declaring independence, and proponents of independence faced serious rhetorical obstacles. In the first place, some people were still clinging to the forlorn hope that reconciliation was possible and that the King would mediate. In the second place, there were long-standing economic ties to Britain because most American trade was with Britain and the British West Indies. In the third place, most Americans were of British descent and spoke the English language. Speakers and writers routinely referred to Britain as "home." Most American religious denominations had originated in Britain, and colonists had recently joined Britain in fighting the "popish French" Canadians. In short, economic and cultural ties were strong.

Political ties were also strong. Americans still had a deep respect for the British form of government, which was usually called "mixed." The "mixed constitution" was based on the idea that society was divided into three groups: royalty, aristocracy and commoners. Britain's "mixed government" represented all three groups. The monarch represented royalty, the House of Lords represented aristocracy and the House of Commons represented commoners. As late as 1772, when the militant Joseph Warren delivered the Boston Massacre oration, he praised Britain's "mixed constitution" for dividing governmental powers so that each segment had to consent to a bill before it became law. He also emphasized that the audience's colonial government was a "copy" of the British system, with the governor representing royalty, the Senate being analogous to Lords and the House of Representatives being analogous to Commons.

With a long tradition of mistrusting government, many Americans feared that if our political ties to the "mother country" were cut, we would have no way of preserving a "mixed government." The result would be a loss of liberty and freedom.

By the end of 1775, some colonists were ready to break the ties, but others—including some who opposed Parliament's "New Colonial Policy"—were not. A powerful rhetorical effort was needed to persuade Americans that independence was desirable. The effort began on January 9, 1776, when the pamphlet, *Common Sense*, first appeared in Philadelphia. The date is rhetorically significant. The pamphlet's appearance was timed to coincide with the arrival of news about the King's message to Parliament, which the author assumed correctly would contain no hint of reconciliation.

Like other political pamphlets, *Common Sense* did not identify its author. Whereas the author of a typical pamphlet became known through the "grapevine," the authorship of *Common Sense* remained secret for months—even while the author, Thomas Paine (1737-1809) and the publisher, Robert Bell, debated one another in Philadelphia newspapers.

The debate concerned money. Bell and the anonymous author agreed that profits were to be divided equally, but they disagreed about whether there had been any profits. In the course of the public newspaper debate, Paine raised his ethos by saying that he had planned to use his share to buy warm clothing for the soldiers who were now retreating through the snow after their defeat at Quebec.

Quite possibly, Paine's planned philanthropy helped sales, but *Common Sense* was already on its way to becoming the most widely-circulated pamphlet in colonial history. Despite Paine's objections, Bell put out two more printings in January (making a total of three, although for some inexplicable reason the third was called a "second edition"). Then, after Paine put out an "enlarged" edition with a new publisher (William and Thomas Bradford), Bell pirated the Bradford edition for what he called a "third edition." Still later, Bell continued pirating the Bradford text, sometimes binding it with *Large Additions to Common Sense*, consisting of several pro-independence essays of unknown authorship.

While Bell and the Bradford continued churning out new printings of *Common Sense*, Paine authorized other publishers around the country to print copies. No one is absolutely sure how many printings appeared, but Richard Gimbel, in his *A Bibliographical Check List of COMMON SENSE with an Account of its Publication* (New Haven: Yale University Press, 1956), lists for 1776 sixteen printings in Philadelphia, one in Andover (MA), two in Boston, one in Charlestown (SC), one in Lancaster (PA), three in New London (CT), two in New York, one in Newburyport (MA), four in Newport (RI), three in Providence (RI), one in Salem (MA), and one at some unknown place. A newspaper in Hartford, the *Connecticut Courant*, also printed a text. Lack of data about the number of copies per printing makes it impossible for us to know precisely the total number, but most estimates run from 100,000 to 150,000—at a time when the entire American population, including slaves and other non-voters, totalled only around two-and-a-half million. Moreover, tavern owners in those days often purchased copies of popular items so they could be read and discussed by patrons (just as cocktail lounges today have television sets for patrons). Paine's contemporaries were undoubtedly correct in agreeing that *Common Sense* was the most important rhetorical document in the pro-independence movement.

Some textual differences are trivial and others substantial. Trivial ones involve matters such as using a "hath" for a "has" (or vice versa), a singular for a plural (or vice versa) or differences in spelling, capitalization or punctuation. Paine might have made some of these changes when he prepared the "Enlarged Edition," but many seem to have been made by printers, either because they wished to "improve" the text or because they made errors in their haste to get out copies ahead of their competitors.

Substantial differences resulted from Paine's own revisions. In Bell's first three printings, *Common Sense* contains a short introduction followed by four main sections. The first two, "Of the Origin and Design of Government in General; with Concise Remarks on the English Constitution" and "Of Monarchy and Hereditary Succession," are attacks on the "mixed constitution" in general and monarchy in particular. As such, they represent the first American attempt to undermine rhetorically the long-admired British constitution. The third section, reprinted below, contains arguments for independence. The fourth section, "Of the Present Ability of America; with some Miscellaneous Reflections," rambles a bit, but the main argument is that the colonies are better able now to fight for independence than they will be at any time in the future.

In revising the text for the Bradford printing (the "Enlarged Edition"), Paine added a "P.S." to the Introduction and some "calculations" to the fourth section to prove America's naval superiority to Britain's. He also added two more sections, one being a brief "Appendix" that recapitulates his pro-independence arguments. The other refutes an anti-independence pamphlet written by some unnamed Quakers in response to the earlier printings of *Common Sense*. However, Paine made no substantial changes to the first three sections in the "expanded edition."

The "expanded edition" was the one that most printers copied for subsequent editions and was therefore the one most commonly read by Americans in 1776. It (or one of its derivatives) is the one most commonly used by modern-day editors, although some prefer the original Bell version. For our purposes, a choice of texts is not a serious concern because neither the third section nor the "P.S." (after it first appeared in the "enlarged edition") was revised. For convenience, the following text is reproduced from the first volume of Moncure Daniel Conway's 1894 edition of *The Writings of Thomas Paine*.

Excerpt from Common Sense

Introduction

Perhaps the sentiments contained in the following pages, are not *yet* sufficiently fashionable to procure them general Favor; a long Habit of not thinking a Thing wrong, gives it a superficial appearance of being *right*, and raises at first a formidable outcry in defence of Custom. But the Tumult soon subsides. Time makes more Converts than Reason.

As a long and violent abuse of power is generally the means of calling the right of it in question, (and in matters too which might never have been thought of, had not the sufferers been aggravated into the inquiry,) and as the King of England hath undertaken in his *own right*, to support the Parliament in what he calls *Theirs*, and as the good People of this Country are grievously oppressed by the Combination, they have an undoubted privilege to enquire into the Pretensions of both, and equally to reject the Usurpation of *either*.

In the following Sheets, the Author hath studiously avoided every thing which is personal among ourselves. Compliments as well as censure to individuals make no part thereof. The wise and the worthy need not the triumph of a Pamphlet; and those whose sentiments are injudicious or unfriendly will cease of themselves, unless too much pains is bestowed upon their conversions.

The cause of America is in a great measure the cause of all mankind. Many circumstances have, and will arise, which are not local, but universal, and through which the principles of all lovers of mankind are affected, and in the event of which their affections are interested. The laying a country desolate with fire and sword, declaring war against the natural rights of all mankind, and extirpating the defenders thereof from the face of the earth, is the concern of every man to whom nature hath given the power of feeling; of which class, regardless of party censure, is

THE AUTHOR.

P.S. The Publication of this new Edition hath been delayed, with a view of taking notice (had it been necessary) of any attempt to refute the Doctrine of Independence: As no answer hath yet appeared, it is now presumed that none will, the time needful for getting such a Performance ready for the Public being considerably past.

Who the Author of this Production is, is wholly unnecessary to the Public, as the Object for Attention is the *Doctrine itself*, not the *Man*. Yet it may not be unnecessary to say, That he is unconnected with any party, and under no sort of Influence, public or private, but the influence of reason and principle.

Philadelphia, February 14, 1776.

Thoughts on the Present State of American Affairs

In the following pages I offer nothing more than simple facts, plain arguments, and common sense: and have no other preliminaries to settle with the reader, than that he will divest himself of prejudice and prepossession, and suffer his reason and his feelings to determine for themselves: that he will put on, or rather that he will not put off, the true character of a man, and generously enlarge his views beyond the present day.

Volumes have been written on the subject of the struggle between England and America. Men of all ranks have embarked in the controversy, from different motives, and with various designs; but all have been ineffectual, and the period of debate is closed. Arms as the last resource decide the contest; the appeal was the choice of the King, and the Continent has accepted the challenge.

It hath been reported of the late Mr. Pelham (who tho' an able minister was not without his faults) that on his being attacked in the House of Commons on the score that his measures were only of a temporary kind, replied, "*they will last my time.*" Should a thought so fatal and unmanly possess the Colonies in the present contest, the name of ancestors will be remembered by future generations with detestation.

The Sun never shined on a cause of greater worth. 'Tis not the affair of a City, a County, a Province, or a Kingdom; but of a Continent—of at least one eighth part of the habitable Globe. 'Tis not the concern of a day, a year, or an age; posterity are virtually involved in the contest, and will be more or less affected even to the end of time, by the proceedings now. Now is the seed-time of Continental union, faith and honour. The least fracture now will be like a name engraved with the point of a pin on the tender rind of a young oak; the wound would enlarge with the tree, and posterity read it in full grown characters.

By referring the matter from argument to arms, a new æra for politics is struck—a new method of thinking hath arisen. All plans, proposals, &c. prior to the nineteenth of April, *i.e.* to the commencement of hostilities, are like the almanacks of the last year; which tho' proper then, are superceded and useless now. Whatever was advanced by the advocates on either side of the question then, terminated in one and the same point, viz. a union with Great Britain; the only difference between the parties was the method of effecting it; the one proposing force, the other friendship; but it hath so far happened that the first hath failed, and the second hath withdrawn her influence.

As much hath been said of the advantages of reconciliation, which, like an agreeable dream, hath passed away and left us as we were, it is but right that we should examine the contrary side of the argument, and enquire into some of the many material injuries which these Colonies sustain, and always will sustain, by being connected with and dependant on Great-Britain. To examine that connection and dependance, on the principles of nature and common sense, to see what we have to trust to, if separated, and what we are to expect, if dependant.

I have heard it asserted by some, that as America has flourished under her former connection with Great-Britain, the same connection is necessary towards her future happiness, and will always have the same effect. Nothing can be more fallacious than this kind of argument. We may as well assert that because a child has thrived upon milk, that it is never to have meat, or that the first twenty years of our lives is to become a precedent for the next twenty. But even this is admitting more than is true; for I answer roundly, that America would have flourished as much, and probably much more, had no European power taken any notice of her. The commerce by which she hath enriched herself are the necessaries of life, and will always have a market while eating is the custom of Europe.

But she has protected us, say some. That she hath engrossed us is true, and defended the Continent at our expense as well as her own, is admitted; and she would have defended Turkey from the same motive, *viz.* for the sake of trade and dominion.

Alas! we have been long led away by ancient prejudices and made large sacrifices to superstition. We have boasted the protection of Great Britain, without Considering, that her motive was *interest* not *attachment*; and that she did not protect us from *our enemies* on *our account*; but from *her enemies* on *her own account*, from those who had no quarrel with us on any *other account*, and who will always be our enemies on the *same account*. Let Britain waive her pretensions to the Continent, or the Continent throw off the dependance, and we should be at peace with France and Spain, were they at war with Britain. The miseries of Hanover last war ought to warn us against connections.

It hath lately been asserted in parliament, that the Colonies have no relation to each other but through the Parent Country, *i.e.* that Pennsylvania and the Jerseys, and so on for the rest, are sister Colonies by the way of England; this is certainly a very roundabout way of proving relationship, but it is the nearest and only true way of proving enmity (or enemyship, if I may so call it.) France and Spain never were, nor perhaps ever will be, our enemies as *Americans*, but as our being the *subjects of Great Britain*.

But Britain is the parent country, say some. Then the more shame upon her conduct. Even brutes do not devour their young, nor savages make war upon their families; Wherefore, the assertion, if true, turns to her reproach; but it happens not to be true, or only partly so, and the phrase *parent* or *mother country* hath been jesuitically adopted by the King and his parasites, with a low papistical design of gaining an unfair bias on the credulous weakness of our minds. Europe, and not England, is the parent country of America. This new World hath been the asylum for the persecuted lovers of civil and religious liberty from *every part* of Europe. Hither have they fled, not from the tender embraces of the mother, but from the cruelty of the monster; and it is so far true of England, that the same tyranny which drove the first emigrants from home, pursues their descendants still.

In this extensive quarter of the globe, we forget the narrow limits of three hundred and sixty miles (the extent of England) and carry our friendship on a larger scale; we claim brotherhood with every European Christian, and triumph in the generosity of the sentiment.

It is pleasant to observe by what regular gradations we surmount the force of local prejudices, as we enlarge our acquaintance with the World. A man born in any town in England divided into parishes, will naturally associate most with his fellow parishioners (because their interests in many cases will be common) and distinguish him by the name of *neighbour*; if he meet him but a few miles from home, he drops the narrow idea of a street, and salutes him by the name of *townsman*; if he travel out of the county and meet him in any other, he forgets the minor divisions of street and town, and calls him *countryman, i.e. countyman*: but if in their foreign excursions they should associate in France, or any other part of *Europe*, their local remembrance would be enlarged into that of *Englishmen*. And by a just parity of reasoning, all Europeans meeting in America, or any other quarter of the globe, are *countrymen*; for England, Holland, Germany, or Sweden, when compared with the whole, stand in the same places on the larger scale, which the divisions of street, town, and county do on the smaller ones; Distinctions too limited for Continental minds. Not one third of the inhabitants, even of this province, [Pennsylvania], are of English descent. Wherefore, I reprobate the phrase of Parent or Mother Country applied to England only, as being false, selfish, narrow and ungenerous.

But, admitting that we were all of English descent, what does it amount to? Nothing. Britain, being now an open enemy, extinguishes every other name and title: and to say that reconciliation is our duty, is truly farcical. The first king of England, of the present line (William the Conqueror) was a Frenchman, and half the peers of England are descendants from the same country; wherefore, by the same method of reasoning, England ought to be governed by France.

Much hath been said of the united strength of Britain and the Colonies, that in conjunction they might bid defiance to the world: But this is mere presumption; the fate of war is uncertain, neither do the expressions mean any thing; for this continent would never suffer itself to be drained of inhabitants, to support the British arms in either Asia, Africa, or Europe.

Besides, what have we to do with setting the world at defiance? Our plan is commerce, and that, well attended to, will secure us the peace and friendship of all Europe; because it is the interest of all Europe to have America a free port. Her trade will always be a protection, and her barrenness of gold and silver secure her from invaders.

I challenge the warmest advocate for reconciliation to show a single advantage that this continent can reap by being connected with Great Britain. I repeat the challenge; not a single advantage is derived. Our corn will fetch its price in any market in Europe, and our imported goods must be paid for buy them where we will.

But the injuries and disadvantages which we sustain by that connection, are without number; and our duty to mankind at large, as well as to ourselves, instruct us to renounce the alliance: because, any submission to, or dependance on, Great Britain, tends directly to involve this Continent in European wars and quarrels, and set us at variance with nations who would otherwise seek our friendship, and against whom we have neither anger nor complaint. As Europe is our market for trade, we ought to form no partial connection with any part of it. It is the true interest of America to steer clear of European contentions, which she never can do, while, by her dependance on Britain, she is made the makeweight in the scale of British politics.

Europe is too thickly planted with Kingdoms to be long at peace, and whenever a war breaks out between England and any foreign power, the trade of America goes to ruin, *because of her connection with Britain*. The next war may not turn out like the last, and should it not, the advocates for reconciliation now will be wishing for separation then, because neutrality in that case would be a safer convoy than a man of war. Every thing that is right or reasonable pleads for separation. The blood of the slain, the weeping voice of nature cries, 'TIS TIME TO PART. Even the distance at which the Almighty hath placed England and America is a strong and natural proof that the authority of the one over the other, was never the design of Heaven. The time likewise at which the Continent was discovered, adds weight to the argument, and the manner in which it was peopled, encreases the force of it. The Reformation was preceded by the discovery of America: As if the Almighty graciously meant to open a sanctuary to the persecuted in future years, when home should afford neither friendship nor safety.

The authority of Great Britain over this continent, is a form of government, which sooner or later must have an end: And a serious mind can draw no true pleasure by looking forward, under the painful and positive conviction that what he calls'' the present constitution'' is merely temporary. As parents, we can have no joy, knowing that this government is not sufficiently lasting to ensure any thing which we may bequeath to posterity: And by a plain method of argument, as we are running the next generation into debt, we ought to do the work of it, otherwise we use them meanly and pitifully. In order to discover the line of our duty rightly, we should take our children in our hand,

and fix our station a few years farther into life; that eminence will present a prospect which a few present fears and prejudices conceal from our sight.

Though I would carefully avoid giving unnecessary offence, yet I am inclined to believe, that all those who espouse the doctrine of reconciliation, may be included with the following descriptions.

Interested men, who are not to be trusted, weak men who *cannot* see, prejudiced men who will not see, and a certain set of moderate men who think better of the European world than it deserves; and this last class, by an ill-judged determination, will be the cause of more calamities to this Continent than all the other three.

It is the good fortune of many to live distant from the scene of present sorrow; the evil is not sufficiently brought to their doors to make them feel the precariousness with which all American property is possessed. But let our imaginations transport us a few moments to Boston; that sea of wretchedness will teach us wisdom, and instruct us for ever to renounce a power in whom we can have no trust. The inhabitants of that unfortunate city who but a few months ago were in ease and affluence, have now no other alternative than to stay and starve, or turn out to beg. Endangered by the fire of their friends if they continue within the city, and plundered by the soldiery if they leave it, in their present situation they are prisoners without the hope of redemption, and in a general attack for their relief they would be exposed to the fury of both armies.

Men of passive tempers look somewhat lightly over the offences of Great Britain, and, still hoping for the best, and apt to call out, *Come, come, we shall be friends again for all this.* But examine the passions and feelings of mankind to bring the doctrine of reconciliation to the touchstone of nature, and then tell me whether you can hereafter love, honour, and faithfully serve the power that hath carried fire and sword into your land? If you cannot do all these, then are you only deceiving yourselves, and by your delay bringing ruin upon posterity. Your future connection with Britain, whom you can neither love nor honour, will be forced and unnatural, and being formed only on the plan of present convenience, will in a little time fall into a relapse more wretched than the first. But if you say, you can still pass the violations over, then I ask, hath your house been burnt? Hath your property been destroyed before your face? Are your wife and children destitute of a bed to lie on, or bread to live on? Have you lost a parent or a child by their hands, and yourself the ruined and wretched survivor? If you have not, then are you not a judge of those who have. But if you have, and can still shake hands with the murderers, then are you unworthy the name of husband, father, friend, or lover, and whatever may be your rank or title in life, you have the heart of a coward, and the spirit of a sycophant.

This is not inflaming or exaggerating matters, but trying them by those feelings and affections which nature justifies, and without which we should be incapable of discharging the social duties of life, or enjoying the felicities of it. I mean not to exhibit horror for the purpose of provoking revenge, but to awaken us from fatal and unmanly slumbers, that we may pursue determinately some fixed object. 'Tis not in the power of Britain or of Europe to conquer America, if she doth not conquer herself by delay and timidity. The present winter is worth an age if rightly employed, but if lost or neglected the whole Continent will partake of the misfortune; and there is no punishment which that man doth not deserve, be he who, or what, or where he will, that may be the means of sacrificing a season so precious and useful.

'Tis repugnant to reason, to the universal order of things, to all examples from former ages, to suppose that this Continent can long remain subject to any external power. The most sanguine in Britain doth not think so. The utmost stretch of human wisdom cannot, at this time, compass a plan, short of separation, which can promise the continent even a year's security. Reconciliation is *now* a fallacious dream. Nature hath deserted the connection, and art cannot supply her place. For, as Milton wisely expresses, "never can true reconcilement grow where wounds of deadly hate have pierced so deep."

Every quiet method for peace hath been ineffectual. Our prayers have been rejected with disdain; and hath tended to convince us that nothing flatters vanity or confirms obstinacy in Kings more than repeated petitioning—and nothing hath contributed more than that very measure to make the Kings of Europe absolute. Witness Denmark and Sweden. Wherefore, since nothing but blows will do, for God's sake let us come to a final separation, and not leave the next generation to be cutting throats under the violated unmeaning names of parent and child.

To say they will never attempt it again is idle and visionary; we thought so at the repeal of the stamp act, yet a year or two undeceived us; as well may we suppose that nations which have been once defeated will never renew the quarrel.

As to government matters, 'tis not in the power of Britain to do this continent justice: the business of it will soon be too weighty and intricate to be managed with any tolerable degree of convenience, by a power so distant from us, and so very ignorant of us; for if they cannot conquer us, they cannot govern us. To be always running three or four thousand miles with a tale or a petition, waiting four or five months for an answer, which, when obtained, requires five or six more to explain it in, will in a few years be looked upon as folly and childishness. There was a time when it was proper, and there is a proper time for it to cease.

Small islands not capable of protecting themselves are the proper objects for government to take under their care; but there is something absurd, in supposing a Continent to be perpetually governed by an island. In no instance hath nature made the satellite larger than its primary planet; and as England and America, with respect to each other, reverse the common order of nature, it is evident that they belong to different systems. England to Europe: America to itself.

I am not induced by motives of pride, party, or resentment to espouse the doctrine of separation and independence; I am clearly, positively, and conscientiously persuaded that it is the true interest of this Continent to be so; that every thing short of *that* is mere patchwork, that it can afford no lasting felicity,—that it is leaving the sword to our children, and shrinking back at a time when a little more, a little further, would have rendered this Continent the glory of the earth.

As Britain hath not manifested the least inclination towards a compromise, we may be assured that no terms can be obtained worthy the acceptance of the Continent, or any ways equal to the expence of blood and treasure we have been already put to.

The object contended for, ought always to bear some just proportion to the expense. The removal of North, or the whole detestable junto, is a matter unworthy the millions we have expended. A temporary stoppage of trade was an inconvenience, which would have sufficiently ballanced the repeal of all the acts complained of, had such repeals been obtained; but if the whole Continent must take up arms, if every man must be a soldier, 'tis scarcely worth our while to fight against a contemptible ministry only. Dearly, dearly do we pay for the repeal of the acts, if that is all we fight for; for, in a just estimation 'tis as great a folly to pay a Bunker-hill price for law as for land. As I have always considered the independancy of this continent, as an event which sooner or later must arrive, so from the late rapid progress of the Continent to maturity, the event cannot be far off. Wherefore, on the breaking out of hostilities, it was not worth the while to have disputed a matter which time would have finally redressed, unless we meant to be in earnest: otherwise it is like wasting an estate on a suit at law, to regulate the trespasses of a tenant whose lease is just expiring. No man was a warmer wisher for a reconciliation than myself, before the fatal nineteenth of April, 1775, but the moment the event of that day was made known, I rejected the hardened, sullen-tempered Pharaoh of England for ever; and disdain the wretch, that with the pretended title of FATHER OF HIS PEOPLE can unfeelingly hear of their slaughter, and composedly sleep with their blood upon his soul.

But admitting that matters were now made up, what would be the event? I answer, the ruin of the Continent. And that for several reasons.

First. The powers of governing still remaining in the hands of the King, he will have a negative over the whole legislation of this Continent. And as he hath shown himself such an inveterate enemy to liberty, and discovered such a thirst for arbitrary power, is he, or is he not, a proper person to say to these colonies, *You shall make no laws but what I please!?* And is there any inhabitant of America so ignorant as not to know, that according to what is called the *present constitution*, this Continent can make no laws but what the king gives leave to; and is there any man so unwise as not to see, that (considering what has happened) he will suffer no law to be made here but such as suits *his* purpose? We may be as effectually enslaved by the want of laws in America, as by submitting to laws made for us in England. After matters are made up (as it is called) can there be any doubt, but the whole power of the crown will be exerted to keep this continent as low and humble as possible? Instead of going forward we shall go backward, or be perpetually quarrelling, or ridiculously petitioning. We are already greater than the King wishes us to be, and will he not hereafter endeavor to make us less? To bring the matter to one point, Is the power who is jealous of our prosperity, a proper power to govern us? Whoever says *No*, to this question, is an Independant for independency means no more than this, whether we shall make our own laws, or, whether the King, the greatest enemy this continent hath, or can have, shall tell us *there shall be no laws but such as I like.*

But the King, you will say, has a negative in England; the people there can make no laws without his consent. In point of right and good order, it is something very ridiculous that a youth of twenty-one (which hath often happened) shall say to several millions of people older and wiser than himself, ''I forbid this or that act of yours to be law.'' But in this place I decline this sort of reply, though I will never cease to expose the absurdity of it, and only answer that England being the King's residence, and America not so, makes quite another case. The King's negative here is ten times more dangerous and fatal than it can be in England; for there he will scarcely refuse his consent to a bill for putting England into as strong a state of defense as possible, and in America he would never suffer such a bill to be passed.

America is only a secondary object in the system of British politics. England consults the good of this country no further than it answers her own purpose. Wherefore, her own interest leads her to suppress the growth of ours in every case which doth not promote her advantage, or in the least interferes with it. A pretty state we should soon be in under such a second hand government, considering what has happened! Men do not change from enemies to friends by the alteration of a name: And in order to show that reconciliation now is a dangerous doctrine, I affirm, *that it would be policy in the King at this time to repeal the acts, for the sake of reinstating himself in the government of the provinces;* In order that HE MAY ACCOMPLISH BY CRAFT AND SUBTLETY, IN THE LONG RUN, WHAT HE CANNOT DO BY FORCE AND VIOLENCE IN THE SHORT ONE. Reconciliation and ruin are nearly related.

Secondly. That as even the best terms which we can expect to obtain can amount to no more than a temporary expedient, or a kind of government by guardianship, which can last no longer than till the Colonies come of age, so the general face and state of things in the interim will be unsettled and unpromising. Emigrants of property will not choose to come to a country whose form of government hangs but by a thread, and who is every day tottering on the brink of commotion and disturbance; and numbers of the present inhabitants would lay hold of the interval to dispose of their effects, and quit the Continent.

But the most powerful of all arguments is, that nothing but independance, *i.e.* a Continental form of government, can keep the peace of the Continent and preserve it inviolate from civil wars. I dread the event of a reconciliation with Britain now, as it is more than probable that it will be followed by a revolt some where or other, the consequences of which may be far more fatal than all the malice of Britain.

Thousands are already ruined by British barbarity; (thousands more will probably suffer the same fate.) Those men have other feelings than us who have nothing suffered. All they now possess is liberty; what they before enjoyed is sacrificed to its service, and having nothing more to lose they disdain submission. Besides, the general temper of the Colonies, towards a British government will be like that of a youth who is nearly out of his time; they will care very little about her: And a government which cannot preserve the peace is no government at all, and in that case we pay our money for nothing; and pray what is it that Britain can do, whose power will be wholly on paper, should a civil tumult break out the very day after reconciliation? I have heard some men say, many of whom I believe spoke without thinking, that they dreaded an independance, fearing that it would produce civil wars: It is but seldom that our first thoughts are truly correct, and that is the case here; for there is ten times more to dread from a patched up connection than from independance. I make the sufferer's case my own, and I protest, that were I driven from house and home, my property destroyed, and my circumstances ruined, that as a man, sensible of injuries, I could never relish the doctrine of reconciliation, or consider myself bound thereby.

The Colonies have manifested such a spirit of good order and obedience to Continental government, as is sufficient to make every reasonable person easy and happy on that head. No man can assign the least pretence for his fears, on any other grounds, than such as are truly childish and ridiculous, viz., that one colony will be striving for superiority over another.

Where there are no distinctions there can be no superiority; perfect equality affords no temptation. The Republics of Europe are all (and we may say always) in peace. Holland and Switzerland are without wars, foreign or domestic: Monarchical governments, it is true, are never long at rest: the crown itself is a temptation to enterprising ruffians at home; and that degree of pride and insolence ever attendant on regal authority, swells into a rupture with foreign powers in instances where a republican government, by being formed on more natural principles, would negociate the mistake.

If there is any true cause of fear respecting independance, it is because no plan is yet laid down. Men do not see their way out. Wherefore, as an opening into that business I offer the following hints; at the same time modestly affirming, that I have no other opinion of them myself, than that they may be the means of giving rise to something better. Could the straggling thoughts of individuals be collected, they would frequently form materials for wise and able men to improve into useful matter.

Let the assemblies be annual, with a president only. The representation more equal, their business wholly domestic, and subject to the authority of a Continental Congress.

Let each Colony be divided into six, eight, or ten, convenient districts, each district to send a proper number of Delegates to Congress, so that each Colony send at least thirty. The whole number in Congress will be at least 390. Each congress to sit and to choose a President by the following method. When the Delegates are met, let a Colony be taken from the whole thirteen Colonies by lot, after which let the Congress choose (by ballot) a president from out of the Delegates of that Province. In the next Congress, let a Colony be taken by lot from twelve only, omitting that Colony from which the president was taken in the former Congress, and so proceeding on till the whole thirteen shall have had their proper rotation. And in order that nothing may pass into a law but what is satisfactorily just, not less than three fifths of the Congress to be called a majority. He that will promote discord, under a government so equally formed as this, would have joined Lucifer in his revolt.

But as there is a peculiar delicacy from whom, or in what manner, this business must first arise, and as it seems most agreeable and consistent that it should come from some intermediate body between the governed and the governors, that is, between the Congress and the People, let a Continental Conference be held in the following manner, and for the following purpose,

A Committee of twenty six members of congress, *viz.* Two for each Colony. Two Members from each House of Assembly, or Provincial Convention; and five Representatives of the people at large, to be chosen in the capital city or town of each Province, for, and in behalf of the whole Province, by as many qualified voters as shall think proper to attend from all parts of the Province for that purpose; or, if more convenient, the Representatives may be chosen in two or three of the most populous parts thereof. In this conference, thus assembled, will be united the two grand principles of business, *knowledge* and *power.* The Members of Congress, Assemblies, or Conventions, by having had experience in national concerns, will be able and useful counsellors, and the whole, being impowered by the people, will have a truly legal authority.

The conferring members being met, let their business be to frame a Continental Charter, or Charter of the United Colonies; (answering to what is called the Magna Charta of England) fixing the number and manner of choosing Members of Congress, Members of Assembly, with their date of sitting; and drawing the line of business and jurisdiction between them: Always remembering, that our strength is Continental, not Provincial. Securing freedom and property to all men, and above all things, the free exercise of religion, according to the dictates of conscience; with such other matter as it is necessary for a charter to contain. Immediately after which, the said conference to dissolve, and the bodies which shall be chosen conformable to the said charter, to be the Legislators and Governors of this Continent for the time being: Whose peace and happiness, may GOD preserve. AMEN.

Should any body of men be hereafter delegated for this or some similar purpose, I offer them the following extracts from that wise observer on Governments, Dragonetti. "The science," says he, "of the Politician consists in fixing the true point of happiness and freedom. Those men would deserve the gratitude of ages, who should discover a mode of government that contained the greatest sum of individual happiness, with the least national expense." (Dragonetti on "Virtues and Reward.")

But where, say some, is the King of America? I'll tell you, friend, he reigns above, and doth not make havoc of mankind like the Royal Brute of Great Britain. Yet that we may not appear to be defective even in earthly honours, let a day be solemnly set apart for proclaiming the Charter; let it be brought forth placed on the Divine Law, the Word of God; let a crown be placed thereon, by which the world may know, that so far as we approve of monarchy, that in America the law is king. For as in absolute governments the King is law, so in free countries the law ought to be king; and there ought to be no other. But lest any ill use should afterwards arise, let the Crown at the conclusion of the ceremony be demolished, and scattered among the people whose right it is.

A government of our own is our natural right: and when a man seriously reflects on the precariousness of human affairs, he will become convinced, that it is infinitely wiser and safer, to form a constitution of our own in a cool deliberate manner, while we have it in our power, than to trust such an interesting event to time and chance. If we omit it now, some Massanello* may hereafter arise, who, laying hold of popular disquietudes, may collect together the desperate and the discontented, and by assuming to themselves the powers of government, finally sweep away the liberties of the Continent like a deluge. Should the government of America return again into the hands of Britain, the tottering situation of things will be a temptation for some desperate adventurer to try his fortune; and in such a case, what relief can Britain give? Ere she could hear the news, the fatal business might be done; and ourselves suffering like the wretched Britons under the oppression of the Conqueror. Ye that oppose independance now, ye know not what ye do: ye are opening a door to eternal tyranny, by keeping vacant the seat of government. There are thousands and tens of thousands, who would think it glorious to expel from the Continent, that barbarous and hellish power, which hath stirred up the Indians and the Negroes to destroy us; the cruelty hath a double guilt, it is dealing brutally by us, and treacherously by them.

To talk of friendship with those in whom our reason forbids us to have faith, and our affections wounded thro' a thousand pores instruct us to detest, is madness and folly. Every day wears out the little remains of kindred between us and them; and can there be any reason to hope, that as the relationship expires, the affection will encrease, or that we shall agree better when we have ten times more and greater concerns to quarrel over than ever?

Ye that tell us of harmony and reconciliation, can ye restore to us the time that is past? Can ye give to prostitution its former innocence? neither can ye reconcile Britain and America. The last cord now is broken, the people of England are presenting addresses against us. There are injuries which nature cannot forgive; she would cease to be nature if she did. As well can the lover forgive the ravisher of his mistress, as the Continent forgive the murders of Britain. The Almighty hath implanted in us these unextinguishable feelings for good and wise purposes. They are the Guardians of his Image in our hearts. They distinguish us from the herd of common animals. The social compact would dissolve, and justice be extirpated from the earth, or have only a casual existence were we callous to the touches of affection. The robber and the

---

*Thomas Anello, otherwise Massanello, a fisherman of Naples, who after spiriting up his countrymen in the public market place, against the oppression of the Spaniards, to whom the place was then subject, prompted them to revolt, and in the space of a day became King.—*Author.*

murderer would often escape unpunished, did not the injuries which our tempers sustain, provoke us into justice.

O! ye that love mankind! Ye that dare oppose not only the tyranny but the tyrant, stand forth! Every spot of the old world is overrun with oppression. Freedom hath been hunted round the Globe. Asia and Africa have long expelled her. Europe regards her like a stranger, and England hath given her warning to depart. O! receive the fugitive, and prepare in time an asylum for mankind.

To the People of Pennsylvania, *Excerpt from* Letter III

William Smith

Commentary

Thomas Paine became an American hero, but we have almost forgotten the Loyalists, even those who favored the colonial cause until drawing the line at declaring independence. This is explained partly by the cliche, "Winners write history," and partly by the Loyalists' difficulty in getting a hearing. As we noted before, self-styled "Loyalists" were often silenced as early as 1774-75. As the independence movement gathered momentum during 1776, mob violence increased, and many local governments formed "Committees of Safety" or "Committees of Inspection" to silence "traitors." Yet Loyalists were not silenced completely, especially in Philadelphia, until after the Continental Congress voted for independence on July 2, 1776 and adopted the Declaration of Independence two days later.

These events are exemplified by the rhetorical endeavors of Rev. William Smith (1727-1803) during the spring of 1776. Now almost forgotten, he was well known in his own time as an Anglican priest, a political essayist, and an educator who converted the Philadelphia "Academy" (a secondary school) into the "College, Academy and Charitable School of Philadelphia" (now the University of Pennsylvania).

During March and April, 1776, Smith wrote a series of eight newspaper letters "To the People of Pennsylvania" under the pseudonym, Cato. Appropriating the name, Cato, was a good rhetorical move. Even poorly educated Americans knew enough Roman history to have learned about the integrity of the ancient Cato. Moreover, two other "Catos" had written a series of letters, originally published in Britain in 1720, that had been reprinted countless times in America and were highly esteemed.

Of the five Philadelphia newspapers whose files are available at the American Antiquarian Society, three carried all eight of Cato's letters, one carried none of them, and another carried only the first letter. However, *all five* carried a host of rebuttals! Most were signed by "Cassandra" or "The Forester." Much refutation involved irrelevancies, such as "queries" about the identity of "Cato" and attacks on Smith for previous political stands. Some relevant refutation restated the pro-independence arguments originally advanced by Paine, and some involved an issue that did not arise until after Paine's pamphlet first appeared: whether the British government was sending commissioners to negotiate with Congress and, if so, whether they should be received or sent home without a hearing. All of the refutation was vituperative, and the local Committee was urged to silence Cato.

Smith devoted most of his first letter to (1) objecting to the legality of the Committee of Inspection and (2) emphasizing the need for full and open debate on a question as important as independence. He also expressed his long-standing support of the colonial cause, including the actions that Congress was currently taking.

Although Smith did not explicitly say so in his first letter, he implied that he planned to devote the remaining letters to refuting Paine, but his plan was disrupted by (1) publicity surrounding the new issue regarding the commissioners and (2) the large number of anti-Cato rebuttals, which Smith felt obligated to answer. In his second letter, Smith answered Cassandra's blast against receiving the commissioners by expressing optimism that negotiations would lead to reconciliation. Letters three and four were wide-ranging, being devoted partly to answering portions of Paine's pamphlet and partly to answering "The Forester" and other anti-Cato writers. Letters five through eight concentrated on defending the "mixed constitution" against attacks that Paine had launched in the first two sections of *Common Sense*.

Readers who compare the following excerpt from Letter III will see its relevance to the portion of *Common Sense* that appears in this anthology. It is reproduced from the March 23, 1776 issue of *The Pennsylvania Ledger: Or the Virginia, Maryland, Pennsylvania, & New-Jersey Weekly Advertiser* that is available on microfilm at the American Antiquarian Society.

Excerpt from Letter III

I have, in my second letter, freely declared my *political creed*, viz.—"That the true interest of America lies in *reconciliation* with Great-Britain, upon Constitutional Principles, and that I wish it upon none else." I now proceed to give my reasons for this declaration. It is fit, in so great a question, that you should weigh both sides well, and exercise that good sense for which the inhabitants of these Colonies have been hitherto distinguished, and then I shall be under no apprehensions concerning the pernicious, though specious plans, which are every day published in our news papers and pamphlets. The people generally judge right, when the whole truth is plainly laid before them; but through inattention in some, and fondness for novelty in others, when but one side of a proposition is agitated and persevered in, they may gradually deceive themselves, and adopt what cooler reflection and future dear-bought experience may prove to be ruinous.

Agriculture and commerce have hitherto been the happy employments, by which these *middle Colonies* have risen into wealth and importance. By them the face of the country has been changed from a barren wilderness into the hospitable abodes of peace and plenty. Without them, we had either never existed as Americans, or existed only as savages.—The oaks would still have possessed their native spots of earth, and never have appeared in the form of ships and houses. What are now well cultivated fields, or flourishing cities, would have remained only the solitary haunts of wild beasts, or of men equally wild.

That much of our former felicity was owing to the protection of England is not to be denied, and that we might still derive great advantages from her protection and friendship, if not valued at too high a price, is equally certain; nor is it worth enquiring, whether that protection was afforded us more for her own sake than ours? That the former was the case, more especially since the Colonies grew into consequence, I have not the least doubt, but that this is a reason for our rejecting any future connexion with her I must utterly deny. Although I consider her as having, in her late conduct towards us, acted the part of a cruel *Step-dame*, and not of a fostering Parent, I would not therefore quarrel with the benefits I may reap from a connexion with her, and can expect to reap no where else. If by her fleets and armies every nation on the globe is deterred from invading our properties, either on the high seas, in foreign countries, or on our own coasts, ought we not in sound policy to profit by her strength; and, without regarding the motives of her conduct, embrace the opportunity of becoming rich and powerful in her friendship, at an expence far less than it would cost us merely to exist in alliance with any other power?

If our present differences can be accommodated, there is scarce a probability that she will ever renew the late fatal system of policy, or attempt to employ force against us. But should she be so infatuated, at any future period, as to think of subjugating us, either by the arts of corruption, or oppressive exertions of power, can we entertain a doubt but that we shall again with a virtue equal to the present, and with the weapons of defence in our hands (when necessary) convince her that we are willing, by a constitutional connexion with her, to afford and receive reciprocal benefits; but although subjects of the same King, we will not consent to be her slaves. It was on *this ground*, and not for the purpose of trying new forms of government, "or erecting separate Independent States," that America embarked in the present glorious contest. On *this ground*, and upon none else, the *Continental Union* is formed. On this ground, we have a powerful support among the true Sons of Liberty in Great-Britain; and lastly, upon this ground, we have the utmost assurance of obtaining a full redress of our grievances, and an ample security against any future violation of our just rights. And if hereafter, in the fullness of time, it shall be necessary to separate from the land that gave birth to our ancestors, it will be in our state of perfect manhood, when we can fully weild our own arms, and protect our commerce and coasts by our own fleets, without looking to any nation upon earth for assistance.

This I say was our ground, and these our views, universally declared from the origin of this contest, till within a few weeks ago, when some gleams of reconciliation began first to break in upon us. If we now mean to change this ground, and reject all propositions of *peace*, from that moment we are deserted by every advocate of our cause in Great-Britain. We falsify every declaration which the Congress hath heretofore held forth in our behalf. We abandon all prospect of preserving our importance by trade and agriculture, the ancient, sure and experienced road to wealth and happiness.

In short, if thus contradicting all our former public professions, we should now affect *Independency* as our own act, before it appears clearly to the world to have been forced upon us by the cruel hand of the Parent-state.—We could neither hope for *Union* nor *Success* in the attempt. We must be considered as a faithless people in the sight of all mankind, and could scarcely expect the confidence of any nation upon earth or look up to heaven for its approving sentence. On the contrary, every convulsion attendant upon revolutions and innovations of government, untimely attempted or finally defeated, might be our portion; added to the loss of trade for want of protection; the consequent decay of husbandry; bloodshed and desolation; with an exchange of the easy and flourishing condition of farmers and merchants, for a life, at best of hardy poverty as *soldiers* or *hunters*.

To see America reduced to such a situation may be the choice of adventurers who have nothing to lose, or by men exalted by the present confusions into *lucrative* offices, which they can hold no longer than the continuance of the public calamities. But can it be the wish of all that great and valuable body of people in America, who, by honest industry, have acquired a competency, and have experienced a happier life.—Can it be their wish, I say (for such considerations) to have destruction continually before their eyes; and to have enormous debts entailed upon them and their posterity, till at length they have nothing left which they can truly call their own?

I know the answers which will be given to these questions, and am prepared to reply to them, with that temper and gravity which so serious a subject requires. It will be *asserted*—indeed it has been already *asserted*—that the animosities between Great-Britain and the Colonies are now advanced to such a height, that RECONCILIATION is impossible. But *assertions* are nothing, when opposed to the nature of things, the truth of history, and all past experience. The quarrels of nations, being neither *personal* or *private*, cannot stir up mutual hatred among individuals. There never was a war so implacable, even among states naturally rivals and enemies, or among savages themselves, as not to have *peace* for its object as well as end! And, among people naturally friends, and connected by every dearer tie, who knows not that their quarrels (as those of *lovers*) are often but a stronger renewal of *love*? In such cases, the tide of affection reverting to its course is like that of water long bent back, which, at length burst the opposing mounds breaks forward through its native channel, and flows with redoubled vigor and increased velocity, to mix itself with its parent-main!

It has been further asserted—that we are able, with our land forces, to defend ourselves against the whole world; that if commerce be an advantage, we may command what foreign alliances we please; that the moment we declare ourselves an *independent people*, there are nations ready to face the British thunder, and become the carriers of our commodities for the sake of enriching themselves; that, if this were not the case, we can soon build navies to force and protect a trade, that a confederacy of the Colonies into one great *republic* is preferable to *Kingly government*, which is the appointment of the *Devil*, or at least reprobated by GOD; that those denominated *wise men*, in our own and foreign countries, who have been so lavish of their encomiums upon the English constitution, were but egregious *fools*; that it is nothing better than a bungling piece of machinery, standing in need of constant *checks* to regulate and continue its motions; that the nation itself is but one mass of corruption, having at its head a *Royal Brute, a hardened Pharaoh*, delighting in blood; that we can never enjoy liberty in connection with such a country, and therefore all the hardships mentioned above, and a thousand times more, if necessary, are to be endured for the preservation of our rights.

If these things had been as fully proved, as they are boldly asserted by the authors of what is called *Common Sense*, I should here drop my pen; and through the short remainder of life, take my chance of whatever miseries Providence may have in reserve for this land, as I know of none else to which I can retire. But as these doctrines contradict every thing which we have hitherto been taught to believe respecting government, I hope you, my dear countrymen, have yet kept *one ear open* to hear what answer may be given in my future letters.

CATO.

Section III

Founding a Nation
Rhetoric of
Constitutional Ratification

Opening Speech at the Constitutional Convention

Edmund Randolph

Commentary

When Congress was debating whether to declare independence in 1776, the leading opponent, John Dickinson, argued that independence should await formation of a central government. Otherwise thirteen independent States would lack enough unity to ensure their independence against Britain's powerful army. Although many Congressional colleagues were irritated by Dickinson's argument, they recognized that unity was necessary. They quickly drafted the Articles of Confederation. Although Congress functioned as a central government during the war, it was not until 1781 that the last State legislature ratified the Articles and thereby legitimized it.

The Articles permitted Congress to raise armies, borrow money and conduct foreign policy, but it could not levy taxes, interfere with the internal affairs of States or regulate interstate commerce. The Articles did not provide for an executive or judicial branch. Voting was by States, and amendments to the Articles required unanimous consent.

In 1787, many (probably most) Americans were satisfied with the Articles. True, many States had social unrest, which was due mostly to economic dislocations caused by the war, and Massachusetts even had a short-lived rebellion the previous year. Most Americans, though, considered such problems to be of concern to individual States, not a far-away central government. The average voter believed a central government to be necessary, but the long-standing fear of centralized authority (intensified by the recent conflict with Britain) made him happy to keep the central government weak. Besides, the existing system had brought independence, established a system for bringing new States into the Union and kept the peace for several years. Why worry?

Some political leaders saw many reasons to worry. The central government could not pay its war debts because States routinely refused to pay congressional "requisitions." They worried that the debts would never be paid and that some future war might lead to disaster if the central government continued to lack taxing power. They feared that various States might impose trade barriers against one another. They were concerned about the social unrest that had been highlighted by the rebellion in Massachusetts. Such fears were shared by some older Revolutionary leaders, such as John Dickinson and George Washington. These fears were especially widespread among younger politicians, such as Alexander Hamilton and James Madison, who had entered public service during the 1770s and were more accustomed to viewing politics from a national perspective.

Such nationally oriented politicians worked unsuccessfully for several years to strengthen the central government, first by proposing to amend the Articles so as to permit Congress to impose revenue-raising tariffs. This was vetoed by Rhode Island. Then they persuaded Congress to accept Virginia's call for a convention in Annapolis in 1786 to revise the Articles. When only five States sent delegates, they did little more than endorse Hamilton's proposal to have another convention the following year. Congress agreed. With the majority opposed to Hamilton's well-known desire to overhaul the existing Articles, Congress followed Virginia's lead in calling the convention "for the sole and express purpose" of preparing proposals for "revising" the Articles. What we now call the "Constitutional Convention" was empowered only to revise the Articles, not to write a new constitution.

The convention opened in May, 1787. After some routine business, including the election of George Washington as presiding officer, it listened to the first substantive speech. It was delivered by Edmund Randolph (1753-1813), governor of Virginia and a leader of the more nationally oriented politicians. Randolph concluded with a set of resolutions which outlined an entirely new form of government. By accepting (though later revising) them, the delegates essentially ignored their instructions.

Delegates were keenly aware that their disregard of instructions would cause future difficulties. They also knew that getting agreement among delegates required a "bundle of compromises." They would have to negotiate a constitution that strengthened the central government without giving it too much power. They would have to provide for the conflicting interests of various States. Compromise is never easy, but it is especially difficult when outside pressures are brought to bear on negotiators. Therefore, the delegates adopted a rule of secrecy and made no provisions for transcribing the debates.

Fortunately for historians, James Madison took voluminous notes, which Jonathan Elliot later used to compile his *Debates on the Adoption of the Federal Constitution. In the Convention Held at Philadelphia, in 1787; with a Diary of the Debates of the Congress of the Confederation; as Reported by James Madison, a Member, and Deputy from Virginia*. By the time that *Elliot's Debates* (as they are commonly called) were published, Madison was dead, the convention was history, the Constitution was popularly acclaimed, its meaning was being argued and there was a demand for speech texts.

The word *texts* should not be taken too literally. A typical speech, being part of an ongoing debate, was delivered impromptu. Madison rarely got more than an abstract, which Elliot (using a narrative form) reproduced in the third person. Randolph's opening speech, of course, was prepared in advance, but he gave only a written summary to Madison, who later gave it to Elliot. The following is reproduced from the 1859 edition of *Elliot's Debates* (Philadelphia: J.B. Lippincott, pp. 126-27) and is complete except for the resolutions. Although only a summary, it gives a pretty clear picture of pronationalist rhetoric.

Opening Speech at the Constitutional Convention

Mr. RANDOLPH — then opened the main business: —

He expressed his regret that it should fall to him, rather than those who were of longer standing in life and political experience, to open the great subject of their mission. But as the Convention had originated from Virginia, and his colleagues supposed that some proposition was expected from them, they had imposed this task on him.

He then commented on the difficulty of the crisis, and the necessity of preventing the fulfil[l]ment of the prophecies of the American downfall.

He observed, that, in revising the federal system, we ought to inquire, first, into the properties which such a government ought to possess; secondly, the defects of the Confederation; thirdly, the danger of our situation; and, fourthly, the remedy.

1. The character of such a government ought to secure, first, against foreign invasion; secondly, against dissensions between members of the Union, or seditions in particular states; thirdly, to procure to the several states various blessings, of which an isolated situation was incapable; fourthly, it should be able to defend itself against encroachment; and, fifthly, to be paramount to the state constitutions.

2. In speaking of the defects of the Confederation, he professed a high respect for its authors, and considered them as having done all that patriots could do, in the then infancy of the science of constitutions and of confederacies; when the inefficiency of requisitions was unknown — no commercial discord had arisen among any states — no rebellion had appeared, as in Massachusetts — foreign debts had not become urgent — the havoc of paper money had not been foreseen — treaties had not been violated; and perhaps nothing better could be obtained, from the jealousy of the states with regard to their sovereignty.

He then proceeded to enumerate the defects: —

First, that the Confederation produced no security against foreign invasion; Congress not being permitted to prevent a war, nor to support it by their own authority. Of this he cited many examples; most of which tended to show that they could not cause infractions of treaties, or of the law of nations, to be punished; that particular states might, by their conduct, provoke war without control; and that, neither militia nor drafts being fit for defence on such occasions, enlistments only could be successful, and these could not be executed without money.

Secondly, that the federal government could not check the quarrel between states, nor a rebellion in any, not having constitutional power, nor means, to interpose according to the exigency.

Thirdly, that there were many advantages which the United States might acquire, which were not attainable under the Confederation; such as a productive impost, counteraction of the commercial regulations of other nations, pushing of commerce *ad libitum*, &c., &c.

Fourthly, that the federal government could not defend itself against encroachments from the states.

Fifthly, that it was not even paramount to the state constitutions, ratified as it was in many of the states.

3. He next reviewed the danger of our situation; and appealed to the sense of the best friends of the United States — to the prospect of anarchy from the laxity of government every where — and to other considerations.

4. He then proceeded to the remedy; the basis of which, he said, must be the republican principle.

Exchange at the Constitutional Convention Regarding a Proposed Second Convention

Edmund Randolph, George Mason, Charles Pinckney and Elbridge Gerry

Commentary

As the Constitution neared final form, proponents knew that they had few worries in the convention but faced serious problems later. A majority of each delegation favored the document. Most individual delegates were ready to endorse it, and eventually thirty-nine did while only sixteen did not. Yet many difficulties lay ahead. The convention was legally obligated to report to Congress, which could only submit the Constitution to the States. Many signs indicated that ratification would be difficult or impossible in several States. Rhode Island had ignored the convention and would probably not ratify. Of the sixty-five delegates, ten had not attended a single session and others had attended irregularly. Delegates knew that their violation of instructions would lead to charges of conspiring to destroy people's liberties. The majority also knew that some compromises would alienate some States while other compromises would alienate others. The net effect was to endanger ratification everywhere.

Acutely aware of future difficulties, the majority used the last few sessions of the convention to lay the groundwork for future ratification. They inserted an article in the Constitution saying that it would go into effect when ratified by nine States. This not only circumvented the unanimity rule in the existing Articles, but would later force reluctant States to choose between being left out of the new Union or ratifying. Delegates recommended that Congress submit the proposed new Constitution to State ratifying conventions on a "take it or leave it" basis, thus ensuring that no amendments could be made to unravel the bundle of compromises.

These strategies were readily accepted by the majority, but the minority knew a steamroller when they saw one. The same Edmund Randolph who had spoken for a stronger government at the opening of the convention now proposed that State ratifying conventions be authorized to submit amendments, which would then be considered by a second convention. He was followed by a fellow Virginian, George Mason (1725-1792) of Revolutionary fame. They were opposed by Charles Pinckney (1757-1824) of South Carolina, a strong nationalist who had contributed much to the final version of the Constitution. Then another minority member, Elbridge Gerry (1744-1814) of Massachusetts, had his say. Unfortunately, Elliot could provide only a brief summary of this exchange, but it exemplifies the rhetoric that opponents of ratification would later use in the States. It is reproduced from the 1859 edition of *Elliot's Debates*, pp. 552-53.

Exchange Between Edmund Randolph, George Mason, Charles Pinckney and Elbridge Gerry Regarding a Proposed Second Convention

Mr. RANDOLPH, animadverting on the indefinite and dangerous power given by the Constitution to Congress, expressing the pain he felt at differing from the body of the Convention on the close of the great and awful subject of their labors, and anxiously wishing for some accommodating expedient which would relieve him from his embarrassments, made a motion importing,

"That amendments to the plan might be offered by the state conventions, which should be submitted to, and finally decided on by, another General Convention."

Should this proposition be disregarded, it would, he said, be impossible for him to put his name to the instrument. Whether he should oppose it afterwards, he would not then decide; but he would not deprive himself of the freedom to do so in his own state, if that course should be prescribed by his final judgment.

Col. MASON seconded and followed Mr. RANDOLPH in animadversions on the dangerous power and structure of the government, concluding that it would end either in monarchy or a tyranical aristocracy — which, he was in doubt, — but one or other, he was sure. This Constitution had been formed without the knowledge or idea of the people. A second Convention will know more of the sense of the people, and be able to provide a system more consonant to it. It was improper to say to the people, take this or nothing. As the Constitution now stands, he could neither give it his support or vote in Virginia; and he could not sign here what he could not support there. With the expedient of another Convention, as proposed, he could sign.

Mr. PINCKNEY. These declarations, from members so respectable, at the close of this important scene, give a peculiar solemnity to the present moment. He descanted on the consequences of calling forth the deliberations and amendments of the different states, on the subject of government at large. Nothing but confusion and contrariety will spring from the experiment. The states will never agree in their plans, and the deputies to a second Convention, coming together under the discordant impressions of their constituents, will never agree. Conventions are serious things, and ought not to be repeated[.] He was not without objections, as well as others, to the plan. He objected to the contemptible weakness and dependence of the executive. He objected to the power of a majority, only, of Congress, over commerce. But, apprehending the danger of a general confusion, and an ultimate decision by the sword, he should give the plan his support.

Mr. GERRY stated the objections which determined him to withhold his name from the Constitution: 1, the duration and reeligibility of the Senate; 2, the power of the House of Representatives to conceal their Journals; 3, the power of Congress over the places of election; 4, the unlimited power of Congress over their own compensation; 5, that Massachusetts has not a due share of representatives allotted to her; 6, that three fifths of the blacks are to be represented, as if they were freemen; 7, that under the power over commerce, monopolies may be established; 8, the Vice-President being made head of the Senate. He could, however, he said, get over all these, if the rights of the citizens were not rendered insecure — first, by the general power of the legislature to make what laws they may please to call "necessary and proper;" secondly, to raise armies and money without limit; thirdly, to establish a tribunal without juries, which will be a Star Chamber as to civil cases. Under such a view of the Constitution, the best that could be done, he conceived, was to provide for a second General Convention.

Closing Speech at the Constitutional Convention

Benjamin Franklin

Commentary

Not satisfied with defeating Randolph's proposal, proponents of the new Constitution concluded the convention only after another move to help ratification. Worried about the future opposition of strong-willed minority members, such as Mason, and possible opposition from waverers, such as Randolph, they designed a strategy to keep waverers in line, appease the minority as much as possible and undercut the minority's ethos by giving the public an appearance of unanimity. Gouverneur Morris prepared a motion which "in order to gain the dissenting members," according to Elliot, was "put into the hands of Dr. Franklin, that it might have the better chance of success."

With most delegates in their thirties, the few older Revolutionary heroes in attendance had special ethos, but that of Benjamin Franklin (1706-1790) was unique. Now in his eighties, he was a distinguished scientist, writer and diplomat with an unusual ability to conciliate opposing views. Selecting Franklin to speak for and then introduce the motion (note the sequence) was a rhetorical masterstroke.

Although too feeble to speak (or at least wishing to appear so), Franklin had a colleague read the speech on his behalf. His fellow delegates were not his only audience. In violation of the secrecy rule, he gave copies to several delegates. The speech was soon being printed in newspapers all over the country. Thus, his was not only the last major speech of the convention, but also the first rhetorical salvo in the campaign for ratification. It is reproduced from the 1859 edition of *Elliot's Debates*, pp. 554-55.

Closing Speech at the Constitutional Convention

"Mr. President: — I confess that there are several parts of this Constitution which I do not at present approve, but I am not sure I shall never approve them. For, having lived long, I have experienced many instances of being obliged, by better information or fuller consideration, to change opinions, even on important subjects, which I once thought right, but found to be otherwise. It is therefore that, the older I grow, the more apt I am to doubt my own judgment, and to pay more respect to the judgment of others. Most men, indeed, as well as most sects in religion, think themselves in possession of all truth, and that wherever others differ from them, it is so far error. Steele, a Protestant, in a dedication, tells the Pope, that the only difference between our churches, in their opinions of the certainty of their doctrines, is, 'the Church of Rome is infallible, and the Church of England is never in the wrong.' But though many private persons think almost as highly of their own infallibility as that of their sect, few express it so naturally as a certain French lady, who, in a dispute with her sister, said, 'I don't know how it happens, sister, but I meet with nobody but myself that is always in the right — *il n'y a que moi qui a toujours raison.*'

"In these sentiments, sir, I agree to this Constitution, with all its faults, if they are such; because I think a general government necessary for us, and there is no form of government, but what may be a blessing to the people if well administered; and believe further, that this is likely to be well administered for a course of years, and can only end in despotism, as other forms have done before it, when the people shall become so corrupted as to need despotic government, being incapable of any other. I doubt, too, whether any other Convention we can obtain may be able to make a better Constitution. For, when you assemble a number of men to have the advantage of their joint wisdom, you inevitably assemble with those men all their prejudices, their passions, their errors of opinion, their local interests, and their selfish views. From such an assembly can a perfect production be expected? It therefore astonishes me, sir, to find this system approaching so near to perfection as it does; and I think it will astonish our enemies, who are waiting with confidence to hear that our councils are confounded, like those of the builders of Babel; and that our states are on the point of separation, only to meet hereafter for the purpose of cutting one another's throats. Thus I consent, sir, to this Constitution, because I expect no better, and because I am not sure, that it is not the best. The opinions I have had of its errors I sacrifice to the public good. I have never whispered a syllable of them abroad. Within these walls they were born, and here they shall die. If every one of us, in returning to our constituents, were to report the objections he has had to it, and endeavor to gain partisans in support of them, we might prevent its being generally received, and thereby lose all the salutary effects and great advantages resulting naturally in our favor among foreign nations, as well as among ourselves, from our real or apparent unanimity. Much of the strength and efficiency of any government, in procuring and securing happiness to the people, depends on opinion — on the general opinion of the goodness of the government, as well as of the wisdom and integrity of its governors. I hope, therefore, that for our own sakes, as a part of the people, and for the sake of posterity, we shall act heartily and unanimously in recommending this

Constitution (if approved by Congress and confirmed by the conventions) wherever our influence may extend, and turn our future thoughts and endeavors to the means of having it well administered.

"On the whole, sir, I cannot help expressing a wish that every member of the Convention, who may still have objections to it, would with me, on this occasion, doubt a little of his own infallibility, and to make manifest our unanimity, put his name to this instrument." He then moved that the Constitution be signed by the members, and offered the following as a convenient form, viz: —

"Done in Convention by the unanimous consent of *the states* present, the 17th of September, &c. In witness whereof, we have hereunto subscribed our names."

Exchange at the Massachusetts Ratifying Convention

Amos Singletary and Jonathan Smith

Commentary

On September 28, 1787, Congress voted to submit the Constitution to State ratifying conventions according to the convention's recommendations. Now amendments were not in order, and the "nine States" strategy was in place. Moving quickly to obtain ratification before opponents could get organized, proponents called themselves "Federalists" and their opponents "Antifederalists." This terminology was a rhetorical masterstroke because it implied that opponents were against the existing federation, as well as the proposed new Constitution.

All States eventually held ratifying conventions, and the Federalist cause went well at first. Delaware ratified unanimously on December 7, 1787. Despite (not unfounded) charges of riding roughshod over the minority, Pennsylvania ratified on December 12, 1787 by 46-23. Then New Jersey (December 18, 1787) and Georgia (January 1, 1788) ratified unanimously. On January 9, 1788, Connecticut ratified 128-40.

The road to a new nation, however, was getting rougher. Opposition was mounting everywhere. When Massachusetts opened its convention (on the same day that Connecticut ratified), politicians everywhere anxiously awaited the outcome. A large and populous State, Massachusetts had been a Revolutionary leader, and Shay's Rebellion of 1786 had helped precipitate the calling of the Constitutional Convention. Because it followed its traditional practice of electing delegates from the towns, the delegates were more representative of public opinion than most previous conventions. Delegates to subsequent State conventions would therefore note the outcome. Moreover, the outcome was uncertain; later historians who have examined the question believe that opponents had an initial majority.

Eager to avoid later charges of unfairness, Massachusetts delegates agreed to have the proceedings transcribed. Some other conventions also had their debates transcribed, but others did not. Hence, Elliot's *Debates in the Several*

151

State Conventions on the Adoption of the Federal Constitution, as Recommended by the General Convention at Philadelphia, in 1787 (first published in 1836) provides texts that are uneven in quality, some being based on transcriptions and others on various other sources.

The Massachusetts convention also agreed to debate the Constitution article-by-article, section-by-section. Debating even the most minor of items, it was not until Tuesday, January 21, that delegates got to the crucial section 8, article 1, which specified congressional powers. Debate continued through Wednesday and Thursday, but, according to Elliot, it had become "desultory" by Friday.

As indicated by the following exchange, reproduced from the 1881 edition of *Elliot's Debates* (Philadelphia: J.B. Lippincott, vol. 2, pp. 101-104), the debate did not remain desultory. To understand it, readers need to know the following (otherwise insignificant) facts. Both debaters had served in the State legislature, which is known officially as the "General Court," but neither was very well known. Both were from small towns in western Massachusetts (Singletary from Sutton and Smith from Lanesborough). Widgery, who interrupted Smith, was from the eastern part of the State. The reference to events in Bristol County was to the well-known upheaval associated with Shay's Rebellion. The exchange was initiated immediately after Fisher Ames, a Federalist, gave a speech which the transcriber unfortunately did not record completely. Judging from the brief summary in Elliot, Ames appealed for unity by calling on "those who stood forth in 1775 to stand forth now" in support of the Constitution.

Exchange Between Singletary and
Smith at the Massachusetts Ratifying Convention

Hon. Mr. SINGLETARY. Mr. President, I should not have troubled the Convention again, if some gentlemen had not called on them that were on the stage in the beginning of our troubles, in the year 1775. I was one of them. I have had the honor to be a member of the court all the time, Mr. President, and I say that, if any body had proposed such a constitution as this in that day, it would have been thrown away at once. It would not have been looked at. We contended with Great Britain, some said for a threepenny duty on tea; but it was not that; it was because they claimed a right to tax us and bind us in all cases whatever. And does not this Constitution do the same? Does it not take away all we have — all our property? Does it not lay *all* taxes, duties, imposts, and excises? And what more have we to give? They tell us Congress won't lay dry taxes upon us, but collect all the money they want by impost. I say, there has always been a difficulty about impost. Whenever the General Court was going to lay an impost, they would tell us it was more than trade could bear, that it hurt the fair trader, and encouraged smuggling; and there will always be the same objection: they won't be able to raise money enough by impost, and then they will lay it on the land, and take all we have got. These lawyers, and men of learning, and moneyed men, that talk so finely, and gloss over matters so smoothly, to make us poor illiterate people swallow down the pill, expect to get into Congress themselves; they expect to be the managers of this Constitution, and get all the power and all the money into their own hands, and then they will swallow up all us little folks, like the great *Leviathan*, Mr. President; yes, just as the whale swallowed up *Jonah*. This is what I am afraid of; but I won't say any more at present, but reserve the rest to another opportunity.

Hon. Mr. SMITH. Mr. President, I am a plain man, and get my living by the plough. I am not used to speak in public, but I beg your leave to say a few words to my brother ploughjoggers in this house. I have lived in a part of the country where I have known the worth of good government by the want of it. There was a black cloud that rose in the east last winter, and spread over the west. [Here Mr. Widgery interrupted. Mr. President, I wish to know what the gentleman means by the east.] I mean, sir, the county of Bristol; the cloud rose there, and burst upon us, and produced a dreadful effect. It brought on a state of anarchy, and that led to tyranny. I say, it brought anarchy. People that used to live peaceably, and were before good neighbors, got distracted, and took up arms against government. [Here Mr. Kingsley called to order, and asked, what had the history of last winter to do with the Constitution. Several gentlemen, and among the rest the Hon. Mr. Adams, said the gentleman was in order — let him go on in his own way.] I am going, Mr. President, to show you, my brother farmers, what were the effects of anarchy, that you may see the reasons why I wish for good government. People I say took up arms; and then, if you went to speak to them, you had the musket of death presented to your breast. They would rob you of your property; threaten to burn your houses; oblige you to be on your guard night and day; alarms spread from town to town; families were broken up; the tender mother would cry, "O, my son is among them! What shall I do for my child!" Some were taken captive, children taken out of their schools, and carried away. Then we should hear of an action, and the poor prisoners were set in the front, to be killed by their own friends. How dreadful, how distressing was this! Our distress was so great that we should have been glad to snatch at any thing that looked like a government. Had any person, that was able to protect us, come and set up his standard, we should all have flocked to it, even if it had been a monarch; and that monarch might have proved a tyrant; — so that you see that anarchy leads to tyranny, and better have one tyrant than so many at once.

Now, Mr. President, when I saw this Constitution, I found that it was a cure for these disorders. It was just such a thing as we wanted. I got a copy of it, and read it over and over. I had been a member of the Convention to form our own state constitution, and had learnt something of the checks and balances of power, and I found them all here. I did not go to any lawyer, to ask his opinion; we have no lawyer in our town, and we do well enough without. I formed my own opinion, and was pleased with this Constitution.

My honorable old daddy there [pointing to Mr. Singletary] won't think that I expect to be a Congress-man, and swallow up the liberties of the people. I never had any post, nor do I want one. But I don't think the worse of the Constitution because lawyers, and men of learning, and moneyed men, are fond of it. I don't suspect that they want to get into Congress and abuse their power. I am not of such a jealous make. They that are honest men themselves are not apt to suspect other people. I don't know why our constituents have not a good right to be as jealous of us as we seem to be of the Congress; and I think those gentlemen, who are so very suspicious that as soon as a man gets into power he turns rogue, had better look at home.

We are, by this Constitution, allowed to send ten members to Congress. Have we not more than that number fit to go? I dare say, if we pick out ten, we shall have another ten left, and I hope ten times ten; and will not these be a check upon those that go? Will they go to Congress, and abuse their power, and do mischief, when they know they must return and look the other ten in the face, and be called to account for their conduct? Some gentlemen think that our liberty and property are not safe in the hands of moneyed men, and men of learning? I am not of that mind.

Brother farmers, let us suppose a case, now: Suppose you had a farm of 50 acres, and your title was disputed, and there was a farm of 5000 acres joined to you, that belonged to a man of learning, and his title was involved in the same difficulty; would you not be glad to have him for your friend, rather than to stand alone in the dispute? Well, the case is the same. These lawyers, these moneyed men, these men of learning, are all embarked in the same cause with us, and we must all swim or sink together; and shall we throw the Constitution overboard because it does not please us alike? Suppose two or three of you had been at the pains to break up a piece of rough land, and sow it with wheat; would you let it lie waste because you could not agree what sort of a fence to make? Would it not be better to put up a fence that did not please every one's fancy, rather than not fence it at all, or keep disputing about it until the wild beasts came in and devoured it? Some gentlemen say, Don't be in a hurry; take time to consider, and don't take a leap in the dark. I say, Take things in time; gather fruit when it is ripe. There is a time to sow and a time to reap; we sowed our seed when we sent men to the federal Convention; now is the harvest, now is the time to reap the fruit of our labor; and if we won't do it now, I am afraid we never shall have another opportunity.

Speech at the Virginia Ratifying Convention Against Ratification

Patrick Henry

Commentary

As illustrated by the Singletary-Smith exchange, the long-standing fear of a powerful government becoming tyrannical had become central to Antifederalist rhetoric and had forced Federalists to emphasize the checks-and-balance system. Belittling the effectiveness of checks and balances, Antifederalists reminded listeners that the British constitution not only had a division of powers between King and Parliament, but also something this Constitution lacked: a Bill of Rights. Still the British government had become tyrannical.

The absence of a Bill of Rights and their own "take it or leave it" strategy put Federalists in a dilemma. They were going to lose Massachusetts without a Bill of Rights, but they could not now rectify their mistake. Massachusetts Federalists promised to support a series of Constitutional amendments, which would collectively constitute a Bill of Rights after the new government began operating. This strategy gained a narrow victory (187-168) on February 6, 1788, and was repeated in other States.

Despite Massachusetts' favorable vote, the ultimate outcome remained in doubt. Refusing to call a State convention, the Rhode Island legislature voted in February to hold a popular referendum (March 24), which overwhelmingly defeated ratification. Meanwhile, the New Hampshire convention met on February 13 and adjourned after a week-long (and unrecorded) debate. Apparently some delegates who had been instructed by their towns to vote negatively were persuaded by Federalist rhetoric and decided to request an adjournment so that they could talk to their constituents. While they talked, Maryland ratified on April 26 (63-11) and South Carolina followed on May 23 (149-73).

Just before New Hampshire became the ninth State to ratify (June 21, 1788), the Virginia convention opened on June 2. People generally assumed that Virginia would either become the ninth State or start a countertrend. Even if New Hampshire ratified, opinion in New York and North Carolina was divided so closely that Virginia's action would probably tip the balance.

Non-ratification in these three populous, wealthy and large States (whose western claims extended into what are now Ohio, West Virginia, Kentucky and Tennessee) would leave the Union without contiguous territory and much-needed resources. Alexander Hamilton successfully followed a delaying strategy in New York until news of Virginia's ratification tipped the balance (30-27). North Carolina refused to ratify until after the new government began operating, but these facts were unknown when the critical Virginia debate began.

The drama of the Virginia convention was enhanced by the array of talent on both sides. Edmund Randolph had swallowed his disappointment at failing to get a second convention and was ready to lead the Federalists. Other Federalists included John Marshall (known for his military record during the Revolution and his debating skill in the legislature), Henry Lee (better known as Light Horse Harry because of his wartime exploits) and James Madison (known for his work in the State legislature, Congress and the Constitutional Convention). Leading the Antifederalists were two Revolutionary heroes, George Mason, who had already kept his promise of arousing opposition to ratification, and Patrick Henry, who had refused to attend the Constitutional Convention. Although not physically present, George Washington was known to favor ratification, and his symbolic presence was a powerful Federalist argument. Respected for writing the Declaration of Independence, Thomas Jefferson (then serving as a diplomat in France) had been contacted privately, and his ambiguous answers allowed both sides to claim his support.

Eager to avoid future charges of chicanery, both sides agreed to have the debate transcribed. Despite its length (an entire volume of Elliot), the transcript is incomplete because the recorder could not always keep up and occasionally resorted to summarizing.

Both sides agreed to follow the Massachusetts procedure of debating the Constitution item-by-item, but they did more. They agreed to avoid general discussion until after all items had been discussed. This procedure, proposed by George Mason (to the chagrin of many Antifederalists), fit the Federalist strategy. First, it would obviate possible charges of steamrolling. Second, discussing technicalities would allow Federalists to emphasize checks and balances and, thus, erect their defense against general Antifederalist arguments about governmental tyranny, the lack of a Bill of Rights, etc. Federalists realized that a good defense was critical because a few wavering delegates would ultimately decide the outcome in this closely divided convention.

The Federalists also wanted to act quickly, but Antifederalists moved for a one-day postponement on the grounds that many delegates had not yet arrived. They neglected to mention that most of the latecomers were Antifederalists. Randolph opposed the motion on the grounds that the State legislature, of which many delegates were members, was scheduled to meet shortly. Antifederalists won this opening skirmish. The need to investigate some contested elections caused additional delay. It was not until the third day that everyone was ready to begin the debate in the agreed-upon manner.

Well, not everyone. Patrick Henry moved that the legislature's acts appointing delegates to the Annapolis and Philadelphia conventions be read. Passage would not only have caused additional delay but would have underscored an obvious point: delegates to the Constitutional Convention had exceeded their authority.

Aware of what Henry was up to, the presiding officer said that the question of "whether the federal Convention exceeded their powers" was irrelevant because the calling of the present convention made earlier instructions no longer binding. Henry then withdrew his motion, but he had reminded wavering delegates of a bothersome point.

Now, once again, delegates were ready to begin debating the Constitution item-by-item. The clerk read the Preamble and the first two sections of the first article. The first speaker was a Federalist who gave a long discourse on these first two sections involving congressional elections, congressional terms and other narrow items. Unwilling to confine himself to narrow questions, Henry used the general language of the Preamble to launch a general attack. "Who authorized" the writers of the Constitution "to speak the language of, *We, the people,* instead of, *We, the states?*" asked Henry. Such language, he argued, constituted a dangerous change in the Federal-State relationship.

Apparently caught off guard by Henry's speech, Randolph answered it with a short one that failed to refute Henry's arguments (except for one short example of the central government's weakness). He ignored the point that delegates had exceeded their instructions. The best he could do was to call the arguments "intemperate" and "trivial." Randolph seemed more interested in refuting the unspoken, but prevalent, suspicion that he had been a waverer. He reviewed his past actions and said that, under present circumstances, he had no choice but to support ratification. The eight States which had ratified would not reverse their actions and the issue was whether Virginia would support or destroy the Union. Clearly, the "nine States" strategy was coming into play.

Ignoring Randolph's speech, George Mason launched another general attack. The Constitution gave the central government an unlimited, unconditional power to tax, which, he argued, would eventually destroy State governments and create a Federal tyranny that would abolish the people's liberties.

The day was drawing to a close when Mason sat down, and the plan of postponing general debate had obviously gone astray. James Madison concluded the day's proceedings by remarking wryly that he would answer Mason's arguments when the convention got to the relevant section of the Constitution.

Although wishing to get back to the first two sections of article one, which were supposedly under consideration, Federalists knew they had to undo the damage. The arguments presented by Henry and Mason had much persuasive appeal to waverers, and their ethos as Revolutionary heroes was high. On the following day, Pendleton gave up the chair to answer Henry's speech. Then Light Horse Harry spoke. He began by praising Henry's distinguished career, but he added that instead of using his usual good judgment, Henry was getting emotional and talking about fears of a central government which had no basis in fact. (In reading Henry's speech, note his response.)

After listening to Pendleton and Lee, Henry delivered what is generally considered to be his major speech against ratification. It was not his only one. The old curmudgeon eventually lost, but he gave the Federalists a bad time to the bitter end (Virginia ratified, 89-79). The following text is derived from the transcription made by the reporter and printed by Elliot. There are a few ellipses where the transcriber failed to keep up or Henry presented legal citations. It is reproduced photographically from Ernest J. Wrage and Barnet Baskerville, *American Forum: Speeches on Historic Issues, 1788-1900* (New York: Harper Brothers, 1960), pp. 7-22.

Speech at the Virginia
Ratifying Convention Against Ratification

Mr. Chairman: I am much obliged to the very worthy gentleman for his encomium. I wish I was possessed with talents, or possessed of any thing that might enable me to elucidate this great subject. I am not free from suspicion: I am apt to entertain doubts. I rose yesterday to ask a question which arose in my own mind. When I asked that question, I thought the meaning of my interrogation was obvious. The fate of this question and of America may depend on this. Have they said, We, the states? Have they made a proposal of a compact between states? If they had, this would be a confederation. It is otherwise most clearly a consolidated government. The question turns, sir, on that poor little thing—the expression, We, the *people,* instead of the *states,* of America. I need not take much pains to show that the principles of this system are extremely pernicious, impolitic, and dangerous. Is this a monarchy, like England—a compact between prince and people, with checks on the former to secure the liberty of the latter? Is this a confederacy, like Holland—an association of a number of independent states, each of which retains its individual sovereignty? It is not a democracy, wherein the people retain all their rights securely. Had these principles been adhered to, we should not have been brought to this alarming transition, from a confederacy to a consolidated government. We have no detail of these great considerations, which, in my opinion, ought to have abounded before we should recur to a government of this kind. Here is a resolution as radical as that which separated us from Great Britain. It is radical in this transition; our rights and privileges are endangered, and the sovereignty of the states will be relinquished: and cannot we plainly see that this is actually the case? The rights of conscience, trial by jury, liberty of the press, all your immunities and franchises, all pretensions to human rights and privileges, are rendered insecure, if not lost, by this change, so loudly talked of by some, and inconsiderately by others. Is this tame relinquishment of rights worthy of freemen? Is it worthy of that manly fortitude that ought to characterize republicans? It is said eight states have adopted this plan. I declare that if twelve states and a half had adopted it, I would, with manly firmness, and in spite of an erring world, reject it. You are not to inquire how your trade may be increased, nor how you are to become a great and powerful people, but how your liberties can be secured; for liberty ought to be the direct end of your government.

Having premised these things, I shall, with the aid of my judgment and information, which, I confess, are not extensive, go into the discussion of this system more minutely. Is it necessary for your liberty that you should abandon those great rights by the adoption of this system? Is the relinquishment of the trial by jury and the liberty of the press necessary for your liberty? Will the abandonment of your most sacred rights tend to the security of your liberty? Liberty, the greatest of all earthly blessings—give us that precious jewel, and you may take every thing else! But I am fearful I have lived long enough to become an old-fashioned fellow. Perhaps an invincible attachment to the dearest rights of man may, in these refined, enlightened days, be deemed old-fashioned; if so, I am contented to be so. I say, the time has been when every pulse of my heart beat for American liberty, and which, I believe, had a counterpart in the breast of every true American; but suspicions have gone forth—suspicions of my integrity—publicly reported that my professions are not real. Twenty-three years ago was I supposed a traitor to my country? I was then said to be the bane of sedition, because I supported the rights of my country. I may be thought suspicious when I say our privileges and rights are in danger. But, sir, a number of the people of this country are weak enough to think these things are too true. I am happy to find that the gentleman on the other side declares they are groundless. But, sir, suspicion is a virtue as long as its object is the preservation of the public good, and as long as it stays within proper bounds: should it fall on me, I am contented: conscious rectitude is a powerful consolation. I trust there are many who think my professions for the public good to be real. Let your suspicion look to both sides. There are many on the other side, who possibly may have been persuaded to the necessity of these measures, which I conceive to be dangerous to your liberty. Guard with jealous attention the public liberty. Suspect every one who approaches that jewel. Unfortunately, nothing will preserve it but downright force. Whenever you give up that force, you are inevitably ruined. I am answered by gentlemen, that, though I might speak of terrors, yet the fact was, that we were surrounded by none of the dangers I apprehended. I conceive this new government to be one of those dangers: it has produced those horrors which distress many of our best citizens. We are come hither to preserve the poor commonwealth of Virginia, if it can be possibly done: something must be done to preserve your liberty and mine. The Confederation, this same despised government, merits, in my opinion, the highest encomium: it carried us through a long and dangerous war; it rendered us victorious in that bloody conflict with a powerful nation; it has secured us a territory greater than any European monarch possesses: and shall a government which has been thus strong and vigorous, be accused of imbecility, and abandoned for want of energy? Consider what you are about to do before you part with the government. Take longer time in reckoning things; revolutions like this have happened in almost every country in Europe; similar examples are to be found in ancient Greece and ancient Rome—instances of the people losing their liberty by their own carelessness and the ambition of a few. We are cautioned by the honorable gentleman, who presides, against faction and turbulence. I acknowledge that licentiousness is dangerous, and that it ought to be provided against: I acknowledge, also, the new form of government may effectually prevent it: yet there is another thing it will as effectually do—it will oppress and ruin the people.

There are sufficient guards placed against sedition and licentiousness; for, when power is given to this government to suppress these, or for any other purpose, the language it assumes is clear, express, and unequivocal; but when this Constitution speaks of privileges, there is an ambiguity, sir, a fatal ambiguity—an ambiguity which is very astonishing. In the clause under consideration, there is the strangest language that I can conceive. I mean, when it says that there shall not be more representatives than one for every thirty thousand. Now, sir, how easy is it to evade this privilege! "The number shall not exceed one for every thirty thousand." This may be satisfied by one representative from each state. Let our numbers be ever so great, this immense continent may, by this artful expression, be reduced to have but thirteen representatives. I confess this construction is not natural; but the ambiguity of the expression lays a good ground for a quarrel. Why was it not clearly and unequivocally expressed, that they should be entitled to have one for every thirty thousand? This would have obviated all disputes; and was this difficult to be done? What is the inference? When population increases, and a state shall send representatives in this proportion, Congress *may* remand them, because the right of having one for every thirty thousand is not clearly expressed. This possibility of reducing the number to one for each state approximates to probability by that other expression—"but each state shall at least have one representative." Now, is it not clear that, from the first expression, the number might be reduced so much that some states should have no representatives at all, were it not for the insertion of this last expression? And as this is the only restriction upon them, we may fairly conclude that they *may* restrain the number to one from each state. Perhaps the same horrors may hang over my mind again. I shall be told I am continually afraid: but, sir, I have strong cause of apprehension. In some parts of the plan before you, the great rights of freemen are endangered; in other parts, absolutely taken away. How does your trial by jury stand? In civil cases gone—not sufficiently secured in criminal—this best privilege is gone. But we are told that we need not fear; because those in power, being our representatives, will not abuse the powers we put in their hands. I am not well versed in history, but I will submit to your recollection, whether liberty has been destroyed most often by the licentiousness of the people, or by the tyranny of rulers. I imagine, sir, you will find the balance on the side of tyranny. Happy will you be if you miss the fate of those nations, who, omitting to resist their oppressors, or negligently suffering their liberty to be wrested from them, have groaned under intolerable despotism! Most of the human race are now in this deplorable condition; and those nations who have gone in search of grandeur, power, and splendor, have also fallen a sacrifice, and been the victims of their own folly. While they acquired those visionary blessings, they lost their freedom. My great objection to this government is, that it does not leave us the means of defending our rights, or of waging war against tyrants. It is urged by some gentlemen, that this new plan will bring us an acquisition of strength—an army, and the militia of the states. This is an idea extremely ridiculous; gentlemen cannot be in earnest. This acquisition will trample on our fallen liberty. Let my beloved Americans guard against that fatal lethargy that has pervaded the universe. Have we the means of resisting disciplined armies, when our only defence, the militia, is put into the hands of Congress?

The honorable gentleman said that great danger would ensue if the Convention rose without adopting this system. I ask, Where is that danger? I see none. Other gentlemen have told us, within these walls, that the union is gone, or that the union will be gone. Is not this trifling with the judgment of their fellow-citizens? Till they tell us the grounds of their fears, I will consider them as imaginary. I rose to make inquiry where those dangers were; they could make no answer: I believe I never shall have that answer. Is there a disposition in the people of this country to revolt against the dominion of laws? Has there been a single tumult in Virginia? Have not the people of Virginia, when laboring under the severest pressure of accumulated distresses, manifested the most cordial acquiescence in the execution of the laws? What could be more awful than their unanimous acquiescence under general distresses? Is there any revolution in Virginia? Whither is the spirit of America gone? Whither is the genius of America fled? It was but yesterday, when our enemies marched in triumph through our country. Yet the people of this country could not be appalled by their pompous armaments: they stopped their career, and victoriously captured them. Where is the peril, now, compared to that? Some minds are agitated by foreign alarms. Happily for us, there is no real danger from Europe; that country is engaged in more arduous business: from that quarter there is no cause of fear: you may sleep in safety forever for them.

Where is the danger? If, sir, there was any, I would recur to the American spirit to defend us; that spirit which has enabled us to surmount the greatest difficulties: to that illustrious spirit I address my most fervent prayer to prevent our adopting a system destructive to liberty. Let not gentlemen be told that it is not safe to reject this government. Wherefore is it not safe? We are told there are dangers, but those dangers are ideal; they cannot be demonstrated. To encourage us to adopt it, they tell us that there is a plain, easy way of getting amendments. When I come to contemplate this part, I suppose that I am mad, or that my countrymen are so. The way to amendment is, in my conception, shut. Let us consider this plain, easy way. "The Congress, whenever two thirds of both houses shall deem it necessary, shall propose amendments to this Constitution, or on the application of the legislatures of two thirds of the several states, shall call a Convention for proposing amendments, which, in either case, shall be valid to all intents and purposes, as part of this Constitution, when ratified by the legislatures of three fourths of the several states, or by the Conventions in three fourths thereof, as the one or the other mode of ratification may be proposed by the Congress. . . ."

Hence it appears that three fourths of the states must ultimately agree to any amendments that may be necessary. Let us consider the consequence of this. However uncharitable it may appear, yet I must tell my opinion— that the most unworthy characters may get into power, and prevent the introduction of amendments. Let us suppose—for the case is supposable, possible, and probable—that you happen to deal those powers to unworthy hands; will they relinquish powers already in their possession, or agree to amendments? Two thirds of the Congress, or of the state legislatures, are necessary even to propose amendments. If one third of these be unworthy men, they may prevent the application for amendments; but what is destructive and mischievous, is, that three fourths of the state legislatures, or of the state conventions, must concur in the amendments when proposed! In such numerous bodies, there must necessarily be some designing, bad men. To suppose that so large a number as three fourths of the states will concur, is to suppose that they will possess genius, intelligence, and integrity, approaching to miraculous. It would indeed be miraculous that they should concur in the same amendments, or even in such as would bear some likeness to one another; for four of the smallest states, that do not collectively contain one tenth part of the population of the United States, may obstruct the most salutary and necessary amendments. Nay, in these four states, six tenths of the people may reject these amendments; and suppose that amendments shall be opposed to amendments, which is highly probable,— is it possible that three fourths can ever agree to the same amendments? A bare majority in these four small states may hinder the adoption of amendments; so that we may fairly and justly conclude that one twentieth part of the American people may prevent the removal of the most grievous inconveniences and oppression, by refusing to accede to amendments. A trifling minority may reject the most salutary amendments. Is this an easy mode of securing the public liberty? It is, sir, a most fearful situation, when the most contemptible minority can prevent the alteration of the most oppressive government; for it may, in many respects, prove to be such. Is this the spirit of republicanism?

What, sir, is the genius of democracy? Let me read that clause of the bill of rights of Virginia which relates to this: 3d clause:—that government is, or ought to be, instituted for the common benefit, protection, and security of the people, nation, or community. Of all the various modes and forms of government, that is best, which is capable of producing the greatest degree of happiness and safety, and is most effectually secured against the danger of mal-administration; and that whenever any government shall be found inadequate, or contrary to those purposes, a majority of the community hath an indubitable, unalienable, and indefeasible right to reform, alter, or abolish it, in such manner as shall be judged most conducive to the public weal.

This, sir, is the language of democracy—that a majority of the community have a right to alter government when found to be oppressive. But how different is the genius of your new Constitution from this! How different from the sentiments of freemen, that a contemptible minority can prevent the good of the majority!

. . . .

Let me here call your attention to that part which gives the Congress power "to provide for organizing, arming, and disciplining the militia, and for governing such part of them as may be employed in the service of the United States—reserving to the states, respectively, the appointment of the officers, and the authority of training the militia according to the discipline prescribed by Congress." By this, sir, you see that their control over our last and best defence is unlimited. If they neglect or refuse to discipline or arm our militia, they will be useless: the states can do neither—this power being exclusively given to Congress. The power of appointing officers over men not disciplined or armed is ridiculous; so that this pretended little remains of power left to the states may, at the pleasure of Congress, be rendered nugatory. Our situation will be deplorable indeed: nor can we ever expect to get this government amended, since I have already shown that a very small minority may prevent it, and that small minority interested in the continuance of the oppression. Will the oppressor let go the oppressed? Was there ever an instance? Can the annals of mankind exhibit one single example where rulers overcharged with power willingly let go the oppressed, though solicited and requested most earnestly? The application for amendments will therefore be fruitless. Sometimes, the oppressed have got loose by one of those bloody struggles that desolate a country; but a willing relinquishment of power is one of those things which human nature never was, nor ever will be, capable of.

The honorable gentleman's observations, respecting the people's right of being the agents in the formation of this government, are not accurate, in my humble conception. The distinction between a national government and a confederacy is not sufficiently discerned. Had the delegates, who were sent to Philadelphia, a power to propose a consolidated government instead of a confederacy? Were they not deputed by states, and not by the people? The assent of the people, in their collective capacity, is not necessary to the formation of a federal government. The people have no right to enter into leagues, alliances, or confederations; they are not the proper agents for this purpose. States and foreign powers are the only proper agents for this kind of govenment. Show me an instance where the people have exercised this business. Has it not always gone through the legislatures? I refer you to the treaties with France, Holland, and other nations. How were they made? Were they not made by the states? Are the people, therefore, in their aggregate capacity, the proper persons to form a confederacy? This, therefore, ought to depend on the consent of the legislatures, the people having never sent delegates to make any proposition for changing the government. Yet I must say, at the same time, that it was made on grounds the most pure; and perhaps I might have been brought to consent to it so far as to the change of government. But there is one thing in it which I never would acquiesce in. I mean, the changing it into a consolidated government, which is so abhorrent to my mind. . . .

If we admit this consolidated govenment, it will be because we like a great, splendid one. Some way or other we must be a great and mighty empire; we must have an army, and a navy, and a number of things. When the American spirit was in its youth, the language of America was different: liberty, sir, was then the primary object. We are descended from a people whose government was founded on liberty: our glorious forefathers of Great Britain made liberty the foundation of every thing. That country is become a great, mighty, and splendid nation; not because their government is strong and energetic, but, sir, because liberty is its direct end and foundation. We drew the spirit of liberty from our British ancestors: by that spirit we have triumphed over every difficulty. But now, sir, the American spirit, assisted by the ropes and chains of consolidation, is about to convert this country into a powerful and mighty empire. If you make the citizens of this country agree to become the subjects of one great consolidated empire of America, your government will not have sufficient energy to keep them together. Such a government is incompatible with the genius of republicanism. There will be no checks, no real balances, in this government. What can avail your specious, imaginary balances, your rope-dancing, chain-rattling, ridiculous ideal checks and contrivances? But, sir, we are not feared by foreigners; we do not make nations tremble. Would this constitute happiness, or secure liberty? I trust, sir, our political hemisphere will ever direct their operations to the security of those objects. . . .

When I thus profess myself an advocate for the liberty of the people, I shall be told I am a designing man, that I am to be a great man, that I am to be a demagogue; and many similar illiberal insinuations will be thrown out: but, sir, conscious rectitude outweighs those things with me. I see great jeopardy in this new government. I see none from our present one. I hope some gentleman or other will bring forth, in full array, those dangers, if there be any, that we may see and touch them.

I have said that I thought this a consolidated government: I will now prove it. Will the great rights of the people be secured by this government? Suppose it should prove oppressive, how can it be altered? Our bill of rights declares, "that a majority of the community hath an indubitable, unalienable, and indefeasible right to reform, alter, or abolish it, in such manner as shall be judged most conducive to the public weal."

I have just proved that one tenth, or less, of the people of America—a most despicable minority—may prevent this reform or alteration. Suppose the people of Virginia should wish to alter their government; can a majority of them do it? No; because they are connected with other men, or, in other words, consolidated with other states. When the people of Virginia, at a future day, shall wish to alter their government, though they should be unanimous in this desire, yet they may be prevented therefrom by a despicable minority at the extremity of the United States. The founders of your own Constitution made your government changeable: but the power of changing it is gone from you. Whither is it gone? It is placed in the same hands that hold the rights of twelve other states; and those who hold those rights have right and power to keep them. It is not the particular government of Virginia: one of the leading features of that government is, that a majority can alter it, when necessary for the public good. This government is not a Virginian, but an American government. Is it not, therefore, a consolidated government? The sixth clause of your bill of rights tells you, "that elections of members to serve as representatives of the people in Assembly ought to be free, and that all men having sufficient evidence of permanent common interest with, and attachment to, the community, have the right of suffrage, and cannot be *taxed,* or deprived of their property for public uses, without their own consent, or that of their representatives so elected, nor bound by any law to which they have not in like manner assented for the public good." But what does this Constitution say? The clause under consideration gives an unlimited and unbounded power of taxation. Suppose every delegate from Virginia opposes a law laying a tax; what will it avail? They are opposed by a majority; eleven members can destroy their efforts: those feeble ten cannot prevent the passing the most oppressive tax law; so that, in direct opposition to the spirit and express language of your declaration of rights, you are taxed, not by your own consent, but by people who have no connection with you.

The next clause of the bill of rights tells you, "that all power of suspending law, or the execution of laws, by any authority, without the consent of the representatives of the people, is injurious to their rights, and ought not to be exercised." This tells us that there can be no suspension of government or laws without our own consent; yet this Constitution can counteract and suspend any of our laws that contravene its oppressive operation; for they have the power of direct taxation, which suspends our bill of rights; and it is expressly provided that they can make all laws necessary for carrying their powers into execution; and it is declared paramount to the laws and constitutions of the states. Consider how the only remaining defence we have left is destroyed in this manner. Besides the expenses of maintaining the Senate and other house in as much splendor as they please, there is to be a great and mighty President, with very extensive powers—the powers of a king. He is to be supported in extravagant magnificence; so that the whole of our property may be taken by this American government, by laying what taxes they please, giving themselves what salaries they please, and suspending our laws at their pleasure. I might be thought too inquisitive, but I believe

I should take up very little of your time in enumerating the little power that is left to the government of Virginia; for this power is reduced to little or nothing: their garrisons, magazines, arsenals, and forts, which will be situated in the strongest places within the states; their ten miles square, with all the fine ornaments of human life, added to their powers, and taken from the states, will reduce the power of the latter to nothing.

The voice of tradition, I trust, will inform posterity of our struggles for freedom. If our descendants be worthy the name of Americans, they will preserve, and hand down to their latest posterity, the transactions of the present times; and, though I confess my exclamations are not worthy the hearing, they will see that I have done my utmost to preserve their liberty; for I never will give up the power of direct taxation but for a scourge. I am willing to give it conditionally; that is, after non-compliance with requisitions. I will do more, sir, and what I hope will convince the most skeptical man that I am a lover of the American Union—that, in case Virginia shall not make punctual payment, the control of our custom-houses, and the whole regulation of trade, shall be given to Congress, and that Virginia shall depend on Congress even for passports, till Virginia shall have paid the last farthing, and furnished the last soldier. Nay, sir, there is another alternative to which I would consent;—even that they should strike us out of the Union, and take away from us all federal privileges, till we comply with federal requisitions: but let it depend upon our own pleasure to pay our money in the most easy manner for our people. Were all the states, more terrible than the mother country, to join against us, I hope Virginia could defend herself; but, sir, the dissolution of the Union is most abhorrent to my mind. The first thing I have at heart is American liberty: the second thing is American union; and I hope the people of Virginia will endeavor to preserve that union. The increasing population of the Southern States is far greater than that of New England; consequently, in a short time, they will be far more numerous than the people of that country. Consider this, and you will find this state more particularly interested to support American liberty, and not bind our posterity by an improvident relinquishment of our rights. I would give the best security for a punctual compliance with requisitions; but I beseech gentlemen, at all hazards, not to give up this unlimited power of taxation. The honorable gentleman has told us that these powers, given to Congress, are accompanied by a judiciary which will correct all. On examination, you will find this very judiciary oppressively constructed; your jury trial destroyed, and the judges dependent on Congress.

In this scheme of energetic government, the people will find two sets of tax-gatherers—the state and the federal sheriffs. This, it seems to me, will produce such dreadful oppression as the people cannot possibly bear. The federal sheriff may commit what oppression, make what distresses, he pleases, and ruin you with impunity; for how are you to tie his hands? Have you any sufficiently decided means of preventing him from sucking your blood by speculations, commissions, and fees? Thus thousands of your people will be most shamefully robbed: our state sheriffs, those unfeeling bloodsuckers, have, under the watchful eye of our legislature, committed the most horrid and barbarous ravages on our people. It has required the most constant vigilance of the legislature to keep them from totally ruining the people; a repeated succession of laws has been made to suppress their iniquitous speculations and cruel extortions; and as often has their nefarious ingenuity devised methods of evading the force of those laws: in the struggle they have generally triumphed over the legislature.

It is a fact that lands have been sold for five shillings, which were worth one hundred pounds: if sheriffs, thus immediately under the eye of our state legislature and judiciary, have dared to commit these outrages, what would they not have done if their masters had been at Philadelphia or New York? If they perpetrate the most unwarrantable outrage on your person or property, you cannot get redress on this side of Philadelphia or New York; and how can you get it there? If your domestic avocations could permit you to go thither, there you must appeal to judges sworn to support this Constitution, in opposition to that of any state, and who may also be inclined to favor their own officers. When these harpies are aided by excisemen, who may search, at any time, your houses, and most secret recesses, will the people bear it? If you think so, you differ from me. Where I thought there was a possibility of such mischiefs, I would grant power with a niggardly hand; and here there is a strong probability that these oppressions shall actually happen. I may be told that it is safe to err on that side, because such regulations may be made by Congress as shall restrain these officers, and because laws are made by our representatives, and judged by righteous judges: but, sir, as these regulations may be made, so they may not; and many reasons there are to induce a belief that they will not. I shall therefore be an infidel on that point till the day of my death.

This Constitution is said to have beautiful features; but when I come to examine these features, sir, they appear to me horribly frightful. Among other deformities, it has an awful squinting; it squints towards monarchy; and does not this raise indignation in the breast of every true American?

Your President may easily become king. Your Senate is so imperfectly constructed that your dearest rights may be sacrificed by what may be a small minority; and a very small minority may continue forever unchangeably this government, although horridly defective. Where are your checks in this government? Your strongholds will be in the hands of your enemies. It is on a supposition that your American governors shall be honest, that all the good qualities of this government are founded; but its defective and imperfect construction puts it in their power to perpetrate the worst of mischiefs, should they be bad men; and, sir, would not all the world, from the eastern to the western hemisphere, blame our distracted folly in resting our rights upon the contingency of our rulers being good or bad? Show me that age and country where the rights and liberties of the people were placed on the sole chance of their rulers being good men, without a consequent loss of liberty! I say that the loss of that dearest privilege has ever followed, with absolute certainty, every such mad attempt.

If your American chief be a man of ambition and abilities, how easy is it for him to render himself absolute! The army is in his hands, and if he be a man of address, it will be attached to him, and it will be the subject of long meditation with him to seize the first auspicious moment to accomplish his design; and, sir, will the American spirit solely relieve you when this happens? I would rather infinitely—and I am sure most of this Convention are of the same opinion—have a king, lords, and commons, than a government so replete with such insupportable evils. If we make a king, we may prescribe the rules by which he shall rule his people, and interpose such checks as shall prevent him from infringing them; but the President, in the field, at the head of his army, can prescribe the terms on which he shall reign master, so far that it will puzzle any American ever to get his neck from under the galling yoke. I cannot with patience think of this idea. If ever he violates the laws, one of two things will happen: he will come at the head of his army, to carry every thing before him; or he will give bail, or do what Mr. Chief Justice will order him. If he be guilty, will not the recollection of his crimes teach him to make one bold push for the American throne? Will not the immense difference between being master of every thing, and being ignominiously tried and punished, powerfully excite him to make this bold push? But, sir, where is the existing force to punish him? Can he not, at the head of his army, beat down every opposition? Away with your President! we shall have a king: the army will salute him monarch: your militia will leave you, and assist in making him king, and fight against you: and what have you to oppose this force? What will then become of you and your rights? Will not absolute despotism ensue? . . .

What can be more defective than the clause concerning the elections? The control given to Congress over the time, place, and manner of holding elections, will totally destroy the end of suffrage. The elections may be held at one place, and the most inconvenient in the state; or they may be at remote distances from those who have a right of suffrage: hence nine out of ten must either not vote at all, or vote for strangers; for the most influential characters will be applied to, to know who are the most proper to be chosen. I repeat, that the control of Congress over the *manner,* &c., of electing, well warrants this idea. The natural consequence will be, that this democratic branch will possess none of the public confidence; the people will be prejudiced against representatives chosen in such an injudicious manner. The proceedings in the northern conclave will be hidden from the yeomanry of this country. We are told that the yeas and nays shall be taken, and entered on the journals. This, sir, will avail nothing: it may be locked up in their chests, and concealed forever from the people; for they are not to publish what parts they think require secrecy: they *may* think, and *will think,* the whole requires it.

Another beautiful feature of this Constitution is, the publication from time to time of the receipts and expenditures of the public money. This expression, *from time to time,* is very indefinite and indeterminate: it may extend to a century. Grant that any of them are wicked; they may squander the public money so as to ruin you, and yet this expression will give you no redress. I say they may ruin you; for where, sir, is the responsibility? The yeas and nays will show you nothing, unless they be fools as well as knaves; for, after having wickedly trampled on the rights of the people, they would act like fools indeed, were they to publish and divulge their iniquity, when they have it equally in their power to suppress and conceal it. Where is the responsibility—that leading principle in the British government? In that government, a punishment certain and inevitable is provided; but in this, there is no real, actual punishment for the grossest mal-administration. They may go without punishment, though they commit the most outrageous violation on our immunities. That paper may tell me they will be punished. I ask, By what law? They must make the law, for there is no existing law to do it. What! will they make a law to punish themselves?

This, sir, is my great objection to the Constitution, that there is no true responsibility—and that the preservation of our liberty depends on the single chance of men being virtuous enough to make laws to punish themselves.

In the country from which we are descended, they have real and not imaginary responsibility; for their mal-administration has cost their heads to some of the most saucy geniuses that ever were. The Senate, by making treaties, may destroy your liberty and laws for want of responsibility. Two thirds of those that shall happen to be present, can, with the President, make treaties that shall be the supreme law of the land; they may make the most ruinous treaties; and yet there is no punishment for them. Whoever shows me a punishment provided for them will oblige me. So, sir, notwithstanding there are eight pillars, they want another. Where will they make another? I trust, sir, the exclusion of the evils wherewith this system is replete in its present form, will be made a condition precedent to its adoption by this or any other state. The transition, from a general unqualified admission to offices, to a consolidation of government, seems easy; for, though the American states are dissimilar in their structure, this will assimilate them. This, sir, is itself a strong consolidating feature, and is not one of the least dangerous in that system. Nine states are sufficient to establish this government over those nine. Imagine that nine have come into it. Virginia has certain scruples. Suppose she will, consequently, refuse to join with those states; may not she still continue in friendship and union with them? If she sends her annual requisitions in dollars, do you think their stomachs will be so squeamish as to refuse her dollars? Will they not accept her regiments? They would intimidate you into an inconsiderate adoption, and frighten you with ideal evils, and that the Union shall be dissolved. 'Tis a bugbear, sir: the fact is, sir, that the eight adopting states can hardly stand on their own legs. Public fame tells us that the adopting states have already heart-burnings and animosity, and repent their precipitate hurry: this, sir, may occasion exceeding great mischief. When I reflect on these and many other circumstances, I must think those states will be found to be in confederacy with us. If we pay our quota of money annually, and furnish our ratable number of men, when necessary, I can see no danger from a rejection.

The history of Switzerland clearly proves that we might be in amicable alliance with those states without adopting this Constitution. Switzerland is a confederacy, consisting of dissimilar governments. This is an example which proves that governments of dissimilar structures may be confederated. That confederate republic has stood upwards of four hundred years; and, although several of the individual republics are democratic, and the rest aristocratic, no evil has resulted from this dissimilarity; for they have braved all the power of France and Germany during that long period. The Swiss spirit, sir, has kept them together; they have encountered and overcome immense difficulties with patience and fortitude. In the vicinity of powerful and ambitious monarchs, they have retained their independence, republican simplicity, and valor. . . .

The most valuable end of government is the liberty of the inhabitants. No possible advantages can compensate for the loss of this privilege. Show me the reason why the American Union is to be dissolved. Who are those eight adopting states? Are they averse to give us a little time to consider, before we conclude? Would such a disposition render a junction with them eligible; or is it the genius of that kind of government to precipitate people hastily into measures of the utmost importance, and grant no indulgence? If it be, sir, is it for us to accede to such a government? We have a right to have time to consider; we shall therefore insist upon it. Unless the government be amended, we can never accept it. The adopting states will doubtless accept our money and our regiments; and what is to be the consequence, if we are disunited? I believe it is yet doubtful, whether it is not proper to stand by a while, and see the effect of its adoption in other states. In forming a government, the utmost care should be taken to prevent its becoming oppressive; and this government is of such an intricate and complicated nature, that no man on this earth can know its real operation. The other states have no reason to think, from the antecedent conduct of Virginia, that she has any intention of seceding from the Union, or of being less active to support the general welfare. Would they not, therefore, acquiesce in our taking time to deliberate—deliberate whether the measure be not perilous, not only for us, but the adopting states?

Permit me, sir, to say, that a great majority of the people, even in the adopting states, are averse to this government. I believe I would be right to say, that they have been egregiously misled. Pennsylvania has, *perhaps,* been tricked into it. If the other states who have adopted it have not been tricked, still they were too much hurried into its adoption. There were very respectable minorities in several of them; and if reports be true, a clear majority of the people are averse to it. If we also accede, and it should prove grievous, the peace and prosperity of our country, which we all love, will be destroyed. This government has not the affection of the people at present. Should it be oppressive, their affections will be totally estranged from it; and, sir, you know that a government, without their affections, can neither be durable nor happy. I speak as one poor individual; but when I speak, I speak the language of thousands. But, sir, I mean not to breathe the spirit, nor utter the language, of secession.

I have trespassed so long on your patience, I am really concerned that I have something yet to say. The honorable member has said, we shall be properly represented. Remember, sir, that the number of our representatives is but ten, whereof six is a majority. Will those men be possessed of sufficient information? A particular knowledge of particular districts will not suffice. They must be well acquainted with agriculture, commerce, and a great variety of other matters throughout the continent; they must know not only the actual state of nations in Europe and America, the situations of their farmers, cottagers, and mechanics, but also the relative situations and intercourse of those nations. Virginia is as large as England. Our proportion of representatives is but ten men. In England they have five hundred and fifty-eight. The House of Commons, in England, numerous as they are, we are told, are bribed, and have bartered away the rights of their constituents: what, then, shall become of us? Will these few protect our rights? Will they be incorruptible? You say they will be better men than the English commoners. I say they will be infinitely worse men, because they are to be chosen blindfolded: their election (the term, as applied to their appointment, is inaccurate) will be an involuntary nomination, and not a choice.

I have, I fear, fatigued the committee; yet I have not said the one hundred thousandth part of what I have on my mind, and wish to impart. On this occasion, I conceived myself bound to attend strictly to the interest of the state, and I thought her dearest rights at stake. Having lived so long—been so much honored—my efforts, though small, are due to my country. I have found my mind hurried on, from subject to subject, on this very great occasion. We have been all out of order, from the gentleman who opened to-day to myself. I did not come prepared to speak, on so multifarious a subject, in so general a manner. I trust you will indulge me another time. Before you abandon the present system, I hope you will consider not only its defects, most maturely, but likewise those of that which you are to substitute for it. May you be fully apprized of the dangers of the latter, not by fatal experience, but by some abler advocate than I!

Speech at the Virginia Ratifying Convention For Ratification

James Madison

Commentary

When Henry sat down, still another day was drawing to a close, and the convention had yet to consider the first two sections of the first article. Henry's arguments and ethos had created a rhetorical situation which required an effective response. Otherwise, the waverers might be lost for good. Unfortunately for the Federalists, the immediate response came from the exasperated Randolph, whose rhetorical skills left something to be desired. He objected to the "irregular manner" of his opponents. In an arrogant and tactless style, he accused Henry of saying nothing in his second speech that he had not said in his first one, which he (Randolph) had already refuted. Nevertheless, he concluded, he would present a more extended refutation tomorrow.

Although Randolph's next speech was better, the one which most scholars believe carried the day was given by James Madison (1751-1836). Although younger than the Revolutionary hero he was answering, Madison had considerable ethos. An experienced Virginia legislator and congressman, he was known to have contributed much to the final version of the Constitution, and no one suspected him of being a tyrant. Although the fact was not widely known, Madison had gained experience defending the Constitution by collaborating with Alexander Hamilton and John Jay in writing the Federalist Papers, which were designed to mobilize support in sharply divided New York.

Armed with his reputation, constitutional expertise and rhetorical experience, Madison spent the preceding evening preparing his speech. It is reproduced photographically from Ernest J. Wrage and Barnet Baskerville, *American Forum: Speeches on Historic Issues, 1788-1900* (New York: Harper Brothers, 1960), pp. 23-32.

Speech at the Virginia Ratifying
Convention for Ratification

Mr. Chairman: I shall not attempt to make impressions by any ardent professions of zeal for the public welfare. We know the principles of every man will, and ought to be, judged, not by his professions and declarations, but by his conduct; by that criterion I mean, in common with every other member, to be judged; and should it prove unfavorable to my reputation, yet it is a criterion from which I will by no means depart. Comparisons have been made between the friends of this Constitution and those who oppose it: although I disapprove of such comparisons, I trust that, in point of truth, honor, candor, and rectitude of motives, the friends of this system, here and in other states, are not inferior to its opponents. But professions of attachment to the public good, and comparisons of parties, ought not to govern or influence us now. We ought, sir, to examine the Constitution on its own merits solely: we are to inquire whether it will promote the public happiness: its aptitude to produce this desirable object ought to be the exclusive subject of our present researches. In this pursuit, we ought not to address our arguments to the feelings and passions, but to those understandings and judgments which were selected by the people of this country, to decide this great question by a calm and rational investigation. I hope that gentlemen, in displaying their abilities on this occasion, instead of giving opinions and making assertions, will condescend to prove and demonstrate, by a fair and regular discussion. It gives me pain to hear gentlemen continually distorting the natural construction of language; for it is sufficient if any human production can stand a fair discussion.

Before I proceed to make some additions to the reasons which have been adduced by my honorable friend over the way, I must take the liberty to make some observations on what was said by another gentleman [Mr. Henry]. He told us that this Constitution ought to be rejected because it endangered the public liberty, in his opinion, in many instances. Give me leave to make one answer to that observation: Let the dangers which this system is supposed to be replete with be clearly pointed out: if any dangerous and unnecessary powers be given to the general legislature, let them be plainly demonstrated; and let us not rest satisfied with general assertions of danger, without examination. If powers be necessary, apparent danger is not a sufficient reason against conceding them. He has suggested that licentiousness has seldom produced the loss of liberty; but that the tyranny of rulers has almost always effected it. Since the general civilization of mankind, I believe there are more instances of the abridgment of the freedom of the people by gradual and silent encroachments of those in power, than by violent and sudden usurpations; but, on a candid examination of history, we shall find that turbulence, violence, and abuse of power, by the majority trampling on the rights of the minority, have produced factions and commotions, which, in republics, have, more frequently than any other cause, produced despotism.

If we go over the whole history of ancient and modern republics, we shall find their destruction to have generally resulted from those causes. If we consider the peculiar situation of the United States, and what are the sources of that diversity of sentiment which pervades its inhabitants, we shall find great danger to fear that the same causes may terminate here in the same fatal effects which they produced in those republics. This danger ought to be wisely guarded against. Perhaps, in the progress of this discussion, it will appear that the only possible remedy for those evils, and means of preserving and protecting the principles of republicanism, will be found in that very system which is now exclaimed against as the parent of oppression.

I must confess I have not been able to find his usual consistency in the gentleman's argument on this occasion. He informs us that the people of the country are at perfect repose,—that is, every man enjoys the fruits of his labor peaceably and securely, and that every thing is in perfect tranquillity and safety. I wish sincerely, sir, this were true. If this be their happy situation, why has every state acknowledged the contrary? Why were deputies from all the states sent to the general Convention? Why have complaints of national and individual distresses been echoed and reechoed throughout the continent? Why has our general government been so shamefully disgraced, and our Constitution violated? Wherefore have laws been made to authorize a change, and wherefore are we now assembled here? A federal government is formed for the protection of its individual members. Ours has attacked itself with impunity. Its authority has been disobeyed and despised. I think I perceive a glaring inconsistency in another of his arguments. He complains of this Constitution, because it requires the consent of at least three fourths of the states to introduce amendments which shall be necessary for the happiness of the people. The assent of so many he urges as too great an obstacle to the admission of salutary amendments, which, he strongly insists, ought to be at the will of a bare majority. We hear this argument, at the very moment we are called upon to assign reasons for proposing a constitution which puts it in the power of nine states to abolish the present inadequate, unsafe, and pernicious Confederation! In the first case, he asserts that a majority ought to have the power of altering the government, when found to be inadequate to the security of public happiness. In the last case, he affirms that even three fourths of the community have not a right to alter a government which experience has proved to be subversive of national felicity! nay, that the most necessary and urgent alterations cannot be made without the absolute unanimity of all the states! Does not the thirteenth article of the Confederation expressly require that no alteration shall be made without the unanimous consent of all the states? Could any thing in theory be more perniciously improvident and injudicious than this submission of the will of the majority to the most trifling minority? Have not experience and practice actually manifested this theoretical inconvenience to be extremely impolitic? Let me mention one fact, which I conceive must carry conviction to the mind of any one: the smallest state in the Union has obstructed every attempt to reform the government; that little member has repeatedly disobeyed and counteracted the general authority; nay, has even supplied the enemies of its country with provisions. Twelve states had agreed to certain improvements which were proposed, being thought absolutely necessary to preserve the existence of the general government; but as these improvements, though really indispensable, could not, by the Confederation, be introduced into it without the consent of every state, **the refractory dissent of that little state prevented their adoption.** The inconveniences resulting from this requisition, of unanimous concurrence in alterations in the Confederation, must be known to every member in this Convention; it is therefore needless to remind them of them. Is it not self-evident that a trifling minority ought not to bind the majority? Would not foreign influence be exerted with facility over a small minority? Would the honorable gentleman agree to continue the most radical defects in the old system, because the petty state of Rhode Island would not agree to remove them?

He next objects to the exclusive legislation over the district where the seat of government may be fixed. Would he submit that the representatives of this state should carry on their deliberations under the control of any other member of the Union? If any state had the power of legislation over the place where Congress should fix the general government, this would impair the dignity, and hazard the safety, of Congress. If the safety of the Union were under the control of any particular state, would not foreign corruption probably prevail, in such a state, to induce it to exert its controlling influence over the members of the general government? Gentlemen cannot have forgotten the disgraceful insult which Congress received some years ago. When we also reflect that the previous cession of particular states is necessary before Congress can legislate exclusively any where, we must, instead of being alarmed at this part, heartily approve of it.

But the honorable member sees great danger in the provision concerning the militia. This I conceive to be an additional security to our liberty, without diminishing the power of the states in any considerable degree. It appears to me so highly expedient that I should imagine it would have found advocates even in the warmest friends of the present system. The authority of training the militia, and appointing the officers, is reserved to the states. Congress ought to have the power to establish a uniform discipline throughout the states, and to provide for the execution of the laws, suppress insurrections, and repel invasions: these are the only cases wherein they can interfere with the militia; and the obvious necessity of their having power over them in these cases must convince any reflecting mind. Without uniformity of discipline, military bodies would be incapable of action: without a general controlling power to call forth the strength of the Union to repel invasions, the country might be overrun and conquered by foreign enemies: without such a power to suppress insurrections, our liberties might be destroyed by domestic faction, and domestic tyranny be established.

The honorable member then told us that there was no instance of power once transferred being voluntarily renounced. Not to produce European examples, which may probably be done before the rising of this Convention, have we not seen already, in seven states (and probably in an eighth state), legislatures surrendering some of the most important powers they possessed? But, sir, by this government, powers are not given to any particular set of men; they are in the hands of the people; delegated to their representatives chosen for short terms; to representatives responsible to the people, and whose situation is perfectly similar to their own. As long as this is the case we have no danger to apprehend. When the gentleman called our recollection to the usual effects of the concession of powers, and imputed the loss of liberty generally to open tyranny, I wish he had gone on farther. Upon his review of history, he would have found that the loss of liberty very often resulted from factions and divisions; from local considerations, which eternally lead to quarrels; he would have found internal dissensions to have more frequently demolished civil liberty, than a tenacious disposition in rulers to retain any stipulated powers. . . .

The power of raising and supporting armies is exclaimed against as dangerous and unnecessary. I wish there were no necessity of vesting this power in the general government. But suppose a foreign nation to declare war against the United States; must not the general legislature have the power of defending the United States? Ought it to be known to foreign nations that the general government of the United States of America has no power to raise and support an army, even in the utmost danger, when attacked by external enemies? Would not their knowledge of such a circumstance stimulate them to fall upon us? If, sir, Congress be not invested with this power, any powerful nation, prompted by ambition or avarice, will be invited, by our weakness, to attack us; and such an attack, by disciplined veterans, would certainly be attended with success, when only opposed by irregular, undisciplined militia. Whoever considers the peculiar situation of this country, the multiplicity of its excellent inlets and harbors, and the uncommon facility of attacking it,—however much he may regret the necessity of such a power, cannot hesitate a moment in granting it. One fact may elucidate this argument. In the course of the late war, when the weak parts of the Union were exposed, and many states were in the most deplorable situation by the enemy's ravages, the assistance of foreign nations was thought so urgently necessary for our protection, that the relinquishment of territorial advantages was not deemed too great a sacrifice for the acquisition of one ally. This expedient was admitted with great reluctance, even by those states who expected advantages from it. The crisis, however, at length arrived, when it was judged necessary for the salvation of this country to make certain cessions to Spain; whether wisely or otherwise is not for me to say; but the fact was, that instructions were sent to our representative at the court of Spain, to empower him to enter into negotiations for that purpose. How it terminated is well known. This fact shows the **extremities** to which nations will go in cases of imminent danger, and demonstrates the necessity of making ourselves more respectable. The necessity of making dangerous cessions, and of applying to foreign aid, ought to be excluded.

The honorable member then told us that there are heart-burnings in the adopting states, and that Virginia may, if she does not come into the measure, continue in amicable confederacy with the adopting states. I wish as seldom as possible to contradict the assertions of gentlemen; but I can venture to affirm, without danger of being in an error, that there is the most satisfactory evidence that the satisfaction of those states is increasing every day, and that, in that state where it was adopted only by a majority of nineteen, there is not one fifth of the people dissatisfied. There are some reasons which induce us to conclude that the grounds of proselytism extend every where; its principles begin to be better understood; and the inflammatory violence wherewith it was opposed by designing, illiberal, and unthinking minds, begins to subside. I will not enumerate the causes from which, in my conception, the heart-burnings of a majority of its opposers have originated. Suffice it to say, that in all they were founded on a misconception of its nature and tendency. Had it been candidly examined and fairly discussed, I believe, sir, that but a very inconsiderable minority of the people of the United States would have opposed it. With respect to the Swiss, whom the honorable gentleman has proposed for our example, as far as historical authority may be relied on, we shall find their government quite unworthy of our imitation. I am sure, if the honorable gentleman had adverted to their history and government, he never would have quoted their example here; he would have found that, instead of respecting the rights of mankind, their government (at least of several of their cantons) is one of the vilest aristocracies that ever was instituted: the peasants of some of their cantons are more oppressed and degraded than the subjects of any monarch in Europe; nay, almost as much so as those of any Eastern despot. It is a novelty in politics, that from the worst of systems the happiest consequences should ensue. Their aristocratical rigor, and the peculiarity of their situation, have so long supported their union: without the closest alliance and amity, dismemberment might follow; their powerful and ambitious neighbors would immediately avail themselves of their least jarrings. As we are not circumstanced like them, no conclusive precedent can be drawn from their situation. I trust the gentleman does not carry his idea so far as to recommend a separation from the adopting states. This government may secure our happiness; this is at least as probable as that it shall be oppressive. If eight states have, from a persuasion of its policy and utility, adopted it, shall Virginia shrink from it, without a full conviction of its danger and inutility? I hope she will never shrink from any duty; I trust she will not determine without the most serious reflection and deliberation.

I confess to you, sir, were uniformity of religion to be introduced by this system, it would, in my opinion, be ineligible; but I have no reason to conclude that uniformity of government will produce that of religion. This subject is, for the honor of America, perfectly free and unshackled. The government has no jurisdiction over it: the least reflection will convince us there is no danger to be feared on this ground.

But we are flattered with the probability of obtaining previous amendments. This calls for the most serious attention of this house. If amendments are to be proposed by one state, other states have the same right, and will also propose alterations. These cannot but be dissimilar, and opposite in their nature. I beg leave to remark, that the governments of the different states are in many respects dissimilar in their structure; their legislative bodies are not similar; their executive are more different. In several of the states, the first magistrate is elected by the people at large; in others, by joint ballot of the members of both branches of the legislature; and in others, in other different manners. This dissimilarity has occasioned a diversity of opinion on the theory of government, which will, without many reciprocal concessions, render a concurrence impossible. Although the appointment of an executive magistrate has not been thought destructive to the principles of democracy in many of the states, yet, in the course of the debate, we find objections made to the federal executive: it is urged that the President will degenerate into a tyrant. I intended, in compliance with the call of the honorable member, to explain the reasons of proposing this Constitution, and develop its principles; but I shall postpone my remarks till we hear the supplement which, he has informed us, he intends to add to what he has already said.

Give me leave to say something of the nature of the government, and to show that it is safe and just to vest it with the power of taxation. There are a number of opinions; but the principal question is, whether it be a federal or consolidated government. In order to judge properly of the question before us, we must consider it minutely in its principal parts. I conceive myself that it is of a mixed nature; it is in a manner unprecedented; we cannot find one express example in the experience of the world. It stands by itself. In some respects it is a government of a federal nature; in others, it is of a consolidated nature. Even if we attend to the manner in which the Constitution is investigated, ratified, and made the act of the people of America, I can say, notwithstanding what the honorable gentleman has alleged, that this government is not completely consolidated, nor is it entirely federal. Who are parties to it? The people—but not the people as composing one great body; but the people as composing thirteen sovereignties. Were it, as the gentleman asserts, a consolidated government, the assent of a majority of the people would be sufficient for its establishment; and, as a majority have adopted it already, the remaining states would be bound by the act of the majority, even if they unanimously reprobated it. Were it such a government as is suggested, it would be now binding on the people of this state, without having had the privilege of deliberating upon it. But, sir, no state is bound by it, as it is, without its own consent. Should all the states adopt it, it will be then a government established by the thirteen states of America, not through the intervention of the legislatures, but by the people at large. In this particular respect, the distinction between the existing and proposed governments is very material. The existing system has been derived from the dependent derivative authority of the legislatures of the states; whereas this is derived from the superior power of the people. If we look at the manner in which alterations are to be made in it, the same idea is, in some degree, attended to. By the new system, a majority of the states cannot introduce amendments; nor are all the states required for that purpose; three fourths of them must concur in alterations; in this there is a departure from the federal idea. The members to the national House of Representatives are to be chosen by the people at large, in proportion to the numbers in the respective districts. When we come to the Senate, its members are elected by the states in their equal and political capacity. But had the government been completely consolidated, the Senate would have been chosen by the people in their individual capacity, in the same manner as the members of the other house. Thus it is of a complicated nature; and this complication, I trust, will be found to exclude the evils of absolute consolidation, as well as of a mere confederacy. If Virginia was separated from all the states, her power and authority would extend to all cases: in like manner, were all powers vested in the general government, it would be a consolidated government; but the powers of the federal government are enumerated; it can only operate in certain cases; it has legislative powers on defined and limited objects, beyond which it cannot extend its jurisdiction.

But the honorable member has satirized, with peculiar acrimony, the powers given to the general government by this Constitution. I conceive that the first question on this subject is, whether these powers be necessary; if they be, we are reduced to the dilemma of either submitting to the inconvenience or losing the Union. Let us consider the most important of these reprobated powers; that of direct taxation is most generally objected to. With respect to the exigencies of government, there is no question but the most easy mode of providing for them will be adopted. When, therefore, direct taxes are not necessary, they will not be recurred to. It can be of little advantage to those in power to raise money in a manner oppressive to the people. To consult the conveniences of the people will cost them nothing, and in many respects will be advantageous to them. Direct taxes will only be recurred to for great purposes. What has brought on other nations those immense debts, under the pressure of which many of them labor? Not the expenses of their governments, but war. If this country should be engaged in war,—and I conceive we ought to provide for the possibility of such a case,—how would it be carried on? By the usual means provided from year to year? As our imports will be necessary for the expenses of government and other common exigencies, how are we to carry on the means of defence? How is it possible a war could be supported without money or credit? and would it be possible for a government to have credit without having the power of raising money? No; it would be impossible for any government, in such a case, to defend itself. Then, I say, sir, that it is necessary to establish funds for extraordinary exigencies, and to give this power to the general government; for the utter inutility of previous requisitions on the states is too well known. Would it be possible for those countries, whose finances and revenues are carried to the highest perfection, to carry on the operations of government on great emergencies, such as the maintenance of a war, without an uncontrolled power of raising money? Has it not been necessary for Great Britain, notwithstanding the facility of the collection of her taxes, to have recourse very often to this and other extraordinary methods of procuring money? Would not her public credit have been ruined, if it was known that her power to raise money was limited? Has not France been obliged, on great occasions, to use unusual means to raise funds? It has been the case in many countries, and no government can exist unless its powers extend to make provisions for every contingency. If we were actually attacked by a powerful nation, and our general government had not the power of raising money, but depended solely on requisitions, our condition would be truly deplorable: if the revenue of this commonwealth were to depend on twenty distinct authorities, it would be impossible for it to carry on its operations. This must be obvious to every member here; I think, therefore, that it is necessary, for the preservation of the Union, that this power shall be given to the general government.

But it is urged that its consolidated nature, joined to the power of direct taxation, will give it a tendency to destroy all subordinate authority; that its increasing influence will speedily enable it to absorb the state governments. I cannot think this will be the case. If the general government were wholly independent of the governments of the particular states, then, indeed, usurpation might be expected to the fullest extent. But, sir, on whom does this general government depend? It derives its authority from these governments, and from the same sources from which their authority is derived. The members of the federal government are taken from the same men from whom those of the state legislatures are taken. If we consider the mode in which the federal representatives will be chosen, we shall be convinced that the general will never destroy the individual governments; and this conviction must be strengthened by an attention to the construction of the Senate. The representatives will be chosen probably under the influence of the members of the state legislatures; but there is not the least probability that the election of the latter will be influenced by the former. One hundred and sixty members represent this commonwealth in one branch of the legislature, are drawn from the people at large, and must ever possess more influence than the few men who will be elected to the general legislature.

. . . Those who wish to become federal representatives must depend on their credit with that class of men who will be the most popular in their counties, who generally represent the people in the state governments; they can, therefore, never succeed in any measure contrary to the wishes of those on whom they depend. It is almost certain, therefore, that the deliberations of the members of the federal House of Representatives will be directed to the interest of the people of America. As to the other branch, the senators will be appointed by the legislatures; and, though elected for six years, I do not conceive they will so soon forget the source from whence they derive their political existence. This election of one branch of the federal by the state legislatures, secures an absolute dependence of the former on the latter. The biennial exclusion of one third will lessen the facility of a combination, and may put a stop to intrigues. I appeal to our past experience, whether they will attend to the interests of their constituent states. Have not those gentlemen, who have been honored with seats in Congress, *often signalized themselves by their attachment to their seats?* I wish this government may answer the expectation of its friends, and foil the apprehension of its enemies. I hope the patriotism of the people will continue, and be a sufficient guard to their liberties. I believe its tendency will be, that the state governments will counteract the general interest, and ultimately prevail. The number of the representatives is yet sufficient for our safety, and will gradually increase; and, if we consider their different sources of information, the number will not appear too small.

A Perilous and Noble Experiment
Rhetoric of the Young Republic

First State of the Union Address

George Washington

Commentary

The rhetoric of the Young Republic reflected a prevailing belief that the new government was a perilous, yet noble, experiment. The Founders knew it was perilous because they had a strong sense of history. Schools during the eighteenth century stressed classical history, and opinion leaders imbibed Enlightenment ideas in the context of European history. What did history teach? The Greek democracies had collapsed. The Roman Republic had turned into a tyrannical empire. The republican Italian city-states of the Renaissance had succumbed to tyranny; so had modern Holland and Denmark. Except for the United States, there were no republics left in the world. Clearly, republics were frail and fragile. The American experiment was perilous indeed.

Yet the experiment was noble. Armed with a secularized version of the old Puritan millenarianism, Americans knew that God was using them to carry out His historical plan. The Chosen People were to safeguard Liberty and Democracy until, at some future time, they would spread over the entire world.

This ambivalent ideology had numerous rhetorical implications, the first being an absence of some rhetoric which our generation takes for granted. Americans of the Young Republic would have been horrified by campaign rhetoric. They believed that other republics had been destroyed by the collapse of civic virtue — especially by personal ambition and unsavory combinations of ambitious men into "parties" or "factions" (or what we call "self-interest groups"). To be sure, behavior does not always conform to ideals, and early leaders often formed "factions" and deliberately sought public office, but they did so behind the scenes. Nothing would have destroyed a politician's ethos more than to be identified with a "party" and to campaign openly.

Knowing that their perilous experiment was not a pure democracy, à la

185

Greece, but a republic, like that of Rome, a common rhetorical tactic was to identify politicians with mythologized images of the great heroes of the Roman Republic, such as Brutus, Cicero and especially Cincinnatus. The Roman Republic provided for appointing a dictator to a six-month term in times of crisis. When the Republic was about to be overwhelmed by Carthage, the Roman Senate appointed Cincinnatus. Informed of his election while plowing a field, the humble farmer defeated Carthage and returned to his plow only sixteen days after his election. So popular was the image that the first city settled after the Revolution was named Cincinnati, and a group of Revolutionary officers formed the Society of Cincinnati.

No politician was more analogous to Cincinnatus than George Washington (1732-1799). He had left his Virginia plantation to serve in the Continental Congress and command the revolutionary army. When the war was over, he quelled an incipient rebellion among his officers, who were on the verge of marching to Philadelphia to force the government to pay them their wages that were due. He retired to his beloved Mount Vernon, but returned to public life to preside over the Constitutional Convention. Never lifting a finger to gain public office, he was a living legend in his own time. Everyone believed that he accepted the presidency not out of personal ambition, but out of a strong sense of civic duty.

Washington's image as the American Cincinnatus immunized him from controversy as he set about converting the ambiguous language of the Constitution into practical operation. He established many traditions, including the State of the Union address. The Constitution says only that the president "shall, from time to time, give to the Congress information of the state of the Union, and recommend to their consideration such measures as he shall judge necessary and expedient...." Like his successors, Washington sent Congress several written messages about various matters, and these doubtless met the constitutional provision. From a legal perspective, these special messages meet the constitutional provision better than State of the Union addresses, which rarely contain any information that Congress does not already know.

We can only conjecture about Washington's motivations. Perhaps he thought an annual address would be a convenient way of meeting the constitutional requirement, to which he referred explicitly when arranging to give the speech. Perhaps he wished to draw upon tradition as the nation began its new journey. The address is certainly consistent with the British tradition of having a "King's speech" open each parliamentary session and the colonial tradition of having each legislative session begin with a gubernatorial address. Perhaps Washington was simply vain. Whatever his motivation, we know that Washington told the presiding officers of both Houses in early 1790 that he would like to address them. On January 8, 1790, he delivered the first State of the Union address.

It was a solemn occasion. Washington rode to the Capitol in an elegant coach preceded by uniformed aides and followed by a procession which included the Cabinet and the chief justice. He was met by the doorkeepers of the two Houses and taken to his seat. Senators and congressmen rose when he entered and sat when he sat. Then he rose, delivered the message, gave copies to the two presiding officers, bowed to the audience and departed with great dignity.

The tradition which Washington established has undergone some modifications. Thinking that the occasion smacked too much of royalty, Jefferson sent a written message to Congress after he became president. The oral presentations were not restored until Woodrow Wilson addressed Congress. Now delivered on prime-time television, the address is aimed more at the general public than Congress, but the accompanying rituals are similar to those of Washington's time.

The content of State of the Union addresses has changed little. They are invariably optimistic, even in times of crisis. Except in unusual circumstances, the approach is that of a compendium, or "laundry list," in which presidents cover a range of topics rather than going into detail on any specific one. The major change concerns the style of making recommendations. With republics being frail, the checks-and-balances system was taken so seriously that even Washington had to be circumspect. With later Americans expecting presidents to be legislative leaders, recommendations are now made more directly.

The following text is reproduced from Jared Sparks, *The Writings of George Washington; Being His Correspondence, Addresses, Messages, and Other Papers, Official and Private, Selected and Published from the Original Manuscripts*.... (Boston: American Stationers, 1837), vol. 12, pp. 7-11.

First State of the Union Address

FELLOW-CITIZENS OF THE SENATE
AND HOUSE OF REPRESENTATIVES,

I embrace with great satisfaction the opportunity, which now presents itself, of congratulating you on the present favorable prospects of our public affairs. The recent accession of the important State of North Carolina to the constitution of the United States (of which official information has been received), the rising credit and respectability of our country, and the general and increasing good will towards the government of the Union, and the concord, peace, and plenty, with which we are blessed, are circumstances auspicious, in an eminent degree, to our national prosperity.

In resuming your consultations for the general good, you cannot but derive encouragement from the reflection, that the measures of the last session have been as satisfactory to your constituents, as the novelty and difficulty of the work allowed you to hope. Still further to realize their expectations, and to secure the blessings, which a gracious Providence has placed within our reach, will, in the course of the present important session, call for the cool and deliberate exertion of your patriotism, firmness, and wisdom.

Among the many interesting objects, which will engage your attention, that of providing for the common defence will merit particular regard. To be prepared for war is one of the most effectual means of preserving peace.

A free people ought not only to be armed, but disciplined; to which end a uniform and well-digested plan is requisite; and their safety and interest require, that they should promote such manufactories as tend to render them independent on others for essential, particularly for military supplies.

The proper establishment of the troops, which may be deemed indispensable, will be entitled to mature consideration. In the arrangements which may be made respecting it, it will be of importance to conciliate the comfortable support of the officers and soldiers with a due regard to economy.

There was reason to hope, that the pacific measures, adopted with regard to certain hostile tribes of Indians, would have relieved the inhabitants of our southern and western frontiers from their depredations. But you will perceive, from the information contained in the papers, which I shall direct to be laid before you, (comprehending a communication from the commonwealth of Virginia,) that we ought to be prepared to afford protection to those parts of the Union, and, if necessary, to punish aggressors.

The interest of the United States requires, that our intercourse with other nations should be facilitated by such provisions as will enable me to fulfil my duty in that respect, in the manner which circumstances may render most conducive to the public good; and, to this end, that the compensations, to be made to the persons who may be employed, should, according to the nature of their appointments, be defined by law, and a competent fund designated for defraying the expenses incident to the conduct of our foreign affairs.

Various considerations also render it expedient, that the terms, on which foreigners may be admitted to the rights of citizens, should be speedily ascertained by a uniform rule of naturalization.

Uniformity in the currency, weights, and measures of the United States is an object of great importance, and will, I am persuaded, be duly attended to.

The advancement of agriculture, commerce, and manufactures, by all proper means, will not, I trust, need recommendation. But I cannot forbear intimating to you the expediency of giving effectual encouragement, as well to the introduction of new and useful inventions from abroad, as to the exertions of skill and genius in producing them at home; and of facilitating the intercourse between the distant parts of our country by a due attention to the post-office and post-roads.

Nor am I less persuaded, that you will agree with me in opinion, that there is nothing which can better deserve your patronage than the promotion of science and literature. Knowledge is in every country the surest basis of public happiness. In one, in which the measures of government receive their impression so immediately from the sense of the community, as in ours, it is proportionably essential. To the security of a free constitution it contributes in various ways; by convincing those who are intrusted with the public administration, that every valuable end of government is best answered by the enlightened confidence of the people; and by teaching the people themselves to know, and to value their own rights; to discern and provide against invasions of them; to distinguish between oppression and the necessary exercise of lawful authority, between burthens proceeding from a disregard to their convenience and those resulting from the inevitable exigencies of society; to discriminate the spirit of liberty from that of licentiousness, cherishing the first, avoiding the last, and uniting a speedy but temperate vigilance against encroachments, with an inviolable respect to the laws.

Whether this desirable object will be the best promoted by affording aids to seminaries of learning already established, by the institution of a national university, or by any other expedients, will be well worthy of a place in the deliberations of the legislature.

GENTLEMEN OF THE HOUSE OF REPRESENTATIVES,

I saw with peculiar pleasure, at the close of the last session, the resolution entered into by you, expressive of your opinion, that an adequate provision for the support of the public credit is a matter of high importance to the national honor and prosperity. In this sentiment I entirely concur. And to a perfect confidence in your best endeavours to devise such a provision as will be truly consistent with the end, I add an equal reliance on the cheerful coöperation of the other branch of the legislature. It would be superfluous to specify inducements to a measure, in which the character and permanent interests of the United States are so obviously and so deeply concerned, and which has received so explicit a sanction from your declaration.

GENTLEMEN OF THE SENATE
AND HOUSE OF REPRESENTATIVES,

I have directed the proper officers to lay before you respectively such papers and estimates as regard the affairs particularly recommended to your consideration, and necessary to convey to you that information of the state of the Union, which it is my duty to afford.

The welfare of our country is the great object to which our cares and efforts ought to be directed; and I shall derive great satisfaction from a coöperation with you in the pleasing though arduous task of insuring to our fellow-citizens the blessings, which they have a right to expect from a free, efficient, and equal government.

GEORGE WASHINGTON.

Report of Tecumseh's Speech to the Creek Council

Samuel Dale

Commentary

One of many topics mentioned in Washington's State of the Union address was the "depredations" of "certain hostile tribes of Indians." The post-Revolutionary era was marked by rapid westward expansion, especially into what are now Kentucky and Ohio. The long-suffering Shawnees, who had once had a flourishing culture along the Ohio River, now had their backs against the wall. Although Shawnee history cannot be reconstructed in detail, epidemics (caused by contacts with white traders?) impelled them to move south around 1650. After living peacefully with the Creeks, they moved to Pennsylvania, where pressure from the imperialistic Iroquois forced them back to their original home. Claiming them as vassals, the Iroquois sold Shawnee lands in Kentucky to Virginia in 1768. After a military defeat in 1774, the Shawnees acknowledged the sale but were promised that they could retain their lands north of the river. One casualty was Puckeshinwa, who died in the arms of his young son, Chiksika, after extracting a promise that he would never make peace with the Virginians.

Keeping his promise, Chiksika joined war parties which moved in and out of Kentucky and Tennessee during and after the Revolution. He was killed in battle in 1788 in the presence of a younger brother to whom he had been a substitute father, Tecumseh (1768-1813). Too young to have much voice in Shawnee politics, Tecumseh was bitter about what was happening to his nation as well as to his family. During the 1780s, the United States government purchased more Shawnee lands to give to Revolutionary veterans in lieu of cash and to sell to speculators and settlers to raise much-needed revenue. Purchases were sometimes made from Indian tribes who did not actually own the land and sometimes from chiefs who lacked the legal authority to sell it. Armed with "legal" titles, the government claimed all but the northwestern portion of Ohio, to which the Shawnees were forced to move.

Forced into a small area, the supply of game was too limited to provide meat or furs that were needed for trade. In a society where women cultivated crops while men hunted and trapped, males felt increasingly useless. Alcoholism and intratribal violence spread as the old communal way of life broke under the strain. Amidst the social deterioration, some Indian chiefs gladly sold lands to the whites. Sales typically involved an annual annuity, and greedy leaders liked the political power and wealth which came from controlling the annuity payments.

This difficult situation was further complicated when the Shawnees divided into two ideological camps. Years of trading furs for manufactured goods silently introduced white ideas such as private property. Some acculturated Indians converted to Christianity, settled down on privately owned farms and invited white missionaries and agricultural experts to teach them a more viable way of life. Others reveled in nostalgia for the good old days before the whites had come. Some of the latter coalesced into a religious movement led by Tecumseh's brother, Tenskwatawa, whose visions made him known as the Prophet. The Master of Life told the Prophet to reject the old shamans (religious leaders) and chiefs who cooperated with the whites. Indians were to give up alcohol, sexual promiscuity and intratribal fighting. They were to restore the old communal life and gradually abandon trading with whites.

The Prophet's teachings spread like wildfire not only among the Shawnees, but also among other tribes in Michigan, Wisconsin, Illinois and Indiana. Wishing to get farther from the whites and closer to his following, the Prophet accepted the invitation of a Potawatomi chief to build a city at the junction of the Wabash and Tippecanoe rivers in Indiana. While Prophetstown grew rapidly, leaders of several tribes signed the Treaty of Fort Wayne in 1809, selling additional land for additional annuities. The treaty illustrates an old Indian problem: lack of unity among the tribes.

Meanwhile, Tecumseh had become a chief and had an enviable reputation as an orator and warrior. More pragmatic than his visionary brother, he politicized the new religion as he built an Indian confederacy. Stunned by the Treaty of Fort Wayne, he held a tense meeting with the territorial governor, William Henry Harrison. In a short speech, he explicated the premise that undergirded his entire rhetorical campaign: Indian lands belong to Indians as a whole, not to a specific Indian nation. Because the treaty had not been approved by all Indian nations, it was therefore illegal.

By 1811, Tecumseh's rhetorical campaign had brought many northern tribes into his confederacy. With an Anglo-American war in the offing, it was time to persuade southern tribes to join. He went first to the Creeks, from whom his father had taken his wife when the Shawnees had been living with them. Thus he had a rhetorical asset in his kinship relation, but he also had a serious rhetorical problem. The Creeks were highly acculturated and did not want war.

When Tecumseh and his party of warriors arrived, a white Indian agent was present, and Tecumseh delayed meeting with the council of Creek (Muscogee) chiefs until the agent left. Tecumseh was apparently unconcerned about the presence of Sam Dale, a well-known frontiersman, whose account of the meeting was printed in Dale's biography and reprinted in Wallace A. Brice, *History of Fort Wayne, from the Earliest Known Accounts of this Point, to the Present Period* (Fort Wayne: D.W. Jones & Son, 1868); it is from Brice (pp. 192-94) that the following account is reproduced.

The accuracy of Dale's report is obviously open to question. We do not know when he wrote it, but some of his remarks suggest that it was after the fact. He was a translator as well as reporter, and we do not know how good he was. Yet he was familiar with Indians and had no reason to misrepresent what he saw and heard. In any case, his is the only available eyewitness account.

Report of Tecumseh's Speech to the Creek Council

Tecumseh led, the warriors followed, one in the footsteps of the other. The Creeks, in dense masses, stood on one side of the path, but the Shawanoes noticed no one; they marched into the center of the square, and then turned to the left. At each angle of the square, Tecumseh took from his pouch some tobacco and sumach, and dropped on the ground; his warriors performed the same ceremony. This they repeated three times as they marched around the square. Then they approached the flag-pole in the center, circled around it three times, and facing the north, threw tobacco and sumach on a small fire, burning, as usual, near the base of the pole. On this they emptied their pouches. They then marched in the same order to the council, or king's house, (as it was termed in ancient times,) and drew up before it. The Big Warrior and leading men were sitting there. The Shawnee chief sounded his war-whoop — a most diabolical yell — and each of his followers responded. Tecumseh then presented to the Big Warrior a wampum-belt of five different colored strands, which the Creek chief handed to his warriors, and it passed down the line. The Shawnee's pipe was then produced: it was large, long, and profusely decorated with shells, beads, and painted eagle and porcupine-quills. It was lighted from the fire in the center, and slowly passed from the Big Warrior along the line.

All this time not a word had been uttered, everything was as still as death; even the winds slept, and there was only the gentle-falling leaves. At length Tecumseh spoke, at first slowly and in sonorous tones, but he grew impassioned and the words fell in avalanches from his lips, his eye burned with supernatural luster, and his whole frame trembled with emotion; his voice resounded over the multitude — now sinking in low and musical whispers, now rising to its highest key, hurling out his words like a succession of thunderbolts. His countenance varied with his speech; its prevalent expression was a sneer of hatred and defiance; sometimes a murderous smile; for a brief interval sentiment of profound sorrow pervaded it, at the close of a look of concentrated vengeance, such, I suppose, as distinguishes the arch-enemy of mankind.

I have heard many great orators, but I never saw one with the vocal powers of Tecumseh, or the same command of the face. Had I been deaf, the play of his countenance would have told me what he said. Its effect on that wild, superstitious, untutored, and war-like assemblage, may be conceived; not a word was said, but stern warriors, 'the stoics of the woods,' shook with emotion, and a thousand tomahawks were brandished in the air. Even Big Warrior, who had been true to the whites, and remained faithful during the war, was, for the moment, visibly affected, and more than once I saw his huge hand clutch spasmodically the handle of his knife. And this was the effect of his delivery — for, though the mother of Tecumseh was a Creek, and he was familiar with the language, he spoke in the northern dialect, and it was afterward interpreted by an Indian linguist to the assembly. His speech has been reported; but no one has done, or can do it justice. I think I can repeat the substance of what he said, and, indeed, his very words:

"In defiance of the white men of Ohio and Kentucky, I have traveled through their settlements — once our favorite hunting-grounds. No war-whoop was sounded, but there is blood upon our knives. The pale-faces felt the blow, but knew not from whence it came. Accursed be the race that has seized on our country, and made women of our warriors. Our fathers, from their tombs, reproach us as slaves and cowards. I hear them now in the wailing winds. The Muscogee were once a mighty people. The Georgians trembled at our war-whoop; and the maidens of my tribe, in the distant lakes, sung the prowess of your warriors, and sighed for their embraces. Now, your very blood is white, your tomahawks have no edges, your bows and arrows were buried with your fathers. O Muscogees, brethren of my mother! brush from your eyelids the sleep of slavery; once more strike for vengeance — once more for your country. The spirits of the mighty dead complain. The tears drop from the skies. Let the white race perish! They seize your land, they corrupt your women, they trample on your dead! Back! whence they came, upon a trail of blood, they must be driven! Back! back — ay, into the great water whose accursed waves brought them to our shores! Burn their dwellings! Destroy their stock! Slay their wives and children! The red-man owns the country, and the pale-face must never enjoy it! War now! War forever! War upon the living! War upon the dead! Dig their very corpses from the graves! Our country must give no rest to a white man's bones. All the tribes of the North are dancing the war-dance. Two mighty warriors across the seas will send us arms.

"Tecumseh will soon return to his country. My prophets shall tarry with you. They will stand between you and your enemies. When the white man approaches you the earth shall swallow him up. Soon shall you see my arm of fire stretched athwart the sky. I will stamp my foot at Tippecanoe, and the very earth shall shake."

Memorial Day Speech
Including the Tecumseh-Pushmataha Debate at the Joint Meeting of the Choctaw and Chicasaw Councils

Charles D. Carter

Commentary

Although some young warriors became followers of Tecumseh, the Creek council refused to join his confederacy. They were highly acculturated — as they emphasized a quarter-century later in an unsuccessful rhetorical campaign to prevent the government from seizing their lands. They eventually had to move on the infamous "Trail of Tears" to the "Indian Territory," now Oklahoma.

Tecumseh moved on to persuade the Choctaws and Chickasaws, but he lost his rhetorical battle with Pushmataha (1765?-1824), an influential Choctaw chief who had long advocated acculturation. Shortly after their debate, the War of 1812 would erupt. Tecumseh would ally himself with the British and be killed in battle. Pushmataha would become a brigadier general in the American army, die peacefully years later and be buried in the Congressional Cemetery. These events would make both leaders legendary figures among whites as well as Indians. Texts of their famous — but unrecorded — debate appeared in various nineteenth-century books.

What is probably a better version of the debate survived in the oral traditions of their own peoples, all of whom later had to join the Creeks in Oklahoma. Charles D. Carter (1868-1929) used the oral tradition in his epideictic speech at Pushmataha's gravesite on Memorial Day, May 29, 1921. The following is reproduced from the proceedings of the service that were printed in the *Congressional Record* (Appendix), vol. 61, part 9 (1921), pp. 8278-8281.

Carter's speech reflects the opinions of a prominent acculturated Indian about a significant rhetorical event that had happened over a century earlier. Carter was born a Choctaw and reared among the Chickasaws — the two nations Tecumseh had tried to persuade. Rising from humble beginnings, he

joined the Chickasaw council and, in June, 1906, became secretary of the first
Democratic executive committee for the proposed state of Oklahoma. Elected
to Congress shortly thereafter, he served from 1907 to 1927. For our
immediate purpose, Carter's speech provides the best available account of the
debate.

Memorial Day Speech, Including an Account of the Tecumseh-Pushmataha Debate at the Joint Meeting of the Choctaw and Chicasaw Councils

When the busy closing hours of the Sixty-first Congress were dragging
along toward midnight, a page came to me on the floor and told me that Mr.
Adam Byrd, from Mississippi, who was retiring from Congress, was about to
leave for home and desired to see me for a few moments before departing.
Mr. Byrd led me to a secluded spot in the Democratic cloakroom and after a
brief explanation enjoined on me two responsibilities, which he said he felt it
my duty to undertake. The first has no connection with this meeting to-day,
but after finishing that this fine old fellow said in a most serious way,
"Charley, you are an Indian, and I want to talk to you about another Indian.
Old Chief Pushmataha was by long odds the greatest Indian who ever lived.
Our Southland had many brave, heroic pioneers — Dale, Claiborne, Andrew
Jackson, and others — but this primitive, unlettered Indian did as much
during the early part of the nineteenth century toward saving the white
population and the things it stands for as any of these, not even excepting his
bosom friend, Old Hickory himself. Our American people may not be
ungrateful, but they are the most thoughtless, forgetful people in the world,
for they have woefully neglected giving anything like adequate credit for the
valuable services Pushmataha rendered the white people then living south of
the Ohio River and their descendants. While he had much to do with making
my own State possible, I doubt if there is one school-teacher out of fifty in
Mississippi who knows anything about his history. I doubt if there are 10 men
in Congress who even know that his body rests out here in Congressional
Cemetery, and before I came here they did not even do his memory the honor
to put flowers on his grave on Decoration Day. I visit his grave on every
Sunday when the weather will permit, and I see that it is properly decorated
at the proper time. Now, I know you are not going to visit his grave every
Sunday as I have, but I do want you to promise me that you will go out there
occasionally and that you will see that the old chief's grave is given proper
attention on Decoration Day." I had barely time to agree when he took me by
the hand, saying, "Good-bye, and God bless you," went out of the cloakroom,
and I never saw him again, for he died shortly afterwards.

I have done my best to keep this pledge, and no Decoration Day has passed
since that time without appropriate decorations being placed on
Pushmataha's grave, but had Adam Byrd failed to make that farewell call on

me that night, we might not be here to-day doing just honor to the memory of this truly great man. Adam Byrd was right. Pushmataha was a great chief. He was one of the greatest Indians who ever lived. He was more than that. He was one of the greatest characters of his generation. The old chief was a skillful hunter, an intrepid warrior, a close student of nature, a powerful orator, and a persuasive debater in the councils of his tribe. He had an acute sense of justice, not only between man and man but between nations as well. By patient and sagacious statesmanship and wise, far-seeing counsel he successfully steered the Choctaw ship of state through the then turbulent complications without, to use his own proud boast, ever having found it necessary "to raise the tomahawk against the Great White Father at Washington or his children."

The absorbing ambition of Pushmataha was that his people might become the equal of the whites in education and civilization and take their place beside the white man in a business way, in a professional way, and in the councils of the Nation. He was always an advocate of education and industry among his people and contributed much not only of his time, but of his small income, to that end. He was dearly beloved by both the Choctaws and Chickasaws, and after his death one of the executive and judicial districts of his nation in Indian Territory was named in his honor. When the forty-sixth star was added to the constellation of Old Glory the Oklahoma people gave evidence of their appreciation of the memory of this grand old man by naming one of the largest and most beautiful counties of the State for him.

But I must not trespass too greatly upon your time. You are to have the privilege of hearing this great man's life and character discussed by those much better informed and equipped than myself. I will pause only long enough to tell you something of what I believe his own people, the Choctaws, consider one of Pushmataha's greatest achievements. This has to do with the part he took in saving the white man's civilization west of the Alleghenies and specifically his reply to the wonderful address delivered before the Choctaw Council by the great Shawnee orator, Tecumseh. The War of 1812 was impending and the British authorities were doing all in their power to stir up antagonism between the Indians and the Americans. The astute Shawnee chief, Tecumseh, was sent on a tour by British agents to organize all Indians west of the Alleghenies with the purpose to expel the white American beyond the mountains. One of the first tribes he visited was the Choctaw. After his mission had been explained to Pushmataha, the wise old chief advised Tecumseh that he was only one of the three chiefs of the Choctaw Nation; that the Choctaws could only take part in any war upon the decision of the general council of the tribe; and that before this was done they would probably desire to consult their kindred tribe and ally, the Chickasaws. Tecumseh then requested that both tribes be called together in order that he might lay his plan before the council. After a consultation with the other two Choctaw chiefs, Masholatubby and Apuckshinubby, and the principal chief of the Chickasaws, a general council of the two tribes was called.

Tecumseh was classed by many of his contemporaries as the most powerful debater of his generation, and this was saying much, for it was during the day of Clay, Calhoun, and Webster. Realizing the full power of his oratory, Tecumseh surmised if he could get to speak to the Choctaw people in general council they would not be able to resist his magnetic logic and eloquence. The council was assembled, and Tecumseh, with his suite of 30 warriors bedecked in panoply of paint and feathers, filed in before the council fire to deliver his address. We must bear in mind that the Shawnees spoke an entirely different language from the Choctaws and Chickasaws, the Shawnees belonging to the Algonquin stock and speaking their dialect, while the Choctaws and Chickasaws are of the Appalachian stock and spoke the Muskogeon dialect. Therefore it was necessary for each speech to be translated by an interpreter so all might understand.

The great Shawnee chief was thoroughly familiar with past relations between all Indian tribes and the whites, and he began by recounting all the wrongs perpetrated on the Indians by the palefaces since the landing of Columbus. He related how the white man had beguiled the Indians along the Atlantic coast to part with their lands for a few trifling beads and a little fire water, leaving them beggars, vagabonds, peons, and strangers in their own land, to be scorned and despised by their paleface neighbors. He told how the Shawnees and other northern tribes were being stripped of their patrimony. He laid down the principle that the Great Spirit had given the Western Hemisphere to all red people in common and that no particular tribe had anything more than the right of possession to any lands, and therefore asserted any relinquishment of title by one tribe to be null and void, because many of the owners had not joined in the transfer. These wrongs discussed he declared had been made possible by the ingenuity of the whites in attacking only one tribe at a time, but if all Indians would join and combine their forces in one attack at one time, the white man could be driven back over the mountains whence he came; that the golden opportunity was now at hand to join hands with the British and scourge from their revered hunting grounds eternally the hated paleface. He closed his eloquent address with a stirring appeal to the patriotism of the Choctaws and Chickasaws, asking if they would await complete submission or would they now join hands and fight beside the Shawnees and other tribes rather than submit?

Evidently Tecumseh's purpose had been fully accomplished. His magnetic words seemed to arouse every vindictive sentiment within the souls of the Choctaw and Chickasaw warriors; their savage enthusiasm had been stirred to white heat when Pushmataha calmly strode before the council fire and began his wonderful reply to Tecumseh's speech. What a pity that no accurate account of this wonderful debate between these two giant primitive orators was at that time preserved. Lincecum, Pickett, Randall, and other historians have left us brief excerpts, Cushman undertakes to give Pushmataha's speech in full, but his recital does not even do faint justice to the original and in no measure conforms to the Choctaws' account of it. For many years it was handed down from generation to generation by tradition to the Choctaws and Chickasaws, but it can be easily understood how that method might fail to preserve all the virile force and eloquence of this wonderful address. I will undertake to give it to you in part as nearly as I remember hearing it told by some of the old Indians many years ago. Pushmataha began his address as follows:

PUSHMATAHA'S REPLY TO TECUMSEH.

"Omiske, tushkahoma ho chukma hashche yumma! Anumpa tilofasih ish huklo."

("Attention, my good red warriors! Hear ye my brief remarks.")

"The great Shawnee orator has portrayed in vivid picture the wrongs inflicted on his and other tribes by the ravages of the paleface. The candor and fervor of his eloquent appeal breathe the conviction of truth and sincerity, and, as kindred tribes, naturally we sympathize with the misfortunes of his people. I do not come before you in any disputation either for or against these charges. It is not my purpose to contradict any of these allegations against the white man, but neither am I here to indulge in any indiscreet denunciation of him which might bring down upon my people unnecessary difficulty and embarrassment.

"The distinguished Shawnee sums up his eloquent appeal to us with this direct question:

"Will you sit idly by, supinely awaiting complete and abject submission, or will you die fighting beside your brethren, the Shawnees, rather than submit to such ignominy?

"These are plain words and it is well they have been spoken, for they bring the issue squarely before us. Mistake not, this language means war. And war with whom, pray? War with some band of marauders who have committed these depredations against the Shawnees? War with some alien host seeking the destruction of the Choctaws and Chickasaws? Nay, my fellow tribesmen. None of these are the enemy we will be called on to meet. If we take up arms against the Americans we must of necessity meet in deadly combat our daily neighbors and associates in this part of the country near our homes.

"If Tecumseh's words be true, and we doubt them not, then the Shawnees' experience with the whites has not been the same as that of the Choctaws. These white Americans buy our skins, our corn, our cotton, our surplus game, our baskets, and other wares, and they give us in fair exchange their cloth, their guns, their tools, implements, and other things which the Choctaws need but do not make. It is true we have befriended them, but who will deny that these acts of friendship have been abundantly reciprocated? They have given us cotton gins, which simplify the spinning and sale of our cotton; they have encouraged and helped us in the production of our crops; they have taken many of our wives into their homes to teach them useful things, and pay them for their work while learning; they are teaching our children to read and write from their books. You all remember well the dreadful epidemic visited upon us last winter. During its darkest hours these neighbors whom we are now urged to attack responded generously to our needs. They doctored our sick; they clothed our suffering; they fed our hungry; and where is the Choctaw or Chickasaw delegation who has ever gone to St. Stephens with a worthy cause and been sent away empty handed? So in marked contrast with the experience of the Shawnees, it will be seen that the whites and Indians in this section are living on friendly and mutually beneficial terms.

"Forget not, O Choctaws and Chickasaws, that we are bound in peace to the Great White Father at Washington by a sacred treaty and the Great Spirit will punish those who break their word. The Great White Father has never violated that treaty, and the Choctaws have never yet been driven to the necessity of taking up the tomohawk against him or his children. Therefore the question before us to-night is not the avenging of any wrongs perpetrated against us by the whites, for the Choctaws and Chickasaws have no such cause, either real or imaginary, but rather it is a question of carrying on that record of fidelity and justice for which our forefathers ever proudly stood, and doing that which is best calculated to promote the welfare of our own people. Yea, my fellow tribesmen, we are a just people. We do not take up the warpath without a just cause and honest purpose. Have we that just cause against our white neighbors, who have taken nothing from us except by fair bargain and exchange? Is this a just recompense for their assistance to us in our agricultural and other pursuits? Is this to be their gracious reward for teaching our children from their books? Shall this be considered the Choctaws' compensation for feeding our hungry, clothing our needy, and administering to our sick? Have we, O Choctaws and Chickasaws, descended to the low estate of ruthlessly breaking the faith of a sacred treaty? Shall our forefathers look back from the happy hunting grounds only to see their unbroken record for justice, gratitude, and fidelity thus rudely repudiated and abruptly abandoned by an unworthy offspring?

"We Choctaws and Chickasaws are a peaceful people, making our subsistence by honest toil; but mistake not, my Shawnee brethren, we are not afraid of war. Neither are we strangers to war, as those who have undertaken to encroach upon our rights in the past may abundantly testify. We are thoroughly familiar with war in all its details and we know full well all its horrible consequences. It is unnecessary for me to remind you, O Choctaws and Chickasaws, veteran braves of many fierce conflicts in the past, that war is an awful thing. If we go into this war against the Americans, we must be prepared to accept its inevitable results. Not only will it foretoken deadly conflict with neighbors and death to warriors, but it will mean suffering for our women, hunger and starvation for our children, grief for our loved ones, and devastation for our beloved homes. Notwithstanding these difficulties, if the cause be just, we should not hesitate to defend our rights to the last man, but before that fatal step is irrevocably taken, it is well that we fully understand and seriously consider the full portent and consequences of the act.

"Hear me, O Choctaws and Chickasaws, for I speak truly for your welfare. It is not the province of your chiefs to settle these important questions. As a people, it is your prerogative to have either peace or war, and as one of your chiefs, it is mine simply to counsel and advise. Therefore, let me admonish you that this critical period is no time to cast aside your wits and let blind impulse sway; be not driven like dumb brutes by the frenzied harangue of this wonderful Shawnee orator; let your good judgment rule and ponder seriously before breaking bonds that have served you well and ere you change conditions which have brought peace and happiness to your wives, your sisters, and your children. I would not undertake to dictate the course of one single Choctaw warrior. Permit me to speak for the moment, not as your chief but as a Choctaw warrior, weighing this question beside you. As such I shall exercise my calm, deliberate judgment in behalf of those most dear to me and dependent on me, and I shall not suffer my reason to be swept away by this eloquent recital of alleged wrongs which I know naught of. I deplore this war, I earnestly hope it may be averted, but if it be forced upon us I shall take my stand with those who have stood by my people in the past and will be found fighting beside our good friends of St. Stephens and surrounding country. I have finished. I call on all Choctaws and Chickasaws indorsing my sentiments to cast their tomahawks on this side of the council fire with me."

The air resounded with the clash of tomahawks cast on the side of the Choctaw chief and only a few warriors seemed still undecided. Tecumseh seeing the purpose of his mission thwarted and thinking Pushmataha could not understand the Shawnee language, spoke to his warriors in his native tongue, saying: "Pushmataha is a coward and the Choctaw and Chickasaw braves are squaws," but Pushmataha had traveled much and knew a smattering of many Indian dialects. He understood Tecumseh and turning upon the Shawnee with all the fire of his eloquence, he clinched the argument and settled the decision of the few wavering Choctaw braves by saying:

"Halt, Tecumseh! Listen to me. You have come here, as you have often gone elsewhere, with a purpose to involve peaceful people in unnecessary trouble with their neighbors. Our people have had no undue friction with the whites. Why? Because we have had no leaders stirring up strife to serve their selfish, personal ambitions. You heard me say that our people are a peaceful people. They make their way, not by ravages upon their neighbors but by honest toil. In that regard they have nothing in common with you. I know your history well. You are a disturber. You have even been a trouble maker. When you have found yourself unable to pick a quarrel with the white man, you have stirred up strife between different tribes of your own race. Not only that, you are a monarch and unyielding tyrant within your own domain; every Shawnee man, woman, and child must bow in humble submission to your imperious will. The Choctaws and Chickasaws have no monarchs. Their chieftains do not undertake the mastery of their people, but rather are they the people's servants, elected to serve the will of the majority. The majority has spoken on this question and it has spoken against your contention. Their decision has therefore become the law of the Choctaws and Chickasaws, and Pushmataha will see that the will of the majority so recently expressed is rigidly carried out to the letter. If, after this decision, any Choctaw should be so foolish as to follow your imprudent advice and enlist to fight against the

Americans, thereby abandoning his own people and turning against the decision of his own council, Pushmataha will see that proper punishment is meted out to him, which is death. You have made your choice; you have elected to fight with the British. The Americans have been our friends and we shall stand by them. We will furnish you safe conduct to the boundaries of this nation as properly befits the dignity of your office. Farewell, Tecumseh. You will see Pushmataha no more until we meet on the fateful warpath."

Obviously, those two noble sons of the forest and their tribes had reached "the point where the trail divides." The Choctaws and Chickasaws were persuaded to refuse participation in Tecumseh's conspiracy against the Americans and the action of these two powerful tribes prevented many other Indians from siding with the British. The Choctaws and Chickasaws finally joined hands with the Americans and fought from the early battles of the war to the Battle of New Orleans, and Pushmataha arose to the rank of brigadier general in the American Army. The Shawnees joined forces with the British and Tecumseh was slain while leading a forlorn charge under Proctor at the Battle of the Thames.

Excerpts from Memoranda on the Constitutionality of the National Bank

Thomas Jefferson and Alexander Hamilton

Commentary

Although politicians of the Young Republic generally agreed about Indian policy, they disagreed about other matters, including two basic questions which the ambiguous language of the Constitution had not settled definitively and which are still with us. First, how strong should the Federal government be? Second, how strong does the Constitution permit it to be?

Despite universal agreement that "factions" and "parties" were bad, national politicians soon divided into informal "strong government" and "weak government" factions. The former was led by Alexander Hamilton (1755?-1804), who began his career as one of Washington's military aides and then entered New York politics. He was such an outspoken advocate of an all-powerful Federal government that he had only limited influence at the Constitutional Convention. Although he successfully led the fight for ratification in New York, his tactics offended so many people, especially Antifederalists, that he was not elected to any public office in the Federal government.

Yet Hamilton played a major role. Washington appointed him secretary of the treasury, and Hamilton moved quickly to get Congress to pay off the old war debts and make the new government a driving force in the economy. On December 13, 1790, less than two years after the new government had begun operating, he issued a report calling for a National Bank. His proposal was converted into legislation; however, James Madison, then a congressman, opposed passage and gave a long speech in which he argued that a National Bank was unconstitutional.

Madison's speech made a profound impact on Washington, who had much respect for his fellow Virginian's knowledge of the Constitution. He asked Madison to write him a veto message; yet, Washington really wished to sign the legislation. Ten years of wartime service with Hamilton had created bonds of friendship that are unique to old soldiers, and he basically agreed with Hamilton's policies. Hoping to satisfy himself that Madison was wrong, Washington asked Edmund Randolph, then attorney general, for his opinion. Randolph put the president in a deeper quandry by agreeing with Madison.

Washington then arranged a quasi-debate by asking for a memorandum from Thomas Jefferson (1743-1826), then secretary of state, and giving Jefferson's and Randolph's memoranda to Hamilton for a response. All memoranda were to deal exclusively with the constitutional question, not the desirability of the Bank. Although Jefferson had scrupulously avoided arguing in public with a fellow Cabinet officer, Washington knew that Jefferson opposed Hamilton's policies, was Madison's close personal friend and was the informal leader of the "weak government" faction.

In a sense, the memoranda are not rhetorical discourses bec..use they were not made public until later. Yet they are rhetorically important for two reasons. First, the writers knew that persuading Washington was critical because of his influence. If he signed the bill (as he eventually did), he would implicitly reject Madison's argument, support Hamilton's "strong government" philosophy and, thereby, encourage the trend to a more powerful Federal government. If he vetoed, he would do the converse.

Second, both writers foreshadowed two opposing lines of argument that would reappear countless times throughout America's rhetorical history. Both got to the crux of the issue by arguing how to interpret constitutional language. Jefferson's doctrine of "strict construction" and "explicit powers" would reappear, for example, in Calhoun's argument against the constitutionality of protective tariffs and Republican arguments against the constitutionality of much New Deal legislation. Hamilton's doctrine of "loose construction" and "implied and resulting powers" would reappear, for example, in Webster's response to Calhoun and New Dealers' responses to the Republicans.

The following excerpts from these very long memoranda are designed only to show how the two debaters argued their conflicting doctrines. Jefferson's is reproduced from *The Writings of Thomas Jefferson* (Library Edition), editors Andrew A. Lipscomb and Albert Ellery Bergh (Washington: Thomas Jefferson Memorial Association, 1903), vol. 3, pp. 146-49. Hamilton's is from the *Works of Alexander Hamilton,* editor Henry Cabot Lodge (New York: G.P. Putnam's Sons, 1886), vol. 3, pp. 180-84, 187.

Excerpt from Jefferson's Memorandum on the Constitutionality of the National Bank

I consider the foundation of the Constitution as laid on this ground: That "all powers not delegated to the United States, by the Constitution, nor prohibited by it to the States, are reserved to the States or to the people." To take a single step beyond the boundaries thus specially drawn around the powers of Congress, is to take possession of a boundless field of power, no longer susceptible of any definition.

The incorporation of a bank, and the powers assumed by this bill, have not, in my opinion, been delegated to the United States, by the Constitution.

I.   They are not among the powers specially enumerated: for these are: 1st. A power to lay taxes for the purpose of paying the debts of the United States; but no debt is paid by this bill, nor any tax laid. Were it a bill to raise money, its origination in the Senate would condemn it by the Constitution.

2d. "To borrow money." But this bill neither borrows money nor ensures the borrowing it. The proprietors of the bank will be just as free as any other money holders, to lend or not to lend their money to the public. The operation proposed in the bill, first, to lend them two millions, and then to borrow them back again, cannot change the nature of the latter act, which will still be a payment, and not a loan, call it by what name you please.

3d. To "regulate commerce with foreign nations, and among the States, and with the Indian tribes." To erect a bank, and to regulate commerce, are very different acts. He who erects a bank, creates a subject of commerce in its bills; so does he who makes a bushel of wheat, or digs a dollar out of the mines; yet neither of these persons regulates commerce thereby. To make a thing which may be bought and sold, is not to prescribe regulations for buying and selling. Besides, if this was an exercise of the power of regulating commerce, it would be void, as extending as much to the internal commerce of every State, as to its external. For the power given to Congress by the Constitution does not extend to the internal regulation of the commerce of a State, (that is to say of the commerce between citizen and citizen,) which remain exclusively with its own legislature; but to its external commerce only, that is to say, its commerce with another State, or with foreign nations, or with the Indian tribes. Accordingly the bill does not propose the measure as a regulation of trade, but as "productive of considerable advantages to trade." Still less are these powers covered by any other of the special enumerations.

II.   Nor are they within either of the general phrases, which are the two following: —

1. To lay taxes to provide for the general welfare of the United States, that is to say, "to lay taxes for *the purpose* of providing for the general welfare." For the laying of taxes is the *power*, and the general welfare the *purpose* for which the power is to be exercised. They are not to lay taxes *ad libitum for any purpose they please*; but only to *pay the debts or provide for the welfare of the Union*. In like manner, they are not *to do anything they please* to provide for the general welfare, but only to *lay taxes* for that purpose. To consider the latter phrase, not as describing the purpose of the first, but as giving a distinct and independent power to do any act they please, which might be for the good of the Union, would render all the preceding and subsequent enumerations of power completely useless.

It would reduce the whole instrument to a single phrase, that of instituting a Congress with power to do whatever would be for the good of the United States; and, as they would be the sole judges of the good or evil, it would be also a power to do whatever evil they please.

It is an established rule of construction where a phrase will bear either of two meanings, to give it that which will allow some meaning to the other parts of the instrument, and not that which would render all the others useless. Certainly no such universal power was meant to be given them. It was intended to lace them up straitly within the enumerated powers, and those without which, as means, these powers could not be carried into effect. It is known that the very power now proposed *as a means* was rejected as *an end* by the Convention which formed the Constitution. A proposition was made to them to authorize Congress to open canals, and an amendatory one to empower them to incorporate. But the whole was rejected, and one of the reasons for rejection urged in debate was, that then they would have a power to erect a bank, which would render the great cities, where there were prejudices and jealousies on the subject, adverse to the reception of the Constitution.

2. The second general phrase is, "to make all laws *necessary* and proper for carrying into execution the enumerated powers." But they can all be carried into execution without a bank. A bank therefore is not *necessary*, and consequently not authorized by this phrase.

It has been urged that a bank will give great facility or convenience in the collection of taxes. Suppose this were true: yet the Constitution allows only the means which are *"necessary,"* not those which are merely "convenient" for effecting the enumerated powers. If such a latitude of construction be allowed to this phrase as to give any non-enumerated power, it will go to every one, for there is not one which ingenuity may not torture into a *convenience* in some instance *or other*, to *some one* of so long a list of enumerated powers. It would swallow up all the delegated powers, and reduce the whole to one power, as before observed. Therefore it was that the Constitution restrained them to the *necessary* means....

Excerpt from Hamilton's Memorandum on the Constitutionality of the National Bank

The Secretary of the Treasury having perused with attention the papers containing the opinions of the Secretary of State and the Attorney-General, concerning the constitutionality of the bill for establishing a national bank, proceeds, according to the order of the President, to submit the reasons which have induced him to entertain a different opinion.

In entering upon the argument, it ought to be premised that the objections of the Secretary of State and the Attorney-General are founded on a general denial of the authority of the United States to erect corporations. The latter, indeed, expressly admits, that if there be any thing in the bill which is not warranted by the Constitution, it is the clause of incorporation.

Now it appears to the Secretary of the Treasury that this *general principle* is *inherent* in the very *definition* of government, and *essential* to every step of the progress to be made by that of the United States, namely: That every power vested in a government is in its nature *sovereign,* and includes, by *force* of the *term,* a right to employ all the *means* requisite and fairly applicable to the attainment of the *ends* of such power, and which are not precluded by restrictions and exceptions specified in the Constitution, or not immoral, or not contrary to the *essential ends* of political society.

This general and indisputable principle puts at once an end to the *abstract* question, whether the United States have power to erect a *corporation;* that is to say, to give a *legal* or *artificial capacity* to one or more persons, distinct from the *natural.* For it is unquestionably incident to *sovereign power* to erect corporations, and consequently to *that* of the United States, in *relation* to the *objects* intrusted to the management of the government. The difference is this: where the authority of the government is general, it can create corporations in *all cases;* where it is confined to certain branches of legislation, it can create corporations *only* in those cases.

Here, then, as far as concerns the reasonings of the Secretary of State and the Attorney-General, the affirmative of the constitutionality of the bill might be permitted to rest. It will occur to the President, that the principle here advanced has been untouched by either of them.

For a more complete elucidation of the point, nevertheless, the arguments which they had used against the power of the government to erect corporations, however foreign they are to the great and fundamental rule which has been stated, shall be particularly examined. And after showing that they do not tend to impair its force, it shall also be shown that the power of incorporation, incident to the government in certain cases, does fairly extend to the particular case which is the object of the bill.

The first of these arguments is, that the foundation of the Constitution is laid on this ground: "That all powers not delegated to the United States by the Constitution, nor prohibited to it by the States, are reserved to the States, or to the people." Whence it is meant to be inferred, that Congress can in no case exercise any power not included in those enumerated in the Constitution. And it is affirmed, that the power of erecting a corporation is not included in any of the enumerated powers.

The main proposition here laid down, in its true signification, is not to be questioned. It is nothing more than a consequence of this republican maxim, that all government is a delegation of power. But how much is delegated in each case is a question of fact, to be made out by fair reasoning and construction, upon the particular provisions of the Constitution, taking as guides the general principles and general ends of governments.

It is not denied that there are *implied,* as well as *express powers,* and that the *former* are as effectually delegated as the *latter.* And for the sake of accuracy it shall be mentioned that there is another class of powers, which may be properly denominated *resulting powers*. It will not be doubted that if the United States should make a conquest of any of the territories of its neighbors, they would possess sovereign jurisdiction over the conquered territory. This would be rather a result from the whole mass of the powers of the government, and from the nature of political society, than a consequence of either of the powers specially enumerated.

It is essential to the being of the national government, that so erroneous a conception of the meaning of the word *necessary* should be exploded.

It is certain, that neither the grammatical nor popular sense of the term requires that construction. According to both, *necessary* often means no more than *needful, requisite, incidental, useful,* or *conducive to*. It is a common mode of expression to say, that it is *necessary* for a government or a person to do this or that thing, when nothing more is intended or understood, than that the interests of the government or person require, or will be promoted by, the doing of this or that thing. The imagination can be at no loss for exemplifications of the use of the word in this sense. And it is the true one in which it is to be understood as used in the Constitution. The whole turn of the clause containing it indicates, that it was the intent of the Convention, by that clause, to give a liberal latitude to the exercise of the specified powers. The expressions have peculiar comprehensiveness. They are, "to make all *laws* necessary and proper for *carrying into execution* the *foregoing powers,* and *all other powers* vested by the Constitution in the *Government* of the United States, or in any *department* or *officer* thereof."

Farewell Address

George Washington

Commentary

The National Bank controversy was followed by events which illustrate several points. The events show how a fundamental value (in this case, opposition to parties) can be overwhelmed by intense ideological differences and an appropriate rhetoric, how the old Puritan propensity to perceive satanic forces conspiring against the Chosen has been secularized and incorporated into political rhetoric, how movements become institutionalized, and how social divisiveness leads to a unity-building rhetoric.

Movements arise from discontent, and Hamilton's success was making the "weak government" faction increasingly unhappy. Movements need leaders. "Weak government" advocates had two effective ones in Jefferson and Madison. Jefferson's authorship of the Declaration of Independence gave him considerable ethos. Although he was neither an effective organizer nor an outspoken partisan, he was the acknowledged spokesman of the "limited government" philosophy. Madison also had considerable ethos, and he was an effective organizer. Proceeding cautiously and perhaps without knowing the eventual outcome, they formed a political party. We lack enough historical evidence to know all the specifics. We know that in the spring of 1791, not long after their defeat over the National Bank, Madison and Jefferson talked to some anti-Hamiltonians in New York. Shortly thereafter, Madison got an old college friend, Philip Freneau, to start a newspaper in Philadelphia (then the capital), and Jefferson gave Freneau an undemanding job in the State Department. The importance of newspapers had been increasing throughout the eighteenth century, and the Philadelphia papers were generally Hamiltonian. Freneau was soon publishing vitriolic satires about Hamilton, and Hamilton responded with attacks on Freneau and Jefferson.

Political parties were not solidified enough to play a role in the election of 1792. Even if they had been, no one would have dared attack the American Cincinnatus. However Washington's second term was marked by events that led to more disputes, an increasingly bitter partisan rhetoric and a solidifying of political parties. The French Revolution led to a European war which the United States could not entirely ignore, both because of our alliance with France and the need for trade. Hamiltonians took a pro-British line while Jeffersonians took a pro-French one. The rhetoric of the Hamiltonians portrayed the Jeffersonians as French-inspired believers in "mobocracy," while that of the Jeffersonians portrayed the Hamiltonians as British-inspired "royalists." Meanwhile, new "societies" (not "parties") sprang up around the country to support the Jeffersonians. They went by various names (Patriotic, True Republican, Republican, Democratic and Democratic-Republican), the last of which eventually became standard — and not without good rhetorical reasons. The term *Democratic* suggested that the Jeffersonians spoke for the people while *Republican* showed their dedication to the nation's form of government.

In 1793, Jefferson resigned from the Cabinet. A year later, Washington called out the militia to put down the so-called "Whiskey Rebellion" (i.e., collect the recently legislated excise tax) in western parts of the country. Hamiltonians charged not only that "Mad Tom" had stirred up the rebellion, but that he was conspiring to bring the French Revolution to America. Although Washington carefully avoided endorsing conspiratorial allegations, he publicly denounced these "self-created societies."

As the election of 1796 approached, Washington decided that enough was enough. With the two-term tradition still in the future and his own popularity still high, he knew he had to announce publicly his desire not to be re-elected. What happened next is paradoxical. The conciliatory Washington drafted a petulant address in which he not only announced his desire, but also defended his record and criticized the opposition. When he showed it to Hamilton, the latter urged him to moderate his rhetoric. Washington gave the draft to his old friend, who rewrote it so thoroughly that it virtually became a new discourse. Washington liked it, revised it only slightly and gave it to the editor of the *American Daily Advertiser,* who published it on September 19, 1796. It was soon reprinted in newspapers everywhere.

Although containing a few oblique attacks on the opposition, the announcement was designed to justify Washington's desire to return to private life, build unity and offer advice to the young nation. It has played a dual role in America's rhetorical history, being cited by various partisans to identify their cause with the "Father of His Country" and by others to show how the Great Hero desired unity above all else. The text is reproduced photographically from David J. Brewer, *World's Best Orations* (St. Louis: Ferd. P. Kaiser, 1901), vol. 10, pp. 3740-3755.

Farewell Address

Friends and Fellow-Citizens: —

THE period for a new election of a citizen to administer the executive government of the United States being not far distant, and the time actually arrived when your thoughts must be employed in designating the person who is to be clothed with that important trust, it appears to me proper, especially as it may conduce to a more distinct expression of the public voice, that I should now apprize you of the resolution I have formed, to decline being considered among the number of those out of whom a choice is to be made.

I beg you, at the same time, to do me the justice to be assured that this resolution has not been taken without a strict regard to all the considerations appertaining to the relation which binds a dutiful citizen to his country; and that in withdrawing the tender of service, which silence in my situation might imply, I am influenced by no diminution of zeal for your future interest, no deficiency of grateful respect for your past kindness, but am supported by a full conviction that the step is compatible with both.

The acceptance of, and continuance hitherto in, the office to which your suffrages have twice called me have been a uniform sacrifice of inclination to the opinion of duty and to a deference for what appeared to be your desire. I constantly hoped that it would have been much earlier in my power, consistently with motives which I was not at liberty to disregard, to return to that retirement from which I had been reluctantly drawn. The strength of my inclination to do this, previous to the last election, had even led to the preparation of an address to declare it to you; but mature reflection on the then perplexed and critical posture of our affairs with foreign nations, and the unanimous advice of persons entitled to my confidence, impelled me to abandon the idea.

I rejoice that the state of your concerns, external as well as internal, no longer renders the pursuit of inclination incompàtible with the sentiment of duty or propriety, and am persuaded, whatever partiality may be retained for my services, that, in the present circumstances of our country, you will not disapprove my determination to retire.

The impressions with which I first undertook the arduous trust were explained on the proper occasion. In the discharge of this trust, I will only say that I have, with good intentions, contributed towards the organization and administration of the government the best exertions of which a very fallible judgment was capable. Not unconscious in the outset of the inferiority of my qualifications, experience in my own eyes, perhaps still more in the eyes of others, has strengthened the motives to diffidence of myself; and every day the increasing weight of years admonishes me more and more that the shade of retirement is as necessary to me as it will be welcome. Satisfied that if any circumstances have given peculiar value to my services, they were temporary, I have the consolation to believe that, while choice and prudence invite me to quit the political scene, patriotism does not forbid it.

In looking forward to the moment which is intended to terminate the career of my public life, my feelings do not permit me to suspend the deep acknowledgment of that debt of gratitude which I owe to my beloved country for the many honors it has conferred upon me; still more for the steadfast confidence with which it has supported me; and for the opportunities I have thence enjoyed of manifesting my inviolable attachment, by services faithful and persevering, though in usefulness unequal to my zeal. If benefits have resulted to our country from these services, let it always be remembered to your praise, and as an instructive example in our annals, that under circumstances in which the passions, agitated in every direction, were liable to mislead, amidst appearances sometimes dubious, vicissitudes of fortune often discouraging, in situations in which not unfrequently want of success has countenanced the spirit of criticism, the constancy of your support was the essential prop of the efforts, and a guarantee of the plans by which they were effected. Profoundly penetrated with this idea, I shall carry it with me to my grave, as a strong incitement to unceasing vows that heaven may continue to you the choicest tokens of its beneficence; that your union and brotherly affection may be perpetual; that the free Constitution, which is the work of your hands, may be sacredly maintained; that its administration in every department may be stamped with wisdom and virtue; that, in fine, the happiness of the people of these States, under the auspices of liberty, may be made complete by so careful a preservation and so prudent a use of this blessing as will acquire to them the glory of recommending it to the applause, the affection, and adoption of every nation which is yet a stranger to it.

Here, perhaps, I ought to stop. But a solicitude for your welfare, which cannot end but with my life, and the apprehension of danger, natural to that solicitude, urge me, on an occasion like the present, to offer to your solemn contemplation, and to recommend to your frequent review, some sentiments which are the result of much reflection, of no inconsiderable observation, and which appear to me all-important to the permanency of your felicity as a people. These will be offered to you with the more freedom, as you can only see in them the disinterested warnings of a parting friend, who can possibly have no personal motive to bias his counsel. Nor can I forget, as an encouragement to it, your indulgent reception of my sentiments on a former and not dissimilar occasion.

Interwoven as is the love of liberty with every ligament of your hearts, no recommendation of mine is necessary to fortify or confirm the attachment.

The unity of government which constitutes you one people is also now dear to you. It is justly so, for it is a main pillar in the edifice of your real independence, the support of your tranquillity at home, your peace abroad; of your safety; of your prosperity; of that very liberty which you so highly prize. But as it is easy to foresee that, from different causes and from different quarters, much pains will be taken, many artifices em-employed to weaken in your minds the conviction of this truth; as this is the point in your political fortress against which the batteries of internal and external enemies will be most constantly and actively (though often covertly and insidiously) directed, it is of infinite moment that you should properly estimate the immense value of your national union to your collective and individual happiness; that you should cherish a cordial, habitual, and immovable attachment to it; accustoming yourselves to think and speak of it as of the palladium of your political safety and prosperity; watching for its preservation with jealous anxiety; discountenancing whatever may suggest even a suspicion that it can in any event be abandoned; and indignantly frowning upon the first dawning of every attempt to alienate any portion of our country from the rest, or to enfeeble the sacred ties which now link together the various parts.

For this you have every inducement of sympathy and interest. Citizens, by birth or choice, of a common country, that country has a right to concentrate your affections. The name of American, which belongs to you in your national capacity, must always exalt the just pride of patriotism more than any appellation derived from local discriminations. With slight shades of difference, you have the same religion, manners, habits, and political principles. You have in a common cause fought and triumphed together; the independence and liberty you possess are the work of joint counsels, and joint efforts of common dangers, sufferings, and successes.

But these considerations, however powerfully they address themselves to your sensibility, are greatly outweighed by those which apply more immediately to your interest. Here every portion of our country finds the most commanding motives for carefully guarding and preserving the union of the whole.

The North, in an unrestrained intercourse with the South, protected by the equal laws of a common government, finds in the productions of the latter great additional resources of maritime and commercial enterprise and precious materials of manufacturing industry. The South, in the same intercourse, benefiting by the agency of the North, sees its agriculture grow and its commerce expand. Turning partly into its own channels the seamen of the North, it finds its particular navigation invigorated; and, while it contributes, in different ways, to nourish and increase the general mass of the national navigation, it looks forward to the protection of a maritime strength, to which itself is unequally adapted. The East, in a like intercourse with the West, already finds, and in the progressive improvement of interior communications by land and water, will more and more find a valuable vent for the commodities which it brings from abroad, or manufactures at home. The West derives from the East supplies requisite to its growth and comfort, and, what is perhaps of still greater consequence, it must of necessity owe the secure enjoyment of indispensable outlets for its own productions to the weight, influence, and the future maritime strength of the Atlantic side of the Union, directed by an indissoluble community of interest as one nation. Any other tenure by which the West can hold this essential advantage, whether derived from its own separate strength, or from an apostate and unnatural connection with any foreign power, must be intrinsically precarious.

While, then, every part of our country thus feels an immediate and particular interest in union, all the parts combined cannot fail to find in the united mass of means and efforts greater strength, greater resource, proportionably greater security from external danger, a less frequent interruption of their peace by foreign nations; and, what is of inestimable value, they must derive from union an exemption from those broils and wars between themselves, which so frequently afflict neighboring countries not tied together by the same governments, which their own rivalships alone would be sufficient to produce, but which opposite foreign alliances, attachments, and intrigues would stimulate and embitter. Hence, likewise, they will avoid the necessity of those overgrown military establishments which, under any form of government, are inauspicious to liberty, and which are to be regarded as particularly hostile to republican liberty. In this sense it is that your union ought to be considered as a main prop of your liberty, and that the love of the one ought to endear to you the preservation of the other.

These considerations speak a persuasive language to every reflecting and virtuous mind, and exhibit the continuance of the Union as a primary object of patriotic desire. Is there a doubt whether a common government can embrace so large a sphere? Let experience solve it. To listen to mere speculation in such a case were criminal. We are authorized to hope that a proper organization of the whole with the auxiliary agency of governments for the respective subdivisions, will afford a happy issue to the experiment. It is well worth a fair and full experiment. With such powerful and obvious motives to union, affecting all parts of our country, while experience shall not have demonstrated its impracticability, there will always be reason to distrust the patriotism of those who in any quarter may endeavor to weaken its bands.

In contemplating the causes which may disturb our Union, it occurs as matter of serious concern that any ground should have been furnished for characterizing parties by geographical discriminations, Northern and Southern, Atlantic and Western; whence designing men may endeavor to excite a belief that there is a real difference of local interests and views. One of the expedients of party to acquire influence within particular districts is to misrepresent the opinions and aims of other districts. You cannot shield yourselves too much against the jealousies and heartburnings which spring from these misrepresentations; they tend to render alien to each other those who ought to be bound together by fraternal affection. The inhabitants of our Western country have lately had a useful lesson on this head; they have seen, in the negotiation by the Executive, and in the unanimous ratification by the Senate, of the treaty with Spain, and in the universal satisfaction at that event, throughout the United States, a decisive proof how unfounded were the suspicions propagated among them of a policy in the General Government and in the Atlantic States unfriendly to their interests in regard to the Mississippi; they have been witnesses to the formation of two treaties, that with Great Britain, and that with Spain, which secure to them everything they could desire, in respect to our foreign relations, towards confirming their prosperity. Will it not be their wisdom to rely for the preservation of these advantages on the Union by which they were procured? Will they not henceforth be deaf to those advisers, if such there are, who would sever them from their brethren and connect them with aliens?

To the efficacy and permanency of your Union, a government for the whole is indispensable. No alliance, however strict, between the parts can be an adequate substitute; they must inevitably experience the infractions and interruptions which all

alliances in all times have experienced. Sensible of this momentous truth, you have improved upon your first essay, by the adoption of a constitution of government better calculated than your
former for an intimate union, and for the efficacious management of your common concerns. This government, the offspring
of our own choice, uninfluenced and unawed, adopted upon full
investigation and mature deliberation, completely free in its principles, in the distribution of its powers, uniting security with
energy, and containing within itself a provision for its own amendment, has a just claim to your confidence and your support. Respect for its authority, compliance with its laws, acquiescence in
its measures, are duties enjoined by the fundamental maxims of
true liberty. The basis of our political systems is the right of
the people to make and to alter their constitutions of government. But the Constitution which at any time exists, till changed
by an explicit and authentic act of the whole people, is sacredly
obligatory upon all. The very idea of the power and the right
of the people to establish government presupposes the duty of
every individual to obey the established government.

All obstructions to the execution of the laws, all combinations
and associations, under whatever plausible character, with the
real design to direct, control, counteract, or awe the regular deliberation and action of the constituted authorities, are destructive
of this fundamental principle, and of fatal tendency. They serve
to organize faction, to give it an artificial and extraordinary force;
to put, in the place of the delegated will of the nation the will
of a party, often a small but artful and enterprising minority of
the community; and, according to the alternate triumphs of different parties, to make the public administration the mirror of
the ill-concerted and incongruous projects of faction, rather than
the organ of consistent and wholesome plans digested by common
counsels and modified by mutual interests.

However combinations or associations of the above description
may now and then answer popular ends, they are likely, in the
course of time and things, to become potent engines, by which
cunning, ambitious, and unprincipled men will be enabled to
subvert the power of the people and to usurp for themselves the
reins of government, destroying afterwards the very engines
which have lifted them to unjust dominion.

Towards the preservation of your government, and the permanency of your present happy state, it is requisite, not only
that you steadily discountenance irregular oppositions to its acknowledged authority, but also that you resist with care the spirit
of innovation upon its principles, however specious the pretexts.

One method of assault may be to effect, in the forms of the Constitution, alterations which will impair the energy of the system,
and thus to undermine what cannot be directly overthrown. In
all the changes to which you may be invited, remember that time
and habit are at least as necessary to fix the true character of
governments as of other human institutions; that experience is
the surest standard by which to test the real tendency of the
existing constitution of a country; that facility in changes, upon
the credit of mere hypothesis and opinion, exposes to perpetual
change, from the endless variety of hypothesis and opinion; and
remember, especially, that for the efficient management of your
common interests, in a country so extensive as ours, a government of as much vigor as is consistent with the perfect security
of liberty is indispensable. Liberty itself will find in such a government, with powers properly distributed and adjusted, its surest
guardian. It is, indeed, little else than a name, where the government is too feeble to withstand the enterprises of faction, to
confine each member of the society within the limits prescribed
by the laws, and to maintain all in the secure and tranquil enjoyment of the rights of person and property.

I have already intimated to you the danger of parties in the
State, with particular reference to the founding of them on geographical discriminations. Let me now take a more comprehensive view, and warn you in the most solemn manner against the
baneful effects of the spirit of party generally.

This spirit, unfortunately, is inseparable from our nature,
having its root in the strongest passions of the human mind. It
exists under different shapes in all governments, more or less
stifled, controlled, or repressed; but, in those of the popular
form, it is seen in its greatest rankness, and is truly their worst
enemy.

The alternate domination of one faction over another, sharp-
ened by the spirit of revenge, natural to party dissension, which
in different ages and countries has perpetrated the most horrid
enormities, is itself a frightful despotism. But this leads at
length to a more formal and permanent despotism. The disorders
and miseries which result gradually incline the minds of men
to seek security and repose in the absolute power of an individual; and sooner or later the chief of some prevailing faction,
more able or more fortunate than his competitors, turns this disposition to the purposes of his own elevation, on the ruins of
public liberty.

Without looking forward to an extremity of this kind (which
nevertheless ought not to be entirely out of sight), the common

and continual mischiefs of the spirit of party are sufficient to make it the interest and duty of a wise people to discourage and restrain it.

It serves always to distract the public councils and enfeeble the public administration. It agitates the community with ill-founded jealousies and false alarms, kindles the animosity of one part against another, foments occasionally riot and insurrection. It opens the door to foreign influence and corruption, which finds a facilitated access to the government itself through the channels of party passions. Thus the policy and the will of one country are subjected to the policy and will of another.

There is an opinion that parties in free countries are useful checks upon the administration of the government and serve to keep alive the spirit of liberty. This within certain limits is probably true; and in governments of a monarchical cast, patriotism may look with indulgence, if not with favor, upon the spirit of party. But in those of the popular character, in governments purely elective, it is a spirit not to be encouraged. From their natural tendency, it is certain there will always be enough of that spirit for every salutary purpose. And there being constant danger of excess, the effort ought to be by force of public opinion, to mitigate and assuage it. A fire not to be quenched, it demands a uniform vigilance to prevent its bursting into a flame, lest, instead of warming, it should consume.

It is important, likewise, that the habits of thinking in a free country should inspire caution in those intrusted with its administration, to confine themselves within their respective constitutional spheres, avoiding in the exercise of the powers of one department to encroach upon another. The spirit of encroachment tends to consolidate the powers of all the departments in one, and thus to create, whatever the form of government, a real despotism. A just estimate of that love of power, and proneness to abuse it, which predominates in the human heart, is sufficient to satisfy us of the truth of this position. The necessity of reciprocal checks in the exercise of political power, by dividing and distributing it into different depositaries, and constituting each the guardian of the public weal against invasions by the others, has been evinced by experiments ancient and modern; some of them in our country and under our own eyes. To preserve them must be as necessary as to institute them. If, in the opinion of the people, the distribution or modification of the constitutional powers be in any particular wrong, let it be corrected by an amendment in the way which the Constitution designates. But let there be no change by usurpation; for though this, in one instance, may be the instrument of good, it is the customary weapon by which free governments are destroyed. The precedent must always greatly overbalance in permanent evil any partial or transient benefit, which the use can at any time yield.

Of all the dispositions and habits which lead to political prosperity, religion and morality are indispensable supports. In vain would that man claim the tribute of patriotism, who should labor to subvert these great pillars of human happiness, these firmest props of the duties of men and citizens. The mere politician, equally with the pious man, ought to respect and to cherish them. A volume could not trace all their connections with private and public felicity. Let it simply be asked: Where is the security for property, for reputation, for life, if the sense of religious obligation desert the oaths which are the instruments of investigation in courts of justice? And let us with caution indulge the supposition that morality can be maintained without religion. Whatever may be conceded to the influence of refined education on minds of peculiar structure, reason and experience both forbid us to expect that national morality can prevail in exclusion of religious principle.

It is substantially true that virtue or morality is a necessary spring of popular government. The rule, indeed, extends with more or less force to every species of free government. Who that is a sincere friend to it can look with indifference upon attempts to shake the foundation of the fabric?

Promote then, as an object of primary importance, institutions for the general diffusion of knowledge. In proportion as the structure of a government gives force to public opinion, it is essential that public opinion should be enlightened.

As a very important source of strength and security, cherish public credit. One method of preserving it is to use it as sparingly as possible, avoiding occasions of expense by cultivating peace, but remembering also that timely disbursements to prepare for danger frequently prevent much greater disbursements to repel it, avoiding likewise the accumulation of debt, not only by shunning occasions of expense, but by vigorous exertion in time of peace to discharge the debts which unavoidable wars may have occasioned, not ungenerously throwing upon posterity the burden which we ourselves ought to bear. The execution of these maxims belongs to your representatives, but it is necessary that public opinion should co-operate. To facilitate to them the performance of their duty, it is essential that you should practically bear in mind that towards the payment of debts there must be revenue; that to have revenue there must be taxes; that no taxes can be devised which are not more or less inconvenient and unpleasant; that the .intrinsic embarrassment, inseparable from the selection of the proper objects (which is always a choice of difficulties), ought to be a decisive motive for a candid construction of the conduct of the government in making it, and for a spirit of acquiescence in the measures for obtaining revenue, which the public exigencies may at any time dictate.

Observe good faith and justice towards all nations; cultivate peace and harmony with all. Religion and morality enjoin this conduct; and can it be, that good policy does not equally enjoin it ? It will be worthy of a free, enlightened, and at no distant period, a great nation, to give to mankind the magnanimous and too novel example of a people always guided by an exalted justice and benevolence. Who can doubt that, in the course of time and things, the fruits of such a plan would richly repay any temporary advantages which might be lost by a steady adherence to it ? Can it be that Providence has not connected the permanent felicity of a nation with its virtue ? The experiment, at least, is recommended by every sentiment which ennobles human nature. Alas! is it rendered impossible by its vices ?

In the execution of such a plan, nothing is more essential than that permanent, inveterate antipathies against particular nations, and passionate attachments for others, should be excluded; and that, in place of them, just and amicable feelings towards all should be cultivated. The nation which indulges towards another a habitual hatred or a habitual fondness is in some degree a slave. It is a slave to its animosity or to its affection, either of which is sufficient to lead it astray from its duty and its interest. Antipathy in one nation against another disposes each more readily to offer insult and injury, to lay hold of slight causes of umbrage, and to be haughty and intractable, when accidental or trifling occasions of dispute occur. Hence, frequent collisions, obstinate, envenomed, and bloody contests. The nation, prompted by ill-will and resentment, sometimes impels to war the government, contrary to the best calculations of policy. The government sometimes participates in the national propensity, and adopts through passion what reason would reject; at other times it makes the animosity of the nation subservient to projects of hostility instigated by pride, ambition, and other sinister and pernicious motives. The peace often, sometimes perhaps the liberty, of nations, has been the victim.

So likewise, a passionate attachment of one nation for another produces a variety of evils. Sympathy for the favorite nation,

facilitating the illusion of an imaginary common interest in cases
where no real common interest exists, and infusing into one the
enmities of the other, betrays the former into a participation in
the quarrels and wars of the latter without adequate inducement
or justification. It leads also to concessions to the favorite nation
of privileges denied to others which is apt doubly to injure the
nation making the concessions; by unnecessarily parting with what
ought to have been retained, and by exciting jealousy, ill-will,
and a disposition to retaliate, in the parties from whom equal
privileges are withheld. And it gives to ambitious, corrupted, or
deluded citizens (who devote themselves to the favorite nation),
facility to betray or sacrifice the interests of their own country,
without odium, sometimes even with popularity; gilding, with the
appearances of a virtuous sense of obligation, a commendable
deference for public opinion, or a laudable zeal for public good,
the base or foolish compliances of ambition, corruption, or infatu-
ation.

As avenues to foreign influence in innumerable ways, such attachments are particularly alarming to the truly enlightened and
independent patriot. How many opportunities do they afford
to tamper with domestic factions, to practice the arts of seduc-
tion, to mislead public opinion, to influence or awe the public
councils? Such an attachment of a small or weak towards a
great and powerful nation dooms the former to be the satellite
of the latter.

Against the insidious wiles of foreign influence (I conjure you
to believe me, fellow-citizens) the jealousy of a free people ought
to be constantly awake, since history and experience prove that
foreign influence is one of the most baneful foes of republican
government. But that jealousy to be useful must be impartial;
else it becomes the instrument of the very influence to be
avoided, instead of a defense against it. Excessive partiality for
one foreign nation and excessive dislike of another cause those
whom they actuate to see danger only on one side, and serve
to veil and even second the arts of influence on the other. Real
patriots who may resist the intrigues of the favorite are liable to
become suspected and odious, while its tools and dupes usurp
the applause and confidence of the people, to surrender their
interests.

The great rule of conduct for us in regard to foreign nations
is in extending our commercial relations, to have with them as
little political connection as possible. So far as we have already
formed engagements, let them be fulfilled with perfect good faith.
Here let us stop.

Europe has a set of primary interests which to us have none, or a very remote relation. Hence she must be engaged in frequent controversies, the causes of which are essentially foreign to our concerns. Hence, therefore, it must be unwise in us to implicate ourselves by artificial ties in the ordinary vicissitudes of her politics, or the ordinary combinations and collisions of her friendships or enmities.

Our detached and distant situation invites and enables us to pursue a different course. If we remain one people under an efficient government the period is not far off when we may defy material injury from external annoyance; when we may take such an attitude as will cause the neutrality we may at any time resolve upon to be scrupulously respected; when belligerent nations, under the impossibility of making acquisitions upon us, will not lightly hazard the giving us provocation; when we may choose peace or war, as our interest, guided by justice, shall counsel.

Why forego the advantages of so peculiar a situation? Why quit our own to stand upon foreign ground? Why, by interweaving our destiny with that of any part of Europe, entangle our peace and prosperity in the toils of European ambition, rivalship, interest, humor or caprice?

It is our true policy to steer clear of permanent alliances with any portion of the foreign world; so far, I mean, as we are now at liberty to do it; for let me not be understood as capable of patronizing infidelity to existing engagements. I hold the maxim no less applicable to public than to private affairs, that honesty is always the best policy. I repeat it, therefore, let those engagements be observed in their genuine sense. But, in my opinion, it is unnecessary and would be unwise to extend them.

Taking care always to keep ourselves by suitable establishments on a respectable defensive posture, we may safely trust to temporary alliances for extraordinary emergencies.

Harmony, liberal intercourse with all nations, are recommended by policy, humanity, and interest. But even our commercial policy should hold an equal and impartial hand; neither seeking nor granting exclusive favors or preferences; consulting the natural course of things; diffusing and diversifying by gentle means the streams of commerce, but forcing nothing; establishing (with powers so disposed, in order to give trade a stable course, to define the rights of our merchants, and to enable the government to support them) conventional rules of intercourse, the best that present circumstances and mutual opinion will permit, but temporary, and liable to be from time to time abandoned or varied, as experience and circumstances shall dictate; constantly keeping in view that it is folly in one nation to look for disinterested favors from another; that it must pay with a portion of its independence for whatever it may accept under that character; that, by such acceptance, it may place itself in the condition of having given equivalents for nominal favors, and yet of being reproached with ingratitude for not giving more. There can be no greater error than to expect or calculate upon real favors from nation to nation. It is an illusion, which experience must cure, which a just pride ought to discard.

In offering to you, my countrymen, these counsels of an old and affectionate friend, I dare not hope they will make the strong and lasting impression I could wish; that they will control the usual current of the passions, or prevent our nation from running the course which has hitherto marked the destiny of nations. But, if I may even flatter myself that they may be productive of some partial benefit, some occasional good; that they may now and then recur to moderate the fury of party spirit, to warn against the mischiefs of foreign intrigue, to guard against the impostures of pretended patriotism; this hope will be a full recompense for the solicitude for your welfare, by which they have been dictated.

How far in the discharge of my official duties I have been guided by the principles which have been delineated, the public records and other evidences of my conduct must witness to you and to the world. To myself, the assurance of my own conscience is, that I have at least believed myself to be guided by them.

In relation to the still subsisting war in Europe, my proclamation of the twenty-second of April, 1793, is the index of my plan. Sanctioned by your approving voice, and by that of your representatives in both houses of Congress, the spirit of that measure has continually governed me, uninfluenced by any attempts to deter or divert me from it.

After deliberate examination, with the aid of the best lights I could obtain, I was well satisfied that our country, under all the circumstances of the case, had a right to take, and was bound in duty and interest to take, a neutral position. Having taken it, I determined, as far as should depend upon me, to maintain it, with moderation, perseverance, and firmness.

The considerations which respect the right to hold this conduct, it is not necessary on this occasion to detail. I will only observe that, according to my understanding of the matter, that right, so far from being denied by any of the belligerent powers, has been virtually admitted by all.

The duty of holding a neutral conduct may be inferred, without anything more, from the obligation which justice and humanity impose on every nation, in cases in which it is free to act, to maintain inviolate the relations of peace and amity towards other nations.

The inducements of interest for observing that conduct will best be referred to your own reflections and experience. With me a predominant motive has been to endeavor to gain time to our country to settle and mature its yet recent institutions, and to progress without interruption to that degree of strength and consistency which is necessary to give it, humanly speaking, the command of its own fortunes.

Though, in reviewing the incidents of my administration, I am unconscious of intentional error, I am nevertheless too sensible of my defects not to think it probable that I may have committed many errors. Whatever they may be, I fervently beseech the Almighty to avert or mitigate the evils to which they may tend. I shall also carry with me the hope that my country will never cease to view them with indulgence; and that, after forty-five years of my life dedicated to its service with an upright zeal, the faults of incompetent abilities will be consigned to oblivion, as myself must soon be to the mansions of rest.

Relying on its kindness in this as in other things, and actuated by that fervent love towards it, which is so natural to a man who views in it the native soil of himself and his progenitors for several generations, I anticipate with pleasing expectation that retreat in which I promise myself to realize, without alloy, the sweet enjoyment of partaking, in the midst of my fellow-citizens, the benign influence of good laws under a free government, the ever-favorite object of my heart, and the happy reward, as I trust, of our mutual cares, labors, and dangers.

First Inaugural Address

Thomas Jefferson

Commentary

Despite Washington's warning against political parties, the American two-party system soon became a fixture. Despite his plea for unity, divisiveness became more intense. The "strong government" faction solidified into the Federalist party, but supporters of Alexander Hamilton and John Adams disagreed over presidential succession. Although the dispute did not prevent Adams from winning, it allowed their hated enemy, "Mad Tom" Jefferson, to win second place.

Adams' presidency was marked by heightened tension between Federalists and the increasingly powerful Democratic-Republicans. Adams' undeclared war with France was criticized bitterly by Democratic-Republicans. Responding to the fact that several Democratic-Republican leaders were immigrants, the Federalist-controlled Congress passed the Alien Act, which made naturalization more difficult. Congress also passed the Sedition Act, which prohibited the publication of "false, scandalous, and malicious writings against the government, either House of Congress, or the President, with intent to bring them into contempt, to stir up sedition, or to aid and abet a foreign nation in hostile designs against the United States." It led to the arrest of several Democratic-Republican newspaper publishers.

Capitalizing on popular discontent, Madison and Jefferson pronounced the Alien and Sedition Acts unconstitutional in secretly authored resolutions which were passed (in modified form) by the Kentucky and Virginia legislatures. Shortly thereafter came the election of 1800. Recognizing that the new system of political parties prevented the Electoral College from working as originally intended, both parties held congressional caucuses to nominate presidential candidates. Although the prevailing "the office seeks the man" mythology precluded candidates from campaigning, their supporters conducted one of the most vicious campaigns in history. Unwilling to recognize the opposition as legitimate, each party declared itself to be the True Heir of the American Revolution and its Federalist or Democratic-Republican principles. Each declared the other to be subversive conspirators who wished to establish either a British-style monarchy or French mobocracy. Personal attacks were equally shrill as Adams was accused of trying to make himself king and "Mad Tom" was accused of sleeping with a slave mistress and being an atheist.

Tensions were exacerbated by an oversight which the Democratic-Republicans made by agreeing to vote for Thomas Jefferson and Aaron Burr at a time when the Constitution made no provision for electors to specify which of their two votes was for president and which for vice-president. After they tied for first place, the election was thrown into Congress. Although Jefferson eventually won, some Federalists tried to stop what was obviously the public will.

Apparently believing their own rhetoric, Federalist congressmen sincerely believed that the incoming president would soon be turning the Sedition Act on them and instituting a French-style reign of terror. In a last-ditch effort to salvage what they could, Congress created a host of new judgeships, which Adams was filling (supposedly) until the midnight before his term expired. Creating "midnight judges," of course, further embittered Democratic-Republicans.

Presidential inaugurals have traditionally been designed to build unity after the divisiveness of an election campaign, but Jefferson faced an historic first. For the first time in American history, an incumbent president had been defeated. Americans were confronted with the paradox of having a party system without considering the other party legitimate. Many Democratic-Republicans sincerely believed that they should destroy the conspiratorial Federalists, and many Federalists sincerely feared that they would. It was in such a superheated rhetorical atmosphere that Jefferson took the oath of office on March 4, 1801 and then delivered a unity-building speech. It is reproduced from *The Writings of Thomas Jefferson: Being His Autobiography, Correspondence, Reports, Messages, Addresses, and Other Writings, Official and Private,* editor H.A. Washington (Washington: Taylor & Maury, 1854), vol. 8, pp. 1-5.

First Inaugural Address

Friends and Fellow Citizens: —

CALLED upon to undertake the duties of the first executive office of our country, I avail myself to the presence of that portion of my fellow citizens which is here assembled, to express my grateful thanks for the favor with which they have been pleased to look toward me, to declare a sincere consciousness that the task is above my talents, and that I approach it with those anxious and awful presentiments which the greatness of the charge and the weakness of my powers so justly inspire. A rising nation, spread over a wide and fruitful land, traversing all the seas with the rich productions of their industry, engaged in commerce with nations who feel power and forget right, advancing rapidly to destinies beyond the reach of mortal eye — when I contemplate these transcendent objects, and see the honor, the happiness, and the hopes of this beloved country committed to the issue and the auspices of this day, I shrink from the contemplation, and humble myself before the magnitude of the undertaking. Utterly indeed, should I despair, did not the presence of many whom I here see remind me, that in the other high authorities provided by our constitution, I shall find resources of wisdom, of virtue, and of zeal. on which to rely under all difficulties. To you, then, gentlemen, who are charged with the sovereign functions of legislation, and to those associated with you, I look with encouragement for that guidance and support which may enable us to steer with safety the vessel in which we are all embarked amid the conflicting elements of a troubled world.

During the contest of opinion through which we have passed, the animation of discussion and of exertions has sometimes worn an aspect which might impose on strangers unused to think freely and to speak and to write what they think; but this being now decided by the voice of the nation, announced according to the rules of the constitution, all will, of course, arrange themselves under the will of the law, and unite in common efforts for the common good. All, too, will bear in mind this sacred principle, that though the will of the majority is in all cases to prevail, that will, to be rightful, must be reasonable; that the minority possess their equal rights, which equal laws must protect, and to violate which would be oppression. Let us, then, fellow citizens, unite with one heart and one mind. Let us restore to social intercourse that harmony and affection without which liberty and even life itself are but dreary things. And let us reflect that having banished from our land that religious intolerance under which mankind so long bled and suffered, we have yet gained little if we countenance a political intolerance as despotic, as wicked, and capable of as bitter and bloody persecutions. During the throes and convulsions of the ancient world, during the agonizing spasms of infuriated man, seeking through blood and slaughter his long-lost liberty, it was not wonderful that the agitation of the billows should reach even this distant and peaceful shore; that this should be more felt and feared by some and less by others; that this should divide opinions as to measures of safety. But every difference of opinion is not a difference of principle. We have called by different names brethren of the same principle. We are all republicans — we are federalists. If there be any among us who would wish to dissolve this Union or to change its republican form, let them stand undisturbed as monuments of the safety with which error of opinion may be tolerated where reason is left free to combat it. I know, indeed, that some honest men fear that a republican government cannot be strong; that this government is not strong enough. But would the honest patriot, in the full tide of successful experiment, abandon a government which has so far kept us free and firm, on the theoretic and visionary fear that this government, the world's best hope, may by possibility want energy to preserve itself? I trust not. I believe this, on the contrary, the strongest government on earth. I believe it is the only one where every man, at the call of the laws, would fly to the standard of the law, and would meet invasions of the public order as his own personal concern. Sometimes it is said that man cannot be trusted with the government of himself. Can he, then, be trusted with the government of others? Or have we found angels in the forms of kings to govern him? Let history answer this question.

Let us, then, with courage and confidence pursue our own federal and republican principles, our attachment to our union and representative government. Kindly separated by nature and a wide ocean from the exterminating havoc of one quarter of the globe; too high-minded to endure the degradations of the others; possessing a chosen country, with room enough for our descendants to the hundredth and thousandth generation; entertaining a due sense of our equal right to the use of our own faculties, to the acquisitions of our industry, to honor and confidence from our fellow citizens, resulting not from birth but from our actions and their sense of them; enlightened by a benign religion, professed, indeed, and practiced in various forms, yet all of them including honesty, truth, temperance, gratitude, and the love of man; acknowledging and adoring an overruling Providence, which by all its dispensations proves that it delights in the happiness of man here and his greater happiness hereafter; with all these blessings, what more is necessary to make us a happy and prosperous people? Still one thing more, fellow citizens — a wise and frugal government, which shall restrain men from injuring one another, which shall leave them otherwise free to regulate their own pursuits of industry and improvement, and shall not take from the mouth of labor the bread it has earned. This is the sum of good government, and this is necessary to close the circle of our felicities.

About to enter, fellow citizens, on the exercise of duties which comprehend everything dear and valuable to you, it is proper that you should understand what I deem the essential principles of our government, and consequently those which ought to shape its administration. I will compass them within the narrowest compass they will bear, stating the general principle, but not all its limitations. Equal and exact justice to all men, of whatever state or persuasion, religious or political; peace, commerce, and honest friendship, with all nations — entangling alliances with none; the support of the state governments in all their rights, as the most competent administrations for our domestic concerns and the surest bulwarks against anti-republican tendencies; the preservation of the general government in its whole constitutional vigor, as the sheet anchor of our peace at home and safety abroad; a jealous care of the right of election by the people — a mild and safe corrective of abuses which are lopped by the sword of revolution where peaceable remedies are unprovided; absolute acquiescence in the decisions of the majority — the vital principle of republics, from which there is no appeal but to force, the vital principle and immediate parent of despotism; a well-disciplined militia — our best reliance in peace and for the first moments of war, till regulars may relieve them; the supremacy of the civil over the military authority; economy in the public expense that labor may be lightly burdened; the honest payment of our debts and sacred preservation of the public faith; encouragement of agriculture, and of commerce as its handmaid; the diffusion of information and the arraignment of all abuses at the bar of public reason; freedom of religion; freedom of the press; freedom of person under the protection of the *habeas corpus*; and trial by juries impartially selected — these principles form the bright constellation which has gone before us, and guided our steps through an age of revolution and reformation. The wisdom of our sages and the blood of our heroes have been devoted to their attainment. They should be the creed of our political faith — the text of civil instruction — the touchstone by which to try the services of those we trust; and should we wander from them in moments of error or alarm, let us hasten to retrace our steps and to regain the road which alone leads to peace, liberty, and safety.

I repair, then, fellow citizens, to the post you have assigned me. With experience enough in subordinate offices to have seen the difficulties of this, the greatest of all, I have learned to expect that it will rarely fall to the lot of imperfect man to retire from this station with the reputation and the favor which bring him into it. Without pretensions to that high confidence reposed in our first and great revolutionary character, whose preëminent services had entitled him to the first place in his country's love, and destined for him the fairest page in the volume of faithful history, I ask so much confidence only as may give firmness and effect to the legal administration of your affairs. I shall often go wrong through defect of judgment. When right, I shall often be thought wrong by those whose positions will not command a view of the whole ground. I ask your indulgence for my own errors, which will never be intentional; and your support against the errors of others, who may condemn what they would not if seen in all its parts. The approbation implied by your suffrage is a consolation to me for the past; and my future solicitude will be to retain the good opinion of those who have bestowed it in advance, to conciliate that of others by doing them all the good in my power, and to be instrumental to the happiness and freedom of all.

Relying, then, on the patronage of your good will, I advance with obedience to the work, ready to retire from it whenever you become sensible how much better choice it is in your power to make. And may that Infinite Power which rules the destinies of the universe, lead our councils to what is best, and give them a favorable issue for your peace and prosperity.

On Internal Improvement

Henry Clay

Commentary

Democratic-Republicans dominated the federal government after Jefferson's election in 1800. He was reelected in 1804, Madison was elected in 1808 and 1812 and Monroe in 1816 and 1820. Meanwhile, the Federalists became a smaller and smaller minority in Congress.

Despite Democratic-Republican domination, the "small government" ideology was challenged. The proper role of the federal government and its constitutional authority became a rhetorical battleground. President Jefferson negotiated the purchase of Louisiana from France in 1803 while privately admitting that his critics were right in saying he had no constitutional authority to do so. The National Bank, whose charter expired in 1811, was not rechartered because "strict constructionists" successfully argued its unconstitutionality, but the so-called "Second Bank" was chartered in 1816 with President Madison's approval, even though he had argued back in 1791 that the first bank was unconstitutional.

One reason for this disparity between the Democratic-Republicans' "small government" rhetoric and their "big government" actions was the growth of the West. Vermont, Kentucky, and Tennessee were admitted as states while the Federalists still controlled the central government, and many more were added after the Jeffersonians took over: Ohio (1803), Louisiana (1812), Indiana (1816), Mississippi (1817), Illinois (1818), Alabama (1819) and Missouri (1821). Not all Westerners thought alike, but most of them were Democratic-Republicans. Yet many Westerners wanted federal aid in building "internal improvements," such as roads and canals. Although internal improvements had been considered a state responsibility, Westerners succeeded in getting the federal government to finance the Cumberland Road, which originally ran from Cumberland, Maryland to Wheeling, Virginia (now West Virginia) and was later extended into Ohio. Some Westerners joined Northerners in advocating a protective tariff to encourage industrial growth.

Although the Democratic-Republican party did not split formally, it divided informally into the so-called "National Republicans," who favored protective tariffs and federally-financed internal improvements, and "Old Republicans," who argued that such policies were unconstitutional.

A major spokesman for the National Republicans was Henry Clay of Kentucky, who came to Congress in 1811 and was promptly elected Speaker of the House of Representatives. On February 4, 1817, he temporarily left the Speaker's chair so that he could address the House in favor of a bill to establish a fund for internal improvements.

Unfortunately we do not have a verbatim text of Clay's short speech, but we have a reporter's account that is reproduced from Calvin Colton's *Life, Correspondence, and Speeches of Henry Clay* (New York: A. S. Barnes & Co., 1857), vol. V, pp. 108-10. Readers should keep in mind that as a technicality, the House was sitting as a Committee of the Whole (which the House often does for procedural reasons), and this accounts for some of Clay's linguistic choices.

On Internal Improvement

Mr. Clay (in Committee of the Whole) observed, that it was not his intention to enter into the general discussion of the subject; he wished only to say, that be had long thought that there were no two subjects which could engage the attention of the national Legislature, more worthy of its deliberate consideration, than those of internal improvements and domestic manufactures.

As to the constitutional point which had been made, he had not a doubt on his mind; but it was not necessary, in his judgment, to embarrass the passage of the bill with the argument of that point at this time. It was a sufficient answer to say, that the power was not now to be exercised. It was proposed merely to designate the fund, and from time to time, as the proceeds of it came in, to invest them in the funded debt of the United States. It would thus be accumulating; and Congress could, at some future day, examine into the constitutionality of the question, and if it has the power, it would exercise it; if it has not, the Constitution, there could be very little doubt, would be so amended as to confer it. It was quite obvious, however, that Congress might so direct the application of the fund, as not to interfere with the jurisdiction of the several States, and thus avoid the difficulty which had been started. It might distribute it among those objects of private enterprise which called for national patronage in the form of subscriptions to the capital stock of incorporated companies, such as that of the Delaware and Chesapeake canal, and other similar institutions. Perhaps that might be the best way to employ the fund; but, he repeated, this was not the time to go into their inquiry.

With regard to the general importance of the proposition; the effect of internal improvements in cementing the Union; in facilitating internal trade; in augmenting the wealth and the population of the country; he would not consume the time of the committee in discussing those interesting topics, after the able manner in which they had been treated by his friend from South Carolina. In reply to those who thought that internal improvements had better be left to the several States, he would ask, he would put it to the candor of every one, if there were not various objects in which many States were interested, and which, requiring therefore their joint co-operation would, if not taken up by the general government, be neglected, either for the want of resources, or from the difficulty of regulating their respective contributions. Such was the case with the improvement of the navigation of the Ohio at the rapids; the canal from the Hudson to the Lakes; the great turnpike road, parallel with the coast from Maine to Louisiana. These, and similar objects, were stamped with a national character, and they required the wisdom and the resources of the nation to accomplish them. No particular, State felt an individual interest sufficient to execute improvements of such magnitude. They must be patronized, efficaciously patronized, by the general government, or they never would be accomplished.

The practical effect of turnpike roads in correcting the evil, if it be one, of the great expansion of our republic, and in conquering space itself, as was expressed by the gentleman from South Carolina, is about to be demonstrated by the great turnpike-road from Cumberland to Wheeling. That road is partially executed, and will probably be completed in about three years. In the mean time, Maryland is extending a line of turnpike-roads from Baltimore to Cumberland, which is also partially finished, and will be completed in the same period. Three years from the present time we shall have a continued line of turnpike roads from Baltimore to Ohio. The ordinary time requisite to travel from Wheeling to Baltimore, prior to the erection of these roads, was eight days. When the roads are completed the same journey may be performed in three days. The distance, in effect, between these two points, will be diminished in the proportion of five eighths, or, in other words, they will be brought five days nearer to each other. Similar results will follow wherever this species of improvement is effected.

Mr. Clay owned that he felt anxiously desirous for the success of this measure. He was anxious, from its intrinsic merits; from his sincere conviction of its tendency greatly to promote the welfare of our common country. He was anxious from other, perhaps more selfish considerations. He wished the Fourteenth Congress to have the merit of laying the foundations of this great work. He wished this Congress who, in his opinion, had so many other just grounds for the national approbation, notwithstanding the obloquy which had attended a single unfortunate measure, to add this new claim to the public gratitude.

Veto Message

James Madison

Commentary

With the support of Clay and other "National Republicans," Congress passed the "internal improvements" bill only a few days before President Madison's term expired in 1817, only to have Madison veto it on his last day in office. Madison's career had been one of moderation (some scholars say inconsistency) with respect to federal power. He had joined Hamilton in urging ratification of the constitution because he thought the Articles of Confederation made the central government too weak, but he had joined Jefferson in forming the Democratic-Republican party because he thought the Federalists were making the central government too strong. He had joined Jefferson in arguing for the explicit powers doctrine, but his Virginia Resolutions had been written more moderately than Jefferson's Kentucky Resolutions. As a congressman, he had argued in 1791 that the first National Bank was unconstitutional, but as president he had assented to chartering the Second Bank in 1816.

Madison's moderation is also shown by his Veto Message, in which he made a clear distinction between the issues of desirability and constitutionality. In arguing the unconstitutionality of the bill, he analyzed the same phrases in the constitution that the bill's proponents had used during the congressional debate to argue that internal improvements were constitutional.

The Veto Message is reproduced from James D. Richard's *Compilation of the Messages and Papers of the Presidents* (New York: Bureau of National Literature, 1897), vol. II, pp. 569-70.

Veto Message

March 3, 1817.

To the House of Representatives of the United States:

Having considered the bill this day presented to me entitled "An act to set apart and pledge certain funds for internal improvements," and which sets apart and pledges funds "for constructing roads and canals, and improving the navigation of water courses, in order to facilitate, promote, and give security to internal commerce among the several States, and to render more easy and less expensive the means and provisions for the common defense,'' I am constrained by the insuperable difficulty I feel in reconciling the bill with the Constitution of the United States to return it with that objection to the House of Representatives, in which it originated.

The legislative powers vested in Congress are specified and enumerated in the eighth section of the first article of the Constitution, and it does not appear that the power proposed to be exercised by the bill is among the enumerated powers, or that it falls by any just interpretation within the power to make laws necessary and proper for carrying into execution those or other powers vested by the Constitution in the Government of the United States.

''The power to regulate commerce among the several States'' can not include a power to construct roads and canals, and to improve the navigation of water courses in order to facilitate, promote, and secure such a commerce without a latitude of construction departing from the ordinary import of the terms strengthened by the known inconveniences which doubtless led to the grant of this remedial power to Congress.

To refer the power in question to the clause ''to provide for the common defense and general welfare'' would be contrary to the established and consistent rules of interpretation, as rendering the special and careful enumeration of powers which follow the clause nugatory and improper. Such a view of the Constitution would have the effect of giving to Congress a general power of legislation instead of the defined and limited one hitherto understood to belong to them, the terms ''common defense and general welfare'' embracing every object and act within the purview of a legislative trust. It would have the effect of subjecting both the Constitution and laws of the several States in all cases not specifically exempted to be superseded by laws of Congress, it being expressly declared ''that the Constitution of the United States and laws made in pursuance thereof shall be the supreme law of the land, and the judges of every State shall be bound thereby, anything in the constitution or laws of any State to the contrary notwithstanding.'' Such a view of the Constitution, finally, would have the effect of excluding the judicial authority of the United States from its participation in guarding the boundary between the legislative powers of the General and the State Governments, inasmuch as questions relating to the general welfare, being questions of policy and expediency, are unsusceptible of judicial cognizance and decision.

A restriction of the power ''to provide for the common defense and general welfare'' to cases which are to be provided for by the expenditure of money would still leave within the legislative power of Congress all the great and most important measures of Government, money being the ordinary and necessary means of carrying them into execution.

If a general power to construct roads and canals, and to improve the navigation of water courses, with the train of powers incident thereto, be not possessed by Congress, the assent of the States in the mode provided in the bill can not confer the power. The only cases in which the consent and cession of particular States can extend the power of Congress are those specified and provided for in the Constitution.

I am not unaware of the great importance of roads and canals and the improved navigation of water courses, and that a power in the National Legislature to provide for them might be exercised with signal advantage to the general prosperity. But seeing that such a power is not expressly given by the Constitution, and believing that it can not be deduced from any part of it without an inadmissible latitude of construction and a reliance on insufficient precedents; believing also that the permanent success of the Constitution depends on a definite partition of powers between the General and the State Governments, and that no adequate landmarks would be left by the constructive extension of the powers of Congress as proposed in the bill, I have no option but to withhold my signature from it, and to cherishing the hope that its beneficial objects may be attained by a resort for the necessary powers to the same wisdom and virtue in the nation which established the Constitution in its actual form and providently marked out in the instrument itself a safe and practicable mode of improving it as experience might suggest.

JAMES MADISON.

Bunker Hill Monument Address

Daniel Webster

Commentary

Rhetorical appeals for unity notwithstanding, the presidencies of Jefferson and Madison saw considerable divisiveness, especially over foreign policy. Divisiveness intensified during the War of 1812. Madison justified his policies as necessary to prevent Britain's unlawful searches and seizures of American ships. Federalists portrayed these policies as an effort to obliterate the Federalist party and make America subservient to France and its satanic emperor, Napoleon. Some New England Federalists were openly agitating for New England to secede from the Union when news of peace arrived in early 1815.

The subsequent "Era of Good Feeling" (dated roughly as 1815-1825) involved an epideictic, unity-building rhetoric which exemplifies the tenuous relationship which often exists between rhetoric and reality, as well as the extent to which the American Revolution had captured the popular imagination. In reality, the War of 1812 was a draw. Weary of the protracted Napoleonic Wars, Britain was ready to quit. Having suffered the indignity of seeing the White House burned by British troops, so too was the United States. The peace treaty resolved none of the prewar disputes and pretty much left things as they had been before the war.

Rhetorically, however, the war was a great American victory. Unaware that the peace treaty had been signed, British forces launched an attack on New Orleans in January, 1815 and were defeated. In America, news of the victory circulated simultaneously with news of the peace treaty, thus making New Orleans symbolic of the entire war. More than just a victory, the war was a victory in our Second War for Independence. As peace celebrations spread, orators never tired of telling how Britain had been trying to restore its colonial rule, reduce us once again to slavery and reimpose upon us the most hideous kinds of tyranny.

Rhetorical use of the Revolution as a unity-building device was not new, but it was encouraged by "winning" our Second War for Independence. Additionally, the use of such rhetoric was promoted by other factors. Revolutionary heroes were passing into the Great Beyond. The intensely patriotic younger generation, now reaching maturity, looked upon the dwindling band of veterans with awe and gratitude. Despite our presumed rationality, certain numbers, including fifty, assume a magical quality. As 1825 approached, some New Englanders formed the Bunker Hill Monument Association and arranged for an unusually impressive celebration on June 17, 1825 — exactly fifty years after the battle.

A huge crowd (some estimates run as high as 100,000 people) formed in Boston and surrounded the 200 Revolutionary veterans (forty of whom fought at Bunker Hill), who rode in carriages as the crowd walked to Charlestown. Once they arrived at Bunker Hill, veterans were given seats of honor. The elderly Marquis de Lafayette, who had come from France to visit the land for which he had fought in the Revolution, laid the cornerstone of the monument. Then the orator arose to give the address.

The orator was Daniel Webster (1782-1852), who typified those who usually spoke on such occasions. A member of the younger generation which had matured while Revolutionary heroes were leading the nation, he served as congressman from his native New Hampshire (1813-1817), moved to Boston to practice law and returned to Congress in 1823. His speech is reproduced photographically from David J. Brewer, *World's Best Orations* (St. Louis: Ferd. P. Kaiser, 1901), vol. 10, pp. 3828-3846.

Bunker Hill Monument Address

THIS uncounted multitude before me, and around me, proves the feeling which the occasion has excited. These thousands of human faces, glowing with sympathy and joy, and, from the impulses of a common gratitude, turned reverently to heaven, in this spacious temple of the firmament, proclaim that the day, the place, and the purpose of our assembling have made a deep impression on our hearts.

If, indeed, there be anything in local association fit to affect the mind of man, we need not strive to repress the emotions which agitate us here. We are among the sepulchres of our fathers. We are on ground distinguished by their valor, their constancy, and the shedding of their blood. We are here, not to fix an uncertain date in our annals, nor to draw into notice an obscure and unknown spot. If our humble purpose had never been conceived, if we ourselves had never been born, the seventeenth of June, 1775, would have been a day on which all subsequent history would have poured its light, and the eminence where we stand, a point of attraction to the eyes of successive generations. But we are Americans. We live in what may be called the early age of this great continent; and we know that our posterity, through all time, are here to suffer and enjoy the allotments of humanity. We see before us a probable train of great events; we know that our own fortunes have been happily cast; and it is natural, therefore, that we should be moved by the contemplation of occurrences which have guided our destiny before many of us were born, and settled the condition in which we should pass that portion of our existence, which God allows **to men on earth.**

We do not read even of the discovery of this continent without feeling something of a personal interest in the event; without being reminded how much it has affected our own fortunes and our own existence. It is more impossible for us, therefore, than for others, to contemplate with unaffected minds that interesting, I may say, that most touching and pathetic scene, when the great discoverer of America stood on the deck of his shattered bark, the shades of night falling on the sea, yet no man sleeping; tossed on the billows of an unknown ocean, yet the stronger billows of alternate hope and despair tossing his own troubled thoughts; extending forward his harassed frame, straining westward his anxious and eager eyes, till heaven at last granted him a moment of rapture and ecstasy, in blessing his vision with the sight of the unknown world.

Nearer to our times, more closely connected with our fates, and therefore still more interesting to our feelings and affections, is the settlement of our own country by colonists from England. We cherish every memorial of these worthy ancestors; we celebrate their patience and fortitude; we admire their daring enterprise; we teach our children to venerate their piety; and we are justly proud of being descended from men who have set the world an example of founding civil institutions on the great and united principles of human freedom and human knowledge. To us, their children, the story of their labors and sufferings can never be without its interest. We shall not stand unmoved on the shore of Plymouth, while the sea continues to wash it; nor will our brethren, in another early and ancient colony, forget the place of its first establishment, till their river shall cease to flow by it. No vigor of youth, no maturity of manhood, will lead the nation to forget the spots where its infancy was cradled and defended.

But the great event, in the history of the continent, which we are now met here to commemorate; that prodigy of modern times, at once the wonder and the blessing of the world, is the American Revolution. In a day of extraordinary prosperity and happiness, of high national honor, distinction, and power, we are brought together, in this place, by our love of country, by our admiration of exalted character, by our gratitude for signal services and patriotic devotion.

The society, whose organ I am, was formed for the purpose of rearing some honorable and durable monument to the memory of the early friends of American independence. They have thought that for this object no time could be more propitious than the present prosperous and peaceful period; that no place could claim preference over this memorable spot; and that no day could be more auspicious to the undertaking than the anniversary of the battle which was here fought. The foundation of that monument we have now laid. With solemnities suited to the occasion, with prayers to Almighty God for his blessing, and in the midst of this cloud of witnesses, we have begun the work. We trust it will be prosecuted, and that springing from a broad foundation rising high in massive solidity and unadorned grandeur it may remain as long as heaven permits the works of man to last, a fit emblem, both of the events in memory of which it is raised and of the gratitude of those who have reared it.

We know, indeed, that the record of illustrious actions is most safely deposited in the universal remembrance of mankind. We know that if we could cause this structure to ascend, not only till it reached the skies, but till it pierced them, its broad surfaces could still contain but part of that which, in an age of knowledge, hath already been spread over the earth, and which history charges itself with making known to all future times. We know that no inscription on entablatures less broad than the earth itself can carry information of the events we commemorate where it has not already gone; and that no structure which shall not outlive the duration of letters and knowledge among men, can prolong the memorial. But our object is by this edifice to show our own deep sense of the value and importance of the achievements of our ancestors; and by presenting this work of gratitude to the eye to keep alive similar sentiments and to foster a constant regard for the principles of the Revolution. Human beings are composed not of reason only, but of imagination also, and sentiment; and that is neither wasted nor misapplied which is appropriated to the purpose of giving right direction to sentiments and opening proper springs of feeling in the heart. Let it not be supposed that our object is to perpetuate national hostility, or even to cherish a mere military spirit. It is higher, purer, nobler. We consecrate our work to the spirit of national independence, and we wish that the light of peace may rest upon it forever. We rear a memorial of our conviction of that un-measured benefit which has been conferred on our own land and of the happy influences which have been produced by the same events on the general interests of mankind. We come as Americans to mark a spot which must forever be dear to us and our posterity. We wish that whosoever, in all coming time, shall turn his eye hither, may behold that the place is not undistinguished where the first great battle of the Revolution was fought. We wish that this structure may proclaim the magnitude and import-ance of that event to every class and every age. We wish that infancy may learn the purpose of its erection from maternal lips and that weary and withered age may behold it and be solaced by the recollections which it suggests. We wish that labor may look up here and be proud in the midst of its toil. We wish that in those days of disaster which, as they come on all nations, must be expected to come on us also, desponding patriotism may turn its eyes hitherward and be assured that the foundations of our national power still stand strong. We wish that this col-umn rising towards heaven among the pointed spires of so many temples dedicated to God may contribute also to produce in all minds a pious feeling of dependence and gratitude. We wish, finally, that the last object on the sight of him who leaves his native shore, and the first to gladden his who revisits it, may be something which shall remind him of the liberty and the glory of his country. Let it rise till it meet the sun in his com-ing; let the earliest light of the morning gild it, and parting day linger and play on its summit.

We live in a most extraordinary age. Events so various and so important that they might crowd and distinguish centuries are in our times compressed within the compass of a single life. When has it happened that history has had so much to record in the same term of years as since the seventeenth of June, 1775? Our own revolution, which under other circumstances might itself have been expected to occasion a war of half a century, has been achieved; twenty-four sovereign and independent States erected; and a General Government established over them, so safe, so wise, so free, so practical, that we might well wonder its estab-lishment should have been accomplished so soon were it not for the greater wonder that it should have been established at all. Two or three millions of people have been augmented to twelve; and the great forests of the West prostrated beneath the arm of successful industry; and the dwellers on the banks of the Ohio and the Mississippi become the fellow-citizens and neighbors of those who cultivate the hills of New England. We have a commerce that leaves no sea unexplored; navies which take no law from superior force; revenues adequate to all the exigencies of government, almost without taxation; and peace with all nations, founded on equal rights and mutual respect.

Europe, within the same period, has been agitated by a mighty revolution, which, while it has been felt in the individual condition and happiness of almost every man, has shaken to the centre her political fabric, and dashed against one another thrones which had stood tranquil for ages. On this, our continent, our own example has been followed; and colonies have sprung up to be nations. Unaccustomed sounds of liberty and free government have reached us from beyond the track of the sun; and at this moment the dominion of European power in this continent, from the place where we stand to the South pole, is annihilated forever.

In the meantime, both in Europe and America, such has been the general progress of knowledge; such the improvements in legislation, in commerce, in the arts, in letters, and, above all, in liberal ideas and the general spirit of the age, that the whole world seems changed.

Yet, notwithstanding that this is but a faint abstract of the things which have happened since the day of the battle of Bunker Hill, we are but fifty years removed from it; and we now stand here to enjoy all the blessings of our own condition, and to look abroad on the brightened prospects of the world, while we hold still among us some of those who were active agents in the scenes of 1775, and who are now here from every quarter of New England to visit once more, and under circumstances so affecting, I had almost said so overwhelming, this renowned theatre of their courage and patriotism.

Venerable men, you have come down to us from a former generation. Heaven has bounteously lengthened out your lives that you might behold this joyous day. You are now where you stood fifty years ago this very hour, with your brothers and your neighbors, shoulder to shoulder, in the strife for your country. Behold, how altered! The same heavens are, indeed, over your heads; the same ocean rolls at your feet; but all else, how changed! You hear now no roar of hostile cannon, you see no mixed volumes of smoke and flame rising from burning Charlestown. The ground strewed with the dead and the dying; the impetuous charge; the steady and successful repulse; the loud call to repeated assault; the summoning of all that is manly to repeated resistance; a thousand bosoms freely and fearlessly bared in an instant to whatever of terror there may be in war and death; all these you have witnessed, but you witness them no more. All is peace. The heights of yonder metropolis, its towers and roofs which you then saw filled with wives and children and countrymen in distress and terror, and looking with unutterable emotions for the issue of the combat, have presented you to-day with the sight of its whole happy population come out to welcome and greet you with a universal jubilee. Yonder proud ships by a felicity of position appropriately lying at the foot of this mount, and seeming fondly to cling around it, are not means of annoyance to you, but your country's own means of distinction and defense. All is peace; and God has granted you this sight of your country's happiness ere you slumber in the grave forever. He has allowed you to behold and to partake the reward of your patriotic toils; and he has allowed us, your sons and countrymen, to meet you here, and in the name of the present generation, in the name of your country, in the name of liberty, to thank you!

But, alas! you are not all here! Time and the sword have thinned your ranks. Prescott, Putnam, Stark, Brooks, Read, Pomeroy, Bridge! our eyes seek for you in vain amidst this broken band. You are gathered to your fathers, and live only to your country in her grateful remembrance and your own bright example. But let us not too much grieve that you have met the common fate of men. You lived at least long enough to know that your work had been nobly and successfully accomplished. You lived to see your country's independence established and to sheathe your swords from war. On the light of Liberty you saw arise the light of Peace, like —

> «Another morn,
> Risen on mid-noon,» —

and the sky on which you closed your eyes was cloudless.

But — ah! — Him! the first great martyr in this great cause! Him! the premature victim of his own self-devoting heart! Him! the head of our civil councils and the destined leader of our military bands, whom nothing brought hither but the unquenchable fire of his own spirit; him! cut off by Providence in the hour of overwhelming anxiety and thick gloom; falling ere he saw the star of his country rise; pouring out his generous blood like water before he knew whether it would fertilize a land of freedom or of bondage! how shall I struggle with the emotions that stifle the utterance of thy name! Our poor work may perish, but thine shall endure! This monument may molder away; the solid ground it rests upon may sink down to a level with the sea, but thy memory shall not fail! Wheresoever among men a heart shall be found that beats to the transports of patriotism and liberty, its aspirations shall be to claim kindred with thy spirit!

But the scene amidst which we stand does not permit us to confine our thoughts or our sympathies to those fearless spirits who hazarded or lost their lives on this consecrated spot. We have the happiness to rejoice here in the presence of a most worthy representation of the survivors of the whole Revolutionary army.

Veterans, you are the remnant of many a well-fought field. You bring with you marks of honor from Trenton and Monmouth, from Yorktown, Camden, Bennington, and Saratoga. Veterans of half a century, when in your youthful days you put everything at hazard in your country's cause, good as that cause was, and sanguine as youth is, still your fondest hopes did not stretch onward to an hour like this! At a period to which you could not reasonably have expected to arrive; at a moment of national prosperity, such as you could never have foreseen, you are now met here to enjoy the fellowship of old soldiers and to receive the overflowings of a universal gratitude.

But your agitated countenances and your heaving breasts inform me that even this is not an unmixed joy. I perceive that a tumult of contending feelings rushes upon you. The images of the dead, as well as the persons of the living, throng to your embraces. The scene overwhelms you, and I turn from it. May the Father of all mercies smile upon your declining years and bless them! And when you shall here have exchanged your embraces; when you shall once more have pressed the hands which have been so often extended to give succor in adversity, or grasped in the exultation of victory; then look abroad into this lovely land, which your young valor defended, and mark the happiness with which it is filled; yea, look abroad into the whole earth and see what a name you have contributed to give to your country, and what a praise you have added to freedom, and then rejoice in the sympathy and gratitude which beam upon your last days from the improved condition of mankind.

The occasion does not require of me any particular account of the battle of the seventeenth of June, nor any detailed narrative of the events which immediately preceded it. These are familiarly known to all. In the progress of the great and interesting controversy, Massachusetts and the town of Boston had become early and marked objects of the displeasure of the British Parliament. This had been manifested in the act for altering the government of the Province, and in that for shutting up the port of Boston. Nothing sheds more honor on our early history, and nothing better shows how little the feelings and sentiments of the colonies were known or regarded in England than the impression which these measures everywhere produced in America. It had been anticipated that while the other colonies would be terrified by the severity of the punishment inflicted on Massachusetts, the other seaports would be governed by a mere spirit of gain; and that, as Boston was now cut off from all commerce, the unexpected advantage which this blow on her was calculated to confer on other towns would be greedily enjoyed. How miserably such reasoners deceived themselves! How little they knew of the depth, and the strength, and the intenseness of that feeling of resistance to illegal acts of power which possessed the whole American people! Everywhere the unworthy boon was rejected with scorn. The fortunate occasion was seized everywhere to show to the whole world that the colonies were swayed by no local interest, no partial interest, no selfish interest. The temptation to profit by the punishment of Boston was strongest to our neighbors of Salem. Yet Salem was precisely the place where this miserable proffer was spurned in a tone of the most lofty self-respect and the most indignant patriotism. "We are deeply affected," said its inhabitants, "with the sense of our public calamities; but the miseries that are now rapidly hastening on our brethren in the capital of the Province, greatly excite our commiseration. By shutting up the port of Boston some imagine that the course of trade might be turned hither, and to our benefit; but we must be dead to every idea of justice, lost to all feelings of humanity, could we indulge a thought to seize on wealth and raise our fortunes on the ruin of our suffering neighbors." These noble sentiments were not confined to our immediate vicinity. In that day of general affection and brotherhood, the blow given to Boston smote on every patriotic heart, from one end of the country to the other. Virginia and the Carolinas, as well as Connecticut and New Hampshire, felt and proclaimed the cause to be their own. The Continental Congress, then holding its first session in Philadelphia, expressed its sympathy for the suffering inhabitants of Boston, and addresses were received from all quarters assuring them that the cause was a common one, and should be met by common efforts and common sacrifices. The Congress of Massachusetts responded to these assurances; and in an address to the Congress at Philadelphia, bearing the official signature, perhaps among the last of the immortal Warren, not-withstanding the severity of its suffering and the magnitude of the dangers which threatened it, it was declared that this colony " is ready, at all times, to spend and to be spent in the cause of America."

But the hour drew nigh which was to put professions to the proof and to determine whether the authors of these mutual pledges were ready to seal them in blood. The tidings of Lex-ington and Concord had no sooner spread than it was universally felt that the time was at last come for action. A spirit pervaded all ranks, not transient, not boisterous, but deep, solemn, deter-mined,—

> " *Totamque infusa per artus*
> *Mens agitat molem, et magno se corpore miscet.*"

War, on their own soil and at their own doors, was, indeed, a strange work to the yeomanry of New England; but their con-sciences were convinced of its necessity, their country called them to it and they did not withhold themselves from the perilous trial. The ordinary occupations of life were abandoned; the plow was staid in the unfinished furrow; wives gave up their husbands, and mothers gave up their sons to the battles of a civil war. Death might come, in honor, on the field; it might come, in disgrace, on the scaffold. For either and for both they were prepared. The sentiment of Quincy was full in their hearts. " Blandishments," said that distinguished son of genius and patriot-ism, " will not fascinate us, nor will threats of a halter intimi-date; for, under God, we are determined that wheresoever, when-soever, or howsoever we shall be called to make our exit, we will die free men."

The seventeenth of June saw the four New England colonies standing here, side by side, to triumph or to fall together; and there was with them from that moment to the end of the war, what I hope will remain with them forever,—one cause, one country, one heart.

The battle of Bunker Hill was attended with the most im-portant effects beyond its immediate result as a military engage-ment. It created at once a state of open, public war. There could now be no longer a question of proceeding against indi-viduals as guilty of treason or rebellion. That fearful crisis was past. The appeal now lay to the sword, and the only question was whether the spirit and the resources of the people would hold out till the object should be accomplished. Nor were its general consequences confined to our own country. The previous proceedings of the colonies, their appeals, resolutions, and addresses had made their cause known to Europe. Without boasting, we may say that in no age or country has the public cause been maintained with more force of argument, more power of illustration, or more of that persuasion which excited feeling and elevated principle can alone bestow, than the revolutionary State papers exhibit. These papers will forever deserve to be studied, not only for the spirit which they breathe, but for the ability with which they were written.

To this able vindication of their cause, the colonies had now added a practical and severe proof of their own true devotion to it, and evidence also of the power which they could bring to its support. All now saw that if America fell, she would not fall without a struggle. Men felt sympathy and regard as well as surprise when they beheld these infant States, remote, unknown, unaided, encounter the power of England, and in the first considerable battle leave more of their enemies dead on the field, in proportion to the number of combatants, than they had recently known in the wars of Europe.

Information of these events circulating through Europe at length reached the ears of one who now hears me. He has not forgotten the emotion which the fame of Bunker Hill and the name of Warren excited in his youthful breast.

Sir, we are assembled to commemorate the establishment of great public principles of liberty, and to do honor to the distinguished dead. The occasion is too severe for eulogy to the living. But, sir, your interesting relation to this country, the peculiar circumstances which surround you and surround us, call on me to express the happiness which we derive from your presence and aid in this solemn commemoration.

Fortunate, fortunate man! with what measure of devotion will you not thank God for the circumstances of your extraordinary life! You are connected with both hemispheres and with two generations. Heaven saw fit to ordain that the electric spark of liberty should be conducted, through you, from the New World to the Old; and we, who are now here to perform this duty of patriotism, have all of us long ago received it in charge from our fathers to cherish your name and your virtues. You will account it an instance of your good fortune, sir, that you crossed the seas to visit us at a time which enables you to be present at this solemnity. You now behold the field, the renown of which reached you in the heart of France, and caused a thrill in your ardent bosom. You see the lines of the little redoubt thrown up by the incredible diligence of Prescott; defended to the last extremity, by his lion-hearted valor; and within which the cornerstone of our monument has now taken its position. You see where Warren fell, and where Parker, Gardner, McCleary, Moore, and other early patriots fell with him. Those who survived that day, and whose lives have been prolonged to the present hour, are now around you. Some of them you have known in the trying scenes of the war. Behold! they now stretch forth their feeble arms to embrace you. Behold! they raise their trembling voices to invoke the blessing of God on you and yours forever.

Sir, you have assisted us in laying the foundation of this edifice. You have heard us rehearse, with our feeble commendation, the names of departed patriots. Sir, monuments and eulogy belong to the dead. We give them this day to Warren and his associates. On other occasions they have been given to your more immediate companions in arms, to Washington, to Greene, to Gates, Sullivan, and Lincoln. Sir, we have become reluctant to grant these, our highest and last honors, further. We would gladly hold them yet back from the little remnant of that immortal band. "*Serus in cælum redeas.*" Illustrious as are your merits, yet far, oh, very far distant be the day when any inscription shall bear your name, or any tongue pronounce its eulogy!

The leading reflection to which this occasion seems to invite us respects the great changes which have happened in the fifty years since the battle of Bunker Hill was fought. And it peculiarly marks the character of the present age that, in looking at these changes and in estimating their effect on our condition, we are obliged to consider, not what has been done in our own country only, but in others also. In these interesting times, while nations are making separate and individual advances in improvement, they make, too, a common progress; like vessels on a common tide, propelled by the gales at different rates, according to their several structure and management, but all moved forward by one mighty current beneath, strong enough to bear onward whatever does not sink beneath it.

A chief distinction of the present day is a community of opinions and knowledge amongst men, in different nations, existing in a degree heretofore unknown. Knowledge has, in our time, triumphed, and is triumphing over distance, over difference of languages, over diversity of habits, over prejudice, and over bigotry. The civilized and Christian world is fast learning the great lesson, that difference of nation does not imply necessary hostility, and that all contact need not be war. The whole world is becoming a common field for intellect to act in. Energy of mind, genius, power, wheresoever it exists, may speak out in any tongue, and the world will hear it. A great chord of sentiment and feeling runs through two continents, and vibrates over both. Every breeze wafts intelligence from country to country; every wave rolls it; all give it forth, and all in turn receive it. There is a vast commerce of ideas; there are marts and exchanges for intellectual discoveries, and a wonderful fellowship of those individual intelligences which make up the mind and opinion of the age. Mind is the great lever of all things; human thought is the process by which human ends are ultimately answered; and the diffusion of knowledge, so astonishing in the last half-century, has rendered innumerable minds, variously gifted by nature, competent to be competitors, or fellow-workers, on the theatre of intellectual operation.

From these causes, important improvements have taken place in the personal condition of individuals. Generally speaking, mankind are not only better fed and better clothed, but they are able also to enjoy more leisure; they possess more refinement and more self-respect. A superior tone of education, manners, and habits prevails. This remark, most true in its application to our own country, is also partly true when applied elsewhere. It is proved by the vastly augmented consumption of those articles of manufacture and of commerce which contribute to the comforts and the decencies of life,— an augmentation which has far outrun the progress of population. And while the unexampled and almost incredible use of machinery would seem to supply the place of labor, labor still finds its occupation and its reward; so wisely has Providence adjusted men's wants and desires to their condition and their capacity.

Any adequate survey, however, of the progress made in the last half century, in the polite and the mechanic arts, in machinery and manufactures, in commerce and agriculture, in letters, and in science, would require volumes. I must abstain wholly from these subjects, and turn, for a moment, to the contemplation of what has been done on the great question of politics and government. This is the master topic of the age; and during the whole fifty years, it has intensely occupied the thoughts of men. The nature of civil government, its ends and uses, have been canvassed and investigated; ancient opinions attacked and defended; new ideas recommended and resisted, by whatever power the mind of man could bring to the controversy. From the closet and the public halls the debate has been transferred to the field; and the world has been shaken by wars of unexampled magnitude, and the greatest variety of fortune. A day of peace has at length succeeded; and now that the strife has subsided, and the smoke cleared away, we may begin to see what has actually been done, permanently changing the state and condition of human society. And without dwelling on particular circumstances, it is most apparent that, from the before-mentioned causes of augmented knowledge and improved individual condition, a real, substantial, and important change has taken place, and is taking place, greatly beneficial, on the whole, to human liberty and human happiness.

The great wheel of political revolution began to move in America. Here its rotation was guarded, regular, and safe. Transferred to the other continent, from unfortunate but natural causes, it received an irregular and violent impulse; it whirled along with a fearful celerity, till at length, like the chariot wheels in the races of antiquity, it took fire from the rapidity of its own motion, and blazed onward, spreading conflagration and terror around.

We learn from the result of this experiment how fortunate was our own condition, and how admirably the character of our people was calculated for making the great example of popular governments. The possession of power did not turn the heads of the American people, for they had long been in the habit of exercising a great portion of self-control. Although the paramount authority of the parent State existed over them, yet a large field of legislation had always been open to our colonial assemblies. They were accustomed to representative bodies and the forms of free government; they understood the doctrine of the division of power among different branches and the necessity of checks on each. The character of our countrymen, moreover, was sober, moral, and religious; and there was little in the change to shock their feelings of justice and humanity, or even to disturb an honest prejudice. We had no domestic throne to overturn, no privileged orders to cast down, no violent changes of property to encounter. In the American Revolution, no man sought or wished for more than to defend and enjoy his own. None hoped for plunder or for spoil. Rapacity was unknown to it; the ax was not among the instruments of its accomplishment; and we all know that it could not have lived a single day under any well-founded imputation of possessing a tendency adverse to the Christian religion.

It need not surprise us that, under circumstances less auspicious, political revolutions elsewhere, even when well intended, have terminated differently. It is, indeed, a great achievement, it is the master-work of the world, to establish governments entirely popular, on lasting foundations; nor is it easy, indeed, to introduce the popular principle at all into governments to which it has been altogether a stranger. It cannot be doubted, however, that Europe has come out of the contest, in which she has been so long engaged, with greatly superior knowledge, and, in many respects, a highly improved condition. Whatever benefit has been acquired is likely to be retained, for it consists mainly in the acquisition of more enlightened ideas. And although kingdoms and provinces may be wrested from the hands that hold them, in the same manner they were obtained; although ordinary and vulgar power may, in human affairs, be lost as it has been won, yet it is the glorious prerogative of the empire of knowledge, that what it gains it never loses. On the contrary, it increases by the multiple of its own power; all its ends become means; all its attainments help to new conquests. Its whole abundant harvest is but so much seed wheat, and nothing has ascertained, and nothing can ascertain, the amount of ultimate product.

Under the influence of this rapidly-increasing knowledge, the people have begun, in all forms of government, to think and to reason on affairs of state. Regarding government as an institution for the public good, they demand a knowledge of its operations and a participation in its exercise. A call for the representative system, wherever it is not enjoyed, and where there is already intelligence enough to estimate its value, is perseveringly made. Where men may speak out, they demand it; where the bayonet is at their throats, they pray for it.

When Louis XIV. said: "I am the state," he expressed the essence of the doctrine of unlimited power. By the rules of that system, the people are disconnected from the state; they are its subjects; it is their lord. These ideas, founded in the love of power, and long supported by the excess and the abuse of it, are yielding in our age to other opinions; and the civilized world seems at last to be proceeding to the conviction of that fundamental and manifest truth, that the powers of government are but a trust, and that they cannot be lawfully exercised but for the good of the community. As knowledge is more and more extended, this conviction becomes more and more general. Knowledge, in truth, is the great sun in the firmament. Life and power are scattered with all its beams. The prayer of the Grecian combatant, when enveloped in unnatural clouds and darkness, is the appropriate political supplication for the people of every country not yet blessed with free institutions: —

« Dispel this cloud, the light of heaven restore;
  Give me to see — and Ajax asks no more.»

We may hope that the growing influence of enlightened sentiments will promote the permanent peace of the world. Wars, to
maintain family alliances, to uphold or to cast down dynasties,
to regulate successions to thrones, which have occupied so much
room in the history of modern times, if not less likely to happen
at all, will be less likely to become general and involve many
nations, as the great principle shall be more and more established,
that the interest of the world is peace, and its first great statute,
that every nation possesses the power of establishing a government for itself. But public opinion has attained also an influence
over governments which do not admit the popular principle into
their organization. A necessary respect for the judgment of the
world operates, in some measure, as a control over the most unlimited forms of authority. It is owing, perhaps, to this truth,
that the interesting struggle of the Greeks has been suffered to
go on so long, without a direct interference, either to wrest that
country from its present masters, and add it to other powers, or
to execute the system of pacification by force, and, with united
strength, lay the neck of Christian and civilized Greece at the
foot of the barbarian Turk. Let us thank God that we live in
an age when something has influence besides the bayonet, and
when the sternest authority does not venture to encounter the
scorching power of public reproach. Any attempt of the kind I
have mentioned should be met by one universal burst of indignation; the air of the civilized world ought to be made too warm
to be comfortably breathed by any who would hazard it.

It is, indeed, a touching reflection, that while, in the fullness
of our country's happiness, we rear this monument to her honor,
we look for instruction in our undertaking, to a country which is
now in fearful contest, not for works of art or memorials of
glory, but for her own existence. Let her be assured that she
is not forgotten in the world; that her efforts are applauded, and
that constant prayers ascend for her success. And let us cherish
a confident hope for her final triumph. If the true spark of religious and civil liberty be kindled, it will burn. Human agency
cannot extinguish it. Like the earth's central fire, it may be
smothered for a time; the ocean may overwhelm it; mountains
may press it down; but its inherent and unconquerable force will
heave both the ocean and the land, and at some time or another,
in some place or another, the volcano will break out and flame
up to heaven.

Among the great events of the half-century, we must reckon,

certainly, the revolution of South America; and we are not likely to overrate the importance of that revolution, either to the people of the country itself or to the rest of the world. The late Spanish colonies, now independent States, under circumstances less favorable, doubtless, than attended our own revolution, have yet successfully commenced their national existence. They have accomplished the great object of establishing their independence; they are known and acknowledged in the world; and, although in regard to their systems of government, their sentiments on religious toleration, and their provisions for public instruction, they may have yet much to learn, it must be admitted that they have risen to the condition of settled and established States more rapidly than could have been reasonably anticipated. They already furnish an exhilarating example of the difference between free governments and despotic misrule. Their commerce at this moment creates a new activity in all the great marts of the world. They show themselves able by an exchange of commodities to bear a useful part in the intercourse of nations. A new spirit of enterprise and industry begins to prevail; all the great interests of society receive a salutary impulse; and the progress of information, not only testifies to an improved condition, but constitutes itself the highest and most essential improvement.

When the battle of Bunker Hill was fought, the existence of South America was scarcely felt in the civilized world. The thirteen little colonies of North America habitually called themselves the "Continent." Borne down by colonial subjugation, monopoly, and bigotry, these vast regions of the South were hardly visible above the horizon. But in our day there hath been, as it were, a new creation. The Southern Hemisphere emerges from the sea. Its lofty mountains begin to lift themselves into the light of heaven; its broad and fertile plains stretch out in beauty to the eye of civilized man and at the mighty being of the voice of political liberty, the waters of darkness retire.

And now let us indulge an honest exultation in the conviction of the benefit which the example of our country has produced and is likely to produce on human freedom and human happiness. And let us endeavor to comprehend in all its magnitude and to feel in all its importance the part assigned to us in the great drama of human affairs. We are placed at the head of the system of representative and popular governments. Thus far our example shows that such governments are compatible, not only with respectability and power, but with repose, with peace, with security of personal rights, with good laws and a just administration.

We are not propagandists. Wherever other systems are preferred, either as being thought better in themselves or as better suited to existing conditions, we leave the preference to be enjoyed. Our history hitherto proves, however, that the popular form is practicable and that, with wisdom and knowledge, men may govern themselves; and the duty incumbent on us is to preserve the consistency of this cheering example and take care that nothing may weaken its authority with the world. If in our case the representative system ultimately fail, popular governments must be pronounced impossible. No combination of circumstances more favorable to the experiment can ever be expected to occur. The last hopes of mankind, therefore, rest with us; and if it should be proclaimed that our example had become an argument against the experiment, the knell of popular liberty would be sounded throughout the earth.

These are incitements to duty; but they are not suggestions of doubt. Our history and our condition, all that is gone before us and all that surrounds us, authorize the belief that popular governments, though subject to occasional variations, perhaps not always for the better in form, may yet in their general character be as durable and permanent as other systems. We know, indeed, that in our country any other is impossible. The principle of free governments adheres to the American soil. It is bedded in it — immovable as its mountains.

And let the sacred obligations which have devolved on this generation and on us sink deep into our hearts. Those are daily dropping from among us who established our liberty and our government. The great trust now descends to new hands. Let us apply ourselves to that which is presented to us as our appropriate object. We can win no laurels in a war for independence. Earlier and worthier hands have gathered them all. Nor are there places for us by the side of Solon, and Alfred, and other founders of states. Our fathers have filled them. But there remains to us a great duty of defense and preservation; and there is opened to us also a noble pursuit to which the spirit of the times strongly invites us. Our proper business is improvement. Let our age be the age of improvement. In a day of peace let us advance the arts of peace and the works of peace. Let us develop the resources of our land, call forth its powers, build up its institutions, promote all its great interests, and see whether we also, in our day and generation, may not perform something worthy to be remembered. Let us cultivate a true spirit of union and harmony. In pursuing the great objects which our condition points out to us, let us act under a settled conviction, and a habitual feeling that these twenty-four States are one country. Let our conceptions be enlarged to the circle of our duties. Let us extend our ideas over the whole of the vast field in which we are called to act. Let our object be our country, our whole country, and nothing but our country. And by the blessing of God may that country itself become a vast and splendid monument, not of oppression and terror, but of wisdom, of peace, and of liberty, upon which the world may gaze with admiration, forever.

Changing Political Rhetoric of the Jacksonian Era

Excerpt from The American System

Henry Clay

Commentary

The superpatriotism of epideictic oratory during the Era of Good Feeling reflected some extremely important facts about the nation's first half-century. The most obvious one is that the country had survived in spite of its divisions. Political parties were now accepted as normal, but the party system no longer reflected the intense divisiveness of former days. The Federalist party's opposition to the War of 1812 had so weakened it outside of New England that the Democratic-Republican party had no one to attack. It was less of a partisan organization than an extralegal institution which served functions that everyone agreed were necessary, such as nominating candidates.

Yet the superpatriotic oratory hid a multitude of trends that were on the verge of erupting into an even more divisive era and, ultimately, a civil war. The fact that Federalists still dominated New England while Democratic-Republicans dominated elsewhere reflected a deepening sectionalism, and economic trends were changing the sections. The Northeast continued to rely on agriculture and the import-export trade, but industrialization was growing and slavery was outlawed. The South's tobacco trade had been seriously disrupted by the Revolutionary War. Tobacco depleted Southern soil and the cost of maintaining an ever-growing, but less-needed, slave population became burdensome. For a while, it seemed that Southern slavery might die; however, the invention of the cotton gin was followed by the rise of the cotton culture in the new Southwestern States, such as Alabama. Seaboard planters had a profitable market for their surplus slaves. As cotton exports to Europe increased, the slave-based Southern economy boomed. Meanwhile, rapid westward expansion created a new section. By 1819, the thirteen original States had grown to twenty-two. Although the West's egalitarianism made it susceptible to the egalitarian rhetoric of the Democratic-Republicans, the West drifted away from the old Jeffersonian ideal of "limited government" and toward a philosophy that was Hamiltonian in everything but name. Many

Westerners supported the "new" or "national republicanism," which considered roads and other "internal improvements" to be a Federal responsibility. There persisted the old Jeffersonian philosophy of "limited government," now more often called "States rights," especially in Southern coastal States. In short, the nation was dividing into three sections, each with a distinctive economy and a dominant ideology. It was only a matter of time before the sectional reality would erupt into a fierce sectional rhetoric.

Slavery had been prohibited in the Northwest Territory (Ohio, Indiana, Illinois, Michigan and Wisconsin) by Congress during the days of the Articles of Confederation, but Congress had rejected a similar proposal for the Southwestern States. Also, nothing was said about slavery when the Louisiana Territory was purchased from France in 1803, nor was anything said in 1812, when a portion of the territory was admitted as the State of Louisiana and another portion was converted into the Missouri Territory. When Missouri applied for Statehood in 1819, some antislavery Northerners tried to make its admission conditional on gradual emancipation, and a fierce congressional debate erupted.

The debate involved three issues, the first being the morality of slavery. A second involved pragmatic arguments, with Northerners arguing that slavery would keep out small, free farmers who could not compete with slave labor. Southerners answered that emancipation would be unfair to slaveowners who had emigrated or wished to emigrate to Missouri. The third involved constitutionality, with some arguing that congressional power to "admit" States should be interpreted strictly; i.e., Congress could accept or reject applications but could not impose conditions. Arguing from the "implied powers" doctrine, others insisted that the Constitution permitted Congress to impose conditions.

The bitter debate seemed to end in March, 1820 with the "Missouri Compromise," which provided that Missouri would be admitted as a slave State as soon as it prepared a State constitution; Maine, previously part of Massachusetts, would be admitted as a free State; and slavery would be prohibited in the remaining portion of the Louisiana Purchase north of 36° 30′ (Missouri's southern boundary). Everyone assumed that as soon as Congress received the Missouri constitution, admission was a mere formality; however, some congressmen were incensed when they learned that the Missouri constitution prohibited free blacks and mulattos from immigrating into the State. They argued that this violated the Federal Constitution's provision that "the citizens of each State shall be entitled to all the privileges and immunities of citizens in the several States." Once again, the debate grew hot. A "Second Missouri Compromise," which required a pledge from Missouri not to violate the constitutional rights of black citizens, was soon reached.

The second compromise was engineered by the Speaker of the House, Henry Clay (1777-1852). Born in Virginia, Clay emigrated to Kentucky, where he practiced law and entered State politics. The State legislature elected him twice to fill unexpired Senate terms (1806 and 1809-1811). He entered Congress in 1811 as a leading "War Hawk" and was quickly elected speaker. After serving on the diplomatic team which negotiated the peace treaty, he returned to Congress and supported various "new republican" measures, such as rechartering the National Bank and Federal financing of "internal improvements" in the West. Having added the Compromise to his impressive list of political achievements, he cast a lustful eye at the White House, whose occupant, James Monroe, was expected to follow the tradition of retiring after two terms.

As the presidential election of 1824 approached, Clay needed another legislative victory and an opportunity to address the public. The old mythology of "the office seeks the man" precluded an overt campaign. So he seized upon an issue that had been lurking in the background and would ultimately join slavery as one of the most divisive issues in American history: the protective tariff.

The tariff had long been a chief source of Federal revenue, but New Englanders had objected strenuously when rates were increased substantially to finance what they sarcastically called "Mr. Madison's War." In 1816, when the high rates were continued, leading Northern congressmen, such as Daniel Webster, opposed them on the grounds that they disrupted the import-export trade in particular and the national economy in general. Most Southern and Western congressmen supported the high rates, although, as we shall see, sectional attitudes changed dramatically in the years ahead.

The change was already beginning in 1824. With the country in an economic recession, Clay argued for an even higher tariff to protect America's young industries. What Clay ingeniously called the "American System" was supported by congressmen who represented Northern industrial interests, but it was vigorously attacked by Northern shipping interests and Southerners, who assailed it as self-interest legislation. Then, as now, opponents of protectionism argued that high tariffs benefited industry at the expense of shippers and consumers and warned that our trading partners would retaliate, thereby injuring those who relied on exports. The South was especially vocal, arguing that it would never industrialize and, hence, be taxed for the benefit of Northern industry.

On March 30-31, 1824, Clay delivered a lengthy congressional speech that was distributed throughout the country as a pamphlet entitled, *Mr. Clay's Speech in Support of an American System for the Protection of American Industry*. Intending to persuade Congress and the public of the virtues of protectionism and earn him support in the upcoming presidential election, Clay began by emphasizing the current economic difficulties and arguing that protectionism would solve them. He then turned to a refutation of various anti-protectionist arguments. Although the discourse is too long to reproduce in its entirety, the following excerpt, taken from the conclusion (pp. 30-32), illustrates his rhetorical method of converting special interest legislation into something good for everybody. It is reproduced, complete with its numerous printing errors, from the pamphlet which is housed at Amherst College (no publisher, place of publication or date is indicated).

Excerpt from The American System

But all these great interests are confided to the protection of one government — to the fate of one ship; and a most gallant ship it is, with a noble crew. *If we prosper, and are happy, protection must be extended to all; it is due to all. It is the great principle on which obedience is demanded from all. If our essential interests cannot find protection from our own government against the policy of foreign powers, where are they to get it?* We did not unite for sacrifice, but for preservation. The inquiry should be, in reference to the great interests of every section of the Union, (I speak not of minute subdivisions,) what would be done for those interests if that section stood alone and separated from the residue of the Republic? If the promotion of those interests would not injuriously affect any other section, then every thing should be done for them, which would be done if it formed a distinct government. If they come into absolute collision with the interests of another section, a reconciliation, if possible, should be attempted, by mutual concession, so as to avoid a sacrifice of the prosperity of either to that of the other. In such a case all should not be done for one which would be done if it were separated and independent, but something; and, in devising the measure, the good of each part and of the whole should be carefully consulted. This is the only mode by which we can preserve, in full vigour, the harmony of the whole Union. The south entertains one opinion, and imagines that a modification of the existing policy of the country, for the protection of American industry, involves the ruin of the south. The north, the east, the west, hold the opposite opinion, and feel and contemplate, in a long adherence to the foreign policy, as it now exists, their utter destruction. Is it true that the interests of these great sections of our country are irreconcilable with each other? *Are we reduced to the sad and afflicting dilemma of determining which shall fall a victim to the prosperity of the other?* Happily, I think, there is no such distressing alternative. If the north, the west, and the east, formed an independent state, unassociated with the south, can there be a doubt that the restrictive system would be carried to the point of prohibition of every foreign fabric of which they produce the raw material, and which they could manufacture? Such would be their policy, if they stood alone; but they are fortunately connected with the south, which believes its interest to require a free admission of foreign manufactures. Here then is a case for mutual concession, for fair compromise. The bill under consideration presents this compromise. It is a medium between the absolute exclusion and the unrestricted admission of the produce of foreign industry. It sacrifices the interest of neither section to that of the other; neither, it is true, gets all that it wants, nor is subject to all that it fears.

But it has been said that the south obtains nothing in this compromise. Does it lose anything? is the first question. I have endeavoured to prove that it does not, by showing that a mere transfer is effected in the source of the supply of its consumption from Europe to America; and that the loss, whatever it may be, of the sale of its great staple in Europe, is compensated by the new market created in America. But does the south really gain nothing in this compromise? The consumption of the other sections, though somewhat restricted, is still left open by this bill, to foreign fabrics, purchased by southern staples. So far its operation is beneficial to the south, and prejudicial to the industry of the other sections, and that is the point of mutual concession. The south will also gain by the extended consumption of its great staple, produced by an increased capacity to consume it in consequence of the establishment of the home market. But the south cannot exert its industry and enterprise in the business of manufactures! Why not? The difficulties, if not exaggerated, are artificial, and may therefore be surmounted. But can the other sections embark in the planting occupations of the south? The obstructions which forbid them are natural, created by the immutable laws of God, and therefore unconquerable.

Other and animating considerations invite us to adopt the policy of this system. Its importance, in connexion with general defence in time of war, cannot fail to be duly estimated. *Need I recall to our painful recollection the sufferings, for the want of an adequate supply of absolute necessaries, to which the defenders of their country's rights and our entire population were subjected during the late war?* Or remind the committee of the great advantage of a steady and unfailing source of supply, unaffected alike in war and in peace? Its importance, in reference to the stability of our Union, that paramount and greatest of all our interests, cannot fail warmly to recommend it, or at least to conciliate the forbearance of every patriot bosom. Now our people present the spectacle of a vast assemblage of jealous rivals, all eagerly rushing to the sea-board, jostling each other in their way, to hurry off to glutted foreign markets the perishable produce of their labour. The tendency of that policy, in conformity to which this bill is prepared, is to transform these competitors into friends and mutual customers; and, by the reciprocal exchanges of their respective productions, to place the confederacy upon the most solid of all foundations, the basis of common interest. And is not government called upon, by every stimulating motive, to adapt its policy to the actual condition and extended growth of our great republic? At the commencement of our Constitution, almost the whole population of the United States was confined between the Alleghany mountains and the Atlantic ocean. Since that epoch, the western part of New-York, of Pennsylvania, of Virginia, all the western states and territories, have been principally peopled. Prior to that period, we had scarcely any interior. An interior has sprung up as it were by enchantment, and along with it new interests and new relations, requiring the parental protection of government. Our policy should be modified accordingly, so as to comprehend all, and sacrifice none. And are we not encouraged by the success of past experience, in respect to the only article which has been adequately protected? Already have the predictions of the friends of the American system, in even a shorter time than their most sanguine hopes could have anticipated, been completely realized in regard to that article; and consumption is now better and cheaper supplied with coarse cottons, than it was under the prevalence of the foreign system.

Even if the benefits of the policy were limited to certain sections of our country, *would it not be satisfactory to behold American industry, wherever situated, active, animated, and thrifty, rather then perservere in a course which renders us subservient to foreign industry?* But these benefits are twofold, direct and collateral, and in the one shape or the other they will diffuse themselves throughout the Union. All parts of the Union will participate, more or less, in both. As to the direct benefit, it is probable that the North and the East will enjoy the largest share. But the West and the South will also participate in them. Philadelphia, Baltimore, and Richmond, will divide with the Nothern capitals the business of manufacturing. The latter city unites more advantages for its successful prosecution than any other place I know; Zanesville, in Ohio, only excepted. And where the direct benefit does not accrue, that will be enjoyed of supplying the raw material and provisions for the consumption of artisans. Is it not most desirable to put at rest and prevent the annual recurrence of this unpleasant subject so well fitted by the various interests to which it appeals, to excite irritation and to produce discontent? Can that be effected by its rejection? Behold the mass of petitions which lie on our table, earnestly and anxiously entreating the protecting interposition of Congress against the ruinous policy which we are pursuing. Will these petitioners, comprehending all orders of society, entire states and communities, public companies and private individuals, spontaneously assembling, cease in their humble prayers by your leading a deaf ear? Can you expect that these petitioners, and others in countless numbers, that will, if you delay the passage of this bill, *supplicate your mercy, should contemplate their substance gradually withdrawn to foreign countries, their ruin slow, but certain and as inevitable as death itself, without one expiring effort?* You think the measure injurious to you; we believe our preservation depends upon its adoption. Our convictions, nutually honest, are equally strong. What is to be done? *I invoke that saving spirit of mutual concession under which our blessed Constitution was formed, and under which alone it can be happily administered. I appeal to the South — to the high-minded, generous, and patriotic South — with which I have so often co-operated, in attempting to sustain the honour and to vindicate the rights of our country. Should it not offer upon the altar of the public good, some sacrifice of its peculiar opinions? Of what does it complain? A possible temporary enhancement in the objects of consumption. Of what do we complain? A total incapacity, produced by the foreign policy, to purchase at any price, necessary foreign objects of consumption. In such an alternative, inconvenient only to the south; ruinous to us, can we expect too much from Southern magnanimity?* The just and confident expectation of the passage of this bill has flooded the country with recent importations of foreign fabrics. If it should not pass, they will complete the work of destruction of our domestic industry. If it should pass, they will prevent any considerable rise in the price of foreign commodities, until our own industry shall be able to supply competent substitutes.

To the friends of the tariff, I would also anxiously appeal. Every arrangement of its provisions does not suit each of you; you desire some further alterations; you would make it perfect. You want what you will never get. Nothing human is perfect. And I have seen with great surprise, a piece signed by a member of Congress, published in the National Intelligencer, stating that this bill must be rejected, and a judicious tariff brought in as its substitute. A *judicious* tariff! No member of Congress could have signed that piece; or, if he did, the public ought not to be deceived. If this bill do not pass, unquestionably no other can pass at this session, or probably during this Congress. And who will go home and say that he rejected all the benefits of this bill, because molasses has been subjected to the enormous additional duty of five cents per gallon? I call, therefore, upon the friends of the American policy, to yield somewhat of their own peculiar wishes, and not to reject the practicable in the idle pursuit after the unattainable. Let us imitate the illustrious example of the framers of the Constitution, and always remembering that whatever springs from man partakes of his imperfections, depend upon experience to suggest, in future, the necessary amendments.

We have had great difficulties to encounter. 1. The splendid talents which are arrayed in this house against us. 2. We are opposed by the rich and powerful in the land. 3. The Executive government, if any affords us but a cold and equivocal support. 4. The importing and navigating interest, I verily believe from misconception, are adverse to us. 5. The British factors and the British influence are inimical to our success. 6. Long established habits and prejudices oppose us. 7. The reviewers and literary speculators, foreign and domestic. And lastly, the leading presses of the country, including the influence of that which is established in this city, and sustained by the public purse.

From some of these, or other causes, the bill may be postponed, thwarted, defeated. But *the cause is the cause of the country, and it must and will prevail. It is founded in the interest and affections of the people. It is as native as the granite deeply embosomed in our mountains. And, in conclusion, I would pray* GOD, *in his infinite mercy, to avert from our country the evils which are impending over it, and by enlightening our councils, to conduct us into that path which leads to riches, to greatness, to glory.*

(THE END.)

Nashville Republican Report
of the Carthage Celebration

Andrew Jackson

Commentary

Although his protective tariff was enacted, Clay failed to win the presidential election of 1824. Of more long-term significance, especially to future campaign rhetoric, was the manner in which the election was conducted. As early as 1796, the parties recognized the need to keep their supporters in the electoral college from splitting their votes. The nomination of candidates by congressional caucuses became an accepted practice; however, objections were loud against "King Caucus" (a rhetorically apt term in republican America) when Monroe was selected in 1816. Anticipating the death of the caucus system, the Tennessee legislature nominated Andrew Jackson (1767-1845) a year before the election of 1824. The caucus of Democratic-Republican congressmen, which nominated William Crawford, was so thinly attended that other State legislatures followed Tennessee's example. Clay and John Q. Adams were added to the list of candidates. Jackson won a plurality of electoral votes but his lack of a majority threw the election into the House of Representatives, where Clay supported the victorious Adams.

Jackson's supporters alleged that the "popular will" had been "thwarted." When Adams appointed Clay secretary of state (a post that Adams and his two predecessors had occupied immediately prior to becoming president), Jacksonians complained of a "corrupt bargain." They did more than merely complain. They realigned the party system by forming local parties that used various labels, including "Jacksonian," "Jacksonian Democrat," "Jacksonian Republican" and "Democrat" — the last of which was especially popular because of its egalitarian overtones.

Jacksonians also subsidized partisan political newspapers, which never tired of telling readers how the corrupt bargain had thwarted the public will. After seizing control of the House in 1826, Jacksonian congressmen introduced a bill to have a painting of the Battle of New Orleans put in the Capitol Building rotunda, and they introduced a Retrenchment Resolution, which called for economy in government. As legislation, such measures were trivial, but they enabled congressmen to glorify Jackson for saving the nation at New Orleans and to portray Adams as a wasteful and unscrupulous spender of the taxpayers' hard-earned dollars. The congressional debates were reported in Jacksonian newspapers (in appropriately biased fashion), and they laid a solid rhetorical base for the presidential election of 1828.

President Adams, stubbornly clinging to the outdated view that parties were bad, refused to organize one of his own. Thus the Jacksonians had a tremendous advantage when the election of 1828 arrived. They were ready for a campaign featuring character assassination and image-building. Adams was portrayed as a corrupt aristocrat who was the tool of wealthy bankers and other special interests. Jacksonians emphasized that Adams had spent much of his career in the castles and drawing rooms of Europe (and forgot to mention that he had served brilliantly as a diplomat). Jackson, in sharp contrast, was a True American, a Common Man, a dirt farmer who believed in hard work, thrift and other agrarian virtues. He was a military hero, who had joined the militia as a mere boy during the Revolution, been a heroic Indian fighter and was the Hero of New Orleans (but forgot to mention his limited political experience).

Jacksonians diffused their rhetoric through the partisan press. They also utilized a new medium of communication that was well adapted to their egalitarian rhetoric: the local political rally which featured a stump speech. The term *stump speech* was something of a misnomer, because the speeches were usually delivered from a platform, but it had a folksy touch in a day when the vast majority of Americans were farmers who cut trees to clear the land and used the wood for fuel and timber.

The Common Man adhered to the old myth that "the office seeks the man" by remaining secluded in his elegant mansion on his large Tennessee estate. One occasion permitted him to give a short, supposedly non-partisan speech. It was a local Fourth of July celebration near his home. Such celebrations were extremely popular not only because it was an age of intense patriotism, but also because many Americans, especially those in the West, lived on isolated farms and welcomed communal activities. Astute to the rhetorical potential of identifying partisanship with non-partisan celebrations, the *Nashville Republican's* account of the ceremony was reprinted in numerous Jacksonian papers, including the leading one (located in the nation's capital), the *United States Telegraph,* from which the following is reproduced. The report appeared on p. 3 in the July 28, 1828 issue of the semi-weekly edition and is taken from the paper which is housed at the American Antiquarian Society.

Newspaper Report of the Carthage Celebration
(Including a Speech by Andrew Jackson)

The Fourth of July was celebrated in Carthage, highly creditable to the patriotism and hospitality of the citizens of that place.

Gen. Jackson and his company, Governor Houston, the Revolutionary Soldiers of that vicinity, and some others, were invited guetts [sic].

At the distance of eight miles, the General and his company were met by ten gentlemen from Carthage, deputed by the Committee of Arrangements, who accompanied our distinguished guests to the bank of the Cumberland.

On their arrival, they were saluted from the opposite shore, by a handsome discharge of artillery and musketry.

The General having crossed the river, was received and introduced by Col. Robert Allen, the President of the day. Here a line of citizens were formed on each side, extending about a half mile in distance; thro' which the General and his company were escorted by Col. Don C[.] Dixon's company of volunteers, a number of our citizens, and a handsome band of music. This scene was truly interesting, for in this march were to be found many of our grey headed-fathers [sic] of the revolution, following on, besides thousands of others, from the youthful patriot to the time beaten and decrepit sire on the verge of the grave — all was respectful and solemn.

The General reached his lodgings, the house of Mr. William Allen, kindly and handsom[e]ly furnished by the owner, for his reception.

About 11 o'clock the General and company were conducted to a platform, erected near the court house, fronted by a beautiful arbor, under which were seated a large assembly of ladies, and about three thousand spectators.

The scene here was more impressive than all beside — the General having reached the platform, he was introduced by Col. Allen to the few revolutionary heroes assembled there; as our distinguished guest would take them by the hand, their hearts heaved with gratitude and their eyes were filled with the tears of affection — what situation could man be placed in that would inspire him with nobler and higher emotions? — better this, than the heartless devotion of millions of sycophants and flatterers.

This ceremony over — Col. A.W. Overton addressed the General in a very feeling and eloquent manner, to which the General replied. The Rev. Mr. Dillard offered up to the throne of all goodness an appropriate prayer, and Jonathan Pickett, Esq. read the Declaration of American Independence. — After a patriotic air from a fine band of music, the hour of twelve having arrived, Dixon Allen, Esq. delivered an eloquent oration in commemoration of our national birth day.

At about two o'clock, the company moved out to the dinner table situated under a beautiful natural arbour, in the edge of the town, where a sumptious repast was furnished by Mr. John Morris. Between five and six hundred persons sat down to dinner, where all was cheerfulness and harmony, and no jaring sound was heard, to mar the enjoyments of the day. The toasts were all drank with great order and decorum, and too much praise cannot be bestowed on Maj. David Burford, and James D. Allen, Esq. the marshalls of the day, for their assiduous attention. The whole celebration was closed by a splendid Ball in the evening, at which the General attended, where he was greeted by the smiles of about one hundred of our most interesting ladies.

Col. A.W. Overton's Address

GENERAL: — You have been invited by the citizens of Smith county to unite with them, in the celebration of this day — you have accepted the invitation, and now honor them with your presence.

Give me leave, Sir, in the name of your friends here assembled, and in behalf of your fellow-citizens of Smith county, (whose humble organ I am,) to tender you their unfeigned congratulations, and to assure you of a sincere, and cordial welcome among them.

It is not in the abject spirit of adulation, nor in the fulsome language of flattery, that we desire to hail your presence among us. No, Sir, such a degraded offering would be rebuked by the spirit that rules this memorable anniversary. These living monuments of our revolutionary glory, would scorn such vile degeneracy, and the exalted patriotism of our honored guest, would disdain such servility in his countrymen: but as freemen, proud of their independence, rejoicing in the event that announced it to the world, we hail you with the animated welcome of gratitude as its most illustrious preserver.

We delight to contemplate you as the youthful hero who mingled with patriotic ardor, in that glorious struggle which redeemed this land from British domination. We trace you with unfeigned satisfaction, through the successive variety of civil employments to which you have been called, by the voice of your country, and in which you have displayed the warmest and most enlightened zeal for her interest. We remember, with the liveliest sensibility, that when savage massacre had drenched our defenceless frontier with the blood of its citizens — when invasion hovered around our country, in its darkest and most fearful form, you have rushed to the scene of danger, and, by an energy and skill, unparalleled in the annals of warfare, achieved our deliverance from the desolation of the storm.

Around you, General, are many of those brave spirits, who shared, with you, the toils, the danger and the glories of your eventful career — many of your "brethren in arms." Many of your old associates in peace. They have known you long, they have known you intimately, and they proclaim you, with a united voice, a patriot, a *statesman* and *benefactor*, worthy of the warmest gratitude, and highest honours. But the high testimonials you have given of your love of country, your devotion to its interest, its honor and glory, h[a]ve not shielded your reputation from the calumny and detraction of your enemies. — The venal, the vulgar and the vile have lavished it upon you, in the most unfeeling and relentless manner. Even the sanctuary of your fire-side has been invaded — the happiness and comforts of your domestic and private relation have not been spared. It is a calumny unmanly in its motives, unnatural in its objects, an[d] unworthy in its means. It has not, it cannot prevail. Innocence will vindicate itself, and guilt draw down its own condemnation. Truth will triumph; and the authors of such falsehood will feel its dreadful recoil in the infamy, to which the justice of mankind will consign them — and your name, General, shall go down to posterity, doubly hallowed by the severity of its trials.

General Jackson's Reply

Sir — Permit me to offer you my sincere thanks for the complimentary terms in which, as the organ of my fellow citizens of Smith county, you are pleased to greet my arrival amongst them.

I accepted their polite invitation to celebrate with them this day as a neighbor and friend, conscious that in thus manifesting his respect for the birth of liberty, he could not be charged with a desire to court popular favor, nor they with a disposition to gratify a spirit so unworthy. No Sir, the patriotism displayed by many h[e]r[e] [in] this assembly, during the last war, would not bear the imputation and I trust will never authorize it by any act of servility whether to an old commander, or to any other citizen.

I am truly grateful, sir, for the good opinion of my fellow citizens. Obtained without a sacrifice of conscience, and without a violation of the interests of the country, it is the greatest of all earthly rewards, and as such do I regard that which you have so eloquently expressed. Unbiassed [sic] by the hopes of office, and animated by an ardent devotion to the inestimable blessings of liberty, it must consign to infamy the authors of the present system of calumny, and uniting with the great stream of public opinion, cannot fail to bear down the machinations of the demagogue, and bring back the government to its original simplicity. In the advancement of this object, be assured, sir, that I shall bear with patience, the attacks of my enemies, and if it shall be my destiny to be made the instrument in the hands of Providence, by which it is to be affected, I shall rather be humbled than elated by the possession of so high a trust.

Excerpts from South Carolina Exposition and Protest (Original Draft)

John C. Calhoun

Commentary

By conducting an election campaign devoted to personalities, the Jacksonians diverted public attention from what was emerging as the most divisive issue of the day: the protective tariff. Dissatisfied with the tariff of 1824 because it had not eliminated foreign competition, Northeastern textile interests lobbied for an even higher tariff. It passed the House on February 10, 1827 but failed in the Senate when Vice-President John C. Calhoun (1782-1850) cast the deciding vote. After some complex political maneuvering, in which Jacksonians tried to satisfy both North and South by appearing to be for and against the bill, the highest tariff yet legislated in American history passed in the spring of 1828.

Most of the congressional debate was little more than a restatement of earlier arguments. The rhetorical situation was one in which persuasion was nearly impossible. The North was now largely united behind the protectionist principle, and the South was increasingly bitter in arguing that Northern greediness was ruining the South. Only a few legislators, mostly from the West, were open to persuasion, but most of the rhetoric did nothing more than intensify the listeners' pre-existing attitudes. Once the South lost, it bitterly denounced the "Tariff of Abominations."

Calhoun was to emerge as the South's leading spokesman, but he occupied a position that was as awkward as it was enviable. It was enviable because of his distinguished career and reputation. He had entered Congress as a War Hawk in 1811, been secretary of war during Monroe's presidency and been elected vice-president in 1824 with the support of both Adams' and Jackson's followers. It was awkward because his position as vice-president prevented him from participating in the legislative debate. By now Adams' followers had abandoned him, and his re-election depended on not alienating pro-tariff Jacksonians any more than he had already done by his tie-breaking vote of the previous year. He wished to address the issue — and did so in a way that was to prove historically significant.

His procedure was to suggest that the legislature in his home State appoint a special committee on the tariff, and he then drafted the committee's report. Although technically a "draft," his discourse circulated widely as the *South Carolina Exposition and Protest* and was formally adopted by the legislature after some alterations. It was an unusually long and legalistic discourse, even by nineteenth-century standards, and it was even more unusual because of its constitutional argument.

Earlier legislation, notably that concerning the National Bank and the Alien and Sedition Acts, had been declared unconstitutional by Madison and Jefferson, but neither had done anything more than protest. In 1824 and, again, in 1828, opponents of protectionism argued that protective tariffs were unconstitutional, but they did not say what remedy should be used if Congress passed the law. Today, Americans assume that the remedy for unconstitutional legislation lay with the Supreme Court, but the Court's power to declare laws unconstitutional was not taken for granted in Calhoun's day. True, the Supreme Court had done so in the famous *Marbury v. Madison* case (1803), but circumstances surrounding the case were unique. A Federalist Court ruled against a law which had been passed by a Federalist-dominated Congress and which was being used by a Federalist against Madison. By ruling in Madison's favor, the Court effectively precluded protests from Democratic-Republicans. The ruling set a precedent that the Court could declare Federal legislation unconstitutional, but not everyone believed that the Court had such power. Calhoun did not. He argued that it was absurd to say that the remedy for unconstitutional Federal legislation resided with the Federal government. The proper remedy was State action.

Because of its length, only a few excerpts are reproduced here. They are taken from Richard K. Cralle's edition of *Reports and Public Letters of John C. Calhoun* [vol. 6, of *The Works of John C. Calhoun* (New York: D. Appleton, 1856)]. The excerpts (pp. 2-5, 10-12, 29, 34-45) provide an overview of the discourse, but they give only the bare essence of the various arguments, except in the case of the proposed remedy — State interposition.

Excerpts from South Carolina Exposition and Protest (Original Draft)

The committee have bestowed on the subjects referred to them the deliberate attention which their importance demands; and the result, on full investigation, is a unanimous opinion that the act of Congress of the last session, with the whole system of legislation imposing duties on imports, — not for revenue, but the protection of one branch of industry at the expense of others, — is unconstitutional, unequal, and oppressive, and calculated to corrupt the public virtue and destroy the liberty of the country; which propositions they propose to consider in the order stated, and then to conclude their report with the consideration of the important question of the remedy.

The committee do not propose to enter into an elaborate or refined argument on the question of the constitutionality of the Tariff system. The General Government is one of specific powers, and it can rightfully exercise only the powers expressly granted, and those that may be necessary and proper to carry them into effect, all others being reserved expressly to the States or the people. It results, necessarily, that those who claim to exercise power under the Constitution, are bound to show that it is expressly granted, or that it is necessary and proper as a means to some of the granted powers. The advocates of the Tariff have offered no such proof. It is true that the third section of the first article of the Constitution authorizes Congress to lay and collect an impost duty, but it is granted as a tax power for the sole purpose of revenue, — a power in its nature essentially different from that of imposing protective or prohibitory duties. Their objects are incompatible. The prohibitory system must end in destroying the revenue from imports. It has been said that the system is a violation of the spirit, and not the letter of the Constitution. The distinction is not material. The Constitution may be as grossly violated by acting against its meaning as against its letter; but it may be proper to dwell a moment on the point in order to understand more fully the real character of the acts under which the interest of this, and other States similarly situated, has been sacrificed. The facts are few and simple. The Constitution grants to Congress the power of imposing a duty on imports for revenue, which power is abused by being converted into an instrument of rearing up the industry of one section of the country on the ruins of another. The violation, then, consists in using a power granted for one object to advance another, and that by the sacrifice of the original object. It is, in a word, a violation by perversion, — the most dangerous of all because the most insidious and difficult to resist....

In the absence of arguments, drawn from the Constitution itself, the advocates of the power have attempted to call in the aid of precedent. The committee will not waste their time in examining the instances quoted. If they were strictly in point, they would be entitled to little weight. Ours is not a Government of precedents, nor can they be admitted, except to a very limited extent, and with great caution, in the interpretation of the Constitution, without changing, in time, the entire character of the instrument. The only safe rule is the Constitution itself, — or, if that be doubtful, the history of the times. In this case, if doubts existed, the journals of the Convention itself would remove them. It was moved in that body to confer on Congress the very power in question to encourage manufactures, but it was deliberately withheld, except to the extent of granting patent rights for new and useful inventions. ... But, giving the precedents every weight that may be claimed for them, the committee feel confident that, in this case, there are none in point previous to the adoption of the present Tariff system. Every instance which has been quoted, may fairly be referred to the legitimate power of Congress, to impose duties on imports for revenue. It is a necessary incident of such duties to act as an encouragement to manufactures, whenever imposed on articles which may be manufactured in our country. In this incidental manner, Congress has the power of encouraging manufactures; and the committee readily concede that, in the passage of an impost bill, that body may, in modifying the details, so arrange the provisions of the bill, as far as it may be done consistently with its proper object, as to aid manufactures. To this extent Congress may constitutionally go, and has gone from the commencement of the Government, which will fully explain the precedents cited from the early stages of its operation. Beyond this they never proceeded till the commencement of the present system, the inequality and oppression of which they will next proceed to consider.

On entering on this branch of the subject, the committee feel the painful character of the duty which they must perform. They would desire never to speak of our country, as far as the action of the General Government is concerned, but as one great whole, having a common interest, which all the parts ought zealously to promote. Previously to the adoption of the Tariff system, such was the unanimous feeling of this State; but in speaking of its operation, it will be impossible to avoid the discussion of sectional interest, and the use of the sectional language. On its authors, and not on us, who are compelled to adopt this course in self-defence, by injustice and oppression, be the censure.

So partial are the effects of the system, that its burdens are exclusively on one side and its benefits on the other. It imposes on the agricultural interest of the South, including the South-west, and that portion of the country particularly engaged in commerce and navigation, the burden not only of sustaining the system itself, but that also of the Government. . . .

That the manufacturing States, even in their own opinion, bear no share of the burden of the Tariff in reality, we may infer with the greatest certainty from their conduct. The fact that they urgently demand an increase, and consider every addition as a blessing, and a failure to obtain one as a curse, is the strongest confession that, whatever burden it imposes, in reality falls, not on them, but on others. Men ask not for burdens, but benefits.

. . . The assertion, that the encouragement of the industry of the manufacturing States is, in fact, discouragement to ours, was not made without due deliberation. It is susceptible of the clearest proof. We cultivate certain great staples for the supply of the general market of the world: — They manufacture almost exclusively for the home market. Their object in the Tariff is to keep down foreign competition, in order to obtain a monopoly of the domestic market. The effect on us is, to compel us to purchase at a higher price, both what we obtain from them and from others, without receiving a correspondent increase in the price of what we sell.

. . . But this oppression, as great as it is, will not stop at this point. The trade between us and Europe has, heretofore, been a mutual exchange of products. Under the existing duties, the consumption of European fabrics must, in a great measure, cease in our country; and the trade must become, on their part, a cash transaction. He must be ignorant of the principles of commerce, and the policy of Europe, particularly England, who does not see that it is impossible to carry on a trade of such vast extent on any other basis than barter; and that, if it were not so carried on, it would not long be tolerated. We already see indications of the commencement of a commercial warfare, the termination of which no one can conjecture, — though our fate may easily be. The last remains of our great and once flourishing agriculture must be annihilated in the conflict. In the first instance, we will be thrown on the home market, which cannot consume a fourth of our products. ...

The committee having presented its views on the partial and oppressive operation of the system, will proceed to discuss the next position which they proposed, — its tendency to corrupt the Government, and to destroy the liberty of the country.

If there be a political proposition universally true, — one which springs directly from the nature of man, and is independent of circumstances, — it is, that irresponsible power is inconsistent with liberty, and must corrupt those who exercise it. On this great principle our political system rests.

The committee has demonstrated that the present disordered state of our political system originated in the diversity of interests which exists in the country; — a diversity recognized by the Constitution itself, and to which it owes one of its most distinguished and peculiar features, — the division of the delegated powers between the State and General Governments. ... In drawing the line between the powers of the two — the General and State Governments — the great difficulty consisted in determining correctly to which of the two the various political powers ought to belong. This difficult task was, however, performed with so much success that, to this day, there is an almost entire acquiescence in the correctness with which the line was drawn. It would be extraordinary if a system, thus resting with such profound wisdom on the diversity of geographical interests among the States, should make no provision against the dangers to which its very basis might be exposed. The framers of our Constitution have not exposed themselves to the imputation of such weakness. When their work is fairly examined, it will be found that they have provided, with admirable skill, the most effective remedy; and that, if it has not prevented the danger with which the system is now threatened, the fault is not theirs, but ours, in neglecting to make its proper application. In the primary division of the sovereign powers, and in their exact and just classification, as stated, are to be found the first provisions or checks against the abuse of authority on the part of the absolute majority. The powers of the General Government are particularly enumerated and specifically delegated; and all powers not expressly delegated, or which are not necessary and proper to carry into effect those that are so granted, are reserved expressly to the States or the people. The

Government is thus positively restricted to the exercise of those general powers that were supposed to act uniformly on all the parts, — leaving the residue to the people of the States, by whom alone, from the very nature of these powers, they can be justly and fairly exercised, as has been stated.

In order to have a full and clear conception of our institutions, it will be proper to remark that there is, in our system, a striking distinction between *Government* and *Sovereignty*. The separate governments of the several States are vested in their Legislative, Executive, and Judicial Departments; while the sovereignty resides in the people of the States respectively. The powers of the General Government are also vested in its Legislative, Executive, and Judicial Departments, while the sovereignty resides in the people of the several States who created it. But, by an express provision of the Constitution, it may be amended or changed by three fourths of the States; and thus each State, by assenting to the Constitution with this provision, has modified its original right as a sovereign, of making its individual consent necessary to any change in its political condition; and, by becoming a member of the Union, has placed this important power in the hands of three fourths of the States, — in whom the highest power known to the Constitution actually resides. Not the least portion of this high sovereign authority resides in Congress, or any of the departments of the General Government. They are but the creatures of the Constitution, and are appointed but to execute its provisions; and, therefore, any attempt by all, or any of these departments, to exercise any power which, in its consequences, may alter the nature of the instrument, or change the condition of the parties to it, would be an act of usurpation.

If we look to the history and practical operation of the system, we shall find, on the side of the States, no means resorted to in order to protect their reserved rights against the encroachments of the General Government; while the latter has, from the beginning, adopted the most efficient to prevent the States from encroaching on those delegated to them. The 25th section of the Judiciary Act, passed in 1789, — immediately after the Constitution went into operation, — provides for an appeal from the State courts to the Supreme Court of the United States in all cases, in the decision of which, the construction of the Constitution, — the laws of Congress, or treaties of the United States may be involved; thus giving to that high tribunal the right of final interpretation, and the power, in reality, of nullifying the acts of the State Legislatures whenever, in their opinion, they may conflict with the powers delegated to the General Government. A more ample and complete protection against the encroachments of the governments of the several States cannot be imagined; and to this extent the power may be considered as indispensable and constitutional. But, by a strange misconception of the nature of our system, — and, in fact, of the nature of government, — it has been regarded as the ultimate power, not only of protecting the General Government against the encroachments of the governments of the States, but also of the encroachments of the former on the latter; — and as being, in fact, the only means provided by the Constitution of confining all the powers of the system to their proper constitutional spheres; and, consequently, of determining the limits assigned to each. Such a construction of its powers would, in fact, raise one of the departments of the General Government above the parties who created the constitutional compact, and virtually invest it with the authority to alter, at its pleasure, the relative powers of the General and State Governments, on the distribution of which, as established by the Constitution, our whole system rests; — and which, by an express provision of the instrument, can only be altered by three fourths of the States, as has already been shown. It would go farther. Fairly considered, it would, in effect, divest the people of the States of the sovereign authority, and clothe that department with the robe [sic] of supreme power. A position more false and fatal cannot be conceived. Fortunately, it has been so ably refuted by Mr. Madison, in his Report to the Virginia Legislature in 1800, on the Alien and Sedition Acts, as to supersede the necessity of further comments on the part of the committee. Speaking of the right of the State to interpret the Constitution for itself, in the last resort, he remarks: — "It has been objected that the Judicial Authority is to be regarded as the sole expositor of the Constitution. On this objection, it might be observed, — *first* — that there may be instances of usurped power" (the case of the Tariff is a striking illustration of the truth), "which the forms of the Constitution could never draw within the control of the Judicial Department; — *secondly*, — that if the decision of the Judiciary be raised above the authority of the sovereign parties to the Constitution, the decision of the other departments, not carried by the forms of the Constitution before the Judiciary, must be equally authoritative and final with the decision of that department. But the proper answer to the objection is, that the resolution of the General Assembly relates to those great and extraordinary cases in which the forms of the Constitution may prove ineffectual against the infractions dangerous to the essential rights of the parties to it. The resolution supposes that dangerous powers not delegated, may not only be usurped and exercised by the other departments, but that the Judicial Department also may exercise or sanction dangerous powers beyond the grant of the Constitution; and consequently, that the ultimate right of the parties to the Constitution to judge whether the compact has been dangerously violated, must extend to violations by one delegated authority as well as by another; by the Judiciary as well as by the Executive or the Legislative. However true, therefore, it may be that the Judicial Department is, in all questions submitted to it by the forms of the Constitution, to decide in the last resort, this resort must necessarily be considered the last in relation to the authorities of the other departments of the Government; not in relation to the rights of the parties to the constitutional compact, from which the Judicial and all other departments hold their delegated trusts. On any other hypothesis the delegation of judicial power would annul the authority delegating it; and the concurrence of this department with others in usurped powers might subvert for ever, and beyond the possible reach of any rightful remedy, the very Constitution which all were instituted to preserve."

If it be conceded, as it must be by every one who is the least conversant with our institutions, that the sovereign powers delegated are divided between the General and State Governments, and that the latter hold their portion by the same tenure as the former, it would seem impossible to deny to the States the right of deciding on the infractions of their powers, and the proper remedy to be applied for their correction. The right of judging, in such cases, is an essential attribute of sovereignty, — of which the States cannot be divested without losing their sovereignty itself, — and being reduced to a subordinate corporate condition. In fact, to divide power, and to give to one of the parties the exclusive right of judging of the portion allotted to each, is, in reality, not to divide it at all; and to reserve such exclusive right to the General Government (it matters not by what department to be exercised), is to convert it, in fact, into a great consolidated government, with unlimited powers, and to divest the States, in reality, of all their rights. ... But the existence of the right of judging of their powers, so clearly established from the sovereignty of States, as clearly implies a veto or control, within its limits, on the action of the General Government, on contested points of authority; and this very control is the remedy which the Constitution has provided to prevent the encroachments of the General Government on the reserved rights of the States; and by which the distribution of power, between the General and State Governments, may be preserved for ever inviolable, on the basis established by the Constitution. It is thus effectual protection is afforded to the minority, against the oppression of the majority. Nor does this important conclusion stand on the deduction of reason alone. It is sustained by the highest contemporary authority. Mr. Hamilton, in the number of the Federalist already cited, remarks that, — "in a single republic, all the power surrendered by the people is submitted to the administration of a single government; and usurpations are guarded against, by a division of the government into distinct and separate departments. In the compound republic of America, the power surrendered by the people is first divided between two distinct governments, and then the portion allotted to each subdivided among distinct and separate departments. Hence a double security arises to the rights of the people. The different governments will control each other; at the same time that each will be controlled by itself." He thus clearly affirms the control of the States over the General Government, which he traces to the division in the exercise of the sovereign powers under our political system; and by comparing this control to the veto, which the departments in most of our constitutions respectively exercise over the acts of each other, clearly indicates it as his opinion, that the control between the General and State Governments is of the same character. Mr. Madison is still more explicit. In his report, already alluded to, in speaking on this subject, he remarks; — "The resolutions, having taken this view of the Federal compact, proceed to infer that, in cases of a deliberate, palpable, and dangerous exercise of other powers, not granted by the said compact, the States, who are parties thereto, have the right, and are in duty bound to interpose to arrest the evil, and for maintaining, within their respective limits, the authorities, rights, and liberties appertaining to them. .... The Constitution of the United States was formed by the sanction of the States, given by each in its sovereign capacity. It adds to the stability and dignity, as well as to the authority of the Constitution, that it rests on this solid foundation. The States, then, being parties to the constitutional compact, and in their sovereign capacity, it follows of necessity that there can be no tribunal above their authority to decide, in the last resort, whether the compact made by them be violated; and, consequently, as parties to it, they must themselves decide, in the last resort, such questions as may be of sufficient magnitude to require their interposition." To these the no less explicit opinions of Mr. Jefferson may be added; who, in the Kentucky resolutions on the same subject, which have always been attributed to him, states that — "The Government, created by this compact, was not made the exclusive or final judge of the extent of the powers delegated to itself; since that would have made its discretion, and not the Constitution, the measure of its powers; — but, as in all other cases of compact between parties having no common judge, each party has an equal right to judge for itself, as well of infractions as of the mode and measure of redress."

The committee have thus arrived, by what they deem conclusive reasoning, and the highest authority, at the constitutional and appropriate remedy against the unconstitutional oppression under which this, in common with the other staple States, labors, — and the menacing danger which now hangs over the liberty and happiness of our country; — and this brings them to the inquiry, — How is the remedy to be applied by the States? In this inquiry a question may be made, — whether a State can interpose its sovereignty through the ordinary Legislature, but which the committee do not deem it necessary to investigate. It is sufficient that plausible reasons may be assigned against this mode of action, if there be one (and there is one) free from all objections. Whatever doubts may be raised as to the question, — whether the respective Legislatures fully represent the sovereignty of the States for this high purpose, there can be none as to the fact that a Convention fully represents them for all purposes whatever. Its authority, therefore, must remove every objection as to form, and leave the question on the single point of the right of the States to interpose at all. When convened, it will belong to the Convention itself to determine, authoritatively, whether the acts of which we complain be unconstitutional; and, if so, whether they constitute a violation so deliberate, palpable, and dangerous, as to justify the interposition of the State to protect its rights. If this question be decided in the affirmative, the Convention will then determine in what manner they ought to be declared null and void within the limits of the State; which solemn declaration, based on her rights as a member of the Union, would be obligatory, not only on her own citizens, but on the General Government itself; and thus place the violated rights of the State under the shield of the Constitution.

Webster-Hayne Debate on Foot's Resolution
Excerpt from Hayne's Second Speech

Robert Y. Hayne

Commentary

When South Carolina legislators adopted the *Protest*, some were ready to do more than simply declare their authority to nullify unconstitutional congressional legislation. They were ready to *exercise* that authority by calling a convention to nullify the Tariff of Abominations. The majority, however, believed that with Jackson now in the White House, Congress would repeal the tariff, and all would be well.

The tariff continued to be the law of the land, and Southerners could not rally enough congressional support to repeal it. Tensions mounted in the nation's capitol as Southern bitterness intensified and Northerners became increasingly alarmed about the threat of nullification. It was inevitable that a bitter sectional debate was going to occur. The only question was when.

In December, 1829, Senator Foot of Connecticut introduced a resolution to limit the sale of Western lands. The Federal government had long been selling lands, thereby raising revenue for itself and enabling thousands of poor Americans along the seaboard to get a fresh start in the rapidly developing West. Benton of Missouri led Western senators in opposing the resolution. He gave an emotional speech in which he argued that the proposal was an Eastern plot to restrict Western development and to keep oppressed Northeastern industrial workers from finding a new life in the West. Realizing that Southern help was needed to defeat the resolution, he openly invited the South to forge an alliance with the West against the Northeast. The ultimate result was a protracted debate in which Foot's Resolution was almost forgotten as sectional hostilities were expressed. Amidst this verbal free-for-all came one of the most famous Senate debates in American history — the Webster-Hayne debate in January, 1830.

Realizing that the South needed Western help in repealing the tariff, Senator Robert Y. Hayne (1791-1839), one of Calhoun's most outspoken disciples from South Carolina, openly accepted Benton's invitation. On January 19, 1830, he attacked not only Foot's resolution, but also the traditional policy of selling lands for enriching the Federal Treasury. The policy, he said, drained the West of wealth to enrich the central government, and this wealth was used by corrupt forces controlling the government to benefit the North. He said that States should be allowed to control their own lands. This argument led him to a defense of States rights in general and nullification in particular. Throughout his oration, he took potshots at the Northeast, especially its "disloyalty" during the War of 1812.

Although Foot's Resolution was not a high-priority item among Northern senators, they were incensed by attacks on their region. They were alarmed at the prospect of a Western-Southern alliance which, if consummated, would mean repeal of the tariff and relegate the North to minority status. On the day after Hayne's speech, the newly elected (but well-known) senator from Massachusetts, Daniel Webster, gave his first reply to Hayne. His major objective was to woo the West, which he did first by recounting at length the Northeast's undying devotion to that section. Knowing that most Westerners deplored Calhoun's doctrine of nullification, he then launched into a lengthy attack on it.

With the issue of nullification now in the forefront, the Senate debate had become a public debate. Newspapers were reporting it throughout the country. When Hayne arose to give his second speech, the galleries were packed. In a long speech, he ranged over a variety of sectional issues. He charged the North with trying to destroy the South, noting especially Northern opposition to slavery and its recent success in establishing a protective tariff. He concluded by returning to nullification, which he claimed was consistent with the doctrine of two revered ex-presidents, Jefferson and Madison. The following excerpt from his conclusion is reproduced photographically from David J. Brewer, *World's Best Orations* (St. Louis: Ferd. P. Kaiser, 1901), vol. 7, pp. 2441-2448.

Excerpt from Hayne's Second Speech

THE Senator from Massachusetts, in denouncing what he is pleased to call the Carolina doctrine, has attempted to throw ridicule upon the idea that a State has any constitutional remedy, by the exercise of its sovereign authority, against "a gross, palpable, and deliberate violation of the Constitution." He calls it "an idle" or "ridiculous notion," or something to that effect, and adds that it would make the Union "a mere rope of sand." Now, sir, as the gentleman has not condescended to enter into any examination of the question and has been satisfied with throwing the weight of his authority into the scale, I do not deem it necessary to do more than to throw into the opposite scale the authority on which South Carolina relies; and there, for the present, I am perfectly willing to leave the controversy. The South Carolina doctrine, that is to say, the doctrine contained in an exposition reported by a committee of the legislature in December 1828, and published by their authority, is the good old Republican doctrine of 1798 — the doctrine of the celebrated 'Virginia Resolutions' of that year, and of 'Madison's Report' of 1799. It will be recollected that the legislature of Virginia, in December 1798, took into consideration the Alien and Sedition Laws, then considered by all Republicans as a gross violation of the Constitution of the United States, and on that day passed, among others, the following resolutions: —

"The General Assembly doth explicitly and peremptorily declare that it views the powers of the Federal Government as resulting from the compact to which the States are parties, as limited by the plain sense and intention of the instrument constituting that compact, as no further valid than they are authorized by the grants enumerated in that compact; and that in case of a deliberate, palpable, and dangerous exercise of other powers not granted by the said compact, the States who are parties thereto have the right, and are in duty bound, to interpose for arresting the progress of the evil, and for maintaining, within their respective limits, the authorities, rights, and liberties appertaining to them."

In addition to the above resolution, the General Assembly of Virginia "appealed to the other States, in the confidence that they would concur with that Commonwealth that the acts aforesaid [the Alien and Sedition Laws] are unconstitutional, and that the necessary and proper measures would be taken by each for co-operating with Virginia in maintaining, unimpaired, the authorities, rights, and liberties reserved to the States respectively, or to the people."

The legislatures of several of the New England States having, contrary to the expectation of the legislature of Virginia, expressed their dissent from these doctrines, the subject came up again for consideration during the session of 1799–1800, when it was referred to a select committee, by whom was made that celebrated report which is familiarly known as 'Madison's Report,' and which deserves to last as long as the Constitution itself. In that report, which was subsequently adopted by the legislature, the whole subject was deliberately re-examined, and the objections urged against the Virginia doctrines carefully considered. The result was that the legislature of Virginia reaffirmed all the principles laid down in the resolutions of 1798, and issued to the world that admirable report which has stamped the character of Mr. Madison as the preserver of that Constitution which he had contributed so largely to create and establish. I will here quote from Mr. Madison's Report one or two passages which bear more immediately on the point in controversy: —

"The resolution, having taken this view of the Federal compact, proceeds to infer 'that in case of a deliberate, palpable, and dangerous exercise of other powers not granted by the said compact, the States who are parties thereto have the right and are in duty bound, to interpose for arresting the progress of the evil, and for maintaining within their respective limits the authorities, rights, and liberties appertaining to them.'

"It appears to your committee to be a plain principle, founded in common sense, illustrated by common practice, and essential to the nature of compacts, that, where resort can be had to no tribunal, superior to the authority of the parties, the parties themselves must be the rightful judges in the last resort whether the bargain made has been pursued or violated. The Constitution of the United States was formed by the sanction of the States, given by each in its sovereign capacity. It adds to the stability and dignity, as well as to the authority of the Constitution, that it rests upon this legitimate and solid foundation. The States, then, being the parties to the constitutional compact, and in their sovereign capacity, it follows of necessity that there can be no tribunal above their authority, to decide, in the last resort, whether the compact made by them be violated; and, consequently, that, as the parties to it, they must themselves decide, in the last resort, such questions as may be of sufficient magnitude to require their interposition.

"The resolution has guarded against any misapprehension of its object by expressly requiring for such an interposition 'the case of a deliberate, palpable, and dangerous breach of the Constitution, by the exercise of powers not granted by it.' It must be a case, not of a light and transient nature, but of a nature dangerous to the great purposes for which the Constitution was established.

"But the resolution has done more than guard against misconstruction by expressly referring to cases of a deliberate, palpable, and dangerous nature. It specifies the object of the interposition which it contemplates to be solely that of arresting the progress of the evil of usurpation, and of maintaining the authorities, rights, and liberties appertaining to the States, as parties to the Constitution.

"From this view of the resolution it would seem inconceivable that it can incur any just disapprobation from those who, laying aside all momentary impressions, and recollecting the genuine source and object of the Federal Constitution, shall candidly and accurately interpret the meaning of the General Assembly. If the deliberate exercise of dangerous powers, palpably withheld by the Constitution, could not justify the parties to it in interposing, even so far as to arrest the progress of the evil, and thereby to preserve the Constitution itself, as well as to provide for the safety of the parties to it, there would be an end to all relief from usurped power, and a direct subversion of the rights specified or recognized under all the State constitutions, as well as a plain denial of the fundamental principles on which our independence itself was declared.»

But, sir, our authorities do not stop here. The State of Kentucky responded to Virginia, and on the tenth of November, 1798, adopted those celebrated resolutions, well known to have been penned by the author of the Declaration of American Independence. In those resolutions, the legislature of Kentucky declare that —

« The Government created by this compact was not made the exclusive or final judge of the extent of the powers delegated to itself, since that would have made its discretion, and not the Constitution, the measure of its powers; but that, as in all other cases of compact among parties having no common judge, each party has an equal right to judge for itself as well of infractions as of the mode and measure of redress.»

At the ensuing session of the legislature, the subject was reexamined, and on the fourteenth of November, 1799, the resolutions of the preceding year were deliberately reaffirmed, and it was, among other things, solemnly declared: —

« That if those who administer the General Government be permitted to transgress the limits fixed by that compact, by a total disregard to the special delegations of power therein contained, an annihilation of the State governments, and the erection upon their ruins of a general consolidated government, will be the inevitable consequence. That the principles of construction contended for by sundry of the State legislatures, that the General Government is the exclusive judge of the extent of the powers delegated to it, stop nothing short of despotism; since the discretion of those who administer the Government, and not the Constitution, would be the measure of their powers. That the several States who formed that instrument, being sovereign and independent, have the unquestionable right to judge of its infraction, and that a nullification by those sovereignties of all unauthorized acts done under color of that instrument is the rightful remedy.»

Time and experience confirmed Mr. Jefferson's opinion on this all-important point. In the year 1821 he expressed himself in this emphatic manner: —

« It is a fatal heresy to suppose that either our State governments are superior to the Federal, or the Federal to the State; neither is authorized literally to decide which belongs to itself or its copartner in government. In differences of opinion between their different sets of public servants, the appeal is to neither, but to their employers peaceably assembled by their representatives in convention. »

The opinion of Mr. Jefferson on this subject has been so repeatedly and so solemnly expressed, that it may be said to have been among the most fixed and settled convictions of his mind.

In the protest prepared by him for the legislature of Virginia, in December 1825, in respect to the powers exercised by the Federal Government in relation to the tariff and internal improvements, which he declares to be "usurpations of the powers retained by the States, mere interpolations into the compact, and direct infractions of it," he solemnly reasserts all the principles of the Virginia Resolutions of 1798 — protests against "these acts of the Federal branch of the Government as null and void, and declares that, although Virginia would consider a dissolution of the Union as among the greatest calamities that could befall them, yet it is not the greatest. There is one yet greater — submission to a government of unlimited powers. It is only when the hope of this shall become absolutely desperate that further forbearance could not be indulged. »

In his letter to Mr. Giles, written about the same time, he says: —

« I see, as you do, and with the deepest affliction, the rapid strides with which the Federal branch of our Government is advancing towards the usurpation of all the rights reserved to the States, and the consolidation in itself of all powers, foreign and domestic, and that, too, by constructions which leave no limits to their powers, etc. Under the power to regulate commerce, they assume, indefinitely, that also over agriculture and manufactures, etc. Under the authority to establish post-roads, they claim that of cutting down mountains for the construction of roads and digging canals, etc. And what is our resource for the preservation of the Constitution? Reason and argument? You might as well reason and argue with the marble columns encircling them, etc. Are we then to stand to our arms with the hot-headed Georgian? No [and I say no, and South Carolina has said no]; that must be the last resource. We must have patience and long endurance with our brethren, etc., and separate from our companions only when the sole alternatives left are a dissolution of our union with them, or submission to a government without limitation of powers. Between these two evils, when we must make a choice, there can be no hesitation.»

Such, sir, are the high and imposing authorities in support of the « Carolina doctrine,» which is, in fact, the doctrine of the Virginia resolutions of 1798.

Sir, at that day the whole country was divided on this very question. It formed the line of demarcation between the Federal and Republican parties; and the great political revolution which then took place turned upon the very question involved in these resolutions. That question was decided by the people, and by that decision the Constitution was, in the emphatic language of Mr. Jefferson, « saved at its last gasp.» I should suppose, sir, it would require more self-respect than any gentleman here would be willing to assume, to treat lightly doctrines derived from such high sources. Resting on authority like this, I will ask gentlemen whether South Carolina has not manifested a high regard for the Union, when, under a tyranny ten times more grievous than the Alien and Sedition Laws she has hitherto gone no further than to petition, to remonstrate, and to solemnly protest against a series of measures which she believes to be wholly unconstitutional and utterly destructive of her interests. Sir, South Carolina has not gone one step further than Mr. Jefferson himself was disposed to go in relation to the present subject of our present complaints; not a step further than the statesmen from New England were disposed to go under similar circumstances; no further than the Senator from Massachusetts himself once considered as within « the limits of a constitutional opposition.» The doctrine that it is the right of a State to judge of the violations of the Constitution on the part of the Federal Government, and to protect her citizens from the operations of unconstitutional laws, was held by the enlightened citizens of Boston, who assembled in Faneuil Hall on the twenty-fifth of January, 1809. They state, in that celebrated memorial, that « they looked only to the State legislature, who were competent to devise relief against the unconstitutional acts of the General Government. That your power [say they] is adequate to that object is evident from the organization of the confederacy.»

A distinguished Senator from one of the New England States [Mr. Hillhouse], in a speech delivered here on a bill for enforcing the Embargo, declared: —

« I feel myself bound in conscience to declare (lest the blood of those who shall fall in the execution of this measure shall be on my head) that I consider this to be an act which directs a mortal blow at the liberties of my country—an act containing unconstitutional provisions to which the people are not bound to submit, and to which, in my opinion, they will not submit.»

And the Senator from Massachusetts himself, in a speech delivered on the same subject in the other House, said:—

« This opposition is constitutional and legal; it is also conscientious. It rests on settled and sober conviction that such policy is destructive to the interests of the people and dangerous to the being of government. The experience of every day confirms these sentiments. Men who act from such motives are not to be discouraged by trifling obstacles, nor awed by any dangers. They know the limit of constitutional opposition; up to that limit, at their own discretion, they will walk, and walk fearlessly.»

How "the being of the Government" was to be endangered by "constitutional opposition" to the Embargo, I leave to the gentleman to explain.

Thus it will be seen, Mr. President, that the South Carolina doctrine is the Republican doctrine of 1798; that it was promulgated by the fathers of the faith; that it was maintained by Virginia and Kentucky in the worst of times; that it constituted the very pivot on which the political revolution of that day turned; that it embraces the very principles, the triumph of which at that time saved the Constitution at its last gasp, and which New England statesmen were not unwilling to adopt when they believed themselves to be the victims of unconstitutional legislation. Sir, as to the doctrine that the Federal Government is the exclusive judge of the extent as well as the limitations of its powers, it seems to me to be utterly subversive of the sovereignty and independence of the States. It makes but little difference, in my estimation, whether Congress or the Supreme Court are invested with this power. If the Federal Government in all or any of its departments is to prescribe the limits of its own authority, and the States are bound to submit to the decision and are not to be allowed to examine and decide for themselves when the barriers of the Constitution shall be overleaped, this is practically " a government without limitation of powers." The States are at once reduced to mere petty corporations, and the people are entirely at your mercy. I have but one word more to add. In all the efforts that have been made by South Carolina to resist the unconstitutional laws which Congress has extended over them, she has kept steadily in view the preservation of the Union by

the only means by which she believes it can be long preserved —
a firm, manly, and steady resistance against usurpation. The
measures of the Federal Government have, it is true, prostrated
her interests, and will soon involve the whole South in irretrievable ruin. But even this evil, great as it is, is not the chief
ground of our complaints. It is the principle involved in the
contest — a principle, which, substituting the discretion of Congress
for the limitations of the Constitution, brings the States and the
people to the feet of the Federal Government, and leaves them
nothing they can call their own. Sir, if the measures of the Federal Government were less oppressive, we should still strive against
this usurpation. The South is acting on a principle she has always held sacred — resistance to unauthorized taxation. These,
sir, are the principles which induced the immortal Hampden to
resist the payment of a tax of twenty shillings. Would twenty
shillings have ruined his fortune ? No! but the payment of half
twenty shillings, on the principle on which it was demanded,
would have made him a slave. Sir, if in acting on these high
motives — if animated by that ardent love of liberty which has
always been the most prominent trait in the Southern character
— we should be hurried beyond the bounds of a cold and calculating prudence, who is there with one noble and generous sentiment in his bosom that would not be disposed, in the language
of Burke, to exclaim: "You must pardon something to the spirit
of liberty!"

Webster-Hayne Debate on Foot's Resolution
Excerpt from Webster's Second Speech

Daniel Webster

Commentary

A few days after Hayne's second speech, Webster arose in the packed Senate chamber to deliver his final reply. He opened with a little humor. He had Foot's resolution read to the audience and remarked that Hayne's speech, which occupied the greater part of two days, had covered "everything, general or local, whether belonging to national politics, or party politics... save only the resolution before the Senate. He has spoken of everything but the public lands."

What Webster said about Hayne's speech was equally true of his own. He spent a long time reviewing the North's stand on slavery, emphasizing that, although it opposed the expansion of slavery, it had done nothing to interfere with slavery where it currently existed. He reviewed the North's support of the West on internal improvements and the sale of public lands. He discussed the tariff, trying especially to justify his shift from opposing the tariff of 1824 to supporting it in 1828. He claimed that New England had been President Washington's most loyal supporter and justified New England's behavior during the War of 1812. Then, like Hayne, he returned to nullification in his conclusion, which is reproduced photographically from David J. Brewer, *World's Best Orations* (St. Louis: Ferd. P. Kaiser, 1901), vol. 7, pp. 3804-3828.

Excerpt from Webster's Second Speech

There yet remains to be performed, Mr. President, by far the most grave and important duty, which I feel to be devolved on me by this occasion. It is to state and to defend what I conceive to be the true principles of the Constitution under which we are here assembled. I might well have desired that so weighty a task should have fallen into other and abler hands. I could have wished that it should have been executed by those whose character and experience give weight and influence to their opinions, such as cannot possibly belong to mine. But, sir, I have met the occasion, not sought it; and I shall proceed to state my own sentiments, without challenging for them any particular regard, with studied plainness and as much precision as possible.

I understand the honorable gentleman from South Carolina to maintain that it is a right of the State legislatures to interfere, whenever, in their judgment, this Government transcends its constitutional limits, and to arrest the operation of its laws.

I understand him to maintain this right; as a right existing under the Constitution, not as a right to overthrow it on the ground of extreme necessity, such as would justify violent revolution.

I understand him to maintain an authority, on the part of the States, thus to interfere, for the purpose of correcting the exercise of power by the General Government, of checking it and of compelling it to conform to their opinion of the extent of its powers.

I understand him to maintain that the ultimate power of judging of the constitutional extent of its own authority is not lodged exclusively in the General Government or any branch of it; but that, on the contrary, the States may lawfully decide for themselves, and each State for itself, whether in a given case the act of the General Government transcends its power.

I understand him to insist that if the exigency of the case, in the opinion of any State government, require it, such State government may, by its own sovereign authority, annul an act of the General Government which it deems plainly and palpably unconstitutional.

This is the sum of what I understand from him to be the South Carolina doctrine, and the doctrine which he maintains. I propose to consider it and compare it with the Constitution. Allow me to say as a preliminary remark that I call this the South Carolina doctrine only because the gentleman himself has so denominated it. I do not feel at liberty to say that South Carolina, as a State, has ever advanced these sentiments. I hope she has not and never may. That a great majority of her people are opposed to the tariff laws is doubtless true. That a majority somewhat less than that just mentioned conscientiously believe these laws unconstitutional may probably also be true. But that any majority holds to the right of direct State interference, at State discretion, the right of nullifying acts of Congress, by acts of State legislation, is more than I know and what I shall be slow to believe.

That there are individuals besides the honorable gentleman who do maintain these opinions is quite certain. I recollect the recent expression of a sentiment, which circumstances attending its utterance and publication justify us in supposing was not unpremeditated. " The sovereignty of the State — never to be controlled, construed, or decided on, but by her own feelings of honorable justice. "

[Mr. Hayne here rose and said that for the purpose of being clearly understood, he would state that his proposition was in the words of the Virginia Resolution as follows: —

"That this assembly doth explicitly and peremptorily declare that it views the powers of the Federal Government as resulting from the compact to which the States are parties, as limited by the plain sense and intention of the instrument constituting that compact, as no further valid than they are authorized by the grants enumerated in that compact; and that, in case of a deliberate, palpable, and dangerous exercise of other powers, not granted by the said compact, the States who are parties thereto have the right and are in duty bound to interpose, for arresting the progress of the evil and for maintaining within their respective limits the authorities, rights, and liberties appertaining to them."]

I am quite aware, Mr. President, of the existence of the resolution which the gentleman read and has now repeated, and that he relies on it as his authority. I know the source, too, from which it is understood to have proceeded. I need not say that I have much respect for the constitutional opinions of Mr. Madison; they would weigh greatly with me always. But, before the authority of his opinion be vouched for the gentleman's proposition, it will be proper to consider what is the fair interpretation of that resolution to which Mr. Madison is understood to have given his sanction. As the gentleman construes it, it is an authority for him. Possibly he may not have adopted the right construction. That resolution declares that in the case of the dangerous exercise of powers not granted by the General Government, the States may interpose to arrest the progress of the evil. But how interpose, and what does this declaration purport? Does it mean no more than that there may be extreme cases in which the people in any mode of assembling may resist usurpation and relieve themselves from a tyrannical government? No one will deny this. Such resistance is not only acknowledged to be just in America, but in England also. Blackstone admits as much in the theory and practice, too, of the English Constitution. We, sir, who oppose the Carolina doctrine do not deny that the people may, if they choose, throw off any government when it becomes oppressive and intolerable, and erect a better in its stead. We all know that civil institutions are established for the public benefit and that when they cease to answer the ends of their existence they may be changed. But I do not understand the doctrine now contended for to be that which, for the sake of distinctness, we may call the right of revolution. I understand the gentleman to maintain that, without revolution, without civil commotion, without rebellion, a remedy for supposed abuse and transgression of the powers of the General Government lies in a direct appeal to the interference of the State governments.

[Mr. Hayne here rose. He did not contend, he said, for the mere right of revolution, but for the right of constitutional resistance. What he maintained was that, in case of a plain, palpable violation of the Constitution by the General Government, a State may interpose, and that this interposition is constitutional.]

So, sir, I understood the gentleman, and am happy to find that I did not misunderstand him. What he contends for is that it is constitutional to interrupt the administration of the Constitution itself in the hands of those who are chosen and sworn to administer it by the direct inference in form of law of the States in virtue of their sovereign capacity. The inherent right in the people to reform their Government I do not deny; and they have another right and that is to resist unconstitutional laws without overturning the Government. It is no doctrine of mine that unconstitutional laws bind the people. The great question is: Whose prerogative is it to decide on the constitutionality or unconstitutionality of the laws? On that the main debate hinges. The proposition that, in case of a supposed violation of the Constitution by Congress, the States have a constitutional right to interfere and annul the law of Congress, is the proposition of the gentleman: I do not admit it. If the gentleman had intended no more than to assert the right of revolution for justifiable cause, he would have said only what all agree to. But I cannot conceive that there can be a middle course between submission to the laws, when regularly pronounced constitutional on the one hand, and open resistance, which is revolution or rebellion on the other. I say the right of a State to annul a law of Congress cannot be maintained but on the ground of the unalienable right of man to resist oppression; that is to say, upon the ground of revolution. I admit that there is an ultimate violent remedy above the Constitution and in defiance of the Constitution, which may be resorted to when a revolution is to be justified. But I do not admit that under the Constitution, and in conformity with it, there is any mode in which a State government, as a member of the Union, can interfere and stop the progress of the General Government, by force of her own laws, under any circumstances whatever.

This leads us to inquire into the origin of this Government and the source of its power. Whose agent is it? Is it the creature of the State legislatures, or the creature of the people? If the Government of the United States be the agent of the State governments, then they may control it, provided they can agree in the manner of controlling it; if it be the agent of the people, then the people alone can control it, restrain it, modify, or reform it. It is observable enough that the doctrine for which the honorable gentleman contends leads him to the necessity of maintaining, not only that this General Government is the creature of the States, but that it is the creature of each of the States severally; so that each may assert the power for itself of determining whether it acts within the limits of its authority. It is the servant of four and twenty masters, of different wills and different purposes, and yet bound to obey all. This absurdity (for it seems no less) arises from a misconception as to the origin of this Government and its true character. It is, sir, the people's Constitution, the people's Government; made for the people, made by the people, and answerable to the people. The people of the United States have declared that this Constitution shall be the supreme law. We must either admit the proposition, or dispute their authority. The States are, unquestionably, sovereign, so far as their sovereignty is not affected by this supreme law. But the State legislatures, as political bodies, however sovereign, are yet not sovereign over the people. So far as the people have given power to the General Government, so far the grant is unquestionably good, and the Government holds of the people, and not of the State governments. We are all agents of the same supreme power, the people. The General Government and the State governments derive their authority from the same source. Neither can, in relation to the other, be called primary, though one is definite and restricted and the other general and residuary. The National Government possesses those powers which it can be shown the people have conferred on it, and no more. All the rest belong to the State governments or to the people themselves. So far as the people have restrained State sovereignty, by the expression of their will, in the Constitution of the United States, so far, it must be admitted, State sovereignty is effectually controlled. I do not contend that it is, or ought to be, controlled further. The sentiment to which I have referred propounds that State sovereignty is only to be controlled by its own "feeling of justice"; that is to say, it is not to be controlled at all; for one who is to follow his own feelings is under no legal control. Now, however men may think this ought to be, the fact is that the people of the United States have chosen to impose control on State sovereignties. There are those, doubtless, who wish they had been left without restraint; but the Constitution has ordered the matter differently. To make war, for instance, is an exercise of sovereignty; but the Constitution declares that no State shall make war. To coin money is another exercise of sovereign power; but no State is at liberty to coin money. Again, the Constitution says that no sovereign State shall be so sovereign as to make a treaty. These prohibitions, it must be confessed, are a control on the State sovereignty of South Carolina, as well as of the other States, which does not arise "from her own feelings of honorable justice." Such an opinion, therefore, is in defiance of the plainest provisions of the Constitution.

There are other proceedings of public bodies which have already been alluded to, and to which I refer again for the purpose of ascertaining more fully what is the length and breadth of that doctrine, denominated the Carolina doctrine, which the honorable Member has now stood upon this floor to maintain. In one of them I find it resolved that "the tariff of 1828, and every other tariff designed to promote one branch of industry at the expense of others, is contrary to the meaning and intention of the Federal compact; and is such a dangerous, palpable and deliberate usurpation of power, by a determined majority, wielding the General Government beyond the limits of its delegated powers, as calls upon the States which compose the suffering minority, in their sovereign capacity, to exercise the powers which, as sovereigns, necessarily devolve upon them when their compact is violated."

Observe, sir, that this resolution holds the tariff of 1828, and every other tariff, designed to promote one branch of industry at the expense of another, to be such a dangerous, palpable and deliberate usurpation of power, as calls upon the States, in their sovereign capacity, to interfere by their own authority. This denunciation, Mr. President, you will please to observe, includes our old tariff of 1816, as well as all others; because that was established to promote the interest of the manufactures of cotton, to the manifest and admitted injury of the Calcutta cotton trade. Observe, again, that all the qualifications are here rehearsed and charged upon the tariff, which are necessary to bring the case within the gentleman's proposition. The tariff is a usurpation; it is a dangerous usurpation; it is a palpable usurpation; it is a deliberate usurpation. It is such a usurpation, therefore, as calls upon the States to exercise their right of interference. Here is a case, then, within the gentleman's principles, and all his qualifications of his principles. It is a case for action. The Constitution is plainly, dangerously, palpably and deliberately violated; and the States must interpose their own authority to arrest the law. Let us suppose the State of South Carolina to express this same opinion by the voice of her legislature. That would be very imposing; but what then? Is the voice of one State conclusive? It so happens that at the very moment when South Carolina resolves that the tariff laws are unconstitutional, Pennsylvania and Kentucky resolve exactly the reverse. They hold those laws to be both highly proper and strictly constitutional. And now, sir, how does the honorable Member propose to deal with this case? How does he relieve us from this difficulty upon any principle of his? His construction gets us into it; how does he propose to get us out?

In Carolina the tariff is a palpable, deliberate usurpation; Carolina, therefore, may nullify it, and refuse to pay the duties. In Pennsylvania it is both clearly constitutional and highly expedient; and there the duties are to be paid. And yet we live under a Government of uniform laws, and under a Constitution, too, which contains an express provision, as it happens, that all duties shall be equal in all the States. Does not this approach absurdity?

If there be no power to settle such questions, independent of either of the States, is not the whole Union a rope of sand? Are we not thrown back again precisely upon the old confederation?

It is too plain to be argued. Four-and-twenty interpreters of constitutional law, each with a power to decide for itself, and none with authority to bind anybody else, and this constitutional law the only bond of their union! What is such a state of things but a mere connection during pleasure, or, to use the phraseology of the times, during feeling? And that feeling, too, not the feeling of the people, who established the Constitution, but the feeling of the State governments.

In another of the South Carolina addresses, having premised that the crisis requires " all the concentrated energy of passion, " an attitude of open resistance to the laws of the Union is advised. Open resistance to the laws, then, is the constitutional remedy, the conservative power of the State, which the South Carolina doctrines teach for the redress of political evils, real or imaginary. And its authors further say that, appealing with confidence to the Constitution itself to justify their opinions, they cannot consent to try their accuracy by the courts of justice. In one sense, indeed, sir, this is assuming an attitude of open resistance in favor of liberty. But what sort of liberty? The liberty of establishing their own opinions, in defiance of the opinions of all others; the liberty of judging and of deciding exclusively themselves, in a matter in which others have as much right to judge and decide as they; the liberty of placing their own opinions above the judgment of all others, above the laws, and above the Constitution. This is their liberty, and this is the fair result of the proposition contended for by the honorable gentleman. Or it may be more properly said, it is identical with it, rather than a result from it.

In the same publication we find the following: —

"Previously to our Revolution, when the arm of oppression was stretched over New England, where did our Northern brethren meet with a braver sympathy than that which sprang from the bosoms of Carolinians? We had no extortion, no oppression, no collision with the king's ministers, no navigation interests springing up in envious rivalry of England."

This seems extraordinary language. South Carolina no collision with the king's ministers in 1775! No extortion! No oppression! But, sir, it is also most significant language. Does any man doubt the purpose for which it was penned? Can any one fail to see that it was designed to raise in the reader's mind the question whether, at this time, — that is to say, in 1828, — South Carolina has any collision with the king's ministers, any oppression, or extortion to fear from England? Whether, in short, England is not as naturally the friend of South Carolina, as New England with her navigation interests springing up in envious rivalry of England?

Is it not strange, sir, that an intelligent man in South Carolina in 1828 should thus labor to prove that in 1775 there was no hostility, no cause of war between South Carolina and England? That she had no occasion in reference to her own interest, or from a regard to her own welfare, to take up arms in the revolutionary contest? Can any one account for the expression of such strange sentiments and their circulation through the State, otherwise than by supposing the object to be what I have already intimated, to raise the question if they had no "collision" (mai k the expression) with the ministers of King George III., in 1775, what collision have they in 1828 with the ministers of King George IV.? What is there now in the existing state of things to separate Carolina from Old more, or rather, than from New England?

Resolutions, sir, have been recently passed by the legislature of South Carolina. I need not refer to them; they go no further than the honorable gentleman himself has gone,—and, I hope, not so far. I content myself, therefore, with debating the matter with him.

And now, sir, what I have first to say on this subject is that at no time and under no circumstances has New England or any State in New England, or any respectable body of persons in New England, or any public man of standing in New England, put forth such a doctrine as this Carolina doctrine.

The gentleman has found no case, he can find none, to support his own opinions by New England authority. New England has studied the Constitution in other schools and under other teachers. She looks upon it with other regards, and deems more highly and reverently both of its just authority and its utility and excellence. The history of her legislative proceedings may be traced — the ephemeral effusions of temporary bodies, called together by the excitement of the occasion, may be hunted up — they have been hunted up. The opinions and votes of her public men, in and out of Congress, may be explored — it will all be in vain. The Carolina doctrine can derive from her neither countenance nor support. She rejects it now; she always did reject it; and till she loses her senses, she always will reject it. The honorable Member has referred to expressions on the subject of the Embargo law made in this place by an honorable and venerable gentleman [Mr. Hillhouse] now favoring us with his presence. He quotes that distinguished Senator as saying that, in his judgment, the Embargo law was unconstitutional, and that, therefore, in his opinion the people were not bound to obey it. That, sir, is perfectly constitutional language. An unconstitutional law is not binding; but then it does not rest with a resolution or a law of a State legislature to decide whether an act of Congress be or be not constitutional. An unconstitutional act of Congress would not bind the people of this district, although they have no legislature to interfere in their behalf; and, on the other hand, a constitutional law of Congress does bind the citizens of every State, although all their legislatures should undertake to annul it by act or resolution. The venerable Connecticut Senator is a constitutional lawyer of sound principles and enlarged knowledge; a statesman practiced and experienced, bred in the company of Washington, and holding just views upon the nature of our governments. He believed the Embargo unconstitutional, and so did others; but what then? Who did he suppose was to decide that question? The State legislatures? Certainly not. No such sentiment ever escaped his lips. Let us follow up, sir, this New England opposition to the Embargo laws; let us trace it till we discern the principle which controlled and governed New England throughout the whole course of that opposition. We shall then see what similarity there is between the New England school of constitutional opinions and this modern Carolina school. The gentleman, I think, read a petition from some single individual, addressed to the legislature of Massachusetts, asserting the Carolina doctrine,—that is, the right of State interference to arrest the laws of the Union. The fate of that petition shows the sentiment of the legislature. It met no favor. The opinions of Massachusetts were otherwise. They had been expressed in 1798 in answer to the resolutions of Virginia, and she did not depart from them, nor bend them to the times. Misgoverned, wronged, oppressed as she felt herself to be, she still held fast her integrity to the Union. The gentleman may find in her proceedings much evidence of dissatisfaction with the measures of government, and great and deep dislike to the Embargo; all this makes the case so much the stronger for her; for notwithstanding all this dissatisfaction and dislike, she claimed no right, still, to sever asunder the bonds of the Union. There was heat and there was anger in her political feeling. Be it so! Her heat or her anger did not, nevertheless, betray her into infidelity to the Government. The gentleman labors to prove that she disliked the Embargo as much as South Carolina dislikes the tariff, and expressed her dislike as strongly. Be it so; but did she propose the Carolina remedy?—did she threaten to interfere, by State authority, to annul the laws of the Union? That is the question for the gentleman's consideration.

No doubt, sir, a great majority of the people of New England conscientiously believed the Embargo law of 1807 unconstitutional; as conscientiously, certainly, as the people of South Carolina hold that opinion of the tariff. They reasoned thus: Congress has power to regulate commerce; but here is a law, they said, stopping all commerce, and stopping it indefinitely. The law is perpetual; that is, it is not limited in point of time, and must, of course, continue until it shall be repealed by some other law. It is as perpetual therefore, as the law against treason or murder. Now, is this regulating commerce or destroying it? Is it guiding, controlling, giving the rule to commerce, as a subsisting thing; or is it putting an end to it altogether? Nothing is more certain than that a majority in New England deemed this law a violation of the Constitution. The very case required by the gentleman to justify State interference had then arisen. Massachusetts believed this law to be "a deliberate, palpable, and dangerous exercise of a power not granted by the Constitution." Deliberate it was, for it was long continued; palpable, she thought it, as no words in the Constitution gave the power, and only a construction, in her opinion most violent, raised it; dangerous it was, since it threatened utter ruin to her most important interests. Here, then, was a Carolina case. How did Massachusetts deal with it? It was, as she thought, a plain, manifest, palpable violation of the Constitution, and it brought ruin to her doors. Thousands of families, and hundreds of thousands of individuals were beggared by it. While she saw and felt all this, she saw and felt also that, as a measure of national policy, it was perfectly futile; that the country was no way benefited by that which caused so much individual distress; that it was efficient only for the production of evil, and all that evil inflicted on ourselves. In such a case, under such circumstances, how did Massachusetts demean herself? Sir, she remonstrated, she memorialized, she addressed herself to the General Government, not exactly "with the concentrated energy of passion," but with her own strong sense and the energy of sober conviction. But she did not interpose the arm of her own power to arrest the law and break the Embargo. Far from it. Her principles bound her to two things; and she followed her principles, lead where they might. First, to submit to every constitutional law of Congress, and, secondly, if the constitutional validity of the law be doubted, to refer that question to the decision of the proper tribunals. The first principle is vain and ineffectual without the second. A majority of us in New England believed the Embargo law unconstitutional; but the great question was, and always will be, in such cases: Who is to decide this? Who is to judge between the people and the Government? And, sir, it is quite plain that the Constitution of the United States confers on the Government itself, to be exercised by its appropriate department, and under its own responsibility to the people, this power of deciding ultimately and conclusively upon the just extent of its own authority. If this had not been done, we should not have advanced a single step beyond the old confederation.

Being fully of opinion that the Embargo law was unconstitutional, the people of New England were yet equally clear in the opinion,— it was a matter they did not doubt upon,— that the question, after all, must be decided by the judicial tribunals of the United States. Before those tribunals, therefore, they brought the question. Under the provisions of the law they had given bonds to millions in amount, and which were alleged to be forfeited. They suffered the bonds to be sued, and thus raised the question. In the old-fashioned way of settling disputes, they went to law. The case came to hearing and solemn argument; and he who espoused their cause and stood up for them against the validity of the Embargo Act was none other than that great man of whom the gentleman has made honorable mention, Samuel Dexter. He was then, sir, in the fullness of his knowledge and the maturity of his strength. He had retired from long and distinguished public service here, to the renewed pursuit of professional duties; carrying with him all that enlargement and expansion, all the new strength and force, which an acquaintance with the more general subjects discussed in the national councils is capable of adding to professional attainment in a mind of true greatness and comprehension. He was a lawyer and he was also a statesman. He had studied the Constitution, when he filled public station, that he might defend it; he had examined its principles that he might maintain them. More than all men, or at least as much as any man, he was attached to the General Government and to the Union of the States. His feelings and opinions all ran in that direction. A question of Constitutional law, too, was, of all subjects, that one which was best suited to his talents and learning. Aloof from technicality, and unfettered by artificial rule, such a question gave opportunity for that deep and clear analysis, that mighty grasp of principle, which so much distinguished his higher efforts. His very statement was argument; his inference seemed demonstration. The earnestness of his own conviction wrought conviction in others. One was convinced, and believed, and assented, because it was gratifying, delightful, to think and feel and believe in unison with an intellect of such evident superiority.

Mr. Dexter, sir, such as I have described him, argued the New England cause. He put into his effort his whole heart, as well as all the powers of his understanding; for he had avowed, in the most public manner, his entire concurrence with his neighbors on the point in dispute. He argued the cause; it was lost, and New England submitted. The established tribunals pronounced the law constitutional, and New England acquiesced. Now, sir, is not this the exact opposite of the doctrine of the gentleman from South Carolina? According to him, instead of referring to the judicial tribunals, we should have broken up the Embargo by laws of our own; we should have repealed it *quoad* New England; for we had a strong, palpable, and oppressive case. Sir, we believed the Embargo unconstitutional; but still that was matter of opinion, and who was to decide it? We thought it a clear case; but, nevertheless, we did not take the law into our own hands because we did not wish to bring about a revolution, nor to break up the Union: for I maintain that, between submission to the decision of the constituted tribunals and revolution, or disunion, there is no middle ground,— there is no ambiguous condition, half allegiance, and half rebellion. And, sir, how futile, how very futile it is to admit the right of State interference, and then attempt to save it from the character of unlawful resistance by adding terms of qualification to the causes and occasions, leaving all these qualifications, like the case itself, in the discretion of the State governments. It must be a clear case, it is said, a deliberate case; a palpable case; a dangerous case. But then the State is still left at liberty to decide for herself what is clear, what is deliberate, what is palpable, what is dangerous. Do adjectives and epithets avail anything? Sir, the human mind is so constituted that the merits of both sides of a controversy appear very clear and very palpable to those who respectively espouse them; and both sides usually grow clearer as the controversy advances. South Carolina sees unconstitutionality in the tariff; she sees oppression there also; and she sees danger. Pennsylvania, with a vision not less sharp, looks at the same tariff, and sees no such thing in it,— she sees it all constitutional, all useful, all safe. The faith of South Carolina is strengthened by opposition, and she now not only sees, but resolves that the tariff is palpably unconstitutional, oppressive, and dangerous; but Pennsylvania, not to be behind her neighbors, and equally willing to strengthen her own faith by a confident asseveration, resolves, also, and gives to every warm affirmative of South Carolina a plain, downright, Pennsylvania negative. South Carolina, to show the strength and unity of her opinion, brings her assembly to a unanimity within seven voices; Pennsylvania, not to be outdone in this respect more than others, reduces her dissentient fraction to a single vote. Now, sir, again I ask the gentleman what is to be done? Are these States both right? Is he bound to consider them both right? If not, which is in the wrong? or rather, which has the best right to decide? And if he and if I are not to know what the Constitution means and what it is till those two State legislatures and the twenty-two others shall agree in its construction, what have we sworn to when we have sworn to maintain it? I was forcibly struck, sir, with one reflection as the gentleman went on in his speech. He quoted Mr. Madison's resolutions, to prove that a State may interfere, in a case of deliberate, palpable, and dangerous exercise of a power not granted. The honorable Member supposes the tariff law to be such an exercise of power; and that, consequently, a case has arisen in which the State may, if it see fit, interfere by its own law. Now it so happens, nevertheless, that Mr. Madison deems this same tariff law quite constitutional. Instead of a clear and palpable violation, it is, in his judgment, no violation at all. So that, while they use his authority for a hypothetical case, they reject it in the very case before them. All this, sir, shows the inherent — futility — I had almost used a stronger word — of conceding this power of interference to the States, and then attempting to secure it from abuse by imposing qualifications, of which the States themselves are to judge. One of two things is true: either the laws of the Union are beyond the discretion and beyond the control of the States, or else we have no Constitution of General Government, and are thrust back again to the days of the Confederacy.

Let me here say, sir, that if the gentleman's doctrine had been received and acted upon in New England, in the times of the Embargo and Nonintercourse, we should probably not now have been here. The Government would very likely have gone to pieces, and crumbled into dust. No stronger case can ever arise than existed under those laws; no States can ever entertain a clearer conviction than the New England States then entertained; and if they had been under the influence of that heresy of opinion, as I must call it, which the honorable Member espouses, this Union would, in all probability, have been scattered to the four winds. I ask the gentleman, therefore, to apply his principles to that case; I ask him to come forth and declare whether, in his opinion, the New England States would have been justified in interfering to break up the Embargo system under the conscientious opinions which they held upon it? Had they a right to annul that law? Does he admit, or deny? If that which is thought palpably unconstitutional in South Carolina justifies that State in arresting the progress of the law, tell me whether that which was thought palpably unconstitutional also in Massachusetts would have justified her in doing the same thing? Sir, I deny the whole doctrine. It has not a foot of ground in the Constitution to stand on. No public man of reputation ever advanced it in Massachusetts, in the warmest times, or could maintain himself upon it there at any time.

I wish now, sir, to make a remark upon the Virginia Resolutions of 1798. I cannot undertake to say how these resolutions were understood by those who passed them. Their language is not a little indefinite. In the case of the exercise by Congress of a dangerous power not granted to them, the resolutions assert the right, on the part of the State, to interfere and arrest the progress of the evil. This is susceptible of more than one interpretation. It may mean no more than that the States may interfere by complaint and remonstrance, or by proposing to the people an alteration of the Federal Constitution. This would all be quite unobjectionable; or, it may be, that no more is meant than to assert the general right of revolution, as against all governments, in cases of intolerable oppression. This no one doubts; and this, in my opinion, is all that he who framed the resolutions could have meant by it: for I shall not readily believe that he was ever of opinion that a State, under the Constitution, and in conformity with it, could, upon the ground of her own opinion of its unconstitutionality, however clear and palpable she might think the case, annul a law of Congress, so far as it should operate on herself, by her own legislative power.

I must now beg to ask, sir, whence is this supposed right of the States derived?—where do they find the power to interfere with the laws of the Union? Sir, the opinion which the honorable gentleman maintains is a notion, founded in a total misapprehension, in my judgment, of the origin of this Government and of the foundation on which it stands. I hold it to be a popular Government, erected by the people; those who administer it, responsible to the people; and itself capable of being amended and modified, just as the people may choose it should be. It is as popular, just as truly emanating from the people, as the State governments. It is created for one purpose; the State governments for another. It has its own powers; they have theirs. There is no more authority with them to arrest the operation of a law of Congress than with Congress to arrest the operation of their laws. We are here to administer a Constitution emanating immediately from the people, and trusted by them to our administration. It is not the creature of the State governments. It is of no moment to the argument, that certain acts of the State legislatures are necessary to fill our seats in this body. That is not one of their original State powers, a part of the sovereignty of the State. It is a duty which the people, by the Constitution itself, have imposed on the State legislatures, and which they might have left to be performed elsewhere, if they had seen fit. So they have left the choice of President with electors; but all this does not affect the proposition, that this whole Government, President, Senate, and House of Representatives, is a popular Government. It leaves it still all its popular character. The governor of a State (in some of the States) is chosen, not directly by the people, but by those who are chosen by the people, for the purpose of performing, among other duties, that of electing a governor. Is the government of the State, on that account, not a popular government? This government, sir, is the independent offspring of the popular will. It is not the creature of State legislatures; nay, more, if the whole truth must be told, the people brought it into existence, established it, and have hitherto supported it, for the very purpose, amongst others, of imposing certain salutary restraints on State sovereignties. The States cannot now make war; they cannot contract alliances; they cannot make, each for itself, separate regulations of commerce; they cannot lay imposts; they cannot coin money. If this Constitution, sir, be the creature of State legislatures, it must be admitted that it has obtained a strange control over the volitions of its creators.

The people, then, sir, erected this Government. They gave it a Constitution, and in that Constitution they have enumerated the powers which they bestow on it. They have made it a limited Government. They have defined its authority. They have restrained it to the exercise of such powers as are granted; and all others, they declare, are reserved to the States or the people. But, sir, they have not stopped here. If they had, they would have accomplished but half their work. No definition can be so clear as to avoid possibility of doubt; no limitation so precise as to exclude all uncertainty. Who, then, shall construe this grant of the people? Who shall interpret their will, where it may be supposed they have left it doubtful? With whom do they repose this ultimate right of deciding on the powers of the Government? Sir, they have settled all this in the fullest manner. They have left it with the Government itself, in its appropriate branches. Sir, the very chief end, the main design, for which the whole Constitution was framed and adopted, was to establish a Government that should not be obliged to act through State agency, or depend on State opinion and State discretion. The people had had quite enough of that kind of Government under the Confederacy. Under that system the legal action — the application of law to individuals — belonged exclusively to the States. Congress could only recommend — their acts were not of binding force till the States had adopted and sanctioned them. Are we in that condition still? Are we yet at the mercy of State discretion and State construction? Sir, if we are, then vain will be our attempt to maintain the Constitution under which we sit.

But, sir, the people have wisely provided in the Constitution itself, a proper suitable mode and tribunal for settling questions of constitutional law. There are, in the Constitution, grants of powers to Congress, and restrictions on these powers. There are also prohibitions on the States. Some authority must therefore necessarily exist, having the ultimate jurisdiction to fix and ascertain the interpretation of these grants, restrictions, and prohibitions. The Constitution has itself pointed out, ordained, and established that authority. How has it accomplished this great and essential end? By declaring, sir, that "the Constitution and the laws of the United States, made in pursuance thereof, shall be the supreme law of the land, anything in the Constitution or laws of any State to the contrary notwithstanding."

This, sir, was the first great step. By this the supremacy of the Constitution and laws of the United States is declared. The people so will it. No State law is to be valid, which comes in conflict with the Constitution, or any law of the United States passed in pursuance of it. But who shall decide this question of interference? To whom lies the last appeal? This, sir, the Constitution itself decides also by declaring "that the judicial power shall extend to all cases arising under the Constitution and laws of the United States." These two provisions, sir, cover the whole ground. They are in truth the keystone of the arch. With these it is a Constitution; without them it is a Confederacy. In pursuance of these clear and express provisions, Congress established at its very first session in the judicial act a mode for carrying them into full effect and for bringing all questions of constitutional power to the final decision of the Supreme Court. It then, sir, became a Government. It then had the means of self-protection; and but for this it would, in all probability, have been now among things which are past. Having constituted the Government, and declared its powers, the people have further said, that since somebody must decide on the extent of these powers, the Government shall itself decide; subject always, like other popular governments, to its responsibility to the people. And now, sir, I repeat, how is it that a State legislature acquires any power to interfere? Who, or what, gives them the right to say to the people: "We, who are your agents and servants for one purpose, will undertake to decide that your other agents and servants, appointed by you for another purpose, have transcended the authority you gave them!" The reply would be, I think, not impertinent — "Who made you a judge over another's servants? To their own masters they stand or fall."

Sir, I deny this power of State legislatures altogether. It cannot stand the test of examination. Gentlemen may say that in an extreme case a State government might protect the people from intolerable oppression. Sir, in such a case, the people might protect themselves without the aid of the State Governments. Such a case warrants revolution. It must make, when it comes, a law for itself. A nullifying act of a State legislature cannot alter the case, nor make resistance any more lawful. In maintaining these sentiments, sir, I am but asserting the rights of the people. I state what they have declared, and insist on their right to declare it. They have chosen to repose this power in the General Government, and I think it my duty to support it, like other constitutional powers.

For myself, sir, I do not admit the jurisdiction of South Carolina, or any other State, to prescribe my constitutional duty; or to settle, between me and the people, the validity of laws of Congress for which I have voted. I decline her umpirage. I have not sworn to support the Constitution according to her construction of its clauses. I have not stipulated by my oath of office, or otherwise, to come under any responsibility except to the people and those whom they have appointed to pass upon the question, whether laws, supported by my votes, conform to the Constitution of the country. And, sir, if we look to the general nature of the case, could anything have been more preposterous than to make a Government for the whole Union, and yet leave its powers subject, not to one interpretation, but to thirteen or twenty-four interpretations? Instead of one tribunal, established by all, responsible to all, with power to decide for all, shall constitutional questions be left to four-and-twenty popular bodies, each at liberty to decide for itself, and none bound to respect the decisions of others; and each at liberty, too, to give a new construction on every new election of its own members? Would anything with such a principle in it, or rather with such a destitution of all principle, be fit to be called a Government? No, sir. It should not be denominated a Constitution. It should be called, rather, a collection of topics for everlasting controversy; heads of debate for a disputatious people. It would not be a government. It would not be adequate to any practical good, nor fit for any country to live under. To avoid all possibility of being misunderstood, allow me to repeat again in the fullest manner that I claim no powers for the Government by forced or unfair construction. I admit that it is a Government of strictly limited powers; of enumerated, specified, and particularized powers; and that whatsoever is not granted is withheld. But notwithstanding all this, and however the grant of powers may be expressed, its limit and extent may yet, in some cases, admit of doubt; and the General Government would be good for nothing, it would be incapable of long existing if some mode had not been provided in which those doubts, as they should arise, might be peaceably but authoritatively solved.

And now, Mr. President, let me run the honorable gentleman's doctrine a little into its practical application. Let us look at his probable *modus operandi*. If a thing can be done, an ingenious man can tell how it is to be done. Now I wish to be informed how this State interference is to be put in practice without violence, bloodshed, and rebellion. We will take the existing case of the tariff law. South Carolina is said to have made up her opinion upon it. If we do not repeal it (as we probably shall not), she will then apply to the case the remedy of her doctrine. She will, we must suppose, pass a law of her legislature declaring the several acts of Congress, usually called the tariff laws, null and void, so far as they respect South Carolina or the citizens thereof. So far all is a paper transaction, and easy enough. But the collector at Charleston is collecting the duties imposed by these tariff laws—he, therefore, must be stopped. The collector will seize the goods if the tariff duties are not paid. The State authorities will undertake their rescue; the marshal with his posse will come to the collector's aid, and here the contest begins. The militia of the State will be called out to sustain the nullifying act. They will march, sir, under a very gallant leader, for I believe the honorable Member himself commands the militia of that part of the State. He will raise the nullifying act on his standard, and spread it out as his banner! It will have a preamble bearing: "That the tariff laws are palpable, deliberate, and dangerous violations of the Constitution!" He will proceed, with this banner flying, to the customhouse in Charleston: —

> "All the while
> Sonorous metal blowing martial sounds."

Arrived at the customhouse, he will tell the collector that he must collect no more duties under any of the tariff laws. This he will be somewhat puzzled to say, by the way, with a grave countenance, considering what hand South Carolina herself had in that of 1816. But, sir, the collector would probably not desist at his bidding. He would show him the law of Congress, the Treasury instruction, and his own oath of office. He would say he should perform his duty, come what might. Here would ensue a pause: for they say that a certain stillness precedes the tempest. The trumpeter would hold his breath awhile, and before all this military array should fall on the customhouse, collector, clerks and all, it is very probable some of those composing it would request of their gallant commander in chief to be informed a little upon the point of law; for they have doubtless a just respect for his opinions as a lawyer, as well as for his bravery as a soldier. They know he has read Blackstone and the Constitution, as well as Turenne and Vauban. They would ask him, therefore, something concerning their rights in this matter. They would inquire whether it was not somewhat dangerous to resist a law of the United States. What would be the nature of their offense, they would wish to learn, if they by military force and array resisted the execution in Carolina of a law of the United States, and it should turn out, after all, that the law was constitutional? He would answer, of course, treason. No lawyer could give any other answer. John Fries, he would tell them, had learned that some years ago. How then, they would ask, do you propose to defend us? We are not afraid of bullets, but treason has a way of taking people off that we do not much relish. How do you propose to defend us? "Look at my floating banner," he would reply; "see there the nullifying law!" Is it your opinion, gallant commander, they would then say, that if we should be indicted for treason, that same floating banner of yours would make a good plea in bar? "South Carolina is a sovereign State," he would reply. That is true — but would the judge admit our plea? "These tariff laws," he would repeat, "are unconstitutional, palpably, deliberately, dangerously." That all may be so; but if the tribunal should not happen to be of that opinion, shall we swing for it? We are ready to die for our country, but it is rather an awkward business, this dying without touching the ground! After all, that is a sort of hemp tax worse than any part of the tariff.

Mr. President, the honorable gentleman would be in a dilemma like that of another great general. He would have a knot before him which he could not untie. He must cut it with his sword. He must say to his followers, Defend yourselves with your bayonets; and this is war — civil war.

Direct collision, therefore, between force and force is the unavoidable result of that remedy for the revision of unconstitutional laws which the gentleman contends for. It must happen in the very first case to which it is applied. Is not this the plain result? To resist, by force, the execution of a law generally is treason. Can the courts of the United States take notice of the indulgence of a State to commit treason? The common saying that a State cannot commit treason herself is nothing to the purpose. Can she authorize others to do it? If John Fries had produced an act of Pennsylvania annulling the law of Congress, would it have helped his case? Talk about it as we will, these doctrines go the length of revolution. They are incompatible with any peaceable administration of the Government. They lead directly to disunion and civil commotion; and, therefore, it is, that at their commencement, when they are first found to be maintained by respectable men, and in a tangible form, I enter my public protest against them all.

The honorable gentleman argues that if this Government be the sole judge of the extent of its own powers, whether that right of judging be in Congress, or the Supreme Court, it equally subverts State sovereignty. This the gentleman sees, or thinks he sees, although he cannot perceive how the right of judging, in this matter, if left to the exercise of State legislatures, has any tendency to subvert the Government of the Union. The gentleman's opinion may be, that the right ought not to have been lodged with the General Government; he may like better such a Constitution, as we should have under the right of State interference; but I ask him to meet me on the plain matter of fact; I ask him to meet me on the Constitution itself; I ask him if the power is not found there — clearly and visibly found there.

But, sir, what is this danger, and what the grounds of it? Let it be remembered that the Constitution of the United States is not unalterable. It is to continue in its present form no longer than the people who established it shall choose to continue it. If they shall become convinced that they have made an injudicious or inexpedient partition and distribution of power, between the State governments and the General Government, they can alter that distribution at will.

If anything be found in the national Constitution, either by original provision, or subsequent interpretation, which ought not to be in it, the people know how to get rid of it. If any construction be established, unacceptable to them, so as to become, practically, a part of the Constitution, they will amend it, at their own sovereign pleasure: but while the people choose to maintain it, as it is; while they are satisfied with it, and refuse to change it, who has given, or who can give, to the State legislatures a right to alter it, either by interference, construction, or otherwise? Gentlemen do not seem to recollect that the people have any power to do anything for themselves; they imagine there is no safety for them any longer than they are under the close guardianship of the State legislatures. Sir, the people have not trusted their safety, in regard to the General Constitution, to these hands. They have required other security, and taken other bonds. They have chosen to trust themselves, first, to the plain words of the instrument, and to such construction as the Government itself, in doubtful cases, should put on its own powers, under their oaths of office, and subject to their responsibility to them; just as the people of a State trust their own State governments with a similar power. Secondly, they have reposed their trust in the efficacy of frequent elections, and in their own power to remove their own servants and agents, whenever they see cause. Thirdly, they have reposed trust in the judicial power, which, in order that it might be trustworthy, they have made as respectable, as disinterested, and as independent as was practicable. Fourthly, they have seen fit to rely, in case of necessity, or high expediency, on their known and admitted power, to alter or amend the Constitution, peaceably and quietly, whenever experience shall point out defects or imperfections. And, finally, the people of the United States have, at no time, in no way, directly or indirectly, authorized any State legislature to construe or interpret their high instrument of government; much less to interfere, by their own power, to arrest its course and operation.

If, sir, the people, in these respects, had done otherwise than they have done, their Constitution could neither have been preserved, nor would it have been worth preserving. And, if its plain provisions. shall now be disregarded, and these new doctrines interpolated in it, it will become as feeble and helpless a being as its enemies, whether early or more recent, could possibly desire. It will exist in every State, but as a poor dependent on State permission. It must borrow leave to be and it will be no longer than State pleasure or State discretion sees fit to grant the indulgence and to prolong its poor existence.

But, sir, although there are fears, there are hopes also. The people have preserved this, their own chosen Constitution, for forty years and have seen their happiness, prosperity and renown grow with its growth, and strengthen with its strength. They are now, generally, strongly attached to it. Overthrown by direct assault, it cannot be; evaded, undermined, nullified, it will not be, if we, and those who shall succeed us here, as agents and representatives of the people, shall conscientiously and vigi-

lantly discharge the two great branches of our public trust —
faithfully to preserve and wisely to administer it.

Mr. President, I have thus stated the reasons of my dissent to
the doctrines which have been advanced and maintained. I am
conscious of having detained you and the Senate much too long.
I was drawn into the debate with no previous deliberation such
as is suited to the discussion of so grave and important a subject. But it is a subject of which my heart is full, and I have
not been willing to suppress the utterance of its spontaneous sentiments. I cannot, even now, persuade myself to relinquish it
without expressing once more, my deep conviction, that since it
respects nothing less than the Union of the States, it is of most
vital and essential importance to the public happiness. I profess, sir, in my career, hitherto, to have kept steadily in view the
prosperity and honor of the whole country, and the preservation
of our Federal Union. It is to that Union we owe our safety at
home and our consideration and dignity abroad. It is to that
Union that we are chiefly indebted for whatever makes us most
proud of our country. That Union we reached only by the discipline of our virtues in the severe school of adversity. It had
its origin in the necessities of disordered finance, prostrate commerce and ruined credit. Under its benign influence, these great
interests immediately awoke as from the dead and sprang forth
with newness of life. Every year of its duration has teemed
with fresh proofs of its utility and its blessings; and, although
our territory has stretched out wider and wider, and our population spread further and further, they have not outrun its protection or its benefits. It has been to us all a copious fountain of
national, social and personal happiness. I have not allowed myself, sir, to look beyond the Union to see what might lie hidden
in the dark recess behind. I have not coolly weighed the chances
of preserving liberty when the bonds that unite us together shall
be broken asunder. I have not accustomed myself to hang over
the precipice of disunion to see whether, with my short sight, I
can fathom the depth of the abyss below; nor could I regard him
as a safe counselor in the affairs of this Government, whose
thoughts should be mainly bent on considering not how the
Union should be best preserved, but how tolerable might be the
condition of the people when it shall be broken up and destroyed.
While the Union lasts we have high, exciting, gratifying prospects spread out before us, for us and our children. Beyond that
I seek not to penetrate the veil. God grant that in my day, at
least, that curtain may not rise. God grant that, on my vision,
never may be opened what lies behind. When my eyes shall be

turned to behold, for the last time, the sun in heaven, may I not see him shining on the broken and dishonored fragments of a once glorious Union; on States dissevered, discordant, belligerent; on a land rent with civil feuds, or drenched, it may be, in fraternal blood! Let their last feeble and lingering glance rather behold the gorgeous ensign of the Republic, now known and honored throughout the earth, still full high advanced, its arms and trophies streaming in their original lustre, not a stripe erased or polluted, nor a single star obscured, bearing for its motto no such miserable interrogatory as, "What is all this worth?" nor those other words of delusion and folly, "Liberty first and union afterwards"; but everywhere, spread all over in characters of living light, blazing on all its ample folds, as they float over the sea and over the land, and in every wind under the whole heavens, that other sentiment, dear to every true American heart — Liberty and Union, now and forever one and inseparable!

Confession of a Convert

Samuel L. Boicourt

Samuel L. Boicourt

Commentary

Calhoun's doctrine of nullification failed to get much favorable response outside South Carolina, but sectionalism intensified during the 1830s. Increased antislavery rhetoric in the North alienated the South far more than a tariff reduction pacified it. Yet Jacksonian Democrats managed to gain support in all sections. The first, and perhaps most important, reason is that their rhetoric continued to emphasize their dedication to the common man at a time when more and more States were abolishing property qualifications for voting and, thus, turning more and more common men into voters. While the nation's population doubled in the years between 1828 and the Civil War, the number of voters tripled. Second, Jacksonians utilized the most efficient media, forgetting pamphlets (which had been a major medium in the eighteenth century but which common men of the nineteenth century rarely read). They relied on partisan newspapers and stump speeches. Third, Jackson reflected dominant public opinion by generally favoring States rights but vigorously opposing Calhoun's doctrine of nullification. Fourth, the Jacksonian party was well organized at the local and State levels. It began holding national conventions in 1831. The first convention was simply to select a vice-presidential candidate to replace the incumbent Calhoun (who was unacceptable to Jackson). The new system enabled it to survive Jackson's retirement. Now called the "Democratic party" or "The Democracy" (words with egalitarian appeal), it nominated Martin Van Buren for the presidency in 1836, rallied behind him in a well-run campaign and was victorious once again.

Meanwhile, Jackson's opponents had trouble getting organized and adapting to the rhetorical revolution that was going on. Despite his defeat in 1828, John Q. Adams refused to form a political party. Nevertheless congressional leaders who believed in strong government, such as Webster and Clay, formed a new "National Republican" party in 1831-1832 and nominated Clay for president. The party's name reflects its rhetorical traditionalism. Although "republican" was a god term which dated back to the Jeffersonians, "national" reflected the party's commitment to a strong central government much too clearly to attract a majority of the nation's voters. National Republicans focused on the issues, especially the National Bank, which Congress had rechartered shortly before the election but which was killed by Jackson's veto. Jacksonian rhetoric about the "Monster Bank" and its greedy supporters was integrated easily into its common man appeal. National Republicans failed to adapt well to the new media. Although they established some partisan newspapers and did a little stump speaking, they did so to a lesser extent than the Jacksonians and continued to rely heavily on pamphlets.

Gradually adapting to the new situation between the elections of 1832 and 1836, the party changed its name to "Whig," a word that was denotatively meaningless but connotatively rich because of its identification with the "whig patriots" of the Revolution. It downplayed ideology as it sought support from all kinds of anti-Jacksonians, including pro- and antislavery people, pro- and antiprotectionists and both people who were for and against the National Bank. It flirted with egalitarianism as it incorporated remnants of the short-lived Anti-Masonic party, which had devoted itself during the late 1820s and early 1830s to abolishing secret societies. In 1836, the Whigs tried to avoid ideology by nominating for the presidency William Henry Harrison, who was not identified with any particular ideology. The tactic was not totally successful. Some New England protectionists insisted on supporting Daniel Webster while some strong backers of States rights campaigned for Hugh White.

An economic recession during Van Buren's presidency brightened the outlook for the Whigs as the election of 1840 approached. Whig leaders knew that they would have to borrow the rhetorical strategies of their Democratic enemies if they were to win. Being a coalition of people with diametrically opposed ideologies, Whigs were only in accord in that they disagreed with Van Buren's proposal to deposit government funds in government vaults (part of the Sub-Treasury bill). They knew this issue alone would not bring them victory. Consequently, their basic strategy was to divert public attention from anything as trivial as a substantive issue.

The strategy unfolded as they nominated William Henry Harrison (1773-1841) for president and John Tyler for vice-president. Tyler, a former Jacksonian, was nominated to make the ticket more palatable to discontented Democrats.

Although Harrison was the oldest presidential candidate to have been nominated prior to 1840, he was not well known as a politician and even less so as an ideologist. He had served only one term in the House of Representatives and his Senate term (beginning in 1825) was cut short when he resigned to accept a brief diplomatic post. Most of his career had been as governor of the Indiana Territory. He had become famous as an Indian fighter, especially as commander of the territorial militia at the famous Battle of Tippecanoe in 1811 and as commanding general of the Army of the Northwest during the War of 1812. During the 1830s, the elderly gentleman had been living on his estate at the north bend of the Ohio River. This made him a farmer, and Whigs saw the rhetorical potential of doing what their enemies had done earlier with Jackson: portraying him as a common man and a military hero.

Whig strategy was aided by a horrendous mistake made by an Eastern Democratic newspaper, which belittled Harrison's age and Western crudeness. It added: "Give him a barrel of hard cider, and settle a pension for two thousand a year, and take our word for it, he will sit the remainder of his days contented in a log cabin." Seizing upon this quotation, Whigs put pictures of Harrison's "log cabin" on everything in sight, including handbills and ribbons that supporters pinned on their coats. They used slogans such as "Tippecanoe and Tyler too." They blamed Van Buren for the recession and termed the Democrats' use of patronage the "spoils system," but they carefully avoided ideology. Rallies, complete with stump speeches, were highlighted by parades in which imitation log cabins were drawn through the streets on wagons. Cider was distributed, usually in containers shaped like log cabins. Journalists and speakers dubbed Harrison "The Farmer of North Bend," while Van Buren was called "the silk stocking aristocrat." They repeated poems such as, "Let Van from his coolers of silver drink wine/And sit on his cushioned settee/Our man on a buckeye bench can recline/Content with hard cider is he." Whigs printed song books with titles such as *The Tippecanoe Roarer*, and at rallies they sang songs such as "The Log Cabin Two-Step." They published campaign newspapers with titles such as the [Chicago] *Hard Cider Press* and *The* [New York] *Log Cabin*.

Caught off guard by Whig strategy and their own rhetorical blunder, Democrats protested that Whigs were turning the campaign into a farce. Whigs had a sharp retort, as is illustrated by a letter which is reproduced from the American Antiquarian Society's copy of the July 2, 1840 issue of *The* [Steubenville, Ohio] *Log Cabin Farmer*, p. 4.

Confession of a Convert

Louisville, May 19, 1840.

GENTLEMEN: I went on Saturday to the log cabin raising, as true a Van Burenite as ever fobbed a custom-house check, to see what fools intelligent Whigs were going to make of themselves to humbug ignorance.

But when, from Mr. Field's speech, I came to understand that the log cabin and hard cider cry was not got up by the Whigs, but had originated from scoffs and jeers in democratic newspapers, cracked off in derision of an old and estimable defender of his country, for being too poor to live in a palace and drink wine, I felt a little stumped.

Thinks I to myself, does honest poverty merit contempt? If he, who handled millions of public money, had been less honest, might he not have been more rich than some of his scoffers? — But again, thinks I, I am poorer than the General: wonder if I am an object of contempt to my rich brother democrats? And, sirs, I set to and saddled down a log. But now, thinks I again, I came here to hunt fools, and may be I'm making one of myself, and I'll quit and go home.

When I got home, I took a look at a likeness of Van Buren; it didn't seem to look as well as it used to. I took it down, washed its face, wiped its nose, and hung it up again; but all wouldn't do — he still smirked through his whiskers at me, just as a shallow fop does at a shoemaker. So I turned him face about and told him to OUT. And now, sirs, I am going with the 'log cabin dwelling-cider-drinker,' to battle against those palace-dwelling, champaigne-drinking democrats, with full confidence that, under the humble banner of the log cabin, the nation is to be rescued from the dominion of the spoilers. It was under the banner of the infamous cross, sirs, that the world was redeemed from the devil and his imps — a banner assumed by the followers of our blessed Lord in commemoration of the ignominious treatment to which he had been subjected by his unholy scoffers and persecutors.

SAMUEL L. BOICOURT
Shoemaker & Cobbler, Jefferson st., between
Third and Fourth streets.

Speech at Fort Meigs

William Henry Harrison

Commentary

Although the "Log Cabin" campaign is an extreme example, it demonstrates a tendency of campaign rhetoric that still persists: highlighting personal images (that are often inconsistent with reality) while de-emphasizing issues. It also illustrates what was then a new rhetorical genre: campaign speeches delivered by the candidate himself. Jackson had given a short speech in 1828, and Harrison had done a little campaigning on his own behalf in 1836, but 1840 marks the first time that a presidential candidate was an energetic campaign orator.

Harrison ran a risk by campaigning for himself. True, the old opposition to "party spirit" was now dead, and the old myth of "the office seeks the man" was in such ill health that candidates for local office in some of the Western States occasionally debated one another. Yet old myths die hard, and tradition dictated that public officials served as an obligation to the public, not to satisfy personal ambition. Harrison's campaigning had to be conducted carefully if he was to avoid appearing overly ambitious.

Instead of conducting campaign tours like those of our era, Harrison was invited to speak at public commemorations of his great military victories. As Old Tip went to and from these celebrations (not always by the most direct route) he consented to stop along the way to address the common folk. Because his military victories had been in the West, so too was his campaigning. A nationwide audience was reached by having Whig papers transcribe and publish the speeches.

The commemorations received considerable publicity. Although the partisan press doubtless exaggerated attendance figures, they were spectacular events. Harrison's most notable address was given on June 11, 1840, at Fort Meigs, where several thousand people gathered to commemorate one of his major victories during the War of 1812. Newspaper texts varied in a few minor details (probably because of stenographic errors). The following, which is derived from a stenographic report done for the *Detroit Advertiser,* is reproduced from the American Antiquarian Society's

315

copy of the June 27, 1840 edition of *The* [Albany and New York City] *Log Cabin*, pp. 1-2.

Speech at Fort Meigs

FELLOW-CITIZENS: — I am not, upon this occasion, before you in accordance with my own individual views or wishes. It has ever appeared to me, that the office of President of the United States should not be *sought* after by any individual; but that the people should, spontaneously, and with their own free will, accord the honor to the man whom they believed would best perform its important duties. Entertaining these views, I should, fellow-citizens, have remained at home, but for the pressing and friendly invitation which I have received from the citizens of Perrysburgh, and the earnestness with which its acceptance was urged upon me by friends in whom I trusted, and whom I am now proud to see around me. If, however, fellow-citizens, I had not complied with that invitation — if I had remained at home — believe me, my friends, that my spirit would have been with you; for where, in this beautiful land, is there a place, calculated as this is, to recall long past reminiscences, and revive slumbering, but not wholly extinguished, emotions in my bosom?

In casting my eyes around, fellow-citizens, they rest upon the spot where the gallant WAYNE triumphed so gloriously over his enemies, and carried out these principles which it seemed his pleasure to impress upon my mind, and in which it has ever been my happiness humbly to attempt to imitate him. It was there, fellow-citizens, I saw the banner of the United States float in triumph over the flag of the enemy. — There it was where was first laid the foundation of the prosperity of the now wide-spread and beautiful West. It was there I saw the indignant Eagle frown upon the British Lion. It was there I saw the youth of our land carry out the lesson they imbibed from the gallant Wayne — the noblest and the best an American can acquire — to die for his country when called to do so in its defence.

[At this moment the speaker's eye fell upon Gen. Hedges, when he said: "Gen. Hedges, will you come up here? You have stood by my side in the hour of battle, and I cannot bear to see you at such a distance now." Immense cheering followed this considerate recognition, and cries of "raise him up," "place him by the side of Gen. Harrison," had scarcely been uttered, when Gen. Hedges was carried forward to the stand.]

The General continued: It was there I saw interred my beloved companions — the companions of my youth. It was not in accordance with the stern etiquette of military life then to mourn their departure; but I now drop a tear over their graves, at the recollection of their virtues and worth.

In 1793, fellow-citizens, I received my commission to serve under Gen. Wayne. In 1794, I was his aid at the battle of the Miami. Nineteen years afterward, I had the honor of again being associated with many of those who were my companions in arms. Nineteen years afterwards, I found myself Commander-in-Chief of the North-Western Army; but I found no diminution in the bravery of the American soldier. I found the same spirit of valor in all — not in the regular soldier only, but in the enrolled militia and volunteer also.

What glorious reminiscences do the view of all these scenes around me recall to my mind! When I consented to visit this memorable spot, I expected that a thousand pleasant associations (would to God there were no plainful [sic] associations mingled with them) would be recalled — that I should meet thousands of my fellow-citizens here — and among them many of my old companions — met here to rear a new altar to liberty in the place of the one which bad men have prostrated.

[Here the General looked around as if for some water, when cry was raised, "give the General some hard cider." This was done, much to the satisfaction of the multitude.]

And, fellow-citizens, (continued the General,) I will not attempt to conceal from you, that, in coming here I expected that I should receive from you those evidences of regard which a generous people are ever willing to bestow upon those whom they believe to be honest in their endeavors to serve their country. I receive these evidences of regard and esteem as the only reward at all adequate to compensate for the anxieties and anguish which in the past, I experienced upon this spot. Is there any man of sensibility, or possessing a feeling of self-respect, who asks what those feelings were? Do you suppose that the Commander-in-Chief finds his reward in the glitter and splendor of the camp? or in the forced obedience of the masses around him? These are not pleasures under all circumstances — these are not the rewards which a soldier seeks. I ask any man to place himself in my situation, and then say whether the extreme pain and anguish which I endured, and which every person similarly situated must have endured, can meet with any adequate compensation, except by such expressions of the confidence and gratitude of the people, as that with which you, fellow-citizens, have this day honored me? These feelings are common to all commanders of sense and sensibility. The commanders of Europe possess them, although placed at the head of armies reared to war. How much more naturally would those feelings attach to a commander situated as I was? For of what materials was the army composed which was placed under my command? The soldiers who fought and bled and triumphed here, were lawyears [sic], who had thrown up their briefs, — physicians, who had laid aside their instruments — mechanics who had put up their tools — and, in far the largest proportions, agriculturalists, who had left their ploughs in the furrow, although their families depended for their bread upon their exertions, and who hastened to the battle-field to give their lives to their country if it were necessary, to maintain her rights. I could point from where I now stand, to places where I felt this anxiety pressing heavily upon me, as I thought of the fearful consequences of a mistake on my part, or the want of judgment in others. I knew there were wives who had given their husbands to the field — mothers who had clothed their sons for battle: and I knew that these expecting wives and mothers were looking for the [sic] safe return of their husbands and sons. When to this was added the recollection, that the peace of the entire West would be broken up, and the glory of my country tarnished if I failed, you may possibly conceive the anguish which my situation was calculated to produce. Feeling my responsibility, I personally supervised and directed the arrangements of the army under my command. I trusted to no Colonial or other officer. No person had any hand in any disposition of the army. Every step of warfare, whether for good or ill, was taken under my own direction, and of none other, as many who now hear me know. Whether every movement would, or would not, pass the criticism of Bonaparte or Wellington, I know not; but, whether they would induce applause or censure, upon myself it must fall.

But, fellow citizens, still another motive induced me to accept the invitation which had been so kindly extended to me. I knew that here I should meet with many who had fought and bled under my command — that I should have the pleasure of taking them by the hand, and recurring, with them, to the scenes of the past. I expected, too, to meet with a few of the great and good men yet surviving, by whose efforts our freedom was achieved. This pleasure alone would have been sufficient to have induced my visit to this interesting spot upon this equally interesting occasion. I see my old companions here, and I see not a few of the revolutionary veterans around me. Would to God that it had ever been in my power to have made them comfortable and happy — that their sun might go down in peace! But, fellow citizens, they remain unprovided for — monuments of the ingratitude of my country. It was with the greatest difficulty that the existing pension act was passed through Congress. But why was it restricted? Why were the brave soldiers who fought under Wayne excluded? — soldiers who suffered far more than they who fought in the revolution proper. The revolution, in fact, did not terminate until 1794 — until the battle was fought upon the battle-ground upon which my eye now rests (Miami.) War continued with them from the commencement of the revolution until the victory of Wayne, to which I have just alluded. The great highway to the West was the scene of unceasing slaughter. Then why this unjust discrimination? Why are the soldiers who terminated the war of the revolution, in fact, excluded, while those by whom it was begun, or a portion of them, are rewarded? I will tell you why. The poor remnant of Wayne's army had but few advocates, while those who had served in the revolution proper had plenty of friends. Scattered as they were over all parts of the Union, and in large numbers, they could exert an influence at the ballot-box. They could whisper thus in the ears of those who sought their influence at the polls: "Take care, for I have waited long enough for what has been promised. The former plea of poverty can no longer be made; the treasury is now full. Take care! — your seat is in danger." "Oh yes, every thing that has been promised shall be attended to, if you will give me your votes." In this way, fellow citizens, tardy, but partial, justice was done to the soldiers of the revolution. They made friends by their influence at the ballot-box. But it was different with Gen. Wayne's soldiers. They were but few in number, and they had but one or two humble advocates to speak for them in Congress. The result has been, justice has been withheld.

I have said that the soldiers under Wayne experienced greater hardships even than the soldiers of the revolution. This is so. Every one can appreciate the difference between an Indian and a regular war. When wounded in battle, the soldier must have warmth and shelter before he can recover. This could always be secured by the soldier of the revolution. In those days, the latch-string of no door was pulled in; when wounded, he was sure to find shelter and very many of those comforts which are so essential to the sick, but which the soldiers in an Indian war cannot procure. Instead of shelter and warmth, he is exposed to the thousand ills incident to Indian warfare. Yet no relief was extended to those who had thus suffered!

After the war closed under Wayne, I retired; and when I saw a man poorer than all others, wandering about the land, decrepit and decayed by intemperance, it was unnecessary to inquire whether he had ever belonged to Wayne's army. His condition was a guarantee of that — was a sufficient assurance that he had wasted his energies among the unwholesome swamps of the West, in the defence of the rights of his fellow citizens, and for the maintenance of the honor and glory of his country.

Well, fellow citizens, I can only say, that if it should ever be in my power to pay the debt which is due these brave but neglected men, that debt shall first of all be paid. And I am very well satisfied that the government can afford it, *provided the latch-string of the treasury shall ever be more carefully pulled in.* Perhaps you will ask me for some proof of my friendship for old soldiers. If so, I can give it you from the records of Congress. When the fifteen hundred dollar law was repealed, I opposed it, as I opposed changing the pay of members of Congress from six to eight dollars, until we had done justice to, and provided for, these soldiers. You will find my votes upon this question among the records of Congress, and my speech upon it in the published debates of the time.

I will now, fellow citizens, give you my reasons for having refused to give pledges and opinions more freely than I have done since my nomination to the Presidency. Many of the statements published on this subject are by no means correct; but it is true that it is my opinion that no pledge should be made by an individual when in nomination for any office in the gift of the People. And why? Once adopt it, and the battle will no longer be to the strong — to the virtuous — or to the sincere lover of his country; but to him who is prepared to tell the greatest number of lies, and to proffer the largest number of pledges which he never intends to carry out. I suppose that the best guarantee which an American citizen could have of the correctness of the conduct of an individual in the future, would be his conduct in the past, when he had no temptation before him to practice deceit.

Now, fellow citizens, I have not altogether grown grey under the helmet of my country, although I have worn it for some time. A large portion of my life has been passed in the civil departments of government. Examine my conduct there, and the most tenacious democrat — I use the word in its proper sense; I mean not to confine it to parties, for there are good in both — may, doubtless, discover faults, but he will find no single act calculated to derogate from the rights of the people.

However, to prove the reverse of this, I have been called a Federalist. [Here was a loud cry of "The charge is a lie — a base lie. You are no Federalist."] Well, what is a Federalist? I recollect what the word formerly signified, and there are many others present who recollect its former signification also. They know that the Federal party were accused of a design to strengthen the hands of the general government at the expense of the separate States. The accusation could not nor cannot apply to me. I was brought up after the strictest manner of Virginia Anti-Federalism. St. Paul himself was not a greater devotee to the doctrines of the Pharisees than was I, by inclination and a father's precepts and example, to Anti-Federalism. I was taught to believe that, sooner or later, that fatal catastrophe to human liberty would take place — that the general government would swallow up all the State governments, and that one department of the government would swallow up all the other departments. I do not know whether my friend Mr. Van Buren (and he is, and I hope ever will be, my personal friend) has a gullet that can swallow every thing; but I do know, that if his measures are all carried out, he will lay a foundation for others to do so, if he does not.

What reflecting man, fellow-citizens, cannot see this? The Representatives of the People were once the source of power. Is it so now? Nay. It is to the Executive mansion now that every eye is turned — that every wish is directed. The men of office and party, who are governed by the principles of John Randolph, to wit: the five loaves and two fishes, seem to have their ears constantly directed to the great bell at head quarters, to indicate how the little ones shall ring.

But to return, I have but to remark that my anti-Federalism has been tempered by my long service in the employ of my country, and my frequent oaths to support her General Government; but I am as ready to resist the encroachments on State rights as I am to support the legitimate authority of the Executive or General Government.

Now, fellow-citizens, I have very little more to say, except to exhort you to go on, peacefully if you can — and you can — to effect that reform upon which your hearts are fixed. What calamitous consequences will ensue to the world if you fail! If you should fail, how the tyrants of Europe will rejoice! If you fail, how will the friends of freedom, scattered, like the far planets of heaven, over the world, mourn, when they see the beacon-light of liberty extinguished — the light whose rays they had hoped would yet penetrate the whole benighted world!

If you triumph, it will only be done by vigilance and attention. Our personal friends, but political enemies, remind each other that 'Eternal vigilance is the price of Liberty.' While journeying thitherward I observed this motto waving at the head of a procession composed of the friends of the present Administration. From this I inferred that discrimination was necessary in order to know who to watch. Under Jefferson, Madison and

Monroe, the eye of the People was turned to the right source — to the Administration. The Administration, however, now says to the People 'You must not watch us, but you must watch the Whigs! Only do that, and all is safe!' But that, my friends, is not the way. The old-fashioned Republican rule is to watch the Government. See that the Government does not acquire too much power. Keep a check upon your rulers. Do this, and liberty is safe. And if your efforts should result successfully, and I should be placed in the Presidential chair, I shall invite a recurrence to the old Republican rule, to watch the Administration, and to condemn all its acts which are not in accordance with the strictest mode of Republicanism. Our rulers, fellow-citizens, must be watched. Power is insinuating. Few men are satisfied with less power than they are able to procure. If the ladies whom I see around me were near enough to hear me, and of sufficient age to give an experimental answer, they would tell you that no lover is ever satisfied with the first smile of his mistress.

It is necessary, therefore, to watch, not the political opponents of an Administration, but the Administration itself, and to see that it keeps within the bounds of the Constitution and the laws of the land. The Executive of this Union has immense power to do mischief, if he sees fit to exercise that power. He may prostrate the country. Indeed, this country has already been prostrated. It has already fallen from pure Republicanism to a Monarchy in spirit, if not in name. A colebrated[sic] author defines monarchy to be that form of government in which the Executive has at once the command of the army, the execution of the laws, and the control of the purse. Now, how is it with our present Executive? The Constitution gives to him the control of the army and the execution of the laws. He now only awaits the possession of the purse to make him a Monarch. Not a Monarch simply with the power of England, but a Monarch with powers of the Autocrat of Russia. For Gibbon says that an individual possessed of these powers will, unless closely watched, make himself a Despot.

The passage of the Sub-Treasury Bill will give to the President an accumulation of power — the single additional power that the constitution withholds from him — and the possession of which will make him a Monarch. This catastrophe to freedom should be and can be prevented by vigilance, union and perseverance.

["We will do it," resounded from twenty thousand voices, "we will do it!"]

In conclusion, then, fellow-citizens, I would impress it upon all — Democrats and Whigs — *to give up the idea of watching each other, and direct your eye to the Government.* Do that, and your children and your children's children, to the latest posterity, will be as happy and as free as you and your fathers have been.

Rhetoric of Religion, Reform and Counterreform
c. 1800-1850

The Evils of Intemperance

Lyman Beecher

Commentary

Simultaneous with the secularization of the old millenarianism were other religious developments which both united and divided the nation. The Great Awakening of the previous century left a host of controversies. What had been called "enthusiastical" preaching in Whitefield's day was now commonly called "evangelical" or "revival." Another controversy involved "Arminianism," a term that was ambiguous enough to keep "Arminians" from agreeing completely with one another, but it always meant replacing the old Calvinist predestination with a free will theology.

These and other controversies cut through denominations in bewildering ways. For example, an evangelical preacher could be an orthodox Calvinist or an Arminian. An Arminian could be a practicing revivalist or anti-revivalist. Yet what is often called "Evangelical Arminianism" eventually dominated. By the Civil War, the Methodists (formed in this country in 1784) and the Baptists (who had been a relatively small group in colonial days) had almost three-fourths of all church members. Both were Evangelical Arminian, as were some other denominations or segments thereof.

Consistent with the spread of Evangelical Arminianism was a declining interest in the fine points of theology. This is not to suggest that theology was forgotten or that theological disputes did not emerge, but it is to suggest that many preachers de-emphasized theology while talking more and more about piety, honesty and good works. This led to much informal interdenominational cooperation. Preachers and laity from various churches often joined to form missionary societies, religious newspapers, non-denominational religious colleges and similar organizations.

The Free Will-Good Works ideology did not always lead to the same attitudes about social philosophy. Some Free Will Good Works adherents were devoted to a heritage of the old millenarianism that was coming to be called "social perfectibility." They were convinced that sinners could be persuaded to choose social perfection if the choice between perfection and evil was presented clearly — and adherents knew that it was their divinely

325

ordained duty to do the Good Work of presenting the choice. The result was a series of movements, the key rhetorical term for which was "reform."

However not all religious people, not even all adherents of the Free Will-Good Works ideology, favored reform. To some, a preacher's proper function was to save individual souls, not reform society. Besides, some thought man's sinful nature made social perfectibility impossible. Since "reform" is an ambiguous term, what was "reform" to one person was "devil's work" to another, especially to people satisfied with the status quo.

This set the stage for a series of controversies, the rhetoric of which often implied (and sometimes said) that a given reform would either make society perfect or degrade it beyond redemption. One of the earliest reform movements was temperance. Its origin was not religious, but it was quickly embraced by religious groups. What was originally a relatively non-controversial movement soon became a highly controversial one.

The Temperance Movement began in 1785, when a Revolutionary hero, Dr. Benjamin Rush (a signer of the Declaration of Independence and chief physician of the Continental Army) published *The Effect of Ardent Spirits on the Human Mind and Body*. He argued for temperance primarily because of the adverse medical effects of strong drink. In 1788, he published an address to ministers asking them to preach temperance. Both the Methodists and Baptists soon took strong temperance stands.

The first temperance organization, founded in rural New York in 1808, stressed individual, not governmental, action. Members pledged themselves to be temperate and to encourage others to do likewise. Similar organizations followed, and, by 1833, when the first national convention of temperance organizations was held, approximately 6000 existed. One was the American Temperance Society (formed in Boston in 1826), which, as its name implies, was more than a local group. It had branches in other localities and employed lecturers to promote the cause. The convention of 1833 called for a national organization, and three years later the American Temperance Union was formed.

As the movement became larger and better organized, its rhetoric began embracing more controversial ideas. First, in contrast to earlier days when societies took various stands (some pledging members to drink moderately, others to abstain from "ardent spirits," which did not include beer and wine, and others to abstain "totally"), the movement became largely committed to total abstinence. Second, writers and speakers began attributing a variety of social evils, especially poverty and crime, to intemperance. A third change was in the offing: proposals to prohibit by law the sale and distribution of strong drink.

These changes were exemplified by the famous sermons of Lyman Beecher (1775-1863), a Presbyterian minister who ministered in Long Island before moving to Litchfield, Connecticut in 1810. Already well-known as a revivalist, he would later become head of Lane Theological Seminary in Ohio. He was still in Litchfield in 1826, when he delivered a series of six sermons against intemperance.

Despite his prominence, Beecher's sermons would probably have attracted limited national attention if it had not been for an organization which exemplified the interdenominationalism of the time and the interaction between religion and social reform. Founded in 1814 as the New England Tract Society, it announced in its constitution that its object was "to promote the interests of vital godliness and good morals, by the distribution of such Tracts, as shall be calculated to receive the approbation of serious Christians of all denominations." Its strategy was to select a relatively small number of exceptionally good tracts, reduce the per unit cost of publishing by printing large numbers and distributing them on a non-profit basis to "Any Religious or Charitable Society, or any Association of persons for the reformation of morals, or the suppression of vice...." In 1823, it changed its name to the American Tract Society. In 1827, a year after Beecher's sermons had been delivered orally, it published Beecher's *Six Sermons on the Nature, Occasions, Signs, Evils, and Remedy of Intemperance.* Going through five editions during the first twelve months and many more subsequently, the small volume soon became known as the bible of the temperance movement.

The first three sermons were entitled "The Nature and Occasions of Intemperance," "The Signs of Intemperance" and "The Evils of Intemperance." The last three, all on "The Remedy of Intemperance," reflected the changing character of the movement by calling not only for "total abstinence," but also for "THE BANISHMENT OF ARDENT SPIRITS FROM THE LIST OF LAWFUL ARTICLES OF COMMERCE...." Beecher's rhetoric also reflected another change: that of attributing various social evils to intemperance. This was especially true of his third sermon, which is reproduced from an 1827 edition (pp. 47-59) now in the possession of Amherst College.

The Evils of Intemperance

"Woe to him that coveteth an evil covetousness to his house, that he may set his nest on high, that he may be delivered from the power of evil! Thou hast consulted shame to thy house by cutting off many people, and hast sinned against thy soul. For the stone shall cry out of the wall, and the beam out of the timber shall answer it.

"Woe unto him that giveth his neighbor drink, that puttest thy bottle to him, and makest him drunken also, that thou mayest look on their nakedness! Thou art filled with shame for glory: drink thou also, and let thy foreskin be uncovered; the cup of the Lord's right hand shall be turned unto thee, and shameful spewing shall be on thy glory." HABAKKUK 2: 9-11, 15, 16.

In the preceding discourses we have illustrated THE NATURE, THE OCCASIONS, AND THE SYMPTOMS OF INTEMPERANCE.

In this discourse we propose to illustrate THE EVILS OF INTEMPERANCE.

The physical and moral influence of this sin upon its victims has of necessity been disclosed in giving an account of the causes and symptoms of this criminal disease. We shall therefore take a more comprehensive view of the subject, and consider the effect of intemperance upon national prosperity. To this view of the subject the text leads us. It announces the general principle, that communities which rise by a violation of the laws of humanity and equity shall not prosper, and especially that wealth amassed by promoting intemperance, will bring upon the community intemperance and poverty and shame, as a providential retribution.

1. The effects of intemperance upon the health and physical energies of a nation, are not to be overlooked or lightly esteemed.

No fact is more certain than the transmission of temperament and of physical constitution, according to the predominant moral condition of society, from age to age. Luxury produces effeminacy, and transmits to other generations imbecility and disease. Bring up the generation of the Romans who carried victory over the world, and place them beside the effeminate Italians of the present day, and the effect of crime upon constitution will be sufficiently apparent. Excesses unmake the man. The stature dwindles, the joints are loosely compacted, and the muscular fibre has lost its elastic tone. No giant's bones will be found in the cemeteries of a nation over whom for centuries the waves of intemperance have rolled; and no unwieldly iron armor, the annoyance and defence of other days, will be dug up as memorials of departed glory.

The duration of human life, and the relative amount of health or disease, will manifestly vary according to the amount of ardent spirits consumed in the land. Even now, no small proportion of the deaths which annually make up our national bills of mortality, are cases of those who have been brought to an untimely end, and who have, directly or indirectly, fallen victims to the deleterious influence of ardent spirits; fulfilling with fearful accuracy the prediction, the wicked "shall not live out half their days." As the jackal follows the lion to prey upon the slain, so do disease and death wait on the footsteps of inebriation. The free and universal use of intoxicating liquors for a few centuries, cannot fail to bring down our race from the majestic, athletic forms of our fathers to the similitude of a despicable and puny race of men. Already the commencement of the decline is manifest, and the consummation of it, should the causes continue, will not linger.

2. The injurious influence of general intemperance upon national intellect is equally certain, and not less to be deprecated.

To the action of a powerful mind, a vigorous muscular frame is, as a general rule, indispensable. Like heavy ordnance, the mind, in its efforts, recoils on the body, and will soon shake down a puny frame. The mental action and physical reäction must be equal, or, finding her energies unsustained, the mind itself becomes discouraged, and falls into despondency and imbecility. The flow of animal spirits, the fire and vigor of the imagination, the fulness and power of feeling, the comprehension and grasp of thought, the fire of the eye, the tones of the voice, and the electrical energy of utterance, all depend upon the healthful and vigorous tone of the animal system, and by whatever means the body is unstrung, the spirit languishes. Cesar, when he had a fever once, and cried, "Give me some drink, Titinius," was not that god who afterwards overturned the republic and reigned without a rival; and Buonaparte, it has been said, lost the Russian campaign by a fever. The greatest poets and orators who stand on the records of immortality, flourished in the iron age, before the habits of effeminacy had unharnessed the body and unstrung the mind. This is true of Homer and Demosthenes and Milton; and if Virgil and Cicero are to be classed with them, it is not without a manifest abatement of vigor for beauty, produced by the progress of voluptuousness in the age in which they lived.

The giant writers of Scotland are, some of them, men of threescore and ten, who still go forth to the athletic sports of their youthful days with undiminished elasticity. The taper fingers of modern effeminacy never wielded such a pen as these men wield, and never will.

The taste may be cultivated in alliance with effeminacy, and music may flourish, while all that is manly is upon the decline; and there may be some fitful flashes of imagination in poetry, which are the offspring of a capricious, nervous excitability; and perhaps there may be sometimes an unimpassioned stillness of soul in a feeble body, which shall capacitate for simple intellectual discrimination. But that fulness of soul and diversified energy of mind which is indispensable to national talent in all its diversified application, can be found only in alliance with an undebased and vigorous muscular system.

The history of the world confirms this conclusion. Egypt, once at the head of nations, has, under the weight of her own effeminacy, gone down to the dust. The victories of Greece let in upon her the luxuries of the East, and covered her glory with a night of ages. And Rome, whose iron foot trode down the nations and shook the earth, witnessed in her latter days faintness of heart and the shield of the mighty vilely cast away.

3. The effect of intemperance upon the military prowess of a nation, cannot but be great and evil. The mortality in the seasoning of recruits already half destroyed by intemperance, will be double to that experienced among hardy and temperate men.

If, in the early wars of our country, the mortality of the camp had been as great as it has been since intemperance has facilitated the raising of recruits, New England would have been depopulated, Philip had remained lord of his wilderness, or the French had driven our fathers into the sea, extending from Canada to Cape Horn the empire of despotism and superstition. An army whose energy in conflict depends on the excitement of ardent spirits, cannot possess the requisite coolness, nor sustain the shock of a powerful onset, like an army of determined temperate men. It was the religious principle and temperance of Cromwell's army, that made it terrible to the licentious troops of Charles the First.

4. The effect of intemperance upon the patriotism of a nation is neither obscure nor doubtful. When excess has despoiled the man of the natural affections of husband, father, brother, and friend, and thrust him down to

the condition of an animal, we are not to expect of him comprehensive views, and a disinterested regard for his country. His patriotism may serve as a theme of sinister profession or inebriate boasting. But what is the patriotism which loves only in words and in general, and violates in detail all the relative duties on which the welfare of country depends?

The man might as well talk of justice and mercy who robs and murders upon the highway, as he whose example is pestiferous, and whose presence withers the tender charities of life, and perpetuates weeping, lamentation, and woe. A nation of drunkards would constitute a hell.

5. Upon the national conscience or moral principle the effects of intemperance are deadly.

It obliterates the fear of the Lord and a sense of accountability, paralyzes the power of conscience, hardens the heart, and turns out upon society a sordid, selfish, ferocious animal.

6. Upon national industry the effects of intemperance are manifest and mischievous.

The results of national industry depend on the amount of well-directed intellectual and physical power. But intemperance paralyzes and prevents both these springs of human action.

In the inventory of national loss by intemperance, may be set down the labor prevented by indolence, by debility, by sickness, by quarrels and litigation, by gambling and idleness, by mistakes and misdirected efforts, by improvidence and wastefulness, and by the shortened date of human life and activity. Little wastes in great establishments constantly occurring, may defeat the energies of a mighty capital. But where the intellectual and muscular energies are raised to the working point daily by ardent spirits, until the agriculture and commerce and arts of a nation move on by the power of artificial stimulus, that moral power cannot be maintained which will guarantee fidelity, and that physical power cannot be preserved and well directed, which will insure national prosperity. The nation whose immense enterprise is thrust forward by the stimulus of ardent spirits, cannot ultimately escape debility and bankruptcy.

When we behold an individual cut off in youth or in middle age, or witness the waning energies, improvidence, and unfaithfulness of a neighbor, it is but a single instance, and we become accustomed to it; but such instances are multiplying in our land in every direction, and are to be found in every department of labor, and the amount of earnings prevented or squandered is incalculable: to all which must be added the accumulating and frightful expense incurred for the support of those and their families whom intemperance has made paupers. In every city and town the poor-tax, created chiefly by intemperance, is augmenting. The receptacles for the poor are becoming too strait for their accommodation. We must pull them down and build greater to provide accommodations for the votaries of inebriation; for the frequency of going upon the town has taken away the reluctance of pride, and destroyed the motives of providence which the fear of poverty and suffering once supplied. The prospect of a destitute old-age, or of a suffering family, no longer troubles the vicious portion of our community. They drink up their daily earnings, and bless God for the poor-house, and begin to look upon it as, of right, the drunkard's home, and contrive to arrive thither as early as idleness and excess will give them a passport to this sinecure of vice. Thus is the insatiable destroyer of industry marching through the land, rearing poor-houses, and augmenting taxation: night and day, with sleepless activity, squandering property, cutting the sinews of industry, undermining vigor, engendering disease, paralyzing intellect, impairing moral principle, cutting short the date of life, and rolling up a national debt, invisible, but real and terrific as the debt of England; continually transferring larger and larger bodies of men from the class of contributors to the national income to the class of worthless consumers.

Add to the loss sustained by the subtraction of labor and the shortened date of life, the expense of sustaining the poor created by intemperance, and the nation is now taxed annually more than the expense which would be requisite for the maintenance of government, and for the support of all our schools and colleges, and all the religious instruction of the nation. Already a portion of the entire capital of the nation is mortgaged for the support of drunkards. There seems to be no other fast property in the land, but this inheritance of the intemperate: all other riches may make to themselves wings and fly away. But until the nation is bankrupt, according to the laws of the state the drunkard and his family must have a home. Should the pauperism of crime augment in this country as it has done for a few years past, there is nothing to stop the frightful results which have come upon England, where property is abandoned in some parishes because the poor-tax exceeds the annual income. You who are husbandmen are accustomed to feel as if your houses and lands were wholly your own; but if you will ascertain the percentage of annual taxation levied on your property for the support of the intemperate, you will perceive how much of your capital is held by drunkards, by a tenure as sure as if held under mortgages or deeds of warranty. Your widows and children do not take by descent more certainly, than the most profligate and worthless part of the community. Every intemperate and idle man whom you behold tottering about the streets and steeping himself at the stores, regards your houses and lands as pledged to take care of him, annually puts his hands deep into your pockets, and eats his bread in the sweat of your brows, instead of his own: and with marvellous good-nature you bear it. If a robber should break loose on the highway to levy taxation, an armed force would be raised to hunt him from society. But the tippler may do it fearlessly in open day, and not a voice is raised, not a finger is lifted.

The effects of intemperance upon civil liberty may not be lightly passed over.

It is admitted that intelligence and virtue are the pillars of republican institutions, and that the illumination of schools, and the moral power of religious institutions, are indispensable to produce this intelligence and virtue.

But who are found so uniformly in the ranks of irreligion as the intemperate? Who like these violate the Sabbath, and set their mouth against the heavens — neglecting the education of their families and corrupting their morals? Almost the entire amount of national ignorance and crime is the offspring of intemperance. Throughout the land the intemperate are hewing down the pillars and undermining the foundations of our national edifice. Legions have besieged it, and upon every gate the battle-axe rings; and still the sentinels sleep.

Should the evil advance as it has done, the day is not far distant when the great body of the laboring classes of the community, the bones and sinews of the nation, will be contaminated; and when this is accomplished, the right of suffrage becomes the engine of self-destruction. For the laboring classes constitute an immense majority, and when these are perverted by intemperance, ambition needs no better implements with which to dig the grave of our liberties, and entomb our glory.

Such is the influence of interest, ambition, fear, and indolence, that one violent partisan with a handful of disciplined troops may overrule the influence of five hundred temperate men, who act without concert. Already is the disposition to temporize, to tolerate, and even to court the intemperate, too apparent, on account of the apprehended retribution of their perverted suffrage. The whole power of law through the nation sleeps in the statute-book; and until public sentiment is roused and concentrated, it may be doubted whether its execution is possible.

Where is the city, town, or village, in which the laws are not openly violated, and where is the magistry that dares to carry into effect the laws against the vending or drinking of ardent spirits? Here then an aristocracy of bad influence has already risen up, which bids defiance to law, and threatens the extirpation of civil liberty. As intemperance increases, the power of taxation will come more and more into the hands of men of intemperate habits and desperate fortunes; of course the laws gradually will become subservient to the debtor, and less efficacious in protecting the rights of property. This will be a vital stab to liberty, to the security of which property is indispensable. For money is the sinew of war; and when those who hold the property of a nation cannot be protected in their rights, they will change the form of government — peaceably if they may, by violence if they must.

In proportion to the numbers who have no right in the soil and no capital at stake and no moral principle, will the nation be exposed to violence and revolution. In Europe, the physical power is bereft of the right of suffrage, and by the bayonet is kept down; but in this nation, the power which may be wielded by the intemperate and ignorant is tremendous. These are the troops of the future Cesars, by whose perverted suffrages our future elections may be swayed, and ultimately our liberties destroyed. They are the corps of irreligious and desperate men, who have something to hope and nothing to fear from revolution and blood. Of such materials was the army of Catiline composed, who conspired against the liberties of Rome. And in the French revolution, such men as Lafayette were soon swept from the helm by mobs composed of the dregs of creation, to give place to the revolutionary furies which followed.

We boast of our liberties, and rejoice in our prospective instrumentality in disenthralling the world. But our own foundations rest on the heaving sides of a burning mountain, through which, in thousands of places, the fire has burst out and is blazing around us. If they cannot be extinguished, we are undone; our sun is fast setting, and the darkness of an endless night is closing in upon us.

To the Public

William Lloyd Garrison

Commentary

Far more controversial than temperance was the antislavery movement, which originated in colonial times but did not emerge as a highly divisive issue until the early 1830s. The first major antislavery pamphlet, Samuel Sewall's *The Selling of Joseph* (1700), was heavily religious. Sewall refuted proslavery arguments, most of which were religious (e.g., Africans are descendants of Ham, whose offspring were cursed by God, and Abraham owned slaves, which shows that God approves of slavery). His major antislavery argument was that slavery is inconsistent with Christian principles.

The inconsistency of slavery with Christianity was almost the only antislavery argument until around the middle of the eighteenth century, when it was supplemented by arguments based on Natural Law and pragmatics. We see this, for example, in the 1760s, when Virginia was trying to discourage slave importations by imposing high tariffs. Arthur Lee published an antislavery pamphlet in which he said that, although Africans were "a race the most detestable and vile that ever the earth produced," the principles of "Justice and Religion" prohibited their enslavement. He advanced pragmatic arguments by saying that the possibility of slave revolts endangered the community, that land values would increase if they were settled by free laborers, that slavery discouraged the growth of arts and sciences and that it produced vices both in the slave and the master.

During and after the Revolution, the Natural Law argument received increased emphasis, but religious and pragmatic arguments continued to be used. The antislavery movement reached the inception stage with the organization of local and State societies, and, by the end of the eighteenth century, slavery had been largely eradicated in Northern States, usually by legislation which abolished it on a gradual basis. Optimists had good reasons for believing that it would soon die in the South. Disruptions in the tobacco business put planters in serious financial difficulty. The cost of maintaining a growing, but less needed, slave population was becoming burdensome. The religious, natural rights and pragmatic arguments against slavery had considerable persuasive appeal even among slaveowners. Although proslavery writers and speakers argued that slavery was divinely sanctioned and that natural rights did not extend to "inferior" blacks, proslavery rhetoric was muted and defensive. Proslavery rhetors rarely argued, as they would later, that slavery was a "positive good." There was good reason to believe that slavery would eventually die.

By the early nineteenth century, the antislavery movement was almost non-existent, but the spread of the cotton culture caused slavery to again become economically viable. Rejuvenating the antislavery movement was largely the work of Benjamin Lundy, who was reared in a deeply religious Quaker household in New Jersey. He was shocked when he was working in Wheeling, Virginia (now West Virginia) and saw slaves being transported through town on their way to being sold. His youth and economic insecurity precluded his doing anything immediately. By 1815, the 26-year-old Lundy was fairly prosperous and, while in St. Clairsville, Ohio, he organized an antislavery society known as "The Union Humane Society." In January, 1816, he issued a circular urging the formation of more societies and holding general conventions to coordinate their efforts. In January, 1821, while in Mount Pleasant, Ohio, he started an abolitionist newspaper, *The Genius of Universal Emancipation*, which he moved to Tennessee and then (in 1824) to Baltimore.

Lundy's strategy was to persuade Southerners that slavery should be abolished. By 1827, according to his estimates, there were 130 antislavery societies in the country, 106 of which were in the South. There were 6,625 members, of which 5,150 were Southerners. He realized that changing Southern opinion would be difficult, for slavery was now integral to the economic and cultural life of the South. Many Southerners believed that slavery was divinely sanctioned and many doubted that natural rights extended to the "inferior" black. His rhetoric was, therefore, moderate. He carefully avoided condemning slaveowners, employed the same kind of antislavery rhetoric which had been used earlier, urged gradual emancipation with compensation for the slaveowner and endorsed colonization of free blacks.

In 1828, while on a Northern speaking tour to raise money, Lundy met William Lloyd Garrison (1805-1879). Reared in poverty in Newburyport, Massachusetts, Garrison received a meager education, but he imbibed the Puritan and evangelical traditions of New England before being apprenticed to a printer at age thirteen. He later became printer and co-editor of the *National Philanthropist*, a newspaper which specialized in attacking "intemperance and its kindred vices," such as gambling, sabbath-breaking and war. He moved to Bennington, Vermont to edit the *Journal of the Times*, a Jacksonian political paper with a reformist bent. Intent on "social perfectionism," Garrison wrote pieces supporting not only temperance, but also women's rights and pacifism.

At first, Garrison declined Lundy's offer to become associate editor of the *Genius*, but his meeting with Lundy converted him to antislavery. In 1829,

Garrison gave the speech against slavery to which he referred in the following discourse. Later he accepted Lundy's offer of editorship and followed Lundy's lead in approving of gradualism, compensation and colonization, but he soon recanted this moderate approach. He got into trouble by accusing a prominent Baltimore citizen of being a slavetrader. The citizen successfully brought suit, and, unable to pay compensation, Garrison was jailed. Through the intervention of Arthur Tappan, a Northern philanthropist, Garrison was released on June 5, 1830. It was time to return North.

Garrison spent the autumn of 1830 on a speaking tour to get support for a more militant abolitionist movement, and his proposed weekly abolitionist newspaper, *The Liberator*. He abandoned his original plan of publishing the paper in Washington after Lundy moved his there; he chose Boston instead. On January 1, 1831, the first issue appeared. As was customary for a new publication, he included a brief statement, on page one, about the objectives of the paper. The statement foreshadowed the militant rhetoric he would employ. It is reproduced from the first issue, which is housed at the American Antiquarian Society. Titles which were not italicized in the original have been italicized.

To the Public

In the month of August, I issued proposals for publishing "THE LIBERATOR" in Washington city; but the enterprise, though hailed in different sections of the country, was palsied by public indifference. Since that time, the removal of the *Genius of Universal Emancipation* to the Seat of Government has rendered less imperious the establishment of a similar periodical in that quarter.

During my recent tour for the purpose of exciting the minds of the people by a series of discourses on the subject of slavery, every place that I visited gave fresh evidence of the fact, that a greater revolution in public sentiment was to be effected in the free states — *and particularly in New-England* — than at the south. I found contempt more bitter, opposition more active, detraction more relentless, prejudice more stubborn, and apathy more frozen, than among slave owners themselves. Of course, there were individual exceptions to the contrary. This state of things afflicted, but did not dishearten me. I determined, at every hazard, to lift up the standard of emancipation in the eyes of the nation, *within sight of Bunker Hill and in the birth place of liberty.* That standard is now unfurled; and long may it float, unhurt by the spoliations of time or the missiles of a desperate foe — yea, till every chain be broken, and every bondman set free! Let southern oppressors tremble — let their secret abettors tremble — let their northern apologists tremble — let all the enemies of the persecuted blacks tremble.

I deem the publication of my original Prospectus unnecessary, as it has obtained a wide circulation. The principles therein inculcated will be steadily pursued in this paper, excepting that I shall not array myself as the political partisan of any man. In defending the great cause of human rights, I wish to derive the assistance of all religions and of all parties.

Assenting to the "self-evident truth" maintained in the American Declaration of Independence, "that all men are created equal, and endowed by their Creator with certain inalienable rights — among which are life, liberty and the pursuit of happiness," I shall strenuously contend for the immediate enfranchisement of our slave population. In Park-street Church, on the Fourth of July, 1829, in an address on slavery, I unreflectingly assented to the popular but pernicious doctrine of *gradual* abolition. I seize this opportunity to make a full and unequivocal recantation, and thus publicly to ask pardon of my God, of my country, and of my brethren the poor slaves, for having uttered a sentiment so full of timidity, injustice, and absurdity. A similar recantation, from my pen, was published in the *Genius of Universal Emancipation* at Baltimore, in September, 1829. My conscience is now satisfied.

I am aware, that many object to the severity of my language; but is there not cause for severity? I *will be* as harsh as truth, and as uncompromising as justice. On this subject, I do not wish to think, or speak, or write, with moderation. No! no! Tell a man whose house is on fire, to give a moderate alarm; tell him to moderately rescue his wife from the hands of the ravisher; tell the mother to gradually extricate her babe from the fire into which it has fallen; — but urge me not to use moderation in a cause like the present. I am in earnest — I will not equivocate — I will not excuse — I will not retreat a single inch — AND I WILL BE HEARD. The apathy of the people is enough to make every statue leap from its pedestal, and to hasten the resurrection of the dead.

It is pretended, that I am retarding the cause of emancipation by the coarseness of my invective, and the precipitancy of my measures. *The charge is not true.* On this question my influence, — humble as it is, — is felt at this moment to a considerable extent, and shall be felt in coming years — not perniciously, but beneficially — not as a curse, but as a blessing; and posterity will bear testimony that I was right. I desire to thank God, that he enables me to disregard "the fear of man which bringeth a snare," and to speak his truth in its simplicity and power. And here I close with this fresh dedication:

> "Oppression! I have seen thee, face to face,
> And met thy cruel eye and cloudy brow;
> But thy soul-withering glance I fear not now —
> For dread to prouder feelings doth give place
> Of deep abhorrence! Scorning the disgrace
> Of slavish knees that at thy footstool bow,
> I also kneel — but with far other vow
> Do hail thee and thy herd of hirelings base: —
> I swear, while life-blood warms my throbbing veins,
> Still to oppose and thwart, with heart and hand,
> Thy brutalising sway — till Afric's [sic] chains

Are burst, and Freedom rules the rescued land, —
Trampling Oppression and his iron rod:
Such is the vow I take — SO HELP ME GOD!"

BOSTON, January 1, 1831.   WILLIAM LLOYD GARRISON.

Excerpt from Abolition of Negro Slavery

Thomas R. Dew

Commentary

The year 1831 was unusually significant for the antislavery movement not only because *The Liberator* was founded, but also because of dramatic events in the South. Recent years had seen considerable publicity given to efforts by the British Anti-Slavery Society to get slavery abolished in the British West Indies and to the slave rebellions in the Caribbean. In August, 1831, Nat Turner's famous slave insurrection occurred in Virginia. White fear intensified, and, although some whites believed that abolition would eliminate the danger, many believed the converse. Many whites blamed abolitionist rhetoric for inflaming the slaves, who otherwise would remain happy and contented. Insurrections intensified white fears of what would happen if the "inferior" and "uncivilized" blacks were emancipated.

Into this emotional situation came a proposal from western Virginia legislators to abolish slavery in the State. The proposal, which came very close to passing, was debated vigorously during the winter of 1831-1832. With pubic interest high, publishers soon had printed versions of the legislative debates.

Increased technology and economic prosperity had resulted in a marked increase in book production since the Revolution. This led to a new medium of communication: the literary quarterly, which typically consisted of a series of "reviews" of recent books. Unlike the short reviews of our time, however, early nineteenth-century "reviews" were lengthy essays on the same subject as the book. Rhetorical conventions allowed — almost demanded — the "reviewer" to use the book as an excuse for writing his own essay.

Thus, publication of the Virginia debate gave both pro- and antislavery writers an opportunity to present their cases. Antislavery spokesmen overlooked it, but Thomas R. Dew (1802-1846) seized the chance to defend slavery. He wrote a lengthy review of the Virginia debate for the prestigious Philadelphia literary magazine, the *American Quarterly Review,* which was to have a profound influence. After being expanded into pamphlet form, it was distributed widely, especially in the South, where it became the bible of proslavery speakers and writers. The essay also influenced Dew's own career, earning him the reward of becoming the first non-clergyman to hold the presidency of William and Mary College, which was the most prestigious college in the South.

Dew's essay is significant not only because of its influence, but also because it highlighted two important transitions in proslavery rhetoric. First, whereas earlier rhetoric was largely defensive, later rhetoric turned slavery into a "positive good" that benefited everybody, including slaves. Second, whereas earlier rhetoric ignored Thomas Jefferson's antislavery sentiments, later writers and speakers often attacked him.

In some respects, Dew's essay was in the old tradition. Its organizational structure was defensive, with the first sections devoted to the economic and social consequences of abolitionist plans and the last part being a point-by-point refutation of antislavery arguments. Yet the vigor with which Dew developed his arguments and the sarcasm which he heaped upon abolitionists gave a militant tone to the essay.

In his opening sections, Dew argued like the political economist he was, and he assumed (as did most of his readers) that blacks were inferior. Calculating that one-third of Virginia's wealth consisted of slaves, he argued the impracticality of any abolitionist plan. He then divided those plans into ones which called for deportation and those which did not. Deportation, he argued, was totally impractical not only because of the expense, but also because the African climate was unsuitable for civilized society. Existing African populations would resist the colonizers, and America's newly freed slaves would be involved in bloody wars which they would eventually lose. Then they would be enslaved by their African captors. Non-deportation would result in an idle and immoral free black population destroying Southern civilization.

The final section, consisting of Dew's refutation of antislavery arguments, is reproduced from a copy of the *American Quarterly Review* (vol. 12, pp. 247-265, September 1832) which is housed in Forbes Library, Northampton, Massachusetts. Footnotes were not numbered in the original.

Excerpt from Abolition of Negro Slavery

1st. It is said slavery is wrong, in the *abstract* at least, and contrary to the spirit of Christianity. To this we answer as before, that any question must be determined by its circumstances, and if, as really is the case, we cannot get rid of slavery without producing a greater injury to both the masters and slaves, there is no rule of conscience or revealed law of God which *can* condemn us. The physician will not order the spreading cancer to be extirpated, although it will eventually cause the death of his patient, because he would thereby hasten the fatal issue. So if slavery had commenced even contrary to the laws of God and man, and the sin of its introduction rested upon our hands, and it was even carrying forward the nation by slow degrees to final ruin — yet if it were *certain* that an attempt to remove it would only hasten and heighten the final catastrophe — that it was in fact a ''vulnus immedicabile'' on the body politic, which no legislation could safely remove, then, we would not only not be bound to attempt the extirpation, but we would stand guilty of a high offence in the sight of both God and man, if we should rashly make the effort. But the original sin of introduction rests not on our heads, and we shall soon see that all those dreadful calamities which the false prophets of our day are pointing to, will never in all probability occur. With regard to the assertion, that slavery is against the spirit of Christianity, we are ready to admit the general assertion but deny most positively that there is any thing in the Old or New Testament, which would go to show that slavery, when once introduced, ought at all events to be abrogated, or that the master commits any offence in holding slaves. The Children of Israel themselves were slave-holders, and were not condemned for it. When they conquered the land of Canaan they made one whole tribe ''hewers of wood and drawers of water,'' and they were at that very time under the special guidance of Jehovah; they were permitted expressly to purchase slaves of the heathens, and keep them as an inheritance for their posterity — and even the Children of Israel might be enslaved for six years. When we turn to the New Testament, we find not one single passage at all calculated to disturb the conscience of an honest slave-holder. No one can read it without seeing and admiring that the meek and humble Saviour of the world in no instance meddled with the established institutions of mankind — he came to save a fallen world, and not to excite the black passions of men and array them in deadly hostility against each other. From no one did he turn away; his plan was offered alike to all — to the monarch and the subject — the rich and the poor — the master and the slave. He was born in the Roman world, a world in which the most galling slavery existed, a thousand times more cruel than the slavery in our own country — and yet he nowhere encourages insurrection — he nowhere fosters discontent — but exhorts *always* to implicit obedience and fidelity. What a rebuke does the practice of the Redeemer of mankind imply upon the conduct of some of his nominal disciples of the day, who seek to destroy the contentment of the slaves, to rouse their most deadly passions, to break up the deep foundations of society, and to lead on to a night of darkness and confusion! ''Let every man (says Paul,) abide in the same calling wherein he is called. Art thou called *being* a servant? care not for it; but if thou mayest be made free use *it* rather.'' (1 *Corinthians,* vii. 20, 21.) Again; ''Let as many servants as are under the yoke, count their own masters worthy of all honour, that the name of God and his doctrines be not blasphemed; and they that have believing masters, let them not despise *them,* because they are brethren, but rather do them service, because they are faithful and beloved partakers of the benefit. These things teach and exhort.'' (1 *Tim.* vi. 1, 2.)

Servants are even commanded in Scripture to be faithful and obedient to unkind masters. "Servants, (says Peter,) be subject to your masters with all fear; not only to the good and gentle, but to the froward [sic]. For what glory is it if when ye shall be buffeted for your faults ye take it patiently; but if when ye do well and suffer for it, ye take it patiently, this is acceptable with God." (1 *Peter*, ii. 18, 20.) These, and many other passages in the New Testament, most convincingly prove, that slavery in the Roman world was nowhere charged as a fault or crime upon the holder, and everywhere is the most implicit obedience enjoined.[1]

We beg leave, before quitting this topic, to address a few remarks to those who have conscientious scruples about the holding of slaves, and therefore consider themselves under an obligation to break all the ties of friendship and kindred — dissolve all the associations of happier days, to flee to a land where this evil does not exist. We cannot condemn the conscientious actions of mankind, but we must be permitted to say, that if the assumption even of these pious gentlemen be correct, we do consider their conduct as very unphilosophical, and we will go further still, we look upon it as even immoral upon their own principles. Let us admit that slavery is an evil, and what then? why it has been entailed upon us by no fault of ours, and must we shrink from the charge which devolves upon us, and throw the slave in consequence into the hands of those who have no scruples of conscience — those who will not perhaps treat him so kindly? No! this is not philosophy, it is not morality; we must recollect that the unprofitable man was thrown into utter darkness. To the slave-holder has truly been intrusted the five talents. Let him but recollect the exhortation of the Apostle — "Masters, give unto your servants that which is just and equal; knowing that ye also have a master in Heaven;" and in the final day he shall have nothing on this score with which his conscience need be smitten, and he may expect the welcome plaudit — "Well done thou good and faithful servant, thou hast been faithful over a few things, I will make thee ruler over many things; enter thou into the joy of the Lord." Hallam, in his History of the Middle Ages, says that the greatest moral evil flowing from monastic establishments, consisted in withdrawing the good and religious from society, and leaving the remainder unchecked and unrestrained in the pursuit of their vicious practices. Would not such principles as those just mentioned lead to a similar result? We cannot, therefore, but consider them as *whining and sickly,* and highly unphilosophical and detrimental to society.

2dly. *But it is further said that the moral effects of slavery are of the most deleterious and hurtful kind;* and as Mr. Jefferson has given the sanction of his great name to this charge, we shall proceed to examine it with all that respectful deference to which every sentiment of so pure and philanthropic a heart is justly entitled.

"The whole commerce between master and slave," says he, "is a perpetual exercise of the most boisterous passions — the most unremitting despotism on the one part, and degrading submission on the other. Our children see this, and learn to imitate it, for man is an imitative animal — this quality is the germ of education in him. From his cradle to his grave, he is learning what he sees others do. If a parent had no other motive, either in his own philanthropy or self love, for restraining the intemperance of passion towards his slave, it should always be a sufficient one that his child is present. But generally it is not sufficient. The parent storms, the child looks on, catches the lineaments of wrath, puts on the same airs in the circle of smaller slaves, gives a loose to his worst of passions, and thus nursed, educated, and daily exercised in the worst of tyranny, cannot but be stamped by it with odious peculiarities."[2] Now we boldly assert that the fact does not bear Mr. Jefferson out in his conclusions. He has supposed the master in a continual passion — in the constant exercise of the most odious tyranny, and the child, a creature of imitation, looking on and learning. But is not this master sometimes kind and indulgent to his slaves? does he not mete out to them, for faithful service, the reward of his cordial approbation? Is it not his interest to do it? and when thus acting humanely, and speaking kindly, where is the child, the creature of imitation, that he does not look on and learn? We may rest assured, in this intercourse between a good master and his servant, more good than evil *may* be taught the child, the exalted principles of morality and religion may thereby be sometimes indelibly inculcated upon his mind, and instead of being reared a selfish contracted being, with nought but self to look to — he acquires a more exalted benevolence, a greater generosity and elevation of soul, and embraces for the sphere of his generous actions a much wider field. Look to the slave-holding population of our country, and you everywhere find them characterized by noble and elevated sentiment, by humane and virtuous feelings. We do not find among them that cold, contracted, calculating *selfishness*, which withers and repels every thing around it, and lessens or destroys all the multiplied enjoyments of social intercourse. Go into our national councils, and ask for the most generous, the most disinterested, the most conscientious, and the least unjust and oppressive in their principles, and see whether the slave-holder will be past by in the selection. Edwards says that slavery in the West Indies seems to awaken the laudable propensities of our nature, such as "frankness, sociability, benevolence, and generosity. In no part of the globe is the virtue of hospitality more prevalent than in the British sugar islands. The gates of the planter are always open to the reception of his guests — to be a stranger is of itself a sufficient introduction.''

Is it not a fact, known to every man in the South, that the most *cruel masters* are those who have been unaccustomed to slavery. It is well known that northern gentlemen who marry southern heiresses, are much severer masters than southern gentlemen.[3] And yet, if Mr. Jefferson's reasoning were correct, they ought to be much milder: in fact, it follows from his reasoning, that the authority which the father is called on to exercise over his children, must be seriously detrimental; and yet we know that this is not the case; that on the contrary, there is nothing which so much humanizes and softens the heart, as this *very authority*; and there are none, even

among those who have no children themselves, so disposed to pardon the
follies and indiscretion of youth, as those who have seen most of them, and
suffered greatest annoyance. There may be many cruel relentless masters,
and there are unkind and cruel fathers too; but both the one and the other
make all those around them shudder with horror. We are disposed to think
that their example in society tends rather to strengthen, than weaken the
principle of benevolence and humanity.

Let us now look a moment to the slave, and contemplate *his* position. Mr.
Jefferson has described him as hating, rather than loving his master, and as
losing, too, all that *amor patriae* which characterizes the true patriot. We
assert again, that Mr. Jefferson is not borne out by the fact. We are well
convinced that there is nothing but the mere relations of husband and wife,
parent and child, brother and sister, which produce a closer tie, than the
relation of master and servant. We have no hesitation in affirming, that
throughout the whole slave-holding country, the slaves of a good master are
his warmest, most constant, and most devoted friends; they have been
accustomed to look up to him as their supporter, director and defender.
Every one acquainted with southern slaves, knows that the slave rejoices in
the elevation and prosperity of his master; and the heart of no one is more
gladdened at the successful debut of young master or miss on the great
theatre of the world, than that of either the young slave who has grown up
with them, and shared in all their sports, and even partaken of all their
delicacies — or the aged one who has looked on and watched them from
birth to manhood, with the kindest and most affectionate solicitude, and has
ever met from them all, the kind treatment and generous sympathies of
feeling tender hearts.

Gilbert Stuart, in his History of Society, says that the time when the
vassal of the feudal ages was most faithful, most obedient, and most
interested in the welfare of his master, was precisely when his dependance
was most complete, and when, consequently, he relied upon his lord for
every thing. When the feudal tenure was gradually changing, and the law
was interposing between landlord and tenant, the close tie between them
began to dissolve, and with it, the kindness on one side, and the affection,
and gratitude on the other, waned and vanished. From all this, we are
forced to draw one important inference — that it is dangerous to the
happiness and well being of the slave, for either the imprudent
philanthropist to attempt to interpose too often, or the rash legislator to
obtrude his regulating edicts, between master and slave. They only serve to
render the slave more intractable and unhappy, and the master more cruel
and unrelenting. And we call upon the reverend clergy, whose examples
should be pure, and whose precepts should be fraught with wisdom and
prudence, to beware, lest in their zeal for the black, they suffer too much of
the passion and prejudice of the human heart to mingle with those pure
principles by which they should be governed. Let them beware of "what
spirit they are of." "No sound," says Burke, "ought to be heard in the
church, but the healing voice of Christian charity. Those who quit their

proper character, to assume what does not belong to them, are for the most part ignorant of the character they assume, and of the character they leave off. Wholly unacquainted with the world in which they are so fond of meddling, and inexperienced in all its affairs, on which they pronounce with so much confidence, they have nothing of politics but the *passions* they excite. Surely the church is a place where one day's truce ought to be allowed to the dissensions and animosities of mankind.''

In the debate in the Virginia legislature, no speaker *insinuated even,* we believe, that the slaves in Virginia were not treated kindly; and all too agreed that they were most abundantly fed, and we have no doubt but that they form the happiest portion of our society. A merrier being does not exist on the face of the globe than the negro slave of the United States. *Even* Captain Hall himself, with his thick ''crust of prejudice,'' is obliged to allow that they are happy and contented, and the master much less cruel than is generally imagined. We cannot, therefore, agree with Mr. Jefferson, in the opinion that slavery makes the unfeeling tyrant and the ungrateful dependant; and in regard to Virginia especially, we are almost disposed, judging from the official returns of crimes and convictions, to assert, with a statesman who has descended to his tomb (Mr. Giles,) ''that the whole population of Virginia, consisting of three *castes* — of free white, free coloured, and slave coloured population, is the soundest and most moral of any other, according to numbers, in the whole world, as far as is known to me.''

3dly. *It has been contended that slavery is unfavourable to a republican spirit*: but the whole history of the world proves that this is far from being the case. In the ancient republics of Greece and Rome, where the spirit of liberty glowed with most intensity, the slaves were more numerous than the freemen. Aristotle, and the great men of antiquity, believed slavery necessary to keep alive the spirit of freedom. In Sparta, the freeman was even forbidden to perform the offices of slaves, lest he might lose the spirit of independence. In modern times, too, liberty has always been more ardently desired by slave-holding communities. ''Such,'' says Burke, ''were our Gothic ancestors; such, in our days, were the Poles; and such will be all masters of slaves who are not slaves themselves.'' — ''These people of the southern (American) colonies are much more strongly, and with a higher and more stubborn spirit, attached to liberty, than those of the northward.'' And from the time of Burke down to the present day, the southern states have always borne this same honourable distinction. Burke says, ''it is because freedom is to them not only an enjoyment, but a kind of rank and privilege.'' Another, and perhaps more efficient cause, of this, is the perfect spirit of equality so prevalent among the whites of all the slave-holding states. Jack Cade, the English reformer, wished all mankind to be brought to one common level. We believe slavery, in the United States, has accomplished this, in regard to the whites, as nearly as can be expected or even desired in this world. The menial and low offices being all performed by the blacks, there is at once taken away the greatest cause of distinction and separation of the ranks of society. The man to the north will not shake hands familiarly with his servant, and converse, and laugh, and dine with him, no matter how honest and respectable he may be. But go to the south, and you will find that no white man feels such inferiority of rank as to be unworthy of association with those around him. The same thing is observed in the West Indies. ''Of the character common to the white residents of the West Indies, it appears to me,'' says Edwards, ''that the leading feature is an independent spirit, and a display of *conscious equality* throughout all ranks and conditions. The poorest white person seems to consider himself nearly on a level with the richest; and emboldened by this idea, approaches his employer with extended hand, and a freedom, which, in the counries of Europe, is seldom displayed by men in the lower orders of life towards their superiors.'' And it is this spirit of equality which is both the generator and preserver of the genuine spirit of liberty.

4thly. *Insecurity of the whites, arising from plots, insurrections, &c., among the blacks.* This is the evil, after all, let us say what we will, which really operates most powerfully upon the schemers and emancipating philanthropists of those sections where slaves constitute the principal property. Now, if we have shown, as we trust we have, that the scheme of deportation is utterly impraticable, and that emancipation, with permission to remain, will produce all these horrors in *still greater degree,* it follows that this evil of slavery, allowing it to exist in all its latitude, would be no argument for legislative action, and therefore we might well rest contented with this issue; but as we are anxious to exhibit this whole subject in its true bearings, and as we do believe that this evil has been most strangely and causelessly exaggerated, we have determined to examine it a moment, and point out its true extent. It seems to us, that those who insist most upon it, commit the enormous error of looking upon every slave in the whole slave-holding country as actuated by the most deadly enmity to the whites, and possessing all that reckless, fiendish temper, which would lead him to murder and assassinate the moment the opportunity occurs. This is far from being true; the slave, as we have already said, generally loves the master and his family;[4] and few indeed there are, who can coldly plot the murder of men, women, and children; and if they do, there are fewer still who can have the villany to execute. We can sit down and imagine that all the negroes in the south have conspired to rise on a certain night, and murder all the whites in their respective families; we may suppose the secret to be kept, and that they have the physical power to exterminate; and yet, we say the whole is *morally impossible.* No insurrection of this kind can ever occur where the blacks are as much civilized as they are in the United States. Savages and Koromantyn slaves can commit such deeds, because their whole life and education have prepared them, and they glory in the achievement; but the negro of the United States has imbibed the principles, the sentiments, and feelings of the white; in one word, he is civilized — at least, comparatively; his whole education and course of life are at war with such fell [sic] deeds. Nothing, then, but the most subtle and poisonous principles, sedulously infused into his mind, can break his allegiance, and transform him into the midnight murderer. Any man who will attend to the history of the Southampton massacre, must at once see, that the cause of even the partial success of the insurrectionists, was the very circumstance that there was no extensive plot, and that Nat, a demented fanatic, was under the impression that heaven had enjoined him to liberate the blacks, and had made its manifestations by loud noises in the air, an eclipse, and by the greenness of the sun. It was these signs which determined *him*, and ignorance and superstition, together with implicit confidence in Nat, determined a few others, and thus the bloody work began. So fearfully and reluctantly did they proceed to the execution, that we have no doubt but that if Travis, the first attacked, could have waked whilst they were getting into his house, or could have shot down Nat or Will, the rest would have fled, and the affair would have terminated *in limine*.

We have read with great attention the history of the insurrections in St. Domingo, and have no hesitation in affirming, that to the reflecting mind, that whole history affords the most complete evidence of the difficulty and almost impossibility of succeeding in these plots, even under the most favourable circumstances. It would almost have been a *moral miracle*, if that revolution had not succeeded. The French revolution had kindled a blaze throughout the world. The society of the *Amis des Noirs*, (the friends of the blacks,) in Paris, had educated and disciplined many of the mulattoes, who were almost as numerous as the whites in the island. The National Assembly, in its mad career, declared these mulattoes to be equal in all respects to the whites, and gave them the same privileges and immunities as the whites. During the ten years, too, immediately preceding the revolution, more than 200,000 negroes were imported into the island from Africa. It is a well known fact, that newly imported negroes are always greatly more dangerous than those born among us; and of those importations a very large proportion consisted of Koromantyn slaves, from the Gold Coast, who have all the savage ferocity of the North American Indian.[5] And lastly, the whites themselves, disunited and strangely inharmonious, would nevertheless have suppressed the insurrections, although the blacks and mulattoes were nearly *fifteen-fold* their numbers, if it had not been for the constant and too fatal interference of France. The great sin of that revolution rests on the *National Assembly*, and should be an awful warning to every legislature to beware of too much tampering with so deliberate and difficult a subject as an alteration of the fundamental relations of society.

But there is another cause which will render the success of the blacks for ever impossible in the South, as long as slavery exists. It is, that, in modern times especially, wealth and talent must ever rule over *mere* physical force. During the feudal ages, the vassals never made a settled concerted attempt to throw off the yoke of the lord or landed proprietor; and the true reason was, they had neither property nor talent, and consequently the power, under these circumstances, could be placed nowhere else than in the hands of the lords; but so soon as the *tiers etat* arose, with commerce and manufactures, there was something to struggle for, and the *crise des revolutions*, (the crisis of revolutions,) was the consequence. No connected, persevering, and well concerted movement, ever takes place, in modern times, unless for the sake of property. Now, the property, talent, concert, and we may add habit, are all with the whites, and render their continued superiority absolutely certain, if they are not meddled with, no matter what may be the disproportion of numbers. We look upon these insurrections in the same light that we do the murders and robberies which occur in society, and in a slave-holding state, they are a sort of substitute for the latter; the robbers and murderers in what are called free states, are generally the poor and needy, who rob for money; negro slaves rarely murder or rob for this purpose; they have no inducement to do it — the fact is, the whole capital of the South is pledged for their maintenance. Now, there is no doubt but that the common robberies and murders, for money, take off, in the aggregate, more men, and destroy more property than insurrections among the slaves; the former are the result of fixed causes *eternally* at work, the latter of occasional causes which are rarely, *very rarely*, in action. Accordingly, if we should look to the whole of our southern population, and compare the average number of deaths, by the hands of assassins, with the numbers elsewhere, we would be astonished to find them perhaps as few or fewer than in any other population of equal amount on the globe. In the city of London there is, upon an average, a murder or a house-breaking and robbery every night in the year, which is greater than the amount of deaths by murders, insurrections, &c., in our whole southern country; and yet the inhabitant of London walks the streets and sleeps in perfect confidence, and why should not we who are in fact in much less danger?[6] These calamities in London, very properly give rise to the establishment of a police, and the adoption of precautionary measures; and so they should in our country, and every where else. And if the Virginia legislature had turned its attention more to this subject during its last session, we think, with all due deference, it would have redounded much more to the advantage of the state than the intemperate discussion which was gotten up.

But it is agreed on almost all hands, that the danger of insurrection now is not very great; but a time must arrive, it is supposed by many, when the dangers will infinitely increase, and either the one or the other race must necessarily be exterminated. "I do believe," said one in the Virginia legislature, "and such must be the judgment of every reflecting man, that unless something is done in time to obviate it, the day must arrive when scenes of inconceivable horror must inevitably occur, and one of these two races of human beings will have their throats cut by the other." Another gentleman anticipates the dark day when a negro legislature would be in session in the capital of the Old Dominion! Mr. Clay, too, seems to be full of gloomy anticipations of the future. In his Colonization Speech of 1830, he says, "Already the slaves may be estimated at two millions, and the free population at ten; the former being in the proportion of one to five of the latter. Their respective numbers will probably double in periods of thirty-three years. In the year 1863, the number of the whites will probably be twenty, and of the blacks four millions. In 1896, forty and eight; and in the year 1929, about a century, eighty and sixteen millions. What mind is sufficiently extensive in its reach — what nerve sufficiently strong — to contemplate this vast and progressive augmentation, without an awful foreboding of the tremendous consequences!'' If these anticipations are true, then may we, in despair, quietly sit down by the waters of Babylon, and weep over our lot, for we can never remove the blacks. *''Haeret lateri lethalis arundo.''*

But we have none of these awful forebodings. We do not look to the time when the throats of one race must be cut by the other; on the contrary, we have no hesitation in affirming, and we think we can prove it too, that in 1929, taking Mr. Clay's own statistics, we shall be much more secure from plots and insurrections, than we are at this moment. It is an undeniable fact, that in the increase of population, the power and security of the dominant party always increase *much more* than in proportion to the relative augmentation of their numbers. One hundred men can much more easily keep an equal number in subjection than fifty, and a million would rule a million more certainly and securely than any lesser number. The dominant can only be overtur. ed by concert and harmony among the subject party, and the greater the relative numbers on both sides, the more impossible does this concert on the part of the subjected become. A police, too, of the same *relative* numbers, is much more efficient amid a numerous population, than a very sparse one. We will illustrate by example, which cannot fail to strike even the most sceptical. Mr. Gibbon supposes that the hundredth man in any community, is as much as the people can afford to keep in pay for the purposes of a police. Now suppose the community be only one hundred, then one man alone is the police. Is it not evident that the ninety-nine will be able at any moment to destroy him, and throw off all restraint? Suppose the community one thousand, then ten will form the police, which would have a rather better chance of keeping up order among the nine hundred and ninety, than the one in the one hundred, but still this would be insufficient. Let your community swell to one million, and ten thousand would then form the police, and ten thousand troops will strike terror in any city on the face of the globe. Lord Wellington lately asserted in the British Parliament, that Paris, containing a population of a million of souls (the most boisterous and ungovernable,) never required, before the reign of Louis Philip, more than forty-five hundred troops to keep it in the most perfect subjection. It is this very principle which explains the fact so frequently noticed, that revolutions are effected much more readily in small states than in large ones. The little republics of Greece underwent revolutions almost every month — the dominant party was never safe for a moment. — The little states of modern Italy have undergone more changes and revolutions than all the rest of Europe together, and if foreign influence were withdrawn, almost every ship from Europe, even now, would bring the news of some new revolution in those states. If the standing army will remain firm to the government, a successful revolution in most large empires, as France, Germany, and Russia, is almost impossible. The two revolutions in France have been successful, in consequence of the disaffection of the troops, who have joined the popular party.

Let us apply these principles to our own case; and for the sake of simplicity we will take a country of a mixed population of twenty thousand, viz. blacks ten thousand, and whites as many: — the patrol which they can keep out, would, according to our rule, be two hundred — double both sides, and the patrol would be four hundred, quadruple and it would be eight hundred — now a patrol of eight hundred would be much more efficient than the two hundred, though they were, relatively to the numbers kept in order, exactly the same; and the same principle is applicable to the progress of population in the whole slave-holding country. In 1929, our police will be much more efficient than now, if the two castes preserve any thing like the same relative numbers. We believe it would be better for the whites that the negro population should double, if they added only one half more to their numbers, than that they should remain stationary on both sides. Hence an insuperable objection to all these deporting schemes — they cannot diminish the relative proportion of the blacks to the whites, but on the contrary increase it, while they check the augmentation of the population as a whole, and consequently lessen the security of the dominant party. We do not fear the increase of the blacks, for that very increase adds to the wealth of society, and enables it to keep up the police. This is the true secret of the security of the West Indies and Brazil. In Jamaica, the blacks are eight fold the whites; throughout the extensive empire of Brazil, they are three to one. Political prophets have been prophesying for fifty years past, that the day would speedily arrive, when all the West Indies would be in the possession of the negroes; and the danger is no greater now, than it was at the commencement. We sincerely believe the blacks never will get possession, unless through the mad interference of the mother countries, and *even* then we are doubtful whether they can conquer the whites. Now, we have nowhere in the United States, the immense disproportion between the two races observed in Brazil and the West Indies, and we are not like to have it in all time to come. We have no data, therefore, upon which to anticipate that dreadful crisis, which so torments the imagination of some.

But our population returns have been looked to, and it has been affirmed that they show a steady increase of blacks, which will finally carry them in all proportion beyond the whites, and that this will be particularly the case in Eastern Virginia. We have no fears on this score either: even if it were true, the danger would not be very great. With the increase of the blacks, we can afford to enlarge the police; and we will venture to say, that with the hundredth man at our disposal, and faithful to us, we would keep down insurrection in any large country on the face of the globe. But the speakers in the Virginia legislature, in our humble opinion, made most unwarrantable inferences from the census returns. They took a period between 1790 and

1830, and judged exclusively from the aggregate results of that whole time. Mr. Brown pointed out their fallacy, and showed that there was but a small portion of the period in which the blacks had rapidly gained upon the whites, but during the residue they were most rapidly losing their high relative increase, and would, perhaps, in 1840, exhibit an augmentation less than the whites. But let us go a little back — in 1740 the slaves in South Carolina, says Marshall, were three times the whites, the danger from them was greater then than it ever has been since, or ever will be again. There was an insurrection in that year, which was put down with the utmost ease, although instigated and aided by the Spaniards. The slaves in Virginia, at the same period, were much more numerous than the whites. Now suppose some of those *peepers* into futurity could have been present, would they not have predicted the speedy arrival of the time when the blacks, running ahead of the whites in numbers, would have destroyed their security? In 1763, the black population of Virginia was 100,000, and the white 70,000. In South Carolina, the blacks were 90,000, and the whites 40,000. Comparing these with the returns of 1740, our prophets, could they have lived so long, might have found some consolation in the greater relative increase of the whites. Again, when we see in 1830, that the blacks in both states have fallen in numbers below the whites, our prophets, were they alive, might truly be pronounced *false.* (*See Holmes's Annals, and Marshall's Life of Washington,* on this subject.)

We are happy to see that the legislature of Virginia, during the last session, incorporated a company to complete the James river and Kanhawa improvements, and that the city of Richmond has so liberally contributed by her subscriptions, as to render the project almost certain of success. It is this great improvement which is destined to revolutionize the financial condition of the Old Dominion, and speed her on more rapidly in wealth and numbers, than she has ever advanced before: the snail pace at which she has hitherto been crawling, is destined to be converted into the giant's stride, and this very circumstance, of itself, will defeat all the gloomy predictions about the blacks. The first effect of the improvement will be to raise up larger towns in the eastern portion of the state. Besides other manifold advantages which these towns will diffuse, they will have a tendency to draw into them the capital and free labourers of the north, and in this way to destroy the proportion of the blacks. Baltimore is now an exemplification of this fact, which by its mighty agency is fast making Maryland a non-slave-holding state. Again, the rise of cities in the lower part of Virginia, and increased density of population, will render the division of labour more complete, break down the large farms into small ones, and substitute, in a great measure, the garden for the plantation cultivation: consequently, less slave and more free labour will be requisite, and in due time the abolitionists will find this most lucrative system working to their heart's content, increasing the prosperity of Virginia, and diminishing the evils of slavery without those impoverishing effects which all other schemes must *necessarily* have. We hope then that those gentlemen who have so perseveringly engaged in urging forward this great scheme of improvement, will not falter until the work is accomplished, and they will have the consolation of seeing that its moral effects will be no less salutary than the physical.

5thly, and lastly. *Slave labour is unproductive, and the distressed condition of Virginia and the whole South is owing to this cause.* Our limits will not allow us to investigate fully this assertion, but a very partial analysis will enable us to show that the truth of the general proposition upon which the conclusion is based, depends on circumstances, and that those circumstances do not apply to our southern country. The ground assumed by Smith and Storch, who are the most able supporters of the doctrine of the superior productiveness of free labour, is that each one is actuated by a desire to accumulate when free, and this desire produces much more efficient and constant exertions than can possibly be expected from the feeble operation of fear upon the slave. We are, in the main, converts to this doctrine, but must be permitted to limit it by some considerations. It is very evident, when we look to the various countries in which there is free labour alone, that a vast difference in its productiveness is manifested. The English operative we are disposed to consider the most productive labourer in the world, and the Irish labourer, in his immediate neighbourhood, is not more than equal to the southern slave — the Spanish and even Italian labourers are inferior. Now, how are we to account for this great difference? It will be found *mainly* to depend upon the operation of two great principles, and *secondarily* upon attendant circumstances. These two principles are the desire to accumulate and better our condition, and a desire to indulge in idleness and inactivity.

We have already seen that the principle of idleness triumphed over the desire for accumulation among the savages of North and South America, among the African nations, among the blacks of St. Domingo, &c., and nothing but the strong arm of authority could overcome its operation. In southern countries, idleness is very apt to predominate, even under the most favourable circumstances, over the desire to accumulate, and slave labour, consequently, in such countries, is most productive. Again, staple-growing states are, *caeteris paribus,* more favourable to slave labour than manufacturing states. Slaves in such countries may be worked in bodies under the eye of a superintendent, and made to perform more labour than freemen. There is no instance of the successful cultivation of the sugar cane by free labour. St. Domingo, once the greatest sugar-growing island in the world, makes now scarcely enough for her own supply. We very much doubt even whether slave labour be not best for all southern agricultural countries. Humboldt, in his New Spain, says he doubts whether there be a plant on the globe so productive as the banana, and yet these banana districts, strange to tell, are the poorest and most miserable in all South America, because the people only labour a little to support themselves, and spend the rest of their time in idleness. There is no doubt but slave labour would be the most productive kind in these districts. We doubt whether the extreme south of the United States, and the West India islands, would ever have been cultivated to the same degree of perfection as now, by any other than slave labour.

But it is said free labour becomes cheaper than slave labour, and finally extinguishes it, as has actually happened in the West of Europe; this we are ready to admit, but think it was owing to a change in the tillage, and the rise of manufactures and commerce, to which free labour alone is adapted. As a proof of this, we can cite the populous empire of China, and the eastern nations generally, where slave labour has stood its ground against free labour, although the population is denser, and the proportional means of subsistence more scanty than anywhere else on the face of the globe. How is this to be accounted for, let us ask? Does it not prove, that under some circumstances, slave labour is as productive as free? We would as soon look to China to test this principle, as any other nation on earth. Again, looking to the nations of antiquity, if the Scriptural accounts are to be relied on, the number of inhabitants in Palestine must have been more than 6,000,000; at which rate, Palestine was at least, when taking into consideration her limited territory, five times as populous as England.[7] Now we know that the tribes of Judah and Israel both used slave labour, and it must have been exceedingly productive, for we find the two Kings of Judah and Israel bringing into the field no less than 1,200,000 chosen men;[8] and Jehosaphat, the son of Asa, had an army consisting of 1,160,000;[9] and what a prodigious force must he have commanded, had he been sovereign of all the tribes! Nothing but the most productive labour could ever have supported the immense armies which were then led into the field.

Wallace thinks that ancient Egypt must have been thrice as populous as England; and yet so valuable was slave labour, that ten of the most dreadful plagues that ever affected mankind, could not dispose the selfish heart of Pharaoh to part with his Israelitish slaves; and when he lost them, Egypt sunk, never to rise to her pristine grandeur again. Ancient Italy too, not to mention Greece, was exceedingly populous, and perhaps Rome was a larger city than any of modern times — and yet slave labour supported these dense populations, and even rooted out free labour. All these examples prove sufficiently, that under certain circumstances, slave is as productive, and even more productive, than free labour.

But the southern states, and particularly Virginia, have been compared with the non-slave-holding states, and pronounced far behind them in the general increase of wealth and population; and this, it is said, is a decisive proof of the inferiority of slave labour in this country. We are sorry we have not the space for a thorough investigation of this assertion, but we have no doubt of its fallacy. Look to the progress of the colonies before the establishment of the federal government, and you find the slave-holding were the most prosperous and the most wealthy. The north dreaded the formation of the confederated government, *precisely* because of its *poverty*. This is an historic fact. It stood to the south, as Scotland did to England at the period of the Union; and feared lest the south, by its superior wealth, supported by this very *slave labour*, which, all of a *sudden*, has become so unproductive, should abstract the little wealth which it possessed. Again, look to the exports at the present time of the whole confederacy, and what do we see — why, that one-third of the states, and those *slave-holding* too, furnish two-thirds of the whole exports!! But although this is now the case, we are still not prosperous. Let us ask them two simple questions; 1st. How came the south, for two hundred years, to prosper with her slave labour, if so very unproductive and ruinous? and 2dly. How does it happen, that her exports are so great even now, and that her prosperity is nevertheless on the decline? Painful as the accusation may be to the heart of the true patriot, we are forced to assert, that the unequal operation of the federal government has principally achieved it. The north has found that it could not compete with the south in agriculture, and has had recourse to the system of duties, for the purpose of raising up the business of manufactures. This is a business in which the slave labour cannot compete with northern, and in order to carry this system through, a coalition has been formed with the west, by which a large portion of the federal funds are to be spent in that quarter for internal improvements. These duties act as a discouragement to southern industry, which furnishes the exports by which the imports are purchased, and a bounty to northern labour, and the partial disbursements of the funds increase the pressure on the south to a still greater degree. It is not slave labour then which has produced our depression, but it is the action of the federal government which is ruining slave labour.

There is at this moment an exemplification of the destructive influence of government agency in the West Indies. The British West India Islands are now in a more depressed condition than any others, and both the Edinburgh and London Quarterly Reviews charge their depression upon the regulations, taxing sugar, coffee, &c., and preventing them, at the same time, from purchasing bread stuffs, &c. from the United States, which can be furnished by them cheaper than from any other quarter. Some of the philanthropists of Great Britain cry out it is slavery which has done it, and the slaves must be liberated; but they are at once refuted by the fact, that never has island flourished more rapidly than Cuba, in its immediate neighbourhood. And Cuba flourishes because she enjoys free trade, and has procured of late plenty of slaves. It is curious that the population of this island has, for the last thirty years, kept pace with that of Pennsylvania, one of the most flourishing of the states of the confederacy, and her wealth has increased in a still greater ratio.[10] Look again to Brazil, perhaps, at this moment, the most prosperous state of South America, and we find her slaves three times more numerous that the freemen. Mr. Brougham, in his Colonial Policy, says that Cayenne never flourished as long as she was scantily supplied with slaves, but her prosperity commenced the moment she was supplied with an abundance of this *unproductive* labour. Now we must earnestly ask an explanation of these phenomena, upon the principle that slave labour is unproductive.

There are other causes too, which have operated in concert with the federal government, to depress the south. The climate is unhealthy, and upon an average, perhaps one-tenth of the labour is suspended during the sickly months. There is a great deal of travelling too, from this cause, to the north, which abstracts the capital from the south, and spreads it over the north; and added to all this, the *standard of comfort* is much higher in the slave-holding than the non-slave-holding states.[11] All these circumstances together, are surely sufficient to account for the depressed condition of the south, without asserting that slave labour is valueless. But we believe all other causes as "dust in the balance," when compared with the operation of the federal government.

How does it happen that Louisiana, with a greater proportional number of slaves than any other state in the Union, with the most insalubrious climate, with one-fourth of her white population spread over the more northern states in the sickly season, and with a higher *standard of comfort* than perhaps any other state in the Union, is nevertheless one of the most rapidly flourishing in the whole southern country? The true answer is, she has been so fortunately situated as to be able to reap the fruits of federal protection. "Midas's wand" has touched her, and she has reaped the golden harvest. There is no complaint there of the unproductiveness of slave labour.

But it is time to bring this long article to a close; it is upon a subject which we have most reluctantly discussed; but, as we have already said, the example was set from a higher quarter; the seal has been broken, and we therefore determined to enter fully into the discussion. If our positions be true, and it does seem to us they may be sustained by reasoning almost as conclusive as the demonstration of the mathematician, it follows, that the time for emancipation has not yet arrived, and perhaps it never will. We hope sincerely, that the intelligent sons of Virginia will ponder well before they move — before they enter into a scheme which will destroy more than half Virginia's wealth, and drag her down from her proud and elevated station among the mean things of the earth.

NOTES

[1] See Ephesians, vi. 5, 9. Titus, ii. 9, 10. Philemon. Colossians, iii. 22, and iv. 1.

[2] Jefferson's Notes on Virginia.

[3] A similar remark is made by Ramsay, and confirmed by Bryan Edwards, in regard to the West Indies. "Adventurers from Europe are universally more cruel and morose towards the slaves, than the Creole or native West Indian." *(Hist of W. 1. Book 4. Chap. 1.)*

[4] We scarcely know a single family, in which the slaves, especially the domestics, do not manifest the most unfeigned grief at the deaths which occur among the whites.

[5] It was the Koromantyns who brought about the insurrection in Jamaica in 1760. They are a very hardy race; and the Dutch, who are a calculating, money-making people, and withal the most cruel masters in the world, have generally preferred these slaves, because they might be *forced* to do most work; but the consequence of their avarice has been, that they have been more cursed with insurrections than any other people in the West Indies.

[6] We wish that accurate accounts could be published of all the deaths which had occurred from insurrections in the United States, West Indies, and South America, since the establishment of slavery; and that these could be compared to the whole population that have lived since that epoch, and the number of deaths which occur in other equal amounts of population, from popular sedition, robberies, &c., and we would be astonished to see what little cause we have for the slightest apprehension on this score.

[7]See Wallace on the Numbers of Mankind, p. 52, Edinb. Edit.

[8]2 Chron. xiii. 3.

[9]2 Chron. xvii.

[10]See some interesting statistics concerning this island in Mr. Poinsett's Notes on Mexico.

[11]In the Virginia debate, it was said that the slow progress of the Virginia population was a most unerring symptom of her want of prosperity, and the inefficacy of slave labour. Now we protest against this criterion, unless very cautiously applied. Ireland suffers more from want and famine than any other country in Europe, and yet her population advances almost as rapidly as ours, and it is this very increase which curses the country with the plague of famine. In the Highlands of Scotland, they have a very sparse population, scarcely increasing at all; and yet they are much better fed, clothed, &c. than in Ireland. Malthus has proved, that there are two species of checks which repress redundant populations — *positive* and *preventive*. It is the latter which keeps down the Scotch population; while the former, always accompanied with misery, keeps down the Irish. We believe at this time the preventive checks are in full operation in Virginia. The people of that state live much better than the same classes to the north, and they will not get married unless there is a prospect of maintaining their families in the same style they have been accustomed to live in. We believe the preventive checks may commence their operation too soon for the wealth of a state, but they always mark a high degree of civilization — so that the slow progress of population in Virginia turns out to be her highest eulogy.

Declaration of Sentiments

American Anti-Slavery Society

Commentary

The Virginia debates marked the apex of Southern abolitionism. By 1837, not a single antislavery society remained in the South. Many localities outlawed antislavery literature. Mobs, often with the approval of law enforcement officials, attacked suspected abolitionists.

Scholars attribute the rapid collapse of Southern abolitionism to many factors, including the persuasiveness of proslavery rhetoric; white fears of "inferior" blacks; the economic importance of slavery; the extent to which slavery was integral to Southern culture; and the opposition of most Southern churches to social reform. Scholars disagree about a question that is of special interest to rhetorical critics: Did the rhetoric of Northern abolitionists contribute to the collapse of Southern abolitionism? Those who say "yes" argue that the militancy of Northern rhetoric intensified Southern fears and/or politicians used Northern abolitionism as a hate object to unify the South in its quarrels over the tariff and other sectional issues. Those who answer negatively argue that other factors were so powerful that Southern abolitionism had no chance of success anyway.

Regardless of how one answers this difficult question, it is clear that Northern abolitionism expanded as Southern abolitionism was dying. Equally clear is that militant Northern rhetoric was strongly influenced by social perfectionism, revivalism, temperance and the spirit of social reform. However, the movement faced serious problems in the North, including divisiveness from within and opposition from without.

By the end of 1831, Garrison had formed the New England Anti-Slavery Society and was calling for a national organization. During the previous year, two wealthy New York philanthropists, Arthur and Lewis Tappan, had been so impressed by the evangelical sermons of a prominent revivalist, Charles Finney, that they had begun financing various religious and reform projects. After converting to abolitionism, the Tappans formed a committee in 1831 to form a national antislavery society; however, they delayed instituting plans until the British Parliament abolished slavery in the British West Indies. They believed it would be rhetorically advantageous to hold the first convention immediately after British abolition became a reality.

In 1833, passage of the West Indian bill seemed assured, and the New York committee set October 25, 1833 as the date for holding the convention in Philadelphia, home of the nation's oldest antislavery society. All went well until the Pennsylvania society withdrew its support under intense pressure from leading Philadelphia citizens. The committee decided to postpone the convention, but Garrison, who had not been involved in the planning, entered the scene and insisted on holding the convention despite opposition. The New York committee agreed, and the first (and hastily organized) convention of the American Anti-Slavery Society was held in Philadelphia on December 5-6, 1833.

Garrison's insistence was due partly to his impatience, but a rhetorical factor was also at work. He saw the persuasive potential of identifying abolitionism with the American Revolution. He wished to hold the society's first meeting in the place where the Continental Congress had adopted the Declaration of Independence. Under Garrison's leadership, a committee prepared the declaration, which is reproduced from the December 16, 1833 issue of *The Liberator*, p. 198, which is currently housed at the American Antiquarian Society.

Declaration of Sentiments

The Convention, assembled in the City of Philadelphia to organize a National Anti-Slavery Society, promptly seize the opportunity to promulgate the following DECLARATION OF SENTIMENTS, as cherished by them in relation to the enslavement of one-sixth portion of the American people.

More than fifty-seven years have elapsed since a band of patriots convened in this place, to devise measures for the deliverance of this country from a foreign yoke. The corner-stone upon which they founded the TEMPLE OF FREEDOM was broadly this — 'that all men are created equal; that they are endowed by their Creator with certain inalienable rights; that among these are life, LIBERTY, and the pursuit of happiness.' At the sound of their trumpet-call, three millions of people rose up as from the sleep of death, and rushed to the strife of blood; deeming it more glorious to die instantly as freemen, than desirable to live one hour as slaves. — They were few in number — poor in resources; but the honest conviction that TRUTH, JUSTICE, and RIGHT were on their side, made them invincible.

We have met together for the achievement of an enterprise, without which, that of our fathers is incomplete, and which, for its magnitude, solemnity, and probable results upon the destiny of the world, as far transcends theirs, as moral truth does physical force.

In purity of motive, in earnestness of zeal, in decision of purpose, in intrepidity of action, in steadfastness of faith, in sincerity of spirit, we would not be inferior to them.

Their principles led them to wage war against their oppressors, and to spill human blood like water, in order to be free. *Ours* forbid the doing of evil that good may come, and lead us to reject, and to entreat the oppressed to reject, the use of all carnal weapons for deliverance from bondage — relying solely upon those which are spiritual, and mighty through God to the pulling down of strong holds.

Their measures were physical resistance — the marshalling in arms — the hostile array — the moral encounter. *Ours* shall be such only as the opposition of moral purity to moral corruption — the destruction of error by the potency of truth — the overthrow of prejudice by the power of love — and the abolition of slavery by the spirit of repentance.

Their grievances, great as they were, were trifling in comparison with the wrongs and sufferings of those for whom we plead. Our fathers were never slaves — never bought and sold like cattle — never shut out from the light of knowledge and religion — never subjected to the lash of brutal taskmasters.

But those, for whose emancipation we are striving, — constituting at the present time at least one-sixth part of our countrymen, — are recognised by the laws, and treated by their fellow beings, as marketable commodities — as goods and chattels — as brute beasts; — are plundered daily of the fruits of their toil without redress; — really enjoy no constitutional nor legal protection from licentious and murderous outrages upon their persons; — are ruthlessly torn asunder — the tender babe from the arms of its frantic mother — the heart-broken wife from her weeping husband — at the caprice or pleasure of irresponsible tyrants; — and, for the crime of having a dark complexion, suffer the pangs of hunger, the infliction of stripes, and the ignominy of brutal servitude. They are kept in heathenish darkness by laws expressly enacted to make their instruction a criminal offence.

These are the prominent circumstances in the condition of more than TWO MILLIONS of our people, the proof of which may be found in thousands of indisputable facts, and in the laws of the slaveholding States.

Hence we maintain —

That in view of the civil and religious privileges of this nation, the guilt of its oppression is unequalled by any other on the face of the earth; — and, therefore,

That it is bound to repent instantly, to undo the heavy burden, to break every yoke, and to let the oppressed go free.

We further maintain —

That no man has a right to enslave or imbrute his brother — to hold or acknowledge him, for one moment, as a piece of merchandise — to keep back his hire by fraud — or to brutalize his mind by denying him the means of intellectual, social and moral improvement.

The right to enjoy liberty is inalienable. To invade it, is to usurp the prerogative of Jehovah. Every man has a right to his own body — to the products of his own labor — to the protection of law — and to the common advantages of society. It is piracy to buy or steal a native African, and subject him to servitude. Surely the sin is as great to enslave an AMERICAN as an AFRICAN.

Therefore we believe and affirm —

That there is no difference, *in principle*, between the African slave trade and American slavery;

That every American citizen, who retains a human being in involuntary bondage, is (according to Scripture) a MAN-STEALER;

That the slaves ought instantly to be set free, and brought under the protection of law;

That if they had lived from the time of Pharaoh down to the present period, and had been entailed through successive generations, their right to be free could never have been alienated, but their claims would have constantly risen in solemnity;

That all those laws which are now in force, admitting the right of slavery, are therefore before God utterly null and void; being an audacious usurpation of the Divine prerogative, a daring infringement on the law of nature, a base overthrow of the very foundations of the social compact, a complete extinction of all the relations, endearments and obligations of mankind, and a presumptuous transgression of all the holy commandments — and that therefore they ought to be instantly abrogated.

We further believe and affirm —

That all persons of color who possess the qualifications which are demanded of others, ought to be admitted forthwith to the enjoyment of the same privileges, and the exercise of the same prerogatives, as others; and that the paths of preferment, of wealth, and of intelligence, should be opened as widely to them as to persons of a white complexion.

We maintain that no compensation should be given to the planters emancipating their slaves —

Because it would be a surrender of the great fundamental principle that man cannot hold property in man;

Because SLAVERY IS A CRIME, AND THEREFORE IT IS NOT AN ARTICLE TO BE SOLD;

Because the holders of slaves are not the just proprietors of what they claim; — freeing the slaves is not depriving them of property, but restoring it to the right owner; — it is not wronging the master, but righting the slave — restoring him to himself;

Because immediate and general emancipation would only destroy nominal, not real property: it would not amputate a limb or break a bone of the slaves, but by infusing motives into their breasts, would make them doubly valuable to the masters as free laborers; and

Because if compensation is to be given at all, it should be given to the outraged and guiltless slaves, and not to those who have plundered and abused them.

We regard, as delusive, cruel and dangerous, any scheme of expatriation which pretends to aid, either directly or indirectly, in the emancipation of the slaves, or to be a substitute for the immediate and total abolition of slavery.

We fully and unanimously recognise the sovereignty of each State, to legislate exclusively on the subject of the slavery which is tolerated within its limits. We concede that Congress, *under the present national compact*, has no right to interfere with any of the slave States, in relation to this momentous subject.

We also maintain that there are, at the present time, the highest obligations resting upon the people of the free States, to remove slavery by moral and political action, as prescribed in the Constitution of the United States. They are now living under a pledge of their tremendous physical force to fasten the galling fetters of tyranny upon the limbs of millions in the southern States; — they are liable to be called at any moment to suppress a general insurrection of the slaves; — they authorise the slave owner to vote for three-fifths of his slaves as property, and thus enable him to perpetuate his oppression; — they support a standing army at the south for its protection; — and they seize the slave who has escaped into their territories, and send him back to be tortured by an enraged master or a brutal driver.

This relation to slavery is criminal and full of danger: IT MUST BE BROKEN UP.

These are our views and principles — these, our designs and measures. With entire confidence in the overruling justice of God, we plant ourselves upon the Declaration of our Independence, and upon the truths of Divine Revelation, as upon the EVERLASTING ROCK.

We shall organize Anti-Slavery Societies, if possible, in every city, town and village of our land.

We shall send forth Agents to lift up the voice of remonstrance, of warning, of entreaty and rebuke.

We shall circulate, unsparingly and extensively, anti-slavery tracts and periodicals.

We shall enlist the PULPIT and the PRESS in the cause of the suffering and the dumb.

We shall aim at a purification of the churches from all participation in the guilt of slavery.

We shall encourage the labor of freemen over that of the slaves, by giving a preference to their productions; — and

We shall spare no exertions nor means to bring the whole nation to speedy repentance.

Our trust for victory is solely in GOD. *We* may be personally defeated, but our principles never. TRUTH, JUSTICE, REASON, HUMANITY, must and will gloriously triumph. Already a host is coming up to the help of the Lord against the mighty, and the prospect before us is full of encouragement.

Submitting this DECLARATION to the candid examination of the people of this country, and of the friends of liberty all over the world, we hereby affix our signatures to it; — pledging ourselves that, under the guidance and by the help of Almighty God, we will do all that in us lies, consistently with this Declaration of our principles, to overthrow the most execrable system of slavery that has ever been witnessed upon earth — to deliver our land from its deadliest curse — to wipe out the foulest stain which rests upon our national escutcheon — and to secure to the colored population of the United States all the rights and privileges which belong to them as men and as Americans — come what may to our persons, our interests, or our reputations — whether we live to witness the triumph of JUSTICE, LIBERTY and HUMANITY, or perish untimely as martyrs in this great, benevolent and holy cause.

Pastoral Letter

General Association of [Congregational Ministers of] Massachusetts

Commentary

With the Tappans' financial backing and an executive committee to supervise operations, the American Anti-Slavery Society (AASS) began publicizing the cause through the traditional medium of pamphlets, but subsequent events prompted a change. In 1835, the Lane Seminary in Cincinnati held a public debate on slavery that was arranged by students, including the 32-year-old Theodore Weld, who had settled down to ministerial studies after having acquired considerable experience as a revivalist and speaker for temperance and abolitionism. Unhappy trustees ordered students to avoid debating slavery in the future. This caused many "Lane Rebels" to transfer to the new Oberlin College while others, including Weld, became agents of the AASS. Their job was to give speeches and organize local societies in western New York and the Northwestern States.

Agents were so successful during late 1835 and early 1836 that the AASS executive committee decided to abandon pamphleteering in favor of public speaking. Agents were asked to recruit enough new colleagues to reach a total of seventy, a number of symbolic significance because it was generally believed that the number of Christian apostles had been seventy. At the November, 1836 AASS convention, a National Female Anti-Slavery Society (NFASS) was formed. Weld's training session for new members of the seventy, conducted immediately after the convention, included two women: Sarah Grimke (1792-1873) and her younger sister Angelina (who later married Weld).

The Grimke sisters were from a wealthy slaveowning family in South Carolina, but Sarah had become disenchanted early. After a revivalist came to town, she left the family's fashionable Episcopal church to become a Presbyterian. She later converted to the Quakers and moved to the Quaker stronghold of Philadelphia. Angelina followed in her footsteps, but, being more outgoing, she was the first to enter the public arena, something that women were not supposed to do. She sent an antislavery letter to Garrison, who printed it in the September 19, 1835 issue of *The Liberator*, and followed it with a pamphlet entitled, *An Appeal to the Christian Women of the Southern States*. She argued that women were as guilty as men for the sin of slavery and should therefore work to eradicate it. Meanwhile Sarah composed an *Epistle to the Clergy of the Southern States*. Their pamphlets were published in 1836, shortly before they joined the seventy.

Public speaking by women was even more unconventional than writing, and the Grimke sisters, of course, had no experience outside Weld's classroom. Presumably, however, there would be no trouble as they set about their task of promoting local female societies and mobilizing them under the banner of the newly created NFASS. They were to give "parlor speeches" in private homes to small groups of women, help them to form a local society and then move to another locality. They spent the winter of 1835-1836 touring New York and New Jersey, where they attracted larger audiences than anticipated and faced some heckling, but no serious problems developed. After attending the first convention of the NFASS in May, 1837, they spoke to the well-established Boston society and toured the surrounding area to help organize more female societies. The little "parlor speech" was soon a fading memory as they attracted large audiences composed of both sexes.

Large audiences did not mean unqualified approval. The sisters sometimes had trouble getting places in which to speak, and many listeners undoubtedly attended only to see a female speaker. They were frequently heckled. Anti-abolitionists accused the spinsters of seeking black husbands, and some abolitionists declared that public speaking by women was "unchristian." Interest in their tour intensified when *The Liberator* published a series of essays entitled "The Labours of the Misses Grimke," written by Henry C. Wright. His visionary utopianism was matched only by his lack of good sense. Without ever communicating with the Grimkes, he published in July a fictional piece, "A Domestic Scene," in which two sisters, "S. and A.G.," embraced pacifism, women's equality, abolitionism and anarchism (governments being as oppressive as slavery).

Amidst the furor, the Congregational clergy of Massachusetts held their annual meeting in late June, 1837. Their uneasiness about females engaging in controversial public activities added to the sense of apprehension that had been developing. Pastoral authority had gradually been undermined by the growing eqalitarianism, which inspired the laity to demand a greater voice in the conduct of church affairs. This gradual trend might not have been a cause for serious concern if it had not been for the resulting divisiveness that was intensifying in many congregations over the church's role in social reform. Some lay people were insisting that churches work vigorously for social reform and were even demanding that temperance and abolitionist speakers be allowed to use church facilities. Other laity were insisting that churches restrict themselves to the traditional business of saving souls. At their previous convention, the ministers had reasserted their authority and circumvented the reform question by voting unanimously against allowing "itinerant agents" to speak in churches without the pastor's consent. In 1837, they had to deal with a letter from their peers in Scotland asking them to endorse abolitionism. Although they did so unanimously, they worried about recent trends, especially the social reformers' pressure on churches, the growing public activity of women and the intense divisiveness that would occur if abolitionists demanded that women speakers be allowed to use church facilities. To express their concerns, they composed a Pastoral Letter, which was published and read from a countless number of pulpits. It is reproduced from the American Antiquarian Society's copy of the *Minutes of the General Association of Massachusetts, at Their Meeting at North Brookfield, June 28, 1837; with the Narrative of the State of Religion, and the Pastoral Letter* (Boston: Crocker & Brewster, 1837), pp. 19-22.

Pastoral Letter

BRETHREN AND FRIENDS,

Having assembled to consult upon the interests of religion within this commonwealth, we would now, as Pastors and Teachers, in accordance with the custom of this Association, address you on some of the subjects which at the present time appear to us to have an important bearing upon the cause of Christ.

The first topic upon which we would speak, has respect to the perplexed and agitating subjects which are now common amongst us.

All that we would say at present with regard to these subjects, is this: *They should not be forced upon any church as matters for debate, at the hazard of alienation and division.*

Once it would have seemed strange even to hint that members of churches could wish to force a subject for debate upon their Pastor and their brethren of the same church. But we are compelled to mourn over the loss, in a degree, of that deference to the pastoral office, which no minister would arrogate, but which is at once a mark of christian urbanity, and a uniform attendant of the full influence of religion upon individual character. If there be a tendency in zeal upon these subjects to violate the principles and rules of christian intercourse, to interfere with the proper pastoral influence, and to make the church into which we flee from a troubled world for peace, a scene of "doubtful disputations," there must be something wrong in that zeal or in the principles which excite it. If any are constrained to adopt those principles, and to use that zeal, we would affectionately and solemnly caution them not to disturb the influence of those ministers who think that the promotion of personal religion among their people, and the establishment of Christians in the faith and comfort of the Gospel, is the proper object of their ministry.

II. We would call your attention to the importance of maintaining *that respect and deference to the Pastoral office which is enjoined in Scripture,* and which is essential to the best influence of the ministry on you and your children.

One way in which this respect has been in some cases violated, is in encouraging lecturers or preachers on certain topics of reform to present their subjects within the parochial limits of settled pastors without their consent.

Your minister is ordained of God to be your teacher, and is commanded to feed that flock over which the Holy Ghost hath made him overseer. If there are certain topics upon which he does not preach with the frequency, or in the manner that would please *you*, it is a violation of sacred and important rights to encourage a stranger to present them. Deference and subordination are essential to the happiness of society, and peculiarly so in the relation of a people to their pastor. Let them despise or slight him, and he ceases to do *them* good, and they cease to respect those things of which he is at once the minister and the symbol. There is great solemnity in those words: "Obey them that have the rule over you and submit yourselves; for they watch for your souls as they that must give account." It is because we desire the highest influence of the ministry upon you and your children, that we now exhort you to reverence that office which the ascending Redeemer selected from all his gifts as the highest token of his love and care for his people.

III. We invite your attention to the dangers which at present seem to threaten the female character with wide spread and permanent injury.

The appropriate duties and influence of women, are clearly stated in the New Testament. Those duties and that influence are unobtrusive and private, but the sources of mighty power. When the mile, dependant, softening influence of woman upon the sternness of man's opinions is fully exercised, society feels the effects of it in a thousand forms. The power of woman is in her dependence, flowing from the consciousness of that weakness which God has given her for her protection and which keeps her in those departments of life that form the character of individuals and of the nation. There are social influences which females use in promoting piety and the great objects of christian benevolence, which we cannot too highly commend. We appreciate the unostentatious prayers and efforts of woman, in advancing the cause of religion at home and abroad: — in Sabbath schools, in leading religious inquirers to their pastor for instruction, and in all such associated effort as becomes the modesty of her sex; and earnestly hope that she may abound more and more in these labours of piety and love. But when she assumes the place and tone of a man as a public reformer, our care and protection of her seem unnecessary, we put ourselves in self defence against her, she yields the power which God has given her for protection, and her character becomes unnatural. If the vine, whose strength and beauty is to lean upon the trellis work and half conceal its clusters, thinks to assume the independence and the overshadowing nature of the elm, it will not only cease to bear fruit, but fall in shame and dishonour into the dust.

We cannot, therefore, but regret the mistaken conduct of those who encourage females to bear an obtrusive and ostentatious part in measures of reform, and countenance any of that sex who so far forget themselves as to itinerate in the character of public lecturers and teachers.

We especially deplore the intimate acquaintance and promiscuous conversation of females with regard to things "which ought not to be named;" by which that modesty and delicacy which is the charm of domestic life, and which constitute the true influence of women in society are consumed, and the way opened, as we apprehend, for degeneracy and ruin. We say these things, not to discourage proper influences against sin, but to secure such reformation as we believe is scriptural and will be permanent.

IV. We would set before you, as specially important in the present times, *the cultivation of private christian character, and private efforts for the spiritual good of individuals.*

If every Christian will faithfully endeavor so to live and act, so to discipline his natural disposition, and to make such attainments in goodness as to receive a testimony like that which Enoch had before his translation, that he pleases God, true piety will be universal, and pure religion will prevent the incursions of doctrinal and practical errors.

We should remember that while we strive to *do* good, it is of the first importance that we *be* good. The improvement of his individual christian character, should be the first and great object with every one. To exercise the feelings of which the Savior has set us an example, to be like Him in the spirit and temper of our minds, is the surest way to secure the approbation and love of God. Without this, our public efforts in the cause of God and man, however extensive and successful, will profit us nothing.

If Christians will labor *privately* to form individual minds, especially those of the young, to virtue and religion, they will hasten the universal prevalence of religion by the most effectual means. We commend the Sabbath School, and the Bible Class to the members of our churches as opportunities of extensive and enduring influence.

The regular, uniform discharge of the duties of our stations in the fear of God, the influence of faith, hope, and charity, upon the heart and conduct, a growing acquaintance with the Bible as a means of true and safe zeal, an increasing knowledge of the way of salvation by Christ, as a matter of personal experience and hope, should be the aim and end of every member of our churches. That we may be examples to you in these things, pray for us continually. And may grace, mercy, and peace be upon you and yours, and upon the whole Israel of God, Amen.

Response to the Pastoral Letter

Sarah M. Grimke

Commentary

The deeply religious sisters were annoyed by the furor, especially the "unchristian" argument. Even before the Pastoral Letter appeared, Sarah began a series of letters on "The Province of Women." In keeping with rhetorical conventions of the day, the letters gave the appearance of being private by being addressed to the president of the Boston Female Anti-Slavery Society, but they were printed in the *New England Spectator,* a religious newspaper, and reprinted in *The Liberator.* After all fifteen letters were completed, they were collected in a pamphlet under the title, *Letters on the Equality of the Sexes, and the Condition of Woman. Addressed to Mary S. Parker, President of the Boston Female Anti-Slavery Society* (Boston: Isaac Knapp, 1838). The third letter, written to refute the Pastoral Letter, is reproduced from a copy of the pamphlet edition owned by the American Antiquarian Society (pp. 14-22).

The Pastoral Letter of the General Association of Congregational Ministers of Massachusetts

Haverhill, 7th Mo. 1837.

DEAR FRIEND, — When I last addressed thee, I had not seen the Pastoral Letter of the General Association. It has since fallen into my hands, and I must digress from my intention of exhibiting the condition of women in different parts of the world, in order to make some remarks on this extraordinary document. I am persuaded that when the minds of men and women become emancipated from the thraldom of superstition and 'traditions of men,' the sentiments contained in the Pastoral Letter will be recurred to with as much astonishment as the opinions of Cotton Mather and other distinguished men of his day, on the subject of witchcraft; nor will it be deemed less wonderful, that a body of divines should gravely assemble and endeavor to prove that woman has no right to 'open her mouth for the dumb,' than it now is that judges should have sat on the trials of witches, and solemnly condemned nineteen persons and one dog to death for witchcraft.

But to the letter. It says, 'We invite your attention to the dangers which at present seem to threaten the FEMALE CHARACTER with wide-spread and permanent injury.' I rejoice that they have called the attention of my sex to this subject, because I believe if woman investigates it, she will soon discover that danger is impending, though from a totally different source from that which the Association apprehends, — danger from those who, having long held the reins of *usurped* authority, are unwilling to permit us to fill that sphere which God created us to move in, and who have entered into league to crush the immortal mind of woman. I rejoice, because I am persuaded that the rights of woman, like the rights of slaves, need only be examined to be understood and asserted, even by some of those, who are now endeavoring to smother the irrepressible desire for mental and spiritual freedom which glows in the breast of many, who hardly dare to speak their sentiments.

'The appropriate duties and influence of women are clearly stated in the New Testament. Those duties are unobtrusive and private, but the sources of *mighty power*. When the mild, *dependent*, softening influence of woman upon the sternness of man's opinions is fully exercised, society feels the effects of it in a thousand ways.' No one can desire more earnestly than I do, that woman may move exactly in the sphere which her Creator has assigned her; and I believe her having been displaced from that sphere has introduced confusion into the world. It is, therefore, of vast importance to herself and to all the rational creation, that she should ascertain what are her duties and her privileges as a responsible and immortal being. The New Testament has been referred to, and I am willing to abide by its decisions, but must enter my protest against the false translation of some passages by the MEN who did that work, and against the perverted interpretation by the MEN who undertook to write commentaries thereon. I am inclined to think, when we are admitted to the honor of studying Greek and Hebrew, we shall produce some various readings of the Bible a little different from those we now have.

The Lord Jesus defines the duties of his followers in his Sermon on the Mount. He lays down grand principles by which they should be governed, without any reference to sex or condition: — 'Ye are the light of the world. A city that is set on a hill cannot be hid. Neither do men light a candle and put it under a bushel, but on a candlestick, and it giveth light unto all that are in the house. Let your light so shine before men, that they may see your good works, and glorify your Father which is in Heaven.' I follow him through all his precepts, and find him giving the same directions to women as to men, never even referring to the distinction now so strenuously insisted upon between masculine and feminine virtues: this is one of the anti-christian 'traditions of men' which are taught instead of the 'commandments of God.' Men and women were CREATED EQUAL; they are both moral and account-able beings, and whatever if *right* for man to do, is *right* for woman.

But the influence of woman, says the Association, is to be private and unobtrusive; her light is not to shine before man like that of her brethren; but she is passively to let the lords of the creation, as they call themselves, put the bushel over it, lest peradventure it might appear that the world has been benefitted by the rays of *her* candle. So that her quenched light, according to their judgment, will be of more use than if it were set on the candlestick. 'Her influence is the source of mighty power.' This has ever been the flattering language of man since he laid aside the whip as a means to keep woman in subjection. He spares her body; but the war he has waged against her mind, her heart, and her soul, has been no less destructive to her as a moral being. How monstrous, how anti-christian, is the doctrine that woman is to be dependent on man! Where, in all the sacred Scriptures, is this taught? Alas! she has too well learned the lesson which MAN has labored to teach her. She has surrendered her dearest RIGHTS, and been satisfied with the privileges which man has assumed to grant her; she has been amused with the show of power, whilst man has absorbed all the reality into himself. He has adorned the creature whom God gave him as a companion, with baubles and gewgaws, turned her attention to personal attractions, offered incense to her vanity, and made her the instrument of his selfish gratification, a plaything to please his eye and amuse his hours of leisure. 'Rule by obedience and by submission sway,' or in other words, study to be a hypocrite, pretend to submit, but gain your point, has been the code of household morality which woman has been taught. The poet has sung, in sickly strains, the loveliness of woman's dependence upon man, and now we find it re-echoed by those who profess to teach the religion of the Bible. God says, 'Cease ye from man whose breath is in his nostrils, for wherein is he to be accounted of? Man says, depend upon me. God says, 'HE will teach us of his ways.' Man says, believe it not, I am to be your teacher. This doctrine of dependence upon man is utterly at variance with the doctrine of the Bible. In that book I find nothing like the softness of woman, nor the sternness of man: both are equally commanded to bring forth the fruits of the Spirit, love, meekness, gentleness, &c.

But we are told, 'the power of woman is in her dependence, flowing from a consciousness of that weakness which God has given her for her protection.' If physical weakness is alluded to, I cheerfully concede the superiority; if brute force is what my brethren are claiming, I am willing to let them have all the honor they desire; but if they mean to intimate, that mental or moral weakness belongs to woman, more than to man, I utterly disclaim the charge. Our powers of mind have been crushed, as far as man could do it, our sense of morality has been impaired by his interpretation of our duties; but no where does God say that he made any distinction between us, as moral and intelligent beings.

'We appreciate,' say the Association, 'the *unostentatious* prayers and efforts of woman in advancing the cause of religion at home and abroad, in leading religious inquirers TO THE PASTOR for instruction.' Several points here demand attention. If public prayers and public efforts are necessarily ostentatious, then 'Anna the prophetess, (or preacher,) who departed not from the temple, but served God with fastings and prayers night and day,' 'and spake of Christ to all them that looked for redemption in Israel,' was ostentatious in her efforts. Then, the apostle Paul encourages women to be ostentatious in their efforts to spread the gospel, when he gives them directions how they should appear, when engaged in praying, or preaching in the public assemblies. Then, the whole association of Congregational ministers are ostentatious, in the efforts they are making in preaching and praying to convert souls.

But woman may be permitted to lead religious inquirers to the PASTORS for instruction. Now this is assuming that all pastors are better qualified to give instruction than woman. This I utterly deny. I have suffered too keenly from the teaching of man, to lead any one to him for instruction. The Lord Jesus says, — 'Come unto me and learn of me.' He points his followers to no man; and when woman is made the favored instrument of rousing a sinner to his lost and helpless condition, she has no right to substitute any teacher for Christ; all she has to do is, to turn the contrite inquirer to the 'Lamb of God which taketh away the sins of the world.' More souls have probably been lost by going down to Egypt for help, and by trusting in man in the early stages of religious experience, than by any other error. Instead of the petition being offered to God, — 'Lead me in thy truth, and TEACH me, for thou art the God of my salvation,' — instead of relying on the precious promises — 'What man is he that feareth the Lord? him shall HE TEACH in the way that he shall choose' — 'I will instruct thee and TEACH thee in the way which thou shalt go — I will guide thee with mine eye' — the young convert is directed to go to man, as if he were in the place of God, and his instructions essential to an advancement in the path of righteousness. That woman can have but a poor conception of the privilege of being taught of God, what he alone can teach, who would turn the 'religious inquirer aside' from the fountain of living waters, where he might slake his thirst for spiritual instruction, to those broken cisterns which can hold no water, and therefore cannot satisfy the panting spirit. The business of men and women, who are ORDAINED OF GOD to preach, the unsearchable riches of Christ' to a lost and perishing world, is to lead souls to Christ, and not to Pastors for instruction.

The General Association say, that 'when woman assumes the place and tone of man as a public reformer, our care and protection of her seem unnecessary; we put ourselves in self-defence against her, and her character becomes unnatural.' Here again the unscriptural notion is held up, that there is a distinction between the duties of men and women as moral beings; that what is virtue in man, is vice in woman; and women who dare to obey the command of Jehovah, 'Cry aloud, spare not, lift up thy voice like a trumpet, and show my people their transgression,' are threatened with having the protection of the brethren withdrawn. If this is all they do, we shall not even know the time when our chastisement is inflicted; our trust is in the Lord Jehovah, and in him is everlasting strength. The motto of woman, when she is engaged in the great work of public reformation should be, — 'The Lord is my light and my salvation; whom shall I fear? The Lord is the strength of my life; of whom shall I be afraid?' She must feel, if she feels rightly, that she is fulfilling one of the important duties laid upon her as an accountable being, and that her character, instead of being 'unnatural,' is in exact accordance with the will of Him to whom, and to no other, she is responsible for the talents and the gifts confided to her. As to the pretty simile, introduced into the 'Pastoral Lerter,' [sic] 'If the vine whose strength and beauty is to lean upon the trellis work, and half conceal its clusters, thinks to assume the independence and the overshadowing nature of the elm,' &c. I shall only remark that it might well suit the poet's fancy, who sings of sparkling eyes and coral lips, and knights in armor clad; but it seems to me utterly inconsistent with the dignity of a Christian body, to endeavor to draw such an anti-scriptural distinction between men and women. Ah! how many of my sex feel in the dominion, thus unrighteously exercised over them, under the gentle appellation of *protection*, that what they have leaned upon has proved a broken reed at best, and oft a spear.

Thine in the bonds of womanhood.

SARAH M. GRIMKE.

The Murder of Lovejoy

Wendell Phillips

Commentary

Internal divisiveness over the role of women was not the abolitionists' only problem. Another was external opposition, which sometimes included mob action. On October 21, 1835, Garrison was dragged through the streets of Boston. Always alert to rhetorical possibilities, Garrison proceeded to portray himself as a "martyr," a word with religious overtones, and to accuse proslavery spokesmen of violating the American tradition of free expression. Subsequent riots presented similar opportunities to create sympathy for a cause that few Northerners were willing to embrace. The most dramatic one came after the highly publicized killing of Elijah Lovejoy, a Presbyterian minister, on November 7, 1837.

Lovejoy had several previous encounters with mobs. While editing a Presbyterian newspaper, the *St. Louis Observer,* Lovejoy attacked slavery in a city where slaveholding was common. After his press was destroyed, he moved across the river to Alton, Illinois, changed the name of the paper to the *Alton Observer,* continued attacking slavery and had his press destroyed two more times. When still another riot seemed imminent, he organized a group to defend his oft-resurrected press and was killed in the ensuing struggle.

A protest meeting was held in Boston a month later (December 8, 1837), but the character of the meeting was shaped by the controversy which erupted between the time that organizers asked for use of Faneuil Hall and the meeting itself. Unfortunately, many details about the dispute are unknown, but William Ellery Channing's version (as reported in *The Liberator,* December 15, 1837) is probably accurate even though biased and sketchy. According to Channing's account, he did not want Bostonians to protest Lovejoy's killing, per se, but attest to their "abhorrence of the lawless spirit which had prompted to this and kindre[d] deeds, and which had broken out here as well as a[t] a distance." The mayor was presented a petition requesting the use of Faneuil Hall, a municipally owned building that was used for occasional public meetings. It was rich in tradition because it had been used for town meetings during the Revolutionary era. The mayor denied the petition. Using the "free speech" argument, Channing generated enough public pressure to get the mayor to relent; however, considerable controversy erupted, with opponents of the meeting decrying the use of Faneuil Hall for what they considered an abolitionist meeting. They also denounced Channing's involvement in secular matters on the grounds that preachers should confine their public role to religious concerns.

The furor brought a large crowd to the meeting, which Garrison categorized into four groups (without estimating their relative size) consisting of abolitionists, "friends of free discussion and the liberty of the press" (as abolitionists called their non-abolitionist supporters), "curious onlookers" and anti-abolitionists. Assuming the accuracy of this categorization, the rhetorical situation facing the organizers of the meeting was clear. The last group would vote against the resolutions while the first group would vote for them. The "friends of free discussion" and the "curious onlookers" were the ones most open to persuasion, but neither was likely to support resolutions which denounced slavery. The "friends of free discussion" were predisposed to support resolutions which denounced mob violence, and the "curious onlookers" were likely to do so if the rhetoric was well adapted.

According to the account in *The Liberator*, the meeting began with Jonathan Phillips being "called to the chair." Although the account does not say so explicitly, it is evident that organizers of the meeting were acutely aware of the rhetorical situation. Instead of following the normal procedure of first having a prayer, the chair's first act was to read the petition to the mayor. "The object of this meeting," he announced, "is not to favor any *party*; but with our best wisdom, and in the most dispassionate manner, to maintain the spirit of universal freedom, the essential and fundamental principles of civil liberty, which have done so much for our country and for all mankind." Then came the prayer, followed by Channing's speech, which he opened by saying that the purpose of the meeting had been "misrepresented." Channing narrated events leading to the meeting, emphasizing that its purpose was only to support free expression. He acknowledged that he had been criticized for engaging in secular activities, but supporting free expression, he said, was "holy" work, just as the Revolutionary work done years before in the hall had been.

Benjamin Hallett then presented fourteen resolutions, none of which alluded to slavery or specifically mentioned Alton. All dealt in general terms with civil and religious liberty and/or mob violence. For example, the fifth said "That among our rights, we hold none more dear than the freedom of speech and the press, that we look to this as the guardian of all other rights, and the chief spring of human improvements; so that to wrest it from the citizen, by violence and murder, is to inflict the deepest wound in the republic."

George Hilliard, a prominent lawyer, delivered a seconding speech stressing the same themes. He did not mention slavery, though he specifically deplored Alton and concluded by saying that the nation had recently seen a series of mob actions, each worse than the one before.

The Liberator reported that Wendell Phillips (1811-1884) was to have spoken next, but Phillips said later that he had not planned to speak. Whatever the plans, they went awry. As soon as Hilliard sat down, James Austin, the attorney general of Massachusetts, arose. Observing that the announcement of the meeting said that there would be "free discussion" of the resolutions, he asked if it would be in order for him to speak. The chair had no choice but to recognize him.

Austin argued against the resolutions in a long speech that was well calculated to persuade listeners who had not already made up their minds. He first observed that it was improper for preachers to involve themselves in controversial secular matters. He then turned to the resolutions. He said that, except for their incredible verbosity, there was nothing fundamentally wrong with the resolutions. "But," he asked, "why are we now called together, solemnly to re-affirm them?" It was not necessary to do so. It was time to "strip off the disguise" and look at the real purpose of the meeting, which was to express sympathy for Lovejoy.

Lovejoy, continued the attorney general, did not deserve sympathy for two reasons. First, he had endangered the public safety of the people of Missouri. Austin emphasized that Missourians, unlike the more fortunate people of Massachusetts, lived in constant fear of slave rebellion. The fact that Lovejoy had moved to Illinois had not changed the situation. His paper had continued to circulate in Missouri, where citizens had every right to consider Lovejoy's attacks on slavery as encouraging slave rebellion. The right of free expression had to be subordinated to the public's right to protect itself. Second, Lovejoy had initiated the violence. When the mob arrived, he was ready with a mob of his own and a gun in his hand. Lovejoy, "a minister of the gospel," fired first. Moving into his peroration, Austin said that abolitionists had not learned the simple lesson that people will exercise their right of self-protection when threatened. Thus, said the speaker in Biblical language, Lovejoy had died "like the fool dieth." To identify the Missouri mob with the Revolution, Austin closed by reminding his audience that they were in Faneuil Hall, where a mob had assembled in 1773 to throw tea into the harbor to protect the public safety.

So much applause erupted that abolitionists later claimed that their opponents tried to break up the meeting. Irrespective of the accuracy of the charge, antiabolitionists were delighted, and it is safe to conjecture that some "curious onlookers" found the speech highly persuasive. A powerful refutation was needed immediately.

In the confusion, Wendell Phillips managed to get recognized, perhaps because the presiding officer was a relative. After order was somewhat (but not completely) restored, the youngster delivered an impromptu speech. He had previously given only one short speech at a small abolitionist gathering. His reputation (as opposed to that of his distinguished family) was merely that of a young lawyer with a meagre practice. He was a David doing rhetorical battle with Goliath.

Like the other speeches of the evening, Phillips' was transcribed and published in *The Liberator*, and it was reprinted shortly afterwards in the *Advocate*. Although abolitionists often referred to it as a rhetorical masterpiece, it was not published again until 1863, when it appeared in the first collection of Phillips' public discourses. The later text is substantially different. It was the first to carry a title, and it contains a host of minor stylistic revisions. It has even more substantial differences: a much-expanded refutation of Austin's arguments and a longer peroration. Although we can only conjecture, it seems doubtful that these changes, made a quarter-century after the fact, were designed to correct whatever errors the transcriber might have made. They were more likely designed to give posterity a more polished version and Phillips succeeded. Anthologists ordinarily use the later version. Assuming that the original is a more accurate version of what Phillips actually said, the following is reproduced from *The Liberator*, December 15, 1837, pp. 202-203, which is housed at the American Antiquarian Society.

The Murder of Lovejoy

MR[.] CHAIRMAN: — We are met for the free discussion of these resolutions, and the events which gave rise to them [cries of question, hear him, go on, no gagging, etc.] I hope I shall be permitted to express my surprise at the sentiments of the last speaker; — surprise not only at such sentiments from such a man, but at the applause they have elicited in these walls. A comparison has been drawn between the events of the Revolution and the tragedy at Alton. We have heard it asserted in this Hall, that Great Britain had a right to tax the Colonies, and we have heard the mob at Alton, got up to murder Lovejoy, compared to that band of our patriot fathers, who threw the tea overboard! [great applause.] Fellow citizens, is this true? [No, no.] The mob at Alton were met to wrest from a citizen his just rights; to resist the laws. We have been told that our fathers did the same; and the glorious mantle of Revolutionary precedent has been thrown over the mobs of our days. For to make out their title to such defence, it has been asserted that the British Parliament had a *right* to tax these Colonies. It is manifest that without such an assertion, the gentleman's parallel would have fallen to the ground; — for Lovejoy had stationed himself within constitutional bulwarks. The men who assailed him went against and over the laws. The *mob,* as the gentleman terms it, which assembled in the Old South, to destroy the tea, were met to resist not the laws, but illegal exactions; not the King's prerogative, but the King's usurpation. To find any other account, you must read our Revolutionary history upside down. Our State archives are loaded with arguments of John Adams, to prove the taxes laid by the British Parliament unconstitutional — beyond their power. It was not till this was made out, that the people of New England rushed to arms. The arguments of the Council Chamber and the House of Representatives preceded and sanctioned the contest. To draw the conduct of our ancestors into a precedent for mobs; for a right to resist laws we ourselves have enacted, is an insult to their memory. The difference between the excitements of those days and our own, which the gentleman, in kindness to the latter, has overlooked, is simply this. The men of that day went for the right. They were the people rising to sustain the laws and constitution of the Province. The rioters of our day go for their own wills, right or wrong. Sir, when I heard the gentleman lay down principles which place the rioters, incendiaries and murderers of Mt. Benedict and Alton, side by side with OTIS and HANCOCK, with QUINCY and ADAMS, I thought those pictured lips [pointing to the portraits in the Hall] would have broken into voice to rebuke the recreant American — the slanderer of the dead. [great applause and counter applause.] The gentleman said that he should sink into insignificance, if he dared to gainsay the principles of these resolutions. Sir, for the sentiments he has uttered, on soil consecrated by the prayers of Puritans and the blood of Patriots, the earth should have yawned and swallowed him up! [Here the agitation continued for some time, before the speaker could be heard.]

Another ground has been taken to excuse the mob, and throw doubt and discredit on the conduct of Lovejoy and his associates. Allusion has been made to what the lawyers understand very well, the 'conflict of laws.' We are told that nothing but the Mississippi River rolls between St. Louis and Alton; and the conflict of laws somehow or other, gives the citizens of the former a right to find fault with the defender of the press for publishing his opinions so near their limits. How the laws of the two States could be said to come into conflict in such circumstances, I question whether any lawyer in this audience can explain or understand. — No matter whether the line that divides one sovereign State from another, be an imaginary one, or ocean wide, the moment you cross it, the State you leave is blotted out of existence, so far as you are concerned. The Czar might as well claim to control the deliberations of Faneuil Hall, as the laws of Missouri demand reverence, or the shadow of obedience from the inhabitants of Illinois.

I must find some fault with the statement which has been made of the events at Alton. It has been asked why Lovejoy and his friends did not appeal to the executive; trust their defence to the police of the city. It has been hinted that from hasty and ill-judged excitement, the men within the building provoked a quarrel, and that he fell in the course of it, one mob resisting another. Recollect, sir, that they acted with the approbation and sanction of the Mayor. There was no executive to appeal to. — The Mayor acknowledged he could not protect them. They asked him if it was lawful for them to defend themselves? [sic] He told them it was, and sanctioned their assembling in arms to do so. — They were not then a mob; they were not merely citizens defending their own property, they were in some sense the *posse comitatus*, adopted for the occasion into the police of the city, acting under the order of a magistrate. It was civil authority resisting lawless violence. Where then was the imprudence? Is the doctrine to be sustained here, that it is *imprudent* for men lawfully to defend and protect life, liberty and property?

It has been stated, perhaps inadvertently, that Lovejoy or his comrades

fired first. This is denied by parties present there. Guns were first fired by the
mob. But suppose the party assailed did fire first. They had a right so to do;
not only the right which every citizen has to defend himself, but the higher
right which every civil officer has to resist violence. Even if Lovejoy fired the
first gun, it would not lessen his claim to our sympathy, or destroy his title to
be considered a martyr in the cause of free discussion. The whole question is,
did he act within the Constitution and the laws? The men who fell in State
street on the 5th March, 1770, did more than they say Lovejoy did. They
were the *first* assailants. Upon some slight quarrel, they pelted the troops with
every missile within reach. Did this bate one jot of the eulogy with which
Hancock and Warren hallowed their memory, hailing them as the first
martyrs in the cause of civil liberty?

If, sir, I had adopted what are called peace principles, I should lament the
circumstances of this case. But if I believe in self defence in support of
constitutional rights, then I must brand as base hypocrisy the conduct of those
who assemble year after year on the 4th of July, to fight over the battles of the
Revolution, and yet 'damn with faint praise,' or load with obloquy, the
memory of this man, because he shed his blood in defence of life, liberty,
property, and the freedom of the press!

The fact is, Lovejoy and his associates were assembled under civil
authority, — in arms by its sanction, — they bore insult and violence patiently.
After fire arms had been repeatedly used against them, they fired on the mob.
So doing they acted legally, in the spirit of our institutions, and after the
example of their founders. The patriot can find nothing in the affair to regret
but this; that within the limits of our country, civil authority should have been
so prostrated as to oblige a citizen to arm in his own defence.

But it is said Lovejoy was presumptuous and imprudent — he 'died as the
fool dieth.' And a right reverend clergyman of the city, has told us that no
citizen has a right to publish opinions disagreeable to the community! If any
mob follows such publication, on *him* rests its guilt! He must wait, forsooth,
till the people come up to it, and agree with him! This libel on liberty goes on
to say, that the want of right to speak as we think, is an evil inseparable from
republican institutions! If this be so, what are they worth? Welcome the
despotism of the Sultan, where one knows what he may publish and what he
may not, rather than the tyranny of this many headed monster, the mob,
where we know not what we may do or say, till some fellow citizen has tried it,
and paid for the lesson with his life. This clerical absurdity chooses as a check
for the abuses of the Press, not the *law*, but the dread of the mob. By so
doing, it deprives not only the individual and the minority of his rights, but
the majority also; for the expression of *their* opinion may sometimes provoke
disturbance from the minority. A few men may make a mob as well as many.
Consequently the majority have no right, as Christian men, to utter their
sentiments, if there is any supposition that it may lead to a mob! Is this the
doctrine for our pulpits, for our presses, and for Faneuil Hall?

Imprudent to defend the liberty of the Press! — Why? because the defence
was unsuccessful? — Does success gild crime into patriotism? and the want of

it change heroic self-devotion to imprudence? Was Hampden imprudent when he drew the sword and threw away the scabbard? yet he was unsuccessful. After a short exile, the race he hated sat again upon the throne.

Imagine yourself present when the first news of Bunker Hill battle reached a New England town. The tale would have run thus — 'The Patriots are routed — the troops victorious — Warren lies dead upon the field.' With what scorn would that *Tory* have been received, who should have charged Warren with *imprudence!* who should have said that he was 'out of place' in that battle; that he died as the *fool dieth!* [great applause.] How would the intimation have been received, that Warren and his associates should have waited a better time? But if success be indeed the only criterion of prudence, Respice unem — wait till the end.

Presumptuous to assert the freedom of the press on American ground! Is the assertion of such freedom before the age? So much before it as to leave one no right to make it, because it displeases the community? Who utters this libel on his country? It is this very thing which entitles Lovejoy to greater praise. The disputed right which provoked the Revolution; taxation without representation, is far beneath that for which he died. [Here there was a strong and general expression of disapprobation which was happily turned by the speaker. One word, said he.] As much as *thought* is better than money, so much is the cause in which Lovejoy died, nobler than a mere question of taxes. James Otis thundered in these Halls, when the King did but touch his *pocket.* What mortal pen could have written down his burning eloquence, had England offered to put a gag upon his lips? [Great applause.]

Sir, I reverence the patriots of those stirring times. I reverence the clergymen who did not so far forget their country in their immediate profession, as to deem it a duty to separate themselves from the struggle — the Mayhews and Coopers, who remembered they were *citizens* before they were ministers.

The question that stirred the revolution touched our civil interests. *This* concerns us not only as citizens, but as immortal beings. Wrapped up in its fate, saved or lost with it, are not only the voice of the statesman, but the instructions of the pulpit, and the progress of our faith.

The right to speak as they thought was never denied our fathers. It has been fought for and gained on English ground, — was brought over by the Puritans, — the motive which drew them to the rocky shores, — the privilege which endeared these barren hills. The liberty of the press was too holy, too evident to be disputed, when Milton's lips had been closed but a single century. Had the king invaded that, instead of the Custom House, who can imagine the storm which would have shaken these colonies?

I am glad, sir, to see this crowded house. It is good for us to be here. Faneuil Hall has the right, it is her duty to strike the key note for these United States. I am glad for one reason, that remarks, such as those to which I have alluded, have been uttered here. The passage of these resolutions in spite of them, will show more clearly, more decisively, the deep indignation with which Boston regards this outrage.

Declaration of Sentiments

Seneca Falls Convention

Commentary

Despite its rapid growth during the 1830s, abolitionism became increasingly divided. Inspired by their millenarian heritage, Wendell Phillips and other Garrisonians were outspoken in favor of pacifism, women's equality and other reforms. Increasingly frustrated by the failure of churches and political parties to denounce slavery, they launched into virulent attacks on established institutions while glorifying a vaguely defined Utopia. These tactics offended many other abolitionists, some of whom decided in 1840 to abolish the AASS and start over. Getting wind of their plans, Garrison recruited supporters to attend the 1840 convention. He not only prevented dissolution of the society, but also filled all vacant offices and committee memberships with female Garrisonians. The anti-Garrisonians promptly withdrew to form the American and Foreign Anti-Slavery Society. The split was now official.

Although the role of women was only one factor causing the split, it was a major issue. It was highlighted by another event in 1840. Many American societies sent women delegates to London for a worldwide antislavery convention, where they were relegated to viewing the proceedings from the gallery.

During the next few years, Lucretia Mott, Elizabeth Stanton, Martha Wright and Mary Ann McClintock talked informally about holding a convention to discuss women's rights. The first women's convention (at which some men were present) was held in Seneca Falls, New York in 1848. Although the immediate motivation of the meeting involved recent changes in New York law regarding the right of women to hold property, there is little doubt that the controversy within the abolitionist movement over the role of women also motivated the organizers. Some, such as Mott, were active abolitionists, and others, such as Stanton (whose husband was an active abolitionist) were marginally involved.

Female participation in abolitionism and other reform movements had a profound effect on the Seneca Falls rhetoric, as the authors of the *History of*

Woman Suffrage, writing four decades later, confessed (vol. 1, p. 68):

> On Sunday morning they met in Mrs. McClintock's parlor to write their declaration, resolutions, and to consider subjects for speeches. As the convention was to assemble in three days, the time was short for such productions; but having no experience in the *modus operandi* of getting up conventions, nor in that kind of literature, they were quite innocent of the herculean labors they proposed. On the first attempt to frame a resolution; to crowd a complete thought, clearly and concisely, into three lines; they felt as helpless and hopeless as if they had been suddenly asked to construct a steam engine. And the humiliating fact may as well now be recorded that before taking the initiative step, those ladies resigned themselves to a faithful perusal of various masculine productions. The reports of Peace, Temperance, and Anti-Slavery conventions were examined....

Like the AASS did at its first convention, the women issued a "Declaration of Sentiments" which analogized their cause with the American Revolution by drawing upon the Declaration of Independence. It is reproduced from the *History* (vol. 1, pp. 70-71).

Declaration of Sentiments

When, in the course of human events, it becomes necessary for one portion of the family of man to assume among the people of the earth a position different from that which they have hitherto occupied, but one to which the laws of nature and of nature's God entitle them, a decent respect to the opinions of mankind requires that they should declare the causes that impel them to such a course.

We hold these truths to be self-evident: that all men and women are created equal; that they are endowed by their Creator with certain inalienable rights; that among these are life, liberty, and the pursuit of happiness; that to secure these rights governments are instituted, deriving their just powers from the consent of the governed. Whenever any form of government becomes destructive of these ends, it is the right of those who suffer from it to refuse allegiance to it, and to insist upon the institution of a new government, laying its foundation on such principles, and organizing its powers in such form, as to them shall seem most likely to effect their safety and happiness. Prudence, indeed, will dictate that governments long established should not be changed for light and transient causes; and accordingly all experience hath shown that mankind are more disposed to suffer, while evils are sufferable, than to right themselves by abolishing the forms to which they were accustomed. But when a long train of abuses and usurpations, pursuing invariably the same object evinces a design to reduce them under absolute despotism, it is their duty to throw off such government, and to provide new guards for their future security. Such has been the patient sufferance of the women under this government, and such is now the necessity which constrains them to demand the equal station to which they are entitled.

The history of mankind is a history of repeated injuries and usurpations on the part of man toward woman, having in direct object the establishment of an absolute tyranny over her. To prove this, let facts be submitted to a candid world.

He has never permitted her to exercise her inalienable right to the elective franchise.

He has compelled her to submit to laws, in the formation of which she had no voice.

He has withheld from her rights which are given to the most ignorant and degraded men — both natives and foreigners.

Having deprived her of this first right of a citizen, the elective franchise, thereby leaving her without representation in the halls of legislation, he has oppressed her on all sides.

He has made her, if married, in the eye of the law, civilly dead.

He has taken from her all right in property, even to the wages she earns.

He has made her, morally, an irresponsible being, as she can commit many crimes with impunity, provided they be done in the presence of her husband. In the covenant of marriage, she is compelled to promise obedience to her husband, he becoming, to all intents and purposes, her master — the law giving him power to deprive her of her liberty, and to administer chastisement.

He has so framed the laws of divorce, as to what shall be the proper causes, and in case of separation, to whom the guardianship of the children shall be given, as to be wholly regardless of the happiness of women — the law, in all cases, going upon a false supposition of the supremacy of man, and giving all power into his hands.

After depriving her of all rights as a married woman, if single, and the owner of property, he has taxed her to support a government which recognizes her only when her property can be made profitable to it.

He has monopolized nearly all the profitable employments, and from those she is permitted to follow, she receives but a scanty remuneration. He closes against her all the avenues to wealth and distinction which he considers most honorable to himself. As a teacher of theology, medicine, or law, she is not known.

He has denied her the facilities for obtaining a thorough education, all colleges being closed against her.

He allows her in Church, as well as State, but a subordinate position, claiming Apostolic authority for her exclusion from the ministry, and, with some exceptions, from any public participation in the affairs of the Church.

He has created a false public sentiment by giving to the world a different code of morals for men and women, by which moral delinquencies which exclude women from society, are not only tolerated, but deemed of little account in man.

He has usurped the prerogative of Jehovah himself, claiming it as his right to assign for her a sphere of action, when that belongs to her conscience and to her God.

He has endeavored, in every way that he could, to destroy her confidence in her own powers, to lessen her self-respect, and to make her willing to lead a dependent and abject life.

Now, in view of this entire disfranchisement of one-half the people of this country, their social and religious degradation — in view of the unjust laws above mentioned, and because women do feel themselves aggrieved, oppressed, and fraudulently deprived of their most sacred rights, we insist that they have immediate admission to all the rights and privileges which belong to them as citizens of the United States.

In entering upon the great work before us, we anticipate no small amount of misconception, misrepresentation, and ridicule; but we shall use every instrumentality within our power to effect our object. We shall employ agents, circulate tracts, petition the State and National legislatures, and endeavor to enlist the pulpit and the press in our behalf. We hope this Convention will be followed by a series of Conventions embracing every part of the country.

Protest

Harry Blackwell and Lucy Stone

Commentary

The Seneca Falls convention received more publicity than organizers had anticipated. They had confined their pre-convention publicity to the nearby area, and very few women's advocates from elsewhere had attended. The most prominent non-attending advocate was Lucy Stone (1818-1893) of Massachusetts, a graduate of Oberlin (then the only co-educational college) and a paid lecturer for the Antislavery Society. Texts of her antislavery speeches are non-existent because she spoke from sketchy notes, but we know that she offended her employers by drawing analogies between black slavery and women's "slavery." Even many antislavery leaders who favored women's rights opposed linking the two subjects for fear linkage would damage the antislavery cause.

Stone and her employers negotiated an agreement whereby Stone continued speaking for the Antislavery Society on weekends and confined her advocacy of women's rights to weekday speeches which the Society did not sponsor. Her three most oft-repeated lectures were on women's "Social and Industrial Disabilities," "Legal and Political Disabilities" and "Moral and Religious Disabilities."

Aware of the attention-gaining value of Seneca Falls, Stone decided to organize an annual *national* convention. She met with eight other women at an antislavery convention in the spring of 1850 to prepare plans. The result was the first annual National Woman's Rights Convention (October 23, 1850), which many historians consider the beginning of women's rights as a national movement. For reasons that will become apparent later, readers should note that the convention was held in Worcester, Massachusetts and that the presiding officer was Sarah Earle, wife of the editor of the *Worcester Spy*, a widely read and highly respected newspaper that dated back to the pre-Revolutionary era.

While Stone continued lecturing on antislavery and women's rights, she was courted by Henry Blackwell (1825-1909), a successful young businessman. Although not an active speaker, he had been giving time to the antislavery cause. After meeting Stone in 1853, he also began attending the annual women's rights conventions, where he occasionally spoke.

As Blackwell and Stone planned their wedding in 1855, he agreed that his bride-to-be should retain her surname, something that was unheard of. He also told Stone that they should use their wedding as an opportunity to protest legislation that placed women in an inferior legal position. With Stone's enthusiastic approval and assistance, he wrote a *Protest* that they signed after reading it aloud together at their wedding in Worcester. If the *Protest* had reached only the few people who attended their wedding, it would have been rhetorically insignificant, but the sympathetic editor of the *Worcester Spy* gave it a substantial audience by printing a complete text along with a letter from the prominent officiating minister, Thomas Wentworth Higginson, who urged that ''others may be induced to do likewise.'' The following text is reproduced from the one in Alice Stone Blackwell's *Lucy Stone: Pioneer of Woman's Rights* (Boston: Little, Brown, 1930), pp. 166-68.

Protest

''While we acknowledge our mutual affection by publicly assuming the relationship of husband and wife, yet, in justice to ourselves and a great principle, we deem it a duty to declare that this act on our part implies no sanction of, nor promise of voluntary obedience to, such of the present laws of marriage as refuse to recognize the wife as an independent, rational being, while they confer upon the husband an injurious and unnatural superiority, investing him with legal powers which no honorable man would exercise, and which no man should possess. We protest especially against the laws which give to the husband:

''1. The custody of the wife's person.

''2. The exclusive control and guardianship of their children.

''3. The sole ownership of her personal and use of her real estate, unless previously settled upon her, or placed in the hands of trustees, as in the case of minors, lunatics, and idiots.

''4. The absolute right to the product of her industry.

''5. Also against laws which give to the widower so much larger and more permanent an interest in the property of his deceased wife than they give to the widow in that of the deceased husband.

''6. Finally, against the whole system by which 'the legal existence of the wife is suspended during marriage,' so that, in most States, she neither has a legal part in the choice of her residence, nor can she make a will, nor sue or be sued in her own name, nor inherit property.

''We believe that personal independence and equal human rights can never be forfeited, except for crime; that marriage should be an equal and permanent partnership, and so recognized by law; that until it is so recognized, married partners should provide against the radical injustice of present laws, by every means in their power.

"We believe that, where domestic difficulties arise, no appeal should be made to legal tribunals under existing laws, but that all difficulties should be submitted to the equitable adjustment of arbitrators mutually chosen.

"Thus, reverencing law, we enter our earnest protest against rules and customs which are unworthy of the name, since they violate justice, the essence of all law."

What to the Slave Is the Fourth of July?
Excerpt from an Oration, at Rochester, July 5, 1852

Frederick Douglass

Commentary

The reformers' desire to identify their causes with the American Revolution was not limited to analogizing their declarations with the Declaration of Independence. Abolitionists regularly held Fourth of July celebrations at which orators declared that the American Revolution would not be complete until slavery was abolished. One such celebration was held in Rochester, New York on July 5 (the Fourth being a Sunday), 1852. The speaker was Frederick Douglass (1817?-1895), whose ethos was unique for two reasons. First, he was a former slave who had accomplished the impossible task of becoming a well-known public figure. As a youngster, he learned to read and write. He purchased a copy of *The Columbian Orator*, a popular anthology of rhetorical masterpieces that Douglass used in the same way that it was used in the schools: to learn history and political theory and to help develop rhetorical skills. He escaped in 1838, changed his name from Bailey to Douglass to hide his real identity and settled in New Bedford, Massachusetts. His hopes of finding work at his skilled trade (ship caulking) were dashed because of racial prejudice. He worked as an unskilled laborer until 1841, when he was asked to speak about his experiences as a slave while attending an abolitionist convention. He so impressed his listeners that he was hired full time by the Massachusetts Anti-Slavery Society to go on speaking tours.

Douglass' rich voice, handsome physique and superb command of the English language gave him the attributes which ordinarily would make a speaker very persuasive, but these same qualities made some of his early listeners doubt that he was a fugitive slave. It was partly to enhance his credibility that he published his *Narrative of the Life of Frederick Douglass[,] An American Slave* (1845), which contained factual material, such as the names of his owners, that reviewers could verify. It appeared at a time when the narrative form was becoming increasingly popular, as evidenced by the sales of novels and travelogues and by the popularity of evangelical sermons,

387

which relied more on Biblical narrative than direct argument. Thus his narrative of a runaway slave had good market potential. He carefully blended his accounts of whippings and other cruelties with those which showed how slavery destroyed the human spirit in order to make his narrative form argumentative in purpose. The book was an instant success, going through four editions in the first year. This raised the possibility of his being reclaimed by his owner and returned to slavery. He fled to Britain, where he lectured on temperance and abolitionism while friends purchased his freedom. Returning to America in 1847, he moved to Rochester, founded a weekly newspaper, continued his abolitionist speaking and was the only male to participate actively in the Seneca Falls convention. His speech supporting the resolution calling for women's suffrage (the only resolution which divided the convention) was credited with getting it adopted. Most, if not all, of these facts were well known to his listeners when he delivered his Fourth of July oration in 1852.

Equally well known was the second factor which made his ethos unique: his restrained response to recent attacks by Garrisonians. The attacks grew out of Douglass' changing attitudes and a growing controversy within the abolitionist movement about secessionism, political activity and the constitutionality of slavery. The AASS had splintered in 1840, and the Massachusetts society was under Garrisonian control when Douglass began working for it in 1841. In 1844, Garrison persuaded the AASS to adopt the slogan "No Union with Slaveholders," to denounce the Constitution as a "compact with the devil" and to proclaim the withdrawal of abolitionists from politics until "a righteous government shall supersede the institution of tyranny." Once again, the AASS splintered, with Garrison's opponents arguing that Garrison's constitutional interpretation was wrong and that Northern secession would be a meaningless gesture because it would not eliminate slavery. Amidst the debate within the abolitionist movement, Douglass stood originally with Garrison. When Douglass published his *Narrative* in 1845, Garrison wrote the preface, using the opportunity to proclaim one of his favorite slogans, NO UNION WITH SLAVEHOLDERS! Douglass later changed his mind, but he stayed out of the internecine warfare both because of his friendship with Garrison and his desire to keep the movement as united as possible. In 1851, Garrison persuaded the AASS to endorse an official list of newspapers which adhered to his views regarding the Constitution and political action. Being a newspaper publisher, Douglass now felt obligated to state his views, but he wished to do so as inoffensively as possible. In a brief editorial, he argued that Garrison's position rested not on a strict interpretation of the Constitution, but on the historical circumstances surrounding it. The Constitution, he claimed, did not sanction slavery. He maintained that abolitionists should use their "political" as well as their "moral" power. He was extremely tactful, saying that political action should be used only by those "whose conscience permits." He concluded by using religious terminology to express his "veneration" for "Brother Garrison," which was "only inferior in degree to that which we owe to our conscience and to our God."

Despite his tact, Garrisonians refused to ignore Douglass' heresy. Nor would they respond to his rhetoric as a mere difference of opinion. Instead, Garrison, Phillips and others launched a series of public *ad hominem* attacks that were as vicious as they were false. For example, Douglass' wife was said to be upset over her husband's alleged involvement with a female assistant. After a few months of silence, Douglass denied the charges, but he never got into the gutter with his accusers. His audience was well aware of these events when Douglass delivered his oration in 1852, and one of the significant aspects of the speech is that he said nothing about them or any other issue that was dividing the movement.

Although the oration was published as a pamphlet shortly after delivery, it did not reach a large national audience until an extract from it was published in 1855 in the appendix of his second autobiography, *My Bondage and My Freedom*. Because we do not know the composition of the reading audience, we cannot know how many readers were aware of Garrison's hostility towards Douglass, but they would have learned little about it from reading the book. Douglass devoted only a page-and-a-half to the break. He confined himself to arguing that the general welfare clause of the Constitution permitted abolitionist legislation, and he again expressed his respect for the Garrisonians. The extract from the 1852 oration, of course, said nothing about the feud. Although identified as an extract, it was given its own title and stands as a complete discourse. It is reproduced from the autobiography (New York: Miller, Orton & Mulligan, 1855), pp. 441-445.

What to the Slave Is the Fourth of July?
Extract from an Oration, at Rochester, July 5, 1852

FELLOW-CITIZENS — Pardon me, and allow me to ask, why am I called upon to speak here to-day? What have I, or those I represent, to do with your national independence? Are the great principles of political freedom and of natural justice, embodied in that Declaration of Independence, extended to us? and am I, therefore, called upon to bring our humble offering to the national altar, and to confess the benefits, and express devout gratitude for the blessings, resulting from your independence to us?

Would to God, both for your sakes and ours, that an affirmative answer could be truthfully returned to these questions! Then would my task be light, and my burden easy and delightful. For who is there so cold that a nation's sympathy could not warm him? Who so obdurate and dead to the claims of gratitude, that would not thankfully acknowledge such priceless benefits? Who so stolid and selfish, that would not give his voice to swell the hallelujahs of a nation's jubilee, when the chains of servitude had been torn from his limbs? I am not that man. In a case like that, the dumb might eloquently speak, and the "lame man leap as an hart."

But, such is not the state of the case. I say it with a sad sense of the disparity between us. I am not included within the pale of this glorious anniversary! Your high independence only reveals the immeasurable distance between us. The blessings in which you this day rejoice, are not enjoyed in common. The rich inheritance of justice, liberty, prosperity, and independence, bequeathed by your fathers, is shared by you, not by me. The sunlight that brought life and healing to you, has brought stripes and death to me. This Fourth of July is *yours*, not *mine*. *You* may rejoice, *I* must mourn. To drag a man in fetters into the grand illuminated temple of liberty, and call upon him to join you in joyous anthems, were inhuman mockery and sacrilegious irony. Do you mean, citizens, to mock me, by asking me to speak to-day? If so, there is a parallel to your conduct. And let me warn you that it is dangerous to copy the example of a nation whose crimes, towering up to heaven, were thrown down by the breath of the Almighty, burying that nation in irrecoverable ruin! I can to-day take up the plaintive lament of a peeled and woe-smitten people.

"By the rivers of Babylon, there we sat down. Yea! we wept when we remembered Zion. We hanged our harps upon the willows in the midst thereof. For there, they that carried us away captive, required of us a song; and they who wasted us required of us mirth, saying, Sing us one of the songs of Zion. How can we sing the Lord's song in a strange land? If I forget thee, O Jerusalem, let my right hand forget her cunning. If I do not remember thee, let my tongue cleave to the roof of my mouth."

Fellow-citizens, above your national, tumultuous joy, I hear the mournful wail of millions, whose chains, heavy and grievous yesterday, are to-day rendered more intolerable by the jubilant shouts that reach them. If I do forget, if I do not faithfully remember those bleeding children of sorrow this day, "may my right hand forget her cunning, and may my tongue cleave to the roof of my mouth!" To forget them, to pass lightly over their wrongs, and to chime in with the popular theme, would be treason most scandalous and shocking, and would make me a reproach before God and the world. My subject, then, fellow-citizens, is AMERICAN SLAVERY. I shall see this day and its popular characteristics from the slave's point of view. Standing there, identified with the American bondman, making his wrongs mine, I do not hesitate to declare, with all my soul, that the character and conduct of this nation never looked blacker to me than on this Fourth of July. Whether we turn to the declarations of the past, or to the professions of the present, the conduct of the nation seems equally hideous and revolting. America is false to the past, false to the present, and solemnly binds herself to be false to the future. Standing with God and the crushed and bleeding slave on this occasion, I will, in the name of humanity which is outraged, in the name of liberty which is fettered, in the name of the constitution and the bible, which are disregarded and trampled upon, dare to call in question and to denounce, with all the emphasis I can command, everything that serves to perpetuate slavery — the great sin and shame of America! "I will not equivocate; I will not excuse;" I will use the severest language I can command; and yet not one word shall escape me that any man, whose judgment is not blinded by prejudice, or who is not at heart a slaveholder, shall not confess to be right and just.

But I fancy I hear some one of my audience say, it is just in this circumstance that you and your brother abolitionists fail to make a favorable impression on the public mind. Would you argue more, and denounce less, would you persuade more and rebuke less, your cause would be much more likely to succeed. But, I submit, where all is plain there is nothing to be argued. What point in the anti-slavery creed would you have me argue? On what branch of the subject do the people of this country need light? Must I undertake to prove that the slave is a man? That point is conceded already. Nobody doubts it. The slaveholders themselves acknowledge it in the enactment of laws for their government. They acknowledge it when they punish disobedience on the part of the slave. There are seventy-two crimes in the state of Virginia, which, if committed by a black man, (no matter how ignorant he be,) subject him to the punishment of death; while only two of these same crimes will subject a white man to the like punishment. What is this but the acknowledgement that the slave is a moral, intellectual, and responsible being. The manhood of the slave is conceded. It is admitted in the fact that southern statute books are covered with enactments forbidding, under severe fines and penalties, the teaching of the slave to read or write. When you can point to any such laws, in reference to the beasts of the field, then I may consent to argue the manhood of the slave. When the dogs in your streets, when the fowls of the air, when the cattle on your hills, when the fish of the sea, and the reptiles that crawl, shall be unable to distinguish the slave from a brute, then will I argue with you that the slave is a man!

For the present, it is enough to affirm the equal manhood of the negro race. Is it not astonishing that, while we are plowing, planting, and reaping, using all kinds of mechanical tools, erecting houses, constructing bridges, building ships, working in metals of brass, iron, copper, silver, and gold; that, while we are reading, writing, and cyphering, acting as clerks, merchants, and secretaries, having among us lawyers, doctors, ministers, poets, authors, editors, orators, and teachers; that, while we are engaged in all manner of enterprises common to other men — digging gold in California, capturing the whale in the Pacific, feeding sheep and cattle on the hillside, living, moving, acting, thinking, planning, living in families as husbands, wives, and children, and, above all, confessing and worshiping the christian's God, and looking hopefully for life and immortality beyond the grave, — we are called upon to prove that we are men!

Would you have me argue that man is entitled to liberty? that he is the rightful owner of his own body? You have already declared it. Must I argue the wrongfulness of slavery? Is that a question for republicans? Is it to be settled by the rules of logic and argumentation, as a matter beset with great difficulty, involving a doubtful application of the principle of justice, hard to be understood? How should I look to-day in the presence of Americans, dividing and subdividing a discourse, to show that men have a natural right to freedom, speaking of it relatively and positively, negatively and affirmatively? To do so, would be to make myself ridiculous, and to offer an insult to your understanding. There is not a man beneath the canopy of heaven that does not know that slavery is wrong *for him.*

What! am I to argue that it is wrong to make men brutes, to rob them of their liberty, to work them without wages, to keep them ignorant of their relations to their fellow-men, to beat them with sticks, to flay their flesh with the lash, to load their limbs with irons, to hunt them with dogs, to sell them at auction, to sunder their families, to knock out their teeth, to burn their flesh, to starve them into obedience and submission to their masters? Must I argue that a system, thus marked with blood and stained with pollution, is wrong? No; I will not. I have better employment for my time and strength than such arguments would imply.

What, then, remains to be argued? Is it that slavery is not divine; that God did not establish it; that our doctors of divinity are mistaken? There is blasphemy in the thought. That which is inhuman cannot be divine. Who can reason on such a proposition! They that can, may; I cannot. The time for such argument is past.

At a time like this, scorching irony, not convincing argument, is needed. Oh! had I the ability, and could I reach the nation's ear, I would to-day pour out a fiery stream of biting ridicule, blasting reproach, withering sarcasm, and stern rebuke. For it is not light that is needed, but fire; it is not the gentle shower, but thunder. We need the storm, the whirlwind, and the earthquake. The feeling of the nation must be quickened; the conscience of the nation must be roused; the propriety of the nation must be startled; the hypocrisy of the nation must be exposed; and its crimes against God and man must be proclaimed and denounced.

What to the American slave is your Fourth of July? I answer, a day that reveals to him, more than all other days in the year, the gross injustice and cruelty to which he is the constant victim. To him, your celebration is a sham; your boasted liberty, an unholy license; your national greatness, swelling vanity; your sounds of rejoicing are empty and heartless; your denunciations of tyrants, brass-fronted impudence; your shouts of liberty and equality, hollow mockery; your prayers and hymns, your sermons and thanksgivings, with all your religious parade and solemnity, are to him mere bombast, fraud, deception, impiety, and hypocrisy — a thin veil to cover up crimes which would disgrace a nation of savages. There is not a nation on the earth guilty of practices more shocking and bloody, than are the people of these United States, at this very hour.

Go where you may, search where you will, roam through all the monarchies and despotisms of the old world, travel through South America, search out every abuse, and when you have found the last, lay your facts by the side of the every-day practices of this nation, and you will say with me, that, for revolting barbarity and shameless hypocrisy, America reigns without a rival.

The Rhetoric of Sectionalism and Civil War

Excerpts from Senate Speeches on the Compromise of 1850

The "Great Triumvirate":
Henry Clay, John C. Calhoun,
and Daniel Webster

Commentary

By 1850, the antislavery movement was attracting considerable public support, but students should avoid the common mistake of equating "antislavery" with "abolitionism." Abolitionists wished to abolish slavery *where it currently existed* whereas other antislavery people wished only to keep slavery from *spreading into the newly acquired territories*. Many territories had recently been acquired. The Republic of Texas had been annexed (1845). Oregon had been divided by treaty between Britain and the U.S. (1846). The war with Mexico (1846-48) had added most of what is now the southwestern portion of the U.S.

The Mexican War had been controversial, and the question of whether to allow slavery in the new territories was even more so. While the war was still in progress, David Wilmot, an antislavery congressman, proposed that slavery be prohibited in future acquisitions. Although defeated, the "Wilmot Proviso" aroused passions in both North and South. Passions were intensified on February 19, 1847, when John C. Calhoun argued in a highly publicized Senate speech that Congress had no constitutional authority to prohibit slaveholders from emigrating to the territories. In March, 1848, when the Senate ratified the peace treaty, a hot debate accompanied another defeat of the Wilmot Proviso. In the presidential election of 1848, "Barnburners" deserted their fellow Democrats to join other antislavery politicians in forming a new "Free Soil" party, which ran on the slogan, "Free Soil, Free Speech, Free Labor, and Free Men."

The short-lived Free Soil party gained little support. Ironically, many Whigs had opposed the Mexican War, but they won the presidential election of 1848 with a war hero, Zachary Taylor. Heroism, not ideology, dominated the campaign rhetoric, but there were long-standing ideological differences between the two major parties. Whigs tended to reflect a "big government" philosophy (protective tariffs and internal improvements), while Democrats tended toward the old Jeffersonian ideal of limited government and states' rights.

The parties were becoming increasingly sectional. Although Whigs had some support in the South, their strength was in the industrialized North, where protective tariffs and other "big government" policies were popular. Conversely, the Southern economy was agrarian, being based largely on slave-produced cotton exports. Southern farmers saw tariffs as "taxes" that they paid to benefit the North. The North-South split widened as many Northern Whigs took an antislavery position that was unacceptable to Southern Whigs.

As congressmen treated one another to verbal insults, the question of whether to prohibit slavery in the new territories remained unresolved for over a year after the war. Yet the territories required some kind of government. This was especially true of California, where the population was growing rapidly as the Gold Rush gathered momentum. In the fall of 1849, impatient Californians applied for Statehood after approving a State constitution that prohibited slavery. When Congress met in December, President Taylor urged in his State of the Union message that California be admitted. A few moderate Southerners hinted that they might agree if the South got something substantial in return, but Southern extremists declared that compromise was impossible. William Seward, an antislavery Whig Senator, agreed: compromise was impossible.

Other slavery-related issues greeted the new congressional session of 1849-50. The normally routine business of electing a House Speaker took three weeks and 63 ballots because the leading Whig candidate was too antislavery for some and not antislavery enough for others. Declaring that the Underground Railroad was part of a conspiracy to destroy the South, Southerners introduced a more stringent Fugitive Slave bill. Northerners presented petitions from various State legislatures calling for passage of the Wilmot Proviso, abolition of slavery in the District of Columbia and abolition of the interstate slave trade. Even setting the Texas-New Mexico boundary involved slavery; for with slavery already legal in Texas, the bigger the state, the more slavery. Senator Calhoun organized a meeting which published an address of the "Southern Delegates in Congress to their Constituents" that suggested the South was on the verge of legislative defeat and might have to protect itself by secession.

By mid-January, 1850, it was clear that something dramatic was about to happen, and many astute observers feared the worst. The North, they predicted, would win on California, the Wilmot Proviso and possibly other measures. Then would come secession and civil war. In the highly charged emotional atmosphere, compromise was impossible.

Or was it? The 72-year-old Henry Clay had returned recently to the Senate, where he had begun his national career 44 years before. If anyone had the ethos to arrange a compromise, it was he. His long-standing advocacy of "big government" measures and hints of a personal distaste of slavery endeared him to Northern Whigs. Yet he was a Kentucky slaveholder with strong links to the South. He was famous as a compromiser, having engineered the Missouri Compromise of 1820, which solved an earlier fight over slavery, and the tariff reduction of 1832, which ended South Carolina's effort to nullify the "Tariff of Abominations." Now in obvious poor health and too old to run again for the presidency, even his severest critics had to admit that Clay's effort to arrange a compromise was motivated by his love of the Union, not personal ambition.

Henry Clay (1777-1852) was one of the so-called "Great Triumvirate," each of whom was nearing the end of his life. Clay, along with John C. Calhoun (1782-1850) and Daniel Webster (1782-1852) had received the nickname 18 years earlier, when they were all Senators opposed to "King Andrew" Jackson. Jackson's supporters gave them the nickname to identify them with the Triumvirs who had helped destroy the ancient Roman Republic (royalist symbols were used as "negative rhetoric" by all sides during the Jacksonian era). By 1850, the nickname had acquired an aura of respect and admiration, even among those who disliked one or more Triumvirs.

Why were the "Triumvirs" so highly regarded, even by their enemies? The usual explanation is of special interest to students of rhetorical history. The presidents between Jackson (1829-37) and Lincoln (1861-65) are generally characterized as "weak." Political leadership was in the legislative branch, especially the Senate, and oratorical skill was an essential attribute of legislative leadership. Unlike today, legislators had few committee meetings to attend, and they actually listened to the speeches given by their peers. With no movies or football games to attend, voters also took an interest in legislative speeches. They packed the Capitol galleries during important debates, and legislative speeches were often printed in newspapers and pamphlets. In 1850, Senators Clay, Calhoun and Webster were generally regarded as the leading legislative orators.

Despite their common hatred of Jackson, the "Triumvirs" were too different to unite. Sectionally, they differed, with Calhoun being from the South, Clay from the West and Webster from New England. Although Calhoun had originally favored tariffs and internal improvements, he had converted to the cause of limited government while Clay and Webster consistently favored "big government." Yet Clay and Webster were personal rivals who competed repeatedly for the Whig presidential nomination. Their similarities and differences were highlighted as they spoke on the slavery-related questions in 1850.

On January 29, 1850, Clay arose to deplore the recent verbal violence. He talked in general terms about the need for compromise. He announced that he was going to present eight resolutions that would collectively constitute a "compromise," but he kept his audience in suspense as he presented and justified them individually. Sometimes his argument was legalistic and historical, but he always emphasized that one section's gain was not much of a loss to the other. The resolutions (1) called for admission of California as a free State; (2) declared that because slavery did not exist by law in the rest of the new acquisitions and was unlikely to be introduced there, territorial governments should be established without "any restriction or condition on the subject of slavery;" (3) fixed the boundaries of Texas; (4) proposed that the Federal Government assume Texas' debts in return for the State's accepting the boundaries as fixed in the third resolution; (5) declared that abolishing slavery in the District of Columbia was "inexpedient" unless Maryland, which had ceded the land in the first place, agreed; (6) declared it "expedient" to abolish the slave trade in the District of Columbia; (7) called for a tougher fugitive slave law; and (8) declared that Congress had no legal authority to interfere with the interstate slave trade.

Clay concluded by resorting to the Washington symbol. After reminding the Senate of a previously presented petition asking Congress to purchase Mount Vernon, he announced that today the man who had asked him to present the petition had given him a "sacred relic," a fragment from Washington's coffin! This, Clay solemnly said, was a portent, "a warning voice, coming from the grave to the Congress now in session to beware, to pause, to reflect before they lend themselves to any purposes which shall destroy the Union which was cemented by his exertions and example." He then had all the resolutions read and asked that debate be postponed for a week!

Opponents wished to debate immediately, but what could they do? A few extremists "regretted" the delay, but only a young "Fire Eater," Jefferson Davis, insisted on an immediate debate. He declared in an emotional tirade that the South was getting nothing out of the so-called compromise, but he said that the South, "in the spirit of compromise," might agree to extending the old 36° 30' line (which divided the Louisiana Purchase into free and slave territories under the Missouri Compromise) to the Pacific (which would have divided California into two sections). Clay ignored Davis' counterproposal and observed wryly that, although he thought he could handle Davis in debate, he preferred waiting.

The debate, which began on February 5, ultimately resulted in the Compromise of 1850, which was similar to (though not exactly like) what Clay originally proposed. Clay opened the debate with a speech that was similar to his first one. He began by imploring God "to calm the violence and rage of party spirit." He organized the speech around the eight resolutions, justifying each one with legalistic and historical arguments while emphasizing how each section gained a lot without losing much. Knowing that opposition to the first resolution came from Southerners, he reminded them that he had joined them in arguing that Congress had no constitutional authority to place restrictions on slavery before admitting Missouri to the Union. Logical consistency, he said, precluded the South from trying to place restrictions on California. Knowing that the second resolution was opposed by Senators from both sections, he addressed both. He told the North that prohibiting slavery in the new territories was unnecessary because the area's desolate climate made it unsuitable for slavery. He told the South that insisting on allowing slavery was pointless because Congress could not undo what God and Nature had already done. As he moved to the resolutions regarding Texas, his fatigue was apparent, and a friend moved to adjourn. This parliamentary maneuver gave Clay the floor the next day when business resumed.

Continuing his lengthy speech on February 6, Clay argued the Texas resolutions on legalistic grounds. Turning to the resolutions regarding the District of Columbia, he acknowledged that Congress had the constitutional authority to abolish slavery, but he said fairness demanded that such action should be approved by Maryland, which had given the land to the Federal Government. He then addressed the South, saying that it would lose little by abolishing the slave trade in the District.

Clay turned next to the fugitive slave resolution, which was probably the most abhorrent to the North. Combining legalistic and "fairness" arguments, he reminded the North that the Constitution required states to return runaway slaves and said that the South had every right to expect the North to abide by the Constitution. Current law was being evaded, and fairness demanded that the North go along with a more stringent one. Legalistic argument also pervaded his justification of the last resolution.

Although he had spoken for almost two days, Clay still needed to respond to the alternative compromise of extending the 36° 30' line, which several Southerners, including the President and Jefferson Davis, had implied was acceptable. Clay said he had considered the proposal but had decided against it because (1) antislavery congressmen, who opposed legalizing slavery south of the line, would keep it from passing and (2) "non-action is best for the South." Non-action was most consistent with the Southern argument that Congress should not legislate about slavery in the territories. Moreover, legalizing slavery was pointless in the southwest because God and Nature had already decreed that slavery was unsuitable in these desolate territories. Adding ethos to logos, Clay said modestly that his role in the Missouri Compromise had been exaggerated.

By now, the old man's speech had been going on for almost two days, and he was obviously tired. "I am taxing both the physical and intellectual powers which a kind Providence has bestowed upon me too much," he said, "and I will endeavor soon to conclude; for I do not desire to trespass upon the time and patience of the Senate." A friend offered to move adjournment if Clay desired, but the old man declined: "No, sir; no, sir; if the Senate will bear with me, I think I can go through with it better to-day than I could tomorrow." With that, he began his peroration, which is reprinted from David J. Brewer, *World's Best Orations* (St. Louis: Ferd. P. Kaiser, 1901), vol. 4, pp. 1273-82.

Excerpt from Clay's Speech

Mr. President:—

This Union is threatened with subversion. I desire to take a very rapid glance at the course of public measures in this Union presently. I wanted, however, before I did that, to ask the Senate to look back upon the career which this country has run from the adoption of the Constitution down to the present day. Was there ever a nation upon which the sun of heaven has shone which has exhibited so much of prosperity as our own? At the commencement of this Government, our population amounted to about four millions. It has now reached upwards of twenty millions. Our territory was limited chiefly and principally to that bordering upon the Atlantic Ocean, and that which includes the southern shores of the interior lakes of our country. Our territory now extends from the northern provinces of Great Britain to the Rio Grande and the Gulf of Mexico; from the Atlantic Ocean on the one side to the Pacific on the other—the largest extent of territory under one government existing upon earth, with only two solitary exceptions. Our tonnage, from being nothing, has risen to a magnitude and amount to rival that of the nation which has been proudly called the mistress of the ocean. We have gone through many wars; one with that very nation from whom in 1776, we broke off, as weak and feeble colonies, when we asserted our independence as a member of the family of nations. And, sir, we came out of that struggle—unequal as it was, armed as she was at all points in consequence of the long struggles of Europe, and unarmed as we were at all points, in consequence of the habits and nature of our country and its institutions—we came out of that war without the loss of any honor whatever; we emerged from it gloriously. In every Indian war—we have been engaged in many of them—our arms have been triumphant. And without speaking at all as to the causes of the recent war with Mexico, whether they were right or wrong, and abstaining from the expression of any opinion as to the justice or propriety of the war when it commenced, all must unite in respect to the gallantry of our arms and the glory of our triumphs. There is no page—there are no pages of history which record more brilliant successes. With respect to the one in command of an important portion of our army, I need say nothing in praise of him who has been borne by the voice of his country to the highest station in it, mainly on account of his glorious military career. But of another military commander, less fortunate in other respects, I must take the opportunity of saying that for skill, for science, for strategy, for bold and daring fighting, for chivalry of individuals and of masses, that portion of the Mexican War which was conducted by the gallant Scott, as chief commander, stands unrivaled either by the deeds of Cortes himself or by those of any other commander in ancient or modern times.

Our prosperity is unbounded. Nay, Mr. President, I sometimes fear that it is the very wantonness of our prosperity that leads us to these threatening ills of the moment, that restlessness and these erratic schemes throughout the whole country, some of which have even found their way into legislative halls. We want, I fear, the chastising wand of Heaven to bring us back to a sense of the immeasurable benefits and blessings which have been bestowed upon us by Providence. At this moment, with the exception of here and there a particular department in the manufacturing business of the country, all is prosperous and happy—both the rich and poor. Our nation has grown to a magnitude in power and in greatness to command the respect, if it does not call for the apprehensions, of all the powers of the earth with which we can come in contact. Sir, do I depict with colors too lively the prosperity which has resulted to us from the operation of the Constitution under which we live? Have I exaggerated in any degree?

Now, let me go a little into detail as to the sway in the councils of the nation, whether of the North or of the South, during the sixty years of unparalleled prosperity that we enjoy. During the first twelve years of the administration of the government Northern councils rather prevailed, and out of them sprung the Bank of the United States; the assumption of the State debts; bounties to the fisheries; protection to the domestic manufactures—I allude to the Act of 1789; neutrality in the wars with Europe; Jay's Treaty; Alien and Sedition Laws; and a *quasi* war with France. I do not say, sir, that those leading and prominent measures which were adopted during the administration of Washington and the elder Adams were carried exclusively by Northern councils. They could not have been, but were carried mainly by the sway which Northern councils had obtained in the affairs of the country.

So, also, with the latter party for the last fifty years. I do not mean to say that Southern counsels alone have carried the measures which I am about to enumerate. I know they could not exclusively have carried them; but I say they have been carried by their preponderating influence, with co-operation, it is true, and large co-operation, in some instances, from the Northern section of the Union.

And what are those measures during the fifty years that Southern counsels have preponderated? The Embargo and other commercial restrictions of nonintercourse and nonimportation; war with Great Britain; the Bank of the United States overthrown; protection to domestic manufactures enlarged and extended (I allude to the passage of the Act of 1815 or 1816); the Bank of the United States re-established; the same bank put down; re-established by Southern counsels and put down by Southern counsels; Louisiana acquired; Florida bought; Texas annexed; war with Mexico; California and other Territories acquired from Mexico by conquest and purchase; protection superseded and free trade established; Indians removed west of the Missouri; fifteen new States admitted into the Union. I may very possibly have omitted some of the important measures which have been adopted during the latter period or time to which I have referred—the last fifty years; but these, I believe, are the most prominent.

I do not deduce from the enumeration of the acts of the one side or the other any just cause of reproach to the one side or the other, although one side or the other has predominated in the two periods to which I have referred. It has been at least the work of both, and neither need justly reproach the other; but I must say in all candor and sincerity that least of all ought the South to reproach the North, when we look at the long list of measures we have had under our sway in the councils of the nation, and which have been adopted as the policy of the Government, when we reflect that even opposite doctrines have been prominently advanced by the South and carried at different times. A Bank of the United States was established under the administration of Mr. Madison, with the co-operation of the South. I do not, when I speak of the South or North, speak of the entire South or North—I speak of the prominent and larger proportions of the South or North. It was during Mr. Madison's administration that the Bank of the United States was established. The friend [Mr. Calhoun] whose sickness I again deplore, as it prevents us from having his attendance here upon this occasion, was the chairman of the committee of the House of Representatives, and carried the measure through Congress. I voted for it with all my heart, although I had been instrumental in putting down the old Bank of the United States. I had changed my mind; and I co-operated in the establishment of the bank of 1816. The same bank was again put down by Southern counsels, with General Jackson at their head, at a later period. Then, with respect to the policy of protection, the South, in 1815—I mean the prominent and leading men of the South, Lowndes, Calhoun, and others—united in extending a certain measure of protection to the domestic manufacturers of the South, as well as of the North. You find, a few years afterwards, that the South opposes the most serious objection to this policy, at least one member of the Union staking upon that objection the dissolution of the Union.

Let us take another view; and of these several views no one is brought forward in any spirit of reproach, but in a spirit of conciliation—not to provoke or exasperate, but to quiet and produce harmony and repose, if possible. What have been the territorial acquisitions made by this country, and to what interests have they conduced? Florida, where slavery exists, has been introduced. All the most valuable parts of Louisiana have also added to the extent and consideration of the slaveholding portion of the Union; for although there is a large extent of that territory north of 36° 30', yet, in point of intrinsic value and importance, I would not give the single State of Louisiana for the whole of it. All Louisiana, with the exception of what lies north of 36° 30', including Oregon, to which we have obtained title mainly upon the ground of its being a part of the acquisition of Louisiana—all Texas, all the territories which have been acquired by the Government of the United States during the past sixty years of the operation of that Government, have been slave territories—theatres of slavery—with the exception I have mentioned lying north of the line of 36° 30'. But how was it in the case of a war made essentially by the South, growing out of the annexation of Texas, which was a measure pressed by the South upon the councils of the country, and which led to the war with Mexico? I do not say of the whole South; but a major portion of the South pressed the annexation of Texas upon the country, and that led to a war with Mexico, and to the ultimate acquisition of these territories which now constitute the bone of contention between the members of the confederacy. And now, when, for the first time, any free territory,—after these great acquisitions in Florida, Louisiana, and Texas had been made and redounded to ·the benefit of the South,—now, when, for the first time, free territories are attempted to be introduced,—territories without the institution of slavery,—I put it to the hearts of my countrymen of the South, if it is right to press matters to the disastrous consequences that have been intimated no longer ago than this very morning, upon the presentation of the resolutions from North Carolina.

[A Senator here offered to move an adjournment.]

Mr. President, I hope the Senate will only have the goodness, if I don't tire out their patience, to permit me to go on. I would prefer concluding to-day. I begin to see land. I shall pretty soon arrive at the end. I had much rather occupy half an hour now than leave what I have to say for to-morrow—to trespass upon the patience of the Senate another day.

Such is the Union, and such are its glorious fruits. We are told now, and it is rung throughout this entire country, that the Union is threatened with subversion and destruction. Well, the first question which naturally arises is, supposing the Union to be dissolved,—having all the causes of grievance which are complained of,—How far will a dissolution furnish a remedy for those grievances? If the Union is to be dissolved for any existing causes, it will be dissolved because slavery is interdicted or not allowed to be introduced into the ceded territories; because slavery is threatened to be abolished in the District of Columbia, and because fugitive slaves are not returned, as in my opinion they ought to be, and restored to their masters. These, I believe, will be the causes, if there be any causes, which can lead to the direful event to which I have referred.

Well, now, let us suppose that the Union has been dissolved. What remedy does it furnish for the grievances complained of in its united condition? Will you be able to push slavery into the ceded Territories? How are you to do it, supposing the North—all the States north of the Potomac, and which are opposed to it—in possession of the navy and army of the United States? Can you expect, if there is a dissolution of the Union, that you can carry slavery into California and New Mexico? You cannot dream of such a purpose. If it were abolished in the District of Columbia, and the Union were dissolved, would the dissolution of the Union restore slavery in the District of Columbia? Are you safer in the recovery of your fugitive slaves, in a state of dissolution or of severance of the Union, than you are in the Union itself? Why, what is the state of the fact in the Union? You lose some slaves. You recover some others. Let me advert to a fact which I ought to have introduced before, because it is highly creditable to the courts and juries of the free States. In every case, so far as my information extends, where an appeal has been made to the courts of justice for the recovery of fugitives, or for the recovery of penalties inflicted upon persons who have assisted in decoying slaves from their masters and aiding them in escaping from their masters—as far as I am informed, the courts have asserted the rights of the owner, and the juries have promptly returned adequate verdicts in favor of the owner. Well, this is some remedy. What would you have if the Union were dissevered? Why, sir, then the severed parts would be independent of each other—foreign countries! Slaves taken from the one into the other would be then like slaves now escaping from the United States into Canada. There would be no right of extradition; no right to demand your slaves; no right to appeal to the courts of justice to demand your slaves which escape, or the penalties for decoying them. Where one slave escapes now, by running away from his owner, hundreds and thousands would escape if the Union were severed in parts—I care not where nor how you run the line, if independent sovereignties were established.

Well, finally, will you, in a state of dissolution of the Union, be safer with your slaves within the bosom of the States than you are now? Mr. President, that they will escape much more frequently from the border States, no one will doubt.

But, I must take the occasion to say that, in my opinion, there is no right on the part of one or more of the States to secede from the Union. War and the dissolution of the Union are identical and inseparable. There can be no dissolution of the Union, except by consent or by war. No one can expect, in the existing state of things, that that consent would be given, and war is the only alternative by which a dissolution could be accomplished. And, Mr. President, if consent were given—if possibly we were to separate by mutual agreement and by a given line, in less than sixty days after such an agreement had been executed, war would break out between the free and slaveholding portions of this Union—between the two independent portions into which it would be erected in virtue of the act of separation. Yes, sir, sixty days—in less than sixty days, I believe, our slaves from Kentucky would be fleeing over in numbers to the other side of the river, would be pursued by their owners, and the excitable and ardent spirits who would engage in the pursuit would be restrained by no sense of the rights which appertain to the independence of the other side of the river, supposing it, then, to be the line of separation. They would pursue their slaves; they would be repelled, and war would break out. In less than sixty days war would be blazing forth in every part of this now happy and peaceable land.

But how are you going to separate them? In my humble opinion, Mr. President, we should begin at least with three confederacies—the Confederacy of the North, the Confederacy of the Atlantic Southern States (the slaveholding States), and the Confederacy of the Valley of the Mississippi. My life upon it, sir, that vast population that has already concentrated, and will concentrate, upon the headwaters and tributaries of the Mississippi, will never consent that the mouth of that river shall be held subject to the power of any foreign State whatever. Such, I believe, would be the consequences of a dissolution of the Union. But other confederacies would spring up, from time to time, as dissatisfaction and discontent were disseminated over the country. There would be the Confederacy of the Lakes—perhaps the Confederacy of New England and of the Middle States.

But, sir, the veil which covers these sad and disastrous events that lie beyond a possible rupture of this Union is too thick to be penetrated or lifted by any mortal eye or hand.

Mr. President, I am directly opposed to any purpose of secession, of separation. I am for staying within the Union, and defying any portion of this Union to expel or drive me out of the Union. I am for staying within the Union, and fighting for my rights—if necessary, with the sword—within the bounds and under the safeguard of the Union. I am for vindicating these rights; but not by being driven out of the Union rashly and unceremoniously by any portion of this confederacy. Here I am within it, and here I mean to stand and die; as far as my individual purposes or wishes can go—within it to protect myself, and to defy all power upon earth to expel me or drive me from the situation in which I am placed. Will there not be more safety in fighting within the Union than without it?

Suppose your rights to be violated; suppose wrongs to be done you, aggressions to be perpetrated upon you; cannot you better fight and vindicate them, if you have occasion to resort to that last necessity of the sword, within the Union, and with the sympathies of a large portion of the population of the Union of these States differently constituted from you, than you can fight and vindicate your rights, expelled from the Union, and driven from it without ceremony and without authority?

I said that I thought that there was no right on the part of one or more of the States to secede from this Union. I think that the Constitution of the thirteen States was made, not merely for the generation which then existed, but for posterity, undefined, unlimited, permanent, and perpetual—for their posterity, and for every subsequent State which might come into the Union, binding themselves by that indissoluble bond. It is to remain for that posterity now and forever. Like another of the great relations of private life, it was a marriage that no human authority can dissolve or divorce the parties from; and, if I may be allowed to refer to this same example in private life, let us say what man and wife say to each other: "We have mutual faults; nothing in the form of human beings can be perfect. Let us then be kind to each other, forbearing, conceding; let us live in happiness and peace."

Mr. President, I have said what I solemnly believe—that the dissolution of the Union and war are identical and inseparable; that they are convertible terms.

Such a war, too, as that would be, following the dissolution of the Union! Sir, we may search the pages of history, and none so furious, so bloody, so implacable, so exterminating, from the wars of Greece down, including those of the Commonwealth of England, and the Revolution of France—none, none of them raged with such violence, or was ever conducted with such bloodshed and enormities, as will that war which shall follow that disastrous event—if that event ever happens—of dissolution.

And what would be its termination? Standing armies and navies, to an extent draining the revenues of each portion of the dissevered empire, would be created; exterminating wars would follow—not a war of two nor three years, but of interminable duration—an exterminating war would follow, until some Philip or Alexander, some Caesar or Napoleon, would rise to cut the Gordian knot, and solve the problem of the capacity of man for self-government, and crush the liberties of both the dissevered portions of this Union. Can you doubt it? Look at history—consult the pages of all history, ancient or modern; look at human nature—look at the character of the contest in which you would be engaged in the supposition of a war following the dissolution of the Union, such as I have suggested—and I ask you if it is possible for you to doubt that the final but perhaps distant termination of the whole will be some despot treading down the liberties of the people?—that the final result will be the extinction of this last and glorious light, which is leading all mankind, who are gazing upon it, to cherish hope and anxious expectation that the liberty which prevails here will sooner or later be advanced throughout the civilized world? Can you, Mr. President, lightly contemplate the consequences? Can you yield yourself to a torrent of passion, amidst dangers which I have depicted in colors far short of what would be the reality, if the event should ever happen?

I conjure gentlemen—whether from the South or the North, by all they hold dear in this world—by all their love of liberty—by all their veneration for their ancestors—by all their regard for posterity—by all their gratitude to him who has bestowed upon them such unnumbered blessings—by all the duties which they owe to mankind, and all the duties they owe to themselves—by all these considerations I implore them to pause—solemnly to pause—at the edge of the precipice before the fearful and disastrous leap is taken in the yawning abyss below, which will inevitably lead to certain and irretrievable destruction.

And, finally, Mr. President, I implore, as the best blessing which heaven can bestow upon me on earth, that if the direful and sad event of the dissolution of the Union shall happen, I may not survive to behold the sad and heart-rending spectacle.

Commentary

Almost a month elapsed before the next Triumvir spoke, although "spoke" is a somewhat inaccurate word. On March 4, the old and sickly Calhoun, who died before the month ended, sat behind the young Senator James Mason of Virginia while Mason read the speech that Calhoun had written. After he had proposed "interposition" (or what opponents called "nullification") back in 1828, Calhoun had been accused of being a disunionist, and the charge had been revived since he had hinted at secession a few years previously.

Calhoun hoped to preserve the Union, but he insisted that it be preserved in a way that would protect the South as he knew it. A few months before his speech, he had finished his *Disquisition on Government*, a lengthy monograph that was both theoretical and practical. In keeping with the eighteenth-century view that governments tend to become oppressive, Calhoun argued that neither democratic rule nor the U.S. constitution can prevent majorities from oppressing minorities. The North, he said, has become a majority that is oppressing the South. The solution, he concluded, is to amend the constitution to establish a "concurrent majority" so that legislation cannot take effect without majority support in both North and South.

The *Disquisition* was not published until after Calhoun's death, but a similar line of argument pervaded his March 4 speech. He began by asking, "How can the Union be preserved?" In answer, he skimmed over Clay's so-called compromise, saying other Senators had sufficiently analyzed its defects, but he ridiculed Clay's use of the Washington symbol: "He was one of us—a slaveholder and a planter." The only compromise proposal Calhoun discussed in detail was the extension of the 36° 30' line to the Pacific, but he rejected it as a modified Wilmot Proviso that the South could never accept.

The only way to save the Union, Calhoun concluded, was for the North to give the South "justice." The South, he asserted, "has no compromise to offer, but the constitution; and no concession or surrender to make. She has already surrendered so much that she has little left to surrender.''

Calhoun's call for ''justice'' rested on an explicit analysis of the ''cause by which the Union is endangered.'' By his analysis, the ''cause'' boiled down to a combination of Northern domination and Northern antislavery sentiment. He began this analysis by saying the Union was originally divided into two sections, the North and the South, but originally they were in ''equilibrium.'' With the passage of time, however, the North became more populous and took over all the branches of the Federal Government. Yet the destruction of the equilibrium was not caused simply by population growth, as Calhoun explicated in the following excerpt taken from Alexander K. McClure's *Famous American Statesmen & Orators, Past and Present, with Biographical Sketches and Their Famous Orations* (New York: F. F. Lovell, 1902), vol. 3, pp. 333-40.

Excerpt from Calhoun's Speech

Had this destruction been the operation of time without the interference of government, the South would have had no reason to complain; but such was not the fact. It was caused by the legislation of this government, which was appointed as the common agent of all and charged with the protection of the interests and security of all.

The legislation by which it has been effected may be classed under three heads.

The first is that series of acts by which the South has been excluded from the common territory belonging to all the States as members of the federal Union—which have had the effect of extending vastly the portion allotted to the northern section, and restricting within narrow limits the portion left the South.

The next consists in adopting a system of revenue and disbursements by which an undue proportion of the burden of taxation has been imposed upon the South, and an undue proportion of its proceeds appropriated to the North; and the last is a system of political measures by which the original character of the government has been radically changed. I propose to bestow upon each of these, in the order they stand, a few remarks, with the view of showing that it is owing to the action of this government that the equilibrium between the two sections has been destroyed, and the whole powers of the system centred in a sectional majority.

The first of the series of acts by which the South was deprived of its due share of the Territories originated with the confederacy which preceded the existence of this government. It is to be found in the provision of the Ordinance of 1787. Its effect was to exclude the South entirely from that vast and fertile region which lies between the Ohio and the Mississippi rivers, now embracing five States and one Territory. The next of the series is the Missouri Compromise, which excluded the South from that large portion of Louisiana which lies north of 36° 30', excepting what is included in the State of Missouri. The last of the series excluded the South from the whole of the Oregon Territory.

All these, in the slang of the day, were what are called slave Territories, and not free soil; that is, Territories belonging to slaveholding powers and open to the immigration of masters with their slaves.

By these several acts the South was excluded from 17,238,025 square miles— an extent of country considerably exceeding the entire valley of the Mississippi. To the South was left the portion of the Territory of Louisiana lying south of 36° 30', and the portion north of it included in the State of Missouri, with the portion lying south of 36° 30', including the States of Louisiana and Arkansas, and the territory lying west of the latter and south of 36° 30', called the Indian country. These, with the Territory of Florida, now the State, make, in the whole, 283,503 square miles. To this must be added the territory acquired with Texas. If the whole should be added to the southern section it would make an increase of 325,520, which would make the whole left to the South 609,023. But a large part of Texas is still in contest between the two sections, which leaves it uncertain what will be the real extent of the portion of territory that may be left to the South.

I have not included the territory recently acquired by the treaty with Mexico. The North is making the most strenuous efforts to appropriate the whole to herself, by excluding the South from every foot of it. If she should succeed, it will add to that from which the South has already been excluded 526,078 square miles, and would increase the whole which the North has appropriated to herself to 1,764,023, not including the portion that she may succeed in excluding us from in Texas. To sum up the whole, the United States, since they declared their independence, have acquired 2,373,046 square miles of territory, from which the North will have excluded the South, if she should succeed in monopolizing the newly acquired territories, about three-fourths of the whole, leaving to the South but about one-fourth.

Such is the first and great cause that has destroyed the equilibrium between the two sections in the government.

The next is the system of revenue and disbursements which has been adopted by the government. It is well known that the government has derived its revenue mainly from duties on imports. I shall not undertake to show that such duties must necessarily fall mainly on the exporting States, and that the South, as the great exporting portion of the Union, has in reality paid vastly more than her due proportion of the revenue; because I deem it unnecessary, as the subject has on so many occasions been fully discussed. Nor shall I, for the same reason, undertake to show that a far greater portion of the revenue has been disbursed at the North, than its due share; and that the joint effect of these causes has been to transfer a vast amount from South to North, which, under an equal system of revenue and disbursements, would not have been lost to her. If to this be added that many of the duties were imposed, not for revenue, but for protection,—that is, intended to put money, not in the treasury, but directly into the pocket of the manufacturers,—some conception may be formed of the immense amount which in the long course of sixty years has been transferred from South to North. There are no data by which it can be estimated with any certainty; but it is safe to say that it amounts to hundreds of millions of dollars. Under the most moderate estimate it would be sufficient to add greatly to the wealth of the North, and thus greatly increase her population by attracting immigration from all quarters to that section.

This, combined with the great primary cause, amply explains why the North has acquired a preponderance in every department of the government by its disproportionate increase of population and States. The former, as has been shown, has increased, in fifty years, 2,400,000 over that of the South. This increase of population during so long a period is satisfactorily accounted for by the number of immigrants, and the increase of their descendants, which have been attracted to the northern section from Europe and the South, in consequence of the advantages derived from the causes assigned. If they had not existed—if the South had retained all the capital which has been extracted from her by the fiscal action of the government; and if it had not been excluded by the Ordinance of 1787 and the Missouri Compromise, from the region lying between the Ohio and the Mississippi rivers, and between the Mississippi and the Rocky Mountains north of 36° 30'—it scarcely admits of a doubt that it would have divided the immigration with the North, and by retaining her own people would have at least equalled the North in population under the census of 1840, and probably under that about to be taken. She would also, if she had retained her equal rights in those territories, have maintained an equality in the number of States with the North, and have preserved the equilibrium between the two sections that existed at the commencement of the government. The loss, then, of the equilibrium is to be attributed to the action of this government.

But while these measures were destroying the equilibrium between the two sections, the action of the government was leading to a radical change in its character, by concentrating all the power of the system in itself. The occasion will not permit me to trace the measures by which this great change has been consummated. If it did, it would not be difficult to show that the process commenced at an early period of the government; and that it proceeded almost without interruption, step by step, until it absorbed virtually its entire powers; but without going through the whole process to establish the fact it may be done satisfactorily by a very short statement.

That the government claims, and practically maintains, the right to decide in the last resort as to the extent of its powers, will scarcely be denied by any one conversant with the political history of the country. That it also claims the right to resort to force to maintain whatever power it claims, against all opposition, is equally certain. Indeed it is apparent, from what we daily hear, that this has become the prevailing and fixed opinion of a great majority of the community. Now, I ask, what limitation can possibly be placed upon the powers of a government claiming and exercising such rights? And, if none can be, how can the separate governments of the States maintain and protect the powers reserved to them by the constitution—or the people of the several States maintain those which are reserved to them, and among others, the sovereign powers by which they ordained and established, not only their separate State constitutions and governments, but also the constitution and government of the United States? But, if they have no constitutional means of maintaining them against the right claimed by this government, it necessarily follows that they hold them at its pleasure and discretion, and that all the powers of the system are in reality concentrated in it. It also follows that the character of the government has been changed in consequence, from a federal republic, as it originally came from the hands of its framers, into a great national consolidated democracy. It has indeed, at present, all the characteristics of the latter, and not one of the former, although it still retains its outward form.

The result of the whole of those causes combined is that the North has acquired a decided ascendancy over every department of this government, and through it a control over all the powers of the system. A single section governed by the will of the numerical majority has now, in fact, the control of the government and the entire powers of the system. What was once a constitutional federal republic is now converted, in reality, into one as absolute as that of the autocrat of Russia, and as despotic in its tendency as any absolute government that ever existed.

As, then, the North has the absolute control over the government, it is manifest that on all questions between it and the South, where there is a diversity of interests, the interest of the latter will be sacrificed to the former, however oppressive the effects may be; as the South possesses no means by which it can resist, through the action of the government. But if there was no question of vital importance to the South, in reference to which there was a diversity of views between the two sections, this state of things might be endured without the hazard of destruction to the South. But such is not the fact. There is a question of vital importance to the southern section, in reference to which the views and feelings of the two sections are as opposite and hostile as they can possibly be.

I refer to the relation between the two races in the southern section, which constitutes a vital portion of her social organization. Every portion of the North entertains views and feelings more or less hostile to it. Those most opposed and hostile regard it as a sin, and consider themselves under the most sacred obligation to use every effort to destroy it.

Indeed, to the extent that they conceive that they have power, they regard themselves as implicated in the sin, and responsible for not suppressing it by the use of all and every means. Those less opposed and hostile regard it as a crime—an offence against humanity, as they call it; and, although not so fanatical, feel themselves bound to use all efforts to effect the same object; while those who are least opposed and hostile regard it as a blot and a stain on the character of what they call the "nation," and feel themselves accordingly bound to give it no countenance or support. On the contrary, the southern section regards the relation as one which cannot be destroyed without subjecting the two races to the greatest calamity, and the section to poverty, desolation, and wretchedness; and accordingly they feel bound by every consideration of interest and safety to defend it.

Commentary

The third Triumvir, Daniel Webster, spoke on March 7, only three days after Calhoun. Webster had originally hoped to avoid debating, partly because he feared that anything he said might hurt his chances of getting the Whigs' presidential nomination in 1852. Despite his age, he still hoped to live in the White House. No one knows for certain why he changed his mind about speaking, but he probably thought he could help his presidential chances by publishing a speech that would portray him as a compromiser. This would put him in tune with public opinion because by the time he spoke, sentiment seemed to be shifting toward compromise both within the Senate and the country at large. Even the "great" oration of Calhoun had apparently failed to persuade any but the most militant Southerners by its uncompromising stand.

Yet Webster had to be careful about how he portrayed himself as a compromiser. With Calhoun's speech still in his listeners' minds, he needed to answer Calhoun, but he could not insult the dying Calhoun without alienating his admirers. Nor could the would-be president be seen as simply following in the footsteps of his old rival Clay.

The length of Webster's speech precludes printing a complete text, but a brief summary and two excerpts will (hopefully) show how he tried to achieve his rhetorical objectives. Our summary is especially interesting because of what Webster did not do as well as what he did. Although he emphasized his support for compromise, he did not specifically endorse Clay's resolutions.

After his introduction, Webster followed Calhoun in devoting most of his speech to history, during which he frequently disagreed with Calhoun. The first excerpt consists of Webster's introduction, which readers are encouraged to analyze in terms of a pro-compromise ethos. The second consists of a portion of Webster's history, which students are urged to analyze in terms of how well it fulfilled the orator's rhetorical objectives. Both excerpts are reprinted from *Writings and Speeches of Daniel Webster*, National Edition (Boston: Little, Brown, 1903), vol. 10, pp. 57-8, 61-72. The National Edition, like many other published versions, calls the speech, "The Constitution and the Union," but the oration is often called "The Seventh of March Speech."

Excerpts from Webster's Speech

Mr. PRESIDENT,—I wish to speak to-day, not as a Massachusetts man, nor as a Northern man, but as an American, and a member of the Senate of the United States. It is fortunate that there is a Senate of the United States; a body not yet moved from its propriety, not lost to a just sense of its own dignity and its own high responsibilities, and a body to which the country looks, with confidence, for wise, moderate, patriotic, and healing counsels. It is not to be denied that we live in the midst of strong agitations, and are surrounded by very considerable dangers to our institutions and government. The imprisoned winds are let loose. The East, the North, and the stormy South combine to throw the whole sea into commotion, to toss its billows to the skies, and disclose its profoundest depths. I do not affect to regard myself, Mr. President, as holding, or as fit to hold, the helm in this combat with the political elements; but I have a duty to perform, and I mean to perform it with fidelity, not without a sense of existing dangers, but not without hope. I have a part to act, not for my own security or safety, for I am looking out for no fragment upon which to float away from the wreck, if wreck there must be, but for the good of the whole, and the preservation of all; and there is that which will keep me to my duty during this struggle, whether the sun and the stars shall appear, or shall not appear for many days. I speak to-day for the preservation of the Union. "Hear me for my cause." I speak to-day, out of a solicitous and anxious heart, for the restoration to the country of that quiet and that harmony which make the blessings of this Union so rich, and so dear to us all. These are the topics that I propose to myself to discuss; these are the motives, and the sole motives, that influence me in the wish to communicate my opinions to the Senate and the country; and if I can do any thing, however little, for the promotion of these ends, I shall have accomplished all that I expect.

Now, Sir, I propose, perhaps at the expense of some detail and consequent detention of the Senate, to review historically this question, which, partly in consequence of its own importance, and partly, perhaps mostly, in consequence of the manner in which it has been discussed in different portions of the country, has been a source of so much alienation and unkind feeling between them.

We all know, Sir, that slavery has existed in the world from time immemorial. There was slavery, in the earliest periods of history, among the Oriental nations. There was slavery among the Jews; the theocratic government of that people issued no injunction against it. There was slavery among the Greeks; and the ingenious philosophy of the Greeks found, or sought to find, a justification for it exactly upon the grounds which have been assumed for such a justification in this country; that is, a natural and original difference among the races of mankind, and the inferiority of the black or colored race to the white. The Greeks justified their system of slavery upon that idea, precisely. They held the African and some of the Asiatic tribes to be inferior to the white race; but they did not show, I think, by any close process of logic, that, if this were true, the more intelligent and the stronger had therefore a right to subjugate the weaker.

The more manly philosophy and jurisprudence of the Romans placed the justification of slavery on entirely different grounds. The Roman jurists, from the first and down to the fall of the empire, admitted that slavery was against the natural law, by which, as they maintained, all men, of whatsoever clime, color, or capacity, were equal; but they justified slavery, first, upon the ground and authority of the law of nations, arguing, and arguing truly, that at that day the conventional law of nations admitted that captives in war, whose lives, according to the notions of the times, were at the absolute disposal of the captors, might, in exchange for exemption from death, be made slaves for life, and that such servitude might descend to their posterity. The jurists of Rome also maintained, that, by the civil law, there might be servitude or slavery, personal and hereditary; first, by the voluntary act of an individual, who might sell himself into slavery; secondly, by his being reduced into a state of slavery by his creditors, in satisfaction of his debts; and, thirdly, by being placed in a state of servitude or slavery for crime. At the introduction of Christianity, the Roman world was full of slaves, and I suppose there is to be found no injunction against that relation between man and man in the teachings of the Gospel of Jesus Christ or of any of his Apostles. The object of the instruction imparted to mankind by the founder of Christianity was to touch the heart, purify the soul, and improve the lives of individual men. That object went directly to the first fountain of all the political and social relations of the human race, as well as of all true religious feeling, the individual heart and mind of man.

Now, Sir, upon the general nature and influence of slavery there exists a wide difference of opinion between the northern portion of this country and the southern. It is said on the one side, that, although not the subject of any injunction or direct prohibition in the New Testament slavery is a wrong; that it is founded merely in the right of the strongest; and that it is an oppression, like unjust wars, like all those conflicts by which a powerful nation subjects a weaker to its will; and that, in its nature, whatever may be said of it in the modifications which have taken place, it is not according to the meek spirit of the Gospel. It is not "kindly affectioned"; it does not "seek another's, and not its own"; it does not "let the oppressed go free." These are sentiments that are cherished, and of late with greatly augmented force, among the people of the Northern States. They have taken hold of the religious sentiment of that part of the country, as they have, more or less, taken hold of the religious feelings of a considerable portion of mankind. The South, upon the other side, having been accustomed to this relation between the two races all their lives, from their birth, having been taught, in general, to treat the subjects of this bondage with care and kindness, and I believe, in general, feeling great kindness for them, have not taken the view of the subject which I have mentioned. There are thousands of religious men, with consciences as tender as any of their brethren at the North, who do not see the unlawfulness of slavery; and there are more thousands, perhaps, that, whatsoever they may think of it in its origin, and as a matter depending upon natural right, yet take things as they are, and, finding slavery to be an established relation of the society in which they live, can see no way in which, let their opinions on the abstract question be what they may, it is in the power of the present generation to relieve themselves from this relation. And candor obliges me to say, that I believe they are just as conscientious, many of them, and the religious people, all of them, as they are at the North who hold different opinions.

The honorable Senator from South Carolina* the other day alluded to the separation of that great religious community, the Methodist Episcopal Church. That separation was brought about by differences of opinion upon this particular subject of slavery. I felt great concern, as that dispute went on, about the result.

---

*Mr. Calhoun.

I was in hopes that the difference of opinion might be adjusted, because I looked upon that religious denomination as one of the great props of religion and morals throughout the whole country, from Maine to Georgia, and westward to our utmost western boundary. The result was against my wishes and against my hopes. I have read all their proceedings and all their arguments; but I have never yet been able to come to the conclusion that there was any real ground for that separation; in other words, that any good could be produced by that separation. I must say I think there was some want of candor and charity. Sir, when a question of this kind seizes on the religious sentiments of mankind, and comes to be discussed in religious assemblies of the clergy and laity, there is always to be expected, or always to be feared, a great degree of excitement. It is in the nature of man, manifested by his whole history, that religious disputes are apt to become warm in proportion to the strength of the convictions which men entertain of the magnitude of the questions at issue. In all such disputes, there will sometimes be found men with whom every thing is absolute; absolutely wrong, or absolutely right. They see the right clearly; they think others ought so to see it, and they are disposed to establish a broad line of distinction between what is right and what is wrong. They are not seldom willing to establish that line upon their own convictions of truth and justice; and are ready to mark and guard it by placing along it a series of dogmas, as lines of boundary on the earth's surface are marked by posts and stones. There are men who, with clear perceptions, as they think, of their own duty, do not see how too eager a pursuit of one duty may involve them in the violation of others, or how too warm an embracement of one truth may lead to a disregard of other truths equally important. As I heard it stated strongly, not many days ago, these persons are disposed to mount upon some particular duty, as upon a war-horse, and to drive furiously on and upon and over all other duties that may stand in the way. There are men who, in reference to disputes of that sort, are of opinion that human duties may be ascertained with the exactness of mathematics. They deal with morals as with mathematics; and they think what is right may be distinguished from what is wrong with the precision of an algebraic equation. They have, therefore, none too much charity towards others who differ from them. They are apt, too, to think that nothing is good but what is perfect, and that there are no compromises or modifications to be made in consideration of difference of opinion or in deference to other men's judgment. If their perspicacious vision enables them to detect a spot on the face of the sun, they think that a good reason why the sun should be struck down from heaven. They prefer the chance of running into utter darkness to living in heavenly light, if that heavenly light be not absolutely without any imperfection. There are impatient men; too impatient always to give heed to the admonition of St. Paul, that we are not to "do evil that good may come"; too impatient to wait for the slow progress of moral causes in the improvement of mankind. They do not remember that the doctrines and the miracles of Jesus Christ have, in eighteen hundred years, converted only a small portion of the human race; and among the nations that are converted to Christianity, they forget how many vices and crimes, public and private, still prevail, and that many of them, public crimes especially, which are so clearly offences against the Christian religion, pass without exciting particular indignation. Thus wars are waged, and unjust wars. I do not deny that there may be just wars. There certainly are; but it was the remark of an eminent person, not many years ago, on the other side of the Atlantic, that it is one of the greatest reproaches to human nature that wars are sometimes just. The defence of nations sometimes causes a just war against the injustice of other nations. In this state of sentiment upon the general nature of slavery lies the cause of a great part of those unhappy divisions, exasperations, and reproaches which find vent and support in different parts of the Union.

But we must view things as they are. Slavery does exist in the United States. It did exist in the States before the adoption of this Constitution, and at that time. Let us, therefore, consider for a moment what was the state of sentiment, North and South, in regard to slavery, at the time this Constitution was adopted. A remarkable change has taken place since; but what did the wise and great men of all parts of the country think of slavery then? In what estimation did they hold it at the time when this Constitution was adopted? It will be found, Sir, if we will carry ourselves by historical research back to that day, and ascertain men's opinions by authentic records still existing among us, that there was then no diversity of opinion between the North and the South upon the subject of slavery. It will be found that both parts of the country held it equally an evil, a moral and political evil. It will not be found that, either at the North or at the South, there was much, though there was some, invective against slavery as inhuman and cruel. The great ground of objection to it was political; that it weakened the social fabric; that, taking the place of free labor, society became less strong and labor less productive; and therefore we find from all the eminent men of the time the clearest expression of their opinion that slavery is an evil. They ascribed its existence here, not without truth, and not without some acerbity of temper and force of language, to the injurious policy of the mother country, who, to favor the navigator, had entailed these evils upon the Colonies. I need hardly refer, Sir, particularly to the publications of the day. They are matters of history on the record. The eminent men, the most eminent men, and nearly all the conspicuous politicians of the South, held the same sentiments; that slavery was an evil, a blight, a scourge, and a curse. There are no terms of reprobation of slavery so vehement in the North at that day as in the South. The North was not so much excited against it as the South; and the reason is, I suppose, that there was much less of it at the North, and the people did not see, or think they saw, the evils so prominently as they were seen, or thought to be seen, at the South.

Then, Sir, when this Constitution was framed, this was the light in which the Federal Convention viewed it. That body reflected the judgment and sentiments of the great men of the South. A member of the other house, whom I have not the honor to know, has, in a recent speech, collected extracts from these public documents. They prove the truth of what I am saying, and the question then was, how to deal with it, and how to deal with it as an evil. They came to this general result. They thought that slavery could not be continued in the country if the importation of slaves were made to cease, and therefore they provided that, after a certain period, the importation might be prevented by the act of the new government. The period of twenty years was proposed by some gentleman from the North, I think, and many members of the Convention from the South opposed it as being too long. Mr. Madison especially was somewhat warm against it. He said it would bring too much of this mischief into the country to allow the importation of slaves for such a period. Because we must take along with us, in the whole of this discussion, when we are considering the sentiments and opinions in which the constitutional provision originated, that the conviction of all men was, that, if the importation of slaves ceased, the white race would multiply faster than the black race, and that slavery would therefore gradually wear out and expire. It may not be improper here to allude to that, I had almost said, celebrated opinion of Mr. Madison. You observe, Sir, that the term *slave*, or *slavery*, is not used in the Constitution. The Constitution does not require that "fugitive slaves" shall be delivered up. It requires that persons held to service in one State, and escaping into another, shall be delivered up. Mr. Madison opposed the introduction of the term *slave*, or *slavery*, into the Constitution; for he said that he did not wish to see it recognized by the Constitution of the United States of America that there could be property in men.

Now, Sir, all this took place in the Convention in 1787; but connected with this, concurrent and contemporaneous, is another important transaction, not sufficiently attended to. The Convention for framing this Constitution assembled in Philadelphia in May, and sat until September, 1787. During all that time the Congress of the United States was in session at New York. It was a matter of design, as we know, that the Convention should not assemble in the same city where Congress was holding its sessions. Almost all the public men of the country, therefore, of distinction and eminence, were in one or the other of these two assemblies; and I think it happened, in some instances, that the same gentlemen were members of both bodies. If I mistake not, such was the case with Mr. Rufus King, then a member of Congress from Massachusetts. Now, at the very time when the Convention in Philadelphia was framing this Constitution, the Congress in New York was framing the Ordinance of 1787, for the organization and government of the territory northwest of the Ohio. They passed that Ordinance on the 13th of July, 1787, at New York, the very month, perhaps the very day, on which these questions about the importation of slaves and the character of slavery were debated in the Convention at Philadelphia. So far as we can now learn, there was a perfect concurrence of opinion between these two bodies; and it resulted in this Ordinance of 1787, excluding slavery from all the territory over which the Congress of the United States had jurisdiction, and that was all the territory northwest of the Ohio. Three years before, Virginia and other States had made a cession of that great territory to the United States; and a most munificent act it was. I never reflect upon it without a disposition to do honor and justice, and justice would be the highest honor, to Virginia, for the cession of her northwestern territory. I will say, Sir, it is one of her fairest claims to the respect and gratitude of the country, and that, perhaps, it is only second to that other claim which belongs to her; that from her counsels, and from the intelligence and patriotism of her leading statesmen, proceeded the first idea put into practice of the formation of a general constitution of the United States. The Ordinance of 1787 applied to the whole territory over which the Congress of the United States had jurisdiction. It was adopted two years before the Constitution of the United States went into operation; because the Ordinance took effect immediately on its passage, while the Constitution of the United States, having been framed, was to be sent to the States to be adopted by their Conventions; and then a government was to be organized under it. This Ordinance, then, was in operation and force when the Constitution was adopted, and the government put in motion, in April, 1789.

Mr. President, three things are quite clear as historical truths. One is, that there was an expectation that, on the ceasing of the importation of slaves from Africa, slavery would begin to run out here. That was hoped and expected. Another is, that, as far as there was any power in Congress to prevent the spread of slavery in the United States, that power was executed in the most absolute manner, and to the fullest extent. An honorable member,* whose health does not allow him to be here to-day—

A SENATOR. He is here.

I am very happy to hear that he is; may he long be here, and in the enjoyment of health to serve his country! The honorable member said, the other day, that he considered this Ordinance as the first in the series of measures calculated to enfeeble the South, and deprive them of their just participation in the benefits and privileges of this government. He says, very properly, that it was enacted under the old Confederation, and before this Constitution went into effect; but my present purpose is only to say, Mr. President, that it was established with the entire and unanimous concurrence of the whole South. Why, there it stands! The vote of every State in the Union was unanimous in favor of the Ordinance, with the exception of a single individual vote, and that individual vote was given by a Northern man. This Ordinance prohibiting slavery for ever northwest of the Ohio has the hand and seal of every Southern member in Congress. It was therefore no aggression of the North on the South. The other and third clear historical truth is, that the Convention meant to leave slavery in the States as they found it, entirely under the authority and control of the States themselves.

This was the state of things, Sir, and this the state of opinion, under which those very important matters were arranged, and those three important things done; that is, the establishment of the Constitution of the United States with a recognition of slavery as it existed in the States; the establishment of the ordinance for the government of the Northwestern Territory, prohibiting, to the full extent of all territory owned by the United States, the introduction of slavery into that territory, while leaving to the States all power over slavery

---

*Mr. Calhoun.

in their own limits; and creating a power, in the new government, to put an
end to the importation of slaves, after a limited period. There was entire
coincidence and concurrence of sentiment between the North and the South,
upon all these questions, at the period of the adoption of the Constitution. But
opinions, Sir, have changed, greatly changed; changed North and changed
South. Slavery is not regarded in the South now as it was then. I see an
honorable member of this body paying me the honor of listening to my
remarks;* he brings to my mind, Sir, freshly and vividly, what I have learned
of his great ancestor, so much distinguished in his day and generation, so worthy
to be succeeded by so worthy a grandson, and of the sentiments he expressed
in the Convention in Philadelphia.**

Here we may pause. There was, if not an entire unanimity, a general
concurrence of sentiment running through the whole community, and especially
entertained by the eminent men of all parts of the country. But soon a change
began, at the North and the South, and a difference of opinion showed itself;
the North growing much more warm and strong in its support. Sir, there is
no generation of mankind whose opinions are not subject to be influenced by
what appear to them to be their present emergent and exigent interests. I impute
to the South no particularly selfish view in the change which has come over
her. I impute to her certainly no dishonest view. All that has happened has
been natural. It has followed those causes which always influence the human
mind and operate upon it. What, then, have been the causes which have created
so new a feeling in favor of slavery in the South, which have changed the whole
nomenclature of the South on that subject, so that, from being thought and
described in the terms I have mentioned and will not repeat, it has now become
an institution, a cherished institution, in that quarter; no evil, no scourge, but
a great religious, social, and moral blessing, as I think I have heard it latterly
spoken of? I suppose this, Sir, is owing to the rapid growth and sudden extension
of the COTTON plantations of the South. So far as any motive consistent with
honor, justice, and general judgment could act, it was the COTTON interest
that gave a new desire to promote slavery, to spread it, and to use its labor.
I again say that this change was produced by causes which must always produce
like effects. The whole interest of the South became connected, more or less,
with the extension of slavery. If we look back to the history of the commerce
of this country in the early years of this government, what were our exports?
Cotton was hardly, or but to a very limited extent, known. In 1791 the first
parcel of cotton of the growth of the United States was exported, and amounted
only to 19,200 pounds.*** It has gone on increasing rapidly, until the whole
crop may now, perhaps, in a season of great product and high prices, amount
to a hundred millions of dollars. In the years I have mentioned, there was more
of wax, more of indigo, more of rice, more of almost every article of export from

---

*Mr. Mason of Virginia.

**See Madison Papers, Vol. III, pp. 1390, 1428, *et seq.*

***Seybert's Statistics, p. 92. A small parcel of cotton found its way to Liverpool from
the United States in 1784, and was refused admission, on the ground that it could not
be the growth of the United States.

the South, than of cotton. When Mr. Jay negotiated the treaty of 1794 with England, it is evident from the twelfth article of the treaty, which was suspended by the Senate, that he did not know that cotton was exported at all from the United States.

Well, Sir, we know what followed. The age of cotton became the golden age of our Southern brethren. It gratified their desire for improvement and accumulation, at the same time that it excited it. The desire grew by what it fed upon, and there soon came to be an eagerness for other territory, a new area or new areas for the cultivation of the cotton crop; and measures leading to this result were brought about rapidly, one after another, under the lead of Southern men at the head of the government, they having a majority in both branches of Congress to accomplish their ends. The honorable member from South Carolina* observed that there has been a majority all along in favor of the North. If that be true, Sir, the North has acted either very liberally and kindly, or very weakly; for they never exercised that majority efficiently five times in the history of the government, when a division or trial of strength arose. Never. Whether they were out-generalled, or whether it was owing to other causes, I shall not stop to consider; but no man acquainted with the history of the Union can deny that the general lead in the politics of the country, for three fourths of the period that has elapsed since the adoption of the Constitution, has been a Southern lead.

In 1802, in pursuit of the idea of opening a new cotton region, the United States obtained a cession from Georgia of the whole of her western territory, now embracing the rich and growing States of Alabama and Mississippi. In 1803 Louisiana was purchased from France, out of which the States of Louisiana, Arkansas, and Missouri have been framed, as slave-holding States. In 1819 the cession of Florida was made, bringing in another region adapted to cultivation by slaves. Sir, the honorable member from South Carolina thought he saw in certain operations of the government, such as the manner of collecting the revenue, and the tendency of measures calculated to promote emigration into the country, what accounts for the more rapid growth of the North than the South. He ascribes that more rapid growth, not to the operation of time, but to the system of government and administration established under this Constitution. That is matter of opinion. To a certain extent it may be true; but it does seem to me that, if any operation of the government can be shown in any degree to have promoted the population, and growth, and wealth of the North, it is much more sure that there are sundry important and distinct operations of the government, about which no man can doubt, tending to promote, and which absolutely have promoted, the increase of the slave interest and the slave territory of the South. It was not time that brought in Louisiana; it was the act of men. It was not time that brought in Florida; it was the act of men. And lastly, Sir, to complete those acts of legislation which have contributed so much to enlarge the area of the institution of slavery, Texas, great and vast and illimitable Texas, was added to the Union as a slave State in 1845; and that, Sir, pretty much closed the whole chapter, and settled the whole account.

---

*Mr. Calhoun.

House Divided

Abraham Lincoln

Commentary

Despite the Compromise of 1850, sectionalism intensified during the ensuing decade. Northern abolitionists denounced the Fugitive Slave Law as violating "Higher Law," (the moral law that was higher than man-made statutes or even the Constitution). Harriet Beecher Stowe's novel, *Uncle Tom's Cabin*, depicted the horrors of slavery in a narrative form that touched the emotions of her readers. Abolitionist rhetoric was filled with stories of Southern cruelty and (of special relevance to interpreting Lincoln's "House Divided" speech) charges of a "Slavepower Conspiracy." Such rhetoric increased Northern antipathy to slavery, but its only function in the South was to convince readers that Northern abolitionists were a group of crazy militants who did not understand how well slaves were treated and who were intent on destroying the Southern way of life.

Despite the intense rhetoric, not all Northerners were antislavery. Some regarded blacks as inferior beings who were probably better off being slaves. The entire question seemed too remote for many people to worry about. Not all antislavery people were abolitionists. Many wished only to keep slavery from spreading, not to interfere with it where it already existed. Most Southerners were proslavery, but secessionist sentiment pretty well evaporated after the compromise.

In short; public attitudes were mixed, but it was a volatile mixture which could lead to an explosion. Dramatic political events soon led to one. Never united ideologically, the old Whig party was destroyed by sectionalism, and Democrats had no trouble electing Franklin Pierce as president in 1852. (Readers of the "House Divided" speech should note Pierce's first name and the first names of others involved in subsequent events.) As early as 1844, Democrats had declared their belief in limiting presidents to one term. This idea encouraged a scramble among would-be presidents looking ahead to 1856.

A leading candidate was Stephen Douglas of Illinois, whose Northern residence required him to do something to gain Southern support for the nomination. In 1854, he introduced the Kansas-Nebraska bill. It provided that two new territorial governments be created in part of the old Louisiana Purchase, both of which were north of 36° 30'. Each would permit slavery while in territorial status and decide for itself whether to permit slavery when it became a State. Douglas and his supporters argued that the bill was consistent with the new spirit of compromise because Kansas would probably enter the Union as a slave State while Nebraska would come in free, thus preserving the sectional balance in the Senate, and the question of slavery in the territories would be removed from Congress, where it was always divisive, and allow the people to decide for themselves. The second argument related to their slogan, "Popular Sovereignty," which had considerable rhetorical appeal because of its egalitarian overtones. Opponents argued that the bill would result in the spread of slavery and that repealing the old Missouri Compromise would heighten, not reduce, the controversy over slavery.

Passage of the bill failed to have its intended effects. In 1856, Douglas lost the presidential nomination to James Buchanan, who easily defeated the candidate of the new Republican party, which had grown out of the ashes of the Whig party. The promise of an end to slavery agitation did not materialize. Free Soilers organized the New England Emigrant Society, which financed poor Northerners who wished to settle in Kansas. These Northerners were soon fighting with slaveowners who immigrated from the South. Before long, newspapers were filled with lurid (and often exaggerated) accounts of "Bleeding Kansas." The legal situation in Kansas became confused as proslavery forces organized a territorial legislature that was recognized by President Pierce but which was plagued by charges of having been elected only because Missourians crossed the border to stuff the ballot boxes. Antislavery forces organized a "representative" legislature, while proslavers met in Lecompton, drafted a State constitution which permitted slavery and applied for admission to the Union. The new president, James Buchanan, urged Congress to accept it. Douglas, in a move which lost him Southern support, led a successful fight to reject it until a fair referendum could be held.

Equally dramatic was the case of Dred Scott, a slave who was taken by his owner from Missouri to army posts in the free State of Illinois and the free territory of Minnesota and then returned to Missouri. Scott later sued for his freedom on the grounds that his residence in free areas had made him free and that, once free, he could not be returned to slavery. The case eventually reached the Supreme Court. A majority of the Court decided to rule against Scott but was faced with developing a line of argument to justify its decision. Although the historical evidence is not conclusive, justices apparently gave some thought to arguing on narrow, technical grounds, saying that army posts were an exception to State and congressional prohibitions of slavery and/or that Scott waived his right to freedom when he returned voluntarily to Missouri. Instead of using such arguments, which could have tempered adverse criticism, Chief Justice Roger Taney wrote a decision employing three broad-based arguments. First, because Scott was black, he had no right to sue in Federal courts, and the lower court had erred in hearing the case; the Federal Constitution was reserved for whites. Second, the Missouri Compromise, which prohibited slavery north of 36 ° 30′ was unconstitutional; Congress had no constitutional authority to prohibit slavery in any of the territories (Taney conveniently ignored Scott's residence in Illinois). Lastly, Scott's legal status was determined by the laws of Missouri, which did not recognize him as having become free despite his temporary residence in free areas.

Not since 1803 had the Supreme Court ruled a congressional law unconstitutional. That alone would have made the Court's decision controversial, but both the content and timing of the decision added to a storm of criticism that was highlighted by allegations of a conspiracy. If the Court could deny the constitutionality of one antislavery law, it would rule others unconstitutional. If Scott could be taken into free areas and still remain a slave because Missouri law said he was, a second "Dred Scott" decision would permit slaveowners to keep slaves in free States. The Court had heard the case before the election of 1856, and its failure to render an early decision allegedly helped the Democrats. In his inaugural address, Buchanan said he would enforce the decision, whatever it was, and urged citizens to abide by it. The Court announced its decision two days later, which led to charges that Buchanan already knew what the Court was going to do and was trying to legitimize its unpopular pronouncement. In short, antislavery critics claimed the whole affair was part of a grand conspiracy to spread slavery throughout the nation.

Not long afterwards came an event which political observers thought would be inconsequential but which turned out to be anything but that. Senator Douglas was up for re-election to the Senate in 1858, and his victory was a foregone conclusion. A nationally known incumbent, his "popular sovereignty" rhetoric had considerable appeal to Illinois voters. The Republican party was too new to have built a solid constituency. To make matters even worse for his opponents, Douglas' ethos among Republicans had risen sharply because he had led the Senate fight against the Lecompton constitution. Some Eastern Republicans even advised their Illinois brethren not to contest Douglas' re-election, and rumors circulated that Douglas was on the verge of abandoning the Democrats to join the new party.

Douglas' opponent was Abraham Lincoln (1809-1865), who was prominent in legal circles because of his unusually successful legal practice but who was not very well known to the general public. He had served eight years in the State legislature as a Whig and had been elected to Congress in 1846, but he had not run for re-election because defeat seemed certain. He had recently helped organize the State Republican party and was rewarded — if one can call it that — by being nominated for the Senate race. Lincoln faced three rhetorical problems: he was much less well known than the popular Douglas, he had to cut into the Democratic vote and he had to keep wavering Republicans in line. As things turned out, Lincoln lost the election (conducted by the State legislature) but won the popular referendum (both by close votes). The skill with which he conducted his campaign thrust him into the national limelight.

It was the third of his problems that was especially important when Lincoln arose on June 16, 1858 to deliver his acceptance speech to the State Republican convention. Now known as the "House Divided" speech, some historians interpret it as two speeches in one. They see the brief first section (which contains the famous "house divided" line) as an abstract statement of moral principle and the second as a partisan charge that Douglas was part of the "slavepower conspiracy." Others, including this writer, interpret the speech as a unified discourse, with the first part being introductory to the second conspiratorial part, and the totality being designed to make Douglas' position on slavery unpalatable to voters in general and his immediate audience of Republicans in particular. Unlike most scholars, this writer considers the "house divided" line to be a rhetorical mistake because it was easily taken out of context to give credence to Douglas' charge that Lincoln was predicting civil war.

Regardless of how the speech is interpreted, understanding Lincoln's word choices requires remembering that Republicans frequently referred to "popular sovereignty" as "squatter sovereignty"; the informal references to "Stephen, Franklin, Roger, and James" are to major politicians whose roles were sketched above; references to "Judge Douglas" are to the senator (who served earlier as a State Supreme Court justice; and McClean and Curtis were the two dissenting judges in the Dred Scott decision. The text is reproduced photographically from David J. Brewer, *World's Best Orations* (St. Louis: Ferd. P. Kaiser, 1901), vol. 7. pp. 2777-2785.

House Divided

Mr. President, and Gentlemen of the Convention:—

IF WE could first know where we are, and whither we are tending, we could better judge what to do, and how to do it.

We are now far into the fifth year since a policy was initiated with the avowed object and confident promise of putting an end to slavery agitation. Under the operation of that policy, that agitation has, not only not ceased, but has constantly augmented. In my opinion, it will not cease until a crisis shall have been reached and passed. " A house divided against itself cannot stand." I believe this Government cannot endure permanently half slave and half free. I do not expect the Union to be dissolved,— I do not expect the house to fall,— but I do expect it will cease to be divided. It will become all one thing or all the other. Either the opponents of slavery will arrest the further spread of it, and place it where the public mind shall rest in the belief that it is in the course of ultimate extinction; or its advocates will push it forward, till it shall become alike lawful in all the States, old as well as new — North as well as South.

Have we no tendency to the latter condition?

Let any one who doubts carefully contemplate that now almost complete legal combination — piece of machinery, so as to speak — compounded of the Nebraska doctrine and the Dred Scott decision. Let him consider not only what work the machinery is adapted to do, and how well adapted, but also let him study the history of its construction, and trace, if he can, or rather fail, if he can, to trace the evidence of design and concert of action among its chief architects, from the beginning.

The new year of 1854 found slavery excluded from more than half the States by State constitutions, and from most of the national territory by congressional prohibition. Four days later commenced the struggle which ended in repealing that congressional prohibition. This opened all the national territory to slavery, and was the first point gained.

But, so far, Congress only had acted, and an indorsement by the people, real or apparent, was indispensable, to save the point already gained and give chance for more.

This necessity had not been overlooked, but had been provided for, as well as might be, in the notable argument of "Squatter Sovereignty," otherwise called "sacred right of self-government," which latter phrase, though expressive of the only rightful basis of any government, was so perverted in this attempted use of it as to amount to just this: That if any one man choose to enslave another, no third man shall be allowed to object. That argument was incorporated into the Nebraska Bill itself, in the language which follows: —

"It being the true intent and meaning of this act not to legislate slavery into any Territory or State, nor to exclude it therefrom, but to leave the people thereof perfectly free to form and regulate their domestic institutions in their own way, subject only to the Constitution of the United States."

Then opened the roar of loose declamation in favor of "Squatter Sovereignty," and "sacred right of self-government." "But," said opposition members, "let us amend the bill so as to expressly declare that the people of the Territory may exclude slavery." "Not we," said the friends of the measure; and down they voted the amendment.

While the Nebraska Bill was passing through Congress, a law case involving the question of a negro's freedom, by reason of his owner having voluntarily taken him first into a Free State and then into a Territory covered by the congressional prohibition, and held him as a slave for a long time in each, was passing through the United States Circuit Court for the District of Missouri; and both Nebraska Bill and lawsuit were brought to a decision in the same month of May 1854. The negro's name was "Dred Scott," which name now designates the decision finally made in the case. Before the then next presidential election, the law case came to, and was argued in, the Supreme Court of the United States; but the decision of it was deferred until after the election. Still, before the election, Senator Trumbull, on the floor of the Senate, requested the leading advocate of the Nebraska Bill to state his opinion whether the people of a Territory can constitutionally exclude slavery from their limits; and the latter answers: "That is a question for the Supreme Court."

The election came, Mr. Buchanan was elected, and the indorsement, such as it was, secured. That was the second point gained. The indorsement, however, fell short of a clear popular majority by nearly four hundred thousand votes, and so, perhaps, was not overwhelmingly reliable and satisfactory. The outgoing President, in his last annual message, as impressively as possible, echoed back upon the people the weight and authority of the indorsement. The Supreme Court met again; did not announce their decision, but ordered a reargument. The presidential inauguration came, and still no decision of the court; but the incoming President in his Inaugural Address, fervently exhorted the people to abide by the forthcoming decision, whatever it might be. Then, in a few days, came the decision.

The reputed author of the Nebraska Bill finds an early occasion to make a speech at this capital, indorsing the Dred Scott decision, and vehemently denouncing all opposition to it. The new President, too, seizes the early occasion of the Silliman letter to indorse and strongly construe that decision, and to express his astonishment that any different view had ever been entertained.

At length a squabble springs up between the President and the author of the Nebraska Bill, on the mere question of fact, whether the Lecompton Constitution was or was not, in any just sense, made by the people of Kansas; and in that quarrel the latter declares that all he wants is a fair vote for the people, and that he cares not whether slavery be voted down or voted up. I do not understand his declaration that he cares not whether slavery be voted down or voted up, to be intended by him other

than as an apt definition of the policy he would impress upon
the public mind — the principle for which he declares he has
suffered so much, and is ready to suffer to the end.   And well
may he cling to that principle.   If he has any parental feeling,
well may he cling to it.   That principle is the only shred left
of his original Nebraska doctrine.   Under the Dred Scott decision
"Squatter Sovereignty" squatted out of existence, tumbled down
like temporary scaffolding — like the mold at the foundry, served
through one blast and fell back into loose sand — helped to carry
an election, and then was kicked to the winds.   His late joint
struggle with the Republicans against the Lecompton Constitution involves nothing of the original Nebraska doctrine.   That
struggle was made on a point — the right of a people to make
their own constitution — upon which he and the Republicans have
never differed.

The several points of the Dred Scott decision, in connection
with Senator Douglas's "care-not" policy, constitute the piece of
machinery, in its present state of advancement.   This was the
third point gained.   The working points of that machinery are : —

First, that no negro slave, imported as such from Africa,
and no descendant of such slave, can ever be a citizen of any
State, in the sense of that term as used in the Constitution of
the United States.   This point is made in order to deprive the
negro, in every possible event, of the benefit of that provision of
the United States Constitution, which declares that : "The citizens
of each State shall be entitled to all privileges and immunities
of citizens in the several States."

Second, that "subject to the Constitution of the United
States," neither Congress nor a Territorial legislature can exclude slavery from any United States Territory.   This point is
made in order that individual men may fill up the Territories
with slaves, without danger of losing them as property, and thus
to enhance the chances of permanency to the institution through
all the future.

Third, that whether the holding a negro in actual slavery in
a free State makes him free, as against the holder, the United
States courts will not decide, but will leave to be decided by the
courts of any slave State the negro may be forced into by the
master.   This point is made, not to be pressed immediately; but,
if acquiesced in for a while, and apparently indorsed by the people at an election, then to sustain the logical conclusion that
what Dred Scott's master might lawfully do with Dred Scott, in
the free State of Illinois, every other master may lawfully do
with any other one, or one thousand slaves, in Illinois, or in any

other free State.

Auxiliary to all this, and working hand in hand with it, the Nebraska doctrine, or what is left of it, is to educate and mold public opinion, at least Northern public opinion, not to care whether slavery is voted down or voted up. This shows exactly where we now are; and partially, also, whither we are tending.

It will throw additional light on the latter, to go back, and run the mind over the string of historical facts already stated. Several things will now appear less dark and mysterious than they did when they were transpiring. The people were to be left "perfectly free," subject only to the Constitution. What the Constitution had to do with it, outsiders could not then see. Plainly enough now, it was an exactly fitted niche, for the Dred Scott decision to afterward come in, and declare the perfect freedom of the people to be just no freedom at all. Why was the amendment, expressly declaring the right of the people, voted down? Plainly enough now: the adoption of it would have spoiled the niche for the Dred Scott decision. Why was the court decision held up? Why even a Senator's individual opinion withheld, till after the presidential election? Plainly enough now: the speaking out then would have damaged the perfectly free argument upon which the election was to be carried. Why the outgoing President's felicitation on the indorsement? Why the delay of a re-argument? Why the incoming President's advance exhortation in favor of the decision? These things look like the cautious patting and petting of a spirited horse, preparatory to mounting him, when it is dreaded that he may give the rider a fall. And why the hasty after-indorsement of the decision by the President and others?

We cannot absolutely know that all these exact adaptations are the result of preconcert. But when we see a lot of framed timbers, different portions of which we know have been gotten out at different times and places, and by different workmen — Stephen, Franklin, Roger, and James, for instance — and when we see these timbers joined together, and see they exactly make the frame of a house or a mill, all the tenons and mortices exactly fitting, and all the lengths and proportions of the different pieces exactly adapted to their respective places, and not a piece too many or too few, — not omitting even scaffolding — or, if a single piece be lacking, we see the place in the frame exactly fitted and prepared yet to bring such piece in — in such a case, we find it impossible not to believe that Stephen and Franklin and Roger and James all understood one another from the be-

ginning, and all worked upon a common plan or draft drawn up
before the first blow was struck.

It should not be overlooked that, by the Nebraska Bill, the
people of a State, as well as a Territory, were to be left "perfectly free," "subject only to the Constitution." Why mention a
State? They were legislating for Territories, and not for or
about States. Certainly the people of a State are and ought to
be subject to the Constitution of the United States; but why is
mention of this lugged into this merely Territorial law? Why
are the people of a Territory and the people of a State therein
lumped together, and their relation to the Constitution therein
treated as being precisely the same? While the opinion of the
court, by Chief-Justice Taney, in the Dred Scott case, and the
separate opinions of all the concurring judges, expressly declare
that the Constitution of the United States neither permits Congress nor a Territorial legislature to exclude slavery from any
United States Territory, they all omit to declare whether or not
the same Constitution permits a State, or the people of a State,
to exclude it. Possibly this is a mere omission; but who can
be quite sure, if McLean or Curtis had sought to get into the
opinion a declaration of unlimited power in the people of a State
to exclude slavery from their limits, just as Chase and Mace
sought to get such declaration, in behalf of the people of a Territory, into the Nebraska Bill — I ask, who can be quite sure
that it would not have been voted down in the one case as it
had been in the other? The nearest approach to the point of
declaring the power of a State over slavery is made by Judge
Nelson. He approaches it more than once, using the precise
idea, and almost the language, too, of the Nebraska Act. On
one occasion, his exact language is, "except in cases where the
power is restrained by the Constitution of the United States, the
law of the State is supreme over the subject of slavery within
its jurisdiction." In what cases the power of the States is so
restrained by the United States Constitution is left an open
question, precisely as the same question, as to the restraint on
the power of the Territories, was left open in the Nebraska Act.
Put this and that together, and we have another nice little niche,
which we may ere long see filled with another Supreme Court
decision, declaring that the Constitution of the United States
does not permit a State to exclude slavery from its limits. And
this may especially be expected if the doctrine of "care not
whether slavery be voted down or voted up," shall gain upon
the public mind sufficiently to give promise that such a decision
can be maintained when made.

Such a decision is all that slavery now lacks of being alike lawful in all the States. Welcome, or unwelcome, such decision is probably coming, and will soon be upon us, unless the power of the present political dynasty shall be met and overthrown. We shall lie down pleasantly dreaming that the people of Missouri are on the verge of making their State free, and we shall awake to the reality instead, that the Supreme Court has made Illinois a slave State. To meet and overthrow the power of that dynasty is the work now before all those who would prevent that consummation. This is what we have to do. How can we best do it?

There are those who denounce us openly to their own friends, and yet whisper us softly, that Senator Douglas is the aptest instrument there is with which to effect that object. They wish us to infer all from the fact that he now has a little quarrel with the present head of the dynasty; and that he has regularly voted with us on a single point, upon which he and we have never differed. They remind us that he is a great man, and that the largest of us are very small ones. Let this be granted. But "a living dog is better than a dead lion." Judge Douglas, if not a dead lion, for this work, is at least a caged and toothless one. How can he oppose the advances of slavery? He does not care anything about it. His avowed mission is impressing the "public heart" to care nothing about it. A leading Douglas Democratic newspaper thinks Douglas's superior talent will be needed to resist the revival of the African slave trade. Does Douglas believe an effort to revive that trade is approaching? He has not said so. Does he really think so? But if it is, how can he resist it? For years he has labored to prove it a sacred right of white men to take negro slaves into the new Territories. Can he possibly show that it is less a sacred right to buy them where they can be bought cheapest? And unquestionably they can be bought cheaper in Africa than in Virginia. He has done all in his power to reduce the whole question of slavery to one of a mere right of property; and as such, how can he oppose the foreign slave trade — how can he refuse that trade in that "property" shall be "perfectly free"—unless he does it as a protection to the home production? And as the home producers will probably not ask the protection, he will be wholly without a ground of opposition.

Senator Douglas holds, we know, that a man may rightfully be wiser to-day than he was yesterday — that he may rightfully change when he finds himself wrong. But can we, for that reason, run ahead, and infer that he will make any particular change, of which he, himself, has given no intimation? Can we safely base our action upon any such vague inference? Now, as ever, I wish not to misrepresent Judge Douglas's position, question his motives, or do aught that can be personally offensive to him. Whenever, if ever, he and we can come together on principle so that our cause may have assistance from his great ability, I hope to have interposed no adventitious obstacle. But clearly, he is not now with us — he does not pretend to be — he does not promise ever to be.

Our cause, then, must be intrusted to, and conducted by, its own undoubted friends — those whose hands are free, whose hearts are in the work — who do care for the result. Two years ago the Republicans of the nation mustered over thirteen hundred thousand strong. We did this under the single impulse of resistance to a common danger, with every external circumstance against us. Of strange, discordant, and even hostile elements, we gathered from the four winds, and formed and fought the battle through, under the constant hot fire of a disciplined, proud, and pampered enemy. Did we brave all them to falter now? — now, when that same enemy is wavering, dissevered, and belligerent? The result is not doubtful. We shall not fail — if we stand firm, we shall not fail. Wise counsels may accelerate, or mistakes delay it, but, sooner or later, the victory is sure to come.

Excerpts from The Lincoln-Douglas Debate at Freeport

Abraham Lincoln and Stephen A. Douglas

Commentary

With the old "the office seeks the man" myth now dead, it was not unique for Lincoln and Douglas to stump the State during the 1858 campaign, but it was unique for two senatorial candidates to hold formal debates. Such debating has never been repeated in our history. The so-called presidential debates have been little more than glorified press conferences. Lincoln and Douglas agreed to a genuine debate format in which one of them opened with a one-hour speech, the other replied for an hour-and-a-half and the opening speaker had a half-hour rejoinder. They alternated positions during the seven debates.

Although senatorial candidates had never debated before, similar (though less formal) debates had been held so frequently by local office seekers in Illinois that if Douglas had refused the challenge from Lincoln's camp, his ethos might have been damaged. It is probably for this reason that he accepted, as he had little else to gain. Stephen Douglas (1813-1861), a former State legislator and State Supreme Court justice and now a famous senator, was much better known than his rival.

Partly because of their novelty and partly because of Douglas' national prominence, the debates attracted considerable attention. Each was attended by thousands of people. The State's two major newspapers, the *Chicago Press and Tribune* (Republican) and *Chicago Times* (Democrat), published complete texts provided by their teams of shorthand reporters. Other papers, both in and out of the State, published summaries and excerpts and also reported the parades and hoopla surrounding the debates. A few months after the election, the debates were published in book form.

Douglas accepted the challenge only after getting Lincoln's grudging agreement to let Douglas be the opening speaker in the first debate. With this opportunity to take the offensive, Douglas began by attacking the Republican party as sectional. Developing the point historically, Douglas said that the old Whig and Democratic parties had ideological differences about the National Bank and the protective tariff but that these differences cut across sectional lines. Both parties had supported the Compromise of 1850 and his Kansas-Nebraska Act. In contrast, the Democratic party remained national in scope while Lincoln and other selfish office seekers had conspired to "abolitionize" both parties and create a sectional "Black Republican" party.

Portraying the "Black Republicans" as a party of extremists, Douglas quoted at length from the "abolition platform" it adopted at its first State convention in 1854. He integrated personal attacks on Lincoln (who, while in the State legislature, "could ruin more liquor than all the boys of the town together"). He attacked Lincoln's "house divided" remark, which was contrary to the views of "our fathers," who had "made this Government divided into free States and slave States, and left each State perfectly free to do as it pleased on the subject of slavery." He claimed that his "popular sovereignty" was consistent with the views of "our fathers" whereas Lincoln's abolitionism was not. Douglas also claimed that Lincoln opposed the Dred Scott decision because he and his fellow abolitionists "are in favor of the citizenship of the negro" whereas Douglas was "in favor of confining citizenship to white men, men of European birth and descent, instead of conferring it upon negroes, Indians, and other inferior races."

In short, Douglas' basic rhetorical strategy was to portray Lincoln as an extreme abolitionist whose views were inconsistent with those of the Founding Fathers. One of his tactics was to ask Lincoln a series of questions which he hoped would force Lincoln into the dilemma of either pronouncing extreme opinions or appearing inconsistent with public statements of the "Black Republicans" who had nominated him.

Lincoln was on the defensive in most of his reply. Obviously trying to disassociate himself from the 1854 platform, he denied having helped draft it. He defended his "house divided" remark, claiming that Douglas had misinterpreted it and that his conspiratorial allegations were true. He then launched a counterattack on Douglas' historical argument. The founding fathers had not created a nation that was half free and half slave. They had inherited an institution which they disliked, and they had tried to stop its spread in the belief that confinement would lead to its "ultimate extinction" — a belief that Lincoln asserted was consistent with his own and inconsistent with Douglas'. Lincoln glossed over most of Douglas' questions — as Douglas emphasized in his rejoinder and as Democratic newspapers gleefully pointed out.

The second, and ultimately most significant, debate was held a week later in Freeport (August 27, 1858). As he prepared for it, Lincoln knew that, although his listening audience would be different from that of the first debate, newspaper coverage of the first one required him to answer Douglas' questions or run the risk of appearing evasive. He also knew that his turn as opening speaker would allow him to take the offensive, which he did in a way that forced Douglas into enunciating his famous "Freeport Doctrine" that ruined whatever chance he had of getting Southern support in his unsuccessful bid for the presidency in 1860. Both debaters ranged over a number of points, with Lincoln reasserting at length his earlier charges that Douglas was part of a conspiracy to force slavery on the free States, and Douglas reasserting in great detail his earlier charge that Lincoln had contributed to the party's "abolition platform." The following excerpts illustrate primarily how they responded to one another's questions. They are reproduced photographically from David J. Brewer, *World's Best Orations* (St. Louis: Ferd. P. Kaiser, 1901), vol. 5, pp. 1912-1918; and vol. 7, pp. 2785-2791.

Excerpt from The Freeport Debate: Lincoln's Opening

Ladies and Gentlemen : —

ON SATURDAY last Judge Douglas and myself first met in public discussion. He spoke one hour, I an hour and a half, and he replied for half an hour. The order is now reversed. I am to speak an hour, he an hour and a half, and then I am to reply for half an hour. I propose to devote myself during the first hour to the scope of what was brought within the range of his half-hour speech at Ottawa. Of course there was brought within the scope in that half-hour speech something of his own opening speech. In the course of that opening argument, Judge Douglas proposed to me seven distinct interrogatories. In my speech of an hour and a half, I attended to some other parts of his speech, and incidentally, as I thought, answered one of the interrogatories then. I then distinctly intimated to him that I would answer the rest of his interrogatories on condition only that he should agree to answer as many for me. He made no intimation at the time of the proposition, nor did he in his reply allude at all to that suggestion of mine. I do him no injustice in saying that he occupied at least half of his reply in dealing with me as though I had refused to answer his interrogatories. I now propose that I will answer any of the interrogatories upon condition that he will answer questions from me not exceeding the same number. I give him an opportunity to respond. The Judge remains silent. I now say that I will answer his interrogatories, whether he answers mine or not; and that after I have done so I shall propound mine to him.

I have supposed myself, since the organization of the Republican party at Bloomington, in May 1856, bound as a party man by the platforms of the party, **then and since. If, in any** interrogatories which I shall answer, I go beyond the scope of what is within these platforms, it will be perceived that no one is responsible but myself.

Having said thus much I will take up the Judge's interrogatories as I find them printed in the Chicago Times, and answer them *seriatim*. In order that there may be no mistake about it, I have copied the interrogatories in writing, and also my answers to them. The first of these interrogatories is in these words: —

Question 1.—I desire to know whether Lincoln to-day stands, as he did in 1854, in favor of the unconditional repeal of the Fugitive Slave Law.

Answer.—I do not now, nor ever did, stand in favor of the unconditional repeal of the Fugitive Slave Law.

Q. 2. I desire him to answer whether he stands pledged to-day, as he did in 1854, against the admission of any more slave States into the Union, even if the people want them.

A.—I do not now, nor ever did, stand pledged against the admission of any more slave States into the Union.

Q. 3.—I want to know whether he stands pledged against the admission of a new State into the Union with such a Constitution as the people of that State may see fit to make.

A.—I do not stand pledged against the admission of a new State into the Union, with such a Constitution as the people of that State may see fit to make.

Q. 4.—I want to know whether he stands to-day pledged to the abolition of slavery in the District of Columbia.

A.—I do not stand to-day pledged to the abolition of slavery in the District of Columbia.

Q. 5.—I desire him to answer whether he stands pledged to the prohibition of the slave trade between the different States.

A.—I do not stand pledged to the prohibition of the slave trade between the different States.

Q. 6.—I desire to know whether he stands pledged to prohibit slavery in all the Territories of the United States, north as well as south of the Missouri Compromise line.

A.—I am impliedly, if not expressly, pledged to a belief in the right and duty of Congress to prohibit slavery in all the United States Territories.

Q. 7.—I desire him to answer whether he is opposed to the acquisition of any new territory unless slavery is first prohibited therein.

A.—I am not generally opposed to honest acquisition of territory; and, in any given case, I would or would not oppose such acquisition, accordingly as I might think such acquisition would or would not aggravate the slavery question among ourselves.

Now, my friends, it will be perceived upon an examination of these questions and answers, that so far I have only answered that I was not pledged to this, that, or the other. The Judge has not framed his interrogatories to ask me anything more than this, and I have answered in strict accordance with the interrogatories, and have answered truly that I am not pledged at all upon any of the points to which I have answered. But I am not disposed to hang upon the exact form of his interrogatory. I am rather disposed to take up at least some of these questions, and state what I really think upon them.

As to the first one, in regard to the Fugitive Slave Law, I have never hesitated to say, and I do not now hesitate to say, that I think, under the Constitution of the United States, the people of the Southern States are entitled to a congressional Fugitive Slave Law. Having said that, I have had nothing to say, in regard to the existing Fugitive Slave Law, further than that I think it should have been framed so as to be free from some of the objections that pertain to it, without lessening its efficiency. And inasmuch as we are not now in an agitation in regard to an alteration or modification of that law, I would not be the man to introduce it as a new subject of agitation upon the general question of slavery.

In regard to the other question, of whether I am pledged to the admission of any more slave States into the Union, I state to you very frankly that I would be exceedingly sorry ever to be put in a position of having to pass upon that question. I should be exceedingly glad to know that there would never be another slave State admitted into the Union; but I must add that if slavery shall be kept out of the Territories during the territorial existence of any one given territory, and then the people shall, having a fair opportunity and a clear field, when they come to adopt the Constitution, do such an extraordinary thing as adopt a slave Constitution, uninfluenced by the actual presence of the institution among them, I see no alternative, if we own the country, but to admit them into the Union.

The third interrogatory is answered by the answer to the second, it being, as I conceive, the same as the second.

The fourth one is in regard to the abolition of slavery in the District of Columbia. In relation to that, I have my mind very distinctly made up. I should be exceedingly glad to see slavery abolished in the District of Columbia. I believe that Congress possesses the constitutional power to abolish it. Yet, as a member of Congress, I should not, with my present views, be in favor of endeavoring to abolish slavery in the District of Columbia, unless it would be upon these conditions: First, that the abolition should be gradual; second, that it should be on a vote of the majority of qualified voters in the district; and, third, that compensation should be made to unwilling owners. With these three conditions I confess I would be exceedingly glad to see Congress abolish slavery in the District of Columbia, and, in the language of Henry Clay: "Sweep from our capital that foul blot upon our nation."

In regard to the fifth interrogatory, I must say here that, as to the question of the abolition of the slave trade between the different States, I can truly answer, as I have, that I am pledged to nothing about it. It is a subject to which I have not given that mature consideration that would make me feel authorized to state a position so as to hold myself entirely bound by it. In other words, that question has never been prominently enough before me to induce me to investigate whether we really have the constitutional power to do it. I could investigate it if I had sufficient time to bring myself to a conclusion upon that subject, but I have not done so, and I say so frankly to you here and to Judge Douglas. I must say, however, that if I should be of opinion that Congress does possess the constitutional power to abolish the slave trade among the different States, I should still not be in favor of the exercise of that power unless upon some conservative principle, as I conceive it, akin to what I have said in relation to the abolition of slavery in the District of Columbia.

My answer as to whether I desire that slavery should be prohibited in all the Territories of the United States is full and explicit within itself and cannot be made clearer by any comments of mine. So I suppose in regard to the question whether I am opposed to the acquisition of any more territory unless slavery is first prohibited therein, my answer is such that I could add nothing by way of illustration, or making myself better understood, than the answer which I have placed in writing.

Now in all this, the Judge has me, and he has me on the record. I suppose he had flattered himself that I was really entertaining one set of opinions for one place and another set for another place — that I was afraid to say at one place what I uttered at another. What I am saying here I suppose I say to a vast audience as strongly tending to Abolitionism as any audience in the State of Illinois, and I believe I am saying that which, if it would be offensive to any persons and render them enemies to myself, would be offensive to persons in this audience.

I now proceed to propound to the Judge the interrogatories, so far as I have framed them. I will bring forward a new installment when I get them ready. I will bring them forward now, only reaching to number four.

The first one is: —

Question 1.— If the people of Kansas shall, by means entirely unobjectionable in all other respects, adopt a State constitution, and ask admission into the Union under it, before they have the requisite number of inhabitants according to the English Bill,— some ninety-three thousand,— will you vote to admit them?

Q. 2.— Can the people of a United States Territory, in any lawful way, against the wish of any citizen of the United States, exclude slavery from its limits prior to the formation of a State constitution?

Q. 3.— If the Supreme Court of the United States shall decide that States cannot exclude slavery from their limits, are you in favor of acquiescing in, adopting, and following such decision as a rule of political action?

Q. 4.— Are you in favor of acquiring additional territory, in disregard of how such acquisition may affect the nation on the slavery question?

As introductory to these interrogatories which Judge Douglas propounded to me at Ottawa, he read a set of resolutions which he said Judge Trumbull and myself had participated in adopting in the first Republican State Convention, held at Springfield in October 1854. He insisted that I and Judge Trumbull, and perhaps the entire Republican party, were responsible for the doctrines contained in the set of resolutions which he read, and I understand that it was from that set of resolutions that he deduced the interrogatories which he propounded to me, using these resolutions as a sort of authority for propounding those questions to me. Now I say here to-day that I do not answer his interrogatories because of their springing at all from that set of resolutions which he read. I answered them because Judge Douglas thought fit to ask them. I do not now, nor never did, recognize any responsibility upon myself in that set of resolutions. When I replied to him on that occasion, I assured him that I never had anything to do with them. I repeat here to-day that I never, in any possible form, had anything to do with that set of resolutions. It turns out, I believe, that those resolutions were never passed in any convention held in Springfield. It turns out that they were never passed at any convention or any public meeting that I had any part in. I believe it turns out in addition to all this that there was not, in the fall of 1854, any convention holding a session at Springfield calling itself a Republican State Convention; yet it is true there was a convention, or assemblage of men calling themselves a convention, at Springfield, that did pass some resolutions. But so little did I really know of the proceedings of that convention, or what set of resolutions they had passed, though having a general knowledge that there had been such an assemblage of men there, that when Judge Douglas read the resolutions I really did not know but they had been the resolutions passed then and there. I did not question that they were the resolutions adopted, for I could not bring myself to suppose that Judge Douglas could say what he did upon this subject without knowing that it was true. I contented myself, on that occasion, with denying, as I truly could, all connection with them, not denying or affirming whether they were passed at Springfield. Now it turns out that he had got hold of some resolutions passed at some convention or public meeting in Kane County. I wish to say here that I don't conceive that in any fair and just mind this discovery relieves me at all. I had just as much to do with the convention in Kane County as that at Springfield. I am just as much responsible for the resolutions at Kane County as those at Springfield, the amount of the responsibility being exactly nothing in either case — no more than there would be in regard to a set of resolutions passed in the moon.

I allude to this extraordinary matter in this canvass for some further purpose than anything yet advanced. Judge Douglas did not make his statement upon that occasion as matters that he believed to be true, but he stated them roundly as being true, in such form as to pledge his veracity for their truth. When the whole matter turns out as it does, and when we consider who Judge Douglas is — that he is a distinguished Senator of the United States — that he has served nearly twelve years as such — that his character is not at all limited as an ordinary Senator of the United States, but that his name has become of world-wide renown — it is most extraordinary that he should so far forget all the suggestions of justice to an adversary, or of prudence to himself, as to venture upon the assertion of that which the slightest investigation would have shown him to be wholly false. I can only account for his having done so upon the supposition that that evil genius which has attended him through his life, giving to him an apparent astonishing prosperity, such as to lead very many good men to doubt there being any advantage in virtue over vice — I say I can only account for it on the supposition that that evil genius has at last made up its mind to forsake him.

And I may add that another extraordinary feature of the Judge's conduct in this canvass — made more extraordinary by this incident — is that he is in the habit, in almost all the speeches he makes, of charging falsehood upon his adversaries, myself and others. I now ask whether he is able to find in anything that Judge Trumbull, for instance, has said, or in anything that I have said, a justification at all compared with what we have, in this instance, for that sort of vulgarity.

Excerpt from The Freeport Debate: Douglas' Reply

Ladies and Gentlemen: —

I AM glad that at last I have brought Mr. Lincoln to the conclusion that he had better define his position on certain political questions to which I called his attention at Ottawa. He there showed no disposition, no inclination, to answer them. I did not present idle questions for him to answer merely for my gratification. I laid the foundation for those interrogatories by showing that they constituted the platform of the party whose nominee he is for the Senate. I did not presume that I had the right to catechise him as I saw proper, unless I showed that his party, or a majority of it, stood upon the platform and were in favor of the propositions upon which my questions were based. I desired simply to know, inasmuch as he had been nominated as the first, last, and only choice of his party, whether he concurred in the platform which that party had adopted for its government. In a few moments I will proceed to review the answers which he has given to these interrogatories; but in order to relieve his anxiety, I will first respond to these which he has presented to me. Mark you, he has not presented interrogatories which have ever received the sanction of the party with which I am acting, and hence he has no other foundation for them than his own curiosity.

First, he desires to know if the people of Kansas shall form a constitution by means entirely proper and unobjectionable, and ask admission into the Union as a State, before they have the requisite population for a Member of Congress, whether I will vote for that admission. Well, now, I regret exceedingly that he did not answer that interrogatory himself before he put it to me, in order that we might understand, and not be left to infer on which side he is. Mr. Trumbull, during the last session of Congress, voted from the beginning to the end against the admission of Oregon, although a free State, because she had not the requisite population for a Member of Congress. Mr. Trumbull would not consent, under any circumstances, to let a State, free or slave, come into the Union until it had the requisite pop-

ulation. As Mr. Trumbull is in the field fighting for Mr. Lincoln, I would like to have Mr. Lincoln answer his own question,
and tell me whether he is fighting Trumbull on that issue or
not. But I will answer his question. In reference to Kansas, it
is my opinion that as she has population enough to constitute a
slave State, she has people enough for a free State. I will not
make Kansas an exceptionable case to the other States of the
Union. I hold it to be a sound rule of universal application to
require a Territory to contain the requisite population for a Member of Congress before it is admitted as a State into the Union.
I made that proposition in the Senate in 1856, and I renewed it
during the last session in a bill providing that no Territory of the
United States should form a constitution and apply for admission,
until it had the requisite population. On another occasion I proposed that neither Kansas or any other territory should be admitted until it had the requisite population. Congress did not
adopt any of my propositions containing this general rule, but did
make an exception of Kansas. I will stand by that exception.
Either Kansas must come in as a free State, with whatever population she may have, or the rule must be applied to all the
other territories alike. I therefore answer at once, that it having
been decided that Kansas has people enough for a slave State, I
hold that she has enough for a free State. I hope Mr. Lincoln
is satisfied with my answer; and now I would like to get his
answer to his own interrogatory — whether or not he will vote to
admit Kansas before she has the requisite population. I want to
know whether he will vote to admit Oregon before that territory
has the requisite population. Mr. Trumbull will not, and the
same reason that commits Mr. Trumbull against the admission of
Oregon commits him against Kansas, even if she should apply
for admission as a free State. If there is any sincerity, any
truth, in the argument of Mr. Trumbull in the Senate against
the admission of Oregon, because she had not 93,420 people,
although her population was larger than that of Kansas, he
stands pledged against the admission of both Oregon and Kansas,
until they have 93,420 inhabitants. I would like Mr. Lincoln to
answer this question. I would like him to take his own medicine. If he differ with Mr. Trumbull, let him answer his argument against the admission of Oregon, instead of poking questions at me.

The next question propounded to me by Mr. Lincoln is: Can
the people of the territory in any lawful way, against the wishes
of any citizen of the United States, exclude slavery from their
limits prior to the formation of a State constitution ? I answer

emphatically, as Mr. Lincoln has heard me answer a hundred times from every stump in Illinois, that in my opinion the people of a territory can, by lawful means, exclude slavery from their limits prior to the formation of a State constitution. Mr. Lincoln knew that I had answered that question over and over again. He heard me argue the Nebraska Bill on that principle all over the State in 1854, in 1855, and in 1856, and he has no excuse for pretending to be in doubt as to my position on that question. It matters not what way the Supreme Court may hereafter decide as to the abstract question whether slavery may or may not go into a territory under the Constitution; the people have the lawful means to introduce it or exclude it as they please, for the reason that slavery cannot exist a day or an hour anywhere, unless it is supported by local police regulations. Those police regulations can only be established by the local legislature; and if the people are opposed to slavery, they will elect representatives to that body who will by unfriendly legislation effectually prevent the introduction of it into their midst. If, on the contrary, they are for it, their legislation will favor its extension. Hence, no matter what the decision of the Supreme Court may be on that abstract question, still the right of the people to make a slave Territory or a free Territory is perfect and complete under the Nebraska Bill. I hope Mr. Lincoln deems my answer satisfactory on that point.

In this connection, I will notice the charge which he has introduced in relation to Mr. Chase's amendment. I thought that I had chased that amendment out of Mr. Lincoln's brain at Ottawa, but it seems that still haunts his imagination, and he is not yet satisfied. I had supposed that he would be ashamed to press that question further. He is a lawyer, and has been a Member of Congress, and has occupied his time and amused you by telling you about parliamentary proceeding. He ought to have known better than to try to palm off his miserable impositions upon this intelligent audience. The Nebraska Bill provided that the legislative power and authority of the said Territory should extend to all rightful subjects of legislation, consistent with the organic act and the Constitution of the United States. It did not make any exception as to slavery, but gave all the power that it was possible for Congress to give without violating the Constitution to the territorial legislature, with no exception or limitation on the subject of slavery at all. The language of that bill which I have quoted gave the full power and the full authority over the subject of slavery, affirmatively and negatively, to introduce it or exclude it, so far as the Constitution of the United States would permit. What more could Mr. Chase give by his amendment? Nothing. He offered his amendment for the identical purpose for which Mr. Lincoln is using it, to enable demagogues in the country to try and deceive the people.

His amendment was to this effect. It provided that the legislature should have the power to exclude slavery; and General Cass suggested: "Why not give the power to introduce as well as exclude?" The answer was: "They have the power already in the bill to do both." Chase was afraid his amendment would be adopted if he put the alternative proposition, and so make it fair both ways, but would not yield. He offered it for the purpose of having it rejected. He offered it, as he has himself avowed over and over again, simply to make capital out of it for the stump. He expected that it would be capital for small politicians in the country, and that they would make an effort to deceive the people with it; and he was not mistaken, for Lincoln is carrying out the plan admirably. Lincoln knows that the Nebraska Bill, without Chase's amendment, gave all the power which the Constitution would permit. Could Congress confer any more? Could Congress go beyond the Constitution of the country? We gave all a full grant with no exception in regard to slavery one way or the other. We left that question, as we left all others, to be decided by the people for themselves, just as they pleased. I will not occupy my time on this question. I have argued it before all over Illinois. I have argued it in this beautiful city of Freeport; I have argued it in the North, the South, the East, and the West, avowing the same sentiments and the same principles. I have not been afraid to avow my sentiments up here for fear I would be trotted down into Egypt.

The third question which Mr. Lincoln presented is: "If the Supreme Court of the United States shall decide that a State of this Union cannot exclude slavery from its own limits, will I submit to it?" I am amazed that Lincoln should ask such a question. "A schoolboy knows better." Yes, a schoolboy does know better. Mr. Lincoln's object is to cast an imputation upon the Supreme Court. He knows that there never was but one man in America, claiming any degree of intelligence or decency, who ever for a moment pretended such a thing. It is true that the Washington Union, in an article published on the seventeenth of last December, did put forth that doctrine, and I denounced the article on the floor of the Senate in a speech which Mr. Lincoln now pretends was against the President. The Union had claimed that slavery had a right to go into the free States, and that any provisions in the Constitution or laws of the Free States to the contrary were null and void. I denounced it in the Senate, as I said before, and I was the first man who did. Lincoln's friends, Trumbull and Seward and Hale and Wilson and the whole black Republican side of the Senate were silent. They left it to me to denounce it. And what was the reply made to me on that occasion? Mr. Toombs, of Georgia, got up and undertook to lecture me on the ground that I ought not to have deemed the article worthy of notice and ought not to have replied to it; that there was not one man, woman, or child south of the Potomac, in any slave State, who did not repudiate any such pretension. Mr. Lincoln knows that that reply was made on the spot, and yet now he asks this question. He might as well ask me: "Suppose Mr. Lincoln should steal a horse, would you sanction it?" and it would be as genteel in me to ask him, in the event he stole a horse, what ought to be done with him. He casts an imputation upon the Supreme Court of the United States by supposing that they would violate the Constitution of the United States. I tell him that such a thing is not possible. It would be an act of moral treason that no man on the bench could ever descend to. Mr. Lincoln himself would never in his partisan feelings so far forget what was right as to be guilty of such an act.

The fourth question of Mr. Lincoln is: "Are you in favor of acquiring additional territory, in disregard as to how such acquisition may affect the Union on the slavery question?" This question is very ingeniously and cunningly put.

The Black Republican creed lays it down expressly, that under no circumstances shall we acquire any more territory unless slavery is first prohibited in the country. I ask Mr. Lincoln whether he is in favor of that proposition. Are you [addressing Mr. Lincoln] opposed to the acquisition of any more territory, under any circumstances, unless slavery is prohibited in it? That he does not like to answer. When I ask him whether he stands up to that article in the platform of his party he turns, Yankee fashion, and, without answering it, asks me whether I am in favor of acquiring territory without regard to how it may affect the Union on the slavery question. I answer that whenever it becomes necessary, in our growth and progress, to acquire more territory, that I am in favor of it, without reference to the question of slavery; and when we have acquired it, I will leave the people free to do as they please, either to make it slave or free territory, as they prefer. It is idle to tell me or you that we have territory enough. Our fathers supposed that we had enough when our territory extended to the Mississippi River, but a few years' growth and expansion satisfied them that we needed more, and the Louisiana Territory, from the west branch of the Mississippi to the British possessions, was acquired. Then we acquired Oregon, then California and New Mexico. We have enough now for the present, but this is a young and a growing nation. It swarms as often as a hive of bees; and as new swarms are turned out each year, there must be hives in which they can gather and make their honey. In less than fifteen years, if the same progress that has distinguished this country for the last fifteen years continue, every foot of vacant land between this and the Pacific Ocean owned by the United States will be occupied. Will you not continue to increase at the end of fifteen years as well as now? I tell you, increase and multiply and expand is the law of this nation's existence. You cannot limit this great Republic by mere boundary lines, saying: "Thus far shalt thou go, and no further." Any one of you gentlemen might as well say to a son twelve years old that he is big enough, and must not grow any larger, and in order to prevent his growth put a hoop around him to keep him to his present size. What would be the result? Either the hoop must burst and be rent asunder, or the child must die. So it would be with this great nation. With our natural increase, growing with a rapidity unknown in any other part of the globe, with the tide of emigration that is fleeing from despotism in the Old World to seek refuge in our own, there is a constant torrent pouring into this country that requires more land, more territory upon which to settle; and just as fast as our interests and our destiny require additional territory in the North, in the South, or on the islands of the ocean, I am for it, and when we acquire it, will leave the people, according to the Nebraska Bill, free to do as they please on the subject of slavery and every other question.

I trust now that Mr. Lincoln will deem himself answered on his four points. He racked his brain so much in devising these four questions that he exhausted himself, and had not strength enough to invent the others. As soon as he is able to hold a council with his advisers, Lovejoy, Farnsworth, and Fred Douglas, he will frame and propound others. ["Good, good!"] You Black Republicans who say good, I have no doubt think that they are all good men. I have reason to recollect that some people in this country think that Fred Douglas is a very good man. The last time I came here to make a speech, while talking from the stand to you, people of Freeport, as I am doing to-day, I saw a carriage, and a magnificent one it was, drive up and take a position on the outside of the crowd; a beautiful young lady was sitting on the box-seat, whilst Fred Douglas and her mother reclined inside, and the owner of the carriage acted as driver. I saw this in your own town. ["What of it?"] All I have to say of it is this, that if you, Black Republicans, think that the negro ought to be on a social equality with your wives and daughters, and ride in a carriage with your wife, whilst you drive the team, you have a perfect right to do so. I am told that one of Fred Douglas's kinsmen, another rich black negro, is now traveling in this part of the State making speeches for his friend Lincoln as the champion of black men. ["What have you to say against it?"] All I have to say on that subject is, that those of you who be-lieve that the negro is your equal and ought to be on an equal-ity with you socially, politically, and legally, have a right to entertain these opinions, and, of course, will vote for Mr. Lincoln.

Excerpt from The Character of Washington

Edward Everett

Commentary

Although Douglas and Lincoln presented diametrically opposed versions of what the Founding Fathers thought about slavery, both used the same rhetorical strategy of identifying their own views with those of the Fathers. They were not alone in basing their rhetoric on the public's reverence for historical heroes. We have already seen that reformers identified their causes with the Declaration of Independence and that Clay argued for the Compromise of 1850 with a fragment of Washington's coffin.

Given the persuasive power of hero symbols, it is not surprising that they were used during the late 1850s by a loosely knit group of people who increasingly referred to themselves as "Unionists." Coming from different sections, belonging to different political parties and holding to different ideologies about divisive issues such as the tariff and slavery, they were united only by their insistence that differences should be de-emphasized now that secession and civil war were genuine possibilities. Their rhetoric included pragmatic arguments, especially the European analogy. If the country divided into two sections, the precedent of secession would lead to further divisions, and eventually we, like Europe, would be a collection of small nations fighting with one another. Their chief argument was that the Founding Fathers wished us to remain united.

Given their diversity, no Unionist can be regarded as typical, but Edward Everett (1794-1865) was as typical as any, and he was one of the best known. Originally a preacher and college professor (the first American to earn a Ph.D., which was bestowed by a German university), he entered Congress in 1825 and continued his political career as a Whig before serving briefly as president of Harvard. His gentlemanly distaste of "party spirit" made him a poor legislative debater, and he would not consider taking to the stump during election campaigns. He advanced his political career by keeping himself in the public eye. At a time when the lecture platform was increasingly popular, he often lectured about scholarly subjects. He was even more famous as an epideictic orator, being especially active on historical occasions, such as the Fourth of July. He hated abolitionism because of its divisiveness to the Union. In 1852, a coalition of anti-abolitionist Massachusetts Whigs and Democrats elected him United States senator to offset Charles Sumner, a recently elected political abolitionist. Everett spoke against the Kansas-Nebraska bill, arguing that passage would intensify sectionalism. After passage, the discouraged Everett, convinced that secession was now inevitable, resigned from the Senate. Gradually overcoming his discouragement, he decided to become active in the Unionist cause. Meanwhile, the Ladies Mount Vernon Association began raising money to purchase Mount Vernon and convert it into a national memorial. Joining forces with them, Everett wrote a series of newspaper articles entitled "Mount Vernon Papers," which dealt with his European travels and which netted $10,000. He raised approximately $70,000 by going on a lecture tour with a speech on "The Character of Washington," which he delivered 137 times throughout the entire country during 1856-1859.

The text of the lecture varied, sometimes because he revised it, sometimes because the aging man's memory failed and mostly because he skillfully adapted some aspect of Washington's life to the particular locality. The general plan, however, was always the same. After a long, chronologically organized biography of Washington, Everett amplified Lord Brougham's assertion that Washington was "the greatest man of our own or of any age." He analyzed the qualities that made Washington great, arguing that instead of having one "dazzling" quality, Washington "united all the qualities required for the honorable and successful conduct of the greatest affairs." He contrasted Washington with other so-called "greats," such as the "debauched" Alexander, and recounted Washington's fame in Europe.

Had Everett concluded at this point, the unity-building function of his speech would have been only indirect. He ended, however, with more direct appeals (or what he privately called "union sentiments"), which are reproduced from Edward Everett, *Orations and Speeches on Various Occasions,* 9th edition (Boston: Little, Brown, 1878), vol. 4, pp. 49-51.

Excerpt from The Character of Washington

But to us citizens of America, it belongs above all others to show respect to the memory of Washington, by the practical deference which we pay to those sober maxims of public policy which he has left us, — a last testament of affection in his Farewell Address. Of all the exhortations which it contains, I scarce need say to you that none are so emphatically uttered, none so anxiously repeated, as those which enjoin the preservation of the Union of these States. On this, under Providence, it depends in the judgment of Washington whether the people of America shall follow the Old World example, and be broken up into a group of independent military powers, wasted by eternal border wars, feeding the ambition of petty sovereigns on the life-blood of wasted principalities, — a custom-house on the bank of every river, a fortress on every frontier hill, a pirate lurking in the recesses of every bay, — or whether they shall continue to constitute a confederate republic, the most extensive, the most powerful, the most prosperous in the long line of ages. No one can read the Farewell Address without feeling that this was the thought and this the care which lay nearest and heaviest upon that noble heart; and if — which Heaven forbid — the day shall ever arrive when his parting counsels on that head shall be forgotten, on that day, come it soon or come it late, it may as mournfully as truly be said, that Washington has lived in vain. Then the vessels as they ascend and descend the Potomac may toll their bells with new significance as they pass Mount Vernon; they will strike the requiem of constitutional liberty for us, — for all nations.

But it cannot, shall not be; this great woe to our beloved country, this catastrophe for the cause of national freedom, this grievous calamity for the whole civilized world, it cannot, shall not be. No, by the glorious 19th of April, 1775; no, by the precious blood of Bunker Hill, of Princeton, of Saratoga, of King's Mountain, of Yorktown; no, by the undying spirit of '76; no, by the sacred dust enshrined at Mount Vernon; no, by the dear immortal memory of Washington, — that sorrow and shame shall never be. Sooner let the days of colonial vassalage return; rather let the Frenchman and savage again run the boundary with the firebrand and scalping-knife, from the St. Lawrence to the Mississippi, than that sister States should be arrayed against each other, or brother's hands be imbrued in brother's blood.

A great and venerated character like that of Washington, which commands the respect of an entire population, however divided on other questions, is not an isolated fact in History to be regarded with barren admiration, — it is a dispensation of Providence for good. It was well said by Mr. Jefferson in 1792, writing to Washington to dissuade him from declining a renomination: "North and South will hang together while they have you to hang to." Washington in the flesh is taken from us; we shall never behold him as our fathers did; but his memory remains, and I say, let us hang to his memory. Let us make a national festival and holiday of his birthday; and ever, as the 22d of February returns, let us remember, that while with these solemn and joyous rites of observance we celebrate the great anniversary, our fellow-citizens on the Hudson, on the Potomac, from the Southern plains to the Western lakes, are engaged in the same offices of gratitude and love. Nor we, nor they alone, — beyond the Ohio, beyond the Mississippi, along that stupendous trail of immigration from East to West, which, bursting into States as it moves westward, is already threading the Western prairies, swarming through the portals of the Rocky Mountains and winding down their slopes, the name and the memory of Washington on that gracious night will travel with the silver queen of heaven through sixty degrees of longitude, nor part company with her till she walks in her brightness through the golden gate of California, and passes serenely on to hold midnight court with her

Australian stars. There and there only, in barbarous archipelagos, as yet untrodden by civilized man, the name of Washington is unknown; and there, too, when they swarm with enlightened millions, new honors shall be paid with ours to his memory.

Cooper Union Address

Abraham Lincoln

Commentary

As the popularity of Everett's "Washington" attests, Unionist attitudes remained strong even as sectionalism intensified. Public attitudes were extremely ambivalent, even among Republicans. Some were less interested in slavery than in old Whig ideas, such as protective tariffs. While some Republicans were militant political abolitionists, others were only Free Soilers. Republican divisiveness was illustrated, for example, in 1860, when some Republican congressmen voted to admit Oregon as a State because its constitution prohibited slavery while others voted negatively because it also prohibited free blacks and mulattoes from residing in the State.

In 1859, as Republican leaders looked ahead to next year's presidential election, they knew they would have to be extremely careful. They were at a disadvantage by being a sectional party. They would split their own ranks if they nominated someone who was too militant or too moderate on the slavery question. Their best-known potential nominee was William Seward. Although he was not as militant as many people thought, Democrats were already trying to discredit him with the "higher law" argument he had used against the Compromise of 1850 and which militants were using to justify violating the Fugitive Slave Act. John Brown's famous raid on Harper's Ferry in the fall of 1859 gave the Democrats additional ammunition. Although most abolitionists regarded the raid as a crime, Democrats were having considerable success identifying Brown with abolitionism and abolitionism with "Black Republicans." With their national convention only a few months away, many Republican leaders were getting nervous. They wanted someone more moderate than Seward. But who?

A distinct possibility was Abraham Lincoln, who had been catapulted into the national limelight by his debates with Douglas. The election results had been impressive. Although the Illinois legislature had re-elected Douglas, the margin had been close (54-46) and the popular referendum had favored Lincoln (125,430-121,609). Also impressive were Lincoln's subsequent encounters with Douglas. Although not debating formally, both had made

450

special efforts to answer each other's arguments while stumping Ohio in support of party candidates during the State election of 1859. Douglas had felt compelled to answer Lincoln and defend "popular sovereignty" in an article published in *Harper's*. Especially impressive was the skill with which Lincoln had pushed Douglas into defending the proposition that Congress lacked constitutional authority to prohibit slavery in the territories but territorial residents could do so. The first part of the doctrine was not universally popular in the North, and the second part was despised in the South where Douglas was already in trouble because of Lecompton and Freeport. In short, Lincoln's focus on the territorial issue made him seem sufficiently antislavery to gain Republican support without making him seem too extreme. Douglas was the most likely Democratic nominee. Lincoln, having pushed him into a difficult position, rose in favor. Few Eastern Republicans had ever met Lincoln, and some leaders decided it was time to take a closer look at this Westerner. All they needed was an appropriate occasion.

With public lectures now extremely popular, the philanthropist, Peter Cooper, had established in New York City the Cooper Union Institute, which promoted adult education and opened its facilities to various groups which wished to sponsor lectures. The Young Men's Central Republican Union of New York City obtained use of the auditorium and invited Lincoln to present a lecture on February 27, 1860. Although ostensibly a lecturer, Lincoln actually delivered a campaign address for the party's nomination to a predominately Republican audience. Tall, raw-boned and dressed in loose-fitted clothing, Lincoln's physical appearance was unimpressive. The speech was so well received that it is generally credited with earning him the presidential nomination. It is reproduced from *Complete Works of Abraham Lincoln*, 2nd edition, editors John G. Nicolay and John Hay (New York: Lamb Publishing Co., 1905), vol. 5, pp. 293-328.

Cooper Union Address to Young Men's Central Republican Union of New York City, 1860

MR. PRESIDENT AND FELLOW-CITIZENS OF NEW YORK: The facts with which I shall deal this evening are mainly old and familiar; nor is there anything new in the general use I shall make of them. If there shall be any novelty, it will be in the mode of presenting the facts, and the inferences and observations following that presentation. In his speech last autumn at Columbus, Ohio, as reported in the "New-York Times," Senator Douglas said:

> Our fathers, when they framed the government under which we live, understood this question just as well, and even better, than we do now.

I fully indorse this, and I adopt it as a text for this discourse. I so adopt it because it furnishes a precise and an agreed starting-point for a discussion between Republicans and that wing of the Democracy headed by Senator Douglas. It simply leaves the inquiry: What was the understanding those fathers had of the question mentioned?

What is the frame of government under which we live? The answer must be, "The Constitution of the United States." That Constitution consists of the original, framed in 1787, and under which the present government first went into operation, and twelve subsequently framed amemdments, the first ten of which were framed in 1789.

Who were our fathers that framed the Constitution? I suppose the "thirty-nine" who signed the original instrument may be fairly called our fathers who framed that part of the present government. It is almost exactly true to say they framed it, and it is altogether true to say they fairly represented the opinion and sentiment of the whole nation at that time. Their names, being familiar to nearly all, and accessible to quite all, need not now be repeated.

I take these "thirty-nine," for the present, as being "our fathers who framed the government under which we live." What is the question which, according to the text, those fathers understood "just as well, and even better, than we do now?"

It is this: Does the proper division of local from Federal authority, or anything in the Constitution, forbid our Federal Government to control as to slavery in our Federal Territories?

Upon this, Senator Douglas holds the affirmative, and Republicans the negative. This affirmation and denial form an issue; and this issue — this question — is precisely what the text declares our fathers understood "better than we." Let us now inquire whether the "thirty-nine," or any of them, ever acted upon this question; and if they did, how they acted upon it — how they expressed that better understanding. In 1784, three years before the Constitution, the United States then owning the Northwestern Territory, and no other, the Congress of the Confederation had before them the question of prohibiting slavery in that Territory; and four of the "thirty-nine" who afterward framed the Constitution were in that Congress, and voted on that question. Of these, Roger Sherman, Thomas Mifflin, and Hugh Williamson voted for the prohibition, thus showing that, in their understanding, no line dividing local from Federal authority, nor anything else, properly forbade the Federal Government to control as to slavery in Federal territory. The other of the four, James McHenry, voted against the prohibition, showing that for some cause he thought it improper to vote for it.

In 1787, still before the Constitution, but while the convention was in session framing it, and while the Northwestern Territory still was the only Territory owned by the United States, the same question of prohibiting slavery in the Territory again came before the Congress of the Confederation; and two more of the "thirty-nine" who afterward signed the Constitution were in that Congress, and voted on the question. They were William Blount and William Few; and they both voted for the prohibition — thus showing that in their understanding no line dividing local from Federal Authority, nor anything else, properly forbade the Federal Government to control as to slavery in Federal territory. This time the prohibition became a law, being part of what is now well known as the ordinance of '87.

The question of Federal control of slavery in the Territories seems not to have been directly before the convention which framed the original Constitution; and hence it is not recorded that the "thirty-nine," or any of them, while engaged on that instrument, expressed any opinion on that precise question.

In 1789, by the first Congress which sat under the Constitution, an act was passed to enforce the ordinance of '87, including the prohibition of slavery in the Northwestern Territory. The bill for this act was reported by one of the "thirty-nine" — Thomas Fitzsimmons, then a member of the House of Representatives from Pennsylvania. It went through all its stages without a word of opposition, and finally passed both branches without ayes and nays, which is equivalent to a unanimous passage. In this Congress there were sixteen of the thirty-nine fathers who framed the original Constitution. They were John Langdon, Nicholas Gilman, Wm. S. Johnson, Roger Sherman, Robert Morris, Thos. Fitzsimmons, William Few, Abraham Baldwin, Rufus King, William Paterson, George Clymer, Richard Bassett, George Read, Pierce Butler, Daniel Carroll and James Madison.

This shows that, in their understanding, no line dividing local from Federal authority, nor anything in the Constitution, properly forbade Congress to prohibit slavery in the Federal territory; else both their fidelity to correct principle, and their oath to support the Constitution, would have constrained them to oppose the prohibition.

Again, George Washington, another of the "thirty-nine," was then President of the United States and as such approved and signed the bill, thus completing its validity as a law, and thus showing that, in his understanding, no line dividing local from Federal authority, nor anything in the Constitution, forbade the Federal Government to control as to slavery in Federal territory.

No great while after the adoption of the original Constitution, North Carolina ceded to the Federal Government the country now constituting the State of Tennessee; and a few years later Georgia ceded that which now constitutes the States of Mississippi and Alabama. In both deeds of cession it was made a condition by the ceding States that the Federal Government should not prohibit slavery in the ceded country. Besides this, slavery was then actually in the ceded country. Under these circumstances, Congress, on taking charge of these countries, did not absolutely prohibit slavery within them. But they did interfere with it — take control of it — even there, to a certain extent. In 1798 Congress organized the Territory of Mississippi. In the act of organization they prohibited the bringing of slaves into the Territory from any place without the United States, by fine, and giving freedom to slaves so brought. This act passed both branches of Congress without yeas and nays. In that Congress were three of the "thirty-nine" who framed the original Constitution. They were John Langdon, George Read, and Abraham

Baldwin. They all probably voted for it. Certainly they would have placed their opposition to it upon record if, in their understanding, any line dividing local from Federal authority, or anything in the Constitution, properly forbade the Federal Government to control as to slavery in Federal territory.

In 1803 the Federal Government purchased the Louisiana country. Our former territorial acquisitions came from certain of our own States; but this Louisiana country was acquired from a foreign nation. In 1804 Congress gave a territorial organization to that part of it which now constitutes the State of Louisiana. New Orleans, lying within that part, was an old and comparatively large city. There were other considerable towns and settlements, and slavery was extensively and thoroughly intermingled with the people. Congress did not, in the Territorial Act, prohibit slavery; but they did interfere with it — take control of it — in a more marked and extensive way than they did in the case of Mississippi. The substance of the provision therein made in relation to slaves was:

1st. That no slave should be imported into the Territory from foreign parts.

2d. That no slave should be carried into it who had been imported into the United States since the first day of May, 1798.

3d. That no slave should be carried into it, except by the owner, and for his own use as a settler; the penalty in all the cases being a fine upon the violator of the law, and freedom to the slave.

This act also was passed without ayes or nays. In the Congress which passed it there were two of the "thirty-nine." They were Abraham Baldwin and Jonathan Dayton. As stated in the case of Mississippi, it is probable they both voted for it. They would not have allowed it to pass without recording their opposition to it if, in their understanding, it violated either the line properly dividing local from Federal authority, or any provision of the Constitution.

In 1819-20 came and passed the Missouri question. Many votes were taken, by yeas and nays, in both branches of Congress, upon the various phases of the general question. Two of the "thirty-nine" — Rufus King and Charles Pinckney — were members of that Congress. Mr. King steadily voted for slavery prohibition and against all compromises, while Mr. Pinckney as steadily voted against slavery prohibition and against all compromises. By this, Mr. King showed that, in his understanding, no line dividing local from Federal authority, nor anything in the Constitution, was violated by Congress prohibiting slavery in Federal territory; while Mr. Pinckney, by his votes, showed that, in his understanding, there was some sufficient reason for opposing such prohibition in that case.

The cases I have mentioned are the only acts of the "thirty-nine," or of any of them, upon the direct issue, which I have been able to discover.

To enumerate the persons who thus acted as being four in 1784, two in 1787, seventeen in 1789, three in 1798, two in 1804, and two in 1819-20, there would be thirty of them. But this would be counting John Langdon, Roger Sherman, William Few, Rufus King, and George Read each twice, and Abraham Baldwin three times. The true number of those of the "thirty-nine" whom I have shown to have acted upon the question which, by the text, they understood better than we, is twenty-three, leaving sixteen not shown to have acted upon it in any way.

Here, then, we have twenty-three out of our thirty-nine fathers "who framed the government under which we live," who have, upon their official responsibility and their corporal oaths, acted upon the very question which the text affirms they "understood just as well, and even better, than we do now;" and twenty-one of them — a clear majority of the whole "thirty-nine" — so acting upon it as to make them guilty of gross political impropriety and wilful perjury if, in their understanding, any proper division between local and Federal authority, or anything in the Constitution they had made themselves, and sworn to support, forbade the Federal Government to control as to slavery in the Federal Territories. Thus the twenty-one acted; and, as actions speak louder than words, so actions under such responsibility speak still louder.

Two of the twenty-three voted against congressional prohibitions of slavery in the Federal Territories, in the instances in which they acted upon the question. But for what reasons they so voted is not known. They may have done so because they thought a proper division of local from Federal authority, or some provision or principle of the Constitution, stood in the way; or they may, without any such question, have voted against the prohibition on what appeared to them to be sufficient grounds of expediency. No one who has sworn to support the Constitution can conscientiously vote for what he understands to be an unconstitutional measure, however expedient he may think it; but one may and ought to vote against a measure which he deems constitutional if, at the same time, he deems it inexpedient. It, therefore, would be unsafe to set down even the two who voted against the prohibition as having done so because, in their understanding, any proper division of local from Federal authority, or anything in the Constitution, forbade the Federal Government to control as to slavery in Federal territory.

The remaining sixteen of the "thirty-nine," so far as I have discovered, have left no record of their understanding upon the direct question of Federal control of slavery in the Federal Territories. But there is much reason to believe that their understanding upon that question would not have appeared different from that of their twenty-three compeers, had it been manifested at all.

For the purpose of adhering rigidly to the text, I have purposely omitted whatever understanding may have been manifested by any person, however distinguished, other than the thirty-nine fathers who framed the original Constitution; and, for the same reason, I have also omitted whatever understanding may have been manifested by any of the "thirty-nine" even on any other phase of the general question of slavery. If we should look into their acts and declarations on those other phases, as the foreign slave-trade, and the morality and policy of slavery generally, it would appear to us that on the direct question of Federal control of slavery in Federal Territories, the sixteen, if they had acted at all, would probably have acted just as the twenty-three did. Among that sixteen were several of the most noted antislavery men of those times, — as Dr. Franklin, Alexander Hamilton, and Gouverneur Morris, — while there was not one now known to have been otherwise, unless it may be John Rutledge, of South Carolina.

The sum of the whole is that of our thirty-nine fathers who framed the original Constitution, twenty-one — a clear majority of the whole — certainly understood that no proper division of local from Federal authority, nor any part of the Constitution, forbade the Federal Government to control slavery in the Federal Territories; while all the rest had probably the same understanding. Such, unquestionably, was the understanding of our fathers who framed the original Constitution; and the text affirms that they understood the question "better than we."

But, so far, I have been considering the understanding of the question manifested by the framers of the original Constitution. In and by the original instrument, a mode was provided for amending it; and, as I have already stated, the present frame of "the government under which we live" consists of that original, and twelve amendatory articles framed and adopted since. Those who now insist that Federal control of slavery in Federal Territories violates the Constitution, point us to the provisions which they suppose it thus violates; and, as I understand, they all fix upon provisions in these amendatory articles, and not in the original instrument. The Supreme Court, in the Dred Scott case, plant themselves upon the Fifth Amendment, which provides that no person shall be deprived of "life, liberty, or property without due process of law"; while Senator Douglas and his peculiar adherents plant themselves upon the Tenth Amendment, providing that "the powers not delegated to the United States by the Constitution" "are reserved to the States respectively, or to the people."

Now, it so happens that these amendments were framed by the first Congress which sat under the Constitution — the identical Congress which passed the act, already mentioned, enforcing the prohibition of slavery in the Northwestern Territory. Not only was it the same Congress, but they were the identical, same individual men who, at the same session, and at the same time within the session, had under consideration, and in progress toward maturity, these constitutional amendments, and this act prohibiting slavery in all the territory the nation then owned. The constitutional amendments were introduced before, and passed after, the act enforcing the ordinance of '87; so that, during the whole pendency of the act to enforce the ordinance, the constitutional amendments were also pending.

The seventy-six members of that Congress, including sixteen of the framers of the original Constitution, as before stated, were preëminently our fathers who framed that part of "the government under which we live" which is now claimed as forbidding the Federal Government to control slavery in the Federal Territories.

Is it not a little presumptuous in any one at this day to affirm that the two things which that Congress deliberately framed, and carried to maturity at the same time, are absolutely inconsistent with each other? And does not such affirmation become impudently absurd when coupled with the other affirmation, from the same mouth, that those who did the two things alleged to be inconsistent, understood whether they really were inconsistent better than we — better than he who affirms that they are inconsistent?

It is surely safe to assume that the thirty-nine framers of the original Constitution, and the seventy-six members of the Congress which framed the amendments thereto, taken together, do certainly include those who may be fairly called "our fathers who framed the government under which we live." And so assuming, I defy any man to show that any one of them ever, in his whole life, declared that, in his understanding, any proper division of local from Federal authority, or any part of the Constitution, forbade the Federal Government to control as to slavery in the Federal Territories. I go a step further. I defy any one to show that any living man in the whole world ever did, prior to the beginning of the present century (and I might almost say prior to the beginning of the last half of the present century), declare that, in his understanding, any proper division of local from Federal authority, or any part of the Constitution, forbade the Federal Government to control as to slavery in the Federal Territories. To those who now so declare I give not only "our fathers who framed the government under which we live," but with them all other living men within the century in which it was framed, among whom to search, and they shall not be able to find the evidence of a single man agreeing with them.

Now, and here, let me guard a little against being misunderstood. I do not mean to say we are bound to follow implicitly in whatever our fathers did. To do so would be to discard all the lights of current experience — to reject all progress, all improvement. What I do say is that if we would supplant the opinions and policy of our fathers in any case, we should do so upon evidence so conclusive, and argument so clear, that even their great authority, fairly considered and weighed, cannot stand; and most surely not in a case whereof we ourselves declare they understood the question better than we.

If any man at this day sincerely believes that a proper division of local from Federal authority, or any part of the Constitution, forbids the Federal Government to control as to slavery in the Federal Territories, he is right to say so, and to enforce his position by all truthful evidence and fair argument which he can. But he has no right to mislead others, who have less access to history, and less leisure to study it, into the false belief that "our fathers who framed the government under which we live" were of the same opinion — thus substituting falsehood and deception for truthful evidence and fair argument. If any man at this day sincerely believes "our fathers who framed the government under which we live" used and applied principles, in other cases, which ought to have led them to understand that a proper division of local from Federal authority, or some part of the Constitution, forbids the Federal Government to control as to slavery in the Federal Territories, he is right to say so. But he should, at the same time, brave the responsibility of declaring that, in his opinion, he understands their principles better than they did themselves; and especially should he not shirk that responsibility by asserting that they "understood the question just as well, and even better, than we do now."

But enough! Let all who believe that "our fathers who framed the government under which we live understood this question just as well, and even better, than we do now," speak as they spoke, and act as they acted upon it. This is all Republicans ask — all Republicans desire — in relation to slavery. As those fathers marked it, so let it be again marked, as an evil not to be extended, but to be tolerated and protected only because of and so far as its actual presence among us makes that toleration and protection a necessity. Let all the guaranties those fathers gave it be not grudgingly, but fully and fairly, maintained. For this Republicans contend, and with this, so far as I know or believe, they will be content.

And now, if they would listen, — as I suppose they will not, — I would address a few words to the Southern people.

I would say to them: You consider yourselves a reasonable and a just people; and I consider that in the general qualities of reason and justice you are not inferior to any other people. Still, when you speak of us Republicans, you do so only to denounce us as reptiles, or, at the best, as no better than outlaws. You will grant a hearing to pirates or murderers, but nothing like it to "Black Republicans." In all your contentions with one another, each of you deems an unconditional condemnation of "Black Republicanism" as the first thing to be attended to. Indeed, such condemnation of us seems to be an indispensable prerequisite — license, so to speak — among you to be admitted or permitted to speak at all. Now can you or not be prevailed upon to pause and to consider whether this is quite just to us, or even to yourselves? Bring forward your charges and specifications, and then be patient long enough to hear us deny or justify.

You say we are sectional. We deny it. That makes an issue; and the burden of proof is upon you. You produce your proof; and what is it? Why, that our party has no existence in your section — gets no votes in your section. The fact is substantially true; but does it prove the issue? If it does, then in case we should, without change of principle, begin to get votes in your section, we should thereby cease to be sectional. You cannot escape this conclusion; and yet, are you willing to abide by it? If you are, you will probably soon find that we have ceased to be sectional, for we shall get votes in your section this very year. You will then begin to discover, as the truth plainly is, that your proof does not touch the issue. The fact that we get no votes in your section is a fact of your making, and not of ours. And if there be fault in that fact, that fault is primarily yours, and remains so until you show that we repel you by some wrong principle or practice. If we do repel you by any wrong principle or practice, the fault is ours; but this brings you to where you ought to have started — to a discussion of the right or wrong of our principle. If our principle, put in practice, would wrong your section for the benefit of ours, or for any other object, then our principle, and we with it, are sectional, and are justly opposed and denounced as such. Meet us, then, on the question of whether our principle, put in practice, would wrong your section; and so meet us as if it were possible that something may be said on our side. Do you accept the challenge? No! Then you really believe that the principle which "our fathers who framed the government under which we live" thought so clearly right as to adopt it, and indorse it again and again, upon their official oaths, is in fact so clearly wrong as to demand your condemnation without a moment's consideration.

Some of you delight to flaunt in our faces the warning against sectional parties given by Washington in his Farewell Address. Less than eight years before Washington gave that warning, he had, as President of the United States, approved and signed an act of Congress enforcing the prohibition of slavery in the Northwestern Territory, which act embodied the policy of the government upon that subject up to and at the very moment he penned that warning; and about one year after he penned it, he wrote Lafayette that he considered that prohibition a wise measure, expressing in the same connection his hope that we should at some time have a confederacy of free States.

Bearing this in mind, and seeing that sectionalism has since arisen upon this same subject, is that warning a weapon in your hands against us, or in our hands against you? Could Washington himself speak, would he cast the blame of that sectionalism upon us, who sustain his policy, or upon you, who repudiate it? We respect that warning of Washington, and we commend it to you, together with his example pointing to the right application of it.

But you say you are conservative — eminently conservative — while we are revolutionary, destructive, or something of the sort. What is conservatism? Is it not adherence to the old and tried, against the new and untried? We stick to, contend for, the identical old policy on the point in controversy which was adopted by "our fathers who framed the government under which we live"; while you with one accord reject, and scout, and spit upon that old policy, and insist upon substituting something new. True, you disagree among yourselves as to what that substitute shall be. You are divided on new propositions and plans, but you are unanimous in rejecting and denouncing the old policy of the fathers. Some of you are for reviving the foreign slave-trade; some for a congressional slave code for the Territories; some for Congress forbidding the Territories to prohibit slavery within their limits; some for maintaining slavery in the Territories through the judiciary; some for the "gur-reat pur-rinciple" that "if one man would enslave another, no third man should object," fantastically called "popular sovereignty"; but never a man among you is in favor of Federal prohibition of slavery in Federal Territories, according to the practice of "our fathers who framed the government under which we live." Not one of all your various plans can show a precedent or an advocate in the century within which our government originated. Consider, then, whether your claim of conservatism for yourselves, and your charge of destructiveness against us, are based on the most clear and stable foundations.

Again, you say we have made the slavery question more prominent than it formerly was. We deny it. We admit that it is more prominent, but we deny that we made it so. It was not we, but you, who discarded the old policy of the fathers. We resisted, and still resist, your innovation; and thence comes the greater prominence of the question. Would you have that question reduced to its former proportions? Go back to that old policy. What has been will be again, under the same conditions. If you would have the peace of the old times, readopt the precepts and policy of the old times.

You charge that we stir up insurrections among your slaves. We deny it; and what is your proof? Harper's Ferry! John Brown!! John Brown was no Republican; and you have failed to implicate a single Republican in his Harper's Ferry enterprise. If any member of our party is guilty in that matter, you know it, or you do not know it. If you do know it, you are inexcusable for not designating the man and proving the fact. If you do not know it, you are inexcusable for asserting it, and especially for persisting in the assertion after you have tried and failed to make the proof. You need not be told that persisting in a charge which one does not know to be true, is simply malicious slander.

Some of you admit that no Republican designedly aided or encouraged the Harper's Ferry affair, but still insist that our doctrines and declarations necessarily lead to such results. We do not believe it. We know we hold no doctrine, and make no declaration, which were not held to and made by "our fathers who framed the government under which we live." You never dealt fairly by us in relation to this affair. When it occurred, some important State elections were near at hand, and you were in evident glee with the belief that, by charging the blame upon us, you could get an advantage of us in those elections. The elections came, and your expectations were not quite fulfilled. Every Republican man knew that, as to himself at least, your charge was a slander, and he was not much inclined by it to cast his vote in your favor. Republican doctrines and declarations are accompanied with a continual protest against any interference whatever with your slaves, or with you about your slaves. Surely, this does not encourage them to revolt. True, we do, in common with "our fathers who framed the government under which we live," declare our belief that slavery is wrong; but the slaves do not hear us declare even this. For anything we say or do, the slaves would scarcely know there is a Republican party. I believe they would not, in fact, generally know it but for your misrepresentations of us in their hearing. In your political contests among yourselves, each faction charges the other with sympathy with Black Republicanism; and then, to give point to the charge, defines Black Republicanism to simply be insurrection, blood, and thunder among the slaves.

Slave insurrections are no more common now than they were before the Republican party was organized. What induced the Southampton insurrection, twenty-eight years ago, in which at least three times as many lives were lost as at Harper's Ferry? You can scarcely stretch your very elastic fancy to the conclusion that Southampton was "got up by Black Republicanism." In the present state of things in the United States, I do not think a general, or even a very extensive, slave insurrection is possible. The indispensable concert of action cannot be attained. The slaves have no means of rapid communication; nor can incendiary freemen, black or white, supply it. The explosive materials are everywhere in parcels; but there neither are, nor can be supplied, the indispensable connecting trains.

Much is said by Southern people about the affection of slaves for their masters and mistresses; and a part of it, at least, is true. A plot for an uprising could scarcely be devised and communicated to twenty individuals before some one of them, to save the life of a favorite master or mistress, would divulge it. This is the rule; and the slave revolution in Hayti was not an exception to it, but a case occurring under peculiar circumstances. The gunpowder plot of British history, though not connected with slaves, was more in point. In that case, only about twenty were admitted to the secret; and yet one of them, in his anxiety to save a friend, betrayed the plot to that friend, and, by consequence, averted the calamity. Occasional poisonings from the kitchen, and open or stealthy assassinations in the field, and local revolts extending to a score or so, will continue to occur as the natural results of slavery; but no general insurrection of slaves, as I think, can happen in this country for a long time. Whoever much fears, or much hopes, for such an event, will be alike disappointed.

In the language of Mr. Jefferson, uttered many years ago, "It is still in our power to direct the process of emancipation and deportation peaceably, and in such slow degrees, as that the evil will wear off insensibly; and their places be, *pari passu*, filled up by free white laborers. If, on the contrary, it is left to force itself on, human nature must shudder at the prospect held up."

Mr. Jefferson did not mean to say, nor do I, that the power of emancipation is in the Federal Government. He spoke of Virginia; and, as to the power of emancipation, I speak of the slaveholding States only. The Federal Government, however, as we insist, has the power of restraining the extension of the institution — the power to insure that a slave insurrection shall never occur on any American soil which is now free from slavery.

John Brown's effort was peculiar. It was not a slave insurrection. It was an attempt by white men to get up a revolt among slaves, in which the slaves refused to participate. In fact, it was so absurd that the slaves, with all their ignorance, saw plainly enough it could not succeed. That affair, in its philosophy, corresponds with the many attempts, related in history, at the assassination of kings and emperors. An enthusiast broods over the oppression of a people till he fancies himself commissioned by Heaven to liberate them. He ventures the attempt, which ends in little else than his own execution. Orsini's attempt on Louis Napoleon, and John Brown's attempt at Harper's Ferry, were, in their philosophy, precisely the same. The eagerness to cast blame on old England in the one case, and on New England in the other, does not disprove the sameness of the two things.

And how much would it avail you, if you could, by the use of John Brown, Helper's Book, and the like, break up the Republican organization? Human action can be modified to some extent, but human nature cannot be changed. There is a judgment and a feeling against slavery in this nation, which cast at least a million and a half of votes. You cannot destroy that judgment and feeling — that sentiment — by breaking up the political

organization which rallies around it. You can scarcely scatter and disperse an
army which has been formed into order in the face of your heaviest fire; but if
you could, how much would you gain by forcing the sentiment which created
it out of the peaceful channel of the ballot-box into some other channel?
What would that other channel probably be? Would the number of John
Browns be lessened or enlarged by the operation?

But you will break up the Union rather than submit to a denial of your
constitutional rights.

That has a somewhat reckless sound; but it would be palliated, if not fully
justified, were we proposing, by the mere force of numbers, to deprive you of
some right plainly written down in the Constitution. But we are proposing no
such thing.

When you make these declarations you have a specific and well-understood
allusion to an assumed constitutional right of yours to take slaves into the
Federal Territories, and to hold them there as property. But no such right is
specifically written in the Constitution. That instrument is literally silent
about any such right. We, on the contrary, deny that such a right has any
existence in the Constitution, even by implication.

Your purpose, then, plainly stated, is that you will destroy the government,
unless you be allowed to construe and force the Constitution as you please, on
all points in dispute between you and us. You will rule or ruin in all events.

This, plainly stated, is your language. Perhaps you will say the Supreme
Court has decided the disputed constitutional question in your favor. Not
quite so. But waiving the lawyer's distinction between dictum and decision,
the court has decided the question for you in a sort of way. The court has
substantially said, it is your constitutional right to take slaves into the Federal
Territories, and to hold them there as property. When I say the decision was
made in a sort of way, I mean it was made in a divided court, by a bare
majority of the judges, and they not quite agreeing with one another in the
reasons for making it; that it is so made as that its avowed supporters disagree
with one another about its meaning, and that it was mainly based upon a
mistaken statement of fact — the statement in the opinion that "the right of
property in a slave is distinctly and expressly affirmed in the Constitution."

An inspection of the Constitution will show that the right of property in a
slave is not "distinctly and expressly affirmed" in it. Bear in mind, the judges
do not pledge their judicial opinion that such right is impliedly affirmed in
the Constitution; but they pledge their veracity that it is "distinctly and
expressly" affirmed there — "distinctly," that is, not mingled with anything
else — "expressly," that is, in words meaning just that, without the aid of any
inference, and susceptible of no other meaning.

If they had only pledged their judicial opinion that such right is affirmed in
the instrument by implication, it would be open to others to show that neither
the word "slave" nor "slavery" is to be found in the Constitution, nor the word
"property" even, in any connection with language alluding to the things slave,
or slavery; and that wherever in that instrument the slave is alluded to, he is
called a "person"; and wherever his master's legal right in relation to him is

alluded to, it is spoken of as "service or labor which may be due" — as a debt payable in service or labor. Also it would be open to show, by contemporaneous history, that this mode of alluding to slaves and slavery, instead of speaking of them, was employed on purpose to exclude from the Constitution the idea that there could be property in man.

To show all this is easy and certain.

When this obvious mistake of the judges shall be brought to their notice, is it not reasonable to expect that they will withdraw the mistaken statement, and reconsider the conclusion based upon it?

And then it is to be remembered that "our fathers who framed the government under which we live" — the men who made the Constitution — decided this same constitutional question in our favor long ago: decided it without division among themselves when making the decision; without division among themselves about the meaning of it after it was made, and, so far as any evidence is left, without basing it upon any mistaken statement of facts.

Under all these circumstances, do you really feel yourselves justified to break up this government unless such a court decision as yours is shall be at once submitted to as a conclusive and final rule of political action? But you will not abide the election of a Republican president! In that supposed event, you say, you will destroy the Union; and then, you say, the great crime of having destroyed it will be upon us! That is cool. A highwayman holds a pistol to my ear, and mutters through his teeth, "Stand and deliver, or I shall kill you, and then you will be a murderer!"

To be sure, what the robber demanded of me — my money — was my own; and I had a clear right to keep it; but it was no more my own than my vote is my own; and the threat of death to me, to extort my money, and the threat of destruction to the Union, to extort my vote, can scarcely be distinguished in principle.

A few words now to Republicans. It is exceedingly desirable that all parts of this great Confederacy shall be at peace, and in harmony one with another. Let us Republicans do our part to have it so. Even though much provoked, let us do nothing through passion and ill temper. Even though the Southern people will not so much as listen to us, let us calmly consider their demands, and yield to them if, in our deliberate view of our duty, we possibly can. Judging by all they say and do, and by the subject and nature of their controversy with us, let us determine, if we can, what will satisfy them.

Will they be satisfied if the Territories be unconditionally surrendered to them? We know they will not. In all their present complaints against us, the Territories are scarcely mentioned. Invasions and insurrections are the rage now. Will it satisfy them if, in the future, we have nothing to do with invasions and insurrections? We know it will not. We so know, because we know we never had anything to do with invasions and insurrections; and yet this total abstaining does not exempt us from the charge and the denunciation.

The question recurs, What will satisfy them? Simply this: we must not only let them alone, but we must somehow convince them that we do let them alone. This, we know by experience, is no easy task. We have been so trying to convince them from the very beginning of our organization, but with no success. In all our platforms and speeches we have constantly protested our purpose to let them alone; but this has had no tendency to convince them. Alike unavailing to convince them is the fact that they have never detected a man of us in any attempt to disturb them.

These natural and apparently adequate means all failing, what will convince them? This, and this only: cease to call slavery wrong, and join them in calling it right. And this must be done thoroughly — done in acts as well as in words. Silence will not be tolerated — we must place ourselves avowedly with them. Senator Douglas's new sedition law must be enacted and enforced, suppressing all declarations that slavery is wrong, whether made in politics, in presses, in pulpits, or in private. We must arrest and return their fugitive slaves with greedy pleasure. We must pull down our free-State constitutions. The whole atmosphere must be disinfected from all taint of opposition to slavery, before they will cease to believe that all their troubles proceed from us.

I am quite aware they do not state their case precisely in this way. Most of them would probably say to us, "Let us alone; do nothing to us, and say what you please about slavery." But we do let them alone, — have never disturbed them, — so that, after all, it is what we say which dissatisfies them. They will continue to accuse us of doing, until we cease saying.

I am also aware they have not as yet in terms demanded the overthrow of our free-State constitutions. Yet those constitutions declare the wrong of slavery with more solemn emphasis than do all other sayings against it; and when all these other sayings shall have been silenced, the overthrow of these constitutions will be demanded, and nothing be left to resist the demand. It is nothing to the contrary that they do not demand the whole of this just now. Demanding what they do, and for the reason they do, they can voluntarily stop nowhere short of this consummation. Holding, as they do, that slavery is morally right and socially elevating, they cannot cease to demand a full national recognition of it as a legal right and a social blessing.

Nor can we justifiably withhold this on any ground save our conviction that slavery is wrong. If slavery is right, all words, acts, laws, and constitutions against it are themselves wrong, and should be silenced and swept away. If it is right, we cannot justly object to its nationality — its universality; if it is wrong, they cannot justly insist upon its extension — its enlargement. All they ask we could readily grant, if we thought slavery right; all we ask they could as readily grant, if they thought it wrong. Their thinking it right and our thinking it wrong is the precise fact upon which depends the whole controversy. Thinking it right, as they do, they are not to blame for desiring its full recognition as being right; but thinking it wrong, as we do, can we yield to them? Can we cast our votes with their view, and against our own? In view of our moral, social, and political responsibilities, can we do this?

Wrong as we think slavery is, we can yet afford to let it alone where it is, because that much is due to the necessity arising from its actual presence in the nation; but can we, while our votes will prevent it, allow it to spread into the national Territories, and to overrun us here in these free States? If our sense of duty forbids this, then let us stand by our duty fearlessly and effectively. Let us be diverted by none of those sophistical contrivances wherewith we are so industriously plied and belabored — contrivances such as groping for some middle ground between the right and the wrong: vain as the search for a man who should be neither a living man nor a dead man; such as a policy of "don't care" on a question about which all true men do care; such as Union appeals beseeching true Union men to yield to Disunionists, reversing the divine rule, and calling, not the sinners, but the righteous to repentance; such as invocations to Washington, imploring men to unsay what Washington said and undo what Washington did.

Neither let us be slandered from our duty by false accusations against us, nor frightened from it by menaces of destruction to the government, nor of dungeons to ourselves. Let us have faith that right makes might, and in that faith let us to the end dare to do our duty as we understand it.

First Inaugural Address

Jefferson Davis

Commentary

Although the Republican convention of 1860 featured a spirited battle between supporters of Seward and Lincoln, the party remained united during the campaign. In contrast, Democrats split along sectional lines. Southerners nominated John Breckenridge and declared that slavery could not be prohibited in the territories, not even by residents. Northerners nominated Douglas and declared that "popular sovereignty" permitted territorial residents to prohibit slavery. Remnants of the old Whig party and some other Unionists formed a Constitutional Union party and nominated John Bell of Tennessee for president and Edward Everett of Massachusetts for vice-president. They produced a platform which was a model of brevity: "The Constitution of the country, the union of the states, and the enforcement of the laws."

Many observers believed that the splintering would result in Breckenridge winning the South, Bell and Douglas splitting the border States, and Douglas and Lincoln splitting the North and West. Thus the election would be thrown into the House, where a moderate acceptable to the South would be elected. What these prognosticators overlooked was that many Northerners and Westerners were less interested in slavery than other matters. Some, especially in Pennsylvania, desired another protective tariff. Many Westerners and prospective immigrants to the West were less concerned about public issues than their personal inability to purchase farmland. Carefully appealing to such groups, Republicans promised a protective tariff and free homesteads in the West. Although Republican promises netted Lincoln only 40% of the popular vote (Lincoln: 1,857,610; Douglas: 1,365,967; Breckinridge: 847,953; Bell: 590,631), he won a clear majority of electoral votes (Lincoln: 180; Breckinridge: 79; Bell: 39; Douglas: 12).

The unexpected victory of a "Black Republican" struck fear into Southern hearts. Secessionists quickly capitalized on it with a conspiratorial rhetoric. Reviewing the past, they pointed to various Northern oppressions, such as the protective tariff and Federal subsidies to Northern shippers. They emphasized (in exaggerated terms) the North's historic opposition to slavery. With a Black Republican in the White House, the final chapter in stealing the territories would be written, fugitive slaves would never be returned, slave insurrections would be encouraged and the Southern way of life would be destroyed.

Southern Unionists employed the best rhetoric they could, but events and emotional hysteria overwhelmed them. One of their arguments was that the situation was not as desperate as secessionists portrayed because the South would still have considerable power in Congress. This argument lost its potency as more and more States seceded. A second argument was that Congress would arrange a satisfactory compromise, and when Congress met in December, both Houses appointed special committees. When they failed to work out a compromise, this argument fell by the wayside and made it difficult for Unionists to answer a now-strengthened secessionist appeal: actual secession, in contrast to a mere threat, would encourage the North to back down. A third Unionist argument was that secession would lead to war. Southerners (including Unionists) were convinced that secession was perfectly legal and many concluded that the North would permit the South to go in peace. Besides, the South could easily repel an invasion.

A bandwagon was soon rolling. On December 20, 1860, South Carolina seceded; it was followed in January by Mississippi, Florida, Alabama, Georgia and Louisiana. Texas needed only to complete a few formalities before it would become the seventh State to depart. On February 4, 1861, delegates from the seceding States met in Montgomery, Alabama to prepare a provisional constitution and establish a provisional government for the Confederate States of America. By unanimous vote, they elected Jefferson Davis (1808-1888) provisional president. On February 18, the former military officer and Mississippi senator delivered his inaugural address.

It was an unusually dramatic occasion. Davis knew that his speech would be reported widely, thus giving him several reading audiences as well as the immediate listening audience. One was the Confederate citizenry, which included a minority of former Unionists. Another audience consisted of slaveholding States, some of which would later join the Confederacy and some would not. A third consisted of free States. All of them, but especially the third, needed to be persuaded that the new nation desired peace but that it should (and would) be prepared to fight if its independence was threatened. The speech is reproduced photographically from David J. Brewer, *World's Best Orations* (St. Louis: Ferd. P. Kaiser, 1901), vol. 5, pp. 1656-1660.

First Inaugural Address

Gentlemen of the Congress of the Confederate States of America, Friends and Fellow-Citizens : —

CALLED to the difficult and responsible station of Chief Executive of the provisional government which you have instituted, I approach the discharge of the duties assigned to me with a humble distrust of my abilities, but with a sustaining confidence in the wisdom of those who are to guide and aid me in the administration of public affairs, and an abiding faith in the virtue and patriotism of the people.

Looking forward to the speedy establishment of a permanent government to take the place of this, and which, by its greater moral and physical power, will be better able to combat with the many difficulties which arise from the conflicting interests of separate nations, I enter upon the duties of the office to which I have been chosen with the hope that the beginning of our career, as a Confederacy, may not be obstructed by hostile opposition to our enjoyment of the separate existence and independence which we have asserted, and, with the blessing of Providence, intend to maintain. Our present condition, achieved in a manner unprecedented in the history of nations, illustrates the American idea that governments rest upon the consent of the governed, and that it is the right of the people to alter or abolish governments whenever they become destructive of the ends for which they were established.

The declared purpose of the compact of union from which we have withdrawn was "to establish justice, insure domestic tranquillity, provide for the common defense, promote the general welfare, and secure the blessings of liberty to ourselves and our posterity"; and when in the judgment of the sovereign States now composing this Confederacy it had been perverted from the purposes for which it was ordained, and had ceased to answer the ends for which it was established, a peaceful appeal to the ballot box declared that so far as they were concerned, the Government created by that compact should cease to exist. In this they merely asserted a right which the Declaration of Independence of 1776 had defined to be inalienable. Of the time and occasion for its exercise, they as sovereigns were the final judges, each for itself. The impartial and enlightened verdict of mankind will vindicate the rectitude of our conduct, and he, who knows the hearts of men, will judge of the sincerity with which we labored to preserve the government of our fathers in its spirit. The right solemnly proclaimed at the birth of the States and which has been affirmed and reaffirmed in the bills of rights of States subsequently admitted into the Union of 1789, undeniably recognizes in the people the power to resume the authority delegated for the purposes of government. Thus the sovereign States, here represented, proceeded to form this Confederacy, and it is by abuse of language that their act has been denominated a revolution. They formed a new alliance, but within each State its government has remained, and the rights of person and property have not been disturbed. The agent, through whom they communicated with foreign nations, is changed; but this does not necessarily interrupt their international relations.

Sustained by the consciousness that the transition from the former Union to the present Confederacy has not proceeded from a disregard on our part of just obligations, or any failure to perform any constitutional duty; moved by no interest or passion to invade the rights of others; anxious to cultivate peace and commerce with all nations, if we may not hope to avoid war, we may at least expect that posterity will aquit us of having needlessly engaged in it. Doubly justified by the absence of wrong on our part, and by wanton aggression on the part of others, there can be no cause to doubt that the courage and patriotism of the people of the Confederate States will be found equal to any measures of defense which honor and security may require.

An agricultural people, whose chief interest is the export of a commodity required in every manufacturing country, our true policy is peace and the freest trade which our necessities will permit. It is alike our interest, and that of all those to whom we would sell and from whom we would buy, that there should be the fewest practicable restrictions upon the interchange of commodities. There can be but little rivalry between ours and any manufacturing or navigating community, such as the northeastern States of the American Union. It must follow, therefore, that a mutual interest would invite good-will and kind offices. If, however, passion or the lust of dominion should cloud the judgment or inflame the ambition of those States, we must prepare to meet the emergency, and to maintain, by the final arbitrament of the sword, the position which we have assumed among the nations of the earth. We have entered upon the career of independence, and it must be inflexibly pursued. Through many years of controversy with our late associates, the Northern States, we have vainly endeavored to secure tranquillity and to obtain respect for the rights to which we are entitled. As a necessity, not a choice, we have resorted to the remedy of separation; and henceforth our energies must be directed to the conduct of our own affairs and the perpetuity of the Confederacy which we have formed. If a just perception of mutual interest shall permit us peaceably to pursue our separate political career, my most earnest desire will have been fulfilled; but if this be denied to us, and the integrity of our territory and jurisdiction be assailed, it will but remain for us, with firm resolve, to appeal to arms and invoke the blessings of Providence on a just cause.

As a consequence of our new condition, and with a view to meet anticipated wants, it will be necessary to provide for the speedy and efficient organization of branches of the Executive Department, having special charge of foreign intercourse, finance, military affairs, and the postal service.

For purposes of defense, the Confederate States may, under ordinary circumstances, rely mainly upon the militia; but it is deemed advisable in the present condition of affairs that there should be a well-instructed and disciplined army, more numerous than would usually be required on a peace establishment. I also suggest that for the protection of our harbors and commerce on the high seas a navy adapted to those objects will be required. These necessities have doubtless engaged the attention of Congress.

With a Constitution differing only from that of our fathers in so far as it is explanatory of their well-known intent, freed from the sectional conflicts which have interfered with the pursuit of the general welfare, it is not unreasonable to expect that States from which we have recently parted may seek to unite their fortunes with ours under the Government which we have instituted. For this your Constitution makes adequate provision; but beyond this, if I mistake not the judgment and will of the people, a re-union with the States from which we have separated is neither practicable nor desirable. To increase the power, develop the resources, and promote the happiness of the Confederacy, it is requisite that there should be so much homogeneity that the welfare of every portion shall be the aim of the whole. Where this does not exist, antagonisms are engendered which must and should result in separation.

Actuated solely by the desire to preserve our own rights and promote our own welfare, the separation of the Confederate States has been marked by no aggression upon others and followed by no domestic convulsion. Our industrial pursuits have received no check; the cultivation of our fields has progressed as heretofore; and even should we be involved in war, there would be no considerable diminution in the production of the staples which have constituted our exports, and in which the commercial world has an interest scarcely less than our own. This common interest of the producer and consumer can only be interrupted by an exterior force, which should obstruct its transmission to foreign markets—a course of conduct which would be as unjust towards us as it would be detrimental to manufacturing and commercial interests abroad. Should reason guide the action of the Government from which we have separated, a policy so detrimental to the civilized world, the Northern States included, could not be dictated by even the strongest desire to inflict injury upon us; but if otherwise, a terrible responsibility will rest upon it, and the suffering of millions will bear testimony to the folly and wickedness of our aggressors. In the meantime, there will remain to us, besides the ordinary means before suggested, the well-known resources for retaliation upon the commerce of the enemy.

Experience in public stations of subordinate grades to this which your kindness has conferred has taught me that care and toil and disappointment are the price of official elevation. You will see many errors to forgive, many deficiencies to tolerate, but you shall not find in me either a want of zeal or fidelity to the cause that is to me highest in hope and of most enduring affection. Your generosity has bestowed upon me an undeserved distinction — one which I neither sought nor desired. Upon the continuance of that sentiment, and upon your wisdom and patriotism I rely to direct and support me in the performance of the duty required at my hands.

We have changed the constituent parts but not the system of our Government. The Constitution formed by our fathers is that of these Confederate States in their exposition of it; and in the judicial construction it has received, we have a light which reveals its true meaning.

Thus instructed as to the just interpretation of the instrument, and ever remembering that all offices are but trusts held for the people and that delegated powers are to be strictly construed, I will hope by due diligence in the performance of my duties, though I may disappoint your expectations, yet to retain, when retiring, something of the good-will and confidence which welcomed my entrance into office.

It is joyous, in the midst of perilous times, to look around upon a people united in heart, where one purpose of high resolve animates and actuates the whole — where the sacrifices to be made are not weighed in the balance against honor and right and liberty and equality. Obstacles may retard — they cannot long prevent — the progress of a movement sanctified by its justice and sustained by a virtuous people. Reverently let us invoke the God of our fathers to guide and protect us in our efforts to perpetuate the principles which, by his blessing, they were able to vindicate, establish, and transmit to their posterity; and with a continuance of his favor, ever gratefully acknowledged, we may hopefully look forward to success, to peace, and to prosperity.

First Inaugural Address

Abraham Lincoln

Commentary

Because the change to January inaugurations had not yet been made, Lincoln's inaugural came two weeks after Davis' (March 4, 1861), and the occasion was even more dramatic. While the Confederate States had been seceding, the outgoing president had done nothing. In general, inaction created few practical problems (for example, a Southern postmaster could simply transfer his allegiance to the Confederacy and go about his business). One problem was serious: the presence of United States soldiers on army posts located in the Confederacy was unacceptable to Confederate leaders, but they were willing to await Lincoln's actions before acting.

Meanwhile, Northern speakers and writers engaged in some frenzied rhetoric about what to do. It was a rhetoric characterized by a shift in the central issue from what it had been a few months earlier. Slavery, which had long been a central issue, was rarely discussed. The new issue was whether States had a legal right to secede, and some curious alliances arose. Militant Garrisonians, who had long advocated Northern secession, joined with anti-abolitionists in saying that secession was legal and that the Confederate states should be allowed to go in peace. Other militant abolitionists joined with other anti-abolitionists in declaring secession to be illegal and to advocate war. The former, of course, presupposed a compact theory of the Constitution whereas the latter did not. Instead of arguing the central issue, most simply announced their premise as if it were God-given Truth and used it to support whatever policy they advocated.

Equally fascinating is that the president-elect did not make any public statements until he gave a few short speeches en route to Washington, but he avoided the central issue. All sorts of rumors were in the air when he arose to deliver his inaugural. Lincoln and his Black Republicans were going to free the slaves by force. He was going to make war on the Confederacy. He was going to let the Confederate States leave in peace. He was going to propose a compromise to try to get the Confederacy to return to the Union. He was against any sort of compromise. He was going to let the Confederacy have

Federal properties located in the South. He was not going to let the Confederacy have Federal properties. He was going to negotiate with the Confederacy about Federal properties. Lincoln was going to be assassinated. War was inevitable. There was not going to be a war.

In this incredibly tense situation, Lincoln delivered his first inaugural, which is reproduced from *Complete Works of Abraham Lincoln*, 2nd edition, editors John G. Nicolay and John Hay (New York: Lamb Publishing Co., 1905), vol. 6, pp. 169-185.

First Inaugural Address

FELLOW-CITIZENS of the United States: In compliance with a custom as old as the government itself, I appear before you to address you briefly, and to take in your presence the oath prescribed by the Constitution of the United States to be taken by the President "before he enters on the execution of his office."

I do not consider it necessary at present for me to discuss those matters of administration about which there is no special anxiety or excitement.

Apprehension seems to exist among the people of the Southern States that by the accession of a Republican administration their property and their peace and personal security are to be endangered. There has never been any reasonable cause for such apprehension. Indeed, the most ample evidence to the contrary has all the while existed and been open to their inspection. It is found in nearly all the published speeches of him who now addresses you. I do but quote from one of those speeches when I declare that "I have no purpose, directly or indirectly, to interfere with the institution of slavery in the States where it exists. I believe I have no lawful right to do so, and I have no inclination to do so." Those who nominated and elected me did so with full knowledge that I had made this and many similar declarations, and had never recanted them.

And, more than this, they placed in the platform for my acceptance, and as a law to themselves and to me, the clear and emphatic resolution which I now read:

> *Resolved,* That the maintenance inviolate of the rights of the States, and especially the right of each State to order and control its own domestic institutions according to its own judgment exclusively, is essential to that balance of power on which the perfection and endurance of our political fabric depend, and we denounce the lawless invasion by armed force of the soil of any State or Territory, no matter under what pretext, as among the gravest of crimes.

I now reiterate these sentiments; and, in doing so, I only press upon the public attention the most conclusive evidence of which the case is susceptible, that the property, peace, and security of no section are to be in any wise endangered by the now incoming administration. I add, too, that all the protection which, consistently with the Constitution and the laws, can be given, will be cheerfully given to all the States when lawfully demanded, for whatever cause — as cheerfully to one section as to another.

There is much controversy about the delivering up of fugitives from service or labor. The clause I now read is as plainly written in the Constitution as any other of its provisions:

> No person held to service or labor in one State, under the laws thereof, escaping into another, shall in consequence of any law or regulation therein be discharged from such service or labor, but shall be delivered up on claim of the party to whom such service or labor may be due.

It is scarcely questioned that this provision was intended by those who made it for the reclaiming of what we call fugitive slaves; and the intention of the lawgiver is the law. All members of Congress swear their support to the whole Constitution — to this provision as much as to any other. To the proposition, then, that slaves whose cases come within the terms of this clause "shall be delivered up," their oaths are unanimous. Now, if they would make the effort in good temper, could they not with nearly equal unanimity frame and pass a law by means of which to keep good that unanimous oath?

There is some difference of opinion whether this clause should be enforced by national or by State authority; but surely that difference is not a very material one. If the slave is to be surrendered, it can be of but little consequence to him or to others by which authority it is done. And should any one in any case be content that his oath shall go unkept on a merely unsubstantial controversy as to how it shall be kept?

Again, in any law upon this subject, ought not all the safeguards of liberty known in civilized and humane jurisprudence to be introduced, so that a free man be not, in any case, surrendered as a slave? And might it not be well at the same time to provide by law for the enforcement of that clause in the Constitution which guarantees that "the citizen of each State shall be entitled to all privileges and immunities of citizens in the several States"?

I take the official oath to-day with no mental reservations, and with no purpose to construe the Constitution or laws by any hypercritical rules. And while I do not choose now to specify particular acts of Congress as proper to be enforced, I do suggest that it will be much safer for all, both in official and private stations, to conform to and abide by all those acts which stand unrepealed, than to violate any of them, trusting to find impunity in having them held to be unconstitutional.

It is seventy-two years since the first inauguration of a President under our National Constitution. During that period fifteen different and greatly distinguished citizens have, in succession, administered the executive branch of the government. They have conducted it through many perils, and generally with great success. Yet, with all this scope of precedent, I now enter upon the same task for the brief constitutional term of four years under great and peculiar difficulty. A disruption of the Federal Union, heretofore only menaced, is now formidably attempted.

I hold that, in contemplation of universal law and of the Constitution, the Union of these States is perpetual. Perpetuity is implied, if not expressed, in the fundamental law of all national governments. It is safe to assert that no government proper ever had a provision in its organic law for its own termination.

Continue to execute all the express provisions of our National Constitution, and the Union will endure forever — it being impossible to destroy it except by some action not provided for in the instrument itself.

Again, if the United States be not a government proper, but an association of States in the nature of contract merely, can it, as a contract, be peaceably unmade by less than all the parties who made it? One party to a contract may violate it — break it, so to speak; but does it not require all to lawfully rescind it?

Descending from these general principles, we find the proposition that, in legal contemplation the Union is perpetual confirmed by the history of the Union itself. The Union is much older than the Constitution. It was formed, in fact, by the Articles of Association in 1774. It was matured and continued by the Declaration of Independence in 1776. It was further matured, and the faith of all the then thirteen States expressly plighted and engaged that it should be perpetual, by the Articles of Confederation in 1778. And, finally, in 1787 one of the declared objects for ordaining and establishing the Constitution was "to form a more perfect Union."

But if the destruction of the Union by one or by a part only of the States be lawfully possible, the Union is less perfect than before the Constitution, having lost the vital element of perpetuity.

It follows from these views that no State upon its own mere motion can lawfully get out of the Union; that resolves and ordinances to that effect are legally void; and that acts of violence, within any State or States, against the authority of the United States, are insurrectionary or revolutionary, according to circumstances.

I therefore consider that, in view of the Constitution and the laws, the Union is unbroken; and to the extent of my ability I shall take care, as the Constitution itself expressly enjoins upon me, that the laws of the Union be faithfully executed in all the States. Doing this I deem to be only a simple duty on my part; and I shall perform it so far as practicable, unless my rightful masters, the American people, shall withhold the requisite means, or in some authoritative manner direct the contrary. I trust this will not be regarded as a menace, but only as the declared purpose of the Union that it will constitutionally defend and maintain itself.

In doing this there needs to be no bloodshed or violence; and there shall be none, unless it be forced upon the national authority. The power confided to me will be used to hold, occupy, and possess the property and places belonging to the government, and to collect the duties and imposts; but beyond what may be necessary for these objects, there will be no invasion, no using of force against or among the people anywhere. Where hostility to the United States, in any interior locality, shall be so great and universal as to prevent competent resident citizens from holding the Federal offices, there will be no attempt to force obnoxious strangers among the people for that object. While the strict legal right may exist in the government to enforce the exercise of these offices, the attempt to do so would be so irritating, and so nearly impracticable withal, that I deem it better to forego for the time the uses of such offices.

The mails, unless repelled, will continue to be furnished in all parts of the Union. So far as possible, the people everywhere shall have that sense of perfect security which is most favorable to calm thought and reflection. The course here indicated will be followed unless current events and experience shall show a modification or change to be proper, and in every case and exigency my best discretion will be exercised according to circumstances actually existing, and with a view and a hope of a peaceful solution of the national troubles and the restoration of fraternal sympathies and affections.

That there are persons in one section or another who seek to destroy the Union at all events, and are glad of any pretext to do it, I will neither affirm nor deny; but if there be such, I need address no word to them. To those, however, who really love the Union may I not speak?

Before entering upon so grave a matter as the destruction of our national fabric, with all its benefits, its memories, and its hopes, would it not be wise to ascertain precisely why we do it? Will you hazard so desperate a step while there is any possibility that any portion of the ills you fly from have no real existence? Will you, while the certain ills you fly to are greater than all the real ones you fly from — will you risk the commission of so fearful a mistake?

All profess to be content in the Union if all constitutional rights can be maintained. Is it true, then, that any right, plainly written in the Constitution, has been denied? I think not. Happily the human mind is so constituted that no party can reach to the audacity of doing this. Think, if you can, of a single instance in which a plainly written provision of the Constitution has ever been denied. If by the mere force of numbers a majority should deprive a minority of any clearly written constitutional right, it might, in a moral point of view, justify revolution — certainly would if such a right were a vital one. But such is not our case. All the vital rights of minorities and of individuals are so plainly assured to them by affirmations and negations, guarantees and prohibitions, in the Constitution, that controversies never arise concerning them. But no organic law can ever be framed with a provision specifically applicable to every question which may occur in practical administration. No foresight can anticipate, nor any document of reasonable length contain, express provisions for all possible questions. Shall fugitives from labor be surrendered by national or by State authority? The Constitution does not expressly say. *May* Congress prohibit slavery in the Territories? The Constitution does not expressly say. *Must* Congress protect slavery in the Territories? The Constitution does not expressly say.

From questions of this class spring all our constitutional controversies, and we divide upon them into majorities and minorities. If the minority will not acquiesce, the majority must, or the government must cease. There is no other alternative; for continuing the government is acquiescence on one side or the other.

If a minority in such case will secede rather than acquiesce, they make a precedent which in turn will divide and ruin them; for a minority of their own will secede from them whenever a majority refuses to be controlled by such minority. For instance, why may not any portion of a new confederacy a year or two hence arbitrarily secede again, precisely as portions of the present Union now claim to secede from it? All who cherish disunion sentiments are now being educated to the exact temper of doing this.

Is there such perfect identity of interests among the States to compose a new Union, as to produce harmony only, and prevent renewed secession?

Plainly, the central idea of secession is the essence of anarchy. A majority held in restraint by constitutional checks and limitations, and always changing easily with deliberate changes of popular opinions and sentiments, is the only true sovereign of a free people. Whoever rejects it does, of necessity, fly to anarchy or to despotism. Unanimity is impossible; the rule of a minority, as a permanent arrangement, is wholly inadmissible; so that, rejecting the majority principle, anarchy or despotism in some form is all that is left.

I do not forget the position, assumed by some, that constitutional questions are to be decided by the Supreme Court; nor do I deny that such decisions must be binding, in any case, upon the parties to a suit, as to the object of that suit, while they are also entitled to very high respect and consideration in all parallel cases by all other departments of the government. And while it is obviously possible that such decision may be erroneous in any given case, still the evil effect following it, being limited to that particular case, with the chance that it may be overruled and never become a precedent for other cases, can better be borne than could the evils of a different practice.

At the same time, the candid citizen must confess that if the ploicy [sic] of the government, upon vital questions affecting the whole people, is to be irrevocably fixed by decisions of the Supreme Court, the instant they are made, in ordinary litigation between parties in personal actions, the people will have ceased to be their own rulers, having to that extent practically resigned their government into the hands of that eminent tribunal. Nor is there in this view any assault upon the court or the judges. It is a duty from which they may not shrink to decide cases properly brought before them, and it is no fault of theirs if others seek to turn their decisions to political purposes.

One section of our country believes slavery is right, and ought to be extended, while the other believes it is wrong, and ought not to be extended. This is the only substantial dispute. The fugitive-slave clause of the Constitution, and the law for the suppression of the foreign slave-trade, are each as well enforced, perhaps, as any law can ever be in a community where the moral sense of the people imperfectly supports the law itself. The great body of the people abide by the dry legal obligation in both cases, and a few break over in each. This, I think, cannot be perfectly cured; and it would be worse in both cases after the separation of the sections than before. The foreign slave-trade, now imperfectly suppressed, would be ultimately revived, without restriction, in one section, while fugitive slaves, now only partially surrendered, would not be surrendered at all by the other.

Physically speaking, we cannot separate. We cannot remove our respective sections from each other, nor build an impassable wall between them. A husband and wife may be divorced, and go out of the presence and beyond the reach of each other; but the different parts of our country cannot do this. They cannot but remain face to face, and intercourse, either amicable or hostile, must continue between them. Is it possible, then, to make that intercourse more advantageous or more satisfactory after separation than before? Can aliens make treaties easier than friends can make laws? Can treaties be more faithfully enforced between aliens than laws can among friends? Suppose you go to war, you cannot fight always; and when, after much loss on both sides, and no gain on either, you cease fighting, the identical old questions as to terms of intercourse are again upon you.

This country, with its institutions, belongs to the people who inhabit it. Whenever they shall grow weary of the existing government, they can exercise their constitutional right of amending it, or their revolutionary right to dismember or overthrow it. I cannot be ignorant of the fact that many worthy and patriotic citizens are desirous of having the National Constitution amended. While I make no recommendation of amendments, I fully recognize the rightful authority of the people over the whole subject, to be exercised in either of the modes prescribed in the instrument itself; and I should, under existing circumstances, favor rather than oppose a fair opportunity being afforded the people to act upon it. I will venture to add that to me the convention mode seems preferable, in that it allows amendments to originate with the people themselves, instead of only permitting them to take or reject propositions originated by others not specially chosen for the purpose, and which might not be precisely such as they would wish to either accept or refuse. I understand a proposed amendment to the Constitution — which amendment, however, I have not seen — has passed Congress, to the effect that the Federal Government shall never interfere with the domestic institutions of the States, including that of persons held to service. To avoid misconstruction of what I have said, I depart from my purpose not to speak of particular amendments so far as to say that, holding such a provision to now be implied constitutional law, I have no objection to its being made express and irrevocable.

The chief magistrate derives all his authority from the people, and they have conferred none upon him to fix terms for the separation of the States. The people themselves can do this also if they choose; but the executive, as such, has nothing to do with it. His duty is to administer the present government, as it came to his hands, and to transmit it, unimpaired by him, to his successor.

Why should there not be a patient confidence in the ultimate justice of the people? Is there any better or equal hope in the world? In our present differences is either party without faith of being in the right? If the Almighty Ruler of Nations, with his eternal truth and justice, be on your side of the North, or on yours of the South, that truth and that justice will surely prevail by the judgment of this great tribunal of the American people.

By the frame of the government under which we live, this same people have wisely given their public servants but little power for mischief; and have, with equal wisdom, provided for the return of that little to their own hands at very short intervals. While the people retain their virtue and vigilance, no administration, by any extreme of wickedness or folly, can very seriously injure the government in the short space of four years.

My countrymen, one and all, think calmly and well upon this whole subject. Nothing valuable can be lost by taking time. If there be an object to hurry any of you in hot haste to a step which you would never take deliberately, that object will be frustrated by taking time; but no good object can be frustrated by it. Such of you as are now dissatisfied, still have the old Constitution unimpaired, and, on the sensitive point, the laws of your own framing under it; while the new administration will have no immediate power, if it would, to change either. If it were admitted that you who are dissatisfied hold the right side in the dispute, there still is no single good reason for precipitate action. Intelligence, patriotism, Christianity, and a firm reliance on Him who has never yet forsaken this favored land, are still competent to adjust in the best way all our present difficulty.

In your hands, my dissatisfied fellow-countrymen, and not in mine, is the momentous issue of civil war. The government will not assail you. You can have no conflict without being yourselves the aggressors. You have no oath registered in heaven to destroy the government, while I shall have the most solemn one to "preserve, protect, and defend it."

I am loath to close. We are not enemies, but friends. We must not be enemies. Though passion may have strained, it must not break our bonds of affection. The mystic chords of memory, stretching from every battle-field and patriot grave to every living heart and hearthstone all over this broad land, will yet swell the chorus of the Union when again touched, as surely they will be, by the better angels of our nature.

Gettysburg Address

Abraham Lincoln

Commentary

Despite its importance in causing the Civil War, slavery played a minor role in prowar rhetoric. Confederates talked about saving Southern liberties while Northerners talked about saving the Union. Lincoln set the stage for the "Save the Union" appeal in his prowar addresses during the spring and summer of 1861. After the Confederate attack on Fort Sumter (April 12), Lincoln issued a proclamation calling upon each State to mobilize its militia to put down the "insurrection." His proclamation, of course, forced those slave States that were still in the Union to make a final decision. The proclamation, though, said nothing about slavery. Similarly, when Congress met in special session on July 4 (a date with obvious symbolic significance) to hear Lincoln's request for military appropriations, Lincoln said nothing about slavery but reiterated his earlier arguments against the legality of secession.

Once the war was in full swing, neither government had an official agency to promote the war. Two private organizations arose in the North to meet the need. As their names suggest, both emphasized the "Save the Union" appeal. One was the "Loyal Publication Society," which distributed prowar pamphlets and broadsides. The second was a loosely knit group of "Union Clubs." The Republican party, in a brilliant rhetorical move to lessen its identification with abolitionism and to portray Democrats as disloyal, renamed itself the "Union Party" during the war.

The "Save the Union" appeal was far more persuasive in the North than an abolitionist appeal would have been. Many Northerners who were willing to support the war to save the Union were strongly opposed to abolitionism. As time went by and casualties mounted, many such people became increasingly bitter toward Lincoln for being too much of an abolitionist. Conversely, many abolitionists became increasingly critical of Lincoln for not being enough of an abolitionist.

Early in the war, Congress emancipated slaves in the District of Columbia and the territories. On January 1, 1863, Lincoln issued his famous

Emancipation Proclamation, which freed the slaves in those areas still in rebellion. This angered anti-abolitionists, but it did not satisfy militant abolitionists, who emphasized that slavery remained untouched in those areas under Union control. Attacks on Lincoln were not limited to the slave question. Some who initially supported the war became discouraged as victory seemed remote and casualties rose. They formed "Peace Societies," which advocated a negotiated settlement with the Confederacy. Meanwhile, "Copperheads," who had opposed the war from the beginning, intensified their attacks on Lincoln. Looking ahead to the election of 1864, Democrats (and even some Republicans) talked about the necessity of replacing the "blundering" Lincoln, who had failed to bring the quick and easy victory that had been expected.

Most historians believe that anti-Lincoln attitudes were so intense that he would have lost the election if Union armies had not won some major victories during 1863. The most important one was at Gettysburg in early July, but not even the Gettysburg victory could stem the growing anti-war sentiment. A draft riot broke out in New York City only a few days after Gettysburg, and a series of anti-black riots spread throughout the North. Lincoln remained a much-criticized president — a point that must be kept in mind as one studies his famous dedicatory address at Gettysburg on November 19, 1863. It has now become so mythologized that critics can easily forget the circumstances under which it was delivered.

The idea of establishing a cemetery was partly to deal with the practical, albeit unpleasant, problem of disposing of the dead. It also had symbolic significance: organizers of the program wished not only to commemorate the dead but also to emphasize the role of the *States* in supporting the war. (Some governors would be up for re-election too.) Although not anti-Lincoln, organizers did not want the unpopular president to play a role. They invited him to attend simply as a courtesy. When he surprised them by accepting the invitation, they reluctantly asked him to deliver "a few appropriate remarks" to dedicate the cemetery at the end of an already arranged (and very long) program.

The ceremony began with a procession from the town to the cemetery, and the unexpectedly large crowd had trouble finding seats. The resulting confusion got the program behind schedule. Music was played, there was a very long prayer and the former Constitutional Unionist, Edward Everett, delivered the main oration. Everett's speech, running approximately two hours, was divided into two parts. In the first, he narrated the battle. In the second, he was argumentative. He argued the illegality of secession, maintained that permitting secession would lead to further disruptions in the Union and (in what he considered the best part of the speech) refuted the common antiwar argument that the hatreds generated by the war would prevent the Union from ever functioning effectively again. More music was played. Lincoln arose to dedicate the cemetery only after the large crowd (estimated at 15,000) had been sitting for a long time in the hot sun under uncomfortable conditions.

The mythology surrounding the speech includes a wide variety of contradictory assertions about response. There is no hard evidence about how the listening audience reacted except for a few responses contained in personal letters and diaries. Recent research provides solid evidence about newspaper response. Copperheads worked overtime attacking the speech, primarily because of its alleged abolitionism, but most papers, including even some anti-Lincoln ones, either publicized it without comment or had a few nice things to say. It was printed frequently, especially in rural weeklies (which is what most people read). The speech is reproduced photographically from A. Craig Baird, *American Public Addresses, 1740-1952* (New York: McGraw-Hill, 1956), p. 115.

Gettysburg Address

Four score and seven years ago our fathers brought forth on this continent, a new nation, conceived in Liberty, and dedicated to the proposition that all men are created equal.

Now we are engaged in a great civil war, testing whether that nation or any nation so conceived and so dedicated, can long endure. We are met on a great battle-field of that war. We have come to dedicate a portion of that field, as a final resting place for those who here gave their lives that that nation might live. It is altogether fitting and proper that we should do this.

But, in a larger sense, we can not dedicate—we can not consecrate—we can not hallow—this ground. The brave men, living and dead, who struggled here, have consecrated it, far above our poor power to add or detract. The world will little note, nor long remember what we say here, but it can never forget what they did here. It is for us the living, rather, to be dedicated here to the unfinished work which they who fought here have thus far so nobly advanced. It is rather for us to be here dedicated to the great task remaining before us—that from these honored dead we take increased devotion to that cause for which they gave the last full measure of devotion—that we here highly resolve that these dead shall not have died in vain—that this nation, under God, shall have a new birth of freedom—and that government of the people, by the people, for the people, shall not perish from the earth.

Post-Civil War America
Rhetoric of Reconstruction

Second Inaugural Address

Abraham Lincoln

Commentary

As Union armies won more victories and the presidential election of 1864 grew even closer, abolitionism was joined by another issue: how to deal with the Confederate States after victory was achieved. The issue was pervaded by emotionalism. Most wars generate hatred, but the Civil War did so to an unusual degree. For the first time in American history, a military draft was instituted. Casualties were incredibly high, with over 600,000 men in the two armies losing their lives at a time when the total population barely exceeded thirty million. It is true that more deaths came from illness than combat, but a Northerner who lost a son or brother or friend was in no mood to make subtle distinctions. The Southern "slaveocracy" was responsible.

Fearful that his fellow Republicans in Congress would vent their hatreds on the vanquished South, Lincoln announced his "Ten Per Cent" plan in December, 1863, only a few weeks after Gettysburg. It allowed Southern State governments to resume operation as soon as one-tenth of the number of 1860 voters took an oath of loyalty to the United States. Clearly, Lincoln wished to keep Congress out of the picture. Believing that the South had never legally left the Union, he was in a position to argue that Congress had no authority over the seceding States.

A group of so-called "Radical Republicans" wanted a much tougher policy, partly for emotional reasons and partly for a mixture of idealistic and selfish ones. Idealistically, they wanted slavery to be abolished and blacks to be protected from future discrimination by white-dominated Southern State governments. Selfishly, they sought party domination. Knowing that Southern whites would never vote for Black Republicans, they looked for ways to enfranchise Southern blacks while disenfranchising Southern whites. They made their first move in July, 1864 by passing the Wade-Davis bill, which prohibited a Confederate State from being readmitted to the Union until slavery was abolished and a majority of 1860 voters took a loyalty oath. Lincoln killed the plan with a pocket veto causing the bill's authors to issue a public statement denouncing Lincoln's policy and declaring that Congress —

not the president — had jurisdiction over Confederate States.

The split within Republican ranks was downplayed during the election. Lincoln mollified Radicals after the election by lobbying quietly for the Thirteenth Amendment to the Constitution, which abolished slavery. Radicals knew that the amendment, which cleared Congress in January, 1865, would not have passed without Lincoln's efforts.

When Lincon arose to deliver his second inaugural on March 4, 1865, the public was eagerly awaiting the forthcoming Confederate surrender. Political leaders knew that the surrender would inevitably put Lincoln and the Radicals at loggerheads over two fundamental questions: What conditions should the seceding states be required to meet before being allowed to function as legal entities and Who had the authority to answer the first question, Congress or the president? The occasion, which traditionally demands a short, unity-building inaugural address, prevented Lincoln from delivering a long, argumentative speech in defense of his policy. However, it was a perfect occasion for him to set a conciliatory tone, which he hoped would build public support for his policy in the days ahead.

Lincoln's speech is reproduced photographically from A. Craig Baird, *American Public Addresses, 1740-1952* (New York: McGraw-Hill, 1956), pp. 116-117.

Second Inaugural Address

FELLOW-COUNTRYMEN: At this second appearing to take the oath of the presidential office there is less occasion for an extended address than there was at the first. Then a statement somewhat in detail of a course to be pursued seemed fitting and proper. Now, at the expiration of four years, during which public declarations have been constantly called forth on every point and phase of the great contest which still absorbs the attention and engrosses the energies of the nation, little that is new could be presented. The progress of our arms, upon which all else chiefly depends, is as well known to the public as to myself, and it is, I trust, reasonably satisfactory and encouraging to all. With high hope for the future, no prediction in regard to it is ventured.

On the occasion corresponding to this four years ago all thoughts were anxiously directed to an impending civil war. All dreaded it, all sought to avert it. While the inaugural address was being delivered from this place, devoted altogether to *saving* the Union without war, insurgent agents were in the city seeking to *destroy* it without war—seeking to dissolve the Union and divide effects by negotiation. Both parties deprecated war, but one of them would *make* war rather than let the nation survive, and the other would *accept* war rather than let it perish, and the war came.

One eighth of the whole population was colored slaves, not distributed generally over the Union, but localized in the southern part of it. These slaves constituted a peculiar and powerful interest. All knew that this interest was somehow the cause of the war. To strengthen, perpetuate, and extend this interest was the object for which the insurgents would rend the Union even by war, while the Government claimed no right to do more than to restrict the territorial enlargement of it. Neither party expected for the war the magnitude or the duration which it has already attained. Neither anticipated that the *cause* of the conflict might cease with or even before the conflict itself should cease. Each looked for an easier triumph, and a result less fundamental and astounding. Both read the same Bible and pray to the same God, and each invokes His aid against the other. It may seem strange that any men should dare to ask a just God's assistance in wringing their bread from the sweat of other men's faces, but let us judge not, that we be not judged. The prayers of both could not be answered. That of neither has been answered fully. The Almighty has His own purposes. "Woe unto the world because of offenses; for it must needs be that offenses come, but woe to that man by whom the offense cometh." If we shall suppose that American slavery is one of those offenses which, in the providence of God, must needs come, but which, having continued through His appointed time, He now wills to remove, and that He gives to both North and South this terrible war as the woe due to those by whom the offense came, shall we discern therein any departure from those divine attributes which the believers in a living God always ascribe to Him? Fondly do we hope, fervently do we pray, that this mighty scourge of war may speedily pass away. Yet, if God wills that it continue until all the wealth piled by the bondsman's two hundred and fifty years of unrequited toil shall be sunk, and until every drop of blood drawn with the lash shall be paid by another drawn with the sword, as was said three thousand years ago, so still it must be said, "The judgments of the Lord are true and righteous altogether."

With malice toward none, with charity for all, with firmness in the right as God gives us to see the right, let us strive on to finish the work we are in, to bind up the nation's wounds, to care for him who shall have borne the battle and for his widow and his orphan, to do all which may achieve and cherish a just and lasting peace among ourselves and with all nations.

Congressional Speech in Favor of Radical Republican Reconstruction Policy (Abridged)

Thaddeus Stevens

Commentary

In less than two months after Lincoln's second inaugural, the Confederacy had surrendered and Lincoln had been assassinated. The issue of how to deal with the seceding States now occupied center stage, but Radicals expected no trouble with the new president. Although Andrew Johnson was a Tennessee slaveholder and a former Democrat, he had never been part of the Southern "aristocracy." He had advanced politically with a "common man" rhetoric that appealed more to small farmers than to owners of large plantations. He was the only senator from a Confederate State to remain loyal to the Union. He had been made vice-president by the Union party to attract prowar Democratic voters. Although vice-presidents lack a public forum, he had made enough snide comments in private about the Southern aristocracy to convince Radicals that he would cooperate.

Radicals were soon disappointed. On May 29, 1865, while Congress was not in session, Johnson issued a Proclamation of Amnesty pardoning most Confederate officials on condition that they take a loyalty oath. He appointed provisional governors for the seceded States and arranged to get their governments functioning under a plan similar to Lincoln's.

When Congress returned in December, 1865, Radicals were alarmed. Although the Thirteenth Amendment had now been ratified by the requisite number of States, many former Confederate States had enacted "Black Codes," which Radicals claimed were slave laws under another name. In addition, all of the old Confederacy had disenfranchised blacks. Most Northern Democrats and many moderate Republicans (many of whom came from States which had traditionally disenfranchised blacks) were ready to support the president. Congressional delegations from several former Confederate States were ready to take their seats. Radicals knew that the 1865-1866 session was critical. They knew that Democrats would oppose them and that moderate Republicans, who held the balance of power, might go either way. Success required two closely related strategies: keep the Southern delegations from being seated and develop a rhetoric that would appeal to moderate Republicans.

On the first day of the congressional session, Radicals proposed that Congress create a special committee to study whether former Confederate States were ready for readmission to the Union and to deny seats to congressmen from those States until after Congress had acted on the committee's report. This proposal appealed to moderate Republicans for several reasons. Then, as now, congressmen were jealous of their power in relationship to that of the president, and creating a special congressional committee put "reconstruction" into their hands. Then, as now, congressmen liked to postpone decisions when they unsure what to do. Being worried about the "Black Codes" and undecided about whether to support Johnson or the Radicals, moderates were glad to turn the matter over to a committee.

Having prevented the Southern delegations from being seated, the Radicals were in a reasonably good position, but their task was complicated on the second day of the session. Conciliatory sentiment was revived after Congress heard the president's message, which called for moderation in dealing with the Union's former enemy. Radicals knew that the president had to be answered in a way that would appeal to moderate Republicans, and the task fell to Thaddeus Stevens (1792-1868). Now over 70, Stevens had represented Pennsylvania in the House since 1849, but his sarcastic manner and outspoken abolitionism had previously weakened his influence. By 1865, his congressional seniority had given him a position of leadership. The combination of his debating skill and the new rhetorical situation quickly propelled him into the most powerful Radical leader (or, according to his enemies, a "dictator"). His speech of December 18, 1865, given in response to the president, is reproduced photographically from the abbreviated version in Ernest J. Wrage and Barnet Baskerville, *American Forum: Speeches on Historic Issues, 1788-1900* (New York: Harper and Brothers, 1960), pp. 204-212.

Congressional Speech in Favor of Radical Republican Reconstruction Policy (Abridged)

A candid examination of the power and proper principles of reconstruction can be offensive to no one, and may possibly be profitable by exciting inquiry. One of the suggestions of the message which we are now considering has special reference to this. Perhaps it is the principle most interesting to the people at this time. The President assumes, what no one doubts, that the late rebel States have lost their constitutional relations to the Union, and are incapable of representation in Congress, except by permission of the Government. It matters but little, with this admission, whether you call them States out of the Union, and now conquered territories, or assert that because the Constitution forbids them to do what they did do, that they are therefore only dead as to all national and political action, and will remain so until the Government shall breathe into them the breath of life anew and permit them to occupy their former position. In other words, that they are not out of the Union, but are only dead carcasses lying within the Union. In either case, it is very plain that it requires the action of Congress to enable them to form a State government and send representatives to Congress. Nobody, I believe, pretends that with their old constitutions and frames of government they can be permitted to claim their old rights under the Constitution. They have torn their constitutional States into atoms, and built on their foundations fabrics of a totally different character. Dead men cannot raise themselves. Dead States cannot restore their own existence "as it was." Whose especial duty is it to do it? In whom does the Constitution place the power? Not in the judicial branch of Government, for it only adjudicates and does not prescribe laws. Not in the Executive, for he only executes and cannot make laws. Not in the Commander-in-Chief of the armies, for he can only hold them under military rule until the sovereign legislative power of the conqueror shall give them law.

There is fortunately no difficulty in solving the question. There are two provisions in the Constitution, under one of which the case must fall. The fourth article says:

"New States may be admitted by the Congress into this Union."

In my judgment this is the controlling provision in this case. Unless the law of nations is a dead letter, the late war between two acknowledged belligerents severed their original compacts, and broke all the ties that bound them together. The future condition of the conquered power depends on the will of the conqueror. They must come in as new States or remain as conquered provinces. Congress—the Senate and House of Representatives, with the concurrence of the President—is the only power that can act in the matter. But suppose, as some dreaming theorists imagine, that these States have never been out of the Union, but have only destroyed their State governments so as to be incapable of political action; then the fourth section of the fourth article applies, which says:

"The United States shall guaranty to every State in this Union a republican form of government."

Who is the United States? Not the judiciary; not the President; but the sovereign power of the people, exercised through their representatives in Congress, with the concurrence of the Executive. It means the political Government—the concurrent action of both branches of Congress and the Executive. The separate action of each amounts to nothing, either in admitting new States or guarantying republican governments to lapsed or outlawed States.

Whence springs the preposterous idea that either the President, or the Senate, or the House of Representatives, acting separately, can determine the right of States to send members or Senators to the Congress of the Union?

To prove that they are and for four years have been out of the Union for all legal purposes, and being now conquered, subject to the absolute disposal of Congress, I will suggest a few ideas and adduce a few authorities. If the so called "confederate States of America" were an independent belligerent, and were so acknowledged by the United States and by Europe, or had assumed and maintained an attitude which entitled them to be considered and treated as a belligerent, then, during such time, they were precisely in the condition of a foreign nation with whom we were at war; nor need their independence as a nation be acknowledged by us to produce that effect. . . .

[Mr. Stevens quotes several legal authorities to support his position that all legal bonds between the Federal Government and the seceding states were broken by the act of war and the recognition of these states as belligerents.]

After such clear and repeated decisions it is something worse than ridiculous to hear men of respectable standing attempting to nullify the law of nations, and declare the Supreme Court of the United States in error, because, as the Constitution forbids it, the States could not go out of the Union in fact. A respectable gentleman was lately reciting this argument, when he suddenly stopped and said, "Did you hear of that atrocious murder committed in our town? A rebel deliberately murdered a Government official." The person addressed said, "I think you are mistaken." "How so? I saw it myself." "You are wrong, no murder was or could be committed, for the law forbids it."

The theory that the rebel States, for four years a separate power and without representation in Congress, were all the time here in the Union, is a good deal less ingenious and respectable than the metaphysics of Berkeley, which proved that neither the world nor any human being was in existence. If this theory were simply ridiculous it could be forgiven; but its effect is deeply injurious to the stability of the nation. I cannot doubt that the late confederate States are out of the Union to all intents and purposes for which the conqueror may choose so to consider them.

But on the ground of estoppel, the United States have the clear right to elect to adjudge them out of the Union. They are estopped both by matter of record and matter *in pais*. One of the first resolutions passed by seceded South Carolina in January, 1861, is as follows:

Resolved, unanimously, That the separation of South Carolina from the Federal Union is final, and she has no further interest in the Constitution of the United States; and that the only appropriate negotiations between her and the Federal Government are as to their mutual relations as foreign States.

Similar resolutions appear upon all their State and confederate government records. The speeches of their members of congress, their generals and executive officers, and the answers of their government to our shameful sueings for peace, went upon the defiant ground that no terms would be offered or received except upon the prior acknowledgment of the entire and permanent independence of the confederate States. After this, to deny that we have a right to treat them as a conquered belligerent, severed from the Union in fact, is not argument but mockery. Whether it be our interest to do so is the only question hereafter and more deliberately to be considered.

But suppose these powerful but now subdued belligerents, instead of being out of the Union, are merely destroyed, and are now lying about, a dead corpse, or with animation so suspended as to be incapable of action, and wholly unable to heal themselves by any unaided movements of their own. Then they may fall under the provision of the Constitution which says "the United States shall guaranty to every State in the Union a republican form of government." Under that power can the judiciary, or the President, or the Commander-in-Chief of the Army, or the Senate or House of Representatives, acting separately, restore them to life and readmit them into the Union? I insist that if each acted separately, though the action of each was identical with all the others, it would amount to nothing. Nothing but the joint action of the two Houses of Congress and the concurrence of the President could do it. If the Senate admitted their Senators, and the House their members, it would have no effect on the future action of Congress. The Fortieth Congress might reject both. Such is the ragged record of Congress for the last four years. . . .

Congress alone can do it. But Congress does not mean the Senate or the House of Representatives, and President, all acting severally. Their joint action constitutes Congress. Hence a law of Congress must be passed before any new State can be admitted; or any dead ones revived. Until then no member can be lawfully admitted into either House. Hence it appears with how little knowledge of constitutional law each branch is urged to admit members separately from these destroyed States. The provision that "each House shall be the judge of the elections, returns, and qualifications of its own members," has not the most distant bearing on this question. Congress must create States and declare when they are entitled to be represented. Then each House must judge whether the members presenting themselves from a recognized State possess the requisite qualifications of age, residence, and citizenship; and whether the election and returns are according to law. The Houses, separately, can judge of nothing else. It seems amazing that any man of legal education could give it any larger meaning.

It is obvious from all this that the first duty of Congress is to pass a law declaring the condition of these outside or defunct States, and providing proper civil governments for them. Since the conquest they have been governed by martial law. Military rule is necessarily despotic, and ought not to exist longer than is absolutely necessary. As there are no symptoms that the people of these provinces will be prepared to participate in constitutional government for some years, I know of no arrangement so proper for them as territorial governments. There they can learn the principles of freedom and eat the fruit of foul rebellion. Under such governments, while electing members to the Territorial Legislatures, they will necessarily mingle with those to whom Congress shall extend the right of suffrage.

In Territories Congress fixes the qualifications of electors; and I know of no better place nor better occasion for the conquered rebels and the conqueror to practice justice to all men, and accustom themselves to make and to obey equal laws.

As these fallen rebels cannot at their option reënter the heaven which they have disturbed, the garden of Eden which they have deserted, and flaming swords are set at the gates to secure their exclusion, it becomes important to the welfare of the nation to inquire when the doors shall be reopened for their admission.

According to my judgment they ought never to be recognized as capable of acting in the Union, or of being counted as valid States, until the Constitution shall have been so amended as to make it what its framers intended; and so as to secure perpetual ascendency to the party of the Union; and so as to render our republican Government firm and stable forever. The first of those amendments is to change the basis of representation among the States from Federal numbers to actual voters. Now all the colored freemen in the slave States, and three-fifths of the slaves, are represented, though none of them have votes. The States have nineteen representatives of colored slaves. If the slaves are now free then they can add, for the other two-fifths, thirteen more, making the slave representation thirty-two. I suppose the free blacks in those States will give at least five more, making the representation of non-voting people of color about thirty-seven. The whole number of representatives now from the slave States is seventy. Add the other two-fifths and it will be eighty-three.

If the amendment prevails, and those States withhold the right of suffrage from persons of color, it will deduct about thirty-seven, leaving them but forty-six. With the basis unchanged, the eighty-three southern members, with the Democrats that will in the best times be elected from the North, will always give them a majority in Congress and in the Electoral College. They will at the very first election take possession of the White House and the halls of Congress. I need not depict the ruin that would follow. Assumption of the rebel debt or repudiation of the Federal debt would be sure to follow. The oppression of the freedmen; the reamendment of their State constitutions, and the reëstablishment of slavery would be the inevitable result. That they would scorn and disregard their present constitutions, forced upon them in the midst of martial law, would be both natural and just. No one who has any regard for freedom of elections can look upon those governments, forced upon them in duress, with any favor. If they should grant the right of suffrage to persons of color, I think there would always be Union white men enough in the South, aided by the blacks, to divide the representation, and thus continue the Republican ascendency. If they should refuse to thus alter their election laws it would reduce the representatives of the late slave States to about forty-five and render them powerless for evil.

It is plain that this amendment must be consummated before the defunct

States are admitted to be capable of State action, or it never can be.

The proposed amendment to allow Congress to lay a duty on exports is precisely in the same situation. Its importance cannot well be overstated. It is very obvious that for many years the South will not pay much under our internal revenue laws. The only article on which we can raise any considerable amount is cotton. It will be grown largely at once. With ten cents a pound export duty it would be furnished cheaper to foreign markets than they could obtain it from any other part of the world. The late war has shown that. Two million bales exported, at five hundred pounds to the bale, would yield $100,000,000. This seems to be the chief revenue we shall ever derive from the South. Besides, it would be a protection to that amount to our domestic manufactures. Other proposed amendments—to make all laws uniform; to prohibit the assumption of the rebel debt—are of vital importance, and the only thing that can prevent the combined forces of copperheads and secessionists from legislating against the interests of the Union whenever they may obtain an accidental majority.

But this is not all that we ought to do before these inveterate rebels are invited to participate in our legislation. We have turned, or are about to turn, loose four million slaves without a hut to shelter them or a cent in their pockets. The infernal laws of slavery have prevented them from acquiring an education, understanding the commonest laws of contract, or of managing the ordinary business of life. This Congress is bound to provide for them until they can take care of themselves. If we do not furnish them with homesteads, and hedge them around with protective laws; if we leave them to the legislation of their late masters, we had better have left them in bondage. Their condition would be worse than that of our prisoners at Andersonville. If we fail in this great duty now, when we have the power, we shall deserve and receive the execration of history and of all future ages.

Two things are of vital importance.

1. So to establish a principle that none of the rebel States shall be counted in any of the amendments of the Constitution until they are duly admitted into the family of States by the law-making power of their conqueror. For more than six months the amendment of the Constitution abolishing slavery has been ratified by the Legislatures of three-fourths of the States that acted on its passage by Congress, and which had Legislatures, or which were States capable of acting, or required to act, on the question.

I take no account of the aggregation of whitewashed rebels, who without any legal authority have assembled in the capitals of the late rebel States and simulated legislative bodies. Nor do I regard with any respect the cunning byplay into which they deluded the Secretary of State by frequent telegraphic announcements that "South Carolina had adopted the amendment;" "Alabama has adopted the amendment, being the twenty-seventh State," &c. This was intended to delude the people, and accustom Congress to hear repeated the names of these extinct States as if they were alive;

when, in truth, they have now no more existence than the revolted cities of Latium, two-thirds of whose people were colonized and their property confiscated, and their right of citizenship withdrawn by conquering and avenging Rome.

2. It is equally important to the stability of this Republic that it should now be solemnly decided what power can revive, recreate, and reinstate these provinces into the family of States, and invest them with the rights of American citizens. It is time that Congress should assert its sovereignty, and assume something of the dignity of a Roman senate. It is fortunate that the President invites Congress to take this manly attitude. After stating with great frankness in his able message his theory, which, however, is found to be impracticable, and which I believe very few now consider tenable, he refers the whole matter to the judgment of Congress. If Congress should fail firmly and wisely to discharge that high duty it is not the fault of the President.

This Congress owes it to its own character to set the seal of reprobation upon a doctrine which is becoming too fashionable, and unless rebuked will be the recognized principle of our Government. Governor Perry and other provisional governors and orators proclaim that "this is the white man's Government." The whole copperhead party, pandering to the lowest prejudices of the ignorant, repeat the cuckoo cry, "This is the white man's Government." Demagogues of all parties, even some high in authority, gravely shout, "This is the white man's Government." What is implied by this? That one race of men are to have the exclusive right forever to rule this nation, and to exercise all acts of sovereignty, while all other races and nations and colors are to be their subjects, and have no voice in making the laws and choosing the rulers by whom they are to be governed. Wherein does this differ from slavery except in degree? Does not this contradict all the distinctive principles of the Declaration of Independence? When the great and good men promulgated that instrument, and pledged their lives and sacred honors to defend it, it was supposed to form an epoch in civil government. Before that time it was held that the right to rule was vested in families, dynasties, or races, not because of superior intelligence or virtue, but because of a divine right to enjoy exclusive privileges.

Our fathers repudiated the whole doctrine of the legal superiority of families or races, and proclaimed the equality of men before the law. Upon that they created a revolution and built the Republic. They were prevented by slavery from perfecting the superstructure whose foundation they had thus broadly laid. For the sake of the Union they consented to wait, but never relinquished the idea of its final completion. The time to which they looked forward with anxiety has come. It is our duty to complete their work. If this Republic is not now made to stand on their great principles, it has no honest foundation, and the Father of all men will still shake it to its center. If we have not yet been sufficiently scourged for our national sin to teach us to do justice to all God's creatures, without distinction of race or color, we must expect the still more heavy vengeance of an offended Father, still increasing his inflictions as he increased the severity of the plagues of Egypt until the tyrant consented to do justice. And when that tyrant repented of his reluctant consent, and attempted to reënslave the people, as our southern tyrants are attempting to do now, he filled the Red sea with broken chariots and drowned horses, and strewed the shores with dead carcasses.

Mr. Chairman, I trust the Republican party will not be alarmed at what I am saying. I do not profess to speak their sentiments, nor must they be held responsible for them. I speak for myself, and take the responsibility, and will settle with my intelligent constituents.

This is not a "white man's Government," in the exclusive sense in which it is used. To say so is political blasphemy, for it violates the fundamental principles of our gospel of liberty. This is man's Government; the Government of all men alike; not that all men will have equal power and sway within it. Accidental circumstances, natural and acquired endowment and ability, will vary their fortunes. But equal rights to all the privileges of the Government is innate in every immortal being, no matter what the shape or color of the tabernacle which it inhabits.

If equal privileges were granted to all, I should not expect any but white men to be elected to office for long ages to come. The prejudice engendered by slavery would not soon permit merit to be preferred to color. But it would still be beneficial to the weaker races. In a country where political divisions will always exist, their power, joined with just white men, would greatly modify, if it did not entirely prevent, the injustice of majorities. Without the right of suffrage in the late slave States, (I do not speak of the free States,) I believe the slaves had far better been left in bondage. I see it stated that very distinguished advocates of the right of suffrage lately declared in this city that they do not expect to obtain it by congressional legislation, but only by administrative action, because, as one gallant gentleman said, the States had not been out of the Union. Then they will never get it. The President is far sounder than they. He sees that administrative action has nothing to do with it. If it ever is to come, it must be constitutional amendments or congressional action in the Territories, and in enabling acts.

How shameful that men of influence should mislead and miseducate the public mind! They proclaim, "This is the white man's Government," and the whole coil of copperheads echo the same sentiment, and upstart, jealous Republicans join the cry. Is it any wonder ignorant foreigners and illiterate natives should learn this doctrine, and be led to despise and maltreat a whole race of their fellow-men?

Sir, this doctrine of a white man's Government is as atrocious as the infamous sentiment that damned the late Chief Justice to everlasting fame; and, I fear, to everlasting fire.

Congressional Speech in Favor of Johnson's Reconstruction Policy (Abridged)

Henry Jarvis Raymond

Commentary

Just as Johnson's message required a response from Stevens, so too did Stevens' speech require an answer from one of Johnson's supporters. The rhetorical situation required that the respondent be a loyal Republican with well-established party credentials. The rhetorical task was to persuade moderate Republicans. The task fell to Henry Jarvis Raymond (1820-1869).

Although new to Congress, Raymond had the necessary credentials. Active in New York politics since the late 1840s, he had helped form the Republican party in 1856. He had been a co-founder and writer for a major Republican newspaper in New York City. Extremely active in 1864, he had helped Johnson obtain the vice-presidential nomination and had campaigned vigorously not only for himself, but also for the entire Union party ticket. His record of party loyalty had resulted in his recent selection as chairman of the Republican National Committee. He had, therefore, considerable ethos among his fellow Republican congressmen when he arose on December 21, 1865 to answer Stevens. His speech is reproduced photographically from the abbreviated version in Ernest J. Wrage and Barnett Baskerville, *American Forum: Speeches on Historic Issues, 1788-1900* (New York: Harper and Brothers, 1960), pp. 214-219.

Congressional Speech in Favor of Johnson's Reconstruction Policy (Abridged)

*M*r. *Chairman:* I should be glad, if it meet the sense of those members who are present, to make some remarks upon the general question now before the House; but I do not wish to trespass at all upon their disposition in regard to this matter. I do not know, however, that there will be a better opportunity to say what little I have to say than is now offered; and if the House shall indicate no other wish, I will proceed to say it. . . . I am glad to assume and to believe that there is not a member of this House, nor a man in this country, who does not wish, from the bottom of his heart, to see the day speedily come when we shall have this nation—the great American Republic—again united, more harmonious in its action than it has ever been, and forever one and indivisible. We in this Congress are to devise the means to restore its union and its harmony, to perfect its institutions, and to make it in all its parts and in all its action, through all time to come, too strong, too wise, and too free ever to invite or ever to permit the hand of rebellion again to be raised against it.

Now sir, in devising those ways and means to accomplish that great result, the first thing we have to do is to know the point from which we start, to understand the nature of the material with which we have to work—the condition of the territory and the States with which we are concerned. I had supposed at the outset of this session that it was the purpose of this House to proceed to that work without discussion, and to commit it almost exclusively, if not entirely, to the joint committee raised by the two Houses for the consideration of that subject. But, sir, I must say that I was glad when I perceived the distinguished gentleman from Pennsylvania [Mr. Stevens], himself the chairman on the part of this House of that great committee on reconstruction, lead off in a discussion of this general subject, and thus invite all the rest of us who choose to follow him in the debate. In the remarks which he made in this body a few days since, he laid down, with the clearness and the force which characterize everything he says and does, his point of departure in commencing this great work. I had hoped that the ground he would lay down would be such that we could all of us stand upon it and cooperate with him in our common object. I feel constrained to say, sir—and I do it without the slightest disposition to create or to exaggerate differences—that there were features in his exposition of the condition of the country with which I cannot concur. I cannot for myself start from precisely the point which he assumes.

In his remarks on that occasion he assumed that the States lately in rebellion were and are out of the Union. Throughout his speech—I will not trouble you with reading passages from it—I find him speaking of those States as "outside of the Union," as "dead States," as having forfeited all their rights and terminated their State existence. I find expressions still more definite and distinct; I find him stating that they "are and for four years have been out of the Union for all legal purposes;" as having been for four years a "separate power," and "a separate nation."

His position therefore is that these States, having been in rebellion, are now out of the Union, and are simply within the jurisdiction of the Constitution of the United States as so much territory to be dealt with precisely as the will of the conqueror, to use his own language, may dictate. Now, sir, if that position is correct, it prescribes for us one line of policy to be pursued very different from the one that will be proper if it is not correct. His belief is that what we have to do is to create new States out of this territory at the proper time—many years distant—retaining them meantime in a territorial condition, and subjecting them to precisely such a state of discipline and tutelage as Congress or the Government of the United States may see fit to prescribe. If I believed in the premises which he assumes, possibly, though I do not think probably, I might agree with the conclusion he has reached.

But, sir, I cannot believe that this is our condition. I cannot believe that these States have ever been out of the Union, or that they are now out of the Union. I cannot believe that they ever have been, or are now, in any sense a separate Power. If they were, sir, how and when did they become so? They were once States of this Union—that every one concedes; bound to the Union and made members of the Union by the Constitution of the United States. If they ever went out of the Union it was at some specific time and by some specific act. I regret that the gentleman from Pennsylvania [Mr. Stevens] is not now in his seat. I should have been glad to ask him by what specific act, and at what precise time, any one of those States took itself out of the American Union. Was it by the ordinance of secession? I think we all agree that an ordinance of secession passed by any State of this Union is simply a nullity, because it encounters in its practical opera-tion the Constitution of the United States, which is the supreme law of the land. It could have no legal, actual force or validity. It could not operate to effect any actual change in the relations of the State adopting it to the national Government, still less to accomplish the removal of that State from the sovereign jurisdiction of the Constitution of the United States.

Well, sir, did the resolutions of these States, the declarations of their officials, the speeches of members of their Legislatures, or the utterances of their press accomplish the result? Certainly not. They could not possibly work any change whatever in the relations of these States to the General Government. All their ordinances and all their resolutions were simply declarations of a purpose to secede. Their secession, if it ever took place, certainly could not date from the time when their intention to secede was first announced. After declaring that intention, they proceeded to carry it into effect. How? By war. By sustaining their purpose by arms against the force which the United States brought to bear against it. Did they sustain it? Were their arms victorious? If they were, then their secession was an accomplished fact. If not, it was nothing more than an abortive attempt—a purpose unfulfilled. This, then, is simply a question of fact, and we all know what the fact is. They did not succeed. They failed to maintain their ground by force of arms—in other words, they failed to secede.

But the gentleman from Pennsylvania [Mr. Stevens] insists that they did secede, and that this fact is not in the least affected by the other fact that the Constitution forbids secession. He says that the law forbids murder, but that murders are nevertheless committed. But there is no analogy between the two cases. If secession had been accomplished, if these States had gone out, and overcome the armies that tried to prevent their going out, then the prohibition of the Constitution could not have altered the fact. In the case of murder the man is killed, and murder is thus committed in spite of the law. The fact of killing is essential to the committal of the crime; and the fact of going out is essential to secession. But in this case there was no such fact. I think I need not argue any further the position that the rebel States have never for one moment, by any ordinances of secession, or by any successful war, carried themselves beyond the rightful jurisdiction of the Constitution of the United States. They have interrupted for a time the practical enforcement and exercise of that jurisdiction; they rendered it impossible for a time for this Government to enforce obedience to its laws; but there has never been an hour when this Government, or this Congress, or this House, or the gentleman from Pennsylvania himself, ever conceded that those States were beyond the jurisdiction of the Constitution and laws of the United States.

During all these four years of war Congress has been making laws for the government of those very States, and the gentleman from Pennsylvania has voted for them, and voted to raise armies to enforce them. Why was this done if they were a separate nation? Why, if they were not part of the United States? Those laws were made for them as States. Members have voted for laws imposing upon them direct taxes, which are apportioned, according to the Constitution, only "among the several States" according to their population. In a variety of ways—to some of which the gentleman who preceded me has referred—this Congress has by its action assumed and asserted that they were still States in the Union, though in rebellion, and that it was with the rebellion that we were making war, and not with the States themselves as States, and still less as a separate, as a foreign, Power.

The gentleman from Pennylvania [Mr. Stevens] spoke of States forfeiting their State existence by the fact of rebellion. Well, I do not see how there can be any such forfeiture involved or implied. The individual citizens of those States ᵥ ᵣnt into the rebellion. They thereby incurred certain penalties under the laws and Constitution of the United States. What the States did was to endeavor to interpose their State authority between the individuals in rebellion and the Government of the United States, which assumed, and which would carry out the assumption, to declare those individuals traitors for their acts. The individuals in the States who were in rebellion, it seems to me, were the only parties who under the Constitution and laws of the United States could incur the penalties of treason. I know of no law, I know of nothing in the Constitution of the United States, I know of nothing in any recognized or established code of international law, which can punish a State as a State for any act it may perform. It is certain that our Constitution assumes nothing of the kind. It does not deal with States, except in one or two instances, such as elections of members of Congress, and the election of electors of President and Vice President.

Indeed, the main feature which distinguishes the Union under the Constitution from the old Confederation is this, that whereas the old Confederation did deal with States directly, making requisitions upon them for supplies and relying upon them for the execution of its laws, the Constitution of the United States, in order to form a more perfect Union, made its laws binding on the individual citizens of the several States, whether living in one State or in another. Congress, as the legislative branch of this Government, enacts a law which shall be operative upon every individual within its jurisdiction. It is binding upon each individual citizen, and if he resists it by force he is guilty of a crime and is punished accordingly, anything in the constitution or laws of his State to the contrary notwithstanding. But the States themselves are not touched by the laws of the United States or by the Constitution of the United States. A State cannot be indicted; a State cannot be tried; a State cannot be hung for treason. The individuals in a State may be so tried and hung, but the State as an organization, as an organic member of the Union, still exists, whether its individual citizens commit treason or not.

Mr. Chairman, I am here to act with those who seek to complete the restoration of the Union, as I have acted with those through the last four years who have sought to maintain its integrity and prevent its destruction. I shall say no word and do no act and give no vote to recognize its division, or to postpone or disturb its rapidly-approaching harmony and peace. I have no right and no disposition to lay down rules by which others shall govern and guide their conduct; but for myself I shall endeavor to act upon this whole question in the broad and liberal temper which its importance demands. We are not conducting a controversy in a court of law. We are not seeking to enforce a remedy for private wrongs, nor to revenge or retaliate private griefs. We have great communities of men, permanent interests of great States, to deal with, and we are bound to deal with them in a large and liberal spirit. It may be for the welfare of this nation that we shall cherish toward the millions of our people lately in rebellion feelings of hatred and distrust; that we shall nurse the bitterness their infamous treason has naturally and justly engendered, and make that the basis of our future dealings with them. Possibly we may best teach them the lessons of liberty, by visiting upon them the worst excesses of despotism. Possibly they may best learn to practice justice toward others, to admire and emulate our republican institutions, by suffering at our hands the absolute rule we denounce in others. It may be best for us and for them that we discard, in all our dealings with them, all the obligations and requirements of the Constitution, and assert as the only law for them the unrestrained will of conquerors and masters.

I confess I do not sympathize with the sentiments or the opinions which would dictate such a course. I would exact of them all needed and all just guarantees for their future loyalty to the Constitution and laws of the United States. I would exact from them, or impose upon them through the constitutional legislation of Congress, and by enlarging and extending, if necessary, the scope and powers of the Freedmen's Bureau, proper care and protection for the helpless and friendless freedmen, so lately their slaves. I would exercise a rigid scrutiny into the character and loyalty of the men whom they may send to Congress, before I allowed them to participate in the high prerogative of legislating for the nation. But I would seek to allay rather than stimulate the animosities and hatred, however just they may be, to which the war has given rise. But for our own sake as well as for theirs I would not visit upon them a policy of confiscation which has been discarded in the policy and practical conduct of every civilized nation on the face of the globe.

I believe it important for us as well as for them that we should cultivate friendly relations with them, that we should seek the promotion of their interests as part and parcel of our own. We have been their enemies in war, in peace let us show ourselves their friends. Now that slavery has been destroyed—that prolific source of all our alienations, all our hatreds, and all our disasters—there is nothing longer to make us foes. They have the same interests, the same hopes, the same aspirations that we have. They are one with us; we must share their sufferings and they will share our advancing prosperity. They have been punished as no community was ever punished before for the treason they have committed. I trust, sir, the day will come ere long when all traces of this great conflict will be effaced, except those which mark the blessings that follow in its train.

I hope and believe we shall soon see the day when the people of the southern States will show us, by evidences that we cannot mistake, that they have returned, in all sincerity and good faith, to their allegiance to the Union; that they intend to join henceforth with us in promoting its prosperity, in defending the banner of its glory, and in fighting the battles of democratic freedom, not only here, but wherever the issue may be forced upon our acceptance. I rejoice with heartfelt satisfaction that we have in these seats of power—in the executive department and in these halls of Congress—men who will cooperate for the attainment of these great and beneficent ends. I trust they will act with wisdom; I know they will act from no other motives than those of patriotism and love of their fellow-men.

Post-Civil War America
Rhetoric of Voting Rights

Petition to Congress for Woman Suffrage

Elizabeth Cady Stanton and Susan B. Anthony

Commentary

Although we can only conjecture about which of Stevens' arguments persuaded moderate Republicans to support the Radical policy, it was probably his appeal to Republican self-interest. Yet Radicals were not in a position to move too far during the 1865-1866 congressional session. Racial prejudice prevailed in the North as well as in the South, which was reflected by numerous State laws which disenfranchised blacks. States rights sentiment was strong in the North as well as in the South, and few people believed that the Federal government had any constitutional authority to overturn State legislation, regardless of discrimination. Finally, blacks were not even "citizens" under the still relevant Dred Scott decision.

Moving cautiously, Radicals persuaded Congress in January, 1866 to empower the Freedman's Bureau (established originally to give economic assistance to ex-slaves) to set aside State laws which it viewed as racially discriminatory. (Note: This law in no way affected Northern States.) In March, Congress moved a little further, passing a "Civil Rights" law, which declared blacks to be "Citizens" and required State governments to treat equally "citizens of every race and color." In vetoing both bills, Johnson argued that Congress had no constitutional authority to overturn State legislation.

Although Radicals managed to override Johnson's veto, they knew that the laws would never withstand a challenge in court. In fact, their anticipation of constitutional challenges encouraged them to begin drafting a constitutional amendment (the Fourteenth) during the winter of 1865-1866, even as they presented their legislation. The amendment, which was introduced in the spring of 1866, effectively overturned the Dred Scott decision by defining "citizens" as "all persons born or naturalized in the United States, and subject to the jurisdiction thereof." It also specified that "no State shall make or enforce any law which shall abridge the privileges or immunities of citizens of the United States; nor shall any State deprive any person of life, liberty, or property, without due process of law; nor deny to any person within its jurisdiction the equal protection of the laws." The precise meaning of this sentence has been, and still is, debated, but it obviously meant something which weakened States rights.

As Radicals drafted the amendment, they knew that the prevalence of States rights sentiment would make congressional passage difficult and State ratification even more difficult. Not wishing to complicate their task by specifically enfranchising blacks but wishing to gain control in the ex-Confederacy, they included a carefully worded section. It penalized States which disenfranchised blacks — but in a way which hurt only those States with a large black population (i.e., the South). The section specified that "when the right to vote . . . is denied [by a State] to any of the male inhabitants of such State . . . or in any way abridged, except for participation in rebellion, or other crime, the basis of [congressional] representation therein shall be reduced in the proportion which the number of such male citizens shall bear to the whole number of male citizens twenty-one years of age in such State."

The traditional disenfranchisement of women made it easy for congressmen to overlook a word which appears three times in the above-cited passage: *male*. Leaders of the women's movement did not overlook it. To the contrary, they began lobbying Congress for female enfranchisement as soon as they heard rumors that a fourteenth amendment was being drafted. They faced a host of insurmountable problems. First, the vast majority of Americans, including women, did not favor female enfranchisement. Even the Seneca Falls convention had divided over the question. Second, the women's movement could not disentangle itself from the racial question. Although many women's conventions had been held during the 1850s, their leaders had been active in the abolitionist movement. Many former abolitionists, especially males, privately urged female leaders not to complicate chances of getting the Fourteenth Amendment ratified. During the early months of 1866, while the amendment was being drafted, even such stalwarts for women's rights as Frederick Douglass and Wendell Phillips privately told female leaders that "this is the negro's hour." Finally, the women's movement was in disarray. The last women's convention had been held in 1860, and the movement had gone into eclipse during the war. It is true that Elizabeth Stanton (1815-1902), one of the conveners of the Seneca Falls Convention, and her younger friend, Susan B. Anthony (1820-1906), had led the Women's National Loyal League (formed in 1863). It is also true that the League had endorsed female suffrage. The endorsement, though, had split the League, as many of its members wished only to support the war effort. The League had worked effectively for the Thirteenth Amendment, but it had since been disbanded.

Despite the difficulties, many members of the movement began petitioning Congress during the winter of 1865-1866 to include women in the Fourteenth

Amendment. Stanton and Anthony tried to organize the petition drive. Part of their effort was to publicize a standard petition, which they urged their supporters to use. Their "form letter" illustrates not only their rhetorical appeal, but also a rhetorical practice that is now used extensively by various causes and self-interest groups: making it easy for supporters to inundate Congress with petitions by providing a standard form for them. The petition is reproduced from Elizabeth Cady Stanton, Susan B. Anthony and Matilda Joslyn Gage, *The History of Woman Suffrage* (New York: Fowler and Wells, 1882), vol. 2, p. 91.

Petition to Congress for Woman Suffrage

FORM OF PETITION. — *To the Senate and House of Representatives:* — The undersigned women of the United States, respectfully ask an amendment of the Constitution that shall prohibit the several States from disfranchising any of their citizens on the ground of sex.

In making our demand for Suffrage, we would call your attention to the fact that we represent fifteen million people — one-half the entire population of the country — intelligent, virtuous, native-born American citizens; and yet stand outside the pale of political recognition. The Constitution classes us as "free people," and counts us *whole* persons in the basis of representation; and yet are we governed without our consent, compelled to pay taxes without appeal, and punished for violations of law without choice of judge or juror. The experience of all ages, the Declarations of the Fathers, the Statute Laws of our own day, and the fearful revolution through which we have just passed, all prove the uncertain tenure of life, liberty, and property so long as the ballot — the only weapon of self-protection — is not in the hand of every citizen.

Therefore, as you are now amending the Constitution, and, in harmony with advancing civilization, placing new safeguards round the individual rights of four millions of emancipated slaves, we ask that you extend the right of Suffrage to Woman — the only remaining class of disfranchised citizens — and thus fulfill your constitutional obligation "to guarantee to every State in the Union a Republican form of Government." As all partial application of Republican principles must ever breed a complicated legislation as well as a discontented people, we would pray your Honorable Body, in order to simplify the machinery of Government and ensure domestic tranquillity, that you legislate hereafter for persons, citizens, tax-payers, and not for class or caste. For justice and equality your petitioners will ever pray.

Call for the Anniversary Convention of the American Equal Rights Association

Lucretia Mott

Commentary

The women's petition drive is a study in paradox. Most of their closest congressional friends, the Radicals, refused to present petitions for fear that any hint of their being for female suffrage would kill chances of passing the Fourteenth Amendment. Most of the petitions were presented by Democrats, largely to embarrass the Radicals and to emphasize that the Fourteenth Amendment was supported by radicals.

Equally paradoxical was the women's difficulty in reviving their movement. Stanton and Anthony organized a National Women's Rights Central Committee. They talked with Wendell Phillips about revising the American Anti-Slavery Society's constitution at its convention in May, 1866 so as to commit it to female, as well as black, suffrage. The AASS was also in disarray because Garrison, its long-time president, favored abolishing it now that slavery was dead. Phillips, its new president, argued that it should continue until black suffrage became a reality. Whether Phillips and the women misunderstood one another or whether (as seems more likely) Phillips engaged in chicanery is debatable. In any case, Stanton and Anthony came to the AASS convention thinking that constitutional revision was a mere formality, but Phillips ruled the proposal out-of-order because the constitutional requirement of a three-month notice for amendments had not been met.

Angry and frustrated, several women leaders immediately formed an American Equal Rights Association (AERA). Holding its first, and hastily organized, convention in May, 1866, it declared itself in favor of female and black suffrage. Lucrecia Mott (1793-1880) was elected president. The oldest of the women leaders, she exemplifies the long-standing interaction between religion and reform. After gaining speaking experience at religious meetings, she had helped organize the AASS in 1833. She had been forced to sit in the balcony at the London convention of world antislavery societies in 1840 and had been the moving force in organizing the Seneca Falls Convention in 1848.

Although Mott was too old to do much of the AERA's work, the call for its anniversary convention (May, 1867) was issued in her name. It is reproduced from Elizabeth Cady Stanton, Susan B. Anthony and Matilda Joslyn Gage, *History of Woman Suffrage* (New York: Fowler and Wells, 1882), vol. 2, pp. 182-183.

Call for the Anniversary Convention
of the American Equal Rights Association

THE first Annual Meeting of the AMERICAN EQUAL RIGHTS ASSOCIATION will be held in the City of New York, at the Church of the Puritans, on Thursday and Friday, the 9th and 10th of May, 1867, commencing on Thursday morning, at 10 o'clock.

The object of this Association is to "secure Equal Rights to all American citizens, especially the Right of Suffrage, irrespective of race, color, or sex." American Democracy has interpreted the Declaration of Independence in the interest of slavery, restricting suffrage and citizenship to a *white male minority.*

The black man is still denied the crowning right of citizenship, even in the nominally free States, though the fires of civil war have melted the chains of chattelism, and a hundred battle fields attest his courage and patriotism. Half our population are disfranchised on the ground of sex; and though compelled to obey the laws and taxed to support the government, they have no voice in the legislation of the country.

This Association, then, has a mission to perform, the magnitude and importance of which can not be over-estimated. The recent war has unsettled all our governmental foundations. Let us see that in their restoration, all these unjust proscriptions are avoided. Let Democracy be defined anew, as *the government of the people,* AND THE WHOLE PEOPLE.

Let the gathering, then, at this anniversary be, in numbers and character, worthy, in some degree, the demands of the hour. The black man, even the black soldier, is yet but half emancipated, nor will he be, until full suffrage and citizenship *are secured to him in the Federal Constitution.* Still more deplorable is the condition of the black woman; and legally, that of the white woman is no better! Shall the sun of the nineteenth century go down on wrongs like these, in this nation, consecrated in its infancy to justice and freedom? Rather let our meeting be pledge as well as prophecy to the world of mankind, that the redemption of at least one great nation is near at hand.

There will be four sessions — Thursday, May 9th, at 10 o'clock A.M. and 8 o'clock P.M.; Friday, May 13th, at 10 A.M., and 8 P.M. The speakers will be Elizabeth Cady Stanton, Gen. Rufus Saxton, Frances D. Gage, Parker

Pillsbury, Robert Purvis, Mary Grew, Ernestine L. Rose, Charles Lenox Remond, Frederick Douglass, Lucy Stone, Henry B. Blackwell, Rev. Olympia Brown, Sojourner Truth (Mrs. Stowe's "Lybian Sybil"), Rev. Samuel J. May, and others.

On behalf of the American Equal Rights Association,

LUCRETIA MOTT, President.

SUSAN B. ANTHONY, Cor. Secretary.
HENRY B. BLACKWELL, Rec. Secretary.
New York, 12th March, 1867.

Speech to the Anniversary Convention of the American Equal Rights Association

Sojourner Truth

Commentary

In the year between the AERA's founding (1866) and its anniversary convention in 1867, two unprecedented rhetorical events occurred. First, a woman ran for Congress. Spotting a loophole in New York law which permitted women to hold public office even though they could not vote, Anthony announced her candidacy in a public letter that declared her support for free trade and universal suffrage. She said that Democrats, who had traditionally opposed protective tariffs, were "sound" on trade but unsound on "personal rights." Republicans, who followed the old Whig policy of supporting protectionism, were just the reverse. Her candor might have been commendable, but it would have alienated voters in both parties even if she had been a male.

The second unprecedented rhetorical event was that President Johnson took to the stump to support congressional candidates who favored his policies. Never before had a president campaigned openly for congressional candidates. The Radicals, however, gained such an overwhelming victory that the next congressional session saw a series of tough Reconstruction laws and the overriding of presidential vetoes. Beginning in early 1867, Congress divided the old Confederacy into five military districts, each governed by an army officer. They legislated a plan in which States could return to the Union only after being "reconstructed"; i.e., after they met a set of stringent conditions, including ratification of the Fourteenth Amendment.

These developments put the AERA in a difficult position when it held its anniversary convention. Anthony's candidacy had not been taken seriously. Their effort to delete *male* from the Fourteenth Amendment had failed. With Radical Reconstruction laws now on the books, the Fourteenth Amendment had a better chance of being ratified, but this put AERA leaders in an ambivalent position. They were pleased at the progress of the Fourteenth Amendment, but they were distressed both by its failure to specifically enfranchise blacks and at its inclusion of the word *male*. They knew they had to devise a new strategy, but disagreements had already arisen. Stanton and Anthony were producing an extremely militant rhetoric (e.g., jumping to the defense of women accused of crimes without first getting all the facts). They favored working for an amendment to the Federal Constitution that would include both blacks and women. Others, led by Lucy Stone, favored a more temperate rhetoric and doubted the practicality of insisting on a Federal amendment that required female suffrage. This group thought it might be better to work for amendments to State constitutions in those States where prospects were brighter. Not all of these differences had erupted when the anniversary convention was held, but the strains were already present. Those who attended the anniversary convention had good reasons to be pessimistic.

The rhetorical situation obviously demanded a rhetoric that would rekindle optimism and enthusiasm while downplaying strains within the movement. The meeting was called to order by Robert Purvis, who proceeded to "congratulate the friends of this Association on the healthful, hopeful, animating, inspiring signs of the times." The president, Lucretia Mott, took the chair and asked Anthony for her secretarial report. Saying nothing about their defeats, Anthony gave a glowing account of the organization's work in various States during the preceding year. After several resolutions were discussed briefly, Mott introduced Sojourner Truth (1797?-1883) to give an inspirational speech.

Truth's age (approximately 70), unusual physique (she was approximately 6 feet tall and very muscular), and colorful career had made her a living legend among feminists and abolitionists. Although later biographers are unsure about some of the following so-called facts, the general outline is probably accurate. In any case, they were believed by those who heard her speak. Born a slave in New York, she was freed when the State abolished slavery, but her former master illegally sold some of her children into Southern slavery. Truth recovered at least one of them through legal action. Active in a religious cult, she continued using her former master's name until she received her new one in a vision. Although illiterate, she published an autobiography, which she peddled at abolitionist and women's meetings. She frequently addressed such meetings, often in dramatic ways. For example, she once uncovered her breasts to prove her femininity after a newspaper had accused the muscular woman of being a man in disguise.

Armed with her inspirational ethos, Truth delivered the speech which is reproduced from Elizabeth Cady Stanton, Susan B. Anthony and Matilda Joslyn Gage, *History of Woman Suffrage* (New York: Fowler and Wells, 1882), vol. 2, pp. 193-194.

Speech to the Anniversary Convention of
the American Equal Rights Association

My friends, I am rejoiced that you are glad, but I don't know how you will feel when I get through. I come from another field — the country of the slave. They have got their liberty — so much good luck to have slavery partly destroyed; not entirely. I want it root and branch destroyed. Then we will all be free indeed. I feel that if I have to answer for the deeds done in my body just as much as a man, I have a right to have just as much as a man. There is a great stir about colored men getting their rights, but not a word about the colored women; and if colored men get their rights, and not colored women theirs, you see the colored men will be masters over the women, and it will be just as bad as it was before. So I am for keeping the thing going while things are stirring; because if we wait till it is still, it will take a great while to get it going again. White women are a great deal smarter, and know more than colored women, while colored women do not know scarcely anything. They go out washing, which is about as high as a colored woman gets, and their men go about idle, strutting up and down; and when the women come home, they ask for their money and take it all, and then scold because there is no food. I want you to consider on that, chil'n. I call you chil'n; you are somebody's chil'n, and I am old enough to be mother of all that is here. I want women to have their rights. In the courts women have no right, no voice; nobody speaks for them. I wish woman to have her voice there among the pettifoggers. If it is not a fit place for women, it is unfit for men to be there.

I am above eighty years old; it is about time for me to be going. I have been forty years a slave and forty years free, and would be here forty years more to have equal rights for all. I suppose I am kept here because something remains for me to do; I suppose I am yet to help to break the chain. I have done a great deal of work; as much as a man, but did not get so much pay. I used to work in the field and bind grain, keeping up with the cradler; but men doing no more, got twice as much pay; so with the German women. They work in the field and do as much work, but do not get the pay. We do as much, we eat as much, we want as much. I suppose I am about the only colored woman that goes about to speak for the rights of the colored women. I want to keep the thing stirring, now that the ice is cracked. What we want is a little money. You men know that you get as much again as women when you write, or for what you do. When we get our rights we shall not have to come to you for money, for then we shall have money enough in our own pockets; and may be you will ask us for money. But help us now until we get it. It is a good consolation to know that when we have got this battle once fought we shall not be coming to you any more. You have been having our rights so long, that you think, like a slave-holder, that you own us. I know that it is hard for one who has held the reins for so long to give up; it cuts like a knife. It will feel all the better when it closes up again. I have been in Washington about three years, seeing about these colored people. Now colored men have the right to vote. There ought to be equal rights now more than ever, since colored people have got their freedom. I am going to talk several times while I am here; so now I will do a little singing. I have not heard any singing since I came here.

[Sojourner sang, "We are going home."] There, children, in heaven we shall rest from all our labors; first do all we have to do here. There I am determined to go, not to stop short of that beautiful place, and I do not mean to stop till I get there, and meet you there, too.

Senate Speech Introducing the Fifteenth Amendment

William M. Stewart

Commentary

Despite its optimistic rhetoric during its anniversary convention of May, 1867, the AERA was fighting for a lost cause. By the end of the year, Radical Republicans also had reason to worry. Democratic strength increased in several State elections which raised fears about the upcoming presidential and congressional elections of 1868. Black enfranchisement was rejected by several Northern States, and only limited success was being achieved in getting the Fourteenth Amendment ratified. The Radicals promptly devised a strategy which called for reconstructing and controlling the ex-Confederacy to offset losses in the North and for minimizing the extent of those losses.

In the ex-Confederacy, Republicans worked through the Freedmen's Bureau to remind blacks that the Republicans were responsible for emancipation, to promise more economic aid and to warn that Democrats wished to restore slavery. They worked rapidly to reconstruct the States. Knowing that whites outnumbered blacks in the ex-Confederacy by approximately two to one, Republicans used Federal Reconstruction laws to disenfranchise many whites. Many more were disenfranchised by local registration boards, which were usually appointed by the military governors and supported by the army units stationed in the former Confederate states. For the 1868 election, 672,000 whites and 703,000 blacks were registered in the Confederacy.

Republican tactics in the South were overwhelmingly successful. Seven States were reconstructed in time for the 1868 election. All seven ratified the Fourteenth Amendment and were under Republican domination. Democrats, of course, swept the white vote with calls for a "white man's party," but they could not overcome the statistical disparity.

Fearing a Northern backlash against its expansion of Federal power on behalf of Southern blacks, Republicans tried to divert Northern attention from the issue by exploiting memories of the recent war. Their presidential candidate was a war hero, General Ulyssus S. Grant. They called Democrats the "party of rebellion" and called themselves the "party of union." Just to be safe, they also tried to show moderation on questions of race and States rights by declaring in their platform that "the question of suffrage in all the loyal States properly belongs to the people of those States."

After carrying the election of 1868, Radicals promptly forgot their platform. They proposed a fifteenth amendment to the Constitution, which said that the "right of citizens of the United States to vote shall not be denied or abridged by the United States or by any State on account of race, color, or previous condition of servitude."

In the Senate, the proposal was reported out of the Judiciary Committee on January 28, 1869 by its chairman, William M. Stewart (1827-1909). Originally from Ohio, Stewart immigrated to California and then to Nevada, which elected him to the Senate as soon as it became a State. His short speech is reproduced from *Great Debates in American History,* editor Marion Mills Miller (New York: Current Literature Publishing Co., 1913), vol. 8, p. 98.

Senate Speech Introducing the Fifteenth Amendment

This great question is the culmination of a contest which has lasted for thirty years. It is the logical result of the rebellion, of the abolition of slavery, and of the conflicts in this country during and before the war. Every person in the country has discussed it; it has been discussed in every local paper, by every local speaker; it has been discussed at the firesides; and now we are to place the grand result, I hope, in the Constitution of the United States. And let me remind my fellow-Senators that it is well that this work be now done, for we have realized the force of the very pointed sentence which was read here from the Swiss address, that "undetermined questions have no pity for the repose of mankind." This question can never rest until it is finally disposed of. This amendment is a declaration to make all men, without regard to race or color, equal before the law. The arguments in favor of it are so numerous, so convincing, that they carry conviction to every mind. The proposition itself has been recognized by the good men of this nation; and it is important, as the new Administration enters upon the charge of the affairs of this country, that it should start on this high and noble principle that all men are free and equal, that they are really equal before the law. We cannot stop short of this.

It must be done. It is the only measure that will really abolish slavery. It is the only guaranty against peon laws and against oppression. It is that guaranty which was put in the Constitution of the United States originally, the guaranty that each man shall have a right to protect his own liberty. It repudiates that arrogant, self-righteous assumption, that one man can be charged with the liberties and destinies of another. You may put this in the form of legislative enactment; you may empower Congress to legislate; you may empower the States to legislate, and they will agitate the question. Let it be made the immutable law of the land; let it be fixed; and then we shall have peace. Until then there is no peace. I want a vote. I will not occupy time. The proposition itself is more eloquent than man can be. It is a declaration too high, too grand, too noble, too just, to be ornamented by oratory.

Excerpts from The Senate Debate on the Fifteenth Amendment

Adonijah S. Welch, Thomas A. Hendricks, Henry W. Corbett, Simon Cameron, Samuel Pomeroy, Garrett Davis, Joseph S. Fowler, Oliver Morton, James R. Doolittle and Charles Drake

Commentary, Including *Excerpts from*
The Senate Debate on the
Fifteenth Amendment

Despite Stewart's plea for a quick vote, the Senate engaged in a lengthy debate on the Fifteenth Amendment. It was a chaotic debate, partly because both sides indulged in party partisanship without too much regard for its relevance to the issue under consideration. For example, Democrats accused Republicans of violating their campaign promise, a charge that was true but had no relevance to the merits of the Fifteenth Amendment. When Republicans used the natural rights argument to justify the amendment, Democrats argued that if Republicans really believed in natural rights, they would support woman suffrage, but the point was made less for its relevance than for partisan advantage (Democrats being united in their opposition to woman suffrage). Throughout the debate, Republicans frequently accused Democrats of being Confederate sympathizers, thus resorting to *ad hominem* argument instead of addressing issues raised by their opponents.

Another reason for the chaos is that several emotionally charged ideological issues emerged, and speakers often discussed only the one(s) which bothered them the most. Debaters sometimes ignored what previous speakers had said and at other times they responded only to some of the previous speaker's points. They even went so far as to debate proposed changes to the Fifteenth Amendment after the proposals had been defeated and were no longer pending. To bring some order out of chaos, the following excerpts are arranged to highlight three major ideological issues: the capabilities of various races, especially blacks and Chinese, the role of women and the proper role of the central government. Unless otherwise noted, the excerpts are reproduced from *Great Debates in American History*, editor Marion Mills Miller (New York: Current Literature Publishing Co., 1913).

The capability of blacks (then more commonly called "negroes" or "Africans") was debated frequently. For example, Adonijah S. Welch (1821-1889) arose to refute the assertion that "the African race in this country is inferior in respect to intelligence and virtue." Welch was what Southern whites scornfully called a "carpetbagger." A former Northerner and Union army veteran, he had moved to Florida in 1865 and been elected senator immediately after the State was reconstructed. (Miller, vol. 8, pp. 140-142.)

> Intelligence and virtue are not the distinctive characteristics of races; they are not peculiar to any race; they are not monopolized by nor wholly excluded from any people on the round earth. Intelligence and virtue are individual possessions, inconstant qualities, varying *ad infinitum* among the individuals of every people. Those constant qualities which mark the different races are mainly physical, consisting of peculiarities of color, feature, figure, and the like; but, as these peculiarities are not the qualifications for the voter, nor indicate the presence or absence of such qualifications, they cannot, without absurdity, be assumed as the ground for withholding or bestowing the right of suffrage. I do not share the prejudice of Senators against race; my prejudices are for or against individuals according to their merits or demerits.
>
> But suppose the question of the inferiority or superiority of races be admitted as possible or pertinent to this discussion, we need not shrink from such conclusions as can be reached. In what respects, let us ask, are the Southern negroes, for example, inferior to the Southern whites? They are certainly in social position far below a large class of white citizens, but they are, on the other hand, the social peers of another class found everywhere throughout the South. But social distinctions, whatever they are, do not confer political privileges in this free land; otherwise American women, who are our social superiors, would outrank us all. Then, again, as to intelligence the freedman holds the same relative position as in regard to social standing. We grant that he is inferior intellectually to the educated whites. It is the legitimate fruit of slavery and not a defect of race. But, if he be inferior to one class, he is most assuredly equal or even superior to that other class known as the poor whites; and, if his intelligence in general be limited, it is encouraging to know that there are many exceptions, instances of learning and culture, which indicate capacity. The present Secretary of State of Florida is a gentleman of talent and learning, and yet he is an African pure and simple. The important question, however, is not as to the comparative, intellectual, or social status of

the negro, for intelligence and refinement and social elevation alone do not avail to make the genuine American citizen. The crowning virtue of American citizenship is patriotism. Nothing is more clearly written in the history of the immediate past than that intellect becomes the instrument of treason when patriotism is wanting. Just here the Southern negro appears to decided advantage. He possesses this indispensable virtue. Intellectually and socially below the dominant class, but equal, at least, to the poorer class of Southern whites, he is, if we except the Southern loyalists, who are limited in number, infinitely superior to them all as a patriot; and I weigh my words well when I say that, if his ignorance were as rayless as the darkest midnight, if he never had a dozen thoughts in all his life and never changed their course, his steady, unflinching love of this Union would render him a far safer depositary of the right of suffrage than he who has compassed all knowledge and all science and hates his country.

Welch's remarks prompted an immediate exchange. Welch's antagonist was the better-known Thomas A. Hendricks (1819-1885), an Indiana Democrat who had served in the House from 1851-1855, been in the Senate since 1863 and been a leading contender for his party's presidential nomination the previous year. (Miller, vol. 8, p. 142.)

I think the negro does not now bring to the mass of the intelligence of this country an addition. I do not think he ever will. That race in its whole history has furnished no evidence of its capacity to lift itself up. It has never laid the foundation for its own civilization. Any elevation that we find in that race is when we find it coming in contact with the white race. While the tendency of the white race is upward, the tendency of the colored race is downward; and I have always supposed it is because in that race the physical predominates over the moral and intellectual qualities.

SENATOR WELCH. — May I ask the Senator, are the qualities of the voter — which are qualifications — in the individual or in the race? Is the white villain, if there is such a character, qualified to vote, while the intelligent negro — for there are intelligent negroes — is unqualified to vote?

SENATOR HENDRICKS. — The amendment that is pending before the Senate is not considering the race in regard to the individuals that make it. This is a proposition to extend the suffrage to an entire race. I am speaking of that race, whether it is a wise thing to bring into the political government of this country this race, which has shown in its history an incapacity to elevate itself or to establish a civilization for itself.

Can you tell me of any useful invention by the race, one single invention of greater importance to the world than the club with which the warrior beats to death his neighbor? Not one.

Although the capability of blacks was the most frequently debated racial issue, the broad wording of the Fifteenth Amendment prohibited States from disenfranchising any race, and this worried the two senators from Oregon, who knew that thousands of Chinese immigrants were coming to the Pacific Coast to work on railroad construction and feared that they would eventually become citizens. A proposal to permit States to disenfranchise Chinese was defended by Henry W. Corbett (1827-1903), a native New Yorker who had moved to Oregon in 1851 and had been elected to the Senate as a Republican in 1867. (Miller, vol. 8, pp. 130-131.)

> With the experience of the past few years on the Pacific coast we have found that this class of people are not beneficial to the advancement of those Christian institutions that lie at the foundation of our Government. The presence of large numbers of them in our midst is not beneficial to the observance of the Sabbath day. It is not encouraging to the Sabbath-school, which is the nursery of our children, and which is to fit them for enlightened and powerful and good statesmen. The question now is whether for our own race, whether for the benefit of our posterity, we shall not make this exception as against the Chinese.
>
> This question reaches beyond the common rights of man under a Christian nation such as was founded upon Plymouth Rock. It reaches the very foundation of our Christian institutions. Allow Chinese suffrage, and you may soon find established pagan institutions in our midst which may eventually supersede those Christian influences which have so long been the pride of our country.
>
> Those nations that have worshiped heathen gods have been overthrown and superseded by Christian nations, and I think it is very fair to presume that the overruling providence of God may curse us in the same way, and that we may eventually be overthrown by that class of people who come to our Pacific shores if we do not guard the priceless legacy which has been intrusted to us.

A different attitude toward the Chinese was expressed by Simon Cameron (1799-1889) of Pennsylvania. Although he had once served in the Senate as a Democrat (1845-1849), he abandoned his party after the Kansas-Nebraska Act and served as a Republican senator (1857-1861). After brief stints as secretary of war and minister to Russia, he returned to the Senate in 1867. (Miller, vol. 8, p. 155.)

> I will welcome every man, whatever may be the country from which he comes, who by his industry can add to our national wealth. Our friends from the Pacific coast are afraid of that simple, frugal people, lest they should destroy their liberties. I have no such fears. These Senators tell us, at the same time, that Chinamen will never become citizens. If they will not become citizens, what harm will they do us under this amendment to the Constitution? We are told that they come here and labor and send all the result of their toil to their own country. They do send a great deal; but what they send is not a tithe of the wealth which they give to us by their industry and their frugal habits.
>
> Mr. President, I must express my surprise at this talk about the poor Chinaman. I never heard of his doing any harm to anybody in America. He has enriched the Pacific slope by his toil. He has made that great railroad which is the miracle of the world by his patient industry. Whoever heard before of a people doing so much work in so short a space of time and getting so little reward for it as they have done? We might just as well say that the Irishmen who came into Pennsylvania and New York and Indiana and Illinois and Iowa, and gave their labor to make the canals

and the railroads which have enriched those States, should be prevented from becoming citizens. The Chinese who are now here will probably return to their own country; most of them, however, in their coffins, for their bodies are always carried away after their dissolution; but their children, who remain here, will after a while imitate our people, adopt our institutions, and become citizens of our country, and by their toil add to the wealth of the country.

Whereas blacks and Chinese were often alleged to be inferior, women were not. To the contrary, both sides on the controversy over female suffrage argued from the premise of women's moral superiority. The argument of Samuel Pomeroy (1816-1891) might be an exception to the general rule or it might be a rhetorical paralipsis (an argument that is presented under the guise of not being presented). In any case, Pomeroy was a central figure in the debate. Originally from Massachusetts, Pomeroy was a long-time reformer who helped organize the New England Emigrant Aid Society and then moved to Kansas, where he was elected to the Senate after Statehood. He was the conduit by which petitions from the American Equal Rights Association were presented, and Pomeroy himself moved that the Fifteenth Amendment be amended to enfranchise women. After a general discussion of natural rights, Pomeroy commented specifically on female suffrage. (Miller, vol. 8, p. 111-112.)

> I ask the ballot for woman, not on account of her weakness or on account of her strength; not because she may be above or below a man; that has nothing to do with the question. I ask it because she is a citizen of the Republic, amenable to its laws, taxed for its support, and a sharer in its destiny. There are no reasons for giving the ballot to a man that do not apply to a woman with equal force. She may use it or neglect it, as many men do; still it should be hers whenever she chooses to exercise the right. This would tend to its elevation and purification; for when the sacredness of the ballot is preserved it would not soil a woman's heart, hand, or dress, or the place of voting any more than when she uses the Bible and the prayer-book in the congregation of humble worshipers. In all the walks of life, retired or public, she adds grace, elegance, and purity to every step of her pathway, to every work of her hand, and to every love of her heart. I am for the enfranchisement fully and without restrictions of every man in the land who has the rights and discharges faithfully the duties of a citizen of the Republic, no matter how depressed or oppressed he may have been. The way of his elevation is by the way of the ballot, and that should be as fixed and as settled as the fundamental law itself. But I would put in the form of law precisely the same provision for every woman in the land; for it is as safe in her hands as in his; it will be used with as much intelligence and with as good results. And, besides all that, the distinctive character of our republican Government on the basis of the original design can be perpetuated in no other way. The highest justice is the only safety. Let it come, then, by one comprehensive amendment striking out all inequalities among citizens, and the dream of the fathers of a free and pure Republic shall be realized, and there shall be peace throughout the land and good will among men.

The issue of female suffrage kept reappearing even after Pomeroy's motion had been defeated and was no longer pending. Expressed more clearly than in Pomeroy's speech, the moral superiority of women was alleged by both sides in subsequent speeches. One exchange was initiated when Garrett Davis of Kentucky (1801-1872) concluded a lengthy speech against the Fifteenth Amendment (based largely on States rights philosophy) by attacking female suffrage. Just why Davis discussed a moot issue is not clear, but conservatism, emotionalism, party partisanship and sectional hostilities were probably involved. In prewar days, Davis had been a Whig congressman (1839-1847), and, after the party's collapse, he joined other "Old Line Whigs" in supporting whatever Unionist cause was available. He campaigned for the Constitutional Union ticket in 1860, worked against secession when Kentucky was considering the issue and was elected as a Unionist in 1861 to fill the senatorial vacancy created by Breckenridge's departure for the Confederacy. Although a Unionist, he adhered to the States rights philosophy, and he was re-elected as a Democrat in 1866. The conclusion of his speech is reproduced from the *Appendix to the Congressional Globe*, 40th Cong., 3rd sess., pp. 289-290.

> Mr. President, a few more words. In the course of every generation the people of large sections of the United States become terribly disordered in their mental and moral structure about various questions, and these evidences of derangement and disordered intellect and morals are always sure to originate in Boston. They want suffrage; they are not satisfied with that, but they want woman suffrage. Now, Mr. President, I have but a few words to say on that matter. I say that woman now occupies her proper domain. She is the priestess of the altar of the household. She is the source of all the morality and virtue that blesses the world. It is of the utmost importance that this ministering priestess shall be preserved pure. He is a most mistaken man, if not a positive misanthrope, who would bring to that altar the defilements of party politics. There is nothing which partisan politics touches that it does not contaminate and degrade. In Heaven's name let woman, whose proper performance of her great functions and influences in her domain are more important than all the offices performed by man, not be subjected to this defilement.
>
> Why go to the hustings, why go to the polls, to the seething crowd that in uncounted numbers is pushing to the polls amid the influences of passion and liquor, vulgarity, blackguardism, bullying, and threatening? Do you want to drag pure woman into such a conjunction as that? No, Mr. President; a good and a pure woman would turn with loathing and disgust from any such contact. Bad women ought never to be allowed to have a vote. It will be a day of woe, of incomparable woe, when the ballot is forced upon American women. I trust that that sad day will never come.

Joseph S. Fowler (1820-1902) responded to Davis' remarks. A long-time reformer who had worked for women's education, Fowler had moved to Tennessee from his native Ohio in prewar days to teach mathematics and practice law before becoming president of Howard Female College (1856-1861). He fled North after secession but came back to his adopted State after it was overrun by Union armies. He worked in the Reconstruction government and was elected to the Senate in 1866. (Miller, vol. 8, p. 139.)

> In a time like the present, when it is thought best to make an amendment to the Constitution, let it not be said the American Congress has been influenced to such a step, not by the universal love of mankind, not by an enlarged patriotism, but from suspicion and distrust of our own race and fellow-citizens. Let it embrace all, not a part. Let it protect the white man as well as the colored. I would go still further, and embrace all who are the subjects of law. I would found it on the spiritual worth and inviolability of the individual. It should embrace women as well as men. There is no argument in favor of the suffrage of men that will not apply equally as well to women. She is equally well fitted to decide what measures are calculated to promote her own interests. If any man were asked whose advice was the wisest and truest on all matters of business and politics he would unhesitatingly answer his wife's, his mother's, or his sister's. It is all a delusion and a sham to talk of excluding women from the ballot and admitting all the civilized and uncivilized men of the world.
>
> When men base their support of suffrage upon the natural rights of man, upon the worth of the individual, and then exclude woman, they do not believe the doctrine they assert. It is a direct contradiction of terms. When they admit the African and the Indian, and exclude their mothers and sisters, it is a startling exhibition of prejudice and the force of custom.
>
> If elections are conducted improperly and rudely it is because the refining and humanizing influence of woman has not been brought to purify them. Let the husband and father go with his wife and daughters to the polls as he does to church, and the rudest men will be taught self-respect and integrity of purpose. It will make the polls as refined and solemn as the lecture or the school.

A third ideological controversy involved the proper role of the Federal government vis-a-vis the States. This historic issue, which is still with us, dates back to the Hamilton-Jefferson debate over the constitutionality of the National Bank, and it deserved a more lucid and philosophical discussion than it got. With most of the advocates of the Fifteenth Amendment being Republicans in the Hamiltonian tradition and with most opponents being States rights Democrats and anti-black, the issue was usually intertwined with racial attitudes, party conflicts, sectionalism and earlier disputes over slavery and the recent war. One of the clearest philosophical debates was initiated by Oliver Morton (1823-1877), but Morton's rhetoric was obviously partisan. The Republican wartime governor of Indiana, Morton entered the Senate in 1867, and his speech, delivered in response to a States rights speech given by the Democratic Senator Salusbury of Delaware, identified Democrats with secession and slavery more than it justified the philosophy of a strong central government. (Miller, vol. 8, pp. 144-145.)

> The Senator told us to-day frankly that we were not one people. He said in the Senate of the United States, after the culmination of a war that cost this nation six hundred thousand lives, that we were not a nation. He gave us to understand that we were as many separate nationalities as we have

States; that one State is different from another as one nation in Europe is different from another. He denied expressly that we were a nation. He gave us to understand that he belonged to the tribe of the Delawares, an independent and sovereign tribe living on a reservation up here near the city of Philadelphia [laughter], but he denied his American nationality. The whole argument from first to last has proceeded upon that idea, that this is a mere confederacy of States; to use the language of the Senator to-day, a partnership of States. What is the deduction? If that is true there was the right of secession; the South was right and we were wrong. He did not draw that deduction, but it is one that springs inevitably from his premises.

Sir, the heresy of secession is not dead; it lives. It lives after this war, although it ought to have been settled by the war. It exists even as snow sometimes exists in the lap of summer when it is concealed behind the cliffs and the hedges and in the clefts of the rocks. It has come forth during this debate. We have heard the very premises, the very arguments, the very historical references upon which the right of secession was urged for thirty years. The whole fallacy lies in denying our nationality. I assert that we are one people and not thirty-seven different peoples; that we are one nation, and as such we have provided for ourselves a national Constitution, and that Constitution has provided the way by which it may be amended.

Mr. President, much has been said in regard to the inconsistent position of the Republican party, and a clause has been read from the Chicago platform in support of that charge. That clause was put into the platform not with reference to an amendment of the Constitution, not estopping the party from amending the Constitution; but with reference to an understanding throughout the country that Congress might attempt to regulate the subject of suffrage in the States. It was with reference to congressional regulation that that clause was put in the platform, but it was not declared directly or by implication that we should not amend the Constitution so as to limit the States in the exercise of that power.

Mr. President, the Republican party has its errors; it has committed its faults; and yet but for that party this Capitol would now be the Capitol of a hostile slaveholding confederacy.

One word in regard to the so-called Democratic party. The Democratic party for more than twenty years has lived upon the negro question. It has been its daily food, and, if the negro question shall now be withdrawn from politics, the Democracy, as a party, will literally starve to death. We need not, therefore, be surprised to find them resisting this constitutional amendment which will forever withdraw the subject from politics, and will strike down that prejudice to which the Democratic party has appealed for years. The Democratic party has not for years appealed to the reason of the people, but it has appealed to their prejudices upon the subject of race. It has sought, and, to some extent obtained, power upon that subject. It is still following the fortunes of slavery after slavery is dead. It cherished slavery while it lived, and now that slavery is dead it has taken to its embrace its odious and putrescent corpse. The Democratic party is now performing the office of Old Mortality by trying to revive inscriptions upon the moldering and dishonored tomb of slavery.

An immediate response to Morton came from James R. Doolittle (1815-1897). His political career illustrates the practical difficulties of a brilliant legal scholar who insisted on logical consistency. Adhering to the Jeffersonian view that strong governments inevitably become tyrannical, Doolittle believed that the Federal Constitution gave the central government only certain, severely limited powers. Believing, like Lincoln, that one of those powers was to stop the spread of slavery (but not to abolish slavery where it already existed), Doolittle was a "Barnburner" Democrat who temporarily abandoned his party to support the Free Soilers in 1848. After the election, he returned to his party in his native New York and continued to be a Democrat after moving to Wisconsin in 1851. His belief in the congressional power to stop the spread of slavery, however, estranged him from the Douglas philosophy which dominated the northern Democracy during the 1850s. Entering the Senate as a Republican in 1857, he was a strong supporter of Lincoln, was re-elected as a Republican and supported the Thirteenth Amendment. Adhering to the Lincoln-Johnson view that the Confederate States had not legally left the Union, he became estranged from Republicanism as Radicals tightened their control. After passage of the Fifteenth Amendment, he returned to the Democrats, which destroyed him politically, and he spent the last years of his life propounding his "divided sovereignty" philosophy as a law professor at the University of Chicago.

Doolittle's legalistic speech also illustrates his practical difficulties. He was interrupted by Morton, who expressed the Hamiltonian view, and he had an exchange with a Radical senator from Missouri, Charles Drake (1811-1892), who misrepresented Doolittle's philosophy. (Miller, vol. 8, pp. 146-148.)

JAMES R. DOOLITTLE [Wisc.]. — The Senator from Indiana seems to think that no statesman can bear in mind two ideas at the same time; that there can be no such thing as States rights maintained by anybody under the Constitution unless that person is a secessionist; and that, on the other hand, no man can maintain that there is any such thing as rights in the Federal Government under the Constitution without being in favor of an absolute concentrated government at Washington. Sir, these two ideas must go together in our system of government, and the time is coming when they must be discussed, when the rights of the States under the Constitution must be acknowledged. It is just as much a war on the Constitution to deny the States the rights which belong to them as it is a war on the Constitution to maintain the doctrine of secession.

SENATOR MORTON. — I have always denied State sovereignty; and I do now. I deny the doctrine that the States are separate and independent nations. We are one people. But, sir, the States have certain rights, rights that are guaranteed to them by the Constitution of the United States, just as we have rights secured to us both by the Federal and State Constitutions. We have State rights, but have no State sovereignty, and never had.

SENATOR DOOLITTLE. — Mr. President, the honorable Senator says there is no State sovereignty. I contend that by every decision of the Supreme Court of the United States, by every declaration made by every writer upon our system of government in the beginning, whether a Federalist or Republican, it was always maintained that the States had an attribute of sovereignty, not absolute, but under the Constitution, because under the Constitution they have parted with their absolute sovereignty; nor has the United States Government any sovereignty under the Constitution which is absolute. All the power which the United States Government has under the Constitution is limited. Sovereignty is limited by the Constitution. State sovereignty is limited by the Constitution; the United States sovereignty is limited by the Constitution; and the great difficulty of our times is that men cannot think or will not think that the two sovereignties exist at the same time under our government, the one limited by the other.

Why, Mr. President, from earliest childhood every man in this body has been taught that we live in the solar system where the planets that revolve around the sun are controlled by two forces: one a force tending toward the center by the force of gravitation — the centripetal force; and the other is the centrifugal force, by which they are driven in their orbits around the center. Mr. President, if either one of these forces were taken away it would absolutely destroy the system. In our solar system, if the centrifugal force were taken away and nothing but the centripetal force left to act, every planet would be drawn to the center, to the sun. On the other hand, if the centripetal force were destroyed in our solar system, and no force permitted to operate but the centrifugal force, all the planets would be driven in a tangent away from our system into illimitable space. Sir, it is the operation of these two forces, the one which tends to the center, the other which tends to the circumference, which keeps these planets moving in their orbits, which maintains our system, which keeps it from destruction; and the destruction of either of these forces is the destruction of the solar system.

Now, sir, come to our system of government; these two forces are planted in it of necessity. These two ideas have been here from the beginning. There have been men who represented the one and represented the other from the beginning. There have been men who have contended always for the absolute sovereignty of this central Government, and other men who have contended always for the absolute sovereignty of the States; and both of them have contended for a falsehood from the beginning. There is no absolute sovereignty in this Government; nor is there any absolute sovereignty in the States; but, under the operation of our system, devised by our fathers, wise as if they had been inspired from on high and had wisdom almost like Him who created the solar system under which we live, these two grand ideas, two great forces in government, were put in operation at one and the same time, each limiting the other, each operating upon the other, both working together, and working out that harmonious system in which alone we live and move and have our being; and that man or statesman, call himself what he may, whether a fire-eating secessionist of the South who comes into this body or elsewhere and maintains the absolute sovereignty of the State, with its right to withdraw from the Union, to retire from the system, to overturn the Government; or that other statesman, Republican though he may call himself, who comes into this body or elsewhere and maintains that this Government only has absolute sovereignty, and that it has the power to seize to itself all the powers of the Government — whichever one of these men undertakes to do this is making war on the Government and war on the system under which we live.

Mr. President, without going into a detailed history, what has occurred since the close of the war? In my judgment, in many of the acts which have been entered upon, the Constitution of the United States has itself been violated. I believe, as much as I believe in my existence here, that in the law which was passed establishing military tribunals and military government in the States of the South, abolishing all civil government, denying all right of trial by jury, this party in power in the Congress of the United States have just as much violated the Constitution in that regard as it ever was violated by any party in the history of the Government.

CHARLES D. DRAKE [Mo.]. — Mr. President, the whole argument of the gentleman and of all the other Senators on the other side who have spoken on this subject proceeds upon the doctrine that George H. Pendleton laid down in 1864, that, if every State in this Union should unite in ratifying the constitutional amendment abolishing slavery except one, slavery would not be abolished in that one State. They limit the power of amendment in the Constitution in that way.

SENATOR DOOLITTLE. — The Senator will allow me to interrupt him. I hope the honorable Senator does not mean to include me in that category from anything I have said. I believe that I made the first speech in this body in favor of the amendment abolishing slavery.

SENATOR DRAKE. — I say, Mr. President, that the whole doctrine of the opponents of this measure in this debate has been to the purport that, let any number of States ratify this amendment, it would have no binding force upon the other States, but only upon those States that ratify it. I say to the gentlemen who talk so about the rights of States, that there is not a State in this Union that has one single right but that which it derives from the Constitution, and there is not one right except that of equal senatorial representation which cannot be taken away from any State by a constitutional amendment passed by two-thirds of Congress and ratified by three-fourths of the States.

Excerpts from Is it a Crime for a Citizen of the United States to Vote?

Susan B. Anthony

Commentary including excerpts

After adoption of the fifteenth amendment, woman suffrage was no longer linked with black suffrage. Many leaders of the women's movement were bitter about the limited support they received from proponents of black suffrage, but they were now on their own. What rhetorical strategies should they employ? Different answers to the question led to a phenomenon that is common to movements: splintering. Lucy Stone and her husband, Henry Blackwell, favored a state-by-state strategy that focused exclusively on suffrage. Instead of focusing solely on suffrage, Elizabeth Stanton and, to a lesser extent, Susan Anthony discoursed about a broader range of reforms, and they became increasingly discouraged with a state-by-state strategy. Their discouragement was due largely to the overwhelming defeat of woman suffrage by popular referendum in Kansas in 1867.

All four of the above-mentioned leaders stumped the state during the Kansas campaign, but Anthony and Stanton made the tactical error of appearing on public platforms with George Train, a wealthy eccentric whose buffoonery made the cause appear ridiculous. Then they ignored Stone's advice by accepting money from Train to start a paper called *Revolution*. The name was chosen to identify woman suffrage with the much-revered American Revolution, but it soon became identified with radicalism as Stanton published essays castigating traditional marriage relationships and advocating easy divorce laws. She opposed abortion and legalized prostitution, both of which she argued were caused by male domination. Although not favoring free love, the paper defended its proponents, which led to charges that Stanton and Anthony were free love advocates. The short-lived paper died in 1870, the same year that Blackwell and Stone founded the less radical *Woman's Journal*.

Meanwhile, in 1869, the American Equal Rights Association divided into the National Woman Suffrage Association (NWSA), led by Anthony and Stanton, and the American Woman Suffrage Association (AWSA), led by Stone and Blackwell. The word, "suffrage," in the formal name of the NWSA implied an emphasis on voting rights, but the writings and speeches of its president, Elizabeth Stanton, dealt with a wider range of subjects.

Although sympathetic to the ideas of her friend Stanton, Anthony was a pragmatist who soon limited her rhetoric to suffrage. Doubting the chances of securing popular or legislative support, she tried to get the federal courts to overthrow state restrictions. This is a strategy that is widely used at the present time. For example, school segregation, school prayer and state laws prohibiting abortion were recently "outlawed" by the U.S. Supreme Court, much to the dismay of those who believe in the older concepts of states' rights and judicial restraint. However, the strategy's success in the post-Civil War period, when these older concepts still prevailed, was problematic, as Anthony soon learned.

Anthony might have got the idea for her strategy from Victoria Woodhull, but if so, it is ironic. Anthony despised Woodhull for too many reasons to discuss here, but she undoubtedly knew about Woodhull's "new departure" strategy for obtaining suffrage. Arguing that the fourteenth amendment had granted suffrage to all citizens, Woodhull said that instead of working for a new amendment to grant women the vote, they could vote already under the fourteenth. Almost no one was persuaded by Woodhull's argument, partly because she had such low ethos. She preached and practiced spiritualism, free love and other radical ideas.

Irrespective of where she got the idea, Anthony initiated her strategy during the presidential election of 1872 by registering and voting in her home town of Rochester. New York law prohibited women from voting, but she apparently overwhelmed the young (and nervous) election officials with a simple rhetorical syllogism: Major premise: The constitution permits citizens to vote. Minor premise: The constitution says I am a citizen. Therefore: I can vote.

Two weeks after the election, Anthony was arrested for violating the state election law. Not surprisingly, her syllogism failed to persuade the court to declare the state law unconstitutional. Nevertheless, her strategy was not a total loss. Her trial and subsequent court appeals were given considerable newspaper publicity, much of which created sympathy for Anthony because of the trial judge's domineering conduct (he refused to let Anthony testify, and he decided the case instead of letting the jury do so).

In addition, Anthony used the six months between her arrest (November 1872) and her trial (June 1873), to deliver a speech entitled, "Is it a Crime for a Citizen of the United States to Vote?" The title was well adapted to public audiences because the immediate reaction of an average American, even one opposed to woman suffrage, would be "Of course not."

Anthony delivered the speech 40 times throughout New York. A complete text appeared in the *History of Woman Suffrage* (vol. 2, pp. 630-46) which Anthony, Stanton and Matilda Gage began publishing a few years later (the four volumes appeared intermittently). Because of its length, we shall simply summarize the speech and reprint a few excerpts. The speech is not easy to summarize because it was not organized tightly, but Anthony's introduction was a clear statement of her thesis:

> I stand before you to-night, under indictment for the alleged crime of having
> voted illegally at the last Presidential election. I shall endeavor this evening
> to prove to you that in voting, I not only committed no crime, but simply
> exercised my "citizen's right," guaranteed to me and all United States
> citizens by the National Constitution, beyond the power of any State to
> deny.

Anthony's thesis was an implicit denial of the states' rights doctrine. Although
many Americans still adhered to it, Anthony did not deal with the doctrine
until later in the speech, and even then she assumed it was wrong rather than
arguing the point.

Despite failing to deal with the states' rights doctrine, Anthony's entire speech
was legalistic, much of it involving arguments over the proper definition of
words. Her first point, that all "citizens" have the legal right to vote, was
documented with quotations from the Federal constitution, the "Fathers" who
wrote it and various State constitutions. She also emphasized that the word,
"citizens," did not specifically exclude women.

Anthony cited a section of the New York constitution, "No member of this
State shall be disfranchised, unless by the 'law of the land,' or the judgment
of his peers," which she interpreted as follows:

> "The law of the land," is the United States Constitution; and there is no
> provision in that document that can be fairly construed into a permission
> to the States to deprive any class of their citizens of their right to vote.
> Hence New York can get no power from that source to disfranchise one
> entire half of her members. Nor has "the judgment of their peers" been
> pronounced against women exercising their right to vote. No disfranchised
> person is allowed to be judge or juror—and none but disfranchised persons
> can be women's peers; nor has the Legislature passed laws excluding them
> on account of idiocy or lunacy; nor yet the courts convicted them of bribery,
> larceny, or any infamous crime. Clearly, then, there is no constitutional
> ground for the exclusion of women from the ballot-box in the State of New
> York. No barriers whatever stand to-day between women and the exercise
> of their right to vote save those of precedent and prejudice.

Continuing her argument that women were included in the definition of
"citizens," Anthony cited legal evidence to show that state tax laws applied
to women. She also cited case law and quotations from legal authorities to show
that "people" and "persons" are "citizens" if they are born or naturalized
within the U.S. Then she summarized her line of argument:

> The only question left to be settled now, is: Are women persons? And I
> hardly believe any of our opponents will have the hardihood to say they
> are not. Being persons, then, women are citizens, and no State has a right
> to make any new law, or to enforce any old law, that shall abridge their
> privileges or immunities. Hence, every discrimination against women in
> the constitutions and laws of the several States, is to-day null and void,
> precisely as is every one against negroes. Is the right to vote one of the
> privileges or immunities of citizens? I think the disfranchised ex-rebels,
> and the ex-state prisoners will all agree with me, that it is not only one

of them, but *the one without which all the others are nothing*. Seek first the kingdom of the ballot, and all things else shall be given thee, is the political injunction.

This summary could not serve as a final one because of a serious rhetorical problem: many of her listeners knew that she had tried unsuccessfully to alter the language of the fourteenth and fifteenth amendments, but there was no reason for her to have done so if the line of argument in this speech was valid. Anthony did not explicate the reasons for her earlier actions, but she argued at length that the two amendments reaffirmed a woman's right to vote. In discussing the fourteenth, she assumed that the audience knew that the word "male" appeared in the second section. She claimed that the first section "was meant to be a prohibition of the States to deny or abridge their [black men's] right to vote . . . [and] it did the same for all persons, white women included, born or naturalized in the United States, for the amendment does not say all male persons of African descent, but all persons are citizens." Then she turned to the second section of the fourteenth and to the fifteenth:

> The second section is simply a threat to punish the States, by reducing their representation on the floor of Congress, should they disfranchise any class of male citizens, and does not allow of the inference that the States may disfranchise from any, or all other causes; nor in anywise weaken or invalidate the universal guarantee of the first section. What rule of law or logic would allow the conclusion, that the prohibition of a crime to one person, on severe pains and penalties, was a sanction of that crime to any and all other persons save that one? But, however much the doctors of the law may disagree, as to whether people and citizens, in the original constitution, were one and the same, or whether the privileges and immunities in the XIV. Amendment include the right of suffrage, the question of the right of the citizen to vote is settled forever by the XV. Amendment: "The citizen's right to vote shall not be denied by the United States, nor any State thereof; on account of race, color, or previous condition of servitude."
>
> How can the State deny or abridge the right of the citizen, if the citizen does not possess it? There is no escape from the conclusion, that to vote is the citizen's right, and the specifications of race, color, or previous condition of servitude can, in no way, impair the force of the emphatic assertion, that the citizen's right to vote shall not be denied or abridged. . . .
>
> But if you insist that the XV. Amendment's emphatic interdiction against robbing United States citizens of their right to vote, "on account of race, color, or previous condition of servitude," is a recognition of the right, either of the United States or any State, to rob citizens of that right for any or all other reasons, I will prove to you that the class of citizens for which I now plead, and to which I belong, may be, and are, by all the principles of our Government, and many of the laws of the States, included under the term "previous condition of servitude."

Anthony then discussed the "servitude" of women by documentating women's inferior legal status, such as the husband's control over children and the inability of women to testify in court. As she began her peroration, Anthony again clarified her new strategy for women's rights:

We no longer petition Legislature or Congress to give us the right to vote. We appeal to the women everywhere to exercise their too long neglected "citizen's right to vote." We appeal to the inspectors of election everywhere to receive the votes of all United States citizens, as it is their duty to do. We appeal to United States commissioners and marshals to arrest the inspectors who reject the names and votes of United States citizens, as it is their duty to do, and leave those alone who, like our eighth ward inspectors, perform their duties faithfully and well. We ask the juries to fail to return verdicts of "guilty" against honest, law-abiding, tax-paying United States citizens for offering their votes at our elections; or against intelligent, worthy young men, inspectors of election, for receiving and counting such citizens' votes. We ask the judges to render true and unprejudiced opinions of the law. . . . And it is on this line that we propose to fight our battle for the ballot—peaceably, but nevertheless persistently to complete triumph, when all United States citizens shall be recognized as equals before the law.

Testimony to the Select Committee on Woman Suffrage
United States Senate, March 7, 1884

Susan B. Anthony

Commentary

The judiciary's rejection of Anthony's constitutional argument meant that woman suffrage could be achieved only through some kind of legislative strategy. Doubting the effectiveness of Stone's state-by-state strategy, Anthony drafted the woman suffrage measure that eventually became the nineteenth amendment to the federal constitution. It was first introduced by her friend, Senator A. A. Sargent of California in 1878, and was reintroduced frequently until it was finally passed by both houses of Congress (1918-19) and ratified by the necessary two-thirds of the state legislatures in 1920.

For the first few years, the proposed amendment was referred to each House's Judiciary Committee. NWSA held its annual convention in Washington so that it would be convenient for Anthony to lead a pilgrimage of NWSA leaders to Capitol Hill to present petitions to the two committees, which usually allowed suffragists to present oral testimony as well as to present written petitions. The rhetorical appeals were similar to those contained in analogous discourses that appeared earlier in this anthology.

Typically, the committee would receive the petitions, take the testimony, make a report to the House or Senate, and then nothing would happen. However, "nothing" might be an exaggeration. Sympathetic congressmen would often use their franking privileges to distribute printed copies of reports and testimony, and newspapers would usually publicize the suffragists' testimony.

Attitudes changed slowly, but in 1882, both houses of Congress appointed a Select Committee on Woman Suffrage. Both committees reported favorably on woman suffrage, but both reports were shelved without being debated. The House went back to burying the "Anthony Amendment" in the Judiciary Committee, but the Senate retained its Select Committee, which reported favorably again in 1884 and 1886. However, it was not until 1886 that the Senate was willing to debate the measure.

Complaining that the Senate had never voted on a proposal that had been pending for over twenty years, Senator Blair of New Hampshire managed to get the Select Committee's report on the Senate floor (December 8, 1886). A full-scale debate began on January 25, 1887. As part of his pro-suffrage strategy, Blair read into the *Congressional Record* the testimony that NWSA leaders had presented to the Senate's Select Committee in 1884 and the Judiciary Committee in 1880. (Unfortunately, historians sometimes get the two sets of testimony confused.) As usual, the testimony in 1884 was delivered by leaders who were attending the annual NWSA convention. A dozen leaders testified. Anthony, who introduced each of the speakers, delivered the final speech.

Anthony's 1884 testimony focused on two anti-suffrage arguments that had gained weight over the years, although the focus was implicit rather than explicit. One was the argument that women would vote in a bloc. The fear of bloc voting could probably be traced back to the woman suffrage movement's earlier identification with antislavery, but it had a basis in fact during the post-Civil War period, especially with regard to the then-current crusade to prohibit the manufacture and sale of liquor. Many woman suffragists were also active in the Women's Christian Temperance Union (founded in 1874). Although many "prohibitionists" favored woman suffrage because they expected "bloc voting," most so-called "wets" opposed woman suffrage for the same reason.

A second anti-suffrage argument was based on the traditional states' rights philosophy. Suffrage, said states' righters, was a matter for states to decide, not the federal government.

Anthony's 1884 testimony is reproduced below in full from the *Congressional Record* (49th Congress, 2nd Session, vol. 18, pt. 1 [December 6, 1886-January 25, 1887], p. 996).

Senate Testimony (1884)

Miss ANTHONY. I wish I could state the avocations and professions of the various women who have spoken in our convention during the last three days. I do not wish to speak disparagingly in regard to the men in Congress, but I doubt if a man on the floor of either House could have made a better speech than some of those which have been made by women during this convention. Twenty-six States and Territories are represented with live women, traveling all the way from Kansas, Arkansas, Oregon and Washington Territory. It does seem to me that after all these years of coming up to this Capitol an impression should be made upon the minds of legislators that we are never to be silenced until we gain the demand. We have never had in the whole thirty years of our agitation so many States represented in any convention as we have had this year.

This fact shows the growth of public sentiment. Mrs. Duniway is here all the way from Oregon, and you say, when Mrs. Duniway is doing so well up there, and is so hopeful of carrying the State of Oregon, why do not you all rest satisfied with that plan of gaining the suffrage? My answer is that I do not wish to see the women of the thirty-eight States of this Union compelled to leave their homes and canvass each State, school district by school district. It is asking too much of a moneyless class of people, disfranchised by the constitution of every State in the Union. The joint earnings of the marriage copartnership in all the States belong legally to the husband. If the wife goes outside the home to work, the law in most of the States permits her to own and control the money thus earned. We have not a single State in the Union where the wife's earnings inside the marriage copartnership are owned by her. Therefore, to ask the vast majority of women who are thus situated, without an independent dollar of their own, to make a canvass of the States is asking to[o] much.

Mrs. GOUGAR. Why did they not ask the negro to do that?

Miss ANTHONY. Of course the negro was not asked to go begging the white man from school district to school district to get his ballot. If it was known that we could be driven to the ballot-box like a flock of sheep, and all vote for one party, there would be a bid made for us; but that is not done, because we can not promise you any such thing; because we stand before you and honestly tell you that the women of this nation are educated equally with the men, and that they, too, have political opinions. There is not a woman on our platform, there is scarcely a woman in this city of Washington, whether the wife of a Senator or a Congressman—I do not believe you can find a score of women in the whole nation—who have not opinions on the pending Presidential election. We all have opinions; we all have parties. Some of us like one party and one candidate and some another.

Therefore we can not promise you that women will vote as a unit when they are enfranchised. Suppose the Democrats shall put a woman-suffrage plank in their platform in their Presidential convention, and nominate an open and avowed friend of woman suffrage to stand upon that platform; we can not pledge you that all the women of this nation will work for the success of that party, nor can I pledge you that they will all vote for the Republican party if it should be the one to take the lead in their enfranchisement. Our women will not toe a mark anywhere; they will think and act for themselves, and when they are enfranchised they will divide upon all political questions, as do intelligent, educated men.

I have tried the experiment of canvassing four States prior to Oregon, and in each State with the best canvass that it was possible for us to make we obtained a vote of one-third. One man out of every three men voted for the enfranchisement of the women of their households, while two voted against it. But we are proud to say that our splendid minority is always composed of the very best men of the State, and I think Senator PALMER will agree with me that the forty thousand men of Michigan who voted for the enfranchisement of the women of his State were really the picked men in intelligence, in culture, in morals, in standing, and in every direction.

It is too much to say that the majority of the voters in any State are superior, educated, and capable, or that they investigate every question thoroughly, and cast the ballot thereon intelligently. We all know that the majority of the voters of any State are not of that stamp. The vast masses of the people, the laboring classes, have all they can do in their struggle to get food and shelter for their families. They have very little time or opportunity to study great questions of constitutional law.

Because of this impossibility for women to canvass the States over and over to educate the rank and file of the voters we come to you to ask you to make it possible for the Legislatures of the thirty-eight States to settle the question, where we shall have a few representative men assembled before whom we can make our appeals and arguments.

This method of settling the question by the Legislatures is just as much in the line of States' rights as is that of the popular vote. The one question before you is, will you insist that a majority of the individual voters of every State must be converted before its women shall have the right to vote, or will you allow the matter to be settled by the representative men in the Legislatures of the several States? You need not fear that we shall get suffrage too quickly if Congress shall submit the proposition, for even then we shall have a hard time in going from Legislature to Legislature to secure the two-thirds votes of three-fourths of the States necessary to ratify the amendment. It may take twenty years after Congress has taken the initiative step to make action by the State Legislatures possible.

I pray you, gentlemen, that you will make your report to the Senate speedily. I know you are ready to make a favorable one. Some of our speakers may not have known this as well as I. I ask you to make a report and to bring it to a discussion and a vote on the floor of the Senate.

You ask me if we want to press this question to a vote provided there is not a majority to carry it. I say yes, because we want the reflex influence of the discussion and of the opinions of Senators to go back into the States to help us to educate the people of the States.

Senator LAPHAM. It would require a two-thirds vote in both the House and the Senate to submit the amendment to the State Legislatures for ratification.

Miss ANTHONY. I know that it requires a two-thirds vote of both Houses. But still, I repeat, even if you can not get the two-thirds vote, we ask you to report the bill and bring it to a discussion and a vote at the earliest day possible. We feel that this question should be brought before Congress at every session. We ask this little attention from Congressmen whose salaries are paid from the taxes; women do their share for the support of this great Government. We think we are entitled to two or three days of each session of Congress in both the Senate and House. Therefore I ask of you to help us to a discussion in the Senate this session. There is no reason why the Senate, composed of seventy-six of the most intelligent and liberty-loving men of the nation, shall not pass the resolution by a two-thirds vote. I really believe it will do so if the friends of this committee and on the floor of the Senate will champion the measure as earnestly as if it were to benefit themselves instead of their mothers and sisters.

Gentlemen, I thank you for this hearing granted, and I hope the telegraph wires will soon tell us that your report is presented, and that a discussion is inaugurated on the floor of the Senate.

The Solitude of Self

Elizabeth Cady Stanton

Commentary

The Senate rejected woman suffrage in 1887, and although committee hearings were held occasionally, no votes were taken again until 1914, when suffrage was again defeated. After the "Anthony Amendment" was finally ratified in 1920, the women's movement went into eclipse until the 1960s, when a new movement, variously called "feminism" or "women's liberation," began alleging the widespread existence of sexual discrimination in the workplace, sexual harassment on college campuses, male domination at home and similar complaints.

The new feminism is reminiscent of Elizabeth Stanton (1815-1902), whose rhetoric was so wide-ranging that some historians suspect she might have abandoned suffrage if her friend Anthony had not prevented it. At Anthony's insistence, Stanton served as National Woman Suffrage Association (NWSA) president until it merged with the American Woman Suffrage Association (AWSA) in 1890 (thereby healing the split within the movement). She then became president of the new National American Woman Suffrage Association (NAWSA).

The new NAWSA continued NWSA's practice of holding annual conventions in Washington so that leaders could present suffragist petitions to Congress and testify before any committees that might be holding hearings. According to the report of the 1892 convention in the *Woman's Journal* (founded earlier by Blackwell and Stone and now NAWSA's official newspaper), the House Judiciary Committee hearings were "unexpected." They were held on Monday morning, January 18, 1892, just as the convention was having its first main session. NAWSA's four major leaders (Stanton, Stone, Hooker and Anthony) missed the convention's opening session in order to testify. Perhaps because the hearings were "unexpected" (although this is not certain), Stanton's testimony consisted of the speech she delivered later to the convention.

Now 76 years old, Stanton insisted on not being re-elected NAWSA president, and her convention speech was regarded as a farewell address. It reached a wider audience of suffragists by being printed in the *Woman's Journal*

539

and some lesser-known suffragist papers under the title, "The Solitude of Self." Some historians say that Stanton repeated it on Wednesday to the Senate Select Committee on Woman Suffrage, but this is probably inaccurate. According to the *Journal*, time limitations were stringent, and NAWSA sent 18 delegates to give "brief" addresses. The 18 were listed in the *Journal*, and Stanton was not among them. The published version of the Senate Committee hearings do not include anything by Stanton, only statements by the 18, who were introduced by Anthony with the following remarks: "Mr. Chairman, we have here at this national gathering representatives from twenty-six States, though we do not propose within the limited time at your disposal to make twenty-six speeches, much as we would like to do it. Inasmuch as in the hearing last Monday morning before the Judiciary Committee of the House the veterans were heard, we propose this morning to present to you the younger women who are at work in the several States."

Even if Stanton did not address Senators, she had at least two more audiences: (1) Printed versions of the House hearings were circulated by sympathetic congressmen, thereby giving Stanton's speech a public reading audience; (2) the speech was resurrected by latter-day feminists, thereby giving it more recent audiences. The first resurrection was in 1910, when NAWSA published the speech as a pamphlet under the editorship of Harriet Stanton Blatch. It has appeared more recently in several anthologies, some of which have a "feminist" bent. Indeed, many recent feminists interpret the speech less as a persuasive discourse designed for her contemporaries than as a feminist discourse for more recent times.

Although interpretations of the speech vary considerably, textual variations are slight. The first two published texts were those in the *Journal* and the House hearings, and subsequent editions are based on one or the other. Most of the differences are a few minor stylistic ones. The only significant differences are (1) the first paragraph in the hearings is missing in the *Journal*; (2) the second paragraph of the quotation near the end of the hearings text is not set off in the *Journal* as part of the quotation, thereby giving the mistaken (?) impression that they were Stanton's words, not the person she was quoting; and (3) the hearings text does not carry the now-well-known title which is in the *Journal*, "The Solitude of Self."

In order to make available Stanton's introduction at the hearings, the following text is reproduced from *Hearing of the Woman Suffrage Association Before the* [House] Committee on the Judiciary, Monday, January 18, 1892.

Address of Mrs. Elizabeth Cady Stanton

Mr. Chairman and gentlemen of the committee: We have been speaking before Committees of the Judiciary for the last twenty years, and we have gone over all the arguments in favor of a sixteenth amendment which are familiar to all you gentlemen; therefore, it will not be necessary that I should repeat them again.

The point I wish plainly to bring before you on this occasion is the individuality of each human soul: our Protestant idea, the right of individual conscience and judgment—our republican idea, individual citizenship. In discussing the rights of woman, we are to consider, first, what belongs to her as an individual, in a world of her own, the arbiter of her own destiny, an imaginary Robinson Crusoe with her woman Friday on a solitary island. Her rights under such circumstances are to use all her faculties for her own safety and happiness.

Secondly, if we consider her as a citizen, as a member of a great nation, she must have the same rights as all other members, according to the fundamental principles of our Government.

Thirdly, viewed as a woman, an equal factor in civilization, her rights and duties are still the same—individual happiness and development.

Fourthly, it is only the incidental relations of life, such as mother, wife, sister, daughter, that may involve some special duties and training. In the usual discussion in regard to woman's sphere, such men as Herbert Spencer, Frederic Harrison, and Grant Allen uniformly subordinate her rights and duties as an individual, as a citizen, as a woman, to the necessities of these incidental relations, some of which a large class of women may never assume. In discussing the sphere of man we do not decide his rights as an individual, as a citizen, as a man by his duties as a father, a husband, a brother, or a son, relations some of which he may never fill. Moreover he would be better fitted for these very relations and whatever special work he might choose to do to earn his bread by the complete development of all his faculties as an individual.

Just so with woman. The education that will fit her to discharge the duties in the largest sphere of human usefulness will best fit her for whatever special work she may be compelled to do.

The isolation of every human soul and the necessity of self-dependence must give each individual the right to choose his own surroundings.

The strongest reason for giving women all the opportunities for higher education, for the full development of her faculties, forces of mind and body; for giving her the most enlarged freedom of thought and action; a complete emancipation from all forms of bondage, of custom, dependence, superstition; from all the crippling influences of fear, is the solitude and personal responsibility of her own individual life. The strongest reason why we ask for woman a voice in the government under which she lives; in the religion she is asked to believe; equality in social life, where she is the chief factor; a place in the trades and professions, where she may earn her bread, is because of her birthright to self-sovereignty; because, as an individual, she must rely on herself. No matter how much women prefer to lean, to be protected and supported, nor how much men desire to have them do so, they must make the voyage of life alone, and for safety in an emergency they must know something of the laws of navigation. To guide our own craft, we must be captain, pilot, engineer; with chart and compass to stand at the wheel; to watch the wind and waves and know when to take in the sail, and to read the signs in the firmament over all. It matters not whether the solitary voyager is man or woman. Nature having endowed them equally, leaves them to their own skill and judgment in the hour of danger, and, if not equal to the occasion, alike they perish.

To appreciate the importance of fitting every human soul for independent action, think for a moment of the immeasurable solitude of self. We come into the world alone, unlike all who have gone before us; we leave it alone under circumstances peculiar to ourselves. No mortal ever has been, no mortal ever will be like the soul just launched on the sea of life. There can never again be just such a combination of prenatal influences; never again just such environments as make up the infancy, youth, and manhood of this one. Nature never repeats herself, and the possibilities of one human soul will never be found in another. No one has ever found two blades of ribbon grass alike, and no one will ever find two human beings alike. Seeing, then, what must be the infinite diversity in human character, we can in a measure appreciate the loss to a nation when any large class of the people is uneducated and unrepresented in the government. We ask for the complete development of every individual, first, for his own benefit and happiness. In fitting out an army we give each soldier his own knapsack, arms, powder, his blanket, cup, knife, fork and spoon. We provide alike for all their individual necessities, then each man bears his own burden.

Again we ask complete individual development for the general good; for the consensus of the competent on the whole round of human interests; on all questions of national life, and here each man must bear his share of the general burden. It is sad to see how soon friendless children are left to bear their own burdens before they can analyze their feelings; before they can even tell their joys and sorrows, they are thrown on their own resources. The great lesson that nature seems to teach us at all ages is self-dependence, self-protection, self-support. What a touching instance of a child's solitude; of that hunger of the heart for love and recognition, in the case of the little girl who helped to dress a Christmas tree for the children of the family in which she served. On finding there was no present for herself she slipped away in the darkness and spent the night in an open field sitting on a stone, and when found in the morning was weeping as if her heart would break. No mortal will ever know the thoughts that passed through the mind of that friendless child in the long hours of that cold night, with only the silent stars to keep her company. The mention of her case in the daily papers moved many generous hearts to send her presents, but in the hours of her keenest suffering she was thrown wholly on herself for consolation.

In youth our most bitter disappointments, our brightest hopes and ambitions are known only to ourselves; even our friendship and love we never fully share with another; there is something of every passion in every situation we conceal. Even so in our triumphs and our defeats. The successful candidate for the Presidency and his opponent each have a solitude peculiarly his own, and good form forbids either to speak of his pleasure or regret. The solitude of the king on his throne and the prisoner in his cell differs in character and degree, but it is solitude nevertheless.

We ask no sympathy from others in the anxiety and agony of a broken friendship or shattered love. When death sunders our nearest ties, alone we sit in the shadow of our affliction. Alike mid the greatest triumphs and darkest tragedies of life we walk alone. On the divine heights of human attainments, eulogized and worshiped as a hero or saint, we stand alone. In ignorance, poverty, and vice, as a pauper or criminal, alone we starve or steal; alone we suffer the sneers and rebuffs of our fellows; alone we are hunted and hounded through dark courts and alleys, in by-ways and highways; alone we stand in the judgment seat; alone in the prison cell we lament our crimes and misfortunes; alone we expiate them on the gallows. In hours like these we realize the awful solitude of individual life, its pains, its penalties, its responsibilities; hours in which the youngest and most helpless are thrown on their own resources for guidance and consolation. Seeing then that life must ever be a march and a battle, that each soldier must be equipped for his own protection, it is the height of cruelty to rob the individual of a single natural right.

To throw obstacles in the way of a complete education is like putting out the eyes; to deny the rights of property, like cutting off the hands. To deny political equality is to rob the ostracised of all self-respect; of credit in the market place; of recompense in the world of work; of a voice in those who make and administer the law; a choice in the jury before whom they are tried, and in the judge who decides their punishment. Shakespeare's play of Titus and Andronicus contains a terrible satire on woman's position in the nineteenth century—"Rude men" (the play tells us) "seized the king's daughter, cut out her tongue, cut off her hands, and then bade her go call for water and wash her hands." What a picture of woman's position. Robbed of her natural rights, handicapped by law and custom at every turn, yet compelled to fight her own battles, and in the emergencies of life to fall back on herself for protection.

The girl of sixteen, thrown on the world to support herself, to make her own place in society, to resist the temptations that surround her and maintain a spotless integrity, must do all this by native force or superior education. She does not acquire this power by being trained to trust others and distrust herself. If she wearies of the struggle, finding it hard work to swim upstream, and allows herself to drift with the current, she will find plenty of company, but not one to share her misery in the hour of her deepest humiliation. If she tries to retrieve her position, to conceal the past, her life is hedged about with fears lest willing hands should tear the veil from what she fain would hide. Young and friendless, *she* knows the bitter solitude of self.

How the little courtesies of life on the surface of society, deemed so important from man towards woman, fade into utter insignificance in view of the deeper tragedies in which she must play her part alone, where no human aid is possible.

The young wife and mother, at the head of some establishment with a kind husband to shield her from the adverse winds of life, with wealth, fortune and position, has a certain harbor of safety, secure against the ordinary ills of life. But to manage a household, have a desirable influence in society, keep her friends and the affections of her husband, train her children and servants well, she must have rare common sense, wisdom, diplomacy, and a knowledge of human nature. To do all this she needs the cardinal virtues and the strong points of character that the most successful statesman possesses.

An uneducated woman, trained to dependence, with no resources in herself must make a failure of any position in life. But society says women do not need a knowledge of the world; the liberal training that experience in public life must give, all the advantages of collegiate education; but when for the lack of all this, the woman's happiness is wrecked, alone she bears her humiliation; and the solitude of the weak and the ignorant is indeed pitiable. In the wild chase for the prizes of life they are ground to powder.

In age, when the pleasures of youth are passed, children grown up, married and gone, the hurry and bustle of life in a measure over, when the hands are weary of active service, when the old armchair and the fireside are the chosen resorts, then men and women alike must fall back on their own resources. If they cannot find companionship in books, if they have no interest in the vital questions of the hour, no interest in watching the consummation of reforms, with which they might have been identified, they soon pass into their dotage. The more fully the faculties of the mind are developed and kept in use, the longer the period of vigor and active interest in all around us continues. If from a lifelong participation in public affairs a woman feels responsible for the laws regulating our system of education, the discipline of our jails and prisons, the sanitary condition of our private homes, public buildings, and thoroughfares, an interest in commerce, finance, our foreign relations, in any or all these questions, her solitude will at least be respectable, and she will not be driven to gossip or scandal for entertainment.

The chief reason for opening to every soul the doors to the whole round of human duties and pleasures is the individual development thus attained, the resources thus provided under all circumstances to mitigate the solitude that at times must come to everyone. I once asked Prince Krapotkin, a Russian nihilist, how he endured his long years in prison, deprived of books, pen, ink, and paper. "Ah," he said, "I thought out many questions in which I had a deep interest. In the pursuit of an idea I took no note of time. When tired of solving knotty problems I recited all the beautiful passages in prose or verse I had ever learned. I became acquainted with myself and my own resources. I had a world of my own, a vast empire, that no Russian jailor of Czar could invade." Such is the value of liberal thought and broad culture when shut off from all human companionship, bringing comfort and sunshine within even the four walls of a prison cell.

As women ofttimes share a similar fate, should they not have all the consolation that the most liberal education can give? Their suffering in the prisons of St. Petersburg; in the long, weary marches to Siberia, and in the mines, working side by side with men, surely call for all the self-support that the most exalted sentiments of heroism can give. When suddenly roused at midnight, with the startling cry of "fire! fire!" to find the house over their heads in flames, do women wait for men to point the way to safety? And are the men, equally bewildered and half suffocated with smoke, in a position to do more than try to save themselves?

At such times the most timid women have shown a courage and heroism in saving their husbands and children that has surprised everybody. Inasmuch, then, as woman shares equally the joys and sorrows of time and eternity, is it not the height of presumption in man to propose to represent her at the ballot box and the throne of grace, to do her voting in the state, her praying in the church, and to assume the position of high priest at the family altar?

Nothing strengthens the judgment and quickens the conscience like individual responsibility. Nothing adds such dignity to character as the recognition of one's self-sovereignty; the right to an equal place, everywhere conceded; a place earned by personal merit, not an artificial attainment, by inheritance, wealth, family, and position. Seeing, then, that the responsibilities of life rest equally on man and woman, that their destiny is the same, they need the same preparation for time and eternity. The talk of sheltering woman from the fierce storms of life is the sheerest mockery, for they beat on her from every point of the compass, just as they do on man, and with more fatal results, for he has been trained to protect himself, to resist, to conquer. Such are the facts in human experience, the responsibilities of individual sovereignty. Rich and poor, intelligent and ignorant, wise and foolish, virtuous and vicious, man and woman, it is ever the same, each soul must depend wholly on itself.

Whatever the theories may be of woman's dependence on man, in the supreme moments of her life he can not bear her burdens. Alone she goes to the gates of death to give life to every man that is born into the world. No one can share her fears, no one can mitigate her pangs; and if her sorrow is greater than she can bear, alone she passes beyond the gates into the vast unknown.

From the mountain tops of Judea, long ago, a heavenly voice bade His disciples "Bear ye one another's burdens," but humanity has not yet risen to that point of self-sacrifice, and if ever so willing, how few the burdens are that one soul can bear for another. In the highways of Palestine; in prayer and fasting on the solitary mountain top; in the Garden of Gethsemane; before the judgment seat of Pilate; betrayed by one of His trusted disciples at His last supper; in His agonies on the cross, even Jesus of Nazareth, in these last sad days on earth, felt the awful solitude of self. Deserted by man, in agony he cries, "My God! My God! why hast Thou forsaken me?" And so it ever must be in the conflicting scenes of life, in the long, weary march, each one walks alone. We may have many friends, love, kindness, sympathy, and charity to smoothe our pathway in everyday life, but in the tragedies and triumphs of human experience each mortal stands alone.

But when all artificial trammels are removed, and women are recognized as individuals, responsible for their own environments, thoroughly educated for all positions in life they may be called to fill; with all the resources in themselves that liberal thought and broad culture can give; guided by their own conscience and judgment; trained to self-protection by a healthy development of the muscular system and skill in the use of weapons of defense, and stimulated to self-support by a knowledge of the business world and the pleasure that pecuniary independence must ever give; when women are trained in this way they will, in a measure, be fitted for those hours of solitude that come alike to all, whether prepared or otherwise. As in our extremity we must depend on ourselves, the dictates of wisdom point to complete individual development.

In talking of education how shallow the argument, that each class must be educated for the special work it proposes to do, and all those faculties not needed in this special walk must lie dormant and utterly wither for want of use, when perhaps, these will be the very faculties needed in life's greatest emergencies. Some say, Where is the use of drilling girls in the languages, the sciences, in law, medicine, theology? As wives, mothers, housekeepers, cooks, they need a different curriculum from boys who are to fill all positions. The chief cooks in our great hotels and ocean steamers are men. In our large cities men run the bakeries; they make our bread, cake and pies. They manage the laundries; they are now considered our best milliners and dressmakers. Because some men fill these departments of usefulness, shall we regulate the curriculum in Harvard and Yale to their present necessities? If not, why this talk in our best colleges of a curriculum for girls who are crowding into the trades and professions; teachers in all our public schools, rapidly filling many lucrative and honorable positions in life? They are showing, too, their calmness and courage in the most trying hours of human experience.

You have probably all read in the daily papers of the terrible storm in the Bay of Biscay when a tidal wave made such havoc on the shore, wrecking vessels, unroofing houses, and carrying destruction everywhere. Among other buildings the woman's prison was demolished. Those who escaped saw men struggling to reach the shore. They promptly by clasping hands made a chain of themselves and pushed out into the sea, again and again, at the risk of their lives, until they had brought six men to shore, carried them to a shelter, and did all in their power for their comfort and protection.

What special school training could have prepared these women for this sublime moment in their lives? In times like this humanity rises above all college curriculums and recognizes Nature as the greatest of all teachers in the hour of danger and death. Women are already the equals of men in the whole realm of thought, in art, science, literature, and government. With telescopic vision they explore the starry firmament and bring back the history of the planetary world. With chart and compass they pilot ships across the mighty deep, and with skillful finger send electric messages around the globe. In galleries of art the beauties of nature and the virtues of humanity are immortalized by them on canvas and by their inspired touch dull blocks of marble are transformed into angels of light.

In music they speak again the language of Mendelssohn, Beethoven, Chopin, Schumann, and are worthy interpreters of their great thoughts. The poetry and novels of the century are theirs, and they have touched the keynote of reform in religion, politics, and social life. They fill the editor's and professor's chair, and plead at the bar of justice, walk the wards of the hospital, and speak from the pulpit and the platform; such is the type of womanhood that an enlightened public sentiment welcomes to-day, and such the triumph of the facts of life over the false theories of the past.

Is it, then, consistent to hold the developed woman of this day within the same narrow political limits as the dame with the spinning wheel and knitting needle occupied in the past? No! no! Machinery has taken the labors of woman as well as man on its tireless shoulders; the loom and the spinning wheel are but dreams of the past; the pen, the brush, the easel, the chisel, have taken their places, while the hopes and ambitions of women are essentially changed.

We see reason sufficient in the outer conditions of human beings for individual liberty and development, but when we consider the self dependence of every human soul we see the need of courage, judgment, and the exercise of every faculty of mind and body, strengthened and developed by use, in woman as well as man.

Whatever may be said of man's protecting power in ordinary conditions, mid all the terrible disasters by land and sea, in the supreme moments of danger, alone woman must ever meet the horrors of the situation; the Angel of Death even makes no royal pathway for her. Man's love and sympathy enter only into the sunshine of our lives. In that solemn solitude of self, that links us with the immeasurable and the eternal, each soul lives alone forever. A recent writer says:

> I remember once, in crossing the Atlantic, to have gone upon the deck of the ship at midnight, when a dense black cloud enveloped the sky, and the great deep was roaring madly under the lashes of demoniac winds. My feeling was not of danger or fear (which is a base surrender of the immortal soul), but of utter desolation and loneliness; a little speck of life shut in by a tremendous darkness. Again I remember to have climbed the slopes of the Swiss Alps, up beyond the point where vegetation ceases, and the stunted conifers no longer struggle against the unfeeling blasts. Around me lay a huge confusion of rocks, out of which the gigantic ice peaks shot into the measureless blue of the heavens, and again my only feeling was the awful solitude.
>
> And yet, there is a solitude, which each and every one of us has always carried with him more inaccessible than the ice-cold mountains, more profound than the midnight sea; the solitude of self. Our inner being, which we call ourself, no eye nor touch of man or angel has ever pierced. It is more hidden than the caves of the gnome; the sacred adytum of the oracle; the hidden chamber of eleusinian mystery, for to it only omniscience is permitted to enter.

Such is individual life. Who, I ask you, can take, dare take, on himself the rights, the duties, the responsibilities of another human soul?

Post-Civil War America
Rhetoric of Regional Conciliation and Racial Conflict

The New South

Henry W. Grady

Commentary

The Radical Reconstruction program could not endure. Southern whites gradually regained control of the ex-Confederate States. In 1877, the last army units were withdrawn, bringing Reconstruction to an end. Part of the reason for this dramatic development is that Northern attitudes changed. Wartime hatreds mellowed, newspaper stories of Southern "rebelliousness" diminished and attention turned to other pressing issues. Stories of Southern Radical corruption and oppression circulated in the North. Even many former abolitionists decided it was time to let "the South's natural leaders" resume control.

Yet Northern attitudes were ambivalent. Attitudes change slowly, and Northerners had not forgotten the old rhetoric of the "slavepower conspiracy" or the horrors of the recent war, which they still blamed the South for starting. Many Northern capitalists saw opportunities for investing in the South, which was struggling to revive its wartorn economy, but they feared that the Radicals might be right: perhaps the South was still "disloyal" and was simply biding its time until it could strike again.

The ambivalence was exemplified by the occasion at which Henry W. Grady (1850-1889) delivered his famous "The New South" oration. As a conciliatory move, the New England Society of New York City invited Grady to speak at its meeting on December 21, 1886. Grady was the first Southerner to have ever been invited to speak to the Society, which was organized in 1805. The audience, composed of 300 business and professional men, included several leading capitalists such as J. Pierpont Morgan. Some were considering Southern investments and all wondered about what Grady would say concerning their former enemy.

Although not known personally to his audience, Grady's reputation for regional conciliation preceded him. True, he came from a prominent Georgia family, and his father had been killed while in the Confederate army. Since 1879, Grady had been editor and part owner of the *Atlanta Constitution*, a medium through which he had been preaching the gospel of "the new South" — a slogan that was coming into use but was not yet as famous as Grady would soon make it. He had been urging his Southern readers to support agricultural diversification, industrialization and conciliation with the North.

If the choice of speaker was appropriate for the Society's goal of promoting regional conciliation, the arrangement of the program was not. Grady was the third of several speakers. The first was a famous Presbyterian preacher, Thomas Dewitt Talmage, who delivered an emotionally charged description of the return of the victorious Union armies after the war. The second was General William T. Sherman, famous for many reasons (including his outspoken contempt for journalists) but mostly for his march through Grady's native state. He began by saying, "I know the Civil War is uppermost in your minds," and, when he finished, the audience stood to sing a popular war song, "Marching Through Georgia."

Grady adapted so well to this difficult rhetorical situation that the audience was on its feet cheering even before he finished. Scores of newspapers were lavish in their praise, and "the new South" quickly became a popular slogan.

Although Grady had prepared his speech in advance, he had not written it verbatim. He made several impromptu revisions to meet the exigencies of the situation. A newspaper reporter transcribed the speech, which was published in several papers and, in slightly revised form, in the Society's yearbook for 1886. The following text, which derives from the yearbook, is reproduced photographically from A. Craig Baird, *American Public Addresses, 1740-1952* (New York: McGraw-Hill, 1956), pp. 181-188.

The New South

"There was a South of slavery and secession—that South is dead. There is a South of union and freedom—that South, thank God, is living, breathing, growing every hour." These words, delivered from the immortal lips of Benjamin H. Hill, at Tammany Hall in 1866, true then, and truer now, I shall make my text to-night.

Mr. President and Gentlemen: Let me express to you my appreciation of the kindness by which I am permitted to address you. I make this abrupt acknowledgment advisedly, for I feel that if, when I raise my provincial voice in this ancient and august presence, I could find courage for no more than the opening sentence, it would be well if, in that sentence, I had met in a rough sense my obligation as a guest, and had perished, so to speak, with courtesy on my lips and grace in my heart. [*Laughter.*] Permitted through your kindness to catch my second wind, let me say that I appreciate the significance of being the first Southerner to speak at this board, which bears the substance, if it surpasses the semblance, of original New England hospitality [*Applause*], and honors a sentiment that in turn honors you, but in which my personality is lost, and the compliment to my people made plain. [*Laughter.*]

I bespeak the utmost stretch of your courtesy to-night. I am not troubled about those from whom I come. You remember the man whose wife sent him to a neighbor with a pitcher of milk, and who, tripping on the top step, fell, with such casual interruptions as the landing afforded, into the basement; and while picking himself up had the pleasure of hearing his wife call out: "John, did you break the pitcher?"

"No, I didn't," said John, "but I be dinged if I don't!" [*Laughter.*]

So, while those who call to me from behind may inspire me with energy if not with courage, I ask an indulgent hearing from you. I beg that you will bring your full faith in American fairness and frankness to judgment upon what I shall say. There was an old preacher once who told some boys of the Bible lesson he was going to read in the morning. The boys finding the place, glued together the connecting pages. [*Laughter.*] The next morning he read on the bottom of one page: "When Noah was one hundred and twenty years old he took unto himself a wife, who was"—then turning the page—"one hundred and forty cubits long [*Laughter*], forty cubits wide, built of gopher-wood [*Laughter*], and covered with pitch inside and out." [*Loud and continued laughter.*] He was naturally puzzled at this. He read it again, verified it, and then said: "My friends, this is the first time I ever met this in the Bible, but I accept it as an evidence of the assertion that we are fearfully and wonderfully made." [*Immense laughter.*] If I could get you to hold such faith to-night I could proceed cheerfully to the task I otherwise approach with a sense of consecration.

Pardon me one word, Mr. President, spoken for the sole purpose of getting into the volumes that go out annually freighted with the rich eloquence of your speakers—the fact that the Cavalier as well as the Puritan was on the continent in its early days, and that he was "up and able to be about." [*Laughter.*] I have read your books carefully and I find no mention of that fact, which seems to me an important one for preserving a sort of historical equilibrium if for nothing else.

Let me remind you that the Virginia Cavalier first challenged France on this continent—that Cavalier John Smith gave New England its very name, and was so pleased with the job that he has been handing his own name around ever since—and that while Miles Standish was cutting off men's ears for courting a girl without her parents' consent, and forbade men to kiss their wives on Sunday, the Cavalier was courting everything in sight, and that the Almighty had vouchsafed great increase to the Cavalier colonies, the huts in the wilderness being full as the nests in the woods.

But having incorporated the Cavalier as a fact in your charming little books I shall let him work out his own salvation, as he has always done with engaging gallantry, and we will hold no controversy as to his merits. Why should we? Neither Puritan nor Cavalier long survived as such. The virtues and traditions of both happily still live for the inspiration of their sons and the saving of the old fashion. [*Applause.*] But both Puritan and Cavalier were lost in the storm of the first Revolution; and the American citizen, supplanting both and stronger than either, took possession of the Republic bought by their common blood and fashioned to wisdom, and charged himself with teaching men government and establishing the voice of the people as the voice of God. [*Applause.*]

My friend Dr. Talmadge has told you that the typical American has yet to come. Let me tell you that he has already come. [*Applause.*] Great types like valuable plants are slow to flower and fruit. But from the union of these colonist Puritans and Cavaliers, from the straightening of their purposes and the crossing of their blood, slow perfecting through a century, came he who stands as the first typical American, the first who comprehended within himself all the strength and gentleness, all the majesty and grace of this Republic—Abraham Lincoln. [*Loud and continued applause.*] He was the sum of Puritan and Cavalier, for in his ardent nature were fused the virtues of both, and in the depths of his great soul the faults of both were lost. [*Renewed applause.*] He was greater than Puritan, greater than Cavalier, in that he was American [*Renewed applause.*] and that in his homely form were first gathered the vast and thrilling forces of his ideal government—charging it with such tremendous meaning and so elevating it above human suffering that martyrdom, though infamously aimed, came as a fitting crown to a life consecrated from the cradle to human liberty. [*Loud and prolonged cheering.*] Let us, each cherishing the traditions and honoring his fathers, build with reverent hands to the type of this simple but sublime life, in which all types are honored; and in our common glory as Americans there will be plenty and to spare for your forefathers and for mine. [*Renewed cheering.*]

In speaking to the toast with which you have honored me, I accept the term, "The New South," as in no sense disparaging to the Old. Dear to me, sir, is the home of my childhood and the traditions of my people. I would not, if I could, dim the glory they won in peace and war, or by word or deed take aught from the splendor and grace of their civilization —never equaled and, perhaps, never to be equaled in its chivalric strength and grace. There is a New South, not through protest against the Old, but because of new conditions, new adjustments and, if you please, new ideas and aspirations. It is to this that I address myself, and to the consideration of which I hasten lest it become the Old South before I get to it. Age does not endow all things with strength and virtue, nor are all new things to be despised. The shoemaker who put over his door "John Smith's shop. Founded in 1760," was more than matched by his young rival across the street who hung out this sign: "Bill Jones. Established 1886. No old stock kept in this shop."

Dr. Talmadge has drawn for you, with a master's hand, the picture of your returning armies. He has told you how, in the pomp and circumstance of war, they came back to you, marching with proud and victorious tread, reading their glory in a nation's eyes! Will you bear with me while I tell you of another army that sought its home at the close of the late war—an army that marched home in defeat and not in victory—in pathos and not in splendor, but in glory that equaled yours, and to hearts as loving as ever welcomed heroes home. Let me picture to you the footsore Confederate soldier, as, buttoning up in his faded gray jacket the parole which was to bear testimony to his children of his fidelity and faith, he turned his face southward from Appomattox in April, 1865. Think of him as ragged, half-starved, heavy-hearted, enfeebled by want and wounds; having fought to exhaustion, he surrenders his gun, wrings the hands of his comrades in silence, and lifting his tear-stained and pallid face for the last time to the graves that dot the old Virginia hills, pulls his gray cap over his brow and begins the slow and painful journey. What does he find—let me ask you, who went to your homes eager to find in the welcome you had justly earned, full payment for four years' sacrifice—what does he find when, having followed the battle-stained cross against overwhelming odds, dreading death not half so much as surrender, he reaches the home he left so prosperous and beautiful? He finds his house in ruins, his farm devastated, his slaves free, his stock killed, his barns empty, his trade destroyed, his money worthless; his social system, feudal in its magnificence, swept away; his people without law or legal status, his comrades slain, and the burdens of others heavy on his shoulders. Crushed by defeat, his very traditions are gone; without money, credit, employment, material or training; and, besides all this, confronted with the gravest problem that ever met human intelligence—the establishing of a status for the vast body of his liberated slaves.

What does he do—this hero in gray with a heart of gold? Does he sit down in sullenness and despair? Not for a day. Surely God, who had stripped him of his prosperity, inspired him in his adversity. As ruin was never before so overwhelming, never was restoration swifter. The soldier stepped from the trenches into the furrow; horses that had charged Federal guns march before the plow, and fields that ran red with human blood in April were green with the harvest in June; women reared in luxury cut up their dresses and made breeches for their husbands, and, with a patience and heroism that fit women always as a garment, gave their hands to work. There was little bitterness in all this. Cheerfulness and frankness prevailed. "Bill Arp" struck the keynote when he said: "Well, I killed as many of them as they did of me, and now I am going to work." (*Laughter and applause.*) Or the soldier returning home after defeat and roasting some corn on the roadside, who made the remark to his comrades: "You may leave the South if you want to, but I am going to Sandersville, kiss my wife and raise a crop, and if the Yankees fool with me any more I will whip 'em again." [*Renewed applause.*] I want to say to General Sherman—who is considered an able man in our hearts, though some people think he is a kind of careless man about fire—that from the ashes he left us in 1864 we have raised a brave and beautiful city; that somehow or other we have caught the sunshine in the bricks and mortar of our homes, and have builded therein not one ignoble prejudice or memory. [*Applause.*]

But in all this what have we accomplished? What is the sum of our work? We have found out that in the general summary the free negro counts more than he did as a slave. We have planted the schoolhouse on the hilltop and made it free to white and black. We have sowed towns and cities in the place of theories and put business above politics. [*Applause.*] We have challenged your spinners in Massachusetts and your iron-makers in Pennsylvania. We have learned that the $400,000,000 annually received from our cotton crop will make us rich, when the supplies that make it are home-raised. We have reduced the commercial rate of interest from twenty-four to six per cent, and are floating four per cent bonds. We have learned that one Northern immigrant is worth fifty foreigners, and have smoothed the path to southward, wiped out the place where Mason and Dixon's line used to be, and hung our latch-string out to you and yours. [*Prolonged cheers.*] We have reached the point that marks perfect harmony in every household, when the husband confesses that the pies which his wife cooks are as good as those his mother used to bake; and we admit that the sun shines as brightly and the moon as softly as it did "before the war." [*Laughter.*] We have established thrift in city and country. We have fallen in love with work. We have restored comfort to homes from which culture and elegance never departed. We have let economy take root and spread among us as rank as the crabgrass which sprang from Sherman's cavalry camps, until we are ready to lay odds on the Georgia Yankee, as he manufactures relics of the battlefield in a one-story shanty and squeezes pure olive oil out of his cotton-seed, against any down-easter that ever swapped wooden nutmegs for flannel sausages in the valleys of Vermont. [*Loud and continuous laughter.*] Above all, we know that we have achieved in these "piping times of peace" a fuller independence for the South than that which our fathers sought to win in the forum by their eloquence or compel on the field by their swords. [*Loud applause.*]

It is a rare privilege, sir, to have had part, however humble, in this work. Never was nobler duty confided to human hands than the uplifting and upbuilding of the prostrate and bleeding South, misguided perhaps, but beautiful in her suffering, and honest, brave and generous always. [*Applause.*] In the record of her social, industrial, and political illustrations we await with confidence the verdict of the world.

But what of the negro? Have we solved the problem he presents or progressed in honor and equity towards the solution? Let the record speak to the point. No section shows a more prosperous laboring population than the negroes of the South; none in fuller sympathy with the employing and land-owning class. He shares our school fund, has the fullest protection of our laws and the friendship of our people. Self-interest, as well as honor, demand that he should have this. Our future, our very existence depend upon our working out this problem in full and exact justice. We understand that when Lincoln signed the Emancipation Proclamation, your victory was assured; for he then committed you to the cause of human liberty, against which the arms of man cannot prevail [*Applause*]; while those of our statesmen who trusted to make slavery the cornerstone of the Confederacy doomed us to defeat as far as they could, committing us to a cause that reason could not defend or the sword maintain in the sight of advancing civilization. [*Renewed applause.*] Had Mr. Toombs said, which he did not say, that he would call the roll of his slaves at the foot of Bunker Hill, he would have been foolish, for he might have known that whenever slavery became entangled in war it must perish, and that the chattel in human flesh ended forever in New England when your fathers—not to be blamed for parting with what didn't pay—sold their slaves to our fathers—not to be praised for knowing a paying thing when they saw it. [*Laughter.*] The relations of the Southern people with the negro are close and cordial. We remember with what fidelity for four years he guarded our defenceless women and children, whose husbands and fathers were fighting against his freedom. To his eternal credit be it said that whenever he struck a blow for his own liberty he fought in open battle, and when at last he raised his black and humble hands that the shackles might be struck off, those hands were innocent of wrong against his helpless charges, and worthy to be taken in loving grasp by every man who honors loyalty and devotion. [*Applause.*] Ruffians have maltreated him, rascals have misled him, philanthropists established a bank for him, but the South, with the North, protects against injustice to this simple and sincere people. To liberty and enfranchisement is as far as law can carry the negro. The rest must be left to conscience and common sense. It should be left to those among whom his lot is cast, with whom he is indissolubly connected and whose prosperity depends upon their possessing his intelligent sympathy and confidence. Faith has been kept with him in spite of caluminous assertions to the contrary by those who assume to speak for us or by frank opponents. Faith will be kept with him in the future, if the South holds her reason and integrity. [*Applause.*]

But have we kept faith with you? In the fullest sense, yes. When Lee surrendered—I don't say when Johnston surrendered, because I understand he still alludes to the time when he met General Sherman last as the time when he "determined to abandon any further prosecution of the struggle"—when Lee surrendered, I say, and Johnston quit, the South became, and has since been, loyal to this Union. We fought hard enough to know that we were whipped, and in perfect frankness accepted as final the arbitrament of the sword to which we had appealed. The South found her jewel in the toad's head of defeat. The shackles that had held her in narrow limitations fell forever when the shackles of the negro slave were broken. [*Applause.*] Under the old regime the negroes were

slaves to the South, the South was a slave to the system. The old plantation, with its simple police regulation and its feudal habit, was the only
type possible under slavery. Thus we gathered in the hands of a splendid
and chivalric oligarchy the substance that should have been diffused
among the people, as the rich blood, under certain artificial conditions,
is gathered at the heart, filling that with affluent rapture, but leaving
the body chill and colorless. [*Applause.*]

The Old South rested everything on slavery and agriculture, unconscious that these could neither give nor maintain healthy growth. The
New South presents a perfect democracy, the oligarchs leading in the
popular movement—a social system compact and closely knitted, less
splendid on the surface but stronger at the core—a hundred farms for
every plantation, fifty homes for every palace, and a diversified industry
that meets the complex needs of this complex age.

The New South is enamored of her new work. Her soul is stirred with
the breath of a new life. The light of a grander day is falling fair on her
face. She is thrilling with the consciousness of growing power and
prosperity. As she stands upright, full-statured and equal among the
people of the earth, breathing the keen air and looking out upon the
expanding horizon, she understands that her emancipation came because
in the inscrutable wisdom of God her honest purpose was crossed and her
brave armies were beaten. [*Applause.*]

This is said in no spirit of time-serving or apology. The South has
nothing for which to apologize. She believes that the late struggle between the States was war and not rebellion, revolution and not conspiracy, and that her convictions were as honest as yours. I should be
unjust to the dauntless spirit of the South and to my own convictions if I
did not make this plain in this presence. The South has nothing to take
back. In my native town of Athens is a monument that crowns its central
hills—a plain, white shaft. Deep cut into its shining side is a name dear
to me above the names of men, that of a brave and simple man who died
in brave and simple faith. Not for all the glories of New England—from
Plymouth Rock all the way—would I exchange the heritage he left me in
his soldier's death. To the foot of that shaft I shall send my children's
children to reverence him who ennobled their name with his heroic
blood. But, sir, speaking from the shadow of that memory, which I
honor as I do nothing else on earth, I say that the cause in which he
suffered and for which he gave his life was adjudged by higher and fuller
wisdom than his or mine, and I am glad that the omniscient God held the
balance of battle in His Almighty hand, and that human slavery was
swept forever from American soil—the American Union saved from the
wreck of war. [*Loud applause.*]

This message, Mr. President, comes to you from consecrated ground.
Every foot of the soil about the city in which I live is sacred as a battle-
ground of the Republic. Every hill that invests it is hallowed to you by
the blood of your brothers, who died for your victory, and doubly hal-

lowed to us by the blood of those who died hopeless, but undaunted, in defeat—sacred soil to all of us, rich with memories that make us purer and stronger and better, silent but stanch witnesses in its red desolation of the matchless valor of American hearts and the deathless glory of American arms—speaking an eloquent witness in its white peace and prosperity to the indissoluble union of American States and the imperishable brotherhood of the American people. [*Immense cheering.*]

Now, what answer has New England to this message? Will she permit the prejudices of war to remain in the hearts of the conquerors, when it has died in the hearts of the conquered? [*Cries of "No! No!"*] Will she transmit this prejudice to the next generation, that in their hearts, which never felt the generous ardor of conflict, it may perpetuate itself? [*"No! No!"*] Will she withhold, save in strained courtesy, the hand which straight from his soldier's heart Grant offered to Lee at Appomattox? Will she make the vision of a restored and happy people, which gathered above the couch of your dying captain, filling his heart with grace, touching his lips with praise and glorifying his path to the grave; will she make this vision on which the last sight of his expiring soul breathed a benediction, a cheat and a delusion? [*Tumultuous cheering and shouts of "No! No!"*] If she does, the South, never abject in asking for comradeship, must accept with dignity its refusal; but if she does not; if she accepts in frankness and sincerity this message of goodwill and friendship, then will the prophecy of Webster, delivered in this very Society forty years ago amid tremendous applause, be verified in its fullest and final sense, when he said: "Standing hand to hand and clasping hands, we should remain united as we have been for sixty years, citizens of the same country, members of the same government, united, all united now and united forever. There have been difficulties, contentions, and controversies, but I tell you that in my judgment

> Those opposed eyes,
> Which like the meteors of a troubled heaven,
> All of one nature, of one substance bred,
> Did lately meet in th' intestine shock,
> Shall now, in mutual well-beseeming ranks,
> March all one way.

[*Prolonged applause.*]

Excerpt from Oration on the Life, Character and Public Service of the Hon. John C. Calhoun

L. Q. C. Lamar

Commentary

Although many white Southerners agreed that a "new South" was necessary, they found it psychologically difficult to adapt to radically changed circumstances. They had lost the war, had their slaves freed, seen their economy ruined and suffered the humiliation of Reconstruction. They needed a rhetoric that would restore their self-esteem.

Ceremonial occasions served as a major vehicle for such rhetoric. Epideictic orators spoke at a countless number of reunions of the United Confederate Veterans (formed in 1889) and other veterans' meetings. They also addressed thousands of listeners when monuments were commemorated to the "Great Heroes" of the "Lost Cause." They explained that the war had been fought not to protect slavery (which had been foisted on the South by greedy Yankee traders), but to defend the Constitution and to protect liberty — which they had ultimately succeeded in doing despite the loss of the war. They also developed an idealized image of the Old South, in which "darkies" sang as they worked in the beautiful fields of cotton. "Cavaliers" were as noble and "ladies" as genteel as the most heroic figures of the Middle Ages. Slaves and masters loved one another, and everyone was happy.

The following illustration of the myth of the Old South is taken from an oration delivered on April 26, 1887 at the unveiling of a statue of John C. Calhoun. The speaker's unusual name, Lucius Quintus Cincinnatus Lamar (1825-1893), was apparently given to him because his father was exceptionally fond of classical literature. An outspoken secessionist as early as 1850, he had served in the Confederate army and diplomatic corps. After the war, he was a law professor at the University of Mississippi until resigning in protest after the governor packed the board of trustees with Radicals. After being elected to Congress in 1872, Lamar worked for regional conciliation, most notably when he delivered a eulogy for the political abolitionist and Radical, Charles Sumner, in 1874. He later served in the Senate, and, at the time of his speech on Calhoun, he was secretary of the interior. The excerpt is reproduced from *A History of the Calhoun Monument at Charleston, S. C.* (Charleston: Lucas, Richardson & Co., 1888), pp. 64-65.

Excerpt from Oration on the Life, Character and Public Service of the Hon. John C. Calhoun

When not in the actual discharge of his official duties he spent his time in retirement at his private home at Fort Hill. He was occupied in agriculture, in which he took the deepest interest. Would that I had the power to portray a Southern planter's home! The sweet and noble associations, the pure, refining and elevating atmosphere of a household presided over by a Southern matron; the tranquil yet active occupations of a large land owner — full of interest and high moral responsibilities; the alliance between man's intellect and nature's laws of production; the hospitality, heartfelt, simple and generous. The Southern planter was far from being the self-indulgent, indolent, coarse and overbearing person that he has sometimes been pictured. He was, in general, careful, patient, provident, industrious, forbearing, and yet firm and determined. These were the qualities which enabled him to take a race of untamed savages, with habits that could only inspire disgust, with no arts, no single tradition of civilization, and out of such a people to make the finest body of agricultural and domestic laborers that the world has ever seen; and, indeed, to elevate them in the scale of rational existence to such a height as to cause them to be deemed fit for admission into the charmed circle of American freedom, and to be clothed with the rights and duties of American citizenship.

The Southern planter penetrated the dense forests, the tangled brake, the gloomy wilderness of our river swamps, where pestilence had its abode, and there, day by day and year by year, amidst exposure, hardship and sickness, his foresight, his prudence, his self-reliance, his adaptation of means to ends were called into requisition. In the communion with himself, in the opportunities for continued study, and in the daily and yearly provision for a numerous body of dependents — for all of whom he felt himself responsible, about whom his anxieties were ever alive, whose tasks he apportioned and whose labors he directed — he was educated in those faculties and personal qualities which enabled him to emerge from his solitude and preside in the County Court, or become a member of his State Legislature; to discharge the duties of local magistracy, or to take his place in the National councils.

The solution of the enigma of the so-called slave power may be sought here.

Its basis lay in that cool, vigorous judgment and unerring sense applicable to the ordinary affairs and intercourse of men which the Southern mode of life engendered and fostered. The habits of industry, firmness of purpose, fidelity to dependents, self-reliance, and the sentiment of justice in all the various relations of life which were necessary to the management of a well-ordered plantation, fitted men to guide legislatures and command armies.

In confirmation of what I say, I have only to point to the fact that it was in such communities as these that a Washington, a Jackson, a Taylor, a Lee, and a host of others, acquired those qualities which enabled them, in the position in which their country placed them, to add such undying lustre to the American name. It was in such communities that men like Jefferson, Madison, Monroe, Polk, Lowndes, Calhoun, Clay, Macon, Marshall, Taney and many others whom I could mention, acquired those characteristics which their countrymen, both North and South, instinctively discerned whenever they were "called upon to face some awful moment to which Heaven has joined great issues, good or bad, for human kind."

Cotton States Exposition Address

Booker T. Washington

Commentary

Southern white ambivalence about the need for a New South and the love of a mythologized Old South was reflected in disparate racial views. Almost all agreed that blacks were inferior and should be disenfranchised, but they differed on the causes of the inferiority. So-called "culturalists" argued that it was due to generations of slavery and inadequate education. Some paternalistic culturalists supported programs that were designed to help blacks become educated and economically self-sufficient. Others believed in the innate, biological inferiority of blacks. Drawing upon the new biological theory of evolution, some speakers and writers argued that blacks were lower on the evolutionary scale. Many whites, especially those of the lower classes, were uninterested in scientific argument. They *knew* that blacks were inferior.

Prejudice prevailed long before emancipation, but whites being faced with postwar economic dislocations and a host of other problems used the newly freed blacks as scapegoats. They favored rigid enforcement of segregation laws. They opposed the education of blacks, claiming that it made them "uppity" as well as encouraged their natural tendency to be lazy. In its extreme form, their prejudice was reflected in the growing number of lynchings.

The situation for Southern blacks would have been desperate even in the absence of racial prejudice. The postwar economy was in a shambles. Many of the old plantations were broken up and fell into the hands of merchants who rented land to small tenant farmers or sharecroppers. Many lived more or less at a subsistence level. The price of their major cash crop, cotton, declined disastrously. Even white sharecroppers had great difficulty improving their situation. Faced with inadequate education and prejudice, few blacks could do more than till a small plot of rented land, live in a shack and go further into debt as they maintained an incredibly low standard of living.

How should blacks respond to their desperate situation? Who should be their leaders? Frederick Douglass (1817?-1895) had long been the acknowledged leader, but he was nearing the end of his career by the time Reconstruction ceased. Leadership gradually passed to Booker T. Washington (1856?-1915), who was born a slave in Virginia. After emancipation, the youngster worked as a day laborer while attending night school. In 1875, he graduated from Hampton Institute, a technical school established after the war by a Union general. After short stints as a school teacher and postgraduate student, Washington returned to Hampton in 1879. In 1881, he became principal of the Tuskegee Normal and Industrial Institute in Alabama, where he remained until his death.

Although Washington opposed disenfranchisement and segregation, he seldom spoke publicly against them. He viewed economic advancement as the key to black progress. It was not only a desirable goal, but also the means of lessening white hostility. Economic advancement was, in turn, dependent on education, especially technical education.

The same basic philosophy pervaded the many speeches and writings which Washington presented to blacks and whites, but the emphasis differed with the two audiences. Speaking frequently to black students and off-campus groups of black adults, he stressed the importance of technical education and preached the old Puritan doctrine of hard work. Nothing would be accomplished by protesting discrimination. Racial harmony would come only after blacks advanced themselves to the point at which they would gain white respect, and whites then would recognize that the two races were interdependent. In his many fund-raising efforts and other discourses addressed to white audiences, Washington emphasized that white advancement was inextricably linked to black progress. He presented evidence of what blacks were doing to improve themselves. Keenly aware of the criticism that education made blacks lazy and rebellious, he described the Tuskegee program and justified its technical orientation as the best method of promoting advancement.

Washington's best-known speech, delivered at the opening of the Cotton States Exposition on September 18, 1895, was unusual in that it was delivered to both races. Held in Atlanta, the Exposition was organized by New South promoters to publicize Southern economic progress and attract investment. It was attended by hundreds of prominent citizens, as well as thousands of common people of both races. Washington was the only black speaker, and his oration received nationwide publicity. The text is reproduced photographically from A. Craig Baird, *American Public Addresses, 1740-1952* (New York: McGraw-Hill, 1956), pp. 189-192.

Cotton States Exposition Address

MR. PRESIDENT AND GENTLEMEN OF THE BOARD OF DIRECTORS AND CITIZENS: One-third of the population of the South is of the Negro race.

No enterprise seeking the material, civil, or moral welfare of this section can disregard this element of our population and reach the highest success. I but convey to you, Mr. President and Directors, the sentiment of the masses of my race when I say that in no way have the value and manhood of the American Negro been more fittingly and generously recognized than by the managers of this magnificent Exposition at every stage of its progress. It is a recognition that will do more to cement the friendship of the two races than any occurrence since the dawn of our freedom.

Not only this, but the opportunity here afforded will awaken among us a new era of industrial progress. Ignorant and inexperienced, it is not strange that in the first years of our new life we began at the top instead of at the bottom; that a seat in Congress or the state legislature was more sought than real estate or industrial skill; that the political convention or stump speaking had more attractions than starting a dairy farm or truck garden.

A ship lost at sea for many days suddenly sighted a friendly vessel. From the mast of the unfortunate vessel was seen a signal, "Water, water; we die of thirst!" The answer from the friendly vessel at once came back, "Cast down your bucket where you are." And a third and fourth signal for water was answered, "Cast down your bucket where you are." The captain of the distressed vessel, at last heeding the injunction, cast down his bucket, and it came up full of fresh, sparkling water from the mouth of the Amazon River. To those of my race who depend on bettering their condition in a foreign land or who underestimate the importance of cultivating friendly relations with the Southern white man, who is their next-door neighbour, I would say: "Cast down your bucket where you are"—cast it down in making friends in every manly way of the people of all races by whom we are surrounded.

Cast it down in agriculture, mechanics, in commerce, in domestic service, and in the professions. And in this connection it is well to bear in mind that whatever other sins the South may be called to bear, when it comes to business, pure and simple, it is in the South that the Negro is given a man's chance in the commercial world, and in nothing is this Exposition more eloquent than in emphasizing this chance. Our greatest danger is that in the great leap from slavery to freedom we may overlook the fact that the masses of us are to live by the productions of our hands, and fail to keep in mind that we shall prosper in proportion as we learn to dignify and glorify common labour and put brains and skill into the common occupations of life; shall prosper in proportion as we learn to draw the line between the superficial and the substantial, the ornamental gew-gaws of life and the useful. No race can prosper till it learns that there is as much dignity in tilling a field as in writing a poem. It is at the bottom of life we must begin, and not at the top. Nor should we permit our grievances to overshadow our opportunities.

To those of the white race who look to the incoming of those of foreign birth and strange tongue and habits for the prosperity of the South, were I permitted I would repeat what I say to my own race, "Cast down your bucket where you are." Cast it down among the eight millions of Negroes whose habits you know, whose fidelity and love you have tested in days when to have proved treacherous meant the ruin of your firesides. Cast down your bucket among these people who have, without strikes and labour wars, tilled your fields, cleared your forests, builded your railroads and cities, and brought forth treasures from the bowels of the earth, and helped make possible this magnificent representation of the progress of the South. Casting down your bucket among my people, helping and encouraging them as you are doing on these grounds, and to education of head, hand, and heart, you will find that they will buy your surplus land, make blossom the waste places in your fields, and run your factories. While doing this, you can be sure in the future, as in the past, that you and your families will be surrounded by the most patient, faithful, law-abiding, and unresentful people that the world has seen. As we have proved our loyalty to you in the past, in nursing your children, watching by the sick-bed of your mothers and fathers, and often following them with tear-dimmed eyes to their graves, so in the future, in our humble way, we shall stand by you with a devotion that no foreigner can approach, ready to lay down our lives, if need be, in defence of yours, interlacing our industrial, commercial, civil, and religious life with yours in a way that shall make the interests of both races one. In all things that are purely social we can be as separate as the fingers, yet one as the hand in all things essential to mutual progress.

There is no defence or security for any of us except in the highest intelligence and development of all. If anywhere there are efforts tending to curtail the fullest growth of the Negro, let these efforts be turned into stimulating, encouraging, and making him the most useful and intelligent citizen. Effort or means so invested will pay a thousand per cent interest. These efforts will be twice blessed—"blessing him that gives and him that takes."

There is no escape through law of man or God from the inevitable:—

> The laws of changeless justice bind
> Oppressor with oppressed;
> And close as sin and suffering joined
> We march to fate abreast.

Nearly sixteen millions of hands will aid you in pulling the load upward; or they will pull against you the load downward. We shall constitute one-third and more of the ignorance and crime of the South, or one-third its intelligence and progress; we shall contribute one-third to the business and industrial prosperity of the South, or we shall prove a veritable body of death, stagnating, depressing, retarding every effort to advance the body politic.

Gentlemen of the Exposition, as we present to you our humble effort at an exhibition of our progress, you must not expect overmuch. Starting thirty years ago with ownership here and there in a few quilts and pumpkins and chickens (gathered from miscellaneous sources), remember the path that has led from these to the inventions and production of agricultural implements, buggies, steam-engines, newspapers, books, statuary, carving, paintings, the management of drug-stores and banks, has not been trodden without contact with thorns and thistles. While we take pride in what we exhibit as a result of our independent efforts, we do not for a moment forget that our part in this exhibition would fall far short of your expectations but for the constant help that has come to our educational life, not only from the Southern states, but especially from Northern philanthropists, who have made their gifts a constant stream of blessing and encouragement.

The wisest among my race understand that the agitation of questions of social equality is the extremest folly, and that progress in the enjoyment of all the privileges that will come to us must be the result of severe and constant struggle rather than of artificial forcing. No race that has anything to contribute to the markets of the world is long in any degree ostracised. It is important and right that all privileges of the law be ours, but it is vastly more important that we be prepared for the exercises of these privileges. The opportunity to earn a dollar in a factory just now is worth infinitely more than the opportunity to spend a dollar in an opera-house.

In conclusion, may I repeat that nothing in thirty years has given us more hope and encouragement, and drawn us so near to you of the white race, as this opportunity offered by the Exposition; and here bending, as it were, over the altar that represents the results of the struggles of your race and mine, both starting practically empty-handed three decades ago, I pledge that in your effort to work out the great and intricate problem which God has laid at the doors of the South, you shall have at all times the patient, sympathetic help of my race; only let this be constantly in mind, that, while from representations in these buildings of the product of field, of forest, of mine, of factory, letters, and art, much good will come, yet far above and beyond material benefits will be that higher good, that, let us pray God, will come, in a blotting out of sectional differences and racial animosities and suspicions, in a determination to administer absolute justice, in a willing obedience among all classes to the mandates of law. This, this, coupled with our material prosperity, will bring into our beloved South a new heaven and a new earth.

Of Mr. Booker T. Washington and Others

W. E. B. DuBois

Commentary

In the same year that Washington delivered his Atlanta address, the young W.E.B. DuBois (1868-1963) received his Ph.D. degree. Originally from western Massachusetts, DuBois (according to his own account) was unaware of racial prejudice until philanthropists sent him to Fisk, a Southern black university, instead of to a Northern school. Incensed by racial prejudice while at Fisk, from which he graduated in 1888, he was happy to return North for additional study. He entered Harvard at a time when it was revolutionizing itself along the lines of German universities. DuBois was fascinated by the new social science, and he resolved to use its scientific method to study the race problem. After two years of postdoctoral work in Europe, he failed to find a job at a Northern university. The disappointed scholar settled down to teaching and historical-sociological scholarship at the all-black Atlanta University.

DuBois originally planned to devote himself to scholarship, but he changed in two ways. First, he entered the public arena. He founded the Niagara Movement in 1905, helped form the National Association for the Advancement of Colored People (NAACP) in 1909 and served as editor of the NAACP's major publication, *The Crisis* (1909-1934). Second, he lost faith in the prospect of persuading white Americans to give up discrimination. The embittered DuBois eventually converted to communism and went into self-imposed exile in Africa.

At the turn of the century, DuBois was still in a state of transition. He was beginning to enter the public arena, but he still had faith in persuading white America. He believed that Washington's program was inadequate, but criticizing Washington was rhetorically risky. A few blacks were saying, mostly in private, that Washington had "sold out," but Washington's reputation was well established. In 1903, DuBois' first major rhetorical effort was published and quickly went through several editions. It was a collection of essays entitled *The Souls of Black Folks: Essays and Sketches*. The essay which contained DuBois' first public attack on Washington's program is reproduced from the Fourth Edition (Chicago: A.C. McClurg, 1904), pp. 41-59.

Of Mr. Booker T. Washington and Others

EASILY the most striking thing in the history of the American Negro since 1876 is the ascendancy of Mr. Booker T. Washington. It began at the time when war memories and ideals were rapidly passing; a day of astonishing commercial development was dawning; a sense of doubt and hesitation overtook the freedmen's sons, — then it was that his leading began. Mr. Washington came, with a simple definite programme, at the psychological moment when the nation was a little ashamed of having bestowed so much sentiment on Negroes, and was concentrating its energies on Dollars. His programme of industrial education, conciliation of the South, and submission and silence as to civil and political rights, was not wholly original; the Free Negroes from 1830 up to war-time had striven to build industrial schools, and the American Missionary Association had from the first taught various trades; and Price and others had sought a way of honorable alliance with the best of the Southerners. But Mr. Washington first indissolubly linked these things; he put enthusiasm, unlimited energy, and perfect faith into this programme, and changed it from a by-path into a veritable Way of Life. And the tale of the methods by which he did this is a fascinating study of human life.

It startled the nation to hear a Negro advocating such a programme after many decades of bitter complaint; it startled and won the applause of the South, it interested and won the admiration of the North; and after a confused murmur of protest, it silenced if it did not convert the Negroes themselves.

To gain the sympathy and coöperation of the various elements comprising the white South was Mr. Washington's first task; and this, at the time Tuskegee was founded, seemed, for a black man, well-nigh impossible. And yet ten years later it was done in the word spoken at Atlanta: "In all things purely social we can be as separate as the five fingers, and yet one as the hand in all things essential to mutual progress." This "Atlanta Compromise" is by all odds the most notable thing in Mr. Washington's career. The South interpreted it in different ways: the radicals received it as a complete surrender of the demand for civil and political equality; the conservatives, as a generously conceived working basis for mutual understanding. So both approved it, and to-day its author is certainly the most distinguished Southerner since Jefferson Davis, and the one with the largest personal following.

Next to this achievement comes Mr. Washington's work in gaining place and consideration in the North. Others less shrewd and tactful had formerly

essayed to sit on these two stools and had fallen between them; but as Mr.
Washington knew the heart of the South from birth and training, so by
singular insight he intuitively grasped the spirit of the age which was
dominating the North. And so thoroughly did he learn the speech and
thought of triumphant commercialism, and the ideals of material prosperity,
that the picture of a lone black boy poring over a French grammar amid the
weeds and dirt of a neglected home soon seemed to him the acme of
absurdities. One wonders what Socrates and St. Francis of Assisi would say to
this.

And yet this very singleness of vision and thorough oneness with his age is a
mark of the successful man. It is as though Nature must needs make men
narrow in order to give them force. So Mr. Washington's cult has gained
unquestioning followers, his work has wonderfully prospered, his friends are
legion, and his enemies are confounded. To-day he stands as the one
recognized spokesman of his ten million fellows, and one of the most notable
figures in a nation of seventy millions. One hesitates, therefore, to criticise a
life which, beginning with so little, has done so much. And yet the time is
come when one may speak in all sincerity and utter courtesy of the mistakes
and shortcomings of Mr. Washington's career, as well as of his triumphs,
without being thought captious or envious, and without forgetting that it is
easier to do ill than well in the world.

The criticism that has hitherto met Mr. Washington has not always been of
this broad character. In the South especially has he had to walk warily to
avoid the harshest judgments, — and naturally so, for he is dealing with the
one subject of deepest sensitiveness to that section. Twice — once when at the
Chicago celebration of the Spanish-American War he alluded to the color-
prejudice that is "eating away the vitals of the South," and once when he
dined with President Roosevelt — has the resulting Southern criticism been
violent enough to threaten seriously his popularity. In the North the feeling
has several times forced itself into words, that Mr. Washington's counsels of
submission overlooked certain elements of true manhood, and that his
educational programme was unnecessarily narrow. Usually, however, such
criticism has not found open expression, although, too, the spiritual sons of
the Abolitionists have not been prepared to acknowledge that the schools
founded before Tuskegee, by men of broad ideals and self-sacrificing spirit,
were wholly failures or worthy of ridicule. While, then, criticism has not
failed to follow Mr. Washington, yet the prevailing public opinion of the land
has been but too willing to deliver the solution of a wearisome problem into
his hands, and say, "If that is all you and your race ask, take it."

Among his own people, however, Mr. Washington has encountered the
strongest and most lasting opposition, amounting at times to bitterness, and
even to-day continuing strong and insistent even though largely silenced in
outward expression by the public opinion of the nation. Some of this
opposition is, of course, mere envy; the disappointment of displaced
demagogues and the spite of narrow minds. But aside from this, there is
among educated and thoughtful colored men in all parts of the land a feeling

of deep regret, sorrow, and apprehension at the wide currency and ascendancy which some of Mr. Washington's theories have gained. These same men admire his sincerity of purpose, and are willing to forgive much to honest endeavor which is doing something worth the doing. They coöperate with Mr. Washington as far as they conscientiously can; and, indeed, it is no ordinary tribute to this man's tact and power that, steering as he must between so many diverse interests and opinions, he so largely retains the respect of all.

But the hushing of the criticism of honest opponents is a dangerous thing. It leads some of the best of the critics to unfortunate silence and paralysis of effort, and others to burst into speech so passionately and intemperately as to lose listeners. Honest and earnest criticism from those whose interests are most nearly touched, — criticism of writers by readers, of government by those governed, of leaders by those led, — this is the soul of democracy and the safeguard of modern society. If the best of the American Negroes receive by outer pressure a leader whom they had not recognized before, manifestly there is here a certain palpable gain. Yet there is also irreparable loss, — a loss of that peculiarly valuable education which a group receives when by search and criticism it finds and commissions its own leaders. The way in which this is done is at once the most elementary and the nicest problem of social growth. History is but the record of such group-leadership; and yet how infinitely changeful is its type and character! And of all types and kinds, what can be more instructive than the leadership of a group within a group? — that curious double movement where real progress may be negative and actual advance be relative retrogression. All this is the social student's inspiration and despair.

Now in the past the American Negro has had instructive experience in the choosing of group leaders, founding thus a peculiar dynasty which in the light of present conditions is worth while studying. When sticks and stones and beasts form the sole environment of a people, their attitude is largely one of determined opposition to and conquest of natural forces. But when to earth and brute is added an environment of men and ideas, then the attitude of the imprisoned group may take three main forms, — a feeling of revolt and revenge; an attempt to adjust all thought and action to the will of the greater group; or, finally, a determined effort at self-realization and self-development despite environing opinion. The influence of all of these attitudes at various times can be traced in the history of the American Negro, and in the evolution of his successive leaders.

Before 1750, while the fire of African freedom still burned in the veins of the slaves, there was in all leadership or attempted leadership but the one motive of revolt and revenge, — typified in the terrible Maroons, the Danish blacks, and Cato of Stono, and veiling all the Americas in fear of insurrection. The liberalizing tendencies of the latter half of the eighteenth century brought, along with kindlier relations between black and white, thoughts of ultimate adjustment and assimilation. Such aspiration was especially voiced in the earnest songs of Phyllis, in the martyrdom of Attucks, the fighting of Salem and Poor, the intellectual accomplishments of Banneker and Derham, and the political demands of the Cuffes.

Stern financial and social stress after the war cooled much of the previous humanitarian ardor. The disappointment and impatience of the Negroes at the persistence of slavery and serfdom voiced itself in two movements. The slaves in the South, aroused undoubtedly by vague rumors of the Haytian revolt, made three fierce attempts at insurrection, — in 1800 under Gabriel in Virginia, in 1822 under Vesey in Carolina, and in 1831 again in Virginia under the terrible Nat Turner. In the Free States, on the other hand, a new and curious attempt at self-development was made. In Philadelphia and New York color-prescription led to a withdrawal of Negro communicants from white churches and the formation of a peculiar socio-religious institution among the Negroes known as the African Church, — an organization still living and controlling in its various branches over a million of men.

Walker's wild appeal against the trend of the times showed how the world was changing after the coming of the cotton-gin. By 1830 slavery seemed hopelessly fastened on the South, and the slaves thoroughly cowed into submission. The free Negroes of the North, inspired by the mulatto immigrants from the West Indies, began to change the basis of their demands; they recognized the slavery of slaves, but insisted that they themselves were freemen, and sought assimilation and amalgamation with the nation on the same terms with other men. Thus, Forten and Purvis of Philadelphia, Shad of Wilmington, Du Bois of New Haven, Barbadoes of Boston, and others, strove singly and together as men, they said, not as slaves; as "people of color," not as "Negroes." The trend of the times, however, refused them recognition save in individual and exceptional cases, considered them as one with all the despised blacks, and they soon found themselves striving to keep even the rights they formerly had of voting and working and moving as freemen. Schemes of migration and colonization arose among them; but these they refused to entertain, and they eventually turned to the Abolition movement as a final refuge.

Here, led by Remond, Nell, Wells-Brown, and Douglass, a new period of self-assertion and self-development dawned. To be sure, ultimate freedom and assimilation was the ideal before the leaders, but the assertion of the manhood rights of the Negro by himself was the main reliance, and John Brown's raid was the extreme of its logic. After the war and emancipation, the great form of Frederick Douglass, the greatest of American Negro leaders, still led the host. Self-assertion, especially in political lines, was the main programme, and behind Douglass came Elliot, Bruce, and Langston, and the Reconstruction politicians, and, less conspicuous but of greater social significance Alexander Crummell and Bishop Daniel Payne.

Then came the Revolution of 1876, the suppression of the Negro votes, the changing and shifting of ideals, and the seeking of new lights in the great night. Douglass, in his old age, still bravely stood for the ideals of his early manhood, — ultimate assimilation *through* self-assertion, and on no other terms. For a time Price arose as a new leader, destined, it seemed, not to give up, but to re-state the old ideals in a form less repugnant to the white South. But he passed away in his prime. Then came the new leader. Nearly all the former ones had become leaders by the silent suffrage of their fellows, had sought to lead their own people alone, and were usually, save Douglass, little known outside their race. But Booker T. Washington arose as essentially the leader not of one race but of two, — a compromiser between the South, the North, and the Negro. Naturally the Negroes resented, at first bitterly, signs of compromise which surrendered their civil and political rights, even though this was to be exchanged for larger chances of economic development. The rich and dominating North, however, was not only weary of the race problem, but was investing largely in Southern enterprises, and welcomed any method of peaceful coöperation. Thus, by national opinion, the Negroes began to recognize Mr. Washington's leadership; and the voice of criticism was hushed.

Mr. Washington represents in Negro thought the old attitude of adjustment and submission; but adjustment at such a peculiar time as to make his programme unique. This is an age of unusual economic development, and Mr. Washington's programme naturally takes an economic cast, becoming a gospel of Work and Money to such an extent as apparently almost completely to overshadow the higher aims of life. Moreover, this is an age when the more advanced races are coming in closer contact with the less developed races, and the race-feeling is therefore intensified; and Mr. Washington's programme practically accepts the alleged inferiority of the Negro races. Again, in our own land, the reaction from the sentiment of war time has given impetus to race-prejudice against Negroes, and Mr. Washington withdraws many of the high demands of Negroes as men and American citizens. In other periods of intensified prejudice all the Negro's tendency to self-assertion has been called forth; at this period a policy of submission is advocated. In the history of nearly all other races and peoples the doctrine preached at such crises has been that manly self-respect is worth more than lands and houses, and that a people who voluntarily surrender such respect, or cease striving for it, are not worth civilizing.

In answer to this, it has been claimed that the Negro can survive only through submission. Mr. Washington distinctly asks that black people give up, at least for the present, three things, —

First, political power,

Second, insistence on civil rights,

Third, higher education of Negro youth, —

and concentrate all their energies on industrial education, the accumulation of wealth, and the conciliation of the South. This policy has been courageously and insistently advocated for over fifteen years, and has been triumphant for perhaps ten years. As a result of this tender of the palm-branch, what has been the return? In these years there have occurred:

1. The disfranchisement of the Negro.

2. The legal creation of a distinct status of civil inferiority for the Negro.

3. The steady withdrawal of aid from institutions for the higher training of the Negro.

These movements are not, to be sure, direct results of Mr. Washington's teachings; but his propaganda has, without a shadow of doubt, helped their speedier accomplishment. The question then comes: Is it possible, and probable, that nine millions of men can make effective progress in economic lines if they are deprived of political rights, made a servile caste, and allowed only the most meagre chance for developing their exceptional men? If history and reason give any distinct answer to these questions, it is an emphatic *No*. And Mr. Washington thus faces the triple paradox of his career:

1. He is striving nobly to make Negro artisans business men and property-owners; but it is utterly impossible, under modern competitive methods, for workingmen and property-owners to defend their rights and exist without the right of suffrage.

2. He insists on thrift and self-respect, but at the same time counsels a silent submission to civic inferiority such as is bound to sap the manhood of any race in the long run.

3. He advocates common-school and industrial training, and depreciates institutions of higher learning; but neither the Negro common-schools, nor Tuskegee itself, could remain open a day were it not for teachers trained in Negro colleges, or trained by their graduates.

This triple paradox in Mr. Washington's position is the object of criticism by two classes of colored Americans. One class is spiritually descended from Toussaint the Savior, through Gabriel, Vesey, and Turner, and they represent the attitude of revolt and revenge; they hate the white South blindly and distrust the white race generally, and so far as they agree on definite action, think that the Negro's only hope lies in emigration beyond the borders of the United States. And yet, by the irony of fate, nothing has more effectually made this programme seem hopeless than the recent course of the United States toward weaker and darker peoples in the West Indies, Hawaii, and the Philippines, — for where in the world may we go and be safe from lying and brute force?

The other class of Negroes who cannot agree with Mr. Washington has hitherto said little aloud. They deprecate the sight of scattered counsels, of internal disagreement; and especially they dislike making their just criticism of a useful and earnest man an excuse for a general discharge of venom from small-minded opponents. Nevertheless, the questions involved are so fundamental and serious that it is difficult to see how men like the Grimkes, Kelly Miller, J.W.E. Bowen, and other representatives of this group, can much longer be silent. Such men feel in conscience bound to ask of this nation three things:

1. The right to vote.
2. Civic equality.
3. The education of youth according to ability.

They acknowledge Mr. Washington's invaluable service in counselling patience and courtesy in such demands; they do not ask that ignorant black men vote when ignorant whites are debarred, or that any reasonable restrictions in the suffrage should not be applied; they know that the low social level of the mass of the race is responsible for much discrimination against it, but they also know, and the nation knows, that relentless color-prejudice is more often a cause than a result of the Negro's degradation; they seek the abatement of this relic of barbarism, and not its systematic encouragement and pampering by all agencies of social power from the Associated Press to the Church of Christ. They advocate, with Mr. Washington, a broad system of Negro common schools supplemented by thorough industrial training; but they are surprised that a man of Mr. Washington's insight cannot see that no such educational system ever has rested or can rest on any other basis than that of the well-equipped college and university, and they insist that there is a demand for a few such institutions throughout the South to train the best of the Negro youth as teachers, professional men, and leaders.

This group of men honor Mr. Washington for his attitude of conciliation toward the white South; they accept the "Atlanta Compromise" in its broadest interpretation; they recognize, with him, many signs of promise, many men of high purpose and fair judgment, in this section; they know that no easy task has been laid upon a region already tottering under heavy burdens. But, nevertheless, they insist that the way to truth and right lies in straightforward honesty, not in indiscriminate flattery; in praising those of the South who do well and criticising uncompromisingly those who do ill; in taking advantage of the opportunities at hand and urging their fellows to do the same, but at the same time in remembering that only a firm adherence to their higher ideals and aspirations will ever keep those ideals within the realm of possibility. They do not expect that the free right to vote, to enjoy civic rights, and to be educated, will come in a moment; they do not expect to see the bias and prejudices of years disappear at the blast of a trumpet; but they are absolutely certain that the way for a people to gain their reasonable rights is not by voluntarily throwing them away and insisting that they do not want them; that the way for a people to gain respect is not by continually belittling and ridiculing themselves; that, on the contrary, Negroes must insist continually, in season and out of season, that voting is necessary to modern manhood, that color discrimination is barbarism, and that black boys need education as well as white boys.

In failing thus to state plainly and unequivocally the legitimate demands of their people, even at the cost of opposing an honored leader, the thinking classes of American Negroes would shirk a heavy responsibility, — a responsibility to themselves, a responsibility to the struggling masses, a responsibility to the darker races of men whose future depends so largely on this American experiment, but especially a responsibility to this nation, — this common Fatherland. It is wrong to encourage a man or a people in evil-doing; it is wrong to aid and abet a national crime simply because it is unpopular not to do so. The growing spirit of kindliness and reconciliation between the North and South after the frightful differences of a generation ago ought to be a source of deep congratulation to all, and especially to those whose mistreatment caused the war; but if that reconciliation is to be marked by the industrial slavery and civic death of those same black men, with permanent legislation into a position of inferiority, then those black men, if they are really men, are called upon by every consideration of patriotism and loyalty to oppose such a course by all civilized methods, even though such opposition involves disagreement with Mr. Booker T. Washington. We have no right to sit silently by while the inevitable seeds are sown for a harvest of disaster to our children, black and white.

First, it is the duty of black men to judge the South discriminatingly. The present generation of Southerners are not responsible for the past, and they should not be blindly hated or blamed for it. Furthermore, to no class is the indiscriminate endorsement of the recent course of the South toward Negroes more nauseating than to the best thought of the South. The South is not "solid"; it is a land in the ferment of social change, wherein forces of all kinds are fighting for supremacy; and to praise the ill the South is to-day perpetrating is just as wrong as to condemn the good. Discriminating and broad-minded criticism is what the South needs, — needs it for the sake of her own white sons and daughters, and for the insurance of robust, healthy mental and moral development.

To-day even the attitude of the Southern whites toward the blacks is not, as so many assume, in all cases the same; the ignorant Southerner hates the Negro, the workingmen fear his competition, the money-makers wish to use him as a laborer, some of the educated see a menace in his upward development, while others — usually the sons of the masters — wish to help him to rise. National opinion has enabled this last class to maintain the Negro common schools, and to protect the Negro partially in property, life, and limb. Through the pressure of the money-makers, the Negro is in danger of being reduced to semi-slavery, expecially in the country districts; the workingmen, and those of the educated who fear the Negro, have united to disfranchise him, and some have urged his deportation; while the passions of the ignorant are easily aroused to lynch and abuse any black man. To praise this intricate whirl of thought and prejudice is nonsense; to inveigh indiscriminately against "the South" is unjust; but to use the same breath in praising Governor Aycock, exposing Senator Morgan, arguing with Mr. Thomas Nelson Page, and denouncing Senator Ben Tillman, is not only sane, but the imperative duty of thinking black men.

It would be unjust to Mr. Washington not to acknowledge that in several instances he has opposed movements in the South which were unjust to the Negro; he sent memorials to the Louisiana and Alabama constitutional conventions, he has spoken against lynching, and in other ways has openly or silently set his influence against sinister schemes and unfortunate happenings. Notwithstanding this, it is equally true to assert that on the whole the distinct impression left by Mr. Washington's propaganda is, first, that the South is justified in its present attitude toward the Negro because of the Negro's degradation; secondly, that the prime cause of the Negro's failure to rise more quickly is his wrong education in the past; and, thirdly, that his future rise depends primarily on his own efforts. Each of these propositions is a dangerous half-truth. The supplementary truths must never be lost sight of: first, slavery and race-prejudice are potent if not sufficient causes of the Negro's position; second, industrial and common-school training were necessarily slow in planting because they had to await the black teachers trained by higher institutions, — it being extremely doubtful if any essentially different development was possible, and certainly a Tuskegee was unthinkable before 1880; and, third, while it is a great truth to say that the Negro must strive and strive mightily to help himself, it is equally true that unless his striving be not simply seconded, but rather aroused and encouraged, by the initiative of the richer and wiser environing group, he cannot hope for great success.

In his failure to realize and impress this last point, Mr. Washington is especially to be criticised. His doctrine has tended to make the whites, North and South, shift the burden of the Negro problem to the Negro's shoulders and stand aside as critical and rather pessimistic spectators; when in fact the burden belongs to the nation, and the hands of none of us are clean if we bend not our energies to righting these great wrongs.

The South ought to be led, by candid and honest criticism, to assert her better self and do her full duty to the race she has cruelly wronged and is still wronging. The North — her co-partner in guilt — cannot salve her conscience by plastering it with gold. We cannot settle this problem by diplomacy and suaveness, by "policy" alone. If worse come to worst, can the moral fibre of this country survive the slow throttling and murder of nine millions of men?

The black men of America have a duty to perform, a duty stern and delicate, — a forward movement to oppose a part of the work of their greatest leader. So far as Mr. Washington preaches Thrift, Patience, and Industrial Training for the masses, we must hold up his hands and strive with him, rejoicing in his honors and glorying in the strength of this Joshua called of God and of man to lead the headless host. But so far as Mr. Washington apologizes for injustice, North or South, does not rightly value the privilege and duty of voting, belittles the emasculating effects of caste distinctions, and opposes the higher training and ambition of our brighter minds, — so far as he, the South, or the Nation, does this, — we must unceasingly and firmly oppose them. By every civilized and peaceful method we must strive for the rights which the world accords to men, clinging unwaveringly to those great words which the sons of the Fathers would fain forget: "We hold these truths to be self-evident: That all men are created equal; that they are endowed by their Creator with certain unalienable rights; that among these are life, liberty, and the pursuit of happiness."

Post-Civil War America
Rhetorical Responses
to Socioeconomic Changes

Speech to the Order of the Knights of Labor

Terence Powderly

Commentary

The nation's trend toward industrialization was of long standing, and so were many related political controversies, as exemplified by earlier speeches in this anthology about protective tariffs by Clay and Calhoun. However, the trend accelerated after the Civil War. In 1860, the U.S. ranked fourth internationally in industrial production, but it ranked first by 1894; by 1914, it outproduced the next three ranking nations combined.

Increased industrialization created other dramatic socio-economic changes. Urbanization soared. In 1860, only 17 percent of the population lived in towns of over 2,500 people, but this increased to 40 percent by 1900. By 1890, Philadelphia and Chicago each had over a million inhabitants, and New York had twice as many.

The work environment also changed dramatically. In the eighteenth and early nineteenth centuries, when the country was largely agricultural, the few ''industrial workers'' were mostly skilled craftsmen (such as blacksmiths and carpenters) who often worked alongside their employers and looked forward to owning their own shops after gaining more experience and saving some money for investment. The factory system, which began replacing a large percentage of skilled craftsmen with unskilled workers, was introduced in the early nineteenth century. Yet as late as 1870, about half of the nation's manufactured products were made in small handicraft shops. By 1890, the percentage had dropped to 20.

The psychological effects of these changes are difficult to discern, but this writer is not alone in conjecturing that a combination of large factories and large cities led to a great deal of alienation and hostility. Unfortunately, these psychological effects are present today, but they were exacerbated in the post-Civil War period by several factors. A labor surplus led to high unemployment, low wages and poor working conditions. The rapidity of change was overwhelming, both in material terms (for example, inadequate sanitation in the cities) and in psychological terms (businessmen were seen as the enemy, for instance). The large number of immigrants had trouble adjusting to a new environment. So did native Americans, most of whom had rural backgrounds and came to the city only because the frontier was closing and farmland was becoming less available.

The resulting unrest resulted in the rise of labor unions, each with its distinctive rhetoric. The earliest successful union was the Order of the Knights of Labor, whose membership in 1885 was a mere 80,000 and a year later skyrocketed to 700,000. Then its membership declined, and within a few years it became a relic of the past while its chief competitor, the American Federation of Labor, prospered. Why?

The early success of the Knights is easily explainable by its ability to capitalize on the labor unrest discussed above. Understanding its rapid decline requires a look at the inconsistencies and inadequacies of its (1) organizational structure, (2) proposals for improving labor's status and (3) rhetoric. Originally a secret society with passwords and ceremonies reminiscent of older societies such as the Masons, the first local group was formed in 1869, but the national organization was not created until 1878. Even then, it remained secret. Although secrecy was gradually abandoned, thereby permitting more aggressive recruiting of members, its semi-secrecy made it easy for opponents to persuade the public that the Knights were conspiratorial and subversive. The Knights' heritage of secrecy also left it disinclined to initiate a strong rhetorical campaign or even to answer publicly what were often untrue attacks.

Although its actions were kept as secret as possible, the Knights had a policy of near-open membership qualifications, which was antithetical to the growing popular belief in socio-economic classes with conflicting interests. The public was increasingly convinced that employers and workers were enemies, and workers were even beginning to see conflicts among themselves, especially between craftsmen and unskilled laborers. Even skilled laborers were beginning to perceive different economic interests between one craft and another. Yet the Knights admitted anyone who was or had been a wage-earner except for people who were presumed to be unproductive (bankers, lawyers, stockbrokers, professional gamblers and liquor dealers). Even employers could join, although few actually did. In view of its rivalry with the American Federation of Labor, readers should note that local groups were not organized around skilled trades. Unskilled workers and craftsmen from various trades banded together. All producers supposedly had the same economic interests.

The assumed consistency of economic interests was inconsistent with the Knights' proposals for improving labor's status. The program was largely the brainchild of Terence Powderly (1849-1924), who guided the Knights for almost its entire period of growth and decline (1879-1893). Powderly's program for improving labor's status rested on a belief in divergent interests between owners and workers. However, he was confident that when disputes arose, they could be settled through reasoned discourse and negotiation or, failing that, arbitration. Strikes and other types of coercion were disallowed. Only later did Powderly grudgingly assent to coercion.

Far better than settling periodic disputes between workers and owners, Powderly believed, was abolition of the wage system. Although lacking a Puritan heritage (his parents were Irish Catholic immigrants), Powderly envisioned an idealized future that is reminiscent of the Puritan's long-awaited Millennium. He outlined this vision in his first presidential address to a secret meeting of the Knights' national assembly in 1880. The assembly consisted of delegates from the various local Knight groups. The text remained unavailable until his manuscript autobiography, entitled *The Path I Trod*, edited by Harry J. Carman, Henry David and Paul N. Guthrie, was published by the Columbia University Press (New York, 1940). The following text is a reproduction of the one in the autobiography (pp. 268-70).

Speech to the Order of the Knights of Labor, 1880

Abolish the Wage System

So long as the present order of things exist [sic], just so long will the attempt to effect lasting peace between the man who buys labor and the man who sells labor be fruitless.

So long as it is to the interest of one kind of men to purchase labor at the lowest possible figure, and so long as it is to the interest of another kind of men to sell labor to the highest possible bidder, just so long will there exist an antagonism between the two which all the speakers and writers on labor cannot remove.

So long as a pernicious system leaves one man at the mercy of another, so long will labor and capital be at war, and no strike can deliver a blow sufficiently hard to break the hold with which unproductive capital today grasps labor by the throat.

In what direction should we turn to see our way clear to a solution of the difficulty? Far be it from me to say that I can point out the way; would that I could with certainty do it! I can only offer a suggestion, which comes to me as the result of experience, and that suggestion is to abolish the

Wage System

This is the system which carries with it into the workshop, the mine and factory a host of evils, which, if repeated, would exhaust the whole vocabulary of murmurings which fill the complaint-book of Labor.

This is the system which, serpentlike, pushes itself along wherever those bands of commercial iron and steel are laid, carrying discontent in its train.

This is the system which enables a half dozen men to sit at their tables in any of our large centers of trade, and, without thought of the welfare of the country, apart from their own interests, issue the mandates which direct the movements of the whole industrial population of the United States.

This is the system which makes every railroad superintendent, every factory or mine superintendent, an autocrat at whose nod or beck the poor, unrequited slave who labors must bow the head and bend the knee in humble suppliance.

To point out a way to utterly destroy this system would be a pleasure to me. I can only direct your attention to it and leave the rest to your wisdom; and I firmly believe that I have pointed out the most vicious of all evils which afflict labor today.

But are we prepared to lay siege to this bulwark of oppression? Remember that for centuries it has been slowly, yet steadily, creeping onward, making each year new and deeper inroads upon labor, until today it stands so well intrenched and powerful that even the staunchest heart in the ranks of labor's defenders shrinks at the thought of breaking down the barriers of fear, ignorance, and superstition, to which its existence has given birth.

The wage system, at its inception, was but an experiment, and for a time doubts were entertained as to its adoption; but the avaricious eye of the Shylock of labor saw in it a weapon with which he could control the toiler, and today that system has so firm a hold upon us that every attempt at shaking off the fetters, by resorting to a strike, only makes it easier for the master to say to his slave, You must work for lower wages.

We must teach our members, then, that the remedy for the redress of the wrongs we complain of does not lie in the suicidal strike; but in thorough, effective organization. Without organization we cannot accomplish anything; through it we hope to forever banish that curse of modern civilization—wage slavery.

But how? Surely not by forming an association and remaining a member; not by getting every other worthy man to become a member and remain one; not by paying the dues required of us as they fall due. These are all important factors in the method by which we hope to regain our independence, and are vitally important; they are the elements necessary to complete organization.

Organization once perfected, what must we do? I answer, study the best means of putting your organization to some practicable use by embarking in a system of

Coöperation

which will eventually make every man his own master—every man his own employer; a system which will give the laborer a fair proportion of the products of his toil. It is to coöperation, then, as the lever of labor's emancipation, that the eyes of the workingmen and women of the world should be directed, upon coöperation their hopes should be centered, and to it do I now direct your attention. I am deeply sensible of the importance, of the magnitude, of the undertaking in which I invite you to engage. I know that it is human nature to grow cold, apathetic, and finally indifferent when engaged in that which requires deep study and persistent effort, unattended by excitement; men are apt to believe that physical force is the better way of redressing grievances, being the shorter remedy; but even that requires patience and fortitude as well as strength. . . .

To the subject of coöperation, then, do I invite your attention, and I liken it unto the Revolutionary War. If you decide upon carrying it out at this convention, it will be the Bunker Hill of Industrial Independence; but you must also bear in mind, though the longest term allotted to man be yours to live, you will not see during that term the complete triumph of your hopes. The War for American Independence had its Bunker Hills and its Washingtons, but it also had its Valley Forges and its Benedict Arnolds. The enthusiasm of the hour will avail us nothing, and coöperation requires every Washington of labor to be up and doing. The laboring man needs education in this great social question, and the best minds of the Order must give their precious thought to this system. There is no good reason why labor cannot, through coöperation, own and operate mines, factories, and railroads. By coöperation alone can a system of

Colonization

be established in which men may band together for the purpose of securing the greatest good to the greatest number, and place the man who is willing to toil upon his own homestead.

Trade Unionism Versus Socialism

Samuel Gompers

Commentary

The Knights of Labor lost members during the 1890s to their chief competitor, the American Federation of Labor (AFL). From its inception in 1886 until his death, the AFL was identified in the public mind with its president, Samuel Gompers (1850-1924). Gompers dominated the AFL, but he had many enemies. Businessmen usually opposed him because they did not want their workers unionized. The general public was suspicious for many reasons, including beliefs that unions were anti-business, were trying to destroy the individual liberties of workers, and were under the control of subversive and violent foreign immigrants.

In the early days of the AFL, both businessmen and the public often associated Gompers and the AFL with socialism, but this rhetorical problem declined as Gompers' opposition to socialism became increasingly well known. Thus the speech on "Trade Unionism Versus Socialism," although delivered to the 1903 AFL convention, should be analyzed in terms of the public audience as well as the audience of union delegates. The speech was hailed in the journal of the well-known National Civic Federation (an organization composed mostly of leading industrialists). It also printed a picture of Gompers with the caption, "Socialism's Ablest Foe."

Socialists were a serious rival from the AFL's inception until about the 1920s. Most socialist leaders were not members of the AFL, but they attacked Gompers via speeches and publications. A few socialists were AFL members, and they tried unsuccessfully to change the union's policies from those that Gompers advocated. The fundamental disagreements were three. First, socialists wished to establish "industrial unions" composed of workers within a particular industry (mining or steel, for instance), whereas the AFL organized "trade unions" composed of particular crafts, each of which should be autonomous. For example, Gompers belonged to the Cigarmakers' Union, which was one of several trade unions that affiliated with the "federation." Implicit in the first issue was a second: socialists wished to unionize unskilled, as well as skilled, workers; whereas the AFL was primarily (some would say exclusively) concerned with recruiting skilled tradesmen. Third, socialists urged all laborers and other "oppressed people" to join together in a political party that would overthrow the capitalist system, abolish private property and nationalize industry—by revolution if necessary. The AFL, although sometimes engaging in political activities such as lobbying for particular legislation and endorsing specific candidates, was unalterably opposed to forming a labor party or subsuming the AFL to either existing party. It endorsed the capitalist system and, in theory if not always in fact, opposed violence.

Gompers was contemptuous of all abstract theories, whether they were Powderly's visionary worker co-operatives or the socialists' revolutionary doctrines. He frequently used the term "bread and butter unionism" to describe his pragmatic philosophy. He meant simply that trade unions should get the best possible wages and working conditions. If negotiations would not work, then strikes and boycotts should be used.

Gompers' first major dispute with socialists was in 1890. Problems began when the Central Labor Union (CLU) of New York City was taken over by socialists. Some anti-socialists then formed the New York Federation of Labor (NYFL), which received an AFL charter. The CLU and the NYFL resolved their differences, and the NYFL returned its AFL charter. Later, the NYFL requested that its charter be reactivated, but Gompers refused because one of the NYFL's affiliated "unions" was the Socialist Labor Party. Gompers argued that only trade unions could belong to the AFL. Socialists appealed his decision, but Gompers was upheld at the AFL convention in 1890.

The rivalry intensified. In 1893, a socialist member of the AFL, Thomas Morgan, proposed that the AFL form a "political labor movement," but Gompers successfully opposed it. Meanwhile, the Socialist Labor Party (SLP), which was a political party, not a union, was falling under the control of Daniel DeLeon. Recognizing that efforts to wrest control of the AFL from Gompers were failing, DeLeon in 1895 formed the Socialist Trade and Labor Alliance (STLA) that would hopefully replace the "conservative" AFL. DeLeon called it the "new unionism." Gompers called it "dual unionism." Gompers opposed the STLA not only because it was a union based on socialist philosophy, but also because he feared that any competition between unions would weaken the union movement. A good example of his opposition to "dual unionism" was his refusal to compete with the railroad unions (called "brotherhoods"), even though the large and powerful brotherhoods were organized on a craft basis but refused to join the AFL.

DeLeon's STLA eventually collapsed as his control of the socialist movement declined, but socialists formed another competitor to the AFL, the Western Federation of Miners (WFM). In 1902, the AFL demanded that the WFM join the AFL, and the WFM replied by forming, and then affiliating with, a broader union, the American Labor Union (ALU). The new "dual union" claimed jurisdiction over all unions in the United States, endorsed industrial unionism and adopted the platform of the Socialist party.

In 1903, shortly before the AFL's annual convention, the WFM went on strike against mines in Colorado. The strike was publicized highly, partly because violence erupted. It was broken after WFM leaders were arrested and the governor refused to obey a judge's order to release them. Then violence accelerated. Technically, the AFL was not involved, but a resolution was introduced at the convention to extend sympathy to the WFM. Other pro-socialist resolutions, similar to ones that had been defeated regularly at AFL conventions, were also introduced. It was in opposition to these motions that Gompers gave the following speech. The text is reproduced from the January 1904 issue of the AFL's magazine, the *American Federationist*, vol. 40, pp. 44-45.

Trade Unionism Versus Socialism

Mr. Chairman and fellow-delegates. I am always impressed with an earnest man's utterances, and to me a man who makes a statement and gives me an assurance, my disposition has always been to be credulous and to believe him. When an organization makes a declaration, my disposition is to believe it. I am always inclined to believe a man or an aggregation of men to be honest, but when I discover that a man has made professions of one thing and his actions belie his words, then I am like the Missourian; after that, so far as he is concerned, he must show me.

Vice-President Duncan has not the opportunity to reply to his critics, because of his calling attention to the conduct of the men who clothed themselves in the mantle of socialism, and assumed a position of superiority, mentally, in honesty, in work, and in ennobling purposes. It is because their professions are in entire discord with their actions in this convention that it is necessary to call their position in question.

I shall not refer at this time to their very many detailed acts of treachery to the trade union movement; but I shall refer to some of the declarations made upon the floor of this convention by delegates participating in this discussion and show you that though they may believe themselves to be trade unionists they are at heart and logically the antagonists of our movement.

I want to say, and I am sure it will come as a shock to the brother, for between Mr. Hayes and myself—I mean Max Hayes—personally there has, I think, existed a very close and sympathetic bond of friendship, but here we differ—I am a trade unionist; he thinks he is.

Delegate Hayes, I firmly believe, was ill when he came to this convention. He could not accept a duty which was meant as a compliment, and has been so regarded by other men, to perform committee work; but if ever a man made an effort and showed that he was sacrificing his vitality he did in making his address upon a speculative theory which, undoubtedly, he thought more important than the doing of the essential work of the convention.

Our friends, the socialists, always when with us have an excellent conception of the trouble in our industrial life. They say, as we say, and as every intelligent man or woman says, that there are miseries which surround us. We recognize the poverty, we know the sweatshop, we can play on every string of the harp, and touch the tenderest chords of human sympathy; but while we recognize the evil and would apply the remedy, our socialist friends would look forward to the promised land, and wait for ''the sweet by and by.'' Their statements as to economic ills are right; their conclusions and their philosophy are all askew.

The action of the committee has been found fault with because they did not bring in a substitute for the resolutions presented, but instead took a course that will bring this matter fairly and squarely before the convention. At the last convention in New Orleans, through placing us in a false position, the resolution upon this question came within an ace of being adopted, but this year the committee has made this question a plain, broad proposition.

The vote that will be recorded here today against the report of the committee will be fairly and squarely recorded in favor of socialism; and the vote that is recorded in favor of the committee's report will be against socialism. And it will be recognized as such throughout the land.

There has not been a legislative body before which the other officers of the Federation or I myself have appeared, nor an association of employers, nor individual employers with whom we have met in conference but that we have been confronted with this socialistic amendment, so-called, which came near being passed at New Orleans. It has made, and will make, our work doubly difficult, because these employers have refused and do refuse to confer for the adjustment of difficulties and disputes when they are led to believe by declaration that property is in danger of confiscation.

We have been asked how many trade unionists there are in Congress. I venture to say that there are more trade unionists in Congress and in our state legislatures holding clear cards than there are elsewhere in similar positions the world over. Do you suppose the socialists want trade unionists elected to Congress and to the legislatures?

(Delegate J. Keyes. ''No.'')

Of course, no. Of course, Socialist Brother Keyes, ''no.'' I am proud of you, Brother Keyes, for your honesty in admitting it. But what Brother Keyes has just admitted on the floor is very true of every other socialist in the convention. As a matter of fact, wherever there has been a trade unionist candidate for any political office if there have been half a dozen socialists in town they have always tried to defeat the trade unionists.

Now, there has been a remark made about the passage of the military law by Congress. I agree it would have been a good thing if we could have prevented the passage of that law, but the delegate said that if we even had a minority in Congress it could not have become law. I point him to the fact that in Germany they have the largest number of any party in the parliament of that country, and yet they have the most tyrannical military laws of any country on the globe.

It is all very well to make a declaration, but the facts are another thing. We are told we ought not to rely upon an indiscreet remark by a socialist here and there; but if not, then why rely upon the remarks of trade unionists here and there? Yes, an indiscreet remark— but the difficulty here and outside of the conventions of the A. F. of L. is to find a socialist who is not all the time guilty of making indiscreet remarks. He is at it all the time.

When the Socialist Trade and Labor Alliance, backed by Mr. DeLeon— and I will not ask pardon for mentioning his name, because if a man is consistent he is entitled to have his name mentioned—

(Delegate J. Mahlon Barnes rose to speak. Delegate Carey, of Haverhill, also called out: "I object.")

You don't know what I am going to say. You were members of that party when the Socialist Alliance was started.

(Delegate Max Hayes: "Let me explain." Cries of "Sit down" and "Hear him.")

I am stating the facts, that is all. They broke away because of the domination of this man DeLeon, and started out to form a new Socialist party, and declared what Delegate White declared here on the floor of the convention to-day was their policy, that the trade unionist must be unhampered and fought from within.

(Delegate Hayes: "That is more than any republican or democrat would say.")

For that reason I am not with those parties, and one of the reasons I am not with your party is because I want to be in line with the declaration that the trade union policy, the movement and the work, must be unhampered by your political nostrums.

When the Socialists formed the American Labor Union in rivalry to the A. F. of L., I took occasion to continually say in the *AMERICAN FEDERATIONIST* that it was but another attempt to form another Socialist trade and labor alliance without its practical courage to openly declare its enmity to the American trade union movement.

Is it not a fact that no matter what we achieve, we are belittled by the Socialists? Even the Labor Day we have achieved for all the people of our country—the proposition comes in here to abolish it and to make Labor Day in line with the Labor Day of continental Europe, May 1st. The A. F. of L. in 1879 addressed a letter to the French workingmen, suggesting to them to celebrate the 1st of May when the carpenters were to inaugurate the eight-hour day; and from that suggestion, made by your humble servant, they have made the 1st of May of each year their holiday, and how do they celebrate it, usually on the Sunday before or the Sunday after. They take no holiday, but they sometimes celebrate in the evening of May 1st.

In no country on the globe has labor ever taken a day for itself without asking consent, or begging or apologizing for itself, except in this country. And yet the Socialists want us to give up our own Labor Day and celebrate on May 1st, I suppose in the evening.

The secretary of the Socialist party has severed his connection with the reformed (?) Socialist party, because of his being opposed to the hostile tactics of that party to the trade unions; and, being at heart a trade unionist, he was forced out of his position. Since that time he has given to the world the real reasons why he was forced out—because he dared to stand up in defense of trade unions and against the policy of antagonizing the trade unions and hoisting up the American Labor Union.

Is it not true, to a very great extent, that your Socialistic American Labor Union, except the miners and a very few others, is made up very largely of expelled members of the trade unions who broke faith with their fellow-workmen? Do you Socialists here deny it? Your official papers say so, and your socialist organizers' reports admit it. Are your socialist unions not boycotting the International Boot and Shoe Workers' Union label and the International Papermakers' Union label, and other international unions, and where they do not boycott them, hold the threat over the heads of some other unions, compelling them either to submit, or forcing them to waver in their fealty and loyalty to the movement?

The cigarmakers' union of Denver has had this condition of things confront it. They were threatened with a socialist boycott of their label, and their president and those poor fellows, many of whom can not labor elsewhere, must submit to the dictates of the Socialist organization, for they have no other alternative except to get out of Denver. Because they can not otherwise work and support themselves, they must submit, or be boycotted by Socialists out of the beneficent climate of Denver, and driven elsewhere, to pine away from the ravages of that dread disease from which so many suffer and by reason of which they sought that climate for the relief afforded.

Men of labor, if you were in the office of the A. F. of L. for a time and you knew the things that transpire in the labor movement in a general and in a specific way, for they are all focussed there, and we know what is going on and we know the enemies of the labor movement—you would have your opinion clear cut upon this subject. Why, we have spent more money in organizing in Colorado itself than in any other state, notwithstanding that, industrially considered, it ought to cost very little.

I want to tell you Socialists that I have studied your philosophy; read your works upon economics, and not the meanest of them; studied your standard works, both in English and German—have not only read, but studied them. I have heard your orators and watched the work of your movement the world over. I have kept close watch upon your doctrines for thirty years; have been closely associated with many of you, and know how you think and what you propose. I know, too, what you have up your sleeve. And I want to say that I am entirely at variance with your philosophy. I declare it to you, I am not only at variance with your doctrines, but with your philosophy.

Economically, you are unsound; socially, you are wrong; industrially, you are an impossibility.

Working Class Politics

Eugene V. Debs

Commentary

Gompers' rhetorical attacks on socialism continued for years, but his emphasis shifted from DeLeon to Eugene V. Debs (1855-1926). The change resulted simply from splintering within the socialist movement that increased Debs' influence at DeLeon's expense. From approximately the beginning of the twentieth century until his death, Debs was identified in the public mind as *the* spokesman for socialism.

Debs had not always been a socialist. Starting work as a railroad fireman, he became national secretary and treasurer of the Brotherhood of Locomotive Firemen in 1880. Converted to a belief in industrial unionism (but not socialism), he formed the American Railway Union (ARU) in 1893. A year later, the ARU went on strike against the Pullman Company, and despite Debs' advice to the contrary, non-Pullman ARU members refused to work on trains unless the Pullman cars were detached. This broadening of the strike led to violence, and the federal government got an injunction against the strike on the legal grounds that strikers were obstructing the U.S. mails and interfering with interstate commerce. The strike was broken, and Debs was jailed for disobeying the injunction.

During Debs' term in jail, two events profoundly affected his future. First, he became a nationally-known figure because of much controversial publicity about the strike, his arrest and the legitimacy of the injunction. Second, he converted to socialism.

After his conversion, Debs did not abandon interest in the union movement, but his primary focus shifted to political socialism. In 1897, he founded the Social Democratic Party of America. In 1900, his party merged with an anti-DeLeon faction from the Socialist Labor Party to form the Socialist Party of America. Prior to his speech on "Working Class Politics," delivered in 1910, Debs was the party's presidential candidate in 1900 (receiving 96,000 votes), in 1904 (420,000 votes) and 1908 (420,973 votes). Socialist leaders were delighted at the better-than-expected showing in 1904 and depressed by the failure to improve in 1908. Determined to broaden the socialist base, Debs participated vigorously in the local and congressional elections of 1910. Before turning to the following speech, which was part of that campaign, a brief digression about some interesting aspects of Debs' later career.

Debs received almost 900,000 votes for president in 1912, over twice as many as he had received in 1908 and almost six percent of the total popular vote. The improvement is somewhat remarkable in view of the fact that there were three major candidates in the field, two of whom were appealing to ''reform-minded'' voters: Theodore Roosevelt (Progressive), Woodrow Wilson (Democrat) and William Taft (Republican). Debs declined his party's presidential nomination in 1916, but he was drafted for a congressional race, in which he outscored the Democratic candidate but lost overwhelmingly to the Republican. His opposition to U.S. entry into World War I was so vigorous that he was imprisoned for violating the Espionage Act. After the war, even many anti-socialists urged President Wilson to pardon him, but Wilson adamantly refused. In 1920, Debs won almost a million votes for president while sitting in a federal prison. Not until after Harding won that election was Debs pardoned.

Back to 1910. Socialists won only one congressional seat, but it was their first. They also won several seats in state legislatures and elected mayors in two cities (Schenectady and Milwaukee). Although Debs feared that many candidates had ''deserted their principles'' to attract ''reform'' voters, it is safe to conjecture that his ethos as *the* spokesman for socialism affected the results. His activity in 1910 was highlighted by the speech he gave on September 18 in Cook County, Illinois.

Debs spoke without manuscript or notes, but an admirer (who probably gave the speech its title) transcribed at least part of it and published ''extracts'' in *The International Socialist Review* (November 1910), vol. 11, pp. 257. They are reproduced below.

Working Class Politics

We live in the capitalist system, so-called because it is dominated by the capitalist class. In this system the capitalists are the rulers and the workers the subjects. The capitalists are in a decided minority and yet they rule because of the ignorance of the working class.

So long as the workers are divided, economically and politically, they will remain in subjection, exploited of what they produce and treated with contempt by the parasites who live out of their labor.

The economic unity of the workers must first be effected before there can be any progress toward emancipation. The interests of the millions of wage workers are identical, regardless of nationality, creed or sex, and if they will only open their eyes to this simple, self-evident fact, the greatest obstacle will have been overcome and the day of victory will draw near.

The primary need of the workers is industrial unity and by this I mean their organization in the industries in which they are employed as a whole instead of being separated into more or less impotent unions according to their crafts. Industrial unionism is the only effective means of economic organization and the quicker the workers realize this and unite within one compact body for the good of all, the sooner will they cease to be the victims of ward-heeling labor politicians and accomplish something of actual benefit to themselves and those dependent upon them. In Chicago where the labor grafters, posing as union leaders, have so long been permitted to thrive in their iniquity, there is especially urgent need of industrial unionism, and when this is fairly under way it will express itself politically in a class conscious vote of and for the working class.

So long as the workers are content with conditions as they are, so long as they are satisfied to belong to a craft union under the leadership of those who are far more interested in drawing their own salaries and feathering their own nests with graft than in the welfare of their followers, so long, in a word, as the workers are meek and submissive followers, mere sheep, they will be fleeced, and no one will hold them in greater contempt than the very grafters and parasites who fatten out of their misery.

It is not Gompers, who banquets with Belmont and Carnegie, and Mitchell, who is paid and pampered by the plutocrats, who are going to unite the workers in their struggle for emancipation. The civic federation, which was organized by the master class and consists of plutocrats, politicians and priests, in connivance with so-called labor leaders, who are used as decoys to give that body the outward appearance of representing both capital and labor, is the staunch supporter of trade-unions and the implacable foe of industrial unionism and Socialism, and this in itself should be sufficient to convince every intelligent worker that the trade union under its present leadership and, as now used, is more beneficial to the capitalist class than it is to the workers, seeing that it is the means of keeping them disunited and pitted against each other, and as an inevitable result, in wage slavery.

The workers themselves must take the initiative in uniting their forces for effective economic and political action; the leaders will never do it for them. They must no longer suffer themselves to be deceived by the specious arguments of their betrayers, who blatantly boast of their unionism that they may traffic in it and sell out the dupes who blindly follow them. I have very little use for labor leaders in general and none at all for the kind who feel their self-importance and are so impressed by their own wisdom that where they lead their dupes are expected to blindly follow without a question. Such "leaders" lead their victims to the shambles and deliver them over for a consideration and this is possible only among craft-divided wage-slaves who are kept apart for the very purpose that they may feel their economic helplessness and rely upon some "leader" to do something for them.

Economic unity will be speedily followed by political unity. The workers once united in one great industrial union will vote a united working class ticket. Not only this, but only when they are so united can they fit themselves to take control of industry when the change comes from wage-slavery to economic freedom. It is precisely because it is the mission of industrial unionism to unite the workers in harmonious cooperation in the industries in which they are employed, and by their enlightened inter-dependence and self-imposed discipline prepare them for industrial mastery and self-control when the hour strikes, thereby backing up with their economic power the verdict they render at the ballot box, it is precisely because of this fact that every Socialist, every class-conscious worker should be an industrial unionist and strive by all the means at his command to unify the workers in the all-embracing bonds of industrial unionism.

The Socialist party is the party of the workers, organized to express in political terms their determination to break their fetters and rise to the dignity of free men. In this party the workers must unite and develop their political power to conquer and abolish the capitalist political state and clear the way for industrial and social democracy.

But the new order can never be established by mere votes alone. This must be the result of industrial development and intelligent economic and political organization, necessitating both the industrial union and the political party of the workers to achieve their emancipation.

In this work, to be successfully accomplished, woman must have an equal part with man. If the revolutionary movement of the workers stands for anything it stands for the absolute equality of the sexes and when this fact is fully realized and the working woman takes her place side by side with the working man all along the battlefront the great struggle will soon be crowned with victory.

Standard Oil and Foreign Missions

Washington Gladden

Commentary

Labor union leaders were not the only polemicists to write and speak about socio-economic change. So did many preachers and college professors. One prominent preacher was Washington Gladden (1836-1918), who helped Professor Richard Ely organize the American Economic Association (AEA) in 1885. Formation of the AEA reflected the increasing amount of specialization in American colleges (many specialized scholarly societies were formed at about the same time), but it also reflected Ely's and Gladden's ideology.

At the time of AEA's founding, many professors subscribed to the *laissez faire* theories of Adam Smith and other "classical" economists; they disapproved of governmental interference in the market place. However, a growing number of economists, especially those who had studied in Germany, believed in governmental "activism." When Ely spoke to the organizational meeting of the AEA, he vehemently attacked the laissez faire philosophy and urged the AEA to support governmental activism. Even many who agreed with him opposed committing a scholarly association to a particular point of view—thus starting a debate that still persists.

Ely was partially successful in getting the AEA committed to an anti-laissez faire philosophy because of the way he "stacked" the meeting. He did not invite professors who adhered to laissez faire, but he invited non-academicians who believed in governmental activism. Among the latter group was Gladden, who was famous as a "reform" preacher. Many historians label him the founder of the "social gospel" movement, but calling him the founder is questionable because of the ambiguities surrounding the term *social gospel*.

The term did not become current until after 1900, when Gladden's career was drawing to a close, and his central message—the Christian duty to promote reform—was neither new nor unique. it had been propounded long before the Civil War by temperance workers and abolitionists such as the Grimke sisters. It was also propounded by many of Gladden's contemporaries in the late nineteenth century, when it was usually called *social Christianity* or *Christian socialism*.

In addition, a wide variety of ideologies went under the name social gospel. At one extreme was the Salvation Army (founded in Britain in 1865 and brought to the United States in 1880), which provided charities for the downtrodden but which was silent on governmental economic policy. At the other extreme was George Herron, who denounced almost all established institutions, especially private property and marriage. Most proponents of the social gospel were somewhere in between, urging something more than private charities but something less than socialism. Yet even the middle-of-the-roaders had no agreed-upon program. Some made ethical pronouncements about labor and capital loving one another, while others preached against the evil practices of the "robber barons"; some advocated that workers become the owners of industry, while others made general statements about the virtue of governmental intervention; and, finally, some were more specific, urging support for labor unions and advocating reform legislation such as laws to set minimum wages and maximum working hours. Despite the ambiguities, the social gospel movement was important between the Civil War and World War I, and Gladden was one of its most prominent representatives.

Gladden's early life shows the influence of Puritan millenarianism as modified by the nineteenth-century doctrine of social perfectibility. Reared in a strongly religious home, Gladden underwent a conversion experience while working as an apprentice, became a Congregational minister and held two short-lived pastorates in the industrial towns of North Adams and Springfield, Massachusetts. At a time when the lecture movement was growing, he delivered a "course" of public lectures to an audience consisting mostly of day laborers. He discussed three industrial systems, the first and worst of which was slavery (which had been abolished only a decade previously). The second was the existing wage system, which was better than slavery but which led to current evils. Although acknowledging that labor unions might improve the situation, he deplored the conflict between labor and capital, which he argued would never disappear until the third system was instituted. This third system was the cooperative system, under which workers would own the factories. He exhorted his audience to form worker cooperatives. The lectures were published as a book in 1976, thus gaining him a wider audience, which included Ely and his reform-minded colleagues.

In 1882, Gladden moved to a pastorate in Columbus, Ohio, where he remained until retirement. He produced a torrent of rhetorical discourses, some about theology and some about the social gospel. His speeches were read from manuscript, and some did double- or even triple-duty. Many sermons and lectures became magazine articles, and some reappeared in his book-length collection of essays. One collection, *The New Idolatry and Other Discussions* (New York: McClure, Phillips & Co.) was published in November, 1905, only two months after an intense controversy had come to a head. Gladden did not narrate the controversy because, as he said in the preface, it was "still fresh in the public mind."

Because the controversy is no longer fresh, some background is in order. In 1894, eleven years before the controversy, Henry D. Lloyd published a vitriolic attack on the Standard Oil Company in a book entitled *Wealth Against Commonwealth*. Although not mentioning the book, Gladden published in 1895 an essay entitled "Tainted Money," in which he argued that much "wealth has been gained by the most daring violations of the laws" and asked, "Is this clean money? Can any man, can any institution, knowing its origin, touch it without being defiled?" Answering his rhetorical question in the negative, Gladden argued that churches and schools should not accept gifts of "tainted money" from "robber barons." Several years passed. In 1904, Ida Tarbell published another attack on Standard Oil in her *History of the Standard Oil Company*. Most scholars agree that it was Tarbell's verbal onslaught which caused the company's founder, John D. Rockefeller, to become the first American industrialist to hire a public relations man to clean up his image. They disagree, though, on whether Rockefeller was a sincere philanthropist or gave money as a way to gain public approval. In any case, in the spring of 1905, he donated $100,000 to the American Board of Commissioners for Foreign Missions. The Board was an auxiliary of the National Council of Congregational Churches, of which Gladden was moderator. Gladden created a sensation by publicly stating that the gift (large even by today's standards and huge by those of 1905) should be refused.

The controversy reached its climax in September, when the Board held its annual meeting. A committee proposed that the Board endorse a "Statement of Principles," the first of which declared:

> Organized as a corporation to carry on foreign missionary work and to receive gifts for that purpose, the American Board has not been given the authority to discriminate between those who offer such gifts, and thereby to judge the character or reputation of the donors. It is not a beneficiary from the gift, but only an agent or a trustee for others.

Gladden countered with a substitute resolution which stated that "the officers of this Board should neither invite nor solicit donations to its funds from persons whose gains have been made by methods morally reprehensible or socially injurious." After considerable debate, both resolutions were laid on the table, thus technically meaning that neither side had won. With the acceptance of Rockefeller's gift, however, Gladden had lost.

Despite his defeat, Gladden presented his case to the public in *The New Idolatry*. He reprinted his earlier essay "Tainted Money" for the express purpose of showing his consistency on the issue. He printed a sermon delivered the previous spring in which he deplored the rule of "Mammon" in contemporary society, declared that churches were becoming captives of the "employer class" and warned that churches were losing touch with "common people." He also printed the committee's "Statement of Principles," his own resolution and his speech to the Board. Finally, he printed the essay which is reproduced below (pp. 33-52).

Standard Oil and Foreign Missions

IT seems important to those who feel that a mistake has been made in soliciting and accepting a large gift from Mr. Rockefeller to the American Board that the grounds of their opposition should be more fully set forth than has been possible hitherto. As the discussion has been going on some things have grown more clear. At first the acceptance of the gift was approved by many on the ground that it was unsolicited. It was admitted that it would have been a mistake to ask for it, but the voluntary proffer could not be rejected. It now transpires that it was not a voluntary proffer, that it was diligently sought for the space of three years. Those who approved the erroneous statements first given out, may be ready now to reconsider.

It is also needful to make it entirely clear that those who disapprove of this alliance are not acting upon mere gossip or rumour, but that they rest their judgment on well-accredited evidence. To bring these facts succinctly before the people of our churches is one purpose of the present paper.

Certain elementary moral principles appear to be repudiated in the explicit statement of the prudential committee: "Our responsibility begins with the receipt of a gift." The contention is that, no matter what may be the character of the giver, his gifts should be welcomed with thanks. It can hardly be possible that the committee means to stand on this rule. At any rate, it is very important that a clear statement be made respecting the principles which should govern the receipt of gifts from doubtful sources. Our benevolent societies cannot knowingly accept gifts which are the proceeds of lawlessness, nor must they knowingly be the partners of those who are winning gains by methods which, though not yet punished by the law, are yet notoriously and indubitably extortionate and dishonourable. In the complexities of modern commerce it is often possible to take advantage of the necessities of men or of their weakness, and extort from them their property without incurring the penalty of any law. But property thus acquired is held by no better moral title than the booty of the highwayman, and the principle which forbids complicity in unjust gains applies to this no less rigorously.

It may be agreed that gifts coming from sources unassailed may be accepted without questioning. It is not necessary that a missionary society should undertake the duties of a moral inquisitor; it ought to assume, unless there is evidence to the contrary, that gifts laid on its altars have been honestly acquired. But when the question is raised, and there is reasonable ground for believing that the money has been iniquitously obtained and does not rightfully belong to the one who offers it, the society must refuse to receive it until the doubt is resolved. There is a moral obligation here which cannot be shirked. It may sometimes be a difficult and disagreeable duty; that is no reason why it should not be faithfully performed.

The prudential committee lays down this maxim: "Our responsibility begins with the receipt of a gift." By this it means, as its argument shows, that its responsibility begins after the gift has been received. Let us amend by saying, "The responsibility of a missionary society begins in the act of receiving a gift, if that gift is unsolicited." And surely it will not be maintained that a missionary society has no responsibility for the character of a gift which it has spent three years in soliciting.

With matters of fact the prudential committee and its defenders deal no more satisfactorily than with matters of principle. Referring to the reasons given by the protestants why this gift should be refused, the committee says that if it does not feel warranted in passing judgment upon "questions which have never been settled, either before the courts or at the bar of public opinion." This must mean that neither the courts nor public opinion have furnished any adequate reasons for believing that the fortune out of which this donation comes has been flagitiously acquired. It is true that certain accusations against this company are now being investigated by the officers of the United States Government, and that legal or legislative proceedings of one sort or another against the company are now pending in thirteen or fourteen states, and it is true that these questions have not been settled.

But it is not true that no charges against this company have been proved in court. More than once the courts of the United States and the states have rendered judgment against it, setting the seal of their condemnation upon its offences. The facts concerning these court proceedings have been spread before the people in newspaper reports; they have been discussed in magazines and in public addresses; the common people, as a rule, are well informed concerning them. Much of the popular knowledge of the operations of this company comes from two sources: Mr. Henry D. Lloyd's "Wealth vs. Commonwealth," and Miss Ida M. Tarbell's "History of the Standard Oil Company," and those who argue that nothing has been proved against the Standard Oil Company are wont to disparage these books as reckless in their method or partisan in their temper.

Most of those who thus judge them have never read them. Those who have read them know that all their important statements are based on official documents, on testimony presented before legislative and congressional committees, on copies of contracts and other business instruments, and on the records of courts. In all these cases the authorities are cited. Every man who can read the English language can verify them. About one-third of each of Miss Tarbell's solid volumes is made up of such documentary evidence. To represent either of these books as the careless or slanderous assaults of ignorant persons is less than just. Neither of these writers is capable of such injustice. Each of them wrote with a deep sense of social responsibility.

Mr. Lloyd's volume exhibits more feeling; it is the testimony of a knightly soul aflame against oppression. But none who knew this man, who spent his life in the service of humanity and laid it down as a sacrifice in a great battle against wrong, needs to be told that in all his passionate devotion to the highest ideals, he could never have wantonly slandered any man. Miss Tarbell's style is more restrained. From beginning to end her book gives the impression of being a dispassionate exposition. The evidence is fairly weighed; the investigation is judicial.

The conclusive proof that these revelations are true is found in the fact that no action has been brought against either of these writers. The statements made by both of them respecting the methods and operations of this company are damning. It is incredible that these men would have rested under such charges if the charges could have been disproved. Mr. Lloyd was not an irresponsible person; he was a man of wealth and position. Miss Tarbell spread her indictment before the public in the pages of a great magazine, whose publishers could have been severely punished if what she stated was libellous. There was money enough to prosecute slanderers, and shrewd lawyers enough to have exposed their malice, and courts not at all loath to do them justice. The fact that not a finger has been raised to punish them is evidence that their indictment cannot be overthrown.

Not only from these books, and from the authorities to which they refer, but from a great variety of other sources open to the people of the United States, may be drawn abundant materials for a judgment respecting the Standard Oil Company and its methods. It is thus a matter of common knowledge that the Standard Oil Company has been frequently convicted, sometimes out of its own mouth, of transgressions of the laws of the land. A fearless judge of the United States District Court denounced their system of rebates as "gross, illegal and inexcusable," and said of it: "The discrimination complained of in this case is so wanton and oppressive that it could hardly have been accepted by an honest man having a due regard for the rights of others." The plea of the apologists for the company always is that their system of rebates was not illegal until the interstate commerce law had forbidden it. But Judge Baxter brushes that sophistry aside. He declares that the charter of every railway involves "the obligation to carry for every person offering business under like circumstances at the same rate. All unjust discriminations are in violation of sound public policy, and are forbidden by law.... If it were not so, the managers of railways in collusion with others in command of large capital could control the business of the country, at least to the extent that the business was dependent on railroad transportation for its success, and make and unmake the fortunes of men at will."

This is precisely what the Standard Oil Company is charged with doing through all its history, and the solemn declaration of a judge of the United States Court that it is "greatly abhorrent to all fair minds" finds an echo in every honest heart. It was but a small amount that the company was compelled by this decision to disgorge, but the words of Judge Baxter apply with equal force to the great bulk of the transactions of this company with the railroads for a period of ten or twelve years, and he describes a kind of operation under which they extorted from their competitors, through the railroads, many millions of dollars. It was by help of this "wanton and oppressive" exercise of power that this stupendous monopoly was built up. The Standard Oil Company, with its present power to rule and ruin the business of the country, could not have existed but for this illegal and outrageous use of the railroads in the extermination of competitors. There was never any appeal from Judge Baxter's judgment in this case, and if anything can be "settled by the courts" it was settled then that it was by the help of flagitious methods that this fortune has been reared. However persistently, in accepting gifts, we may shut our eyes to these facts, millions of the American people are fully informed concerning them.

There are other facts not less notorious. It is known that the managers of this combination, after doing business illegally as a trust for ten years, were compelled by a decree of the Supreme Court of Ohio to dissolve their organization and go out of business. Their entire procedure during all that time had been in violation of law. They found in New Jersey, of course, a "legal" outfit for carrying on their depredations.

On various occasions they have been constrained to make distinct confession respecting the nature of their business. In 1879 when their leaders were under indictment for conspiracy, they refused to answer questions put to them by an investigating committee on the plea that if they told the truth they would incriminate themselves; and again, in 1898, when ordered by the Supreme Court of Ohio to produce their books in court, the secretary of the Standard Oil Company of Ohio made oath that he could not do so without incriminating both the company and himself.

The American people know of all these things and many more like unto them. More than this, they are fully aware that the business methods of the company, even when not technically illegal, are often utterly dishonourable. Competitive business at its best estate is apt to be hard and merciless, but it recognizes certain principles of decency and fair play. It is a game, and it is played to win; but the rules of the game are fairly observed by honourable competitors. It is the simple truth to say that the Standard Oil Company from the beginning has violated all these rules. It has played continually with stacked cards and loaded dice. On the football field or in the prize ring such unsportsmanlike behaviour would be execrated.

There is a kind of competition which the German law makes criminal. This is the kind of competition which this company has always practised. The system of rebates is, of course, the most abhorrent of these practices. It is often said that the acceptance of rebates has been nearly universal on the part of large shippers, but the kind of rebates extorted by this company — rebates not only on its own shipments, but on all those of its competitors, ordinary concerns could never have collected. Other gigantic combinations are now enforcing the same kind of tribute from independent dealers, but it is palpable that only those aggregations of wealth which are able to dominate the railroads could compel them to collect tribute for their benefit from their competitors. There is nothing more startling or more ominous in American history than the fact that such a tremendous injustice has been permitted to go on year after year, with no interference by the Government. Of this kind of extortion Mr. Rockefeller has the credit of being the inventor. It was a weapon that he forged and wielded most mercilessly in the destruction of his competitors. Others have since learned the art, but the credit of originating it must be given to him. Is it not entirely clear that no man, with the most elementary notions of justice, could ever have conceived of it?

Besides this colossal wrong many practices of the utmost baseness have characterized this business. The subsidizing of local railway freight agents, by whom full reports have been sent to the Standard of all shipments arriving at the station from competing companies; the bribery of the employees of competitors to reveal to the Standard the secrets of their employers' business; especially the contemptible manner in which prices are always cut to kill competition, and then raised as soon as it is killed, and every poor oil pedlar anywhere in the land selling other than Standard oil is dogged and driven from his livelihood by this giant — these are illustrations of a kind of thing which does not deserve to bear the name of business. In Miss Tarbell's chapter on "Cutting to Kill" will be found photographic reproductions of the kind of "reports" made to this company and many letters from dealers all over the land reciting their experience.

Let no man say that such methods as these are characteristic of American commerce. What do the reputable business men mean who come forward to defend or to apologize for this brigandage? Do they wish to associate themselves with an enormity of this nature? Do they want us to believe that they are doing business after this fashion? Is it Pharisaism to claim a higher standard of business morality than that which rules in such transactions?

Such are a few of the notorious facts upon which the American people have made up their judgment respecting the business of the Standard Oil Company. If iniquitous gains are not to be welcomed into the Lord's treasury, a serious mistake must have been made in soliciting these.

It is sometimes said that this man and this company are only the products of bad social conditions. But history shows that they are producers more than products. They have done more to create these evil social conditions than any score of other agencies.

We are often asked why we single out this man for reprobation. If the answer has not already been given it is enough to say that we did not single him out; it was the prudential committee who singled him out by soliciting his donation. We object to this gift because it is now before us for judgment. It is said that there are others from whom a gift would be equally objectionable. Even if that were true, no gifts have been offered by these others, and it will be time to decide about them when they are offered. Each case must stand on its own merits.

That there may be others with whom the churches ought to refuse alliance is probable. The methods which the Standard Oil Company has found so successful are being adopted by other great companies, and this is the alarming fact.

This vast power of concentrated wealth, which is exerted, with a growing disregard of human welfare for the aggrandizement of the few by the oppression of the many, has filled the minds of the people with a mighty indignation. It is not true that all rich men are robbers, but the facts which have come to light within the last year respecting some of the aggregations of wealth are sufficiently disquieting. The Standard Oil Company is not the only gigantic monopoly which evinces an unsocial purpose, and there is no intention on the part of those who resist these aggressions to confine their warfare to this one organization. But this is the mightiest and probably the worst of these anti-social forces; its operations are better known than those of any of its kindred; the case against it is clearer than against any other monopoly. If the churches of Christ are to separate themselves from the iniquity of conscienceless and predatory wealth, there can be no better place than this to begin. If we accept in our Christian work the alliance of the Standard Oil Company, we can refuse no other alliance with oppressors and despoilers of the people; to say that we will not testify against this iniquity because others are nearly or quite as heinous is practically to say that we will testify against no iniquity, that in the presence of all this wrong we will shut our eyes and seal our lips.

Is it not plain that the association into which the Church is being drawn in its solicitation of this gift must be full of injury to the cause which it represents and embarrassing and humiliating to the people upon whom it depends for support? Surely, there are those with whom we cannot be profitably yoked together, and we beseech our churches, before it is too late, to consider well the harm which this alliance is sure to work in several directions.

The Church which accepts the Standard Oil Company as its yoke-fellow can hardly hope to keep the respect of right-minded young men and women. Tens of thousands of these have been studying social problems in our colleges and universities, and their minds are clear upon the bearing of these social questions. The Church which, for money, is ready to condone social injustice will lose its hold on these young people. They are able to understand the law of Christ, and they have studied the record of this iniquity, and they know that there can be no agreement between them. They will either be repelled from the Church, as too many of them have already been, or else, drawn by the example of those who ought to be better guides into complaisance with what they know to be wrong, their moral standards will be lowered and their characters undermined. Let no man dismiss this as a chimera; the Church is in great danger of inflicting terrible injury upon the youth of this generation, and thus of striking a fatal blow at her own life.

The effect upon the working people of the land and upon the whole of the non-churchgoing class must also be well considered. There are many explanations, some of which are more or less plausible, of the increasing absence of the industrious self-respecting working people from our churches, but the one great cause is the almost universal belief that the churches of the country are in too close relations with unscrupulous and predaceous wealth. A good many of us have been trying hard to correct this impression and to remove the causes of it. We have felt that the separation between the churches and these honest, hard-working people, who are the bone and sinew of our population, is the opprobrium of our Christianity. We had hoped that our Congregational Churches were making some progress toward a better understanding with them, but the effect of the acceptance of this gift will be to widen and deepen the chasm between the churches and those whom they most need to reach. It is fatuous to doubt it. From all over the land, already, the testimony is pouring in, showing that this is sure to happen. By the working people, the average people, everywhere, the protest against the acceptance of the gift was met with a glad outcry of hope and thanksgiving; while the tidings that it has been overruled has called forth bitter words of despairing indignation.

If the Church wishes to regain its hold upon the people who heard its Master gladly, it must keep itself free from such alliances as these.

The truth is that the great masses of the American people have a very clear and positive opinion respecting the sources from which this gift has come. No casuistry will change their minds. They never can be persuaded that friendship with such malign powers is not suspicious and shameful. They will insist on believing that churches as well as men are known by the company they keep, and they will never be convinced that a church which cultivates the society and co-operation of such men is a true representative of Jesus Christ.

Finally, the national aspects of this question press upon our attention. This nation is facing a crisis in its history. Our easy-going optimism may ignore it, but the battle is on between corporate greed and industrial freedom. Enormous aggregations of capital are seeking to gather up and control not only the railways and the mines and the food supply of the people, but the Government itself. This power already lays a heavy hand on industry and enterprise. Thoughtful men confront the future with sober faces. If we want to save our nation from the vast oppressions that are sure to provoke reactions, we must gird ourselves for a determined struggle. In all this warfare the Christian churches ought to be at the front, leaders in the fight for equal opportunity, witnesses for the liberty with which the Son makes us free.

Now, it is undeniable that among the powers and influences which have led the nation into the peril which now threatens us — the peril arising from aggregations of selfish wealth — none has been more potent or more ruthless than that which it is now proposed to take into partnership in our missionary work. It is an impossible suggestion. As Christian patriots we cannot think of it. We must keep our churches from all entangling alliances with the enemies of our country, no matter in what guise they may appear. Failure here will be the costliest blunder that the Church has ever made.

The Forgotten Man (Abridged)

William Graham Sumner

Commentary

Although Ely invited the non-academician, Washington Gladden, to the organizational meeting of the American Economic Association, he was careful to avoid inviting a fellow German-trained academician, William Graham Sumner (1840-1910). Ely privately told friends that he wanted none of "the Sumner crowd" in the AEA. The reasons are not difficult to discern. The well-known, controversial and outspoken Sumner represented the epitome of laissez faire philosophy. He was rhetorically active in writing and speaking against any sort of governmental interference in the economy, whether it be the protectionism that the trustees of his university favored or the reforms that Ely and Gladden espoused.

Like Ely, Sumner was both a scientist and a moralist. The son of a day laborer, Sumner learned the virtues of hard work and thrift at an early age. Through parental sacrifice, he was able to attend college. Then he borrowed money to study in Germany. Although fascinated by the social sciences, he proceeded to prepare for the ministry. After short stints as a Yale tutor and Episcopal minister, he returned to Yale in 1872 as Professor of Political and Social Science. Like Ely and other specialists, Sumner opposed the tutorial system (even while he was a tutor) and wished to put social studies on a scientific basis. Like Ely, Sumner engaged in some historical economic research. Unlike those in the Ely group, Sumner was influenced by Herbert Spencer's theory of Social Darwinism, which maintained that social progress depends on allowing social "laws" to work unimpeded: let the "fittest" survive and the "unfit" fall by the wayside. Social Darwinism has generally been scorned by later social scientists, mostly on the grounds that it represents a heartless lack of concern for the "unfit."

Sumner's academic career was divided into two periods. In his later years, he moved away from economics, worked out his Social Darwinism in more detail and avoided the public arena while he wrote for his fellow sociologists.

It was during his early years, especially the 1870s and 1880s, that he wrote books and essays and delivered lectures addressed to the general public about current public issues. His rhetorical discourses, although containing elements of Social Darwinism, were dominated by a single, moralistic appeal: governmental interference in the economy ultimately hurts the honest, hard-working, average American.

Sumner was an active supporter of civil service "reform," arguing that improved civil service would lessen governmental corruption, for corruption, he argued, is ultimately paid for by honest, hard-working, average Americans. When the Greenback party emerged to advocate paper money, Sumner supported the gold standard, arguing that paper money was an artificial inducement for inflation, which hurts honest, hard-working, average Americans. When Congress was legislating subsidies for shipbuilders, Sumner argued that economic laws should be allowed to work as they will. If shippers could purchase foreign ships at a cheaper price, they would save money for themselves and, ultimately, the consumer. Investment capital could then be diverted into more efficient industries, thereby creating jobs for honest, hard-working, average Americans. Especially scornful of the protective tariff (which got him into trouble with the Yale trustees), Sumner published in 1885 a book entitled *Protectionism, the -Ism Which Teaches that Waste Makes Wealth*. He announced in the preface, "Protectionism arouses my moral indignation...and forces me to take part in a popular agitation." Protective tariffs, he argued, were simply another subsidy which, like all subsidies, benefited a special interest group at the expense of honest, hard-working, average Americans.

Sumner was equally scornful of proposals to subsidize the poor. He expounded his views in his most famous lecture, which was first delivered in 1883 and repeated many times thereafter. In addition, it was published as an essay several times after his death. The following abridged version is reproduced photographically from Ernest J. Wrage and Barnett Baskerville, *American Forum: Speeches on Historic Issues, 1788-1900* (New York: Harper & Brothers, 1960), pp. 229-243.

The Forgotten Man (Abridged)

I propose in this lecture to discuss one of the most *subtile* and widespread social fallacies. It consists in the impression made on the mind for the time being by a particular fact, or by the interests of a particular group of persons, to which attention is directed while other facts or the interests of other persons are entirely left out of account. I shall give a number of instances and illustrations of this in a moment, and I cannot expect you to understand what is meant from an abstract statement until these illustrations are before you, but just by way of a general illustration I will put one or two cases.

Whenever a pestilence like yellow fever breaks out in any city, our attention is especially attracted towards it, and our sympathies are excited for the sufferers. If contributions are called for, we readily respond. Yet the number of persons who die prematurely from consumption every year greatly exceeds the deaths from yellow fever or any similar disease when it occurs, and the suffering entailed by consumption is very much greater. The suffering from consumption, however, never constitutes a public question or a subject of social discussion. If an inundation takes place anywhere, constituting a public calamity (and an inundation takes place somewhere in the civilized world nearly every year), public attention is attracted and public appeals are made, but the losses by great inundations must be insignificant compared with the losses by runaway horses, which, taken separately, scarcely obtain mention in a local newspaper. In hard times insolvent debtors are a large class. They constitute an interest and are able to attract public attention, so that social philosophers discuss their troubles and legislatures plan measures of relief. Insolvent debtors, however, are an insignificant body compared with the victims of commonplace misfortune, or accident, who are isolated, scattered, ungrouped and ungeneralized, and so are never made the object of discussion or relief. In seasons of ordinary prosperity, persons who become insolvent have to get out of their troubles as they can. They have no hope of relief from the legislature. The number of insolvents during a series of years of general prosperity, and their losses, greatly exceed the number and losses during a special period of distress.

These illustrations bring out only one side of my subject, and that only partially. It is when we come to the proposed measures of relief for the evils which have caught public attention that we reach the real subject which deserves our attention. As soon as A observes something which seems to him to be wrong, from which X is suffering, A talks it over with B, and A and B then propose to get a law passed to remedy the evil and help X. Their law always proposes to determine what C shall do for X or, in the better case, what A, B and C shall do for X. As for A and B, who get a law to make themselves do for X what they are willing to do for him, we have nothing to say except that they might better have done it without any law, but what I want to do is to look up C. I want to show you what manner of man he is. I call him the Forgotten Man. Perhaps the appellation is not strictly correct. He is the man who never is thought of. He is the victim of the reformer, social speculator and philanthropist, and I hope to show you before I get through that he deserves your notice both for his character and for the many burdens which are laid upon him.

No doubt one great reason for the phenomenon which I bring to your attention is the passion for reflection and generalization which marks our period. Since the printing press has come into such wide use, we have all been encouraged to philosophize about things in a way which was unknown to our ancestors. They lived their lives out in positive contact with actual cases as they arose. They had little of this analysis, introspection, reflection and speculation which have passed into a habit and almost into a disease with us. Of all things which tempt to generalization and to philosophizing, social topics stand foremost. Each one of us gets some experience of social forces. Each one has some chance for observation of social phenomena. There is certainly no domain in which generalization is easier. There is nothing about which people dogmatize more freely. Even men of scientific training in some department in which they would not tolerate dogmatism at all will not hesitate to dogmatize in the most reckless manner about social topics. The truth is, however, that science, as yet, has won less control of social phenomena than of any other class of phenomena. The most complex and difficult subject which we now have to study is the constitution of human society, the forces which operate in it, and the laws by which they act, and we know less about these things than about any others which demand our attention. In such a state of things, over-hasty generalization is sure to be extremely mischievous. You cannot take up a magazine or newspaper without being struck by the feverish interest with which social topics and problems are discussed, and if you were a student of social science, you would find in almost all these discussions evidence, not only that the essential preparation for the discussion is wanting, but that the disputants do not even know that there is any preparation to be gained. Consequently we are bewildered by contradictory dogmatizing. We find in all these discussions only the application of pet notions and the clashing of contradictory "views." Remedies are confidently proposed for which there is no guarantee offered except that the person who prescribes the remedy says that he is sure it will work. We hear constantly of "reform," and the reformers turn out to be people who do not like things as they are and wish that they could be made nicer. We hear a great many exhortations to make progress from people who do not know in what direction they want to go. Consequently social reform is the most barren and tiresome subject of discussion amongst us, except aesthetics.

I suppose that the first chemists seemed to be very hardhearted and unpoetical persons when they scouted the glorious dream of the alchemists that there must be some process for turning base metals into gold. I suppose that the men who first said, in plain, cold assertion, there is no fountain of eternal youth, seemed to be the most cruel and cold-hearted adversaries of human happiness. I know that the economists who say that if we could transmute lead into gold, it would certainly do us no good and might do great harm, are still regarded as unworthy of belief. Do not the money articles of the newspapers yet ring with the doctrine that we are getting rich when we give cotton and wheat for gold rather than when we give cotton and wheat for iron?

Let us put down now the cold, hard fact and look at it just as it is. There is no device whatever to be invented for securing happiness without industry, economy, and virtue. We are yet in the empirical stage as regards

all our social devices. We have done something in science and art in the
domain of production, transportation and exchange. But when you come
to the laws of the social order, we know very little about them. Our laws
and institutions by which we attempt to regulate our lives under the laws
of nature which control society are merely a series of haphazard experiments.
We come into collision with the laws and are not intelligent enough to
understand wherein we are mistaken and how to correct our errors. We
persist in our experiments instead of patiently setting about the study of
the laws and facts in order to see where we are wrong. Traditions and
formulae have a dominion over us in legislation and social customs which
we seem unable to break or even to modify.

For my present purpose I ask your attention for a few moments to the
notion of liberty, because the Forgotten Man would no longer be forgotten
where there was true liberty. You will say that you know what liberty is.
There is no term of more common or prouder use. None is more current,
as if it were quite beyond the need of definition. Even as I write, however,
I find in a leading review a new definition of civil liberty. Civil liberty the
writer declares to be "the result of the restraint exercised by the sovereign
people on the more powerful individuals and classes of the community,
preventing them from availing themselves of the excess of their power to
the detriment of the other classes." You notice here the use of the words
"sovereign people" to designate a class of the population, not the nation
as a political and civil whole. Wherever "people" is used in such a sense,
there is always fallacy. Furthermore, you will recognize in this definition
a very superficial and fallacious construction of English constitutional history.
The writer goes on to elaborate that construction and he comes out at
last with the conclusion that "a government by the people can, in no case,
become a paternal government, since its lawmakers are its mandataries and
servants carrying out its will, and not its fathers or its masters." This, then,
is the point at which he desires to arrive, and he has followed a familiar
device in setting up a definition to start with which would produce the
desired deduction at the end.

In the definition the word "people" was used for a class or section of the
population. It is now asserted that if *that* section rules, there can be no
paternal, that is, undue, government. That doctrine, however, is the very
opposite of liberty, and contains the most vicious error possible in politics.
The truth is that cupidity, selfishness, envy, malice, lust, vindictiveness, are
constant vices of human nature. They are not confined to classes or to
nations or particular ages of the world. They present themselves in the
palace, in the parliament, in the academy, in the church, in the workshop,
and in the hovel. They appear in autocracies, theocracies, aristocracies,
democracies, and ochlocracies all alike. They change their masks somewhat
from age to age and from one form of society to another. All history is
only one long story to this effect: men have struggled for power over their
fellow-men in order that they might win the joys of earth at the expense

of others and might shift the burdens of life from their own shoulders upon those of others. It is true that, until this time, the proletariat, the mass of mankind, have rarely had the power and they have not made such a record as kings and nobles and priests have made of the abuses they would perpetrate against their fellow-men when they could and dared. But what folly it is to think that vice and passion are limited by classes, that liberty consists only in taking power away from nobles and priests and giving it to artisans and peasants and that these latter will never abuse it! They will abuse it just as all others have done unless they are put under checks and guarantees, and there can be no civil liberty anywhere unless rights are guaranteed against all abuses, as well from proletarians as from generals, aristocrats, and ecclesiastics.

Now what has been amiss in all the old arrangements? The evil of the old military and aristocratic governments was that some men enjoyed the fruits of other men's labor; that some persons' lives, rights, interests and happiness were sacrificed to other persons' cupidity and lust. What have our ancestors been striving for, under the name of civil liberty, for the last five hundred years? They have been striving to bring it about that each man and woman might live out his or her life according to his or her own notions of happiness and up to the measure of his or her own virtue and wisdom. How have they sought to accomplish this? They have sought to accomplish it by setting aside all arbitrary personal or class elements and introducing the reign of law and the supremacy of constitutional institutions like the jury, the habeas corpus, the independent judiciary, the separation of church and state, and the ballot. Note right here one point which will be important and valuable when I come more especially to the case of the Forgotten Man: whenever you talk of liberty, you must have *two* men in mind. The sphere of rights of one of these men trenches upon that of the other, and whenever you establish liberty for the one, you repress the other. Whenever absolute sovereigns are subjected to constitutional restraints, you always hear them remonstrate that their liberty is curtailed. So it is, in the sense that their power of determining what shall be done in the state is limited below what it was before and the similar power of other organs in the state is widened. Whenever the privileges of an aristocracy are curtailed, there is heard a similar complaint. The truth is that the line of limit or demarcation between classes as regards civil power has been moved and what has been taken from one class is given to another.

We may now, then, advance a step in our conception of civil liberty. It is the status in which we find the true adjustment of rights between classes and individuals. Historically, the conception of civil liberty has been constantly changing. The notion of rights changes from one generation to another and the conception of civil liberty changes with it. If we try to formulate a true definition of civil liberty as an ideal thing towards which the development of political institutions is all the time tending, it would be this: Civil liberty is the status of the man who is guaranteed by law and civil institutions the exclusive employment of all his own powers for his own welfare.

This definition of liberty or civil liberty, you see, deals only with concrete and actual relations of the civil order. There is some sort of a poetical and metaphysical notion of liberty afloat in men's minds which some people dream about but which nobody can define. In popular language it means that a man may do as he has a mind to. When people get this notion of liberty into their heads and combine with it the notion that they live in a free country and ought to have liberty, they sometimes make strange demands upon the state. If liberty means to be able to do as you have a mind to, there is no such thing in this world. Can the Czar of Russia do as he has a mind to? Can the Pope do as he has a mind to? Can the President of the United States do as he has a mind to? Can Rothschild do as he has a mind to? Could a Humboldt or a Faraday do as he had a mind to? Could a Shakespeare or a Raphael do as he had a mind to? Can a tramp do as he has a mind to? Where is the man, whatever his station, possessions, or talents, who can get any such liberty? There is none. There is a doctrine floating about in our literature that we are born to the inheritance of certain rights. That is another glorious dream, for it would mean that there was something in this world which we got for nothing. But what is the truth? We are born into no right whatever but what has an equivalent and corresponding. duty right alongside of it. There is no such thing on this earth as something for nothing. Whatever we inherit of wealth, knowledge, or institutions from the past has been paid for by the labor and sacrifice of preceding generations; and the fact that these gains are carried on, that the race lives and that the race can, at least within some cycle, accumulate its gains, is one of the facts on which civilization rests. The law of the conservation of energy is not simply a law of physics; it is a law of the whole moral universe, and the order and truth of all things conceivable by man depends upon it. If there were any such liberty as that of doing as you have a mind to, the human race would be condemned to everlasting anarchy and war as these erratic wills crossed and clashed against each other. True liberty lies in the equilibrium of rights and duties, producing peace, order, and harmony. As I have defined it, it means that a man's right to take power and wealth out of the social product is measured by the energy and wisdom which he has contributed to the social effort.

Now if I have set this idea before you with any distinctness and success, you see that civil liberty consists of a set of civil institutions and laws which are arranged to act as impersonally as possible. It does not consist in majority rule or in universal suffrage or in elective systems at all. These are devices which are good or better just in the degree in which they secure liberty. The institutions of civil liberty leave each man to run his career in life in his own way, only guaranteeing to him that whatever he does in the way of industry, economy, prudence, sound judgment, etc., shall redound to his own welfare and shall not be diverted to some one else's benefit. Of course it is a necessary corollary that each man shall also bear the penalty of his own vices and his own mistakes. If I want to be free from any other man's dictation, I must understand that I can have no other man under my control.

Now with these definitions and general conceptions in mind, let us turn to the special class of facts to which, as I said at the outset, I invite your attention. We see that under a régime of liberty and equality before the law, we get the highest possible development of independence, self-reliance, individual energy, and enterprise, but we get these high social virtues at the expense of the old sentimental ties which used to unite baron and retainer, master and servant, sage and disciple, comrade and comrade. We are agreed that the son shall not be disgraced even by the crime of the father, much less by the crime of a more distant relative. It is a humane and rational view of things that each life shall stand for itself alone and not be weighted by the faults of another, but it is useless to deny that this view of things is possible only in a society where the ties of kinship have lost nearly all the intensity of poetry and romance which once characterized them. The ties of sentiment and sympathy also have faded out. We have come, under the régime of liberty and equality before the law, to a form of society which is based not on status, but on free contract. Now a society based on status is one in which classes, ranks, interests, industries, guilds, associations, etc., hold men in permanent relations to each other. Custom and prescription create, under status, ties, the strength of which lies in sentiment. Feeble remains of this may be seen in some of our academical societies to-day, and it is unquestionably a great privilege and advantage for any man in our society to win experience of the sentiments which belong to a strong and close association, just because the chances for such experience are nowadays very rare. In a society based on free contract, men come together as free and independent parties to an agreement which is of mutual advantage. The relation is rational, even rationalistic. It is not poetical. It does not exist from use and custom, but for reasons given, and it does not endure by prescription but ceases when the reason for it ceases. There is no sentiment in it at all. The fact is that, under the régime of liberty and equality before the law, there is no place for sentiment in trade or politics as public interests. Sentiment is thrown back into private life, into personal relations, and if ever it comes into a public discussion of an impersonal and general public question it always produces mischief.

Now you know that "the poor and the weak" are continually put forward as objects of public interest and public obligation. In the appeals which are made, the terms "the poor" and "the weak" are used as if they were terms of exact definition. Except the pauper, that is to say, the man who cannot earn his living or pay his way, there is no possible definition of a poor man. Except a man who is incapacitated by vice or by physical infirmity, there is no definition of a weak man. The paupers and the physically incapacitated are an inevitable charge on society. About them no more need be said. But the weak who constantly arouse the pity of humanitarians and philanthopists are the shiftless, the imprudent, the negligent, the impractical, and the inefficient, or they are the idle, the intemperate, the extravagant, and the vicious. Now the troubles of these persons are constantly forced upon public attention, as if they and their interests deserved especial consideration, and a great portion of all organized and unorganized effort for the common welfare consists in attempts to relieve these classes of people. I do not wish to be understood now as saying that nothing ought to be done for these people by those who are stronger and wiser. That is not my point. What I want to do is to point out the thing which is overlooked and the error which is made in all these charitable efforts. The notion is accepted as if it were not open to any question that if you help the inefficient and vicious you may gain something for society or you may not, but that you lose nothing. This is a complete mistake. Whatever capital you divert to the support of a shiftless and good-for-nothing person is so much diverted from some other employment, and that means from somebody else. I would spend any conceivable amount of zeal and eloquence if I possessed it to try to make people grasp this idea. Capital is force. If it goes one way it cannot go another. If you give a loaf to a pauper you cannot give the same loaf to a laborer. Now this other man who would have got it but for the charitable sentiment which bestowed it on a worthless member of society is the Forgotten Man. The philanthropists and humanitarians have their minds all full of the wretched and miserable whose case appeals to compassion, attacks the sympathies, takes possession of the imagination, and excites the emotions. They push on towards the quickest and easiest remedies and they forget the real victim.

Now who is the Forgotten Man? He is the simple, honest laborer, ready to earn his living by productive work. We pass him by because he is independent, self-supporting, and asks no favors. He does not appeal to the emotions or excite the sentiments. He only wants to make a contract and fulfill it, with respect on both sides and favor on neither side. He must get his living out of the capital of the country. The larger the capital is, the better living he can get. Every particle of capital which is wasted on the vicious, the idle, and the shiftless is so much taken from the capital available to reward the independent and productive laborer. But we stand with our backs to the independent and productive laborer all the time. We do not remember him because he makes no clamor; but I appeal to you whether he is not the man who ought to be remembered first of all, and whether, on any sound social theory, we ought not to protect him against the burdens of the good-for-nothing. In these last years I have read hundreds of articles and heard scores of sermons and speeches which were really glorifications of the good-for-nothing, as if these were the charge of society, recommended by right reason to its care and protection. We are addressed all the time as if those who are respectable were to blame because some are not so, and as if there were an obligation on the part of those who have done their duty towards those who have not done their duty. Every man is bound to take care of himself and his family and to do his share of the work of society. It is totally false that one who has done so is bound to bear the care and charge of those who are wretched because they have not done so. The silly popular notion is that the beggars live at the expense of the rich, but the truth is that those who eat and produce not, live at the expense of those who labor and produce. The next time that you are tempted to subscribe a dollar to a charity, I do not tell you not to do it, because after you have fairly considered the matter, you may think it right to do it, but I do ask you to stop and remember the Forgotten Man and understand that if you put your dollar in the savings bank it will go to swell the capital of the country which is available for division amongst those who, while they earn it, will reproduce it with increase.

Let us now go on to another class of cases. There are a great many schemes brought forward for "improving the condition of the working classes." I have shown already that a free man cannot take a favor. One who takes a favor or submits to patronage demeans himself. He falls under obligation. He cannot be free and he cannot assert a station of equality with the man who confers the favor on him. The only exception is where there are exceptional bonds of affection or friendship, that is, where the sentimental relation supersedes the free relation. Therefore, in a country which is a free democracy, all propositions to do something for the working classes have an air of patronage and superiority which is impertinent and out of place. No one can do anything for anybody else unless he has a surplus of energy to dispose of after taking care of himself. In the United States, the working classes, technically so called, are the strongest classes. It is they who have a surplus to dispose of if anybody has. Why should anybody else offer to take care of them or to serve them? They can get whatever they think worth having and, at any rate, if they are free men in a free state, it is ignominious and unbecoming to introduce fashions of patronage and favoritism here. A man who, by superior education and experience of business, is in a position to advise a struggling man of the wages class, is certainly held to do so and will, I believe, always be willing and glad to do so; but this sort of activity lies in the range of private and personal relations.

I now, however, desire to direct attention to the public, general, and impersonal schemes, and I point out the fact that, if you undertake to lift anybody, you must have a fulcrum of point of resistance. All the elevation you give to one must be gained by an equivalent depression on some one else. The question of gain to society depends upon the balance of the account, as regards the position of the persons who undergo the respective operations. But nearly all the schemes for "improving the condition of the working man" involve an elevation of some working men at the expense of other working men. When you expend capital or labor to elevate some persons who come within the sphere of your influence, you interfere in the conditions of competition. The advantage of some is won by an equivalent loss of others. The difference is not brought about by the energy and effort of the persons themselves. If it were, there would be nothing to be said about it, for we constantly see people surpass others in the rivalry of life and carry off the prizes which the others must do without. In the cases I am discussing, the difference is brought about by an interference which must be partial, arbitrary, accidental, controlled by favoritism and personal preference. I do not say, in this case, either, that we ought to do no work of this kind. On the contrary, I believe that the arguments for it quite outweigh, in many cases, the arguments against it. What I desire, again, is to bring out the forgotten element which we always need to remember in order to make a wise decision as to any scheme of this kind. I want to call to mind the Forgotten Man, because, in this case also, if we recall him and go to look for him, we shall find him patiently and perseveringly, manfully and independently struggling against adverse circumstances without complaining or begging. If, then, we are led to heed the groaning and complaining of others and to take measures for helping these others, we shall, before we know it, push down this man who is trying to help himself.

Let us take another class of cases. So far we have said nothing about the abuse of legislation. We all seem to be under the delusion that the rich pay the taxes. Taxes are not thrown upon the consumers with any such directness and completeness as is sometimes assumed; but that, in ordinary states of the market, taxes on houses fall, for the most part, on the tenants and that taxes on commodities fall, for the most part, on the consumers, is beyond question. Now the state and municipality go to great expense to support policemen and sheriffs and judicial officers, to protect people against themselves, that is, against the results of their own folly, vice, and recklessness. Who pays for it? Undoubtedly the people who have not been guilty of folly, vice, or recklessness. Out of nothing comes nothing. We cannot collect taxes from people who produce nothing and save nothing. The people who have something to tax must be those who have produced and saved.

When you see a drunkard in the gutter, you are disgusted, but you pity him. When a policeman comes and picks him up you are satisfied. You say that "society" has interfered to save the drunkard from perishing. Society is a fine word, and it saves us the trouble of thinking to say that society acts. The truth is that the policeman is paid by somebody, and when we talk about society we forget who it is that pays. It is the Forgotten Man again. It is the industrious workman going home from a hard day's work, whom you pass without noticing, who is mulcted of a percentage of his day's earnings to hire a policeman to save the drunkard from himself. All the public expenditure to prevent vice has the same effect. Vice is its own curse. If we let nature alone, she cures vice by the most frightful penalties. It may shock you to hear me say it, but when you get over the shock, it will do you good to think of it: a drunkard in the gutter is just where he ought to be. Nature is working away at him to get him out of the way, just as she sets up her processes of dissolution to remove whatever is a failure in its line. Gambling and less mentionable vices all cure themselves by the ruin and dissolution of their victims. Nine-tenths of our measures for preventing vice are really protective towards it, because they ward off the penalty. "Ward off," I say, and that is the usual way of looking at it; but is the penalty really annihilated? By no means. It is turned into police and court expenses and spread over those who have resisted vice. It is the Forgotten Man again who has been subjected to the penalty while our minds were full of the drunkards, spendthrifts, gamblers, and other victims of dissipation. Who is, then, the Forgotten Man? He is the clean, quiet, virtuous, domestic citizen, who pays his debts and his taxes and is never heard of out of his little circle. Yet who is there in the society of a civilized state who deserves to be remembered and considered by the legislator and statesman before this man?

Another class of cases is closely connected with this last. There is an apparently invincible prejudice in people's minds in favor of state regulation. All experience is against state regulation and in favor of liberty. The freer the civil institutions are, the more weak or mischievous state regulation is. The Prussian bureaucracy can do a score of things for the citizen which no governmental organ in the United States can do; and, conversely, if we want to be taken care of as Prussians and Frenchmen are, we must give up something of our personal liberty.

Now we have a great many well-intentioned people among us who believe that they are serving their country when they discuss plans for regulating the relations of employer and employee, or the sanitary regulations of dwellings, or the construction of factories, or the way to behave on Sunday, or what people ought not to eat or drink or smoke. All this is harmless enough and well enough as a basis of mutual encouragement and missionary enterprise, but it is almost always made a basis of legislation. The reformers want to get a majority, that is, to get the power of the state and so to make other people do what the reformers think it right and wise to do. A and B agree to spend Sunday in a certain way. They get a law passed to make C pass it in their way. They determine to be teetotallers and they get a law passed to make C be a teetotaller for the sake of D who is likely to drink too much. Factory acts for women and children are right because women and children are not on an equal footing with men and cannot, therefore, make contracts properly. Adult men, in a free state, must be left to make their own contracts and defend themselves. It will not do to say that some men are weak and unable to make contracts any better than women. Our civil institutions assume that all men are equal in political capacity and all are given equal measure of political power and right, which is not the case with women and children. If, then, we measure political rights by one theory and social responsibilities by another, we produce an immoral and vicious relation. A and B, however, get factory acts and other acts passed

regulating the relation of employers and employee and set armies of commissioners and inspectors traveling about to see to things, instead of using
their efforts, if any are needed, to lead the free men to make their own
conditions as to what kind of factory buildings they will work in, how
many hours they will work, what they will do on Sunday and so on. The
consequence is that men lose the true education in freedom which is needed
to support free institutions. They are taught to rely on government officers
and inspectors. The whole system of government inspectors is corrupting
to free institutions. In England, the liberals used always to regard state
regulation with suspicion, but since they have come into power, they
plainly believe that state regulation is a good thing—if *they* regulate—because, of course, they want to bring about good things. In this country each
party takes turns, according as it is in or out, in supporting or denouncing
the non-interference theory.

Now, if we have state regulation, what is always forgotten is this: Who
pays for it? Who is the victim of it? There always is a victim. The workmen
who do not defend themselves have to pay for the inspectors who defend
them. The whole system of social regulation by boards, commissioners,
and inspectors consists in relieving negligent people of the consequences of
their negligence and so leaving them to continue negligent without correction. That system also turns away from the agencies which are close,
direct, and germane to the purpose, and seeks others. Now, if you relieve
negligent people of the consequences of their negligence, you can only
throw those consequences on the people who have not been negligent.
If you turn away from the agencies which are direct and cognate to the
purpose, you can only employ other agencies. Here, then, you have your
Forgotten Man again. The man who has been careful and prudent and
who wants to go on and reap his advantages for himself and his children
is arrested just at that point, and he is told that he must go and take care of
some negligent employees in a factory or on a railroad who have not
provided precautions for themselves or have not forced their employers to
provide precautions, or negligent tenants who have not taken care of their
own sanitary arrangements, or negligent householders who have not provided against fire, or negligent parents who have not sent their children
to school. If the Forgotten Man does not go, he must hire an inspector
to go. No doubt it is often worth his while to go or send, rather than leave
the thing undone, on account of his remoter interest; but what I want
to show is that all this is unjust to the Forgotten Man, and that the reformers and philosophers miss the point entirely when they preach that it is
his duty to do all this work. Let them preach to the negligent to learn
to take care of themselves. Whenever A and B put their heads together and
decide what A, B and C must do for D, there is never any pressure on A
and B. They consent to it and like it. There is rarely any pressure on D
because he does not like it and contrives to evade it. The pressure all comes
on C. Now, who is C? He is always the man who, if let alone, would make

a reasonable use of his liberty without abusing it. He would not constitute any social problem at all and would not need any regulation. He is the Forgotten Man again, and as soon as he is brought from his obscurity you see that he is just that one amongst us who is what we all ought to be.

[Through a series of examples, Sumner goes on to decry claims to preferential treatment for various social and economic groups, all of which impose an unjust burden upon the Forgotten Man.]

It is plain enough that the Forgotten Man and the Forgotten Woman are the very life and substance of society. They are the ones who ought to be first and always remembered. They are always forgotten by sentimental-ists, philanthropists, reformers, enthusiasts, and every description of specu-lator in sociology, political economy, or political science. If a student of any of these sciences ever comes to understand the position of the For-gotten Man and to appreciate his true value, you will find such student an uncompromising advocate of the strictest scientific thinking on all social topics, and a cold and hard-hearted skeptic towards all artificial schemes of social amelioration. If it is desired to bring about social improvements, bring us a scheme for relieving the Forgotten Man of some of his burdens. He is our productive force which we are wasting. Let us stop wasting his force. Then we shall have a clean and simple gain for the whole society. The Forgotten Man is weighted down with the cost and burden of the schemes for making everybody happy, with the cost of public beneficence, with the support of all the loafers, with the loss of all the economic quackery, with the cost of all the jobs. Let us remember him a little while. Let us take some of the burdens off him. Let us turn our pity on him instead of on the good-for-nothing. It will be only justice to him, and society will greatly gain by it. Why should we not also have the satisfaction of thinking and caring for a little while about the clean, honest, industrious, independent, self-supporting men and women who have not inherited much to make life luxurious for them, but who are doing what they can to get on in the world without begging from anybody, especially since all they want is to be let alone, with good friendship and honest respect? Certainly the philanthropists and sentimentalists have kept our attention for a long time on the nasty, shiftless, criminal, whining, crawling, and good-for-nothing people, as if they alone deserved our attention.

The Forgotten Man is never a pauper. He almost always has a little capital because it belongs to the character of the man to save something. He never has more than a little. He is, therefore, poor in the popular sense, although in the correct sense he is not so. I have said already that if you learn to look for the Forgotten Man and to care for him, you will be very skeptical toward all philanthropic and humanitarian schemes. It is clear now that the interest of the Forgotten Man and the interest of "the poor," "the weak," and the other petted classes are in antagonism. In fact, the warning to you to look for the Forgotten Man comes the minute that the orator or writer begins to talk about the poor man. That minute the Forgotten Man is in danger of a new assault, and if you intend to meddle in the matter at all, then is the minute for you to look about for him and to give him your aid. Hence, if you care for the Forgotten Man, you will be sure to be charged with *not* caring for the poor. Whatever you do for any of the petted classes wastes capital. If you do anything for the Forgotten Man, you must secure him his earnings and savings, that is, you legislate for the security of capital and for its free employment; you must oppose paper money, wildcat banking and usury laws and you must maintain the inviolability of contracts. Hence you must be prepared to be told that you favor the capitalist class, the enemy of the poor man.

What the Forgotten Man really wants is true liberty. Most of his wrongs and woes come from the fact that there are yet mixed together in our institutions the old mediaeval theories of protection and personal dependence and the modern theories of independence and individual liberty. The consequence is that the people who are clever enough to get into positions of control, measure their own rights by the paternal theory and their own duties by the theory of independent liberty. It follows that the Forgotten Man, who is hard at work at home, has to pay both ways. His rights are measured by the theory of liberty, that is, he has only such as he can conquer. His duties are measured by the paternal theory, that is, he must discharge all which are laid upon him, as is always the fortune of parents. People talk about the paternal theory of government as if it were a very simple thing. Analyze it, however, and you see that in every paternal relation there must be two parties, a parent and a child, and when you speak metaphorically, it makes all the difference in the world who is parent and who is child. Now, since we, the people, are the state, whenever there is any work to be done or expense to be paid, and since the petted classes and the criminals and the jobbers cost and do not pay, it is they who are in the position of the child, and it is the Forgotten Man who is the parent. What the Forgotten Man needs, therefore, is that we come to a clearer understanding of liberty and to a more complete realization of it. Every step which we win in liberty will set the Forgotten Man free from some of his burdens and allow him to use his powers for himself and for the commonwealth.

Acres of Diamonds

Russell Conwell

Commentary

Still another rhetorical response to socio-economic change came from another preacher-academician, Russell Conwell (1843-1925). More active rhetorically than Ely, Gladden and Sumner combined, Conwell wrote forty-four books. At the height of his career, he delivered between 150 and 200 public lectures a year, in addition to his regular Sunday preaching. His most famous lecture was "Acres of Diamonds," delivered over 6000 times. The precise number is unknown. Indeed, many details about Conwell's life are unknown, and many questionable or inaccurate ones are often presented as fact.

Biographical difficulties arise partly from the fact that laudatory biographies began appearing when Conwell was around sixty years of age, and authors tended to mix legend with fact. Conwell was generous in giving interviews and even wrote some autobiographical sketches. He was careless, though, about details. Looking back on a long and active life, Conwell himself was inaccurate. Full-length biographies ceased appearing after his death, but historians and anthologists often wrote sketches based largely on earlier biographies and Conwell's published recollections. The best-known sketches provide a good outline of Conwell's career, but they often perpetuate inaccurate details, including some about his famous "Acres" speech. In 1981, Temple University distributed a few photocopies of Joseph C. Carter's typescript, *The "Acres of Diamonds" Man: A Memorial Archive of Russell H. Conwell, A Truly Unique Institutional Creator*. Although laudatory and devoid of much analysis, this well-researched biography is the chief source for the following sketch.[1]

Despite Conwell's youth, the nineteen-year-old farm boy from western Massachusetts gave a recruiting speech before being commissioned as a

---

[1] The editor also acknowledges his indebtedness to his son-in-law, Rev. Leon Momaney, for assistance. Rev. Momaney graduated from Gordon-Conwell Theological Seminary.

captain in the Union army (which one biographer mistakenly says was the first delivery of "Acres"). After suffering the considerable stress of war, he earned a law degree, but the young combat veteran was restless. He moved from Albany to Minneapolis to Boston and alternated between legal practice, running a newspaper and working in real estate. His restlessness found a creative outlet in the Boston *Traveller*, a newspaper which specialized in travelogues. Able to finance his travels by writing, Conwell toured Europe in 1867-1868 and the ex-Confederacy in 1869. In 1868, he signed on with James Redpath, who was soon to become the nation's leading booking agent for lecturers. Conwell's reputation grew, primarily because of his lecture on "The Lessons of Travel." It was further enhanced during 1870 by a series of "Around the World" articles which he wrote for the *Traveller* and several lectures (including "Lessons") which he delivered as he circled the globe. Of more long-term importance was his acquisition of a huge inventory of unusual stories about faraway places, legends, anecdotes and other illustrative materials, including the "acres of diamonds" story that soon became his trademark.

The rhetorical importance of his huge inventory of stories cannot be overemphasized. Conwell stated explicitly that he considered specific illustrations to be more persuasive than abstract argument. Unlike Ely and Sumner, who argued from scientific economic principles, Conwell's lectures were a string of stories with a little argument woven in. His discourses epitomized the narrative form of argument.

It is Conwell's reliance on narrative form (together with scanty records) that makes it so difficult for us to know precisely when "Acres of Diamonds" originated or how many times it was delivered. With post-Civil War Americans entranced by stories of faraway places, Conwell became one of Redpath's busiest lecturers after returning from his world tour. He later recalled that his inclusion of the "acres" story in "Lessons of Travel" was so popular that people began calling it "Acres of Diamonds" and that he changed the title accordingly. This is certainly plausible, but we also know that he was giving "Lessons" as late as the 1890s, long after "Acres" had become his major lecture. According to another recollection, he first gave "Acres" at a reunion of his old regiment in 1870. We know that this is partly, if not totally, incorrect. The first reunion was in 1873, and, according to a newspaper summary of his speech, he reported on what had happened to members of the regiment since the war. He told of meeting a former comrade in the Middle East, and it is possible that he related the "acres" story which he had picked up at the same time. The newspaper account, however, does not say so. All we can be sure of is that Conwell began using the story early in the 1870s and, somewhere along the line (probably fairly early), started entitling one of his lectures "Acres of Diamonds."

Meanwhile, Conwell's life changed in other ways. His first wife died, he remarried a very religious woman, underwent a conversion experience and attended a nearby seminary part time. In 1880, he became a lay preacher for a nearly defunct Baptist church in Lexington, Massachusetts, revitalized it and was ordained in 1881. In 1882, he transferred to Grace Baptist Church in Philadelphia, where he remained the rest of his life. Considering Conwell a human dynamo and having some internal troubles (the details of which are unknown), Grace recruited Conwell by offering not only a good salary but also by permitting him to continue lecturing for Redpath.

The objective evidence of Conwell's success at Grace is so impressive that we can readily understand his becoming a living legend. First, membership and church attendance skyrocketed. From around 300 when he arrived in 1882, membership rose to 900 by 1886 and to 1200 by 1889. When Conwell arrived in 1882, a new building had just been completed, but it was soon so crowded that non-members had to have tickets. In 1889, construction began on what was commonly called "the Temple." Completed in 1891 with a seating capacity of 4200, the ticket arrangement soon had to be reinstituted. Membership stabilized at around 3600, making Grace the largest Protestant church in the country. Second, Grace became what was commonly called an "institutional" church. It ran summer camps and youth clubs, founded a hospital, and supported Conwell's pet project, a night school which became Temple University.

Conwell's success was unquestionably due partly to his social philosophy, which is often called *The Gospel of Wealth* (a term originated by Andrew Carnegie). Conwell was an avid defender of wealth, so much so that later scholars often overlook an equally important part of the "gospel": philanthropy. People had a right, indeed an obligation, to become as rich as they could, if they did so honestly; yet, they also had a Christian duty to help others. Help, however, was not for everyone. It was for those who worked to help themselves. It was in this spirit that he founded Temple. Determined to help enterprising, but financially pressed, young men and women who could not afford to become full-time students, Temple offered night courses and low tuition. Sometime in the 1880s, Conwell began using the proceeds from "Acres" to help needy students. Although the amounts cited by laudatory biographers (running from one to eight million) are probably too high, the total amount was unquestionably large.

Just as we cannot be precise about the amount of money "Acres" raised, we are unsure about the precise number of deliveries. The official figure of 6,152 is probably close to the mark. His second wife, who married Conwell in 1873, kept careful track, but Conwell admitted that he could only estimate the number of previous deliveries. On May 21, 1914, his presentation at Grace Church was publicized as number 5000; another gala occasion was held in 1921 for 6000. When Conwell celebrated his eighty-second birthday in 1924, the media began speculating about how many times he would deliver the speech before retirement and underscored the official number each time he spoke. He delivered it at Temple University on November 13, 1924, only a few weeks before his death.

The speech presents rhetorical critics with a textual problem. Conwell never spoke from manuscript, and he testified that when he was scheduled to speak in a given locality, he tried to arrive early, talk to local inhabitants and adapt the speech to local circumstances. Given his sensitivity to the immediate occasion, a speech delivered over 6000 times during a half-century would inevitably vary. Published texts also vary. The first appeared in a local newspaper on August 6, 1886. It was a transcription of the lecture delivered three days before at Chautauqua, a summer resort famous for its annual lecture series. It was reprinted in *Gleams of Grace,* a small collection of Conwell sermons that Grace Church published in 1887 as it began its fund-raising campaign for the new "Temple." From 1890-1893, Conwell published several editions of a book entitled *Acres of Diamonds,* each having a different subtitle (such as "How Men Get Rich Honestly"). Although containing similar material as published versions of the lecture, the books are obviously too long to be considered speech texts. Alarmed by such a famous speech being unavailable in print, Albert Hatcher Smith published, "with Mr. Conwell's permission," a summary of the speech in his biography (1899).

A plethora of texts began appearing shortly thereafter. Some were published in obscure places that this writer has not located, but many were circulated widely. Thomas B. Reed's anthology, *Modern Eloquence* (1900), which went through several editions, includes "Acres." A year later, when Reed formed the Modern Eloquence Corporation, he printed the same text as a pamphlet. Agnes Rush Burr used a different text in her biography of Conwell (1905, 1917). In 1915, and again in 1943, Harper's published still a different text (along with a short biography by Robert Shackleton and an autobiographical note). This was abridged for the Wrage and Baskerville anthology, *American Forum* (1960). The 5000th delivery was transcribed and serialized in the *Temple Review* during 1914. Although not widely circulated at the time, it is the text used in the most recent editions (Revell, 1960; Pyramid, 1966).

While the aforementioned versions allow somewhat cursory comparisons, several differences are obvious. The length varies. Some, but not all, begin with remarks about how the speech violates the "rules of oratory" — an intriguing remark for rhetorical critics in view of Conwell's popularity and the fact that he wrote a book on public speaking. In some, but not all, versions, Conwell recounts the early history of the lecture (invariably giving some incorrect dates). The Burr text contains some mildly anti-labor union remarks which the others do not. Illustrations differ slightly, and those which are used repeatedly are sometimes developed differently.

Despite textual differences, Conwell's basic rhetorical method never changed. He always began with the "acres" story or told it immediately after some preliminary remarks. Then followed a string of shorter stories. More or less the same points were interwoven with the illustrations. The basic idea, as stated in Harper's edition, "has continuously been precisely the same. The idea is that in this country of ours every man has the opportunity to make more of himself than he does in his own environment, with his own skills, with his own energy, and with his own friends."

Given the textual problems, selecting a version for this anthology was admittedly somewhat arbitrary. One that typified the speech as given on the lecture circuit was preferred rather than one which exemplified that given at a special celebration (e.g., the Temple version) or which apparently was written for publication (e.g., Reed's text). Given the fact that approximately half the deliveries predate the more readily accessible twentieth-century texts, I decided to use the earlier (but not readily available) version. It is reproduced from *"Gleams of Grace." Eight Sermons by Russell H. Conwell (Pastor of Grace Baptist Church, Philad'a, Pa.) To Which is Added the Chautauqua Report of His Celebrated Popular Lecture, "Acres of Diamonds"* (Business Men's Association of Grace Baptist Church, "For the benefit of the 'Building Fund' for the New Church Structure"; for sale by J.B. Lippincott, Philadelphia, 1887), pp. 83-100. To make for easier reading, the many errors in the *Gleams* text are not marked with the usual [sic] designation.

Acres of Diamonds

MY DEAR FRIENDS: I assure you that I esteem it no little honor to be called once more to this platform where so many of the most distinguished men and women of the world have stood. The acres of diamonds of which I propose to speak to-day are to be found in your homes, or near to them, and not in some distant land. I cannot better introduce my thought than by the relation of a little incident that occurred to a party of American travelers beyond the Euphrates river. We passed across the great Arabian desert, coming out at Bagdad, passed down the river to the Arabian gulf, and on our way down we hired an Arabian guide to show us all the wonderful things connected with the ancient history and scenery; and that guide was very much like the barbers which men find in this country to-day, that is, he thought it was not only his duty to guide us, but also to entertain us with stories both curious and weird, and ancient and modern, many of which I have forgotten, and I am glad I have, but there is one I remember to-day: The old guide led the camel along by his halter, telling various stories, and once he took his Turkish cap from his head and swung it high in the air to give me to understand that he had something especially important to communicate, and then he told me this beautiful story:

There once lived on the banks of the Indus river an ancient Persian by the name of Al Hafed, He owned a lovely cottage on a magnificent hill, from which he could look down upon the glittering river and the glorious sea; he had wealth in abundance, fields, grain, orchards, money at interest, a beautiful wife and lovely children, and he was contented. Contented because he was wealthy, and wealthy because he was contented. And one day there visited this Al Hafed an ancient priest, and that priest sat down before the fire and told him how diamonds were made, and said the old priest, "If you had a diamond the size of your thumb you could purchase a dozen farms like this, and if you had a handful you could purchase the whole county." Al Hafed was at once a poor man; he had not lost anything, he was poor because he was discontented, and he was discontented because he thought he was poor. He said: "I want a mine of diamonds; what is the use of farming a little place like this? I want a mine and I will have it." He could hardly sleep that night, and early in the morning he went and wakened the priest, and said: "I want you to tell me where you can find diamonds." Said the old priest: If you want diamonds, go and get them."

"Won't you please tell me where I can find them?"

"Well, if you go and find high mountains, with a deep river running between them, over white sand, in this white sand you will find diamonds."

"Well," said he, "I will go."

So he sold his farm, collected his money, and went to hunt for diamonds. He began, very properly, with the Mountains of the Moon, and came down through Egypt and Palestine. Years passed. He came over through Europe, and, at last, in rags and hunger he stood a pauper on the shores of the great Bay of Barcelona, and when that great tidal wave came rolling in through the Pillars of Hercules he threw himself into the incoming tide, and sank beneath its foaming crest never again to rise in this life.

Here the guide stopped to fix some dislocated baggage, and I said to myself, "What does he mean by telling me this story! It was the first story I ever read in which the hero was killed in the first chapter." But he went on: "The man who purchased Al Hafed's farm led his camel one day out to the stream in the garden to drink. As the camel buried his nose in the water the man noticed a flash of light from the white sand, and reached down and picked up a black stone with a strange eye of light in it which seemed to reflect all the hues of the rainbow. He said, "It's a wonderful thing," and took it in his house where he put it on his mantel and forgot all about it. A few days afterwards the same old priest came to visit Al Hafed's successor. He noticed a flash of light from the mantel, and taking up the stone, exclaimed:

"Here is a diamond! Has Al Hafed returned!!"

"Oh, no, that is not a diamond, that is nothing but a stone that we found out in the garden."

"But," said the priest, "that is a diamond!" and together they rushed out into the garden, and stirred up the white sands with their fingers, and there came up other more beautiful gems, and more valuable than the first. And that was the guide's story. And it is, in the main, historically true. Thus were discovered the wonderful mines of Golconda. Again the guide swung his cap, and said: "Had Al Hafed remained at home and dug in his own cellar or garden, or under his own wheat fields, he would have found Acres of Diamonds." And this discovery was the founding of the line of the Great Moguls, whose magnificent palaces are still the astonishment of all travelers. He did not need to add the moral. But that I may teach by illustration, I want to tell you the story that I then told him:

We were sort of exchanging works; he would tell me a story and I would tell him one, and so I told him about the man in California, living on his ranch there, who read of the discovery of gold in the southern part of the State. He became dissatisfied and sold his ranch and started for new fields in search of gold. His successor, Colonel Sutter, put a mill on the little stream below the house, and one day when the water was shut off his little girl went down to gather some of the white sand in the race way; and she brought some of it in the house to dry it. And while she was sifting it through her fingers, a gentleman, a visitor there, noticed the first shining sands of gold ever discovered in Upper California. That farm that the owner sold to go somewhere else to find gold has added eighteen millions of dollars to the circulating medium of the world; and they told me there sixteen years ago that the owner of one-third of the farm received a twenty-dollar gold piece for every fifteen minutes of his life.

That reminds me of what Professor Agassiz told his summer class in mineralogy in reference to Pennsylvania. I live in Pennsylvania, but, being a Yankee, I enjoy telling this story. This man owned a farm, and he did just what I would do if I owned a farm in that State — sold it. Before he sold it he concluded that he would go to Canada to collect coal oil. The professors will tell you that this stuff was first found in connection with living springs, floating on the water. This man wrote to his cousin in Canada, asking for employment collecting this oil. The cousin wrote back that he did not understand the work. The farmer then studied all the books on coal oil and when he knew all about it, and the theories of the geologists concerning it from the formation of primitive coal beds to the present day, he removed to Canada to work for his cousin, first selling his Pennsylvania farm for eight hundred and thirty-three dollars. The old farmer who purchased his estate, went back of the barn one day to fix a place for the horses to drink, and found that the previous owner had already arranged that matter. He had fixed some plank edgewise, running from one bank towards the other, and resting edgewise a few inches into the water, the purpose being to throw over to one side a dreadful looking scum that the cattle would not put their noses in, although they would drink the water below it. That man had been damming back for twenty-one years, the substance; the discovery of which the official geologist pronounced to be worth to the State the sum of a hundred millions of dollars. Yet that man had sold his farm for eight hundred and thirty-three dollars. He sold one of the best oil-producing farms and went somewhere else to find — nothing.

That story brought to my mind the incident of the young man in Massachusetts. There was a young man in college studying mining and mineralogy, and while he was a student they employed him for a time as a tutor and paid him fifteen dollars a week for the special work. When he graduated they offered him a professorship and forty-five dollars a week. When this offer came, he went home and said to his mother,

"Mother, I know too much to work for forty-five dollars a week; let us go out to California, and I will stake out gold mines and copper and silver mines, and we will be rich."

His mother said it was better to stay there. But as he was an only son he had his way, and they sold out and started. But they only went to Wisconsin, where he went into the employ of the Superior Copper Mining Company, at a salary of fifteen dollars a week. He had scarcely left the old estate before the farmer who had bought it was digging potatoes and bringing them through the yard in a large basket. The farms there are almost all stone wall, and the gate was narrow, and as he was working his basket through, pulling first one side then the other, he noticed in that stone wall a block of native silver about eight inches square. This professor of mining and mineralogy was born on that place, and when he sold out he sat on that very stone while he was making the bargain. He had passed it again and again. He had rubbed it with his sleeve until it had reflected his countenance and said: "Come, now, here is a hundred thousand dollars for digging — dig me."

I should enjoy exceedingly telling these stories, but I am not here to relate incidents so much as to bring lessons that may be helpful to you. I love to laugh at the mistakes of these men until the thought comes to me, "How do you know what that man in Wisconsin is doing — and that man in Canada?" It may be that he sits by his hearth to-day and shakes his sides and laughs at us for making the same mistakes and feels that after all he is in comparatively good company. We have all made the same mistakes. Is there anyone here that has not? If there is one that says you have never made such a blunder, I can argue with you that you have. You may not have had the acres of diamonds and sold them. You may not have had wells of oil and sold them, and yet you may have done so. A teacher in the Wilkesbarre schools came to me after one of my lectures and told me that he owned a farm of fifty acres, that he sold for five dollars an acre, and a few weeks before my lecture it was sold for thirty-eight thousand dollars, because they had found a silver mine on it.

You say you never have made any such mistakes. Are you rich to-day? Are you worth five million dollars? Of course not!

Why not? "I never had opportunity to get it."

Now you and I can talk. Let us see!

Were you ever in the mercantile business? Why didn't you get rich? "Because I couldn't, there was so much competition and all that." Now my friend, didn't you carry on your store just as I carried on my father's store? I don't like to tell how I conducted my father's store. But when he went away to purchase goods he would sometimes leave me in charge; and a man would come in and say: Do you keep jacknives? "No, we don't keep jacknives." Then another would come in and ask: "Do you keep jacknives?" "No, we don't."!! And still another. "No, we don't keep jacknives; why are you all bothering me about jacknives!!!"

Did you keep store in that way? Do you ask me what was the fault? The difficulty was that I never had learned by bitter experience the foundations of business success; and that it is the same foundation that underlies all true success, the foundation that underlies Christianity and morality. That it is the whole of man's life to live for others; and he that can do the most to elevate, enrich and inspire others, shall reap the greatest reward himself. Not only so says the Holy Book, but so says business common sense. I will go into your store and ask: Do you know neighbor A. that lives over a couple of squares from your store? "Yes, he deals here." Where did he come from? "I don't know." Has he any children? "I don't know." Does he have a school in his district? Does he go to church? "I don't know." Is he a married man? "I don't know." What ticket does he vote? "I don't know, and I don't care!" Is that the way you do business? If it is then you have been conducting your business as I carried on my father's store! And you do not succeed and are poor? I understand it. You can't succeed and I am glad of it, and I will give five dollars to see your failure announced in the newspaper tomorrow morning. The only way to succeed is to take an interest in the people around you, and honestly work for their welfare.

"But," you say, "I have no capital." I am glad you haven't. I am sorry for the rich men's sons. Young man, if you have no capital, there is hope for you. According to the statistics collected in the city of Boston twenty years ago, ninety-six of every one hundred successful merchants were born poor; and trustworthy statistics also show, that of the rich men's sons not one in a thousand dies rich. I am sorry for the rich men's sons unless their fathers be wise enough to bring them up like poor children. If you haven't any capital, life is full of hope to you.

A.T. Stewart started out with a dollar and a half to begin on and he lost all but sixty-two and a half cents the first afternoon. That was before he was a school teacher. He purchased things the people did not want. He said "I will never do that again," and he went around to the doors and found what the people wanted and invested his sixty-two and a half cents safely for he knew what people wanted, and went on until he was worth forty-two millions of dollars; and what man has done men can do again. You may say: "I can't be acquainted with every man in the county and know his wife and children in order to succeed." If you know a few fairly well you may judge the world by them. John Jacob Astor is said by one of his latest biographers to have had a mortgage on a millinery establishment. I always think when I reach this point that the ladies will say:

"Fools rush in where angels fear to tread."

They could not pay the interest on the mortgage and he foreclosed and took possession. He went into partnership with the same man who failed and kept the old clerks and retained the old stock. He went out and set down on a bench in Union Park. What was he doing there? He was watching the women as they passed by, and when he saw a lady with her shoulders thrown back, and her head up as if she didn't care if all the world was looking at her, he studied that bonnet and before it was out of sight he knew every feather and ribbon and all about the frame, and — and — some men may be able to describe a bonnet, but I cannot. I don't believe there are words in the English language to do it. Then he went to the store and said:

"Put such and such a bonnet in the window for I know that there is one woman that likes it."

And then he would go and watch for another style and return and have that put in the window with the other. And success came. Some years ago I went into that store to find out about it for myself, and there I found the descendents of that man doing business, and it is the largest millinery firm in the world, with branch houses in all the large cities on the globe. That success was made because Astor studied into the matter and knew what the women wanted before he had the articles made.

But you say, "I cannot do it." You can do it. You say you have no capital — but you have a jacknife. I could not sleep if I did not have a jacknife in my pocket — a Yankee cannot. In Massachusetts, there lived a man who was a carpenter, and who was out of work. He sat around the stove until his wife told him to go out doors, and he did — every man in Massachusetts is compelled by law to obey his wife. He sat down on the shore of the bay and whittled a soaked oak shingle, until he made a chain that his children quarreled over. Then he whittled another.

Then a neighbor, coming in, advised him to whittle toys, for sale. "I can't make toys," said he. "Yes, you can." "But I wouldn't know what to make?" There is the whole thing; not in having the machinery or the capital, but in knowing what the people want; and so his friend said to the carpenter: "Why don't you ask your own children? See what they like, and perhaps other children will like the same thing." He concluded to do so; and, when his little girl came down, he said: "Mary, what kind of a toy would you like to have me make?" "Oh, a little doll cradle, and carriage, and horse," and a dozen other things. He began with his jacknife and made up these rough, unpainted toys. A friend of his sold them in a Boston shoe store at first, and brought back twenty-five and fifty cents at a time, and then his wife began to be better natured. The wife always does get better natured when there is a prospect of money to divide. She came out and split up the wood while he made up the toys. The last case I had as a lawyer before I entered the ministry that man was on the stand, and I said to him: "When did you commence to whittle those toys?" "In 1870." "How much are the patents on those toys worth?" His answer was, their actual value, to him, was $78,000; and it was a little less than seven years after the time when he began with his jacknife; and to-day I know that he is worth a hundred thousand dollars, and he has received it all from having consulted his own children, and judging from them what other people's children wanted, and trying to supply the demand. If a man takes an interest in people, and knows what they need, and endeavors to supply it, he must succeed.

Some of you who sit before me, thinking you are poor, are actually in possession of wealth. Like the Baltimore lady, who, fourteen years after her father's failure, found a costly diamond bracelet she had lost seventeen years before.

Many of you smile at the thought that you are in the actual possession of wealth. A shoemaker in Massachusetts sat around in the house until his wife drove him out with a broom, and then he went out into the back yard and sat down on an ash barrel. Near by was a beautiful mountain stream, but I don't suppose that he thought of Tennyson's beautiful poem —

> "Chatter, chatter, as I flow,
>   To join the brimming river;

> Men may come, and men may go,
>   But I go on forever.'

It was not a poetical situation, sitting on an ash barrel and his wife in the kitchen with a mop. Then he saw a trout flash in the stream and hide under the bank, and he reached down and got the fish, and took it into the house; and his wife took it, and sent it to a friend in Worcester. The friend wrote back that he would give five dollars for another such a trout, and our shoemaker and his wife immediately started out to find it, man and wife now perfectly united. A five-dollar bill in prospect. They went up the stream to its source, and followed it down to the brimming river, but there was not another trout to be found. Then he went to the minister. That minister didn't know how trout grew, but he told them to go to the public library, and, under a pile of dime novels, he would find Seth Green's book, and that would give them the information they wanted. They did so, and found out all about the culture of trout, and began operations. They afterwards moved to the banks of the Connecticut river, and then to the Hudson, and now that man sends trout, fresh and packed in ice, all over the country, and is a rich man. His wealth was in that back yard just as much twenty years before. But he did not discover it until his repeated failures had made his wife imperious.

I remember meeting, in Western Pennsylvania, a distinguished professor who began as a country school teacher. He was determined to know his district, and he learned that the father of one of the boys was a maker of wagon wheels. He studied up all about making wagon wheels, and when that man's boy came to school he told him all about it; and the boy went home and told his father: "I know more about wagon wheels than you do!" "That teacher is teaching that boy wonderfully," said the father. He told a farmer's boy all about the value of fertilizer for the soil, and he went home and told his father, and the old gentleman said: "How that boy is learning." That teacher is now the president of a college, and is a D.D., an LL.D., and a Ph.D. He taught what the people wanted to know, and that made him successful.

Once I went up into the mountain region of New Hampshire to lecture, and I suffered a great deal from the cold. When I came back to Harvard, I said to a friend, who was a scientific man, of great culture: "Professor, I am never going into New Hampshire to lecture again, never!" "Why?" "Because I nearly shivered the teeth out of my head." "And why did you shiver?" "Because the weather was cold." "Oh, no, no!" said my friend. "Then it was because I did not have bedclothes enough!" "No, no, it wasn't that." "Well," I said, "you are a scientific man, and I wish you would tell me, then, just why I shivered?" "Well, sir," he replied, "it was because you didn't know any better." Said he: "Didn't you have in your pocket a newspaper?" "Oh, yes." "Well, why didn't you spread that over your bed? If you had you would have been as warm as the richest man in America, under all his silk coverlids; and you shivered because you did not know enough to put the two-cent paper over your bed."

How many women want divorces — and ought to have them, too. How many divorces originate something like this: A workingman comes in haste to his supper, and sits down to eat potatoes that are about as hard as the rocks beside which they grew. He will chop them up and eat them in a hurry, and they won't digest well. They make him cross. He frets and scolds, and perhaps he swears, he scarcely knows why, and then there is trouble. If the good woman had only known enough of science to put in a pinch of salt, they would have come out mealy and luscious and eatable, and ready to laugh themselves to pieces in edible joy, and he would have eaten them down in peace and satisfaction and with good digestion, and he would have arisen from the table with a smile on his face, and there would have been joy in that family; and all because of a pinch of salt. The lack in appreciating the value of little things often keeps us in poverty.

I want to ask the audience, Who are the great inventors of the world? Many will answer that it is a peculiar race of men, with intellects like lightning flashes and heads like bushel measures. But, in fact, inventors are usually ordinary practical thinkers. You may invent as much as they, if you study on the question, What does the world need? It is not so difficult to prepare a machine, after all, as it is to find out just what people want. The Jacquard loom was invented by a working woman. So was the printing roller. So was the second best cotton gin. So was the mowing machine. I am out of all patience with myself because I did not invent the telephone. I had the same opportunity that the other boy had; I put my ear down to the rail and heard the rumbling of the engine through the miles of track, and arose and threw snow-balls — the other boy arose and asked Why? He discovered that it was caused by the generation of electricity by the wheels, and, when he saw Edison's speaking machine, he had the whole matter at a glance.

There was a congressman once who resolved to talk sense; of course, he was an exception to the general rule. He was one day walking through the Treasury department, when a clerk said to him that it was a fine day. As he met other clerks, they remarked the same thing, and at last our congressman said: "Why do you tell me that it is a fine day. I know that already. Now, if you could tell me what the weather will be to-morrow, it would be of some importance." A clerk caught the idea and began to think it over, and entered into correspondence with the professor at Cincinnatti. That was the origin of our signal service. Soon we will know what the weather will be a week ahead. Yes, not many years hence, we will decide what weather we will have by a popular vote. How simple all these mighty improvements and inventions seem when we study the simple steps of their evolution! Yet civilized men and women are greater to-day than ever before. We often think all great men are dead, and the longer they are dead the greater they appear to have been. But, in fact, men are greater, and women are nobler, than ever before. We are building on the foundations of the past, and we must be exceeding small if we are not greater than they who laid them. The world knows nothing of its greatest men. Some young man may say: "I am going to be great." "How?" "How?" "By being elected to an office." Shall the man be greater than the men who elect him? Shall the servant be greater than his master? That a man is in public office is no evidence of greatness. Even if you are great when you are in office, they will not call you great till after you die. Another young man says: "I am going to be great when there comes a war." But success in war is not always an evidence of greatness. Historians are apt to credit a successful man with more than he really does, and with deeds that were performed by subordinates. General Thomas was one of the greatest generals of the war, yet an incident in his life illustrates this thought. After the battle of Nashville, the soldiers, seeing him, cheered the hero, and shouted, "Hurrah for the hero of Lookout Mountain." This was distasteful to the General, and he ordered it to be stopped. Said he: "Talk about the hero of Lookout Mountain! Why, I was ordered by General Grant to keep my troops at the foot of the mountain, and the enemy began to drop their shells among us, and I ordered my men to retreat, but they would not do it; and they charged and captured the works against my positive orders. Now they talk about the hero of Lookout Mountain!"

Yet as he was in command of that corps he would naturally be credited with the victory of that charge, while the daring private or subordinate may never be mentioned in history. You can be as great at home and in private life as you can on fields of awful carnage. Greatness, in its noblest sense knows no social or official rank.

I can see again a company of soldiers in the last war going home to be received by their native town officers. Did you ever think you would like to be a king or queen? Go and be received by your town officers, and you will know what it means. I shall never see again so proud a moment as that when, at the head of a company of troops, we were marching home to be received. I was but a boy in my teens. I can hear now distinctly the band playing, and see the people that were waiting. We marched into their town hall and were seated in the center. Then I was called to take a position on the platform with the town officers. Then came the address of welcome. The old gentleman had never made a speech before, but he had written this, and walked up and down the pasture until he had committed is *[sic]* to memory. But he had brought it with him and spread it out on the desk. The delivery of the speech by that good but nervous town official went something like this:

Fellow Citizens — fellow citizens. We are — we are — we are very happy — we are — we are very happy to welcome back to our native town — these soldiers. Fellow citizens, we are very happy to welcome back to our native town these soldiers who have — who have — who have fought — who have fought and bled — and come back to their native town again. We are — we are — we are especially — especially pleased to see with us to-day this young hero. This young hero — to see this young hero," — in imagination we have seen — (remember that he said "in imagination,") we have seen him leading his troops on to battle. We have seen his — his — his shining sword, flashing in the sunshine, as he shouted to his troops, 'Come on!'"

Oh, dear, dear! dear, what did he know about war? That Captain with his shining sword flashing in air, shouting to his troops, COME ON! He never did it, never. If there had not often been a double line of flesh and blood between him and the enemy he would not have been there that day to be received. If he had known anything about war he would have known what any soldier in this audience can tell you that it was next to a crime for an officer of Infantry in time of danger to go ahead of his men! Do you suppose he is going out there to be shot in front by the enemy and in the back by his own men? That is no place for him. And yet the hero of the reception hour was that boy. There stood in that house, unnoticed, men who had carried that boy on their backs through deep rivers, men who had given him their last draught of coffee; men who had run miles to get him food. And some were not there; some were sleeping their last sleep in their unknown graves. They had given their lives for the nation, but were scarcely noticed in the good man's speech. And the boy was the hero of the reception hour. Why? For no other reason under Heaven but because he was an officer and these men were only private soldiers. Human nature often estimates men's greatness by the office they hold; yet office cannot make men great, nor noble, nor brave.

Any man may be great, but the best place to be great is at home. They can make their kind better; they can labor to help their neighbors and instruct and improve the minds of the men, women and children around them; they can make holier their own locality; they can build up the schools and churches around them, and they can make their own homes bright and sweet. These are the elements of greatness, it is here greatness begins, and if a man is not great in his own home or in his own school district he will never be great anywhere.

Political Rhetoric and Socioeconomic Changes from Reconstruction to World War I

Old-time Political Speeches

Albert Beveridge

Commentary

While professors and preachers responded to socio-economic changes from clearly stated, albeit markedly different, ideological perspectives, the importance of ideology declined in political rhetoric. True, Democrats continued their prewar opposition to protective tariffs while Republicans continued to support protectionism. Democrats were generally more supportive of States rights. Both parties, though, fell under the control of professional politicians who were more interested in the spoils of office than ideology. The spoils of office often involved large-scale corruption, as politics no longer seemed to attract many of the nation's best minds. The implications for political rhetoric were many. Ignoring ideological issues, candidates for public office charged their opponents with corruption while portraying themselves as far more honest than they probably were. With their inbred cynicism, candidates routinely appealed for votes on the basis of economic self-interest in a far more blatant and open manner than in prewar days. The lack of a solid, philosophically based political rhetoric was a national misfortune. The nation needed a thoughtful approach to rapid socio-economic changes. It drifted into a policy of increased governmental involvement without considering carefully the merits of the policy or the best kinds of involvement. Small wonder that thoughtful citizens such as Ely and Sumner were worried.

Despite widespread public cynicism, party loyalties remained strong. Southern whites remained solidly Democratic, while blacks remained Republican. The North remained predominately Republican, and, as Civil War veterans and other Northerners moved west, they took their loyalties with them. Only the new immigrants were up for grabs. While those who moved West tended to become Republican, the Democratic "machines" in the industrial-urban areas attracted most of them to their ranks.

Explaining the persistence of old party loyalties is not easy, but the non-ideological rhetoric undoubtedly played a role. Both parties campaigned on the old emotional issues from the Civil War and Reconstruction eras.

Southern Democrats reminded voters that they were the "white man's party" and castigated "Black Republicans." Northern and Western Republicans reminded voters that they were the "party of union" and castigated Democrats for being the "party of rebellion."

The partisan rhetoric flowed through several media, the most important of which were better suited to reinforcing party loyalties than changing them. The day of political pamphlets had passed. Although campaign biographies and magazines were now more important, the major media were still those of the prewar era: newspapers and stump speeches. Most newspapers were as rabidly partisan as they had been in antebellum days, and, because voters usually subscribed to their party's papers, their loyalties were reinforced. Similarly, political rallies were major social events. Voters usually attended only their party's rallies, where they heard stump speeches that reinforced their loyalties.

Unfortunately, texts of stump speeches are rarely extant. Like their antebellum predecessors, speakers rarely spoke from manuscript or had their orations transcribed, but we can get their flavor from observers' accounts, such as the one written by Albert J. Beveridge (1862-1927). He was a famous political orator who wrote a book on public speaking a few years before his death. He opened it with some reminiscences of the stump speaking he had heard in Illinois as a boy. His recollections are reproduced from *The Art of Public Speaking* (Boston: Houghton Mifflin, 1924), pp. 3-9.

Old-time Political Speeches

THE first political speech I ever heard was typical of the oratory upon which most of us were brought up. Also it showed that, if he had lived, Abraham Lincoln might, perhaps, have been overthrown by the post-war politicians; for Lincoln's supreme idea was the reconstruction of the South on the basis of brotherhood and good-will — genuine reunion; whereas the rally-round-the-flag politicians wanted the South treated as a conquered province — genuine disunion.

So the words for which, above all others, the American people and the world now love and revere Lincoln, "with malice toward none, with charity for all ... let us ... bind up the Nation's wounds" — not only the wounds of the North, the East, the West, but the wounds of the whole Nation — did not fit the plans of those who, for political purposes, wished to keep the war going long after it was over.

Therefore they fanned the embers of hatred. They kept old war passions alive, and even incubated new ones. Thus came a recrudescence of that emotional speechmaking which in America was one aftereffect of the French Revolution — speechmaking which violates every principle of oratory, and which has done much to destroy that noble art in the United States.

The only Republicans in the county where we lived in my childhood were

Union soldiers, among the most ardent of whom were my father and brothers; and when we had a political rally all of them came to the county seat, a little country town whose dirt streets were axle-deep with mud or ankle-deep with dust. On the edge of the village — for it was no more — was a grove of oak and walnut trees, where we Republicans held our meetings. The Democrats held theirs a mile away on the other side of the county seat in a wood made up mostly of hickory trees.

In the early seventies, when I was a very small boy, there was a Republican gathering in our Republican grove. The speaker was a well-known politician of the period and a typical post-war stump-speaker, who grew more furious at "the rebels" as the war receded in time.

Long, thick, inky-black hair flowed over his collar, and immense black mustaches added to his formidable and ferocious appearance. The August sun made the surrounding prairies shimmer with heat and even in the shade of the trees men mopped their brows, women fanned crying babies, and all were as uncomfortable as they were enthusiastic.

I sat between my parents on the front plank which, at either end and in the middle, rested on logs. The speaker, escorted by the committee, mounted the flag-draped platform, was introduced, threw off his coat and vest, tore his collar and tie from his neck, replaced them with a red bandanna handkerchief which made him look more militant than ever, ran his fingers through his mane and began:

"Comrades! And you, the mothers, wives, and sweethearts of my comrades! Who murdered our comrades? Rebels! Democrats!" (Tremendous cheering. A voice "Give 'm hell, John." More cheering.) "Who tried to shoot the Stars and Stripes from the heavens? Rebels! Democrats!" So the orator in a crimson torrent raged on, waving the flag, pounding the table, gesticulating wildly, shaking his head like an infuriated bull and working himself up to boiling heat, physically as well as emotionally. At last came a picturesque and blood-curdling climax.

It was a great speech everybody said, and so the little, barefoot boy believed it to be. After singing "Marching through Georgia," the farmers and their families got into their big wagons, some with fifers and drummers from out townships, and started homeward, hurrahing for our candidates. All were as happy as they were patriotic.

The very next week, under the protection of a Democratic farmer who lived near us, I went to a Democratic meeting in the hickory grove. We took our politics seriously and none of my family would attend; but I wanted so badly to hear the Democratic speech, that my parents finally consented, although with reluctance and misgiving.

As to violent delivery, exaggerated statement, and lack of argument, the Democratic speech was identical with the Republican speech I had heard a few days earlier — all was denunciation, only the thesis was reversed. We Republicans, it seemed, were rascals, scoundrels, and ought to be in jail, every last one of us. Again there was the acrobatic rage of the speaker, again the shedding of garments, again the lurid adjectives, again the senseless cheering, again the shouted encouragement from excited partisans to "give 'm hell," again the general acclaim that it was a great speech, again the small-boy's acceptance that it was a great speech.

I was angered and mystified — how could we Republicans be such a bad lot? and, besides, had not our Republican speaker called these Democrats "rebels"? It did not connect up, but, still, I was hot for my clan. However, it was a great speech; there could be no doubt about that outstanding fact. So was the verbal and emotional tempest, I had heard the week before, a great speech.

The greatness of these two speeches was the one thing upon which everybody agreed. The partisans of neither side repeated any arguments of either speaker — there were none to repeat — but there was ardent rivalry as to which speech was the greater. The word "great" was worked by everybody until the sweat of exhaustion poured from every letter of it.

Such were the performances that, for several decades after the Civil War, were called oratory. Even to-day we sometimes hear the same kind of public speaking, especially during political campaigns — the same furious delivery, the same extreme misstatement, the same unfairness, the same animosity, the same ignoring of fact and reason.

Populist Songs
"The Independent Man" and
"Good-bye, My Party, Good-bye"

Mrs. J. T. Kellie and Anonymous

Commentary

As the two political parties accused each other of corruption and rhetorically refought the Civil War and Reconstruction, they left corruption unsolved and ideology neglected. So-called third parties stepped into the vacuum, but they faced overwhelming problems. Radical parties stated their ideologies with so much clarity that they alienated most of the voting public. Moderate ones also had problems, some of their own making and some that were inherent in the political situation. Many third parties were hastily organized immediately before an upcoming presidential election. Their lack of organization at local and State levels precluded their conducting effective campaigns. They usually concentrated on one or two issues which interested only a segment of the voting public. Party loyalties were strong and even sympathetic voters often were reluctant to abandon their party. Many thought it better to work in their party than to waste ballots on one that could not possibly win.

Yet third parties played a significant rhetorical role. They brought issues to public attention. If they succeeded in gaining support, one or both of the major parties assimilated their ideas, usually toning them down in the process of legislating and enforcing them. Agitation then died down, and the third party disappeared, but public policy was affected.

This process began even before the end of Reconstruction. Dismayed by the corruption of the Grant administration, some reform-minded Republicans formed a "Liberal Republican" party in 1872 and campaigned for honesty in government. The same election saw formation of the National Labor Union, which nominated a presidential candidate and ran on a platform calling for civil service, railroad regulation, an eight-hour day and similar reforms. Although returning to their party, Liberal Republicans remained concerned about governmental corruption. They helped organize the National Civil Service Reform League and lobbied for civil service legislation that was passed in 1883. They probably would have been content with their success if Republicans had not nominated the corrupt James Blaine the following year.

In the presidential election of 1884, they endorsed the Democratic candidate, Grover Cleveland, while trying to separate themselves from the Democrats by hastily devising an "Independent" party. By bolting, they helped elect the first Democratic president since 1856.

The most successful third party arose in the 1890s as a response to the economic problems of farmers, but the movement had a long and checkered history. Then, as now, farmers faced a serious problem of indebtedness. Although homesteaders got free land from the government, the rapid growth of technology required capital investments for farm machinery. With crops being harvested only once a year, farmers often borrowed money to meet living and operating expenses. Sometimes they borrowed from banks and mortgaged their farms, and sometimes they sold unharvested crops for future delivery to commodity dealers or speculators.

In the early postwar era, when farm prices were high, indebtedness was simply regarded as a necessary business expense. After the "panic of '73," when commodity prices tumbled, banks began foreclosing on farm land. The Federal government had moved to what its supporters called a "sound money" policy and what its critics called a "hard money policy." Wartime expenses had been met by supplementing gold and silver currency with large issues of paper notes, commonly called "greenbacks." Virtually all economists, regardless of ideology, agreed that paper money was inflationary, and various Federal laws began moving the country to a gold standard. One law (later called the "crime of 1873") included a provision for demonetizing silver.

Acknowledging that greenbacks were inflationary, Greenback party orators argued during the 1876 campaign that inflation was needed to raise farm prices and bring back prosperity. In 1878, the party worked vigorously in State elections. It issued a platform calling not only for more greenbacks, but also for another inflationary proposal that would later dominate the farm movement: the unlimited coinage of silver, which was coming out of newly discovered mines in the West in ever-increasing amounts. The party won fifteen congressional seats and got enough support from the two major parties to slow the pace at which the government was moving to the gold standard. Then the European demand for American farm commodities rose sharply, and prices went up. Its single issue gone, the Greenback party collapsed.

During the 1880s, farm prices resumed their downward spiral, and the farmers' alliance movement spread rapidly. It grew out of older local and State organizations that originally promoted social and educational activities. As discontent mounted and political activity increased, these organizations tried to enhance their political influence by merging into regional associations. By 1889, three regional "alliances" existed: the Northern (actually Western, with most of its members being in the Plains States), the Southern (a white group) and the Colored (a black organization under white control). Their rhetoric varied, but they always called for inflationary proposals, especially more greenbacks and silver. In 1889, the Southern Alliance attempted to form a national organization. Realizing that urban support was needed, it enlisted the support of labor unions. One strategy was to rename itself the "Farmers' and Laborers' Union of America." Another was to invite the other alliances and the two major unions (the young American Federation of Labor or AFL and the old Knights of Labor) to hold their annual conventions simultaneously in St. Louis, where negotiating teams could work out a merger.

The effort failed. Declaring that farm organizations consisted of employers, the AFL declined to attend. The others attended but failed to merge. Knights leaders feared that they would be submerged in an organization dominated by farmers. Equally reluctant Northern Alliance negotiators argued about many aspects of the proposed organization, some as trivial as its name and some as substantive as the role of blacks. Although Southerners yielded on most issues, Northerners still refused. Many Alliance members were Civil War veterans. One Alliance paper in Kansas, noting that the Southern Alliance was larger and that many of its leaders were former Confederate officers, called the proposed merger "another rebel yell." Equally important was a disagreement over strategy. Many Northerners wished to form a third party. White Southerners, fearing that a split in the white vote would return their States to "Black Republicanism," insisted on working through existing parties.

The differences were emotional and strategic, not ideological. The unmerged organizations issued statements (commonly called the "St. Louis Demands") that were similar in style and substance. In a militant style which featured the word *demands*, they called for more governmental activity than even Hamilton had suggested. They demanded more greenbacks, government ownership of railroads and a prohibition of land ownership by aliens and others who did not actually till the soil.

Proceeding in their own ways, the Alliances worked intensively to influence the State elections of 1890. The Southern Alliance worked for the nomination of Democratic candidates who supported the St. Louis Demands. Third parties sprang up in the West under different names: "Alliance" in Minnesota, "Independent" in Nebraska and "People's" in Kansas.

In an atmosphere reminiscent of the Log Cabin campaign, third parties conducted political rallies complete with parades, picnics, banners and songs. Stump orators fulminated against the satanic forces that were oppressing poor farmers: greedy bankers (who charged outrageous interest rates and foreclosed when farmers could not meet their payments), commodity speculators (who sat in their fancy offices in Eastern cities making money for doing nothing except robbing the hard-working farmers), railroads (who charged high prices to transport farm produce to the Eastern markets and let stand idle the huge land grants they had received from the government) and the monied East (where speculators, railroad magnates and other plutocrats lived in luxury at the expense of indebted farmers).

The rhetorical attacks on Satan had considerable appeal in rural America, which had strong ideological links to the Puritan view of history as a battle between Christ and Antichrist and to the Puritan work ethic, but they were insufficient to pull voters away from their traditional party loyalties.

Strategists, therefore, worked specifically to destroy the old loyalties, which in States such as Kansas were to the "Grand Old Party" of Lincoln. Mary Elizabeth Lease, a Kansas lawyer who delivered 160 campaign speeches, capsulized the appeal by imitating the well-known Gettysburg Address: "Wall Street owns the country. It is no longer a government of the people, by the people and for the people, but a government of Wall Street, by Wall Street and for Wall Street." Banners displayed slogans such as, "We voted with our party no matter where it went. We voted with our party till we haven't a cent." Lyrics were set to the music of popular tunes, published in songbooks and sung at political rallies. "The Independent Man," written by Mrs. J.T. Kellie and sung to the tune of "The Girl I Left Behind Me," was popularized by the Nebraska Independent party. "Good-bye, My Party, Good-bye," sung to the tune of "Good-bye, My Lover, Good-bye," was often credited by contemporaries with having won Kansas for the People's party. They are reproduced from John D. Hicks, *The Populist Revolt: A History of the Farmers' Alliance and the People's Party* (Minneapolis: Univ. of Minnesota Press, 1931), pp. 168-169.

Populist Songs: "The Independent Man" and "Good-bye, My Party, Good-bye"

THE INDEPENDENT MAN

"I was a party man one time
   The party would not mind me
So now I'm working for myself,
   The party's left behind me.

"A true and independent man
   You ever more shall find me —
I work and vote, and ne'er regret
   The party left behind me."

GOOD-BYE, MY PARTY, GOOD-BYE

It was no more than a year ago,
      Good-bye, my party, good-bye
That I was in love with my party so,
      Good-bye, my party, good-bye
To hear aught else I never would go;
      Good-bye, my party, good-bye.
Like the rest I made a great blow;
      Good-bye, my party, good-bye.

Chorus:

> Bye, party, bye, lo; bye, party, bye, lo;
> Bye, party, bye, lo; good-bye, my party, good-bye.

I was often scourged with the party lash,
>   Good-bye, my party, good-bye.
The bosses laid on with demands for cash;
>   Good-bye, my party, good-bye.
To do aught else I deemed it rash,
>   Good-bye, my party, good-bye.
So I had to take it or lose my hash,
>   Good-bye, my party, good-bye.

Chorus:

I was raised up in the kind of school,
>   Good-bye, my party, good-bye.
That taught to bow to money rule,
>   Good-bye, my party, good-bye.
And it made of me a "Kansas Fool,"
>   Good-bye, my party, good-bye.
When they found I was a willing tool,
>   Good-bye, my party, good-bye.

Chorus:

The old party is on the downward track,
>   Good-bye, my party, good-bye.
Picking its teeth with a tariff tack,
>   Good-bye, my party, good-bye.
With a placard pinned upon his back,
>   Good-bye, my party, good-bye.
That plainly states, "I will never go back";
>   Good-bye, my party, good-bye.

Chorus:

Cross of Gold

William Jennings Bryan

Commentary

The Alliances' foray into politics in 1890 was very successful. Even before the elections, the sympathetic Republican senator, John Sherman, pushed through Congress two laws favored by the Alliances: an anti-trust law, which Alliance leaders hoped would curb railroad monopolies, and the Silver Purchase Act, which provided for the limited issuance of silver certificates, with sixteen ounces of silver being equivalent in value to one of gold. In the elections, third parties did unusually well, winning several congressional seats and State governments in the West. Many sympathetic Republicans and Democrats were also elected.

Although many Alliance leaders were satisfied with their progress, impatient militants joined with a wide assortment of reformers to organize the National People's Party, commonly known as the Populists. It did unusually well for a third party in the presidential election of 1892. Its candidate, James B. Weaver, won almost ten percent of the popular vote and twenty-two electoral votes. In general, Populist votes came at the expense of the Republicans, thus giving Democrats control of both Houses of Congress as well as the White House (for the first time since antebellum days). With Populism strong among Southern Democrats, the situation looked promising.

Then the roof collapsed. Recession hit the country in 1893. Businesses went bankrupt, over 100 railroads failed, stock prices dropped, farm prices tumbled and unemployment skyrocketed. Disorder spread quickly. "General" Jacob Coxey led an "army" of unemployed workers to Washington to petition Congress for a public works program. His "army" was dispersed, and Coxey arrested. When the Pullman Company cut wages, the newly formed American Railway Union conducted a strike which spread to other railroad companies. President Cleveland broke the strike with Federal troops.

A congressional combination of Democrats and Republicans joined in a reform program that was vastly different from the reforms that Populists wanted. A higher tariff was enacted, with protectionists arguing that it would curtail imports and create jobs. Populists answered that this was another example of the Monied East exploiting the rest of the country. The Silver Purchase Act was repealed, with "gold bugs" arguing that the immediate cause of the depression was the lack of confidence in the nation's inflationary monetary system. Populists countered that more, not less, silver was needed to bolster the economy.

Repeal of the Silver Purchase Act highlighted the monetary issue, which was one of the few Populist ideas that sympathetic Democrats could espouse. Many Populist demands, such as nationalizing railroads, were unacceptable to some "Populist Democrats," but all agreed on the virtues of "bimetallism"; i.e., a monetary system based on both gold and silver at the old ratio of sixteen to one. Going far beyond the now-defunct Silver Purchase Act, "Silver Democrats" demanded the "free and unlimited coinage of silver," language that is often, but mistakenly, interpreted as redundant. "Free" meant that miners should be allowed to have silver bullion minted without charge. "Unlimited" meant that no ceiling should be placed on the amount of silver which could circulate.

In the months before the presidential election of 1896, Silver Democrats worked feverishly to get elected as convention delegates. When the convention opened on July 7, 1896, it was clear that the silverites, controlling most of the Southern and Western delegations, were in charge. It was also clear that this would be the most divided Democratic convention since 1860. The normally routine business of selecting a temporary chairman became a divisive issue, with the silverite candidate defeating a gold bug by the decisive vote of 556-349. Controlling the credentials committee, silverites took care of their own in the bitter struggles for the contested delegations. Controlling the platform committee, silverites prepared a platform which not only called for bimetallism, but also condemned Cleveland and his supporters on other issues. By indirect, but unsubtle, language, it faulted the president for his handling of the railroad strike. With equally unsubtle language directed at Democrats who had collaborated with Republicans on the tariff, it denounced protectionism as a breeder of trusts and an assault on the common man. The president's supporters realized they were in the minority. Angry and stubborn, they offered a minority report which not only endorsed the gold standard, but also complimented the president for "his honesty, economy, courage and fidelity." Silverite "Pitchfork Ben" Tillman (who earned his nickname by promising Georgia voters that he would stick Cleveland "in his fat old ribs" with a pitchfork) announced that he would introduce a motion for an explicit condemnation of Cleveland as "undemocratic and tyrannical." As the first day of the convention drew to a close, tensions were high.

Cooler heads on both sides negotiated a method to control the convention. They agreed to a prearranged formal debate covering both the platform (technically, a motion to substitute the gold plank for the silver one) and the resolutions regarding Cleveland. It was to last only an hour and twenty minutes. Pitchfork Ben would begin with a fifty-minute speech and be followed by three gold bugs, Senator David Hill of New York, ex-Governor

William Russell of Massachusetts and Postmaster General W.F. Vilas of Wisconsin. Then William Jennings Bryan (1860-1925) would close with a short speech for silver.

In a sense, the debate was mere ritual. None of the delegates was open to persuasion on any of the issues except Tillman's motion to condemn Cleveland. Most silverites favored an explicit condemnation on principle, but many feared that it would divide the party so much that winning the election would be impossible, especially since Republicans had cautiously endorsed bimetallism at their recent convention. The Republican platform said the gold standard should be maintained only until an international agreement for bimetallism could be obtained. By the time the debate began on the afternoon of July 8, most delegates were ready to vote and get on with a question that silverites had not yet considered carefully: Who should be their presidential nominee?

As things turned out, the debate was not mere ritual. It caused an uproar, and it settled the question of who should be nominated. As planned, the first speech was by Tillman, who alienated many silverites as well as gold bugs. He spoke of the Civil War, praised South Carolina's secessionism and declared that the monetary question was a sectional issue dividing North and South. He was frequently interrupted by boos and hisses. When he finished, Senator Jones of Arkansas, although an unscheduled speaker, addressed the convention long enough to say that, despite his being a Confederate veteran, he completely disavowed Tillman's sectionalism. This calmed the crowd, but it soon became inattentive and restless as the much-despised gold bugs gave their speeches and the incredible heat made delegates increasingly uncomfortable. Only the desire to be present for the final vote motivated delegates to suffer through the speeches.

Then came Bryan's rhetorical triumph. He captured attention immediately and suggested indirectly that silverites should not vote to condemn the president. He held attention throughout the body of the speech, not by rehashing old silver arguments that everybody had heard before, but by vigorously answering gold bug arguments. As he neared the end, silver delegates applauded every sentence. They went wild after his emotional peroration. As expected, the gold bugs' motions to substitute their gold plank and to commend the president failed (303-628 and 357-564). The silver platform passed (628-301). Tillman unexpectedly withdrew his motion saying he would not "strike a fallen foe." Except possibly for the Tillman motion being withdrawn (but even that is not very probable), these results cannot be ascribed to Bryan's speech. What can be ascribed to his speech is that, on the following day, the "silver-tongued orator" was nominated.

That Bryan's speech earned him the nomination is indicated not only by the enthusiastic response his oration received, but also by the fact that nothing else can explain his nomination. He came to the convention with no substantial support for the nomination. He was only 36 years of age. Most of his career had been as a local lawyer, first in his native Illinois and then in Lincoln, Nebraska. He had limited political experience, having served only two terms in Congress (1891-1895), and he had lost a Senate race in 1894. Recently, he had edited the *Omaha World-Herald* and travelled extensively to help organize Silver Democrats. Only a few delegates knew him, however, and he had only a modest reputation. The text of his speech is reproduced photographically from A. Craig Baird, *American Public Addresses, 1740-1952* (New York: McGraw-Hill, 1956), pp. 194-200.

Cross of Gold

I would be presumptuous, indeed, to present myself against the distinguished gentlemen to whom you have listened if this were a mere measuring of abilities; but this is not a contest between persons. The humblest citizen in all the land, when clad in the armor of a righteous cause, is stronger than all the hosts of error. I come to speak to you in defense of a cause as holy as the cause of liberty—the cause of humanity.

When this debate is concluded, a motion will be made to lay upon the table the resolution offered in commendation of the administration, and also the resolution offered in condemnation of the administration. We object to bringing this question down to the level of persons. The individual is but an atom; he is born, he acts, he dies; but principles are eternal; and this has been a contest over a principle.

Never before in the history of this country has there been witnessed such a contest as that through which we have just passed. Never before in the history of American politics has a great issue been fought out as this issue has been, by the voters of a great party. On the fourth of March, 1895, a few Democrats, most of them members of Congress, issued an address to the Democrats of the nation, asserting that the money question was the paramount issue of the hour; declaring that a majority of the Democratic party had the right to control the action of the party on this paramount issue; and concluding with the request that the believers in the free coinage of silver in the Democratic party should organize, take charge of, and control the policy of the Democratic party. Three months later, at Memphis, an organization was perfected, and the silver Democrats went forth openly and courageously proclaiming their belief, and declaring that, if successful, they would crystallize into a platform the declaration which they had made. Then began the conflict. With a zeal approaching the zeal which inspired the Crusaders who followed Peter the Hermit, our silver Democrats went forth from victory unto victory until they are now assembled, not to discuss, not to debate, but to enter up the judgement already rendered by the plain people of this country. In this contest brother has been arrayed against brother, father against son. The warmest ties of love, acquaintance and association have been disregarded; old leaders have been cast aside when they have refused to give expression to the sentiments of those whom they would lead, and new leaders have sprung up to give direction to this cause of truth. Thus has the contest been waged, and we have assembled here under as binding and solemn instructions as were ever imposed upon representatives of the people.

We do not come as individuals. As individuals we might have been glad to compliment the gentleman from New York [Senator Hill], but we know that the people for whom we speak would never be willing to put him in a position where he could thwart the will of the Democratic party. I say it was not a question of persons, it was a question of principle, and it is not with gladness, my friends, that we find ourselves brought into conflict with those who are now arrayed on the other side.

The gentleman who preceded me [ex-Governor Russell] spoke of the State of Massachusetts; let me assure him that not one present in all this convention entertains the least hostility to the people of the State of Massachusetts, but we stand here representing the people who are the equals, before the law, of the greatest citizens in the State of Massachusetts. When you [*turning to the gold delegates*] come before us and tell us that we are about to disturb your business interests, we reply that you have disturbed our business interests by your course.

We say to you that you have made the definition of a business man too limited in its application. The man who is employed for wages is as much a business man as his employer, the attorney in a country town is as much a business man as the corporation counsel in a great metropolis; the merchant at the cross-roads store is as much a business man as the merchant of New York; the farmer who goes forth in the morning and toils all day—who begins in the spring and toils all summer—and who by the application of brain and muscle to the natural resources of the country creates wealth, is as much a business man as the man who goes upon the board of trade and bets upon the price of grain; the miners who go down a thousand feet into the earth, or climb two thousand feet upon the cliffs, and bring forth from their hiding places the precious metals to be poured into the channels of trade are as much business men as the few financial magnates who, in a back room, corner the money of the world. We come to speak for this broader class of business men.

Ah, my friends, we say not one word against those who live upon the Atlantic coast, but the hardy pioneers who have braved all the dangers of the wilderness, who have made the desert to blossom as the rose—the pioneers away out there [*pointing to the West*], who rear their children near to Nature's heart, where they can mingle their voices with the voices of the birds—out there where they have erected school houses for the education of their young, churches where they praise their Creator, and cemeteries where rest the ashes of their dead—these people, we say, are as deserving of the consideration of our party as any people in this country. It is for these that we speak. We do not come as aggressors. Our war is not a war of conquest; we are fighting in the defense of our homes, our families, and posterity. We have petitioned, and our petitions have been scorned; we have entreated, and our entreaties have been disregarded; we have begged, and they have mocked when our calamity came. We beg no longer; we petition no more. We defy them.

The gentleman from Wisconsin has said that he fears a Robespierre. My friends, in this land of the free you need not fear that a tyrant will spring up from among the people. What we need is an Andrew Jackson to stand, as Jackson stood, against the encroachments of organized wealth.

They tell us that this platform was made to catch votes. We reply to them that changing conditions make new issues; that the principles on which Democracy rests are as everlasting as the hills, but that they must be applied to new conditions as they arise. Conditions have arisen, and we are here to meet those conditions. They tell us that the income tax ought not be brought in here; that it is a new idea. They criticize us for our criticism of the Supreme Court of the United States. My friends, we have not criticized; we have simply called attention to what you already know. If you want criticisms, read the dissenting opinions of the court. There you will find criticisms. They say that we passed an unconstitutional law; we deny it. The income tax law was not unconstitutional when it was passed; it was not unconstitutional when it went before the Supreme Court for the first time; it did not become unconstitutional until one of the judges changed his mind, and we cannot be expected to know when a judge will change his mind. The income tax is just. It simply intends to put the burdens of government upon the backs of the people. I am in favor of an income tax. When I find a man who is not willing to bear his share of the burdens of the government which protects him, I find a man who is unworthy to enjoy the blessings of a government like ours.

They say that we are opposing national bank currency; it is true. If you will read what Thomas Benton said, you will find he said that, in searching history, he could find but one parallel to Andrew Jackson; that was Cicero, who destroyed the conspiracy of Cataline and saved Rome. Benton said that Cicero only did for Rome what Jackson did for us when he destroyed the bank conspiracy and saved America. We say in our platform that we believe that the right to coin and issue money is a function of government. We believe it. We believe that it is a part of sovereignty, and can no more with safety be delegated to private individuals than we could afford to delegate to private individuals the power to make penal statutes or levy taxes. Mr. Jefferson, who was once regarded as good Democratic authority, seems to have differed in opinion from the gentleman who has addrest us on the part of the minority. Those who are opposed to this proposition tell us that the issue of paper money is a function of the bank, and that the Government ought to go out of the banking business. I stand with Jefferson rather than with them, and tell them, as he did, that the issue of money is a function of government, and that banks ought to go out of the governing business.

They complain about the plank which declares against life tenure in office. They have tried to strain it to mean that which it does not mean. What we oppose by that plank is the life tenure which is being built up in Washington, and which excludes from participation in official benefits the humbler members of society.

Let me call your attention to two or three important things. The gentleman from New York says that he will propose an amendment to the platform providing that the proposed change in our monetary system shall not affect contracts already made. Let me remind you that there is no intention of affecting those contracts which according to present laws are made payable in gold; but if he means to say that we cannot change our monetary system without protecting those who have loaned money before the change was made, I desire to ask him where, in law or in morals, he can find justification for not protecting the debtors when the act of 1873 was passed, if he now insists that we must protect the creditors.

He says he will also propose an amendment which will provide for the suspension of free coinage if we fail to maintain the parity within a year. We reply that when we advocate a policy which we believe will be successful, we are not compelled to raise a doubt as to our own sincerity by suggesting what we shall do if we fail. I ask him, if he would apply his logic to us, why he does not apply it to himself. He says he wants this country to try to secure an international agreement. Why does he not tell us what he is going to do if he fails to secure an international agreement? There is more reason for him to do that than there is for us to provide against the failure to maintain the parity. Our opponents have tried for twenty years to secure an international agreement, and those are waiting for it most patiently who do not want it at all.

And now, my friends, let me come to the paramount issue. If they ask us why it is that we say more on the money question than we say upon the tariff question, I reply that, if protection has slain its thousands, the gold standard has slain its tens of thousands. If they ask us why we do not embody in our platform all the things that we believe in, we reply that when we have restored the money of the Constitution all other necessary reforms will be possible; but that until this is done there is no other reform that can be accomplished.

Why is it that within three months such a change has come over the country? Three months ago, when it was confidently asserted that those who believe in the gold standard would frame our platform and nominate our candidate, even the advocates of the gold standard did not think that we could elect a President. And they had good reason for their doubt, because there is scarcely a State here today asking for the gold standard which is not in the absolute control of the Republican party. But note the change. Mr. McKinley was nominated at St. Louis upon a platform which declared for the maintenance of the gold standard until it can be changed into bimetalism by international agreement. Mr. McKinley was the most popular man among the Republicans, and three months ago everybody in the Republican party prophesied his election. How is it to-day? Why, the man who was once pleased to think that he looked like Napoleon—that man shudders to-day when he remembers that he was nominated on the anniversary of the battle of Waterloo. Not only that, but as he listens he can hear with ever-increasing distinctness the sounds of the waves as they beat upon the lonely shores of St. Helena.

Why this change? Ah, my friends, is not the reason for the change evident to any one who will look at the matter? No private character, however pure, no personal popularity, however great, can protect from the avenging wrath of an indignant people a man who will declare that he is in favor of fastening the gold standard upon this country, or who is willing to surrender the right of self-government and place the legislative control of our affairs in the hands of foreign potentates and powers.

We go forth confident that we shall win. Why? Because upon the paramount issue of this campaign there is not a spot of ground upon which the enemy will dare to challenge battle. If they tell us that the gold standard is a good thing, we shall point to their platform and tell them that their platform pledges the party to get rid of the gold standard and substitute bimetalism. If the gold standard is a good thing, why try to get rid of it? I call your attention to the fact that some of the very people who are in this convention to-day and who tell us that we ought to declare in favor of international bimetalism—thereby declaring that the gold standard is wrong and that the principle of bimetalism is better—these very people four months ago were open and avowed advocates of the gold standard, and were then telling us that we could not legislate two metals together, even with the aid of all the world. If the gold standard is a good thing, we ought to declare in favor of its retention and not in favor of abandoning it; and if the gold standard is a bad thing, why should we wait until other nations are willing to help us to let go? Here is the line of battle, and we care not upon which issue they force the fight; we are prepared to meet them on either issue or on both. If they tell us that the gold standard is the standard of civilization, we reply to them that this, the most enlightened of all the nations of the earth, has never declared for a gold standard and that both the great parties this year are declaring against it. If the gold standard is the standard of civilization, why, my friends, should we not have it? If they come to meet us on that issue we can present the history of our nation. More than that; we can tell them that they will search the pages of history in vain to find a single instance where the common people have ever declared themselves in favor of the gold standard. They can find where the holders of fixt investments have declared for a gold standard, but not where the masses have.

Mr. Carlisle said in 1878 that this was a struggle between "the idle holders of idle capital" and "the struggling masses, who produce the wealth and pay the taxes of the country"; and, my friends, the question we are to decide is: Upon which side will the Democratic party fight; upon the side of "the idle holders of idle capital" or upon the side of "the struggling masses"? That is the question which the party must answer first, and then it must be answered by each individual hereafter. The sympathies of the Democratic party, as shown by the platform, are on the side of the struggling masses who have ever been the foundation of the Democratic party. There are two ideas of government. There are those who believe that, if you will only legislate to make the well-to-do prosperous, their prosperity will leak through on those below. The Democratic idea, however, that if you legislate to make the masses prosperous, their prosperity will find its way up through every class which rests upon them.

You come to us and tell us that the great cities are in favor of the gold standard; we reply that the great cities rest upon our broad and fertile prairies. Burn down your cities and leave our farms, and your cities will spring up again as if by magic; but destroy our farms and the grass will grow in the streets of every city in the country.

My friends, we declare that this nation is able to legislate for its own people on every question, without waiting for the aid or consent of any other nation on earth; and upon that issue we expect to carry every State in the Union. I shall not slander the inhabitants of the fair State of Massachusetts nor the inhabitants of the State of New York by saying that, when they are confronted with the proposition, they will declare that this nation is not able to attend to its own business. It is the issue of 1776 over again. Our ancestors, when but three millions in number, had the courage to declare their political independence of every other nation; shall we, their descendants, when we have grown to seventy millions, declare that we are less independent than our forefathers? No, my friends, that will never be the verdict of our people. Therefore we care not upon what lines the battle is fought. If they say bimetalism is good, but that we cannot have it until the other nations help us, we reply that, instead of having a gold standard because England has, we will restore bimetalism, and then let England have bimetalism because the United States has it. If they dare to come out in the open field and defend the gold standard as a good thing, we will fight them to the uttermost. Having behind us the producing masses of this nation and the world, supported by the commercial interests, the laboring interests, and the toilers everywhere, we will answer their demand for a gold standard by saying to them: You shall not press down upon the brow of labor this crown of thorns, you shall not crucify mankind upon a cross of gold.

The March of the Flag (Abridged)

Albert Beveridge

Commentary

The electoral campaign of 1896 amounted to a political and rhetorical revolution. First, the campaign was the first issue-oriented one in over a generation. The standard rhetorical reminders of the Civil War era were forgotten as both sides argued the relative merits of gold and bimetallism. Second, both parties used methods which, though different, foreshadowed the mass persuasion that we now take for granted. Campaigning more vigorously than any predecessor, Bryan travelled 18,000 miles, mostly by rail. He delivered 600 speeches in 475 localities in twenty-seven states. With the "office seeks the man" myth not yet dead, William McKinley stayed at home implying that he was a statesman while his opponent was greedy for office. Audiences appeared "spontaneously" to ask the great man to address them from his front porch (while his campaign manager quietly arranged for extensive press coverage of these "spontaneous" rhetorical events). Third, the Democrats effectively co-opted the People's party, which also nominated Bryan, and employed a class-conscious, common man rhetoric. Although Democrats had used a common man appeal ever since Jeffersonians attacked the Hamiltonian "aristocrats," they had traditionally supported limited government. With the limited government ideology still strong, Populist enthusiasm for governmental activism gave Democrats a case of ideological schizophrenia that still persists.

McKinley's victory was followed by an improved economy. As domestic conditions stabilized, public attention turned to Cuba. One of the few remaining outposts of the once-powerful Spanish empire, Cuba had a history of rebellions, the most recent having erupted in 1895. Responding harshly, Spanish soldiers herded thousands of Cubans into concentration camps, where untold numbers died from brutality, illness and poor living conditions. American expansionists had long cast a lustful eye on Cuba. Although none dared argue openly for an expansionist war, newspaper stories of Spanish brutality gave them a strong humanitarian argument for some undefined "diplomatic intervention." Other arguments supported intervention, including the destruction of American property in Cuba, the danger to American businessmen and tourists, and the possibility that Spanish weakness would result in Cuba being occupied by some imperialist power. Although public opinion strongly supported diplomatic intervention, there was little support for war until the battleship *Maine* was sunk in Havana harbor on February 15, 1898. By April, the Spanish-American war had begun.

Fearing that public hysteria would give expansionists a field day, congressional anti-expansionists carefully amended the declaration of war so that it prohibited the annexation of Cuba; however, they overlooked the possibility of other Spanish possessions falling into American hands. When the preliminary peace protocol was signed on August 12, 1898, American soldiers occupied Puerto Rico and the Navy controlled the seas around Manila. Even before negotiations for the final treaty began on October 1, a public debate erupted over whether the United States should keep the Philippines.

The debate was highlighted by an accident of chronology. Peace negotiations began just as State and congressional campaigns were getting into high gear. Many candidates saw the issue as one which could sweep them into office. Among them was Albert J. Beveridge (1862-1927), a young Indianapolis lawyer (whose book on public speaking was a quarter-century in the future). He lusted for the Senate seat that would become vacant the following year. Indiana was one of the few States which still had its legislature elect senators. Although no one had announced his candidacy, would-be senators were trying to get themselves in the public eye while privately lining up support. Beveridge's reputation as an orator gave him a significant advantage. He had begun stumping for Republican candidates while he was in college and had become more active after opening his law office in 1887. By 1898, he already had many Republicans indebted to him, and his oratorical reputation earned him an invitation to give the major address at the opening campaign rally on September 16, 1898.

Beveridge's speech not only helped him get the Senate seat, but also made him a major spokesman for annexing the Philippines. It was cheered wildly by the hundreds who heard it, and it was printed (in slightly variant forms) as a campaign document that was used by expansionist candidates in Indiana and neighboring States. The following text derives ultimately from Beveridge's collected speeches and is reproduced photographically from the abridged version in Ernest J. Wrage and Barnet Baskerville, *American Forum: Speeches on Historic Issues, 1788-1900* (New York: Harper & Brothers, 1960), pp. 352-357.

The March of the Flag (Abridged)

It is a noble land that God has given us; a land that can feed and clothe the world; a land whose coastlines would inclose half the countries of Europe; a land set like a sentinel between the two imperial oceans of the globe, a greater England with a nobler destiny.

It is a mighty people that He has planted on this soil; a people sprung from the most masterful blood of history; a people perpetually revitalized by the virile, man-producing working-folk of all the earth; a people imperial by virtue of their power, by right of their institutions, by authority of their Heaven-directed purposes—the propagandists and not the misers of liberty.

It is a glorious history our God has bestowed upon His chosen people; a history heroic with faith in our mission and our future; a history of statesmen who flung the boundaries of the Republic out into unexplored lands and savage wilderness; a history of soldiers who carried the flag across blazing deserts and through the ranks of hostile mountains, even to the gates of sunset; a history of a multiplying people who overran a continent in half a century; a history of prophets who saw the consequences of evils inherited from the past and of martyrs who died to save us from them; a history divinely logical, in the process of whose tremendous reasoning we find ourselves to-day.

Therefore, in this campaign, the question is larger than a party question. It is an American question. It is a world question. Shall the American people continue their march toward the commercial supremacy of the world? Shall free institutions broaden their blessed reign as the children of liberty wax in strength, until the empire of our principles is established over the hearts of all mankind?

Have we no mission to perform, no duty to discharge to our fellow-man? Has God endowed us with gifts beyond our deserts and marked us as the people of His peculiar favor, merely to rot in our own selfishness, as men and nations must, who take cowardice for their companion and self for their deity —as China has, as India has, as Egypt has?

Shall we be as the man who had one talent and hid it, or as he who had ten talents and used them until they grew to riches? And shall we reap the reward that waits on our discharge of our high duty; shall we occupy new markets for what our farmers raise, our factories make, our merchants sell— aye, and, please God, new markets for what our ships shall carry?

Hawaii is ours; Porto Rico is to be ours; at the prayer of her people Cuba finally will be ours; in the islands of the East, even to the gates of Asia, coaling stations are to be ours at the very least; the flag of a liberal government is to float over the Philippines, and may it be the banner that Taylor unfurled in Texas and Fremont carried to the coast.

The Opposition tells us that we ought not to govern a people without their consent. I answer, The rule of liberty that all just government derives its authority from the consent of the governed, applies only to those who are capable of self-government. We govern the Indians without their consent, we govern our territories without their consent, we govern our children without their consent. How do they know that our government would be without their consent? Would not the people of the Philippines prefer the just, humane, civilizing government of this Republic to the savage, bloody rule of pillage and extortion from which we have rescued them?

And, regardless of this formula of words made only for enlightened, self-governing people, do we owe no duty to the world? Shall we turn these peoples back to the reeking hands from which we have taken them? Shall we abandon them, with Germany, England, Japan, hungering for them? Shall we save them from those nations, to give them a self-rule of tragedy?

They ask us how we shall govern these new possessions. I answer: Out of local conditions and the necessities of the case methods of government will grow. If England can govern foreign lands, so can America. If Germany can govern foreign lands, so can America. If they can supervise protectorates, so can America. Why is it more difficult to administer Hawaii than New Mexico or California? Both had a savage and an alien population; both were more remote from the seat of government when they came under our dominion than the Philippines are to-day.

Will you say by your vote that American ability to govern has decayed; that a century's experience in self-rule has failed of a result? Will you affirm by your vote that you are an infidel to American power and practical sense? Or will you say that ours is the blood of government; ours the heart of dominion; ours the brain and genius of administration? Will you remember that we do but what our fathers did—we but pitch the tents of liberty farther westward, farther southward—we only continue the march of the flag?

The march of the flag! In 1789 the flag of the Republic waved over 4,000,000 souls in thirteen states, and their savage territory which stretched to the Mississippi, to Canada, to the Floridas. The timid minds of that day said that no new territory was needed, and, for the hour, they were right. But Jefferson, through whose intellect the centuries marched; Jefferson, who dreamed of Cuba as an American state; Jefferson, the first Imperialist of the Republic—Jefferson acquired that imperial territory which swept from the Mississippi to the mountains, from Texas to the British possessions, and the march of the flag began!

The infidels to the gospel of liberty raved, but the flag swept on! The title to that noble land out of which Oregon, Washington, Idaho and Montana have been carved was uncertain; Jefferson, strict constructionist of constitutional power though he was, obeyed the Anglo-Saxon impulse within him, whose watchword then and whose watchword throughout the world to-day is, "Forward!": another empire was added to the Republic, and the march of the flag went on!

Those who deny the power of free institutions to expand urged every argument, and more, that we hear, to-day; but the people's judgment approved the command of their blood, and the march of the flag went on!

A screen of land from New Orleans to Florida shut us from the Gulf, and over this and the Everglade Peninsula waved the saffron flag of Spain; Andrew Jackson seized both, the American people stood at his back, and, under Monroe, the Floridas came under the dominion of the Republic, and the march of the flag went on! The Cassandras prophesied every prophecy of despair we hear today; but the march of the flag went on!

Then Texas responded to the bugle calls of liberty, and the march of the flag went on! And, at last, we waged war with Mexico, and the flag swept over the southwest, over peerless California, past the Gate of Gold to Oregon on the north, and from ocean to ocean its folds of glory blazed.

And, now, obeying the same voice that Jefferson heard and obeyed, that Jackson heard and obeyed, that Monroe heard and obeyed, that Seward heard and obeyed, that Grant heard and obeyed, that Harrison heard and obeyed, our President to-day plants the flag over the islands of the seas, outposts of commerce, citadels of national security, and the march of the flag goes on!

Distance and oceans are no arguments. The fact that all the territory our fathers bought and seized is contiguous, is no argument. In 1819 Florida was farther from New York than Porto Rico is from Chicago today; Texas, farther from Washington in 1845 than Hawaii is from Boston in 1898; California, more inaccessible in 1847 than the Philippines are now. Gibraltar is farther from London than Havana is from Washington; Melbourne is farther from Liverpool than Manila is from San Francisco.

The ocean does not separate us from lands of our duty and desire—the oceans join us, rivers never to be dredged, canals never to be repaired. Steam joins us; electricity joins us—the very elements are in league with our destiny. Cuba not contiguous! Porto Rico not contiguous! Hawaii and the Philippines not contiguous! The oceans make them contiguous. And our navy will make them contiguous.

But the Opposition is right—there is a difference. We did not need the western Mississippi Valley when we acquired it, nor Florida, nor Texas, nor California, nor the royal provinces of the far northwest. We had no emigrants to people this imperial wilderness, no money to develop it, even no highways to cover it. No trade awaited us in its savage fastnesses. Our productions were not greater than our trade. There was not one reason for the land-lust of our statesmen from Jefferson to Grant, other than the prophet and the Saxon within them. But, to-day, we are raising more than we can consume, making more than we can use. Therefore we must find new markets for our produce.

And so, while we did not need the territory taken during the past century at the time it was acquired, we do need what we have taken in 1898, and we need it now. The resources and the commerce of these immensely rich dominions will be increased as much as American energy is greater than Spanish sloth. In Cuba, alone, there are 15,000,000 acres of forest unacquainted with the ax, exhaustless mines of iron, priceless deposits of manganese, millions of dollars' worth of which we must buy, to-day, from the Black Sea districts. There are millions of acres yet unexplored.

The resources of Porto Rico have only been trifled with. The riches of the

Philippines have hardly been touched by the finger-tips of modern methods. And they produce what we consume, and consume what we produce—the very predestination of reciprocity—a reciprocity "not made with hands, eternal in the heavens." They sell hemp, sugar, coconuts, fruits of the tropics, timber of price like mahogany; they buy flour, clothing, tools, implements, machinery and all that we can raise and make. Their trade will be ours in time. Do you indorse that policy with your vote?

Cuba is as large as Pennsylvania, and is the richest spot on the globe. Hawaii is as large as New Jersey; Porto Rico half as large as Hawaii; the Philippines larger than all New England, New York, New Jersey and Delaware combined. Together they are larger than the British Isles, larger than France, larger than Germany, larger than Japan.

If any man tells you that trade depends on cheapness and not on government influence, ask him why England does not abandon South Africa, Egypt, India. Why does France seize South China, Germany the vast region whose port is Kiouchou?

Our trade with Porto Rico, Hawaii and the Philippines must be as free as between the states of the Union, because they are American territory, while every other nation on earth must pay our tariff before they can compete with us. Until Cuba shall ask for annexation, our trade with her will, at the very least, be like the preferential trade of Canada with England. That, and the excellence of our goods and products; that, and the convenience of traffic; that, and the kinship of interests and destiny, will give the monopoly of these markets to the American people.

The commercial supremacy of the Republic means that this Nation is to be the sovereign factor in the peace of the world. For the conflicts of the future are to be conflicts of trade—struggles for markets—commercial wars for existence. And the golden rule of peace is impregnability of position and invincibility of preparedness. So, we see England, the greatest strategist of history, plant her flag and her cannon on Gibraltar, at Quebec, in the Bermudas, at Vancouver, everywhere.

So Hawaii furnishes us a naval base in the heart of the Pacific; the Ladrones another, a voyage further on; Manila another, at the gates of Asia—Asia, to the trade of whose hundreds of millions American merchants, manufacturers, farmers, have as good right as those of Germany or France or Russia or England; Asia, whose commerce with the United Kingdom alone amounts to hundreds of millions of dollars every year; Asia, to whom Germany looks to take her surplus products; Asia, whose doors must not be shut against American trade. Within five decades the bulk of Oriental commerce will be ours.

There are so many real things to be done—canals to be dug, railways to be laid, forests to be felled, cities to be builded, fields to be tilled, markets to be won, ships to be launched, peoples to be saved, civilization to be proclaimed and the flag of liberty flung to the eager air of every sea. Is this an hour to waste upon triflers with nature's laws? Is this a season to give our destiny over to word-mongers and prosperity-wreckers? No! It is an hour to remember our duty to our homes. It is a moment to realize the opportunities fate has opened to us. And so it is an hour for us to stand by the Government.

Wonderfully has God guided us. Yonder at Bunker Hill and Yorktown His providence was above us. At New Orleans and on ensanguined seas His hand sustained us. Abraham Lincoln was His minister and His was the altar of freedom the Nation's soldiers set up on a hundred battle-fields. His power directed Dewey in the East and delivered the Spanish fleet into our hands, as He delivered the elder Armada into the hands of our English sires two centuries ago. The American people can not use a dishonest medium of exchange; it is ours to set the world its example of right and honor. We can not fly from our world duties; it is ours to execute the purpose of a fate that has driven us to be greater than our small intentions. We can not retreat from any soil where Providence has unfurled our banner; it is ours to save that soil for liberty and civilization.

Acceptance Speech, 1900 (Abridged)

William Jennings Bryan

Commentary

The campaign rhetoric of 1898 was only the beginning of a long debate about the Philippines. When the Senate convened in December, 1898, the peace treaty was not yet before it, but already Vest of Missouri tried to forestall annexation. He introduced a resolution saying that "under the Constitution of the United States no power is given to the Federal Government to acquire territory to be held and governed permanently as colonies." During the lengthy debate, Vest based his argument on the old Jeffersonian concept of "explicit powers," but the steady growth of Federal power since the Civil War made it unappealing even to many anti-imperialists. In January, the treaty came before the Senate. After a long debate, it was ratified on February 6, 1899. Far from being over, the public debate intensified as American soldiers put down a Filipino revolt and charges of American brutality circulated. Local "Anti-Imperialist Leagues" soon coalesced into a national organization, thereby encouraging more debate.

Running through the public debate were opposing interpretations of our Revolutionary and Millenarian heritages, as well as different racial attitudes. Anti-imperialists cited the Declaration of Independence, emphasized that government rests on "the consent of the governed" and argued that Filipinos had not consented to be our colony. Expansionists replied that the concept of "consent" applied only to those who were capable of giving consent. While racists argued that Filipinos would never be capable of giving consent, moderates argued that centuries of authoritarian Spanish rule made Filipinos incapable at the present time. Anti-Imperialists argued that suppressing the Filipino army violated America's divinely ordained mission of being the model of Liberty and Justice to the world. Expansionists replied that it was America's divinely ordained duty to bring "our little brown brother" the blessings of Christianity, teach him the ways of democracy and protect him from being colonized by some brutal colonial power who would surely step into the vacuum if America withdrew.

The debate cut through party lines, but Democrats generally opposed annexation. Some Democrats sincerely opposed annexation while others saw an issue that could reunite a badly divided party, as there was still hostility between the Eastern and Southern-Western wings as a result of their conflict in 1896. Easterners were angry when the convention of 1900 renominated Bryan and announced again its support of free silver. The gold bugs' hero, ex-President Cleveland, announced his opposition to annexation. Although Bryan had favored ratifying the peace treaty in order to bring the war to an official end, he too had spoken clearly against annexation. Seizing upon a concept which could unite the party, the Democratic platform of 1900 emphasized that imperialism would be the paramount issue of the campaign and promised that, if elected, they would free the Philippines after establishing a stable government. When the Notification Committee informed Bryan of his nomination on August 8, 1900, he devoted his acceptance speech to the new issue. In contrast to our day, when acceptance speeches are delivered to the convention, the old custom still prevailed. Notification came about a month after the nomination. Although ostensibly a response to the committee, the acceptance speech was heard by a huge crowd. It was printed and circulated widely. It is reproduced photographically from the abridged version in Ernest J. Wrage and Barnet Baskerville, *American Forum: Speeches on Historic Issues, 1788-1900* (New York: Harper & Brothers, 1960), pp. 358-368.

Acceptance Speech, 1900 (Abridged)

*M*r. *Chairman and Members of the Notification Committee:* I shall, at an early day, and in a more formal manner, accept the nomination which you tender, and shall at that time discuss the various questions covered by the Democratic platform. It may not be out of place, however, to submit a few observations at this time upon the general character of the contest before us and upon the question which is declared to be of paramount importance in this campaign.

When I say that the contest of 1900 is a contest between Democracy on the one hand and plutocracy on the other I do not mean to say that all our opponents have deliberately chosen to give to organized wealth a predominating influence in the affairs of the Government, but I do assert that on the important issues of the day the Republican party is dominated by those influences which constantly tend to substitute the worship of mammon for the protection of the rights of man.

[Bryan continues his observations upon "the general character of the contest" by contrasting the Republican and Democratic parties. He then explains that he voted for the Philippine treaty because he thought it better to end the war first, and then to give the Filipinos their independence. He then takes up the question of imperialism.]

Those who would have this Nation enter upon a career of empire must consider, not only the effect of imperialism on the Filipinos, but they must also calculate its effects upon our own nation. We cannot repudiate the principle of self-government in the Philippines without weakening that principle here.

Lincoln said that the safety of this Nation was not in its fleets, its armies, or its forts, but in the spirit which prizes liberty as the heritage of all men, in all lands, everywhere, and he warned his countrymen that they could not destroy this spirit without planting the seeds of despotism at their own doors.

Even now we are beginning to see the paralyzing influence of imperialism. Heretofore this Nation has been prompt to express its sympathy with those who were fighting for civil liberty. While our sphere of activity has been limited to the Western Hemisphere, our sympathies have not been bounded by the seas. We have felt it due to ourselves and to the world, as well as to those who were struggling for the right to govern themselves, to proclaim the interest which our people have, from the date of their own independence, felt in every contest between human rights and arbitrary power.

Three-quarters of a century ago, when our nation was small, the struggles of Greece aroused our people, and Webster and Clay gave eloquent expression to the universal desire for Grecian independence. In 1898 all parties manifested a lively interest in the success of the Cubans, but now when a war is in progress in South Africa, which must result in the extension of the monarchical idea, or in the triumph of a republic, the advocates of imperialism in this country dare not say a word in behalf of the Boers.

Sympathy for the Boers does not arise from any unfriendliness towards England; the American people are not unfriendly toward the people of any nation. This sympathy is due to the fact that, as stated in our platform, we believe in the principles of self-government and reject, as did our forefathers, the claims of monarchy. If this nation surrenders its belief in the universal application of the principles set forth in the Declaration of Independence, it will lose the prestige and influence which it has enjoyed among the nations as an exponent of popular government.

Our opponents, conscious of the weakness of their cause, seek to confuse imperialism with expansion, and have even dared to claim Jefferson as a supporter of their policy. Jefferson spoke so freely and used language with such precision that no one can be ignorant of his views. On one occasion he declared: "If there be one principle more deeply rooted than any other in the mind of every American, it is that we should have nothing to do with conquest." And again he said: "Conquest is not in our principles; it is inconsistent with our government."

The forcible annexation of territory to be governed by arbitrary power differs as much from the acquisition of territory to be built up into States as a monarchy differs from a democracy. The Democratic party does not oppose expansion when expansion enlarges the area of the Republic and incorporates land which can be settled by American citizens, or adds to our population people who are willing to become citizens and are capable of discharging their duties as such.

The acquisition of the Louisiana territory, Florida, Texas and other tracts which have been secured from time to time enlarged the Republic and the Constitution followed the flag into the new territory. It is now proposed to seize upon distant territory already more densely populated than our own country and to force upon the people a government for which there is no warrant in our Constitution or our laws.

Even the argument that this earth belongs to those who desire to cultivate it and who have the physical power to acquire it cannot be invoked to justify the appropriation of the Philippine Islands by the United States. If the islands were uninhabited American citizens would not be willing to go there and till the soil. The white race will not live so near the equator. Other nations have tried to colonize in the same latitude. The Netherlands have controlled Java for three hundred years and yet today there are less than sixty thousand people of European birth scattered among the twenty-five million natives.

After a century and a half of English domination in India, less than one-twentieth of one per cent of the people of India are of English birth, and it requires an army of seventy thousand British soldiers to take care of the tax collectors. Spain had asserted title to the Philippine Islands for three centuries and yet when our fleet entered Manila bay there were less than ten thousand Spaniards residing in the Philippines.

A colonial policy means that we shall send to the Philippine Islands a few traders, a few taskmasters and a few office-holders and an army large enough to support the authority of a small fraction of the people while they rule the natives.

If we have an imperial policy we must have a great standing army as its natural and necessary complement. The spirit which will justify the forcible annexation of the Philippine Islands will justify the seizure of other islands and the domination of other people, and with wars of conquest we can expect a certain, if not rapid, growth of our military establishment.

[Mr. Bryan warns against the dangers of a large standing army. He then discusses the future status of the Filipino, implying that since he is not to be a citizen, he must necessarily be a subject.]

What is our title to the Philippine Islands? Do we hold them by treaty or by conquest? Did we buy them or did we take them? Did we purchase the people? If not, how did we secure title to them? Were they thrown in with the land? Will the Republicans say that inanimate earth has value but that when that earth is molded by the divine hand and stamped with the likeness of the Creator it becomes a fixture and passes with the soil? If governments derive their just powers from the consent of the governed, it is impossible to secure title to people, either by force or by purchase.

We could extinguish Spain's title by treaty, but if we hold title we must hold it by some method consistent with our ideas of government. When we made allies of the Filipinos and armed them to fight against Spain, we disputed Spain's title. If we buy Spain's title we are not innocent purchasers.

There can be no doubt that we accepted and utilized the services of the Filipinos, and that when we did so we had full knowledge that they were fighting for their own independence, and I submit that history furnishes no example of turpitude baser than ours if we now substitute our yoke for the Spanish yoke.

Let us consider briefly the reasons which have been given in support of an imperialistic policy. Some say that it is our duty to hold the Philippine Islands. But duty is not an argument; it is a conclusion. To ascertain what our duty is, in any emergency, we must apply well-settled and generally accepted principles. It is our duty to avoid stealing, no matter whether the thing to be stolen is of great or little value. It is our duty to avoid killing a human being, no matter where the human being lives or to what race or class he belongs.

Every one recognizes the obligation imposed upon individuals to observe both the human and the moral law, but as some deny the application of those laws to nations, it may not be out of place to quote the opinions of others. Jefferson, than whom there is no higher political authority, said: "I know of but one code of morality for men, whether acting singly or collectively."

Franklin, whose learning, wisdom and virtue are a part of the priceless legacy bequeathed to us from the revolutionary days, exprest the same idea in even stronger language when he said:

Justice is strictly due between neighbor nations as between neighbor citizens. A highwayman is as much a robber when he plunders in a gang as when single; and the nation that makes an unjust war is only a great gang.

Many may dare to do in crowds what they would not dare to do as individuals, but the moral character of an act is not determined by the number of those who join it. Force can defend a right, but force has never yet created a right. If it was true, as declared in the resolutions of intervention, that the Cubans "are and of right ought to be free and independent" (language taken from the Declaration of Independence), it is equally true that the Filipinos "are and of right ought to be free and independent."

The right of the Cubans to freedom was not based upon their proximity to the United States, nor upon the language which they spoke, nor yet upon the race or races to which they belonged. Congress by a practically unanimous vote declared that the principles enunciated at Philadelphia in 1776 were still alive and applicable to the Cubans. Who will draw a line between the natural rights of the Cubans and the Filipinos? Who will say that the former has a right to liberty and that the latter has no rights which we are bound to respect? And, if the Filipinos "are and of right ought to be free and independent," what right have we to force our government upon them without their consent? Before our duty can be ascertained their rights must be determined, and when their rights are once determined it is as much our duty to respect those rights as it was the duty of Spain to respect the rights of the people of Cuba or the duty of England to respect the rights of the American colonists. Rights never conflict; duties never clash. Can it be our duty to usurp political rights which belong to others? Can it be our duty to kill those who, following the example of our forefathers, love liberty well enough to fight for it?

Some poet has described the terror which overcame a soldier who in the midst of the battle discovered that he had slain his brother. It is written "All ye are brethren." Let us hope for the coming of the day when human life—which when once destroyed cannot be restored—will be so sacred that it will never be taken except when necessary to punish a crime already committed, or to prevent a crime about to be committed.

It is said that we have assumed before the world obligations which make it necessary for us to permanently maintain a government in the Philippine Islands. I reply first, that the highest obligation of this nation is to be true to itself. No obligation to any particular nations, or to all the nations combined, can require the abandonment of our theory of government, and the substitution of doctrines against which our whole national life has been a protest. And, second, that our obligation to the Filipinos, who inhabit the islands, is greater than any obligation which we can owe to foreigners who have a temporary residence in the Philippines or desire to trade there.

It is argued by some that the Filipinos are incapable of self-government and that, therefore, we owe it to the world to take control of them. Admiral Dewey, in an official report to the Navy Department, declared the Filipinos more capable of self-government than the Cubans and said that he based his opinion upon a knowledge of both races. But I will not rest the case upon the relative advancement of the Filipinos. Henry Clay, in defending the right of the people of South America to self-government said:

> It is the doctrine of thrones that man is too ignorant to govern himself. Their partizans assert his incapacity in reference to all nations; if they cannot command universal assent to the proposition, it is then demanded to particular nations; and our pride and our presumption too often make converts of us. I contend that it is to arraign the disposition of Providence himself to suppose that he has created beings incapable of governing themselves, and to be trampled on by kings. Self-government is the natural government of man.

Clay was right. There are degrees of proficiency in the art of self-government, but it is a reflection upon the Creator to say that he denied to any people the capacity for self-government. Once admit that some people are capable of self-government and that others are not and that the capable people have a right to seize upon and govern the incapable, and you make force—brute force—the only foundation of government and invite the reign of a despot. I am not willing to believe that an all-wise and an all-loving God created the Filipinos and then left them thousands of years helpless until the islands attracted the attention of European nations.

Republicans ask, "Shall we haul down the flag that floats over our dead in the Philippines?" The same question might have been asked, when the American flag floated over Chapultepec and waved over the dead who fell there; but the tourist who visits the City of Mexico finds there a national cemetery owned by the United States and cared for by an American citizen.

Our flag still floats over our dead, but when the treaty with Mexico was signed American authority withdrew to the Rio Grande, and I venture the opinion that during the last fifty years the people of Mexico have made more progress under the stimulus of independence and self-government than they would have made under a carpet-bag government held in place by bayonets. The United States and Mexico, friendly republics, are each stronger and happier than they would have been had the former been cursed and the latter crushed by an imperialistic policy disguised as "benevolent assimilation."

"Can we not govern colonies?" we are asked. The question is not what we can do, but what we ought to do. This nation can do whatever it desires to do, but it must accept responsibility for what it does. If the Constitution stands in the way, the people can amend the Constitution. I repeat, the nation can do whatever it desires to do, but it cannot avoid the natural and legitimate results of its own conduct.

The young man upon reaching his majority can do what he pleases. He can disregard the teachings of his parents; he can trample upon all that he has been taught to consider sacred; he can disobey the laws of the State, the laws of society and the laws of God. He can stamp failure upon his life and make his very existence a curse to his fellow men, and he can bring his father and mother in sorrow to the grave; but he cannot annul the sentence, "The wages of sin is death."

And so with the nation. It is of age and it can do what it pleases; it can spurn the traditions of the past; it can repudiate the principles upon which the nation rests; it can employ force instead of reason; it can substitute might for right; it can conquer weaker people; it can exploit their lands, appropriate their property and kill their people; but it cannot repeal the moral law or escape the punishment decreed for the violation of human rights. . . .

Some argue that American rule in the Philippine Islands will result in the better education of the Filipinos. Be not deceived. If we expect to maintain a colonial policy, we shall not find it to our advantage to educate the people. The educated Filipinos are now in revolt against us, and the most ignorant ones have made the least resistance to our domination. If we are to govern them without their consent and give them no voice in determining the taxes which they must pay, we dare not educate them, lest they learn to read the Declaration of Independence and Constitution of the United States and mock us for our inconsistency.

The principal arguments, however, advanced by those who enter upon a defense of imperialism are:

First—That we must improve the present opportunity to become a world power and enter into international politics.

Second—That our commercial interests in the Philippine Islands and in the Orient make it necessary for us to hold the islands permanently.

Third—That the spread of the Christian religion will be facilitated by a colonial policy.

Fourth—That there is no honorable retreat from the position which the nation has taken.

The first argument is addrest to the nation's pride and the second to the nation's pocket-book. The third is intended for the church member and the fourth for the partizan.

It is sufficient answer to the first argument to say that for more than a century this nation has been a world power. For ten decades it has been the most potent influence in the world. Not only has it been a world power, but it has done more to shape the politics of the human race than all the other nations of the world combined. Because our Declaration of Independence was promulgated others have been promulgated. Because the patriots of 1776 fought for liberty others have fought for it. Because our Constitution was adopted other constitutions have been adopted.

The growth of the principle of self-government, planted on American soil, has been the overshadowing political fact of the nineteenth century. It has made this nation conspicuous among the nations and given it a place in history such as no other nation has ever enjoyed. Nothing has been able to check the onward march of this idea. I am not willing that this nation shall cast aside the omnipotent weapon of truth to seize again the weapons of physical warfare. I would not exchange the glory of this Republic for the glory of all the empires that have risen and fallen since time began.

The permanent chairman of the last Republican National Convention presented the pecuniary argument in all its baldness when he said:

We make no hypocritical pretense of being interested in the Philippines solely on account of others. While we regard the welfare of those people as a sacred trust, we regard the welfare of the American people first. We see our duty to ourselves as well as to others. We believe in trade expansion. By every legitimate means within the province of government and constitution we mean to stimulate the expansion of our trade and open new markets.

This is the commercial argument. It is based upon the theory that war can be rightly waged for pecuniary advantage, and that it is profitable to purchase trade by force and violence.

The pecuniary argument, the more effective with certain classes, is not likely to be used so often or presented with so much enthusiasm as the religious argument. If what has been termed the "gunpowder gospel" were urged against the Filipinos only it would be a sufficient answer to say that a majority of the Filipinos are now members of one branch of the Christian church; but the principle involved is one of much wider application and challenges serious consideration.

The religious argument varies in positiveness from a passive belief that Providence delivered the Filipinos into our hands, for their good and our glory, to the exultation of the minister who said that we ought to "thrash the natives (Filipinos) until they understand who we are," and that "every bullet sent, every cannon shot and every flag waved means righteousness."

We cannot approve of this doctrine in one place unless we are willing to apply it everywhere. If there is poison in the blood of the hand it will ultimately reach the heart. It is equally true that forcible Christianity, if planted under the American flag in the far-away Orient, will sooner or later be transplanted upon American soil.

If true Christianity consists in carrying out in our daily lives the teachings of Christ, who will say that we are commanded to civilize with dynamite and proselyte with the sword? He who would declare the divine will must prove his authority either by Holy Writ or by evidence of a special dispensation.

Imperialism finds no warrant in the Bible. The command, "Go ye into all the world and preach the gospel to every creature," has no Gatling gun attachment. When Jesus visited a village of Samaria and the people refused to receive him, some of the disciples suggested that fire should be called down from Heaven to avenge the insult; but the Master rebuked them and said: "Ye know not what manner of spirit ye are of; for the Son of Man is not come to destroy men's lives, but to save them." Suppose he had said: "We will thrash them until they understand who we are," how different would have been the history of Christianity! Compare, if you will, the swaggering, bullying, brutal doctrine of imperialism with the golden rule and the commandment, "Thou shalt love thy neighbor as thyself."

Love, not force, was the weapon of the Nazarene; sacrifice for others, not the exploitation of them, was His method of reaching the human heart. A missionary recently told me that the Stars and Stripes once saved his life because his assailant recognized our flag as a flag that had no blood upon it.

Let it be known that our missionaries are seeking souls instead of sovereignty; let it be known that instead of being the advance guard of conquering armies, they are going forth to help and uplift, having their loins girt about with truth and their feet shod with the preparation of the gospel of peace, wearing the breastplate of righteousness and carrying the sword of the spirit; let it be known that they are citizens of a nation which respects the rights of the citizens of other nations as carefully as it protects the rights of its own citizens, and the welcome given to our missionaries will be more cordial than the welcome extended to the missionaries of any other nation.

The argument made by some that it was unfortunate for the nation that it had anything to do with the Philippine Islands, but that the naval victory at Manila made the permanent acquisition of those islands necessary, is also unsound. We won a naval victory at Santiago, but that did not compel us to hold Cuba.

The shedding of American blood in the Philippine Islands does not make it imperative that we should retain possession forever; American blood was shed at San Juan Hill and El Caney, and yet the President has promised the Cubans independence. The fact that the American flag floats over Manila does not compel us to exercise perpetual sovereignty over the islands; the American flag floats over Havana to-day, but the President has promised to haul it down when the flag of the Cuban Republic is ready to rise in its place. Better a thousand times that our flag in the Orient give way to a flag representing the idea of self-government than that the flag of this Republic should become the flag of an empire.

There is an easy, honest, honorable solution of the Philippine question. It is set forth in the Democratic platform and it is submitted with confidence to the American people. This plan I unreservedly indorse. If elected, I will convene Congress in extraordinary session as soon as inaugurated and recommend an immediate declaration of the nation's purpose, first, to establish a stable form of government in the Philippine Islands, just as we are now establishing a stable form of government in Cuba; second, to give independence to the Filipinos as we have promised to give independence to the Cubans; third, to protect the Filipinos from outside interference while they work out their destiny, just as we have protected the republics of Central and South America, and are, by the Monroe doctrine, pledged to protect Cuba.

A European protectorate often results in the plundering of the ward by the guardian. An American protectorate gives to the nation protected the advantage of our strength, without making it the victim of our greed. For three-quarters of a century the Monroe doctrine has been a shield to neighboring republics and yet it has imposed no pecuniary burden upon us. After the Filipinos had aided us in the war against Spain, we could not honorably turn them over to their former masters; we could not leave them to be the victims of the ambitious designs of European nations, and since we do not desire to make them a part of us or to hold them as subjects, we propose the only alternative, namely, to give them independence and guard them against molestation from without.

When our opponents are unable to defend their position by argument they fall back upon the assertion that it is destiny, and insist that we must submit to it, no matter how much it violates our moral precepts and our principles of government. This is a complacent philosophy. It obliterates the distinction between right and wrong and makes individuals and nations the helpless victims of circumstance.

Destiny is the subterfuge of the invertebrate, who, lacking the courage to oppose error, seeks some plausible excuse for supporting it. Washington said that the destiny of the republican form of government was deeply, if not finally, staked on the experiment entrusted to the American people. How different Washington's definition of destiny from the Republican definition!

I can conceive of a national destiny surpassing the glories of the present and the past—a destiny which meets the responsibilities of to-day and measures up to the possibilities of the future. Behold a republic, resting securely upon the foundation stones quarried by revolutionary patriots from the mountain of eternal truth—a republic applying in practise and proclaiming to the world the self-evident propositions that all men are created equal; that they are endowed by their Creator with inalienable rights; that governments are instituted among men to secure these rights, and that governments derive their just powers from the consent of the governed. Behold a republic in which civil and religious liberty stimulate all to earnest endeavor and in which the law restrains every hand uplifted for a neighbor's injury—a republic in which every citizen is a sovereign, but in which no one cares or dares to wear a crown. Behold a republic standing erect while empires all around are bowed beneath the weight of their own armaments—a republic whose flag is loved while other flags are only feared. Behold a republic increasing in population, in wealth, in strength and in influence, solving the problems of civilization and hastening the coming of an universal brotherhood—a republic which shakes thrones and dissolves aristocracies by its silent example and gives light and inspiration to those who sit in darkness. Behold a republic gradually but surely becoming the supreme moral factor in the world's progress and the accepted arbiter of the world's disputes—a republic whose history, like the path of the just, "is as the shining light that shineth more and more unto the perfect day."

The Man with the Muck Rake

Theodore Roosevelt

Commentary

McKinley's overwhelming reelection in 1900 was only one sign of imperialism's popularity. Another was the rise of Theodore Roosevelt (1858-1919), an avowed expansionist who had achieved public renown for his wartime exploits. Roosevelt's career also exemplifies two other important trends: renewed political activity by patrician families and the rise of the "progressive" movement. Unlike the Founding Fathers, who believed that upper-class families were duty-bound to participate in politics, the "old wealth" of Roosevelt's youth generally considered politics a dirty business.

As patricians such as Roosevelt moved into politics, they often considered themselves progressives; however, the word *progress* is easier to define connotatively than denotatively. *Progress* was (and still is) a rhetorically appealing term because of its connotations. The heritage of millenarianism and social perfectability, rapid population increase, new technologies, astounding economic growth — such factors made Americans believe unquestioningly in progress. Thus the "progressive" label gave politicians and political programs considerable rhetorical appeal.

Denotatively, however, *progressive* is difficult to define. The progressive movement is usually dated from around 1900 to the 1920s, but the term *progressive* was not exclusive to that era. Furthermore, progressives disagreed on many issues. Some favored expansionism, and some did not. Some were former Populists, while others were former gold bugs. Some were Republicans, while others were Democrats. Some were idealistic, whereas others were so pragmatic that they have been charged with capitalizing on a popular concept rather than being *real* progressives. Despite the definitional difficulties, progressives held two general ideas in common. First, progress depended on an active Federal government. Unlike their laissez faire critics, who believed in progress without Federal activity, progressives favored a variety of Federal programs. Second, they favored reforms, especially those that would supposedly eradicate political corruption and weaken "boss control" of the parties. They embraced civil service, party primaries, initiative, referendum and recall.

Roosevelt's early career shows these trends at work even though *progressive* was not yet a god word. He started going to the local Republican meetings as soon as he returned to his New York home after graduating from college. Although only twenty-two years of age, local bosses orchestrated his bid for the State legislature. The wealthy "silk stocking" district was predominately Republican, but the only people who came to party meetings were the vulgar Irish bosses. With corruption a major issue, they were desperate for a "clean government" candidate. Given his youth and family connections — and the fact that he was the only "silk stocking" politician in the group — Roosevelt was the obvious choice. Although serving only three terms (1882-1884) and alienating party regulars, Roosevelt got a "clean government" image by exposing corruption and pushing a civil service bill. Personal tragedies and illness pulled him away from politics temporarily (except for a woefully unsuccessful campaign for mayor of New York City in 1886), but his "clean government" image and family connections got him a series of political appointments: U.S. Civil Service Commission (1889-1895), police commissioner of New York City (1895-1897) and assistant secretary of the Navy (1897-1898). After becoming a war hero, he was swept into the governorship and promptly alienated party bosses, who decided the best way of getting rid of the popular governor was to get him the vice-presidential nomination in 1900. They could not predict that McKinley would be assassinated, that Roosevelt would serve out McKinley's second term and be elected on his own in 1904.

Roosevelt's presidency highlighted some trends that have since become integral to our contemporary rhetorical scene. First, Roosevelt believed in the concept of a strong president (or what critics call the "imperial president"). True, earlier presidents had occasionally tried to influence congressional legislation, but they usually did so by having private chats with congressional leaders. Roosevelt was one of the first to utilize a new tactic. Calling the presidency a "bully pulpit," he spoke directly to the public in hopes that the public would influence Congress to support his position. Second, he initiated the presidential press conference, albeit in a way that was vastly different from the highly publicized conferences of our time. He met privately and infrequently with a few members of the press, but the fact remains that he initiated a new rhetorical genre. Third, he confronted a relatively new rhetorical situation: ideological diversity within his own party combined with ideological similarities between segments of both parties. True, earlier party leaders had often faced a similar problem, as is indicated by the demise of the Whigs and the Democratic feuds of 1860 and 1896, but early Democrats had generally subscribed to Jefferson's idea of limited government while Federalists, Northern Whigs and Republicans had generally adhered to Hamilton's idea of a strong central government. By Roosevelt's time, progressivism had infiltrated both parties, but both had strong conservative elements. Success depended on sounding progressive enough to get support from progressives in both parties without sounding progressive enough to alienate conservative Republicans. Roosevelt's technique was encapsulated accurately, if unsympathetically, by a cartoonist who pictured him as a chef pouring ingredients into a bowl marked "A Teddy Speech" while saying, "The more you mix in, the easier to satisfy everyone." Ingredients included "Progressivism," "Conservative Views," "Radical Spice," "Pure Democracy," "Initiative/Referendum/Recall" and "Any Old View."

Roosevelt's rhetorical recipe is exemplified by a speech given in response to what we now call investigative journalism. His presidency saw a plethora of magazine articles and books such as Lincoln Steffens' *Shame of the Cities*, which exposed political corruption; Button J. Hendrick's *Story of Life Insurance*, which exposed unsound practices in the industry; articles by Ray Stannard Baker about exploitation of blacks; and Upton Sinclair's novel, *The Jungle*, which portrayed unsanitary conditions in slaughterhouses. Roosevelt had mixed feelings. These writings did not attack him personally, and they helped influence public opinion to favor governmental regulations which Roosevelt favored; however, he got increasingly nervous about their sensationalism. Then appeared a series of magazine articles by David Graham Phillips entitled "The Treason of the Senate," in which several senators, including some of Roosevelt's personal friends and legislative supporters, were depicted as corporate agents. It was time to deliver a public response.

The opportunity came when Roosevelt was asked to deliver a speech on April 15, 1906, at the laying of the cornerstone of the new congressional office building. Although Roosevelt knew that the occasion was important enough to receive considerable press coverage, he decided to take no chances. The White House leaked word to the press a few days before the ceremony that the president was going to make an especially important statement. His highly publicized speech, which introduced the word *muckraking* into the popular vocabulary, is reproduced photographically from A. Craig Baird, *American Public Addresses, 1740-1952* (New York: McGraw-Hill, 1956), pp. 211-219.

The Man with the Muck Rake

Over a century ago Washington laid the corner stone of the Capitol in what was then little more than a tract of wooded wilderness here beside the Potomac. We now find it necessary to provide by great additional buildings for the business of the government.

This growth in the need for the housing of the government is but a proof and example of the way in which the nation has grown and the sphere of action of the national government has grown. We now administer the affairs of a nation in which the extraordinary growth of population has been outstripped by the growth of wealth in complex interests. The material problems that face us today are not such as they were in Washington's time, but the underlying facts of human nature are the same now as they were then. Under altered external form we war with the same tendencies toward evil that were evident in Washington's time, and are helped by the same tendencies for good. It is about some of these that I wish to say a word today.

In Bunyan's "Pilgrim's Progress" you may recall the description of the Man with the Muck Rake, the man who could look no way but downward, with the muck rake in his hand; who was offered a celestial crown for his muck rake, but who would neither look up nor regard the crown he was offered, but continued to rake to himself the filth of the floor.

In "Pilgrim's Progress" the Man with the Muck Rake is set forth as the example of him whose vision is fixed on carnal instead of spiritual things. Yet he also typifies the man who in this life consistently refuses to see aught that is lofty, and fixes his eyes with solemn intentness only on that which is vile and debasing.

Now, it is very necessary that we should not flinch from seeing what is vile and debasing. There is filth on the floor, and it must be scraped up with the muck rake; and there are times and places where this service is the most needed of all the services that can be performed. But the man who never does anything else, who never thinks or speaks or writes, save of his feats with the muck rake, speedily becomes, not a help but one of the most potent forces for evil.

There are in the body politic, economic and social, many and grave evils, and there is urgent necessity for the sternest war upon them. There should be relentless exposure of and attack upon every evil man, whether politician or business man, every evil practice, whether in politics, business, or social life. I hail as a benefactor every writer or speaker, every man who, on the platform or in a book, magazine, or newspaper, with merciless severity makes such attack, provided always that he in his turn remembers that the attack is of use only if it is absolutely truthful.

The liar is no whit better than the thief, and if his mendacity takes the form of slander he may be worse than most thieves. It puts a premium upon knavery untruthfully to attack an honest man, or even with hysterical exaggeration to assail a bad man with untruth.

An epidemic of indiscriminate assault upon character does no good, but very great harm. The soul of every scoundrel is gladdened whenever an honest man is assailed, or even when a scoundrel is untruthfully assailed.

Now, it is easy to twist out of shape what I have just said, easy to affect to misunderstand it, and if it is slurred over in repetition not difficult really to misunderstand it. Some persons are sincerely incapable of understanding that to denounce mud slinging does not mean the endorsement of whitewashing; and both the interested individuals who need whitewashing and those others who practice mud slinging like to encourage such confusion of ideas.

One of the chief counts against those who make indiscriminate assault upon men in business or men in public life is that they invite a reaction which is sure to tell powerfully in favor of the unscrupulous scoundrel who really ought to be attacked, who ought to be exposed, who ought, if possible, to be put in the penitentiary. If Aristides is praised overmuch as just, people get tired of hearing it; and overcensure of the unjust finally and from similar reasons results in their favor.

Any excess is almost sure to invite a reaction; and, unfortunately, the reaction, instead of taking the form of punishment of those guilty of the excess, is apt to take the form either of punishment of the unoffending or of giving immunity, and even strength, to offenders. The effort to make financial or political profit out of the destruction of character can only result in public calamity. Gross and reckless assaults on character, whether on the stump or in newspaper, magazine, or book, create a morbid and vicious public sentiment, and at the same time act as a profound deterrent to able men of normal sensitiveness and tend to prevent them from entering the public service at any price.

As an instance in point, I may mention that one serious difficulty encountered in getting the right type of men to dig the Panama canal is the certainty that they will be exposed, both without, and, I am sorry to say, sometimes within, Congress, to utterly reckless assaults on their character and capacity.

At the risk of repetition let me say again that my plea is not for immunity to, but for the most unsparing exposure of, the politician who betrays his trust, of the big business man who makes or spends his fortune in illegitimate or corrupt ways. There should be a resolute effort to hunt every such man out of the position he has disgraced. Expose the crime, and hunt down the criminal; but remember that even in the case of crime, if it is attacked in sensational, lurid, and untruthful fashion, the attack may do more damage to the public mind than the crime itself.

It is because I feel that there should be no rest in the endless war against the forces of evil that I ask the war be conducted with sanity as well as with resolution.

The men with the muck rakes are often indispensable to the well being of society; but only if they know when to stop raking the muck, and to look upward to the celestial crown above them, to the crown of worthy endeavor. There are beautiful things above and round about them; and if they gradually grow to feel that the whole world is nothing but muck, their power of usefulness is gone.

If the whole picture is painted black there remains no hue whereby to single out the rascals for distinction from their fellows. Such painting finally induces a kind of moral color blindness; and people affected by it come to the conclusion that no man is really black, and no man really white, but they are all gray.

In other words, they neither believe in the truth of the attack, nor in the honesty of the man who is attacked; they grow as suspicious of the accusation as of the offense; it becomes well nigh hopeless to stir them either to wrath against wrongdoing or to enthusiasm for what is right; and such a mental attitude in the public gives hope to every knave, and is the despair of honest men.

To assail the great and admitted evils of our political and industrial life with such crude and sweeping generalizations as to include decent men in the general condemnation means the searing of the public conscience. There results a general attitude either of cynical belief in and indifference to public corruption or else of a distrustful inability to discriminate between the good and the bad. Either attitude is fraught with untold damage to the country as a whole.

The fool who has not sense to discriminate between what is good and what is bad is well nigh as dangerous as the man who does discriminate and yet chooses the bad. There is nothing more distressing to every good patriot, to every good American, than the hard, scoffing spirit which treats the allegation of dishonesty in a public man as a cause for laughter. Such laughter is worse than the crackling of thorns under a pot, for it denotes not merely the vacant mind, but the heart in which high emotions have been choked before they could grow to fruition.

There is any amount of good in the world, and there never was a time when loftier and more disinterested work for the betterment of mankind was being done than now. The forces that tend for evil are great and terrible, but the forces of truth and love and courage and honesty and generosity and sympathy are also stronger than ever before. It is a foolish and timid, no less than a wicked thing, to blink the fact that the forces of evil are strong, but it is even worse to fail to take into account the strength of the forces that tell for good.

Hysterical sensationalism is the poorest weapon wherewith to fight for lasting righteousness. The men who with stern sobriety and truth assail the many evils of our time, whether in the public press, or in magazines, or in books, are the leaders and allies of all engaged in the work for social and political betterment. But if they give good reason for distrust of what they say, if they chill the ardor of those who demand truth as a primary virtue, they thereby betray the good cause and play into the hands of the very men against whom they are nominally at war.

In his Ecclesiastical Polity that fine old Elizabethan divine, Bishop Hooker, wrote:

He that goeth about to persuade a multitude that they are not so well governed as they ought to be shall never want attentive and favorable hearers, because they know the manifold defects whereunto every kind of regimen is subject, but the secret lets and difficulties, which in public proceedings are innumerable and inevitable, they have not ordinarily the judgment to consider.

This truth should be kept constantly in mind by every free people desiring to preserve the sanity and poise indispensable to the permanent success of self-government. Yet, on the other hand, it is vital not to permit this spirit of sanity and self-command to degenerate into mere mental stagnation. Bad though a state of hysterical excitement is, and evil though the results are which come from the violent oscillations such excitement invariably produces, yet a sodden acquiescence in evil is even worse.

At this moment we are passing through a period of great unrest—social, political, and industrial unrest. It is of the utmost importance for our future that this should prove to be not the unrest of mere rebelliousness against life, of mere dissatisfaction with the inevitable inequality of conditions, but the unrest of a resolute and eager ambition to secure the betterment of the individual and the nation.

So far as this movement of agitation throughout the country takes the form of a fierce discontent with evil, of a determination to punish the authors of evil, whether in industry or politics, the feeling is to be heartily welcomed as a sign of healthy life.

If, on the other hand, it turns into a mere crusade of appetite against appetite, of a contest between the brutal greed of the "have nots" and the brutal greed of the "haves," then it has no significance for good, but only for evil. If it seeks to establish a line of cleavage, not along the line which divides good men from bad, but along that other line, running at right angles thereto, which divides those who are well off from those who are less well off, then it will be fraught with immeasurable harm to the body politic.

We can no more and no less afford to condone evil in the man of capital than evil in the man of no capital. The wealthy man who exults because there is a failure of justice in the effort to bring some trust magnate to account for his misdeeds is as bad as, and no worse than, the so-called labor leader who clamorously strives to excite a foul class feeling on behalf of some other labor leader who is implicated in murder. One attitude is as bad as the other, and no worse; in each case the accused is entitled to exact justice; and in neither case is there need of action by others which can be construed into an expression of sympathy for crime.

It is a prime necessity that if the present unrest is to result in permanent good the emotion shall be translated into action, and that the action shall be marked by honesty, sanity, and self-restraint. There is mighty little good in a mere spasm of reform. The reform that counts is that which comes through steady, continuous growth; violent emotionalism leads to exhaustion.

It is important to this people to grapple with the problems connected with the amassing of enormous fortunes, and the use of those fortunes, both corporate and individual, in business. We should discriminate in the sharpest way between fortunes well won and fortunes ill won; between those gained as an incident to performing great services to the community as a whole and those gained in evil fashion by keeping just

within the limits of mere law honesty. Of course, no amount of charity
in spending such fortunes in any way compensates for misconduct in
making them.

As a matter of personal conviction, and without pretending to discuss
the details or formulate the system, I feel that we shall ultimately have
to consider the adoption of some such scheme as that of a progressive
tax on all fortunes, beyond a certain amount, either given in life or devised or bequeathed upon death to any individual—a tax so framed as to
put it out of the power of the owner of one of these enormous fortunes
to hand on more than a certain amount to any one individual; the tax,
of course, to be imposed by the national and not the state government.
Such taxation should, of course, be aimed merely at the inheritance or
transmission in their entirety of those fortunes swollen beyond all healthy
limits.

Again, the national government must in some form exercise supervision
over corporations engaged in interstate business—and all large corporations engaged in interstate business—whether by license or otherwise, so
as to permit us to deal with the far reaching evils of overcapitalization.

This year we are making a beginning in the direction of serious effort
to settle some of these economic problems by the railway rate legislation.
Such legislation, if so framed, as I am sure it will be, as to secure definite
and tangible results, will amount to something of itself; and it will
amount to a great deal more in so far as it is taken as a first step in the
direction of a policy of superintendence and control over corporate
wealth engaged in interstate commerce; this superintendence and control not to be exercised in a spirit of malevolence toward the men who
have created the wealth, but with the firm purpose both to do justice to
them and to see that they in their turn do justice to the public at large.

The first requisite in the public servants who are to deal in this shape
with corporations, whether as legislators or as executives, is honesty. This
honesty can be no respecter of persons. There can be no such thing as
unilateral honesty. The danger is not really from corrupt corporations;
it springs from the corruption itself, whether exercised for or against corporations.

The eighth commandment reads, "Thou shalt not steal." It does not
read, "Thou shalt not steal from the rich man." It does not read, "Thou
shalt not steal from the poor man." It reads simply and plainly, "Thou
shalt not steal."

No good whatever will come from that warped and mock morality
which denounces the misdeeds of men of wealth and forgets the misdeeds practiced at their expense; which denounces bribery, but blinds
itself to blackmail; which foams with rage if a corporation secures favors
by improper methods, and merely leers with hideous mirth if the corporation is itself wronged.

The only public servant who can be trusted honestly to protect the rights of the public against the misdeeds of a corporation is that public man who will just as surely protect the corporation itself from wrongful aggression.

If a public man is willing to yield to popular clamor and do wrong to the men of wealth or to rich corporations, it may be set down as certain that if the opportunity comes he will secretly and furtively do wrong to the public in the interest of a corporation.

But in addition to honesty, we need sanity. No honesty will make a public man useful if that man is timid or foolish, if he is a hot-headed zealot or an impracticable visionary. As we strive for reform we find that it is not at all merely the case of a long uphill pull. On the contrary, there is almost as much of breeching work as of collar work. To depend only on traces means that there will soon be a runaway and an upset.

The men of wealth who today are trying to prevent the regulation and control of their business in the interest of the public by the proper government authorities will not succeed, in my judgment, in checking the progress of the movement. But if they did succeed they would find that they had sown the wind and would surely reap the whirlwind, for they would ultimately provoke the violent excesses which accompany a reform coming by convulsion instead of by steady and natural growth.

On the other hand, the wild preachers of unrest and discontent, the wild agitators against the entire existing order, the men who act crookedly, whether because of sinister design or from mere puzzle headedness, the men who preach destruction without proposing any substitute for what they intend to destroy, or who propose a substitute which would be far worse than the existing evils—all these men are the most dangerous opponents of real reform. If they get their way they will lead the people into a deeper pit than any into which they could fall under the present system. If they fail to get their way they will still do incalculable harm by provoking the kind of reaction which in its revolt against the senseless evil of their teaching would enthrone more securely than ever the evils which their misguided followers believe they are attacking.

More important than aught else is the development of the broadest sympathy of man for man. The welfare of the wage worker, the welfare of the tiller of the soil, upon these depend the welfare of the entire country; their good is not to be sought in pulling down others; but their good must be the prime object of all our statesmanship.

Materially we must strive to secure a broader economic opportunity for all men, so that each shall have a better chance to show the stuff of which he is made. Spiritually and ethically we must strive to bring about clean living and right thinking. We appreciate that the things of the body are important; but we appreciate also that the things of the soul are immeasurably more important.

The foundation stone of national life is, and ever must be, the high individual character of the average citizen.

First Inaugural Address

Woodrow Wilson

Commentary

Announcing that he would not seek reelection in 1908, Roosevelt supported William Howard Taft. The latter's presidency was increasingly criticized by progressives of both parties. In 1910, Democrats won control of Congress because their usual Southern strength was supplemented by an unusually large number of progressive Democratic victories in the Midwest. Immediately after the election, a National Republican Progressive League was formed to prevent Taft's renomination in 1912. After a bitter convention battle resulted in Taft's renomination, a new "Progressive" party nominated Roosevelt. This dramatic struggle between former allies and Roosevelt's flair for getting newspaper publicity resulted in the press paying little attention to the Democratic candidate, Woodrow Wilson (1856-1924).

With Republican ranks split, Wilson had an excellent chance of winning. He had to sound progressive enough to keep Democratic progressives from voting for Roosevelt while sounding conservative enough to keep conservatives from turning to Taft. His task was made easier because he was relatively unknown. Most of his career had been spent as a college professor of history and political science, during which time he had achieved considerable renown among his professional colleagues. He had spoken rarely on current public issues (though as a debate coach, he had trained students to do so). His book on *Congressional Government* (1885) endorsed the concept of a strong president, but it gave no hint as to whether a president should be progressive or conservative. After becoming president of Princeton in 1902, Wilson gave a few public speeches that suggested a Jeffersonian belief in limited government. He criticized governmental regulations of business, objected to Bryan's control of the Democratic party and criticized labor unions. He did not attract public attention, though, until 1906, when he tried unsuccessfully to abolish Princeton's undergraduate eating clubs and substitute a college system similar to that of British universities. The press portrayed him as fighting single-handedly against aristocratic snobbery and elitism.

Thinking Wilson to be sufficiently conservative, Democratic party leaders successfully ran the new egalitarian for governor of New Jersey in 1910. They were surprised when the new governor wrested control of the party from them and got some national attention by pushing progressive legislation such as workmen's compensation, direct primaries and governmental regulations of business. Although his new, progressive image earned him support at the Democratic convention in 1912, his nomination (which did not come until the forty-sixth ballot) was due less to his being enthusiastically supported than it was to his being unacceptable to no one. Best known for his image of a scholarly egalitarian, he was progressive enough for progressives and conservative enough for conservatives.

While Taft and Roosevelt split the Republican vote, Wilson ran a campaign designed to keep ideologically diverse Democrats in line. He promised vigorous enforcement of anti-trust laws but ignored Roosevelt's charges that he was a "conservative Tory." He, therefore, sounded a little progressive without sounding too progressive. He campaigned with a promise of a "New Freedom," a rhetorically appealing term to both conservatives and progressives, but he did not alienate anyone by defining it.

When Wilson arose to deliver his inaugural address on March 4, 1913, an unusually large crowd attended. Some observers estimated the audience at 100,000, and, of course, the speech was reported widely in the press. One of Wilson's rhetorical tasks was the typical one for inaugurals — to unify the country after a divisive election campaign. Wilson, however, believed in being a strong president, and he wished to set an ideological tone for the policies he would pursue. The text is reproduced photographically from A. Craig Baird, *American Public Addresses, 1740-1952* (New York: McGraw-Hill, 1956), pp. 221-224.

First Inaugural Address

There has been a change of government. It began two years ago, when the House of Representatives became Democratic by a decisive majority. It has now been completed. The Senate about to assemble will also be Democratic. The offices of President and Vice President have been put into the hands of Democrats. What does the change mean? That is the question that is uppermost in our minds to-day. That is the question I am going to try to answer, in order, if I may, to interpret the occasion.

It means much more than the mere success of a party. The success of a party means little except when the Nation is using that party for a large and definite purpose. No one can mistake the purpose for which the Nation now seeks to use the Democratic Party. It seeks to use it to interpret a change in its own plans and point of view. Some old things with which we had grown familiar, and which had begun to creep into the very habit of our thought and of our lives, have altered their aspect as we have latterly looked critically upon them, with fresh, awakened eyes; have dropped their disguises and shown themselves alien and sinister. Some new things, as we look frankly upon them, willing to comprehend their real character, have come to assume the aspect of things long believed in and familiar, stuff of our own convictions. We have been refreshed by a new insight into our own life.

We see that in many things that life is very great. It is incomparably great in its material aspects, in its body of wealth, in the diversity and sweep of its energy, in the industries which have been conceived and built up by the genius of individual men and the limitless enterprise of groups of men. It is great, also, very great, in its moral force. Nowhere else in the world have noble men and women exhibited in more striking forms the beauty and the energy of sympathy and helpfulness and counsel in their efforts to rectify wrong, alleviate suffering, and set the weak in the way of strength and hope. We have built up, moreover, a great system of government, which has stood through a long age as in many respects a model for those who seek to set liberty upon foundations that will endure against fortuitous change, against storm and accident. Our life contains every great thing, and contains it in rich abundance.

But the evil has come with the good, and much fine gold has been corroded. With riches has come inexcusable waste. We have squandered a great part of what we might have used, and have not stopped to conserve the exceeding bounty of nature, without which our genius for enterprise would have been worthless and impotent, scorning to be careful, shamefully prodigal as well as admirably efficient. We have been proud of our industrial achievement, but we have not hitherto stopped thoughtfully enough to count the human cost, the cost of lives snuffed out, of energies overtaxed and broken, the fearful physical and spiritual cost to the men and women and children upon whom the dead weight and burden of it all has fallen pitilessly the years through. The groans and agony of it all had not yet reached our ears, the solemn, moving undertone of our life, coming up out of the mines and factories and out of every home where the struggle had its intimate and familiar seat. With the great Government went many deep secret things which we too long delayed to look into and scrutinize with candid, fearless eyes. The great Government we loved has too often been made use of for private and selfish purposes, and those who used it had forgotten the people.

At last a vision has been vouchsafed us of our life as a whole. We see the bad with the good, the debased and decadent with the sound and vital. With this vision we approach new affairs. Our duty is to cleanse, to reconsider, to restore, to correct the evil without impairing the good, to purify and humanize every process of our common life without weakening or sentimentalizing it. There has been something crude and heartless and unfeeling in our haste to succeed and be great. Our thought has been "Let every man look out for himself, let every generation look out for itself," while we reared giant machinery which made it impossible that any but those who stood at the levers of control should have a chance to look out for themselves. We had not forgotten our morals. We remembered well enough that we had set up a policy which was meant to serve the humblest as well as the most powerful, with an eye single to the standards of justice and fair play, and remembered it with pride. But we were very heedless and in a hurry to be great.

We have come now to the sober second thought. The scales of heedlessness have fallen from our eyes. We have made up our minds to square every process of our national life again with the standards we so proudly set up at the beginning and have always carried at our hearts. Our work is a work of restoration.

We have itemized with some degree of particularity the things that ought to be altered and here are some of the chief items: A tariff which cuts us off from our proper part in the commerce of the world, violates the just principles of taxation, and makes the Government a facile instrument in the hands of private interests; a banking and currency system based upon the necessity of the Government to sell its bonds fifty years ago and perfectly adapted to concentrating cash and restricting credits; an industrial system which, take it on all its sides, financial as well as administrative, holds capital in leading strings, restricts the liberties and limits the opportunities of labor, and exploits without renewing or conserving the natural resources of the country; a body of agricultural activities never yet given the efficiency of great business undertakings or served as it should be through the instrumentality of science taken directly to the farm, or afforded the facilities of credit best suited to its practical needs; watercourses undeveloped, waste places unreclaimed, forests untended, fast disappearing without plan or prospect of renewal, unregarded waste heaps at every mine. We have studied as perhaps no other nation has the most effective means of production, but we have not studied cost or economy as we should either as organizers of industry, as statesmen, or as individuals.

Nor have we studied and perfected the means by which government may be put at the service of humanity, in safeguarding the health of the Nation, the health of its men and its women and its children, as well as their rights in the struggle for existence. This is no sentimental duty. The firm basis of government is justice, not pity. These are matters of justice. There can be no equality or opportunity, the first essential of justice in the body politic, if men and women and children be not shielded in their lives, their very vitality, from the consequences of great industrial and social processes which they can not alter, control, or singly cope with. Society must see to it that it does not itself crush or weaken or damage its own constituent parts. The first duty of law is to keep sound the society it serves. Sanitary laws, pure food laws, and laws determining conditions of labor which individuals are powerless to determine for themselves are intimate parts of the very business of justice and legal efficiency.

These are some of the things we ought to do, and not leave the others undone, the old-fashioned, never-to-be-neglected, fundamental safeguarding of property and of individual right. This is the high enterprise of the new day: To lift everything that concerns our life as a Nation to the light that shines from the hearthfire of every man's conscience and vision of the right. It is inconceivable that we should do this as partisans; it is inconceivable we should do it in ignorance of the facts as they are or in blind haste. We shall restore, not destroy. We shall deal with our economic system as it is and as it may be modified, not as it might be if we had a clean sheet of paper to write upon; and step by step we shall make it what it should be, in the spirit of those who question their own wisdom and seek counsel and knowledge, not shallow self-satisfaction or the excitement of excursions whither they can not tell. Justice, and only justice, shall always be our motto.

And yet it will be no cool process of mere science. The Nation has been deeply stirred, stirred by a solemn passion, stirred by the knowledge of wrong, of ideals lost, of government too often debauched and made an instrument of evil. The feelings with which we face this new age of right and opportunity sweep across our heartstrings like some air out of God's own presence, where justice and mercy are reconciled and the judge and the brother are one. We know our task to be no mere task of politics but a task which shall search us through and through, whether we be able to understand our time and the need of our people, whether we be indeed their spokesmen and interpreters, whether we have the pure heart to comprehend and the rectified will to choose our high course of action.

This is not a day of triumph; it is a day of dedication. Here muster, not the forces of party, but the forces of humanity. Men's hearts wait upon us; men's lives hang in the balance; men's hopes call upon us to say what we will do. Who shall live up to the great trust? Who dares fail to try? I summon all honest men, all patriotic, all forward-looking men, to my side. God helping me, I will not fail them, if they will but counsel and sustain me!

Political Rhetoric from "The War to End All Wars" to World War II

War Message

Woodrow Wilson

Commentary

The Wilson era saw further momentum toward a strong presidency and progressivism. A result of rhetorical significance was that the president's annual state of the Union address, which had been delivered to Congress in writing since Jefferson's time, was now delivered orally. The net effect was to give the president's rhetoric more national attention than it had formerly received.

Perhaps the most significant development of the Wilson era was our involvement in World War I. Although some historians believe our participation was inevitable, early rhetoric shows that public opinion was against our entering the war. Ever since the War of 1812, America had remained neutral during European wars, and Fourth of July orators had routinely contrasted the Chosen Nation with the aggressive and tyrannical European nations. Historians agree that the public wished to continue its traditional policy of neutrality after the European war erupted in the summer of 1914.

Yet there was also an undercurrent of sympathy for the Allies. It was not universal, with many German-Americans favoring the "old country" and many Irish-Americans retaining their old anti-British attitudes. However, America had a strong British heritage, Britain was a major trading partner and the press had closer links to Britain and France than to Germany and Austria. Allied stories of German atrocities were circulated widely even though some of them (such as chopping off the hands of Belgian children) were as false as they were horrifying. In short, ambivalence prevailed; yet the general climate was one of favoring the Allies but staying neutral.

The common, but not universal, shift toward involvement was probably due to German submarine warfare. With its navy being inferior to that of Britain, Germany enforced its blockade of Britain with submarines. They did not always take the time (as their critics said) or have the time (as their defenders said) to allow passengers and crews of Allied mercantile ships to flee on lifeboats before sinking them. Sinking (rather than capturing) mercantile ships was new, which resulted in British claims and German counterclaims being publicized widely in America. Britain claimed that Germany was violating international law by sinking unarmed passenger ships and killing innocent civilians. Germany claimed that the so-called passenger ships actually carried war material. The United States became involved because Americans were sometimes aboard British ships. Other diplomatic disputes arose over German treatment of American ships that were trading with the Allies. The issue came to a climax when Germany sank the British passenger ship *Lusitania* on May 7, 1915. Among the 1200 civilians who died were 128 Americans. Although historical data later substantiated the German claim that the ship was carrying munitions, Americans generally believed the British denial.

The *Lusitania* affair intensified the growing debate. Secretary of State William Jennings Bryan resigned rather than follow Wilson's directive to send a diplomatic protest to Germany. He took to the stump to justify his action. A host of "peace societies" produced a plethora of antiwar rhetoric. Best known were the Carnegie Endowment for International Peace and the World Peace Foundation, both formed in 1910, but others included the American Society for the Judicial Settlement of International Disputes, the Church Peace Union, the Women's Peace Party, the Anti-Militarist League and the National Peace Council. Although rarely commenting on the specific disputes with Germany, they strongly implied that stubborn insistence on American rights under international law was not worth the risk of getting into a war.

Meanwhile, a public debate arose over military preparedness. Led by two heroes of the Spanish-American War, General Leonard Wood and ex-president Roosevelt (who objected to Wilson's "milk and water policy"), a host of speakers and writers argued that the country was unprepared for the war which might come. Two organizations, the American Legion and the National Security League, were formed to advocate preparedness. Although not alone in his beliefs, Bryan wrote against preparedness in his new paper, *The Commoner*. Congress began authorizing increased military expenditures by 1916; however, most congressmen justified their votes by saying that, although they favored neutrality, they voted for preparedness "just in case." That public opinion still favored neutrality is indicated by Wilson's campaign slogan in the 1916 electoral campaign, "He kept us out of war."

As so often happens during times of intense controversy, some significant events got relatively little attention. The most important was a set of resolutions introduced by Senator Gore and Representative McLemore in early 1916. The resolutions prohibited Americans from travelling on ships belonging to belligerents. They were justified on the grounds that such travel was unnecessary and raised the threat that American deaths would drag the country into war. Although opponents argued that such restrictions limited American rights under international law, the speaker of the House privately told Wilson that the resolutions would pass the House by a ratio of 2-1. Strongly opposed to the resolutions, Wilson worked quietly but assiduously to defeat them by telling Democratic congressmen that the issue was one of party loyalty. The resolutions failed in the House 276-142 and in the Senate 68-14.

The early months of 1917 saw three events which pushed the United States in the direction of war. One was the Russian Revolution. Habitually inclined to see the world in Puritanical terms of Good versus Evil, Wilson naively saw the fall of the czar as the beginning of Russian democracy and now saw the war as Democracy versus Absolutism. Although events in far-off Russia made only a limited impact on public opinion, the other two events did. One was Germany's announcement in February that it would engage in "unrestricted submarine warfare," which was followed by the sinking of some American ships. Another was the "Zimmermann Letter," a diplomatic dispatch from the German foreign secretary to his ambassador in Mexico that was inter- cepted by British intelligence and given to the United States. The dispatch said only that the ambassador should propose an alliance with Mexico in case of war between Germany and the United States and should promise Mexico a return of territory lost in 1848. However, the dispatch was publicized in the United States as a German effort to promote a Mexican invasion.

On March 21, 1917, newspapers announced that Wilson had called Congress into special session. Everyone knew what to expect when Wilson arose to speak on the evening of April 2, 1917. Astute observers realized that he would get widespread congressional and public support but that he needed to persuade reluctant supporters and do what he could to mollify opponents. His speech is reproduced photographically from A. Craig Baird, *American Public Addresses, 1740-1952* (New York: McGraw-Hill, 1956), pp. 225-232.

War Message

I have called the Congress into extraordinary session because there are serious, very serious, choices of policy to be made, and made im- mediately, which it was neither right nor constitutionally permissible that I should assume the responsibility of making.

On the third of February last I officially laid before you the extraordi- nary announcement of the Imperial German Government that on and after the first day of February it was its purpose to put aside all restraints of law or of humanity and use its submarines to sink every vessel that sought to approach either the ports of Great Britain and Ireland or the western coasts of Europe or any of the ports controlled by the enemies of Germany within the Mediterranean. That had seemed to be the object of the German submarine warfare earlier in the war, but since April of last year the Imperial Government had somewhat restrained the com- manders of its undersea craft in conformity with its promise then given to us that passenger boats should not be sunk and that due warning would be given to all other vessels which its submarines might seek to destroy, when no resistance was offered or escape attempted, and care taken that their crews were given at least a fair chance to save their lives in their open boats. The precautions taken were meager and haphazard enough, as was proved in distressing instance after instance in the progress of the cruel and unmanly business, but a certain degree of restraint was observed. The new policy has swept every restriction aside. Vessels of every kind, whatever their flag, their character, their cargo, their destination, their errand, have been ruthlessly sent to the bottom without warning and without thought of help or mercy for those on board, the vessels of friendly neutrals along with those of belligerents. Even hospital ships and ships carrying relief to the sorely bereaved and stricken people of Belgium, though the latter were provided with safe conduct through the proscribed areas by the German Government itself and were distinguished by unmistakable marks of identity, have been sunk with the same reckless lack of compassion or of principle.

I was for a little while unable to believe that such things would in fact be done by any government that had hitherto subscribed to the humane practices of civilized nations. International law had its origin in the attempt to set up some law which would be respected and observed upon the seas, where no nation had right of dominion and where lay the free highways of the world. . . . This minimum of right the German Government has swept aside under the plea of retaliation and necessity and because it had no weapons which it could use at sea except these which it is impossible to employ as it is employing them without throwing to the winds all scruples of humanity or of respect for the understandings that were supposed to underlie the intercourse of the world. I am not now thinking of the loss of property involved, immense and serious as that is, but only of the wanton and wholesale destruction of the lives of noncombatants, men, women, and children, engaged in pursuits which have always, even in the darkest periods of modern history, been deemed innocent and legitimate. Property can be paid for; the lives of peaceful and innocent people cannot be. The present German submarine warfare against commerce is a warfare against mankind.

It is a war against all nations. American ships have been sunk, American lives taken, in ways which it has stirred us very deeply to learn of, but the ships and people of other neutral and friendly nations have been sunk and overwhelmed in the waters in the same way. There has been no discrimination. The challenge is to all mankind. Each nation must decide for itself how it will meet it. The choice we make for ourselves must be made with a moderation of counsel and a temperateness of judgment befitting our character and our motives as a nation. We must put excited feeling away. Our motive will not be revenge or the victorious assertion of the physical might of the nation, but only the vindication of right, of human right, of which we are only a single champion.

When I addressed the Congress on the twenty-sixth of February last I thought that it would suffice to assert our neutral rights with arms, our right to use the seas against unlawful interference, our right to keep our people safe against unlawful violence. But armed neutrality, it now appears, is impracticable. Because submarines are in effect outlaws when used as the German submarines have been used against merchant shipping, it is impossible to defend ships against their attacks as the law of nations has assumed that merchantmen would defend themselves against privateers or cruisers, visible craft giving chase upon the open sea. It is common prudence in such circumstances, grim necessity indeed, to endeavor to destroy them before they have shown their own intention. They must be dealt with upon sight, if dealt with at all. The German Government denies the right of neutrals to use arms at all within the areas of the sea which it has proscribed, even in the defense of rights which no modern publicist has ever before questioned their right to defend. The intimation is conveyed that the armed guards which we have placed on our merchant ships will be treated as beyond the pale of law and subject to be dealt with as pirates would be. Armed neutrality is ineffectual enough at best; in such circumstances and in the face of such pretensions it is worse than ineffectual: it is likely only to produce what it was meant to prevent; it is practically certain to draw us into the war without either the rights or the effectiveness of belligerents. There is one choice we cannot make, we are incapable of making: we will not choose the path of submission and suffer the most sacred rights of our Nation and our people to be ignored or violated. The wrongs against which we now array ourselves are no common wrongs; they cut to the very roots of human life.

With a profound sense of the solemn and even tragical character of the step I am taking and of the grave responsibilities which it involves, but in unhesitating obedience to what I deem my constitutional duty, I advise that the Congress declare the recent course of the Imperial German Government to be in fact nothing less than war against the government and people of the United States; that it formally accept the status of belligerent which has thus been thrust upon it; and that it take immediate steps not only to put the country in a more thorough state of defense but also to exert all its power and employ all its resources to bring the Government of the German Empire to terms and end the war.

What this will involve is clear. It will involve the utmost practicable coöperation in counsel and action with the governments now at war with Germany, and, as incident to that, the extension to those governments of the most liberal financial credit, in order that our resources may so far as possible be added to theirs. It will involve the organization and mobilization of all the material resources of the country to supply the materials of war and serve the incidental needs of the Nation in the most abundant and yet the most economical and efficient way possible. It will involve the immediate full equipment of the navy in all respects but particularly in supplying it with the best means of dealing with the enemy's submarines. It will involve the immediate addition to the armed forces of the United

States already provided for by law in case of war at least five hundred thousand men, who should, in my opinion, be chosen upon the principle of universal liability to service, and also the authorization of subsequent additional increments of equal force so soon as they may be needed and can be handled in training. It will involve also, of course, the granting of adequate credits to the Government, sustained, I hope, so far as they can equitably be sustained by the present generation, by well conceived taxation.

I say sustained so far as may be equitable by taxation because it seems to me that it would be most unwise to base the credits which will now be necessary entirely on money borrowed. It is our duty, I most respectfully urge, to protect our people so far as we may against the very serious hardships and evils which would be likely to arise out of the inflation which would be produced by vast loans.

In carrying out the measures by which these things are to be accomplished we should keep constantly in mind the wisdom of interfering as little as possible in our own preparation and in the equipment of our own military forces with the duty—for it will be a very practical duty—of supplying the nations already at war with Germany with the materials which they can obtain only from us or by our assistance. They are in the field and we should help them in every way to be effective there.

I shall take the liberty of suggesting, through the several executive departments of the Government, for the consideration of your committees, measures for the accomplishment of the several objects I have mentioned. I hope that it will be your pleasure to deal with them as having been framed after very careful thought by the branch of the Government upon which the responsibility of conducting the war and safeguarding the Nation will most directly fall.

While we do these things, these deeply momentous things, let us be very clear, and make very clear to all the world what our motives and our objects are. My own thought has not been driven from its habitual and normal course by the unhappy events of the last two months, and I do not believe that the thought of the Nation has been altered or clouded by them. I have exactly the same things in mind now that I had in mind when I addressed the Senate on the twenty-second of January last; the same that I had in mind when I addressed the Congress on the third of February and on the twenty-sixth of February. Our object now, as then, is to vindicate the principles of peace and justice in the life of the world as against selfish and autocratic power and to set up amongst the really free and self-governed peoples of the world such a concert of purpose and of action as will henceforth insure the observance of those principles. Neutrality is no longer feasible or desirable where the peace of the world is involved and the freedom of its peoples, and the menace to that peace and freedom lies in the existence of autocratic governments backed by organized force which is controlled wholly by their will, not by the will of their people. We have seen the last of neutrality in such circumstances. We are at the beginning of an age in which it will be insisted that the same standards of conduct and of responsibility for wrong done shall be observed among nations and their governments that are observed among the individual citizens of civilized states.

We have no quarrel with the German people. We have no feeling towards them but one of sympathy and friendship. It was not upon their impulse that their government acted in entering this war. It was not with their previous knowledge or approval. It was a war determined upon as wars used to be determined upon in the old, unhappy days when peoples were nowhere consulted by their rulers and wars were provoked and waged in the interest of dynasties or of little groups of ambitious men who were accustomed to use their fellow men as pawns and tools. Self-governed nations do not fill their neighbor states with spies or set the course of intrigue to bring about some critical posture of affairs which will give them an opportunity to strike and make conquest. Such designs can be successfully worked out only under cover and where no one has the right to ask questions. Cunningly contrived plans of deception or aggression, carried, it may be, from generation to generation, can be worked out and kept from the light only within the privacy of courts or behind the carefully guarded confidences of a narrow and privileged class. They are happily impossible where public opinion commands and insists upon full information concerning all the nation's affairs.

A steadfast concert for peace can never be maintained except by a partnership of democratic nations. No autocratic government could be trusted to keep faith within it or observe its covenants. It must be a league of honor, a partnership of opinion. Intrigue would eat its vitals away; the plottings of inner circles who could plan what they would and render account to no one would be a corruption seated at its very heart. Only free peoples can hold their purpose and their honor steady to a common end and prefer the interests of mankind to any narrow interest of their own.

Does not every American feel that assurance has been added to our hope for the future peace of the world by the wonderful and heartening things that have been happening within the last few weeks in Russia? Russia was known by those who knew it best to have been always in fact democratic at heart, in all the vital habits of her thought, in all the intimate relationships of her people that spoke their natural instinct, their habitual attitude towards life. The autocracy that crowned the summit of her political structure, long as it had stood and terrible as was the reality of its power, was not in fact Russian in origin, character, or purpose; and now it has been shaken off and the great, generous Russian people have been added in all their naïve majesty and might to the forces that are fighting for freedom in the world, for justice, and for peace. Here is a fit partner for a League of Honor.

One of the things that has served to convince us that the Prussian autocracy was not and could never be our friend is that from the very outset of the present war it has filled our unsuspecting communities and even our offices of government with spies and set criminal intrigues everywhere afoot against our national unity of counsel, our peace within and without, our industries and our commerce. Indeed it is now evident that its spies were here even before the war began; and it is unhappily not a matter of conjecture but a fact proved in our courts of justice that the intrigues which have more than once come perilously near to disturbing the peace and dislocating the industries of the country have been carried on at the instigation, with the support, and even under the personal direction of official agents of the Imperial Government accredited to the Government of the United States. Even in checking these things and trying to extirpate them we have sought to put the most generous interpretation possible upon them because we knew that their source lay, not in any hostile feeling or purpose of the German people towards us (who were, no doubt, as ignorant of them as we ourselves were), but only in the selfish designs of a Government that did what it pleased and told its people nothing. But they have played their part in serving to convince us at last that that Government entertains no real friendship for us and means to act against our peace and security at its convenience. That it means to stir up enemies against us at our very doors the intercepted note to the German Minister at Mexico City is eloquent evidence.

We are accepting this challenge of hostile purpose because we know that in such a Government, following such methods, we can never have a friend; and that in the presence of its organized power, always lying in wait to accomplish we know not what purpose, there can be no assured security for the democratic Governments of the world. We are now about to accept gauge of battle with this natural foe to liberty and shall, if necessary, spend the whole force of the nation to check and nullify its pretensions and its power. We are glad, now that we see the facts with no veil of false pretense about them to fight thus for the ultimate peace of the world and for the liberation of its peoples, the German peoples included: for the rights of nations great and small and the privilege of men everywhere to choose their way of life and of obedience. The world must be made safe for democracy. Its peace must be planted upon the tested foundations of political liberty. We have no selfish ends to serve. We desire no conquest, no dominion. We seek no indemnities for ourselves, no material compensation for the sacrifices we shall freely make. We are but one of the champions of the rights of mankind. We shall be satisfied when those rights have been made as secure as the faith and the freedom of nations can make them.

Just because we fight without rancor and without selfish object, seeking nothing for ourselves but what we shall wish to share with all free peoples, we shall, I feel confident, conduct our operations as belligerents without passion and ourselves observe with proud punctilio the principles of right and of fair play we profess to be fighting for.

I have said nothing of the Governments allied with the Imperial Government of Germany because they have not made war upon us or challenged us to defend our right and our honor. The Austro-Hungarian Government has, indeed, avowed its unqualified indorsement and acceptance of the reckless and lawless submarine warfare adopted now without disguise by the Imperial German Government, and it has therefore not been possible for this Government to receive Count Tarnowski, the Ambassador recently accredited to this Government by the Imperial and Royal Government of Austria-Hungary; but that Government has not actually engaged in warfare against citizens of the United States on the seas, and I take the liberty, for the present at least, of postponing a discussion of our relations with the authorities at Vienna. We enter this war only where we are clearly forced into it because there are no other means of defending our rights.

It will be all the easier for us to conduct ourselves as belligerents in a high spirit of right and fairness because we act without animus, not in enmity towards a people or with the desire to bring any injury or disadvantage upon them, but only in armed opposition to an irresponsible government which has thrown aside all considerations of humanity and of right and is running amuck. We are, let me say again, the sincere friends of the German people, and shall desire nothing so much as the early reëstablishment of intimate relations of mutual advantage between us,—however hard it may be for them, for the time being, to believe that this is spoken from our hearts. We have borne with their present Government through all these bitter months because of that friendship,—exercising a patience and forbearance which would otherwise have been impossible. We shall, happily, still have an opportunity to prove that friendship in our daily attitude and actions towards the millions of men and women of German birth and native sympathy who live amongst us and share our life, and we shall be proud to prove it towards all who are in fact loyal to their neighbors and to the Government in the hour of test. They are, most of them, as true and loyal Americans as if they had never known any other fealty or allegiance. They will be prompt to stand with us in rebuking and restraining the few who may be of a different mind and purpose. If there should be disloyalty, it will be dealt with with a firm hand of stern repression; but, if it lifts its head at all, it will lift it only here and there and without countenance except from a lawless and malignant few.

It is a distressing and oppressive duty, Gentlemen of the Congress, which I have performed in thus addressing you. There are, it may be, many months of fiery trial and sacrifice ahead of us. It is a fearful thing to lead this great peaceful people into war, into the most terrible and disastrous of all wars, civilization itself seeming to be in the balance.

But the right is more precious than peace, and we shall fight for the things which we have always carried nearest our hearts,—for democracy, for the right of those who submit to authority to have a voice in their own Governments, for the rights and liberties of small nations, for a universal dominion of right by such a concert of free peoples as shall bring peace and safety to all nations and make the world itself at last free. To such a task we can dedicate our lives and our fortunes, everything that we are and everything that we have, with the pride of those who know that the day has come when America is privileged to spend her blood and her might for the principles that gave her birth and happiness and the peace which she has treasured. God helping her, she can do no other.

Senate Speech on Free Speech in Wartime (Abridged)

Robert LaFollette

Commentary

Although most Americans supported the war, a minority did not. As a result, several significant rhetorical developments took place. First, Wilson organized a "Committee of Public Information" (CPI) about a week after the declaration (April 14, 1917). The name of the CPI was a bit misleading. For the first time in American history, the government had an organization (not just a committee) to produce and circulate prowar rhetoric (not just information). Working assiduously through all communication media, the CPI not only circulated war news to the press, but also wrote editorials that were distributed to newspapers with requests that they be printed. It published its own daily *Official Bulletin*. Its artists produced prowar posters and films. It recruited 75,000 speakers, gave them a name which reminded Americans of their Revolutionary heritage ("Four Minute Men"), provided them with a basic speech that could be adapted to local circumstances and had them speak at theatres during intermissions and at factories during lunch breaks.

Wilson also tried to suppress antiwar rhetoric. In June, 1917, Congress passed the "Espionage Act," thus employing another label that was slightly misleading. In addition to outlawing espionage, the law prohibited statements designed to interfere with military recruiting or military operations. The law was first used against the Socialist party, which met shortly after the declaration of war to proclaim it "a crime against the people of the United States and against the nations of the world." In July, 1917, Kate O'Hare, a prominent Socialist, was indicted after giving an antiwar speech, and other arrests followed quickly. In August, a dozen Socialist publications were banned from the mails. On September 7, Federal agents conducted nationwide raids on local offices of the Socialist party and the radical International Workers of the World.

Although the government confined its suppression of antiwar advocates to radical organizations, the summer of 1917 saw a rising hysteria directed against anyone suspected of disloyalty. Some pacifist clergymen were assaulted (both verbally and physically), countless school boards dropped German from the high school curriculum and salespeople often refused to serve people with antiwar opinions.

Among those who were assailed for disloyalty with increasing intensity during the summer was Robert LaFollette (1855-1925). A long-time Republican progressive, LaFollette had served as governor of Wisconsin and had been elected to the Senate in 1906. He had refused to endorse Roosevelt in 1912, either because he wanted the presidential nomination for himself (as his critics charged) or because he believed Roosevelt to be insufficiently progressive (as he claimed). In any case, he had supported Wilson until the president began moving toward war. After Germany declared unrestricted submarine warfare, LaFollette organized a Senate filibuster to prevent legislation that would have allowed American merchant ships to arm themselves. He earned, thereby, the undying enmity of Wilsonians. He earned even more enmity by voting against the declaration of war and still more by introducing (August 11, 1917) a Senate resolution calling for a public statement of Allied war aims. By referring to secret treaties between the Allies, the preamble to the resolution implied that the Allies were secretly engaged in a war of conquest. LaFollette's resolution was denounced vigorously both in and out of the Senate.

He earned still more enmity by opposing the War Revenue Act. In his last Senate speech on the subject (September 10, 1917), he used economic arguments, claiming that the measure was unfair because it taxed average citizens rather than "war profits" and the nation should finance the war on a "pay as you go" basis rather than burden future generations with a huge debt. Amidst the hysteria, however, LaFollette's economic arguments were overlooked. He was accused of trying to sabotage the war effort in general and the war bond drive in particular.

On the same day that he delivered the Senate speech, he received an invitation to speak in St. Paul ten days later at the end of a three-day meeting of the Nonpartisan League. a progressive organization that had taken an antiwar stand. With limited time for preparation, he decided to speak on the War Revenue Act. When he arrived on September 19, he learned that Senator Borah had spoken on the same subject the previous evening. Isolating himself for a day-and-a-half, LaFollette prepared a typescript about a subject that had been weighing on his mind all summer: the suppression of free speech. However, when he showed it to the officials who had invited him to speak, they asked him not to deliver it, saying secret service agents were on the scene, newspapers would misinterpret it and the League would get into trouble. After toying with the idea of not speaking at all, LaFollette delivered an extemporaneous speech to a cheering audience of about 10,000 supporters. It was transcribed independently by three stenographers — an important point in view of later events.

The bulk of the speech was about the War Revenue Act, but, in his introduction, LaFollette ingratiated himself with his audience by recounting their common work on behalf of progressivism and peace. This led to some interruptions by several questioners, most of them friendly but a few hostile. His impromptu responses became the focus of unfriendly — and misleading — newspaper accounts. He explicitly stated that the United States had legitimate grievances against Germany (though he added that they were not worth fighting for), but the Associated Press misquoted him as saying, "We had no grievances against Germany." Perhaps more important was his response to a hostile question, "How about the *Lusitania?* Responding with an analogy, LaFollette said that a neutral who travels on a belligerent ship loaded with munitions is risking his life as much as if he sat near an arsenal in a belligerent country. He went on to say that Bryan, who had been secretary of state at the time, told Wilson four days before the *Lusitania* sailed that it was carrying munitions and that Americans should be warned to stay off the ship. The press had a field day. First, it turned LaFollette's statement into the central theme of the speech, as is illustrated by the *New York Times,* headline, "LaFollette Defends Lusitania Sinking." Second, his charge against Wilson was denounced as a lie.

On September 22, only a day after news reports first appeared, the Minnesota governor ordered the State Public Safety Commission to investigate the speech. Declaring publicly that the speech was "disloyal and seditious," it dispatched a petition to the Senate asking that LaFollette be expelled. Roosevelt implicitly endorsed expulsion by declaring publicly that LaFollette belonged in the German Reichstag, not in the United States Senate. On September 23, LaFollette delivered the substance of his undelivered St. Paul speech on free expression to a church in Toledo which had recently been organized by an antiwar preacher, but the press was too excited about what he had allegedly said in St. Paul to give it any attention.

On September 29, the Minnesota petition arrived at the Senate. It was sent to the Committee on Privileges and Elections, as were subsequent petitions. After meeting on October 3, 4 and 5, the committee announced it would investigate LaFollette's charges regarding Wilson's knowledge of munitions being aboard the *Lusitania.* Speculating about who might be called to testify on this question, the press ignored the fact that the committee also intended to investigate the authenticity of newspaper versions of LaFollette's St. Paul speech, a problem that LaFollette's aides had quietly brought to the committee's attention.

The press also reported on October 5 that LaFollette had obtained a gentlemen's agreement to be recognized the following day on a point of personal privilege for the purpose of giving a three-hour speech. The galleries were packed with an audience which, in view of recent publicity, undoubtedly expected LaFollette to discuss his St. Paul speech, the impending investigation, the *Lusitania* affair and the movement to have him expelled from the Senate. Except for fleeting and indirect references, he did not. Instead, he drew upon his Toledo speech (undelivered in St. Paul) to address the general problem of free expression during war.

Most of the exclusions from the following abbreviated text involve LaFollette's extensive historical argument, in which he read lengthy excerpts from speeches by Lincoln, Webster, Clay and other opponents of the Mexican war. His explicit argument was that Americans have traditionally respected free speech, but he implicitly identified himself with historical heroes. The abbreviated version is reproduced photographically from A. Craig Baird, *American Public Addresses, 1740-1952* (New York: McGraw-Hill, 1956), pp. 244-248.

Senate Speech on Free Speech in Wartime (Abridged)

MR. PRESIDENT: I rise to a question of personal privilege.

I have no intention of taking the time of the Senate with a review of the events which led to our entrance into the war except in so far as they bear upon the question of personal privilege to which I am addressing myself.

Six Members of the Senate and fifty Members of the House voted against the declaration of war. Immediately there was let loose upon those Senators and Representatives a flood of invective and abuse from newspapers and individuals who had been clamoring for war, unequaled, I believe, in the history of civilized society.

Prior to the declaration of war every man who had ventured to oppose our entrance into it had been condemned as a coward or worse, and even the President had by no means been immune from these attacks.

Since the declaration of war the triumphant war press has pursued those Senators and Representatives who voted against war with malicious falsehood and recklessly libelous attacks, going to the extreme limit of charging them with treason against their country.

This campaign of libel and character assassination directed against the Members of Congress who opposed our entrance into the war has been continued down to the present hour, and I have upon my desk newspaper clippings, some of them libels upon me alone, some directed as well against other Senators who voted in opposition to the declaration of war. One of these newspaper reports most widely circulated represents a Federal judge in the state of Texas as saying, in a charge to a grand jury—I read the article as it appeared in the newspaper and the headline with which it is introduced:

DISTRICT JUDGE WOULD LIKE TO TAKE SHOT AT
TRAITORS IN CONGRESS

(By Associated Press leased wire)

Houston, Texas, October 1, 1917. Judge Waller T. Burns, of the United States district court, in charging a Federal grand jury at the beginning of the October term today, after calling by name Senators Stone of Missouri, Hardwick of Georgia, Vardaman of Mississippi, Gronna of North Dakota, Gore of Oklahoma, and LaFollette of Wisconsin, said:

"If I had a wish, I would wish that you men had jurisdiction to return bills of indictment against these men. They ought to be tried promptly and fairly, and I believe this court could administer the law fairly; but I have a conviction, as strong as life, that this country should stand them up against an adobe wall tomorrow and give them what they deserve. If any man deserves death, it is a traitor. I wish that I could pay for the ammunition. I would like to attend the execution, and if I were in the firing squad I would not want to be the marksman who had the blank shell." . . .

If this newspaper clipping were a single or exceptional instance of lawless defamation, I should not trouble the Senate with a reference to it. But, Mr. President, it is not.

In this mass of newspaper clippings which I have here upon my desk, and which I shall not trouble the Senate to read unless it is desired, and which represent but a small part of the accumulation clipped from the daily press of the country in the last three months, I find other Senators, as well as myself, accused of the highest crimes of which any man can be guilty—treason and disloyalty—and, sir, accused not only with no evidence to support the accusation, but without the suggestion that such evidence anywhere exists. It is not claimed that Senators who opposed the declaration of war have since that time acted with any concerted purpose either regarding war measures or any others. They have voted according to their individual opinions, have often been opposed to each other on bills which have come before the Senate since the declaration of war, and, according to my recollection, have never all voted together since that time upon any single proposition upon which the Senate has been divided.

I am aware, Mr. President, that in pursuance of this campaign of vilification and attempted intimidation, requests from various individuals and certain organizations have been submitted to the Senate for my expulsion from this body, and that such requests have been referred to and considered by one of the committees of the Senate.

If I alone had been made the victim of these attacks, I should not take one moment of the Senate's time for their consideration, and I believe that other Senators who have been unjustly and unfairly assailed, as I have been, hold the same attitude upon this that I do. *Neither the clamor of the mob nor the voice of power will ever turn me by the breadth of a hair from the course I mark out for myself, guided by such knowledge as I can obtain and controlled and directed by a solemn conviction of right and duty.*

But, sir, it is not alone Members of Congress that the war party in this country has sought to intimidate. The mandate seems to have gone forth to the sovereign people of this country that they must be silent while those things are being done by their Government which most vitally concern their well-being, their happiness, and their lives. Today and for weeks past honest and law-abiding citizens of this country are being terrorized and outraged in their rights by those sworn to uphold the laws and protect the rights of the people. I have in my possession numerous affidavits establishing the fact that people are being unlawfully arrested, thrown into jail, held incommunicado for days, only to be eventually discharged without ever having been taken into court, because they have committed no crime. Private residences are being invaded, loyal citizens of undoubted integrity and probity arrested, cross-examined, and the most sacred constitutional rights guaranteed to every American citizen are being violated.

It appears to be the purpose of those conducting this campaign to throw the country into a state of terror, to coerce public opinion, to stifle criticism, and suppress discussion of the great issues involved in this war.

I think all men recognize that in time of war the citizen must surrender some rights for the common good which he is entitled to enjoy in time of peace. *But, sir, the right to control their own Government according to constitutional forms is not one of the rights that the citizens of this country are called upon to surrender in time of war.*

Rather in time of war the citizen must be more alert to the preservation of his right to control his Government. He must be most watchful of the encroachment of the military upon the civil power. He must beware of those precedents in support of arbitrary action by administration officials which, excused on the plea of necessity in war time, become the fixed rule when the necessity has passed and normal conditions have been restored.

More than all, the citizen and his representative in Congress in time of war must maintain his right of free speech. More than in times of peace it is necessary that the channels for free public discussion of governmental policies shall be open and unclogged. I believe, Mr. President, that I am now touching upon the most important question in this country today—and that is the right of the citizens of this country and their representatives in Congress to discuss in an orderly way frankly and publicly and without fear, from the platform and through the press, every important phase of this war; its causes, and manner in which it should be conducted, and the terms upon which peace should be made. The belief which is becoming widespread in this land that this most fundamental right is being denied to the citizens of this country is a fact, the tremendous significance of which those in authority have not yet begun to appreciate. I am contending, Mr. President, for the great fundamental right of the sovereign people of this country to make their voice heard and have that voice heeded upon the great questions arising out of this war, including not only how the war shall be prosecuted but the conditions upon which it may be terminated with a due regard for the rights and the honor of this Nation and the interests of humanity.

I am contending for this right because the exercise of it is necessary to the welfare, to the existence, of this Government, to the successful conduct of this war, and to a peace which shall be enduring and for the best interest of this country.

Suppose success attends the attempt to stifle all discussion of the issues of this war, all discussions of the terms upon which it should be concluded, all discussion of the objects and purposes to be accomplished by it, and concede the demand of the war-mad press and war extremists that they monopolize the right of public utterance upon these questions unchallenged, what think you would be the consequences to this country not only during the war but after the war?

Mr. President, our Government, above all others, is founded on the right of the people freely to discuss all matters pertaining to their Government, in war not less than in peace. It is true, sir, that Members of the House of Representatives are elected for two years, the President for four years, and the Members of the Senate for six years, and during their temporary official terms these officers constitute what is called the Government. But back of them always is the controlling sovereign power of the people, and when the people can make their will known, the faithful officer will obey that will. Though the right of the people to express their will by ballot is suspended during the term of office of the elected official, nevertheless the duty of the official to obey the popular will continue throughout his entire term of office. How can that popular will express itself between elections except by meetings, by speeches, by publications, by petitions, and by addresses to the representatives of the people? Any man who seeks to set a limit upon those rights, whether in war or peace, aims a blow at the most vital part of our Government. And then as the time for election approaches and the official is called to account for his stewardship—not a day, not a week, not a month, before the election, but a year or more before it, if the people choose—they must have the right to the freest possible discussion of every question upon which their representative has acted, of the merits of every measure he has supported or opposed, of every vote he has cast and every speech that he has made. And before this great fundamental right every other must, if necessary, give way, for in no other manner can representative government be preserved.

Progressive Government

Franklin D. Roosevelt

Commentary

Herbert Hoover had been in the White House only a few months when the Great Depression began in the autumn of 1929. By the presidential election year of 1832, the gross national income dropped from eighty-three to forty billion dollars. Industrial production was halved and unemployment tripled. While agricultural overproduction cut farm income in half, urban food riots broke out.

The severity of the Great Depression makes it easy to say, as many scholars do, that subsequent political events — Hoover's overwhelming defeat in 1932 by Franklin D. Roosevelt (1882-1945); the growth of governmental activism, which went beyond what earlier progressives had ever imagined; and an end to Republican domination of the Federal government — were inevitable. The doctrine of inevitability might be correct, but it should not blind us to two sets of rhetorical considerations. First, rhetorical factors, in addition to economic factors, also help to explain the results of the 1932 election, and, second, Roosevelt employed several rhetorical strategies which, although now commonplace, were revolutionary in 1932. A discussion of the first set of considerations is somewhat ironic. Progressive Republicans had helped create public expectations for governmental activism, and, shortly after the Depression began, Republicans responded with legislation which created the Reconstruction Finance Corporation (RFC). The RFC loaned billions of dollars to help businesses rehire unemployed workers, but Hoover's rhetoric could not persuade voters that the RFC would solve the problem. He appeared insensitive to the crisis as he talked about "rugged individualism" and was quoted (slightly inaccurately) as saying, "Prosperity is just around the corner."

Hoover's uninspirational rhetoric gave Democrats an obvious advantage in the 1932 election, but their demographic, religious and ideological schizophrenia presented serious problems. They had been hurt during the 1920s by internal struggles between the Northeast (heavily urban, Catholic, opposed to prohibition and inclined toward "big government") and the Solid

South (predominantly rural, Protestant, in favor of prohibition and inclined toward "limited government"). If the struggle for the nomination in 1932 had highlighted these differences, the party could have been torn apart and the election lost.

Roosevelt's background gave him a mixture of assets and liabilities in his quest for the schizophrenic party's nomination. Although his distant cousin, Theodore, was now dead, the Roosevelt name was still magic. It was his kinship to Theodore which had prompted party leaders to run the otherwise-unknown FDR for the State legislature back in 1910; however, in 1912, while Teddy was running on the Progressive ticket, FDR publicly endorsed Wilson. Rewarded with an appointment as assistant secretary of the Navy, FDR was identified as a Wilsonian. After his bout with polio, which earned FDR considerable public sympathy but raised questions about his stamina, he worked for Al Smith and succeeded Smith as governor of New York in 1928. His association with Smith (an Irish Catholic "machine" politician from the city and an opponent of prohibition), worried the predominantly "dry" Southern and rural Democrats. Roosevelt's progressive record as governor of New York endeared him to progressive Democrats but worried conservatives. This balance of assets and liabilities was ironic: Smith, who had the support of most Northeastern Democrats, was FDR's chief competitor for the nomination. Roosevelt had to seek support from outside his own area, but he had to avoid alienating Smith's supporters in the process. He had to do so in a way that would attract party conservatives, as well as progressives.

After announcing his candidacy in February, 1932, FDR began a campaign for the nomination that was marked by ambiguity and a progressive rhetoric that was crafted carefully so as not to alienate conservatives. The former Wilsonian hinted that the League of Nations was a dead issue, and he equivocated about prohibition. He opened his first campaign speech (April 7, 1932) by saying that other Democratic candidates, as well as Republicans, were overemphasizing aid to big business. Without mentioning Smith by name, Roosevelt deprecated Smith's proposal for a public works program. Then he outlined a policy for helping the *forgotten man*, a term that one of his speechwriters, Raymond Moley, later confessed had been appropriated from the Social Darwinist, William Sumner. He proposed, in very general terms, aid to farmers, aid to small (but not large) banks, aid to homeowners and a tariff "revision." Its content was progressive, but its ambiguity at a time of economic crisis made it appealing to normally conservative voters.

Roosevelt's first campaign speech brings us to the second set of rhetorical considerations — his use of strategies that constituted a rhetorical revolution. The first was his use of radio, a new medium that was unsuitable for the old-fashioned oratorical style of many politicians but appropriate for Roosevelt's conversational style. After Roosevelt, successful politicians had to learn how to utilize the electronic media, first radio and then television. A second rhetorical revolution was a new genre of acceptance speech. Instead of following the tradition of waiting to be notified by a committee, Roosevelt flew to the convention to accept the nomination. His immediate rhetorical purpose was to appear dynamic, an important tactic in view of his physical handicap, but subsequent nominees followed his lead, and, thus, a new rhetorical tradition was born. Third, FDR employed a group of speechwriters, mostly college professors who were often scorned by professional politicians as "brain trusters." Roosevelt was not the first speaker to use speechwriters (some observers believe that Coolidge was the first president to use them), but he was the first major politician to deliver discourses that were produced by a committee. The system is now commonplace.

Having won the nomination, Roosevelt conducted a campaign in the general election that was less ambiguous than the one which had won him the nomination, but it was filled with logical inconsistencies. In his acceptance speech, he embraced the Democratic platform, which called for a series of progressive measures, including the public works program Roosevelt had deprecated earlier. One of the most fraudulent rhetorical documents in history, the platform not only failed to say how the programs would be financed, but also sounded fiscally conservative. It castigated Republicans for overspending, promised a balanced budget and pledged a twenty-five percent reduction in Federal spending. Ignoring the inconsistency, FDR concluded his acceptance speech by promising a "New Deal," thus appealing to the nation's traditional belief in progress.

As the campaign swung into high gear, Roosevelt continued promising vaguely defined progressive programs, while also promising a balanced budget and reduced spending. Some brain trusters worried that his rhetoric sounded too much like Hoover's. Robert Straus asked permission to write a speech that would clearly differentiate between the two candidates' ideologies. Roosevelt was uninterested until newspaper editorialists began ridiculing Hoover for reusing one of his favorite terms, "rugged individualism." FDR authorized Straus to write the speech, which was originally entitled "Individualism: Romantic and Realistic," but he refrained from delivering it.

Roosevelt was invited to address the Commonwealth Club of San Francisco on September 23, 1932. He originally intended to deliver a short encomium to San Francisco, but advisers warned that such a hackneyed speech would be inappropriate for an elite audience which met regularly to hear serious speeches on serious subjects. It was a nonpartisan club, which made a direct appeal for votes inappropriate.

This rhetorical situation prompted Roosevelt to give the Straus speech, which various brain trusters had helped revise and retitle. Forty years later, one brain truster, Rexford Tugwell, claimed that the speech was a "dividing line" in FDR's campaign because favorable audience response encouraged a "bolder" advocacy of progressivism thereafter. The claim is dubious because, a month after the Commonwealth Club speech, Roosevelt made his famous Pittsburgh address in which he ignored progressivism while pledging a balanced budget and reduced Federal spending. Nevertheless, the

Commonwealth Club speech is important historically. More philosophical than the usual campaign speech, its title and content constitute an unusually clear statement of Roosevelt's New Deal ideology. It is reproduced from Ernest J. Wrage and Barnet Baskerville, *Contemporary Forum: American Speeches on Twentieth-Century Issues* (1962; rpt. Seattle: University of Washington Press, 1969), pp. 146-156.

Progressive Government

I count it a privilege to be invited to address the Commonwealth Club. It has stood in the life of this city and State, and, it is perhaps accurate to add, the Nation, as a group of citizen leaders interested in fundamental problems of Government, and chiefly concerned with achievement of progress in Government through nonpartisan means.

The privilege of addressing you, therefore, in the heat of a political campaign, is great. I want to respond to your courtesy in terms consistent with your policy.

I want to speak not of politics but of government. I want to speak not of parties, but of universal principles. They are not political, except in that large sense in which a great American once expressed a definition of politics — that nothing in all of human life is foreign to the science of politics.

I do want to give you, however, a recollection of a long life spent, for a large part, in public office. Some of my conclusions and observations have been deeply accentuated in these past few weeks. I have traveled far — from Albany to the Golden Gate. I have seen many people, and heard many things, and today, when, in a sense, my journey has reached the half-way mark, I am glad of the opportunity to discuss with you what it all means to me.

Sometimes, my friends, particularly in years such as these, the hand of discouragement falls upon us. It seems that things are in a rut, fixed, settled, that the world has grown old and tired and very much out of joint. This is the mood of depression, of dire and weary depression.

But then we look around us in America, and everything tells us that we are wrong. America is new. It is in the process of change and development. It has the great potentialities of youth, and particularly is this true of the great West, and of this coast, and of California.

I would not have you feel that I regard this in any sense a new community. I have traveled in many parts of the world, but never have I felt the arresting thought of the change and development more than here, where the old, mystic East would seem to be near to us, where the currents of life and thought and commerce of the whole world meet us. This factor alone is sufficient to cause man to stop and think of the deeper meaning of things when he stands in this community.

But, more than that, I appreciate that the membership of this club consists of men who are thinking in terms beyond the immediate present, beyond their own immediate tasks, beyond their own individual interests. I want to invite you, therefore, to consider with me in the large some of the relationships of government and economic life that go deep into our daily lives, our happiness, our future and our security.

The issue of Government has always been whether individual men and women will have to serve some system of government or economics, or whether a system of government and economics exists to serve individual men and women. This question has persistently dominated the discussion of government for many generations. On questions relating to these things men have differed, and for time immemorial it is probable that honest men will continue to differ.

The final word belongs to no man; yet we can still believe in change and in progress. Democracy, as a dear old friend of mine in Indiana, Meredith Nicholson, has called it, is a quest, a never-end seeking for better things, and in the seeking for these things and the striving for them, there are many roads to follow. But, if we map the course of these roads, we find that there are only two general directions.

When we look about us, we are likely to forget how hard people have worked to win the privilege of Government. The growth of the national governments of Europe was a struggle for the development of a centralized force in the nation, strong enough to impose peace upon ruling barons. In many instances the victory of the central government, the creation of a strong central government, was a haven of refuge to the individual. The people preferred the master far away to the exploitation and cruelty of the smaller master near at hand.

But the creators of national government were perforce ruthless men. They were often cruel in their methods, but they did strive steadily toward something that society needed and very much wanted — a strong central State, able to keep the peace, to stamp out civil war, to put the unruly nobleman in his place, and to permit the bulk of individuals to live safely.

The man of ruthless force had his place in developing a pioneer country, just as he did in fixing the power of the central government in the development of the nations. Society paid him well for his services and its development. When the development among the nations of Europe, however, had been completed, ambition and ruthlessness, having served their term, tended to overstep their mark.

There came a growing feeling that government was conducted for the benefit of a few who thrived unduly at the expense of all. The people sought a balancing — a limiting force. There came gradually, through town councils, trade guilds, national parliaments, by constitution and by popular participation and control, limitations on arbitrary power.

Another factor that tended to limit the power of those who ruled was the rise of the ethical conception that a ruler bore a responsibility for the welfare of his subjects.

The American colonies were born in this struggle. The American Revolution was a turning point in it. After the Revolution the struggle continued and shaped itself in the public life of the country. There were those who, because they had seen the confusion which attended the years of war for American independence, surrendered to the belief that popular Government was essentially dangerous and essentially unworkable. They were honest people, my friends, and we cannot deny that their experience had warranted some measure of fear.

The most brilliant, honest and able exponent of this point of view was Hamilton. He was too impatient of slow-moving methods. Fundamentally he believed that the safety of the Republic lay in the autocratic strength of its government, that the destiny of individuals was to serve that government, and that fundamentally a great and strong group of central institutions, guided by a small group of able and public-spirited citizens, could best direct all government.

But Mr. Jefferson, in the summer of 1776, after drafting the Declaration of Independence, turned his mind to the same problem and took a different view. He did not deceive himself with outward forms. Government to him was a means to an end, not an end in itself; it might be either a refuge and a help or a threat and a danger, depending on the circumstances. We find him carefully analyzing the society for which he was to organize a government: "We have no paupers. The great mass of our population is of laborers, our rich who cannot live without labor, either manual or professional, being few and of moderate wealth. Most of the laboring class possess property, cultivate their own lands, have families and from the demand for their labor, are enabled to exact from the rich and the competent such prices as enable them to feed abundantly, clothe above mere decency, to labor moderately and raise their families."

These people, he considered, had two sets of rights, those of "personal competency" and those involved in acquiring and possessing property. By "personal competency" he meant the right of free thinking, freedom of forming and expressing opinions, and freedom of personal living, each man according to his own lights. To insure the first set of rights, a Government must so order its functions as not to interfere with the individual. But even Jefferson realized that the exercise of the property rights might so interfere with the rights of the individual that the Government, without whose assistance the property rights could not exist, must intervene, not to destroy individualism, but to protect it.

You are familiar with the great political duel which followed; and how Hamilton and his friends, building toward a dominant, centralized power, were at length defeated in the great election of 1800 by Mr. Jefferson's party. Out of that duel came the two parties, Republican and Democratic, as we know them today.

So began, in American political life, the new day, the day of the individual against the system, the day in which individualism was made the great watchword of American life.

The happiest of economic conditions made that day long and splendid. On the Western frontier, land was substantially free. No one who did not shirk the task of earning a living was entirely without opportunity to do so. Depressions could, and did, come and go; but they could not alter the fundamental fact that most of the people lived partly by selling their labor and partly by extracting their livelihood from the soil, so that starvation and dislocation were practically impossible. At the very worst there was always the possibility of climbing into a covered wagon and moving West where the untilled prairies afforded a haven for men to whom the East did not provide a place. So great were our natural resources that we could offer this relief not only to our own people, but to the distressed of all the world. We could invite immigration from Europe and welcome it with open arms. Traditionally, when a depression came a new section of land was opened in the West. And even our temporary misfortune served our manifest destiny.

It was in the middle of the nineteenth century that a new force was released and a new dream created. The force was what is called the industrial revolution, the advance of steam and machinery and the rise of the forerunners of the modern industrial plant.

The dream was the dream of an economic machine, able to raise the standard of living for everyone; to bring luxury within the reach of the humblest; to annihilate distance by steam power and later by electricity, and to release everyone from the drudgery of the heaviest manual toil.

It was to be expected that this would necessarily affect government. Heretofore, government had merely been called upon to produce conditions within which people could live happily, labor peacefully, and rest secure. Now it was called upon to aid in the consummation of this new dream.

There was, however, a shadow over the dream. To be made real it required use of the talents of men of tremendous will and tremendous ambition, since by no other force could the problems of financing and engineering and new developments be brought to a consummation.

So manifest were the advantages of the machine age, however, that the United States fearlessly, cheerfully and, I think, rightly accepted the bitter with the sweet. It was thought that no price was too high to pay for the advantages which we could draw from a finished industrial system. The history of the last half century is accordingly in large measure a history of a group of financial Titans, whose methods were not scrutinized with too much care, and who were honored in proportion as they produced the results, irrespective of the means they used. The financiers who pushed the railroads to the Pacific were always ruthless, often wasteful, and frequently corrupt; but they did build railroads, and we have them today.

It has been estimated that the American investor paid for the American railway system more than three times over in the process; but despite this fact the net advantage was to the United States. As long as we had free land, as long as population was growing by leaps and bounds, as long as our industrial plants were insufficient to supply our own needs, society chose to give the ambitious man free play and unlimited reward, provided only that he produced the economic plant so much desired.

During this period of expansion there was equal opportunity for all, and the business of government was not to interfere but to assist in the development of industry.

This was done at the request of business men themselves. The tariff was originally imposed for the purpose of "fostering our infant industry," a phrase I think the older among you will remember as a political issue not so long ago.

The railroads were subsidized, sometimes by grants of money, oftener by grants of land. Some of the most valuable oil lands in the United States were granted to assist the financing of the railroad which pushed through the Southwest.

A nascent merchant marine was assisted by grants of money, or by mail subsidies, so that our steam shipping might ply the seven seas.

Some of my friends tell me that they do not want the Government in business. With this I agree, but I wonder whether they realize the implications of the past.

For while it has been American doctrine that the government must not go into business in competition with private enterprises, still it has been traditional, particularly in Republican administrations, for business urgently to ask the government to put at private disposal all kinds of government assistance. The same man who tells you that he does not want to see the government interfere in business — and he means it and has plenty of good reasons for saying so — is the first to go to Washington and ask the government for a prohibitory tariff on his product.

When things get just bad enough — as they did two years ago — he will go with equal speed to the United States Government and ask for a loan. And the Reconstruction Finance Corporation is the outcome of it.

Each group has sought protection from the Government for its own special interests without realizing that the function of Government must be to favor no small group at the expense of its duty to protect the rights of personal freedom and of private property of all its citizens.

In retrospect we can now see that the turn of the tide came with the turn of the century. We were reaching our last frontier; there was no more free land and our industrial combinations had become great uncontrolled and irresponsible units of power within the State.

Clear-sighted men saw with fear the danger that opportunity would no longer be equal; that the growing corporation, like the feudal baron of old, might threaten the economic freedom of individuals to earn a living. In that hour our antitrust laws were born.

The cry was raised against the great corporations. Theodore Roosevelt, the first great Republican Progressive, fought a Presidential campaign on the issue of "trust busting" and talked freely about malefactors of great wealth. If the Government had a policy it was rather to turn the clock back, to destroy the large combinations and to return to the time when every man owned his individual small business.

This was impossible. Theodore Roosevelt, abandoning the idea of "trust busting," was forced to work out a difference between "good" trusts and "bad" trusts. The Supreme Court set forth the famous "rule of reason" by which it seems to have meant that a concentration of industrial power was permissible if the method by which it got its power, and the use it made of that power, were reasonable.

Woodrow Wilson, elected in 1912, saw the situation more clearly. Where Jefferson had feared the encroachment of political power on the lives of individuals, Wilson knew that the new power was financial. He saw, in the highly centralized economic system, the despot of the twentieth century, on whom great masses of individuals relied for their safety and their livelihood, and whose irresponsibility and greed (if they were not controlled) would reduce them to starvation and penury.

The concentration of financial power had not proceeded as far in 1912 as it has today, but it had grown far enough for Mr. Wilson to realize fully its implications. It is interesting, now, to read his speeches. What is called "radical" today (and I have reason to know whereof I speak) is mild compared to the campaign of Mr. Wilson. "No man can deny," he said, "that the lines of endeavor have more and more narrowed and stiffened; no man who knows anything about the development of industry in this country can have failed to observe that the larger kinds of credit are more and more difficult to obtain unless you obtain them upon terms of uniting your efforts with those who already control the industry of the country, and nobody can fail to observe that every man who tries to set himself up in competition with any process of manufacture which has taken place under the control of large combinations of capital will presently find himself either squeezed out or obliged to sell and allow himself to be absorbed."

Had there been no World War — had Mr. Wilson been able to devote eight years to domestic instead of to international affairs — we might have had a wholly different situation at the present time. However, the then distant roar of European cannon, growing ever louder, forced him to abandon the study of this issue. The problem he saw so clearly is left with us as a legacy; and no one of us on either side of the political controversy can deny that it is a matter of grave concern to the government.

A glance at the situation today only too clearly indicates that equality of opportunity as we have known it no longer exists. Our industrial plant is built. The problem just now is whether, under existing conditions, it is not overbuilt.

Our last frontier has long since been reached, and there is practically no more free land. More than half of our people do not live on the farms or on lands and cannot derive a living by cultivating their own property.

There is no safety valve in the form of a Western prairie to which those thrown out of work by the Eastern economic machines can go for a new start. We are not able to invite the immigration from Europe to share our endless plenty. We are now providing a drab living for our own people.

Our system of constantly rising tariffs has at last reacted against us to the point of closing our Canadian frontier on the north, our European markets on the east, many of our Latin-American markets to the south, and a goodly proportion of our Pacific markets on the west, through the retaliatory tariffs of those countries.

It has forced many of our great industrial institutions, who exported their surplus production to such countries, to establish plants in such countries, within the tariff walls. This has resulted in the reduction of the operation of their American plants and opportunity for employment.

Just as freedom to farm has ceased, so also the opportunity in business has narrowed. It still is true that men can start small enterprises, trusting to native shrewdness and ability to keep abreast of competitors; but area after area has been preempted altogether by the great corporations, and even in the fields which still have no great concerns the small man starts under a handicap.

The unfeeling statistics of the past three decades show that the independent business man is running a losing race. Perhaps he is forced to the wall; perhaps he cannot command credit; perhaps he is "squeezed out," in Mr. Wilson's words, by highly organized corporate competitors, as your corner grocery man can tell you.

Recently a careful study was made of the concentration of business in the United States. It showed that our economic life was dominated by some 600-odd corporations who controlled two-thirds of American industry. Ten million small business men divided the other third. More striking still, it appeared that, if the process of concentration goes on at the same rate, at the end of another century we shall have all American industry controlled by a dozen corporations and run by perhaps a hundred men. Put plainly, we are steering a steady course toward economic oligarchy, if we are not there already.

Clearly, all this calls for a re-appraisal of values. A mere builder of more industrial plants, a creator of more railroad systems, an organizer of more corporations, is as likely to be a danger as a help.

The day of the great promoter or the financial Titan, to whom we granted anything if only he would build or develop, is over. Our task now is not discovery or exploitation of natural resources or necessarily producing more goods.

It is the soberer, less dramatic business of administering resources and plants already in hand, of seeking to reestablish foreign markets for our surplus production, of meeting the problem of underconsumption, of adjusting production to consumption, of distributing wealth and products more equitably, of adapting existing economic organizations to the service of the people. The day of enlightened administration has come.

Just as in older times the central Government was first a haven of refuge and then a threat, so now in a closer economic system the central and ambitious financial unit is no longer a servant of national desire but a danger. I would draw the parallel one step farther. We did not think because national government had become a threat in the eighteenth century that therefore we should abandon the principle of national government. Nor today should we abandon the principle of strong economic units called corporations merely because their power is susceptible of easy abuse. In other times we dealt with the problem of an unduly ambitious central government by modifying it gradually into a constitutional democratic government. So today we are modifying and controlling our economic units.

As I see it, the task of Government in its relation to business is to assist the development of an economic declaration of rights, an economic constitutional order. This is the common task of statesman and business man. It is the minimum requirement of a more permanently safe order of things.

Happily, the times indicate that to create such an order not only is the proper policy of government, but it is the only line of safety for our economic structures as well.

We know now that these economic units cannot exist unless prosperity is uniform — that is, unless purchasing power is well distributed throughout every group in the nation. That is why even the most selfish of corporations for its own interest would be glad to see wages restored and unemployment aided and to bring the Western farmer back to his accustomed level of prosperity and to assure a permanent safety to both groups.

That is why some enlightened industries themselves endeavor to limit the freedom of action of each man and business group within the industry in the common interest of all; why business men everywhere are asking a form of organization which will bring the scheme of things into balance, even though it may in some measure qualify the freedom of action of individual units within the business.

The exposition need not further be elaborated. It is brief and incomplete, but you will be able to expand it in terms of your own business or occupation without difficulty.

I think everyone who has actually entered the economic struggle — which means everyone who was not born to safe wealth — knows in his own experience and his own life that we have now to apply the earlier concepts of American government to the conditions of today.

The Declaration of Independence discusses the problem of government in terms of a contract. Government is a relation of give and take — a contract, perforce, if we would follow the thinking out of which it grew. Under such a contract rulers were accorded power, and the people consented to that power on consideration that they be accorded certain rights. The task of statesmanship has always been the re-definition of these rights in terms of a changing and growing social order. New conditions impose new requirements upon government and those who conduct government.

I held, for example, in proceedings before me as Governor, the purpose of which was the removal of the Sheriff of New York, that under modern conditions it was not enough for a public official merely to evade the legal terms of official wrongdoing. He owed a positive duty as well. I said, in substance, that if he had acquired large sums of money, he was, when accused, required to explain the sources of such wealth. To that extent this wealth was colored with a public interest. I said that public servants should, even beyond private citizens, in financial matters be held to a stern and uncompromising rectitude.

I feel that we are coming to a view, through the drift of our legislation and our public thinking in the past quarter century, that private economic power is, to enlarge an old phrase, a public trust as well. I hold that continued enjoyment of that power by any individual or group must depend upon the fulfillment of that trust. The men who have reached the summit of American business life know this best; happily, many of these urge the binding quality of this greater social contract.

The terms of that contract are as old as the Republic, and as new as the new economic order.

Every man has a right to life; and this means that he has also a right to make a comfortable living. He may by sloth or crime decline to exercise that right, but it may not be denied him. We have no actual famine or dearth; our industrial and agricultural mechanism can produce enough and to spare. Our government, formal and informal, political and economic, owes to everyone an avenue to possess himself of a portion of that plenty sufficient for his needs, through his own work.

Every man has a right to his own property; which means a right to be assured to the fullest extent attainable, in the safety of his savings. By no other means can men carry the burdens of those parts of life which in the nature of things afford no chance of labor — childhood, sickness, old age.

In all thought of property, this right is paramount; all other property rights must yield to it.

If, in accord with this principle, we must restrict the operations of the speculator, the manipulator, even the financier, I believe we must accept the restriction as needful not to hamper individualism but to protect it.

These two requirements must be satisfied, in the main, by the individuals who claim and hold control of the great industrial and financial combinations which dominate so large a part of our industrial life. They have undertaken to be not business men but princes — princes of property. I am not prepared to say that the system which produces them is wrong. I am very clear that they must fearlessly and competently assume the responsibility which goes with the power. So many enlightened business men know this that the statement would be little more than a platitude were it not for an added implication.

This implication is, briefly, that the responsible heads of finance and industry, instead of acting each for himself, must work together to achieve the common end.

They must, where necessary, sacrifice this or that private advantage, and in reciprocal self-denial must seek a general advantage. It is here that formal government — political government, if you choose — comes in.

Whenever in the pursuit of this objective the lone wolf, the unethical competitor, the reckless promoter, the Ishmael or Insull, whose hand is against every man's, declines to join in achieving an end recognized as being for the public welfare, and threatens to drag the industry back to a state of anarchy, the government may properly be asked to apply restraint.

Likewise, should the group ever use its collective power contrary to the public welfare, the government must be swift to enter and protect the public interest.

The government should assume the function of economic regulation only as a last resort, to be tried only when private initiative, inspired by high responsibility, with such assistance and balance as government can give, has finally failed. As yet there has been no final failure, because there has been no attempt; and I decline to assume that this nation is unable to meet the situation.

The final term of the high contract was for liberty and the pursuit of happiness.

We have learned a great deal of both in the past century. We know that individual liberty and individual happiness mean nothing unless both are ordered in the sense that one man's meat is not another man's poison.

We know that the old "rights of personal competency" — the right to read, to think, to speak, to choose and live a mode of life — must be respected at all hazards.

We know that liberty to do anything which deprives others of those elemental rights is outside the protection of any compact, and that government in this regard is the maintenance of a balance, within which every individual may have a place if he will take it; in which every individual may find safety if he wishes it; in which every individual may attain such power as his ability permits, consistent with his assuming the accompanying responsibility.

All this is a long, slow task. Nothing is more striking than the simple innocence of the men who insist, whenever an objective is present, on the prompt production of a patent scheme guaranteed to produce a result.

Human endeavor is not so simple as that. Government includes the art of formulating a policy, and using the political technique to attain so much of that policy as will receive general support; persuading, leading, sacrificing, teaching always, because the greatest duty of a statesman is to educate.

But in the matters of which I have spoken we are learning rapidly in a severe school. The lessons so learned must not be forgotten even in the mental lethargy of a speculative upturn.

We must build toward the time when a major depression cannot occur again; and if this means sacrificing the easy profits of inflationist booms, then let them go; and good riddance.

Faith in America, faith in our tradition of personal responsibility, faith in our institutions, faith in ourselves demands that we recognize the new terms of the old social contract.

We shall fulfill them, as we fulfilled the obligation of the apparent Utopia which Jefferson imagined for us in 1776, and which Jefferson, Roosevelt and Wilson sought to bring to realization.

We must do so, lest a rising tide of misery, engendered by our common failure, engulf us all.

But failure is not an American habit; and in the strength of great hope we must all shoulder our common load.

First Inaugural Address

Franklin D. Roosevelt

Commentary

Aided by Hoover's lackluster campaign rhetoric and the economic depression, Roosevelt won the presidential election of 1932 by an overwhelming electoral vote of 472-59. On March 4, 1933, he delivered his inaugural address, both the context and purpose of which were unusual. From the standpoint of later generations, the context was unusual because Roosevelt's inauguration was the last to be held in March, a subsequent constitutional amendment having changed the date to January. From the standpoint of his immediate audience, the context was unusual because the three-year-old depression was bringing the economy to near collapse.

Roosevelt had not yet devised a detailed plan for combatting the depression, but he knew that the most important purpose of his address was to raise public morale. Achieving this objective was not easy in view of the depth of despair that prevailed, and the task was complicated by his second rhetorical purpose: to persuade the audience that a strong president was needed. Many (perhaps most) of today's readers take it for granted that a "strong president" is desirable, but Roosevelt's audience had conflicting views. Two recent executives, Theodore Roosevelt and Woodrow Wilson, had been "strong presidents," but both had been criticized bitterly for intruding into what had traditionally been regarded as Congressional prerogatives and responsibilities.

It was with these two difficult rhetorical objectives in mind that the address was prepared. For many years, it was generally believed that Roosevelt himself wrote the speech, but recent research shows clearly that it was largely the work of his speech writer, Raymond Moley. Irrespective of its authorship, the address was Roosevelt's. He delivered it not only to the unusually large audience that crowded into Washington, but also to the general public via radio and newspapers.

The newspaper text, like most such texts, was simply a reproduction of the press release that was given to reporters shortly before the speech was presented. It is not significantly different from the one that Roosevelt actually delivered, but there are some stylistic variations. Inasmuch as many more people heard the speech (either in Washington or via radio) than read it, the oral text is reproduced below. It was prepared by Halford Ross Ryan and first appeared in print in the third edition of his *Contemporary American Public Discourse* (Waveland Press, 1992), pp. 13-17.

First Inaugural Address

President Hoover, Mr. Chief Justice, my friends. This is a day of national consecration, and I am certain that on this day my fellow Americans expect that on my induction into the Presidency I will address them with a candor and a decision which the present situation of our· people impels. This is preeminently the time to speak the truth, the whole truth, frankly and boldly. Nor need we shrink from honestly facing conditions in our country today. This great nation will endure as it has endured, will revive, and will prosper. So, first of all, let me assert my firm belief that the only thing we have to fear is fear itself — nameless, unreasoning, unjustified terror which paralyzes needed efforts to convert retreat into advance.

In every dark hour of our national life, a leadership of frankness and of vigor has met with that understanding and support of the people themselves which is essential to victory. And I am convinced that you will again give that support to leadership in these critical days.

In such a spirit on my part and on yours we face our common difficulties. They concern, thank God, only material things. Values have shrunk to fantastic levels, taxes have risen, our ability to pay has fallen, government of all kinds is faced by serious curtailment of income, the means of exchange are frozen in the currents of trade, the withered leaves of industrial enterprise lie on every side, farmers find no markets for their produce, and the savings of many years in thousands of families are gone. More important, a host of unemployed citizens face the grim problem of existence, and an equally great number toil with little return. Only a foolish optimist can deny the dark realities of the moment.

And yet our distress comes from no failure of substance. We are stricken by no plague of locusts. Compared with the perils which our forefathers conquered, because they believed and were not afraid, we have still much to be thankful for. Nature still offers her bounty, and human efforts have multiplied it. Plenty is at our doorstep, but a generous use of it languishes in the very sight of the supply. Primarily, this is because the rulers of the exchange of mankind's goods have failed through their own stubbornness and their own incompetence, have admitted their failure, and have abdicated. Practices of the unscrupulous money-changers stand indicted in the court of public opinion, rejected by the hearts and minds of men.

True, they have tried, but their efforts have been cast in the pattern of an outworn tradition. Faced by failure of credit, they have proposed only the lending of more money. Stripped of the lure of profit by which to induce our people to follow their false leadership, they have resorted to exhortations, pleading tearfully for restored confidence. They only know the rules of a generation of self-seekers. They have no vision, and when there is no vision the people perish.

Yes, the money-changers have fled from their high seats in the temple of our civilization. We may now restore that temple to the ancient truths [applause]. The measure of that restoration lies in the extent to which we apply social values more noble than mere monetary profit. Happiness lies not in the mere possession of money; it lies in the joy of achievement, in the thrill of creative effort. The joy, the moral stimulation, of work no longer must be forgotten in the mad chase of evanescent profits. These dark days, my friends, will be worth all they cost us if they teach us that our true destiny is not to be ministered unto but to minister to ourselves, to our fellowmen [applause].

Recognition of that falsity of material wealth as the standard of success goes hand in hand with the abandonment of the false belief that public office and high political position are to be valued only by the standards of pride of place and personal profit. And there must be an end to conduct in banking and in business which too often has given to a sacred trust the likeness of callous and selfish wrongdoing [applause]. Small wonder that confidence languishes, for it thrives only on honesty, on honor, on the sacredness of obligations, on faithful protection, and on unselfish performance. Without them, it cannot live.

Restoration calls, however, not for changes in ethics alone. This nation is asking for action, and action now [applause].

Our greatest primary task is to put people to work [applause]. This is no unsolvable problem if we face it wisely and courageously. It can be accomplished in part by direct recruiting by the government itself, treating the task as we would treat the emergency of a war but at the same time, through this employment, accomplishing great—greatly needed projects to stimulate and reorganize the use of our great natural resources.

Hand in hand with that we must frankly recognize the overbalance of population in our industrial centers and by engaging on a national scale in a redistribution endeavor to provide a better use of the land for those best fitted for the land [applause]. Yes, the task can be helped by definite efforts to raise the values of agricultural products and with this the power to purchase the output of our cities. It can be helped by preventing realistically the tragedy of the growing loss through forecl—foreclosure of our small homes and our farms. It can be helped by insistence that the Federal, the state, and the local government act forthwith on the demand that their cost be drastically reduced [applause]. It can be helped by the unifying of relief activities which today are often scattered, uneconomical, unequal. It can be helped by national planning for and supervision of all forms of transportation and of communications and other utilities that have a definitely public character. There are many ways in which it can be helped, but it can never be helped by merely talking about it [applause].

We must act, and we must act quickly.

And finally, in our progress towards a resumption of work we require two safeguards against a return of the evils of the old order. There must be a strict supervision of all banking and credits and investments [applause]. There must be an end to speculation with other people's money [applause]. And there must be provision for an adequate but sound currency [applause].

These, my friends, are the lines of attack. I shall presently urge upon a new Congress, in special session, detailed measures for their fulfillment, and I shall seek the immediate assistance of the forty-eight states.

Through this program of action we address ourselves to putting our own national house in order and making income balance outgo. Our international trade relations, though vastly important, are in point of time and necessity secondary to the establishment of a sound national economy [applause]. I favor as a practical policy the putting of first things first. I shall spare no effort to restore world trade by international economic readjustment, but the emergency at home cannot wait on that accomplishment. The basic thought that guides these specific means of national recovery is not nationally — narrowly nationalistic. It is the insistence, as a first consideration, upon the interdependence of the various elements in and parts of the United States of America, a recognition of the old and permanently important manifestation of the American spirit of the pioneer. It is the way to recovery. It is the immediate way. It is the strongest assurance that recovery will endure.

In the field of world policy I would dedicate this nation to the policy of the "good neighbor" — the neighbor who resolutely respects himself and, because he does so, respects the rights of others — the neighbor who respects his obligations and respects the sanctity of his agreements in and with a world of neighbors [applause].

If I read the temper of our people correctly, we now realize as we have never realized before our interdependence on each other, that we cannot merely take but we must give as well, that if we are to go forward, we must move as a trained and loyal army, willing to sacrifice for the good of a common discipline, because without such discipline no progress can be made, no leadership becomes effective. We are, I know, ready and willing to submit our lives and our property to such discipline because it makes possible a leadership which aims at the larger good. This I propose to offer, pledging that the larger purposes will bind upon us, bind upon us all as a sacred obligation, with a unity of duty hitherto evoked only in times of armed strife.

With this pledge taken, I assume unhesitatingly the leadership of this great army of our people dedicated to a disciplined attack upon our common problems.

Action in this image, action to this end, is feasible under the form of government which we have inherited from our ancestors. Our constitution is so simple, so practical, that it is possible always to meet extraordinary needs by changes in emphasis and arrangement without loss of essential form. That is why our constitutional system has proved itself the most superbly enduring political mechanism the modern world has ever seen. It has met every stress of vast expansion of territory, of foreign wars, of bitter internal strife, of world relations. And it is to be hoped that the normal balance of executive and legislative authority may be wholly equal, wholly adequate, to meet the unprecedented task before us. But it may be that an unprecedented demand and need for undelayed action may call for temporary departure from that normal balance of public procedure. I am prepared under my constitutional duty to recommend the measures that a stricken nation in the midst of a stricken world may require. These measures, or such other measures as the Congress may build out of its experience and wisdom, I shall seek within my constitutional authority to bring to speedy adoption. But in the event that the Congress shall fail to take one of these two courses, in the event that the national emergency is still critical, I shall not evade the clear course of duty that will then confront me. I shall ask the Congress for the one remaining instrument to meet the crisis: broad executive power to wage a war against the emergency, as great as the power that would be given to me if we were in fact invaded by a foreign foe [applause].

For the trust reposed in me I return the courage and the devotion that befit the time. I can do no less.

We face the arduous days that lie before us in the warm courage of national unity, with the clear consciousness of seeking old and precious moral values, with the clean satisfaction that comes from the stern performance of duty by old and young alike. We aim at the assurance of a rounded, a permanent national life. We do not distrust the essen—the future of essential democracy. The people of the United States have not failed. In their need they have registered a mandate that they want direct, vigorous action. They have asked for discipline and direction under leadership. They have made me the present instrument of their wishes. In the spirit of the gift, I take it.

In this dedication [applause], in this dedication of a nation, we humbly ask the blessing of God. May he protect each and every one of us. May he guide me in the days to come.

The Arsenal of Democracy

Franklin D. Roosevelt

Commentary

The Great Depression increased the persuasiveness of Roosevelt's New Deal rhetoric, but memories of the Great War hindered his persuasiveness on behalf of what his supporters called "internationalism" and critics called "interventionism." During the 1920s and 1930s, many factors encouraged Americans to return to their traditional belief in isolationism. With the single exception of Finland, European countries defaulted on their war debts to the United States. Schools began teaching a "revisionist" history, which claimed that the Allies and Germany were equally guilty of starting the war, and scholarly studies of war propaganda reinforced the prevalent belief that we had been dragged into the war by slick British propagandists and munitions makers. After *Fortune* magazine published an exposé of war profiteering in March, 1934, the Senate authorized an investigation which concluded that munitions makers were "merchants of death." Meanwhile, a plethora of antiwar rhetoric, such as the novel *All Quiet on the Western Front*, depicted the horrors of war. As late as 1937, an opinion poll reported that seventy-one percent of the public answered "yes" to the question "Do you think it was a mistake for the United States to enter the World War?" If another war erupted, Americans were determined to avoid their earlier mistake.

The determination was so strong that the first Neutrality Act (August 24, 1935) was passed with virtually no debate. It empowered the president to declare "such fact" when a foreign war erupted, whereupon the manufacture and sale of munitions would be placed under a National Munitions Control Board and their sale to belligerents prohibited. The president was also empowered to proclaim that American citizens who travelled on ships belonging to belligerents did so at their own risk. Although privately unhappy with the legislation, Roosevelt publicly endorsed it. He invoked it in 1935 in regard to the Italian-Ethiopian war and again in 1936 after the start of the Spanish Civil War. In 1937, however, Roosevelt refused to invoke the act after Japan invaded China. On October 5, when dedicating a bridge in Chicago, he gave his now-famous "Quarantine" speech. Using a figurative analogy,

Roosevelt said that "an epidemic of world lawlessness is spreading" and that law-abiding nations should cooperate to "quarantine" the "disease." The meaning of "quarantine" was left ambiguous, but the speech set the stage for an increasingly bitter debate about foreign policy.

The first round of the debate erupted at the end of the year. On December 12, 1937, Japanese aircraft attacked an American gunboat accompanying three merchant ships in China, and two of the ships were sunk. Fearful that the incident might lead to war, Congressman Ludlow of Indiana promptly introduced a constitutional amendment which provided that, except in case of actual invasion, Congress could not declare war until after a national referendum. Roosevelt's opposition caused the House to defeat the proposal, but only by the narrow margin of 209-188. His major argument — that the proposal would encourage aggressors to attack Americans and thereby increase the risk of war — indicates his awareness of American determination to stay out of war.

Attention soon shifted to Germany, where Hitler's rise to power in 1933 was followed by a series of events which most Americans deplored: the establishment of a dictatorship, violations of the peace treaty (including the enlargement of the army and the fortification of the French border), proclamations of German racial superiority, and the persecution of Jews and Gypsies. By 1938, Germany began expanding. In March, Austria was annexed. In September, Germany, Italy, Britain and France signed the famous Munich Agreement, which permitted Germany to annex the Sudetenland, a strip of Czechoslovakian land along the German border. These actions created a more favorable climate for Roosevelt's state of the Union address of January 4, 1939, in which he warned of "threats of aggression," called for increased military appropriations and said that the Neutrality Act might help aggressors more than those being attacked. He was laying the rhetorical foundation for interventionism if war erupted.

War soon came. Encouraged by the failure of France and Britain to resist his "peaceful" conquest of Czechoslovakia (March, 1939), Hitler signed a nonaggression pact with the Soviets (August 23, 1939). On September 1, the "nonaggressors" invaded Poland, and, two days later, France and Britain declared war on Germany. World War II had begun.

Although most Americans were pro-Ally, they generally wished to remain neutral. This ambivalence was reflected in a subsequent debate. In a "Fireside Chat" on September 3, Roosevelt invoked the Neutrality Act but added that "Even a neutral cannot be asked to close his mind or his conscience." Addressing a special session of Congress, he stated that he wished he had not signed the Neutrality Act. As Congress debated the act, proponents of repeal argued that we should help the Allies while opponents argued for strict neutrality. The result was a legislative compromise — an amended Neutrality Act which prohibited American ships from entering "danger zones" but allowed war material to be sold to belligerents on a cash-and-carry basis.

In mid-1940, the European military situation was dramatically altered

and so, too, was the subsequent American rhetoric. Germany conquered
Denmark and Norway. It stormed through the Low Countries on the way to
Paris, while Italy invaded France from the south. Britain withdrew its army
from the European continent, and, on June 22, France surrendered. Britain
now stood alone as Germany launched one airstrike after another.
Meanwhile, in June, 1940, a Committee to Defend America by Aiding the
Allies was formed. In words that sounded suspiciously like the hysterical
rhetoric of the War to End All Wars, its speakers denounced "isolationists" as
a pro-German "fifth column" that was deceiving Americans and preparing
the way for a Nazi takeover. In September, a counterorganization, called the
America First Committee, was formed. Matching its opponents' *ad hominem*
rhetoric, its popular spokesman, Charles Lindberg (a folk hero since flying
nonstop across the Atlantic in 1926), warned that "powerful elements" were
using slick propaganda to deceive Americans and draw us into a war that was
of no concern to us.

Meanwhile, Roosevelt was nominated for an unprecedented third term. He
declared publicly that he would stay out of the actual campaign. He did not
mention his secret negotiations to lend Britain fifty destroyers in return for
the leasing of British bases in America, as Britain's defense was deemed vital
to the defense of the United States. The deal was not announced until
September 3, 1940, after negotiations were complete. Opponents charged
that the deal violated the Neutrality Act. Supporters relied on two old, nearly
forgotten, laws which empowered the president "to dispose of vessels of the
Navy and unneeded naval material" and argued that the Neutrality Act had
not been violated because the ships had not been built specifically for
belligerents. The refutation seemed weak even to many of Roosevelt's
supporters. The incident came into greater focus when the third-term
tradition was being broken, and it helped to fuel charges that Roosevelt was
seeking to make himself a dictator.

Nervous about the persuasive potential of his opponents' rhetoric,
Roosevelt forgot his promise not to campaign. His speech on October 30,
1940 was characterized by two important rhetorical tactics. First, Roosevelt
equated isolationists with those who had obstructed his domestic policies,
thereby capitalizing on the popularity of his domestic program. He, thus,
obscured some relevant facts: his Republican opponent was an
internationalist and many noninterventionists were old progressives who
supported the New Deal. Second, he reassured American mothers and fathers
with a promise that those who dislike Roosevelt still love to quote: "I have said
this before, but I shall say it again and again and again: Your boys are not
going to be sent into any foreign war."

Safely reelected (though by a somewhat narrower margin than previously;
namely, 26,800,000 to 22,304,000), Roosevelt asked Congress in mid-
December for approval to extend the lend-lease program. As a storm of
debate erupted, Roosevelt tried to build public pressure on Congress by
delivering a radio address on the evening of December 29, 1940. It is
reproduced from Ernest J. Wrage and Barnet Baskerville, *Contemporary*

Forum: American Speeches on Twentieth-Century Issues (1962; rpt. Seattle: University of Washington Press, 1969), pp. 246-254.

The Arsenal of Democracy

My friends: This is not a fireside chat on war. It is a talk on national security; because the nub of the whole purpose of your President is to keep you now, and your children later, and your grandchildren much later, out of a last-ditch war for the preservation of American independence and all of the things that American independence means to you and to me and to ours.

Tonight, in the presence of a world crisis, my mind goes back eight years to a night in the midst of a domestic crisis. It was a time when the wheels of American industry were grinding to a full stop, when the whole banking system of our country had ceased to function.

I well remember that while I sat in my study in the White House, pre-paring to talk with the people of the United States, I had before my eyes the picture of all those Americans with whom I was talking. I saw the workmen in the mills, the mines, the factories; the girl behind the counter; the small shopkeeper; the farmer doing his Spring plowing; the widows and the old men wondering about their life's savings.

I tried to convey to the great mass of American people what the banking crisis meant to them in their daily lives.

Tonight I want to do the same thing, with the same people, in this new crisis which faces America.

We met the issue of 1933 with courage and realism. We face this new crisis — this new threat to the security of our nation — with the same courage and realism.

Never before since Jamestown and Plymouth Rock has our American civilization been in such danger as now.

For on September 27, 1940 — this year — by an agreement signed in Berlin, three powerful nations, two in Europe and one in Asia, joined themselves together in the threat that if the United States of America interfered with or blocked the expansion program of these three nations — a program aimed at world control — they would unite in ultimate action against the United States.

The Nazi masters of Germany have made it clear that they intend not only to dominate all life and thought in their own country, but also to enslave the whole of Europe, and then to use the resources of Europe to dominate the rest of the world.

It was only three weeks ago that their leader stated this: "There are two worlds that stand opposed to each other." And then in defiant reply to his opponents he said this: "Others are correct when they say: 'With this world we cannot ever reconcile ourselves.'... I can beat any other power in the world." So said the leader of the Nazis.

In other words, the Axis not merely admits but the Axis proclaims that there can be no ultimate peace between their philosophy — their philosophy of government — and our philosophy of government.

In view of the nature of this undeniable threat, it can be asserted, properly and categoricaily, that the United States has no right or reason to encourage talk of peace until the day shall come when there is a clear intention on the part of the aggressor nations to abandon all thought of dominating or conquering the world.

At this moment the forces of the States that are leagued against all peoples who live in freedom are being held away from our shores. The Germans and the Italians are being blocked on the other side of the Atlantic by the British and by the Greeks, and by thousands of soldiers and sailors who were able to escape from subjugated countries. In Asia the Japanese are being engaged by the Chinese nation in another great defense.

In the Pacific Ocean is our fleet.

Some of our people like to believe that wars in Europe and in Asia are of no concern to us. But it is a matter of most vital concern to us that European and Asiatic war-makers should not gain control of the oceans which lead to this hemisphere.

One hundred and seventeen years ago the Monroe Doctrine was conceived by our government as a measure of defense in the face of a threat against this hemisphere by an alliance in Continental Europe. Thereafter, we stood guard in the Atlantic, with the British as neighbors. There was no treaty. There was no "unwritten agreement."

And yet there was the feeling, proven correct by history, that we as neighbors could settle any disputes in peaceful fashion. And the fact is that during the whole of this time the Western Hemisphere has remained free from aggression from Europe or from Asia.

Does any one seriously believe that we need to fear attack anywhere in the Americas while a free Britain remains our most powerful naval neighbor in the Atlantic? And does any one seriously believe, on the other hand, that we could rest easy if the Axis powers were our neighbors there?

If Great Britain goes down, the Axis powers will control the Continents of Europe, Asia, Africa, Australasia, and the high seas — and they will be in a position to bring enormous military and naval resources against this hemisphere. It is no exaggeration to say that all of us in all the Americas would be living at the point of a gun — a gun loaded with explosive bullets, economic as well as military.

We should enter upon a new and terrible era in which the whole world, our hemisphere included, would be run by threats of brute force. And to survive in such a world, we would have to convert ourselves permanently into a militaristic power on the basis of war economy.

Some of us like to believe that even if Britain falls, we are still safe, because of the broad expanse of the Atlantic and of the Pacific.

But the width of those oceans is not what it was in the days of clipper ships. At one point between Africa and Brazil the distance is less than it is from Washington to Denver, Colorado, five hours for the latest type of bomber.

And at the north end of the Pacific Ocean, America and Asia almost touch each other.

Why, even today we have planes that could fly from the British Isles to New England and back again without refueling. And remember that the range of the modern bomber is ever being increased.

During the past week many people in all parts of the nation have told me what they wanted me to say tonight. Almost all of them expressed a courageous desire to hear the plain truth about the gravity of the situation. One telegram, however, expressed the attitude of the small minority who want to see no evil and hear no evil, even though they know in their hearts that evil exists. That telegram begged me not to tell again of the ease with which our American cities could be bombed by any hostile power which had gained bases in this Western Hemisphere. The gist of that telegram was: "Please, Mr. President, don't frighten us by telling us the facts."

Frankly and definitely there is danger ahead — danger against which we must prepare. But we well know that we cannot escape danger, or the fear of danger, by crawling into bed and pulling the covers over our heads.

Some nations of Europe were bound by solemn nonintervention pacts with Germany. Other nations were assured by Germany that they need never fear invasion. Nonintervention pact or not, the fact remains that they were attacked, overrun, thrown into modern slavery at an hour's notice or even without any notice at all.

As an exiled leader of one of these nations said to me the other day, "the notice was a minus quantity. It was given to my government two hours after German troops had poured into my country in a hundred places." The fate of these nations tells us what it means to live at the point of a Nazi gun.

The Nazis have justified such actions by various pious frauds. One of these frauds is the claim that they are occupying a nation for the purpose of "restoring order." Another is that they are occupying or controlling a nation on the excuse that they are "protecting it" against the aggression of somebody else.

For example, Germany has said that she was occupying Belgium to save the Belgians from the British. Would she then hesitate to say to any South American country: "We are occupying you to protect you from aggression by the United States"?

Belgium today is being used as an invasion base against Britain, now fighting for its life. And any South American country, in Nazi hands, would always constitute a jumping off place for German attack on any one of the other republics of this hemisphere.

Analyze for yourselves the future of two other places even nearer to Germany if the Nazis won. Could Ireland hold out? Would Irish freedom be permitted as an amazing pet exception in an unfree world? Or the islands of the Azores, which still fly the flag of Portugal after five centuries? You and I think of Hawaii as an outpost of defense in the Pacific. And yet the Azores are closer to our shores in the Atlantic than Hawaii is on the other side.

There are those who say that the Axis powers would never have any desire to attack the Western Hemisphere. That is the same dangerous form of wishful thinking which has destroyed the powers of resistance of so many conquered peoples. The plain facts are that the Nazis have proclaimed, time and again, that all other races are their inferiors and therefore subject to their orders. And most important of all, the vast resources and wealth of this American hemisphere constitute the most tempting loot in all of the round world.

Let us no longer blind ourselves to the undeniable fact that the evil forces which have crushed and undermined and corrupted so many others are already within our own gates. Your government knows much about them and every day is ferreting them out.

Their secret emissaries are active in our own and in neighboring countries. They seek to stir up suspicion and dissension, to cause internal strife. They try to turn capital against labor, and vice versa. They try to reawaken long slumbering racial and religious enmities which should have no place in this country. They are active in every group that promotes intolerance. They exploit for their own ends our own natural abhorrence of war.

These trouble-breeders have but one purpose. It is to divide our people, to divide them into hostile groups and to destroy our unity and shatter our will to defend ourselves.

There are also American citizens, many of them in high places, who, unwittingly in most cases, are aiding and abetting the work of these agents. I do not charge these American citizens with being foreign agents. But I do charge them with doing exactly the kind of work that the dictators want done in the United States.

These people not only believe that we can save our own skins by shutting our eyes to the fate of other nations. Some of them go much further than that. They say that we can and should become the friends and even the partners of the Axis powers. Some of them even suggest that we should imitate the methods of the dictatorships. But Americans never can and never will do that.

The experience of the past two years has proven beyond doubt that no nation can appease the Nazis. No man can tame a tiger into a kitten by stroking it. There can be no appeasement with ruthlessness. There can be no reasoning with an incendiary bomb. We know now that a nation can have peace with the Nazis only at the price of total surrender.

Even the people of Italy have been forced to become accomplices of the Nazis; but at this moment they do not know how soon they will be embraced to death by their allies.

The American appeasers ignore the warning to be found in the fate of Austria, Czechoslovakia, Poland, Norway, Belgium, the Netherlands, Denmark and France. They tell you that the Axis powers are going to win anyway; that all of this bloodshed in the world could be saved, that the United States might just as well throw its influence into the scale of a dictated peace and get the best out of it that we can.

They call it a "negotiated peace." Nonsense! Is it a negotiated peace if a gang of outlaws surrounds your community and on threat of extermination makes you pay tribute to save your own skins?

Such a dictated peace would be no peace at all. It would be only another armistice, leading to the most gigantic armament race and the most devastating trade wars in all history. And in these contests the Americas would offer the only real resistance to the Axis powers. With all their vaunted efficiency, with all their parade of pious purpose in this war, there are still in their background the concentration camp and the servants of God in chains.

The history of recent years proves that the shootings and the chains and the concentration camps are not simply the transient tools but the very altars of modern dictatorships. They may talk of a "new order" in the world, but what they have in mind is only a revival of the oldest and worst tyranny. In that there is no liberty, no religion, no hope.

The proposed "new order" is the very opposite of a United States of Europe or a United States of Asia. It is not a government based upon the consent of the governed. It is not a union of ordinary, self-respecting men and women to protect themselves and their freedom and their dignity from oppression. It is an unholy alliance of power and pelf to dominate and to enslave the human race.

The British people and their allies today are conducting an active war against this unholy alliance. Our own future security is greatly dependent on the outcome of that fight. Our ability to "keep out of war" is going to be affected by that outcome.

Thinking in terms of today and tomorrow, I make the direct statement to the American people that there is far less chance of the United States getting into war if we do all we can now to support the nations defending themselves against attack by the Axis than if we acquiesce in their defeat, submit tamely to an Axis victory, and wait our turn to be the object of attack in another war later on.

If we are to be completely honest with ourselves, we must admit that there is risk in any course we may take. But I deeply believe that the great majority of our people agree that the course that I advocate involves the least risk now and the greatest hope for world peace in the future.

The people of Europe who are defending themselves do not ask us to do their fighting. They ask us for the implements of war, the planes, the tanks, the guns, the freighters which will enable them to fight for their liberty and for our security. Emphatically we must get these weapons to them, get them to them in sufficient volume and quickly enough so that we and our children will be saved the agony and suffering of war which others have had to endure.

Let not the defeatists tell us that it is too late. It will never be earlier. Tomorrow will be later than today.

Certain facts are self-evident.

In a military sense Great Britain and the British Empire are today the spearhead of resistance to world conquest. And they are putting up a fight which will live forever in the story of human gallantry.

There is no demand for sending an American expeditionary force outside our own borders. There is no intention by any member of your government to send such a force. You can therefore, nail, nail any talk about sending armies to Europe as deliberate untruth.

Our national policy is not directed toward war. Its sole purpose is to keep war away from our country and away from our people.

Democracy's fight against world conquest is being greatly aided, and must be more greatly aided, by the rearmament of the United States and by sending every ounce and every ton of munitions and supplies that we can possibly spare to help the defenders who are in the front lines. And it is no more unneutral for us to do that than it is for Sweden, Russia and other nations near Germany to send steel and ore and oil and other war materials into Germany every day in the week.

We are planning our own defense with the utmost urgency, and in its vast scale we must integrate the war needs of Britain and the other free nations which are resisting aggression.

This is not a matter of sentiment or of controversial personal opinion. It is a matter of realistic, practical military policy, based on the advice of our military experts who are in close touch with existing warfare. These military and naval experts and the members of the Congress and the Administration have a single-minded purpose — the defense of the United States.

This nation is making a great effort to produce everything that is necessary in this emergency — and with all possible speed. And this great effort requires great sacrifice.

I would ask no one to defend a democracy which in turn would not defend every one in the nation against want and privation. The strength of this nation shall not be diluted by the failure of the government to protect the economic well-being of its citizens.

If our capacity to produce is limited by machines, it must ever be remembered that these machines are operated by the skill and the stamina of the workers. As the government is determined to protect the rights of the workers, so the nation has a right to expect that the men who man the machines will discharge their full responsibilities to the urgent needs of defense.

The worker possesses the same human dignity and is entitled to the same security of position as the engineer or the manager or the owner. For the workers provide the human power that turns out the destroyers, and the planes and the tanks.

The nation expects our defense industries to continue operation without interruption by strikes or lockouts. It expects and insists that management and workers will reconcile their differences by voluntary or legal means, to continue to produce the supplies that are so sorely needed.

And on the economic side of our great defense program, we are, as you know, bending every effort to maintain stability of prices and with that the stability of the cost of living.

Nine days ago I announced the setting up of a more effective organization to direct our gigantic efforts to increase the production of munitions. The appropriation of vast sums of money and a well-coordinated executive direction of our defense efforts are not in themselves enough. Guns, planes, ships and many other things have to be built in the factories and the arsenals of America. They have to be produced by workers and managers and engineers with the aid of machines which in turn have to be built by hundreds of thousands of workers throughout the land.

In this great work there has been splendid cooperation between the government and industry and labor. And I am very thankful.

American industrial genius, unmatched throughout all the world in the solution of production problems, has been called upon to bring its resources and its talents into action. Manufacturers of watches, of farm implements, of linotypes and cash registers and automobiles, and sewing machines and lawn mowers and locomotives, are now making fuses and bomb packing crates and telescope mounts and shells and pistols and tanks.

But all of our present efforts are not enough. We must have more ships, more guns, more planes — more of everything. And this can be accomplished only if we discard the notion of "business as usual." This job cannot be done merely by superimposing on the existing productive facilities the added requirements of the nation for defense.

Our defense efforts must not be blocked by those who fear the future consequences of surplus plant capacity. The possible consequences of failure of our defense efforts now are much more to be feared.

And after the present needs of our defense are past, a proper handling of the country's peacetime needs will require all of the new productive capacity, if not still more.

No pessimistic policy about the future of America shall delay the immediate expansion of those industries essential to defense. We need them.

I want to make it clear that it is the purpose of the nation to build now with all possible speed every machine, every arsenal, every factory that we need to manufacture our defense material. We have the men — the skill — the wealth — and above all, the will.

I am confident that if and when production of consumer or luxury goods in certain industries requires the use of machines and raw materials that are essential for defense purposes, then such production must yield, and will gladly yield, to our primary and compelling purpose.

So I appeal to the owners of plants — to the managers — to the workers — to our own government employes — to put every ounce of effort into producing these munitions swiftly and without stint. With this appeal I give you the pledge that all of us who are officers of your government will devote ourselves to the same whole-hearted extent to the great task that lies ahead.

As planes and ships and guns and shells are produced, your government, with its defense experts, can then determine how best to use them to defend this hemisphere. The decision as to how much shall be sent abroad and how much shall remain at home must be made on the basis of our overall military necessities.

We must be the great arsenal of democracy. For us this is an emergency as serious as war itself. We must apply ourselves to our task with the same resolution, the same sense of urgency, the same spirit of patriotism and sacrifice as we would show were we at war.

We have furnished the British great material support and we will furnish far more in the future.

There will be no "bottlenecks" in our determination to aid Great Britain. No dictator, no combination of dictators, will weaken that determination by threats of how they will construe that determination.

The British have received invaluable military support from the heroic Greek Army and from the forces of all the governments in exile. Their strength is growing. It is the strength of men and women who value their freedom more highly than they value their lives.

I believe that the Axis powers are not going to win this war. I base that belief on the latest and the best of information.

We have no excuse for defeatism. We have every good reason for hope — hope for peace, yes, and hope for the defense of our civilization and for the building of a better civilization in the future.

I have the profound conviction that the American people are now determined to put forth a mightier effort than they have ever yet made to increase our production of all the implements of defense, to meet the threat to our democratic faith.

As President of the United States, I call for that national effort. I call for it in the name of this nation which we love and honor and which we are privileged and proud to serve. I call upon our people with absolute confidence that our common cause will greatly succeed.

America's Present Emergency

Burton K. Wheeler

Commentary

Leaders of the America First Committee realized that Roosevelt's popularity and rhetorical skill required a prompt response to his call for a lend-lease program. They also realized that Roosevelt's tactic of equating isolationists with anti-New Deal conservatives required a respondent whose reputation would refute the equation. None met the requirement better than Burton K. Wheeler (1882-1975), a prominent Democratic senator from Montana. After a term in Congress (1911-1913), Wheeler served as a Wilson-appointed district attorney (1913-1918) and had been an outspoken progressive senator since being elected back in 1922. He had, in fact, been such an extreme progressive that he had been LaFollette's running mate on the Progressive ticket in 1924.

A leading spokesman for the America First Committee, Wheeler responded to Roosevelt's "Arsenal" speech a day later on radio. The speech is reproduced from Ernest J. Wrage and Barnet Baskerville, *Contemporary Forum: American Speeches on Twentieth-Century Issues* (1962; rpt. Seattle: University of Washington Press, 1969), pp. 255-262.

America's Present Emergency

The views I express to you tonight are not the views of the *Star*, which has generously afforded me an opportunity to speak to you. They are not the views of any international banker, nor are they dictated by interventionists or warmongers. The thoughts I am about to express are not based upon any fear of wild boasts of American conquest by Stalin, Hitler, or Mussolini. I know that neither they nor their ideologies will capture the people of the United States or our imagination to the point that we would adopt fascism, communism, or nazi-ism as American doctrine.

You and I are Americans — and as Americans, of course, we are interested in the well-being of the people of all the world. Coming as we do from the four corners of the earth, we know that our business, our race, and our religion color our reaction to any European war. We know that today wars in Europe or Asia affect us economically, politically, and emotionally.

We sympathize with the oppressed and persecuted everywhere.

We also realize that we have great problems at home — that one-third of our population is ill-fed, ill-housed, and ill-clad — and we have been told repeatedly, upon the highest authority, that unless and until this situation is corrected, our democracy is in danger. I fully subscribe to this view.

Believing as I do in this thesis, I cannot help but feel that we should settle our own problems before we undertake to settle the problems of Asia, Africa, Australasia, South America, and Europe.

As Americans, interested first in America, what is our present stake? Our stakes are our independence, our democracy, and our trade and commerce. Every red-blooded American would fight to preserve them.

What is the best way to preserve them? There are two schools of thought. One group feels — as they felt before the last World War — that England is our first line of defense and that we must go to England's aid every time she declares war, and that some European dictator is after rich loot in the United States, perhaps our gold buried in the hills of Kentucky. This group wants to repeal our Neutrality Act and the Johnson Act. They want to loan our ships, our guns, and our planes — even though it may involve us in the European conflict. They profess to believe it is necessary for the preservation of our country, our religion, and civilization.

We were told the same things in almost the same terms before the last war.

The other group feels that we should build our defenses to meet any emergency that may arise. But we do not believe that the preservation of the American people or our democracy depends upon any foreign nation. It is hard for us to visualize a nation of 130,000,000 people so weak that we cannot defend ourselves when our forefathers in the Thirteen Original Colonies — poor, divided, and weak — were not only able to conquer an army already in our midst but to build the greatest democracy the world has ever known.

Just as I love the United States so do I dislike Hitler and all that he symbolizes. My sympathy for the British is both deep and genuine, and is exceeded only by the depth and sincerity of my Americanism. No anti-British feeling dictates my opposition to the evasion or repeal of the Johnson and Neutrality Acts. I am opposed to American convoy of British ships. I oppose all these because they lead us down that road with only one ending — total, complete, and futile war. And William Allen White, chairman of the Committee to Defend America by Aiding the Allies, agrees that the convoying of British ships by American vessels and the repeal of the Neutrality and Johnson Acts would mean war for us.

Remember, if we lease war materials today, we will lend or lease American boys tomorrow. Last night we heard the President promise that there would be no American expeditionary force, but we received no promise that our ships and sailors and our planes and pilots might not at some time within the near future be cast into the cauldron of blood and hate that is Europe today.

Our independence can only be lost or compromised if Germany invades the Western Hemisphere north of the equator. This would be fantastic, as it would require the transportation of at least 2,000,000 men, with planes, tanks, and equipment in one convoy across the Atlantic. This would require two or three thousand transports plus a fleet larger than our Navy, plus thousands of fighter-escorted bombers. Such a fleet cannot possibly be available. Certainly it cannot be trained efficiently before our 2-ocean Navy is ready. It is not possible for the German Navy to prepare an effective plan for such an invasion which our Navy and Army, with our air force, cannot defeat. Remember, Hitler has already been 7 months in vainly trying to cross 20 miles. If Hitler's army can't cross the narrow English Channel in 7 months, his bombers won't fly across the Rockies to bomb Denver tomorrow.

The only threat to our independence would be to join in some "union of free nations," so-called, in which we would be but a unit and outnumbered and outgeneraled by our good neighbors across the sea.

Democracy! We cannot hold our democracy except by prosperity and improvement in the mechanics of democracy. This will not be aided by joining the war.

The cost of this war will come out of the millions of poor people — the common folk of the world who will toil for generations to pay the cost of the destruction.

War inevitably means back-breaking debt, blighted lives, bedeviled futures. War means the end of civil liberties — the end of free speech, free press, free enterprise. It means dictatorship and slavery — all the things we abhor in nazi-ism, communism, and fascism. It means Stalin or Hitler will have achieved their boasts for a totalitarian world without conquering America.

The President in his speech last night ridiculed the idea of a peace in Europe. Conceding all that he so eloquently said about "outlaws," the "concentration camps," and the "servants of God in chains" — what about Russia and Joseph Stalin's communism? And have we not recognized Hitler and Franco? Did we not at least acquiesce in Mussolini and all his works?

If we follow the logic of Mr. Roosevelt, then we ought immediately to break off diplomatic relations with Russia, Italy, Germany, Japan, and other nations whose domestic and foreign policies we abhor.

And where do we go from there?

Regardless of when or who is proclaimed victor in the present war — it cannot last forever. Peace, fleeting though it may be, will eventually come to Europe. At some time in the future representatives of England and Germany will sit around a table — sometime they will agree upon peace — and until that day, the world suffers. Each of us, from the President of the United States to the most humble citizen, should exert his every effort for peace, now.

Removal of Hitler, even the defeat of the German armies, will not destroy that which Hitler symbolizes. Hitlerism can be destroyed and banished from

Europe only by destroying that which caused or maintains nazi-ism.

Ask yourselves who and what were responsible for the real birth and growth of Hitlerism.

Lord Lothian, until his recent death wartime Ambassador from Great Britain to the United States, said of nazi-ism — I quote him: "In great measure it was rebellion against the discriminations of the treaty of Versailles...." That wasn't some Nazi sympathizer; that was your friend, Lord Lothian, speaking.

I firmly believe the German people want peace just as any people prefer peace to war — and the offer of a just, reasonable, and generous peace will more quickly and effectively crumble Hitlerism and break the morale of the German people than all the bombers that could be dispatched over Berlin.

A just peace is difficult, if not impossible, to abstractly define while war rages. It is too completely dependent on the attitude of the belligerents.

A working basis for a just peace might involve among other factors the following:

1. Restoration of Germany's 1914 boundaries with an autonomous Poland and Czechoslovakia.
2. Restoration of independent France, Holland, Norway, Belgium, and Denmark.
3. Restoration of Alsace-Lorraine to France.
4. Restoration of German colonies.
5. Protection of all racial and religious minorities in all countries.
6. Internationalization of the Suez Canal.
7. No indemnities or reparations.
8. Arms limitation.

The United States is no longer trudging along the road to war. We are running. Some feel that we have gone so fast and so far that there can be no stopping — no return to complete peace except via war. But we are at peace and we can remain at peace if either one of two lines of action is pursued. First, Americans in greater number must firmly resolve and express themselves, that we will fight no offensive war. And, secondly, we can remain at peace if the horrible European debacle of death and destruction ends in the near future.

Though today we stand as close to the brink of war as we stood in January of 1917, some people still oppose a European peace. Warmongers, sordid romanticists, reckless adventurers, and some whose sympathies and sentiments are stronger than their reasoning powers would plunge this Nation into war; plunge us into a war from which we could gain nothing; plunge us into a war that would destroy democracy — that would bring deep, harrowing anguish to millions of hearts. And how would they bring this to pass? They would take us in today as they did in 1917.

The right Honorable Sir Gilbert Parker, writing for *Harper's Magazine* of March 1918, said of American entry into the last war:

Practically since the day war broke out between England and the Central Powers, I became responsible for American publicity.... We established connection with the man in the street through cinema pictures of the Army and Navy, as well as through interview, articles, pamphlets, etc.... We had reports from important Americans constantly, and established association, by personal correspondence, with influential and eminent people of every profession in the United States, beginning with university and college presidents, professors, and scientific men, and running through all the ranges of the population.

We had our documents and literature sent to great numbers of public libraries, Y.M.C.A. societies, universities, colleges, historical societies, clubs, and newspapers. It is hardly necessary to say that the work was one of extreme difficulty and delicacy.

Do Sir Gilbert's words in any way explain the warmongering telegram to the President urging greater aid to Britain? Has British propaganda again reached the college and university professors? Twenty-nine educators signed the highly publicized wire that urged steps that would take the United States into war on the side of Britain.

And have you and I, "the man on the street," felt the insidious force of war propaganda through the movies?

Is there another Sir Gilbert Parker in the United States? Perhaps not, but there are a lot of foreign slackers — European royalty, princes and potentates, and their idolaters — who, instead of being wined and dined in high places in Washington and urging us to go to war, ought to be home fighting the battles for liberty and Christianity they so glibly tell us about. Poor things! As usual, they were forced to leave their country while their subjects had to remain to do the fighting.

My friends, it is this satanically clever propaganda that appeals to the Christianity, the idealism, the humanity, and the loyalty of the American people that takes us to war. It is this that we must resist. It is this that we must cast aside if we truly love our country and democracy. We must remain at peace and dedicate ourselves to effecting peace for a war-torn world.

We have reached a strange situation in America when those who advocate peace — who do not follow the party line — are branded appeasers or unwitting tools of the dictators. This still is a democracy, and American citizens whose beliefs vary from those of the Government ought not to be howled down or intimidated by threats of the F.B.I. Free speech still belongs to all the people, not to just a few at the top.

I do not believe that the great majority of our people are eager to be embraced by war — and I call upon them not to be afraid to say so. I, for one, believe the policy advocated by the interventionists is insane because it will lead to total war, and war is insanity.

I say so now and I intend to continue to say so, even if at the end I stand alone.

Americans! Do not let yourselves be swayed by mass hysteria. Do not travel again the road that you took in 1917. You hanged Bob La Follette in effigy because he opposed war, and lived to repent your action and put him in the Hall of Fame. Fifteen years after that war, when the secret treaties were exposed, you realized that you had been duped. Has history suddenly changed?

Are the facts of yesterday no longer facts? Has this war a sweeter odor than the last? Don't let yourselves be misled by the so-called notables. Numerically they are few — a few hundred — even though they command the newspaper headlines. But they do not speak for the mass of Americans. They do not represent labor, the farmer, the youth, the mothers or the fathers of America. The great mass of our people are inarticulate, but it is time you were heard. You must not be driven like sheep to the slaughtering pens.

There is a war that I call upon you to enter — a noble war which the royalty of Europe and our Tory friends at home are unwilling to face — a war to end economic inequality and poverty and disease in this, the richest land in the world.

America's war ought to be a war against industrial unemployment and low farm prices.

Whether the stroke of 12 will usher in a really happy new year tomorrow night depends upon you — and upon your sincere loyalty to Christian ideals. "Peace on earth to men of good will" is a sacred cause for which we should pray and work. Let your Representatives in Washington know that you have not surrendered the independence of America to warmongers and interventionists — and God will bless America.

War Message

Franklin D. Roosevelt

Commentary

America's entry into World War II was marked by irony. Except for some momentary flurries of public excitement after the gunboat incident in 1937 and Japan's joining the Axis alliance in 1940, Asian affairs went virtually unnoticed while Americans debated European policy. During 1938-1941, few Americans knew about diplomatic protests regarding Japanese treatment of American property and citizens in occupied China, Roosevelt's efforts to persuade American bankers not to loan money to Japan, or Japan's insistence that it be given a free hand in establishing a "New Order" in Asia and that America cease selling war material to China. As early as January, 1941, the American ambassador in Tokyo warned Roosevelt that Japan might launch a surprise attack, and several officials privately predicted war. These facts were unknown to journalists, let alone the public. The press was not aware of Roosevelt's concern over the Japanese occupation of French Indochina. It paid little attention to the diplomatic negotiations which proceeded sporadically during 1941. The subject was not even brought up at a presidential press conference until a few days before the Japanese attack on Pearl Harbor. Even then, the subject was treated lightly. Oblivious to the gathering storm, Americans were stunned when they heard radio announcements on the morning of December 7, 1941 that Pearl Harbor had been attacked.

Roosevelt was not the first president to deliver a war message, but he faced a unique rhetorical situation when he addressed Congress on December 8. Because his war message was broadcast via radio, it was the first one which the American public heard. Perhaps more important, his audience was in a greater state of shock than previous audiences had been. The war was unexpected, American territory had been attacked directly, a terrible defeat had occurred and rumors were spreading like wildfire. Some rumors were true (Japan was invading the Philippines) and some false (Japan was attacking California). All of them heightened fear and uncertainty.

The uniqueness of the rhetorical situation absolved Roosevelt of certain rhetorical requirements while intensifying others. Unlike his predecessors, he did not have to justify a declaration of war with a long argumentative discourse. On the other hand, he had to do more than his predecessors in clarifying the situation and arousing optimism. His speech is reproduced photographically from Halford Ross Ryan, *American Rhetoric from Roosevelt to Reagan,* Second Edition (Prospect Heights, Illinois: Waveland Press, 1987), pp. 24-25.

War Message

Yesterday, December 7, 1941 — a date which will live in infamy — the United States of America was suddenly and deliberately attacked by naval and air forces of the Empire of Japan.

The United States was at peace with that nation and, at the solicitation of Japan, was still in conversation with its Government and its Emperor looking toward the maintenance of peace in the Pacific.

Indeed, one hour after Japanese air squadrons had commenced bombing Oahu, the Japanese Ambassador to the United States and his colleague delivered to the Secretary of State a formal reply to a recent American message. While this reply stated that it seemed useless to continue the existing diplomatic negotiations, it contained no threat or hint of war or armed attack.

It will be recorded that the distance of Hawaii from Japan makes it obvious that the attack was deliberately planned many days or even weeks ago. During the intervening time, the Japanese Government has deliberately sought to deceive the United States by false statements and expressions of hope for continued peace.

The attack yesterday on the Hawaiian Islands has caused severe damage to American naval and military forces. Very many American lives have been lost. In addition, American ships have been reported torpedoed on the high seas between San Francisco and Honolulu.

Yesterday the Japanese Government also launched an attack against Malaya.

Last night Japanese forces attacked Hongkong.

Last night Japanese forces attacked Guam.

Last night Japanese forces attacked the Philippine Islands.

Last night the Japanese attacked Wake Island.

This morning the Japanese attacked Midway Island.

Japan has, therefore, undertaken a surprise offensive extending through-out the Pacific area. The facts of yesterday speak for themselves. The people of the United States have already formed their opinions and well understand the implications to the very life and safety of our nation.

As Commander in Chief of the army and navy I have directed that all measures be taken for our defense.

Always will we remember the character of the onslaught against us.

No matter how long it may take us to overcome this premeditated invasion, the American people in their righteous might will win through to absolute victory.

I believe I interpret the will of the Congress and of the people when I assert that we will not only defend ourselves to the uttermost but will make very certain that this form of treachery shall never endanger us again.

Hostilities exist. There is no blinking at the fact that our people, our territory and our interests are in grave danger.

With confidence in our armed forces — with the unbounding determination of our people — we will gain the inevitable triumph — so help us God.

I ask that the Congress declare that since the unprovoked and dastardly attack by Japan on Sunday, December 7, a state of war has existed between the United States and the Japanese Empire.

Section XIV

The Rhetoric of
Post-World War II America

The Truman Doctrine

Harry Truman

Commentary

World War II, unlike its predecessor, was not explicitly called "the war to end all wars," but the same idea was conveyed by an abundance (over-abundance?) of public language such as "lasting peace," "never again" and "making the world safe for democracy." Such wartime rhetoric, together with our nation's millenarian heritage, persuaded most Americans that the end of World War II would bring peace and prosperity forever and ever (or at least into the foreseeable future).

Unfortunately, public expectations were not consistent with postwar reality. Although democratic governments were re-established in the countries of Western Europe that had been liberated by Anglo-American forces, the Soviet Union established dictatorial Communist regimes in the countries of Central Europe that it had supposedly "liberated." In Asia, the Soviets established a Communist regime in North Korea, and Soviet troops occupied northern Iran. Communist revolutionists tried unsuccessfully to seize Malaya, but succeeded in capturing the Chinese mainland. Manchuria (the most highly industrialized portion of China) was robbed of industrial machinery for Soviet use.

How should the United States react? Answers varied. Henry Wallace, who had been Vice-President during Roosevelt's third presidential term and later served in President Truman's cabinet, spoke against what he called Truman's "get tough" policy. Although somewhat critical of Soviet actions, Wallace advocated a vaguely-defined policy of "co-operation." His rhetoric was welcomed by pro-Soviet left-wingers who were sympathetic to "revolution," but they were few in number. The appeal of revolutionary Socialism, which had not been very strong even in Debs' day, had dissipated by the 1940s. Moreover, the socialist movement had splintered badly since Debs' time, and only the Communist offshoot was pro-Soviet. Not surprisingly, Wallace was dismissed from Truman's cabinet, and his effort to win the presidency on a Communist-backed "Progressive" party ticket in 1948 attracted little support.

To most Americans, Wallace's proposed policy of "co-operation" with the Soviet Union was unpersuasive.

Another proposed policy, which came to be called "Fortress America," was advocated by many people who had been isolationists in prewar days. Not all proponents agreed on all details of the policy, but they generally agreed that the Communist threat was serious and should be met without getting heavily involved in global affairs unless American security was threatened directly. They believed that Soviet aggression against the U.S. could be deterred by (1) building a military force that emphasized naval and air force strength and (2) sending military aid to the non-Communist Chinese government. Isolationism had a long tradition, as exemplified by U.S. refusal to join the League of Nations after World War I and by Burton Wheeler's prewar speech that appeared earlier in this anthology. Isolationism, however, had been eroded by the experience of World War II, which along with our millenarian tradition, persuaded many Americans that the U.S. was duty-bound to play a larger role in global affairs. This is exemplified by the limited opposition to our entering the United Nations, which stands in marked contrast to our refusal to join the League a generation earlier.

A third policy, which ultimately prevailed, was often called "containment" (a term devised in 1947 by George Kennan, Chairman of the State Department's Policy Planning Staff) or the "Truman doctrine." Its proponents, like those who advocated "co-operation" or "Fortress America," did not agree on all details, and critics alleged that the policy was adopted belatedly and applied inconsistently. Nevertheless, the general outline was clear: the U.S. should try to prevent ("contain") further Communist expansion.

The following speech was delivered by President Harry S. Truman (1884-1972) to a joint session of Congress on March 12, 1947. Today's readers might find it somewhat paradoxical. On one hand, Truman only alluded to the general state of global affairs and did not discuss containment as a broad strategic concept. He discussed only the specific situation in Greece and Turkey. On the other hand, his proposal for economic assistance was immediately termed the "Truman Doctrine," and historians generally regard it as the earliest rhetorical expression of "containment."

The following is a reproduction of the text which appeared first in the March 15, 1947 issue of *Vital Speeches*, pp. 322-24, and was reprinted in the second edition of *American Rhetoric from Roosevelt to Reagan* (Prospect Heights, IL: Waveland Press, 1987).

The Truman Doctrine

The gravity of the situation which confronts the world today necessitates my appearance before a joint session of the Congress. The foreign policy and the national security of this country are involved.

One aspect of the present situation, which I wish to present to you at this time for your consideration and decision, concerns Greece and Turkey.

The United States has received from the Greek Government an urgent appeal for financial and economic assistance. Preliminary reports from the American Economic Mission now in Greece and reports from the American Ambassador in Greece corroborate the statement of the Greek Government that assistance is imperative if Greece is to survive as a free nation.

I do not believe that the American people and the Congress wish to turn a deaf ear to the appeal of the Greek Government.

Greece is not a rich country. Lack of sufficient natural resources has always forced the Greek people to work hard to make both ends meet. Since 1940, this industrious and peace-loving country has suffered invasion, four years of cruel enemy occupation, and bitter internal strife.

When forces of liberation entered Greece they found that the retreating Germans had destroyed virtually all the railways, roads, port facilities, communications and merchant marine. More than a thousand villages had been burned. Eighty-five per cent of the children were tubercular. Livestock, poultry and draft animals had almost disappeared. Inflation had wiped out practically all savings.

As a result of these tragic conditions, a military minority, exploiting human want and misery, was able to create political chaos which, until now, has made economic recovery impossible.

Greece is today without funds to finance the importation of those goods which are essential to bare subsistence. Under these circumstances the people of Greece cannot make progress in solving their problems of reconstruction. Greece is in desperate need of financial and economic assistance to enable it to resume purchases of food, clothing, fuel and seeds. These are indispensable for the subsistence of its people and are obtainable only from abroad. Greece must have help to import the goods necessary to restore internal order and security so essential for economic and political recovery.

The Greek Government has also asked for the assistance of experienced American administrators, economists and technicians to insure that the financial and other aid given to Greece shall be used effectively in creating a stable and self-sustaining economy and in improving its public administration.

The very existence of the Greek state is today threatened by the terrorist activities of several thousand armed men, led by Communists, who defy the Government's authority at a number of points, particularly along the northern boundaries. A commission appointed by the United Nations Security Council is at present investigating disturbed conditions in northern Greece and alleged border violations along the frontier between Greece on the one hand and Albania, Bulgaria and Yugoslavia on the other.

Meanwhile, the Greek Government is unable to cope with the situation. The Greek Army is small and poorly equipped. It needs supplies and equipment if it is to restore the authority of the Government throughout Greek territory.

Greece must have assistance if it is to become a self-supporting and self-respecting democracy.

The United States must supply that assistance. We have already extended to Greece certain types of relief and economic aid but these are inadequate.

There is no other country to which democratic Greece can turn.

No other nation is willing and able to provide the necessary support for a democratic Greek Government.

The British Government, which has been helping Greece, can give no further financial or economic aid after March 31. Great Britain finds itself under the necessity of reducing or liquidating its commitments in several parts of the world, including Greece.

We have considered how the United Nations might assist in this crisis. But the situation is an urgent one requiring immediate action, and the United Nations and its related organizations are not in a position to extend help of the kind that is required.

It is important to note that the Greek Government has asked for our aid in utilizing effectively the financial and other assistance we may give to Greece, and in improving its public administration. It is of the utmost importance that we supervise the use of any funds made available to Greece, in such a manner that each dollar spent will count toward making Greece self-supporting, and will help to build an economy in which a healthy democracy can flourish.

No government is perfect. One of the chief virtues of a democracy, however, is that its defects are always visible and under democratic processes can be pointed out and corrected. The Government of Greece is not perfect. Nevertheless it represents 85 per cent of the members of the Greek Parliament who were chosen in an election last year. Foreign observers, including 692 Americans, considered this election to be a fair expression of the views of the Greek people.

The Greek Government has been operating in an atmosphere of chaos and extremism. It has made mistakes. The extension of aid by this country does not mean that the United States condones everything that the Greek Government has done or will do. We have condemned in the past, and we condemn now, extremist measures of the Right or the Left. We have in the past advised tolerance, and we advise tolerance now.

Greece's neighbor, Turkey, also deserves our attention.

The future of Turkey as an independent and economically sound State is clearly no less important to the freedom-loving peoples of the world than the future of Greece. The circumstances in which Turkey finds itself today are considerably different than those of Greece. Turkey has been spared the disasters that have beset Greece. And during the war, the United States and Great Britain furnished Turkey with material aid.

Nevertheless, Turkey now needs our support.

Since the war Turkey has sought financial assistance from Great Britain and the United States for the purpose of effecting that modernization necessary for the maintenance of its national integrity.

That integrity is essential to the preservation of order in the Middle East.

The British Government has informed us that, owing to its own difficulties, it can no longer extend financial or economic aid to Turkey.

As in the case of Greece, if Turkey is to have the assistance it needs, the United States must supply it. We are the only country able to provide that help.

I am fully aware of the broad implications involved if the United States extends assistance to Greece and Turkey, and I shall discuss these implications with you at this time.

One of the primary objectives of the foreign policy of the United States is the creation of conditions in which we and other nations will be able to work out a way of life free from coercion. That was a fundamental issue in the war with Germany and Japan. Our victory was won over countries which sought to impose their will, and their way of life, upon other nations.

To ensure the peaceful development of nations, free from coercion, the United States has taken a leading part in establishing the United Nations. The United Nations is designed to make possible lasting freedom and independence for all its members. We shall not realize our objectives, however, unless we are willing to help free people to maintain their free institutions and their national integrity against aggressive movements that seek to impose upon them totalitarian regimes. This is no more than a frank recognition that totalitarian regimes imposed on free peoples, by direct or indirect aggression, undermine the foundations of international peace and hence the security of the United States.

The peoples of a number of countries of the world have recently had totalitarian regimes forced upon them against their will. The Government of the United States has made frequent protests against coercion and intimidation in violation of the Yalta agreement, in Poland, Rumania, and Bulgaria. I must also state that in a number of other countries there have been similar developments.

At the present moment in world history nearly every nation must choose between alternative ways of life. The choice is too often not a free one.

One way of life is based upon the will of the majority, and is distinguished by free institutions, representative government, free elections, guarantees of individual liberty, freedom of speech and religion, and freedom from political oppression.

The second way of life is based upon the will of a minority forcibly imposed upon the majority. It relies upon terror and oppression, a controlled press and radio, fixed elections, and the suppression of personal freedoms.

I believe that it must be the policy of the United States to support free peoples who are resisting attempted subjugation by armed minorities or by outside pressures. I believe that we must assist free peoples to work out their own destinies in their own way. I believe that our help should be primarily through economic and financial aid which is essential to economic stability and orderly political processes.

The world is not static, and the status quo is not sacred. But we cannot allow changes in the status quo in violation of the Charter of the United Nations by such methods as coercion, or by such subterfuges as political infiltration. In helping free and independent nations to maintain their freedom, the United States will be giving effect to the principles of the Charter of the United Nations.

It is necessary only to glance at a map to realize that the survival and integrity of the Greek nation are of grave importance in a much wider situation. If Greece should fall under the control of an armed minority, the effect upon its neighbor,

Turkey, would be immediate and serious. Confusion and disorder might well spread throughout the entire Middle East.

Moreover, the disappearance of Greece as an independent State would have a profound effect upon those countries in Europe whose peoples are struggling against great difficulties to maintain their freedoms and their independence while they repair the damages of war. It would be an unspeakable tragedy if these countries, which have struggled so long against overwhelming odds, should lose that victory for which they sacrificed so much. Collapse of free institutions and loss of independence would be disastrous not only for them but for the world. Discouragement and possibly failure would quickly be the lot of neighboring peoples striving to maintain their freedom and independence.

Should we fail to aid Greece and Turkey in this fateful hour, the effect will be far-reaching to the West as well as to the East. We must take immediate and resolute action.

I therefore ask the Congress to provide authority for assistance to Greece and Turkey in the amount of $400,000,000 for the period ending June 30, 1948. In requesting these funds, I have taken into consideration the maximum amount of relief assistance which would be furnished to Greece out of the $350,000,000 which I recently requested that the Congress authorize for the prevention of starvation and suffering in countries devastated by the war.

In addition to funds, I ask the Congress to authorize the detail of American civilian and military personnel to Greece and Turkey, at the request of those countries, to assist in the tasks of reconstruction, and for the purpose of supervising the use of such financial and material assistance as may be furnished. I recommend that authority also be provided for the instruction and training of selected Greek and Turkish personnel.

Finally, I ask that the Congress provide authority which will permit the speediest and most effective use, in terms of needed commodities, supplies and equipment, of such funds as may be authorized.

If further funds, or further authority, should be needed for purposes indicated in this message, I shall not hesitate to bring the situation before the Congress. On this subject the executive and legislative branches of the Government must work together.

This is a serious course upon which we embark. I would not recommend it except that the alternative is much more serious.

The United States contributed $341,000,000,000 toward winning World War II. This is an investment in world freedom and world peace. The assistance that I am recommending for Greece and Turkey amounts to little more than one-tenth of 1 percent of this investment. It is only common sense that we should safeguard this investment and make sure that it was not in vain.

The seeds of totalitarian regimes are nurtured by misery and want. They spread and grow in the evil soil of poverty and strife. They reach their full growth when the hope of a people for a better life has died. We must keep that hope alive.

The free peoples of the world look to us for support in maintaining their freedoms. If we falter in our leadership, we may endanger the peace of the world—and we shall surely endanger the welfare of our own nation.

Great responsibilities have been placed upon us by the swift movement of events. I am confident that the Congress will face these responsibilities squarely.

Excerpt from Speech to the Ohio Society of New York

Robert A. Taft

Commentary

Congressional endorsement of Truman's proposal for aid to Greece and Turkey was only one application of the "containment" strategy. Economic assistance was given to Western Europe under the "Marshall Plan," and the U.S. led in forming a military alliance known as the "North Atlantic Treaty Organization" (NATO). A common thread running through the proponents' rhetoric in behalf of each measure was that it would strengthen our "friends" and "allies" against Communist aggression.

Many of Truman's actions were endorsed by Congressional legislation, but some were taken without the consent of Congress. The most noteworthy was when President Truman announced that U.S. troops would be sent under United Nations authorization to help South Korea resist the attack launched by North Korea on June 25, 1950. Calling this a "police action," Truman did not ask Congress for a declaration of war.

Senator Robert A. Taft (1889-1953) was one of Truman's most vocal critics. First elected to the U.S. Senate in 1938, Taft's reputation as the leading Republican spokesman led to his being called "Mr. Republican." He had opposed Roosevelt's foreign and domestic policies in prewar days. Although after the war he supported some "liberal" domestic policies, such as federal aid to education, he delivered a barrage of speeches in which he attacked Truman's foreign policy. His criticisms follow. (1) Many of Truman's actions, such as the Korean War, were taken without the Congressional authorization that the Constitution requires. (2) During the transition between war and peace, Roosevelt and Truman made secret (and therefore unconstitutional) agreements with the Soviet Union, especially those at the Yalta and Potsdam conferences, which permitted much of the Soviet expansionism that was belatedly recognized as dangerous. (3) By failing to support the Nationalist Chinese government (led by Chiang Kai-shek), Truman and his foreign policy advisers ensured its defeat by Communist revolutionaries and its resultant retreat to the island of

Formosa (now Taiwan). (4) By failing to state clearly U.S. vital interests in Asia, Truman and his advisers virtually invited North Korea's attack on South Korea. (5) Now that we were in the Korean War, the U.S. should insist on reunifying the peninsula rather than negotiating an agreement that would permit Communist North Korea to continue its existence. These criticisms were developed in detail in a book entitled *A Foreign Policy for Americans* that was published mid-way through the Korean War.

The book is too long to duplicate here, but Taft's foreign policy ideas were summarized in a speech he delivered to the Ohio Society of New York on January 15, 1951, shortly after he had been re-elected easily in a Senate race in which he had emphasized his objections to Truman's foreign policy. An excerpt was printed in the *Congressional Record* (January 23, 1951, 82nd Congress, 1st session, vol. 97, pt. 1, p. 562) and is reproduced below.

Speech to the Ohio Society of New York

The election in Ohio also showed a substantial lack of confidence in the conduct of foreign policy by the present Administration. Since the election it has been claimed that this lack of confidence played no part in the result. But certainly no voter had any doubt that I was opposed to the administration's foreign policy up to that moment. In every county in Ohio, I pointed out that the present threat of Russian aggression upon which our whole present national danger is based was brought about by the secret agreements of Tehran, Yalta, and Potsdam, and by our course since that time in the Far East. I pointed out that at Yalta and Potsdam, we set Russia up in a powerful position in central Europe, in Berlin, and Eastern Germany, in Prague and Czechoslovakia, in Vienna and eastern Austria, from which they dominate central Europe and threaten the safety of Western Europe and of the United States. I pointed out that these agreements had handed over Manchuria to Russia in violation of the open-door policy upon which our whole eastern policy had been based for 50 years. I pointed out that this agreement had been made without even telling Chiang Kai-shek, who had been our ally for 5 years, until months after it had been made. I pointed out that this had led to the arming of the Chinese Communists by Russia and the constant promotion of their cause, while we welcomed the Chinese Communists as agrarian reformers entitled to American support. I pointed out that General Marshall had insisted that Chiang take Communists into his cabinet and, when this fatal course was refused, cut off all arms from the Nationalist armies at the most crucial time. I pointed out that we failed to arm the South Koreans, although we said we would do so, giving them only small arms against tanks, planes, and heavy artillery furnished to North Korea by the Russians.

A war in Korea was morally justified as an international move against aggression. But the President undertook it without legal authority and in direct violation of the statute which specified that Congress must pass on the troops to be furnished the United Nations under the Charter.

The war in Korea has revealed the inherent weakness of the United Nations which I have pointed out from the beginning, and made it clear that because of the veto we cannot possibly rely on the United Nations as a weapon against Russian aggression. While it may still be a diplomatic weapon, we would only repeat the disaster resulting from the aggression of the Chinese Communists if we relied upon it in determining our military policy.

Since we can no longer rely upon the United Nations, it is obvious that we cannot for some years hope to resist Chinese aggression in Korea, and it seems to me that we should retire as we have already retired from Hungnam.

Instead of that, we are now contemplating the most complete appeasement since Munich. The acceptance by our confused State Department of the UN cease-fire plan is another tragic error in our far-eastern policy. We obtain nothing except the right to make a withdrawal, which we apparently could make ourselves if we decided to do so. Paragraph 3 of the plan provides that all non-Korean armed forces will be withdrawn by appropriate stages from Korea. In other words, we sneak away from Korea, leaving the Korean Communists in full control, by the gracious leave of the Communists. At the same time we agree to sit down with the British, the Russians, and the Chinese Communists to discuss the admission of Communist China into the United Nations, and also the disposition of Formosa.

To admit that an outrageous aggression such as that of the Chinese Communists can be the basis for admission into the United Nations is not only an abject acceptance of American defeat, but it destroys the whole moral basis of the United Nations. To discuss the surrender of Formosa to the United Nations is a weakening of our entire military position in the Far East, a betrayal of the Nationalist Government of China, and a surrender of the only considerable armed force in the Far East which remains to oppose further Communist aggression.

The proposal is even worse when we consider that the Nationalist Government is not to be represented in the conference, nor is the established Government of the Republic of Korea to be recognized, although it was set up under UN auspices and recognized by the UN. Of course, it would be far better to retire under our own power as at Hungnam to a defensible position in Japan, Okinawa, and Formosa, and retain complete freedom as to the admission of Communist China and the disposition of Formosa.

This cease-fire plan is the most complete surrender to which the United States has ever agreed. Of course, it encourages aggression, and it is only a question of time before the Communist armies, released by the cease-fire in Korea, and the hamstringing of Chiang's army, will march on down into Indochina and southeastern Asia. It has long seemed obvious to me that, if we wish to prevent the spread of communism, we must release Chiang's army from its present neutrality and furnish such arms as may be necessary for him to create a diversion against Chinese Communist advance in southeast Asia. If this brings war between the United States and the Chinese Communists, it is nothing different from what we now have—in fact, it would be a much less dangerous war to us, much less fatal to our men, and much less expensive in material.

Statement on the Annual Budget Message

Dwight D. Eisenhower

Commentary

Taft's rhetorical attacks on Truman were partly designed to earn him the Republican party's presidential nomination in 1952. However, the party was split between so-called "conservatives," such as Taft, and "moderates," who were sympathetic (or at least half-way sympathetic) to the "liberal" domestic policies being pushed by Roosevelt's heirs in the Democratic party. "Moderates" were also sympathetic to Truman's foreign policy. After a hard fight in the convention, the nomination went to Dwight Eisenhower, who easily won the election.

A host of factors account for Eisenhower's overwhelming election in 1952 and his re-election four years later. Perhaps most important was his ethos as a War Hero and as an Internationalist. He had commanded Allied forces in Europe during World War II, and after a short stint as president of Columbia University he had served as Truman's Chief of Staff and NATO commander.

As president, Eisenhower negotiated an end to the Korean War and continued his predecessor's foreign policy of containment. He called his domestic policy "Modern Republicanism," a policy that favored some "liberal" programs but avoided putting too much power into the hands of the Federal government at the expense of the States. It was a partial return to the Jeffersonian doctrine of States' Rights that had been abandoned during Roosevelt's "New Deal" and Truman's "Fair Deal."

To Eisenhower, one of the most worrisome aspects of the New Deal-Fair Deal era was what he regarded as financial irresponsibility. Prior to the New Deal, *all* parties had agreed on balancing the Federal budget and repaying debts. Indeed, one of the arguments for adopting the Constitution in 1788 was that the Federal government needed to pay off its Revolutionary War debts. As time went by, the Federal Government usually balanced the budget or ran a surplus (for the express purpose of paying off debts) except in times of war or economic depression. Balancing the Federal budget was a non-debatable

757

issue even in the election of 1932, when Democrats, as well as Republicans, promised reduced spending. Even during the New Deal era, Federal deficits were usually justified by saying that deficit spending would stimulate the economy but that once the depression ended, Federal surpluses would be necessary to pay off the debt.

Only three of Eisenhower's budgets avoided a deficit. Critics within the Republican party charged that he was a "Me too" Republican; one who was too sympathetic to the kinds of New Deal-Fair Deal proposals that were being advocated by "liberal" Democrats. Supporters claimed that the deficits resulted from the needs for (1) military expenditures and (2) funding a plethora of domestic programs that had been enacted by the Democrat-controlled Congress. Eisenhower himself complained that many spending measures of which he disapproved were inserted into legislation that he was "compelled by circumstances to sign." To stop this practice he advocated (first in 1958) a line-item veto. Congress, which has a long tradition of slipping "pet projects" into bills that must be enacted if the government is to function, turned down the proposal, as it has done many times since.

On January 19, 1959, Eisenhower sent his last Annual Budget Message to Congress (for Fiscal Year 1960, which would begin on October 1). Concerned about prior deficits and a host of legislative proposals that he considered unaffordable, he had already met with Republican Congressional leaders to develop legislative strategies for killing what he called "foolish proposals" that would unnecessarily add to expenditures. He also realized the necessity of persuading the public that "thrift is not a bad word."

In keeping with his effort to persuade the public, Eisenhower delivered the following speech via the mass media. It was successful in the short run (the Fiscal 1960 budget ran a small surplus) and unsuccessful in the long run (the Federal budget has been balanced only once since 1960). The speech is reproduced from the *Public Papers of the President. Dwight D. Eisenhower* for 1959 (Washington: U.S. Government Printing Office, 1960), pp. 112-3.

Statement by the President on the Annual Budget Message

Fellow Citizens:

Today I have sent to the Congress the Budget of the United States.

The Budget is the annual governmental plan for spending your Federal tax money, which amounts to one dollar out of every five that all our people earn. It comprises the proposals of the Government for assuring the safety of our Nation, the well-being of our people and their continuing prosperity. The program that I have sent to the Congress will, at the same time, allow us to live within our means.

The Budget is in balance.

This is important, because if the Government does not live within its means, every American suffers. When the Government continues to run deficits, inflation is the end result. And inflation means rising costs to every housewife, a falling value to every pay envelope, and a threat to the prosperous functioning of our economy. Every citizen, no matter where he lives or what he does, has a vital stake in preventing inflation.

The President has the duty of representing all the interests of the entire nation in his Budget recommendations.

But it is Congress—and Congress alone—that must enact the legislation to carry out these recommendations.

The program in this Budget provides for:

—Accelerated modern weapons development and a strong and adequate national defense program;

—Increases for dramatic exploration of outer space;

—The greatest investment for public works programs in the Nation's history;

—Additional help to local communities to improve the health, education and welfare of citizens.

Many more programs are provided for in this balanced budget.

In the Government, as in your family, it is not possible to do all that everyone would like to do—all at the same time. A budget is a way to schedule priorities. And whatever choices are made, there will be objections from pressure groups that would put their own interests before the common welfare—that would like to see the Government spend more for their special projects. The Budget is not designed for special interests; the real purpose is to promote the good of all America.

I intend to do everything within my power to keep our country strong, our economy expanding, and Federal spending at a level that will make these objectives possible of attainment. I hope you will help.

Thank you.

Speech to the Greater Houston Ministerial Association

John F. Kennedy

Commentary

As Eisenhower's second presidential term drew to an end, several political and technological changes were combining to change campaign rhetoric. One was the presidential primary. Although "progressives" had managed to get primaries adopted in some States as early as the beginning of the twentieth century, delegates to national party conventions were not bound by the results (either by law or public opinion). Would-be nominees sometimes delivered a few speeches prior to the conventions, but they relied primarily on supporters to work behind the scenes to influence convention delegates and the "bosses" who often controlled them. For all practical purposes, the primary system emerged after World War II. With it came much more demanding rhetorical tasks for candidates. They now must announce their candidacy, organize a campaign staff and speak in numerous State primaries. They must raise millions of dollars to hire political consultants and media experts.

The primary system raises a host of questions. Are primaries more democratic, as the old "progressives" expected them to be? Is rhetorical astuteness the best criterion for nominating presidential candidates? Is the system too expensive? Do the demands of campaigning require officeholders to neglect their current duties? Have primaries caused the quality of rhetorical discourse to decline?

A second change involves so-called scientific public opinion polling, which Gallup and Roper first used to predict a presidential election in 1936. After misjudging the 1948 election, pollsters fell into temporary disrepute, but by the 1950s, candidates began using pollsters to help plan their campaigns. What are the effects of polling? Do poll results encourage candidates to be ambiguous on divisive issues? Do they encourage candidates to address immediate issues while disregarding less obvious, but perhaps more important, long-term problems?

A third change is in the area of television, which began to reach the average American home in the 1950s. National political conventions were first televised in 1952. Many candidates had trouble adapting to the new medium. For example, Adlai Stevenson kept looking down at his speech texts so that the glare of the television lights emphasized his shiny bald head. Even today, some candidates have difficulties. Is the nation well served by demanding that successful candidates have a good "television personality?"

Americans now get the bulk of their news via television, which reports events in short segments that often seem more entertaining and sensational than informative. Although campaigners probably give more speeches today than ever before, most members of their "audience" get only a clip on the nightly news, which, unfortunately, can often be taken out of context. Does this encourage speakers to avoid developing a complicated line of argument in preference to using simple-minded, but appealing, one-liners? Journalists often create issues by emphasizing certain topics on the nightly news, questioning candidates about them and reporting reactions to what a candidate said. Do journalists have too much influence? Does the journalistic emphasis on immediate events obscure the basic ideological issues that are often at stake but rarely debated? Although there may be disagreement about the answers, there is general agreement on the importance of television.

The presidential election of 1960 highlighted the changes mentioned above. Under the old nomination system, the only serious candidates would have been well-known politicians or war heroes. A lesser-known person would have been nominated only if the convention were divided. In 1960, the leading contenders for the Democratic nomination were two well-known senators, Hubert Humphrey (a major liberal spokesman) and Lyndon B. Johnson (the Senate majority leader). Yet the nomination went to John Fitzgerald Kennedy (1917-1963), a young, inexperienced senator with an undistinguished legislative record. He was selected, not as a compromise, but because of his rhetorical astuteness in the primaries, which included judicious use of public opinion polls, a television personality and a satisfactory response to an issue raised by journalists.

Although 1960 illustrates changes, Kennedy's entry into politics in 1946 illustrates a phenomenon which shows continuity with the past: the persuasive value of family names. His paternal grandfather, Kennedy, had been a political boss of the old saloonkeeper variety, and his maternal grandfather, Fitzgerald, had been one of Boston's most popular mayors. Back from military service and lacking political experience, Kennedy won a congressional seat in 1946. Instead of building a notable legislative record, he joined the so-called Tuesday through Thursday Club—he worked in Congress for three days and spent most of the week giving speeches around Massachusetts. After being elected senator in 1952, he continued to concentrate on building his public image rather than building a legislative record. Not surprisingly, he was criticized for entering the primary races. Humphrey complained about the vast sums of money the wealthy Kennedy was spending. Johnson remarked sarcastically that he was tending to his senatorial duties while Kennedy was not. Other Democratic elders grumbled about the young man's brashness. Ignoring his opponents' complaints, Kennedy entered only those primaries where poll results indicated a reasonable chance of success. His campaigns were well organized, well financed and—as his success demonstrated—very persuasive.

One primary which Kennedy entered because of favorable polls was West Virginia's, but two things had changed by the time the primary campaign began. First, the West Virginia primary had become crucial; Kennedy and Humphrey were close in national polls and in the number of delegates won in earlier primaries. Secondly, polls now had Kennedy losing in West Virginia. His decline was due largely to an issue which Kennedy's opponents had not raised overtly but which the national press had begun discussing: Kennedy's Catholicism. Only once before, in 1928, had a major party (the Democrats) nominated a Catholic (Al Smith). Smith probably would have lost anyway, but his Catholicism undoubtedly hurt him. With the predominantly Democratic State of West Virginia being dominated by evangelical Protestantism, Kennedy's chances looked dim. They were not brightened when Humphrey's supporters began singing a campaign song to the tune of a popular evangelical hymn, "Give Me That Old Time Religion."

Kennedy employed television to defuse the religious issue. He ran a series of short television advertisements dealing with religion, but the coup de grace was a televised, half-hour interview with a man who had a name that was much loved by Democrats: Franklin Delano Roosevelt, Jr. Kathleen Hall Jamieson summarizes the interview in her brilliant book, *Packaging the Presidency* (New York: Oxford University Press, 1984): "Using questions prepared for him by Kennedy's staff, FDR Jr. asked the candidate: Would Kennedy's church influence him in the White House? Would the pope tell him what to do? What was Kennedy's attitude toward restriction of the rights of Protestants in such countries as Spain and Italy? . . . FDR Jr. summarized and then blessed Kennedy's answers."

Why Republicans ignored the religious issue in the general election is debatable, but it is clear that they did not need to raise it. Journalists did it for them. Kennedy remained silent until poll results indicated that he would gain more than he would lose by addressing it. Accepting an invitation to answer questions posed by its members, Kennedy appeared before the Greater Houston Ministerial Association on September 12, 1960. His opening statement and the subsequent question-answer period were taped, and both excerpts and the entire rhetorical event were frequently televised. Even now, Kennedy's advisers claim that the purpose of the telecasts was only to reach audiences that might be worried about Kennedy's Catholicism, but Jamieson's tabulation of complete telecasts (those which included his entire speech and the subsequent interchange) suggests that he also tried to mobilize the Catholic vote by playing them mostly in Catholic areas where Republican strength had been rising. In short, Kennedy's speech had more than one audience and one purpose. He tried to persuade Catholics to consider his religion while trying to persuade Protestants to overlook it. The following text of his opening statement is reproduced from Halford Ross Ryan, *Contemporary American Public Discourse,* Third Edition (Prospect Heights, Illinois: Waveland Press, 1992), pp. 173-176.

Speech to the Greater Houston Ministerial Association

I am grateful for your generous invitation to state my views.

While the so-called religious issue is necessarily and properly the chief topic here tonight, I want to emphasize from the outset that I believe that we have far more critical issues in the 1960 election: the spread of Communist influence, until it now festers only ninety miles off the coast of Florida —the humiliating treatment of our President and Vice President by those who no longer respect our power—the hungry children I saw in West Virginia, the old people who cannot pay their doctor's bills, the families forced to give up their farms—an America with too many slums, with too few schools, and too late to the moon and outer space.

These are the real issues which should decide this campaign. And they are not religious issues—for war and hunger and ignorance and despair know no religious barrier.

But because I am a Catholic, and no Catholic has ever been elected President, the real issues in this campaign have been obscured—perhaps deliberately. In some quarters less responsible than this. So it is apparently necessary for me to state once again—not what kind of church I believe in, for that should be important only to me, but what kind of America I believe in.

I believe in an America where the separation of church and state is absolute—where no Catholic prelate would tell the President (should he be a Catholic) how to act and no Protestant minister would tell his parishioners for whom to vote—where no church or church school is granted any public funds or political preference—and where no man is denied public office merely because his religion differs from the President who might appoint him or the people who might elect him.

I believe in an America that is officially neither Catholic, Protestant nor Jewish—where no public official either requests or accepts instructions on public policy from the Pope, the National Council of Churches or any other ecclesiastical source—where no religious body seeks to impose its will directly or indirectly upon the general populace or the public acts of its officials—and where religious liberty is so indivisible that an act against one church is treated as an act against all.

For, while this year it may be a Catholic against whom the finger of suspicion is pointed, in other years it has been, and may someday be again, a Jew—or a Quaker—or a Unitarian—or a Baptist. It was Virginia's harassment of Baptist preachers, for example, that led to Jefferson's statute of religious freedom. Today, I may be the victim—but tomorrow it may be you — until the whole fabric of our harmonious society is ripped apart at a time of great national peril.

Finally, I believe in an America where religious intolerance will someday end — where all men and all churches are treated as equal — where every man has the same right to attend or not to attend the church of his choice — where there is no Catholic vote, no anti-Catholic vote, no bloc voting of any kind — and where Catholics, Protestants and Jews, both the lay and the pastoral level, will refrain from those attitudes of disdain and division which have so often marred their works in the past, and promote instead the American ideal of brotherhood.

That is the kind of America in which I believe. And it represents the kind of Presidency in which I believe — a great office that must be neither humbled by making it the instrument of any religious group, nor tarnished by arbitrarily withholding it, its occupancy from the members of any religious group. I believe in a President whose views on religion are his own private affair, neither imposed upon him by the nation or imposed by the nation upon him as a condition to holding that office.

I would not look with favor upon a President working to subvert the First Amendment's guarantees of religious liberty (nor would our system of checks and balances permit him to do so). And neither do I look with favor upon those who would work to subvert Article VI of the Constitution by requiring a religious test — even by indirection — for if they disagree with that safeguard, they should be openly working to repeal it.

I want a chief executive whose public acts are responsible to all and obligated to none — who can attend any ceremony, service or dinner his office may appropriately require him to fulfill — and whose fulfillment of his Presidential office is not limited or conditioned by any religious oath, ritual or obligation.

This is the kind of America I believe in — and this is the kind of America I fought for in the South Pacific and the kind my brother died for in Europe. No one suggested then that we might have a "divided loyalty," that we did "not believe in liberty" or that we belonged to a disloyal group that threatened "the freedoms for which our forefathers died."

And in fact this is the kind of America for which our forefathers did die when they fled here to escape religious test oaths, that denied office to members of less favored churches, when they fought for the Constitution, the Bill of Rights, the Virginia Statute of Religious Freedom — and when they fought at the shrine I visited today — the Alamo. For side by side with Bowie and Crockett died Fuentes and McCafferty and Bailey and Bedillio and Carey — but no one knows whether they were Catholics or not. For there was no religious test there.

I ask you tonight to follow in that tradition, to judge me on the basis of fourteen years in the Congress — on my declared stands against an ambassador to the Vatican, against unconstitutional aid to parochial schools, and against any boycott of the public schools (which I attended myself) — and instead of doing this do not judge me on the basis of these pamphlets and publications we have all seen that carefully select quotations out of context from the statements of Catholic Church leaders, usually in other countries, frequently in other centuries, and rarely relevant to any situation here — and always omitting, of course, that statement of the American bishops in 1948 which strongly endorsed church-state separation.

I do not consider these other quotations binding upon my public acts — why should you? But let me say, with respect to other countries, that I am wholly opposed to the state being used by any religious group, Catholic or Protestant, to compel, prohibit or prosecute the free exercise of any other religion. And that goes for any persecution at any time, by anyone, in any country.

And I hope that you and I condemn with equal fervor those nations which deny their Presidency to Protestants and those which deny it to Catholics. And rather than cite the misdeeds of those who differ, I would also cite the record of the Catholic Church in such nations as France and Ireland — and the independence of such statesmen as de Gaulle and Adenauer.

But let me stress again that these are my views — for, contrary to common newspaper usage, I am not the Catholic candidate for President. I am the Democratic party's candidate for President who happens also to be a Catholic.

I do not speak for my church on public matters — and the church does not speak for me.

Whatever issue may come before me as President, if I should be elected — on birth control, divorce, censorship, gambling, or any other subject — I will make my decision in accordance with these views, in accordance with what my conscience tells me to be in the national interest, and without regard to outside religious pressure or dictate. And no power or threat of punishment could cause me to decide otherwise.

But if the time should ever come — and I do not concede any conflict to be remotely possible — when my office would require me to either violate my conscience, or violate the national interest, then I would resign the office, and I hope any other conscientious public servant would do likewise.

But I do not intend to apologize for these views to my critics of either Catholic or Protestant faith, nor do I intend to disavow either my views or my church in order to win this election. If I should lose on the real issues, I shall return to my seat in the Senate satisfied that I tried my best and was fairly judged.

But if this election is decided on the basis that 40,000,000 Americans lost their chance of being President on the day they were baptized, that it is the whole nation that will be the loser in the eyes of Catholics and non-Catholics around the world, in the eyes of history, and in the eyes of our own people.

But if, on the other hand, I should win this election, I shall devote every effort of mind and spirit to fulfilling the oath of the Presidency — practically identical, I might add, with the oath I have taken for fourteen years in the

Congress. For, without reservation, I can, and I quote "solemnly swear that I will faithfully execute the office of President of the United States and will to the best of my ability preserve, protect and defend the Constitution, so help me God."

Inaugural Address

John F. Kennedy

Commentary

Kennedy's inaugural address highlighted another change from the pre-World War II era: America's internationalism. We do not know why Kennedy took the unusual step of devoting an inaugural address exclusively to international affairs. Some scholars speculate that he was responding to a speech given only a few days before by the Soviet leader, who promised to overwhelm the United States in the current struggle between communism and "capitalist imperialism." If so, Kennedy's speech should be studied as a statement to the world (especially the Soviets), as well as one addressed to Americans. Whatever his reason, his speech exemplified our new-found internationalism and our old belief in being a Chosen Nation. Although not actually using the Puritan terminology, he painted a millenarian vision of the world becoming free and prosperous under American leadership. The speech is from Halford Ross Ryan, *Contemporary American Public Discourse*, Third Edition (Prospect Heights, Illinois: Waveland Press, 192), pp. 194-197, but a few changes have been made so that the speech conforms to the videotape version that is available in *Great Speeches*, vol. I (produced by Alliance Video for Great Speeches, Inc., 1985).

Inaugural Address

Vice President Johnson, Mr. Speaker, Mr. Chief Justice, President Eisenhower, Vice President Nixon, President Truman, Reverend Clergy, fellow citizens: We observe today not a victory of party but a celebration of freedom — symbolizing an end as well as a beginning — signifying renewal as well as change. For I have sworn before you and Almighty God the same solemn oath our forebears prescribed nearly a century and three-quarters ago.

The world is very different now. For man holds in his mortal hands the power to abolish all forms of human poverty and all forms of human life. And yet the same revolutionary beliefs for which our forebears fought are still at issue around the globe — the belief that the rights of man come not from the generosity of the state but from the hand of God.

We dare not forget today that we are the heirs of that first revolution. Let the word go forth from this time and place, to friend and foe alike, that the torch has been passed to a new generation of Americans — born in this century, tempered by war, disciplined by a hard and bitter peace, proud of our ancient heritage — and unwilling to witness or permit the slow undoing of those human rights to which this nation has always been committed, and to which we are committed today at home and around the world.

Let every nation know, whether it wishes us well or ill, that we shall pay any price, bear any burden, meet any hardship, support any friend, oppose any foe to assure the survival and the success of liberty.

This much we pledge — and more.

To those old allies whose cultural and spiritual origins we share, we pledge the loyalty of faithful friends. United, there is little we cannot do in a host of cooperative ventures. Divided, there is little we can do — for we dare not meet a powerful challenge at odds and split asunder.

To those new states whom we welcome to the ranks of the free, we pledge our word that one form of colonial control shall not have passed away merely to be replaced by a far more iron tyranny. We shall not always expect to find them supporting our view. But we shall always hope to find them strongly supporting their own freedom — and to remember that, in the past, those who foolishly sought power by riding the back of the tiger ended up inside.

To those people in the huts and villages of half the globe struggling to break the bonds of mass misery, we pledge our best efforts to help them help themselves, for whatever period is required — not because the Communists may be doing it, not because we seek their votes, but because it is right. If a free society cannot help the many who are poor, it cannot save the few who are rich.

To our sister republics south of our border, we offer a special pledge — to convert our good words into good deeds — in a new alliance for progress — to assist free men and free governments in casting off the chains of poverty. But this peaceful revolution of hope cannot become the prey of hostile powers. Let all our neighbors know that we shall join with them to oppose aggression or subversion anywhere in the Americas. And let every other power know that this hemisphere intends to remain the master of its own house.

To that world assembly of sovereign states, the United Nations, our last best hope in an age where the instruments of war have far outpaced the instruments of peace, we renew our pledge of support — to prevent it from becoming merely a forum for invective — to strengthen its shield of the new and the weak — and to enlarge the area in which its writ may run.

Finally, to those nations who would make themselves our adversary, we offer not a pledge but a request: that both sides begin anew the quest for peace, before the dark powers of destruction unleashed by science engulf all humanity in planned or accidental self-destruction.

We dare not tempt them with weakness. For only when our arms are sufficient beyond doubt can we be certain beyond doubt that they will never be employed.

But neither can two great and powerful groups of nations take comfort from our present course — both sides overburdened by the cost of modern weapons, both rightly alarmed by the steady spread of the deadly atom, yet both racing to alter that uncertain balance of terror that stays the hand of mankind's final war.

So let us begin anew — remembering on both sides that civility is not a sign of weakness, and sincerity is always subject to proof. Let us never negotiate out of fear. But let us never fear to negotiate.

Let both sides explore what problems unite us instead of belaboring those problems which divide us.

Let both sides, for the first time, formulate serious and precise proposals for the inspection and control of arms — and bring the absolute power to destroy other nations under the absolute control of all nations.

Let both sides seek to invoke the wonders of science instead of its terrors. Together let us explore the stars, conquer the deserts, eradicate disease, tap the ocean depths and encourage the arts and commerce.

Let both sides unite to heed in all corners of the earth the command of Isaiah — to "undo the heavy burdens...[and] let the oppressed go free."

And if a beach-head of co-operation may push back the jungle of suspicion, let both sides join in creating a new endeavor not a new balance of power, but a new world of law, where the strong are just and the weak secure and the peace preserved.

All this will not be finished in the first 100 days. Nor will it be finished in the first 1,000 days, not in the life of this Administration, nor even perhaps in our lifetime on this planet. But let us begin.

In your hands, my fellow citizens, more than mine, will rest the final success or failure of our course. Since this country was founded, each generation of Americans has been summoned to give testimony to its national loyalty. The graves of young Americans who answered the call to service surround the globe.

Now the trumpet summons us again — not as a call to bear arms, though arms we need — not as a call to battle, though embattled we are — but a call to bear the burden of a long twilight struggle year in and year out, "rejoicing in hope, patient in tribulation" — a struggle against the common enemies of man: tyranny, poverty, disease and war itself.

Can we forge against these enemies a grand and global alliance, north and south, east and west, that can assure a more fruitful life for all mankind? Will you join in that historic effort?

In the long history of the world, only a few generations have been granted the role of defending freedom in its hour of maximum danger. I do not shrink from this responsibility — I welcome it. I do not believe that any of us would exchange places with any other people or any other generation. The energy, the faith, the devotion which we bring to this endeavor will light our country and all who serve it — and the glow from that fire can truly light the world.

And so, my fellow Americans: ask not what your country can do for you — ask what you can do for your country.

My fellow citizens of the world: ask not what America will do for you, but what together we can do for the freedom of man.

Finally, whether you are citizens of America or citizens of the world, ask of us here the same high standards of strength and sacrifice which we ask of you. With a good conscience our only sure reward, with history the final judge of our deeds, let us go forth to lead the land we love, asking His blessing and His help, but knowing that here on earth God's work must truly be our own.

How to Save Lives and Political Face in Vietnam

George McGovern

Commentary

Whether Kennedy's American audience in 1961 was really prepared to "pay any price" to help our friends around the world is debatable, but his inaugural address was well received. Would it be well received today? Or is "Internationalism" now in decline? Is a form of pre-World War II "isolationism" returning? Although we can only speculate about the answers, it is clear that rhetoric about foreign policy has changed in many ways. One significant change is that the persuasive potential of the "folly of appeasement" argument has declined since the post-World War II years. Why? Memories of the appeasement at Munich shortly before World War II have faded. Moreover, most Americans feel much more secure now that the Soviet Union has collapsed.

Vietnam has also changed debates about foreign policy. In the 1980s, for example, proponents of aid to Nicaragua argued that the best way to *prevent* another Vietnam was to help anticommunist forces, while opponents argued that help would *lead to* another Vietnam. Similarly, as this is written in 1994, opponents of sending American troops to Bosnia argue that such action would lead to another Vietnam.

In addition to incorporating a new argument into foreign policy rhetoric, the Vietnam experience illustrates a troublesome rhetorical pattern of public indifference, the public's rallying behind the president after a dramatic incident, and, finally, the public's involvement in a debate that grows in emotional intensity. The pattern seems to be recent, but it began emerging even before World War II, when the public was indifferent to Asian affairs until after the Japanese attack on Pearl Harbor. The pattern was more evident in regard to Korea, a situation which the public ignored until after North Korea's attack on the South in 1950. Public opinion rallied behind Truman. As the war dragged on, critics did not attack American involvement, per se, but they argued that Truman's "incompetence" had caused the war and prevented us from winning it.

The pattern was clear in the case of Vietnam. Few Americans realized that, after Japan's withdrawal from Indochina at the end of World War II, Vietnamese nationalists, including both communists and noncommunists, resisted French efforts to reconquer the former colony. Few Americans realized that the French persuaded Truman to give them financial assistance in "protecting" the "free world." The public did not take notice until 1954, when France lost the war and signed an agreement which divided Indochina into several nations, including a communist-controlled North Vietnam and a noncommunist South Vietnam. Persuaded by his military advisers that the southeast Asian mainland was not vital to American interests and that a war could not be won there, President Eisenhower approved (without signing) the agreement and sent economic aid to the South. To most Americans, the matter was settled.

Subsequently, while the public returned to ignoring the situation, President Kennedy sent a few military advisers to prop up the South Vietnamese government, which came under criticism from noncommunists and military pressure from the communist-led Vietcong who received support from the North. After Kennedy's death in 1963, his successor, Lyndon Johnson, sent more advisers, and the press gave increasing attention to the deteriorating situation. Just as the election campaign of 1964 was shifting into high gear, a dramatic incident rallied the public behind the president. On August 2 and 4, North Vietnamese patrol boats allegedly attacked American naval ships in the Gulf of Tonkin. Johnson ordered an airstrike on North Vietnamese naval bases and drew upon the "folly of appeasement" argument in a public speech about the necessity of meeting force with force. Congress was easily persuaded to pass the "Gulf of Tonkin" resolution, which empowered the president to "repel any attack."

During the election campaign, the Republican nominee, Barry Goldwater, advocated more bombing, while Johnson promised not to get American boys killed in a foreign war. After his reelection, Johnson sent more soldiers to Vietnam. Although internal debates among policymakers are still not fully known, we know that a few frustrated military advisers proposed an "enclave" strategy, in which American troops would hold a few strategic, defensible areas until the Vietcong's lack of success forced them to negotiate. Johnson, however, insisted on a search-and-destroy strategy, which led to more troops, more casualties—and an increasingly hysterical debate. Forgetting Eisenhower's view that Southeast Asia was not essential to American security, proponents of the war claimed that the fall of Vietnam would mean the beginning of one communist victory after another. They supplemented this argument with the "folly of appeasement" argument: a dishonorable retreat would destroy American credibility with both our allies and our enemies.

Antiwar rhetoric during the Vietnam War was characterized by many arguments that had been used during previous wars (for example, we have no reason to be involved; our allies are equally at fault; American liberties are being threatened by militarism; the resources being wasted could be used better here at home; and we are not winning). However, the antiwar rhetoric was somewhat different from that of earlier wars. Much of it emanated from college campuses, and mass demonstrations often included riots and illegal occupancy of campus buildings. Antiwar rhetoric was unusually inflammatory, involving much unprintable language and explicit charges that Johnson had lied. The movement was linked to various countercultures, including mild-mannered "flower children" and the more boisterous "hippies."

It is difficult to determine whether public opinion turned against the war because of the rhetoric or because of other factors, such as the war weariness that inevitably develops when wars drag on without being won, the frequent televised newscasts which included graphic pictures of death and destruction, frequent news reports of the South Vietnamese government's deficiencies and, finally, the failure of prowar speakers to persuade people that a communist victory threatened America. In any case, Vietnam became unpopular.

On July 27, 1965, when the antiwar movement was in its early stages, George McGovern (1922-) delivered a speech to a sparsely attended Senate session. Despite its being largely ignored by the press, it is rhetorically significant for several reasons. It illustrates the rhetorical method by which prowar arguments of "honor" and "credibility" were refuted. It highlights a contrast between the moderate antiwar rhetoric of the early days and the later, more emotional, rhetoric. It also highlights McGovern's minimal reputation in 1965 and his later prominence. A veteran of World War II, McGovern had spent the early postwar years as a student and then as a professor. In 1956 and 1958, he was elected a Democratic congressman from South Dakota. After McGovern's unsuccessful senatorial race in 1960, Kennedy appointed him director of the Food for Peace program. Elected to the Senate in 1962, he had not assumed a major senatorial role by 1965, and most of his work had involved agricultural issues. His only speeches on international affairs had been one in 1963 in favor of a smaller military budget and some short ones early in 1965 arguing the failure of Johnson's Vietnam policy. His July 27 speech was interrupted by two like-minded colleagues, and the three yielded the floor to one another to reinforce each other's arguments. Only his words prior to the interchange are reproduced below and were obtained from the *Congressional Record*, 89th Congress, vol. 111, p. 18308.

How to Save Lives and Political Face in Vietnam

Mr. McGOVERN. Mr. President, it now appears that the United States is faced with the distinct possibility of a major land war in Asia. Seventy-five thousand U.S. troops are already there, and it is reported that this number may reach 200,000 by the end of the year and perhaps many more than that by next spring. That would be a force on the scale of the Korean war with the added dimension of a much more elusive enemy. We do not know whether or not such a major American campaign would draw in the main body of the North Vietnam Army — a well-equipped, disciplined force of 350,000 men. If that army were to become involved in the war in the south, a much larger commitment of American forces — perhaps a million men — would be required if our side were to prevail. Also unpredictable is the reaction of China and Russia. Neither do we know what kind of political system would emerge even if we were somehow able to wear down the guerrillas and their allies.

We are talking here, however, of a major war involving thousands of American casualties, the expenditure of billions of dollars, vast bloodshed and destruction for the Vietnamese people, and an uncertain outcome. There are other possible side results of such a war that may be even more serious in the long run than the war itself, including:

First. The worsening of relations between the world's two major nuclear powers, the Soviet Union and the United States.

Second. The strengthening of the most belligerent leadership elements in the Communist world and the weakening of the moderate forces.

Third. The growing conviction in Asia whether justified or not that the United States is a militaristic power with a low regard for the lives of Asiatics and an excessive concern over other people's ideologies and political struggles.

Fourth. The derailment of efforts toward world peace and the improvement of life in the developing countries, to say nothing of its impact on our own hopes for a better society.

The proponents of a large U.S. military effort in Vietnam base their case on the domino theory and their fear of the paper tiger charge. This theory, first propounded by the late John Foster Dulles more than a decade ago, has been the guiding light of the foreign policy establishment ever since.

According to the domino theory, if South Vietnam goes Communist, this will topple Thailand or Cambodia which will then topple Burma, Malaysia, and so on through the list of Asiatic [sic] powers including the Philippines, India, Pakistan, Australia, New Zealand, and Japan.

It is not always made clear whether the dominoes are expected to fall because of Chinese aggression or because each country in turn infects its neighbor with the virus of communism. Be that as it may, as the theory goes, the United States must stand firm in South Vietnam to prevent the dominoes from falling no matter what the cost.

The related paper tiger theory holds that unless the United States stands firm, we will lose face in the eyes of Asiatics and American power in the Pacific will collapse.

This was the rationale that led Mr. Dulles and President Eisenhower to take up the French mantle after France was expelled from French Indochina by Ho Chi Minh in 1954 and other U.S. aid to President Diem to build an anti-Communist barrier in South Vietnam.

Despite the fact that numerous governments have come and gone in Saigon since the fall of Diem in 1963, we have been holding on to that bastion at a steadily mounting cost ever since until we now stand on the brink of a major land war in Asia.

The questions now before us are:

First. Do we continue to accelerate the struggle toward a major war?

Second. Do we call it off and withdraw our forces? or,

Third. Do we consolidate our present position, keep our casualties at a minimum and hold out indefinitely for a negotiated settlement?

A POLICY OF MODERATION — HOLDING THE LINE

I strongly recommend the third course. I urge that we stop the bombing attacks in both North and South Vietnam. Bombing is largely ineffective in a guerrilla war and more often than not kills the wrong people. We should also stop the jungle land skirmishes which subject our soldiers to ambush. Instead, let us consolidate our troops in a holding action in the cities and well-defended enclaves along the coast. We can hold the cities and the coastal enclaves with few casualties and with little likelihood that the Vietcong will attack frontally. Such a plan would provide a haven for anti-Communist progovernment citizens including the religious groups. It would demonstrate that we are not going to be pushed out, thus giving consolation to those who hold the domino theory and fear the paper tiger label. We would by this policy respect our commitment to the various governments in Saigon that have held power since 1954. It is the best strategy for saving both lives and political face — the two most sensitive factors to be considered now.

Furthermore, it is based on the realities of the present political and military map of Vietnam. While we are in control of the cities and the coast, the guerrillas control most of the rural and village areas. To dislodge them would be to destroy in the process thousands of the innocent civilians we are trying to save.

A recent news report described the despair of American officers who arrived in the village of Bagia which our forces recaptured from the Vietcong after 3 days of U.S. bombing, machinegun, and rocket attacks. What the officers found were weeping women holding their dead children or nursing their wounds and burns. The village church and the school had been destroyed; the people who had been considered progovernment were filled with bitterness toward their rescuers. Meanwhile, the handful of Vietcong guerrillas in the village, who were responsible for our attack in the first place, had melted into the jungle and were never found. Surveying the human tragedy in this village an American officer said:

> This is why we're going to lose this stupid damn war.
> It's senseless, just senseless.

A policy of restricting our military efforts in Vietnam to a holding action in the cities and the coastal enclaves will avoid this kind of self-defeating jungle warfare, which we are ill-equipped to fight, but which the other side is best equipped to fight. We can supply, feed and defend the urban and coastal areas with a modest effort and minimum loss of life. This is a strategy that calls primarily for restraint and patience until such time as the Vietcong get it through their heads that we will not be pushed out. I have been critical of our unilateral involvement in Vietnam. I think the original commitment and its acceleration was a mistake. But we made the commitment, and I would be prepared to support the kind of holding action outlined above for as many years as is necessary to reach an acceptable settlement of the struggle.

I Have a Dream

Martin Luther King, Jr.

Commentary

Just as the old millenarian vision is reflected in much of the Chosen Nation's rhetoric about foreign affairs, so too does it remain central to rhetoric about domestic policy. Recent reformers, like those of bygone days, tend to paint a vision of a perfect society. Other rhetorical continuities with the past include frequent religious appeals and references to the heroes who wrote the Declaration of Independence.

Yet continuities have been accompanied by changes. One such change involves the role of the judiciary. In general, earlier courts hindered, rather than promoted, political reform, as evidenced by rulings in the 1930s which declared some New Deal legislation unconstitutional. By the 1950s, an activist Supreme Court began initiating social change, most notably by ruling that racial segregation laws were unconstitutional.

Another change involves the alleged beneficiaries of reform. Progressives, Populists and New Dealers said they were working for farmers, small businessmen and other average Americans. Recent "change advocates" say they work for those who have been "left behind," especially blacks, Hispanics and women.

Other changes involve the rhetorical methods of change advocates. First, terms such as *activist, change agent* and *liberal* are now more common than older ones such as *reformer* and *progressive*. In addition, the Founding Fathers (the favorite of old-time reformers) now share the rhetorical spotlight with more recent heroes — especially Lincoln, the "Great Emancipator." Likewise, there is an increased application of the principles and statistics of social science. Following the lead of Ely and other "social gospellers," modern activists rely heavily on scientific data. The term *civil rights*, which entered America's rhetorical lexicon when Radical Republicans proposed civil rights legislation to end racial segregation shortly after the Civil War, is also employed to a greater extent. It reappeared when the American Civil Liberties Union used it against suppressions of free speech after World War I, but, in the 1960s, *civil rights* became a key rhetorical term. Lastly, like militant abolitionists of the 1850s, who justified violations of the Fugitive Slave Act by saying the act was against higher law, recent activists often use civil disobedience.

The racial equality movement illustrates the changes and continuities inherent in recent American rhetoric. Prior to 1954, the Supreme Court had espoused the separate-but-equal doctrine, which held that racial segregation was constitutional if equal accommodations were available to both white and black races. The Court reversed itself on May 17, 1954 *(Brown v. Board of Education of Topeka, Kansas)*. Drawing upon social scientific data, the Court argued that separate schools were inherently unequal. Furthermore, it ruled in 1955 that public schools must desegregate with "deliberate speed."

In the same month that the *Brown* decision was announced, Martin Luther King, Jr. (1929-1968) assumed the pastorate of an all-black Baptist church in Montgomery, Alabama. During his first two years, he was busy completing his doctoral dissertation and developing a preaching method that evolved from an intellectual sermon (complete with quotations from authors as varied as Aquinas and Ghandi) into an intellectual-emotional blend reminiscent of the old evangelical style. While deeply involved in these activities, he was not oblivious to mounting racial tensions. "White Citizens' Councils" were springing up all over the South to resist school desegregation. Several Southern politicians signed the "Southern Manifesto," which condemned the Supreme Court for its decision. On the other side, civil rights activists noted that the *Brown* decision applied only to schools, and they looked for court cases to test the separate-but-equal doctrine in nonacademic situations.

In early 1956, a little-known black woman, Rosa Parks, was arrested in Montgomery, Alabama for refusing to give up her bus seat to a white. Local black leaders decided not only to use her arrest as a test case, but also to initiate a bus boycott until the company hired black drivers and desegregated its seating. The boycott was conducted by a newly formed organization that was named to reflect America's traditional belief in progress: the "Montgomery Improvement Association." King was elected president.

The unexpected success of the boycott propelled King into the national spotlight. He went on speaking tours, and, in 1957, he helped organize the Southern Christian Leadership Conference (SCLC). To avoid splintering the civil rights movement, SCLC leaders de-emphasized their objections to existing organizations, but some said privately that the NAACP (founded in 1909) was too elitist and noted that the National Urban League (1911) and the Congress of Racial Equality (1942) confined their activities to Northern cities. Concentrating on the South, the SCLC used Lincoln's birthday in 1958 to launch a black voter registration drive. It also supported various sit-ins and boycotts of segregated facilities. King resigned his pastorate in January, 1960 to become associate pastor of his father's church in Atlanta and to devote more time to SCLC activities.

By 1963, the Southern racial situation was more tense than ever, especially in Alabama. The new governor, George Wallace, had campaigned on the slogan: "Segregation today, segregation tomorrow, segregation forever." Soon after taking office, he dramatically resisted the enrollment of a black student at the University of Alabama until Kennedy federalized the National Guard. The outspoken segregationist "Bull" Connors lost his race for mayor of Birmingham. Claiming that he still retained his post as police commissioner, Connors virtually took over the town government while the newly elected mayor waited until the State supreme court ruled on the legality of Connors' claim. Again exploiting the Lincoln image, King announced on the centennial of the Emancipation Proclamation that he would lead a demonstration in Birmingham. After being arrested, he answered sympathetic critics who urged more moderation by issuing his "Letter from a Birmingham Jail."

Birmingham was a turning point for the civil rights movement and for King personally. Connors unwittingly created sympathy for the movement by his brutal (and televised) treatment of demonstrators. On May 23, 1963, the Alabama Supreme Court ruled against Connors, and the new mayor quickly instituted important desegregation measures. On June 11, Kennedy delivered a televised speech and eight days later sent Congress a civil rights bill. Shortly thereafter, a *Newsweek* poll showed that eighty-eight percent of ordinary blacks and ninety-five percent of black leaders considered King their most effective leader.

King was not the only leader. A prominent elder statesman was A. Philip Randolph, retired president of the all-black Brotherhood of Sleeping Car Porters. Before the advent of air travel, when Pullman sleeping cars were the chic way to travel, Pullman was the largest single employer of blacks, and Randolph was the only black labor union official of any prominence. He promoted the tactic of mass demonstrations as early as 1940, when he planned a "March on Washington" to pressure Roosevelt to require defense contractors to employ blacks. Although the march did not materialize, he conducted rallies in Chicago and New York during the war. By 1962-1963, he was planning a "March on Washington for Jobs and Freedom." Randolph got support from various black leaders. Aware of the jealousy which some leaders had of King, he hoped that the rally would help pull the divergent groups together.

On June 22, 1963, only three days after sending his civil rights bill to Congress, Kennedy met with several black leaders to try to dissuade them from holding the march. He argued that it would hurt the bill's chances of passing. They were not dissuaded, but they did agree to hold the rally in front of the Lincoln Memorial instead of the Capitol, as originally planned.

The highly publicized march was held on August 28, 1963. Leaders, who had worried about attaining their goal of 100,000 participants, were delighted when nearly a quarter of a million demonstrators appeared. Ceremonies began at 1:30 p.m. with the singing of the "Star Spangled Banner," which was followed by a series of speakers from various organizations, each of whom had an eight-minute time limit. Almost two hours elapsed and the audience was getting restless before Randolph reignited interest by introducing King. King's speech was received enthusiastically by the immediate audience, got considerable television coverage and was circulated in printed form.

What was the content of King's address? Printed texts vary, and King did not exactly say what most printed texts have him saying. Haig Bosmajian discussed many errors in eighteen printed texts after comparing them to two commercial recordings made on the scene. [See "The Inaccuracies in the Reprintings of Martin Luther King's 'I Have a Dream' Speech," *Communication Education* 31 (April, 1982), 107-114]. Some errors involve word substitutions (e.g., "cities" for "villages") or word deletions, but some involve the deletion, modification or addition of entire sentences.

Explaining the changes is difficult because the usual reasons (printer's errors, someone's desire to improve a speech or an unsympathetic editor's desire to damage it) do not hold in this case. The changes are too extensive to be mere errors. Instead of improving the speech, they damage it by obscuring certain stylistic devices (e.g., word repetition) which characterized King's evangelical style; yet, most of the eighteen texts were published by scholars and/or civil rights workers friendly to King. All that is known is that numerous published versions contain textual errors.

The text which appears here contains none of the errors noted by Bosmajian. It is based on an audio recording purchased from National Archives and a video tape recording available from *Great Speeches*, vol. I (produced by Alliance Video for Great Speeches, Inc., 1985 and is reprinted by permission of the Joan Daves Agency. To facilitate reading, it does not include the frequent audience responses (applause and verbalizations, such as "yes"), but it does include King's few nonfluencies. To the best of the editor's knowledge, it is the most accurate available printed text of what King actually said.

I Have a Dream

I am happy to join with you today in what will go down in history as the greatest demonstration for freedom in the history of our nation.

Five score years ago, a great American, in whose symbolic shadow we stand today, signed the Emancipation Proclamation. This momentous decree came as a great beacon light of hope to millions of Negro slaves, who had been seared in the flames of withering injustice. It came as a joyous daybreak to end the long night of their captivity.

But one hundred years later, the Negro still is not free. One hundred years later, the life of the Negro is still sadly crippled by the manacles of segregation and the chains of discrimination. One hundred years later, the Negro lives on a lonely island of poverty in the midst of a vast ocean of material prosperity. One hundred years later, the Negro is still languished in the corners of American society and finds himself an exile in his own land.

So we've come here today to dramatize a shameful condition. In a sense we've come to our nation's capital to cash a check. When the architects of our

Republic wrote the magnificent words of the Constitution and the Declaration of Independence, they were signing a promissory note to which every American was to fall heir. This note was a promise that all men — yes, black men as well as white men — would be guaranteed the unalienable rights of life, liberty, and the pursuit of happiness.

It is obvious today that America has defaulted on this promissory note insofar as her citizens of color are concerned. Instead of honoring this sacred obligation, America has given the Negro people a bad check, a check which has come back marked "insufficient funds." But we refuse to believe that the bank of justice is bankrupt. We refuse to believe that there are insufficient funds in the great vaults of opportunity of this nation. So we've come to cash this check — a check that will give us upon demand the riches of freedom and the security of justice.

We have also come to this hallowed spot to remind America of the fierce urgency of now. This is no time to engage in the luxury of cooling off or to take the tranquilizing drug of gradualism. Now is the time to make real the promises of democracy. Now is the time to rise from the dark and desolate valley of segregation to the sunlit path of racial justice. Now is the time to lift our nation from the quicksands of racial injustice to the solid rock of brotherhood. Now is the time to make justice a reality for all of God's children.

It would be fatal for the nation to overlook the urgency of the moment. This sweltering summer of the Negro's legitimate discontent will not pass until there is an invigorating autumn of freedom and equality. Nineteen sixty-three is not an end, but a beginning. Those who hope that the Negro needed to blow off steam and will now be content will have a rude awakening if the nation returns to business as usual. There will be neither rest nor tranquillity in America until the Negro is granted his citizenship rights. The whirlwinds of revolt will continue to shake the foundations of our nation until the bright day of justice emerges.

But that is something that I must say to my people who stand on the warm threshold which leads into the palace of justice. In the process of gaining our rightful place we must not be guilty of wrongful deeds. Let us not seek to satisfy our thirst for freedom by drinking from the cup of bitterness and hatred.

We must forever conduct our struggle on the high plane of dignity and discipline. We must not allow our creative protest to degenerate into physical violence. Again and again we must rise to the majestic heights of meeting physical force with soul force. The marvelous new militancy which has engulfed the Negro community must not lead us to a distrust of all white people, for many of our white brothers, as evidenced by their presence here today, have come to realize that their destiny is tied up with our destiny. And they have come to realize that their freedom is inextricably bound to our freedom. We cannot walk alone.

And as we walk, we must make the pledge that we shall always march ahead. We cannot turn back. There are those who are asking the devotees of civil rights, "When will you be satisfied?" We can never be satisfied as long as the Negro is the vic — victim of the unspeakable horrors of police brutality. We can never be satisfied as long as our bodies, heavy with the fatigue of travel, cannot gain lodging in the motels of the highways and the hotels of the cities. We cannot be satisfied as long as the Negro's basic mobility is from a smaller ghetto to a larger one. We can never be satisfied as long as our children are stripped of their selfhood and robbed of their dignity by signs stating "For Whites Only." We cannot be satisfied as long as a Negro in Mississippi cannot vote and a Negro in New York believes he has nothing for which to vote. No, no, we are not satisfied, and we will not be satisfied until justice rolls down like waters and righteousness like a mighty stream.

I am not mi — unmindful that some of you have come here out of great trials and tribulations. Some of you have come fresh from narrow jail cells. Some of you have come from areas where your crest — quest for freedom left you battered by the storms of persecution and staggered by the winds of police brutality. You have been the veterans of creative suffering. Continue to work with the faith that unearned suffering is redemptive.

Go back to Mississippi, go back to Alabama, go back to South Carolina, go back to Georgia, go back to Louisiana, go back to the slums and ghettos of our Northern cities, knowing that somehow this situation can and will be changed. Let us not wallow in the valley of despair.

I say to you today, my friends, so even though we face the difficulties of today and tomorrow, I still have a dream. It is a dream deeply rooted in the American dream.

I have a dream that one day this nation will rise up and live out the true meaning of its creed: "We hold these truths to be self-evident; that all men are created equal."

I have a dream that one day on the red hills of Georgia the sons of former slaves and the sons of former slaveowners will ba — be able to sit down together at the table of brotherhood.

I have a dream that one day even the state of Mississippi, a state sweltering with the heat of injustice, sweltering with the heat of oppression, will be transformed into an oasis of freedom and justice.

I have a dream that my four little children will one day live in a nation where they will not be judged by the color of their skin but by the content of their character.

I have a dream today.

I have a dream that one day, down in Alabama, with its vicious racists, with its governor having his lips dripping with the words of interposition and nullification, one day right there in Alabama little black boys and black girls will be able to join hands with little white boys and white girls as sisters and brothers.

I have a dream today.

I have a dream that one day every valley shall be exalted, every hill and mountain shall be made low, the rough places will be made plain and the crooked places will be made straight, and the glory of the Lord shall be revealed, and all flesh shall see it together.

This is our hope. This is the faith that I go back to the South with. With this faith we will be able to hew out of the mountain of despair a stone of hope. With this faith we will be able to transform the jangling discords of our nation into a beautiful symphony of brotherhood. With this faith we will be able to work together, to pray together, to struggle together, to go to jail together, to stand up for freedom together, knowing that we will be free one day.

This will be the day...this will be the day when all of God's children will be able to sing with new meaning: "My country 'tis of thee, sweet land of liberty, of thee I sing. Land where my fathers died, land of the Pilgrims' pride, from every mountainside, let freedom ring," and if America is to be a great nation, this must become true.

So let freedom ring. From the prodigious hilltops of New Hampshire, let freedom ring. From the mighty mountains of New York, let freedom ring, from the heightening Alleghenies of Pennsylvania!

Let freedom ring from the snowcapped Rockies of Colorado!

Let freedom ring from the curvaceous slopes of California!

But not only that.

Let freedom ring from Stone Mountain of Georgia!

Let freedom ring from Lookout Mountain of Tennessee!

Let freedom ring from every hill and mole hill of Mississippi.

From every mountainside, let freedom ring, and when this happens... when we allow freedom [to] ring, when we let it ring from every village and every hamlet, from every state and every city, we will be able to speed up that day when all of God's children, black men and white men, Jews and Gentiles, Protestants and Catholics, will be able to join hands and sing in the words of the old Negro spiritual, "Free at last! Free at last! Thank God Almighty, we are free at last!"

Separation vs. Integration: A Debate

James Farmer and Malcolm X

Commentary

King's dream of an integrated, interracial society was shared by most, but not all, black activists during the 1960s. Differences of opinion were highlighted by a debate held at Cornell University on March 7, 1962, a year before King's "I Have a Dream" speech. The debate was sponsored by the Cornell United Religious Work (CURW), an interdenominational student religious organization, which printed a text of the debate in its magazine, *Dialogue*, vol. 2 (May 1962), pp. 14-18. This text is reproduced here.

Sponsorship of the debate by a student religious group exemplifies the high level of student involvement in the civil rights movement during the post-World War II period, especially by students with a "social gospel" orientation. As we saw earlier, Washington Gladden led a generation of preacher-reformers around 1900; and their "social gospel" continued to influence the churches, especially young theology students. This is exemplified by James Farmer (1920-) and the Congress of Racial Equality (CORE). The son of a college professor who held a theology degree, Farmer earned a theology degree in 1941 from Howard University, where he studied with Howard Thurman, a prominent Methodist clergyman and vice-chairman of the Fellowship of Reconciliation (FOR), a pacifist organization that had been founded during the First World War. Instead of entering the ministry after graduation, Farmer activated his pacifism at a time when the United States was about to enter World War II by going to work for FOR. Assigned to the Chicago area, he soon joined five University of Chicago students, most of whom were pacifists and studying theology, in organizing CORE.

Like other pacifists of that era, CORE's members were strongly influenced by Mohandas Gandhi, the famous Hindu who was combatting British colonialism in India by a strategy of "passive resistance." In a leaflet printed even before it was a "Congress" (it was originally a "committee"), CORE said its "one purpose" was "to eliminate racial discrimination" and its "one method" would be "interracial, non-violent direct action." It announced it would concentrate on ending discrimination in places of public accommodation, and its "direct action" would include "such techniques as negotiation, mediation, demonstration, and picketing." It used the threat of a white boycott to achieve one of its first successes—gaining service for blacks at the university barbershop—and it used an interracial "sit-in" to gain service for blacks at a local restaurant.

CORE's "direct action" was more militant than the strategies of the older National Association for the Advancement of Colored People (NAACP), which relied primarily on lawsuits to end segregation; but both groups were interracial and committed to desegregation. Despite some tensions between them, the two organizations worked harmoniously, as exemplified by Farmer's joining the NAACP staff in 1959. Farmer had previously been on FOR's staff, which illustrates how CORE, unlike the better-known NAACP, relied primarily on volunteer, part-time workers.

CORE's early activities were confined mostly to a few northern cities, and it was not involved in the Montgomery bus boycott in 1956. However, the boycott energized CORE psychologically because this was a type of "direct action" that it had been using for eighteen years. It made plans to intensify its activity and to move into the South. Farmer became full-time National Director in 1961 and led a highly-publicized "Freedom Ride." A Supreme Court decision of December 1960 had desegregated interstate travel facilities; but with the decision being frequently ignored, the "Freedom Riders" traveled on interstate buses in the South in an effort to desegregate waiting rooms, restaurants and rest rooms as well as the buses themselves. They also held rallies along the way.

A combination of events skyrocketed the "Ride" into public attention: (1) the violence with which Riders were often met by white segregationists (one Rider needed fifty stitches after being hit with a metal pipe, for example); (2) the non-violent response of the Riders (who had pledged themselves to "passive resistance"); (3) the frequency with which Riders were arrested (usually for "disturbing the peace"); and (4) the rapid escalation of participants and events. By the time they got to Jackson, Mississippi, so many Riders were under arrest that the local jails could not accommodate them; but with a new application of Gandhi's "jail in" tactic, many Riders refused to be released on bail. The Federal government tried unsuccessfully to persuade CORE to "cool off" while sending hundreds of marshals to protect Riders.

At the time of the Cornell debate, the Freedom Ride had made Farmer one of the best-known black activists of the time; and CORE was at the zenith of its popularity and influence. Many historians believe CORE's activities contributed significantly to eventual passage of the Civil Rights law and a significant decline in segregation. Historians also agree that CORE contributed to a more militant attitude on the part of blacks, especially youngsters. Farmer was delighted that more blacks were actively fighting discrimination, but he worried about increased violence and the growing popularity among blacks of the "separation" ideal.

The idea of separation was not new, only more popular. It had been articulated much earlier by Marcus Garvey, who founded the United Negro

Improvement Association in 1920 and advocated a "Return to Africa." Its growing popularity was exemplified by the increasing influence of Malcolm X (1925-1965), whose father, Earl Little, had been one of Garvey's followers. Little was a Baptist minister who preached racial pride as well as religion. His militancy resulted in his house in Lansing, Michigan being burned, apparently by members of the Ku Klux Klan. He then moved to Omaha, Nebraska, where his militancy continued. In 1931, when Malcolm was only six years old, Earl Little died after being run over by a street car. Although there was no concrete evidence, Malcolm believed his father had been murdered. A few years later, Malcolm's mother was placed in a mental hospital, and the family disintegrated. Malcolm went back to Michigan to attend school; but he soon moved to the East, where he got a railroad job but was imprisoned for drug dealing. This unusual background inculcated a strong anti-white attitude.

While in prison, Malcolm Little converted to the Nation of Islam, and changed his surname to "X" from his "slave name" Little. When he was released from prison in 1952, the Nation of Islam had only about 400 members. Its leader, Elijah Muhammad, commissioned Malcolm X and a few other young converts to recruit more members. By 1959, membership had grown dramatically (although estimates varied from 40,000 to 100,000), and sixty-nine temples had been established in twenty-seven states. Most of the new "Black Muslim" temples were in the East, where Malcolm X was headquartered; and he was generally regarded as the Nation's leading spokesman despite his not being the official leader.

This dramatic growth of what Malcolm X called "Black Nationalism" attracted considerable attention, especially after a 1959 television documentary entitled "The Hate that Hate Produced," which convinced many Americans that he was advocating violence against whites. Whether he actually favored violence is a debatable question; but there is no doubt about three points: (1) His ideas were markedly different from those of Martin Luther King (whom Malcolm X once called "an ignorant Negro preacher") and CORE. (2) Both Malcolm X and Farmer faced serious difficulties soon after the debate. Malcolm X broke with Elijah Muhammad in 1964. He announced in his "Declaration of Independence" that although he still retained his Moslem religion and still agreed with Muhammad that the ultimate solution for blacks was to go "back home, to our own African homeland," he was forming a new "Muslim Mosque, Inc." to work for "Black Nationalism." Less than a year later he was assassinated. Meanwhile, Farmer faced internal criticisms; and he resigned as National Director of CORE, at which time the organization dropped its commitment to non-violence. (3) Both Farmer and Malcolm were leading black spokesmen when they engaged in the following debate.

Separation or Integration: James Farmer

When the Freedom Riders left from Montgomery, Alabama, to ride into the conscience of America and into Jackson, Mississippi, there were many persons who said to us, "Don't go into Mississippi, go anyplace you like, go to the Union of South Africa, but stay out of Mississippi." They said, "What you found in Alabama will be nothing compared to what you will meet in Mississippi." I remember being told a story by one minister who urged us not to go. he said, "Once upon a time there was a Negro who had lived in Mississippi, lived for a long time running from county to county. Finally he left the state, and left it pretty fast, as Dick Gregory would put it, not by Greyhound, but by bloodhound, and he went to Illinois to live, in Chicago. And unable to find a job there, after several weeks of walking the street unemployed, he sat down and asked God what he should do. God said, "Go back to Mississippi." He said, "Lord you surely don't mean it, you're jesting. You don't mean for me to go back to Mississippi. There is segregation there!" The Lord said, "Go back to Mississippi." The man looked up and said, "Very well, Lord, if you insist, I will do it. I will go. But will you go with me?" The Lord said, "As far as Cincinnati."

The Freedom Riders felt that they should go all the way because there is something wrong with our nation and we wanted to try to set it right. As one of the nation's scholars wrote at the turn of the century, "The problem of the twentieth century will be the problem of the color-line, of the relations between the lighter and the darker peoples of the earth, Asia and Africa, in America, and in the islands of the sea." What prophetic words, indeed. We have seen the struggle for freedom all over the world. We have seen it in Asia; we have seen it in the islands of the sea; we have seen it in Africa, and we are seeing it in America now. I think the racist theories of Count DeGobineu, Lothrop Stoddard and others have set the pattern for a racism that exists within our country. There are theories that are held today, not only by those men and their followers and successors, but by Ross Barnett, John Patterson devotees and followers of the Klan and the White Citizens Councils, and Lincoln Rockwell of the American Nazi Party.

These vicious racist theories hold that Negroes are inferior and whites are superior innately. Ordained by God, so to speak. No more vicious theory has existed in the history of mankind. I would suggest to you that no theory has provided as much human misery throughout the centuries as the theory of races—The theories that say some people are innately inferior and that others are innately superior. Although we have some of those theories in our country, we also have a creed of freedom and of democracy. As Pearl Buck put it, "Many Americans suffer from a split personality. One side of that personality is believing in democracy and freedom, as much as it is possible for a man to believe. The other side of this personality is refusing, just as doggedly, to practice that democracy and that freedom, in which he believes." That was the split personality. Gunnar Myrdal, in his book, *The American Dilemma*, indicated that this was basically a moral problem, and that we have this credo which Americans hold to, of freedom, and democracy, and equality, but still we refuse to practice it. Gunnar Myrdal indicated that this is sorely troubling the American conscience.

All of us are a part of this system, **all** a part of it. We have all developed certain prejudices, I have mine, you have yours. It seems to me that it is extremely dangerous when any individual claims to be without prejudice, when he really does have it. I'm prejudiced against women drivers. I think they are a menace to civilization, and the sooner they are removed from the highways, the safer we will all be, but I know that's nothing but a prejudice. I have seen women drivers who are better drivers than I am, but does that destroy my prejudice? No. What I do then, is to separate her from the group of women drivers and say, "Why she is an exception." Or maybe I say she is driving very well because she feels guilty. She knows that other women in the past have had accidents, and so she drives cautiously.

I remember several years ago when I was a youth, attending a church youth conference, and a young fellow from Mississippi and I became very good friends. The last day of the conference as we walked along the road he put his arm on my shoulder and said, "Jim, I have no race prejudice." "No," said I. "Absolutely not," said he. I raised my eyebrows. "As a matter of fact," he went on, "I was thirteen years old before I knew I was any better than a Negro." Well sometimes a supposed absence of racial prejudice runs quite along those lines. Now prejudice is a damaging thing to Negroes. We have suffered under it tremendously. It damages the lives of little children. I remember when I first came into contact with segregation; it was when I was a child in Mississippi when my mother took me downtown, and on the way back this hot July day I wanted to stop and get a coke, and she told me I couldn't get a coke. I had to wait until I got home."Well why can't I, there's a little boy going in," said I, "I bet he's going to get a coke." He was. "Well, why can't I go?" "Because he's white," she said, "and you're colored." It's not important what happened to me, the fact is that the same thing over and over again happens to every mother's child whose skin happens to be dark. If the damage that is done to Negroes is obvious, the damage that is done to whites in America is equally obvious, for they're prejudiced. I lived in Texas a large part of my life; remember driving through the state, and after dusk had fallen being followed by cars of whites who forced me off the road and said to me, "Don't you know that your kind is not supposed to be in this town after sundown." I wondered what was happening to these people; how their minds were being twisted, as mine and others like me had had our minds twisted by this double-edged sword of prejudice. It is a disease indeed. It is an American disease. It is an American dilemma.

The Nation Suffers for Segregation

The damage to Negroes is psychological, it is also economic. Negroes occupy the bottom of the economic ladder, the poorest jobs, the lowest paying jobs. Last to be hired, and first to be fired, so that today the percentage of unemployed Negroes is twice as high as that of whites. There has been political damage as well. In the south we find that comparatively few Negroes are registered to vote. Many are apathetic even when they could register. The percentage who are registered in the north is almost equally as low. As a result, comparatively few Negroes are elected to political office. Thus, the damage to the Negroes as a result of the disease of segregation has been psychological, economic, social, and political. I would suggest to you that the same damages have occurred to whites. Psychological damages are obvious. Economic—the nation itself suffers economically, as a result of denying the rights of full development to one-tenth of its population. Skills, talents, and abilities are crushed in their cradle, are not allowed to develop. Snuffed out. Thus, the nation's economy has suffered. People who could be producing are instead walking the streets. People who could be producing in better jobs and producing more are kept in the lower jobs, sweeping the floors and serving other persons. The whole nation has been damaged by segregation. Now, all of us share the guilt too. I myself am guilty. I am guilty because I spent half my life in the South. During those years I participated in segregation, cooperated with it, and supported it.

We are all intricately involved in the system of segregation. We have not yet extricated ourselves. Negroes are involved, and guilty, and share the blame to the extent they themselves have, by their deeds and their acts, allowed segregation to go on for so long. I do not believe that guilt is a part of my genes or your genes. It hinges upon the deeds that you have done. If you have supported segregation, then you are guilty. If you continue to support it, then your guilt is multiplied. But that is your guilt, that is mine. We share the guilt for the disease of segregation, and its continued existence. All too long, Negro Americans have put up with the system of segregation, North and South. Incidentally, it is not a Southern problem, it is a Northern one as well. Segregation exists in housing and in jobs, and in schools. We have put up with it, have done nothing about it.

The day before the Freedom Riders left Washington, D.C. to ride into the South, I visited my father who was in the hospital on what proved to be his deathbed. I told him I was going on a Freedom Ride to the South. He wanted to know what it was and I told him. "Where are you going?" he asked, and I told him. He said, "Well, I'm glad that you're going, son, and I hope you survive. I realize you may not return, but," said he, "I'm glad you're going because when I was a child in South Carolina and Georgia, we didn't like segregation either, but we thought that's the way things always had to be and the way they always would be, so we put up with it, took part in it, decided to exist and to stay alive. I am glad," said he, "that there are lots of people today who are no longer willing to put up with the evil of segregation, but want to do something about it and know that something can be done." How right he was indeed.

The masses of Negroes are through putting up with segregation: they are tired of it. They are tired of being pushed around in a democracy which fails to practice what it preaches. The Negro students of the South who have read the Constitution, and studied it, have read the amendments to the Constitution, and know the rights that are supposed to be theirs—they are coming to the point where they themselves want to do something about achieving these rights, not depend on somebody else. The time has passed when we can look for pie in the sky, when we can depend upon someone else on high to solve the problem for us. The Negro students want to solve the problem themselves. Masses of older Negroes want to join them in that. We can't wait for the law. The Supreme Court decision in 1954 banning segregated schools has had almost eight years of existence, yet, less than eight percent of the Negro kids are in integrated schools. That is far too low. Now the people themselves want to get involved, and they are. I was talking with one of the student leaders of the South only last week; he said, "I myself desegregated a lunch counter, not somebody else, not some big man, some powerful man, but me, little me. I walked the picket line and I sat in and the walls of segregation toppled. Now all people can eat there." One young prize fighter was a cellmate of mine in the prisons of Mississippi as a Freedom Rider; he had won his last fight and had a promising career. I saw him three weeks ago and asked him, "How are you coming along?" He said, "Not very well. I lost the last fight and I am through with the prize ring. I have no more interest in it. The only fight I want now," said he, "is the freedom fight. Because I, a little man, can become involved in it, and can help to win freedom." So that's what's happening; you see, we are going to do something about freedom now, we are not waiting for other people to do it. The student sit-ins have shown it; we are winning. As a result of one year of the student sit-ins, the lunch counters were desegregated in more than 150 cities. The walls are tumbling down.

Direct Action Brings Results

Who will say that lunch counters which are scattered all over the country are not important? Are we not to travel? Picket lines and boycotts brought Woolworth's to its knees. In its annual report of last year, Woolworth's indicated that profits had dropped and one reason for the drop was the nationwide boycott in which many Northern students, including Cornellians, participated. The picketing and the nationwide demonstrations are the reason that the walls came down in the South, because people were in motion with their own bodies marching with picket signs, sitting in, boycotting, withholding their patronage. In Savannah, Georgia, there was a boycott, in which ninety-nine percent of the Negroes participated. They stayed out of the stores. They registered to vote. The store owners then got together and said, "We want to sit down and talk; gentlemen, you have proved your point. You have proved that you can control Negroes' purchasing power and that you can control their votes. We need no more proof, we are ready to hire the people that you send." Negroes are hired in those stores now as a result of this community-wide campaign. In Lexington, Kentucky, the theatres were opened up by CORE as a result of picketing and boycotting. Some of the theaters refused to admit Negroes, others would let Negroes sit up in the balcony. They boycotted that one, picketed the others. In a short period of time, the theatre owners sat down to negotiate. All of the theatres there are open now. Using the same technique, they provided scores of jobs in department stores, grocery stores, and more recently as city bus drivers.

Then came the Freedom Rides, 325 people were jailed in Jackson, Mississippi, others beaten, fighting for freedom non-violently. They brought down many many barriers. They helped to create desegregation in cities throughout the South. The ICC order was forthcoming as a result of the Freedom Rides and a more recent Supreme Court ruling. CORE sent test teams throughout the South after the ICC order went into effect. The test teams found that in hundreds of cities throughout the South, where terminals had been previously segregated, they now were desegregated and Negroes were using them. Mississippi is an exception, except for two cities; Louisiana is an exception, except for one pocket of the state; but by and large the Rides were successful. And then on Route 40. How many Negroes and interracial groups have driven Route 40 to Washington or to New York and carried their sandwiches, knowing that they could not eat between Wilmington and Baltimore. The Freedom Rides there, and some Cornell students participated in those Freedom Rides, brought down the barriers in more than half of those restaurants and each weekend, Rides are taking place aimed at others. By Easter we will have our Easter dinner in any place we choose on Route 40. At least 53 out of the 80 are now desegregated. In voter registration projects, we have registered 17,000 Negroes in South Carolina, previously unregistered. The politicians, segregationists, it's true, now call up our leaders and say, "I would like to talk to you because I don't believe in segregation as much as my opponent," or, "We would like to sit down and talk," or, "Can you come by my house and let's talk about this thing." Because they are realizing that now they have to be responsible to the votes of Negroes as well as the handful of whites, these are the things that are being done by people themselves in motion. Not waiting for someone else to do it, not looking forward to pie in the sky at some later date, not expecting a power on high to solve the problem for them; but working to solve it themselves and winning.

Integration Repudiates Racist Theories

What are our objectives; segregation, separation? Absolutely not! The disease and the evils that we have pointed to in our American culture have grown out of segregation and its partner, prejudice. We are for integration, which is the repudiation of the evil of segregation. It is a rejection of all the racist theories of DeGobineu, Lothrop Stoddard and all the others. It matters not whether they say that whites are superior to Negroes and Negroes are inferior, or if they reverse the coin and say that Negroes are superior and whites are inferior. The theory is just as wrong, just as much a defiance of history. We reject those theories. We are working for the right of Negroes to enter all fields of activity in American life. To enter business if they choose, to enter the professions, to enter the sciences, to enter the arts, to enter the academic world. To be workers, to be laborers if they choose. Our objective is to have each individual accepted on the basis of his individual merit and not on the basis of his color. On the basis of what he is worth himself.

This has given a new pride to a large number of people. A pride to the people in Mississippi, who themselves saw others, white and Negro, joining them in the fight for freedom; 41 local citizens went into the jails of Mississippi joining the Freedom Riders. They have come out now and they have started their own non-violent Jackson movement for freedom. They are sitting in. They are picketing, they are boycotting and it is working. In Macomb, Mississippi, local citizens are now seeking to register to vote, some of them registering. In Huntsville, Alabama, as a result of CORE's campaign there (and we are now under injunction), for the past six weeks local Negro citizens have been sitting in every day at lunch counters. One of the white CORE leaders there in Huntsville was taken out of his house at gunpoint, undressed and sprayed with mustard oil. That's the kind of treatment they have faced, but they will not give up because they know they are right and they see the effects of their efforts; they see it in the crumbling walls in interstate transportation and in other public facilities.

We are seeking an open society, an open society of freedom where people will be accepted for what they are worth, will be able to contribute fully to the total culture and the total life of the nation.

Now we know the disease, we know what is wrong with America, we know now that the CORE position is in trying to right it. We must do it in interracial groups because we do not think it is possible to fight against caste in a vehicle which in itself is a representative of caste. We know that the students are still sitting in, they are still fighting for freedom. What we want Mr. X, the representative of the Black Muslims and Elijah Muhammad, to tell us today, is what his program is, what he proposes to do about killing this disease. We know the disease, physician, what is your cure? What is your program and how do you hope to bring it into effect? How will you achieve it? It is not enough to tell us that it may be a program of a black state. The Communists had such a program in the thirties and part of the forties, and they dropped it before the fifties as being impractical. So we are not only interested in the terminology. We need to have it spelled out, if we are being asked to follow it, to believe in it, what does it mean? Is it a separate Negro society in each city? As a Harlem, a South Side Chicago? Is it a separate state in one part of the country? Is it a separate nation in Africa, or elsewhere? Then we need to know how is it to be achieved. I assume that before a large part of land could be granted to Negroes or to Jews or to anybody else in the country it would have to be approved by the Senate of the United States.

You must tell us, Mr. X, if you seriously think that the Senate of the United States which has refused or failed for all these years to pass a strong Civil Rights Bill, you must tell us if you really think that this Senate is going to give us, to give you, a black state. I am sure that Senator Eastland would so vote, but the land that he would give us would probably be in the bottom of the sea. After seeing Alabama and Mississippi, if the power were mine, I would give you those states, but the power is not mine, I do not vote in the Senate. Tell us how you expect to achieve this separate black state.

Now it is not enough for us to know that you believe in black businesses, all of us believe that all Americans who wish to go into business should go into business. We must know, we need to know, if we are to appraise your program, the kind of businesses, how they are to be established; will we have a General Motors, a General Electric? Will I be able to manufacture a Farmer Special? Where am I going to get the capital from? You must tell us if we are going to have a separate interstate bus line to take the place of Greyhound and Trailways. You must tell us how this separate interstate bus line is going to operate throughout the country if all of us are confined within one separate state.

You must tell us these things, Mr. X, spell them out. You must tell us also what the relationship will be between the black businesses which you would develop and the total American economy. Will it be a competition? Will it be a rival economy, a dual economy or will there be cooperation between these two economies?

Our program is clear. We are going to achieve our goals of integration by non-violent direct action on an interracial level with whites and Negroes jointly cooperating to wipe out a disease which has afflicted and crippled all of them, white and black alike. The proof of the pudding is the eating. We have seen barriers fall as the result of using these techniques. We ask you, Mr. X, what is your program?

Separation or Integration: Malcolm X

In the name of Allah, the Beneficent, the Merciful, to whom all praise is due whom we forever thank for giving America's 20 million so-called Negroes the most honorable Elijah Muhammad as our leader and our teacher and our guide.

I would point out at the beginning that I wasn't born Malcolm Little. Little is the name of the slave master who owned one of my grandparents during slavery, a white man, and the name Little was handed down to my grandfather, to my father and on to me. But after hearing the teachings of the Honorable Elijah Muhammad and realizing that Little is an English name, and I'm not an Englishman, I gave the Englishman back his name; and since my own had been stripped from me, hidden from me, and I don't know it, I use X; and someday, as we are taught by the Honorable Elijah Muhammad, every black man, woman and child in America will get back the same name, the same language, and the same culture that he had before he was kidnapped and brought to this country and stripped of these things.

I would like to point out in a recent column by James Reston on the editorial page of the *New York Times*, December 15, 1961, writing from London, Mr. Reston, after interviewing several leading European statesmen, pointed out that the people of Europe, or the statesmen in Europe, don't feel that America or Europe have anything to worry about in Russia; that the people in Europe foresee the time when Russia, Europe, and America will have to unite together to ward off the threat of China and the non-white world. And if this same statement was made by a Muslim, or by the honorable Elijah Muhammad, it would be classified as racist; but Reston who is one of the leading correspondents in this country and writing for one of the most respected newspapers, points out that the holocaust that the West is facing is not something from Russia, but threats of the combined forces of the dark world against the white world.

Why do I mention this? Primarily because the most crucial problem facing the white world today is the race problem. And the most crucial problem facing white America today is the race problem. Mr. Farmer pointed out beautifully and quoted one writer actually as saying that the holocaust that America is facing is primarily still based upon race. This doesn't mean that when people point these things out that they are racist; this means that they are facing the facts of life that we are confronted with today. One need only to look at the world troubles in its international context, national context, or local context, and one will always see the race problem right there, a problem that it is almost impossible to duck around.

It so happens that you and I were born at a time of great change, when changes are taking place. And if we can't react intelligently to these changes, then we are going to be destroyed. When you look into the United Nations set-up, the way it is, we see that there is a change of power taking place, a change of position, a change of influence, a change of control. Wherein, in the past, white people used to exercise unlimited control and authority over dark mankind, today they are losing their ability to dictate unilateral terms to dark mankind. Whereas, yesterday dark nations had no voice in their own affairs, today, the voice that they exercise in their own affairs is increasing, which means in essence that the voice of the white man or the white world is becoming more quiet every day, and the voice of the non-white world is becoming more loud every day. These are the facts of life and these are the changes that you and I, this generation, have to face up to on an international level, a national level, or a local level before we can get a solution to the problems that confront not only the white man, but problems that confront also the black man, or the non-white man.

When we look at the United Nations and see how these dark nations get their independence—they can out-vote the Western block or what is known as the white world—and to the point where up until last year the U.N. was controlled by the white powers, or Western powers, mainly Christian powers, and the secretaryship used to be in the hands of a white European Christian; but now when we look at the general structure of the United Nations we see a man from Asia, from Burma, who is occupying the position of Secretary, who is a Buddhist, by the way, and we find the man who is occupying the seat of President is a Moslem from Africa, namely Tunisia. Just in recent times all of these changes are taking place, and the white man has got to be able to face up to them, and the black man has to be able to face up to them, before we can get our problem solved, on an international level, a national level, as well as on the local level.

In terms of black and white, what this means is that the unlimited power and prestige of the white world is decreasing, while the power and prestige of the non-white world is increasing. And just as our African and Asian brothers wanted to have their own land, wanted to have their own country, wanted to exercise control over themselves and govern themselves—they didn't want to be governed by whites or Europeans or outsiders, they wanted control over something among the black masses here in America. I think it would be mighty naive on the part of the white man to see dark mankind all over the world stretching out to get a country of his own, a land of his own, an industry of his own, a society of his own, even a flag of his own, it would be mighty naive on the part of the white man to think that same feeling that is sweeping through the dark world is not going to leap 9000 miles across the ocean and come into the black people here in this country, who have been begging you for 400 years for something that they have yet to get.

In the areas of Asia and Africa where the whites gave freedom to the non-whites a transition took place, of friendliness and hospitality. In the areas where the non-whites had to exercise violence, today there is hostility between them and the white man. In this, we learn that the only way to solve a problem that is unjust, if you are wrong, is to take immediate action to correct it. But when the people against whom these actions have been directed have to take matters in their own hands, this creates hostility, and lack of friendliness and good relations between the two.

An Era of Great Change

I emphasize these things to point up the fact that we are living in an era of great change; when dark mankind wants freedom, justice, and equality. It is not a case of wanting integration, or separation, it is a case of wanting freedom, justice, and equality.

Now if certain groups think that through integration they are going to get freedom, justice, equality and human dignity, then well and good, we will go along with the integrationists. But if integration is not going to return human dignity to dark mankind, then integration is not the solution to the problem. And oft times we make the mistake of confusing the objective with the means by which the objective is to be obtained. It is not integration that Negroes in America want, it is human dignity. They want to be recognized as human beings. And if integration is going to bring us recognition as human beings, then we will integrate. But if integration is not going to bring us recognition as human beings, then integration "out the window," and we have to find another means or method and try that to get our objectives reached.

The same hand that has been writing on the wall in Africa and Asia is also writing on the wall right here in America. The same rebellion, the same impatience, the same anger that exists in the hearts of the dark people in Africa and Asia is existing in the hearts and minds of 20 million black people in this country who have been just as thoroughly colonized as the people in Africa and Asia. Only the black man in America has been colonized mentally, his mind has been destroyed. And today, even though he goes to college he comes out and still doesn't even know he is a black man; he is ashamed of what he is, because his culture has been destroyed, his identity has been destroyed;

he has been made to hate his black skin, he has been made to hate the texture of his hair, he has been made to hate the features that God gave him. Because the honorable Elijah Muhammad is coming along today and teaching us the truth about black people to make us love ourselves, instead of realizing that it is you who taught us to hate ourselves and our own kind, you accuse the honorable Elijah Muhammad of being a hate teacher and accuse him of being a racist. He is only trying to undo the white supremacy that you have indoctrinated the entire world with.

I might point out that it makes America look ridiculous to stand up in world conferences and refer to herself as the leader of the free world. Here is a country, Uncle Sam, standing up and pointing a finger at the Portuguese, and at the French, and at other colonizers, and there are 20 million black people in this country who are still confined to second-class citizenship, 20 million black people in this country who are still segregated and Jim-Crowed, as my friend, Dr. Farmer has already pointed out. And despite the fact that 20 million black people here yet don't have freedom, justice and equality, Adlai Stevenson has the nerve enough to stand up in the United Nations and point the finger at South Africa, and at Portugal and at some of these other countries. All we say is that South Africa preaches what it practices and practices what it preaches; America preaches one thing and practices another. And we don't want to integrate with hypocrites who preach one thing and practice another.

The good point in all of this is that there is an awakening going on among whites in America today, and this awakening is manifested in this way: two years ago you didn't know that there were black people in this country who didn't want to integrate with you; two years ago the white public had been brainwashed into thinking that every black man in this country wanted to force his way into your community, force his way into your schools, or force his way into your factories; two years ago you thought that all you would have to do is give us a little token integration and the race problem would be solved. Why? Because the people in the black community who didn't want integration were never given a voice, were never given a platform, were never given an opportunity to shout out the fact that integration would never solve the problem. And it has only been during the past year that the white public has begun to realize that the problem will never be solved unless a solution is devised acceptable to the black masses—as well as the black bourgeoisie—the upper class or middle class Negro. And when the whites began to realize that these integration-minded Negroes were in the minority, rather than in the majority, then they began to offer an open forum and give those who want separation an opportunity to speak their mind too.

Middle-class Settles for Integration

We who are black in the black belt, or black community, or black neighborhood can easily see that our people who settle for integration are usually the middle-class so-called Negroes, who are in the minority. Why? Because they have confidence in the white man; they have absolute confidence that you will change. They believe that they can change you, they believe that there is still hope in the American dream. But what to them is an American dream to us is an American nightmare, and we don't think that it is possible for the American white man in sincerity to take the action necessary to correct the unjust conditions that 20 million black people here are made to suffer morning, noon, and night. And because we don't have any hope or confidence or faith in the American white man's ability to bring about a change in the injustices that exist, instead of asking or seeking to integrate into the American society we want to face the facts of the problem the way they are, and separate ourselves. And in separating ourselves this doesn't mean that we are anti-white or anti-American, or anti-anything. We feel, that if integration all these years hasn't solved the problem yet, then we want to try something new, something different and something that is in accord with the conditions as they actually exist.

The honorable Elijah Muhammad teaches us that there are over 725 million Moslems or Muslims on this earth. I use both words interchangeably. I use the word Moslem for those who can't undergo the change, and I use the word Muslim for those who can. He teaches us that the world of Islam stretches from the China Sea to the shores of West Africa and that the 20 million black people in this country are the lost-found members of the nation of Islam. He teaches that before we were kidnapped by your grandfathers and brought to this country and put in chains, our religion was Islam, our culture was Islamic, we came from the Muslim world, we were kidnapped and brought here out of the Muslim world. And after being brought here we were stripped of our language, stripped of our ability to speak our mother tongue, and it's a crime today to have to admit that there are 20 million black people in this country who not only can't speak their mother tongue, but don't even know they ever had one. This points up the crime of how thoroughly and completely the black man in America has been robbed by the white man of his culture, of his identity, of his soul, of his self. And because he has been robbed of his self, he is trying to accept your self. Because he doesn't know who he is, now he want to be who you are. Because he doesn't know what belongs to him, he is trying to lay claim to what belongs to you. You have brainwashed him and made him a monster. He is black on the outside, but you have made him white on the inside. Now he has a white heart and a white brain, and he's breathing down your throat and down your neck because he thinks he's a white man the same as you are. He thinks that he should have your house, that he should have your factory, he thinks that he should even have your school, and most of them even think that they should have your woman, and most of them are after your woman.

So-Called Negroes Are Lost Sheep

The honorable Elijah Muhammad teaches us that the black people in America, the so-called Negroes, are the people who are referred to in the Bible as the lost sheep, who are to be returned to their own in the last days. He says that we are also referred to in the Bible, symbolically, as the lost tribe. he teaches us in our religion, that we are those people whom the Bible refers to who would be lost until the end of time. Lost in a house that is not theirs, lost in a land that is not theirs, lost in a country that is not theirs, and who will be found in the last days by the Messiah who will awaken them and enlighten them, and teach them that which they had been stripped of, and then this would give them the desire to come together among their own kind and go back among their own kind.

And this, basically, is why we who are followers of the honorable Elijah Muhammad don't accept integration; we feel that we are living at the end of time, by this, we feel that we are living at the end of the world. Not the end of the earth, but the end of the world. He teaches us that there are many worlds. The planet is an earth, and there is only one earth, but there are many worlds on this earth, the Eastern World and the Western World. There is a dark world and a white world. There is the world of Christianity, and the world of Islam. All of these are worlds and he teaches us that when the book speaks of the end of time, it doesn't mean the end of the earth, but it means the end of time for certain segments of people, or a certain world that is on this earth. Today, we who are here in America who have awakened to the knowledge of ourselves; we believe that there is no God but Allah, and we believe that the religion of Islam is Allah's religion, and we believe that this Christian country will have to accept Allah as God, accept the religion of Islam as God's religion, or otherwise God will come in and wipe it out. And we don't want to be wiped out with the American white man, we don't want to integrate with him, we want to separate from him.

Separation is the Best Solution

The method by which the honorable Elijah Muhammad is straightening out our problem is not teaching us to force ourselves into your society, or force ourselves even into your political, economic or any phase of your society, but he teaches us that the best way to solve this problem is for complete separation. He says that since the black man here in America is actually the property that was stolen from the East by the American white man, since you have awakened today and realized that this is what we are, we should be separated from you, and your government should ship us back from where we came from, not at our expense, because we didn't pay to come here. We were brought here in chains. So the honorable Elijah Muhammad and the Muslims who follow him, we want to go back to our own people. We want to be returned to our own people.

But in teaching this among our people and the masses of black people in this country, we discover that the American government is the foremost agency in opposing any move by any large number of black people to leave here and go back among our own kind. The honorable Elijah Muhammad's words and work is harassed daily by the F.B.I. and every other government agency which use various tactics to make the so-called Negroes in every community think that we are all about to be rounded up, and they will be rounded up too if they will listen to Mr. Muhammad; but what the American government has failed to realize, the best way to open up a black man's head today and make him listen to another black man is to speak against that black man. But when you begin to pat a black man on the back, no black man in his right mind will trust that black man any longer. And it is because of this hostility on the part of the government toward our leaving here that the honorable Elijah Muhammad says then, if the American white man or the American government doesn't want us to leave, and the government has proven its inability to bring about integration or give us freedom, justice and equality on a basis, equally mixed up with white people, then what are we going to do? If the government doesn't want us to go back among our own people, or to our own people, and at the same time the government has proven its inability to give us justice, the honorable Elijah Muhammad says if you don't want us to go and we can't stay here and live in peace together, then the best solution is separation. And this is what he means when he says that some of the territory here should be set aside, and let our people go off to ourselves and try and solve our own problem.

Some of you may say, Well, why should you give us part of this country? The honorable Elijah Muhammad says that for 400 years we contributed our slave labor to make the country what it is. If you were to take the individual salary or allowances of each person in this audience it would amount to nothing individually, but when you take it collectively all in one pot you have a heavy load. Just the weekly wage. And if you realize that from anybody who could collect all of the wages from the persons in this audience right here for one month, why they would be so wealthy they couldn't walk. And if you see that, then you can imagine the result of millions of black people working for nothing for 310 years. And that is the contribution that we made to America. Not Jackie Robinson, not Marian Anderson, not George Washington Carver, that's not our contribution; our contribution to American society is 310 years of free slave labor for which we have not been paid one dime. We who are Muslims, followers of the honorable Elijah Muhammad, don't think that an integrated cup of coffee is sufficient payment for 310 years of slave labor.

Rebuttal: James Farmer

I think that Mr. X's views are utterly impractical and that his so-called "black state" cannot be achieved. There is no chance of getting it unless it is to be given to us by Allah. We have waited for a long time for God to give us other things and we have found that the God in which most of us happen to believe helps those who help themselves. So we would like you to tell us, Mr. X, just what steps you plan to go through to get this black state. Is it one that is going to be gotten by violence, by force? Is it going to be given to us by the Federal government? Once a state is allocated, then are the white people who happen to live there to be moved out forcibly, or Negroes who don't want to go to your black state going to be moved in forcibly? And what does this do to their liberty and freedom?

Now Mr. X suggests that we Negroes or so-called Negroes, as he puts it, ought to go back where we came from. You know, this is a very interesting idea. I think the solution to many of the problems, including the economic problem of our country, would be for all of us to go back where we came from and leave the country to the American Indians. As a matter of fact, maybe the American Indian can go back to Asia, where I understand the anthropologists tell us he came from, and I don't know who preceded him there. But if we search back far enough I am sure that we can find some people to people or populate this nation. Now the overwhelming number of Negroes in this country consider it to be their country; their country more than Africa: I was in Africa three years ago, and while I admire and respect what is being done there, while there is certainly a definite sense of identification, and sympathy with what is going on there, the fact is that the cultures are so very different. Mr. X, I am sure that you have much more in common with me or with several people whom I see sitting here than you do with the Africans, than you do with Tom Mboya. Most of them could not understand you, or you they, because they speak Swahili or some other language and you would have to learn those languages.

I tell you that we are Americans. This is our country as much as it is white American. Negroes came as slaves, most of us did. Many white people came as indentured servants; indentured servants are not free. Don't forget it wasn't all of you who were on that ship, The Mayflower.

Now separation of course has been proposed as the answer to the problem, rather than integration. I am pleased however that Malcolm, oh pardon me, Mr. X, indicated that if integration works, and if it provides dignity, then we are for integration. Apparently he is almost agreeing with us there. He is sort of saying as King Agrippa said to St. Paul, "Almost Thou Persuadest Me." I hope that he will be able to come forth and make the additional step and join me at the integrationist side of this [t]able. In saying that separation really is the answer and even the most effective solution to this problem, he draws a distinction between separation and segregation, saying that segregation is forced ghettoism while separation is voluntary ghettoism. Well now, I would like to ask Mr. X whether it would be voluntary for Negroes to be segregated as long as we allow discrimination in housing throughout our country to exist. If you live in a black state and cannot get a house elsewhere, then are you voluntarily separated, or are you forcibly segregated?

Black Men and White Women

Now Mr. X suggests that actually the Negroes in this country want the white man's women. Now this is a view, of course, which is quite familiar to you; I've heard it before, there are some Negroes who are married to white people, and I, just before I came up, was looking over a back issue of the paper of the Muslims, and saw in there an indication that I myself have a white wife. And it was suggested that therefore I have betrayed my people in marrying a white woman. Well you know I happen to have a great deal of faith in the virtues and the abilities and capacities of Negroes. Not only Negroes, but all of the people too. In fact, I have so much faith in the virtues of Negroes that I do not even think those virtues are so frail that they will be corrupted by contact with other people.

Mr. X also indicated that Negroes imitate whites. It is true, we do, he is right. We fix our hair and try to straighten it; I don't do mine. I haven't had a conk in my life, I think they call it a process now, etc. But this is a part of the culture of course. After the black culture was taken away from us, we had to adapt the culture that was here, adopt it, and adapt to it. But it is also true that white people try to imitate Negroes, with their jazz, with their hair curlers, you know, and their man-tans. I think, Mr. X, that perhaps the grass is always greener on the other side of the fence. Now when we create integration, perhaps it won't be so necessary for us to resort to these devices.

The basic bourgeoisie—is it only the middle class that wants integration? Were the sit-in students black bourgeoisie? They didn't fit into the definition in E. Franklin Frazier's book on the black bourgeoisie. Quite to the contrary, these students were lower class people. Many of them were workers working to stay in school. In the Freedom Rides, were they black bourgeoisie? No, we didn't have exceptions there, we had some people who were unemployed. These are not the black bourgeoisie who want integration. Quite to the contrary, very frequently, the middle class developed a vested interest in the maintenance of segregation. Because if they have a store, and if segregation is eliminated, then I'll be in open competition with the white stores. And thus it is most often true as Frazier pointed out in his book, that the middle class tends to be opposed to desegregation. Now I would wonder also in the building of black businesses if we are not going to be building another black bourgeoisie? If Negroes may not perhaps be giving up one master for another, a white one for a black one? Are we going to build a new Negro middle class, and say that no matter how tyrannical it may prove to be it is my own and therefore, I like it?

Now we of course know that the Negro is sick, the white man is sick, we know that psychologically we have been twisted by all of these things; but still, Mr. X, you have not told us what the solution is except that it is separation, in your view. You have not spelled it out. Well, now, this sickness, as I tried to indicate in my first presentation, springs from segregation. It is segregation that produces prejudice, as much as prejudice produces segregation. In Detroit, at the time of the race riot, the only rioting, the only fighting, was in the all-Negro and all-white sections of the city, where separation was complete. In those several sections of the city where Negroes and whites lived together, next door to each other, there was no fighting because there the people were neighbors or friends. Now you propose separation as the solution to this problem, as the cure to the disease. Here we have a patient that is suffering from a disease caused by mosquitoes, and the physician proposes as a cure that the man go down and lie in a damp swamp and play with wiggletails.

Rebuttal: Malcolm X

I hadn't thought, or intended anyway, to get personal with Mr. Farmer in mentioning his white wife; I thought that perhaps it would probably have been better left unsaid, but it's better for him to say than for me to say it, because then you would think I was picking on him. I think you will find if you were to have gone into Harlem a few years back you would have found on the juke boxes, records by Belafonte, Eartha Kitt, Pearl Bailey, all of these persons were very popular singers in the so-called Negro community a few years back. But since Belafonte divorced Marguerite and married a white woman it doesn't mean that Harlem is anti-white, but you can't find Belafonte's records there; or maybe he just hasn't produced a hit. All of these entertainers who have become involved in intermarriage, and I mean Lena Horne, Eartha Kitt, Sammy Davis, Belafonte, they have a large white following, but you can't go into any Negro community across the nation and find records by these artists that are hits in the so-called Negro community. Because, subconsciously, today the so-called Negro withdraws himself from the entertainers who have crossed the line. And if the masses of black people won't let a Negro who is involved in an intermarriage play music for him, he can't speak for him.

The only way you can solve the race problem as it exists, is to take into consideration the feelings of the masses, not the minority; the majority not the minority. And it is proof that the masses of white people don't want Negroes forcing their way into their neighborhood and the masses of black people don't think it's any solution for us to force ourselves into the white neighborhood, so the only ones who want integration are the Negro minority, as I say, the bourgeoisie and the white minority, the so-called white liberals. And that same white liberal who professes to want integration whenever the Negro moves to his neighborhood, he is the first one to move out. And I was talking with one today who said he was a liberal and I asked him where did he live, and he lived in an all-white neighborhood and probably might for the rest of his life. This is conjecture, but I think it stands true. The Civil War was fought 100 years ago, supposedly to solve this problem. After the Civil War was fought, the problem still existed. Along behind that, the thirteenth and fourteenth Amendments were brought about in the Constitution supposedly to solve the problem; after the Amendments, the problem was still right here with us.

Most Negroes think that the Civil War was fought to make them citizens; they think that it was fought to free them from slavery because the real purposes of the Civil War are clothed in hypocrisy. The real purposes of the Amendments are clothed in hypocrisy. the real purpose behind the Supreme Court Desegregation decision was clothed in hypocrisy. And any time integrationists, NAACP, CORE, Urban League, or what have you, will stand up and tell me to spell out how we are going to bring about separation, and here they are integrationists, a philosophy which is supposed to have the support of the Senate, Congress, President, and the Supreme Court, and still with all of that support and hypocritical agreeing, eight years after the desegregation decision, you still don't have what the court decided on.

So we think this, that when whites talk integration they are being hypocrites, and we think that the Negroes who accept token integration are also being hypocrites, because they are the only ones who benefit from it, the handful of hand-picked high-class, middle-class Uncle Tom Negroes. They are hand-picked by whites and turned loose in a white community and they're satisfied. But if all of the black people went into the white community, over night you would have a race war. If four or five little black students going to school in New Orleans bring about the riots that we saw down there, what do you think would happen if all of the black people tried to go to any school that they want, you would have a race war. So our approach to it, those of us who follow the honorable Elijah Muhammad, we feel that it is more sensible than running around here waiting for the whites to allow us inside their attic or inside their basement.

Anti-Discrimination Groups Discriminate

Every Negro group that we find in the Negro community that is integrated is controlled by the whites who belong to it, or it is led by the whites who belong to it. NAACP has had a white president for 53 years, it has been in existence for 53 years; Roy Wilkins is the Executive Secretary, but Spingarn, a white man, has been the president for the past 23 years, and before him, his brother, another white man was president. They have never had a black president. Urban League, another so-called Negro organization, doesn't have a black president, it has a white president. Now this doesn't mean that that's racism, it only means that the same organizations that are accusing you of practicing discrimination, when it comes to leadership they're practicing discrimination themselves.

The honorable Elijah Muhammad says, and points out to us that in this book (*Anti-Slavery*) written by a professor from the University of Michigan, Dwight Lowell Dumond, a person who is an authority on the race question or slave question, his findings were used by Thurgood Marshall in winning the Supreme Court Desegregation decision. And in the preface of this book, it says that second-class citizenship is only a modified form of slavery. Now I'll tell you why I'm dwelling on this; everything that you have devised yourself to solve the race problem has been hypocrisy, because the scientists who delved into it teach us or tell us that second-class citizenship is only a modified form of slavery, which means the Civil War didn't end slavery and the Amendments didn't end slavery. They didn't do it because we still have to wrestle the Supreme Court and the Congress and the Senate to correct the hypocrisy that's been practiced against us by whites for the past umteen years.

And because this was done, the American white man today subconsciously still regards the black man as something below himself. And you will never get the American white man to accept the so-called Negro as an integrated part of his society until the image of the Negro the white man has is changed, and until the image that the Negro has of himself is also changed.

A Time for Choosing

Ronald Reagan

Commentary

The chronological proximity of the "civil rights" and anti-Vietnam war movements might have been an historical accident, but observers who see an ideological connection point out that many "activists" worked in both movements (much like many pre-Civil War "reformers" were involved in both woman suffrage and abolitionism). Moreover, the 1960s also saw the resurgence of the women's movement, many of whose adherents also protested racial segregation and the Vietnam war. Thus, some observers saw the 1960s as a decade of protest by "liberals" and "radicals."

Although this writer does not deny the plethora of protest rhetorics during the 1960s, he would like to caution readers against uncritical acceptance of two common oversimplifications. First, although superficial pundits have a habit of dividing history into nice, neat segments that are a decade in length (such as "The Roaring Twenties," "The Depressed Thirties," "The Bland Fifties") history is not that neat.

Second, not all of the protest rhetorics of the 1960s were "liberal" or "radical." There were countermovements, as exemplified by Concerned Women for America, an anti-feminist organization that is even larger than the pro-feminist National Organization for Women. Perhaps more important, "conservatives" also launched protests. Their leader was Barry Goldwater, who was reported by the *New York Times* to be the most sought-after speaker on college campuses during 1964 (the nearest competitor being Malcolm X).

Goldwater's conservative movement can be dated (somewhat arbitrarily) from the 1960 presidential election. Although the Republican nominee, Richard Nixon, was barely defeated in the general election, his nomination at the Republican convention was hotly contested. The intra-party contest was partly over personalities, but it was also a battle (that still persists) over ideological and geographical control of the party. The dispute has been described in different ways: "Liberals vs. Conservatives;" "Moderates vs. Extremists;" "Accommodators vs. True Believers;" "Eastern Establishment vs. the West;" "Elitists vs. Populists."

No matter what the label, the battle reflects historical trends that changed both political parties. Pre-Civil War Republicans were a "big government" party in the Hamiltonian tradition, while Democrats were in the Jeffersonian tradition of "small government." Republicans virtually monopolized the "reform" tradition by supporting temperance and opposing slavery. After the war, Republicans continued to support "big government" measures, such as railroad subsidies and protective tariffs, while most Democrats did not. Although both parties became increasingly corrupt, the limited efforts for political "reform" usually came from Republicans.

By around 1900, the "progressive" movement, which advocated legislative programs that promoted "big government," influenced both parties, but it also helped divide each party. In 1912, the intra-party battle among Republicans resulted in Teddy Roosevelt leaving the party to run on a third-party ticket called "Progressive," and Wilson ran as a "progressive" Democrat. By the 1930s, Northern Democrats generally supported the "big government" ideology of the New Deal, while Southern Democrats remained Jeffersonians. One of Franklin Roosevelt's most amazing accomplishments was to keep the party more-or-less united. His successors, Truman, Kennedy and Johnson, were also fairly successful in keeping the party together, but the "big government" philosophy was getting so strong that a few "small government" Democrats began to question their own party loyalty. Meanwhile, most Republicans continued in the Hamiltonian tradition, but Jefferson's "small government" ideology gained ground.

By the 1930s, political language began to change, although this writer confesses that he cannot explain why. The word, "liberal," gradually replaced "progressive." Perhaps the final blow to the godlike qualities of "progressive" came in 1948, after the word was appropriated by the unpopular Progressive party that nominated Henry Wallace for president. The word, "conservative," began to take on two contradictory meanings: (1) a "big government" ideology in the Hamiltonian tradition (advocating, for example, subsidies to business); and (2) a "small government" philosophy in the Jeffersonian tradition.

As the Republican convention of 1960 approached, the outspoken Senator Barry Goldwater of Arizona knew exactly what he meant when he called himself a "conservative." He believed in "small government," but he doubted whether like-minded Republicans were numerous enough to take over the party. However, he knew they were strong enough to prevent the nomination of Nelson Rockefeller, an Eastern "liberal." According to his autobiography, Goldwater endorsed Nixon's nomination because of Nixon's "conservative" record and pre-convention promises to support "conservative" measures. Goldwater was outraged when Nixon endorsed a "liberal" platform at the convention to gain Rockefeller's support. Nevertheless, his fear of breaking up the Republican party and his intense dislike of Democratic "liberalism" prompted him to campaign for Nixon. In an impromptu convention speech, Goldwater urged his fellow conservatives to do likewise, but he added: "Let's grow up, conservatives. Let's, if we want to, take this party back—and I think we can some day."

In a sense, "some day" was 1964, but in another sense it was 1980. Republican conservatives worked successfully to nominate Goldwater in 1964, but he was defeated overwhelmingly in the general election. Yet conservatives remained in control of the party and won the presidency in 1980 with Ronald Reagan (1911-   ). It would take us too far afield to try to analyze why Goldwater lost so overwhelmingly and Reagan was so popular, but Reagan's speech, "A Time for Choosing," delivered about a week before the 1964 election, tells us a great deal if we study it in terms of both its immediate and long-term contexts.

Among the many tactical errors that Goldwater now confesses to making in 1964 was a decision to avoid letting the campaign go into debt. Modern political campaigns are very expensive, and paying for them "after the fact" has become standard procedure. Goldwater's reluctance to go into debt put his campaign in a financial bind that was exacerbated by the refusal of many wealthy "Eastern liberals" to contribute. Goldwater later said (probably correctly) that a good long-term effect of this situation was that conservative party workers learned how to become "populists" as they got small contributions from large numbers of "average people" instead of big contributions from a few Eastern "elitists." They learned to communicate with "average people," and they compiled lists of small contributors and prospective volunteer workers for use in later campaigns.

Reagan's rhetoric in 1964 suddenly thrust him into the foreground of the Republican party, although he had not changed his party registration from Democrat to Republican until 1962 and had never been a candidate for public office. His limited political experience, however, was offset by rhetorical skills of long standing. A professional movie actor, Reagan had become a popular after-dinner speaker as early as the 1930s. He increased his activity on what he called the "mashed potato circuit" after becoming president of the Screen Actors Guild. In 1954, he became host of the television program, *General Electric Theatre*, with the understanding that he would also assist the corporation's public relations enterprise by speaking regularly at luncheon clubs, banquets and business conventions. Although these were nonpartisan occasions, his most frequent speech, entitled "Encroaching Control: Keep Government Poor and Remain Free," set forth the "small government" philosophy. In 1962, the former Democrat campaigned for the California state Republican ticket, and in 1964 he became co-chairman of the California Citizens for Goldwater-Miller Committee.

After delivering a fund-raising speech in Los Angeles, Reagan was asked by party leaders to repeat it on national television on October 27, 1964, only a week before the election. This was Reagan's first political speech on national television. The speech had no title. An announcer said simply that Reagan was going to give an address in behalf of Goldwater.

The speech obviously did not save Goldwater, but favorable reaction among conservatives was overwhelming. Goldwater called it the "best speech of the campaign." It was rebroadcast during the final week of the campaign by numerous Republican committees throughout the nation. It raised vast amounts of money, although this writer cannot be precise (he has seen estimates from supposedly reliable sources ranging from eight million to three-quarters of a million dollars). It so impressed a group of conservative California businessmen that early in 1965 they asked Reagan to run for governor and engaged a public relations firm to manage his campaign. The firm distributed mimeographed copies of the speech under the title, "A Time for Choosing," and Reagan delivered an expanded version of the speech when he opened his successful gubernatorial campaign at the 1965 convention of the California Republican Assembly.

The following text is reproduced from Ronald Reagan's *Speaking My Mind: Selected Speeches* (New York: Simon and Schuster, 1989), pp. 25-36.

A Time for Choosing

Thank you very much. Thank you, and good evening. The sponsor has been identified, but unlike most television programs, the performer hasn't been provided with a script. As a matter of fact, I have been permitted to choose my own words and discuss my own ideas regarding the choice that we face in the next few weeks.

I have spent most of my life as a Democrat. I recently have seen fit to follow another course. I believe that the issues confronting us cross party lines. Now, one side in this campaign has been telling us that the issues of this election are the maintenance of peace and prosperity. The line has been used "We've never had it so good!"

But I have an uncomfortable feeling that this prosperity isn't something upon which we can base our hopes for the future. No nation in history has ever survived a tax burden that reached a third of its national income. Today thirty-seven cents out of every dollar earned in this country is the tax collector's share, and yet our government continues to spend 17 million dollars a day more than the government takes in. We haven't balanced our budget twenty-eight out of the last thirty-four years. We have raised our debt limit three times in the last twelve months, and now our national debt is one and a half times bigger than all the combined debts of all the nations of the world. We have 15 billion dollars in gold in our treasury—we don't own an ounce. Foreign dollar claims are 27.3 billion dollars, and we have just had announced that the dollar of 1939 will now purchase forty-five cents in its total value.

As for the peace that we would preserve, I wonder who among us would like to approach the wife or mother whose husband or son has died in Vietnam and ask them if they think this is a peace that should be maintained indefinitely. Do they mean peace, or do they mean we just want to be left in peace? There can be no real peace while one American is dying someplace in the world for the rest of us. We are at war with the most dangerous enemy that has ever faced mankind in his long climb from the swamp to the stars, and it has been said if we lose that war, and in so doing lose this way of freedom of ours, history will record with the greatest astonishment that those who had the most to lose did the least to prevent its happening. Well, I think it's time we ask ourselves if we still know the freedoms that were intended for us by the Founding Fathers.

Not too long ago two friends of mine were talking to a Cuban refugee, a businessman who had escaped from Castro, and in the midst of his story one of my friends turned to the other and said, "We don't know how lucky we are." And the Cuban stopped and said, "How lucky you are! I had someplace to escape to." In that sentence he told us the entire story. If we lose freedom here, there is no place to escape to. This is the last stand on earth.

And this idea that government is beholden to the people, that it has no other source of power except the sovereign people, is still the newest and most unique idea in all the long history of man's relation to man. This is the issue of this election. Whether we believe in our capacity for self-government or whether we abandon the American Revolution and confess that a little intellectual elite in a far-distant capital can plan our lives for us better than we can plan them ourselves.

You and I are told increasingly that we have to choose between a left or right, but I would like to suggest that there is no such thing as a left or right. There is only an up or down—up to man's age-old dream—the ultimate in individual freedom consistent with law and order—or down to the ant heap of totalitarianism, and regardless of their sincerity, their humanitarian motives, those who would trade our freedom for security have embarked on this downward course.

In this vote-harvesting time they use terms like the "Great Society," or as we were told a few days ago by the President, we must accept a "greater government activity in the affairs of the people." But they have been a little more explicit in the past and among themselves—and all of the things that I now will quote have appeared in print. These are not Republican accusations. For example, they have voices that say "the cold war will end through our acceptance of a not undemocratic socialism." Another voice says that the profit motive has become outmoded, it must be replaced by the incentives of the welfare state; or our traditional system of individual freedom is incapable of solving the complex problems of the twentieth century.

Senator Fulbright has said at Stanford University that the Constitution is outmoded. He referred to the president as our moral teacher and our leader, and he said he is hobbled in his task by the restrictions in power imposed on him by this antiquated document. He must be freed so that he can do for us what he knows is best.

And Senator Clark of Pennsylvania, another articulate spokesman, defines liberalism as "meeting the material needs of the masses through the full power of centralized government." Well, I for one resent it when a representative of the people refers to you and me—the free men and women of this country—as "the masses." This is a term we haven't applied to ourselves in America. But beyond that, "the full power of centralized government"—this was the very thing the Founding Fathers sought to minimize. They knew that governments don't control *things*. A government can't control the economy without controlling people. And they knew when a government sets out to do that, it must use force and coercion to achieve its purpose. They also knew, those Founding Fathers, that outside of its legitimate functions, government does nothing as well or as economically as the private sector of the economy.

Now, we have no better example of this than the government's involvement in the farm economy over the last thirty years. Since 1955 the cost of this program has nearly doubled. One-fourth of farming in America is responsible for 85 percent of the farm surplus. Three-fourths of farming is out on the free market and has known a 21 percent increase in the per capita consumption of all its produce. You see, that one-fourth of farming is regulated and controlled by the federal government. In the last three years we have spent forty-three dollars in the feed grain program for every dollar bushel of corn we don't grow.

Senator Humphrey last week charged that Barry Goldwater as president would seek to eliminate farmers. He should do his homework a little better, because he will find out that we have had a decline of 5 million in the farm population under these government programs. He will also find that the Democratic administration has sought to get from Congress an extension of the farm program to include that three-fourths that is now free. He will find that they have also asked for the right to imprison farmers who wouldn't keep books as prescribed by the federal government. The secretary of agriculture asked for the right to seize farms through condemnation and resell them to other individuals. And contained in that same program was a provision that would have allowed the federal government to remove 2 million farmers from the soil.

At the same time there has been an increase in the Department of Agriculture employees. There is now one for every thirty farms in the United States, and still they can't tell us how sixty-six shiploads of grain headed for Austria disappeared without a trace, and Billie Sol Estes never left shore!

Every responsible farmer and farm organization has repeatedly asked the government to free the farm economy, but who are farmers to know what is best for them? The wheat farmers voted against a wheat program. The government passed it anyway. Now the price of bread goes up; the price of wheat to the farmers goes down.

Meanwhile, back in the city, under urban renewal the assault on freedom carries on. Private property rights are so diluted that public interest is almost anything that a few government planners decide it should be. In a program that takes from the needy and gives to the greedy, we see such spectacles as in Cleveland, Ohio, a million-and-a-half-dollar building completed only three years ago must be destroyed to make way for what government officials call a "more compatible use of the land." The President tells us he is now going to start building public housing units in the thousands where heretofore we have only built them in the hundreds. But FHA and the Veterans Administration tell us that they have 120,000 housing units they've taken back through mortgage foreclosures.

For three decades we have sought to solve the problems of unemployment through government planning, and the more the plans fail, the more the planners plan. The latest is the Area Redevelopment Agency. They have just declared Rice County, Kansas, a depressed area. Rice County, Kansas, has two hundred oil wells, and the 14,000 people there have over thirty million dollars on deposit in personal savings in their banks. When the government tells you you are depressed, lie down and be depressed!

We have so many people who can't see a fat man standing beside a thin one without coming to the conclusion that the fat man got that way by taking advantage of the thin one! So they are going to solve all the problems of human misery through government and government planning. Well, now if government planning and welfare had the answer, and they've had almost thirty years of it, shouldn't we expect government to read the score to us once in a while? Shouldn't they be telling us about the decline each year in the number of people needing help? . . . the reduction in the need for public housing?

But the reverse is true. Each year the need grows greater, the program grows greater. We were told four years ago that seventeen million people went to bed hungry each night. Well, that was probably true. They were all on a diet! But now we are told that 9.3 million families in this country are poverty-stricken on the basis of earning less than $3,000 a year. Welfare spending is ten times greater than in the dark depths of the Depression. We are spending 45 billion dollars on welfare. Now do a little arithmetic, and you will find that if we divided the 45 billion dollars up equally among those 9 million poor families, we would be able to give each family $4,600 a year, and this added to their present income should eliminate poverty! Direct aid to the poor, however, is running only about $600 per family. It seems that someplace there must be some overhead.

So now we declare "war on poverty," or "you, too, can be a Bobby Baker!" How do they honestly expect us to believe that if we add 1 billion dollars to the 45 billion we are spending . . . one more program to the thirty-odd we have—and remember, this new program doesn't replace any, it just duplicates existing programs . . . do they believe that poverty is suddenly going to disappear by magic? Well, in all fairness I should explain that there is one part of the new program that isn't duplicated. This is the youth feature. We are now going to solve the dropout problem, juvenile delinquency, by reinstituting something like the old CCC camps, and we are going to put our young people in camps, but again we do some arithmetic, and we find that we are going to spend each year just on room and board for each young person that we help $4,700 a year! We can send them to Harvard for $2,700! Don't get me wrong. I'm not suggesting that Harvard is the answer to juvenile delinquency!

But seriously, what are we doing to those we seek to help? Not too long ago, a judge called me here in Los Angeles. He told me of a young woman who had come before him for a divorce. She had six children, was pregnant with her seventh. Under his questioning, she revealed her husband was a laborer earning $250 a month. She wanted a divorce so that she could get an $80 raise. She is eligible for $330 a month in the Aid to Dependent Children Program. She got the idea from two women in her neighborhood who had already done that very thing.

Yet anytime you and I question the schemes of the do-gooders, we are denounced as being against their humanitarian goals. They say we are always "against" things, never "for" anything. Well, the trouble with our liberal friends is not that they are ignorant, but that they know so much that isn't so! We are for a provision that destitution should not follow unemployment by reason of old age, and to that end we have accepted social security as a step toward meeting the problem.

But we are against those entrusted with this program when they practice deception regarding its fiscal shortcomings, when they charge that any criticism of the program means that we want to end payments to those people who depend on them for a livelihood. They have called it insurance to us in a hundred million pieces of literature. But then they appeared before the Supreme Court and they testified that it was a welfare program. They only use the term "insurance" to sell it to the people. And they said social security dues are a tax for the general use of the government, and the government has used that tax. There is no fund, because Robert Byers, the actuarial head, appeared before a congressional committee and admitted that social security as of this moment is $298 billion in the hole! But he said there should be no cause for worry because as long as they have the power to tax, they could always take away from the people whatever they needed to bail them out of trouble! And they are doing just that.

A young man, twenty-one years of age, working at an average salary . . . his social security contribution would, in the open market, buy him an insurance policy that would guarantee $220 a month at age sixty-five. The government promises 127! He could live it up until he is thirty-one and then take out a policy that would pay more than social security. Now, are we so lacking in business sense that we can't put this program on a sound basis so that people who do require those payments will find that they can get them when they are due . . . that the cupboard isn't bare? Barry Goldwater thinks we can.

At the same time, can't we introduce voluntary features that would permit a citizen to do better on his own, to be excused upon presentation of evidence that he had made provisions for the nonearning years? Should we not allow a widow with children to work, and not lose the benefits supposedly paid for by her deceased husband? Shouldn't you and I be allowed to declare who our beneficiaries will be under these programs, which we cannot do? I think we are for telling our senior citizens that no one in this country should be denied medical care because of a lack of funds. But I think we are against forcing all citizens, regardless of need, into a compulsory government program, especially when we have such examples, as announced last week, when France admitted that their medicare program was now bankrupt. They've come to the end of the road.

In addition, was Barry Goldwater so irresponsible when he suggested that our government give up its program of deliberate planned inflation so that when you do get your social security pension, a dollar will buy a dollar's worth, and not forty-five cents' worth?

I think we are for the international organization, where the nations of the world can seek peace. But I think we are against subordinating American interests to an organization that has become so structurally unsound that today you can muster a two-thirds vote on the floor of the General Assembly among nations that represent less than 10 percent of the world's population. I think we are against the hypocrisy of assailing our allies because here and there they cling to a colony, while we engage in a conspiracy of silence and never open our mouths about the millions of people enslaved in Soviet colonies in the satellite nations.

I think we are for aiding our allies by sharing of our material blessings with those nations which share in our fundamental beliefs, but we are against doling out money government to government, creating bureaucracy, if not socialism, all over the world. We set out to help 19 countries. We are helping 107. We spent $146 billion. With that money, we bought a 2-million-dollar yacht for Haile Selassie. We bought dress suits for Greek undertakers, extra wives for Kenya government officials. We bought a thousand TV sets for a place where they have no electricity. In the last six years, fifty-two nations have bought $7 billion of our gold, and all fifty-two are receiving foreign aid from us. No government ever voluntarily reduces itself in size. Government programs, once launched, never disappear. Actually, a government bureau is the nearest thing to eternal life we'll ever see on this earth!

Federal employees number 2.5 million, and federal, state, and local, one out of six of the nation's work force is employed by government. These proliferating bureaus with their thousands of regulations have cost us many of our constitutional safeguards. How many of us realize that today federal agents can invade a man's property without a warrant? They can impose a fine without a formal hearing, let alone a trial by jury, and they can seize and sell his property in auction to enforce the payment of that fine. In Chicot County, Arkansas, James Wier overplanted his rice allotment. The government obtained a $17,000 judgment, and a U.S. marshal sold his 950-acre farm at auction. The government said it was necessary as a warning to others to make the system work! Last February 19th, at the University of Minnesota, Norman Thomas, six times candidate for president on the Socialist Party ticket, said, "If Barry Goldwater became president, he would stop the advance of socialism in the United States." I think that's exactly what he will do!

As a former Democrat, I can tell you Norman Thomas isn't the only man who has drawn this parallel to socialism with the present administration. Back in 1936, Mr. Democrat himself, Al Smith, the great American, came before the American people and charged that the leadership of his party was taking the party of Jefferson, Jackson, and Cleveland down the road under the banners of Marx, Lenin, and Stalin. And he walked away from his party, and he never returned to the day he died, because to this day, the leadership of that party has been taking that party, that honorable party, down the road in the image of the labor socialist party of England. Now it doesn't require expropriation or confiscation of private property or business to impose socialism upon a people. What does it mean whether you hold the deed or the title to your business or property if the government holds the power of life and death over that business or property? Such machinery already exists. The government can find some charge to bring against any concern it chooses to prosecute. Every businessman has his own tale of harassment. Somewhere a perversion has taken place. Our natural, inalienable rights are now considered to be a dispensation from government, and freedom has never been so fragile, so close to slipping from our grasp as it is at this moment. Our Democratic opponents seem unwilling to debate these issues. They want to make you and I think that this is a contest between two men . . . that we are to choose just between two personalities. Well, what of this man they would destroy . . . and in destroying, they would destroy that which he represents, the ideas that you and I hold dear.

Is he the brash and shallow and trigger-happy man they say he is? Well, I have been privileged to know him "when." I knew him long before he ever dreamed of trying for high office, and I can tell you personally I have never known a man in my life I believe so incapable of doing a dishonest or dishonorable thing.

This is a man who in his own business, before he entered politics, instituted a profit-sharing plan, before unions had ever thought of it. He put in health and medical insurance for all his employees. He took 50 percent of the profits before taxes and set up a retirement plan, and a pension plan for all his employees. He sent monthly checks for life to an employee who was ill and couldn't work. He provided nursing care for the children of mothers who work in the stores. When Mexico was ravaged by the floods from the Rio Grande, he climbed in his airplane and flew medicine and supplies down there.

An ex-GI told me how he met him. It was the week before Christmas during the Korean War, and he was at the Los Angeles airport trying to get a ride home to Arizona, and he said that there were a lot of servicemen there and no seats available on the planes. Then a voice came over the loudspeaker and said, "Any men in uniform wanting a ride to Arizona, go to runway such-and-such," and they went down there, and there was a fellow named Barry Goldwater sitting in his plane. Every day in the weeks before Christmas, all day long, he would load up the plane, fly to Arizona, fly them to their homes, then fly back over to get another load.

During the hectic split-second timing of a campaign, this is a man who took time out to sit beside an old friend who was dying of cancer. His campaign managers were understandably impatient, but he said, "There aren't many left who care what happens to her. I'd like her to know that I care." This is a man who said to his nineteen-year-old son, "There is no foundation like the rock of honesty and fairness, and when you begin to build your life upon that rock, with the cement of the faith in God that you have, then you have a real start!" This is not a man who could carelessly send other people's sons to war. And that is the issue of this campaign that makes all of the other problems I have discussed academic, unless we realize that we are in a war that must be won.

Those who would trade our freedom for the soup kitchen of the welfare state have told us that they have a utopian solution of peace without victory. They call their policy "accommodation." And they say if we only avoid any direct confrontation with the enemy, he will forget his evil ways and learn to love us. All who oppose them are indicted as warmongers. They say we offer simple answers to complex problems. Well, perhaps there is a simple answer . . . not an easy one . . . but a simple one, if you and I have the courage to tell our elected officials that we want our *national* policy based upon what we know in our hearts is morally right.

We cannot buy our security, our freedom from the threat of the bomb by committing an immorality so great as saying to a billion human beings now in slavery behind the Iron Curtain, "Give up your dreams of freedom because to save our own skin, we are willing to make a deal with your slave-masters." Alexander Hamilton said, "A nation which can prefer disgrace to danger is prepared for a master, and deserves one!" Let's set the record straight. There is no argument over the choice between peace and war, but there is only one guaranteed way you can have peace . . . and you can have it in the next second . . . surrender!

Admittedly there is a risk in any course we follow other than this, but every lesson in history tells us that the greater risk lies in appeasement, and this is the specter our well-meaning liberal friends refuse to face . . . that their policy of accommodation is appeasement, and it gives no choice between peace and war, only between fight or surrender. If we continue to accommodate, continue to back and retreat, eventually we have to face the final demand—the ultimatum. And what then? When Nikita Khrushchev has told his people he knows what our answer will be? He has told them that we are retreating under the pressure of the cold war, and someday when the time comes to deliver the ultimatum, our surrender will be voluntary because by that time we will have been weakened from within spiritually, morally, and economically. He believes this because from our side he has heard voices pleading for "peace at any price" or "better Red than dead," or as one commentator put it, he would rather "live on his knees than die on his feet." And therein lies the road to war, because those voices don't speak for the rest of us. You and I know and do not believe that life is so dear and peace so sweet as to be purchased at the price of chains and slavery. If nothing in life is worth dying for, when did this begin—just in the face of this enemy?—or should Moses have told the children of Israel to live in slavery under the pharaohs? Should Christ have refused the cross? Should the patriots at Concord Bridge have thrown down their guns and refused to fire the shot heard round the world? The martyrs of history were not fools, and our honored dead who gave their lives to stop the advance of the Nazis didn't die in vain! Where, then, is the road to peace? Well, it's a simple answer after all.

You and I have the courage to say to our enemies, "There is a price we will not pay." There is a point beyond which they must not advance! This is the meaning in the phrase of Barry Goldwater's "peace through strength!" Winston Churchill said that "the destiny of man is not measured by material computation. When great forces are on the move in the world, we learn we are spirits—not animals." And he said, "There is something going on in time and space, and beyond time and space, which, whether we like it or not, spells duty." You and I have a rendezvous with destiny. We will preserve for our children this, the last best hope of man on earth, or we will sentence them to take the last step into a thousand years of darkness.

We will keep in mind and remember that Barry Goldwater has faith in us. He has faith that you and I have the ability and the dignity and the right to make our own decisions and determine our own destiny.

Thank you.

Testimony Before Senate Hearings on the Equal Rights Amendment, May 6, 1970

Gloria Steinem

Commentary

Other protest rhetoric of the 1960s came from the women's movement, which had gone into eclipse after ratification of the woman suffrage amendment in 1920. The eclipse lasted over forty years; and most historians date the movement's rejuvenation as either 1963, when Betty Friedan published *The Feminine Mystique*, or 1966, when the National Organization of Women (NOW) was founded.

The eclipse, however, was not total. In 1923, Daniel Anthony, a nephew of Susan B. Anthony, submitted to Congress a proposed amendment to the Federal Constitution that read: "Men and women shall have equal rights throughout the United States and every place subject to its jurisdiction." Women's organizations responded to Anthony's "equal rights amendment" (ERA) by dividing into what one historian, William L. O'Neill, calls "hard core feminists" and "social feminists." The "hard core" lobbied to have Anthony's regularly-rejected proposal reintroduced annually. "Social feminists," consisting of groups such as the League of Women Voters and the National Consumers' League, opposed it.

The opponents' line of argument rested on the premise that women are entitled to certain legally-protected special privileges, such as government-mandated maximum working hours and the legal right to alimony in divorce cases. Legal language is often debated in court when a statute or constitution is applied to a specific case, and an "equal rights" provision would have been no exception. If it had been adopted, some divorced man who had been ordered by a lower court to pay alimony would probably have appealed to a higher court, using the argument: "Forcing divorced men to pay alimony is unconstitutional because it denies our equality of rights on account of our sex." Would such an argument have prevailed? Opponents of Anthony's proposal feared it would. They argued that protective legislation for women would probably be ruled unconstitutional if ERA became part of the Constitution.

Congress paid little attention to Anthony's proposal until the late 1960s, when it considered an ERA proposal that was similar to, but not exactly like, Anthony's. The new version was divided into three sections: "(1) Equality of rights under the law shall not be denied or abridged by the United States or by any state on account of sex. (2) The Congress shall have the power to enforce, by appropriate legislation, the provisions of this article. (3) This amendment shall take effect two years after the date of ratification."

The newly energized women's movement worked almost unanimously for ERA. Excepting the National Council of Catholic Women, no well-known women's organization opposed ERA during the Congressional debates even though Senator Sam Ervin articulated the traditional "special protection" argument in his unsuccessful efforts to amend it. Arguing that ERA could be interpreted by courts to take away certain protections, he introduced amendments, such as those saying that ERA "shall not impair" laws "which exempt women from compulsory military service" or "impose upon fathers responsibility for the support of their children" or establish special industrial protections. His proposals were defeated overwhelmingly.

On May 6, 1970, Gloria Steinem (1934-   ) testified in behalf of ERA before the Senate Subcommittee on Constitutional Amendments. She had emerged as a major leader of the women's movement, and she remains so at the time of this writing. She was a free-lance journalist who had been active in political causes such as protesting the Vietnam War. She had helped found the *New York Magazine* two years prior to her testimony, and in 1970 she was a co-founder of the Women's Action Alliance.

A few days after her testimony, Steinem delivered the commencement speech at Vassar. Entitled "Women Freeing the Men, Too," the speech contained a few snide remarks about how the "male-chauvinist Congress" had delayed ERA for forty-seven years; but her line of argument in the speech was essentially the same as that in her testimony. In both rhetorical situations, she implicitly attacked the premise on which the ERA opponents' "special protection" argument was based. In her oral testimony she read a prepared statement but added a few "ad lib" remarks. Both the oral and written versions were printed in the *Hearings of the Subcommittee on Constitutional Amendments of the Committee on the Judiciary*, 91st Congress, 1970, pp. 331-37. Because the "ad libs" would not be meaningful to readers unfamiliar with what previous speakers had said, the written version is reproduced here, complete with spelling abnormalities.

Testimony of Gloria Steinem

My name is Gloria Steinem. I am a writer and editor. I have worked in several political campaigns, and am currently a member of the Policy Council of the Democratic National Committee.

During twelve years of working for a living, I've experienced much of the legal and social discrimination reserved for women in this country. I have been refused service in public restaurants, ordered out of public gathering places, and turned away from apartment rentals: all for the clearly-stated, sole reason that I am a woman. And all without the legal remedies available to blacks and other minorities. I have been excluded from professional groups, writing assignments on so-called "unfeminine" subjects such as politics, full participation in the Democratic Party, jury duty, and even from such small male privileges as discounts on airline fares. Most important to me, I have been denied a society in which women are encouraged, or even allowed, to think of themselves as first-class citizens and responsible human beings.

However, after two years of researching the status of American women, I have discovered that I am very, very lucky. Most women, both wage-earners and housewives, routinely suffer more humiliation and injustice than I do.

As a freelance writer, I don't work in the male-dominated hierarchy of an office. (Women, like blacks and other visibly-different minorities, do better in individual professions such as the arts, sports, or domestic work; anything in which they don't have authority over white males.) I am not one of the millions of women who must support a family. Therefore, I haven't had to go on welfare because there are no day care centers for my children while I work, and I haven't had to submit to the humiliating welfare inquiries about my private and sexual life, inquiries from which men are exempt. I haven't had to brave the sex bias of labor unions and employers, only to see my family subsist on a median salary 40 percent less than the male median salary.

I hope this committee will hear the personal, daily injustices suffered by many women—professionals and day laborers, women house-bound by welfare as well as suburbia. We have all been silent for too long. We won't be silent anymore.

The truth is that all our problems stem from the same sex-based myths. We may appear before you as white radicals or the middle-aged, middleclass or black soul sisters, but we are *all* sisters in fighting against these out-dated myths. Like racial myths, they have been reflected in our laws. Let me list a few:

That Women Are Biologically Inferior to Men

In fact, an equally good case can be made for the reverse. Women live longer than men, even when the men are not subject to business pressures. Women survived Nazi concentration camps better, keep cooler heads in emergencies currently studied by disaster researchers, are protected against heart attacks by their female sex hormones, and are so much more durable at every stage of life that nature must conceive 20 to 50 percent more males in order to keep some balance going.

Man's hunting activities are forever being pointed to as tribal proof of superiority. But while he was hunting, women built houses, tilled the fields, developed animal husbandry, and perfected language. Men, being all alone in the bush, often developed into a creature as strong as women, fleeter of foot, but not very bright.

However, I don't want to prove the superiority of one sex to another. That would only be repeating a male mistake. English scientists once definitively proved, after all, that the English were de[s]cended from the angels, while the Irish were descended from the apes: it was the rationale for England's domination of Ireland for more than a century. The point is that science is used to support current myth and economics almost as much as the church was.

What we do know is that the difference *between* two races or two sexes is much smaller than the differences to be found *within* each group. Therefore, in spite of the slide show on female inferiorities that I understand was shown to you yesterday, the law makes much more sense when it treats individuals, not groups bundled together by some condition of birth.

A word should be said about Dr. Freud, the great 19th Century perpetuator of female inferiority. Many of the differences he assumed to be biological, and therefore changeless, have turned out to be societal, and have already changed. Penis Envy, for instance, is clinically disappearing. Just as black people envied white skin, 19th Century women envied penises. A secondclass group envies whatever it is that makes another group first class.

That Women Are Already Treated Equally in This Society

I'm sure there has been ample testimony to prove that equal pay for equal work, equal chance for advancement, and equal training or encouragement is obscenely scarce in every field, even those—like food and fashion industries— that are supposedly "feminine."

A deeper result of social and legal injustice, however, is what sociologists refer to as "Internalized Aggression." Victims of aggression absorb the myth of their own inferiority, and come to believe that their group is in fact secondclass.

Women suffer this secondclass treatment from the moment they are born. They are expected to *be* rather than achieve, to function biologically rather than learn. A brother, whatever his intellect, is more likely to get the family's encouragement and education money, while girls are often pressured to conceal ambition and intelligence, to "Uncle Tom."

I interviewed a New York public school teacher who told me about a black teenager's desire to be a doctor. With all the barriers in mind, she suggested he be a veterinarian instead.

The same day, a high school teacher mentioned a girl who wanted to be a doctor. The teacher said, "How about a nurse—"

Teachers, parents, and the Supreme Court may exude a protective, well-meaning rationale, but limiting the individual's ambition is doing no one a favor. Certainly not this country. It needs all the talent it can get.

That American Women Hold Great Economic Power

51 percent of all shareholders in this country are women. That's a favorite male-chauvinist statistic. However, the number of shares they hold is so small that the total is only 18 percent of all shares. Even those holdings are often controlled by men.

Similarly, only 5 percent of all the people in the country who receive $10,000 a year or more, earned or otherwise, are women. And that includes all the famous rich widows.

The constantly-repeated myth of our economic power seems less testimony to our real power than to the resentment of what little power we do have.

That Children Must Have Full-Time Mothers

American mothers spend more time with their homes and children than those of any other society we know about. In the past, joint families, servants, a prevalent system in which grandparents raised the children, or family field work in the agrarian systems—all these factors contributed more to child care than the labor-saving devices of which we are so proud.

The truth is that most American children seem to be suffering from too much Mother, and too little Father. Part of the program of Women's Liberation is a return of fathers to their children. If laws permit women equal work and pay opportunities, men will then be relieved of their role as sole breadwinner. Fewer ulcers, fewer hours of meaningless work, equal responsibility for his own children: these are a few of the reasons that Women's Liberation is Men's Liberation, too.

As for the psychic health of the children, studies show that the quality of time spent by parents is more important than the quantity. The most damaged children were not those whose mothers worked, but those whose mothers preferred to work but stayed home out of role-playing desire to be a ''good mother.''

That the Women's Movement is Not Political, Won't Last, or Is Somehow Not ''Serious''

When black people leave their 19th Century roles, they are feared. When women dare to leave theirs, they are ridiculed. We understand this, and accept the burden of ridicule. It won't keep us quiet anymore.

Similarly, it shouldn't deceive male observers into thinking this is somehow a joke. We are 51 percent of the population, we are essentially united on these issues across boundaries of class or race or age, and we may well end by changing this society more than the civil rights movement. That is an apt parallel. We, too, have our right wing and left wing, our separatists, gradualists, and Uncle Toms. But we are changing our own consciousness, and that of the country. Engels noted the relationship of the authoritarian, nuclear family to capitalism: the father as capitalist, the mother as means of production, and the children as labor. He said the family would change as the economic system did, and that seems to have happened, whether we want to admit it or not. Women's bodies will no longer be owned by the state for the production of workers and soldiers: birth control and abortion are facts of everyday life. The new family is an egalitarian family.

Gunnar Myrdal noted thirty years ago the parallel between women and Negroes in this country. Both suffered from such restricting social myths as:

smaller brains, passive natures, inability to govern themselves (and certainly not white men), sex objects only, childlike natures, special skills and the like. When evaluating a general statement about women, it might be valuable to substitute "black people" for "women"—just to test the prejudice at work.

And it might be valuable to do this Constitutionally as well. Neither group is going to be content as a cheap labor pool anymore. And neither is going to be content without full Constitutional rights.

Finally, I would like to say one thing about this time in which I am testifying.

I had deep misgivings about discussing this topic when National Guardsmen are occupying our campuses, the country is being turned against itself in a terrible polarization, and America is enlarging an already inhuman and unjustifiable war. But it seems to me that much of the trouble this country is in has to do with the Masculine Mystique; with the myth that masculinity somehow depends on the subjugation of other people. It is a bi-partisan problem: both our past and current Presidents seem to be victims of this myth, and to behave accordingly.

Women are not more moral than men. We are only uncorrupted by power. But we do not want to imitate men, to join this country as it is, and I think our very participation will change it. Perhaps women elected leaders—and there will be many more of them—will not be so likely to dominate black people or yellow people or men; anybody who looks different from us.

After all, we won't have our masculinity to prove.

Excerpts from Testimony Before the House of Representatives on the Equal Rights Amendment, October 20, 1983

Phyllis Schlafly

Commentary

Two years after Steinem's testimony, in March 1972, Congress sent ERA to the States for ratification, and imposed a seven-year time limit. (Time limits are not always imposed, but they have become more common in recent times.) Within a year, twenty-eight States ratified ERA, and Congresswoman Martha Griffiths confidently predicted, "ERA will be part of the Constitution before the year's out." Some historians believe that overconfidence was a major reason why ERA eventually lost. Supporters failed to campaign for it at the State level.

In contrast, opponents were slow to combat ERA in Congress but fast at the State level. Their major leader, Phyllis Schlafly (1924-   ), said that her first reaction was that "ERA was something between innocuous and mildly helpful"; but her attention was elsewhere at the time pro-ERA sentiment was increasing in the late 1960s and early 1970s. In 1964, she had supported Goldwater's presidential campaign with a book entitled, *A Choice Not an Echo*. Since then, she had continued to oppose the "liberal" and "elitist" wing of the Republican party by her work within the party and by her public rhetoric. She had co-authored several books on foreign policy and military strategy. In 1967, she had founded a newsletter, *The Phyllis Schlafly Report*, that circulated widely among conservatives. It was not until 1971, when declining a friend's invitation to participate in a debate on ERA, that she agreed to accept her friend's plea to study the probable effects of ERA. A lawyer by training, Schlafly knew that court interpretations rest heavily on the legislative history of a legal measure and on previous court decisions (or precedents), so she studied the legislative history of ERA and the decisions of State courts in States that had ERA provisions in their Constitutions.

Schlafly soon became a dedicated opponent of ERA, but it was too late to do much to try to persuade Congress. It was not until February 1972, only a month before ERA cleared Congress, that she devoted an issue of *The Phyllis*

Schlafly Report to arguing against ERA. However, it was not too late to fight ERA at the State level. In October, 1972, she founded STOP ERA and appointed State chairs, who organized "grass roots" efforts to dissuade State legislatures from ratifying ERA.

Although efforts varied from State to State, Schlafly was the acknowledged leader of anti-ERA forces, and her rhetoric guided the movement. She used four basic arguments. First, she maintained that existing legislation against discrimination made ERA unnecessary. Second, she argued that the second section of ERA would effectively destroy States' Rights. Some observers believe that this argument was especially effective with State legislators. Third, she indulged in *ad hominem* rhetoric, pointing out that ERA was supported by lesbians, left-wing radicals and users of obscene language. Schlafly's fourth, and major, argument was a reiteration and extension of the "special protection" argument that "social feminists" and Senator Ervin had employed earlier.

ERA died for lack of a sufficient number of State ratifications, but it was reintroduced in Congress in 1983. The rhetoric in 1983 was basically the same as it was earlier, except that even some proponents acknowledged that some alterations should be made in the ERA language to prevent courts from applying ERA in unintended ways. Using such acknowledgements as an opening wedge, Schlafly began her testimony to the House Subcommittee on Civil and Constitutional Rights (October 20, 1983) with a series of proposed amendments to ERA language that were similar to those advocated unsuccessfully by Senator Ervin a decade earlier (such as "This article shall not be construed to deprive wives or widows of any right or benefit granted by any state, or to interfere with state laws that obligate husbands to support their wives," and "This article shall not require the sex-integration of private schools, churches, hospitals, prisons, or public accomodations, or require treating males and females the same where differences tend to accomodate personal modesty").

The major portion of Schlafly's testimony was entitled "The Effect of Equal Rights Amendments in State Constitutions." She began by observing that many States had recently amended their constitutions, and she distinguished between what she called "authentic" State ERA amendments (which were similar to the proposed Federal ERA) and "equal protection" provisions. She then articulated the assumption that Federal courts would probably interpret a Federal ERA in basically the same ways that State courts have interpreted "authentic" State ERA provisions. Excerpts are reproduced from *Hearings Before the Subcommittee on Civil and Constitutional Rights of the Committee on the Judiciary, House of Representatives, Ninety-eighth Congress, First Session, on H. J. Res*[olution] 1, Equal Rights Amendment, Serial No. 115 (1983), pp. 433-37, 450-55. (Her footnotes are omitted; brackets and ellipses are hers.)

Testimony of Phyllis Schlafly

Effect on Family Law

When proponents were presenting their case for passage of the Federal Equal Rights Amendment to Congress in 1971 and 1972, they used as their principal legal statement about its anticipated effects an article of some one hundred pages in the *Yale Law Journal*. The article was quite frank in proclaiming that the adoption of a Federal ERA "will give strength and purpose to efforts to bring about a far-reaching change which, for some, may prove painful."

The chief victims of these "painful" effects of the "far-reaching change" will be wives and mothers. This is the inescapable conclusion to be drawn from the family law litigation in the states that have adopted authentic State ERAs.

In Washington, which has a State ERA, the court admonished wives to face up to what ERA means:

> It is to be remembered that while the 61st amendment to the Constitution of the State of Washington, approved November 7, 1972, is commonly referred to as the Equal Rights Amendment, it firmly requires equal responsibilities as well. This amendment is the touchstone of the developing case and statute law in the area of marriage dissolution.

The holding in this case, *Smith v. Smith*, was that ERA requires equal responsibilities of parents for child support and that the ex-husband can get his support obligations reduced to meet the ERA standard.

Wives have traditionally had in this country a great variety of extensive rights based on their marital status, as a result of our public policy to respect the family as the basic unit of society, and as a statutory and common-law balance to the biological fact that only women have babies. These rights, which vary from state to state, include the wife's right of financial support in an ongoing marriage, the right of separate maintenance and payment of attorney's fees during divorce litigation, the right to alimony after divorce, the right to a presumption of custody of her children, rights against her husband's alienation of his property during his life or by will, and a variety of special benefits accorded to widows.

Such benign discrimination is wholly in harmony with the Equal Protection Clause and was seldom challenged prior to the 1970s. The U.S. Supreme Court in *Kahn v. Shevin* made clear the current constitutionality and relevancy of such preferential statutes designed for the benefit of wives and widows. The Court held that, consistent with the Equal Protection Clause, a legislature can make a rational classification of widows as a class of people who need a special benefit. The Court upheld Florida's property tax exemption for widows. The challenge to the Florida statute was strongly supported by pro-ERA lawyers.

The states that have State ERAs are blazing the trail of the "painful" effects of applying an absolute standard of equality to the marital and parental relationships. They provide a window into which we can look to see what "equality of rights" means when applied to the husband-wife relationship.

Maryland is a State ERA state. In *Coleman v. Maryland*, the Court of Special Appeals held that the statute which makes it a crime for a husband to fail to support his wife is unconstitutional under the State ERA. The court said that this statute "establishes a distinction solely upon the basis of sex" and "such distinctions are now absolutely forbidden" by the State ERA.

The court discussed the social policy and the history of the law which made it the duty of the husband to support his wife, calling it "warp and woof of the prevailing ethos" of the nineteenth century. All that is changed now, according to the court; "that view has been subjected to a series of violent cultural shocks. The Equal Rights Amendment of 1972 more accurately reflects the ethos or zeitgeist of this time." The court held that the support statute "is no longer the public policy of this state."

Newspapers which had been strong supporters of ERA were made very uncomfortable by this decision, calling it "an unfortunate conflict" of sexual justice, but admitted that the court had "no alternative" under the State ERA. The newspapers accurately pointed out that, while imprisonment for nonsupport is seldom imposed, the threat of imprisonment is a most valuable and necessary tool "to impress upon husbands their financial responsibility." It is almost the only tool available to reduce the welfare rolls because, in the absence of this law and the remedies available under it, a large group of women become the financial responsibility of the taxpayers.

Pennsylvania is a State ERA state and, because of the State ERA, wives have lost their common law and statutory right to have their necessaries paid for by their husbands.

This common law right has been a right of wives for centuries and is an essential ingredient of the concept of the right of the wife to be supported in her home. The Pennsylvania statute read as follows:

> In all cases where debts may be contracted for necessaries for the support and maintenance of the family of any married woman, it shall be lawful for the creditor in such case to institute suit against the husband and wife for the price of such necessaries, and after obtaining a judgment, have an execution against the husband alone.

In *Albert Einstein Medical Center v. Gold*, the issue was whether, under the law which obligated the husband to pay for his wife's necessaries, the State ERA would obligate the wife to pay for her husband's necessaries. The *Gold* court held the law unconstitutional under the State ERA but, instead of invalidating it, extended the husband's liability to the wife and required her to pay for her husband's medical and hospital expenses.

In *Gold*, the court apparently could not resist this caveat to wives:

> The matter before us is yet another example of the impact of the Equal Rights Amendment upon the lives of all citizens of the Commonwealth and, once again, demonstrates that those who seek to expand the equal rights concept must be prepared to accept the burdens as well as the benefits of such expansion.

The court did not say what the "benefits" are, but *Gold* and the subsequent "necessaries" cases described below surely make clear some of the burdens.

Two years later in *Albert Einstein Medical Center v. Nathans*, the court faced the same law in its traditional circumstances: the question of payment for a wife's necessaries. The "necessaries" involved in this case were medical and hospital services provided to the wife in an ongoing marriage which were conceded to be "necessary for her health, well-being and comfort." The court simply nullified the common law and statutory responsibility of a husband to pay for his wife's "necessaries," noting that these include not only medical care, but also food, clothing, and shelter.

The court waxed very righteous in applying the absolute standard under the State ERA. The court held that "all legal distinctions based on the male or female role in the marital relationship are rendered inoperative by the [State ERA] amendment" and that the common law concept obligating the husband to pay for his wife's necessaries is "repugnant to the Equal Rights Amendment." The court took judicial notice of what it called "medical and scientific advances which have increased both production and population . . . have made birth control a desirable social objective, and have been factors liberating her [a wife] from the common law requirements that tethered her to her husband and to her husband's home."

'Painful' Effects of ERA

Thus, it is clear that whichever way a State ERA is interpreted by the courts—to extend liability to both sexes as in *Gold* or to nullify the husband's liability as in *Nathans*—the Pennsylvania wife suffers the "painful" effects of the "far-reaching change" forced upon her by the State ERA.

Effect on Schools

Two cases in State ERA states have established the new rule that girls must be permitted to compete with boys in all sports, even contact sports such as football.

In *Commonwealth v. Pennsylvania Interscholastic Athletic Association*, the court held unconstitutional under the State ERA a bylaw of the Pennsylvania Interscholastic Athletic Association (PIAA) which prohibited girls from competing against boys in interscholastic competitions. Even though neither of the parties requested it, the court extended its decision to cover football and wrestling. "It is apparent," the court said, "that there can be no valid reason for excepting those two sports from our order in this case."

Granting summary judgment as a matter of law, the court held that the mandate of the State ERA is absolute and must apply to all school sports regardless of any rational arguments that might be presented in behalf of exceptions.

The PIAA had sought to justify its bylaw on the ground that it gave girls "greater opportunities for participation if they compete exclusively with members of their own sex." The PIAA never got its day in court to make its argument.

In *Darrin v. Gould*, the Supreme Court of the State of Washington likewise held that it is sex discrimination under the State ERA to deny girls the right to play on the high school football team. The court cited the "broad, sweeping, mandatory language" of the State ERA that compelled this result.

The argument was made in this case that allowing girls to compete with boys in contact sports such as football will result in boys being allowed to compete on girls' teams, thereby disrupting the girls' athletic programs. The court simply dismissed this as "opinion evidence" or "conjectural evidence" which cannot support a public policy contrary to the State ERA mandate.

One judge concurred reluctantly, "exclusively upon the basis that the result is dictated by the broad and mandatory language" of the State ERA. He questioned whether the people fully contemplated the result, but said that whether the people understood what they did or not, "in sweeping language they embedded the principle of the ERA in our constitution, and it is beyond the authority of this court to modify the people's will. So be it."

Title IX of the Federal Education Amendments of 1972 bans discrimination on account of sex in schools and colleges, but makes a number of statutory and regulatory exceptions to the absolute mandate. One of these exemptions is for the contact sports: boxing, wrestling, football, basketball, ice hockey, and rugby. If the Federal ERA is placed in the U.S. Constitution, it will wipe out all statutory and regulatory exceptions under *Marbury v. Madison*: "a law repugnant to the Constitution is void."

Vorchheimer v. School District of Philadelphia raises an interesting question about the tactics of proponents of the absolute standard for enforcement of ERA. The School District of Philadelphia maintains two sex-segregated public high schools as part of an otherwise coeducational, public school system, one called Philadelphia High School for Girls and the other Central High School (for boys). The trial court found as Fact #27 that "The courses offered at Girls are similar and of equal quality to those offered at Central." Susan Vorchheimer brought suit to force the boys' school to admit her.

The fatal defect in her suit, however, was that she brought it under the Equal Protection Clause of the Fourteenth Amendment and under the Equal Education Opportunities Act of 1974, neither of which requires the sex-integration of all schools. The court upheld Philadelphia's right to maintain two voluntary sex-segregated schools. The U.S. Supreme Court, dividing 4 to 4, let this decision stand.

The mystery is why Susan Vorchheimer's lawyer and her ERA friends, who now complain about the decision all over the country, did not invoke the Pennsylvania State ERA, under which, using the absolute standard, she certainly would have won. Perhaps Miss Vorchheimer's friends were not yet ready to let the country know that the Equal Rights Amendment will make all single-sex schools unconstitutional—and thereby bring their long tradition of academic excellence to a close in the name of "equal rights."

In contrast to the absolute standard used by Pennsylvania under its State ERA, the courts in the equal-protection states continue to hand down decisions that allow a rational difference of treatment based on sex. Thus, in *Mercer v. North Forest Independent School District*, the Texas Court of Civil Appeals held that the two-tiered approach used by the U.S. Supreme Court in equal protection cases is the proper method by which to judge the Texas so-called ERA. A boy had challenged the constitutionality of public school regulations which restricted the hair length of boys but not girls. The court stated: "We cannot agree with the Supreme Court of Washington that the ERA admits of no exceptions to its prohibition of sex discrimination.''

It is clear that the non-ERA states and the equal-protection states will be able to maintain diversity in education and common-sense differences of treatment based on sex. The authentic ERA, State or Federal, will use a constitutional whip to force all schools, classes and school activities, athletics and regulations into the gender-free mold.

Effect on Insurance

The insurance industry is built on a distribution of risk among groups in which the average cost of the benefits can be statistically and reliably predicted. Everybody in the group pays a certain small premium so that no one in the group will be financially ruined by unforeseen and unwanted circumstances such as an untimely death, a major automobile accident, or a fire that destroys a home. If the insurance company could look into the future and know which individuals would have automobile accidents, it would obviously sell insurance only to those who would never need it. It is because we cannot predict which individuals will have the accidents or will die early that insurance costs are based on statistical averages of identifiable groups.

Among the facts on which insurance is based are those which prove differences based on sex. Statistical tables used by insurance companies provide such massive and reliable evidence of differences between the sexes that it is unnecessary to recite it here.

Among these differences are the facts, to cite just two examples, that, on the average, young men under age 25 have many more automobile accidents than young women and that women live longer than men. These statistical facts result in differentials in the prices paid by insureds. Young women under age 25 pay a much lower automobile accident insurance premium than young men under age 25. One recent study made by the industry shows that, if the insurance companies were required to charge males and females the same rate, young men would pay 8 percent less but young women would have to pay 29 percent more.

The longer life span of women means that women pay lower life insurance premiums than men because they pay into the system for more years before they die. On the other hand, a pension plan which is designed to start paying an annuity at age 65 must be cost-equalized in one of two ways: by charging women more during the pay-in years before age 65, or by paying them a smaller benefit during the pay-out years after age 65.

Since insurance is regulated by state law, thus involving sufficient state action to bring it under any State or Federal ERA, what will be the effect of ERA on the insurance industry? No ERA State has answered this question yet, but the U.S. Supreme Court gave the probable answer in *Los Angeles Dept. of Water and Power v. Manhart*.

In *Manhart*, the issue was whether the city of Los Angeles could charge women more for payments into a pension plan because they live more years after retirement than male employees. The city justified the differential on the grounds that (a) it was needed to equalize the take-home benefits after retirement, and (b) the differential was based on a factor "other than sex" which was protected by the so-called Bennett Amendment. The legislative history of the Bennett Amendment, including the explicit statements of one of the sponsors, Senator Hubert Humphrey, showing the congressional intent to allow sex differentials based on longstanding differences of treatment in retirement determined by valid sex differences, was set forth in the case.

Nevertheless, the Court held that the result was the classification of males and females by sex, and that is "sex discrimination" which is prohibited by Title VII of the Civil Rights Act. Conceding that "retroactive liability could be devastating for a pension fund," the Court denied retroactive relief but invalidated the differentials in payments into the pension plan.

Manhart applies only to the limited area of pensions governed by Title VII. All pensions, however, could be held subject to the State or Federal ERA whenever the challenge is brought. The results cannot help but be hurtful to women and costly to everyone. Since it is self-evident that insurance companies will have to cover their costs under any formula, the "marriage" of *Manhart* to ERA threatens the pocketbooks of all those who buy insurance.

Speech to the National Association of Evangelicals (the "Evil Empire" Speech)

Ronald Reagan

Commentary

In his first inaugural address (1981) Ronald Reagan (1911-   ) expressed the conservative philosophy with an oft-quoted antithesis: "In this present crisis, government is not the solution to our problem; government is the problem." He reiterated the conservative philosophy as he addressed numerous public audiences.

Frequent presidential speeches to public audiences, as distinguished from a few messages to Congress (usually in written form), characterize what political scientists often call the "rhetorical presidency." In former times, even "strong" presidents pushed their programs through Congress by talking privately with legislators, but "rhetorical presidents" (to use the common metaphor) "go over the heads" of Congress by addressing the public. The beginnings go back to Theodore Roosevelt, who used the presidency as his "bully pulpit," and it accelerated, albeit sporadically, during the twentieth century. Many scholars, as well as pundits, call Reagan the "Great Communicator" and consider him the epitome of the "rhetorical president."

One of the many speeches delivered by the "rhetorical president" to public audiences was one to a convention of the National Association of Evangelicals on March 8, 1983. The speech was publicized highly at the time because he called the Soviet Union an "evil empire" in the course of his argument against a "nuclear freeze" proposal that was then being debated widely. However, most of the speech dealt with what are often called "social" or "moral" issues which are still very controversial.

The following text is reproduced from *Public Papers of the Presidents of the United States: Ronald Reagan, 1983*, (U.S. Government Printing Office, 1984), book 1, pp. 359-364.

Speech to the Annual Convention of the National Association of Evangelicals in Orlando, Florida, March 8, 1983

Reverend clergy all, Senator Hawkins, distinguished members of the Florida congressional delegation, and all of you:

I can't tell you how you have warmed my heart with your welcome. I'm delighted to be here today.

Those of you in the National Association of Evangelicals are known for your spiritual and humanitarian work. And I would be especially remiss if I didn't discharge right now one personal debt of gratitude. Thank you for your prayers. Nancy and I have felt their presence many times in many ways. And believe me, for us they've made all the difference.

The other day in the East Room of the White House at a meeting there, someone asked me whether I was aware of all the people out there who were praying for the President. And I had to say, "Yes, I am. I've felt it. I believe in intercessionary prayer." But I couldn't help but say to that questioner after he'd asked the question that—or at least say to them that if sometimes when he was praying he got a busy signal, it was just me in there ahead of him. [*Laughter*] I think I understand how Abraham Lincoln felt when he said, "I have been driven many times to my knees by the overwhelming conviction that I had nowhere else to go."

From the joy and the good feeling of this conference, I go to a political reception. [*Laughter*] Now, I don't know why, but that bit of scheduling reminds me of a story—[*laughter*]—which I'll share with you.

An evangelical minister and a politician arrived at Heaven's gate one day together. And St. Peter, after doing all the necessary formalities, took them in hand to show them where their quarters would be. And he took them to a small, single room with a bed, a chair, and a table and said this was for the clergyman. And the politician was a little worried about what might be in store for him. And he couldn't believe it then when St. Peter stopped in front of a beautiful mansion with lovely grounds, many servants, and told him that these would be his quarters.

And he couldn't help but ask, he said, "But wait, how—there's something wrong—how do I get this mansion while that good and holy man only gets a single room?" And St. Peter said, "You have to understand how things are up here. We've got thousands and thousands of clergy. You're the first politician who ever made it." [*Laughter*]

But I don't want to contribute to a stereotype. [*Laughter*] So, I tell you there are a great many God-fearing, dedicated, noble men and women in public life, present company included. And yes, we need your help to keep us ever mindful of the ideas and the principles that brought us into the public arena in the first place. The basis of those ideals and principles is a commitment to freedom and personal liberty that, itself, is grounded in the much deeper realization that freedom prospers only where the blessings of God are avidly sought and humbly accepted.

The American experiment in democracy rests on this insight. Its discovery was the great triumph of our Founding Fathers, voiced by William Penn when he said: "If we will not be governed by God, we must be governed by tyrants." Explaining the inalienable rights of men, Jefferson said, "The God who gave us life, gave us liberty at the same time." And it was George Washington who said that "of all the dispositions and habits which lead to political prosperity, religion and morality are indispensable supports."

And finally, that shrewdest of all observers of American democracy, Alexis de Tocqueville, put it eloquently after he had gone on a search for the secret of America's greatness and genius—and he said: "Not until I went into the churches of America and heard her pulpits aflame with righteousness did I understand the greatness and the genius of America. . . . America is good. And if America ever ceases to be good, America will cease to be great."

Well, I'm pleased to be here today with you who are keeping America great by keeping her good. Only through your work and prayers and those of millions of others can we hope to survive this perilous century and keep alive this experiment in liberty, this last, best hope of man.

I want you to know that this administration is motivated by a political philosophy that sees the greatness of America in you, her people, and in your families, churches, neighborhoods, communities—the institutions that foster and nourish values like concern for others and respect for the rule of law under God.

Now, I don't have to tell you that this puts us in opposition to, or at least out of step with, a prevailing attitude of many who have turned to a modern-day secularism, discarding the tried and time-tested values upon which our very civilization is based. No matter how well intentioned, their value system is radically different from that of most Americans. And while they proclaim that they're freeing us from superstitions of the past, they've taken upon themselves the job of superintending us by government rule and regulation. Sometimes their voices are louder than ours, but they are not yet a majority.

An example of that vocal superiority is evident in a controversy now going on in Washington. And since I'm involved, I've been waiting to hear from the parents of young America. How far are they willing to go in giving to government their prerogatives as parents?

Let me state the case as briefly and simply as I can. An organization of citizens, sincerely motivated and deeply concerned about the increase in illegitimate births and abortions involving girls well below the age of consent, sometime ago established a nationwide network of clinics to offer help to these girls and, hopefully, alleviate this situation. Now, again, let me say, I do not fault their intent. However, in their well-intentioned effort, these clinics have decided to provide advice and birth control drugs and devices to underage girls without the knowledge of their parents.

For some years now, the Federal Government has helped with funds to subsidize these clinics. In providing for this, the Congress decreed that every effort would be made to maximize parental participation. Nevertheless, the drugs and devices are prescribed without getting parental consent or giving notification after they've done so. Girls termed "sexually active"—and that has replaced the word "promiscuous"—are given this help in order to prevent illegitimate birth or abortion.

Well, we have ordered clinics receiving Federal funds to notify the parents such help has been given. One of the Nation's leading newspapers has created the term "squeal rule" in editorializing against us for doing this, and we're being criticized for violating the privacy of young people. A judge has recently granted an injunction against an enforcement of our rule. I've watched TV panel shows discuss this issue, seen columnists pontificating on our error, but no one seems to mention morality as playing a part in the subject of sex.

Is all of Judeo-Christian tradition wrong? Are we to believe that something so sacred can be looked upon as a purely physical thing with no potential for emotional and psychological harm? And isn't it the parents' right to give counsel and advice to keep their children from making mistakes that may affect their entire lives?

Many of us in government would like to know what parents think about this intrusion in their family by government. We're going to fight in the courts. The right of parents and the rights of family take precedence over those of Washington-based bureaucrats and social engineers.

But the fight against parental notification is really only one example of many attempts to water down traditional values and even abrogate the original terms of American democracy. Freedom prospers when religion is vibrant and the rule of law under God is acknowledged. When our Founding Fathers passed the first amendment, they sought to protect churches from government interference. They never intended to construct a wall of hostility between government and the concept of religious belief itself.

The evidence of this permeates our history and our government. The Declaration of Independence mentions the Supreme Being no less that four times. "In God We Trust" is engraved on our coinage. The Supreme Court opens its proceedings with a religious invocation. And the Members of Congress open their sessions with a prayer. I just happen to believe the schoolchildren of the United States are entitled to the same privileges as Supreme Court Justices and Congressmen.

Last year, I sent the Congress a constitutional amendment to restore prayer to public schools. Already this session, there's growing bipartisan support for the amendment, and I am calling on Congress to act speedily to pass it and to let our children pray.

Perhaps some of you read recently about the Lubbock school case, where a judge actually ruled that it was unconstitutional for a school district to give equal treatment to religious and nonreligious student groups, even when the group meetings were being held during the students' own time. The first amendment never intended to require government to discriminate against religious speech.

Senators Denton and Hatfield have proposed legislation in the Congress on the whole question of prohibiting discrimination against religious forms of student speech. Such legislation could go far to restore freedom of religious speech for public school students. And I hope the Congress considers these bills quickly. And with your help, I think it's possible we could also get the constitutional amendment through the Congress this year.

More than a decade ago, a Supreme Court decision literally wiped off the books of 50 States statutes protecting the rights of unborn children. Abortion on demand now takes the lives of up to 1-1/2 million unborn children a year. Human life legislation ending this tragedy will some day pass the Congress, and you and I must never rest until it does. Unless and until it can be proven that the unborn child is not a living entity, then its right to life, liberty, and the pursuit of happiness must be protected.

You may remember that when abortion on demand began, many, and, indeed, I'm sure many of you, warned that the practice would lead to a decline in respect for human life, that the philosophical premises used to justify abortion on demand would ultimately be used to justify other attacks on the sacredness of human life—infanticide or mercy killing. Tragically enough, those warnings proved all too true. Only last year a court permitted the death by starvation of a handicapped infant.

I have directed the Health and Human Services Department to make clear to every health care facility in the United States that the Rehabilitation Act of 1973 protects all handicapped persons against discrimination based on handicaps, including infants. And we have taken the further step of requiring that each and every recipient of Federal funds who provides health care services to infants must post and keep posted in a conspicuous place a notice stating that "discriminatory failure to feed and care for handicapped infants in this facility is prohibited by Federal law." It also lists a 24-hour, toll-free number so that nurses and others may report violations in time to save the infant's life.

In addition, recent legislation introduced in the Congress by Representative Henry Hyde of Illinois not only increases restrictions on publicly financed abortions, it also addresses this whole problem of infanticide. I urge the Congress to begin hearings and to adopt legislation that will protect the right of life to all children, including the disabled or handicapped.

Now, I'm sure that you must get discouraged at times, but you've done better than you know, perhaps. There's a great spiritual awakening in America, a renewal of the traditional values that have been the bedrock of America's goodness and greatness.

One recent survey by a Washington-based research council concluded that Americans were far more religious than the people of other nations; 95 percent of those surveyed expressed a belief in God and a huge majority believed the Ten Commandments had real meaning in their lives. And another study has found that an overwhelming majority of Americans disapprove of adultery, teenage sex, pornography, abortion, and hard drugs. And this same study showed a deep reverence for the importance of family ties and religious belief.

I think the items that we've discussed here today must be a key part of the Nation's political agenda. For the first time the Congress is openly and seriously debating and dealing with the prayer and abortion issues—and that's enormous progress right there. I repeat: America is in the midst of a spiritual awakening and a moral renewal. And with your Biblical keynote, I say today, "Yes, let justice roll on like a river, righteousness like a never-failing stream."

Now, obviously, much of this new political and social consensus I've talked about is based on a positive view of American history, one that takes pride in our country's accomplishments and record. But we must never forget that no government schemes are going to perfect man. We know that living in this world means dealing with what philosophers would call the phenomenology of evil or, as theologians would put it, the doctrine of sin.

There is sin and evil in the world, and we're enjoined by Scripture and the Lord Jesus to oppose it with all our might. Our nation, too, has a legacy of evil with which it must deal. The glory of this land has been its capacity for transcending the moral evils of our past. For example, the long struggle of minority citizens for equal rights, once a source of disunity and civil war, is now a point of pride for all Americans. We must never go back. There is no room for racism, anti-Semitism, or other forms of ethnic and racial hatred in this country.

I know that you've been horrified, as have I, by the resurgence of some hate groups preaching bigotry and prejudice. Use the mighty voice of your pulpits and the powerful standing of your churches to denounce and isolate these hate groups in our midst. The commandment given us is clear and simple: "Thou shalt love they neighbor as thyself."

But whatever sad episodes exist in our past, any objective observer must hold a positive view of American history, a history that has been the story of hopes fulfilled and dreams made into reality. Especially in this century, America has kept alight the torch of freedom, but not just for ourselves but for millions of others around the world.

And this brings me to my final point today. During my first press conference as President, in answer to a direct question, I pointed out that, as good Marxist-Leninists, the Soviet leaders have openly and publicly declared that the only morality they recognize is that which will further their cause, which is world revolution. I think I should point out I was only quoting Lenin, their guiding spirit, who said in 1920 that they repudiate all morality that proceeds from supernatural ideas—that's their name for religion—or ideas that are outside class conceptions. Morality is entirely subordinate to the interests of class war. And everything is moral that is necessary for the annihilation of the old, exploiting social order and for uniting the proletariat.

Well, I think the refusal of many influential people to accept this elementary fact of Soviet doctrine illustrates an historical reluctance to see totalitarian powers for what they are. We saw this phenomenon in the 1930's. We see it too often today.

This doesn't mean we should isolate ourselves and refuse to seek an understanding with them. I intend to do everything I can to persuade them of our peaceful intent, to remind them that it was the West that refused to use its nuclear monopoly in the forties and fifties for territorial gain and which now proposes 50-percent cut in strategic ballistic missiles and the elimination of an entire class of land-based, intermediate-range nuclear missiles.

At the same time, however, they must be made to understand we will never compromise our principles and standards. We will never give away our freedom. We will never abandon our belief in God. And we will never stop searching for a genuine peace. But we can assure none of these things America stands for through the so-called nuclear freeze solutions proposed by some.

The truth is that a freeze now would be a very dangerous fraud, for that is merely the illusion of peace. The reality is that we must find peace through strength.

I would agree to a freeze if only we could freeze the Soviets' global desires. A freeze at current levels of weapons would remove any incentive for the Soviets to negotiate seriously in Geneva and virtually end our chances to achieve the major arms reductions which we have proposed. Instead, they would achieve their objectives through the freeze.

A freeze would reward the Soviet Union for its enormous and unparalleled military buildup. It would prevent the essential and long overdue modernization of United States and allied defenses and would leave our aging forces increasingly vulnerable. And an honest freeze would require extensive prior negotiations on the systems and numbers to be limited and on the measures to ensure effective verification and compliance. And the kind of a freeze that has been suggested would be virtually impossible to verify. Such a major effort would divert us completely from our current negotiations on achieving substantial reductions.

A number of years ago, I heard a young father, a very prominent young man in the entertainment world, addressing a tremendous gathering in California. It was during the time of the cold war, and communism and our own way of life were very much on people's minds. And he was speaking to that subject. And suddenly, though, I heard him saying, "I love my little girls more than anything—" And I said to myself, "Oh, no, don't. You can't— don't say that." But I had underestimated him. He went on: "I would rather see my little girls die now, still believing in God, than have them grow up under communism and one day die no longer believing in God."

There were thousands of young people in that audience. They came to their feet with shouts of joy. They had instantly recognized the profound truth in what he had said, with regard to the physical and the soul and what was truly important.

Yes, let us pray for the salvation of all those who live in that totalitarian darkness—pray they will discover the joy of knowing God. But until they do, let us be aware that while they preach the supremacy of the state, declare its omnipotence over individual man, and predict its eventual domination of all peoples on the Earth, they are the focus of evil in the modern world.

It was C. S. Lewis who, in his unforgettable "Screwtape Letters," wrote: "The greatest evil is not done now in those sordid 'dens of crime' that Dickens loved to paint. It is not even done in concentration camps and labor camps. In those we see its final result. But it is conceived and ordered (moved, seconded, carried and minuted) in clear, carpeted, warmed, and well-lighted offices, by quiet men with white collars and cut fingernails and smooth-shaven cheeks who do not need to raise their voice."

Well, because these "quiet men" do not "raise their voices," because they sometimes speak in soothing tones of brotherhood and peace, because, like other dictators before them, they're always making "their final territorial demand," some would have us accept them at their word and accommodate ourselves to their aggressive impulses. But if history teaches anything, it teaches that simple-minded appeasement or wishful thinking about our adversaries is folly. It means the betrayal of our past, the squandering of our freedom.

So, I urge you to speak out against those who would place the United States in a position of military and moral inferiority. You know, I've always believed that old Screwtape reserved his best efforts for those of you in the church. So, in your discussions of the nuclear freeze proposals, I urge you to beware the temptation of pride—the temptation of blithely declaring yourselves above it all and label both sides equally at fault, to ignore the facts of history and the aggressive impulses of an evil empire, to simply call the arms race a giant misunderstanding and thereby remove yourself from the struggle between right and wrong and good and evil.

I ask you to resist the attempts of those who would have you withhold your support for our efforts, this administration's efforts, to keep America strong and free, while we negotiate real and verifiable reductions in the world's nuclear arsenals and one day, with God's help, their total elimination.

While America's military strength is important, let me add here that I've always maintained that the struggle now going on for the world will never be decided by bombs or rockets, by armies or military might. The real crisis we face today is a spiritual one; at root, it is a test of moral will and faith.

Whittaker Chambers, the man whose own religious conversion made him a witness to one of the terrible traumas of our time, the Hiss-Chambers case, wrote that the crisis of the Western World exists to the degree in which the West is indifferent to God, the degree to which it collaborates in communism's attempt to make man stand alone without God. And then he said, for Marxism-Leninism is actually the second oldest faith, first proclaimed in the Garden of Eden with the words of temptation, "Ye shall be as gods."

The Western World can answer this challenge, he wrote, "but only provided that its faith in God and the freedom He enjoins is as great as communism's faith in Man."

I believe we shall rise to the challenge. I believe that communism is another sad, bizarre chapter in human history whose last pages even now are being written. I believe this because the source of our strength in the quest for human freedom is not material, but spiritual. And because it knows no limitation, it must terrify and ultimately triumph over those who would enslave their fellow man. For in the words of Isaiah: "He giveth power to the faint; and to them that have no might He increased strength. . . . But they that wait upon the Lord shall renew their strength; they shall mount up with wings as eagles; they shall run, and not be weary. . . ."

Yes, change your world. One of our Founding Fathers, Thomas Paine, said, "We have it within our power to begin the world over again." We can do it, doing together what no one church could do by itself.

God bless you, and thank you very much.

Inaugural Address (1993)

William Clinton

Commentary

The election of 1992 showed that public discontent was widespread. Not only did the presidential incumbent (George Bush) lose, but a third party candidate (Ross Perot) did well enough to keep the winner, William Clinton (1946-   ), from receiving a majority of the popular votes.

Political pundits attributed much of the discontent to an economic recession, for which Bush was blamed by some fellow Republicans as well as by Democrats. However, there were signs of widespread disenchantment with politics in general; one was frequent use of the ambiguous word, "change," by all of Bush's opponents. Moreover, many signs indicate that alienation, far from being limited to the 1992 election, has been increasing in recent decades. One sign is that winners of two recent presidential elections, Carter in 1976 and Reagan in 1980, portrayed themselves as "outsiders." Other indications of alienation are the high turnover rate in recent congressional elections, the low voter turnout in elections at all levels of government, and the growing movement to enact term limitations.

If, in fact, alienation is widespread, it raises a host of disturbing questions. Among those of special interest to rhetorical historians are: Does rhetorical discourse contribute to the alienation? If so, how? What, if anything, can be done to correct the situation?

Despite widespread alienation, many of our rhetorical traditions continue. One is the presidential inaugural. As is customary, the newspaper text of Clinton's speech was based on a press release that was distributed prior to delivery. Clinton made only a few minor departures from the press release, but for the sake of providing an "oral" text, the following is based on a videotape recording.

Inaugural Address

My Fellow Citizens, today we celebrate the mystery of American renewal. This ceremony is held in the depth of winter, but by the words we speak and the faces we show the world, we force the spring—a spring reborn in the world's oldest democracy that brings forth the vision and courage to reinvent America.

When our Founders boldly declared America's independence to the world and our purposes to the Almighty, they knew that America to endure would have to change—not change for change sake but change to preserve America's ideals: life, liberty, the pursuit of happiness. Though we march to the music of our time, our mission is timeless. Each generation of Americans must define what it means to be an American.

On behalf of our nation, I salute my predecessor, President Bush, for his half-century of service to America. [*Applause*] And I thank the millions of men and women whose steadfastness and sacrifice triumphed over depression, fascism and communism. Today, a generation raised in the shadows of the cold war assumes new responsibilities in a world warmed by the sunshine of freedom but threatened still by ancient hatreds and new plagues. Raised in unrivaled prosperity, we inherit an economy that is still the world's strongest but is weakened by business failures, stagnant wages, increasing inequality and deep divisions among our own people.

When George Washington first took the oath I have just sworn to uphold, news traveled slowly across the land by horseback and across the ocean by boat. Now the sights and sounds of this ceremony are broadcast instantaneously to billions around the world. Communications and commerce are global, investment is mobile, technology is almost magical, and ambition for a better life is now universal. We earn our livelihood in America today in peaceful competition with people all across the earth. Profound and powerful forces are shaking and remaking our world, and the urgent question of our time is whether we can make change our friend and not our enemy.

This new world has already enriched the lives of millions of Americans who are able to compete and win in it. But when most people are working harder for less, when others cannot work at all, when the cost of health care devastates families and threatens to bankrupt our enterprises great and small, when the fear of crime robs law-abiding citizens of their freedom, and when millions of poor children cannot even imagine the lives we are calling them to lead, we have not made change our friend. We know we have to face hard truths and take strong steps, but we have not done so. Instead we have drifted, and that drifting has eroded our resources, fractured our economy and shaken our confidence.

Though our challenges are fearsome, so are our strengths. Americans have ever been a restless, questing, hopeful people, and we must bring to our task today the vision and will of those who came before us. From our Revolution to the Civil War, to the Great Depression, to the Civil Rights Movement, our people have always mustered the determination to construct from these crises the pillars of our history. Thomas Jefferson believed that to preserve the very foundations of our nation we would need dramatic change from time to time. Well, my fellow Americans, this is our time. Let us embrace it.

Our democracy must be not only the envy of the world but the engine of our own renewal. There is nothing wrong with America that cannot be cured by what is right with America [*Applause*]; and so today we pledge an end to the era of deadlock and drift, and a new season of American renewal has begun. [*Applause*] To renew America we must be bold. We must do what no generation has had to do before. We must invest more in our own people, in their jobs and in their future, and at the same time cut our massive debt, and we must do so in a world in which we must compete for every opportunity. It will not be easy. It will require sacrifice, but it can be done and done fairly—not choosing sacrifice for its own sake, but for our own sake. We must provide for our nation the way a family provides for its children.

Our Founders saw themselves in the light of posterity. We can do no less. Anyone who has ever watched a child's eyes wander into sleep knows what posterity is. Posterity is the world to come—the world for whom we hold our ideals, from whom we have borrowed our planet and to whom we bear sacred responsibility. We must do what America does best—offer more opportunity to all and demand more responsibility from all. [*Applause*] It is time to break the bad habit of expecting something for nothing from our government or from each other. Let us all take more responsibility not only for ourselves and our families, but for our communities and our country.

To renew America we must revitalize our democracy. This beautiful capital, like every capital since the dawn of civilization, is often a place of intrigue and calculation. Powerful people maneuver for position and worry endlessly about who is in and who is out, who is up and who is down, forgetting those people whose toil and sweat sends us here and pays our way. [*Applause*] Americans deserve better, and in this city today there are people who want to do better; and so I say to all of you here, let us resolve to reform our politics so that power and privilege no longer shout down the voice of the people. Let us put aside personal advantage so that we can feel the pain and see the promise of America. Let us resolve to make our Government a place for what Franklin Roosevelt called bold, persistent experimentation—a government for our tomorrows, not our yesterdays. Let us give this capital back to the people to whom it belongs. [*Applause*]

To renew America we must meet challenges abroad as well as at home. There is no longer a clear division between what is foreign and what is domestic. The world economy, the world environment, the world AIDS crisis, the world arms race—they affect us all.

Today as an old order passes, the new world is more free but less stable. Communism's collapse has called forth old animosities and new dangers. Clearly, America must continue to lead the world we did so much to make. While America rebuilds at home, we will not shrink from the challenges nor fail to seize the opportunities of this new world. Together with our friends and allies we will work to shape change lest it engulf us. When our vital interests are challenged or the will and conscience of the international community is defied, we will act with peaceful diplomacy whenever possible, with force when necessary. The brave Americans serving our nation today in the Persian Gulf, in Somalia, and wherever else they stand are testament to our resolve. But our greatest strength is the power of our ideas, which are still new in many lands. Across the world we see them embraced, and we rejoice. Our hopes, our hearts, our hands are with those on every continent who are building democracy and freedom. Their cause is America's cause.

The American people have summoned the change we celebrate today. You have raised your voices in an unmistakable chorus, you have cast your votes in historic numbers, and you have changed the face of Congress, the Presidency, and the political process itself. Yes, you, my fellow Americans have forced the spring. Now we must do the work the season demands. To that work I now turn with all the authority of my office. I ask the Congress to join with me; but no President, no Congress, no government can undertake this mission alone. My fellow Americans, you too must play your part in our renewal.

I challenge a new generation of young Americans to a season of service—to act on your idealism by helping troubled children, keeping company with those in need, reconnecting our torn communities. There is so much to be done— enough, indeed, for millions of others who are still young in spirit to give of themselves in service, too. In serving, we recognize a simple but powerful truth—we need each other and we must care for one another. Today we do more than celebrate America. We rededicate ourselves to the very idea of America—an idea born in revolution and renewed through two centuries of challenge—an idea tempered by the knowledge that but for fate we, the fortunate and the unfortunate, might have been each other—an idea ennobled by the faith that our nation can summon from its myriad diversity the deepest measure of unity—an idea infused with the conviction that America's long, heroic journey must go forever upward.

And so, my fellow Americans, as we stand at the edge of the 21st century, let us begin anew with energy and hope, with faith and discipline; and let us work until our work is done. The Scripture says: ''And let us not be weary in well-doing, for in due season we shall reap if we faint not.''

From this joyful mountaintop of celebration, we hear a call to service in the valley. We have heard the trumpets, we have changed the guard; and now each in our own way, and with God's help, we must answer the call.

Thank you, and God bless you all.